D0122521

**Child
Development
and Personality**

Under the Editorship of Wayne H. Holtzman and Gardner Murphy

Child
Development
and Personality

THIRD EDITION

PAUL HENRY MUSSEN
University of California, Berkeley

JOHN JANEWAY CONGER
University of Colorado School of Medicine

JEROME KAGAN
Harvard University

Harper & Row, Publishers
New York, Evanston, and London

Photograph on cover by Henle from Monkmeyer
Frontispiece by W. Eugene Smith

Contents

Preface
to the Third Edition

The field of child psychology has changed radically since 1963, the year the second edition of this book was published. The pace of systematic investigation has accelerated markedly, as it has in all scientific disciplines, and the products of research have improved in both quality and quantity. In addition, for many social, historical, and intellectual reasons, the research and theoretical emphases of the field seem to have shifted significantly. Some problems considered to be of major importance a decade ago receive much less attention today; other problem areas of human development that had previously been only minor foci of research efforts have become central. The most prominent among the new research emphases is that dealing with cognition, broadly defined—perception, learning, thinking, problem-solving. Other central issues of contemporary research, related to this increased interest in cognition, are concerned with neonatal and infant capabilities, acquisition and early development of language, the basic capabilities and education of culturally disadvantaged children, and social and personal factors related to school achievement. The behavior and values of adolescents and the formation of so-called "youth culture" have also become more important foci of speculation and research.

The third edition of this text reflects these critical changes and presents a contemporary view of the field of child psychology. The basic objectives of the book are the same as they were in the earlier editions: to give the student a broad, comprehensive view of the child at each stage of his development, delineating the interrelationships among various aspects of development—biological, cognitive, personality, social—and emphasizing the factors influencing development. Research findings are interpreted as being *relative* rather than *absolute*.

The theoretical orientation of the book has shifted somewhat. Contemporary learning theory continues to be useful in analyzing large segments of the individual's behavior, particularly early acquisition of motives and personality characteristics, but we have become acutely aware that the classical principles of learning are not sufficient to explain language acquisition and cognitive development. Psychoanalytic theory is still a fruitful source of suggestions for understanding the development of underlying motives, but the psychoanalytic influence on our conceptualizations of stages of development has diminished. In general, cognitive theory—particularly that derived from the writing of Piaget and his followers—plays a much greater role in our theoretical discussions than it did in the second edition.

The authors gratefully acknowledge the help of many individuals in the preparation of this edition. We are most indebted to Alberta Siegel and John Flavell who read the entire manuscript, encouraged us, and made many thoughtful criticisms and valuable suggestions. Dr. Theodore T. Puck provided invaluable advice about the chapter on genetics.

For secretarial and bibliographic assistance, without which this book could not have been completed, we wish to thank Carol Potter, April Hird, Ann Rosenzweig, Doris Simpson, Henriette Salek, Nancy Smith, and Dorothy Townsend.

P. H. M.
J. J. C.
J. K.

**Child
Development
and Personality**

1
Introduction

In recent years, scientific research has progressed continually and at a spectacular rate. Like other fields of science, child psychology is thriving and expanding, and within a relatively short span of time the field has acquired an entire "new look."

Until about 25 years ago, the subject matter of child psychology was essentially limited to accounts of trends in development—descriptions of age changes in physical, psychological, and behavioral characteristics. Early research in child psychology (and texts based on this research) consisted largely of detailed descriptions of sequences of "steps" in children's acquisition of restricted types of behavior such as walking and talking. Developmental data were seldom related to broad psychological principles or to general theories of human behavior.

Since World War II the scope and definition of the field of developmental psychology, as well as the major directions of research, have changed radically. New theoretical and substantive problems have been formulated. For example, developmental psychologists are currently much more concerned with such problems as the child's acquisition of his first language, the possible effects of early sensory stimulation on later intellectual development, and the processes involved in forming attachments to others. Some issues previously considered to be major ones—e.g., the growth of vocabulary, the acquisition of psychomotor skills—have faded in importance. Others, formerly thought to be of minor significance—e.g., infant perception, development of attention, infants' anxiety about strangers, and children's concept formation—now appear to be central, critical problems. Some prominent theories have lost much of their appeal and no longer seem valid or useful, even though until recently they served as fruitful sources of both explanations of behavior and research ideas. Recently constructed theories and revised versions of older ones offer novel concepts and new approaches to problems.

The methods and tools of research in child psychology have also changed. Some research techniques, such as mothers' reports, doll play, and projective tests, have been proven to have limitations that were not fully understood, and do not seem to be so fruitful. Some of these procedures have been improved, others discarded. New ones have been invented and are widely used—including, among others, improved techniques for measuring infants' visual perception; better controlled, contrived "situational" methods of observing parent-child interactions and/or children's behavior; ingenious tests of conceptual ability; and more objective methods of making naturalistic observations. As would be expected under such circumstances, some old "facts"—generalizations based on earlier studies and exploratory data—no longer seem valid or at best seem to have only limited value. They are being replaced by recent findings—conclusions based on better, more systematic investigations.

This book presents a contemporary view of child psychology, particularly emphasizing significant recent research and the most fruitful modern concepts and theories of human development. Our focus is on the origins and development of those psychological processes that seem most salient for understanding human behavior.

Like other areas of psychology, developmental psychology has as its major goals the description, explanation, and prediction of human behavior—more specifically, the growth and development of human behavior. To achieve these goals, the developmental psychologist draws heavily on basic research findings of other major areas of psychology.

Developmental psychology is not an isolated or independent field. The principles of learning, perception, motivation, and social behavior are as applicable to developmental psychology as they are to other branches of the science. Many aspects of development remain incomprehensible without these generalizations and advances in developmental psychology depend upon progress in the entire realm of psychology. For example, data and generalizations derived from research in such diverse areas as behavior genetics, physiological psychology, and learning and motivation may, and often do, have direct relevance to fundamental problems of developmental psychology. Contributions from these fields are vital for understanding the genetic determinants of behavior, the physiological bases of development, and the acquisition of behavior and personality characteristics.

A number of outstanding developmental psychologists, such as Piaget (e.g., 20, 21) and Werner (27) have formulated theories that deal specifically with the origin and development of basic psychological processes. But, in addition, as will be evident throughout this book, some of the most fruitful theories and research techniques used in the study of developmental psychology are adopted from other fields of psychology, often with modifications. For instance, psychoanalytic theory is concerned primarily with emotional adjustment and maladjustment, but aspects of this theory deal with the *origins* of psychological disturbance and with hypotheses about normal personality development. Likewise, learning theory, formulated largely on the basis of research in laboratories (often with animals), has helped enormously in understanding the development of large segments of human behavior. Cognitive theory, constructed to explain adult perception, thinking, and problem-solving, has been the inspiration for much theorizing and research on the origins and development of these processes. These theories will be elaborated later in this chapter (see pp. 16–18).

Let us consider the other side of the coin, too. Developmental psychology is not only a "taker" from other areas of psychology. The study of developmental psychology is, of course, self-justified. Knowledge of how psychological processes originate, change, and develop is as important and interesting as knowledge of, say, physics, embryology, history, or geography. Moreover, the field of developmental psychology makes major contributions to the total discipline of which it is a part. Many psychological generalizations have been established largely on the basis of laboratory research and experimentation with animals or with human beings in highly artificial, contrived situations. Consequently it may be difficult to determine their value as general explanations of behavior. Their usefulness is substantially increased, however, if the principles can be shown to apply to children's behavior. Thus the area of child psychology provides an important proving ground for assessing the generality of psychological principles.

Furthermore, many aspects of adult behavior cannot be explained adequately without using the data of developmental psychology. Developmental psychologists study children not only to understand children but also because early development strongly affects later functioning. Recent research strongly suggests that there are *critical* or *sensitive periods* during which certain important psychological processes are developing most rapidly. Disturbances during these periods may alter the development of these processes in critical ways. For example, if chimpanzees are raised in darkness during the first year of life, certain cells in the retina will fail to develop and vision will be permanently impaired; the first year, then, is critical for normal visual development (23).

Analogously, the first year of life seems to be a very sensitive—or even a *critical* period—in the development of the child's *trust* of others. If the infant fails to develop this feeling at this period, he may never do so. Events that occur during the first 3 or 4 years appear to be critical for the development of adult schizophrenia, whereas the preadolescent years are critical for the adoption of delinquent behavior. If the critical experiences and critical periods were precisely known, some kind of planned intervention might be instituted to prevent these problems. The fundamental point is that responses acquired early in childhood guide the individual's subsequent personality development and adjustment, thus providing some continuity to individual behavior. Hence, full understanding of adult behavior rests upon knowledge of early development. This is the great contribution of developmental psychology and the theme of the present book.

THE PRACTICAL IMPORTANCE
OF CHILD PSYCHOLOGY

Clearly, the study of child psychology is of great theoretical significance and makes major contributions to the field of psychology. The systematic study of child psychology may also have practical applications, yielding facts that are useful in understanding and diagnosing the individual's behavior—including problem behavior—and in suggesting methods of modifying behavior. For example, the study of age trends in various aspects of behavior provides sets of averages, norms, or standards that can be used in evaluating a particular youngster's development. Does he begin to walk before, after, or at the same time as the average child? Does he understand as many words and speak as clearly as the average child of his age? Similarly, studies of the development of thinking and reasoning ability give information that is useful in comparing the child's progress in these skills with that of the average child of his age. Standards or norms of development derived from systematic research in child psychology are often quite helpful in diagnosing individual psychological problems.

For example, an 8-month-old child is brought to a clinic or to a doctor's office because his parents feel that he is intellectually dull, unresponsive, and uninterested in people or in the environment. Developmental scales may show that, according to the norms or standards of performance for his age group, he is retarded in motor and sensory development. Although it is almost impossible to make an accurate diagnosis of intellectual status in a child this young, such findings do suggest the *possibility* of mental deficiency.

If, in addition to his retardation in sensory and motor development, the child is very small for his age, a thorough medical checkup may be advised. This examination may reveal that the child is suffering from a thyroid deficiency. Previous research has shown that in a special kind of mental defect known as *cretinism,* there is an intimate connection between iodine deficiency in thyroid secretion and intellectual and physical retardation. If the condition is detected early, treatment by the administration of thyroid is, in many cases, highly effective in stimulating both physical growth and psychological development.

In such a case, comparison of the child's ability with norms of motor and sensory development makes it clear that the child is retarded in those areas. Facts derived from previous research showing the relationships among psychological retardation, physical size, and thyroid deficiency are useful in prescribing therapy. In short, the norms serve as a basis for suggesting a diagnosis, and knowledge of the interactions among other factors is valuable in suggesting a method of treatment.

Another illustration of the practical utility of the data of child psychology involves juvenile delinquency, which is both a social problem and a psychological problem—a manifestation of personal maladjustment. Suppose, for example, a 10-year-old boy of normal intelligence begins to steal things from other children and from homes in his neighborhood. Systematic research has shown that delinquent behavior is often rooted in feelings of parental rejection and insecurity and, consequently, in profound resentment and hostility toward parents. Knowledge of the results of such scientific investigations provides the court psychologist with an idea of how to proceed with the case. He will be alert to possible feelings of rejection; if he finds them, he can then look for their sources and work toward alleviating them.

In such instances, techniques of psychological treatment (psychotherapy) may be used with the delinquent child. One of the major aims of such treatment is to allow the child to express his feelings freely and to learn to understand the factors involved in his socially unacceptable behavior. If he can gain insight (emotional understanding), the child may be able to reconstruct his emotional attitudes and behavior.

Scientific findings about the relationship between home environment and personality problems may be applied in attempting to modify the child's behavior and to make it more socially acceptable. The psychologist may attempt to modify the child's environment, if possible, by working with the delinquent's family to help reduce conflict and stress in the home. The child may perceive the changed home situation as less rejecting, and hence there may be less motivation for him to commit delinquent acts.

Another vivid demonstration of the potential social utility of the results of the systematic study of child psychology comes from recent attempts to raise the educational level and the social status of the culturally disadvantaged. Research, which we shall discuss in detail later in the book indicates that the academic difficulties of culturally disadvantaged children in ghetto areas stem largely from extreme deprivation and lack of challenge, novelty, or stimulation in their very early home environments. The motivation required for success in school and in academic pursuits ordinarily develops in the early years, and is largely determined by the nature of the youngster's interactions with the adults in his environment. Therefore, to achieve enduring improvements in school performance and increased interest in education among the culturally disadvantaged, the level of stimulation during their early childhood must be raised. Educators must attempt to provide environments that are stimulating enough to compensate for early deprivations; it is not yet clear whether this can be done after the preschool period.

The findings of systematic child psychology are not limited to the understanding of children's problems. Clinical data and case histories of criminals and psychiatric patients reveal that personal and social maladjustments among adults almost always have their roots in early life experiences. It was Sigmund Freud, the founder of psychoanalysis, who called attention most forcefully to the importance of childhood events. Through his penetrating analyses of the patients with whom he worked, he made abundantly clear the truth of the poet's statement, "The child is father to the man."

In considerable measure, the origins of adult unhappiness and feelings of inadequacy must be sought in the individual's childhood. Therefore, in order to understand the adult's psychological problems with any degree of sophistication, we must learn about his early developmental history.

However, it is not only abnormal behavior that has many of its origins in childhood; much of the normal adult's predominant personality characteristics and behavior patterns can be traced to factors in his earlier life. A man may be shy and withdrawn or friendly and outgoing, generous or stingy, independent in his actions or dependent on others, lazy or ambitious, tense or relaxed, passive or aggressive. All these characteristics are the outcomes of his unique personality development, but particularly they are the result of the intimate experiences of his childhood. Similarly, the broad lifetime goals and overall philosophy of the individual—his choice of vocation and the satisfactions he will seek from it, the kind of person he will want to marry, and his expectations with regard to his children—may become fully understandable only in the light of his entire developmental history.

SOME HISTORICAL PERSPECTIVE

Most sophisticated people take it for granted that the events of early childhood affect the individual's later social and psychological adjustment. Moreover, almost everyone seems to be interested in children and their welfare; in their growth and development; and in their acquisition of skills, abilities, personality, and social characteristics. Contemporary Western culture is truly "child centered," and this has clearly facilitated progress in child psychology. As the culture has become increasingly child centered, child psychology has become a more substantial and vigorous scientific discipline.

But until the seventeenth century—a relatively recent period in the total span of Western history—there was no special emphasis on childhood as a separate phase of the life cycle. Some exceptional scholars and thinkers of ancient days were interested in children's development because they felt intuitively that what happens in childhood has strong impacts on later development. Plato, for example, recognized the importance of early childhood training in the determination of the individual's later vocational aptitudes and adjustments. In his *Republic,* he discussed inherent differences among individuals and recommended that steps be taken to discover each child's outstanding aptitudes, so that specific education and training along the lines of his particular talents might begin early.

By and large, however, until three centuries ago, children in Western Europe were not regarded as a particular class of humans or treated in distinctive ways. Obviously infants needed special care and attention, but once they had been weaned and had achieved a minimum of ability to take care of themselves, they became "small adults"—mingling, working, and playing with mature people. Phillip Aries, a French intellectual historian, documents this dramatically in his fascinating book, *Centuries of Childhood* (1).

> In the middle ages, at the beginning of modern times, and for a long time after that in the lower classes, children were mixed with adults as soon as they were considered capable of doing without their mothers or nannies, not long after a tardy weaning (in other words, at about the age of seven). They immediately went straight into the great community of men, sharing in the work and play of their companions, old and young alike (1, 411).

It is interesting to note that in medieval art, children were depicted as immature adults, and even as late as the fifteenth and sixteenth centuries were shown in nonreligious paintings gathering with adults for purposes of work, relaxation, or sport. Their clothing was not distinctive; rather, they dressed like the men and women of their own social class.

Nor were the behaviors of children expected to differ vastly from those of adults. After the age of 3 or 4, they played the same games as adults, either with other children or adults, and participated fully in community celebrations and festivities. Moreover, in the medieval school there was no graduated system of education by which subjects were introduced in order from easiest to most difficult. Students of all ages from 10 years to 20 or over were mixed together in the same classroom. Children were not thought to be "innocent" and in need of protection from references to sexual matters. Children shared in the wild, violent, libertine life of the times; even in school, they were extremely unruly, disobedient, and violent.

The seventeenth century marked a great change in attitudes toward children and their morals. For reasons not fully understood—but probably linked with the strong religious currents of the Reformation and Counter Reformation—clergymen and humanitarians of this time began to encourage the separation of children from adults and even adolescents. Gradually these thinkers influenced parents, and a whole new family attitude, oriented around the child and his education, appeared.

With the great change in attitudes and morals, the concept of the innocence of childhood—a period of "primitivism, irrationalism and pre-logicalism"—won acceptance. From that time on, children were to be spared all references to sexual matters lest their innocence be corrupted.

> The idea of childish innocence resulted in two kinds of attitudes and behaviors toward childhood: firstly, safeguarding against pollution by life, and particularly by the sexuality tolerated if not approved of among adults; and secondly, strengthening it by developing character and reason (1, 119).

The child became a "special" person. He ceased to be dressed like the grownup. From the seventeenth century on, paintings depict him wearing outfits reserved for his own age group and which set him apart from adults.

Moral education became one of the principal objects of school life. Those concerned with the Reformation believed that all children, even those of the lower classes, should be given the religious instruction that had hitherto been restricted to the privileged few. Moreover, religious or moral education became closely linked with instruction in the utilitarian skills of reading and writing, "which were now regarded as necessary for the exercise of any trade, even a manual job. In this way it was hoped to make pious, serious workers out of what had been depraved adventurers" (1, 303). Education thus became recognized as "the only possible means of instilling a sense of morality into the down-and-outs, of turning them into servants and workers, and hence of providing the country with a good labor force" (1, 310).

While the elite reformers and moralists who occupied high positions in Church and State argued that lower-class children should receive better utilitarian and religious education, they also maintained that the upper-class child should work even harder to cultivate gentle manners. "The well-bred child would be preserved from roughness and immorality which would become the special characteristic of the lower classes" (1, 328).

The insistence of these seventeenth-century authorities on the moral and social importance of systematic education was accompanied by stress on the need for special institutions for educational purposes. During this period, therefore, the structure of school classes also became modified, assuming a form closer to that of the present: grades or forms in separate rooms, yearly promotion, and one class per year, based largely on the pupil's age.

> In the moralists and pedagogues of the 17th century, we see that fondness for childhood and its special nature no longer found expression in amusement and coddling, but in psychological interest and moral solicitude. The child was no longer regarded as amusing or agreeable, but as in need of help and guidance. In order to correct the behavior of children people must first understand them, and the texts of the late 16th and 17th centuries are full of comments on child psychology.
>
> The first concept of childhood—characterized by coddling—had made its appearance in the family circle, in the company of little children. The second, on the contrary, sprang from a source outside the family: churchmen or gentlemen of the robe, few in number before the 16th century, and a far greater number of moralists in the 17th century, eager to insure disciplined, rational manners. They too had become alive to the formerly neglected phenomenon of childhood, but they were unwilling to regard children as charming toys, for they saw them as fragile creatures of God, who needed to be both safeguarded and reformed (1, 133).

Philosophers and Child Psychology

These new concepts of childhood and of education were also the sources of a new, speculative literature of child psychology and development. The earliest writers were primarily philosophers, clergymen, physicians, educators, humanitarians, and reformers, but they dealt with issues that are still critical for the developmental psychologist. For example, they wrote about the inherent characteristics of children (what is congenital or inherited) and the most effective methods of child-rearing and training. Some, conceiving of childhood as "naturally evil," wrote passionately about the child's "native depravity," while others portrayed the child as a "noble savage," biologically endowed with virtues and characteristics that, if allowed expression, would ensure healthy growth and socially responsible behavior.

The British philosopher, John Locke, writing at the very end of the seventeenth century, viewed the child's experience and education as the fundamental determinants of his development—although he did allow for "native propensities." The infant's mind, he wrote, is a *tabula rasa*—a blank slate—and he is therefore receptive to all kinds of learning.

Locke was committed to the ultimate rationality of man.

> The great Principle and Foundation of all Virtue and Worth is placed in this, that a man is able to deny himself his own desires, cross his own inclinations, and purely follow what reason directs as best, though the appetite lean the other way (17, 59).

The object of all education is therefore self-discipline, self-control, and the "power of denying ourselves the satisfaction of our own desires, where reason does not authorize them" (16). To achieve these goals, parents must begin instructing children in self-denial "from their very cradles."

Jean Jacques Rousseau, a French philosopher, writing in the latter half of the eighteenth century, believed that the child is endowed with an innate moral sense. In *Emile* (24) he spoke of the child as a "noble savage" with intuitive knowledge of what is right and wrong, but thwarted by restrictions imposed on him by society.

> Rousseau suggests that no great harm to the child or to society will result if the child grows with little adult supervision and direction! The child will become increasingly fit to live in the world, not by virtue of ceaseless vigilance on the part of his governors, but because nature has endowed him with an order of development that ensures his healthy growth. More than that, the typical interventions of parents and teachers mar and distort the natural succession of the changes of childhood; the child that man raises is almost certain to be inferior to the child that nature raises (13, 74).

Locke's and Rousseau's views of how children develop contrast sharply. Locke's view was essentially that of associationistic psychology: the child's development is determined by his education, and, more specifically, his behavior is shaped or molded by his experiences, by the rewards and punishments provided by the environment.

> I grant that good and evil, reward and punishment, are the only motives to a rational creature; these are the spur and reins, whereby all mankind is set on

work, and guided, and therefore they are to be made use of to children too. For I advise their parents and governors always to carry this in their minds, that children are to be treated as rational creatures (13, 61).

In Rousseau's thinking, the child responded *actively* to the world around him, engaging

his environment, using it to suit his interests. He fits his abilities to the world in play and in the solving of problems, not as a passive recipient of the tutor's instruction . . . but as a busy, testing, motivated explorer. Knowledge is not an invention of adults poured into willing or unwilling vessels; it is a joint construction of the child in nature and the natural world. . . . The active searching child, setting his own problems, stands in contrast to the receptive one, even the one equipped with curiosity, on whom society fixes its stamp (13, 75).

As we shall see later, modern theories of development also differ (as Locke's and Rousseau's did) in their conceptions of the child's relationship to the world. Some modern theorists see the child's development primarily as passive and receptive, responding to the pressures—rewards and punishments—of the environment. For others, the child develops through active, purposeful engagement with his environment, organizing and interpreting his experiences, and attempting to solve problems.

Locke's and Rousseau's writings were important seminal influences in child development, but these philosophers' theories, though penetrating, were speculative and untested. Contemporary theorists and researchers attempt to check their hypotheses by systematic and careful observations and by experiments. "The theories [of the 17th- and 18th-century philosophers] were bound to be somewhat diffuse and contradictory until the child became a fit object for scientific study" (13, 112).

Baby Biographies

As a result of these new general attitudes, children came to be regarded as proper subjects for study. Philosophers, biologists, and educators began to discover their own children, and some of the most curious and courageous attempted to learn about them by the novel procedure of observation. Thus, in 1774, Johann Heinrich Pestalozzi (19), a Swiss educator, published notes based on the careful observations of the development of his 3½-year-old son. His book reflected his own theories, which, like Rousseau's, stressed the innate goodness of the child and the role of the child's own activity in development. Thirteen years later (1787), Dieterich Tiedemann published a kind of diary of infant behavior (25), tracing the sensory, motor, language, and intellectual growth of a single infant during the first 2½ years of life.

In the nineteenth century, a series of "baby biographies" began to appear. The most eminent writer of such a biography was Charles Darwin, the evolutionist, who published a diary of his observations of his son's early development (7). Darwin saw the child as a rich source of information about the nature of man—"by careful observation of the infant and child, one could see the descent of man" (*13*, 115). The fact that such a distinguished scientist and theorist would write a baby biography was impressive; it made the baby biography a legitimate scientific document.

In spite of the brilliance of some of the writers, these early baby biographies are not generally good sources of scientific data. Too often they were based on observations that were unsystematic and made at irregular intervals. Furthermore, like Darwin, most observers had their own special theory about development or education and saw the child they were observing as a living expression of this theory. Also, the writers were usually proud parents, or uncles or aunts, undoubtedly biased and selective in their perceptions. Understandably, they were likely to emphasize the intriguing, positive aspects of early development while neglecting some of the negative factors. Finally, because each account is based on only one case, it is almost impossible to make valid generalizations from any of them.

Nevertheless, like the earlier philosophical works, these biographies were valuable—they contained some information and many hypotheses about the nature of development. In fact, the conclusions drawn from the baby biographies were not nearly as important as their influence in delineating major problems of child psychology (many of them still unsolved) and exciting widespread interest in the scientific study of children.

Beginnings of Scientific Child Psychology

No one in the nineteenth century influenced the history of child psychology more than Charles Darwin. The publication of *On the Origin of Species* (1859) was probably the single most vital force in the establishment of child psychology as a scientific discipline. The notion of the evolution of the species—and especially Darwin's continued search for "signs of man in animal life"—inevitably led to speculation about the development of man and society. "The irreducible contribution of Darwin to the study of children was . . . in his assignment of scientific value to childhood" (*13*, 115).

Stimulated by Darwin's theory

> the search for phylogenetic and societal shades in the child marked the beginning of a science of child behavior. Man was not to be understood by the analysis of his adult functions, an analysis that was rational in conception and closely linked to logic; rather, man was to be understood by a study of his origins—in nature and in the child. When did consciousness dawn? What were the beginnings of morality? How could we know the world of the infant? Questions like these which, in form of more or less sophistication, were to dominate child psychology for many years, derive their sense from a genetic view of man (*13*, 116).

Systematic study of larger groups of children began toward the end of the nineteenth century. A pioneer in such study in the United States was G. Stanley Hall, president of Clark University and one of the founders of American psychology. He was interested in investigating "the contents of children's minds" (9) because, like Darwin, he was convinced that the study of development was crucial to the problem of understanding man. To conduct his studies of larger groups, he devised and refined a new research technique, the questionnaire, which consisted of a series of questions designed to obtain information about children's and adolescents' behavior, attitudes, and interests. Hall collected written responses to questionnaires from both children and parents.

In a sense, Hall's work, which continued into the twentieth century, marks the beginning of systematic child study in the United States. By modern standards, his work would not be considered controlled or highly objective; the problems with which he was concerned have been investigated with much greater scientific sophistication in recent years. Nevertheless, he did employ large numbers of subjects in an effort to obtain representative data, and he attempted to determine the relationships among personality characteristics, adjustment problems, and background experiences. For these reasons, Hall's approach to child psychology certainly represented a distinct methodological advance over the philosophical and biographical approaches discussed above.

CHILD PSYCHOLOGY
AS A SCIENTIFIC DISCIPLINE

The systematic study of children burgeoned in the twentieth century. As the discipline of child psychology became firmly established, it expanded into many new fields, fanned out into many paths, took on many "new looks." Within the broad field of developmental psychology, more specialized topics became the foci of systematic research and theory. For example, early in the present century child psychologists interested in individual variation devised methods of measuring intelligence, which stimulated considerable interest in the nature and growth of intelligence. Freud's papers on psychoanalytic theory, based largely on his clinical experiences and insights, contributed novel and extremely challenging ideas about personality development. Early research on conditioning and learning, by Pavlov in Russia and by Watson in the United States, led to the construction of theories and to experimentation on children's acquisition of habits as well as of knowledge. We shall refer frequently to these early contributions and to the research they have stimulated.

The Nature of Scientific Investigation

Before beginning our discussion of the content of developmental psychology—the most important empirical findings and theories—let us digress slightly to consider briefly the nature of science and scientific investigation. Our aim is to clarify the major differences between contemporary scientific child psychology and the kind of child psychology that is exemplified by philosophical writings and baby biographies.

Science can be defined only very generally; there is no precise definition agreed upon by all scientists. Nor is there any one "scientific method" or pattern of scientific activity applicable to all fields of research. Physicists and chemists generally conduct experiments in well-equipped laboratories; archeologists and astronomers, accumulating important scientific data, seldom work in laboratories. Thus science cannot be defined in terms of specific, concrete techniques, equipment, or content. It is, rather, a way of doing things, a way of looking at nature which involves certain principles and procedures. Here are some of the basic principles in summary form.

1. Controlled Observation and Objective Measurement. Observation is fundamental to all scientific endeavor; it involves focusing on some specific, precisely defined phenomenon (or phenomena) and controlling to some degree the conditions under which the observations are made. The scientist's observations must be as free as possible from subjective bias; in his evaluation of his observations, he must use standard units of measurement if possible, or, if this is not possible, units that can be understood and applied by others. Therefore, instruments potentially provide the most desirable methods of recording natural phenomena. Further, the degree to which the observations can be quantified (translated into numbers) is often a good index of the maturity of a science.

An experiment is a kind of observation that is particularly well-controlled, and in many respects it is the most desirable type. In its simplest form, the experiment consists of holding constant all but one of the variables presumably related to a given phenomenon. This particular variable is then manipulated by the experimenter in accordance with his own plans. The purpose of the experiment is to observe whether, and how, the variable under observation (the dependent variable) changes as the variable being manipulated by the experimenter (the independent variable) is changed.

Suppose, for example, that the psychologist wants to observe the effects of competition on children's performance in arithmetic tests. Do children who compete with each other do better in these tests than children who are not competing? The psychologist might attempt to answer this question by doing an experiment with two groups of children, one called the "experimental group," the other the "control group." Since he is concerned only with the relationship between competition and test performance he must be certain that the two groups are matched or equated in intelligence, arithmetic ability, health, or other factors that might affect performance.

In the experiment proper, the two groups would be subjected to different treatments. A competitive situation could be set up in the experimental group by informing the children that the student getting the highest grade on an arithmetic test would be given a prize. In the control group, no such competitive situation would be created. Both groups would then be given the same arithmetic test, and the difference between the performances of the two groups would be determined.

Here the independent variable was competition, and it was regulated by the experimenter. Other important variables were controlled by initial random assignment of children to the two groups and by matching the groups on variables considered likely to affect performance in arithmetic. Therefore we can be fairly certain that the obtained differences between the two groups must be due to the introduction of competition in one group and its absence in the other.

This example makes clear the unique advantage of experimental method, namely, the direct demonstration of relationships between variables. Without the use of experimental procedures, we cannot be sure which factors may be most important in determining a particular outcome.

> As long as we depend on the observation of occurrences not involving our assistance, the observable happenings are usually the product of so many factors that we cannot determine the contribution of each individual factor to the total result. The scientific experiment isolates the factors one from the other; the interference of man [that is, the experimenter] creates conditions in which one factor is shown at work undisturbed by the others . . . . (22, 97).

Most observations in the physical sciences are experiments, and experimental methods are applied whenever possible and suitable in child psychology. But in this field, as in other areas of social science, there are many problems for which the experimental method is not appropriate or practical.

2. Scientific Statements Must Be Communicable. The language and measurement techniques used by the scientist must involve words and symbols that are so precisely and carefully defined that other investigators in a field can repeat the observations or experiments. Thus, the statement, "Johnny was *upset*" is not the best type of scientific statement because it is ambiguous. There is likely to be disagreement about the meaning of the word "upset." The statement, "Johnny cried for five minutes and showed many uncontrolled arm and leg movements" comes closer to being scientifically acceptable because it is more precise and more objective.

3. Theory. Scientists are not satisfied simply with precise descriptions of phenomena based on careful observation or experimentation; they are also deeply concerned with explaining what they have observed. The scientific approach is therefore characterized by the construction of hypotheses, theories, or "best guesses" about the determinants of the phenomena under study. To a great extent, the scientist's theory guides all phases of his research. A scientific theory will determine the selection of the dependent and independent variables to be studied, i.e., the kinds of data to be collected and the methods for collecting them. After the data are collected, the scientist organizes and interprets them according to a set of principles or theory that allows for logical explanation, and, in some cases, for the prediction of subsequent events.

The ability to predict phenomena is one of the main advantages of theory. For example, because we have a theory (or set of interrelated principles) explaining planetary motion, we can predict when the next eclipse will occur. If we had a good theory to explain why some children do not learn well in school, we could predict school failures before they occurred and might be able to take more effective steps to ameliorate the situation.

4. Science Is Open-Ended and Subject to Revision. A scientific theory or hypothesis must be viewed as the "best possible guess with our present knowledge," but science is an open-ended, self-checking system. After formulating hypotheses and theories, the scientist conducts further observations and experiments to test them. More specifically, scientific hypotheses imply predictions about events, e.g., about the effects of competition on performance in arithmetic. If the prediction is valid, the hypothesis is confirmed; if it is not, the hypothesis must be rejected. In the latter case, the scientist must revise his hypotheses and subject the revised version to further tests. The process of building up scientific knowledge requires continuous formulation of hypotheses, checking them, reformulation, and rechecking. In this way, increasingly satisfactory scientific theories—theories that will account for more and more observed facts—are constructed.

If adherence to these general principles is the major criterion of a science, child psychology can be (at least in theory) as scientific as nuclear physics or the study of the metabolism of viruses. It will be judged scientific to the extent that child psychologists make objective observations, formulate their methods and findings in terms that are communicable to—and repeatable by—others, and construct (and reconstruct, if necessary) theories that will explain and predict children's behavior.

Scientific Status of Developmental Psychology

Judged in the terms discussed above, what is the scientific status of developmental psychology? The question cannot be answered definitively, but it is possible to make brief, tentative assessments of some of its scientific strengths and weaknesses.

American psychology, including child psychology, has been traditionally and stubbornly empirical. The great stress of modern developmental psychology, and its greatest scientific strength, has been objective observation, description, and measurement. The history of the field is one of continuous progress in data collection: better techniques and more careful controls in observation, and increasing objectivity and precision of measurement. More scientific problems are investigated experimentally, and the number of ingenious, carefully controlled experiments rises each year. Consequently, a substantial body of observational data has been accumulated.

A large proportion of the vast literature in the field published since 1900 consists of reports of these data. Norms of physical, intellectual, emotional, and social development have been carefully calculated. Techniques of measuring abilities, particularly intelligence, have been refined and standardized. Within limits, it is possible to predict the child's later intelligence from tests made early in his school career.

Relationships among variables have been studied systematically by observation and experimentation. To give only a few illustrations, the role of genetic or hereditary factors in certain kinds of mental deficiency is well-understood. The relationship between physical maturation and the development of certain motor activities (such as walking or manipulation) has been established. There is a significant body of information on the conditions that affect the rate and efficiency of learning, remembering, and forgetting. Environmental influences on cognitive functioning, including intelligence, have been, and continue to be, popular subjects of research; some significant facts have been discovered. We have learned a great deal (although not nearly as much as we need to know) about the short-term and enduring effects of early deprivation (lack of stimulation) and parental rejection on cognitive functioning and personal adjustment.

The most important and substantial empirical findings in child psychology—in effect, the present state of scientific knowledge in the field—constitute the subject matter of this book. Nevertheless, as the reader will learn, the amount of basic data available is still limited. Moreover, some conclusions are of questionable validity, for techniques of measuring important psychological variables are often not precise enough to yield more than suggestive results.

Progress in child psychology is intimately related to progress in other branches of psychology. Thus increased precision of research tools, better techniques of observation and experimentation, and optimal use of statistical techniques will lead to greater scientific sophistication in all areas of psychology, including child psychology.

THEORY IN DEVELOPMENTAL PSYCHOLOGY

In some ways the present status of theory in child psychology is comparable to that in the physical sciences in the seventeenth century. The scientists of that time knew that combining chemicals produced substances that differed from the components in color, weight, texture, and smell. But they could not explain how this happened; theories of valency and interatomic binding forces had not yet been developed. Analogously, in present-day child psychology there is a vast body of information, but the field is relatively deficient—as are most behavioral sciences—in explanatory theory.

There is no single comprehensive theory encompassing the vast body of accumulated data in the field of developmental psychology. A complete theory would have to include explanatory concepts accounting for the origins, as well as the mechanisms of development and change, of all aspects of psychological functioning—motor, cognitive, emotional, and social. It may be impossible to construct such an ideal theory; certainly no one has accomplished it yet.

However, several kinds of theory have proved particularly useful in developmental psychology—serving to integrate some accumulated data in certain areas of the field and to stimulate new research. But even relatively comprehensive theories of the "grand design" must be regarded as partial theories from the point of view of child psychology, in the sense that they deal only with the special aspects of development.

Psychoanalytic Theory

Psychoanalytic theory, which began with Freud's monumental work, is concerned mostly with personality development, and more specifically, with emotional problems and neuroses. The concepts and hypotheses of psychoanalysis were derived largely from clinical experience with adults. The psychoanalysts' therapeutic activities made them keenly aware of the tremendous impact of the child's early environment in paving the way for later maladjustment. From their investigations of their patients' backgrounds, the analysts derived many hypotheses about the effects of infantile and childhood experiences on later personality.

While the impact of psychoanalysis on psychological thought is probably not so great as it was 20 years ago, psychoanalytic theory has contributed significantly to progress in child psychology. It is the source of many hypotheses about personality development, and it delineated critical areas for scientific investigation. Later on in the book, some of the major concepts and hypotheses of psychoanalysis will be discussed more fully.

Learning Theory

A second kind of theory which has been extremely influential is known as learning or behavior theory. It posits that the most important aspects of behavior are learned: "precisely that behavior which is widely felt to characterize man as a rational being or as a member of a particular nation or social class is learned rather than innate" (8, 25).

Learning has traditionally been one of the most significant and fruitful areas of research and theory in psychology, and there are many facts and hypotheses about the nature of the process and about the conditions most conducive to effective learning. As we shall see, learning begins to play a critical part in the child's development very early in life. It would be impossible to understand the child's growth from helplessness and dependency to maturity and independence without some knowledge of the principles of learning. This does not mean that learning theory can adequately explain *all* of psychological development or all acquired behavior. Findings from several types of significant recent research—particularly in imitative behavior, early language development, and growth of thinking and reasoning—cannot be readily interpreted in terms of the principles of learning; in fact, they challenge some of the traditional conceptions of the learning process. Nevertheless, much of behavioral development can be explained most simply and adequately by means of the principles of learning. These principles, their advantages and limitations, as well as the relative contributions of various theories of learning, will be discussed in detail in Chapter 4.

Cognitive Theory

As we shall also see later, there has recently been a tremendous growth —or perhaps resurgence—of interest in cognitive processes (e.g., thinking, reasoning, and problem-solving) and their development. Cognitive theory has become quite prominent and has been highly influential. The principal source of theory and research in this area is Jean Piaget, the brilliant Swiss psychologist.

Piaget's theories pertain to cognition alone, his central interest being in problems of thought and knowledge—i.e., how the child understands nature and the world about him. In Piaget's theory, the active participation of the child in his environment and his innate tendency toward adaptation are fundamental in effecting development in understanding and in basic knowledge. The child's own resources, his built-in, self-generating mechanisms determine behavioral development. The theory is elegant, complex, ingenious, and provocative.

Comments

Each of these theoretical systems offers tenable—and often, but not always, testable—hypotheses about specific aspects of development. But no single theory unifies all, or even most, of the important knowledge about the origin and development of diverse aspects of behavior. Judged from the point of view of the adequacy of theory, then, present-day child psychology is scientifically immature.

APPLICATION OF SCIENTIFIC FINDINGS

Most scientists conduct their own research to achieve understanding for its own sake. Yet it is inevitable that as their findings become known, society becomes interested in the application of these findings for the advancement of human welfare. Moreover, the time gap between conducting scientific investigations and applying the findings to practical social problems (technology) appears to be decreasing considerably (14)—there is more pressure to apply scientific findings and to do so without delay.

Sound application, of course, depends upon scientifically established knowledge and verified hypotheses rather than on theory alone. For better or for worse, child psychology as a discipline has always been linked with practical action.

> Far more than other specialists in the study of man, theorists of children have been willing to give specific instructions to their fellow citizens about how to run their lives. Shrill, pedantic, or wise, many of the important figures in the history of child study have spoken not only to their professional and academic colleagues, but to parents and teachers as well (13, x).

And, unfortunately, their advice and recommendations have often been based on deeply held theories about development rather than on the results of scientific research.

As a matter of practical necessity, pressing social and personal problems must sometimes be tackled and solutions attempted before there is a substantial body of pertinent verified principles or facts. For example, in recent years, psychologists and educators have faced the need to work very rapidly to improve the educational status of culturally deprived children, such as those raised in Negro ghettoes. With increasing frequency, child psychiatrists, clinical psychologists, and social workers are called upon to work with individuals or in group programs designed to help stem the rising tides of juvenile delinquency and drug abuse among children and adolescents. Actually, there are very few established facts that are relevant and can be immediately and effectively applied for these purposes. Educators are therefore forced to depend on common sense, their own experience, and on any hypotheses that seem applicable—even though they may not have been adequately tested. It is also true that

> the scientist . . . is not necessarily the best judge of the social utility of his own work or of that of science in general. His motives in doing research are irrelevant to the consequences of his work for the community. In fact, it is fair to say that society exploits the poetic fascination that motivates many academic scientists, eventually capitalizing on applications that no one could have foreseen (15, 66).

As responsible citizens, most scientists sincerely hope the results of their research endeavors will eventually be useful in advancing human welfare. Happily, "most of the body of science ultimately achieves practical utility" (26). But scientists realize that this broad objective can be achieved only by applying knowledge that is based on sound basic research. Hence they must be extremely cautious in interpreting research findings to the non-scientific community.

CONTEMPORARY CHILD PSYCHOLOGY: RECENT TRENDS

As we have already seen, collection of empirical data has been emphasized in child psychology ever since its establishment as an independent scientific discipline. But major research foci change from time to time. For a long period during the early part of this century, many child psychologists devoted their research efforts to the establishment of age trends in the development of psychomotor skills and intelligence. At the same time—and related to this interest—studies of human variability and accurate assessment became prominent preoccupations of researchers.

By far the greatest part of this book deals with recent research and theory, reflecting the remarkable progress and drastic shifts that have marked the last 25 years of the history of this field. Some of the changes are broad and pervasive, affecting both goals and research approaches. There are still many investigations that, like earlier studies, are concerned with age trends in particular functions (e.g., thinking and reasoning, or creativity). But much more research is concentrated on the *processes* or *mechanisms* underlying these changes—that is, on the explanations of why these changes occur. In this kind of research, the investigator seeks to establish antecedent-consequent relationships: the conditions or events (antecedents) that precede and presumably lead to behavior changes or developments (consequents).

Not surprisingly, this shift to investigating the determinants of behavioral development has been accompanied by intensified interest in theory. Early research in child development, particularly of the age-trend variety, was purely empirical—usually lacking theoretical bases, and, consequently, largely without theoretical significance. Problems studied in current research projects are generally derived from theory and are typically designed to test some theoretical issues or explanatory hypotheses. The findings of such studies are, therefore, pertinent to the validity or "truth-value" of some theoretical system, and can be integrated with those from other studies—thus gaining in general significance and applicability.

At the same time, and related to these broad changes, new or previously neglected topics (or new versions of old problems) have attracted the attention of child psychologists. We will mention only a few that are currently of major importance. For example, following World War II and for more than a dozen years thereafter—until the later 1950s or early 1960s—studies of socialization and personality development, and factors affecting them, predominated. These topics continue to be significant and fruitful areas of investigation, as is reflected in our strong emphasis on studies of the influences of variables such as social class, ordinal position, and parent-child relationships on the child's personality and behavior.

Research on Cognitive Development

There is now a vigorous rival for first rank in interest and appeal for research workers in child psychology. Research in cognition and cognitive development has burgeoned during the last decade. Late in 1957, the Russians successfully launched Sputnik, the first man-made satellite. Russia's apparent lead in technology alarmed the American public, which, like educators and psychologists, began to feel that American children were not receiving as thorough an education—particularly in mathematics and science—as their Russian peers. Shortly thereafter, public and governmental agencies began a long-overdue, intensive push to improve the educational and social status of the culturally deprived and disadvantaged.

These events, and the social pressures stemming from them, became major spurs to research in cognition. Educational practices had to be improved, which required a better understanding of the development of perception, learning, thinking, language ability, concept formation, techniques of problem-solving, and creativity. In addition, problems of the effects of early stimulation and deprivation on these cognitive processes assumed immense importance. As a result, research in cognitive development has gained tremendously in both quantity and quality in recent years. Compared with cognitive research of 20 years ago, contemporary investigations are much broader in scope, more rigorous, systematic, ingenious, and challenging. Moreover, new studies are closely linked with theories that are particularly (although not exclusively) Piaget's. The latest advances in understanding cognitive development are described in detail in this book, which, compared with earlier editions (first edition, 1956; second edition, 1963), places a much stronger emphasis on this aspect of development.

The current increased interest in the origins and early development of complex behavior has also generated new, comprehensive efforts to describe and understand the behavior and capabilities of infants and young babies. What responses can the infant make? What conditions elicit them? What kinds of stimulation engage his attention? What aspects of infant behavior are readily modified and under what conditions? Does early environmental stimulation have immediate and/or enduring effects on cognitive processes? Are behavior or temperamental characteristics of the infant stable and predictive of his later personality? These are, of course, not new problems—but recently they have received increased attention. Novel, ingenious methods of investigating these problems have been devised, and research has become much more rigorous and systematic. Our new knowledge is described in later chapters (see especially Chapters 5 and 6).

Some Contrasting Points of View

A young, active, vigorous, and dynamic scientific discipline must be tolerant of different points of view about many central issues. Among child psychologists—as among scientists in other fields—there are proponents of sharply divergent approaches to research and contrasting theoretical conceptions of the basic nature of the child and of the mechanisms of development and change. Here we will list only a sample of the important contrasting, and sometimes even diametrically opposite, points of view. Many other contrasting concepts will be delineated in other parts of this book; some of them have a long history, while others have become critical issues only recently.

Research Approaches. *Experimental* approaches may be contrasted with *correlational, nonexperimental* approaches. The latter typically involve investigating the relationships between variables—e.g., between early stimulation and rate of language acquisition, or between parental rejection and later emotional adjustment. As we learned earlier, experimental methods can demonstrate the relationship between antecedent-consequent variables most simply, clearly, and precisely. Thus some child psychologists prefer to limit their research to experiments in which the experimenter manipulates the relevant antecedent conditions.

But there are problems of profound interest to the child psychologist for which the experimental method is simply not appropriate or feasible. For example, suppose he is testing a hypothesis about the relationship between early deprivation of affection and later learning deficits. He could hardly expect parents to reject their children for purposes of his experiment. But the investigator might be able to study a group of children known to have been emotionally deprived and a control group of children who had received emotional support during infancy. He would attempt to control the effects of other possible relevant variables by equating the two groups as closely as possible in factors such as intelligence, age, sex, health, and socioeconomic status. It would then be possible to compare the learning deficits of the two groups and hence to determine whether there is in fact a relationship between early emotional deprivation and later learning difficulties. The study would not be an experiment in the usual sense because the experimenter did not manipulate the independent variable, emotional deprivation. However, the study would be as close to the ideal of an experiment as would be possible under the circumstances.

Longitudinal Approaches and Cross-Sectional Approaches. There are two contrasting broad approaches to the study of children, longitudinal and cross-sectional, each with its distinct advantages and disadvantages. In the *longitudinal approach* the same group of children is studied repeatedly over an extended period of time, often a decade or longer. This approach is especially valuable for investigations in which there is an attempt to discover whether characteristics such as intelligence, dependency, and behavior problems are stable over long periods of time or subject to fluctuations. The longitudinal approach must be used to study the latent or delayed influences of some early experience on later behavior. For example, current theory about personality development suggests that maternal rejection during the first few years of life will lead to disturbed interpersonal relations during childhood and adolescence. The only way to test the validity of this hypothesis is to select mothers who are rejecting during the early period and then to make follow-up studies of their children later on, assessing their subsequent social behavior. Obviously, the longitudinal method is expensive, time-consuming, and difficult to use.

In the second and more common method, the *cross-sectional*, the investigator selects a group of children at one age period, or different groups of children at different ages, and makes his observations at that time period. For example, the growth of reasoning ability can be studied with the cross-sectional method by selecting a group of ten children at each of six ages—2, 4, 6, 8, 10, and 12 years—and comparing the average performances of the six groups in reasoning tests.

On the other hand, an investigator might use the longitudinal method to answer the same question. He would measure the same group of 60 children at 2-year intervals from 2 to 12 years of age and assess the average biennial growth in reasoning ability.

A new method, the *short-term longitudinal* (also called accelerated longitudinal or convergence approach; 5, 6) combines some of the advantages of both longitudinal and cross-sectional methods. Groups of children of overlapping ages are tested periodically. Thus, one group might be tested annually at ages 5, 6, and 7, while another group would be tested at 7, 8, and 9. The two groups provide longitudinal data about performance at five ages, even though the study takes only three years. Moreover, different groups may be compared at the same ages. The method is particularly appropriate for studying transitions from one stage to the next in psychological functions such as reasoning (5, 6).

Contrasting Conceptions of the Nature of Development

Some theories view the child as active in relation to his environment; others see him as passive. Recall that in Locke's view, the child's behavior is molded by experience, that is, by the pressures exerted on him by others and by the environment. Rousseau, on the other hand, regarded the child's development as an active process, the child engaging his environment and developing happily and healthily if he is not interfered with.

In learning-theory and psychoanalytic explanations of behavior, environmental events are the main determinants of the child's behavior and responses. What becomes of him depends on what happens to him. In contrast, Piaget and other cognitive theorists believe that psychological development is essentially self-generating—activated by inherent, innate tendencies toward adaptation. Behavior changes are a product of the child's activity in the environment: his curiosity, searching, probing, and problem-solving. The world impinges on the child, but he perceives the environment in his own way and imposes structure and meaning on it. Stated very simply, the contrasting views regard development as happening to the individual versus development as happening in him.

Is there *continuity* or *discontinuity* in the course of behavioral development? Does the child's behavior progress continuously by gradual accretions, without sudden or sharp jumps or shifts? Or is the course of developmental progress step-like, segmented or divided into stages or levels with dramatic changes of behavior from one stage to the next, these stages following in orderly sequence or progression?

It is impossible on empirical grounds to choose between these alternative conceptions of the course of development. In some theoretical contexts, the notion of stages seems useful and appropriate; in others, it does not.

The term *stage*, used simply to describe observations, as is often done in everyday language, has no scientific or explanatory value. To say that the child is in the "3-year-old stage" is merely to say that he is 3 years old, or acts like a 3-year-old, whatever that vague expression means. The statement that a child refuses to obey his mother because he is in the "negative" stage doesn't really give us any information about what is happening or why.

The concept of stages, as it is used in developmental theory, is not a simple one. Stages are generally postulated when behavioral development appears to advance by means of striking and salutary changes in complex patterns of behavior. A stage is defined in terms of a complicated set of characteristics or segments of behavior that occur together and may therefore be conveniently grouped. A statement about stages of development, e.g., intellectual development, is "an abstracted and highly compressed description of a limited aspect of . . . behavior" (12, 68).

But more than description is involved. To be meaningful, the description

must have a theoretical basis; there must be some theoretical reason for collecting these segments of behavior together. The concept of stages implies
a sequence of development which suggests

the operation of organizing—i.e., theoretical–principles.

Being part of a sequence, the proposed stages of development help us to think
coherently about the course of development and at the same time suggest the
theoretical basis on which behavior is seen as segmented and developing (12, 68).

As we shall see in greater detail in later chapters, both psychoanalytic
theory and Piaget's theory of cognitive development make use of stage
descriptions. In each of these theoretical systems, the stages represent complex patterns of behavior that are parts of an orderly sequence of development, and the specific characteristics of each stage are fully described.

To illustrate, in psychoanalytic theory there is a fixed sequence of stages
of psychosexual development—beginning with the oral stage and progressing
through the anal and phallic stages. In the oral stage, the first year, the
child's chief interest and activity are centered around the biological function
of eating, which is the chief source of gratification at that time. The theory
postulates that the infant's feeding experiences at this stage—e.g., whether
they are relaxed and pleasant or the opposite—will have profound and
enduring effects on his later adjustment and personality, particularly on the
development of characteristics such as friendliness, optimism, and generosity.
Presumably as a result of biological maturation, the oral stage is superseded
first by the anal, and then by the phallic stage. Each of these stages encom-
passes a complicated set of interrelated personality characteristics.

Stages of development are also of central importance in Piaget's influential theory of cognitive development. On the basis of intensive systematic
observations of children in many kinds of thinking and problem-solving
tasks, Piaget and his collaborators conclude that "whereas somatic and perceptual development seem to be continuous, intellectual development seems
to take place in stages" (10, 23). For each stage, the child's capabilities and
his approach to cognitive problems are specified, particularized, and related
to the general theory. "Each stage involves a period of formation (genesis)
and a period of attainment" (10, 23) which is characterized by progressive
organization of cognitive abilities. The order of succession of stages from
early, relatively simple thinking to more mature and more complex abilities
is constant. Early transition from one step to the next, more advanced one
involves a process of integration, in which earlier cognitive abilities become
part of later organizations of cognitive activities (10, 23). The accomplishments of earlier stages are carried into later ones, but they are also integrated
with new elements that appear to arise spontaneously in later stages.

We have not delineated the intricacies of either psychoanalytic or
Piaget's theory here, but these brief statements make it clear that stage descriptions are of great importance in both theoretical systems. In both cases,

there are explicit statements about the behavior and characteristics to be accounted for, and the relationship between the stages and the overall developmental theory.

What both theories need—and unfortunately, what both lack—is an explicit set of rules of transition: statements about the mechanisms by which the child progresses from one stage to the next. It is perhaps ironic that learning theorists, who do not generally make use of stage concepts, seem to be more concerned than stage theorists with the *processes* and *conditions* of change—that is, with specifying the factors related to behavioral change.

Absolute Versus Relativistic Views
of Children's Behavior and Development

Developmental psychologists (again, like other scientists) are apt to generalize about their findings when they discover relationships between variables—e.g., between certain stimuli, such as maternal overprotection, and behavioral responses, such as submissiveness. They are likely to make general interpretative and explanatory statements, often phrasing them in terms that seem to have absolute, fixed, and permanent meaning. But, because behavior and development are governed by such a multiplicity of complex variables, facts and generalizations must often be regarded as *relative*—that is, true and applicable only within certain situational contexts. This point will be illustrated by a few examples of generalizations that need to be modified in the light of the characteristics of the subjects and the specific context in which the stimuli and responses occur.

Evidence from experimental studies indicates that frustration of young children produces increments in aggressive and regressive responses in play. In one investigation, two groups of nursery school children were observed in free-play. Then one group, the experimental one, was frustrated by being forced to work on difficult and tedious tasks for awhile. The other (control) group experienced no such frustration. After a short period, both groups returned to the free-play situation, where they were observed. In this session, the frustrated group manifested significantly more aggressive responses than did the other group. In another experiment, children's play regressed and became less mature following the frustrating experience of playing with intriguing, highly desirable toys and then being deprived of them. From these findings, investigators made the generalization that frustration is likely to lead to aggression or regression.

Certainly the generalization seems applicable in many situations. For example, clinical data demonstrate that children who are severely punished and rejected (i.e., frustrated) react toward their parents with hostility. And, children frustrated by classroom restrictions are likely to manifest a great deal of aggression toward their classmates.

But the concept of frustration must be a relative one; it cannot be judged on the basis of external stimuli alone. To know whether an event is frustrating to an individual we have to know something about his perceptions and expectancies. What one child regards as tedious may not be dull to another; toys that are stimulating and exciting to one subject may be very ordinary and routine to another.

Consider these facts, too. Lower-class Negro mothers frequently slap their young children for misbehaviors that seem very minor to middle-class observers, although there is little reason to believe that these mothers do not love their children. In fact, they may sincerely believe that physical punishment is the most effective way to teach the child appropriate behavior. The lower-class Negro mother, then, may punish her child because she loves him, not because she rejects him.

> Determination of whether a parent is rejecting or not cannot be answered by focussing primarily on the behaviors of the parents. Rejection is not a fixed, invariant quality of behavior *qua* behavior. Like pleasure, pain, or beauty, rejection is in the mind of the rejectee. It is a belief held by the child; not an action by the parent (*11*, 132).

The child's reactions to frustration will clearly depend also on the nature of the situation in which he is frustrated. In the experiments cited, the children were in a highly permissive situation and were entirely free to express aggression. But even highly frustrated children are not likely to behave aggressively in situations in which such behavior is clearly inappropriate or likely to be punished—as, for example, in a classroom with a strict teacher.

In addition, nonpsychological aspects of the social setting may exert very powerful influences on individual or group behavior. Such influences have been explored most systematically by Barker, Wright, and their colleagues in a series of important studies which showed that, to a very large extent, children's natural habitats ("behavior settings") regulate their behavior. For example, regardless of their personal motives, children generally behave in ways appropriate to the settings in which they find themselves— school, church, or drugstore.

> Evidence regarding the profound motivational influence of the nonpsychological environment is at hand in the high conformity of behavior at weddings, on highways, in schools, offices, churches, and factories where there is a great diversity of personal motivation, yet behavioral uniformity. It seems that one can hardly avoid even with the strongest intentions, doing as the Romans do when one is in Rome (*4*, 5).

Another good example of the impact of nonpsychological (e.g., economic and sociological) variables on behavior comes from a recent cross-cultural study of child-rearing practices and their effects. Such studies demonstrate, not surprisingly, that the parents' (particularly the mother's) child-rearing practices are highly influential in determining the course of the child's personality development. It has generally been assumed that socialization practices are guided by the culture's notions of what is beneficial for children's long-range development and/or by parental motives and personality characteristics.

But this may not be the case at all. In fact, the authors of an excellent, well-planned, cross-cultural study concluded:

> It now appears that the pressures impinging upon the growing child are much more in the nature of by-products of the horde of apparently irrelevant considerations that impinge upon the parents. These considerations of household composition, size of family, work load, etc., determine the time and energy that mothers have available to care for children. They determine the range and content of mother-child relations and the context in which these relations must take place (18, 291).

The amount of time a mother spends with her child, for example, is in large measure a function of how much help is available from other women in the community. If there are no others to help, the mother spends less time with her infant. The degree of warmth expressed by mothers is related to privacy in living arrangements. Those in close, crowded quarters have to control emotional expressiveness to prevent quarrels between their children and among others in the household. Similarly, maternal punishment of the child's aggressive behavior depends less on the mother's philosophy about aggression than it does on how many people share the living quarters. In cultures in which living space is cramped, peace must be maintained by punishing, and thus reducing, overt aggression. In short, each mother must deal with these problems of the situation, and "the message that each passes to her children is more a function of these problems than of the theory of child rearing" (18, 291).

Clearly, then, generalizations about psychological development and about the relationships between psychological variables are not permanent, fixed, or absolute. Particularly when applied as explanations of an individual's behavior or behavior in a specific situation, such statements must be regarded as relative—their applicability depending on the individual's perception or interpretation of the situation on the one hand, and the situation itself on the other.

SUMMARY

This book is designed to present a contemporary view of child psychology, emphasizing major theories, concepts, and research findings. In his studies, the developmental psychologist, concerned with the origins and development of basic psychological processes, draws upon and contributes to progress in fields such as perception, learning, personality, and social psychology. The contributions of developmental psychology are practical as well as theoretical. For example, certain aspects of adult behavior can be understood only in terms of the principles of development, and many developmental data are of practical utility in the diagnosis and treatment of psychological problems.

In Western culture, until approximately three hundred years ago, childhood was not regarded as a distinct phase of the life cycle. Not until the seventeenth century did attitudes toward children and their morals begin to change and the child became a "special" person. Philosophers such as Locke and Rousseau began to expound their ideas about the nature and education of children, and their writings significantly influenced subsequent theory and practice in education.

In the eighteenth century, children became subjects for study, particularly for intensive observations, recorded in "baby biographies" by philosophers, educators, and biologists. Darwin's writings, published in the middle of the nineteenth century, marked the beginnings of the science of child behavior. Systematic study of *groups* of children was initiated by G. Stanley Hall at the end of the last century.

Scientific study of children has advanced enormously in the twentieth century. Theories have been proposed; new, basic research problems have been delineated (and reformulated), and research methods have been devised, improved and refined. The psychological theories that have had the greatest impact on present-day child study are learning theory, psychoanalysis, and cognitive theory—particularly the theories of Piaget, the brilliant Swiss psychologist. The major methods of investigation include naturalistic and controlled observation, experimentation, and longitudinal and cross-sectional study.

In recent years there has been increased emphasis on the processes and mechanisms underlying developmental changes, rather than simple descriptions of age changes. Findings from studies of psychological development must be regarded as *relative*—true and applicable within certain situational contexts—not as permanent, fixed, or absolute.

References

1. Aries, P. *Centuries of childhood.* New York: Knopf, 1962.
2. Barker, R. G., & Wright, H. F. *One boy's day: a specimen record of behavior.* New York: Harper & Row, 1951.
3. Barker, R. G., & Wright, H. F. *Midwest and its children.* New York: Harper & Row, 1955.
4. Barker, R. G. Ecology and motivation. In M. R. Jones (Ed.), *Nebraska symposium on motivation, 1960,* Lincoln: Univer. of Nebraska Press, 1960, 1–50.
5. Bell, R. Q. Convergence: an accelerated longitudinal approach. *Child Develpm.,* 1953, 24, 145–152.
6. Bell, R. Q. An experimental test of the accelerated longitudinal approach. *Child Develpm.,* 1954, 25, 281–286.
7. Darwin, C. A. A biographical sketch of an infant. *Mind,* 1877, 2, 285–294.
8. Dollard, J., & Miller, N. *Personality and psychotherapy.* New York: McGraw-Hill, 1950.

9. Hall, G. S. The contents of children's minds on entering school. *Ped. Sem.*, 1891, *1*, 139–173.

10. Inhelder, B. Some aspects of Piaget's genetic approach to cognition. In W. Kessen & C. Kuhlman (Eds.), Thought in the young child. *Monogr. Soc. Res. Child Develpm.*, 1962, 27, No. 2, 19–40.

11. Kagan, J. On the need for relativism. *Amer. Psychologist.* 1967, *22*, No. 2, 131–141.

12. Kessen, W. Stage and structure in the study of children. In W. Kessen & C. Kuhlman (Eds.), Thought in the young child, *Monogr. Soc. Res. Child Develpm.*, 1962, *27*, No. 2, 65–86.

13. Kessen, W. *The child.* New York: Wiley, 1965.

14. Kranzberg, M. The disunity of science-technology. *Amer. Scientist,* 1968, *56*, No. 1.

15. Lederberg, J. Some problems of instant medicine. *Saturday Review,* May 6, 1967, 66–70.

16. Locke, J. *Some thoughts concerning education; 1690.* Sections 38 and 40. London: Cambridge Univer. Press, 1913.

17. Locke, J. Rewards, reputation, and curiosity. Reprinted in W. Kessen, *The child.* New York: Wiley, 1965.

18. Minturn, L., & Lambert, W. *Mothers of six cultures.* New York: Wiley, 1964.

19. Pestalozzi, J. A father's diary, 1774. Cited by R. De Guimps, *Pestalozzi, his life and work.* New York: Appleton-Century-Crofts, 1906.

20. Piaget, J. *The origins of intelligence in children.* New York: International Universities Press, 1952.

21. Piaget, J. *Logic and psychology.* New York: Basic Books, 1957.

22. Reichenbach, H. *The rise of scientific philosophy.* Berkeley: Univer. of California Press, 1951.

23. Riesen, A. H. Arrested vision. *Scientific Amer.,* 1950, *183*, 16–19.

24. Rousseau, J. J. *Emile, or concerning education.* 1762. Book 2. New York: Dutton, 1938.

25. Tiedemann, D. *Beobachtungen ueber die Entwickelung der Seelenfahrigkeiten bei Kindern.* Altenburg: Bonde, 1787.

26. Waterman, A. T. The changing environment of science. *Science,* 1965, *147*, 16.

27. Werner, H. *Comparative psychology of mental development.* Chicago: Follet, 1948 (rev. ed.).

part I
The Prenatal Period

2

Genetic Factors in Development

In our attempt to understand the behavior of the developing child, many factors must be considered. The simplest behavior is often the result of many different influences. Basically, these influences fall into five major categories: (1) genetically determined biological variables; (2) nongenetic biological variables (e.g., lack of oxygen during the birth process; malfunctioning of the pituitary gland); (3) the child's past learning; (4) his immediate social psychological environment (i.e., his parents, siblings, peers, and teachers); and (5) the general social and cultural milieu in which he develops.

The first two influences have been called the *nature* forces; the latter three, the *nurture* or environmental forces. The child's behavior and personality are, at any one time, a product of the continuing interaction of nature and nurture.

Although we normally speak of biological (nature) determinants as separate from environmental determinants, it is important to appreciate that one cannot easily evaluate *how much* each force contributes to a particular psychological event. Both sets of forces interact continually to produce a given effect. Consider the analogy of a snowfall. Cold temperature and a high proportion of moisture in the air are both required to produce snow and it is not possible to say that the cold temperature was 60 percent responsible and the moisture 40 percent responsible for the snowflakes. Although we speak of genetic and environmental determinants of behavior, we always acknowledge that they act in unison; this is as true of the individual cell as it is of the whole person. The chemical action of the genetic material in a particular cell is a function of the material outside the nucleus as well as the chromosomes themselves. Indeed, the effect of a single gene will depend on the specific collection of other genes in that cell. Scientists try to discover the specific genetic and environmental forces that are controlling a specific behavior; scientists do not ask which influence is more important, just as they would not ask about the relative importance of moisture or cold in the snowfall analogy. This realization of the intimate interaction of genes and environment is relatively recent. Scientists of this century, as well as those of the past, have debated the nature-nurture issue, as the following two statements reveal.

> Heredity and not environment is the chief maker of man. . . . Nearly all the misery and nearly all the happiness in the world are due not to environment. . . . The differences among men are due to differences in the germ cells with which they were born (1, 102–103).

Compare this statement with the following:

> Give me a dozen healthy infants, well formed, and my own specified world to bring them up in and I'll guarantee to take any one at random and train him to become any type of specialist I might select—doctor, lawyer, merchant, chief, and yes, even beggar-man and thief, regardless of his talents, peculiarities, tendencies, abilities, vocations, and race of his ancestors. There is no such thing as an inheritance of capacity, talent, temperament, mental constitution, and characteristics (1, 103).

The advances in biology and psychology make both statements naive and lead us to search for the way the combined action of our inherited potentialities and the events we experience make us the way we are.

The science of genetics has experienced dramatic advances during the last 25 years and we are beginning to accumulate a great deal of information about the influence of heredity on mental retardation, and on aspects of seriously abnormal behavior. This chapter will deal with our knowledge of genetic functions and genetic factors; the next chapter with nonhereditary, biological factors that operate during pregnancy and delivery.

BEGINNINGS OF LIFE

The life of each individual begins when a sperm cell from the father penetrates the wall of an ovum, or egg, from the mother. As we shall see in some detail in Chapter 3, the fertilization of an ovum by a sperm sets in motion an intricate process called mitosis. In this process, the original fertilized ovum divides and subdivides until thousands of cells have been produced. Gradually, as the process continues, the resulting cells begin to assume special functions, as parts of the nervous, skeletal, muscular, or circulatory systems. The embryo, which at first resembles a gradually expanding ball, begins to take shape, and the beginnings of head, eyes,

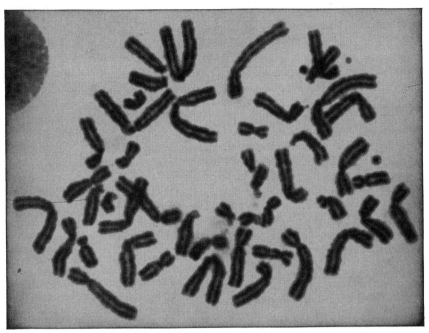

Fig. 2.1. Metaphase spread from normal male cell showing the human chromosomes. (Courtesy of Dr. P. S. Moorhead.)

trunk, arms, and legs appear. Approximately 9 months after fertilization, the fetus is ready for birth.

HEREDITARY TRANSMISSION

Life begins at conception. But what of the forces that, throughout the individual's existence, will influence his development? When do they begin? The answer, again, is at conception. For at the moment that the tiny tadpolelike sperm penetrates the wall of the ovum, it releases 23 minute particles called *chromosomes*. At approximately the same time, the nucleus, the inner core of the ovum, breaks up, releasing 23 chromosomes of its own.

This process is of great interest to us because it has been established through painstaking research, that these chromosomes, which are further subdivided into even smaller particles called *genes*, are the carriers of the child's heredity. All the child's physical heritage from his father and his mother is contained in these 46 chromosomes (see Fig. 2.1).

What Is Transmitted?

Long before the geneticists established the existence of chromosomes and genes, scientists were convinced that many characteristics of a child's parents were transmitted to the child at conception. People have, however, differed about what was transmitted and how. For example, one school of thought, dating back to Lamarck, a French zoologist who published a book called *Philosophie zooligique* in 1773, long maintained a doctrine that preached the inheritance of acquired characteristics. Lamarck felt that individuals improved or weakened their own physical capacities through experience or training, and that the effects of such changes could be transmitted to their offspring. Thus, by developing a diseased lung or poor digestion, a prospective parent would be hurting his child's chances of being healthy. People began to postulate such notions as that the giraffe acquired his long neck because his ancestors had spent a great deal of time reaching into trees for food, or that the snake lost his legs as a result of his forebears' propensity for creeping through crevices (*40*).

Nor were such speculations confined only to obvious physical characteristics. Many people believed that a mother could influence her child's chances of being born with a talent for singing, if she had, in her youth, carefully cultivated her own voice, or that if a father had previously developed an interest in mathematics, this interest was likely to be inherited by his son.

However, such early theories as these, and the inferences based upon them, were dealt a hard blow by Weismann in 1889 (*60*). He presented evidence suggesting that while the rest of the body may change with increasing age or through exercise, illness, or injury, the germ cells (chromosomes and genes) which an individual harbors, and which are passed on to his children at their conception, do not ordinarily change.

In the main, subsequent research has tended to support Weismann's position. However, it has since been determined that under exceptional circumstances, genes may change or be inactivated, as for example, through direct radiation from X ray or from atomic blasts. Nevertheless, genes are not subject to any of the usual influences that either build up or break down our bodies or improve our minds. Thus the genes that a sick but well-educated man of 50 possesses are no different from those that he possessed as a healthy but untutored youth of 17. In short, changes in the rest of the body do not affect the genetic characteristics of the germ cells which are passed on to our children. Hence there is no reason for believing that we can affect our children's genetic constitutions by engaging in physical education or self-improvement campaigns.

What Is a Gene? Until recently the existence of a gene was hypothetical. It was assumed to be a complex chemical the actions of which controlled the development of organs and physiological processes. In 1953, Doctors Watson and Crick suggested a possible structure for the gene and this suggested structure helped us to understand a lot about heredity (*58*). A gene is composed of a chemical called deoxyribonucleic acid or DNA for short. DNA is the molecule of heredity; it contains the genetic code that determines what is transmitted from one generation to the next. A gene is a segment of DNA, and chromosomes are structures in which

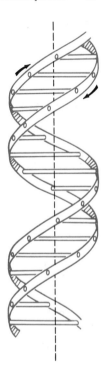

Fig. 2.2. Model of the DNA molecule proposed by Watson and Crick. (From J. D. Watson & F. H. C. Crick, *Nature*, 1953, Vol. 171. By permission.)

the genes are arranged in a linear order together with protein and other chemicals. There are about 1,000,000 genes in a human cell or, on the average, about 20,000 genes per chromosome. The molecule of DNA itself consists of two chains coiled around each other in the shape of a double helix with pairs of structures connecting the chains like steps in a ladder. The best way to imagine what a molecule of DNA is like is to think of a long rubber ladder twisted around its long axis. Each lengthwise strip comprising the vertical sides of the ladder is made up of molecules of sugar and phosphate. Each cross step in the ladder represents a pair of chemicals that are called bases. The bases are paired in a special way so that the base called *adenine* always appears with the base called *thymine,* and the base *guanine* always appears with the base *cytosine* (see Fig. 2.2).

This structure helps us to understand the fundamentals of cell division and heredity transmission. It is necessary that the chromosomes duplicate themselves in the growth of new cells. This ladderlike structure permits the duplication, for the molecule of DNA can unzip itself, split apart, and produce a complement or duplication of itself.

The Mechanisms of Hereditary Transmission

One of the things that must have puzzled parents in prescientific days was why two children of the same parents should be so different physically. The answer lies in the mechanics of hereditary transmission.

1. Original cell (only four chromosomes shown, for simplification).

2. Each chromosome splits in half, lengthwise.

3. The halved chromosomes go to opposite sides and wall forms between them as cell begins to divide.

4. The halved chromosomes grow to full size, resulting in two cells, each a replica of the original.

Fig. 2.3. How a fertilized egg cell multiplies. (From *The New You and Heredity*, by Amram Scheinfeld. Copyright 1950 by Amram Scheinfeld. Published by J. B. Lippincott Company. Also reprinted by permission of Paul R. Reynolds, Inc.)

If each child received all of both parents' genes, we could not explain individual genetic differences between siblings, as all brothers and sisters would then have identical heredities. The fact, however, is that each child inherits only half of each parent's genes. Moreover, different children in a family inherit different combinations of their mother's and father's genes. Thus individual differences between them become not only possible but also necessary.

The way in which this happens will become clear as we proceed. It will be recalled that the original fertilized ovum contains 46 chromosomes. As this cell divides to form two new cells, each of its 46 chromosomes first doubles, then each doubled chromosome divides in half by separating lengthwise down its center (see Fig. 2.3). Through a process known as mitosis, the chromosomes then go to opposite sides of the cell. Thus, when the cell itself divides down the center, the new cells will each contain 46 chromosomes, as did the original cell.

This process is repeated again and again as development proceeds. Even in the completed human being, when the myriad cells of the body have by this time taken on their special functions as tissue, bone, blood, and muscle, each cell still contains a replica of the original 46 chromosomes of the fertilized ovum.

Germ Cells

But if this is true, why don't the sperm and ovum which go to make up a new individual also contain 46 chromosomes each, since certainly they too are cells? It will be recalled that the new individual receives only 23 chromosomes from each parent.

The answer, stripped of genetic complexities, is actually simple. The adult organism contains not one, but two kinds of cells—body cells which go to make up bone, nerves, muscles, and organs; and germ cells, from which the sperm and ova are derived. While the process of chromosome and cell division described above applies to the somatoplasm (the body cells), it does not apply completely to the germ cells. Throughout most of their history, the latter develop just as the body cells do. But at the time of their final division into recognizable sperm or ova, the pattern changes. At this point, the germ cells split, but the chromosomes do not. Instead, the 46 chromosomes, which in reality are 23 pairs of similar chromosomes— one pair-member from each parent—simply divide into two groups. One member of each pair goes to one of the resulting sperm or egg cells, and one to the other (see Fig. 2.4). Thus the ova and sperm have only 23 chromosomes each and the new individual obtains a total of only 46.

We can see, too, why it is that the children of the same parents do not all have to be alike. As may be seen from Fig. 2.5, if Sperm A unites with Ovum D, the new individual will possess a different set of chromosomes than if Sperm B unites with it. (Ovum C is indicated in dotted lines because ordinarily at any one conception only one ovum from the mother is ready for fertilization. The same, of course, is not true of sperm. At any one mating millions of sperm are released—as many as a hundred million in one drop of seminal fluid, any one of which might potentially fertilize the receptive ovum.)

Is Identity Possible?

We have seen how it is possible for individuals in the same family to be different in their genetic make-ups. But is identity between siblings possible? The answer is *no*—except in the case of identical twins who develop from the same fertilized ovum which only later splits into two individuals.[1] If the 46 chromosomes in the germ cells always divided the same way, with one combination going to one sperm or ovum and the rest to the other, identity would be possible. In fact, it could be anticipated frequently. But these 46 chromosomes do not divide in this way. Except that one member of each of the 23 pairs goes to one sperm or ovum and the other member

[1] For an interesting and simple discussion of the way in which identical and fraternal twins are produced, the reader is referred to Scheinfeld (49). Somewhat more technical discussions will be found in general texts by Stern (52) and Gates (16).

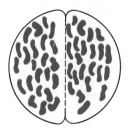

1. Germ cell containing 46 chromosomes

2. The paired chromosomes separate, going to opposite sides of the cell, and the cell divides.

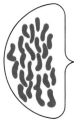 

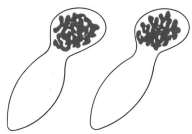

3. There are now two half-cells, with only 23 single chromosomes in each.

4. The chromosomes mass together, and part of the cell contents forms a sheath around them.

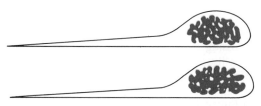

5. The sheath shapes the chromosomes into a tightly packed mass forming the head. The rest of the cell contents is squeezed out behind to form the tail.

Fig. 2.4. How sperms are produced. (From *The New You and Heredity*, by Amram Scheinfeld. Copyright 1950 by Amram Scheinfeld. Published by J. B. Lippincott Company. Also reprinted by permission of Paul R. Reynolds, Inc.)

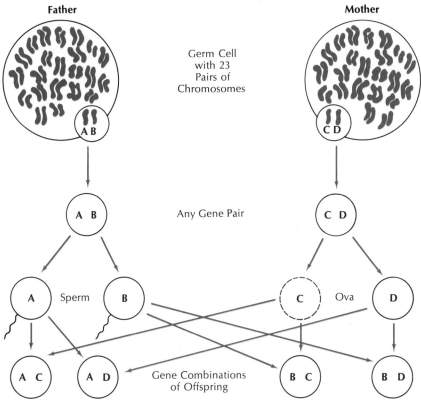

Fig. 2.5. Schematic diagram showing possible gene combinations of offspring resulting from gene pairs of parents.

to the other, the pattern is pretty much random. In other words, the way one pair of chromosomes separates does not influence the way another pair will split.

Moreover, in the formation of the germ cells (the sperm or ova) there is a process called crossing over which further increases the likelihood that each sperm or ovum will be unique and, therefore, that each individual will be unique. When the 23 pairs of chromosomes line up in pairs during the first phases of germ-cell formation (called meiosis), they exchange genetic material as if human beings facing each other might exchange parts of their fingers. One part of one member of the pair exchanges some DNA with the other.

If crossing over did not occur, the total number of different combinations of sperm and ovum is estimated at 64,000,000,000,000 different kinds of children—many times the total number of people on the earth today. But *with* crossing over, the number of possible different offspring is many, many times that number. Thus, except for identical twins, each human being is genetically unique and biologically different from every other person on earth. Let us reflect a minute on what this means for the science of psychology. The physicist or chemist, who is concerned with nonliving things, usually does not work with or theorize about unique substances. A chemist assumes that every molecule of oxygen or silver is exactly like every other molecule. A physicist assumes that every electron is exactly like every other electron. But the biologist and psychologist can not assume that every monkey, rat, or child is exactly like every other one. More seriously, he cannot assume that a nerve cell in one child's brain is exactly like a nerve cell in his brother's brain, for the genetic make-up of the two cells is different. Thus the psychologist is faced with dramatically more variability of the basic forms he is trying to understand. This is one reason why psychology is much less mature as a science than chemistry or physics, and why prediction and understanding of behavior is much more difficult.

Sex Determination

Of the 23 pairs of chromosomes, one pair is called the sex chromosomes and is responsible for determining the sex of the child. In the normal female, both members of this pair are large in size and are called the X chromosomes. In the normal male, one member of the pair is an X chromosome; the second member is smaller in size and is called the Y chromosome. Thus, the body cells of males (except for sperm cells) contain one X and one Y chromosome. One-half of the sperm cells of the male contain an X chromosome; the remaining half contain a Y chromosome. When a female ovum, containing an X chromosome, unites, in conception, with a sperm containing a Y chromosome, a male child is produced. When an ovum unites with a sperm carrying an X chromosome, a female child develops. Since one-half of the sperm cells contain X and one-half Y chromosomes, theoretically the odds are 50–50 that a boy or girl will be conceived. There is actually a slight excess of male over female births (106 boys to 100 girls among whites in the United States) and this may mean that Y sperm are more likely than X sperm to penetrate the ovum (52).

The Mendelian Laws

The elementary principles of gene interaction were first worked out by an Austrian monk, Gregor Mendel, in the privacy of his monastery garden in 1857. Mendel worked with two strains of peas, red-flowering and white-flowering. He found that if he mated plants of a pure red strain with plants of a pure white strain, in the second generation all the offspring would be red. But if he then mated these offspring with each other, the third generation would average three red-flowering peas to one white.

Experiments such as this led Mendel to derive a number of general principles about hereditary transmission, often referred to as the "Mendelian laws."

These are as follows: (1) The units of heredity have remarkable constancy. These units are now known to be the genes, and they are passed from generation to generation and remain unchanged unless altered by mutation. (2) In each individual the genes are found in pairs. When the two genes in a pair are different in their effects, one gene frequently *dominates* over the other so that it might be referred to as "dominant," and the other as "recessive." (In the above example of the two strains of peas, red genes dominate over white, so that when both are present in a gene pair, the pea flower will be red.) Thus the expression of a gene in the color of a flower or hair, or the shape of an organ is complex. (3) When seeds are formed in any individual, the members of each pair of genes *segregate out*, independently of the other pairs, with just one of every two mated genes going from each parent to each offspring (49).

This last principle suggests that the transmission of genes on different chromosomes acts like a biological coin-tossing machine. Imagine a coin-tossing machine in which each coin represents a pair of genes—one gene on each face of the coin and the machine is unbiased. Then imagine 500,000 coins being thrown each time. One toss of 500,000 coins represents a father's contribution and another toss of 500,000 coins represents the mother's contribution. The unique combination of heads and tails from this combined toss of 1,000,000 coins will determine the genetic make-up of the child.

Mendel's results were largely ignored during his own day. It was not until 1900, sixteen years after the brilliant monk's death, that his work, first published in 1865, was rediscovered, and serious attack on the problems of genetic transmission begun. Subsequent work by many geneticists (25, 41, 49, 53) tended to confirm and vindicate Mendel's theories. Their work also demonstrated, however, that the mechanisms of heredity were often a good deal more complex than they had originally appeared.

For example, they showed that genetic prediction is often complicated by the fact that many characteristics depend on complex combinations of gene pairs, rather than on a single pair. In addition, they found that genes do not simply behave dominantly or recessively but in numerous other ways also, and that their effects may vary under different conditions. A discussion of these complexities is not necessary for our purposes. It is enough to say that it would be much easier to weigh the relative importance of hereditary and other factors in determining human characteristics if all these characteristics were as simple in their hereditary aspects as blossom color and other characteristics studied by Mendel in the pea plant. Some, such as eye color, hereditary baldness in men, some forms of diabetes, and certain kinds of night blindness, are almost as simple; but most are not. Eye color, for example, is determined primarily by a combination of one gene from each parent. Certain types of mental deficiency, on the other hand, seem to depend on a number of pairs of genes being present in a particular combination.

DETERMINING THE EXTENT
OF GENETIC INFLUENCES

Although, as we shall see, there is no doubt that many human characteristics are strongly influenced by heredity, it is difficult to determine the nature of this influence. By and large, we cannot directly observe the tiny genes in action. Instead, we are forced to infer their presence from their effects, just as Mendel inferred the presence of red-flowering and white-flowering genes from the colors of the blossoms which were produced.

Moreover, some genetic effects are not seen until late adulthood. Consider the case of a degenerative disease of the nervous system, Huntington's chorea. This disorder, caused by a dominant gene, strikes in generation after generation of the same family and its frequency can be predicted by genetic principles. But it usually does not affect the person until he is 35 years old.

In most cases, however, the situation is less clear. Some newborn babies are more active than others, and these variations may be caused by genetic factors. (For purposes of this illustration, let us ignore the possibility that prenatal influences also play a part.) However, it has also been found that when people are anxious and under psychological stress, they can become active and restless. Certain drugs have the same effect. Thus it is extremely difficult to sort out the separate contribution of drugs, genetic factors, or psychological influences on the activity level of babies.

Actually, as we must infer the importance of both genetic and environmental factors from their effects on the individual, the only sure way of determining whether either set of factors plays an important role in a specific condition is to find some way of holding one constant while varying the other. If the condition then also varies, we know that the factor we have varied plays an important role.

For example, in a number of studies, identical twins have been used to control as much as possible for genetic factors. As they have identical hereditary background, any differences between them may be attributed to environmental influences, e.g., different experiences. Newman, Freeman, and Holzinger (42) have used this method to study the effects upon personality of rearing children (of the same genetic make-up) in different home environments. Some of this work will be discussed shortly.

In other studies, particularly those with animals (in which by controlled mating it is possible to experiment on genetic factors), the physical and psychological environments are held as constant as possible, and the effects of varying heredity are noted (44). In cases where we are unable to hold most of the factors constant, we can only make, at best, intelligent guesses concerning the relative importance of genetic or environmental influences.

PUTTING GENETIC DETERMINANTS INTO PERSPECTIVE

The general question of genetic influence must be asked with respect to specific characteristics. Is it eye color, baldness, intelligence? The relative influences of heredity and environment differ markedly from one characteristic to another.

We must also ask under what conditions the characteristic is being

manifested. This is particularly important in the case of behavioral characteristics. Take, for example, the task of determining the hereditary and
environmental antecedents of diabetes. If a thin diabetic woman tells us
that she never eats candy, while an obese diabetic woman reports eating
a pound of chocolates every day, we would suspect hereditary factors as
more likely in the former than in the latter case.

Or take another example, closer to the concerns of this book. Suppose
that a child fails a reading-readiness test of the type given children prior
to admission to the first grade in school. If the child is suffering from cerebral sclerosis, a form of mental deficiency which is dependent on the coex-
istence of two specific recessive genes, heredity could reasonably be called
an important contributor to his failure. No amount of superior medical care,
and no amount of training by his mother or teacher could overcome the
disabling effects of the disease. On the other hand, if the child shows no
evidence of specific biological deficiency, but has lived an isolated mountain
life with illiterate parents, and later with proper training passes the test,
environment would seem to be the sole determinant of his original failure.

The specific effect of the interaction of hereditary and environmental
forces will differ for different behaviors and different structural characteristics. Moreover, the important question is not *what* behaviors are influenced
by heredity, but *how* the genes are able to exert this influence.

> The traditional questions about heredity and environment may be intrinsically
> unanswerable. Psychologists keep asking *which* type of factor, heredity or en-
> vironment, is responsible for individual differences in a given trait. Later, they
> tried to discover *how much* of the variance was attributable to heredity and how
> much to environment. . . . A more fruitful approach is to be found in the ques-
> tion, "How?" (2, 197).

That is, it is not sufficient to know that a small body frame or high
intelligence are inherited; we must determine the many complicated biological processes that are triggered into action as a result of possessing the
genes associated with body size. Do genes affect growth through influencing
hormonal action, through direct action on bone or muscle, or through a
combination of these actions? When we have the answers to specific questions such as these, we will have a more complete understanding of what
it means to say that a trait is inherited. Unfortunately, there are not many
clues to help us in understanding the ways in which a gene or combination
of genes produces specific behaviors.

One inherited basis for mental retardation provides a good example of
the kind of knowledge that is needed. Many of the foods we eat contain a
chemical called phenylalanine. Most people possess an enzyme that converts
phenylalanine to a harmless by-product. However, a small group of children
have a specific hereditary defect in that they do not possess the enzyme
that converts the phenylalanine; they lack a gene that produces this critical
enzyme. As a result, the concentration of phenylalanine rises above that
which is normal and becomes converted to phenylpyruvic acid. The nerve

cells of the central nervous system become damaged and mental retardation results. This disease is called phenylketonuria, or PKU for short. Once scientists learned the nature of the specific metabolic disorder in PKU, they began to think about ways of helping these children. They invented a diet that contained very low levels of phenylalanine, yet maintained the children's health. As a result, the toxic acid did not accumulate and the children's mental development was almost normal, and certainly far superior to what it would have been had they not taken the special diet. Knowledge of the exact biological mechanism that mediates a genetic defect can occasionally lead to effective cures.

Unfortunately, we do not have many other examples like PKU. In most instances, the specific influence of hereditary factors is unknown and very *indirect*. That is, no motive, behavior, or emotion is ever inherited as such. The inheritance of a physical deformity may eventually lead to feelings of inferiority, but it would be nonsense to say that such feelings are inherited. In actuality, the basic characteristics which we know to be inherited are the ability to produce enzymes and proteins (which help form the structure of cells, tissues, and organs), and the ability to produce products which regulate the amounts of each of these materials which are synthesized by cells under a variety of different conditions. All of these phenomena influence psychological variables in many subtle ways.

To cite a few simple examples, genetic forces determine whether an individual is a man or a woman; they help to determine whether he is tall or short, fat or thin, handsome or ugly, sluggish or high-strung. They may influence his resistance to various diseases, and set limits beyond which his intelligence cannot develop.

Because heredity acts directly only upon the individual's biological characteristics, it cannot itself produce a child's jealousy of its mother or an enthusiasm for space guns and rocket ships. These attributes, necessarily depending in part upon learning through interaction with particular objects in the environment, cannot be entirely and simply determined by heredity. Heredity may play a role, however, since it helps to produce the kind of individual who is doing the learning. For example, it may help to influence whether an individual becomes a heavyweight boxer or a jockey, through its influence on the biological mechanisms determining the person's height and weight.

RESULTS OF HUMAN GENETIC RESEARCH

As a result of the difficulties inherent in much genetic research with humans, there are large gaps in our knowledge of the role of heredity in human development. Nevertheless, progress is being made. A brief summary of the findings from some of the more pertinent studies in this area will be presented here.

Some of this research has employed the so-called twin-study method. In this type of approach, an attempt is made to control environmental influences, thus making it possible to note whether genetic factors alone will produce variations in the phenomenon under study. In the case of intelligence, for example, the performances of identical twins on intelligence tests may be compared with those of fraternal (nonidentical) twins. The working assumption is that the environments of fraternal twins are as similar as those of identical twins. In this way, the possible effects of environmental factors on IQ are considered to be controlled. Consequently, if identical twins are found to resemble each other more closely in IQ than fraternal twins, it is concluded that genetic factors affect intelligence. The greater similarity in the IQ scores of the identical twins is considered to be due to the fact that these twins have exactly the same heredity, whereas fraternal twins do not.

However, a word of caution about such reasoning is necessary. It should be readily evident to the reader that the environmental influences to which two children are exposed do differ, even though they are both raised in the same family. Furthermore, it appears that these environmental influences may differ, at least in some respects, more for fraternal twins or other siblings than for identical twins.

> Several studies have shown that identical twins spend more time together, enjoy more similar reputations, are more likely to be in the same classrooms, have more similar health records, and in many other respects share a more common physical and social environment than that ordinarily experienced by fraternal twins (27).

Thus the assumption in twin studies like the one described above, that the possible effects of environment have been adequately controlled for, may not always be justified. In a few studies, an attempt has been made to avoid this problem by comparing identical twins reared apart with fraternal twins or other siblings reared together. If, in this instance, identical twins still resemble each other more closely than fraternal twins or other siblings, it may be concluded that genetic factors are playing a role. It would be highly improbable in such a case that the environments of the identical twins would be more similar than those of the fraternal twins; hence environmental similarity could not account for the closer resemblance of identical twins. Thus findings of greater similarity among identical twins is considered the partial result of genetic factors.

In evaluating the results of many of the twin studies which follow, the possibility that environmental variations may be accounting for some of the differences observed must be considered. It is also true that in several of these studies, the number of subjects used was quite small; and final judgment should be withheld until an adequate number of cases have been accumulated.

Physical Features

An individual's physical features depend heavily upon his heredity. Birth injury may alter the shape of his face, disease may whiten his hair. But the color of a person's eyes; the shape of his nose; the pigmentation of his skin; the color, curliness, and stiffness of his hair, are typically a function of the genes he has inherited. Some features, such as eye color, depend upon quite simple combinations of genes. Others, such as skin color, are more complex and involve five or six sets of genes acting together.

For the most part, variations in physical features within the American population bear little relation to an individual's biological ability to adapt to the demands of living. An individual with brown eyes can see as well as one with blue. An individual with fair skin may have greater difficulty with sunburn than an individual whose skin has more pigment to protect it. But the principal effects of variation in physical features upon the individual's adjustment are not biological, but social and psychological. As indicated by America's racial strife, people do not always treat a person with black skin the way they treat one with white skin. Nor do they always respond similarly to people with hooked noses and straight noses. Knowledge of the ways in which people with different features are often treated in our society is essential to a proper understanding of personality development, as we shall see later.

Anatomical Traits

Although body form and structure are more subject to nonhereditary influences—such as nutrition, climate, exercise, and even occupation—than are physical features, there is evidence to suggest that hereditary factors are also of great importance. For example, in their classic study of twins, Newman, Freeman, and Holzinger (42) found that among twins who were raised together, identical twins were consistently more alike than nonidentical twins on measures of height, weight, hand length, and hand width. They also found that, except in the case of weight, identical twins reared in different environments resembled each other more than nonidentical twins reared together.

In another study, the physical development of children born to two large-sized parents was compared with the development of children born to two small-sized parents. The measure of parental body size was the width of the rib cage, a characteristic which appears to be genetically influenced and closely related to the amount of muscle and bone the individual possesses. The children born to large parents, in comparison with those born to small ones, were taller and heavier from birth through 17 years of age (15).

Study of adult identical and fraternal twins (average age in the twenties) revealed that some aspects of body form have a genetic component. Specifically, a long, thin body build (known as ectomorphy) showed greater similarity between identical than between fraternal twins, especially for females (43).

Finally certain anatomical malformations may be hereditary—for example, cleft palate and club foot are much more likely to occur in both members of identical twins than in both members of a pair of fraternal twins (7).

On the other hand, environmental factors may exert important influences on some body growth patterns. For example, it has been found that within one generation, the children of Jewish and Japanese immigrants exceeded their parents' height by an average of 2 inches (4). Other research suggests that obesity may be more frequently the result of dietary problems than of glandular disorders or hereditary factors (5). What is more, the antecedents of overeating appear to be intimately related to such psychological factors as "parental overprotection . . . and to deprivation of satisfying outlets and contacts so that for the child, food intake assumes inordinate importance" (56, 276).

Physiological Traits

There is an intimate relationship between physiological and psychological processes. For example, while fear and anger generally elicit rises in blood pressure, dryness of the throat, and increases in pulse rate, there are wide individual differences in the intensity of these reactions. Equally disturbing psychological events may have more severe—and perhaps more persistent—effects on a person with a highly reactive nervous system than on a person with a less reactive one. It is therefore important for the student of personality development to know the extent to which differences in physiological and neurological functioning are genetically determined.

Various investigators have used the twin-study method to investigate the role of genetic factors in determining physiological and neurological functioning. They have, for example, been able to show that while environmental influences are important in determining such physiological functions as blood pressure and pulse rate, genetic factors are important, too. In one study (39) the average difference in blood pressure (expressed in millimeters of mercury) between identical twins was 5.1, as compared with 8.4 for nonidentical twins. Similar findings were obtained for the pulse rate. The closer correspondence between the blood pressures and pulse rates of identical twins suggests that heredity may play a role in determining these characteristics.

In a more elaborate setting, Jost and Sontag (28) studied the similarities in seven neurological and physiological measures by using pairs of identical twins, pairs of "unrelated siblings" (i.e., singletons with the same parents), and pairs of unrelated children. The measures included such factors as breathing rate, blood pressure (systolic and diastolic), salivation, perspiration, and pulse rate. All the measures were combined into one score, an *index of autonomic stability.*

They then correlated[2] the paired individuals in the three groups on the various measures. The scores of each twin were correlated with those of his partner, those of each child with those of his siblings, and those of the unrelated children were correlated with each other. The scores of identical

[2] Mathematically, a correlation coefficient of zero means that there is no relationship between two sets of measures. A coefficient of 1.0, on the other hand, indicates a one-to-one, or perfect, relationship. Partial relationships are expressed by coefficients ranging from zero to 1.0.

twins were consistently much more closely related than those of siblings. Sibling scores in turn were more alike than those of unrelated children. The finding that identical twins resemble each other most closely on these measures suggests "that there is a genetic factor in autonomic nervous system functioning" (28).

The results of such studies may help to explain the development of a number of so-called psychosomatic conditions, such as ulcers or high blood pressure. For example, under psychological stress, some individuals become hypertensive (develop high blood pressure) while others do not react this way. Genetic factors may be involved in predisposing some individuals to such conditions.

Age of First Menstruation. Another physiological trait which seems to be partly a function of heredity, and which has considerable psychological significance, is age of first menstruation (52). It should be obvious that delay in menstruation, or premature menstruation, relative to her contemporaries, would have important implications for the girl's psychological adjustment. In one study (45) it was found that the average difference in age of menstruation was 2.8 months for identical twins, 12 months for nonidentical twins, 12.9 months for non-twin siblings, 18.4 months for mother and daughter, and 18.6 for unrelated women. Of course, as in most genetically influenced characteristics, environmental forces also play a role in age of menstruation.

Longevity. Longevity is, of course, conspicuously influenced by all sorts of environmental factors, including accidents; but genetic influences seem to play a part. A study of the intrapair differences in the life span of deceased twins who died after the age of 60 revealed an average difference in the life span of 36.9 months for identical, and 78.3 months for nonidentical twins. The number of subjects used in this study was small, but the results are suggestive (35).

Physical Defect and Disease

In conditions such as certain types of diabetes, hemophilia (inability of the blood to clot properly when an individual is cut), and some types of visual and hearing defects, hereditary factors have been shown to be highly important. In other conditions, however, the question of hereditary predisposition is the subject of much controversy, although there is little concrete evidence. Such conditions include various allergies, high blood pressure, some kinds of cancer, stomach ulcers, and tuberculosis. Most physical diseases are dependent on a complex combination of hereditary and environmental factors.

Mental Defect and Retardation

There are several genetically determined disorders that lead to gross defect or deterioration in intelligence. One of these, called *infantile amaurotic family idiocy,* results from a peculiar hereditary defect in the nerve cells of the brain and spinal cord. The cells swell and fill with fat, and blindness, paralysis, and mental deficiency result. In most cases, death occurs several years after the onset of the disease. This disorder appears to be caused by the inheritance of a specific recessive gene from both the mother and father, and occurs most often when the parents themselves are close relatives (52).

Another inherited syndrome for which the physiological processes have been worked out in more detail is called *phenylketonuria* or PKU (26). As we indicated earlier, children with this disease lack an enzyme which is necessary for normal metabolic functioning. In the absence of this enzyme, a toxic chemical accumulates in the body and leads to damage to the nervous system and mental deterioration (23, 24). There is a small group of similar diseases in which the child lacks an enzyme that allows him to metabolize a particular chemical in his body. This metabolic failure often results in mental retardation (51).

Genetic Control of Enzymes. The mechanisms for PKU or similar disorders may represent a model for many forms of mental retardation, each of which has a different cause. That is, each gene produces a specific protein, some of which are enzymes, the enzyme specific for phenylalanine being only one of many necessary for healthy biological functioning. It is likely that, in the years ahead, scientists will discover a series of inherited diseases in which the child lacks a specific enzyme necessary to metabolize particular sugars, proteins, or amino acids. Lack of the enzymes will lead to nervous system defects and mental retardation. However, it must be remembered that the vast majority of children classified as mentally retarded are probably *not* the victims of any genetic disorder.

Chromosomal Aberration. Abnormalities in the structure of the chromosomes may be another basis for mental defects. The best example of this is mongolism, which is called Down's syndrome. These children are born with an Oriental cast to their facial appearance—thus the term mongolism. Most of them function at a very low level of intelligence and, although friendly, are usually not capable of complicated mental performance. These children are mentally retarded, apparently as the result of the presence of an extra member of the Number 21 chromosome pair. These children have 47 instead of the normal 46 chromosomes.

Again, extra chromosomes can occur in any one of the 23 pairs of human chromosomes, and some of these abnormalities could lead to defects in development and eventual mental retardation. But the specific cause would be different in each of these cases.

Mental Disorder

The role of genetic factors in the development of mental disorder has been, and continues to be, a source of controversy in the field of psychiatry. There is general agreement that certain forms of mental disorder such as general paresis (syphilis of the central nervous system) are caused by infection or similar agents attacking the body from without. Some other rather rare forms of mental illness (such as Huntington's chorea) result from definite genetic causes—although the specific underlying genetic structure is not known.

There is less agreement when it comes to the vast majority of cases of mental disorder, those falling into the two categories of (1) the "functional" psychoses (severe mental disorders without known organic cause) and (2) the psychoneuroses (the milder forms of mental disorder and maladjustment). Some experts (30, 32, 33, 37) tend to view these disorders as primarily genetic in origin. Others tend to view them as almost entirely dependent on environmental factors, usually early life experiences.

Why is there so little agreement? In order to provide a concrete basis for discussion, let us consider one of the commonest forms of functional psychosis, namely, schizophrenia. This illness, manifested by severe defects in logical thinking and in emotional responsiveness, probably comes closest to the average person's idea of what it means to be "crazy." It accounts for the occupancy of more hospital beds in the United States than any other form of illness, mental or physical.

Schizophrenia has been attributed exclusively to hereditary defects by some authors, and exclusively to disturbances in early parent-child relationships by others (3). Most psychiatrists consider schizophrenia a total reaction of a biological organism to its environment, although they may differ widely concerning the relative importance attributable to heredity and environmental influences in its determination.

There are several reasons for this difference of opinion. For one thing, the diagnosis of most mental disorders, including schizophrenia, is based upon a rather vaguely defined constellation of behavioral symptoms. One cannot apply any simple test (as one can, for example, in the case of tuberculosis) in order to determine the presence or absence of the disorder. As a result, it is often difficult to make a diagnosis of schizophrenia, and disputes over diagnosis are not uncommon, particularly when the presenting symptoms are not severe.

Although there is no simple explanation applicable to all cases of schizophrenia, the case for a genetic factor in some forms of schizophrenia is strong. The classic studies have been performed by Kallmann (31, 33), who obtained information on 1382 twins, 2741 full siblings, 134 half sibs, and 74 step sibs. In all cases, one individual (called the index case) had been hospitalized for schizophrenia. If psychosis is influenced by heredity, then the incidence of schizophrenia would be higher among those persons genetically similar to the index case. That is, the incidence of schizophrenia among those genetically similar would be highest among identical twins, next among fraternal twins, next among full siblings, then half sibs, step sibs, and finally, lowest for nonrelatives. Kallmann's results confirmed this expectation. They were as follows (the figures represent the proportion of cases in which the person related to the index case also became schizophrenic).

Identical twins	85.8	Half siblings	7.0
Fraternal twins	14.7	Step siblings	1.8
Full siblings	14.3	General population	0.9

The individual with some blood ties to the index cases (full sibling) showed higher incidence of the same illness than nonrelated people; and the closer the genetic relation, the higher the incidence. Both identical twins were much more likely to have the disease than both fraternal twins. However, even Kallmann's data suggest the importance of environmental factors. For example, he found that the monozygotic (identical) twins of schizophrenic patients developed the disorder also in about 91 percent of the cases when the twins were raised in the same general environment, but in only 78 percent of cases when raised in different environments.

Some investigators believe that the term schizophrenia refers to more than one disease process and that some forms are more strongly influenced by genetic factors than others. In particular, it is believed that the sudden development of a schizophrenic breakdown, with no trace of this illness in the individual's previous life history, is apt to be minimally influenced by genetic factors. The contribution of genetic factors is assumed to be greater in cases in which individuals have shown pathological symptoms for many years prior to the breakdown. A recent study of 37 pairs of identical twins, one or both of whom were schizophrenic, suggested that when both twins were schizophrenic, there was a greater likelihood of the twins showing a long history of mental illness. This was less likely to be true when only one of the twins became schizophrenic. Moreover, when both twins were schizophrenic, in contrast to only one of them developing the disease, there was a much higher incidence of schizophrenia in the families of the twins (47). The author concluded that there are at least two broad groups of schizophrenia (reactive and process), and that the genetic contribution to the former was minimal, but to the latter, considerable (47).

Schizophrenia in Children. Although most of the work on the genetics of schizophrenia has been with adults, there is some work with children. It is important to realize first that childhood schizophrenia may not be the same disease as adult schizophrenia. Second, there may be at least two different kinds of disorders in children. One disorder has an early onset, and is called autism (see pp. 408–410). The child looks different during the first two years of life. He doesn't speak, and seems to avoid social contact—and as one mother put it, "he lives in a glass ball." The second disorder has a later onset, and is called schizophrenia. The child begins to develop symptoms at about 6 years of age and, unlike the autistic child, the schizophrenic child does speak. However, both of these types of children show some or all of the following characteristics.

1. They both have a serious impairment in their emotional relations with people. They seem unusually aloof and distant and are not involved or attentive to other people.

2. They have odd reactions to their own body; they will assume odd postures and will scratch and mutilate parts of their body.

3. They show an unusual preoccupation with inanimate objects and will study a marble or block for an inordinately long period of time.

4. They show a strong need to maintain sameness in their environment and become upset if there is any change in the room.

5. They seem to have abnormal perceptual experiences. They react in an exaggerated way, either showing no response or an extreme response to certain sensory stimuli.

6. They show excessive and unprovoked anxiety to a variety of events, especially changes in the environment.

7. Speech is deviant and they will often repeat phrases spoken to them. If you say to the child, "Hello, Jimmy, how are you?" the child might repeat "Hello, Jimmy, how are you?"

8. They show odd motor patterns, such as excessive hyperactivity or complete immobility, or assume unusual postures such as rocking their bodies or spinning themselves like a top.

9. They appear to be mentally retarded (9).

As with adult schizophrenics, there are more cases of identical than fraternal twins having the illness (34). That is, among identical twins with schizophrenia, 70 percent have twins who also have the disease, in contrast to only 17 percent among the fraternal twins. However, there is not always such a dramatic difference between identical and fraternal twins in the joint occurrence of schizophrenia. In a Norwegian study of 342 pairs of twins among whom one or both had been hospitalized with psychosis, the agreement figures were only about 35 percent for the identical twins in contrast to 2 percent for the fraternal twins (36). Although 35 percent is high, it is much lower than the figure of 70 percent reported by Kallman (36).

These differences between identical and nonidentical twins suggest that the illness is inherited. However, several studies report that children suffering from childhood psychosis are more likely to have experienced some pre- or perinatal complications. Some of the children may be brain damaged.

> Accumulated data from prenatal and perinatal histories, development courses, neurological histories and examinations, electroencephalography, and systematic studies of neurological functions, perception and cognition provide rather indisputable evidence of impairment of the central nervous system. The disorders and the integration of the neurological functions often occur very early in infancy and are thus first expressed in terms of sensory, perceptual, motor and postural deviations, and later in terms of the more complex cognitive and social failures and protective adjustments which are most usually viewed as the essential attributes of schizophrenic children (18).

In sum, the symptoms of the schizophrenic child resemble those that might be expected from brain damage caused either by genetic defect or events during pregnancy and delivery. Support for a genetic determinant comes from the fact that a higher proportion of illness occurs in both twins of identical than of fraternal pairs, which is the standard argument for genetic determination.

Studies of the chromosomes of psychotic children have indicated, thus far, that the chromosomes do not appear to differ from those of normals. However, some scientists believe that schizophrenics may have a defect, perhaps inherited, in the biochemistry of their central nervous system. The logic of the argument follows. Schizophrenics often have hallucinations, and certain chemicals related to LSD (the psychedelic drug) cause hallucinations in normal people. If the schizophrenic produced abnormal quantities of these chemicals, owing to a biochemical defect, he might have hallucinatory experiences. Regardless of whether this turns out to be true, it illustrates the type of reasoning and knowledge that is necessary if we are to understand how genetic mechanisms might influence biochemistry which in turn might lead to serious mental disorder. At the present time, we cannot say with certainty whether forms of schizophrenia are hereditary. The unraveling of the determinants of schizophrenia illustrates the challenging problems encountered in trying to ascertain the genetic bases of a mental disorder.

Personality

The role of genetic factors on aspects of human behavior other than serious mental disease is not clear. One reason for the ambiguity is the lack of a specific set of behaviors to study. In Down's syndrome or in the hallucinations of a schizophrenic one has a very specific phenomenon to study. The scientist can compare twins on their facial features, low IQ, and abnormality in chromosome numbers. But there are very few personality dimensions that are that specific. Repeated acts of violent aggression toward others is one moderately specific trait, and recent studies suggest that there is a higher proportion of chromosomal anomalies among a criminal than among a normal population. Male inmates of four prisons were screened for height, and chromosomal analyses were performed on all men 6 feet tall or more. Ten percent of these men had an extra chromosome; they had 47 instead of the normal 46 chromosomes. Some of these men had two X's and one Y; others had one X and two Y's (the normal pattern is one X and one Y). Among noncriminal males over 6 feet tall in the general population, the frequency of such an abnormality is about 1 percent (55).

Although most psychologists would agree that the tendency to display repeated acts of violence is a personality trait, they often do not agree as to which personality dimensions are the important ones to study. This lack of agreement leads to slow progress in solving this problem. Second, the behaviors included under the study of personality are less discrete than those in retardation or psychosis. An hallucination is not on a continuum with a nonhallucination; it is a yes or no event. Similarly, an IQ of 25 does not seem to be on a continuum with an IQ of 100; it is a qualitatively different phenomenon. But personality variables such as friendliness, activity, anger, apathy, or shyness are not all-or-none phenomena. Each is present in degrees and blends into a continuum. Therefore, if they are genetically controlled they are probably controlled by a large set of interacting genes. The popular approach in such research is to compare identical and fraternal twins on a variety of personality traits and then determine traits on which the identical twins are more alike than the fraternal twins.

Careful study of all the research on the genetics of personality suggests that at least one dimension may be partially under genetic control. This can be best described as a tendency toward inhibition and social introversion as contrasted with a tendency toward activity and social extraversion. At a more concrete level, this dimension describes a person who is timid, shy, and withdrawn in contrast to one who is active, friendly, and outgoing.

Sets of adolescent twins in Boston and Minneapolis took a standard personality test and results revealed that the identical twins were more alike on social introversion than the fraternals. In national background, the Minneapolis population was predominantly Scandinavian while the Boston population had very few Scandinavians and many Italian, Irish, and Jewish children. Thus both the gene pool and the environmental experiences of the two populations were different. The fact that degree of social introversion was more similar for identical than for fraternal twins suggests that, in both cities, this personality trait may be genetically controlled (19). Other studies (8, 48) also suggest that among a large set of personality traits (e.g., aggressiveness, moodiness, dependency, sexual behavior, shyness), identical twins are usually more similar than fraternal twins—primarily on traits such as soberness versus enthusiasm, avoidance of people versus enjoying social contact, and inhibition versus spontaneity. These traits are part of the more general personality dimension we call introversion-extraversion. Moreover, this trait appears to be stable over a long period of time—more stable than most personality characteristics. A longitudinal study of typical Ohio children followed from birth to adulthood revealed that the tendency to be inhibited with others was remarkably stable from age 10 to adulthood, and surprisingly, showed some stability from age 3 to adulthood (29). Other longitudinal studies report similar results.

Studies of twin infants also reveal that identical twins are more alike than fraternal twins on the tendency to smile and show fear of strangers (12). These sources of evidence are in general agreement and suggest that tendencies to be inhibited and socially withdrawn (in contrast to having a more impulsive and socially spontaneous disposition) may be under genetic control.

This conclusion fits well with findings from genetic studies of animal behavior. In a classic study of the behaviors of dogs, Scott and Fuller studied five breeds over a 13-year period at the Jackson Laboratories in Bar Harbor, Maine (50). The five breeds were African basenjis, beagles, American cocker spaniels, Shetland sheep dogs (shelties), and wire-haired fox terriers. The researchers kept control over nongenetic factors such as diet, environment, and physical conditions, and the animals experienced carefully prescribed interactions with humans as well as with other dogs. Some of the major behavioral differences among the five species were related to fear and inhibition. Cocker spaniels were easiest to train, while the beagles and terriers were the most difficult to train. Moreover, the cocker spaniels were less emotional and less likely to try to escape from a threatening situation than the wire-haired terriers (50).

Genetic influences on preferred reactions to a new situation are seen clearly in the different reactions of terriers and beagles to the same traumatic experience. Members of the two species were raised alone (in isolation). The puppies were taken from their mother at 21 days and placed alone in cages which allowed feeding and watering, but no physical or visual contact with a human being. When these animals were placed in an arena at 16–20 weeks of age, the terriers were much more active than the beagles, and more active than normally reared terriers; the isolated beagles were less active than normally reared beagles. The two species that were exposed to the same isolated, caged environment for 13 weeks showed *different* activity levels in a new situation (13).

Similarly, imposing the same prenatal stress on different strains of pregnant mice resulted in different levels of activity in the offspring (10, 59). There is an important principle contained in these results: The genetic make-up of the animal—or person—determines his preferred behavior to a given stimulus. In order to understand human personality we must discover those classes of preferred behaviors that might be under genetic control. The data suggest that degree of inhibition may be one such behavior.

In addition to the psychological characteristics mentioned here, there are other aspects of animal and human functioning that appear to have a genetic component, and the interested student is referred to Fuller and Thompson (14), Stern (52), and Hirsch (21) for a detailed summary of them.

Intelligence

Of all the human attributes studied thus far, the IQ score seems most clearly to be under some genetic control. The meaning of an IQ score is a complicated matter and discussion of it will be reserved for Chapter 11. For the present we will summarize the most pertinent studies indicating a genetic component in intelligence-test performance and, by inference, in quality of intellectual functioning. In general, identical twins are more similar than fraternal twins in IQ (see 27, 42, 46, 54). Newman, Freeman, and Holzinger found an average difference in IQ of 9.9 points for pairs of fraternal twins but of only 5.9 points for pairs of identical twins (42). Among the characteristics studied in 600 children 10 to 15 years of age, intelligence seemed to be the most strongly influenced by genetic factors— much more than a variety of personality traits (8).

More definitive findings regarding the role of genetic factors in determining intellectual status may be expected from comparisons between fraternal twins reared together and identical twins reared apart. Newman,

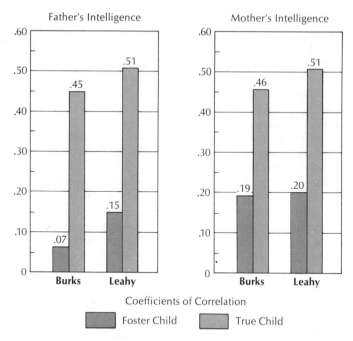

Fig. 2.6. A comparison of foster and true parent-child correlations. (After H. E. Jones, Environmental influences on mental development. In L. Carmichael (Ed.), *Manual of child psychology*. New York: Wiley, 1946. By permission.)

Freeman, and Holzinger (42) found a higher correlation between the IQ's of identical twins raised in different environments (.76) than between those of nonidentical twins reared together (.63). In other words, as it seems highly unlikely that the relevant features in the environments of identical twins reared apart were as similar as those of fraternal twins reared together, one is forced to the conclusion that heredity is one of the important determiners of intellectual performance.

Still another approach to the problem of genetic factors in intellectual performance involves the study of children in foster homes. In general, the average correlation between children's IQ's and those of their natural parents ranges between .50 and .60. This degree of relationship may then be compared with the correlation between foster children's intelligence and that of their foster parents. If we find that the latter correlation is significantly lower than .50 (i.e., that foster children resemble their foster parents much less than natural children resemble their parents), we may infer that hereditary factors account for the greater similarity between true parents and their children.

In one such study, Burks (6) obtained the IQ's of 204 school-age foster children, all of whom had been placed in foster homes before 12 months of age. In addition she obtained the IQ's of the children's foster parents.

MEDIAN CORRELATION

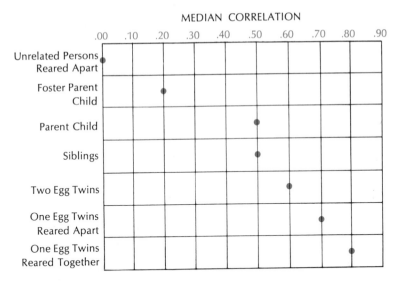

Fig. 2.7. Correlation between the intelligence scores of people having different genetic relationships to each other. (From L. Erlenmeyer-Kimling & L. F. Jarvik. Genetics and intelligence. *Science,* December, 1963, *142,* 1477-1479. Copyright 1963 by the American Association for the Advancement of Science. By permission.)

A control group of 105 children who were living with their true parents was then also set up, and the IQ's of these "true" children and their parents were also obtained. Thus Burks was able to compare the correlations in IQ between foster parents and their children with those between true parents and their children. A similar approach was used by Leahy (*38*). Figure 2.6 shows the results of both these studies, demonstrating that the relationships between children and their own fathers and mothers were higher than those between children and their foster parents.

Another investigator (*22*) compared the relationships between adopted children's IQ's and the estimated intelligence of the children's true and foster parents. The estimate of parental intelligence was based on amount of formal education. Up to age 4, education of either true or foster parent was not significantly related to the IQ of the child. From age 6 on, however, the correlation between the adopted child's IQ and the education of his true mother and father was about +.35, while the corresponding correlation between foster parents' education and child's IQ was approximately zero.

The differences in correlation which are evident in all these studies might well have been greater were it not for the fact that "when placement officers have knowledge of the cultural circumstances of the true parents, this is likely to influence their choice of foster homes" (*27*). In other words, when adoption agencies can estimate the intelligence of the child's true parents, they are likely to try to place the child with a foster family of similar intellectual status. This practice should tend to increase the correlation between the IQ's of children and their foster parents. Despite this, the true parent-child correlations were higher than those between foster parents and their foster children in all the studies.

Figure 2.7 summarizes the results of many studies and indicates the typical relation between IQ scores of individuals differing in their genetic similarity to each other (11). As can be seen from the Figure, identical twins have the most similar IQ scores and unrelated people the least. However, there is a low positive correlation between the IQ's of foster parents and their children (who are not genetically related) and a higher correlation between fraternal twins than siblings (who are equal in genetic similarity). Thus environmental factors are important (as we shall see later) in raising or lowering a child's level of intellectual performance. But environmental forces can be effective only within definite limits set by heredity.

SUMMARY

As the reader must now appreciate, we know little about the exact influences of genetics for most human psychological attributes, especially those that fall on broad continuums such as intelligence or personality. Behavioral correlates of genetic differences in animals lead to some important conclusions that are likely to apply to man. First, genetic differences are likely to lead to differences in preferred reactions to the same situation. One strain of mice "freezes" in a particular situation, another strain runs around frantically. One strain of dogs becomes excited when a bell rings, another remains placid. The same environmental experience seems to have different behavioral effects on populations that have different genetic make-ups. Since males and females have different genetic make-ups we might expect accompanying sex differences—and we are beginning to find them. Girls seem to show less variability in their physical growth than boys, and they also seem more predictable. Girls seem to be more precocious in their psychological development, and prediction of rate of cognitive development over a long period of time is easier for girls than for boys. Each of these sex differences may be under genetic control.

The task is to continue to search for those psychological dimensions that may have major genetic control. But the final proof of hereditary control awaits the discovery of the biological processes that link the actions of the genes with specific psychological characteristics, so that we can understand how the genes helped to produce a particular behavioral consequence.

References

1. Allport, G. *Personality: a psychological interpretation.* New York: Holt, Rinehart and Winston, 1937.
2. Anastasi, A. Heredity, environment and the question "How?" *Psychol. Rev.,* 1958, *65*, 197–208.

3. Bleuler, E. *Dementia praecox or the group of schizophrenias.* New York: International Universities Press, 1950.
4. Boas, F. *Changes in bodily form of descendants of immigrants* (U.S. Senate Document 208). Washington D.C.: U.S. Government Printing Office, 1911.
5. Bronstein, I. P., Wexler, S., Brown, A. W., & Halpern, L. J. Obesity in childhood. *Amer. J. Dis. Child.,* 1942, *63,* 238–251.
6. Burks, B. S. The relative influence of nature and nurture upon mental development: A comparative study of foster parent-foster child resemblance and true parent-true child resemblance. *(27th Yearb. nat. Soc. Stud. Educ.)* Chicago: Univer. Chicago Press, Part I, 1928, 219–316.
7. Carter, C. O. The genetics of common malformations. In M. Fishbein (Ed.). *Congenital malformations,* New York: International Medical Congress, 1964, 306–313.
8. Cattell, R. B., Stice, G. F., & Kristy, N. F. A first approximation to nature-nurture ratios for eleven primary personality factors in objective tests. *J. abnorm. soc. Psychol.,* 1957, *54,* 143–159.
9. Creak, M. Schizophrenia syndrome in childhood. *Cerebral Palsy Bull.,* 1961, *3,* 501.
10. DeFries, J. C. Prenatal maternal stress in mice: differential effects on behavior. *J. Hered.,* 1964, *55,* 289–295.
11. Erlenmeyer-Kimling, L., & Jarvik, L. F. Genetics and intelligence. *Science,* 1963, *142,* 1477–1479.
12. Freedman, D. An ethological approach to the genetic study of human behavior. In S. G. Vandenberg (Ed.), *Methods and goals in human behavior genetics.* New York: Academic Press, 1965, 141–161.
13. Fuller, J. C. Experiential deprivation and later behavior. *Science,* 1967, *158,* 1645–1652.
14. Fuller, J. L., & Thompson, W. R. *Behavior genetics.* New York: Wiley, 1960.
15. Garn, S. M., Clark, A., Landkof, Lina, & Newell, Laura. Parental body build and developmental progress in the offspring. *Science,* 1960, *132,* 1555–1556.
16. Gates, R. R. *Human genetics.* Vol. II. New York: Macmillan, 1946.
17. Goldfarb, W. *Childhood schizophrenia.* Cambridge, Mass.: Harvard Univer. Press, 1961.
18. Goldfarb, W. Childhood psychoses. In P. M. Mussen (Ed.), *Handbook of child psychology.* New York: Wiley, in press.
19. Gottesman, I. I. Personality and natural selection. In S. G. Vandenberg (Ed.), *Methods and goals in human behavior genetics.* New York: Academic Press, 1965, 63–74.
20. Haldane, J. B. S. *Heredity and politics.* New York: Norton, 1938.
21. Hirsch, J. *Behavior genetic analysis.* New York: McGraw-Hill, 1967.
22. Honzik, Marjorie P. Developmental studies of parent-child resemblance in intelligence. *Child Develpm.,* 1957, *28,* 215–228.
23. Horner, F. A., & Streamer, C. W. Phenylketonuria treated from earliest infancy. *Amer. J. Dis. Child.,* 1959, *97,* 345–347.
24. Horner, F. A., Streamer, C. W., Clader, D. E., Hassell, L. L., Binkley, F. L., & Dumars, K. W. Effect of phenylalanine restricted diet in phenylketonuria: II. *Amer. J. Dis. Child.,* 1957, *93,* 615–618.
25. Jennings, H. S. *Genetics.* New York: Norton, 1935.
26. Jervis, G. A. The mental deficiencies. In Arieti, S. (Ed.), *American handbook of psychiatry.* Vol. II. New York: Basic Books, 1959, 1289–1316.

27. Jones, H. E. Environmental influence on mental development. In L. Carmichael (Ed.), *Manual of child psychology.* New York: Wiley, 1946, 582–632.
28. Jost, H., & Sontag, L. W. The genetic factors in autonomic nervous system. *Psychosom. Med.,* 1944, *6,* 308–310.
29. Kagan, J., & Moss, H. A. *Birth to maturity.* New York: Wiley, 1962.
30. Kallmann, F. J. *The genetics of schizophrenia.* New York: Augustin, 1938.
31. Kallmann, F. J. The genetic theory of schizophrenia. *Amer. J. Psychiat.,* 1946, *103,* 309–322.
32. Kallmann, F. J. Genetic aspects of psychosis. In *The history of mental health and disease.* New York: Hoeber, 1952, 283–298.
33. Kallmann, F. J. *Heredity in health and mental disorder.* New York: Norton, 1953.
34. Kallmann, F. J., & Rolff, B. Genetic aspects of preadolescent schizophrenia. *Amer J. Psychiat.,* 1965, *112,* 599–606.
35. Kallmann, F. J., & Sander, G. Twin studies on aging and longevity. *J. Hered.* 1948, *39,* 349–357.
36. Kringlen, I. Schizophrenia in twins. *Psychiatry,* 1966, *29,* 172–184.
37. Landis, C., & Bolles, M. M. *Textbook of abnormal psychology.* New York: Macmillan, 1947.
38. Leahy, A. M. Nature-nurture and intelligence. *Genet. Psychol. Monogr.,* 1935, *17,* 235–308.
39. Malkova, N. N., *Proc. Maxim Gorki med.-biol. res. Inst.,* 1934, No. 3. Cited in Stern, C., *Principles of human genetics.* San Francisco: Freeman, 1960 (2nd ed.).
40. McGraw, M. B. Motivation of behavior. In L. Carmichael (Ed.), *Manual of child psychology.* New York: Wiley, 1946, 332–369.
41. Morgan, T. H. *Scientific basis of evolution.* New York: Norton, 1932.
42. Newman, H. H., Freeman, R. N., & Holzinger, K. J. *Twins: A study of heredity and environment.* Chicago: Univer. Chicago Press, 1937.
43. Osborne, R. H., & DeGeorge, F. V. *Genetic basis of morphological variation.* Cambridge: Harvard Univer. Press, 1959.
44. Parker, M. M. Experimental studies in the psychology of temperament in the adult albino rat. *Abstr. doct. Diss.* Ohio State Univer., 1939, No. 30.
45. Petri, A. Z. *Morph. Anthrop., 33,* 1934. Cited by C. Stern, *Principles of human genetics.* San Francisco: Freeman, 1949.
46. Rosanoff, A. J., Hardy, L. M., & Plesset, J. R. The etiology of mental deficiency with special reference to its occurrence in twins. *Psychol. Monogr.* 1937, *48,* No. 4.
47. Rosenthal, D. Some factors associated with concordance and discordance with respect to schizophrenia in monozygotic twins. *J. nerv. ment. Dis.,* 1959, 129, 1–10.
48. Scarr, S. Genetic factors in activity motivation. *Child Develpm.,* 1966, *37,* 663–673.
49. Scheinfeld, A. *The new you and heredity.* Philadelphia: Lippincott, 1950.
50. Scott, J. P., & Fuller, J. L. *Genetics of the social behavior of the dog.* Chicago: Univer. Chicago Press, 1965.
51. Seegmiller, J. E., Rosenbloom, F. M., & Kelley, W. N. Enzyme defect associated with a sex linked human neurological disorder and excessive purine synthesis. *Science,* 1967, *155,* 1682–1683.
52. Stern, C. *Principles of human genetics.* San Francisco: Freeman, 1960 (2nd ed.).
53. Stockard, C. R. *Physical basis of personality.* New York: Norton, 1931.

54. Stocks, P., & Karn, M. N. A biometric investigation of twins and their brothers and sisters. *Ann. Eugen.,* 1933, *5,* 1–55.
55. Telfer, M. A., Baker, D., Clark, G. R., & Richardson, C. E. Incidence of gross chromosomal errors among tall criminal American males. *Science,* 1968, *159,* 1249–1250.
56. Thompson, H. Physical growth. In L. Carmichael (Ed.), *Manual of child psychology.* New York: Wiley, 1946.
57. Vandenberg, S. G. Multivariate analysis of twin differences. In S. G. Vandenberg (Ed.), *Methods and goals in human behavior genetics.* New York: Academic Press, 1965, 29–43.
58. Watson, J. D., & Crick, F. H. C. Molecular structure of nucleic acids—a structure for deoxyribose nucleic acid. *Nature,* 1953, *171,* 737–738.
59. Weir, M. W., & DeFries, J. C. Prenatal maternal influence on behavior in mice: evidence of a genetic basis. *J. comp. physiol. Psychol.,* 1964, *58,* 412–417.
60. Weismann, A. *Essays upon heredity and kindred biological problems.* New York: Oxford, 1889.

3

Prenatal Development

It is a rather curious fact that while we recognize that the new individual's life begins at conception, we reckon his age from the moment of birth. It would almost seem that we were implicitly saying that the events in a person's life prior to birth are of little importance in determining the future course of his development. This attitude is especially likely to apply to our conceptions of *psychological* development. And yet the environment in which the unborn child grows can be of tremendous importance in influencing later patterns of growth, not only physically, but psychologically as well.

The Chinese have traditionally been somewhat more realistic in their age computations.

> Each of their babies is given at birth a full year's credit on the reckoning of its age. They know, of course, that the span of our prefatory existence is actually only nine months long, but fractions are a bother, and in China every man claims one more year of age than does the European born of the same day and the same year (6, 1).

In view of the magnitude of the growth processes occurring during the prenatal period, the Chinese approach to age reckoning appears somewhat more appropriate than ours.

HOW CONCEPTION OCCURS

Conception occurs when a sperm from the male pierces the cell wall of an ovum or egg from the female. The occasions on which such mating is

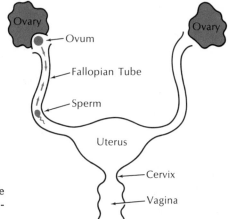

Fig. 3.1. Schematic diagram of female reproductive system showing how conception occurs.

possible are strictly limited physiologically, and are quite independent of the vagaries of human impulse. Figure 3.1 shows a schematic diagram of the female reproductive system. Once every 28 days (usually around the middle of the menstrual cycle) an ovum ripens in one of the two ovaries, is discharged into the corresponding Fallopian tube, or oviduct, and begins its slow journey toward the uterus, propelled by small hairlike cilia which line the tube. In most cases, it takes from three to seven days for the ovum to reach the uterus (23). If the ovum has not been fertilized in the course of this journey, it disintegrates in the uterus after a few days, "and its remains, which are less than a grain of dust, disperse unnoticed" (6).

If, on the other hand, a mating has taken place, one of the many millions of tiny sperm released by the male may find its way up into the oviduct during the time the ovum is making its descent. There it may unite with the ovum and the conception of a new individual may result.

As indicated in Chapter 2, each sperm is a tadpolelike cell. The oval head of the sperm is packed with the 23 chromosomes. Behind the head are special structures that supply the energy the sperm cell needs to travel the distance to reach the ovum. It is estimated that the sperm travel at a velocity of about one-tenth of an inch per minute.

THE EARLIEST PERIOD OF DEVELOPMENT

At the moment of conception, the ovum, the largest cell in the human body, is still very small—only about 1/175 of an inch in diameter (6). The fertilized ovum, called a zygote, begins to grow immediately. Let us briefly summarize this process. When the sperm enters the ovum a process is initiated which results in the fusing of the nucleus of the sperm with the nucleus of the ovum. It will be recalled that each of the nuclei contains 23 chromosomes. The 23 chromosomes from the sperm and the 23 chromosomes from the ovum then line up and split, yielding 23 pairs of chromo-

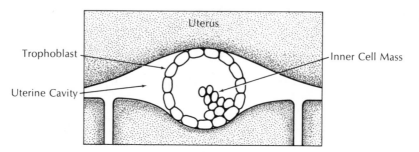

Fig. 3.2. Schematic representation of ovum at early stage of implantation in uterine wall.

somes. The process of development has now begun. The time from the sperm's penetration of the ovum to the development of the first two cells usually takes between 24 and 36 hours.

The process of development from conception to birth is usually divided into three phases. The first phase, called the period of the ovum, lasts from fertilization until the time that the zygote (fertilized ovum) is firmly implanted in the wall of the uterus. This process typically takes about 10 to 14 days.

The second phase—from 2 to 8 weeks—is called the period of the embryo. This period is characterized by a differentiation of all the major organs that will be present in the newborn baby. The last phase—from 8 weeks until delivery (normally 40 weeks) is called the period of the fetus, and is characterized by growth of the organism.

The Period of the Ovum

The fertilized ovum continues to double its cells during its journey from the oviduct, where it was fertilized to the uterus (where it will become implanted).

By the time the fertilized ovum reaches the uterus, it is about the size of a pinhead and has several dozen cells. A small cavity is formed within the mass of cells, resulting in an outer and a separated inner cluster of cells (see Fig. 3.2). The outer layer, called the *trophoblast,* will ultimately develop into accessory tissues which protect and nourish the embryo. The inner cluster of cells will become the embryo itself.

While these developments are taking place, small burrlike tendrils have begun to grow around the outside of the trophoblast. It is by means of these tendrils that in a few more days (around 10 to 14 days after fertilization) the ovum will attach itself to the uterine wall.

In the meantime, however, the uterus itself has begun to undergo changes in preparation for receiving the fertilized ovum (called a *blastocyte* at this stage). At the time of implantation (attachment of the ovum to the uterine wall), the tendrils from the trophoblast burrow into the receptive mucous membrane of the uterus. Extensions of the tendrils reach into the blood spaces which have formed within the maternal tissue. At this time, the period of the ovum comes to an end, and the second phase of prenatal development, the period of the embryo, begins. The new individual has ceased to be an independent, free-floating organism and has established a dependent relationship with the mother.

The Period of the Embryo

Once the growing egg has been successfully lodged in its new home, development is rapid. Its *inner* cell mass, which will become a recognizable embryo, begins to differentiate itself into three distinct layers.

1. The *ectoderm* (outer layer), from which will develop the epidermis or outer layer of the skin, the hair, the nails, parts of the teeth, skin glands, sensory cells—and the nervous system.

2. The *mesoderm* (middle layer), from which will develop the dermis or inner skin layer, the muscles, skeleton, and the circulatory and excretory organs.

3. The *endoderm* (inner layer), from which will develop the lining of the entire gastrointestinal tract, the Eustachian tubes, trachea, bronchia, lungs, liver, pancreas, salivary glands, thyroid glands, and thymus (16, 23).

While the inner cell mass is being differentiated into a recognizable embryo, the outer layers of cells are giving rise to the fetal membranes— the *chorion* and *amnion*. These two membranes, together with a third membrane derived from the uterine wall of the mother (the *decidua capsularis*), extend from the wall of the uterus and enclose the developing embryo (see Fig. 3.3). They form a sac which is filled with a watery fluid (*liquor amnii*) and acts as a buffer to protect the embryo from shocks experienced by the mother. It also helps to provide an even temperature for the embryo and serves to prevent adhesions between the embryo and the amniotic membrane (39).

Simultaneously, other fetal sacs are formed, the most important of which becomes the umbilical cord. It extends from the embryo, and is attached at its opposite end to the section of the uterine wall where the uterus and the chorion are joined. This area is called the *placenta*.

The umbilical cord might well be referred to as the lifeline of the embryo. Through it, two arteries carry blood from the embryo to the placenta, and one vein carries blood to the infant from the placenta. However, the relationship between the child's bloodstream and the mother's is not a direct one. Both the child's and the mother's bloodstreams open into the placenta. But the two systems are always separated by cell walls within the placenta. These cell walls consist of semipermeable membranes which function as extremely fine mesh screens, large enough to permit the passage of gases, salts, and other substances of small molecular size, but too small to allow blood cells to get through.

Although a precise knowledge of all the substances which pass through a normal placenta is lacking, it is known that various nutrient substances from the mother's blood—chiefly sugars, fats, and some protein elements

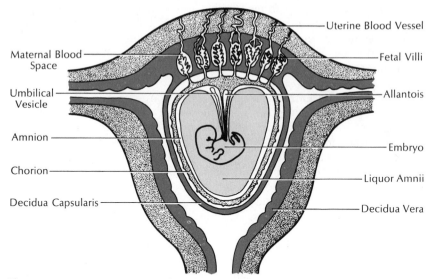

Fig. 3.3. Diagram representing the relationship between the uterus, the membrane, and the embyro during early pregnancy. (From L. Carmichael. Origins and prenatal growth of behavior. In C. Murchison (Ed.), *A handbook of child psychology.* Worchester: Clark Univer. Press, 1933, p. 50 [2nd ed.]. By permission.)

—permeate it. Waste products from the infant, primarily carbon dioxide and other metabolites, can also pass through the placenta. In addition, some vitamins, drugs (including nicotine and alcohol), vaccines, and a few disease germs (notably those of diphtheria, typhoid, influenza, and syphilis) may also get through and affect the embryo's development (6, 10).

It should be noted that there are no direct neural connections between the maternal and embryonic nervous systems; only chemicals can cross the placental barrier.

Despite the fact that there are no nerve fibers joining mother and fetus, a mother's emotional state may indirectly influence the physiological functioning of her child. When the mother is emotionally aroused, a variety of physiological reactions occur, and specific hormones such as adrenalin, as well as other chemical agents, are released into the mother's bloodstream. Some of these substances may pass through the placenta and affect the on-going physiological processes in the unborn child (6, 10).

Development of the Embryo. Much of our knowledge of prenatal development has been derived from the intensive study of embryos and fetuses which, for medical reasons, had to be surgically removed from the uterus.

During the period of the embryo, development is extremely rapid. By 18 days, the embryo has already begun to take some shape. It has established a longitudinal axis and its front, back, left, and right sides, and a

1 NOV 74

DEAR JIMMY:

I am sending you this picture of me to remind
you , that we have a date during Xmas vacation. How
is my most favorite long peckered recruiter anyway. I
don't mean Sgt Perry. How is he anyway? Ihave learned
a lot since I last seen you. I spend more time on my
back on my off time than I do on my feet, and I love it
Well Jimmy I hope this note finds you horny and well, will
be looking forward to seeing you next month.

                    LOVE FROM TH TALL ONE
                    LINDA

head and tail are discernible. By the end of the third week a primitive heart has developed and has begun to beat (17; see Fig. 3.4).

At the end of the first month the embryo is about 1/5 inch long. It has the beginnings of a mouth region, of a gastrointestinal tract, and of a liver. The heart is becoming well developed, and the head and brain regions are becoming more clearly differentiated. At this stage, the embryo is still a very primitive organism. It has as yet no arms or legs, no developed features, and only the most elementary of body systems.

By 8–9 weeks, however, the picture has changed markedly (see Fig. 3.5). The embryo is now about an inch long. Face, mouth, eyes, and ears have begun to take on fairly well-defined form. Arms and legs and even hands and feet with stubby fingers and toes have appeared (16). At this stage the sex organs are just beginning to form. The development of muscle and cartilage also begins, but well-defined neuromotor activity (activation of the muscles by impulses from the nerves) is still absent at this stage (16). The internal organs—intestines, liver, pancreas, lungs, kidneys—take on a definite shape and assume some degree of function. The liver, for example, begins to manufacture red blood cells.

The period of the embryo is characterized by an extremely rapid development of the nervous system. Figures 3.4 and 3.5 show that, during this period, the head is large in relation to other body areas. This suggests that the first eight weeks constitute a sensitive period with respect to the integrity of the nervous system. Mechanical or chemical interference with development at this time (e.g., mother falling downstairs, or an overdose of drugs to the mother) is more likely to cause permanent nervous system damage than a similar disruption at a later date. For example, if the mother should contract German measles during this period, the child is more likely to be mentally deficient than if she should have this illness during the last eight weeks of pregnancy.

The Period of the Fetus

The third period of prenatal development, *the period of the fetus,* extends from the end of the second month until birth. During this time, the various body systems, which have been laid down in rudimentary form earlier, become quite well developed, and begin to function. Up until about 8½ weeks, the fetus has led a relatively passive existence, floating quiescently in the amniotic fluid. At this time, however, it becomes capable of responding to tactile (touch) stimulation (39). The trunk flexes and the head extends. From this point on, motor functions become increasingly more differentiated and complex.

By the end of the third month, the fetus is about 3 inches long and weighs about 3/4 ounce. It has definitely begun to resemble a human being, though the head is disproportionately large (see Figs. 3.6A and 3.6B). Muscles are becoming well developed, and spontaneous movements of the arms and legs may be observed. Eyelids and nails have begun to form, and the fetus' sex can now be distinguished easily. The nervous system is still very incomplete,

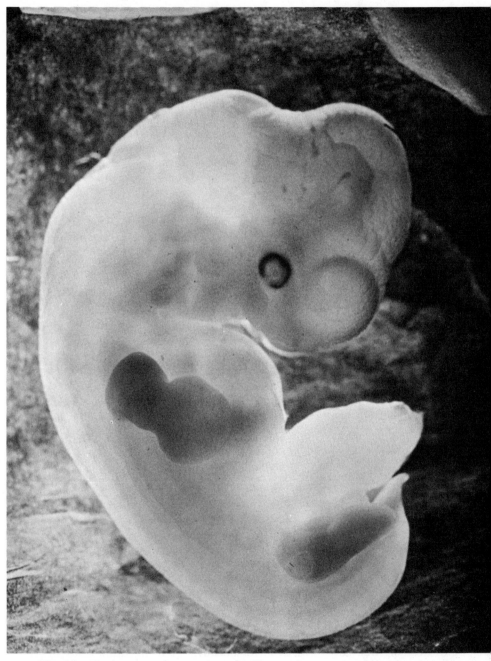

Fig. 3.4. The human embryo at 6 weeks. The eye is seen as a dark-rimmed circle.
© Lennart Nilsson, courtesy LIFE Magazine.

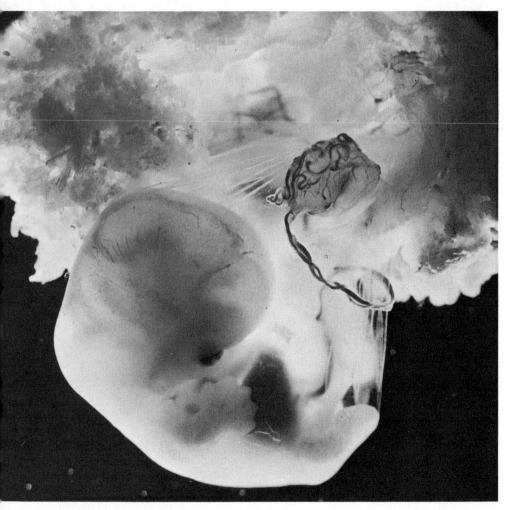

Fig. 3.5. The human embryo at 9 weeks. Hands and fingers are now clear. ©
Lennart Nilsson, courtesy LIFE Magazine.

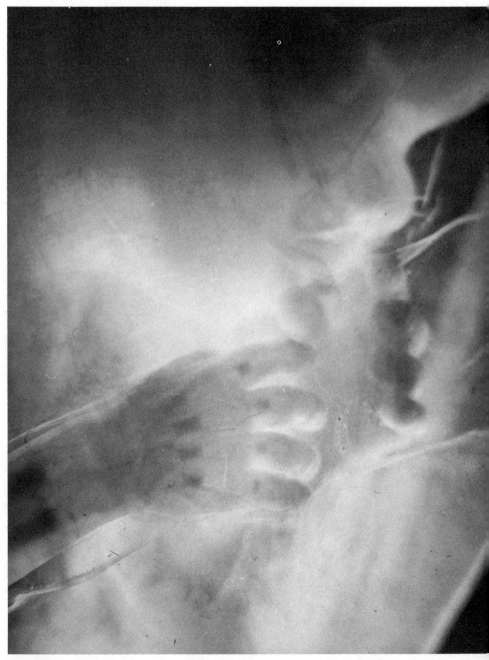

Fig. 3.6A and B (opposite). The 12-week-old human embryo. Reflex movements now appear. The fetus moves its hand to its mouth and makes sucking movements. © Lennart Nilsson, courtesy LIFE Magazine.

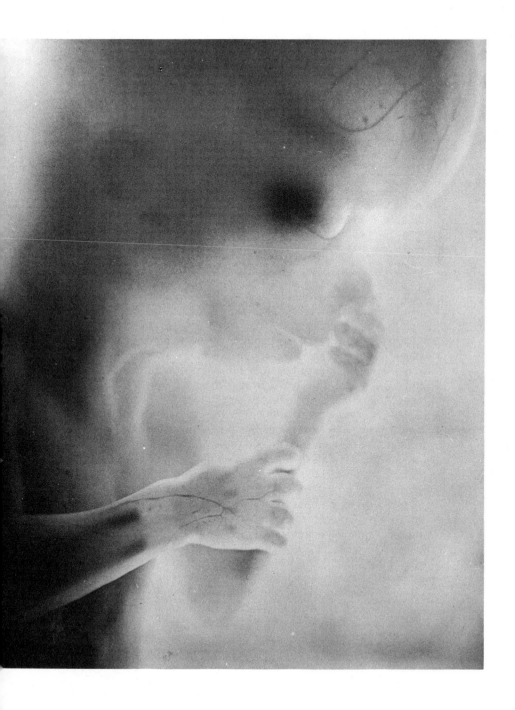

however. During the next four weeks, motor behavior becomes more complex. Gesell has described the status of motor behavior in the fetus during
these weeks:

> He moves his upper lip. When a little more mature he moves his lower lip.
> Later he moves both lips in unison. Still later he opens and closes his mouth.
> He swallows with closed mouth, but at times he also swallows amniotic fluid.
> His tongue moves. . . . He may also rotate his head in association with the
> "oral reflex"; for complex patterns of feeding behavior are in the making.
> Peristaltic waves sweep over his lengthening digestive tube.
>
> Arms and legs occasionally move in diagonal alternation in a manner which
> suggests locomotion, whether aquatic or terrestrial—small movements which
> may, however, displace the position of the fetus. But human arms and hands
> are ultimately meant for manipulation as well as locomotion, and the fetus
> accordingly foreshadows long in advance the patterns of a higher order. He
> elevates the upper arms, he extends his drooping hands. Elbows formerly fixed
> are mobile. He deploys his hands in the median plane: sometimes they almost
> touch the mouth. His movements are less stilted than they were in the previous
> months, when his palms assumed a stiff pat-a-cake attitude or were retracted
> far apart. He now rotates his forearm medially. He opens and closes his
> hands. He moves his thumb independently, or curls it fist-like under the con-
> joint digits, a token of latter opposibility (16, 68).

By the end of 16 weeks, the mother can feel the fetus' movements. At
this point the fetus is about 4½ inches in length. In the period from 16 to
20 weeks, the fetus increases to about 10 inches in length and 8 or 9 ounces
in weight (23). It becomes more human-looking and hair appears on the
head and body. The mouth becomes capable of protrusion, as well as opening and closing—a precursor of later sucking movements (16). Blinking of
the eyes occurs, although the lids are still tightly fused. The hands become capable of gripping in addition to closing (see Fig. 3.7A).

Toward the end of the eighth week, the reproductive system begins
to develop. The gonads (the ovaries and the testes) initially appear as a
pair of blocks of tissue in both sexes. Moreover, it appears that the hormones manufactured by the male's testes are necessary to stimulate the
development of a male reproductive system. If the testes are removed or
fail to perform properly the baby that is born possesses a primarily female
reproductive system. Evidence from rabbits indicates that if the tiny ovary
is removed immediately after its formation, the female fetus develops normally. It appears, therefore, that the anatomy of the female reproductive
system is basic—that is the form that will develop if either testes or ovaries
are removed or do not function.

After 20 weeks (the fifth month) the skin begins to assume adult
form; hair and nails appear, and sweat glands are developed (see Fig. 3.7B).

By 24 weeks of age (6 months) the eyes are completely formed, and
taste buds appear on the tongue. The fetus is now capable of "true inspiration and expiration, and of a thin crying noise should he be prematurely
born" (16, 71; see Fig. 3.7C).

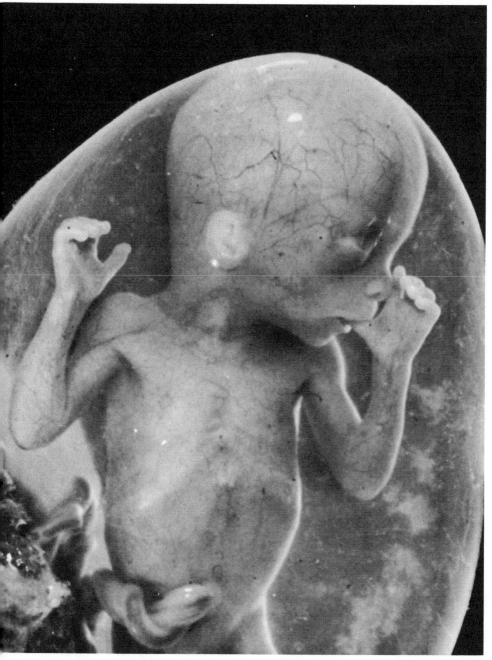

Fig. 3.7A. The 4½-month-old fetus is shown sucking its thumb. © Lennart Nilsson, courtesy LIFE Magazine.

Fig. 3.7B. The 5-month-old fetus in a resting position. © Lennart Nilsson, courtesy LIFE Magazine.

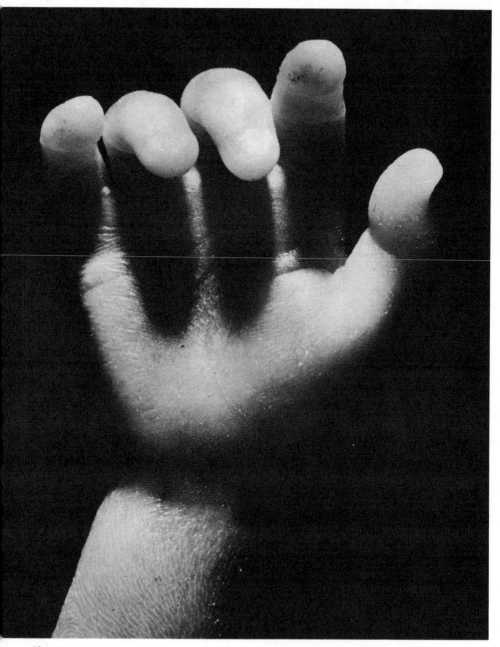

Fig. 3.7C. The 6-month-old fetus with emerging fingernails. © Lennart Nilsson, courtesy LIFE Magazine.

The fetal age of 28 weeks is an important one. It demarcates the zone between viability (the ability to live if born) and nonviability. By this age, the child's nervous, circulatory, and other bodily systems have become sufficiently well structured to stand a chance of being able to function adequately in the extrauterine environment, although, of course, special care is required. At this point, reactions to changes in temperature approximate those of the full-term infant. Experimental studies of infants born at this age indicate that basic tastes, such as sweet, salt, sour, and bitter can be differentiated by the fetus (4). So can basic odors. Visual and auditory reactions also occur, though not so clearly as in the full-term infant. On the other hand, sensitivity to pain seems to be relatively absent in the premature infant.

The period from 28 weeks to birth at full term (40 weeks) is marked by further development of the basic bodily structures and functions. In the outline which follows, Watson and Lowrey (51) have employed some of the available data on premature infants to illustrate the increasingly elaborate behavior which develops between 28 weeks and normal birth.

Fetus at 28-32 weeks
Movements meager, fleeting, poorly sustained
Lack of muscular tone
Mild avoidance responses to bright light and sound
In prone position turns head to side
Palmar stimulation elicits barely perceptible grasp
Breathing shallow and irregular
Sucking and swallowing present but lack endurance
No definite waking and sleeping pattern
Cry may be absent or very weak
Inconstant tonic neck reflex

Fetus at 32-36 weeks
Movement sustained and positive
Muscle tone fair understimulation
Moro reflex (startle reaction) present
Strong but inadequate response to light and sound
In prone position turns head, elevates rump
Definite periods of being awake
Palmar stimulation causes good grasp
Good hunger cry
Fairly well-established tonic neck reflex

Fetus at 36-40 weeks
Movements active and sustained
Muscle tone good
Brief erratic following of objects with eyes
Moro reflex strong
In prone position attempts to lift head
Active resistance to head rotation
Definite periods of alertness
Cries well when hungry and disturbed

Appears pleased when caressed
Hands held as fists much of time, good grasp
Tonic neck reflect more pronounced to one side (usually right) than to the other
Good, strong sucking reflex (51).

PRENATAL ENVIRONMENTAL INFLUENCES

Thus far, we have been discussing what might be called "normal" or typical patterns of prenatal development. But such patterns can only occur when the organism itself and its environment fall within what might be thought of as normal limits.

The chapter on genetic mechanisms emphasized that hereditary factors can affect the individual's development in important ways. We also noted, however, that no trait or characteristic of an individual is entirely hereditarily determined. Heredity may make important contributions to many of the individual's potentialities or limitations, but most of his characteristics are the consequents of complex interactions between genetically transmitted factors and environmental influences. The growth and development of the individual's inherent potential may be actualized, facilitated, and enhanced—or thwarted, mutilated, and limited—depending on the kind of physical, social, and psychological environment he encounters. "The important point to understand . . . is that the same genes may be influenced to express themselves differently and to have different end effects as a consequence of the different environments in which they function" (28, 151).

Ordinarily we think of the prenatal environment as constant and similar for all fetuses. Certainly, the fetus' surroundings are relatively simple in comparison with the complex world he will encounter after birth. Nevertheless, there are many variations in prenatal environment, and the pressures to which one fetus is subjected may differ greatly from those exerted on another. Recent research suggests that the mother's physical and emotional status (and consequently the prenatal environment she provides) may exert important influences on the course of fetal development and the subsequent health and adjustment of the child. Some of the more important prenatal environmental factors which have been investigated will be discussed in the following sections.

Age of Mother

Advances in medical science have made pregnancy and birth much less dangerous and difficult than they ever have been previously. The total incidence of infant mortality (Fig. 3.8) and maternal mortality, regardless of the age of the mother, is now very low. There is some evidence, however, that these mortality rates are higher if the mothers are below 23 or above 29 than if they are between these two ages.

Moreover, mothers under 20 and over 35 years of age tend to have a

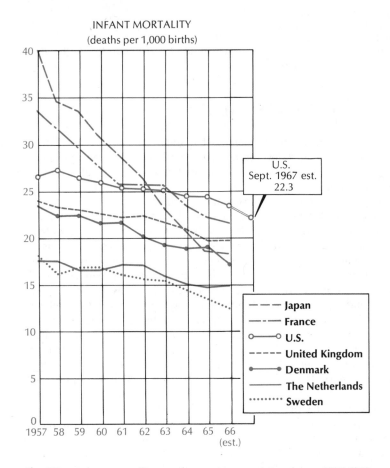

Fig. 3.8. Infant mortality across various nations from 1957-1966. (TIME, December 29, 1967. TIME Chart by V. Puglisi, copyright TIME Inc. 1967.)

higher proportion of retarded youngsters than mothers between 20 and 35 years of age (32). These difficulties may be due to the inadequate development of the reproductive system in some younger women and to progressive decline in reproductive functioning in some older ones.

Women who deliver their first infant when they are 35 or over are also more likely than younger women to experience illnesses during pregnancy and longer and more difficult labor. They are also more likely to require operative delivery and Caesarean sections. The older the woman, the greater the likelihood that these problems will arise, but the absolute incidence of serious complications is small.

The expectant mother should have an adequate diet if she is going to maintain her own general good health during her pregnancy and deliver a healthy infant. This appears entirely reasonable when we remember that the growing fetus' food supply comes ultimately from the mother's blood stream, via the semipermeable membranes of the placenta and the umbilical cord. In one experimental investigation of the consequents of malnutrition during pregnancy, the subjects were 210 pregnant women attending a clinic at the University of Toronto (12, 10). All of them had inadequate diets during their first 4 or 5 months of pregnancy. In the later phases of pregnancy, the diets of 90 of the women were supplemented and made adequate from a nutritional standpoint. The other 120 maintained their nutritionally deficient diets throughout their pregnancies. By comparing these two groups, the investigators could systematically study the influence of good and poor maternal diets upon the course of pregnancy and the condition of the infant during the first few months of life.

The "good-diet" mothers were in better health throughout their pregnancies. Complications such as anemia, toxemia, threatened and actual miscarriages, premature births, and stillbirths were much more frequent in the "poor-diet" group than in the "good-diet" group. On the average, women in the latter group were in labor 5 hours less than the women with inadequate diets.

Compared with the infants born to "poor-diet" mothers, the babies of "good-diet" women had better health records during the first two weeks of postnatal life. They also had a much smaller incidence of major illnesses (pneumonia, rickets, tetany, anemia) and minor diseases (colds, bronchitis) during the entire first 6 months.

Another investigator (50) demonstrated that stillbirths, prematurities, and deaths in early infancy were less common among the babies of mothers with nutritionally adequate diets than among those whose mothers had less adequate diets. Moreover, insufficient protein in the mother's diet may lead to premature birth and neural defects in the infant (3).

The findings suggest that the "fetus obtains its nutritional requirements prior to the maternal organism and draws upon maternal storages. When these storages are depleted to a point of deficiency in the mother, the baby will fail to obtain the necessary elements" (50, 380).

There is support for the hypothesis that severe malnutrition of a pregnant mother may cause mental retardation in her child. In animals, formation of the fatty protection covering nerve fibers (called myelin) is impaired if the fetus is malnourished during the period when the myelin is being formed (1). The human fetus begins to form myelin during the seventh month of pregnancy and it is possible that if the fetus does not receive sufficient nutrition because the mother is malnourished, the formation of the myelin will be impaired. This defect is likely to lead to impaired functioning of the brain and perhaps to retarded mental development (8).

The incidence of malnutrition in Asia, Africa, and Latin America is awesome and growing. If serious malnutrition in a pregnant mother does produce brain damage in the fetus, society must act soon to reduce the incidence of malnutrition all over the world.

Drugs

During the last 5 years doctors and parents have become increasingly concerned about the potentially harmful effects of drugs on the developing fetus. The increased concern comes from two sources. First, scientists no longer believe that there is a completely effective barrier between the mother and the fetus; foreign chemicals in the mother's bloodstream do pass into the fetus' blood stream. Second, there have been many dramatic cases of damage to the fetus as a result of drugs taken by the mother. The most famous of these involved babies born with gross anatomical defects in their limbs, caused by the mothers' taking a drug called thalidomide during the pregnancy. Drugs can affect the development of the embryo and the fetus, but we need much more specific information about the relation between fetal malformation and diet and drug use.

There is more certain knowledge about the effects of drugs taken just prior to or during the delivery of the baby, drugs given to ease the mother's distress and pain. These drugs do affect the fetus and the newborn baby, although the effect may be only temporary.

Newborns whose mothers have been given barbiturate drugs or other preparations during labor may show signs of oversedation and respiratory difficulties. Electroencephalograms (records of cortical electrical activity) of 20 infants whose mothers had been given doses of seconal sodium while in labor showed depressed cortical activity for two days following birth (22). During this time the infants seemed sluggish and drowsy. By the third day, however, these symptoms of mild sedation had worn off and no residuals were noted. Nevertheless, it seems reasonable to believe that a heavy dosing of the mother with drugs "may so overload the fetal bloodstream as to produce asphyxiation of the fetus at birth, with permanent brain damage of such a kind as to lead to mental impairment" (28, 162).

One study has demonstrated that the amount of drugs given the mother during labor will influence the attentiveness of the newborn. Twenty babies, 2 to 4 days old, were shown some pictures in a random order for 1 minute at a time. The babies delivered from mothers who had been given a depressant (such as pentobarbitol) within 90 minutes of delivery looked less at the pictures than the babies delivered of mothers who had no drug within 90 minutes of delivery. Moreover, the closer to the time of delivery the drugs were administered, the less attentive the infant was (47).

Finally, it is possible that the pregnant mother's smoking may effect the fetus because nicotine from her cigarette may trigger chemical reactions that will be transmitted through the placenta. Fetal heart rate is often, but not invariably, accelerated following the mother's smoking—although there is no evidence of enduring heart or circulatory system impairment (44).

Irradiation

Radium or roentgen (X ray) irradiation of the pelvis may be therapeutically necessary for the pregnant woman with a pelvic or ovarian tumor or cancer. Small amounts of this irradiation, such as those used in X ray photography, are not known to damage the fetus, but large therapeutic doses may be injurious or precipitate abortions.

Over one-third of a group of 75 full-term infants whose mothers had therapeutic irradiation during pregnancy manifested mental or physical abnormalities which could not be attributed to any source other than the treatments. Twenty had severe disturbances of the central nervous system, 16 of them being microcephalic. (Microcephaly is a clinical type of feeble-mindedness, in which there is an abnormally small, pointed skull and a very small brain.) Eight others were extremely small, physically deformed, or blind (30, 31).

The most dramatic illustration of the effect of atomic radiation on the fetus was learned following the dropping of an atomic bomb on Hiroshima, Japan. If a mother pregnant less than 20 weeks was within a half mile of the center of the explosion she was very likely to give birth to a physically or mentally abnormal child (37).

Maternal Diseases and Disorders During Pregnancy

There appears to be an effective barrier between the embryo and many of its mother's virus or germ organisms. Hence fetal infection from maternal disease is infrequent. In some rare cases, however, infants have been born with smallpox, measles, chickenpox, or mumps transmitted from the mother (18).

On the other hand, infection with syphilitic spirochetes from the mother is not infrequent. One investigator (10) found spirochetes in 16 fetuses taken from a group of 67 syphilitic mothers—an incidence of 24 percent. These spirochetes may produce abortion or miscarriage. Or, if the child survives, he may be born weak, deformed, or mentally deficient. In some cases, the child may not manifest syphilitic symptoms until several years later. As fetuses under 18 weeks of age are apparently not susceptible to the disease, transmission of the spirochetes may be prevented if treatment of a syphilitic mother begins early in her pregnancy.

Rubella (German measles) contracted by the prospective mother in the first 3 or 4 months of pregnancy may damage the fetus considerably, producing deaf-mutism, cardiac lesions, cataracts, or various forms of mental deficiency. There does not appear to be any direct relation between the severity of maternal infection and the degree of fetal involvement. Mild attacks may produce fetal malformations as grave as those suffered when the mother is ill from 7 to 14 days. Available data indicate that about 12 percent of the mothers with rubella during the first 3 months of pregnancy have defective children (20).

Mothers who were diabetic during their pregnancy often gave birth to infants with physical abnormalities that involve the circulatory and respiratory systems (15).

There are also some general disturbances of the mother during pregnancy that may affect the fetus. One of the most common is called toxemia of pregnancy. This disorder, which is of unknown origin, involves swelling of the mother's limbs, and is associated with a general dysfunction of the mother's kidney and circulatory systems. This illness is more common among lower- than among middle-class mothers, and could be caused by a combination of poor nutrition and subsequent lowering of resistance to infection. It is possible that the toxemia might affect the fetus in a deleterious way.

Pasamanick and his colleagues searched hospital files for information on pregnancy and delivery in mothers of children who developed various types of mental and emotional disturbance during childhood (*32–36*). The evidence suggested that a greater proportion of mentally retarded than of normal children had mothers with physiological disturbances during pregnancy—especially bleeding and toxemia during the late stages of pregnancy.

Rh Factors

If there are genetically determined differences between the blood types of the fetus and its mother, they may be biochemically incompatible. For example, the child's red blood corpuscles may contain a substance which makes his blood agglutinate or "clump" in response to a specially prepared serum, while his mother's blood may lack this substance. In this case, the child, like 85 percent of the white American population, is "Rh positive"; his mother is "Rh negative" (*27*).

The Rh-positive fetus produces certain substances called antigens which enter into the mother's circulation through the placental barrier. Toxic substances (antibodies) are then manufactured in her blood and passed back into the fetus' circulatory system. They may do a great deal of damage there, destroying his red blood cells and preventing them from distributing oxygen normally. There may be tragic consequences, including miscarriage, stillbirth, or death shortly after birth from erythroblastosis (destruction of red blood corpuscles). Or, if the child survives, he may be partially paralyzed or mentally deficient, possibly as a result of brain damage from inadequate oxygen supply during a crucial developmental period (*28*).

Fortunately, these disastrous consequences do not occur in every case of mother-child Rh incompatibility. Erythroblastosis occurs only in about one out of every 200 pregnancies (*28*). First-born children are not usually affected, because it takes time for the mother to develop the antibodies, but subsequent offspring are more likely to suffer if their Rh blood types differ from their mother's.

There are medical techniques now available which, if applied early, minimize the consequences of this incompatibility. "Every [woman] planning marriage should consult her physician to find out the Rh types both of herself and her prospective husband. There are various ways in which the evil factors of clashing Rh factors may be partially averted if doctors know about them beforehand" (*28*, 166).

The blood corpuscles contain other special chemicals besides Rh, known as the A, B, and O substances. These provide the names for the common blood types among humans. Incompatibility between mother and fetus for

A, B, or O substances may have the same consequences as Rh incompatibility (38, 54), although, fortunately, this occurs in a smaller percentage of cases, even when incompatible combinations are present.

Maternal Emotional States

Despite the fact that there are no direct connections between the mother's and the fetus' nervous systems, the mother's emotional state can influence fetal reactions and development. This is true because emotions such as rage, fear, and anxiety bring the mother's autonomic nervous system into action, liberating certain chemicals (acetylcholine and epinephrine) into the blood stream. Furthermore, under such conditions the endocrine glands, particularly the adrenals, secrete different kinds and amounts of hormones. Cell metabolism is also modified. In brief, the composition of the blood changes, and new chemical substances are transmitted through the placenta, producing changes in the fetus' circulatory system (45).

Sontag (42–44), working at the Fels Research Institute in Yellow Springs, Ohio, showed that these changes may be irritating to the fetus. He noted that bodily movements of fetuses increased several hundred percent while their mothers were undergoing emotional stress. If the mother's emotional upset lasted several weeks, fetal activity continued at an exaggerated level throughout the entire period. When these upsets were brief, heightened irritability usually lasted several hours. According to this investigator, prolonged maternal emotional stress during pregnancy may have enduring consequents for the child (43).

Maternal emotional tensions may also play some role in the development of colic in the neonate. Colic is a term applied to a syndrome characterized by a distension of the abdomen, apparent pain, and continuous crying at certain intervals during the day. One investigator (25) has reported that the mothers of colicky babies were more tense and anxious during pregnancy than the mothers of noncolicky babies. The former group also felt more inadequate about their ability to care for the child. Perhaps the mother's chronic concern about her ability to handle the coming baby produced physiological reactions in both mother and baby that predisposed the child to the colic reaction. It is, of course, possible that tense mother-child relations following birth may have led to the development of colic. This study does not permit a differentiation of these alternative explanations, and the student should bear in mind that there are many cases of colic that are not clearly related to maternal tension and anxiety.

Extreme anxiety and tension during pregnancy may also predispose the mother to experience a more difficult labor and delivery. Forty-eight pregnant women were given a questionnaire designed to assess the intensity of their conscious anxiety in many areas. On the basis of official hospital records it was possible to classify each woman's subsequent delivery as "normal" (25 women) or "abnormal" (23 women). The women whose deliveries were abnormal or had complications reported a high amount of anxiety during the pregnancy period (7).

In brief, maternal anxiety and emotional unrest during pregnancy may affect the developing fetus adversely and handicap the newborn infant in his adaptation to the external environment. The long-term consequences of such disturbances are difficult to evaluate, as it is usually impossible to determine whether prenatal or very early postnatal conditions played the more important role in the infant's reactions.

Maternal Attitudes.   The expectant mother's attitude toward her pregnancy may be reflected in her emotional state during this period. A woman who resents being pregnant is more likely to be emotionally upset than one who is happy about the prospect of having a child. For example, in one study (41) a large group of mothers were asked to recall their attitudes during pregnancy. Approximately one-half reported feeling delighted, while one-quarter either felt unhappy or ambivalent when they discovered that they were pregnant. In general, a greater proportion of first pregnancies than of later ones were accompanied by feelings of happiness. Moreover, the longer the time period between pregnancies, the greater the likelihood that the mother would report positive feelings.

The mother's attitude toward her pregnancy is also intimately related to her emotional maturity and personal adjustment. For example, one team of investigators concluded that "marital conflict, whatever its cause, was the major factor in the acceptance or rejection of pregnancies" (21). They also noted that, in some instances, failure to adjust to pregnancy was related to the mother's emotional immaturity and her continued desire to return to the dependent status she enjoyed as a child.

In order to determine the factors related to favorable and unfavorable attitudes toward pregnancy, one investigator administered a questionnaire to a group of 100 expectant women and compared the responses of the 25 with the most positive attitudes with those of the 25 least favorably disposed to having a child (9). Generally speaking, those who felt positive toward pregnancy were well adjusted in marriage, felt financially secure, and were sexually and socially compatible with their husbands. In addition, more of these women had siblings and had experienced close family relationships during childhood. On the other hand, poor marital adjustment, emotional impoverishment during childhood, absence of close relationships with the mother during childhood, poor sex education, and having been forced to take care of younger siblings characterized the women with unfavorable attitudes toward pregnancy.

The mother's attitude toward the pregnancy and her baby seem to be a valid predictor of the mother's behavior with her baby after birth. In one study, mothers who were pregnant with their first child were interviewed during the last 3 months of the pregnancy. They were asked about their attitude toward the baby, their general feeling toward the coming infant, and the degree to which they thought they would seek affection and contact with the baby after its birth. The mothers were then visited in their homes when the babies were 1 month old. Those mothers who had the most positive attitudes toward their unborn children spent the most time in face-to-face contact with them at 1 month (29). A mother's attitude toward her unborn child has psychological meaning and relates to aspects of her personality and behavior. Because extreme rage, anger, or frustration over an unwanted pregnancy could produce physiological reactions that might influence the fetus, we must at least consider the possibility that the psychological status of the pregnant mother can have consequences for the future psychological integrity of the baby.

THE BIRTH PROCESS AND ITS CONSEQUENCES

Thus far we have considered the possible effect of events that occurred during the pregnancy—nutrition of the mother, drugs the mother may have taken, maternal diseases or infections, irradiation, and the mother's emotional state. Each tends to influence the fetus during the organization and growth of its organs and the development of its physiological functions. There is a second set of factors that can affect the fetus adversely. They are related to the mechanics of the delivery process—the ease with which delivery occurs and the rapidity with which the newborn begins to breathe. Although there are many dangers associated with this process, the two major ones involve a breaking of the blood vessels of the brain (called hemorrhaging), caused by strong pressures on the head of the fetus, and lack of sufficient oxygen because of the infant's failure to begin to breathe once he is separated from the maternal source of oxygen. Both of these events— the hemorrhaging and the failure to breathe early—affect the supply of oxygen to the nerve cells of the brain, and, in extreme cases, can lead to damage to nerve cells and subsequent psychological defects. The neurons of the central nervous system require oxygen; if they are deprived of oxygen, some cells may die. If too many neurons die, the infant may suffer serious brain damage or, in the extreme, death.

There is an interesting difference between the effects of lack of oxygen (called anoxia) on the *infant* and on the *adult*. At a general level, the brain can be considered to consist basically of two parts—the *cerebral cortex*, which is the furrowed part responsible for complex perceptions and thought, and the *brain stem*. The brain stem is made up of a series of connected structures, many of which are responsible for motor coordination. Anoxia in a newborn is more likely to cause damage to the cells of the brain stem, rather than the cortex. Anoxia in an adult is more likely to cause damage to the nerve cells of the cortex rather than the brain stem (49). When the cells of the brain stem are damaged, motor defects are likely to occur. The child may show a paralysis of the legs or the arms, a tremor of the face or fingers, or an inability to use his vocal muscles. In the latter case, he may have difficulty learning to speak. The general term cerebral palsy describes a variety of motor defects associated with damage to the brain cells possibly as a result of lack of oxygen during the birth process.

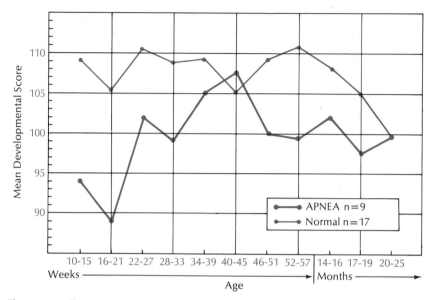

Fig. 3.9. Differences in developmental score between normal and anoxic infants. (From G. A. Stechler. A longitudinal follow-up of neonatal APNEA. *Child Developm.,* copyright 1964 by The Society for Research in Child Development, Inc., *35,* 343. By permission.)

These nervous system defects, although present at birth, are not necessarily hereditary.

There are, therefore, two major factors—hemorrhaging and respiratory delay—which can lead to oxygen deficit to the nerve cells which, in turn, can lead to a varied set of defects, some of which are motor (52). These facts are well known. The more perplexing question is whether children with a mild oxygen deficit, but who do not show obvious motor paralysis or tremors, have a mild degree of brain damage which might influence their future psychological development.

We cannot answer this question with complete confidence, but there are some clues. One way to study this issue is to find a group of infants who experienced mild anoxia during the delivery process and compare them with a group of infants from the same social class and ordinal position who did not experience anoxia. Both groups of infants would be studied continually for 5 to 10 years to determine if they differ in their psychological development. Scientists have performed studies of this type and the results suggest that there may be relatively specific differences in intellectual functioning between the anoxic and normal infants during the first 2 to 3 years. With age, however, the differences disappear or become minimal. By the time the child is 7 or 8 years of age it is difficult to distinguish the mild anoxic from the normal child (5).

In general, the infant with mild anoxia tends to score lower on stand-

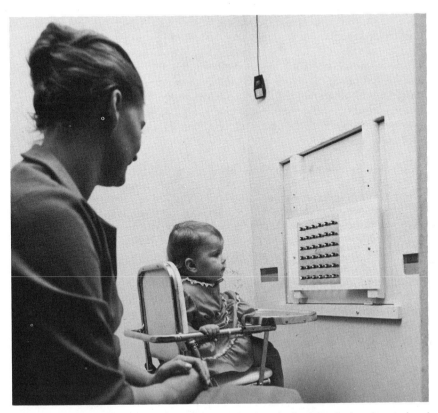

Fig. 3.10. The Infant Laboratory conducted by Dr. Michael Lewis for the study of infant attention. A child (approximately 18-months-old) sits facing the light matrix. Two of the observation windows flanking the matrix are visible, and it is from these windows that the observers record the infant's behavior. (From M. Lewis, B. Bartels, H. Cambell & S. Goldberg. Individual differences in attention. *American Journal of Diseases of Children*, 1967, Vol. 113. By permission.)

ard tests of motor development during the first year, but by 2 years of age the differences between anoxic and normal babies are minimal (46; see Fig. 3.9). Anoxic babies also seem to be less attentive to moving lights during the first year of life (26; see Fig. 3.10).

It will be recalled that infants born to mothers who had heavy sedation during delivery also showed shorter attention spans to photographs during the first 4 days of life. Infants with some depressed functioning of the brain, because of either drugs or anoxia, appear to show shorter periods of sustained attention to visual stimuli during the first months of life.

Finally, anoxic infants, during the first week, are more irritable and show more muscular tension and rigidity than normal infants do (19).

One of the most comprehensive studies of the long-term effects of mild anoxia at birth involved a follow-up assessment of newborns who had suffered anoxia at birth and were tested at both 3 and 7 years of age. At 3 years of age, the anoxic children performed poorly on tests of conceptualization, compared with the normals (14). When these children were tested again at age 7, the differences between the normal and anoxic children were less dramatic and their IQ scores were equal. However, the anoxic children had greater difficulty in copying designs placed before them, and were more distractible than the normals. A child who does not think about what he is drawing or lets his attention shift to events around him is likely to draw a design poorly.

It may be concluded that perinatal anoxia is related to deficits evident at 7 years of age. It is also evident that such deficits which do occur are reasonably minimal for the group as a whole. While there was some tendency for the degree of impairment to be associated with newborn criteria of severity the association is a weak one. A prognosis for any given newborn would be very difficult to make except when there are very severe or numerous complications (5, 33).

In sum, mild anoxia can cause damage to the cells of the brain, which, in turn, may disturb motor behavior and produce shorter periods of attentiveness during the first year. With age, the differences between anoxic and normal children become smaller, and whatever differences still exist are likely to involve motor coordination and, perhaps, distractibility.

PREMATURITY

Premature birth is another phenomenon that seems to be predictive of the child's later development. The definition of prematurity should be in terms of the number of weeks of gestational age. An infant born at less than 37 weeks of gestational age (time since fertilization) is classified premature; one born between 37 and 40 weeks would be classified as normal. However, it is difficult to obtain information on the time of conception, and most scientists use the child's birth weight as the index of prematurity. When birth weight is used, an infant born under 5½ pounds is regarded as premature, and an infant born under 4 pounds is classified as severely premature. It is estimated that 7.6 percent of hospital births in the United States are categorized as premature. The premature infant has wrinkled, transparent skin, a disproportionately large head and tongue, poor muscle tone, and prominent and widely spaced eyes. Studies of the development of premature children reveal that these infants remain smaller in height and weight until about 5 or 6 years of age. Prematures also tend to obtain lower scores on general tests of cognitive and motor development during the first 5 years.

An extensive 5-year study in Scotland followed 1000 infants, some of whom were born prematurely. As late as at 4 years of age, the prematures of all social classes had lower developmental quotients than the normals— but the premature children from the lowest social-class backgrounds had the

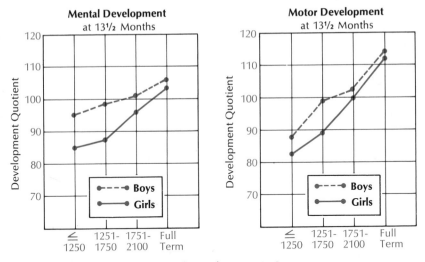

Fig. 3.11. Differences in mental and motor development for three groups of varying prematurity and a normal full-term group. (From M. D. S. Braine, C. B. Heimer, H. Wortis & A. M. Freedman. Factors associated with impairment of the early development of prematures. *Monogr. Soc. Res. Child Develpm.*, copyright 1966 by The Society for Research in Child Development, Inc., *31*, 139. By permission.)

poorest scores of all. On the other hand, there were no dramatic differences in overt behavior between the majority of the prematures and the normal children (*11*).

One study, involving only lower-class Negro infants born either premature or at term, followed the infants until 1 year of age. The prematures were more likely than the full-term babies to suffer anoxia, a loss in weight, and infection during the opening days of life. The premature infants performed much poorer than the normals did on a test of gross motor development when they were 13 months of age; moreover, within the premature group, the lighter the birth weight, the poorer the performance (*2*; see Fig. 3.11).

In sum, the premature child does differ slightly from the normal. He is likely to be more restless and distractable if extremely premature, and display slightly retarded motor and cognitive development during the first year. At the extreme ranges of prematurity, under 4 pounds, the child is more likely to be brain-damaged so that serious psychological defects will follow. Children with milder levels of prematurity do not differ significantly from normals on tests of motor or cognitive development. There is a suggestion that prematures may suffer mild anoxia, loss of weight, and related physiological disturbances during the early weeks of life, and it is possible that the retarded performance is related to these disturbances.

Finally, we cannot rule out the possibility that the behavioral differences between prematures and normals might be caused, in part, by maternal behavior. The premature infant may be overprotected and isolated by his parents. Because his parents may be afraid of harming an organism they regard as delicate or fragile, they may not push him to perform and not encourage his cognitive development as much as they would a normal child.

Relationship to Social Class. Many of the problems associated with pregnancy and delivery are three to four times more frequent among lower- than among middle-class families. Toxemias, infections, prematurity, and anoxia are all more likely to occur in a lower-class mother and her infant than in a middle-class family. In addition, poorer intellectual performance is more common among lower-class than middle-class children, even when there is no evidence of any of the above prenatal or perinatal problems. We have, therefore, a positive association among three phenomena: (1) membership in the lower class; (2) prenatal and perinatal complications; and (3) poor performance on measures of intellectual development. But we do not know whether the poorer intellectual development is caused, in part, by the problems of pregnancy and delivery or is solely the consequent of being raised in a lower-class home. The poorer IQ of the lower-class child could be primarily a function of lack of intellectual stimulation and have little to do with the prenatal or perinatal factors. On the other hand, the poorer performance on tests of intellectual development could be the consequent of prenatal or perinatal trauma. The results suggest that a child exposed to prenatal or perinatal problems does have a greater likelihood of showing slightly retarded mental and motor development during the first year, regardless of his social class. If he is born into a lower-class family, this probability is increased. If he is born to middle-class parents, the probability of intellectual retardation becomes minimal. Many separate factors contribute to intellectual performance. If a child is handicapped by several retarding factors (e.g., maternal malnutrition, toxemia, anoxia, prematurity, and minimal intellectual stimulation), the likelihood that he will show retarded intellectual development is increased.

Two facts must be kept in mind, however. First, the child is extremely malleable, and many children apparently recover from early deficits due either to prematurity or anoxia. Second, less than 10 percent of all births in the nation experience any of the problems discussed in this chapter. Fortunately most infants begin life well within the normal range.

SUMMARY

The unborn infant's development can be influenced negatively by a variety of factors, including the adequacy of the mother's nutrition, drugs, X rays, and infection. In general, the younger the fetus, the more susceptible it is to these untoward factors. The most serious threat to the newborn during the birth process is lack of adequate oxygen which can be caused by both mechanical and chemical factors; this deprivation can damage the cells of the central nervous system. Unfortunately, the majority of the serious problems associated with pregnancy and childbirth are most common among the economically disadvantaged who suffer more from poor health and a lack of proper nutrition than the middle class. Although the premature or anoxic infant is different from the normal child during the early months of life, these differences become smaller with time and, at the moment, it is difficult to state the long-term consequences of mild prematurity or mild anoxia.

References

1. Benton, J. W., Moser, H. W., Dodge, P. R., & Carr, S. Modification of the schedule of myelinization in the rat by early nutritional deprivation. *Pediatrics,* 1966, *38,* 801–804.

2. Braine, M. D. S., Heimer, C. B., Wortis, H., & Freedman, A. M. Factors associated with impairment of the early development of prematures. *Monogr. Soc. Res. Child Develpm.,* 1966, *31,* No. 106, 1–92.

3. Burke, B. S., Beal, V. A., Kirkwood, S. B., & Stuart, H. C. The influence of nutrition during pregnancy upon the conditions of the infant at birth. *J. Nutrition,* 1943, *26,* 569–583.

4. Carmichael, L. The onset and early development of behavior. In L. Carmichael (Ed.), *Manual of child psychology.* New York: Wiley, 1954 (2nd ed.).

5. Corah, N. L., Anthony, E. J., Painter, P., Stern, J. A., & Thurston, D. Effects of perinatal anoxia after 7 years. *Psychol. Monogr.,* 1965, *79,* 1–34.

6. Corner, G. W. *Ourselves unborn: an embryologist's essay on man.* New Haven: Yale Univer. Press, 1944.

7. Davids, A. De Vault, S. & Talmadge, M. Anxiety, pregnancy and childbirth abnormalities. *J. consult. Psychol.,* 1961, *25,* 74–77.

8. Davison, A. N., & Dobbing, J. Myelinization as a vulnerable period in brain development. *Brit. Med. Bull.,* 1966, *22,* 40–45.

9. Despres, M. A. Favorable and unfavorable attitudes toward pregnancy in primiparae. *J. genet. Psychol.,* 1937, *51,* 241–254.

10. Dippel, A. L. The relationship of congenital syphilis to abortion and miscarriage, and the mechanisms of intrauterine protection. *Amer. J. Obst. & Gynec.,* 1944, *47,* 369–379.

11. Drillien, C. M., & Ellis, R. W. B. *The growth and development of the prematurely born infant.* Baltimore: Williams & Wilkins, 1964.

12. Ebbs, J. H., Brown, A., Tisdall, F. F., Moyle, W. J., & Bell, M. The influence of improved prenatal nutrition upon the infant. *Canad. Med. Ass. J.,* 1942, 6–8.

13. Ebbs, J. H., Tisdall, F. F. & Scott, W. A. The influence of prenatal diet on the mother and child. *Milbank Memorial Fund Quart.,* 1942, *20,* 35–36.

14. Ernhart, C. B., Graham, F. K., & Thurston, D. Relationship of neonatal apnea to development at three years. *Arch. Neurol.,* 1960, *2,* 504–510.

15. Gellis, S. S., & Hsia, D. Y. The infant of the diabetic mother. *Amer. J. Dis. Child.,* 1959, *97,* 1.

16. Gesell, A ., *The embryology of behavior.* New York: Harper & Row, 1945.

17. Gesell, A., & Amatruda, C. S. *Developmental diagnosis: normal and abnormal child development.* New York: Hoèber, 1941.

18. Goodpasture, E. W. Virus infection of the mammalian fetus. *Science*, 1942, *95*, 391–396.
19. Graham, Frances K., Matarazzo, Ruth G., & Caldwell, Bettye M. Behavioral differences between normal and traumatized newborns. *Psychol. Monogr.*, 1956, *70*, No. 5.
20. Greenberg, M., Pelliteri, O., & Barton, J. Frequency of defects in infants whose mothers had rubella during pregnancy. *J. Amer. Med. Ass.*, 1957, *165*, 675–678.
21. Hall, D. E., & Mohr, G. J. Prenatal attitudes of primiparae: a contribution to the mental hygiene of pregnancy. *Ment. Hyg.* (N.Y.), 1933, *17*, 226–234.
22. Hughes, J. G., Ehemann, B., & Brown, U. A. Electroencephalography of the newborn. *Amer. J. Dis. Child.*, 1948, *76*, 626–633.
23. Hurlock, E. B. *Child development.* New York: McGraw-Hill, 1950.
24. Knobloch, H., Rider, R. V., Harper, P., & Pasamanick, B. Neuropsychiatric sequelae of prematurity: a longitudinal study. *J. Amer. Med. Ass.*, 1956, *161*, 581–585.
25. Lakin, M. Personality factors in mothers of excessively crying (colicky) infants. *Monogr. Soc. Res. Child Develpm.*, 1957, *22*, No. 64.
26. Lewis, M., Martels, B., Campbell, H., and Goldberg, S. Individual differences in attention. *Amer. J. Dis. Child.*, 1967, *113*, 461–465.
27. McCurdy, R. N. C. *The rhesus danger: its medical, moral and legal aspects.* London: William Heinemann Medical Books, 1950.
28. Montagu, M. F. A. Constitutional and prenatal factors in infant and child health. In M. J. E. Senn (Ed.), *Symposium on the healthy personality.* New York: Josiah Macy, Jr. Found., 1950, 148–175.
29. Moss, H. A. & Robson, K. S. Maternal influences in early social visual behavior. Paper presented at the annual meeting of the American Orthopsychiatric Association, 1967.
30. Murphy, D. P. The outcome of 625 pregnancies in women subjected to pelvic radium roentgen irradiation. *Amer. J. Obst. & Gynec.*, 1929, *18*, 179–187.
31. Murphy, D. P. *Congenital malformation.* Philadelphia: Univer. of Pennsylvania Press, 1947 (2nd ed.).
32. Pasamanick, B., & Lilienfeld, A. M. Association of maternal and fetal factors with development of mental deficiency. 1. Abnormalities in the prenatal and paranatal periods. *J. Amer. Med. Ass.*, 1955, *159*, 155–160.
33. Pasamanick, B., & Lilienfeld, A. M. Maternal and fetal factors in the development of epilepsy. II. Relationship to some clinical features of epilepsy. *Neurology*, 1955, *5*, 77–83.
34. Pasamanick, B., Knobloch, H., & Lilienfeld, A. M. Socioeconomic status and some precursors of neuropsychiatric disorder. *Amer. J. Orthopsychiat.*, 1956, *26*, 594–601.
35. Pasamanick, B., & Kawi, A. A study of the association of prenatal and paranatal factors with the development of tics in children. *J. Pediat.*, 1956, *48*, 596–601.
36. Pasamanick, B., Constantinow, F. K., & Lilienfeld, A. M. Pregnancy experience and the development of childhood speech disorders. *Amer. J. Dis. Child.*, 1956, *91*, 113–118.
37. Plummer, G. Anomalies occurring in children exposed in utero to the atomic bomb in Hiroshima. *Pediatrics*, 1952, *10*, 687.
38. Race, R. R., & Sanger, R. *Blood groups in man.* Springfield, Ill.: Thomas, 1954.
39. Rand, W., Sweeny, M., & Vincent, E. L. *Growth and development of the growing child.* Philadelphia: Saunders, 1946.

40. Scheinfeld, A. *The new you and heredity.* Philadelphia: Lippincott, 1950.
41. Sears, R. R., Maccoby, E. E., & Levin, H. *Patterns of child rearing.* New York: Harper & Row, 1957.
42. Sontag, L. W. The significance of fetal environmental differences. *Amer. J. Obst. & Gynec.,* 1941, *42,* 996–1003.
43. Sontag, L. W. War and fetal maternal relationship. *Marriage and Fam. Living,* 1944, *6,* 1–5.
44. Sontag, L. W., & Wallace, R. F. The effect of cigarette smoking during pregnancy upon the fetal heart rate. *Amer J. Obst. & Gynec.,* 1935, *29,* 3–8.
45. Squier, R., & Dunbar, F. Emotional factors in the course of pregnancy. *Psychosom. Med.,* 1946, *8,* 161–175.
46. Stechler, G. A longitudinal follow-up of neonatal apnea. *Child Develpm.,* 1964, *35,* 333–348.
47. Stechler, G. Newborn attention as affection by medication during labor. *Science,* 1964, *144,* 315–317.
48. Stern, C. *Principles of human genetics.* San Francisco: Freeman, 1960 (2nd ed.).
49. Teuber, H. L., & Rudel, R. G. Behavior after cerebral lesions in children and adults. *Develpm. Med. & Child Neurol.,* 1962, *4,* 3–20.
50. Tompkins, W. T. The clinical significance of nutritional deficiencies in pregnancy. *Bull. N. Y. Acad. Med.,* 1948, *24,* 376–388.
51. Watson, E. H., & Lowrey, G. H. *Growth and development of children.* Chicago: Year Book Publishers, 1954.
52. Windle, W. F. Neuropathology of certain forms of mental retardation. *Science,* 1963, *140,* 1186–1189.

part II
The
First Two
Years

4

Learning
and Development

The importance of learning in the child's development would be difficult to overestimate. The kinds of responses the infant and growing child can learn, and how much he can learn, are limited, of course, by his biological nature and inheritance. No human being can learn to swim *exactly* like a fish, or to run like a gazelle, despite the colloquialisms we use to describe a good swimmer or runner. Similarly, a mongoloid child, disadvantaged by defective chromosomes, will never be able to learn atomic theory or the calculus. Nevertheless, within broad limits many of the characteristics of humans—not only the usual intellectual or performance skills that come readily to mind but also desires, values, fears, and attitudes, even many basic physiological responses—are learned.

Attempts to understand how learning occurs and how the continuing interaction between a biological organism and its environment lead to modifications in the individual's *capacity* to perform, as well as in performance itself, have been the preoccupations of highly talented investigators and theoreticians over many decades. Just in the last few years, impressive—even awesome—advances have been made not only in our knowledge of what can be learned, but, in some instances at least, also in controlling the course of learning within remarkably precise limits. It has been found, for example, that a single nerve cell in the brain of a living animal can be "taught" to increase and decrease its rate of firing of neural impulses (51). We have discovered that a humble flatworm can be conditioned to respond to light with a contraction of its body and, further, that if the worm is then cut in half and allowed to regenerate into two complete new organisms, both will maintain this learned response (51). Skinner and his associates have demonstrated that pigeons can be trained to play competitive ping-pong (31, 68).

At the human level, a number of psychologists working with severely brain-damaged or psychotic children, have shown that children who previously did not respond at all to environmental demands, or who responded very inadequately or inappropriately (despite valiant attempts at conventional treatment), can still be taught, through patiently detailed learning procedures, many of the responses necessary for social living (13, 35, 47, 78).

And yet there is a paradox in all this. It would appear that the more we learn *empirically* about the necessary conditions of learning under varying circumstances, the more difficulty we encounter in developing a systematic theory of learning, one capable of enunciating basic principles which can adequately account for all or even a majority of these many complex and diverse instances of learning. When there is little to explain, explanation is not too difficult, as earlier theories of learning have demonstrated (32).

In contrast, the current explosion in factual information about the development of skills and abilities presents challenges to learning theorists that will not be resolved for many years to come. Consequently, it is not possible to present a complete set of theoretical learning principles, neatly applicable to all acquired behavior. For example, it is difficult to explain the 2-year-old's extremely rapid advances in language (cf. pp. 184–192) or the schoolchild's progress in logical thinking (his shifts from one cognitive "stage" to another) in terms of the established principles of learning that apply to the development and modification of many of the child's responses. Nevertheless, it should be possible to contribute substantially to our knowledge of the role of learning in child development, both by presenting a number of important empirical findings about children's learning and by discussing some of the basic theoretical principles of learning that appear to be at work in the acquisition and development of many aspects of behavior.

WHAT IS LEARNING?

Stated most simply, learning is the process by which behavior, or the potentiality for behavior, is modified as a result of experience. Before continuing, it is useful to consider what is meant by the word, *learning*. Learning represents the establishment of new relationships—bonds or connections—between units that were not previously associated. There may be relationships between (1) stimuli and overt responses; (2) stimuli and internal processes; (3) internal processes and overt responses; or (4) a pair or more of internal processes. Learning refers to the establishment of the new bonds, or the strengthening of already existing associations that were weak.

Stimuli and responses may be of many different kinds. An individual who learns to respond regularly to a stop light by applying his foot to the brake of his car has established an association between a visual stimulus (the light) and a motor response (braking). But stimuli (often called *cues* when they are sufficiently distinctive to serve as a basis for learning) may vary widely. Thus not only such obvious cues as traffic lights but also the sight of a mother's face, or the sound of her voice—even internal stimuli, such as thoughts, images, feelings, and bodily sensations—may all serve as stimuli to which responses can be learned.

Similarly, responses can be of many kinds. They can be motor acts: talking, walking, or hitting a baseball; physiological responses: sweating or changes in heart rate; or thoughts and images. It should be noted that internal responses like thinking and feeling can serve either as cues or responses. This means that any example of ongoing behavior, such as solving a problem or learning a poem, involves a complex, continuous series of cues and responses.

What Learning Is Not

Not all behavior is learned. Some response tendencies exist at birth and even during prenatal life. As we have already noted, the pupillary reflex (contraction of the pupil in response to light) has been observed even in premature infants. Many other responses of infants—swallowing, opening and closing the eyes, shuddering in response to a bitter taste, grasping when pressure is applied to the palm—are unlearned.

While the unlearned nature of such "basic" responses may seem obvious to the reader, there are other instances of unlearned behavior which are by no means so evident. One might assume that the tendency of baby ducklings—even ugly ones—to follow their mothers results from their having learned the value of this response through experience. But such is not the case, as the recent work of animal ethologists has demonstrated (32, 46, 82). The actual fact is that the young duckling, and some other species as well, are born with a tendency to accept a certain range of "mother-figures," characterized by general size, patterns of movement, and sounds. Once any particular "mother" has been accepted and followed, only this particular figure will produce the "following response." Of course, under normal conditions of existence, this figure will be the actual mother. But if these conditions are changed for experimental purposes or by accidents of nature, the "following response" may be obtained to other figures: a toy duck, a goose, or even a distinguished large, and impressive ethologist such as Professor Konrad Lorenz, who has investigated this phenomenon, technically referred to as *imprinting* (29, 46).

Other equally complex and surprising examples of unlearned behavior have been studied by ethologists. For example, it has been determined in the case of the male stickleback fish that a very specific visual stimulus (namely, a red underbelly) in another fish will provoke complex fighting behavior. In contrast, a smaller, nonred underbelly will elicit courting behavior. Even dummies that look very little like another stickleback fish will provoke these responses as long as the essential *key stimulus* is present (*18, 46*).

In many instances, much of the gentle art of mothering appears to be unlearned. Thus animals ranging from the humble rat to birds will build nests in preparation for their young, even though they may never have witnessed such activities themselves.

It is, of course, far more difficult to isolate and study possible examples of complex human behavior that is unlearned, and most of our knowledge to date comes from experimental work with animals. While it appears likely that complex behavior in humans is generally much more dependent on learning and much less dependent on innate response tendencies, the possibility exists that at least some types of human behavior previously assumed to be learned may turn out to be at least partially dependent on such innate response tendencies.

Maturation. Another of learning's "chief competitors" as a modifier of behavior is maturation:

> If a behavior sequence matures through regular stages irrespective of intervening practice, the behavior is said to develop through maturation and not through learning. If training procedures do not speed up or modify the behavior, such procedures are not causally important and the changes do not classify as learning. Relatively pure cases such as the swimming of tadpoles and the flying of birds can be attributed primarily to maturation. Many activities are not as clear-cut, but develop through a complex interplay of maturation and learning. A convenient illustration is the development of language in the child. The child has not learned to talk until old enough, but the language which he learns is that which he hears. In such cases it is an experimental problem to isolate the effects of maturation and of learning. The ambiguity in such cases is one of fact, not of definition (32, 4).

Because maturation proceeds at such a rapid rate in children, it is important to take its possible effects into account in studies of children's learning. Thus, for example, it is not enough to note that a group of young children who were previously unable to climb a set of stairs became able to do so some weeks later after intensive training procedures—the child was also maturing during this period. In order to control for the effects of maturation, it is necessary also to have a *control* group of children of the same age who are not exposed to these intensive training procedures during this period. Only by comparing the subsequent stair-climbing skills of the two groups can we determine the extent to which the development of these skills is a function of specific learning experiences and not simply of physical maturation.

TYPES OF LEARNING

Having discussed briefly what learning is, and what it is not, let us turn our attention to some basic examples of learning in order, first, to consider what the essential components of any learning situation are, and second, what general principles may be derived to help us to understand (and hopefully to control and predict) learning.

Much of our current knowledge regarding learning and its principles stems from studies in which an external stimulus has been associated with an overt external response (e.g., learning to press a lever in response to the stimulus of a light). There are, however, other types of learning that have received increased attention recently, and we will discuss some of the more important of them later in this chapter. While in some instances these other types of learning are more complex, many of the basic principles of learning derived from simple stimulus-response experiments are still applicable to these other forms of learning. Thus it is desirable to consider some of the simpler forms of learning first, in order to establish some of the basic principles of learning.

Classical and Operant Conditioning

Classical Conditioning. The most common, and perhaps the most basic category of learning involves the establishment of an association between an external stimulus and a response, where prior to learning no such connection existed. *Classical conditioning* is the purest example of such learning. In classical conditioning a *reflex response,* which is innately elicited by a specific stimulus (e.g., removing one's hand from a fire or blinking one's eyes in response to a very bright light), is associated with a previously neutral stimulus.

The *response* can be an *overt action* (an eye blink or the withdrawal of a hand) or a *physiological reaction* (salivation or a change in heart rate). But the *response* must be a naturally reflexive reaction to a particular stimulus in classical conditioning.

Most readers have already heard of one famous example of classical conditioning, although they may not have thought of it in these terms. Pavlov's pioneering experiments with salivation in dogs have been discussed far beyond the frontiers of psychology—often with considerable dramatic license. They may be viewed either as an illustration of man's ability to control his fate in an orderly fashion or, with equal inaccuracy, as a sign of an impending Orwellian world of "1984," characterized by thought control, loss of individual freedom, and the development of a race of human robots subject only to the whims of an all-powerful state.

What did Pavlov actually demonstrate? In essence, he showed that a dog can be taught the *response* of salivation to the *stimulus* (or *cue*) of a buzzer (see Fig. 4.1). This was accomplished by pairing the presentation of the sound of the buzzer with the presentation of food. Food is a stimulus that innately (i.e., without learning) elicits the salivation response. Salivation does not ordinarily occur to the cue of a buzzer, but as a result of repeated pairings of the buzzer with the food, the buzzer sound alone becomes capable of eliciting the salivation response. In other words, a connection or association is learned between the cue of the buzzer and the response of salivation, when prior to learning this connection did not exist.

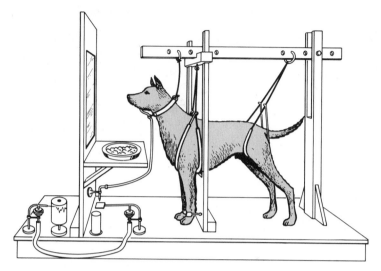

Fig. 4.1. Pavlov's dog. The dog is strapped into a harness in which it has grown used to standing. A tube attached to the dog's salivary gland collects any saliva secreted by the gland, and the number of drops from the tube is recorded on a revolving drum outside the chamber. A laboratory attendant can watch the dog through a one-way mirror and can deliver food to the dog's feedpan by remote control. Thus, there is nothing in the chamber to distract the dog's attention except the food, when it is delivered, and any other stimulus that the attendant wishes to present, such as the sound of a metronome. (After R. M. Yerkes & S. Morgulis. The method of Pavlov in animal behavior. *Psychol. Bull.,* 1909.)

Let us consider a somewhat more complex case. Dorothy Marquis (*50*) has studied the infant's very early learning in relation to feeding. Working with 10 infants between 2 and 9 days of age, she sounded a buzzer in their presence 5 seconds prior to each feeding. Within 5 days after the beginning of this training, 8 of these infants began to exhibit sucking and mouth-opening responses (innate responses to the stimulation of a nipple) as soon as they heard the buzzer. She also noted that the sound of the buzzer tended to reduce crying and general activity. Four control infants heard the sound of the buzzer but were not fed immediately afterward. These infants did not manifest sucking and mouth-opening behaviors in response to the buzzer. In short, the first group of infants learned to suck to the cue of a buzzer as a result of the pairing of the sound of the buzzer with feeding.

It may be noted that in each of the above examples of classical conditioned learning, elicitation of the desired response was automatic. In the case of Pavlov's dog, food is a stimulus that innately produces salivation; similarly, in the case of Marquis' infant, the presence of a bottle in the mouth initiates the inborn sucking reflex.

In classical conditioning a new association is established between an external stimulus and a response that is basically a reflex. Similar associations are continually being established in the young infant. The stimulus of a nipple placed in the infant's mouth elicits sucking movements innately, but the sight of the bottle does not. Yet after several months of bottlefeeding, the infant will begin to make sucking movements when he sees the bottle (45, 50, 76).

Operant Conditioning. Another example of learning that involves a new relation between a stimulus and an overt response is called *operant conditioning* or *operant learning*. Here the overt response that is being connected with a new stimulus is not a reflex. An example would be the familiar task of teaching a dog to "shake hands." No known stimulus innately produces such behavior. Instead, the response itself must be gradually and carefully developed, through a technique known as *instrumental or operant conditioning*. In essence, this technique involves rewarding appropriate responses whenever they happen to occur. In this procedure, the subject's own response is *instrumental* to the production of the reward—it *operates* to bring about the reward, hence the term *instrumental* or *operant conditioning*.

In some learning situations, the experimenter may simply sit around and wait for the proper response to occur by chance. One of the most common operant learning situations employed by psychologists in recent years involves the use of the Skinner box, named after the innovator and most productive investigator of operant conditioning. Typically, this apparatus consists of a small soundproof box containing a little lever, a food cup, and perhaps a light. The task of an animal placed in the box is to press the lever in order to obtain food. The animal may make many irrelevant responses when first placed in the box, such as running around, attempting to climb a wall, or scratching himself. Eventually, however, he is likely to press the lever, if only by chance. When he does so, he is automatically rewarded by a small pellet of food dropped in the food cup. With continued experience in this situation, the animal becomes increasingly quick and adept in lever-pressing, and irrelevant responses tend to disappear.

In other situations, one may not wait for chance alone to produce the proper response, but may take steps to increase the likelihood of the proper response's occurring. This, of course, is one of the skills displayed by experienced trainers—and many mothers as well! In the case of the dog being taught to "shake hands," for example, the proper response may be suggested by passive movement of the paw by the trainer, or it may be elicited by a mild shock to the limb, followed by reward. Of course, even in instrumental conditioning, the desired response must be potentially available in the person's or animal's repertoire of possible responses. Even the most ingenious experimenter cannot teach a dog to pronounce the sounds of the alphabet.

Nevertheless, recent investigators, stimulated in large measure by the pioneering work of Skinner and his associates (67, 69), have produced impressive learning in a wide variety of challenging situations by using operant conditioning techniques. By ingenious arrangements of experimental conditions, and judicious use of rewards—and sometimes punishments— they have been able to "shape" rather elaborate response patterns under often difficult circumstances, such as teaching pigeons to play ping-pong.

In both classical and operant conditioning, the new association can be between a stimulus and an overt response, or a stimulus and a physiological reaction. The major difference between classical conditioning and operant conditioning is that in classical conditioning the response already exists and only has to be connected to a new stimulus. In operant conditioning, the response—particularly one that is complex—must usually be gradually and carefully developed. Initially, a rat placed in a Skinner box does not make the response of pressing the bar. A strong association is gradually established between the sight of the bar and the response of pressing the bar whereas prior to this learning the association was nonexistent or very weak. Children acquire many operant associations of this kind. They learn to open doors, to turn on faucets, to hold baseball bats, to write with pencils, and to ring doorbells.

There are also more complex and difficult uses of operant conditioning. For example, Mednick (51) has described a project conducted in an operant conditioning research laboratory in a mental hospital in Massachusetts:

> Experiments are carried on in specially constructed rooms that happen to be in the basement of the building. Dealing with very seriously disturbed patients, the experimenters have often found it quite difficult simply to get the patients to come down to the experiment rooms. An undergraduate from a nearby university, well versed in operant conditioning procedures, took it upon himself to attempt to bring a patient with a long-standing mental illness to one of these rooms. Illness had reduced this patient to an almost animal state. He had little or no control over defecation or urination; he would often bite individuals who came too close to him; he did not speak. Consequently, he was kept in virtual isolation.

> In order to get him downstairs, the student used an operant conditioning technique called "shaping-up." In this method the experimenter continually rewards acts that come closer and closer to some ultimately desired behavior. Thus, the student waited for the first time the patient turned his head toward the door leading to the basement stairs. At this point he presented the patient with a small piece of candy which the latter quickly ate. (It had been previously determined that the patient liked candy.) Presently, the patient faced the door again, and again the student was there with a piece of candy. After a number of such incidents the patient simply stood facing the door. The candy acted as a *reward* for door-facing and increased the likelihood, or *probability*, of its occurrence. After this phase of training was completed, the student withheld the candy until the patient took a step. When the patient had received candy several times for taking steps, the student again withheld candy until he took steps in the direction of the basement stairs. After a number of days, during which there were many reversals and disappointments, the patient actually

walked down the stairs, entered a basement room, and went through the experimental procedures. This was the first time in some years that the patient had behaved in such an organized manner. (*51*, 3–4).

Recently Lovaas and his associates (47–49) at the University of California at Los Angeles have employed similar techniques of "behavior therapy" in an attempt to increase social responsiveness and to reduce the incidence of self-destructive and self-mutilating behavior in severely withdrawn, psychotic children. Many of these children had been in treatment for extensive periods with no improvement; others had been rejected from treatment because they were poor treatment risks:

> Some of the children were completely unresponsive to social stimuli and evidenced no social or intellectual behavior. They were so oblivious to their surroundings that they behaved as if they were blind and deaf. They were completely engrossed in self-stimulatory behaviors, such as spinning objects, rocking in sitting or standing positions, twirling, flapping their wrists, and gazing at lights and at their cupped hands (*47*, 8).

In a significant percentage of the children, vocal behaviors were limited to occasional vowel sounds having no discernible communicative intent. Others engaged in *echolalia* (simply repeating whatever sounds they hear).

Using a systematic, carefully controlled program of rewards (e.g., food and attention) and punishment (e.g., removal of food and withdrawal of affection), these investigators have been able, in successive stages, to increase the incidence of meaningful speech (e.g. "I want a cookie") and to reduce the incidence of meaningless, echolalic, or psychotic speech (e.g., "spaghetti Irene," "helicopter pillow") (*47, 48*). They have also been able to reduce self-destructive and self-mutilative behavior, and to increase social approaches to adults by using various rewards and punishments, including isolation and electric shock (*47*). Use of such punishment with children has provoked considerable controversy. However, the authors point out that the alternatives with such severely disturbed children may be much more deleterious. Some children had bitten large chunks of flesh from their own bodies, or hit their heads so severely that they broke their nose-bones or detached their retinas. Some had blinded themselves. In this context, the authors view their training procedures, including the use of punishment as "an act of affection" (*47*).

In still other studies (*13, 35, 78*), behavior-modification procedures have been used to promote training in basic social responses among mentally retarded children. In one study (*35*), toilet training proceeded efficiently when successful elimination was rewarded with candy, and in another study (*13*), such self-help activities as eating, dressing, and drying hands were facilitated through similar procedures. Similar methods have been used to improve children's reading skills (*77, 86*) and to reduce overly aggressive behavior among nursery school children (*16*).

BASIC CONDITIONS OF LEARNING

As parents and teachers, as well as psychologists, know learning is not inevitable: It does not always occur even in some situations in which we most expect it. It appears that certain conditions must be satisfied in any given case if learning is to take place. What do we know about the nature of these conditions?

A few basic points seem obvious. In the first place, unless a stimulus is distinctive enough to be discriminable, it will be difficult, if not impossible, to attach a response to it. Further, even a distinctive stimulus (or cue, as such a stimulus is sometimes called) may be of little value unless the subject can be induced to attend to or notice it. One of the many problems in teaching appropriate social responses to autistic or schizophrenic children appears to be the difficulty of getting the child to pay attention to relevant stimuli to which we hope to attach responses, even though these stimuli may be both distinctive and simple. One often gains the impression that the child is so preoccupied with his own internal, private world that he pays little attention to the external stimulus to which he is exposed.

It also appears obvious that if a particular *response* is to be attached to a stimulus, the individual must be capable of making the response. This may be either because it is readily available to him and can easily be evoked by presenting some other appropriate stimulus (as in classical conditioning), or because it is developed and perfected in the course of the current learning experience (as in behavior shaping in operant conditioning).

State of the Child

As implied above, the physiological and psychological state of the subject is also important. Learning of a response to a stimulus does not take place in limbo. It takes place within a living organism, whether animal or man. Obviously, then, the biological state of a child will affect his capacity for learning. Earlier theories of learning often tended to ignore or to minimize the importance of the state of the organism doing the learning (32).

Recent evidence, however, points increasingly to the influence of the subject's biological state upon his learning ability. The factors which affect this biological state may be of many kinds. One which is especially important in the field of child development is the subject's degree of physical maturation. As is made clear elsewhere in this book, an infant may be incapable of a particular bit of learning at one stage of development, even though the stimulus may be distinctive and uncomplicated and the required response relatively simple. A few weeks later, the infant may learn this same stimulus-response association easily. Sometimes, of course, his increased readiness may be aided by other learning which has taken place in the meantime, but very often it is primarily a function of advances in neurophysiological and physical maturation. A good deal of research recently has

centered around the roles of maturation and learning in the child's development of perceptual capabilities (39, 78, 87). Modes of perceiving change
with age, and there have been systematic studies of infant's and child's
capacity for organizing clusters of discrete visual stimuli into patterns, for
attending to stimuli and scanning figures, and for perceiving size and distance relationships (39, 78, 87). In particular, a considerable amount of research has been conducted recently on visual fixation responses in neonates
(cf. p. 158) and more generally on form perception in infancy, including that
of the human face (pp. 160–166). Other studies have shown, for example, that
3-year-olds, in looking at a figure, normally start with the focal part of the
figure and move downward; by the age of 6, children start with the top of
the figure, regardless of focal point (89). Preschool children prefer to scan
in a vertical rather than a horizontal dimension, and can make more accurate differentiations in this axis (89). The child's spontaneous organization
of spatially contiguous stimuli changes with age, 6-year-olds being more
likely than preschoolers to name objects that are spatially adjacent, when
asked to start naming individual objects in a collection. More kindergarten-
age girls than boys start naming objects from the left, possibly indicating
greater readiness for learning to read (23).

Obviously, as these brief examples indicate, a child's ability to learn
tasks requiring attention to certain kinds of stimuli and particular levels of
perceptual readiness will vary with age, either because of increased motivation, additional cognitive ability, or, in most instances, both.

Cognitive theorists and researchers—particularly those most influenced
by Piaget—present some convincing evidence that there are stages in intellectual development and in the progress from simple to more mature, more
complex thinking that basically depend on "spontaneous development"
rather than on learning. Evidence from a number of relevant studies indicates
that training (and learning) do not substantially accelerate the transition from
one stage to another (e.g., 88, 72, 73, 74, 75). For example, until the child
has attained the necessary cognitive level, he cannot acquire or really understand the principles of logical thinking or basic concepts such as conservation
(the idea that certain properties of matter, e.g., mass, are invariant despite
perceptible alterations, e.g., change in shape; cf. pp. 447–458). Summarizing
these experiments, Flavell says, "Almost all the training methods reported
impress one as sound and reasonable and well suited to the executive job
at hand. And yet, most of them have had remarkably little success in producing cognitive change." (20, 377). And, on the basis of a series of their own
experiments, Inhelder and Sinclair, coworkers of Piaget, concluded that the
child's cognitive functioning can be modified "only within certain limits imposed by the laws of development. . . . Learning is subordinate to the laws
of development and development does not consist in a mere successive
accumulation of bits of learning, for development follows . . . laws that are
both logical and biological" (37).

Other biological factors, both stable and transient, may also affect
learning. Thus, the subject's capacity for learning may be affected by brain

damage, physiological disorders, fatigue, or the effects of drugs, as well as by anxiety, elation, or other emotional states. Many examples could be given. For example, children with disturbances in neurophysiological functioning, either as a result of congenital disorders or subsequent disease, may be hyperactive and have great difficulty in maintaining attention for any sustained period of time, thus making learning difficult. Such children may sometimes be helped by the administration of controlled levels of tranquilizing drugs (19). Children in many parts of the world are chronically weak and fatigued, as a result of inadequate nutrition. Consequently, their capacity to learn new associations is adversely affected. Many studies have indicated that while mild levels of anxiety may actually aid learning, or at least not interfere with it appreciably, high levels of anxiety can be extremely disruptive of the subject's proper functioning, and hence may significantly impair learning ability (58, 65).

It appears clear that learning is a function of the nature of the *stimulus,* the nature of the *response,* and the *state of the learning organism.* What other factors may be important? Two which are often cited by most, though not all, theorists are *motivation* and *reinforcement.* The contention of these theorists is that learning is more likely to occur (1) when the organism wants or needs to obtain a certain goal (i.e., when he is *motivated*), and (2) when the response he makes results in acquisition of the goal (i.e., the response is *rewarded* or *reinforced*). While these concepts may seem reasonable, even perhaps obvious, experimental work in learning indicates that the matter is not actually as simple as it may at first appear.

The Role of Reward or Reinforcement

The reader may have noticed that in some of the examples of learning already referred to, the subject was provided with a reward of some sort whenever he made a correct response to a stimulus (e.g., giving an autistic child a bit of food when he made an appropriate social response, as in Lovaas' studies). The presumption here was that a reward or *reinforcement,* if given promptly when the subject makes a correct response to a stimulus, strengthens the stimulus-response bond and increases the likelihood that the proper response will again be made the next time the stimulus is presented. How important actually is reinforcement for learning, and, if it is important, what is its nature?

The first of these questions, namely, the importance of reinforcement in learning, has been a topic of ardent dispute among psychologists for many decades, and the matter is still unresolved (32, 40). In fact, new experimental evidence derived from learning experiments, rather than settling the issue, has, if anything, made the problem even more complex (32). Some psychologists have maintained that reinforcement is not a necessary condition for learning at all, that its apparent importance in some cases is really only incidental in that it helps to insure that the appropriate response will take place in the presence of the stimulus and not under other conditions. Such theorists, pioneered by Edwin Guthrie, are often referred to as *contiguity theorists:* they maintain that *contiguity* alone (i.e., simply the occurrence of the response in the presence of the stimulus) is sufficient to produce learning.

Other psychologists maintain that reinforcement is always necessary for learning, and that instances in which conditioning appears to take place without reinforcement are deceptive. In such cases, they argue, it is not that reinforcement was absent; it is merely that the psychologist was not aware of the reinforcement which actually occurred. While these theorists often differ among themselves in their specific views regarding the ways in which reinforcement or reward operates, as a group they are frequently referred to as *reinforcement theorists.*

Still other psychologists, perhaps a majority, argue that while reinforcement may not be a necessary concomitant of all learning, it is important for many and perhaps most forms of learning—particularly social learning. Among this latter group, one cadre maintains that contiguity alone may be sufficient for classical conditioning, particularly when responses of the autonomic nervous system are involved. As a simple example, let us assume that an increase in heart rate is to be conditioned as a response to the sound of a bell. This may be done by first pairing the sound of the bell with a mild electric shock which itself increases heart rate. Subsequently, when the bell stimulus is presented alone, heart rate increases. Was reinforcement present? These theorists would argue that it was not.

In the case of most forms of instrumental or operant conditioning, however, these theorists would insist that reward or reinforcement is necessary or at least helpful. They would point to many examples that appear to support this view. The learning of a complicated maze by a rat is facilitated if he is rewarded by food at the end of the maze. A child who finally makes the correct response in a complicated learning problem is more likely to repeat the correct response the next time it is presented if he is rewarded for this response, and not for other (incorrect) responses. The reward itself may consist of a piece of candy, a grade of "A," or simply a congratulatory statement such as "Very good"—so long as the "reward" actually is rewarding for the particular child.

Rewards need not be actively perceived as such by the subject in order to function effectively. For example, in recent experiments in psychotherapy, the psychologist or psychiatrist, in listening to a patient, adopts the device of simply saying "uh-huh," or repeating a patient's statement by saying "you feel that . . . ," or otherwise indicating interest when the patient talks about a particular range of personal problems. On the other hand, the therapist does not respond at all or show any interest when the patient happens to talk of other matters. In such situations, it has been found that the subject will tend to talk more and more about the particular range of problems selected by the experimenter and less and less about other matters. No comparable increase takes place if the experimenter does not respond at all or if, instead, he responds only to other topics raised by the patient. The inference is that the patient is learning to talk about a particular range of problems because he is rewarded for discussion of these problems by the psychologist's display of interest in them, even though the patient may not realize either that his behavior is changing or that this change is being reinforced (i.e., rewarded) by the psychologist.

Unfortunately, in our present state of knowledge, none of the issues raised above concerning the role of reinforcement can be definitively settled. In fact, some of the issues have become so complex recently, as a result of new experimental evidence, that it is difficult in a presentation such as this even to state the issues simply and without distortion. However, it is the authors' view that reward or reinforcement does play an important role in the learning of associations between stimuli and overt responses, or between mediational units (i.e., internal processes, such as thoughts or perceptions) and overt responses, but it may be of less importance when the bond is between stimuli and mediational units.

There are basically four different kinds of associations that can be learned. These are associations between:

1. A stimulus and an overt response or physiological reaction.
2. A stimulus and a cognitive or mediational unit (idea, perception).
3. A cognitive unit and an overt response.
4. One cognitive unit and another cognitive unit.

Reinforcements seem to be helpful—often necessary—in promoting associations that involve *overt responses* (categories 1 and 3), but less important when the association involves acquiring a new cognitive unit (e.g., learning that a new fruit is called a kiwi), or *realizing* the logic of multiplication. These new acquisitions seem to require primarily *attention* to the elements of the learning situation.

Perhaps the best example of associations between internal cognitive or mediational units is the phenomenon we call *insight*. Insight in science, art, or poetry involves suddenly perceiving or recognizing an association between two units of thought that have always been separate. When the scientist Kekule had the insight that he could explain the data from his chemistry laboratory by assuming that the six carbon atoms in benzene form a hexagon, he connected his knowledge about the behavior of certain organic molecules with a mental image of a hexagon. *He had learned something;* a new connection or association had been established. A person in psychotherapy may suddenly recognize the association or the relation between his anger toward his mother and the fact that he blames his mother for his own shortcomings. This kind of association may be most applicable to human beings, but it does fit our general definition of learning, which involves the establishment of an association between two units that prior to the learning were not associated or connected.

Obviously much of the informal learning taking place in the child's daily life involves these *mediational units.* Unfortunately, this sort of learning has not, until recently, begun to receive the intensive kind of investigation long accorded to associations between external stimuli and overt responses (which are easier to study), and the role of reinforcement in learning involving mediational units is by no means clear.

As some of the kinds of learning with which we will be concerned in this book involve associations between stimuli and overt behavior, it will be necessary throughout our discussions to examine both the kinds of events that are likely to be reinforcing for children in general and those which may be reinforcing only for specific groups of children, or, indeed, individual children with special needs.

The Nature of Reinforcement.   What do we actually mean by reward or reinforcement? An operational definition is relatively easy and has already been implied in our previous discussion: *a reward is an event that follows a response and increases the likelihood that the response will occur the next time the eliciting stimulus is presented.* In a sense, however, such a definition begs the question. It does not tell us ahead of time whether a particular event is likely to promote learning. We have to wait to find out whether it *has* been facilitated in a particular case; if it has, then "the event" can be viewed as rewarding or reinforcing.

Studies of learning under conditions of intense hunger, thirst, and pain indicate that organisms do indeed learn to do things that reduce tension or overstimulation. However, an increasing amount of empirical evidence is accumulating which suggests that there are also many situations in which increases in stimulation, rather than decreases, are reinforcing and lead to learning *(27, 36, 44)*. One investigator *(41)* has found that rats placed in darkness will press a lever more frequently if lever-pressing produces dim illumination than if it results in no increase in visual stimulation.

Recently Olds and Milner *(56, 57)* discovered that electrical stimulation by an electrode placed in a certain portion of the hypothalamus of an animal's brain could serve as a reward. The animal would learn to perform even quite complicated response patterns if the patterns were followed by such stimulation. In fact, in some experiments animals actually learned to turn on the electrical stimulation themselves. In 1967, Trowill *(84)*, and Miller and DiCara *(54)* demonstrated that electrical stimulation of an appropriate area of the brain could be used as a reward for learning even such basic physiological responses as increases and decreases in heart rate. (These experiments are of particular interest because a number of theorists have maintained that autonomic nervous system responses can be learned only through *classical conditioning*, rather than, as in this case, *instrumental conditioning*.)

Harlow *(24, 25)*, a psychologist at the University of Wisconsin, has found that well-fed, contented monkeys learned to solve complicated mechanical puzzles (involving an assortment of hooks, latches, and hinges) when their manipulative activities were followed merely by the opportunity to view parts of the laboratory (i.e., increased visual stimulation).

In studies of humans, Piaget *(60)* and others have commented on the way in which well-cared-for infants and young children will learn such developmental tasks as playing with a rattle, kicking a string, or standing up in the crib. All of these behaviors produce increased stimulation; yet they are easily learned. Apparently in these cases increases in stimulation facilitate rather than retard learning.

With humans, as with animals, there is evidence which suggests that, under some circumstances, an absence of stimulation can be as disturbing as painfully intense stimulation (14). In one study conducted at McGill University, college students were paid twenty dollars a day to do nothing. They lay for 24 hours a day on a comfortable bed. The temperature was optimal and constant. Eyes, ears, and hands were shielded to minimize stimulus variation. While to busy readers preoccupied with classes and examinations this might appear to be a highly desirable state of affairs, the fact is that, under such conditions, few subjects in this experiment could endure more than 2 or 3 days. They developed a desire for stimulus variation that was almost overwhelming.

The fact that both increases and decreases in stimulation (or tension) sometimes appear rewarding has led still other psychologists, such as J. Mc-Vicker Hunt of the University of Illinois, to postulate that active, normal biological organisms, including children, require a moderate amount of variety in stimulation and such variety will be reinforcing, although the optimal amount may vary from time to time (53).

It is unlikely that such theoretical arguments as these concerning the true nature of reinforcement will be settled in the near future (32, 40). Nevertheless, two things appear evident: (1) reward or reinforcement, as functionally defined, can play a significant role in learning overt responses; (2) we do not need to wait for any final resolution of theoretical problems regarding the nature of reinforcement in order to gain much valuable information about the kinds of events likely to serve as rewards in many kinds of learning situations important to the child's development. Fortunately, much is already known, as we shall see, and much more is being learned each day by psychologists unwilling to wait until all of the theoretical issues are solved before getting on with the job of finding out more about what children can learn at various ages, and what sorts of conditions appear to facilitate appropriate learning and to limit maladaptive learning— including the most effective use of various kinds of rewards. Thus, for example, much progress has been made in the last 5 years in determining the effectiveness of a variety of *social reinforcers* in children's learning.

Reinforcement and Attention.   One speculation on the role of reinforcement is based on the observation that many of the stimuli that are called reinforcements generally seem to influence the attention of the organism. For example, in Pavlov's classical conditioning experiment, the food that serves as the unconditioned stimulus for the salivary reflex attracts the dog's attention to the situation. It tunes him in to what is also occurring at the time or has just occurred, such as the sound of the metronome. Similarly, in operant conditioning in the Skinner box, the arrival of the food pellet operates to attract the rat's attention. Attention is critical in human learning and social rewards focus the attention of the learner. Thus, contiguity of events plus attention to the relevant stimuli may be the essential ingredients in acquiring a new association. Neal Miller has written:

> It may be that the memory engram (i.e. the *association*) is based solely upon associations and that the effects of drive and reward are exerted indirectly by determining which stimuli the organism pays attention to and which responses he performs, thereby determining which ones are available for associations (52).

OBSERVATIONAL LEARNING

Many traditional learning procedures involve the gradual "shaping" of behavior, as in Skinnerian operant conditioning studies in which animals are taught complex behavioral sequences (e.g., teaching pigeons to play ping-pong or mynah birds to speak English phrases or sentences) through a painfully gradual process of rewarding correct or partly correct responses and failing to reward incorrect responses. Much the same thing takes place in some kinds of learning in children and adults. For example, in teaching a young girl ballet dancing or teaching a boy how to swing a golf club, the instructor will reward those portions of a response sequence that are correct with well-timed words of approval, while similarly discouraging incorrect movements. The instructor may also increase the likelihood that a correct response will occur by guiding the passive movement of the student (e.g., guiding the boy's arm through a correct swing with a golf club). Continued, corrective, differentially rewarded practice is an important element in the acquisition of such complex skills.

However, learning many complicated tasks would be extremely difficult if this were the only means by which correct learning could be encouraged. In many human activities, such corrective practice is supplemented by *observation*. Thus, the teacher may interrupt the student's efforts in order to demonstrate a correct response to him. If at least the elements of a correct response are already present in the subject's response repertoire, observation can play a very significant role in promoting learning. Moreover, observational learning also occurs in animals. In some cases, cats will learn to press a lever for food with greater ease if they first watch a well-trained cat perform this response than if they are taught by traditional operant conditioning procedures in which they receive milk each time they make the response (38).

In several recent studies, Bandura (2, 3) and Bandura and Walters (10) and their associates have demonstrated the usefulness of *observational learning* in children. They have also provided a great deal of information regarding factors that influence the likelihood of a subject's subsequently imitating responses acquired through observation.

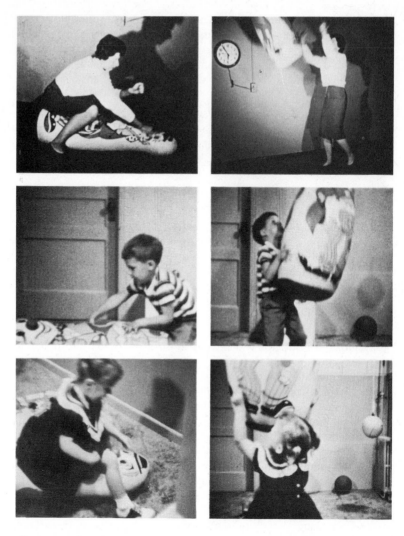

Fig. 4.2A and B (opposite). Photographs of children reproducing the aggressive behavior of the female model they observed on film. (From A. Bandura, D. Ross, & S. A. Ross. Imitation of film-mediated aggressive models. *J. abnorm. soc. Psychol.,* 1963, *66,* 8. Published by the American Psychological Association. By permission.)

In a typical experiment by these investigators, a child is exposed to a real-life or filmed model, either child or adult. The model then performs a series of actions (e.g., pummeling an inflated doll; see Fig. 4.2). Later the child is tested under one or another condition to determine the extent to which he mimics the behavior previously displayed by the model. His

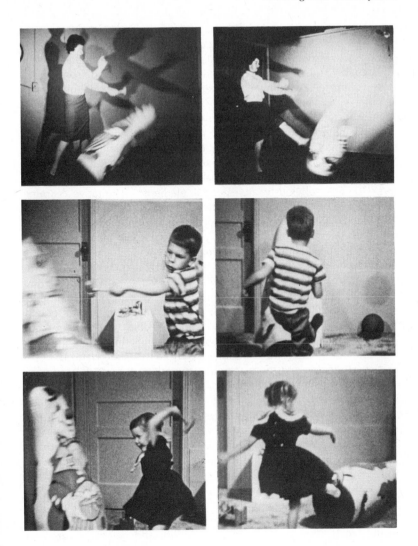

behavior may then be compared with that of *control* subjects who have not observed the model.

In this fashion, many variations in the situation can be examined to determine their effects on the subject's tendency subsequently to mimic the behavior he has observed. Using such techniques, Bandura and his colleagues have demonstrated the effectiveness of observational learning over a very wide range of behaviors. Thus it has been shown that subjects are more likely to imitate the behavior of prestigeful than nonprestigeful models and of models who are similar to the subject themselves (e.g., another child, as compared with a cartoon animal). Children are also more likely to imitate the behavior of models who are rewarded for their actions than those who are punished or not rewarded. Further, certain kinds of responses (e.g., aggressive responses) are more likely to be imitated than others. Presumably, imitation of some kinds of models and of some kinds of responses is more rewarding under certain conditions than imitation of other kinds.

Certain aspects of these ingenious investigations are of particular interest. As we have noted earlier, learning of responses and response sequences requires attention to relevant stimuli in the situation. Bandura notes that "motivational factors or the anticipation of positive or negative reinforcement may augment or reduce the probability of occurrence of observing responses" (10, 59)—obviously an essential element in imitative learning. It may be assumed that the children in these experiments were already generally prepared to make observing responses because such behaviors had been rewarded on numerous occasions in the past, in interactions with peers, in the home, in school, and elsewhere.

However, Bandura and his associates have shown that this general readiness may be increased or decreased by a wide variety of factors. These include: the motivational set of given subjects (e.g., instructions to pay close attention to the model's behavior, promises of future rewards for subsequent accurate imitation of the model's behavior, and the like); the child's readiness to notice certain elements in the model's behavior, on the basis of past experience (Bandura cites one experiment [83] in which advanced police administration students were more attentive to violent aspects of a complex stimulus situation than novice students, presumably because of prior reward for such attention); and the relevance of the model himself, or the activity involved, to the child's own needs and expectations derived from his past experience. Children and adults as well are more likely to be attentive in some situations than others (e.g., a bored husband at a concert with his wife, as compared with that same husband at a baseball game when his favorite team is playing).

Bandura also demonstrated another very important point by taking his experiment one step farther than previous theorists had done in their studies of *imitation learning*. In a variety of experiments, he attempted to differentiate between acquisition of a response capability and actual performance of the response. Thus, in one investigation illustrative of those summarized above, Bandura (4) had shown children films of a model displaying aggressive behavior under various conditions: "In one condition of the experiment, the model was severely punished; in a second, the model was generously rewarded with approval and food reinforcers; while the third condition presented no response-consequences to the model" (10, 57).

As might be expected, a postexposure test of imitative behavior revealed that these various conditions produced differential amounts of imitative behavior. Children in the *model-punished* condition performed significantly fewer imitative responses than those in both the *model-rewarded* and the *no-consequences* groups.

It was at this point that Bandura introduced his novel extension of the experiment. He offered children in all three groups attractive rewards, contingent on their reproducing the model's behavior. He found that the introduction of these positive rewards completely wiped out the previously observed performance differences—that is, children in all three groups imitated equally, revealing an equivalent amount of learning among children in each of the three groups.

Bandura believes that such experiments demonstrate several important points sometimes neglected by other theorists. In the first place, *acquisition* of a particular pattern of imitative responses does not necessarily require actual performance of these responses in the immediate situation. In other words, provided the subject is properly attentive (presumably because observing responses have been rewarded in the past), he may learn a particular pattern of responses demonstrated by the model, and be able to reproduce them in the future even though he has not, in the past, made these particular responses in this particular sequence or in response to this particular stimulus. Thus he emphasizes that actual *performance* of imitative response patterns is not always necessary for learning them. The critical element here appears to be the learning of internal processes in response to the external stimuli.

Bandura also draws an important distinction between the factors affecting *acquisition* and those affecting *performance*. In this experiment, for example, while the tendency to perform imitative responses (without further instructions) was affected by whether or not the model had been rewarded or punished for his acts, *learning to be able to perform the responses* was not so affected. Bandura demonstrated this when all three groups were later promised rewards if they could imitate the model's actions, and comparable results were obtained for the three groups (despite individual differences among children *within* the groups). Additional evidence of modeling effects is provided by experiments employing similar classes of responses (1, *30*) as well as considerably more complicated patterns and sequences of behavior (5, 9). At an even higher level of complexity, it has been shown that children can acquire contingencies for self-reinforcement and self-evaluative responses (6, 11), judgmental orientations (7), self-imposed delay-of-reward patterns (8) and linguistic structures (15) as a function of brief exposure to the behavior of models. Moreover, responses acquired observationally may be retained over an extended period of time (i.e., six months) even though there is little or no occasion to perform the novel patterns of behavior during the interval (30). The findings of other experiments make it clear that the subjects are more likely to behave in socially disapproved ways frequently after they have observed models doing so (e.g., yielding to temptation or violating prohibitions) (63). On the other hand, observation of a model conforming to the social norms seems to strengthen the observer's self-controlling responses and reduce the tendency to yield to temptation (63).

It may appear reasonable to the reader that children and adults learn many possible new patterns of responding to particular stimuli without actually having to perform the responses. It may also appear obvious that factors other than those involved in learning the responses may affect their likelihood of being performed in the future. However, this aspect of learning by observation has tended to be neglected in the past by experimenters whose attention has been focused on the gradual shaping of behavior itself by differential reinforcement of actual overt responses.

Observational learning and learning by conditioning of overt responses, either classically or instrumentally, often supplement each other. One would not, as Bandura notes, permit an adolescent to learn to drive a car, or an army recruit to handle firearms, solely through trial-and-error procedures. On the other hand, it appears clear that in these, as in many other instances of complex learning requiring novel responses, actual corrective practice combined with reward for correct responses is necessary also. For example, simply telling a youth who is learning to shoot a rifle not to blink his eyes when he fires, and not to grab the trigger, will not be sufficient. Observational learning is likely to be of less value when it involves responses that are complex and largely new. In contrast, it appears most effective when it involves fairly simple combinations or responses that have already been acquired, although the new learning situation may require putting these responses together in new or novel sequences, or in response to new stimuli. In contrast, behavior "shaping" appears most effective where the response pattern is sufficiently complex or unusual as to constitute, at least in its totality, new and difficult behavior. As already indicated, optimal learning in many situations requires a skillful combination of the two elements. It is the introduction of just such skillful combinations that has produced so many remarkable educational advances in recent years, as, for example, in the newer forms of language training used in our schools.

MOTIVATION

The term motivation is a generic one that refers to the needs, goals, or desires that provoke the organism to action. It is important at the outset to recognize that motivation is a concept (38, 42, 43).

suggested by certain characteristics of behavior which are a matter both of everyday observation and of experimental manipulation in the laboratory.

The two features of behavior which seem to demand the development of some such concept as that of motivation are 1) certain variations in the behavior of the same individual from time to time, and 2) certain extreme individual differences in response to the same situation, including differences in the apparent speed of learning. If, for example, we observe that a ten year old youngster loiters and dallies along his way to school and, a few hours later, rushes pell-mell on his way to the playground, we are apt to infer that his motives differ on the two occasions. Or if we watch two small children in the presence of a large dog and see that one of them runs in apparent terror to its mother, while the other shows strong interest or at least no alarm, it again seems reasonable to think in terms of different motives and to say that the first child was afraid of the dog (*40, 395*).

Motivation may have several properties. One of these is as an *energizer of behavior*. When an individual is hungry, or thirsty, or in pain, he tends to become active and to make a variety of responses, some of which may lead to learning. The first time a young organism is hungry, these responses may appear quite aimless; they do not seem to be directed toward a particular goal. If, however, an infant in the course of its restlessness finds a bottle or the mother's breast, his responses on the next occasion when he is hungry are likely to be more directed toward this goal. The explanation involves the fact that motivating forces (often called *needs* or *drives*) *have value also as stimuli* (e.g., hunger pangs or the stimulation of pain receptors). The stimulus aspect of needs or drives may thus become attached to responses such as seeking the mother's breast, so that the next time the need is aroused, its stimulus characteristics may provoke these responses.

Motivation may thus range from diffuse, nondirective states of arousal to rather specific expressions of goal-directed energy. While often applying the terms *need* or *drive* to the whole range of motivational forces affecting behavior, a number of theorists prefer to restrict the term *motive* to instances in which activity is not only aroused but is directed toward a goal (e.g., a desire for food, or love for one's mother).

While there is fairly general agreement regarding these two properties of motivation, there is less agreement about a third possible property— namely, the effects of drives or motives in promoting learning. Some psychologists view the principal value of motivation as stemming from its activity-arousing properties, which impel the organism to make responses which may then be learned simply because they took place in the presence of appropriate stimuli (contiguity theorists). Other psychologists, including many reinforcement theorists, tend to view motivation as having a significant additional role in learning, that of providing the necessary conditions for the occurrence of reinforcement. In the case of hunger, for example, reinforcement is viewed as being provided by a reduction in hunger; in the case of an individual with a strong need for achievement, reinforcement is provided by accomplishment of an important goal. For such theorists, *reinforcement satisfies* a need or motive. Others view motives as sensitizing the organism to attend to particular stimuli. A child who *is motivated* to obtain an "A" in arithmetic is more likely to focus his attention on his arithmetic book and the teacher than the child who has no desire for an "A."

Sources of Motivation. There are many kinds of needs and motives which may influence behavior. More specifically there are *innate* needs, or what are commonly termed *primary* needs. These include a variety of biological needs—for food, water, warmth, oxygen—that require gratification if the organism is to survive.

A need is viewed as an internal physiological state of the organism and not as a set of responses. That is, the child has to learn to eat or seek out food when he is *hungry*. It is true that nature sometimes helps in this process by providing the organism with a response that is appropriate to a certain need. Thus, the response of sucking is typically elicited when a nipple is placed in the infant's mouth. However, the infant learns to suck more efficiently with practice and, with age, learns how to drink from a glass and eat with a spoon.

Although needs sometimes impel the child to seek gratification, it should be noted that usually the organism must learn the response that is most effective in gratifying the need. But most responses of humans are elicited not by *needs* but by *motives*.

Motives are acquired desires for particular goals. Children learn motives for affection, power, grades, money, and acceptance by one's friends. These desires—or motives—promote the learning of particular behaviors. Moreover, as with needs, the individual has to learn a set of behaviors to gratify the motive. One of the common sources of tension and anxiety in human beings is the chronic presence of a motive (e.g., love, dominance, social status) but no means of gratifying it. Motives are usually labeled in terms of the *goal* that is sought. But neither presence nor absence of a particular behavior is a very faithful index of the strength of the motive.

Relation Between Motives and Behavior. As motives are conceived of as cognitive in nature, there is no necessary link between a motive and an overt action. A child may have a desperately strong wish to care for his younger sister, yet display no overt attempt to gratify that wish. A 10-year-old may have a strong desire for a close friend, but fail to show any behavior that might bring him into a closer relationship with him. What determines whether the motive will produce goal-related actions? First, the child must have learned responses that effectively gratify the motive. A 6-year-old may have a strong desire to control his older brother, but if he has not learned how to effect this control, we may not see much evidence of this motive in his everyday behavior. The child acquires these goal-gratifying actions through direct reward and punishment, through exposure to models who display the actions, and through exposure to books, radio, and television—all of which describe effective ways to gratify motives. The 3-year-old learns that resisting his mother's requests upsets her, and this experience leads him to use this behavioral tactic more regularly every time he feels hostile toward her. Each time the mother indicates how upsetting her child's stubborn resistance is, she is rewarding his resistant behavior and increasing the likelihood that he will behave this way in the future. The child also learns ways of gratifying motives by watching the successful behavior of others. The child may see a boy successfully dominate another by pushing and by verbal threatening. A child with a motive to dominate his peers may imitate that response in the future because the end result he witnessed matched the goal that he was striving to attain.

A second factor governing the probability of a motive's leading to a related behavior is the child's expectancy that the action will be successful in obtaining the desired goal. A 5-year-old who has been in three foster homes, none of which responded to his requests for affection and help, is likely to stop displaying such requests and become sullen and withdrawn. His desire for adult affection may be still present, but his behavior does not reveal it. The lower the expectancy of gratifying a motive, the less likely it is that the child will issue behavior directed at goal attainment.

Anxiety over displaying the goal-related behavior is a third factor that controls the link between motive and action. A motive in a 2-year-old is likely to lead immediately to behavior aimed at direct gratification because 2-year-olds have not yet learned to delay or inhibit gratification of most of their strong motives. The 5-year-old, by contrast, has learned that he must delay gratification of many of his desires and inhibit certain actions because of anxiety over parental rejection or guilt. Thus the stronger the anxiety over commission of a goal-related act, the less likely the child will display that act when he experiences the motive in an active state.

A final determinant of the probability of goal-directed behavior is the immediate situation or context in which the child becomes aroused. If the child feels strong hostility toward his mother but is sitting in school, he is not likely to behave in a way that will gratify the motive; he is likely to behave in a goal-related way if he is home.

In sum, acquisition of acts that gratify motives, expectancy of goal attainment, anxiety over display of goal-directed responses, and the immediate context all influence the probability that the child will actively attempt to gratify a strong motive.

Motives and Specific Goals.   The reader may rightfully ask, "How can I tell that an individual has a motive for a specific goal?" At present, one of the best techniques available for inferring the presence of a motive involves the observation of the individual's behavior when he has been deprived of the goal. If a person has a motive for achieving a certain goal, then being deprived of the goal should have two behavioral consequences. First, his behavior should change following deprivation, and the new behavior should reflect signs of striving for the goal. Second, a new response that results in obtaining the goal should be learned more effectively after than before deprivation of the goal.

Let us illustrate this principle with the behavior of a 2-year-old. We usually assume that a child of this age has acquired a strong need for his mother; that is, he desires her presence, and perception of her is gratifying. We might also assume that the 2-year-old is not likely to have a burning need to contemplate a Picasso painting hanging on his living-room wall. We can test these assumptions by watching the child's behavior following the removal of mother and painting. We would expect that when the mother left the room the child might cry, thrash about, or search for the lost goal object, i.e., the mother. Such behavior following removal of the Picasso would indeed be surprising.

Let us further suppose that we want to teach the child a new response, such as opening a door. We would expect the child to learn this response much more efficiently if it led to a view of the mother rather than of the painting. Moreover, this response would be learned much faster if the child had been deprived of mother's presence for a half-hour than if this deprivation had lasted only a few minutes. On the other hand, if the response of opening the door led only to perception of the Picasso painting, we would expect no marked difference in the rapidity with which the response was learned. Although these examples may appear contrived, parents make inferences every time their child shows a sudden and abrupt change in behavior—a cry, for example, or increased restlessness. At such times, the mother instinctively asks, "What can he want?" and she searches for some object that she thinks will satisfy the child.

Finally, a motive can be inferred if the child's behavior changes following the introduction of a goal that might be desired. For example, if the father announces he has two tickets to a baseball game, a 4-year-old, who is not motivated for this goal, would probably not react in any way. A 10-year-old, on the other hand, is likely to become *excited*—and this dramatic change in his behavior provides evidence of a potentially strong motive for watching baseball games.

To summarize, then, we infer the presence of a motive for a goal if (1) deprivation of the goal leads to changes in behavior; (2) we can use the goal as "bait" or reward for the learning of new behavior; and (3) presentation of a goal state produces changes in behavior. Finally, we infer a motive if the behavior is discrepant from that which is normative, or expected, in a particular context. That is, if a child sits at his desk in school, one cannot conclude that he is necessarily highly motivated to be in school. The classroom situation calls for the behavior of "sitting at a desk." If, however, his behavior violates or does not conform to what is expected, then we say that he has a special motive. For example, if we see the child running around the classroom most of the day, teasing the teacher, annoying the child in front of him, or constantly raising his hand to every question the teacher asks, we might infer that this child has a motive for the "attention of other children and adults" or, perhaps, a motive to annoy others.

PRIMARY AND SECONDARY REWARDS

Reward or reinforcement is defined in terms of classes of events that facilitate learning. Typically, if a response leads to an event that gratifies a need, that event (called a reward) strengthens the response. Thus, if the cries of a hungry child result in the immediate administration of food, we assume that the response of crying is strengthened because it led to the rewarding goal of food.

Food, water, sleep, and warmth are called primary rewards because they satisfy primary needs. However, there is evidence to suggest that cer-

Fig. 4.3. Secondary reinforcement of a chimpanzee. The chimpanzee has been operantly conditioned by the secondary reinforcement of a poker chip, which he now drops into a vending machine to obtain the primary reinforcement of food. (After J. T. Cowles. Food taken as incentives for learning by chimpanzees. *Psychol. Monogr.* 1937, Vol. 14, No. 5. Published by the American Psychological Association.)

tain kinds of stimulation are innately pleasant or satisfying, although they are not necessary to the survival of the organism. Stimulation of the genital area and tactile contact in infancy are two such classes of pleasant stimulation. These stimuli are regarded as innate or unlearned rewards because any response that is followed by this class of stimulation will be strengthened. Therefore, there may be primary rewards that are not directly related to primary needs (i.e., needs involved in the maintenance of life).

Just as there are learned needs or motives (e.g., fame, approval, money); there are also learned rewards. A transistor radio has no reward value for a baby. The reward value of this object has to be learned. In the case of the motive for academic achievement, the reward may be the acquisition of a good report card. Similarly, in the case of the child's love for the mother, the learned reward will be her presence. A learned reward is defined as a class of stimuli that has acquired positive value because it gratifies a motive. Learned rewards act as incentives, and any response that leads to the acquisition of a learned reward will itself be strengthened.

If a class of stimuli is to acquire reward value, it must be associated with events that have already become rewards (17, 90).

Many experiments have been performed in which animals have been operantly conditioned through secondary reinforcement. Chimpanzees, for example, have been conditioned not only with primary reinforcement provided by food but also with secondary reinforcement provided by poker chips that they can put into a sort of vending machine that delivers food when a chip is dropped into a slot, as shown in Fig. 4.3.

The human parallel, of course, is that for a child, jelly beans may provide strong reinforcement, and money, at the beginning, no reinforcement at all. But, because money can buy jelly beans, it becomes a secondary reinforcing stimulus through association. Many of the things that human beings consider rewards seem to acquire their reinforcement value in this very way.

Once money has acquired reward value for a child, it may be successfully employed as reinforcement—not only for responses such as opening boxes but also for other (perhaps more useful) ones, such as making beds, sweeping sidewalks, or delivering newspapers. It may even serve as some encouragement toward "being a good boy." In the case of adults, it keeps innumerable people busy building cars, walking tightropes, and selling shoes.

Other examples of learned reward in our culture are numerous. Medals, cups, high grades in school, pats on the back, use of the family car, and promotions all may have reward value. Of course, a particular object cannot function as a reward unless there is a motive operating at the moment that will be satisfied by receipt of the object. This is obvious in the case of primary rewards. No one thinks of offering food to a thirsty individual, or sexual objects to one who is hungry, in order to reward him.

This principle is not always clear in the case of learned rewards. For example, we often assume that certain objects are intrinsically rewarding for all children simply because they serve as rewards for most children. However, as children have different kinds of learning experiences, no two of them will have exactly the same motives. Consequently, they will not always be equally satisfied by the same rewards. For example, while praise may well serve as a reward for children who are in need of social approval, it is not likely to serve well for a boy whose overwhelming need is to convince himself and others that he's a "tough guy" and not a "mamma's boy." In the same way, one can hardly expect a rich boy who needs love and acceptance to learn something by offering him money as a reward. It is impossible to get an adolescent farm boy, who has no curiosity about what is going on in the next county, to join the Navy by promising him the delights of travel and adventure. At the level of cultures, it is probably unreasonable to expect that one could convert a starving Indian or Chinese to the American way of life by pointing out the blessings of freedom of speech, religion, and the press. To be rewarding, an object must always be able to serve, at least to some degree, a need or motive operating at the moment.

Social Reinforcement. As we shall see later in this book, much valuable research has been conducted in the last few years aimed at determining the characteristics of learned rewards, derived from the child's social experience, which tend to facilitate learning, both among children generally and among particular groups of children. Such rewards are frequently referred to as *social reinforcers.* It has been found, for example, that reinforcement value may vary with the sex, age, and the kind of role played by an individual who is the rewarding agent in a learning situation (26, 33, 39, 64, 79). In one study, for example, it was found that school-age children are most responsive to rewards from the opposite-sex parent (59). They also work harder at a task when a friend, rather than a stranger, is the reinforcing agent (26). For normal children, mentally retarded peers are less effective as reinforcing agents than are normal peers, but for retarded children, the type of peer makes little difference (81).

Unfortunately, the effectiveness of social reinforcers is turning out to be a more complicated matter than has often been assumed in the past. Thus what may constitute a strong positive reinforcer for some groups of children may have little or no reward value for another group. In some situations, for some children, even criticism may apparently have positive reward value. One complicating factor appears to be that the value of a reward may not be absolute, but may vary with the child's prior *expectations* (39). Thus, the child who is expecting a real dog for Christmas as a reward for doing well in school, will find little reward value in a toy dog on Christmas morning, whereas for the child who may be expecting little or nothing, a toy dog may have considerable reward value.

Thus far we have discussed two general types of learning: *classical* or *respondent conditioning* and *instrumental* or *operant conditioning*, each of which has been illustrated with a number of relatively straightforward examples. We have also discussed the role of four basic factors that appear to be involved in many forms of learning: *stimulus* (or *cue*), *response, motivation*, and *reinforcement* (or *reward*).

There are other, in some instances more complex, forms of learning that will also require at least brief discussion. However, before proceeding to a consideration of them, there are several additional principles affecting all learning that must be mastered before we can analyze in detail the complexities of learned behavior.

Immediacy of Reinforcement

This principle states that, *in general,* the more immediately a reward follows the response, the stronger will be the association between the stimulus and the response and the greater will be the likelihood that presentation of the stimulus again on a future occasion will provoke the response.

Let us assume that we want to teach a child to look both ways before crossing the street. In accordance with the principle just discussed, we should reward the response of looking as soon as it occurs (immediacy of reinforcement). If such a procedure is followed, the presumption is that the child's chances of learning to make the correct response will be much greater than if we delay in giving the reward until after the child is through playing and has come into the house.

The principle of immediacy of reinforcement has played an important role in the development of *programmed instruction*, including the use of teaching machines. These new educational devices are playing an increasingly important role in many forms of education and, indeed, are fast becoming a major commercial industry. While teaching machines were first employed by Sidney Pressey (61, 62) at the Ohio State University many years ago, they received their current impetus largely from the efforts of Skinner to extend the results of his animal studies of operant conditioning to automatic self-instruction in humans (70, 71).

With Pressey's original machine, a student reads the question presented in the aperture of the machine, selects an answer from among several alternatives, and then presses the button corresponding to his chosen answer. If he is correct, the next question appears in the slot; if he makes a mistake, the original question remains until he makes the correct response (32, 62).

Skinner's machine differed from Pressey's "chiefly in that the student was not given the alternatives to choose from, but instead was asked to write his own responses in the spaces provided, and then, as a printed tape advanced, the correct answer appeared for comparison with what he had written" (32, 555).

Many sophisticated extensions of these basic devices have been made by other investigators, including programmed books as well as machines, but the central tenets remain: (1) the organization of the learning task into logical, simplified, sequential steps; and (2) *immediate reward* of correct responses and discouragement of incorrect responses. It is to these elements, plus the opportunity for as much practice as is necessary (adjusted to the student's own pace), that much of the efficacy of programmed instruction in many kinds of learning situations is attributed.

While, in general, the principle of immediacy of reinforcement is a valuable one, recent evidence indicates that it cannot always be as rigidly applied with children as with infrahuman species, "presumably because the gap between the response and reward is bridged in the child by more adequate memory traces and by verbalization regarding the correct stimulus-response relations" (78, 110).

Schedule of Reinforcement

The effects of reinforcement on learning will be influenced not only by the immediacy of reward but also by the schedule or pattern of reward. A child may be praised by his teacher *every time* he does his lessons well or *only occasionally*. In the latter case, the child is receiving only *partial* or *intermittent reinforcement*. In general, experiments both with animals and with humans indicate that learned behavior that is partially reinforced persists longer than behavior which is constantly reinforced.

In most real-life situations, partial reinforcement is the rule rather than the exception. The baby who has learned to say "milk" will not get milk every time, but only on occasions when his mother is present and perhaps not always even then. The boy who swings the baseball bat does not get a home run every time. In adult life, the persistence of behavior learned through partial reinforcement helps explain why a woman who once won a consolation prize in a slogan contest will keep entering contests for years without further reward and why a man who once won a daily double at the race track keeps trying despite a long succession of losing days.

The strength of partial reinforcement probably accounts for the persistence of behavior that once served a purpose but no longer does so. Children sometimes manage to get their own way through temper tantrums or through shouting and often continue this kind of behavior in their own adulthoods, when it is unnecessary and inappropriate. Some children succeed at times in avoiding punishment by assuming a very humble and apologetic attitude and, even when they have become adults, continue to behave as if other people were older and stronger than they. Partial reinforcement is one reason old habits, even bad ones, are often so hard to break.

The Principle of Generalization

What About New Situations? When a hungry child has learned to go to the refrigerator for a snack in his own home, it is likely that if he becomes hungry in his grandmother's home he will also go to the refrigerator. Similarly, when a child has been trained to avoid a hot radiator or stove in his home, he will, fortunately, also tend to avoid other radiators or stoves in other homes. How does this happen? Since the cues in the two homes are not identical, why doesn't he have to learn to make the response all over again in this new situation? The answer to this question requires an additional principle, that of *stimulus generalization*. This principle states that when a response has been learned to one cue or stimulus, it is likely to occur to similar stimuli. The greater the degree of similarity between the original stimuli and those in the new situation, the greater the likelihood that the response will occur.

What determines similarity among stimuli? In the case of objects, the importance of color, size, and shape is obvious. Thus, if a child has learned initially to grasp for a blue-tinted nursing bottle, he is more likely to reach for a purple one than for a red one. After language has been acquired, however, the categorical verbal labels applied to things are frequently the primary determinants of similarity. In other words, what we *call* an object constitutes the most important basis for generalization.

For the adult, the word *dog* refers to everything from a white Afghan to a toy Pekingese. However, in terms of the objective physical quality of the stimulus, a cat is more similar to the toy Pekingese than to the white Afghan. If a response learned to a collie were generalized only to dogs that were physically similar to it, the child would be very limited in the range of animals to which he would respond as he did to the collie. It is quite unlikely that a response learned to a collie would generalize to the toy Pekingese solely on the basis of physical similarity. However, if his parents categorize the collie as a "dog," the word *dog* becomes as much a part of the total stimulus situation as the physical aspects of the animal. Thus, in the future, the child may come to apply the responses he has learned to his pet collie (e.g., patting the animal, expecting him to bark, etc.), not only to other physically similar animals, but also to all animals he labels *dog.* The term *learned* or *mediated generalization* is applied to those cases in which the basis for generalization involves a categorical language label (e.g., dog).

As the child approaches school age, language becomes his most important source of cues, and objects with similar labels (similar meaning) form the basis for many generalizations (66). Therefore, if the child has learned the response of respecting older people, he will be likely to generalize this response to all human beings whom he labels as "older," regardless of their sex, height, weight, color, or physique. As we shall see, this principle of mediated generalization is very critical in development and will be frequently referred to in later discussions.

As already implied, generalization is a very useful and important phenomenon, since no two stimulus situations are ever quite the same. Unless people generalized, they could seldom profit from past experiences. Of course, generalization can have its negative side also. For example, if the child has learned to respond to a particular teacher with resentment because she had been cruel and rejecting toward him, he may generalize this response to other teachers, regardless of whether resentment of them is justified.

Initially, generalization is likely to be extensive. The child who has learned to attach the label "dog" to the family pet is apt to extend this label to all four-footed animals he meets. Thus, the first cow or horse he encounters is likely to be called a dog. Gradually, however, the extent of the generalization will decrease until finally it is (correctly) limited only to dogs. This learned correction to overgeneralization is called *discrimination* (55) and is based on the elimination, or *extinction,* of incorrectly generalized responses.

Extinction

The fact that a response is learned does not mean that it will always remain strong. If the response is not followed by a reward, the association between the stimulus and the response becomes weak, and eventually the stimulus fails to elicit the response. When this happens, we say that the response has undergone *extinction.* Consider a baby who has learned to cry when he is afraid because the mother always came to him when he cried. In this case, the arrival of the mother was the reinforcement. If the mother suddenly stopped coming to the child when he cried, the response of crying would eventually cease—it would have undergone extinction.

However, lack of reward is not the only condition that can result in a decreased likelihood of the occurrence of a response. This statement introduces us to the notion of what is called a *response hierarchy.*

Response Hierarchy

Response hierarchy refers to the fact that in most new situations the child is capable of making a variety of responses. Each of these is of different strength (i.e., has a different probability of occurring). The relative strength of each of these responses determines the response hierarchy. With age, some responses lose in strength and others gain. Thus, response hierarchies change with age. For example, a child learns to reach for a bottle and suck the nipple because these responses are rewarded. These behaviors, therefore, are most likely to occur when the child is hungry. However, when the child is around 2 years of age or earlier, parents usually put pressure on him to give up the infantile habit of nursing from a bottle and encourage him to drink from a glass when he is hungry. The child may begin to anticipate parental displeasure or punishment when he thinks of sucking from the bottle, and a new response, the tendency to drink from a glass, begins to compete with the older one of asking for a bottle. If the motive to avoid parental displeasure becomes strong enough, the child will inhibit the old response and begin drinking from the glass. When alternative responses are available to gratify a need or motive (e.g., asking for a glass or a bottle of milk), the one that actually occurs will be the one with the greatest strength and the least amount of fear or anxiety associated with it.

The concept of hierarchy of response has numerous practical implications. We shall give but one example here. A child of 5 may have learned that the most frequently rewarded method of attracting his parents' attention is by asking questions. This response, therefore, becomes high in his hierarchy of responses in this type of situation. However, let us assume that his parents suddenly become too busy to answer his questions. They may then cease to reward this question-asking response. As a result, this learned response may become weaker and fall to a lower position in the child's response hierarchy. Older responses that have been rewarded earlier in life, such as crying or temper tantrums, may then become the strongest in the response hierarchy and the most likely to occur. A return to older, more primitive forms of responding is called *regression*.

Anticipatory Responses

The reader may recall that, in Dorothy Marquis' experiment on infant feeding (pp. 104–105), the response of sucking became attached to the cue of a buzzer, as the sound of the buzzer was always followed by the presentation of food. Originally, the sucking response would not occur until the food was actually presented. However, as learning proceeded, the sucking response began to occur as soon as the buzzer sounded and before the infant received any food. What happened in the course of the experiment was that the responses of sucking and cessation of crying began to appear earlier in the response sequence—to become anticipatory.

Anticipatory responses are common in learning. A child learning to ride a bicycle originally may lean to one side only after almost falling on the other. Gradually, however, he will learn to lean slightly in an opposite direction as soon as the bicycle begins to fall. In other words, the response of corrective leaning will become anticipatory. Some anticipatory responses are not so useful, however, especially those based on anticipation of pain or anxiety. Let us take the example of a child learning to dive. Originally, he will close his eyes only after he has been stung as he strikes the water. Gradually, however, this response will become more and more anticipatory until, as one diving instructor put it, the child goes to the end of the board, closes his eyes, and hopes! The example, referred to earlier in this chapter, of the boy who shuts his eyes when firing a gun provides still another example of a response which has become anticipatory. Originally, the boy blinked his eyes only after hearing the sound of the gun. Thus, responses associated in time with reward or pain may move forward in the behavior sequence (i.e., become anticipatory) and affect the efficiency of future behavior.

The general principles enunciated above—*immediacy of reinforcement, schedule of reinforcement, generalization* and *discrimination, extinction, response hierarchies,* and *anticipatory responses*—are most clearly applicable to instrumental (or operant) conditioning and to classical conditioning—i.e., to learning associations between external stimuli and overt responses. As such, they have considerable explanatory and predictive value in our attempts to understand children's learning and development. But recall that there are three other kinds of learned associations: those between stimuli and internal processes; those between internal processes and overt responses; and those between a pair or more of internal processes.

Mediational Units. A large part of human learning, particularly the most complex, involves internal processes or responses, which we will refer to as mediational units. For example, a mother points to an apple while the child is watching and says, "That's an apple." The child doesn't have to say anything; no overt response on the child's part is required. If the mother says "apple" several times, the child learns a new association between the external stimulus of the apple and the internal symbolic response *apple*.

In similar fashion, the thought of an apple (internal process) may lead the child to go to the kitchen in search of an apple to eat (overt response). Or the thought of an apple (internal process) may lead to other related thoughts (internal processes) on the basis of prior learning.

Learning Theory and Complex Learning

The learning of complex abilities and content—e.g., ideas, concepts, rules, and principles—involves mediated units and associations between internal processes, as well as the principles of generalization or transfer and discrimination.

Gagné, a learning theorist, has proposed a *cumulative learning theory* or *model* that attempts to account for such learning. He postulates that there are eight types of learning, hierarchically organized; that is, each more simple type of learning is a prerequisite for each successive kind of "higher order" learning. In order of increasing complexity, the eight types are: *signal learning* (learning a response to a signal, as in classical conditioning); *stimulus response learning* (learning a connection between a response and a discriminated stimulus); *chains* (chains of two or more response connections); *verbal associations* (learning of chains that are verbal); *multiple discrimination* (in which the individual "learns to make *n* different identifying responses to as many different stimuli"); *concept learning* (the acquisition of "a capability of making a common response to a class of stimuli that may differ from each other widely in physical appearance"); *principle learning* ("a chain of two or more concepts"); *problem-solving* ("a kind of learning that requires the internal events usually called thinking"). In thinking, two or more previously acquired principles must be combined to produce a new capability (21, 58–59).

Learning is regarded as cumulative because each more complex type of learning depends on recall of more primitive types and humans have a "built-in" capacity for generalization "of specific identical (or highly similar) elements. . . . Of course, 'elements' here means rules, concepts, or any other learned capabilities . . . described." (22) Moreover, ". . . each variety of learning begins with a *different state of the organism* and ends with a *different capability for performance*. It is believed, therefore, that the differences among these varieties of learning far outweigh their similarities" (21, 60).

Gagné's formulation of the development of successively more complex levels of learning represents an attempt to bring together, in one theoretical framework, some basic concepts of learning and cognitive theories. Thus, it attempts to bridge the gap between the simple learning phenomena usually investigated by learning theorists (i.e., stimulus-response connections) and higher thought processes that generally concern cognitive theorists.

TYPES OF NEEDS AND MOTIVES

The neonate's repertoire of needs is limited; it includes the primary needs of hunger, thirst, avoidance of pain, physical contact, stimulation, warmth, defecation, and urination. He must go on to develop the many learned motives that play such a dominant role in his later life. The principles outlined above not only are involved in the learning of motor responses and ideas, but also help us to understand the acquisition of learned needs or motives.

For the most part, learning theory is not helpful in suggesting what specific motives are likely to be of greatest importance in the personality development of children in this culture. However, tentative formulations of the major determinants of child and adolescent behavior may be derived from theories of personality development, from empirical research, and from clinical observations of children.

In approaching this topic, it is important to recognize that children and adults are not always aware of all their motives. When a child is not able to say why he "did what he did" (i.e., he is completely unaware of his motives), we say that his motives were unconscious. For example, the child who protests most loudly the love for his mother may, in fact, be concealing unconscious motives of hostility. It is as though his protestations of love have protected him from the realization of his socially unacceptable, hostile motives. Motives usually become unconscious when they involve thoughts and actions that are inconsistent with the individual's concept of himself and the way he "ought to be." Awareness of such motives would be likely to arouse anxiety, guilt, and self-blame.

A Useful Set of Motives

The following motives appear to be of crucial importance in the child's personality development. In most cases, it is difficult to spell out the details of how these motives have been learned. While some, like anxiety, have been the subject of extensive experimental and clinical investigation, many others have thus far proved difficult to study rigorously.

1. *Motive for physical contact* is the desire for close contact with selected children and adults and is expressed in such behaviors as hugging of others and requests for close body contact.

2. *Motive for positive evaluation from others* is the desire to obtain approval, recognition, and praise. The 3-year-old child who runs to show his painting to the nursery teacher is usually seeking gratification of this motive.

3. *Motive for instrumental aid or help from others* is the desire for assistance in solving problems or overcoming obstacles, and is seen in the child's many requests for assistance in dressing, opening doors and, of course, with homework.

4. *Motive to reduce uncertainty* is the desire to avoid or diminish any situation wherein the child is *not sure* what will happen next or how he should behave. The child, as well as the adult, wants *rules* and familiar signs that tell him of future events. This motive is, of course, closely related to the desire to reduce anxiety, because anxiety involves *uncertainty* about the future.

5. *Motive for autonomy* is the desire to control one's *actions* and be free from the coercive control of one's behavior by another. The expression of this motive is seen in the child's pushing away the parent who wants to help him tie his shoes. The child wishes to do this task by himself—autonomously.

6. *The motive to dominate others,* related to the desire for autonomy, is the desire to play the dominant, rather than the submissive role, in interaction with others; it can be seen in the struggles for power in most groups of children.

7. *Motive to cause harm or anxiety to another*—usually called *hostility*—is the wish that some misfortune come to the person who frustrates the child's motives or threatens his values.

8. *Motive for genital stimulation* is simply the desire for the pleasant sensory qualities of genital stimulation. This motive becomes much more

complex during later childhood when it becomes part of the child's hetero-sexual motives.

9. *Motive for competence* is the desire to perfect certain skills and can be seen in the constructive play of children. Of course, some of the attempts to perfect skills are the product of a desire for approval or the desire to avoid punishment. *But it does not seem possible* to explain all of the child's attempts to learn new tasks and competencies in this way. He seems to derive satisfaction from mastering certain new tasks for their own sake.

10. *Motive to maximize congruence between one's behavior, motives, or thoughts, and previously acquired standards.* This last motive is one of the most pervasive, and it touches many aspects of the child's functioning. The child *establishes standards* of behavior and belief which he invests with value. By age 6, many children have learned that their behavior should match that appropriate for their sex; also, they should be kind to others and they should tell the truth. Once such standards have been incorporated, the child is highly motivated to make his actions and thoughts conform to them. When they do not, he is likely to feel uneasy and one of the major causes of anxiety is deviation from standards.

ANXIETY

It is perhaps unfortunate that feelings that are unpleasant are so common and so perceptually clear. These observations of an introspective nature imply the important role that the emotion of anxiety plays in a theoretical conception of human development. Anxiety has both a cognitive and a feeling aspect. Anxiety is present when the child experiences unpleasant sensations and is in a situation in which he anticipates something painful or uncomfortable may occur, or he is uncertain of future events. Thus the 3-year-old who cringes from his mother when she warns him of his father's reaction to a toilet accident is experiencing the affect of anxiety. The response of cowering or crying in this context is the result of anxiety. The crying of the 6-month-old who is confronted with a strange face is probably not a reaction to the affect of anxiety. The 6-month-old is too immature to interpret his visceral sensations. The crying is a reaction to a discrepant event, not to the anticipation of some painful experience. We should, therefore, use another word for this phenomenon and *fear* is a good candidate.

The conditions that are most likely to produce the emotion of anxiety in the child of 3 years or older are: (1) anticipation of loss of nurturance or affection; (2) anticipation of physical harm; and (3) lack of congruence between a rule or socialization the child has learned and his evaluation of his current beliefs or behaviors. Refinements, elaborations, and subtle combinations of these sources of anxiety give rise to unpleasant affects such as helplessness, depression, guilt, and shame, which appear during the later preschool and early school years.

Although psychologists believe anxiety is an important affect in childhood, there is no agreement as to how to measure it, or how to distinguish among the specific sources of anxiety. There has been no lack of effort in this direction. Psychologists have tried interviews, questionnaires, inkblots, and measures of palmar sweating and heart rate, but none is a completely satisfactory means of measurement. The concept of anxiety is discussed because it is believed to be essential and it is hoped that social scientists will eventually devise more exact methods for measuring its presence and intensity.

Anxiety is of great importance as a determinant of human behavior, for it is most likely to elicit behaviors that conflict with the satisfaction of other motives. A child wants to jump off a diving board like the other children, but he is afraid. He would like to tell his parents how angry their "unreasonable" demands make him, but he fears retribution. Life would be much easier for him if he could admit to himself the way he sometimes secretly feels about his mother, father, or brother, but even actively or consciously thinking such thoughts would produce too much anxiety. Therefore, he learns to avoid these acts and thoughts because such avoidance is rewarding (i.e., it leads to a reduction in the anxiety aroused by the thoughts and behaviors).

How does anxiety begin? What produces the feeling of acute discomfort, the pounding heart and rapid pulse, the sinking feeling in the stomach, the perspiration, the trembling, the exaggerated startle, the dryness of the throat and mouth, and other indicators of anxiety? Objectively, as these illustrations show, the physiological components of anxiety are not learned but are part of the constitutional make-up of the child. What the child learns is an association between a person, object, or situation, and the combined feelings, images, and physiological reactions that characterize anxiety. It is the *arousal* of anxiety that is learned. Thus, a 2-year-old might learn to be afraid of large dogs because his mother becomes hysterical whenever she sees one. Once the connection between the sight of a dog and anxiety has been learned, the child will attempt to avoid dogs. In this way a motive to avoid large dogs can be learned.

Moreover, as anxiety is a learned response, it follows the same principles of learning (such as extinction and generalization) that apply to other behaviors. For example, if the child originally has learned to be afraid of a specific dog, he might generalize this reaction in terms of all objects he has labeled "dog" or "animal." This might include cats, horses, cows, sheep, and even chickens.

Pain as a Determinant of Anxiety

As we pointed out earlier, if learning is to take place—if a new bond between a cue and a response is to be formed—we must somehow find a way of eliciting the response in the first place. In the opinion of a number of psychologists, one class of stimuli that innately produces fear or anxiety is pain (*32, 54*). In such cases, it is not hard to see how anxiety gets started, even in infancy. Infants often experience pain, no matter how solicitious their mothers are. The infant may be stuck with a pin, suffer the acute anguish of colic, or become intensely hungry. Experimental evidence tends to support common observation that hunger pangs rise to greater heights in infants than in adults (*80*). As the infant continues to experience an association between the early, mild feelings of hunger and the more painful later feelings, he will soon learn to anticipate the painful feelings during the early stages of hunger. This anticipation of pain, we are assuming, leads to anxiety. Thus, by allowing infants to become intensely hungry before feeding them, mothers may establish the conditions that lead to feelings of the time of eruption of the first tooth. A very small proportion of infants mother who accidentally sticks her infant with a pin when she changes his diaper, sets up the conditions that permit the child to anticipate pain and, therefore, anxiety, when confronted again with the stimulus of the mother preparing a diaper.

Other Determinants of Anxiety

Stimuli other than pain also produce anxiety, though all too little is known at this point about their nature. Some psychologists suggest that a sudden increase or change in stimulation may produce anxiety.

Hebb (*28*) has suggested that anxiety (or fear) is aroused when a stimulus is discrepant—when a pattern contains both *familiar* and *unfamiliar* elements. For example, he found that chimpanzees show fear reactions when presented with a plaster cast of a chimpanzee head. The head is a familiar stimulus element but the absence of the attached body makes this stimulus incongruous and the animal behaves as if he were afraid. If Hebb's hypothesis is valid, a completely novel stimulus will elicit less fear than one which has some familiar elements embedded in a generally unfamiliar context. That is, as children mature they learn certain rules about the world. They build up definite images or expectations about the environment. They expect that animals will have four feet; birds will have wings; people will have two arms and two eyes; snow will be white, etc. If a child's expectations of what he will see or hear, smell or feel are seriously jarred or disconfirmed (i.e., his expectations are not borne out), he may become anxious.

For example, if a mother should suddenly approach her 8-month-old child while holding a writhing snake rather than a bottle, the child may begin to cry. This anxiety reaction is probably attributable not to an anticipation of being hurt by the snake, but to the presence of an unexpected stimulus in the position of a familiar one—to a psychological surprise. It is to be noted that this kind of anxiety is not likely to occur until the organism has already built up some expectations about the environment. Moreover, this type of anxiety is not likely to occur during the early days of life.

Some Major Sources of Anxiety

While the potential for becoming anxious exists within the physiology of the individual, the types of situations to which anxiety may become attached are a function of a child's learning experiences. It is important to be aware of these differential learning situations, for use of the term *anxiety* alone, without further stipulation of "anxiety over what," is not helpful in understanding or predicting behavior.

Basically *anxiety* is the psychologist's term for that state characterized by an unpleasant feeling tone and either anticipation of an unwanted event or *uncertainty* about the future. The child learns the unpleasant quality of many classes of events and, hence, there are varied causes of anxiety. The following list is not intended to be exhaustive.

Anxiety over Potential Physical Harm. This category of anxiety results from the child's associating certain stimuli with possible pain and danger to his physical well-being (e.g., high places, dangerous animals, fire, deep water). The child may have experienced the pain characteristic of these events or may have been told that these situations lead to pain and physical harm.

Anxiety over Loss of Love. Anxiety over loss of love stems from the anticipation that a source of affection, nurturance, or acceptance (such as mother's love or the friendship of a peer) will be withdrawn or lost. The learning of this class of anxiety may or may not be solely based on the anticipation of pain following loss of a source of love or support. Although this is a common source of anxiety in the child, it is not yet possible to explain the details of its development.

Guilt. Guilt is a special state of anxiety that does not usually appear until about age 3 to 4, and is elicited by the anticipation of violating a rule or standard, or following the violation of an internalized standard or value. In the older child, guilt is characterized by feelings of self-derogation and unworthiness.

Anxiety over Inability to Master the Environment. This anxiety occurs when the individual feels that he is not able to handle the problems and stresses that the environment poses. It is related to, but not identical with, the common term *feelings of inferiority*.

Deviation from Cultural Expectations—Anxiety over Deviant Self-Concept. Every culture has an unwritten list of valued traits, beliefs, and motives that it expects its members to possess. While these characteristics differ with the sex, social class, and the ethnic background of the child, they serve in large measure to define the kind of person the child feels he should be. The individual's concept of himself is, to a large extent, a function of how closely his characteristics approximate the valued traits. When the individual perceives a great discrepancy between his own skills, traits, and temperamental qualities, and those he feels he *should* possess, anxiety is generated. The intensity of the anxiety is related to the degree to which the person perceives himself as deviating from his own and the culture's ideal standards. This source of anxiety is critical in the sex-role development of the child and in the development of self-esteem. These concepts will be discussed in later chapters.

LEARNED MOTIVES AS THE BASIS FOR OTHER MOTIVES

The learning process is like a rapidly expanding building. Once a previously neutral stimulus has acquired the ability to arouse anxiety, for example, it may serve as the basis for learning other anxieties. If a little boy has learned to fear his father, he may later come to fear and withdraw from objects associated with the father, such as the father's friends. Hence, a learned anxiety, such as fear of the father, may serve as a basis not only for learning new instrumental acts but also for acquiring new sources of anxiety.

A child's desire for his mother's love may originally have developed because of her role in meeting his primary needs through such acts as providing warm bottles, rocking and cuddling, changing diapers, removing safety pins, and adding blankets on cold nights. Once developed, however, this motive (i.e., desire for maternal love) may serve as part of the basis for learning further complex motives. For example, if the mother gives love only if the child is being orderly and conscientious, the child may develop a need for orderliness and conscientiousness that will be manifested even when the mother is not around. He may even learn to do many complex acts, such as always putting his toys away carefully, keeping his clothes clean, washing his hands frequently, and always doing what he is told, in order to satisfy the motives that are based on his need for maternal affection.

Finally, many motives of the adolescent and adult are derived from a combination of several, more basic motives. The desire for money in our culture, for example, may be based on the need for social recognition (i.e., gained through ostentatious display of material goods), mastery (i.e., the culture often assesses a man's competence by the amount of money he makes), and dominance (i.e., possession of money allows an individual to dominate others).

The kinds of motives that children learn, the ages at which these motives are likely to emerge, and the circumstances which lead to their emergence, are some of the central concerns of this book.

ENVIRONMENTAL INFLUENCES ON MOTIVATION

Differences among children in the strength and occurrence of various motives are, in part, the result of differences in the value systems of the child's parents and friends, and, consequently, of the behavior they reward. These, in turn, are influenced by broader factors, such as the child's social class, his ethnic and religious affiliations, and his ordinal position in the family. In one family, for example, a child's aggressive behavior with his peers may lead to approval: "He's a regular boy," we hear some admiring parents say, "always into something." Other parents may complain, "That kid is always into something; he's going to drive me crazy. I caught him with a set of tools from his father's workshop this afternoon, and had to spank him and send him to bed."

Americans generally are rewarded for assertive behavior. The Zuni Indian, on the other hand, is genuinely shocked at such behavior and certainly does not reward it in his children (12). In pioneer America, where climate and topography combined to frustrate man in the satisfaction of his primary needs, the development of aggressive behavior was encouraged. In some tropical countries, where food and shelter present few problems, aggressive behavior is little rewarded—at least in part because it is not so necessary for the satisfaction of primary needs (34). Environmental factors such as these, and their influences on the individual's psychological development, will be emphasized throughout the book.

References

1. Bandura, A. Behavioral modification through modeling procedures. In L. Krasner & L. P. Ullman (Eds.), *Research in behavior modification*. New York: Holt, Rinehart and Winston, 1965.
2. Bandura, A. Vicarious processes: a case of no-trial learning. In L. Berkowitz (Ed.), *Advances in social psychology*. Vol. II. New York: Academic Press, 1965.
3. Bandura, A. Social learning through imitation. In M. R. Jones (Ed.), *Nebraska symposium on motivation: 1962*. Lincoln: Univer. of Nebraska Press, 211–269.
4. Bandura, A. The influence of rewarding and punishing consequences to the model in the acquisition and performance of imitative responses. Unpublished manuscript, Stanford University, 1962.
5. Bandura, A., Grusec, J. E., & Menlove, F. The influence of symbolization and incentive-set on observational learning. Unpublished manuscript, Stanford University, 1965.
6. Bandura, A., & Kupers, C. J. Transmission of patterns of self-reinforcement through modeling. *J. abnorm. soc. Psychol.* 1964, *69*, 1–9.
7. Bandura, A., & McDonald, F. J. The influence of social reinforcement and the behavior of models in shaping children's moral judgments. *J. abnorm. soc. Psychol.*, 1963, *67*, 274–281.
8. Bandura, A., & Mischel, W. Modification of self-imposed delay of reward through exposure to live and symbolic models. *J. pers. soc. Psychol.*, 1965, *2*, 698–705.
9. Bandura, A., Ross, D., & Ross, S. A. A comparative test of the status envy, social power, and secondary reinforcement theories of identification learning. *J. abnorm. soc. Psychol.*, 1963, *67*, 527–534.
10. Bandura, A., & Walters, R. H. *Social learning and personality development*. New York: Holt, Rinehart and Winston, 1963.
11. Bandura, A., & Whalen, C. K. The influence of antecedent reinforcement and divergent modeling cues on patterns of self-reward. *J. pers. soc. Psychol.*, 1966, *3*, 373–382.

12. Benedict, R. *Patterns of culture.* New York: Penguin, 1946.
13. Bensberg, G. J., Colwell, C. N., & Cassel, R. H. Teaching the profoundly retarded self-help activities by behavior shaping techniques. *Amer. J. ment. Def.,* 1965, *69,* 674–679.
14. Bexton, W. E., Heron, W., & Scott, T. H. Effects of decreased variation in the sensory environment. *Canad. J. Psychol.,* 1954, *8,* 70–76.
15. Bierman, M. M. The relative efficacy of modeling, reinforcement, and problem-solving set in altering children's grammatical styles. Unpublished doctoral dissertation, Stanford University, 1965.
16. Brown, P., & Elliott, R. Control of aggression in a nursery school class. *J. exp. child Psychol.,* 1965, *2,* 103–107.
17. Cowles, J. T. Food tokens as incentives for learning by chimpanzees. *Comp. Psychol. Monogr.,* 1937, *14,* No. 5.
18. Dethier, V. G., & Stella, E. *Animal behavior.* Englewood Cliffs, N.J.: Prentice-Hall, 1964 (2nd ed.).
19. Eisenberg, L. Psychiatric disorders of childhood: III. Psychotic and brain disorders. In A. M. Freedman & H. I. Kaplan (Eds.), *Comprehensive textbook of psychiatry.* Baltimore: Williams & Wilkins, 1967, 1433–1452.
20. Flavell, J. H. *The developmental psychology of Jean Piaget.* Princeton, N.J.: Van Nostrand, 1963.
21. Gagné, R. M. *The conditions of learning.* New York: Holt, Rinehart and Winston, 1965.
22. Gagné, R. M. Contributions of learning to human development. *Psychol. Rev.,* in press.
23. Gottschalk, J. Bryden, M. P., & Rahnovitch, M. S. Spatial organization of children's responses to a pictorial display. *Child Develpm.,* 1964, *35,* 811–815.
24. Harlow, H. F. Motivation as a factor in the acquisition of new responses. In *Current theory and research in motivation: a symposium.* Lincoln: Univer. of Nebraska Press, 1953, 24–49.
25. Harlow, H. F. Learning and satiation of response in intrinsically motivated complex puzzle performance by monkeys. *J. comp. physiol. Psychol.,* 1950, *43,* 289–294.
26. Hartup, W. W. Friendship status and the effectiveness of peers as reinforcing agents. *J. exp. child Psychol.,* 1964, *1,* 154–162.
27. Hebb, D. O. Drives and the CNS (conceptual nervous system). *Psychol. Rev.,* 1955, *62,* 243–254.
28. Hebb, D. O. On the nature of fear. *Psychol. Rev.,* 1946, *53,* 259–276.
29. Hess, E. H. Ethology. In A. M. Freedman & H. I. Kaplan (Eds.), *Comprehensive textbook of psychiatry.* Baltimore: Williams & Wilkins, 1967, 180–189.
30. Hicks, D. J. Imitation and retention of film-mediated aggressive peer and adult models. *J. pers. soc. Psychol.,* 1965, *2,* 97–100.
31. Hilgard, E. R., & Bower, G. H. *Theories of learning.* New York: Appleton-Century-Crofts, 1966 (3rd ed.),
32. Hilgard, E. R. *Theories of learning.* New York: Appleton-Century-Crofts, 1948.
33. Hill, K. T., & Stevenson, H. W. The effects of social reinforcement vs. non-reinforcement and sex of E on the performance of adolescent girls. *J. Pers.,* 1965, *33,* 30–36.
34. Honigman, J. J. *Culture and personality.* New York: Harper & Row, 1954.
35. Hundziak, M., Maurer, R. A., & Watson, L. S., Jr. Operant conditioning in toilet

training of severely mentally retarded boys. *Amer. J. ment. Def.*, 1965, *70*, 120–124.

36. Hunt, J. McV. Experience in the development of motivation: some reinterpretations. *Child Develpm.*, 1960, *31*, 489–504.

37. Inhelder, B., & Sinclair, H. Learning cognitive structures. In P. Mussen, J. Langer, & M. Covington (Eds.), *New directions in developmental psychology*, in press.

38. John, E. B., Chessler, P., Bartlett, F., & Victor, I. Observation learning in cats. *Science*, 1968, *159*, 1489–1491.

39. Kagan, J. & Henker, B. Developmental psychology. In P. R. Farnsworth, O. McNeman, & Q. McNeman (Eds.), *Ann. Rev. Psychol.* Palo Alto, Calif.: Annual Review, Inc., 1966, *17*, 1–50.

40. Kimble, G. A. *Hilgard and Marquis' conditioning and learning.* New York: Appleton-Century-Crofts, 1961 (2nd ed.).

41. Kish, G. B. A demonstration of learning when the onset of illumination is used as a reinforcing stimulus. *Amer. Psychol.*, 1954, *9*, 406 (Abstr.).

42. Koch, S. The logical character of the motivation concept: I. *Psychol. Rev.*, 1941, *48*, 15–38.

43. Koch, S. The logical character of the motivation concept: II. *Psychol. Rev.*, 1941, *48*, 127–154.

44. Leuba, C. Toward some integration of learning theories: the concept of optimal stimulation. *Psychol. Rev.*, 1955, *1*, 27–33.

45. Lipsitt, L. P. Learning in the first year of life. In L. P. Lipsitt & C. C. Spiker (Eds.), *Advances in child development and behavior.* New York: Academic Press, 1963, 147–195.

46. Lorenz, K. Z. *King Solomon's ring.* London: Methuen, 1952.

47. Lovaas, O. I. A behavior therapy approach to the treatment of childhood schizophrenia. In *Minnesota symposium on child psychology.* Minneapolis: Univer. of Minnesota Press, 1967.

48. Lovaas, O. I., Berberich, J. P., Perloff, B. F., & Schaeffer, B. Acquisition of imitative speech in schizophrenic children. *Science*, 1966, *151*, 705–707.

49. Lovaas, O. I., Freitag, G., Gold, V. J., & Kassorla, I. C. Experimental studies in childhood schizophrenia: analysis of self-destructive behavior. *J. exp. Psychol.*, 1965, *2*, 67–84.

50. Marquis, D. P. Can conditioned responses be established in the newborn infant? *J. genet. Psychol.*, 1931, *39*, 479–492.

51. Mednick, S. A. *Learning.* Englewood Cliffs, N.J.: Prentice-Hall, 1964.

52. Miller, N. E. Laws of learning relevant to its biological bases. *Proceedings of the American Philosophical Association*, 1967, *3*, 315–325.

53. Miller, N. E. Learnable drives and rewards. In S. S. Stevens (Ed.), *Handbook of experimental psychology.* New York: Wiley, 1951, 435–472.

54. Miller, N. E., & DiCara, L. Instrumental learning of heart rate changes in curarized rats: shaping, and specificity to discriminative stimulus. *J. comp. physiol. Psychol.*, 1967, *63*, 12–19.

55. Miller, N. E., & Dollard, J. *Social learning and imitation.* New Haven: Yale Univer. Press, 1941.

56. Olds, J. Adaptive functions of paleocortical and related structures. In H. F. Harlow & C. N. Woolsey (Eds.), *Biological and biochemical bases of behavior.* Madison: Univer. of Wisconsin Press, 1958.

57. Olds, J., & Milner, P. Positive reinforcement produced by electrical stimulation of septal area and other regions of the rat brain. *J. comp. physiol. Psychol.*, 1954, *47*, 419–427.

58. Palermo, D. S., Castaneda, A., & McCandless, B. R. The relationship of anxiety in children to performance in a complex learning task. *Child Develpm.*, 1956, *27*, 333–337.
59. Patterson, G. R., Littman, R. A., & Hinsey, W. C. Parental effectiveness as reinforcers in the laboratory and its relation to child rearing practices and child adjustment in the classroom. *J. Pers.*, 1964, *32*, 180–199.
60. Piaget, J. *The origins of intelligence in children.* New York: International Universities Press, 1952.
61. Pressey, S. L. A simple apparatus which gives tests and scores and teaches. *Sch. Soc.*, 1926, 23, 373–376.
62. Pressey, S. L. A machine for automatic teaching of drill material. *Sch. Soc.*, 1927, *25*, 549–552.
63. Ross, S. A. The effect of deviant and nondeviant models on the behavior of preschool children in a temptation situation. Unpublished doctoral dissertion, Stanford University, 1962.
64. Ruebush, B. K., & Stevenson, H. The effects of mothers and strangers on the performance of anxious and defensive children. *J. Pers.*, 1964, *32*, 587–600.
65. Sarason, I. G. Test anxiety, general anxiety, and intellectual performance. *J. counsel. Psychol.*, 1957, *21*, 485–490.
66. Sigel, I. E. The dominance of meaning. *J. genet. Psychol.*, 1954, *85*, 201–207.
67. Skinner, B. F. *The behavior of organisms.* New York: Appleton-Century-Crofts, 1938.
68. Skinner, B. F. How to teach animals. *Scientific Amer.*, 1951, *185*, 26–29.
69. Skinner, B. F. *Science and human behavior.* New York: Macmillan, 1953.
70. Skinner, B. F. The science of learning in the art of teaching. *Harv. educ. Rev.*, 1954, *24*, 86–97.
71. Skinner, B. F. Teaching machines. *Science,* 1958, *128*, 969–977.
72. Smedslund, J. The acquisition of conservation of substance and weight in children. I. Introduction. *Scand. J. Psychol.*, 1961, *2*, 11–20. (a)
73. Smedslund, J. The acquisition of conservation of substance and weight in children. II. External reinforcement of conservation of weight and of the operations of addition and subtraction. *Scand. J. Psychol.*, 1961, *2*, 71–84. (b)
74. Smedslund, J. The acquisition of conservation of substance and weight in children. III. Extinction of conservation of weight acquired "normally" and by means of empirical controls on a balance scale. *Scand. J. Psychol.*, 1961, *2*, 85–87. (c)
75. Smedslund, J. The acquisition of conservation of substance and weight in children. IV. An attempt at extinction of the visual components of the weight concept. *Scand. J. Psychol.*, 1961, *2*, 153–155. (d)
76. Spelt, D. K. The conditioning of the human fetus in utero. *J. exp. Psychol.*, 1948, *38*, 338–346.
77. Staats, A. W., & Butterfield, W. H. Treatment of nonreading in a culturally deprived juvenile delinquent: An application of reinforcement principles. *Child Develpm.*, 1965, *36*, 925–942.
78. Stevenson, H. W. Developmental psychology. In P. R. Farnsworth, O. McNeman, & Q. McNeman (Eds.), *Ann. Rev. Psychol.* Palo Alto, Calif.: Annual Review, Inc., 1967, *18*, 102–127.
79. Stevenson, H. W., & Odom, R. D. Visual reinforcement with children. *J. exp, child Psychol.*, 1964, *1*, 248–255.
80. Taylor, R. Hunger in the infant. *Amer. J. Dis. Child,* 1917, *14*, 233–257.
81. Terrell, C., & Stevenson, H. W. The effectiveness of normal and retarded peers as reinforcing agents. *Amer. J. ment. Def.*, 1965, *70*, 373–381.

82. Tinbergen, N. Social releasers and the experimental method required for their study. *Wilson Bull.,* 1948, *60,* 6–51.
83. Toch, H. H., & Schulte, R. Readiness to perceive violence as a result of police training. *Brit. J. Psychol.,* 1961, *52,* 389–394.
84. Trowill, J. A. Instrumental conditioning of the heart rate in the curarized rat. *J. comp. physiol. Psychol.,* 1967, *63,* 7–11.
85. Watson, J. B., & Raynor, R. Conditioned emotional reactions. *J. exp. Psychol.,* 1920, *3,* 1–4.
86. Whitlock, C., Sr. Note on reading acquisition: an extension of laboratory principles. *J. exp. child Psychol.,* 1966, *3,* 83–85.
87. Wohlwill, J. F. Perceptual learning. In P. R. Farnsworth, O. McNeman, & Q. McNeman (Eds.), *Ann. Rev. Psychol.* Palo Alto, Calif.: Annual Review, Inc., 1966, *17,* 201–232.
88. Wohlwill, J. F., & Lowe, R. C. An experimental analysis of the development of the conservation of number. *Child Develpm.* 1962, *33,* 153–167.
89. Wohlwill, J. F., & Wiener, M. Discrimination of form orientation in your children. *Child Develpm.,* 1964, *35,* 1113–1125.
90. Wolfe, J. B. Effectiveness of token rewards for chimpanzees. *Comp. Psychol. Monogr.,* 1936, *12,* No. 60.

5

Biological
Changes
in the First Year

The birth of the child is marked by two fundamental changes in his functioning. He is now subjected to states of imbalance, deprivation, or discomfort that must soon be repaired, and he encounters a variety of events and experiences which shape his perception of the environment and his reactions to it. Stated more simply, the newborn experiences states of hunger, heat, cold, and pain from which he was protected during the prenatal period. These states are important psychologically for they force the infant to do something in order to alleviate the discomfort. The infant will typically thrash and cry when hungry, vocalize when excited, thrash his limbs when in pain. These are innate reactions to the sensations he feels, and they typically lead to an important change in the environment. Another person usually comes to tend the child when he cries or thrashes, and with this action the child's development comes under the partial control of the social environment. From the moment a person begins to serve the infant, certain behaviors become selectively strengthened and others weakened—the infant begins his attachment to a human being and is initiated into a system in which human beings are viewed as the basic objects to whom one turns for help and from whom one learns values, motives, and complex behaviors.

The current and next chapters discuss development during the first 18 months, the period that is typically called infancy. At about 2 years, give or take a few months, "infancy" ends because between about 18 and 26 months most children begin to speak meaningful language and are able to comprehend relatively complex communications from others. The child's interactions with the world are changed dramatically at this time, for he then begins to attach symbolic meaning to his experiences. This particular chapter will concentrate on the perceptual-motor and biological developments of the first 18 months. The next chapter will consider the role of the family during this period and the child's developing attachment to those who care for him.

BODY GROWTH IN INFANCY

In view of the numerous variations among infants in size at birth and in rate of growth, averages or norms can give only a general picture of development. On the average, full-term male babies, who are slightly larger in all body dimensions than females, are about 20 inches tall and weigh 7½ pounds at birth. It should be noted, however, that the range of "normal" birth heights and weights is large. For example, newborns from poverty-stricken environments, although similarly proportioned, tend to be smaller than those from more favorable environments (3). This is probably caused by nutritional differences and a greater incidence of maternal infection during pregnancy.

The first year of the child's life brings remarkably rapid and extensive growth changes. Body length increases over one-third, and weight almost triples, so that by the age of 1, the average baby is about 28 or 29 inches tall and weighs about 20 pounds.

In addition, there are vast modifications in body proportions and in skeletal, neural, and muscular structure. Detailed technical discussions of these developments are beyond the scope of this book, but a condensed description of the major changes follows (100).

Body Proportions

Because "the body does not grow as a whole and in all directions at once" (98, 299), the infant's overall body proportions change rapidly, particularly during the second half of the first year. The differential growth rates of the legs and face illustrate the way in which body proportions change. At birth, the infant's legs are about one-fifth as long as they will be when he is an adult, but from about 8 weeks of age they grow at an accelerated rate. In contrast to this, the head and face grow more slowly than the body as a whole, although skull size and shape become significantly modified. The total length of the head and face of the 3-month-old fetal infant is about one-third of his total body length; at birth this height is about one-fourth; in adulthood, about one-tenth (98; see Fig. 5.1).

Skeletal Development

All of the bones of the body originate from soft cartilage tissue which over a period of time becomes ossified or hardened into bone material by the deposition of minerals. Ossification begins during the prenatal period

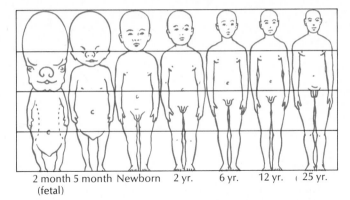

2 month 5 month Newborn   2 yr.   6 yr.   12 yr.   (25 yr.
(fetal)

Fig. 5.1. Changes in form and proportion of the human body during fetal and postnatal life. (From C. M. Jackson. Some aspects of form and growth. in W. J. Robbins, S. Brody, A. F. Hogan, C. M. Jackson, & C. W. Green (Eds.), *Growth*. New Haven: Yale Univer. Press, 1929, p. 118. By permission.)

and continues, for some bones, until late adolescence. As most infants' bones are not ossified to a great extent, they are softer, more pliable, more reactive to muscular pull and pressure, and more susceptible to deformity than those of older children and adults. Fortunately, they are also less subject to breakage.

The timing and rate of ossification differs with the various bones of the body and among individuals. Some of the bones of the hand and wrist ossify very early in life, and by the end of the first year most children have developed three of their total (i.e., adult) complement of 28 hand and wrist bones. Other skeletal parts ossify later. The skull of the newborn infant has six soft spots (fontanelles) which ossify gradually and do not disappear until the child is about 2 years of age. Other bones develop still later (98).

As with other aspects of development, there are marked individual and group differences in rates of ossification and skeletal growth. Sex differences in skeletal development favoring girls are present at birth and increase with age. Negro infants are generally advanced beyond white infants (100). Moreover, broad-framed children tend to have a faster rate of ossification than narrow-framed children. Hereditary factors markedly affect the rate and timing of skeletal development, although illness, allergies, and malnutrition may produce disturbances of ossification.

Teeth

Tiny beginnings of the deciduous or "baby" teeth are present in the fetus from the age of 10 to 13 weeks and calcification has begun by the fifth prentatal month, but there is a great deal of individual variability in the time of eruption of the first tooth. A very small proportion of infants are born with one or more teeth, others do not have any until after they are

1 year old. The first tooth, generally a lower front tooth, erupts at an average age of 7 months. By the time the average child is a year old he has six teeth, but the range is from 0 to 12 months (40). The timing of tooth eruption is unrelated to many aspects of physical development (e.g., height, weight, muscle mass) during infancy and childhood. As in bone growth, girls are slightly advanced over boys in tooth formation and time of eruption. Genetic factors also influence the sequence and timing of tooth eruption, and Oriental and Negro children are generally more advanced than Caucasians (34, 95).

Muscles

Although the neonate has all the muscle fibers he will ever have, they are small in relation to his size. However, there is continuous growth in muscle length, breadth, and thickness until, in adulthood, the weight of the muscles is about forty times what it was at birth. The striped or skeletal (voluntary) muscles of the body are not yet completely under the infant's control during the first year. They fatigue rapidly, and recover easily in the early stages of the development of voluntary responses such as sitting and walking (98).

As with teeth and bones, different muscle groups grow at different rates, and there is a general tendency for the muscles near the head and neck to develop earlier than those of the lower limbs (cephalocaudal development). Finally, infant boys have a greater proportion of muscle tissue than infant girls, and this sex difference holds for males and females at all ages (32, 33).

Finally, it should be noted that there are consistent sex differences in growth dimensions. Girls develop faster than boys and this faster rate of development begins during the fetal period. The body composition of the sexes differs, with infant girls having proportionally more fat and less water than boys. Girls have less muscle tissue and are generally lighter and shorter than boys. But the most intriguing sex difference is that the physical growth of girls is less variable than that of boys. That is, if we pick a particular growth variable, such as number of teeth at age 2, and examine a thousand boys and a thousand girls, the range for number of teeth would be greater for boys than for girls. There would be more boys with many teeth and more boys with few teeth. The range for girls would be smaller (35).

In addition, girls' growth is more stable than that of boys. The rate of skeletal maturity in the 2-year-old girl is a better predictor of her future rate of skeletal development than it is for the boy (1). As we shall see later, this greater stability in bone growth is paralleled by a greater stability in intellectual growth. For example, a girl's vocabulary at age 3 is a better predictor of her adult vocabulary and IQ than a boy's vocabulary is. This interesting parallel between physical and psychological factors is intriguing and suggests the operation of fundamental sex differences in the organization of development. Perhaps before the next edition of this book is written we shall understand this phenomenon more fully.

THE NEWBORN

The Initial Equipment

Surprisingly, the newborn is a remarkably capable organism from the moment he begins to breathe. He can see, hear, and smell, and he is sensitive to pain, touch, and change in position. The only sense modality which may not be functioning immediately at birth is taste, but even this sense develops rather quickly. The infant is biologically ready to experience most of the basic sensations of his species from the moment he is born. This is not true of all mammals. Puppies, as the reader may know, are both blind and deaf at birth.

The newborn's behavioral equipment is also remarkably well developed. He can display a variety of reflexes, some of which are necessary for survival, and many of which are complex. For example, a newborn only 2 hours old will follow a moving light with his eyes if the velocity of the light is optimal; his pupils will dilate in darkness and constrict in light; he will suck a finger or nipple inserted into his mouth; he will turn in the direction in which his cheek or the corner of his mouth is touched. He can cry, cough, turn away, vomit, lift his chin from a prone position, and grasp an object placed in his palm. His body will react to a loud sound, and he can flex and extend his limbs, smack his lips, and chew his fingers (23).

One of the important and interesting responses shown by the newborn is called the Moro reflex. In this response, the infant throws his arms out to the side, extends his fingers and then brings arms back and hands to the midline, as if he were embracing someone. The infant will normally show this reaction to a sudden change in head position, and often shows it to any event that would surprise him. The best way to demonstrate this reflex is to lay the baby on his back and, when he is quiet, simultaneously hit the sides of the pillow or mattress on either side of the infant's head. This sudden change in stimulation typically elicits the Moro reflex. It is believed that the effective cause of this reflex is either a change in the proprioceptive receptors in the muscles in the neck or stimulation from the vestibular system. This reflex is of developmental importance because, in normal infants, it begins to vanish at 3 to 4 months of age, and by 6 months is difficult to elicit. One interpretation of the disappearance is based on the belief that the newborn's behavior is largely controlled by processes in the brain stem rather than by the cerebral cortex. The brain stem, which lies under the cortex, contains centers that are responsible for the basic biological functions of breathing and circulation, as well as basic reflexes. The cerebral cortex is largely responsible for perception, memory, and thought. The cerebral cortex may not be fully functional in the newborn and may only gradually awaken and begin assuming control of the infant's behavior during the opening weeks of life. As the cortex gains control, it begins to inhibit and modulate the

(a)

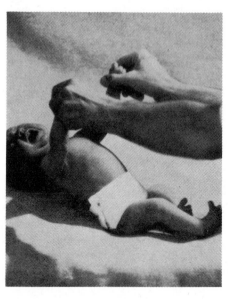

(b)

Fig. 5.2. The traction test. (a) Initial position (b) Response. The infant's hands are grasped as he is pulled slowly to a sitting position. The normal infant resists as in (b). (From H. Prechtl & D. Beintema. The neurological examination of the fullterm newborn infant. *Little Club Clinics in Developmental Medicine*, No. 12. London. Spastics Society Medical Information Unit and William Heinemann Medical Books, Ltd., 1964, p. 46. By permission.)

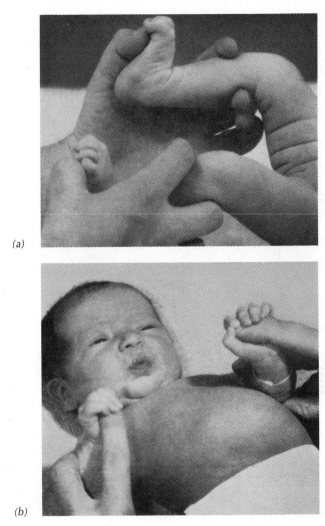

(a)

(b)

Fig. 5.3.   (a) Elicitation of ankle clonus. The examiner presses both thumbs against the soles of the foot; the infant's toes flex around the thumbs. (b) Testing for the palmer grasp. The examiner presses his finger into the infant's palms and infant's fingers flex around the examiner's finger. (From H. Prechtl & D. Beintema. The neurological examination of the fullterm newborn infant. *Little Club Clinics in Developmental Medicine,* No. 12. London: Spastics Society Medical Information Unit and William Heinemann Medical Books, Ltd., 1964, p. 35. By permission.)

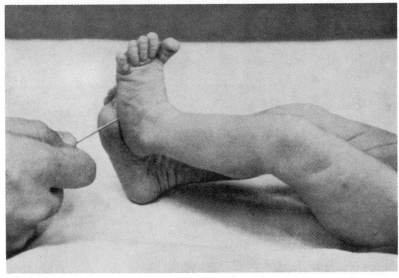

(a)

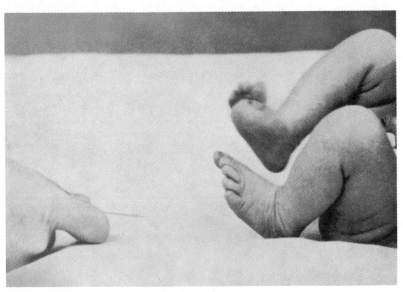

(b)

Fig. 5.4. The withdrawal reflex. (a) Stimulation. The examiner pricks the infant's sole with a pin. (b) Response. The infant withdraws his foot. (From H. Prechtl & D. Beintema. The neurological examination of the fullterm newborn infant. *Little Club Clinics in Developmental Medicine*, No. 12. London: Spastics Society Medical Information Unit and William Heinemann Medical Books, Ltd., 1964, p. 40. By permission.)

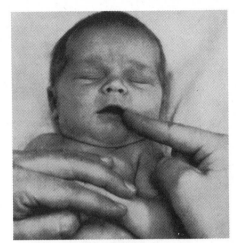

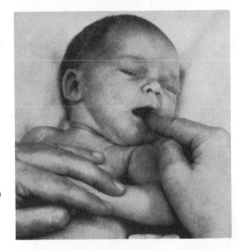

(a)

(b)

(c)

Fig. 5.5. The rooting re-sponse. (a) Stimulation. The examiner tickles the side of the infant's mouth with a finger. (b) Head turning. The infant turns his head in the direction of the finger. (c) Grasping with the mouth. The infant tries to suck the stimu-lating finger. (From H. Prechtl & D. Beintema. The neuro-logical examination of the fullterm newborn infant. *Little Club Clinics in Develop-mental Medicine*, No. 12. London: Spastics Society Medi-cal Information Unit and William Heinemann Medical Books, Ltd., 1964, p. 41. By permission.)

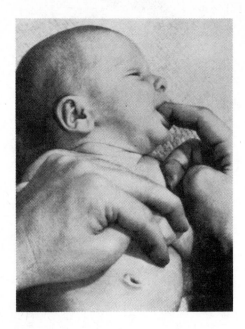

(a)

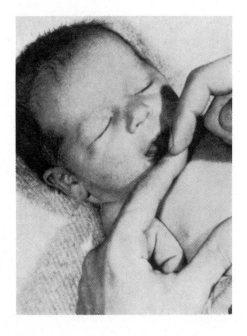

(b)

Fig. 5.6. (a) Testing sucking. The infant sucks the finger placed into his mouth. (b) Elicitation of the jaw-jerk. The examiner delivers a short, sharp tap to the chin and the infant's chin is lifted by contraction of masseteric muscles. (From H. Prechtl & D. Beintema. The neurological examination of the fullterm newborn infant. *Little Club Clinics in Developmental Medicine,* No. 12. London: Spastics Society Medical Information Unit and William Heinemann Medical Books, Ltd., 1964, p. 42. By permission.)

Table 5.1   Reflexes of the Newborn

Effective Stimulus	Reflex
Tap upper lips sharply	Lips protrude
Tap bridge of nose	Eyes close tightly
Bright light suddenly shown to eyes	Closure of eyelids
Clap hands about 18 inches from infant's head	Closure of eyelids
Touch cornea with light piece of cotton	Eyes close
With baby held on back turn face slowly to right side	Jaw and right arm on side of face extend out; the left arm flexes
Extend forearms at elbow	Arms flex briskly
Put fingers into infant's hand and press his palms	Infant's fingers flex and enclose finger
Press thumbs against the ball of infant's feet	Toes flex
Scratch sole of foot starting from toes towards the heels	Big toe bends upward and small toes spread
Prick soles of feet with pin	Infant's knee and foot flex
Tickle area at corner of mouth	Head turns toward side of stimulation
Put index finger into mouth	Sucks
Hold infant in air, stomach down	Infant attempts to lift head and extends legs

lower brain stem centers that are responsible for the Moro reflex. Neurologists would view with some alarm a 10-month-old infant who was still displaying the Moro response to a change in head position, for this would suggest that there might be some deficiency or damage in the infant's central nervous system.

Table 5.1 lists some of the major reflexes of the newborn and the kinds of stimuli that release them (see Figs. 5.3–5.6).

Contemporary psychology views the newborn with considerably more respect than the scientist of the sixteenth century, who saw the infant as relatively insensitive. We have exploded the myth of newborn insensitivity and incompetence.

The second myth we must examine is the often-quoted belief that "the world of the baby is a blooming, buzzing confusion." This idea was probably born from a prejudice that saw the infant as a passive, helpless animal with little power to do very much about his environment. This description of a buzzing and confusing world is a reasonable conclusion for an urban scientist who must have thought that if his own world was a noisy and confused place, it must seem even more chaotic to the more helpless infant.

Recent research on attentional processes suggests that the infant's world may actually be quieter than ours. Humans typically attend to (i.e., perceive) one sensory channel at a time. When we are listening intently to a bird's song, we may not feel a touch, smell a flower, or see a deer. We may not be able to perceive two different auditory messages—one to each ear—coming in at the same time. We choose the one we wish to listen to, and we are temporarily deaf to the other channel (12). We may think we can attend to many channels of sensory information at once because we shift our attention rapidly and frequently from one event to another. This gives us the impression or continuous perception of many things simultaneously. This rapid oscillation of attention is analogous to the electric current in the light bulb that goes on and off sixty times a second. We perceive continuous rather than discontinuous light because the shift in current is so rapid we cannot detect it. It is possible that the newborn can not change his focus of attention as rapidly as the older child can. When the baby is watching his mother he may not hear sounds around him; when he is attending to a hunger pain he may not feel his mother's touch. His world may be made up of single perceptions and, therefore, be less confused, noisy, and buzzing than our own.

The child begins life with some responses he can make, and a sensory system that functions well. He is now ready to acquire new behaviors and ideas. This process proceeds in stages, not all at once, and psychologists are just beginning to see the outline of these stages for each of the systems that are growing.

STAGES OF INFANCY

Newborn Period. The newborn period is considered to cover the first 5 to 7 days. At this time, the infant is recovering from the physiological trauma of delivery and is just beginning to establish an equilibrium with his environment. Infants born to mothers who received heavy doses of drugs during labor are groggier and less alert than babies born to mothers given minimal doses of drugs (94).

Second Stage. The second period of infancy lasts from 1 to 8 weeks of age. The reason that 8 weeks is designated as the approximate end of a phase is because several important changes occur at this time. The infant becomes markedly more visually attentive to the world around him, his vocalizations increase dramatically, and the amount of time he spends crying is markedly reduced.

Third Stage. Between 8 and 12 weeks another set of important events occurs. First, the infant's behavior suggests that he is beginning to appreciate depth and to perceive objects in three dimensions. Before this, the baby reacts with the same amount of smiling and the same duration of looking to two-and three-dimensional forms of human faces. Between 3 and 4 months, however, he will look longer and will smile and vocalize more frequently at a three-dimensional form. In addition, the 3-month-old will begin to lose interest to repetitions of same stimuli. This phenomenon is called habituation (29). The diminished responsivity can involve either decreased looking, decreased smiling, or decreased autonomic reactivity. Finally, as we have noted before, the Moro reflex begins to vanish between 3 and 4 months of age.

Fourth Stage. The next stage lasts from about 4 to 7 months and is characterized by increased smiling to human voices and faces, the peak of such smiling occurring between 3 and 5 months of age. (We shall be discussing the smile in the next chapter.) The second major event occurring during this period is the coordination of eye-hand movements and coordinated visual-motor reaching, which usually occurs at 5½ months.

Fifth Stage. The next period lasts from about 7 to 12 months and is characterized by frequent displays of anxiety in response to surprising or unexpected stimuli, anxiety about the presence of a stranger being only one instance of this reaction.

Sixth Stage. This period lasts from about 12 to 18 months and involves the onset of walking, and increased mobility, as well as the beginning of language comprehension and expression. The infant can now understand simple requests, can use language to obtain desired goals and can react to objects on the basis of their symbolic names rather than only on the basis of their color, shininess, or capacity for being sucked or slapped.

This very brief description given above is presented to give the reader some appreciation for some of the milestones in behavior during the first 18 months. Let us now discuss in more detail specific modalities in both the perceptual and motor domains.

Perceptual Development

The Visual Mode. Discussion of the perceptual development of the infant requires us to consider first the infant's capacities and, second, the determinants of attention to stimuli. What are the characteristics of visual, auditory, olfactory, or tactile stimuli that will attract and hold the infant's attention? This is an important and complicated issue. The infant's early mental development grows from his distribution of attention to events in his environment. If we knew the principles that determined what events the infant usually looks at or listens to we would know more about what he was learning.

Visual Capacities. As indicated earlier, the infant is able to see light, dark, and color at birth and has remarkably good visual acuity.

Although the essential neural mechanisms began to appear in the third week of prenatal life, the neuromuscular apparatus involved in vision is still not perfected when the infant is born. In order to assess the infant's visual sensitivity, we must observe his responses to visual stimuli.

1. The pupillary reflex (contraction of the pupil in response to increased light and dilation in response to decreased light), observed even in premature

infants, reveals that the neonate is sensitive to differences in the intensity of visual stimuli. Although the response is somewhat sluggish at birth, it becomes perfected during the first few days of postnatal life (82, 83). At first, it can be elicited only by strong stimuli, but with increasing age, less intensity is required.

2. Visual pursuit movements. Infants as young as a few days will follow moving lights indicating that the eye muscles are sufficiently coordinated to track stimuli.

3. According to the best available data (69), *coordination* and *convergence* of the two eyes, both essential for fixation and depth perception, are absent at birth but appear in rudimentary form a few hours afterwards.

Real convergence or binocular fixation first occurs at about 7 or 8 weeks. It is initially accomplished by a series of jerking movements which are gradually eliminated, and replaced by smooth, continuous convergence.

4. Because the ciliary muscles of the neonate are not mature enough to permit perfect accommodation (adjustment of the thickness of the lens of the eye to bring the light rays into proper focus on the retina) the newborn does not perceive clear-cut images in the way that a 1-year-old does.

It appears that for the first month the infant does not make any adjustment to objects at varying distances from his eyes (called accommodation). He seems to have a fixed focus at about 8 inches from his face. By 2 months he begins to accommodate to the distance of objects, and by 4 months of age his ability to accommodate is comparable to that of an adult. As early as 16 weeks the infant is capable of making adjustments of his eyes so that he can focus on near and far targets (48).

Although the poor accommodation for the first 8 weeks would make the perception of detailed form at a distance difficult, the newborn clearly shows responsiveness to movement of stimuli and to different intensities of light. A 5-day-old baby sucking on a nipple will momentarily stop sucking if a light begins to move in his visual field (45), and he will look different amounts of time at stimuli of different brightness (49). The infant, therefore, reacts to movement and light intensity from the first days of life.

A third attribute of visual stimulation to which the newborn is reactive is the contrast created by a contour (the edge of a black line on a white background). The infant seems drawn to contours and will focus his attention near the contour more than he will on other parts of the field. If a newborn is shown a black triangle on a white field, his eyes will hover near the sides of the triangle—especially near the vertices of the triangle, the place where the contrast between black and white is maximal (89).

The infant's attention to contour can be used to assess his visual acuity. The young infant typically looks longest at the stimulus that contains the most contour. If we show him two stimuli with differing amounts of contour and he looks longer at one of them, we can conclude that he can detect the differences between them. Robert Fantz performed experiments of this kind and concluded that, as early as 2 weeks of age, the infant can detect the difference between a gray patch and a square composed of stripes

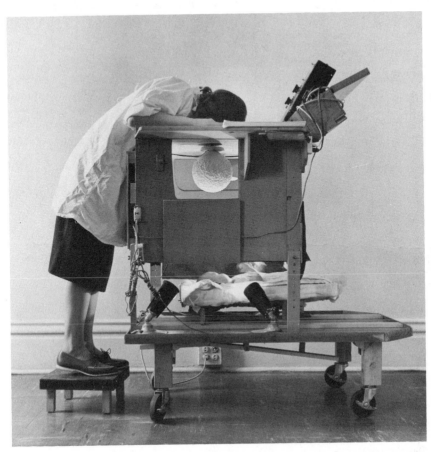

Fig. 5.7. Form perception. (From R. L. Fantz. The origin of form perception. *Scientific Amer.*, May, 1961, *204*, 66. Photographer: David Linton. By permission.)

that are only ⅛ of an inch wide, at a distance of 9 inches from his face. By 3 months of age infants will look longer at (and, therefore, can discriminate) stripes 1/64 of an inch wide than at a gray patch at a distance of only 15 inches (30; see Fig. 5.7).

Before the first half-year of life is over, the human infant's visual acuity is comparable to that of any child or adult. Figure 5.8 shows the relative power of six different stimuli to sustain the gaze of infants from 2 days through 6 months of age. Note that all five stimuli with black and white contours hold the infant's attention longer than the plain gray patch, as early as 2 days of age. Recent work by neurophysiologists indicates that the visual areas of the cortex are responsive to contour edges in particular spatial orientations. This suggests that the longer attention to the stimuli with contours is not based on learning but is the result of a biological characteristic of

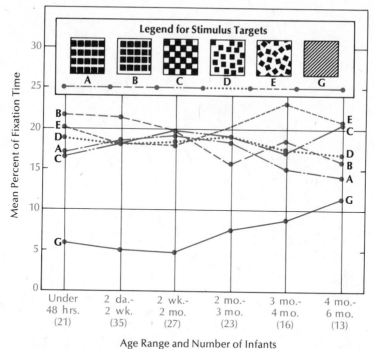

Fig. 5.8. Differences in fixation time for six different patterns for infants of varying ages. (From R. L. Fantz, Visual perception from birth as shown by pattern selectivity. Copyright, The New York Academy of Sciences, 1965, Vol. 118. Reprinted by permission.)

the central nervous system (51). This tendency to look at contour will lead the infant to focus his attention on his mother's eyes because of their inherent black-white contrast.

Now that we can be assured that the infant is capable of detecting varied shapes and forms, a more intriguing question can be asked. What kinds of forms are likely to attract and hold the infant's attention? To what kinds of events does he usually attend?

Stimulus Determinants of Attention

The Role of Complexity. During the infant's first 2 to 3 months of life, stimuli that have a high degree of contour and movement are most likely to attract and hold his attention. Moving objects attract his attention more effectively than stationary ones; forms with black-white contrast attract longer gazes than forms that are of a homogeneous color or contain little contour.

However, these principles cannot explain all of the infant's attentional behavior after 2 to 3 months of age. For example, most infants 4 to 8 weeks old look longer at a striped pattern than at a bull's-eye. But after 8 weeks of age they look longer at the bull's-eye than at the striped stimuli. It may be that a bull's-eye has a special retinal effect that holds the infant's attention.

It is interesting that several species of birds show an avoidance reaction to stimuli that are circular and composed of concentric circles (that is, a bull's-eye pattern) (8). Monkeys also show a strong attentive and subsequent fear reaction to a pair of staring eyes, which are, in effect, two bull's-eyes. Thus, there may be special releaser stimuli that innately hold attention as a function of biologically determined neuromotor patterns (see Chapter 4). We need additional principles to understand the infants' attentional preferences.

One popular hypothesis states that stimuli can be organized on a dimension of complexity, and infants will attend longest to stimuli that are moderately complex. The first question to be raised is, "What does complexity mean?" That is not an easy question to answer. The number of discrete elements in a stimulus is one basis for judging complexity. Thus a checkerboard with sixteen black-and-white squares is more complex than a checkerboard with only nine black-and-white squares. *Variety* is a second basis for complexity. The more different the elements are in an array, the more complex the stimulus. Thus, a circle that contains three stars, three squares, and three triangles is more complex than a circle with nine triangles, although each has nine elements. Experiments in which these definitions of complexity were used have yielded the finding that infants look longer at more complex stimuli as they grow older (10).

But there are alternative interpretations of this finding. It is possible that the primary determinants of sustained attention during the opening weeks of life are movement and contour (i.e., lots of black-and-white contrast), combined with an optimal area or optimal length of a contour edge. In general, experiments have indicated that infants devote the longest attention to stimuli that contained a great deal of black-and-white contrast but are of an optimal area (65, 72).

The complexity hypothesis is still controversial; there is no experiment that clearly demonstrates that infants will attend longer to more complex stimuli when the size of the stimulus and the amount of contour are eliminated as factors.

However, contrast and movement are not the only governors of the infant's attention. One-year-old babies do not always look longest at stimuli that have these characteristics. One study is a good bridge to the next factor to be considered—the effect of meaning and familiarity of the stimulus. Four-month-old children were shown the four faces in Fig. 5.9 (44). The infants looked longer at the stimuli most similar to a human face than they did to the ones with the most contour or the greatest number of elements. More important, two of the faces were of relatively equal complexity with respect to number of elements (Faces 2 and 4), but 2 was more like a face than 4 was. The infants looked longer at 2 than at 4—suggesting that the meaning of a stimulus might be more important than its complexity in holding the infant's attention (44).

The Role of Meaning and Discrepancy. Attentiveness to movement and contrast is unlearned and operates during the earliest weeks. As early as 4 months, however, the relation of the stimulus to an acquired schema the

Stimulus	Degree of Faceness	Amount of Detail	Percent Fixation Time
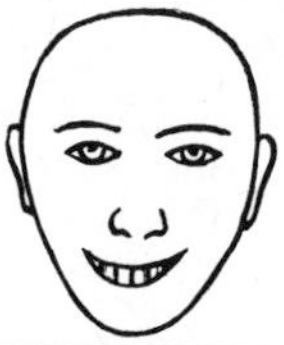	1	3	.33
	2	1	.28
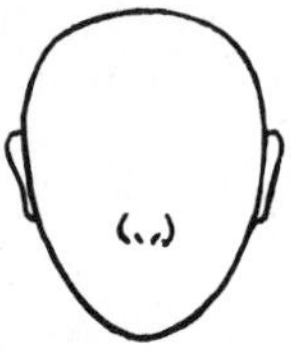	3	4	.19
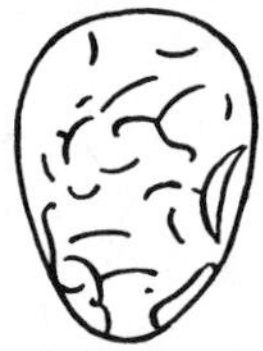	4	2	.20

Fig. 5.9. Differences in flixation time for four different facial stimuli. (From R. A. Haaf & R. Q. Bell. A facial dimension in visual discrimination by human infants. *Child Developm.*, copyright 1967 by The Society of Research in Child Development, Inc., *38*, 895. By permission.)

child has developed becomes a new determinant of attention. Schema is a hypothetical word which stands for some internal representation of an experience; it is a memory.[1] Your mental picture of your childhood home is a schema; your memory of your high school teacher's faces is a schema. A schema, however, is not always a mental picture; it can also be an idea.. We assume that during the first year of life the mental structures the child is acquiring are primarily images. After a sufficient amount of experience with a particular object or event, an infant builds up a schema for it. The schema is not a photographic duplicate of the phe-

[1] Jean Piaget, whose work we shall consider later, uses the word *schema* to stand for the infant's perceptual-motor coordinations (searching for objects; banging objects; pulling a string). *Schemata* is the plural form of schema.

Fig. 5.10.   Shapes shown to one group of 4-month-old infants.

nomenon. Rather, it is probably more like a caricature that highlights the most distinctive elements of the event. The most distinctive elements in a human face are probably the oval outline and the two symmetrically placed eyes; it is possible that a 3-month-old infant's schema for the face emphasizes these elements.

A stimulus discrepancy refers to a relation between an event and a schema. A discrepant stimulus is one that is different from a schema, but is not totally dissimilar. It is related to the schema in some way. A picture of a table is not a discrepancy with respect to the schema of a face, but a picture of a face with no eyes is a discrepancy from the schema of a face. A discrepant stimulus is both similar to and different from the original. It preserves some elements of the original.

Moderate discrepancies from established schemata have the greatest power to attract the infant's attention. One hypothesis states that changes in orientation or pattern of the distinctive features of a schema will be optimal discrepancies, and, as a result, will elicit the most sustained attention.

Four-month-old infants were shown the meaningless black-and-white shapes seen in Fig. 5.10, and another group was shown the faces in Fig. 5.11.

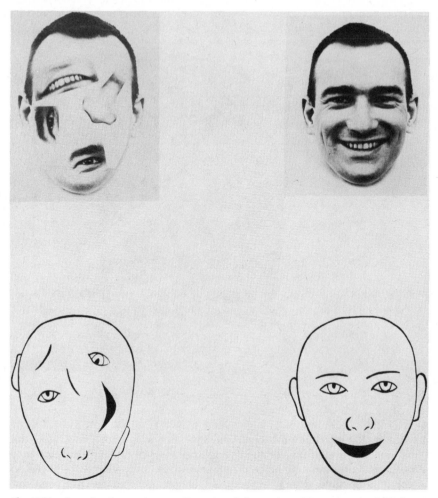

Fig. 5.11. Set of achromatic two-dimensional faces shown to 4-month-old infants.

Although the nonsense shapes have greater contrast than the faces, the faces attracted longer attention. The 4-month infants were reacting to the discrepancy from their established schema for a face. Each of the stimulus faces was clearly different from, yet also similar to, the child's schema for his parent's face. Thus we add to the power of movement and contour a third characteristic of stimuli that can hold attention in the visual mode: *stimuli that are optimally discrepant from established schemata are likely to attract and maintain attention (72).*

The Role of Association. There is still another determinant of attention in the young child that exerts its influence during the second year. This factor is the density or richness of learned associations for a particular type of stimulus. Infants from 4 to 27 months of age were shown the sets of faces dis-

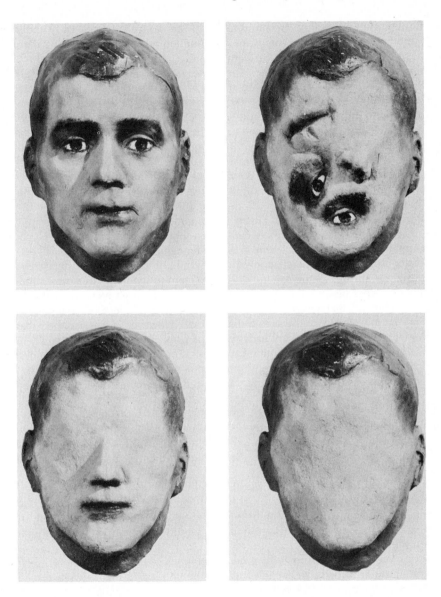

Fig. 5.12.   Clay masks shown to infants 4 to 27 months of age.

played in Fig. 5.12. Duration of looking decreased in infants from 4 through 13 months, but then increased again during the second year of age. The looking time decreased from 4 to 13 months because the faces were less discrepant to the older infants. But why do the looking times increase after one year?

The 2-year-old-child has acquired some language and a fairly sophisticated set of symbolic associations to faces. The faces elicit a nest of symbolic hypotheses and the child maintains his attention while he is activating these hypotheses or "thinking about them." It is as if the child implicitly asks of the scrambled face, "What happened? Who hit him? Where is his nose?" Some of the child's comments to the faces are instructive. One child said, "Who threw the pie at him?" Another remarked, "His nose is broken, mommy." The power of contrast, movement, discrepancy, and richness of associations are probably additive and when the child is 2 years of age the stimulus that has contour-contrast, movement, discrepancy, and elicits associations should hold his attention for the longest period of time. The television commercial or a cartoon contains all four characteristics; perhaps that is why nursery school children study the television screen for so long a time.

Perception of Depth and Three Dimensions

A problem that has always baffled psychologists and philosophers concerns the contribution of learning to the fundamental aspects of visual perception, such as the perception of shape and the perception of depth and perspective. Does the human infant have to learn to see things in three dimensions, or does he have this capacity from birth? Until recently, most psychologists assumed that the infant had to learn to perceive in three dimensions and that his visual world was two-dimensional. However, it was assumed that he learned this capacity very early, perhaps prior to 6 months of age. There is some evidence for the learning hypothesis. For example, prior to 10 weeks, infants attend equally long to a two- or three-dimensional black circle; but after 10 weeks at age he will look longer at a three-dimensional sphere than at a two-dimensional circle of the same area, indicating that the infant is reacting to the third dimension. Up to 10 weeks of age most infants will react similarly to two- and three-dimensional faces (a color photograph of the face, versus actual face of a person), but at 3 months he will smile and vocalize more to the actual face than to the two-dimensional representation (81).

When a solid three-dimensional model of a human head was compared with a similar flat, two-dimensional form, there was a sudden increase in the infant's looking at the former between 2 and 3 months of age. Moreover, this difference occurred whether the infant was looking with both eyes or with only one eye (30).

One of the most provocative demonstrations of depth perception during the first year involves an apparatus called the visual cliff. Infants were placed on a center runway that had a sheet of strong glass extending outward on either side. On one side a textured pattern was placed far below the glass, thus giving the illusion of depth (i.e., an adult would perceive depth in this situation). These investigators called this situation the "visual cliff," for the difference between the two sides appeared as a cliff (see Fig. 5.13).

Both 6-month-old infants and terrestrial animals avoided the side which appeared to have the "drop-off" or cliff. Even if the infant's mother stood at the deep side of the apparatus and entreated her child to cross over

Fig. **5.13.** The visual "cliff." (From E. J. Gibson & R. R. Walk. *Scientific Amer.*, April, 1961, *202*, 65. Photographer: William Vandivert. By permission.)

to her, most infants would not approach, even though the heavy glass (which they were able to touch) would have made the crossing safe (*41*).

If a gray pattern was placed on the deep side, making the perception of depth more difficult, many more infants crossed over the deep side to their mothers. Moreover, when the checkerboard pattern on the deep side was brought close to the surface of the glass, thereby reducing the apparent depth, more infants crossed to their mothers (*99*).

It cannot be concluded that the infant's perception of depth and avoidance of the deep side are unlearned, as these infants were 6 months old when they were tested. They had some opportunity to learn that objects appear at different distances from their eyes. Experience with objects at a distance may influence the learning of depth perception, for infants who are late crawlers and, therefore, have less experience with objects in their environment, are more likely to cross the deep side than infants who are early crawlers (99). Despite the suggested role of experience, there is a strong possibility that the capacity for depth perception is present at birth. Work with animals indicates that some species, such as the chicken and goat, are capable of depth perception during the first day of life and will not cross the deep side when tested immediately following birth.

Because the infant does not seem to be very adept at accommodating to near and far targets before he is 3 to 4 months old, and seems to have a fixed focus at 8 inches, he may not experience perspective very often. The behavior of animals in the visual cliff suggests that the infant may be capable of experiencing depth at birth, but has to develop oculomotor coordination to make effective use of his capabilities.

In sum, the infant is a visually sophisticated organism. He has excellent acuity, gives evidence of depth perception, and learns schemata for human faces as early as 12 weeks of age. By 1 year his visual perceptions may be similar to the adult's—although in most respects lacking the richness of symbolic associations that are characteristic of adults.

Hearing

Unfortunately there has been less research on hearing and auditory perception than on vision, and much less is known about this sensory modality (especially in the period between 2 weeks and 1 year). Most of the research work has been with newborn infants. The newborn is capable of hearing at birth and is sensitive to location of sound as well as to frequency. In order to study the infant's capacity to make a discrimination, a sound of a given frequency, loudness, and duration is presented for a fixed number of trials (say, twenty). By the last trial the infant has become minimally responsive to the tone. (That is, he does not show motor movements, babblings, or heart-rate changes that characterize orientation to the source.) Then the experimenter presents a new tone which differs from the original in one respect—either loudness, frequency, duration, or location—leaving the other three qualities unchanged. If the infant shows a greater response (a motor action, a heart-rate change, a vocalization, a smile, or a change in breathing) on the twenty-first trial, it could be inferred that the infant discriminated the difference between the last two tones. The experiments that use this general strategy have shown that newborns can detect the difference between tones of 200 and 1000 cycles per second, this would approximate the difference between a fog horn and a clarinet (68). In one study a baby reacted differently to tones to 200 and 250 cycles per second (cps), which is approximately equivalent to one step in a musical scale (11).

More provocative is the fact that the newborn appears to be constructed by nature to react differently to sounds of differing frequency or pitch. Low-frequency sounds (200 to 600 cps) tend to cause an increase in motor behavior if the child is normally alert and not hyperactive. These low-frequency sounds also inhibit the distress of the child if he is crying. High-frequency sounds (4000 cps, such as a whistle) lead to freezing behavior and a dramatic alerting reaction that makes one think the infant is asking, "What is it?" (25). These different reactions to sounds of varied frequencies resemble the special reaction 8-week-old infants showed to a bull's-eye, and indicate that (in man, just as in lower animals) nature may have built in special behavioral reactions that are more or less specific to particular kinds of stimuli.

A second aspect of sound that affects the newborn is duration. Sounds of short duration (less than a second) have a minimal effect. Sounds of 5 to 15 seconds have maximal effect on the infant's level of activity (96). If the sound lasts too long (over several minutes), the infant again becomes less responsive (83, 237).

A third quality of sound is its rhythmicity. Newborns become quieter in response to rhythmic sounds than to dysrhythmic sounds. Moreover if the sound of a rhythmic heart beat is compared with a rhythmic click, the rhythmic heart beat quiets the baby more effectively than the rhythmic click. Two interpretations of this difference in effect are possible. The heart beat is of a lower frequency than the click, and low-frequency sounds seem to inhibit distress reactions. On the other hand, at a more speculative level, one might argue that because the infant was exposed to the sound of a heart beat prior to birth—namely, his mother's heart beat—he may have developed a very primitive memory or schema and, therefore, the quieting displayed in response to the rhythmic heart beat is a learned reaction.

Although this latter explanation may seem too speculative, experiments with animals indicate that prenatal learning can occur. One group of chicken eggs was exposed, prior to hatching, to a particular characteristic set of beeping sounds of 200 cps. The second group was raised in quiet. Within 6 hours after hatching, each chick was put in the center of a circular table. On one point of the rim of the table a speaker emitted a sound of 200 cycles and the movement of the chick toward the speaker was measured. At the end of 45 seconds that speaker went off and a second speaker, diametrically opposite the first, emitted a different sound of 2000 cps. The chickens exposed to the tone of 200 cycles prior to hatching moved closer to that tone than to the 2000-cycle tone they never heard. Moreover, the chickens raised with sound followed a toy chick that was emitting a sound of 200 cycles for a longer time than they followed a moving toy chick emitting a novel sound (42).

Thus it is possible that the infant's greater quieting response to the rhythmic heart beat is a learned reaction. The problem with this interpretation is that other studies of newborns reveal no differences in crying or quieting as responses to a heart beat, a metronome's ticking, or a lullaby. Each of these sounds is intermittent and of low frequency, and all three lead to greater cessation of crying than no sound at all (9).

In summary, low-frequency rhythmic sounds tend to stop a baby's crying. Perhaps this is why leaning over a baby and rhythmically repeating, "hel-lo, hel-lo, hel-lo" in a low voice is often very effective in quieting an upset infant.

There may be some analogy between the data on seeing and hearing. Moving lights elicit more attention than nonmoving lights and this may be related to the fact that rhythmic, intermittent sounds quiet more than steady tones do. In both cases there is a break or discontinuity in the stimulus, which presents a *change* to the central nervous system. A moderately long contour elicits greater attention than a very short or a very long contour; a sound duration of 16 seconds leads to more reactivity or quieting than one of 1-second or 50-second duration. This comparability suggests some basic relations between the quality of a stimulus, its degree of contrast, rhythmicity, and duration, and the child's attentional behavior.

The Older Infant. All of the above-described generalizations are relevant to the newborn, through the first week of life. What about the 6- or 12-month-old infant? What is the effect of learning on his attention to auditory stimuli? Do we have any principle that is comparable with the effect of discrepancy in the visual mode? In one study, 8-month-old boys listened to four sets of sentences varying in both meaning and inflection. Some of the sentences were nonsense words read with low inflection or high inflection; the other two sets of sentences contained meaningful, familiar words—such as baby, smile, and daddy. They were read with either high or low inflection. Each infant heard the stimuli three times in a random order. The episode that contained familiar words and was read with high inflection caused more babbling when it stopped than any of the others did—suggesting that the infant was reacting to the meaningful words read with inflection by a strange male voice (64).

The acquired meaningfulness of speech sounds seems to have an effect as early as 8 months of age, before the child seems to understand speech and certainly before he can say any words.

Olfaction

Even less is known about olfactory perception than about hearing. The newborn is capable of responding to odors, turning his head away from unpleasant odors such as ammonia or acetic acid. The newborn can also make some discrimination among objects. A particular complex odor (the combination of two odors) was presented to infants for ten trials and any change in the child's breathing pattern was noted. With each succeeding trial the change in breathing became less noticeable as the child became accustomed to the olfactory stimulus. On the eleventh and twelfth trials, only one of the odors was presented—and thus it was discrepant from the complex odor used during the first ten trials. Most of the infants showed a marked change in breathing, indicating that they detected the difference in the odors (26).

The neonate seems to show little or no discrimination of weak or less distinctive odors, but the presence of odors may provoke more activity than clear air, and greater saturations may stimulate greater activity (24).

Gustation

Neonates do not react differentially to solutions of salt, sugar, citric acid, quinine, and distilled water (as a control) applied to their tongues, thus demonstrating that they have little taste sensitivity. Apparently this sensitivity develops rapidly, however, for within the first two weeks they begin to make pronounced positive (sucking) responses to sugar and negative (grimacing) responses to quinine and citric acid (84).

One experimenter observed that newborn infants would suck when given milk, glucose, acid milk, and sterile water, but would inhibit this response when given salt solutions. Moreover, he noted that the "moderately full baby is a better discriminator than the very hungry infant" (63).

Thermal Sensitivity

The neonate's activity level is elevated when the atmosphere is cold and reduced when it is warm. Experimental studies indicate that infants respond to temperature changes of 5 or 6 degrees in objects (cylinders which can be heated or chilled from a neutral point of 33° C) contacting their legs (20). Cold stimuli (average temperature, 11 or 12° C) applied to the legs elicited extension and flexion, while head movements, acceleration in breathing, and irregular pulse followed cold stimulation of the forehead (84).

Early thermal sensitivity is also reflected in the finding that most infants squirm and suck irregularly if their milk is warmer than 50° C or colder than 23° C (63). There are, of course, large individual differences in sensitivity to warmth and cold.

Static-Kinesthetic Sensitivity

Neonates are highly sensitive to changes in the spatial position of the body. If the baby falls from a sitting position, is held upside down, or jarred, he will make generalized postural adjustments. Body rotation or prone placement on a table may stimulate nystagmus (oscillation of the eyes) or head movements. Newborn infants make alternate "stepping" movements when they are held upright with their feet resting upon a flat surface. These important responses, which subsequently become involved in maintaining upright posture and walking, reveal that the infant reacts to stimulation from sense organs located in his muscles and semicircular canals of the ear (the organs involved in maintaining balance).

Pain

The phenomenon of pain sensitivity is somewhat different from that of other sense modalities. First, unlike vision, hearing, or olfaction, there do not appear to be any localized areas in the brain that receive and integrate pain-producing stimulation. Second, the experience that adults call "pain" is highly dependent upon learning. Elaboration of this point is reserved for a later section.

Although there is little systematic information on pain sensitivity in infants, existing evidence suggests that sensitivity to pain is present to some degree at birth, and becomes sharper during the first few days of post-natal life. For example, the number of pain stimuli (pin pricks) necessary to instigate withdrawal of the stimulated area (the original response to pain) decreases between birth and 8 days (90, 91).

There may be constitutional differences among infants in pain sensitivity (71), females being more sensitive than males. As we shall see later, pain plays an important role in the child's acquisition of fear and, individual variation in sensitivity to pain may partially account for differences in susceptibility to fear in older children.

RESPONSE CAPABILITIES

Sensory capacities allow the child to experience differences in quality of sight, sounds, tastes, smells, and touch, and (as we have seen) the human infant comes into the world with an intact set of sensory receptors for the basic modalities. The infant begins life with a very small set of responses called reflexes, which are not learned. Some of them were discussed in the earlier section on the newborn. Some of these reflexes, such as sucking on a nipple and crying in response to pain are adaptive and necessary to the baby's survival. Others are not necessary for life but reflect the state of the infant's nervous system. Examples of the latter include the Moro response; shuddering in response to bitter taste; head balancing instigated by changes in bodily position; the grasp reflex (closing hand tightly, usually stimulated by contact pressure on finger or palm); the Babinski reflex (extension of the big toe and fanning out of the other toes when the sole of the foot is stroked); and, in the male, penis erection and raising of the testes, elicited by stimulation of the inner thigh.

Coordination of many parts of the body is involved in the newborn infant's more generalized responses, including: (1) trunk movements (squirming, twisting, arching the back, and drawing in the stomach); (2) body jerks; (3) shivering or trembling; and (4) creeping movements. These responses are present during the first days of life. The responses that are not present at birth are divided into two different types—maturational and learned.

Maturational responses develop with no special tutoring in the formal sense. Given the general opportunity to use limbs and body, every child will creep, stand, walk, sit up, and grab objects. The second type of response must be learned in a specific sense, or it will not appear. These responses include the culturally specific actions that children learn, such as opening a refrigerator, turning on a faucet, sitting on a potty, writing, coloring, singing, skating, playing football, and sailing. Let us consider the maturational responses first, for they tell a dramatic story during the first year.

The Maturation of Motor Development

The child's sitting, crawling, and standing exemplify maturational development. They occur during the first 2 years of life as a consequence of the opportunity to use the body plus the maturation of certain neural tissues, expansion and increased complexity of the central nervous system, and growth of bones and muscles. In many instances, these seemingly unlearned behavior patterns improve and become better coordinated, more precise, and more accurate after practice.

In this chapter, the emphasis is only on developments in locomotion, reaching, and grasping. No attempt is made to review the whole vast array of responses of the first year; complete surveys may be found in the works of Gesell and Amatruda (38) and McGraw (75).

Locomotion

Sitting. The response repertoire of the neonate does not include any reflex sitting posture, but the ability to sit develops early (4, 21, 38, 92). On the average, babies are able to sit for a minute, with support, at the age of 3 or 4 months, and by 7 or 8 months, they can do it without support. Once sitting is achieved, there is rapid improvement, so that by 9 months most babies can sit independently for 10 minutes or longer (38).

Crawling and Creeping. Ames (2) analyzed motion pictures of crawling and creeping in 20 infants and concluded that there are 14 stages in the development of these activities (see Fig. 5.14). There are great individual differences in the ages at which infants reach the various stages, but practically all infants go through the same sequence.

The first stage, thrusting one knee forward beside the body, appeared in half the infants at 28 weeks or younger. The median age for crawling (i.e., moving with the abdomen in contact with the floor) was 34 weeks. At this age, the muscles of the trunk, arms, and legs are not sufficiently strong or coordinated to maintain the body weight. The infants began to creep on hands and knees, which requires new coordination and equilibrium, at a median age of 40 weeks, while creeping on hands and feet, the final stage of prone progression, was attained by a median age of 49 weeks. Infants may skip one or two stages of development, but all of them progress through most of the steps (2).

Walking. The ability to walk independently also matures gradually, after a series of preliminary achievements. As in other aspects of development, there is a wide range of ages at which the various stages are attained. The median ages for standing while holding on to furniture, walking when led, pulling up to a stand, standing alone, and walking alone were 42, 45, 47,

Fig. 5.14. The 14 stages of prone progression. (Described by L. B. Ames in The sequential patterning of prone progression in the human infant. *Genet. Psychol. Monogr.*, 1937, Vol. 19. By permission of The Journal Press.)

62, and 64 weeks, respectively, according to Shirley's data on 25 children (*92*; see Fig. 5.15). The transition from one developmental step to the next is not always smooth and "never does the infant pass completely and irretrievably from one stage into another. There is always a merging of patterns and parts of patterns both in the degree of perfection of the action and in the frequency of occurrence. There are often regressions to the less mature response" (*74, 98*).

There is considerable evidence (*21, 74, 75, 91*) that growth changes and maturation of the neural and muscular systems—rather than environmental conditions, experiences, or practice—determine when the child will sit, stand, and walk. For example, Dennis (*21*) kept a pair of female twins on their backs for the first 9 months of their lives, thus preventing any practice in sitting or standing. Despite these restrictions, they were only slightly retarded in these activities, the most marked retardation being in sitting. When they were given their first opportunities to sit alone at the age of 37 weeks, the restricted twins were not able to do so. Several weeks later, however, they were able to sit alone. Although most children by the time they are 40 weeks old can support their body weight while standing with help, the twins were not able to do this at 52 weeks, when they were given their first opportunity to do so. Within 3 days, however, both infants could stand

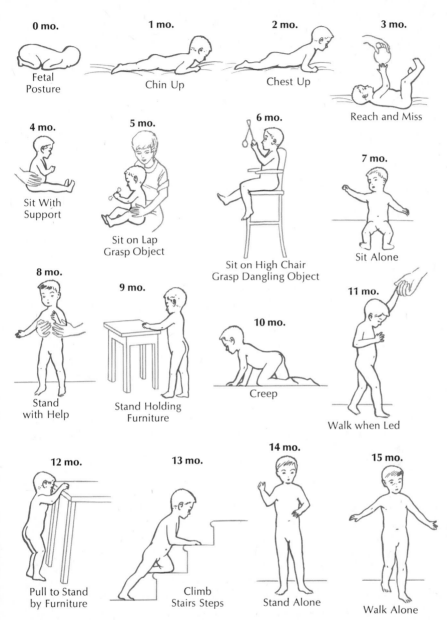

Fig. 5.15. The development of posture and locomotion in infants. (From *The First Two Years* by Mary M. Shirley. Institute of Child Welfare Monograph No. 7. Minneapolis: Univer. of Minnesota Press. © Copyright 1933, renewed 1961 by the University of Minnesota. By permission.)

with help for at least 2 minutes. One twin suffered no retardation in crawling, walking when led, or standing or walking independently.

Generally speaking, although these motor behaviors develop without any special practice or teaching by adults, extreme degrees of environmental restriction on opportunity for motor development may retard the onset of walking (22). Dennis compared the motor development of children (1 to 3 years of age) raised in three different Iranian institutions, only one of which provided its children with opportunities to sit and play in the prone position. The children in this relatively more enriched environment were less retarded in onset of walking than those in the institutions where motor experience was more restricted. Dennis concluded:

> The results of the present study challenge the widely held view that motor development consists of the emergence of a behavioral squence based primarily upon maturation. . . . These facts seem to indicate clearly that experience affects not only the ages at which motor items appear but also their very form (22, 57).

Thus, the role of experience is vital. When a child's opportunity to use his body and to wander freely in a secure space is severely limited (as it may be in an institution), he will walk later than a comparable child who has such freedom.

There are slight differences in onset of walking that may be due to differences in the rate of the child's physical development. African children in Uganda, for example, walk earlier than European children and this precocity in walking is associated with advances in other aspects of motor and physical development during the first year (36). An extensive study of more than 1000 children from five European cities (Brussels, London, Paris, Stockholm, and Zurich) revealed that the Brussels and Stockholm children walked about *1 month* earlier than infants from Paris, London, and Zurich—12½ versus 13½ months (50). Moreover, the Brussels and Stockholm children were taller than the others and more advanced in general motor development at 1 year (50).

How are these differences to be explained? On the one hand, we can argue that children in Uganda, Brussels, and Stockholm are given more freedom and their earlier walking reflects greater opportunity to perfect this skill. On the other hand, as muscle mass in the leg and calf areas and general central nervous system maturation are important in walking, it is possible that genetic or nutritional differences are responsible for such differences among the populations of children. It is not possible at present to decide which of these explanations is better. However, even if it turns out that the Stockholm child develops motor coordination *faster* than the Parisian child because of genetic differences, this is not equivalent to saying the Stockholm child is more intelligent. There is no strong relation between age of walking or rate of physical development during the first 2 years and intelligence during the preschool or early school years.

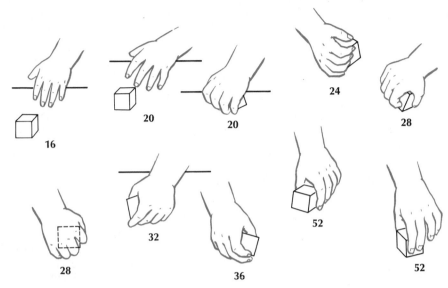

Fig. 5.16. The development of prehension. (From H. M. Halverson. An experimental study of prehension in infants by means of systematic cinema records. *Genet. Psychol. Monogr.*, 1931, Vol. 10. By permission of The Journal Press.)

Manipulation

Like locomotion, manipulative ability evolves through a series of stages. Analysis of motion pictures of infants reaching for and grasping cubes showed that those under 20 weeks of age do not actually reach for objects, although they may follow them with their eyes. Some infants 20 weeks old stretch their arms in the general direction of the object, making slow, awkward, and angular reaching movements that primarily involve shoulder and elbow action. With increased age, the approach becomes more direct, and the wrist and hand participate. By 60 weeks of age, the infant reaches for attractive objects without superfluous movements (*46, 47*).

There are ten stages in the development of prehension, according to Halverson (*46*). The neonate's grasp reflex disappears by the time he is 4 months old. Sixteen-week-old infants make no real contact with an object, but by 20 weeks they can touch and squeeze things in a primitive way without taking hold firmly. Grasping becomes more successful, and unnecessary movements decrease as the child matures. Thus by 28 weeks of age, he uses his palm smoothly in closing in on a cube, but his thumb and fingers are not involved. The forefinger begins to play a part in grasping at about 36 weeks. In the final stages of the development of prehension, thumb and forefinger function together, and other fingers are also used precisely in securing a cube. By the time the child is 60 weeks of age, his grasp is much like an adult's (see Fig. 5.16).

Sensorimotor Coordination and Reaching. One of the interesting maturational developments is a response that typically reaches maturity at about 5 months and has been called *visually directed reaching.* If you place an attractive object in the field of vision of a 1-month-old baby, he will stare at it, but will make no attempt to grab it. By 2½ months of age, he will begin to swipe at it, but will be far off target. By 4 months, the infant will raise his hand in the vicinity of the object, alternate his glance between the hand and object, gradually removing the gap between his hand and the object and then perhaps touching it. By 5 or 5½ months the infant will reach for the object and contact it efficiently. His aim is now perfect.

Although this response goes through a standard set of maturational steps, as walking or standing does, it is subject to dramatic alteration through environmental experiences of enrichment. Infants raised in an unstimulating institution where they were deprived of objects to attend to or reach are retarded in their attainment of visual motor reaching. The progress of infants who are provided with enriched opportunity for reaching and watching attractive objects (e.g., through having attractive mobiles being placed above their heads and being allowed to handle them; see Fig. 5.17) is accelerated; they will show visual motor reaching as early as 4 to 4½ months (101).

If the infant is provided with an opportunity to practice and, therefore, to perfect reaching responses, we see earlier manifestation of that behavior —even though the process is basically maturational. Enriching the stimulus environment does not always lead to acceleration of all the child's mental or motor development. The child must be maturationally ready to reach if the enrichment is to help. The child of 3 to 4 months ordinarily studies and swipes at attractive objects, and providing him with some if he has none will direct his attention to them and stimulate him to reach. However, providing stimulation to accelerate responses that the child is not prepared to display may accomplish nothing and in some cases may lead to a retardation. For example, the institutionalized infants placed in the enriched environment described above showed less attentiveness to the colorful environment during the first 5 weeks. These children were more irritable and fussy than those who did not have the enriched stimulation—as if the enriching stimuli were distressing the child. The presence of a stimulus to which the infant cannot make a response seems to be one cause of distress to the infant. It is possible that the 3-week-old baby is too immature to make any response to the richly colored mobile and becomes more upset than if nothing were present.

Consider a 1-year-old who is not ready to write with a crayon. Giving him crayons or pencils would not necessarily facilitate earlier development of this skill. Indeed, if the child grows tired of the crayons or pencils he may ignore them 2 years later when he has become maturationally ready to use them. The child can be helped to master skills earlier than he ordinarily would through enrichment, but the timing of the enrichment is important. It is almost as bad to present enriching experiences before the child is ready to use them effectively as it is to deprive the child of these stimulations entirely.

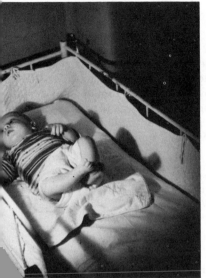
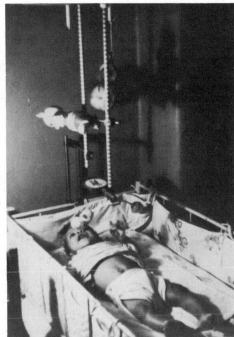
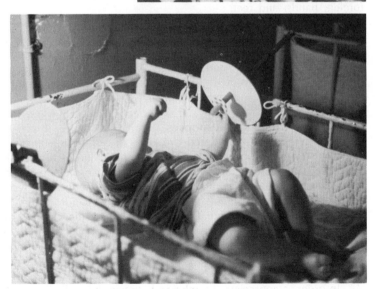

Fig. 5.17.   A situation in which visual motor coordination is tested. (From B. L. White & R. Held. Plasticity of sensory motor development. In J. F. Rosenblith & W. Allinsmith (Eds.), *Readings in child development and educational psychology*. Boston: Allyn and Bacon, copyright © 1966 [2nd ed.]. By permission.)

DEVELOPMENTAL TRENDS

First-year sensory and motor developments reflect several general directional trends. The *cephalocaudal* (or head-to-foot) trend is illustrated in the relatively early accomplishment of head movements, visual fixation, and eye-hand coordination, and the relatively late appearance of standing and walking. The limbs and muscles of the upper part of the body become functionally effective before the lower limbs. In walking, appropriate coordination of the arms precedes that of the legs.

> The principle is well illustrated in the behavior characteristics of the twenty week old infant. His trunk is still so flaccid that he must be propped or strapped in a chair to maintain a sitting posture. When he is so secured, however, his eyes, head, and shoulders exhibit heightened activity and intensified tonus. The pelvic zone and the lower extremities at 20 weeks are, in comparison, very immature (37, 341).

Progress in the development of motor responses during the first year also follows a roughly *proximodistal* direction, i.e., from the central to the peripheral segments of the body. Thus, in reaching, the shoulders and elbows are used before the wrist and fingers. In both prone and erect locomotion, the upper arm and upper leg are brought under control before the forearm, foreleg, hands, and feet.

The trend *from mass to specific* activities or from large to smaller muscles is also evident in the motor advances of the first year. The gross awkward movements of early grasping are replaced by more precise, refined movements of the thumb and forefinger. Locomotion is initially accompanied by excess bodily movements, but these decrease gradually until only the appropriate muscles and limbs are involved.

Acquired Instrumental Responses

We have thus far considered two kinds of responses—reflexes which are automatically elicited by stimuli without learning, and maturational responses which can be retarded or facilitated by experience, but do not have to be learned in the visual sense. Both can be regarded as universal responses that are released by certain stimuli. Our third category includes complex responses that are learned or acquired. They are learned by the child in order to (1) provide him with sensory feedback (the infant will bang a block or a sphere in order to experience some sensations); or (2) gratify a need or motive (the child will learn to cry when he is alone or learn to turn a doorknob to get out of a room, or learn to protest vocally when he is frustrated).

In order to appreciate the relation between the child's learned responses and the needs and motives that they serve, we must review the needs and motives that are present in the first year. Recall that a need is a change in biological or physiological state (i.e., a disruption in equilibrium or homeostasis, according to one view). This changed bodily state often leads immediately to unpleasant sensations—but it need not, as in a Vitamin A deficiency. Most of the time a need leads to some generalized increase or decrease in behavior or reactivity, but, again, it need not, as in iron deficiency.

BASIC NEEDS

The infant is born with a number of basic physiological drives or needs which must be satisfied if he is to survive. Most of these needs are usually taken care of in a self-regulatory manner, without any active participation by the infant. However, two drives, hunger and thirst, are not gratified automatically. For this reason, as we shall see later, they are crucially involved in the infant's earliest learning.

Need for Oxygen

Within the first few days of postnatal life, respiration is stabilized on an adultlike level (83). Reflex mechanisms (regulated by the saturation of oxygen and carbon dioxide in the blood) operate to assure the neonate an oxygen supply adequate for his needs. Consequently, the drive for oxygen rarely becomes high or intense.

Temperature Regulation

Before birth, the child's temperature is likely to remain fairly stable because he is protected by the surrounding amniotic fluid. Once he is outside the uterus, however, his temperature is much more likely to vary in response to changes in the environment. The newborn infant may be exposed to drafts and to changes in the weather. He may kick off his blankets and become cold; or, more likely, according to pediatricians, he may be bundled up too snugly by his anxious parents and become too hot. He is much more subject to fever-producing infections than he was before birth.

Within limits, the child's need to maintain a relatively constant temperature is fulfilled by automatic physiological mechanisms. When these limits are exceeded, however, as in the above examples, the temperature regulation drive becomes intensified, and the child requires external assistance in bringing his temperature back to normal. In short, he needs parents to open or shut windows, add or remove blankets, and, if indicated, to administer proper drugs.

Need for Sleep

At present, there is no completely satisfactory physiological theory to account for the need for rest. Sleep seems to be another device by which the body regulates itself, maintains equilibrium in its chemical constitution and physiological processes, and thus preserves the organism's energy for later activity.

The proportion of time spent in sleep decreases as the child grows

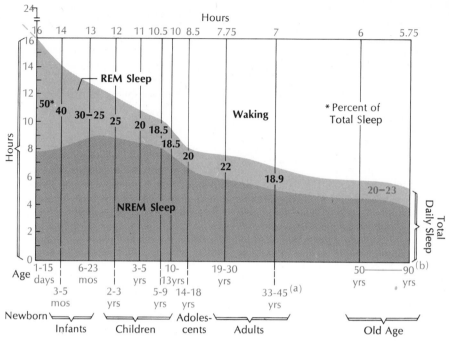

Fig. 5.18. Changes (with age) in amounts of total sleep, REM sleep, and non-REM sleep. (From H. P. Roffwarg, J. N. Muzio & W. C. Dement. Ontogenic development of the human sleep-dream cycle. *Science*, 1966, 152, 608. Revised since publication in *Science* by H. P. Roffwarg. By permission of the author.)

older. Neonates on the average spend 80 percent of their time asleep and 20 percent awake, while 1-year-olds on the average are awake as much of the time as they are asleep (*14*).

The rhythms and depth of sleep also change rapidly during the first year. For the first 3 or 4 weeks, the average infant takes seven or eight short naps a day, but the number is reduced to between two and four longer periods of sleep by 6 weeks of age. By 28 weeks, most children will sleep through the night, and from then until they are about a year old, will require only two or three daytime naps (*39*). Night sleep also becomes less broken as the child matures—to the considerable relief of weary mothers.

There are great individual differences in sleep needs, and any particular child's requirements may vary from time to time. Many factors influence the quality and quantity of sleep. During the earliest months, intestinal upsets, and later on, wetness, bodily discomfort, noise, or emotional factors (violence, excitement, etc.) may interfere with sound rest. The infant's need for sleep or rest seldom becomes intense, as he will ordinarily sleep as much as is necessary and wake when he is rested. Later on, he will have to learn the culturally approved patterns of sleep and wakefulness, but this is not an important problem during the first year.

There are at least two different kinds of sleep. In one, the person displays short rapid movements of his eyes. In the second these eye movements are absent. In adults, dreams are most likely to occur during the rapid eye movement phase (called REM sleep), but it is not likely that the infant is dreaming when he displays these eye movements. Figure 5.18 shows the change in proportion of REM and non-REM sleep during the day from the first days of life through old age. REM sleep is most frequent during the first 5 months (40 percent of sleep time), and decreases with age (88).

Need for Elimination

When the neonate's bowel is full, the anal sphincters open reflexively and the contents are expelled. In the same way, when the bladder is swollen, the urethral sphincter is automatically released. These processes are entirely involuntary in early infancy; the neuromuscular equipment necessary for voluntary control has not yet matured.

There are major alterations in patterns of elimination during the first year. While there are wide individual differences, bowel movements are generally frequent and sporadic during the first few weeks, but by the time the infant is 4 weeks old, the number generally falls to three or four evacuations daily, ordinarily associated with waking. By 8 weeks of age, the average infant usually has only two bowel movements daily, one upon waking and one close to or during a feeding. By 16 weeks, a definite interval between feeding and evacuation has usually been established (39).

During the first few weeks of postnatal existence, the average infant urinates frequently, but gradually the number of micturitions decreases and their volume increases. By 28 weeks of age, intervals of dryness may be as long as one or two hours. At the end of the first year, the baby may still be dry after a long nap and will likely begin to be intolerant of wet diapers.

Learning to withhold elimination until the proper—that is, socially approved—place and time requires the inhibition or suppression of responses which initially occur automatically. In toilet training, voluntary control must be substituted for reflex actions. This presents a complex and difficult learning problem which requires a great deal of skill and patience in handling, as we shall see later.

Hunger and Thirst

These two drives are confounded, i.e., are not easily differentiated, in young infants and hence will be discussed together. From a psychological and social point of view, they are the most important of the neonate's basic drives, for their satisfaction depends on someone else's help rather than on automatic, reflex activities. If the infant's hunger and thirst are not reduced soon, tensions mount, become severe, and provoke a great deal of bodily activity. For this reason, these drives play an important role in the infant's earliest learning. Here we shall review briefly the changes in physiological hunger needs and feeding patterns during the first year. Discussion of the broader social learning implications of the feeding situation, the infant's first interpersonal relationship, is reserved for Chapter 6.

Data on American newborn infants on self-demand schedules (feeding whenever the baby is hungry) indicate that, on the average, neonates take seven or eight feedings per day. By 4 weeks of age, the number has been reduced to five or six. At this time, the average infant's food intake is between 18 and 25 ounces, but this rises to about 35 ounces when he is 6 to 8 weeks old. Within the next few weeks, the number of feedings is further reduced, although total food intake does not change significantly (39).

In our culture, solid foods are often introduced into the infant's menu when he is about 8 weeks of age, and by 20 weeks, cereals and vegetables may form a regular part of his diet. By the time the American child is 1 year old, the three-meal regime has probably become stabilized and he may manifest marked food preferences. The time and manner of weaning the infant to solid foods varies from culture to culture.

Some of the infant's needs lead regularly to the same set of behaviors. When hungry the infant begins to thrash and cry until gratified. When tired, he is likely to fret; when frustrated, he may protest and thrash. Fretting, crying, protesting, and thrashing are prepotent responses that are elicited by many different needs during the first year. As we shall see in the next chapter, the special development of the cry, protest, or fret depends on how the social environment responds to these actions.

VOCALIZATION AND SUBSEQUENT SPEECH DEVELOPMENT

Babbling and vocal sounds are universal responses during infancy. In normal children there does not seem to be a strong relation between frequency of early babbling during the first 3 to 4 months and the amount of vocalizing at 1 or 2 years of age. Babbling in an infant under 6 months usually occurs when the child is excited by something he sees or hears; it is often an accompaniment of motor activity. During the second half of the first year, the child will often quiet while he is listening to a sound. When the sound stops he will begin to babble. This babbling is likely to reflect an excitatory reaction created by processing the sounds he heard.

The utterance of meaningful words is a much different phenomenon. Speech is used to obtain goals, not just to reflect general excitement. Speech requires exposure to people who speak a language, babbling does not. The early vocalization of the infant does pass through certain stages, however. Let us review them briefly.

The infant makes two basic sounds. The first includes all sounds related to crying and is present at birth. A second category of sounds includes those that eventually become part of meaningful speech. According to one author (67) the second type does not emerge until the sixth or eighth week of life and can best be described as a *cooing* sound. Recall that other changes that also occur during the sixth to eighth week include increased visual attention, decreased crying, and signs of depth perception. This cooing sound is different from a cry because, in cooing, the tongue is involved in modu-

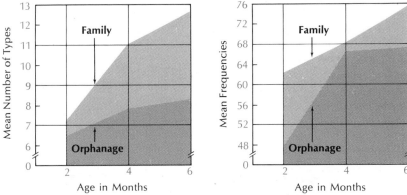

Fig. 5.19. Mean frequencies of vocalizing and mean numbers of types of sound in the vocalizing of infants in home and institutions. (From A. J. Brodbeck & O. C. Irwin. The speech behavior of infants without families. *Child Developm.*, copyright 1946 by The Society for Research in Child Development, Inc., *17*, 149. By permission.)

lating the sound. This usually does not happen when the baby cries. The babbling that occurs during the first 6 weeks is an innate response and is relatively unchanged by experience during this first 2 months. The environment seems to affect the frequency and variety of these baby sounds after the first 8 to 10 weeks. Children raised in homes in which both mother and child engage in reciprocal vocal play with each other vocalize more and with greater variety than infants from homes where such exchange is minimal.

Environment and Language

Babies under 6 months of age living in unstimulating orphanage environments are often retarded both in frequency of vocalizations and number and types of sounds (see Fig. 5.19). Further, during the second half of the first year, infants raised in middle-class homes show more frequent and varied sounds than children of working-class families. This finding suggests that middle-class mothers may do more vocalizing to their infants which, in turn, may stimulate the child's vocal expression (see Fig. 5.20). It has also been found that rewarding the 3-month-old child's utterances by smiling and touching his abdomen after each sound leads to an increase in the amount of infant vocalization (*86*). The infant's babbling behavior apparently can be modified through experience, and can be increased or decreased, depending on the amounts of social stimulation the child's vocalizations receive. As the vocalizations of infants in institutions are less apt to attract the attention of an adult, and are, therefore, not often rewarded, the frequency of such responses among these children is not likely to increase at a normal rate.

Once the elementary speech sounds are acquired, progress in speech consists of using these sounds in a variety of ways and in different combina-

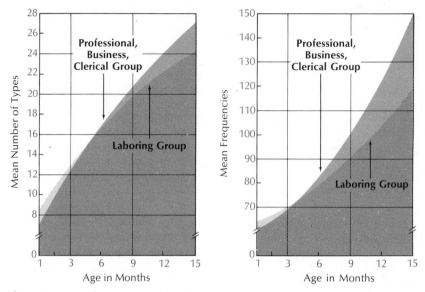

Fig. 5.20. Mean frequencies of vocalizing and mean numbers of types of sounds in the vocalizing of infants of laboring and professional parents and of infants in homes and institutions. (From O. C. Irwin. Infant speech. *J. Speech & Hearing Disorders,* 1943, Vol. 13. By permission.)

tions. Individual differences in the rates of speech development are apparent from earliest infancy.

One of the intriguing questions that has long baffled psychologists is why infants continue to babble to themselves, even though no one responds to their vocalizations. It is believed that the child's perception of his own voice production acts as a stimulant to further vocalization during the latter half of the first year. The primitive sounds of the 1- or 2-month-old baby, however, appear to be independent of either environmental factors or the child's perception of these noises.

The most convincing demonstration of this fact comes from observations of deaf infants born to deaf mute parents. The vocalizations of these infants during the first 8 weeks—which are heard by neither parent nor child—do not differ from those of normal children with parents who can hear the baby's sounds. After 2 months of age, the environment does play a role in shaping the variety and frequency of the infant's sounds. However,

> [most] present day psychologists seem to agree . . . that new sounds are not learned by imitation of the speech of others, but rather that they emerge in the child's spontaneous vocal play as a result of maturation, and that the child imitates only those sounds which have already occurred in its spontaneous babblings. This view holds that imitation of the speech of others serves only to call attention to new combinations of sounds already used (73, 517).

Relation of Babbling to Later Mental Development

Although frequency and variety of babbling during the opening months are not good predictors of the child's later talkativeness or the size of his vocabulary, they are the ingredients from which basic speech sounds will be formed. There appears to be an interesting sex difference in the predictive power of early babbling between 4 and 12 months of age. Infant girls who babble in response to human faces tend to be more attentive and obtain slightly higher intelligence scores at 1, 2, and 3 years of age than girls who babble very little to human faces. This relation does not hold for boys, despite the fact that the 4-month-old boys babble as much as girls. Boys and girls 4 months of age were shown the faces illustrated in the Fig. 5.11. Some children never babbled to the faces; others babbled several seconds to each face. When these infants were seen at 8 months of age, the girls who babbled a lot at 4 months showed more attention to the sound source of a tape-recorded voice than the girls who babbled little. These same infants were seen again at 13 months of age. The girls who had babbled earlier, vocalized and quieted more readily to representations of human forms than the girls who had not babbled at all. At 27 months, the former group played longer and showed more sustained play with toys than the nonbabbling girls. This relation did not obtain for boys.

Two additional, independent longitudinal studies have reported similar and equally interesting results. Infant girls who vocalized frequently in a testing situation between 6 and 12 months of age had higher IQ scores as adults than the infant girls who did not vocalize. However, this relation between early vocalization and IQ did not occur for boys (15).

A similar study of infants in London yielded comparable results. Girls who vocalized a lot at 6 months had better vocabularies at 2 and 3 years of age than the girls who did not vocalize. However, the boys who vocalized a lot had no better vocabulary than those who did not babble at all (77).

How can we interpret this interesting sex difference found in *three separate longitudinal studies?* There are several possibilities. One explanation assumes that the innate neuromotor organization of boys and girls is basically different. If the central nervous system of girls were structured so that girls were more likely than boys to vocalize when they are attentive to and excited by an interesting event, then the vocalizations of the infant girl would be a good measure of the girl's tendency to invest attention in events around her, and perhaps predictive of her future intelligence. If the innate neuromotor organization of boys did not lead them to vocalize when they were attentive to events, then vocalization in the boy should not be related to future intellectual ability.

A second possible explanation also has a biological flavor and assumes that there is greater stability of cognitive development among girls than among boys. In this case, it is assumed that frequent vocalization reflects advanced mental development for both boys and girls. But because a girl's rate of mental development seems to be more stable than that of the boy, the infant vocalization score is a better predictor of future IQ among the girls than boys. It is perhaps not a coincidence that physical growth dimensions—such as height, weight, and rate of bone growth—are more stable from year to year among girls than among boys (1). It is possible that the greater predictive power of infant vocalization for girls is another reflection of a more general tendency toward greater stability in girls' development.

A final potential explanation assumes that mothers treat sons and daughters differently, and argues that mothers who are motivated to encourage their daughter's mental development spend a lot of time vocalizing to them—more time than they would with a son, and more than mothers who are not concerned with their daughter's rate of development. The mother's face-to-face vocalization should lead to increased levels of babbling in the girl. This mother would also be expected to continue to stimulate her daughter and would probably teach her words early and encourage the development of other intellectual skills. The predictive link between early babbling and later cognitive abilities would then be a function of the continuity of the mother's acceleration of her daughter. The absence of a predictive link between infant vocalization and cognitive development in the boys would require the assumption that accelerating mothers do not preferentially engage in as much vocalization with their sons. Preliminary data support this assumption. Observations of the mother-infant interaction in the home reveal that well-educated mothers engage in more distinctive face-to-face vocalization with their daughters than less-well-educated mothers do, whereas there is no comparable difference among the mothers of sons. Moreover, middle-class mothers are more likely to imitate the vocalization of their 3-month-old daughters than those of their sons (78).

It is not possible at the moment to state which of these explanations is the best. Future research will help to make that decision.

Speech Development

In the first year of life, the major language developments include the emergence of about one-half of the major phonemes and some simple morphemes. Phonemes are the fundamental elements of a language and include the basic vowels and consonants. The sounds of p and b are examples of phonemes. Many phonemes occur spontaneously in the child's babbling, but a certain amount of learning is involved in refining the production of the naturally occurring phonemes so that they sound more like the articulations made by adults. The morpheme is the smallest meaningful element in a language. The morphemes ma or no have distinct and relatively unambiguous meaning.

The most systematic research on speech development in early infancy has been conducted by Irwin and his associates at the University of Iowa (18, 19, 53–62). They recorded phonetically the speech sounds made by 40 infants during the first 10 days of life. The vowel sounds uttered were i (as in bit), e (as in bet), a (as in bat), or u (as in but), a being the one all infants made. The aspirate *h* (as in house) was the most frequently used consonant, and *w* and *k* were also noted occasionally. The consonants *m*, *l*, and *b* were not heard during this period.

Throughout infancy, there are marked changes in the nature and number of sounds produced. In a 30-month longitudinal (follow-up) study of speech development, Irwin (53–60) phonetically transcribed monthly samples of the speech sounds uttered by 95 infants during a short test period (30 breaths). Speech development was measured in terms of phoneme types (elemental speech sounds listed in the International Phonetic Alphabet) and phoneme frequency (the number of times each of the types is used by the infant).

The data revealed rapid and far-reaching expansion in the infant's speech repertoire during the first year. As early as "the second quarter of the first year of life infants produce most of the vowel elements and about half of the consonants" (73, 507). The average baby under 2 months of age has 7 phonemes in its speech repertory; at 6 months he has 12, and at a year, 18. (Adult American speech includes 35 phonemes.) The number of sounds uttered also multiplies rapidly during this period. During the first 2 months, infants vocalized an average of 63 sounds (counting all repetitions) in the test period, but at 6 months, the average number rose to 74, and at a year it was about 90 (53, 59, 60).

Throughout the first year, the number of vowel types used exceeds the number of consonant types. The vowel-consonant ratio is 5:1 during the first month, but this discrepancy becomes reduced gradually until after the first year, consonants predominate. Adults have a consonant-vowel ratio of 1.4:1 (56).

About 90 percent of the earliest consonant sounds made by the infant are glottals (aspirate *h* or stops and catches made in the throat), but by the end of the first year, these sounds constitute only about 30 percent of the infant's consonants. Labials (for example, *p*, *b*, *m*, *w*, *wh*), labiodentals (*f* and *v*), and postdentals (*t*, *d*, *n*) are practically nonexistent in the neonate's repertory, but they become quite frequent during the first year (54, 55).

The regularity of trends in sound production provides some evidence that early sound patterns are dependent primarily on maturation and changes in anatomical, neuromuscular systems. For example, the postural change involved in sitting "must affect the shape of the oral cavity, especially by affecting the normal position of the soft palate, which undoubtedly accounts at least in part for the forward movement of the control of muscles involving the later-appearing consonants" (73, 513).

Moreover, children of all nationalities seem to go through the same sequence of speech development. "Children who are hearing only English use German [vowel] sounds, French guttural *r*, and a wide variety of sounds they will not be able to produce as English-speaking adults" (76, 146).

A child cannot learn verbal responses until he is old enough and mature enough to learn them. Maturation sets the pace. With a normal environment the child's

Table 5.2 Developmental Milestones
in Motor and Language Development

At the completion of:	Motor Development	Vocalization and Language
12 weeks	Supports head when in prone position; weight is on elbows; hands mostly open; no grasp reflex	Markedly less crying than at 8 weeks; when talked to and nodded at, smiles, followed by squealing-gurgling sounds usually called *cooing,* which is vowel-like in character and pitch-modulated; sustains cooing for 15-20 seconds
16 weeks	Plays with a rattle placed in his hands (by shaking it and staring at it), head self-supported; tonic neck reflex subsiding	Responds to human sounds more definitely; turns head; eyes seem to search for speaker; occasionally some chuckling sounds
20 weeks	Sits with props	The vowel-like sounds begin to be interspersed with more consonant-sounds; labial fricatives, spirants and nasals are common; acoustically, all vocalizations are very different from the sounds of the mature language of the environment
6 months	Sitting: bends forward and uses hands for support; can bear weight when put into standing position, but cannot yet stand with holding on; reaching: unilateral; grasp: no thumb apposition yet; releases cube when given another	Cooing changing into babbling resembling one-syllable utterances; neither vowels nor consonants have very fixed recurrences; most common utterances sound somewhat like ma, mu, da, or di
8 months	Stands holding on; grasps with thumb apposition; picks up pellet with thumb and finger tips	Reduplication (or more continuous repetitions) becomes frequent; intonation patterns become distinct; utterances can signal emphasis and emotions
10 months	Creeps efficiently; takes side-steps, holding on; pulls to standing position	Vocalizations are mixed with sound-play such as gurgling or bubble-blowing; appears to wish to imitate sounds, but the imitations are never quite successful; beginning to differentiate between words heard by making differential adjustment
12 months	Walks when held by one hand; walks on feet and hands—knees in air; mouthing of objects almost stopped; seats self on floor	Identical sound sequences are replicated with higher relative frequency of occurrence and words (mamma or dadda) are emerging; definite signs of understanding some words and simple commands (show me your eyes)

Table 5.2   *(Continued)*

At the com-pletion of:	Motor Development	Vocalization and Language
18 months	Grasp, prehension and release fully developed; gait stiff, propulsive and precipitated; sits on child's chair with only fair aim; creeps building tower of three cubes	Has a definite repertoire of words—more than three, but less than fifty; still much babbling but now of several syllables with intricate intonation pattern; no attempt at communicating information and no frustration for not being understood; words may include items such as thank you or come here, but there is little ability to join any of the lexical items into spontaneous two-item phrases; understanding is progressing rapidly
24 months	Runs, but falls in sudden turns; can quickly alternate between sitting and stance; walks stairs up or down, one foot forward only	Vocabulary of more than fifty items (some children seem to be able to name everything in environment); begins spontaneously to join vocabulary items into two-word phrases; all phrases appear to be own creations; definite increase in communicative behavior and interest in language
30 months	Jumps up into air with both feet; stands on one foot for about two seconds; takes few steps on tiptoe; jumps from chair; good hand and finger coordination; can move digits independently; manipulation of objects much improved; builds tower of six cubes	Fastest increase in vocabulary with many new additions every day; no babbling at all; utterances have communicative intent; frustrated if not understood by adults; utterances consist of at least two words, many have three or even five words; sentences and phrases have characteristic child grammar, that is, they are rarely verbatim repetitions of an adult utterance; intelligibility is not very good yet, though there is great variation among children; seems to understand everything said to him
3 years	Tiptoes three yards; runs smoothly with acceleration and deceleration; negotiates sharp and fast curves without difficulty; walks stairs by alternating feet; jumps 12 inches; can operate tricycle	Vocabulary of some 100 words; about 80% of utterances are intelligible even to strangers; grammatical complexity of utterances is roughly that of colloquial adult language, although mistakes still occur
4 years	Jumps over rope; hops on right foot; catches ball in arms; walks line	Language is well established; deviations from the adult norm tend to be more in style than in grammar

Source: E. H. Lenneberg. *Biological functions of language.* New York: Wiley, 1967. By permission.

speech awaits a step by step unfolding of the growth process. Consequently we find a succession of developmental stages that are quite similar in all children. By manipulating the environment of the child we can modify or delay his language development, but we shall never teach a baby to utter prepositional phrases before he begins to babble. The successive stages of language development are similar in all normal children (76, 141).

It is difficult to determine when the child actually says his first meaningful word. Parents, anxiously anticipating their offspring's accomplishments, may jump to the conclusion that their baby has begun to talk if he happens to utter a sound vaguely resembling a word. On the basis of systematic observations, different psychologists have reached different conclusions regarding the average age of the onset of talking. When mothers' reports are used as basic data, the appearance of the first word is found at an average age of 11 months (14, 17). While there is a great deal of individual variation, data indicate that the average child generally says his first word sometime around the end of the first year.

Since much of the child's early babbling consists of repetitions of identical or similar syllables, the first words uttered are usually reduplicated monosyllables such as bye-bye, mama, or dada. The first word spoken is characteristically a noun or interjection but often functions as a whole sentence. For example "mamma" may mean, *where is mother* or *I want mother,* or *there is mother,* depending upon the inflection and accompanying behavior.

This discussion of early speech growth has emphasized the child's overt utterances, for these are easily observed. The question of how much language comprehension the child acquires during the first year is more difficult to assess. It is likely that the 1-year-old child understands much more than he can express and, in many cases, is potentially capable of saying words that he has not actually uttered. As we shall see in Chapter 6, the desire to speak and the amount of reward speech receives are important determinants of the frequency and quality of the young child's language products.

Although the child typically utters his first word at 1 year, the expression of short sentences which we might call meaningful speech typically occurs between the ages of 18 and 28 months (see Table 5.2). Most of the meaningful single-word utterances of 1-year-olds are simple words like "mamma," "milk," "here," "go," and "up-baby." These single simple words have a meaning that is called *syncretic*—the words stand for an entire thought or a sentence rather than acting as one specific word. The 1-year-old child who points to his bottle and says "milk" may mean, "I want my milk" or "Give me some milk". The single word refers to an entire idea. We shall go into more detail on the vocabulary and grammatical growth of the child in later chapters (see pp. 247–254).

MENTAL DEVELOPMENT

This discussion of language and speech development brings us to a more general discussion of mental development. Let us be clear what is meant by this term. The development of intellectual processes and mental skills involves three major dimensions. First, the infant acquires various schemata as a result of experience. He establishes images of familiar objects and of the people he has encountered. During the first year these schemata are primarily images. At the end of the second year, language becomes a part of the structure and, therefore, of mental activity. Language allows the child to translate experience and to communicate with others and, of course, to reason.

The second set of structures that are part of mental activity include learned bonds or connections between (1) an external event and a schema, (2) a schema and a response, (3) one schema and another schema, or (4) a stimulus event and an external response. Let us consider an illustration of each of these four types of associations: (1) the child learns an association between the sight of his mother going to the refrigerator (an external event) with the image of a glass of milk (a schema); (2) he learns an association between the image of his mother walking out the front door (a schema) and the act of whining or crying (an overt response); (3) he learns an association between the thought of his father coming in the front door (schema) and the thought of playing with his father in the living room (a second schema); and (4) he learns an association between the sight of a ball (an external event) and bouncing it (an overt response).

Although the child learns many complex responses, there has been some doubt about whether learning can occur in the newborn. Recent research indicates that learning may occur from the first day of life and new responses are established more easily as the child matures. A 3-day-old newborn can learn to turn his head in the direction of the sound of a bell through classical conditioning procedures. The infant lies on his back in a crib and a bell is sounded on the right side of his head. If he does not turn his head to the right when the bell sounds, then the experimenter lightly touches the corner of his mouth on the right side in order to facilitate the infant's turning in that direction. When he turns, he is allowed to suck on a bottle containing milk. This pairing of the sound of a bell with receipt of milk if he turns to the right is repeated 10 times for each feeding session. The 3-day-old requires about 17–18 such feeding sessions (about 177 trials) to learn to turn his head to the right every time the bell sounds, without someone's stimulating the corner of his mouth. He has learned an association between the external stimulus of a bell and the response of turning his head to the right (79). Children who are 85 days old when this learning sequence begins require only 42 trials to learn the association. Infants 20 weeks old require only an average of 27 trials (79). This dramatic difference in ease of learning this conditioned response is due in large measure, to the lack of alertness and minimal attentiveness of the newborn baby, rather than to differences in the ability to make the response of turning the head.

The newborn will also learn to suck more effectively if the response of sucking leads to the receipt of food. Ordinarily, the newborn does not suck a tube placed in its mouth, but if the sucking gets him sugar water, the rate of sucking responses increases dramatically (70).

Learning of an association between an external stimulus and a response is possible from the first days of life. Developmental psychologists must now determine what are the conditioned stimuli that are normally responded to, and the responses that are most easily acquired.

PIAGET'S VIEW OF INTELLECTUAL DEVELOPMENT IN INFANCY

During the first year of life, schemata are not plentiful and much of the infant's learning involves associations between external stimuli or internal sensations and an overt response. The infant learns to hold a bottle; to shake a rattle in order to produce a noise; to suck more efficiently or seek out a ball that rolled out of sight. All of these examples of learned motor behaviors are illustrations of what Professor Jean Piaget calls sensorimotor learning (80). Piaget has had an enormous influence on developmental psychology, and we shall present here a brief description of his conceptions of mental development during this infant period.

Piaget believes that intelligence is the ability to adapt to the environment. The development of the ability to adapt passes through a series of maturational stages. Initially, Piaget distinguished between two major stages in intellectual development: sensorimotor intelligence (approximately 0 to 2 years of age) and conceptual intelligence (age 2 to maturity). During the sensorimotor stage the child's adaptations do not involve extensive use of symbols or language. The ability of the 10-month-old to find a toy under a pillow or to shake a rattle in order to make a noise does not require knowledge of a language. These acts are considered preverbal.

The sensorimotor phase is further differentiated into six developmental stages covering the first 18 months of life (80).

The first four stages of the sensorimotor period are generally achieved during the first year, although for Piaget the ages at which the stages occur are not of primary importance. All children go through the same succession of stages, progressing from earlier to later in the same order, but the rate of progress will vary from child to child.

During the later stages of the sensorimotor period, the child's cognitive functioning becomes more complex, more objective, and increasingly oriented toward reality. Intention, directionality, and goal orientation of behavior, already apparent in the fourth stage of this period, become more marked and definite in the fifth and sixth stages. In addition, the child begins to "react to new situations with a decidedly active and versatile program of experimentation" (80). At the end of the sensorimotor period a primitive kind of representation—imagery—becomes manifest.

During the first stage, that of *reflexes* (birth to 1 month), innate reflexes (such as sucking movements to the stimulus of a nipple) become more efficient. These unlearned responses comprise the major adaptive behavior of the organism. The second stage, called *primary circular reactions,* is characterized by the appearance of repetitions of simple acts that are repeated for their own sake. Examples of primary circular reactions include repetitive sucking, repetitive opening and closing of the fists, and repetitive fingering of a blanket. There seems to be no intent or purpose to this activity, and in contrast to the next stage, the child does not seem to be interested in the effect that his behavior has on the environment.

The succeeding four stages contain more intentional activity, according to Piaget (80). In the third stage, *secondary circular reactions* (4 to 6 months), the child repeats responses which produce interesting results. For example, the child will repeatedly kick his legs in order to produce a swinging motion in a toy suspended over his crib. To a naive observer it appears that the child has accidentally discovered that a certain act (kicking his legs) produces an interesting change in the external environment (the toy swings), and the child repeats the act in order to see the change in the environment. In the earlier stage of primary circular reactions, the act was repeated for its own sake, rather than to produce an interesting stimulus effect.

In the fourth stage, *coordination of secondary reactions* (7 to 10 months), the child begins to solve simple problems. The infant now uses a response he has already mastered as a means of obtaining a specific goal object. For example, he will now knock down a pillow in order to obtain a toy hidden behind it. In the preceding state (secondary circular reactions) the child might repeatedly knock down a pillow merely to watch it fall. In this later stage, he uses this learned response as a means to obtain a desired goal, and not as an end in itself.

During the fifth stage *(tertiary circular reactions)* the child begins to show active trial-and-error experimentation. During this period (11 to 18 months) the child varies his responses toward the same object or tries out new responses to obtain the same goal. For example, the child who has learned to knock down a pillow with his fist to get a toy may then attempt to knock it down with his feet or use a rattle to push it down. The child is now manifesting the essence of problem-solving behavior.

During this stage the infant discovers (generally accidentally) some novel, interesting, and exciting event that he attempts to repeat and prolong, so that he can continue to enjoy it—e.g., kicking a doll hanging above the crib simply to watch it swing. In the secondary circular reaction of Stage three, the repetition is accomplished by rather stereotyped and mechanical actions. But in the fifth stage, the tertiary circular reaction, the child modifies and varies his movements—i.e., accommodates—in a "progressively more deliberate fashion" (80). Act and object (means and end) are clearly differentiated.

> The infant gives the impression—and here is the real significance of the tertiary reaction for intellectual development—of really exploring the object's potentialities, of really varying the act in order to see how this variation affects the object, of really subordinating his actions to an object seen as a thing apart, something "out there" (31, 114).

What is most interesting to the child at this stage is novelty per se, the variations that he can produce in the movements he initiates. He becomes active in trial-and-error exploration of his environment, seeking new means of attaining goals and thus discovering new ways of solving problems. In the activities of the fifth stage, the child begins to manifest the constructive, original elements that Piaget regards as characteristic of intelligence. He describes the actions in this way:

> It is therefore a question of innovating. [The child performs] an "experiment in order to see": the child gropes. The only difference is that, now, the groping is oriented as a function of the goal itself, that is to say, of the problem presented . . . instead of taking place simply "in order to see" (Piaget, quoted in *31*, 118).

Piaget's observations of his son Laurent illustrate this "discovery of new means through active experimentation" graphically. He records:

> I place my watch on a big red cushion (of a uniform color and without a fringe) and place the cushion directly in front of the child. Laurent tries to reach the watch directly and not succeeding, he grabs the cushion which he draws toward him as before. But then, instead of letting go of the support at once, as he has hitherto done, in order to try again to grasp the objective, he recommences with obvious interest, to move the cushion while looking at the watch. Everything takes place as though he noticed for the first time the relationship for its own sake and studied it as such. He thus easily succeeds in grasping the watch (Piaget, quoted in *31*, 117).

Stage six of the sensorimotor period, the final and most advanced stage of this period, is achieved at approximately 18 months. It is characterized by "invention of new means through internal mental combinations" (*80*) and its most striking and significant feature is the development of a primitive form of representation, a kind of imagery that is used in problem solving. When the child at this stage wishes to obtain some end for which he has no habitual, available means, he invents one. But he does this not by overt, fumbling, trial-and-error explorations, as in Stage five. Instead, he operates covertly, by "internal experimentation, an inner exploration of ways and means" (*31*, 119). Piaget gives some vivid illustrations of activity at this stage:

> At 1:6 for the first time Lucienne plays with a doll carriage whose handle comes to the height of her face. She rolls it over the carpet by pushing it. When she comes against a wall, she pulls, walking backward. But as this position is not convenient for her, she pauses and without hesitation goes to the other side to push the carriage again. She therefore found the procedure in one attempt, apparently through analogy to other situations but without training, apprenticeship, or chance.

> In the same kind of inventions, that is to say, in the realm of kinematic representations, the following fact should be cited. At 1:10 Lucienne tries to kneel before a stool but, by leaning against it, pushes it further away. She then raises herself up, takes it and places it against a sofa. When it is firmly set there she leans against it and kneels without difficulty (Piaget, quoted in *31*, 119).

The dual processes of representation and invention are the keystones of the sixth stage. The kind of inventiveness demonstrated by Lucienne in the illustrations above clearly requires symbolic images, the ability to symbolize actions or events *before acting them out in reality*. In short, the child at this stage is capable of imagined representation and, consequently, of a kind of international manipulation of reality.

The accomplishments of this stage are dramatically reflected in the child's acquisition of the ability to "defer imitation," i.e., to reproduce behavior of an absent model from memory. For example, one day, Jacqueline, another of Piaget's children, saw a child throw a temper tantrum. The next day she tried it herself, although she had never had a tantrum before, producing an obvious imitation of the tantrum she had seen twelve hours earlier.

> With the advent of the capacity to represent actions rather than simply to per- form them, the sensory-motor period draws to a close and the child is ready for an analogous but even more extended and tortuous apprenticeship in the use of symbols. . . . This does not, of course, mean that the child no longer continues to develop in the sensory-motor sphere. But it does mean that hence- forth the most advanced *intellectual* adaptations of which a given child is capable will take place in a conceptual-symbolic rather than purely sensory- motor arena (*31*, 121).

The next broad period of cognitive development, the preoperational, is marked by the use of language and symbolic function; both of these proc- esses are built upon systematic use of representation, which begins in Stage six of the sensorimotor period. We will learn more of the preoperational period in Chapter 11.

In the course of his work on the growth of intelligence, Piaget has made some ingenious observations on the development of a variety of internal schemata or concepts that all children acquire. One such concept is the no- tion that an object that is out of sight still exists. The stages the child passes through in acquiring the idea that objects have permanence will be outlined briefly in order to communicate the flavor of Piaget's observations.

During the first 2 or 3 months of life, the child's visual universe, accord- ing to Piaget, is made up of a series of fleeting images without permanence. It is as if the child were on a train watching the world pass before him. He follows a stimulus until it passes out of his line of vision, and he then aban- dons any search for it. Moreover, his attention is easily captured by any new stimulus.

From 3 to 6 months, the child coordinates vision and movements of his arms and hands. He will now grab for objects that he can see, but will not reach for objects outside his immediate visual field. Piaget interprets the child's failure to search for the hidden object as indicating that he does not realize that the hidden object still exists. The infant behaves as if an object out of sight has lost its permanence (i.e., it no longer exists).

During the last 3 months of the first year the child advances one step further. He will now reach for an object that is hidden from view *if he has watched it being hidden.* Thus, if the child sees the mother place a bottle under a blanket he will search for the bottle there.

During the first 6 months of the second year the child becomes capable of accounting for "spatial displacements" of objects. If an object is hidden under a pillow, the child in the preceding stage will search for it, but if he then sees the object being hidden under a second pillow, he will continue to look for it under the first pillow. In this later stage, however, the child will search for the object under the second pillow, indicating a recognition that objects can be displaced.

In the final stage of acquiring the concept of object permanence, the child will search for objects that he has not actually seen being hidden. For example, if the mother shows the child a toy fish in a box, puts the fish and box under a cover, and then removes the box without the fish, the child will search for the fish under the cover, as though he realized that it must be there. This behavior does not occur during the earlier stages, and suggests that the child becomes aware that objects have permanence and do not cease to exist when they disappear from view (80).

From this summary of Piaget's views of mental development in the first year, it can be seen that the coordination of simple motor actions with incoming perceptions (sensorimotor acts) predominate in the mental activity of the child. Precocious development of these behaviors is not necessarily related to the precocious development of vocabulary, comprehension of speech, or the ability to master arithmetic concepts. It cannot be assumed that advanced sensorimotor development at 1 year of age is an index of superior linguistic or numerical ability in later years. Although marked retardation in sensorimotor development at 1 year may be a prognostic sign of retardation in the child, the psychological significance of advanced or precocious sensorimotor development is still largely a mystery.

As a result of Piaget's observations of cognitive process in infants, other investigators have begun to examine the quality of the infants' mental activity. The fruits of these investigations reveal a level of sophistication and complexity that was not expected. One-year-old infants seem to recognize the similarities among objects, suggesting that they possess a form of primitive conceptual skill. Infants 1, 1½, and 2 years of age were seated in an infant chair with a tray. The examiner then placed four yellow cubes (½ inch on each side) and four gray clay balls (the same size as the cubes) on the tray in front of the child. Although the eight objects were arranged in a random and scattered manner in front of the infant, more than 40 percent of the 1-year-olds touched successively either the four clay balls or the four yellow cubes. Over 70 percent of those in the two older age groups displayed this behavior. That is, if the child first touched or manipulated a clay ball, he was likely to touch the remaining three clay balls in succession, without manipulating the yellow cubes. The 1-year-old notices the differences in color and shape between the cubes and balls and, what is more important, is predisposed to treat the identical objects in a special way. When the differences between the objects are subtle, infants do not display this primitive conceptual grouping. Thus, when the objects were four elliptical shapes and four parallelograms (of the same color and size), very few infants touched all four identical objects in succession (87).

INDIVIDUAL DIFFERENCES AMONG INFANTS

Thus far, we have been considering primarily general developmental milestones for the average child. But there are dramatic differences among infants in behavior and physiological reactivity. Some children walk at 10 months, others at 18; some say their first word at 9 months, others not until 29 months. Thus, norms are misleading for they describe averages and the average child really does not exist. Individual differences at 1 or 2 years of age may be the result of either environmental differences or heredity, and the environmental effects could be pre- or postnatal. The differences that exist during the first days and weeks are likely to be biological in nature, and may have an effect on development in one of two ways. These differences may push the child to develop in one particular direction or they may elicit from the mother different reactions toward the infant. Let us consider first some dimensions of difference among young infants and then indicate what they might mean.

Although mothers have always recognized that each of their children was "different from the first day," psychologists have only recently begun to look systematically at these initial, unlearned differences and their potential significance. The term *congenital* refers to characteristics that are present at birth and which, in some cases, may be hereditary. Investigators have studied such characteristics as sensory thresholds, motor activity, and physiological reactions, and it appears that there are marked differences among newborns with respect to these attributes.

Activity

There are wide individual differences in the spontaneous motor activity of infants. Some children show frequent and vigorous thrashing of arms and legs, whereas others lie still and quiet. Some infants sleep restlessly; others show minimal activity during sleep (52, 102). Furthermore, there is some evidence to suggest that infant boys show higher and more vigorous activity levels than girls (66, 97).

It is not unreasonable to assume that some aspects of the child's development during the early years might be influenced by extremely high or low levels of activity. For example, an extremely active and motorically energetic infant might be more apt to become physically aggressive in the preschool years. Some writers have speculated that unusually high degrees of infant activity are a sign of inability to control and modify the effect of strong needs and states of internal tension (27). Highly active children may have difficulty inhibiting direct, aggressive behavior when they encounter the complex frustrations of the preschool and school-age environment. These are only possibilities and have not yet been verified by empirical study.

The child's activity level may also affect his development indirectly by influencing his general interaction with the environment and the way he is handled by others.

> The development of behavior . . . depends upon the responsiveness of the growing organism. An active, irritable infant participates in a wider environment than does a quiet, phlegmatic one, and he invites different reactions from those who share the environment with him. The baby who turns, reaches, and kicks restlessly in his crib; smiles, or coos a great deal; or who nurses actively and long, inevitably exposes himself to situations which differ from those which the placid, unreactive child encounters. What these differences in reactivity may mean for the infant's behavior organization is also importantly determined, of course, by the needs and attitudes of his parents and of the others who respond to him. An exuberant, accepting family may welcome noisy activity in its newest member which quieter, more restrictive parents would consider irritating, frightening, or bad (16, 21).

A mother who is easily irritated by a noisy, active infant may be more punishing toward an active child than toward a placid one. An energetic, athletic father may be cross and irritable with a placid infant but accepting with a more active, responsive one. Thus the child's level of activity may influence the reactions of his parents toward him and, thereby, affect his subsequent development.

In one of the first attempts to study the relation between the behaviors of infancy and later childhood, 31 infants were observed during the first 8 months of life and again from 3 to 6 years of age (27). One investigator studied descriptions of the infant's behavior during the first year and predicted what each child might be like during the preschool years. The accuracy of these predictions was assessed through study of the older child's behavior in a group, his behavior in a play session with a psychiatrist, and through interviews with the parents.

Children who had been awkward in their motor movements and had not displayed vigorous motor activity during infancy were retarded, as preschoolers, in level of motor development and motor coordination (relative to their level of development in other areas) during the preschool years. This specific relationship had been predicted, and suggests that some aspects of infant activity are precursors of future behavior (27).

Sensory Thresholds and Adaptation

At birth, visual, auditory, tactile, olfactory, pain, and gustatory sense organs are all capable of responding to appropriate stimulation. However, infants differ with respect to the amount of stimulation that is required to elicit a response in these sensory modalities. Some infants will turn or move their limbs in response to minimal visual or auditory stimulation, while others require more intense stimulation before they respond.

There is some suggestive (though not conclusive) evidence that newborn females have lower thresholds for pain than males do. That is, neonatal girls will exhibit a flexing of the toe to lower intensities of electrical stimulation upon the toe than are required to elicit this reaction in boys (71).

Moreover, infants who have low thresholds to tactile stimulation (i.e., show a motor response when their skin is lightly stroked) are less likely to exert muscular effort than infants who have high thresholds to tactile stimulation (i.e., do not show a motor response when their skin is lightly stroked; 5). Newborn boys were placed on their stomachs and observers watched to see whether any child attempted to push his head and chest up from the crib. The boys who were most likely to show this "push-up" reaction displayed minimal motor activity when their cheeks were lightly stroked during sleep (5).

These data, together with sex differences in pain threshold, tentatively suggest that differential sensitivity to pain and touch are congenital characteristics.

It should be emphasized that these findings are still inconclusive, and more research is needed to corroborate them. Moreover, even if newborns differ markedly in sensitivity to sound, touch, or pain, it is still possible that these differences are transient and have little or no relation to future behavior.

Moreover, some infants rapidly adapt to a new stimulus (i.e., gradually cease responding), while others continue to respond after many presentations of the same stimulus (11). In one study, 50 babies between 1 and 5 days of age were presented repeatedly with a tone of constant intensity. An observer recorded whether the children, individually, showed a startle pattern (i.e., flexing of the legs and arms simultaneously) to the tone while, at the same time, each child's heart rate was recorded. There were marked differences among the babies in their reaction to the repeated tones. Some showed a startle response to almost all of the tones; others rarely responded. Moreover, of those who responded to the initial presentations, some continued to respond even after 30 presentations. Other babies quickly adapted (or habituated) to the tone and stopped showing a startle after several presentations (11).

The rapidity with which an infant habituates to a stimulus (i.e., grows "bored") seems to have significance for his future behavior. One group of infants were seen at 4, 8, 13, and 27 months of age. Some of the 4-month-olds showed rapid loss of interest to a set of faces presented to them; a second group of infants showed sustained interest throughout the 16 presentations of the faces. The boys who showed rapid loss of interest were slightly shorter, lighter, and smiled less often than the boys who were slow to habituate. When the boys were seen at 8 months of age, the rapidly habituating group showed more restless and distractible play with toys, shifting from one toy to another. The slow-habituating group tended to play with a toy (e.g., a toy bug, or a mallet) for a longer period of time before shifting activities.

The boys who were extreme at the earlier ages retained their style of play through their second birthday. The light, wiry 4-month-boys who lost interest in the faces quickly at 4 months and showed frequent shifts in their play at 8 months displayed shorter periods of sustained attentive play with a train or with blocks than the boys who were slow to adapt to the faces and shifted activities less often during the first year (64). One group can be described as having a *fast tempo;* the other group, a *slower tempo.*

Observation of one slow-tempo boy at 13 months illustrates this dimension. The boy was in a room with his mother and he discovered one of the plastic quoits there. For 10 minutes he rolled the quoit around the room, watching carefully as it rolled after each push he gave it, and laughing as it stopped each time. During most of the 10-minute period he was deeply engrossed in the activity, as if he were perceptually addicted to it. The observers who watched him felt that his concentration was so intense that he would have been insensitive to most stimulus changes that might have occurred around him.

Physiological Reactivity

When a neonate is under tension or stress, his bodily reactions may reflect his lack of physiological or psychological well-being. There are at least four physiological systems that may react to increases in tension: the gastrointestinal tract, the skin, the respiratory (breathing) apparatus, and the cardiovascular system (heart and blood vessels). Newborns differ in the differential responsivity of these systems under stress (43). That is, some infants show large increases in heart rate or large changes in skin temperature when under stress (e.g., hunger), whereas others show less marked physiological changes in similar situations. Some babies characteristically vomit when under tension; others break out with a rash; and still others show marked flushing of the face or skin due to increase in blood pressure and dilation (opening) of the small blood vessels near the skin.

An Overview

In summary, differences among infants in activity, sensitivity to stimulation, and physiological reactions are present during the first week of life. Until additional research has been done, it cannot be known whether an infant's characteristic bodily reactions will be stable over long periods of time. They may be only transient phenomena with little importance for future development. However, if they prove to be constant over the first year, it seems likely that they will influence the child's subsequent development. For example, if early differences in heart rate, stomach reactivity, or skin sensitivity do, in fact, reflect stable constitutional tendencies, then the development of specific psychosomatic symptoms in later life (e.g., ulcers, asthma, allergies) may be, at least in part, related to the ways in which the infant reacts to stress. Whether these infant reaction patterns are hereditary in origin or a result of environmental processes during intrauterine development is a fascinating but still largely unsolved mystery.

SUMMARY

There are several important points to be noted about the first year of life. First, the newborn is a remarkably capable organism with well-functioning sensorimotor systems. He is capable of learning associations between stimuli and responses from the first days of life, and the role of meaning and familiarity of events becomes important before the first half-year is over.

He preferentially attends to visual or auditory stimuli that have sharp on-off characteristics (moving light; intermittent sounds) and are of optimal size or duration. Once he begins to acquire internal representations of these phenomena, his attention is directed to stimuli that resemble the familiar (i.e., discrepant stimuli). Still later in the first year, after he acquires nests of associations to repeated stimuli, he is most likely to maintain prolonged attention, to events that are discrepant and elicit rich nests of associations. His motor actions, like his mental schema, also develop rapidly; by 1 year of age he is displaying planned and well-coordinated actions with arms and legs. Also as the first year draws to a close, he enters the world of meaning—applying language labels to familiar phenomena.

As the first year ends the infant is a rather complicated and knowledgable organism who has already acquired ideas about the world and ways of dealing with it. The next chapter considers his developing relations with one particular set of objects—the adults who care for him.

References

1. Acheson, R. M. Maturation of the skeleton. In F. Falkner (Ed.), *Human development*. Philadelphia: Saunders, 1966, 465–502.
2. Ames, L. B. The sequential patterning of prone progression in the human infant. *Genet. Psychol. Monogr.*, 1937, *19*, 409–460.
3. Bakwin, H., & Bakwin, R. M. Growth of thirty-two external dimensions during the first year of life. *J. Ped.*, 1936, *8*, 177–183.
4. Bayley, N. The development of motor abilities during the first three years. *Monogr. Soc. Res. Child Develpm.*, 1935, No. 1.
5. Bell, R. Q. Relations between behavior manifestations in the human neonate. *Child Develpm.*, 1960, *31*, 463–478.
6. Bergman, P., & Escalona, S. Unusual sensitivities in very young children. *Psychoanalytic Study of Child.* Vol. III-IV. New York: International Universities Press, 1949, 333–352.
7. Berko, J., & Brown, R. Psycholinguistic research methods. In P. Mussen (Ed.), *Handbook of research methods in child development*. New York: Wiley, 1960.
8. Blest, A. D. The function of eyespot patterns in the Lepidoptera. *Behavior*, 1957, *11*, 209–256.

9. Brackbill, Y., Adams, G., Crowell, D. H., & Gray, M. L. Arousal level in newborns and preschool children under continuous auditory stimulation. *J. exp. child Psychol.,* 1966, *3,* 178–188.

10. Brennan, W. M., Ames, E. W., & Moore, E. W. Age differences in infant's attention to patterns of different complexities. *Science,* 1966, *151,* 354–356.

11. Bridger, W. H. Sensory habituation and discrimination in the human neonate. *Amer. J. Psychiat.,* 1961, *117,* 991–996.

12. Broadbent, D. E., *Perception and communication.* New York: Pergamon, 1958.

13. Brodbeck, A. J., & Irwin, O. C. The speech behavior of infants without families. *Child Develpm., 17,* 145–156.

14. Buhler, C. *The first year of life.* (Trans. by Greenberg and Ripin.) New York: Day, 1930.

15. Cameron, J., Livson, N., & Bayley, N. Infant vocalizations and their relationship to mature intelligence. *Science,* 1967, *157,* 331–333.

16. Cameron, N., & Margaret, A. *Behavior pathology.* Boston: Houghton Mifflin, 1951.

17. Cattell, P. *The measurement of intelligence of infants and young children.* New York: The Psychological Corporation, 1940.

18. Chen, H. P., & Irwin, O. C. Infant speech: vowel and consonant types. *J. Speech Disorders,* 1946, *11,* 27–29.

19. Chen, H. P., & Irwin, O. C. Development of speech during infancy: curve of differential percentage. *J. exp. Psychol.,* 1946, *36,* 522–525.

20. Crudden, C. H. Reactions of newborn infants to thermal stimuli under constant tactual conditions. *J. exp. Psychol.,* 1937, *20,* 350–370.

21. Dennis, W. Infant development under conditions of restricted practice and of minimum social stimulation. *Genet. Psychol. Monogr.,* 1941, *23,* 143–191.

22. Dennis, W. Causes of retardation among institutional children: Iran. *J. genet. Psychol.,* 1960, *96,* 47–59.

23. Desmond, M. M., Franklin, R. R., Vallbona, C., Hilt, R. H., Plumb, R., Arnold, H., & Watts, J. The Clinical behavior of the newly born: I. *J. Pediat.,* 1963, *62,* 307–325.

24. Disher, D. R. The reactions of newborn infants to chemical stimuli administered nasally. *Ohio State Univer. Stud. Contr. Psychol.,* 1934, No. 12, 1–52.

25. Eisenberg, R. B., Griffin, E. J., Coursin, D. B., & Hunter, M. A. Auditory behavior in the neonate. *J. Speech & Hearing Res.* 1964, *7,* 245–269.

26. Engen, T., & Lipsitt, L. P. Decrement and recovery of responses to olfactory stimuli in the human neonate. *J. comp. physiol. Psychol.,* 1965, *59,* 312–316.

27. Escalona, S., & Heider, G. M., *Prediction and outcome.* New York: Basic Books, 1959.

28. Fantz, R. L. The origin of form perception. *Scientific Amer.,* 1961, *204,* 66–72.

29. Fantz, R. L. Visual experience in infants: decreased attention to familiar patterns relative to novel ones. *Science,* 1964, *146,* 668–670.

30. Fantz, R. L. Visual perception from birth as shown by pattern selectivity. *Ann. N. Y. Acad. Sci.,* 1965, *118,* 793–814.

31. Flavell, J. H. *The developmental psychology of Jean Piaget.* Princeton, N.J.: Van Nostrand, 1963.

32. Garn, S. M. Roentgenogrammetric determinations of body composition. *Human Biol.,* 1957, *29,* 337–353.

33. Garn, S. M. Fat, body size, and growth in the newborn. *Human Biol.,* 1958, *30,* 265–280.

34. Garn, S. M., & Moorees, C. F. A. Stature, body-build, and tooth emergence in Aleutian Aleut children. *Child Developm.*, 1951, *22*, 261–270.
35. Garn, S. M., & Rohmann, C. G. Variability in the order of ossification of the boney centers of the hand and wrist. *Amer. J. Phys. Anthrop.*, 1960, *18*, 219–229.
36. Geber, M. Development psychomoteur de l'enfant africain. *Courier*, 1956, *6*, 17–29.
37. Gesell, A. The ontogenesis of infant behavior. In L. Carmichael (Ed.), *Manual of child psychology*. New York: Wiley, 1954 (2nd ed.), 335–373.
38. Gesell, A., & Amatruda, C. S. *Developmental diagnosis: normal and abnormal child development*. New York: Hoeber, 1941.
39. Gesell, A., Halverson, H. M., Thompson, H., Ilg, F. L., Costner, B. M., Ames, L. B., & Amatruda, C. S. *The first five years of life: a guide to the study of the preschool child*. New York: Harper & Row, 1940.
40. Gesell, A., & Thompson, H. *The psychology of early growth*. New York: Macmillan, 1938.
41. Gibson, E. J., & Walk, R. R. The "visual cliff." *Scientific Amer.*, 1960, *202*, 2–9.
42. Grier, J. B., Counter, S. A., & Shearer, W. M. Prenatal auditory imprinting in chickens. *Science*, 1967, *155*, 1692–1693.
43. Grossman, H. J., & Greenberg, N. H. Psychosomatic differentiation in infancy. *Psychosom. Med.*, 1957, *19*, 293–306.
44. Haaf, R. A., & Bell, R. Q. A facial dimension in visual discrimination by human infants. *Child Develpm.*, 1967, *38*, 893–899.
45. Haith, M. M. The response of the human newborn to visual movement. *J. exp. child Psychol.*, 1966, *3*, 235–243.
46. Halverson, H. M. An experimental study of prehension in infants by means of systematic cinema records. *Genet. Psychol. Monogr.*, 1931, *10*, 107–286.
47. Halverson, H. M. Complications of the early grasping reactions. *Genet. Psychol. Monogr.*, 1936, *47*, 47–63.
48. Haynes, H., White, B. L., & Held, R. Visual accommodation in human infants. *Science*, 1965, *148*, 528–530.
49. Hershenson, M. Visual discrimination in the human newborn. *J. comp. physiol. Psychol.*, 1964, *58*, 270–276.
50. Hindley, C. B., Filliozat, A. M., Klackenberg, G., Nicolet-Meister, P., & Sand, E. A. Differences in age of walking in five European longitudinal samples. *Human Biol.*, 1966, *38*, 364–379.
51. Hubel, D. H., & Weisel, T. N. Receptive fields, binocular interaction, and functional architecture in the cat's visual cortex. *J. Physiology*, 1962, *160*, 106–154.
52. Irwin, O. C. The amount and nature of activities of newborn infants under constant external stimulating conditions during the first ten days of life. *Genet. Psychol. Monogr.*, 1930, *8*, 1–92.
53. Irwin, O. C. Development of speech during infancy: curve of phonemic frequencies. *J. exp. Psychol.*, 1947, *37*, 187–193.
54. Irwin, O. C. Infant speech: consonant sounds according to place of articulation. *J. Speech Disorders*, 1947, *12*, 397–401.
55. Irwin, O. C. Infant speech: consonant sounds according to manner of articulation. *J. Speech Disorders*, 1947, *12*, 402–404.
56. Irwin, O. C. Infant speech: development of vowel sounds. *J. Speech & Hearing Disorders*, 1948, *13*, 31–34.

57. Irwin, O. C. Infant speech: the effect of family occupational status and of age on sound frequency. *J. Speech & Hearing Disorders*, 1948, *13*, 320–323.
58. Irwin, O. C. Infant speech: speech sound development of sibling and only infants. *J. exp. Psychol.*, 1948, *38*, 600–602.
59. Irwin, O. C. Speech development in the young child: 2. Some factors related to the speech development of the infant and young child. *J. Speech & Hearing Disorders*, 1952, *17*, 269–279.
60. Irwin, O. C., & Chen, H. P. Infant speech: vowel and consonant frequency. *J. Speech & Hearing Disorders*, 1946, *11*, 123–125.
61. Irwin, O. C., & Chen, H. P. Development of speech during infancy: curve of phonemic types. *J. exp. Psychol.*, 1946, *36*, 431–436.
62. Irwin, O. C., & Curry, F. Vowel elements in the crying vocalization of infants under ten days of age. *Child Develpm.*, 1941, *12*, 99–109.
63. Jensen, K. Differential reactions to taste and temperature stimuli in newborn infants. *Genet. Psychol. Monogr.*, 1932, *12*, 363–479.
64. Kagan, J. Continuity in the first year. Unpublished manuscript, 1968.
65. Karmel, B. Z. The effect of complexity, amount of contour, element size, and element arrangement on visual preference behavior in the hooded rat, domestic chick, and human infant. Unpublished doctoral dissertation, George Washington University, 1966.
66. Knop, C. A. The dynamics of newly born babies. *J. Pediat.*, 1946, *29*, 721–728.
67. Lenneberg, E. H. *Biological functions of language.* New York: Wiley, 1967.
68. Leventhal, A. S., & Lipsitt, L. P. Adaptation, pitch discrimination, and sound localization in the neonate. *Child Develpm.*, 1964, *35*, 759–767.
69. Ling, B. C. I. A genetic study of sustained visual fixation and associated behavior in the human infant from birth to six months. *J. genet. Psychol.*, 1942, *61*, 227–277.
70. Lipsitt, L. P. Learning in the human infant. In H. W. Stevenson, E. H. Hess, & H. L. Rheingold (Eds.), *Early behavior.* New York: Wiley, 1967, 225–247.
71. Lipsitt, L. P., & Levy, N. Pain threshold in the human neonate. *Child Develpm.*, 1959, *30*, 547–554.
72. McCall, R. B., & Kagan, J. Attention in the infant: effects of complexity, contour, perimeter and familiarity. *Child Develpm.*, 1967, *38*, 939–952.
73. McCarthy, D. Language development in children. In L. Carmichael (Ed.), *Manual of child psychology.* New York: Wiley, 1954 (2nd ed.), 492–630.
74. McGraw, M. B. *Growth: a study of Johnny and Jimmy.* New York: Appleton-Century-Crofts, 1935.
75. McGraw, M. B. Maturation of behavior. In L. Carmichael (Ed.), *Manual of child psychology.* New York: Wiley, 1946, 332–369.
76. Miller, G. A. *Language and communication.* New York: McGraw-Hill, 1951.
77. Moore, T. Language and intelligence: a longitudinal study of the first eight years. *Human Develpm.*, 1967, *10*, 88–106.
78. Moss, H. A. Sex, age, and state as determinants of mother-infant interaction. *Merrill-Palmer Quart.*, 1967, *13*, 19–36.
79. Papousek, H. Experimental studies of appetitional behavior in human newborns and infants. In H. W. Stevenson, E. H. Hess, & H. L. Rheingold (Eds.), *Early behavior.* New York: Wiley, 1967, 249–277.
80. Piaget, J. *The construction of reality in the child.* New York: Basic Books, 1954.
81. Polak, P. R., Emde, R. N., & Spitz, R. A. The smiling response: II. Visual dis-

crimination and the onset of depth perception. *J. nerv. ment. Dis.,* 1964, *139,* 407–415.

82. Pratt, K. C. The effects of repeated visual stimulation on the activity of newborn infants. *J. genet. Psychol.,* 1934, *44,* 117–126.

83. Pratt, K. C. The neonate. In L. Carmichael (Ed.), *Manual of child psychology.* New York: Wiley, 1954 (2nd ed.), 215–291.

84. Pratt, K. C., Nelson, A. K., & Sun, K. H. The behavior of the newborn infant. *Ohio State Univer. Stud. Contr. Psychol.,* 1930, No. 10.

85. Prechtl, H., & Beintema, D. The neurological examination of the full term newborn infant. *Little Club Clinics in Developmental Medicine,* No. 12, London: Spastics Society Medical Information Unit and William Heinemann Medical Books, 1964.

86. Rheingold, H., Gewirtz., J. L., & Ross, H. Social conditioning of vocalizations in the infant. *J. comp. physiol. Psychol.,* 1959, *52,* 68–73.

87. Ricciuti, H. N. Object grouping and selective ordering behavior in infants 12 to 24 months old. *Merrill-Palmer Quart.,* 1965, *11,* 129–148.

88. Roffwarg, H. P., Muzio, J. N., & Dement, W. C. Ontogenetic development of the human sleep-dream cycle. *Science,* 1966, *152,* 604–619.

89. Salapatek, P., & Kessen, W. Visual scanning of triangles by the human newborn. *J. exp. child Psychol.,* 1966, *3,* 113–122.

90. Sherman, M., & Sherman, I. C. Sensori-motor responses in infants. *J. comp. Psychol.,* 1925, *5,* 53–68.

91. Sherman, M., Sherman, I. C., & Flory, C. D. Infant behavior. *Comp. Psychol. Monogr.,* 1936, *12,* No. 4.

92. Shirley, M. M. The first two years: a study of twenty-five babies. Vol. I. Postural and locomotor development. *Inst. Child Welf. Monogr.,* Ser. No. 6. Minneapolis: Univer. of Minnesota Press, 1933.

93. Spiegler, D. M., & Ourth, L. L. Factors involved in the development of prenatal rhythmic sensitivity. *S.R.C.D.,* New York, March, 1967.

94. Stechler, G. Newborn attention as affected by medication during labor. *Science,* 1964, *144,* 315–317.

95. Steggerda, M., & Hill, J. J. Eruption time of teeth among whites, Negroes, and Indians. *Amer. J. Orthodontics & Oral Surg.,* 1942, *26,* 327–335.

96. Stubbs, E. M. The effect of the factors of duration, intensity, and pitch of sound stimuli on the responses of newborn infants. *Univer. Iowa Stud. Child Welf.,* 1934, 9, No. 4, 75–135.

97. Terman, L. M., & Tyler, L. E. Psychological sex differences. In L. Carmichael (Ed.), *Manual of child psychology.* New York: Wiley, 1954 (2nd ed.).

98. Thompson, H. Physical growth. In L. Carmichael (Ed.), *Manual of child psychology.* New York: Wiley, 1954 (2nd ed.).

99. Walk, R. D. The development of depth perception in animal and human infants. *Monogr. Soc. Res. Child Develpm.,* 1966, *31,* No. 5, pp. 82–108.

100. Watson, E. H., & Lowrey, G. H. *Growth and development of children.* Chicago: Year Book Publishers, 1958 (3rd ed.).

101. White, B. L., & Held, R. Plasticity of sensory motor development. In J. F. Rosenblith & W. Allinsmith (Eds.), *Readings in child development and educational psychology.* Boston: Allyn and Bacon, 1966 (2nd ed.).

102. Wolff, P. H. Observations on newborn infants. *Psychosom. Med.,* 1959, *21,* 110–118.

6

Social
Learning
in the First Year

The previous chapter detailed the development of the infant's sensory, perceptual, and response systems. The response and sensory capabilities given the infant allow him to perceive and react to a wide variety of objects and events. One set of objects to which the infant must react is other people. Moreover, the infant will use human beings to gratify some of his needs and motives all of his life. Knowledge of the development of reactions toward other human beings is basic to understanding the behavior of child and adult. This chapter will deal with that part of the story that occurs during the first year. By concentrating on the experiences of this period, we will try to shed some light on the emerging relationship between infant and adult.

The newborn begins life with very few specific emotional or motivational responses to other people. He has no innate tendencies to love, to hate, to fear, to approach, or to avoid people. His experiences with human beings during this first year lay the foundation for his future attitudes toward them. Extreme neglect or rejection during this period may result in serious damage to the child's future capacity for developing satisfying relations with other people. His learned reactions to the person or persons who care for him, in most cases his mother, form a nucleus for his later behavior toward others.

THE NECESSITY FOR MAKING RESPONSES

We start with a basic premise: From the moment the baby is born, he behaves. Some of his responses are spontaneous; others are reactions to needs. Some of the behaviors are necessary for survival, others are clearly not. As indicated in Chapter 5, the baby spontaneously scans the environment, vocalizes, sucks, smiles, cries, and thrashes. As he approaches the third and fourth months of life he begins to cling to objects and begins to manipulate his fingers, his mother's hair, and toys. What is the role of the caretaker, typically the mother, in this small set of responses? As we noted earlier, the infant's attention is attracted to objects that have high black-and-white contrast and that move. The eyes of the mother fit these two requirements well. The eyes contain good black-white contrast and they dart back and forth regularly and quickly. Moreover, if we view the entire face as the effective stimulus for the infant, then the movement of the lips and tongue and the attraction of the voice make the face a most interesting object—a kind of mobile toy that makes sounds. We would expect the infant to focus his attention on it. Observations of babies verify this expectation, for infants frequently spend long periods of time looking at and scanning their mother's face.

A second spontaneous response, that of babbling, is increased dramatically if it elicits a response, especially from a human being. But most objects do not produce a sound when the infant babbles. Mobiles, cribs, and hands do not "do something back" to the child when he vocalizes. The caretaker does. The infant babbles, the mother smiles and vocalizes back; the infant babbles again and the mother repeats. This sequence proceeds for several minutes with the mother's vocalization and facial reactions maintaining the child's behavior, and often his glee. We have, therefore, a second instance in which a human being is a likely object toward which the infant's responses—in this case babbling—will be directed.

Smiling, like babbling, is a common infant reaction and occurs with great frequency after 8 weeks of age. Of course, it can be seen as early as the first day. Like babbling, the smile is often directed at the mother.

Crying is a third response of which the infant is capable from the first hours. If the infant is separated from his mother by a few feet or more, crying acts as an effective signal to the mother to retrieve or attend to her baby. This is exactly what happens among dogs, monkeys, and apes; the squeal of a young puppy has the same function as the cry of an infant. It guarantees that the infant will not be in distress for a long time. The infant usually cries in response to either internal distress or a strange event. When the caretaker comes to relieve the distress, the infant typically relaxes his muscles and, when held upright, rests his head on the mother's shoulder and holds her neck.

Sucking is a fourth response that involves the caretaker. This is obvious in the case of children who are nursed—but even if the child is bottle-fed, he is usually being cradled in the mother's arms while he is feeding, and the relaxed posture and scanning of the face are selectively directed at the person holding the infant and feeding him.

Other species have slightly different responses that they direct at their mothers. A monkey clings tightly to the hairy underside of the mother, holding her close while she walks or sits. Puppies orient closely to the warm underbelly of the mother and suckle. Precocial birds, like ducks and chickens (i.e., those able to walk at birth), follow their mothers, make sounds at her, and will run to her when frightened or distressed.

Thus for many species, including man, the early unlearned reactions of the infant are usually directed at the biological mother. As a result, the infant, under natural conditions, becomes attached to her, whether the location is a city apartment, a suburban home, or a hut in the mountains of Guatemala.

THE CONCEPT OF ATTACHMENT

The concept of attachment is relatively new in our theorizing about child development, but it has an important connotation that was missing from earlier theoretical discussions. The traditional interpretation of the close relation between an infant and the mother assumed that the relationship was due to a conditioning of positive reward value to the mother. The interpretation was usually stated in the following way. Any new stimulus that is associated with a reward (food, warmth, or a pleasant state, for example) acquires reward value itself. Through learning, the mother, as a stimulus, comes to signify pleasure and contentment in much the same way that the buzzer became a sign of food for Pavlov's dogs. Furthermore, the infant will learn that to approach this source of pleasure will lead to effective gratification of his needs with minimal delay. The child learns the important response of looking for and approaching his mother when he is hungry.

According to the principle of *stimulus generalization,* a response learned to one stimulus is likely to be made to stimuli which are similar to the original one. Other sources of pain and discomfort (e.g., injury, cold, and illness) are sufficiently similar to the pain of hunger that the child should make the same response he made when hungry. That is, the child who approaches his mother when hungry should also approach her for nurturance (gratification of needs) when he is in pain and discomfort for other reasons. Further, because the mother is similar to other people, the infant should, in varying degrees, generalize his approach response to other people. In brief, the initial feeding situation was regarded as the basis for learning whether the mother is rewarding, and whether approaching the mother— and, by generalization, other people—leads to gratification.

If the initial feeding experience was not rewarding because the mother was tense, held her baby in an awkward manner, force-fed him, or handled him roughly, the child would experience some pain in association with the stimulus of the mother, and the sensations of hunger. If the painful stimuli occurred frequently enough and over a long enough period of time the stimulus would acquire a negative or anxiety-arousing value and she would become symbolic of discomfort rather than of pleasure. As an organism's innate reaction to discomfort and pain is withdrawal and avoidance, the infant would learn to avoid rather than to approach the mother. Moreover,

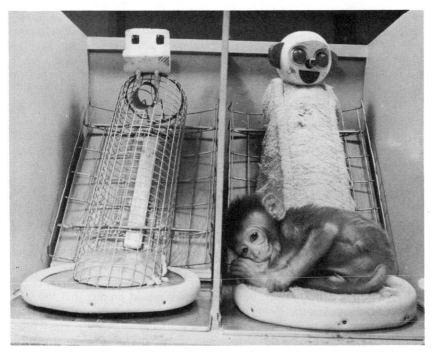

Fig. 6.1. Wire and cloth mother surrogates. (From H. F. Harlow & R. R. Zimmerman, *Science*, 1959, *130*, 422. By permission.)

the infant would not learn that approaching people in a state of discomfort might lead to gratification of his motives. Another infant, for whom the feeding experience has been predominantly pleasant, will be more likely to look to others for gratification of his needs and motives.

The results of several important experiments have complicated this simple social learning view. One of the most important series of studies was conducted by Professor Harry Harlow and his colleagues at the University of Wisconsin. Harlow placed infant monkeys with "mother" monkeys that were constructed of wire mesh. Some of these infants were fed from a bottle attached to the "chest" of a plain wire-mesh mother. Others were similarly "fed" by a wire-mesh mother that differed in just one respect from the other mother—it was covered by terry cloth (see Fig. 6.1). When the monkeys were given the choice of going to either mother, the animals characteristically chose the terry-cloth mother and spent more time clinging to her than to the plain wire-mesh mother. This was also true for infant monkeys fed only from the wire mother, and never fed from the terry-cloth mother. The infant would go to the wire mother only when hungry, feed until satisfied, and then return to the terry-cloth mother for most of the day *(26, 27)*.

Because the pain associated with hunger is reduced by the wire but

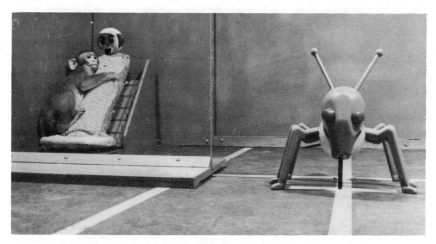

Fig. 6.2. Typical response to cloth mother in the modified open-field test. (From H. F. Harlow & R. R. Zimmerman, *Science*, 1959, *130*, 430. By permission.)

not by the terry-cloth mother, the older theory would predict that the wire mother who supplies the food should be the most rewarding stimulus and, therefore, the one with whom the monkey should spend the most time. The fact that this prediction is incorrect forces us to reassess our basic hypothesis about those events that cause an infant to become attached to another figure.

Further, when a fear-provoking stimulus (a large wooden model of a spider) was placed in the cage with the monkey, he ran to the terry-cloth mother rather than to the wire-mesh mother (see Fig. 6.2). The terry-cloth mother was more effective in reducing the infant monkey's fear than the wire mother was. When the terry-cloth mother was present, the young monkey was more likely to venture out to explore the fear-arousing stimulus. When the young animal was with the wire-mesh mother, he was more fearful and was less likely to explore the open space around the strange and "threatening" object (see Fig. 6.3).

A series of related studies stimulated by Harlow's original work suggest the following conclusions. If the young monkey is to develop normally he must have some interaction with an object to which he can cling during the opening months of life. Another monkey is best—but a terry-cloth surrogate allows the infant to cling and is, therefore, better than the wire surrogate. The clinging response is natural to the monkey, as perhaps scanning and vocalizing are to human infants. In time of stress the monkey runs to the object to which he normally clings. For example, if two chimpanzees are placed in a strange situation, they show increased clinging to each other, as if the clinging reduced fear or distress. As the chimpanzees become familiar with the originally strange situation, the mutual clinging decreases *(33)*. There seems to be a strong similarity between this behavior in the

Fig. 6.3.   Rhesus infant, raised with a cloth surrogate mother, displaying security and exploratory behavior in a strange situation in the mother's presence. From H. Harlow & M. H. Harlow. Learning to love. *Amer. Scientist,* Autumn, 1966, *54,* No. 3, 251. By permission.)

chimpanzee or the monkey and that of a 1-year-old human child who runs to his mother and hides his face in her skirts if a strange person enters the house or an unexpected noise is heard.

Let us consider another example of *attachment* before we come to some conclusions about the meaning of the word. Ethologists working with ducks and chickens have found that if a newly hatched duck first follows a strange object—such as a yellow circle or a human being, rather than its mother—it will continue to follow this object. This phenomenon has been called *imprinting (3),* as we mentioned in an earlier chapter. As with Harlow's terry-cloth-reared monkeys, the duck becomes attached to the object even though it does not alleviate or reduce pain, hunger, or discomfort in any way. In the case of the duck there does not even have to be any tactile contact between it and the object it follows. That is, the object does not have to be reinforcing. How can we explain this phenomenon?

Apparently each species is provided with a special set of responses that it can emit at birth or very soon afterwards. These responses are like reflexes, but they are more complex; the infant will emit them in response

Elliott Erwitt from Magnum

to the first appropriate stimulus that the environment supplies. The objects that elicit these responses are likely to become objects of attachment for the young animal.

In the natural environment of the jungle the young monkey clings to the hairy undersurface of his mother for several months after birth. Nature has supplied the infant monkey with a strong grasping reflex and the monkey becomes attached to those objects that allow him to display this response. The mother is the most effective stimulus for this reaction. The duck or chicken upon hatching typically follows a moving object and, under natural conditions, the biological mother will be the first moving object the young bird encounters. The chicken becomes attached to the mother because the mother allows the natural response of following to occur.

What of the human infant? What are its naturally strong reactions? The infant smiles, babbles, scans, manipulates, and holds, among other things. The mother is often the stimulus that is the target for these responses. The mother talks and stimulates the baby to babble; the mother moves her face and stimulates the child to scan it; the mother allows the baby to play with her hair and fingers and permits the manipulative responses to appear. As a result, the baby gradually becomes attached to the mother.

If the mother—in addition to allowing these responses to occur—also provides food, alleviates pain, and supplies pleasant tactile stimulation, we then have several mechanisms that will lead the child to become closely attached to the human adult—reduction of discomfort caused by hunger, thirst, or pain; the supply of pleasant sensations; and the attachment process in which the adult becomes the object for the infant's behaviors. Let us now say a few words about the hunger-feeding cycle and its contribution to the mother-child relation.

Hunger and the Feeding Situation

It is difficult to differentiate the needs of hunger and thirst in infants—milk will gratify both of them. In order to simplify the discussion, both needs will be referred to as *hunger*. Internal stimuli associated with hunger regularly mount to a high level of intensity several times a day, and the infant is almost completely dependent upon someone else for gratification of this need. If there is a long delay between the first twinges of hunger and their relief the tension may mount considerably. As such delays are unavoidable and occur frequently, hunger is the primary need that is most likely to provoke a high level of sustained discomfort; much of the child's earliest learning will involve this need. Let us consider how hunger might influence the learning of behavior toward the adult.

Consider what happens during the typical hunger-feeding cycle. The 4-month-old infant begins to feel uncomfortable. He begins to thrash and to cry and after several minutes someone comes to feed him. As the caretaker (usually the mother) feeds him, the infant gradually becomes less active. He studies her face as he feeds and experiences simultaneously the alleviation of the hunger and pain, the tactile contact with his mother, the kinesthetic stimulation from the cradled posture he is assuming, and the olfactory and auditory stimulation the mother presents. As these experiences are occurring simultaneously, the child learns two things: He learns first to associate comfortable pleasant sensations with the visual-vocal-auditory stimuli of the mother, and he learns to make the responses of scanning, babbling, smiling, clinging, and body adjustment in response to the person holding him. In short, he learns two kinds of associations—one, an association between the stimuli of the mother and the feelings of pleasure, and second, an association between the stimulus of the mother and the active responses of looking, vocalizing and postural adjustment.

The Relevance of a Feeding Situation. The student will note that we have emphasized the attachment of the child to the mother, the distinctive stimulation the mother gives the child, and the complex social interaction involving the two. We have de-emphasized the specific feeding practices the mother uses—such as whether she nurses or uses a bottle. This de-emphasis of the mode of feeding represents an important theoretical change in psychology's view of what is important in the mother-infant interaction during the first year. There is, however, still some concern with the differences between breast- and bottle-feeding, and we shall consider this issue briefly.

There have been major shifts over time in the proportion of mothers from particular social, ethnic, or personality groups who choose to breast or bottle-feed. During the period from 1930 to 1940 lower-class mothers nursed while middle-class mothers used bottles. In the current decade, the situation is the reverse. College-educated mothers prefer to nurse, while lower-class mothers almost exclusively use bottles. The mother's attitude toward the child and the kinds of social interaction that occur during feeding are more critical than whether the baby is nursed or fed by bottle. Moreover, as many American mothers tend to stop nursing before the child is 5 months of age, the type of feeding becomes even less important. One can argue that nursing is preferable to bottle-feeding because it maximizes the mother's pleasure in the feeding situation and therefore, strengthens her attachment to her child. Moreover, when the mother is nursing, she has a better opportunity to hold the child close to her and give him feelings of support, muscle relaxation, and tactile stimulation. The cradling posture the baby assumes when nursing may allow the child to make more active motor responses toward the mother. These actions can occur with bottle feeding if the child is held securely and is stimulated, talked to, and played with. However, bottle feeding will certainly be psychologically less conducive to attachment if the bottle is propped up and the mother leaves the child alone.

There is also concern with whether the child should be fed on demand (whenever he cries for food) or on a schedule. The advantages of demand feeding are that infants differ in the rate at which they become hungry. Allowing the child to feed when he becomes hungry prevents the build-up of painful hunger tensions. Moreover, if the mother decides to schedule every 3 or 4 hours, it means that the child may be fed before he desires food, while at other times he may eat only after his hunger pains have become intense—so that eating may be uncomfortable. However, it should be remembered that specific feeding practices assume their major importance because they are embedded in the matrix of the mother-child relationship. The practices employed by the mother should make the feeding situation pleasant and rewarding for the mother and allow the child's attachment to be strengthened. It must be remembered that babies are capable of adapting to the schedule of the mother. For example, D. P. Marquis experimentally investigated the problem of adaptation to a feeding schedule within the first 10 days of life (32). She measured the bodily activities (restlessness) of two groups of infants who were on different feeding schedules. Daily changes in restlessness were used as the criterion of adaptation. One group, consisting of 18 infants, was on a 4-hour feeding schedule throughout the 10-day period. Sixteen other infants were on 3-hour schedules for the first 8 days of their lives but were shifted to 4-hour schedules on the ninth day (32).

After a few days, the infants' bodily activities rose sharply immediately before their next scheduled feeding, the increase being greater and more abrupt in the 4-hour group. This provides some evidence that this group had learned to wait four hours for food.

On the day the "3-hour schedule" infants were shifted to the 4-hour schedule, there were marked changes in their activity patterns. At the end of 3 hours, their habitual feeding time, body movements increased abruptly and reached the highest level recorded during the study. Apparently this group had learned to respond to hunger cues at the end of 3 hours. Failure to receive food at this time produced extreme restlessness and activity. It may be concluded that infants just a few days old can modify their behavior in accordance with external demands such as feeding schedules.

Consequences of Attachment to the Caretaker

There are two important consequences of these early experiences of attachment and pleasure with the caretaker. First, the responses the infant makes to the caretaker will generalize to other people. Second, the infant should develop a fairly articulated schema (or mental image) for the caretaker's face, form, and voice.

Generalization of Responses from Caretaker to Another Person. The principle of generalization states that if the infant makes a set of responses to one class of stimuli he is likely to make them to similar objects, but not to objects that are very different from the original. An excellent illustration of this principle comes from a study of monkeys who were raised under a variety of conditions.

One group was initially reared by a human for 3 weeks and then placed alone in wire cages. These animals had no contact with any monkeys until they were 1 year old. A second group was reared by their natural mothers until 1 year of age. A third group was placed in isolation at birth and could neither see nor touch humans or monkeys until they were 6 months old; then they were put in wire cages until they were 1 year old. During the second year of life, all the monkeys lived in wire cages and had regular opportunities to play with other monkeys each day. When the monkeys were between 2 and 3 years of age, each was placed in a circular chamber with a human on one side and a monkey on the other. The monkey could enter either chamber or stay in the center and approach neither the human nor the monkey. The monkeys who were reared by a human for the first 3 weeks, and then isolated for the rest of the first year spent more time with the human than any other group. The early experience with the human apparently led to a preference for a human. The monkeys reared by their mother spent most of their time approaching another monkey. The monkeys reared in complete isolation for the first 6 months spent most of the time in the center of the chamber, approaching neither monkey nor man (43).

This generalization of approach responses from the earliest object of attachment to a similar object also holds for the human infant. The generalization of social responses from a mother substitute to other people has been demonstrated in a rigorous experimental study (41). The investigator selected 16 6-month-old infants who were living in an institution in which many volunteers cared for the child. For 8 of these infants (the experimental babies) the investigator herself played the role of mother 8 hours a day, 5 days a week, for 8 consecutive weeks. During this time, she bathed and diapered them, played with them, smiled at them, and tried to be as good a substitute mother as possible. The other 8 infants (control babies) were cared for in the typical institutional fashion—without individual "mother," but with several women performing these motherly duties in a more routine fashion. Moreover, the experimental babies received *more* nurturance than the controls during the 8-week period. Thus the experimental babies differed from the controls in two ways: they had one person care for them consistently during the 8-week period, and they received more caretaking during this period.

All infants were tested each week during the 8-week experimental period and for 4 additional weeks following the termination of the experimental treatment. The test administered included tests of social responsiveness to three kinds of people (the experimenter, an examiner who gave them other tests, and, at the end of the 8-week period, a stranger), as well as a postural development and cube-manipulation test.

The results revealed that the 8 infants who had been cared for by the mother (i.e., the experimenter) showed much more social responsiveness to the experimenter, the examiner, and the stranger, than the control children did (41; see Fig. 6.4). That is, when these people smiled or talked to the children, the experimentally treated infants were more likely to smile back or show some facial reaction to the adults than the normally treated children, the effect being most marked in response to the experimenter. These results clearly support the hypothesis that acts learned in response to a nurturant and socially stimulating caretaker will generalize to other people. There were no significant differences in the motor development of the two groups as measured by the cube and posture tests. Apparently, the experience of having the consistently nurturant and stimulating mother figure had minimal effect on simple motor skills, but a dramatic effect on social behavior (41). The author believed that the critical factor responsible for the increased social responsiveness of the experimental babies was the reciprocal and playful social stimulation that occurred between child and adult.

The responses of scanning and studying the face, like social responsiveness, can generalize from the mother to a picture of a face. Mothers and their 3-month-old infants were observed in the home and the observers noted how often the mother assumed a face-to-face position with her baby. A week later the infants were brought to the laboratory and shown pictures of human faces, and picture of checkerboards. The infant girls who looked longest at the pictures of faces experienced the most frequent face-to-face contact with their mothers at home. The long scanning was specific to the

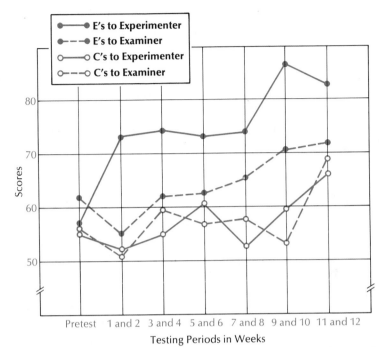

Fig. 6.4. The average social responsiveness of the experimental (E) and control (C) infants to the experimental examiner over 12 testing periods. (From H. L. Reingold. The modification of social responsiveness in institutional babies. *Monogr. Soc. Res. Child Developm.*, copyright 1956 by The Society for Research in Child Development, Inc., *21*, 23. By permission.)

face pictures, because these girls did not look very long at the checkerboards (36).

Establishment of a Schema. A second hypothetical consequence of the infant's attachment to the mother is that the infant develops a finely articulated schema for his mother, especially her face. It is assumed that the infant acquires a mental image of the person who is the object of attachment. As a result, the infant has a tendency to react with fear and to avoid people that differ from the caretaker. This phenomenon is illustrated by detailed study of the imprinting process in ducks, to which we referred earlier. Immediately after hatching, the duck has a strong tendency to approach and to follow a moving object and he will become imprinted on it. However, 13 hours after hatching, the duck begins to show avoidance responses and will not follow a strange object (3). The time for imprinting is over. It appears that it takes about 13 hours for the duck to develop an articulated schema for the first attachment object it encounters. Now any

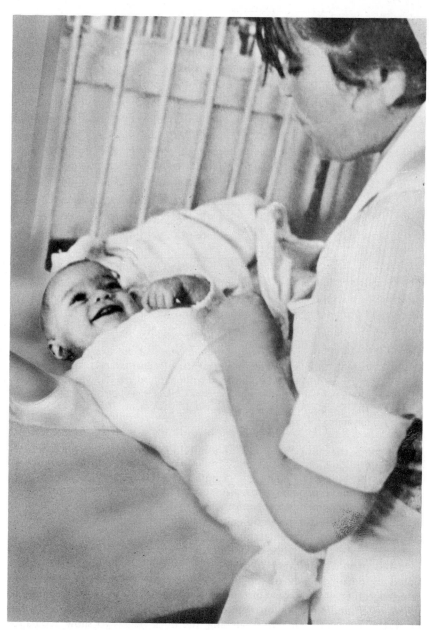

Fig. 6.5. Four-month-old institution infant smiling at caretaker while being dressed. (From J. L. Gewirtz. The cause of infant smiling in four child-rearing environments in Israel. In B. M. Foss (Ed.), *Determinants of infant behavior.* Vol. III. London: Methuen, 1965. By permission of the publisher and The Tavistock Institute of Human Relations.)

object that is discrepant elicits an avoidance reaction and a distress call. Similarly, the infant of 6 to 8 months of age passes through a temporary period during which it shows fear and avoidance of a strange person. This phenomenon is called *stranger anxiety*. At this time, the infant has developed a clear enough schema of the caretaker's face so that he may react to a strange person with some fear and turning away.

But the malleability of the infant's system is seen exquisitely in the fact that this extreme avoidance and fear are short-lived. After sufficient exposure to others the infant does not react with intense fear any more, and may even generalize the approach response it had learned to the original caretaker to new people. Once the child has learned a schema for a particular object the infant may react initially with anxiety to a slightly dissimilar object. But, with continued exposure to the strange object, the period of anxiety passes.

The Smile

An overt sign that the young infant displays when he has acquired a schema of a face is a smile in response to it. At 4 months of age most infants will smile at a still representation of a human face. No movement or voice is necessary, although movement of the face and voice increases the probability that the smile will occur. It appears that 4-month-old infants from various cultural environments are likely to show a smile to a face looking directly at them (see Fig. 6.5).

Gewirtz studied the smiling of three groups of infants raised under different conditions in Israel (17). Institutionalized infants living in residential buildings rarely saw their parents and received routine institutional care. Kibbutz infants lived in collective settlements. They were raised in large houses with professional caretakers but were fed frequently during the first year by their own mothers. Family-reared children were raised in typically Western apartments by their mothers. Figure 6.6 graphs the frequency of smiling to a strange woman's face while the baby lay in the crib. The peak for smiling for the kibbutz- and family-reared infants was a few weeks earlier than the peak for the infants raised in the institution. But the peak age for all infants was very close to 4 months of age (17).

These findings suggest that it takes about 3 to 4 months of exposure to develop some schema for a human face. The smile at 4 months may be the infant's way of saying that he recognizes the facial stimulus. The smile does not always signify a recognition response, however. Many newborn infants smile long before they develop a schema for anything, and 1-year-old babies will smile at someone who smiles back at them. The smile reflects different messages at different ages.

Effect of the Smile on the Mother. The infant's tendency to smile a lot or little can affect the nature of the mother-child relation. The mother typically interprets the smile as a sign that her baby is happy and content and, by inference, that she is an effective mother. If her infant is an in-

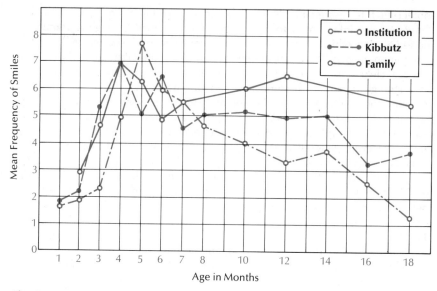

Fig. 6.6. Frequency of smiling among infants raised in three different environments. (From J. L. Gewirtz. The cause of infant smiling in four child-rearing environments in Israel. In B. M. Foss (Ed.), *Determinants of infant behavior.* Vol. III. London: Methuen, 1965. By permission of the publishers and The Tavistock Institute of Human Relations.)

frequent smiler she may begin to doubt her maternal competence and worry about her ability to make her infant contented and pleased. Although frequency of smiling can be increased if an adult responds to the child's smile by picking him up (4), there are unlearned differences among infants in the tendency to smile. Even among family-reared infants who have had considerable exposure to a human face, some will show lots of smiling to a strange face or a clay mask, while others will smile very little. These individual differences are also present in newborns. Some premature babies were consistently high smilers; others rarely smiled (13). Moreover, infant boys who smile frequently tend to be fatter than infrequent smilers, who are often short and wiry. These differences in the readiness to smile may play an important role in the dynamic interaction between the mother and her infant. The smile rewards the mother, and increases her involvement with her infant. The mother behaves as if the smile were a reinforcement for her efforts—the infant's way of rewarding the mother for her good works. If some babies are biologically predisposed to be easy and frequent smilers, they are likely to elicit more approach behavior from their mother than nonsmiling infants.

The Relation of Attachment and Anxiety

As suggested in an earlier chapter, continued experience with a particular object leads to the establishment of a schema for that object; as a result, the infant becomes vulnerable to the experience of fear when he encounters an event that is discrepant from his schema. The infant is subject to many instances of fear, but two major classes of anxiety seem to grow out of a close attachment to an adult. One is called *stranger anxiety;* the other, *separation anxiety.*

Anxiety as a Reaction to Discrepancy. We have suggested that one of the early causes of distress in the infant is an encounter with a stimulus that involves a moderate discrepancy from a schema that the infant has already established. The anxiety to a strange human face—to which we alluded earlier—is a clear example of this phenomenon. Let us consider this common and dramatic event. The child at 8 months is sitting in his high chair, playing with his cereal. A strange woman enters the kitchen and stands facing the baby. The infant studies the stranger for 10 seconds; his face tightens, and suddenly he begins to cry. It is clear that the stranger has elicited the cry, for if the stranger leaves, the child becomes happy again. If the stranger reappears, it is likely that the child will cry again. We call this event *stranger anxiety* and in American children it is typically seen first at about 6 months of age, showing a peak frequency at 8 months, and then gradually vanishing by the time the child is 12 to 15 months old. Moreover, the infant is less likely to show fear to the stranger if he is sitting on his mother's lap rather than sitting a few feet from her—much as Harlow's monkeys were less fearful if they were holding the terry-cloth mother than if they were separated from it (35). Apparently, proximity to the mother inhibits the fear, as if the child felt more secure when held by her.

This display of fear to an object that partially resembles one for which a schema has been formed can also be seen in kittens. In one study 5-week-old kittens were given one of three treatments (8). One group of kittens was handled and played with by a different person 5 days a week for 4 weeks. A second group was given the same handling for the same length of time, but was handled by only one experimenter. The third group of kittens was given no handling at all. At the end of each 5-day period during the 4 weeks of handling, a stranger test was given each kitten. Each kitten was handled by a stranger who did not know to which group a particular kitten belonged. Each week a different stranger was used. The kittens who were either handled by only one experimenter or were not handled at all showed the most fear; they made many attempts to escape or they froze or retreated when called. Apparently the kittens who were exposed to several different people were able to adapt more easily to the stranger because being handled by a stranger was not a *discrepant* experience. The kittens handled by one person showed little fear of the person to whom they had become accustomed; but they, as well as those handled by no one, showed fear to all other strangers—a feline form of "stranger anxiety" —because the strangers were discrepant stimuli (8; see Fig. 6.7).

The sequence of infant smiling in response to a familiar schema at 4 months and anxiety to a strange face at 8 months resembles the imprinting

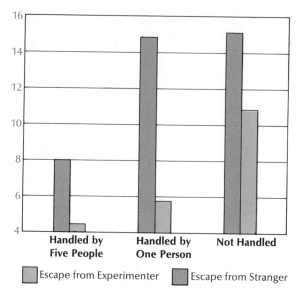

Escape from Experimenter Escape from Stranger

Fig. 6.7. Differences in number of escape attempts among kittens raised under three varied conditions. (Adapted from R. R. Collard. Fear of strangers and play behavior in kittens with varied social experience. *Child Developm.*, copyright 1967 by The Society for Research in Child Development, Inc., *38*, 883. By permission.)

sequence in ducks; you will recall that the ducks approach a moving object for the first 13 hours of life but avoid it after that.

The infant—human or bird—initially shows approach responses to the object encountered most regularly. After a firm schema for that object has developed, they may show some temporary fear to stimuli that resemble the original object. Why is there this period of temporary fear? Why is not the fear permanent? Why does it ever develop at all? Mental development consists, in large measure, of the development of schemata for objects and events. As schemata become established more firmly, the infant encounters stimuli that are a bit discrepant but that do bear a partial resemblance to his particular schema. It is reasonable to guess that the infant's reaction to the discrepant event will depend on whether he has some response to make to it—some way of interpreting it or acting upon it. If the infant has a reaction, he is not likely to become anxious and cry. In fact, he may signify his ability to deal with the strange event by smiling or laughing.

The emergence of stranger anxiety is interpreted as indicating that by 6 to 8 months, most infants have developed such a good schema for their mother's face that the stranger is a discrepancy. The infant is alerted. But he is too immature to make any constructive response to this discrepant stimulus. He cannot deal with the strange person and, as a result, he cries. Five months later he is more mature and is able to do something. He can ask, "Who is that, Mommy?"; he can run to his mother; or he will have been exposed to so many strange faces that his schema for a face will be more generalized. A new face becomes a less discrepant event than it was 5 months earlier.

Separation Anxiety. A second form of anxiety makes its appearance in American infants of about 10 months of age, and begins to vanish by the time the child is 18 months of age. The event that elicits the fear is different from the one that causes stranger anxiety. The child is playing in the living room with some toys; he sees his mother go to the front door and leave. As the door closes he begins to cry. This is separation anxiety. A 7-month-old American infant would typically not cry in this situation. Why then does the 1-year-old? On the surface, this fear does not seem similar to stranger anxiety. The child has seen the mother leave the house many times and, therefore, this event should not be discrepant from an acquired schema. Before considering various interpretations let us compare the experiences of a typical middle-class American infant with those of an infant from another culture.

The American infant spends most of his time in a crib in a room separate from the mother. During at least half of his waking hours he is alone scanning the room, playing with his fingers, watching shadows on the wall, studying a mobile, playing with his crib, watching the curtains. The mother comes to her baby primarily when he cries, when she thinks he is hungry, or when she thinks he needs a diaper changed. The single human being he comes to know better than any other is his mother. However, because his mother is not always near him, he also learns to make responses to objects, such as pieces of blanket and stuffed animals in his crib. Many American infants become intimately attached to their furry animals or pieces of blanket.

Let us now look at a baby raised in a different situation—a small hut in Uganda. Uganda is a small country in the Eastern part of Africa tucked between Kenya on the east and the Republic of the Congo on the west. Uganda babies are typically nursed until they are 2 years old. Most American infants are either not nursed or are weaned from the breast before they are 5 months old. A Uganda mother is usually available to her child and the infant is often fed on demand. Toilet training is begun early and is initiated by the mother, who holds the baby in a squatting position with the mother supporting him and the baby holding onto the mother. Thus the infant makes clinging responses to the mother early in the first year while he is being bowel-trained. The American mother usually lets her baby soil his diapers during the first year, and the baby lies passively in the crib while he is being changed. Also the Uganda mother carries her baby with her most of the day—either straddled across her hip, or held in place on her back by a sling of cotton cloth. The baby goes with the mother most of the day and does not experience the mother's leaving the room or the hut, an event the American baby experiences many times each day.

In sum, the American baby spends most of his first 6 months in a crib alone; the Uganda baby spends most of his time being held by someone (1).

The Uganda baby shows anxiety to separation from the mother as early as 6 months of age—2 to 4 months before a typical middle-class American infant will show this reaction (1). Why should the 6-month Uganda baby cry when his mother leaves when this reaction does not occur in an average American infant until 10 to 12 months? There are several possible interpretations. One involves the earlier notion that a discrepancy from a schema elicits anxiety. As the Uganda infant is usually with his mother, the perception of the mother leaving him is an obviously discrepant event. If he has no other response to make to it he will cry.

Because the American infant is not with his mother continually he requires more time to develop a schema in which the mother is an essential stimulus element of his immediate situation. That is, the infant has some schema for his immediate context and when he is very young the mother is not an essential part of this schema. However, as he matures and the mother becomes a more distinctive object, it becomes more likely that if she is in the room where he is playing, she will be an essential part of his schema for the "room." It is reasonable to assume that the more regular the presence of the mother, the earlier the infant will reach the point where he includes the mother as part of his schema. The Uganda baby is with his mother almost continually, so we would expect him to regard the mother as an essential part of every situation. Her absence presents a discrepancy that elicits anxiety. The American infant does not reach this stage until 10 or 11 months of age.

The above interpretation of separation anxiety rests in part, on the same fundamental principle that was used to explain stranger anxiety—even though these two fears do not look similar on the surface. There is, however, a second possible interpretation with a slightly different flavor that is more closely related to our earlier discussion of attachment.

The infant, like the older child and adult, learns specific responses to particular stimulus situations. After many repetitions of these stimulus-response chains, such responses become habitual. The adult typically sits in the same chair at breakfast every morning, despite the availability of perhaps three other chairs. The 3-year-old child always takes the same furry toy to bed with him despite the availability of newer and more colorful ones. Moreover, if we prevent the person from making the habitual response he may become upset. If the 3-year-old is not allowed to take his favorite furry dog to bed, he is likely to cry, even though other toy dogs are available.

It appears, therefore, that when a response becomes very strong to a particular situation or object (i.e., habitual), disruption of the response can lead to anxiety.

Let us see if this hypothesis applies to separation anxiety. The baby is continually responding to his mother, looking at her, smiling, vocalizing, and clinging to her. The frequency of these actions increases when he is mildly aroused. When the mother leaves, the child is prevented from making these habitual responses; the response sequence is disrupted and he may cry. The Uganda baby, who is continually with his mother, builds up stronger responses earlier than the American infant does; thus he should show separation anxiety earlier.

This interpretation of separation anxiety implies that the closer the attachment of the baby to the mother, the more frequent and intense the separation anxiety. The Uganda baby, we infer, is more closely attached to its mother than the American baby and this inference fits with the fact that he has many more opportunities to scan, cling, hold, manipulate, and play with his mother than an American baby of the same age.

The opportunity to make a response that might bring the infant into closer contact with the mother seems to allay the infant's fear. In a series of studies Rheingold placed 10-month-old children in a strange room under one of four conditions: with the mother, with a stranger, with toys, or completely alone (40). As long as the mother was in the room the infant did not cry. But the infants who were not with their mothers were likely to cry within 1 minute of being placed in the room; the presence of toys or a stranger did not help (40). These observations suggest that the strangeness of the room (an event that is discrepant from the child's schema) produced the fear. But the presence of the mother protected the child from anxiety. The critical importance of the availability of a response that brought the child into visual or physical contact with the mother is illustrated in the following observations. The 10-month-old infant was placed with the mother in a room which had an open door that led to the same strange empty room that had made most of the other infants cry. The infants in this situation often crawled into the empty room *but did not cry when they arrived there.* The infant would look around and then crawl back to his mother in the adjoining room. For a short period of time the infant was alone in the same strange room that had made the other infants cry. The difference was that these babies could do something effective if they became apprehensive—they could crawl back to their mother. The infants who cried in the earlier observations could do nothing.

In sum, it appears that separation anxiety may involve three components—the discrepancy that is produced by being separated from the mother, the disruption of habitual responses to the mother, and the inability to make any relevant response that brings him to his mother. Separation anxiety should vanish when the mother's absence is no longer a discrepant event or when the child can do something about the mother's absence. Both of these changes occur with age. As the child grows, he experiences more frequent separations from his mother and, with maturity, he is able to interpret her absence and reassure himself of her return.

This interpretation of separation anxiety, which is conjectural, differs from a past interpretation that emphasized the conditioning of anxiety to the mother's absence. The older interpretation assumed that the child was most likely to experience pain and distress when his mother was absent and not available to care for him. The conditioned stimulus was the mother's absence and the unconditioned stimulus was the discomfort of hunger, cold, or pain. As a result, the infant learned to become afraid when he saw his mother leave him. The problem with this explanation is that it predicts that infants who are rarely separated from their mothers should be deprived of the opportunity of learning this association, and therefore, should not show separation anxiety. However, the Uganda infants, who are rarely away from their mothers, show earlier and more intense separation anxiety than American infants who do experience periods of maternal absence. Thus the interpretation that assumes that intensity of attachment determines separation anxiety seems more reasonable.

Let us now consider infants raised under conditions of minimal contact with a caretaker, where attachment should be very weak. In order to do this, we must look at infants who are raised in institutional environments.

Lack of a Primary Caretaker: The Institutionalized Child

A child who does not have a primary adult devoted to his care should not become attached to an adult. He should be less likely to show stranger and separation anxiety, and he should be less socially responsive than family-reared children. He should be less likely to smile, vocalize, laugh, or approach adults, and he should be retarded in language.

We know that absence of any relation with a living object has grave consequences for the infant monkey. If a monkey is placed in isolation for the first 6 months of his life, he shows extremely abnormal behavior when he is removed from isolation. He avoids all social contact, appears very fearful, clutches at himself and crouches (27; see Fig. 6.8). If the period of isolation is less than 6 months, the monkey usually recovers and, after a while, begins to approach normal behavior. But if the isolation lasts longer than 6 months or over a year, the social and sexual behavior of the monkey is abnormal indeed. Often these monkeys do not recover and never interact appropriately with others. They show extreme fear and occasional aggression (27).

Even the monkeys who were raised with the terry-cloth mothers described earlier, and who seemed secure with them, were initially fearful with other monkeys and did not show normal social or sexual behavior when they grew up. After a year of living with other monkeys they gradually recovered, but absence of a living mother with whom the infant monkey could interact seriously affected their social behavior. We do not know the critical actions that a live mother performs that produce normal psychological growth. Movement is probably one of these critical factors. Monkeys raised with a terry-cloth mother who was attached to a motor (the terry-cloth mother moved irregularly in the cage) were less fearful and socially more responsive than monkeys raised with stationary terry-cloth mothers (33).

No human child is raised in total isolation, but the effects of lack of a caretaker can be studied in infants raised in an institution. A child raised

Fig. 6.8. The monkey raised in isolation shows unusual posture in the cage. (From H. Harlow & M. H. Harlow. Learning to love. *Amer. Scientist,* Autumn, 1966, *54,* No. 3, 264. By permission.)

in an institutional environment, even a clean and conscientiously administered one, has dramatically less opportunity to become attached to an adult. Hence he should show less anxiety when an adult leaves, develop less well-articulated schema of an adult face, and be less likely to develop stranger anxiety. As the infant does not have the opportunity to engage in face-to-face vocalization, he should be less vocal; and because his crying rarely brings anyone, the frequency of his crying or protesting should decrease gradually.

Research on Institutionalization. During the early 1940s Rene Spitz observed the behavior of young children who spent their first year in institutions where care was inadequate and inconsistent (*45*). During the second half of the first year, 15 percent of the infants began to develop an unusual sequence of behavior. At first they cried continually, but after several months the crying subsided and they began to become indifferent to adults. "The children would lie or sit with wide open, expressionless eyes, frozen, immobile face, and a far away expression as if in a daze, apparently not perceiving what went on in their environment" (*45,* 314). (It is of more than incidental interest that Harlow's juvenile monkeys who were raised on wire surrogate mothers are described in a way that is similar to Spitz' earlier descriptions of the institutionalized infants.)

Some of these children may have been physically ill, either suffering from serious malnutrition or chronic infectious diseases. However, these observations alerted many psychologists and psychiatrists to the possible psychological consequences of institutional living, and better-controlled studies have corroborated the conclusion that institutionalized babies are markedly different from those raised in families.

Provence and Lipton observed 75 babies living in an institutional environment in the United States where nutrition and care were adequate and the infants were not physically ill (37). The description of the institutional environment will help the reader appreciate the conditions under which these infants lived.

> The younger group of infants (age 4 days to 8 months) occupied cribs placed singularly in glass partitioned cubicles. The room was clean, cheerful and light with adequate heat and ventilation. The infants were fed in their cribs with bottles propped. When cereals, fruits and vegetables were added to the diet they were also given in a propped bottle with a large holed nipple rather than given by spoon. . . . Sometimes a stuffed toy was placed in the crib for the baby to look at. After about 4 months of age, simple rattles, beads and so on, were placed on a string suspended across the crib sides and the single playpen which contained other age appropriate toys. . . . Each infant in this group shared the time and attention of the attendant with 7 to 9 other infants in the same age range for the 8 hour period of the day when she was present. For the remaining 16 hours of the day, there was no person in the nursery except at feeding time when an attendant who also had similar duties in other nurseries heated formulas, propped bottles, and changed diapers (37).

Not only were the infants fed without the presence of an adult, but there was minimal variability in their experience. There were no vocalizations from other people, no reciprocal play, no close relationship between a child's crying and the reaction of someone else.

In considering how these babies were different from those raised in families it should be noted, first, that there were *no* major differences between normal and institutionalized babies prior to 3 or 4 months of age. It is only after 4 months that the differences became evident. The institutionalized babies vocalized very little; they showed no cooing, no babbling, and little crying. Moreover, they did not adapt their postures to the arms of an adult, "they felt something like sawdust dolls; they moved, they bent easily at the proper joints, but they felt stiff or wooden" (37).

These infants were not picked up very often and, therefore, one would not expect them to make the kinds of postural adjustments that babies ordinarily make. By 8 months of age most of these infants were markedly less interested in grasping or approaching toys, and they began to lose interest in their external environment. During the second half of the first year, body rocking became very common and was more frequent than would be observed among family-reared babies. Stranger anxiety was rare, and the infants' facial expressions were bland and clearly not so expressive as those of family-reared infants. If they were frustrated, they would cry passively or turn away; rarely would they make an attempt to conquer a frustration. Finally, language was delayed. There were no words at all at 1 year of age and vocalization and language were the behaviors that were most seriously depressed. The following is a description of one of these babies at 45 weeks of age.

> Outstanding were his soberness, his forlorn appearance, and lack of animation. The interest that he showed in the toys was mainly for holding, inspecting and rarely mouthing. When he was unhappy he now had a cry that sounded neither demanding nor angry—just miserable—and it was usually accompanied by his beginning to rock. The capacity for protest which he had earlier was much diminished. He did not turn to adults to relieve his distress or to involve them in a playful or pleasurable interchange. He made no demands. The active approach to the world, which had been one of the happier aspects of his earlier development, vanished. As one made active and persistent efforts at a social interchange he became somewhat more responsive, animated and motorically active, but lapsed into his depressed and energy-less appearance when the adult became less active with him (37, 134–135).

There were two descriptive comments by observers that seemed to convey the impression Teddy made at this time: one was, "the light in Teddy has gone out"; the other was: "if you crank his motor you can get him to go a little; he can't start on his own" (ibid.).

All of the behaviors that were most likely to be learned as a result of interaction with an adult (i.e., clinging, crying to distress, approaching adults for play, and vocalization) were most clearly retarded or absent in the institutionalized children.

Degree of behavioral retardation in institutionalized children was also studied in two types of institutions in Iran (11). In the first, called the deprived setting, the child was never placed on his stomach, and hence could not practice creeping. He was not held in a sitting position while being fed and had no toys with which to play. In addition, only one attendant was provided for every eight children, so that interpersonal contacts of any sort were severely limited. In the second institution, called the enriched setting, the child was often placed on his stomach, was held while eating, had toys and playthings, and in general received considerably greater attention. In this latter setting, one attendant was provided for every three children.

The children in both settings typically entered the institution shortly after birth. During the second year of life, the behavior of the 50 children in the deprived setting was compared with the behavior of the 20 children in the enriched setting. While only 42 percent of the deprived children could sit alone, 90 percent of the enriched children could do so. Secondly, less than 5 percent of the deprived group could stand or walk while holding on to a support, while over 60 percent of the other children could perform these responses. Finally, no child in the deprived institution could walk alone, while 3 of the 20 children in the enriched setting were able to do so.

The lack of opportunity to learn the motor acts of sitting and walking in the deprived setting was primarily responsible for the observed behavioral retardation of children in this group. The deprived children were not allowed to practice creeping or sitting and, consequently, were retarded in these responses. However, the deprived children also showed more head-shaking and repetitive rocking of the body and appeared more unhappy than the enriched children.

Relevant Variables in Institutionalization. In the opinion of some workers, the crucial variable involved in the behavioral correlates of insti-tutionalization is absence of a mother figure. Others tend to blame lack of toys, monotonous sensory environment, poor nutrition, or disease. But neither institutionalization nor mothering is a unitary variable. Institutions vary in the amount of individual attention a child is given, in the degree of sensory and motor stimulation provided, and through the opportunity to play with other children and to learn to manipulate toys and other objects. In the studies cited above, there were marked differences among the insti-tutions involved with respect to all of these variables.

As far as mothering is concerned, among children's own biological mothers there are great interindividual differences in actual procedures of child handling. Furthermore, it can be questioned whether biological mothers are necessarily superior to all mother surrogates in child care. It has not yet been clearly established whether continuous care of the infant by one adult exclusively is more conducive to development of intellectual and emotional health than a setting which includes additional caretakers—so-called multiple-mothering (48). Preliminary studies of infants (15, 16, 38, 39) cared for by more than one mother indicate that divisions of parental responsibility may not necessarily affect either intellectual or emotional development adversely. In fact, one study (39) suggests that such rearing, in the context of a collective Israeli farm, may reduce some of the emotional problems found in overly intense individual family relationships—such as overattachment to the opposite-sex parent, excessive competition, hos-tility toward the same-sex parent, and extreme sibling rivalry. Obviously, much remains to be learned about the different consequences of individual-versus multiple-mothering, as well as the effects of differing patterns of multiple-mothering (e.g., one central mother figure with assistants versus a more equal division of mothering duties).

The potential danger of speaking loosely about the damaging effects of maternal deprivation or institutionalization without attempting to specify further the actual variables involved, is well illustrated in a report (5) on two residential nurseries in the Soviet Union where psychological care is adequate. In these nurseries, which are maintained primarily for research purposes, children are raised from birth to about 3 years of age. At one nursery, the most prominent feature of the child-rearing program is its stress on physical development, including diet, sleep, and, most particularly, an elaborate schedule of daily massages and exercises in which the child is involved beginning at 60 days of age.

At the other, children spend the first 3 years of life in a well-equipped nursery which includes such things as specially designed walkers and play-pens. According to Brackbill,

> [M]ore usual than its furnishings is the nursery's program for verbal-motor stimulation of its children. This is regarded by the staff as a matter of great importance and something that merits their sustained efforts. As a part of the overall plan, every nurse has specific duties that she performs each day with all infants individually. As an example of "verbal duties," the task for Nurse A might be to ask each infant in turn, "Where is the cat?", "Where is the visitor?", "Show me your ear.", "Show me your hand.", and so on. In each case, the child's answer is followed by appropriate reinforcement. When the mother visits—and she is urged to visit often—she has access to the nurse's list of stimulants and is encouraged to further the verbal and motor training herself.

> Attention to verbal and motor development is carried over to the toddler group. But in addition, a new goal is added to their program of upbringing. Staff efforts are now also focused on the child's development of self-help and independence. . . . The one to three year olds are shown how to pick up their toys before midday dinner, how to feed themselves, how to get along socially with their three table companions at dinner time, how to prepare themselves for a nap after dinner (5, 10–11).

No adverse effects of this kind of institutionalization have been evident in the children at either nursery—physically, socially, emotionally, or intellectually.

If one thinks of the negative aspects of institutionalization in terms of such component variables as the absence of close interactions between a child and mother surrogate, minimal opportunities for social learning and development of motor responses, and lack of varied sensory stimulation, then it appears that the Russian nurseries described above meet few of the criteria for an institution. In many respects, in fact, they appear more closely to resemble well-ordered nurturant homes.

Later Consequents of Inadequate Mothering

The studies cited above were limited primarily to infants and very young children, but another investigator, Goldfarb (18–25), focused his attention on the later development of children who had experienced lack of a caretaker. Orphans who had been reared in an institution for the first 3 years of their lives before being transferred to foster homes were compared with others (matched in age and sex) who had been brought up in foster homes since infancy. Subjects were drawn from four age groups, averaging approximately 3½, 6½, 8½, and 12 years. There were extensive case studies, observations, and test data (intelligence, education, achievement, personality, motor coordination, social maturity, and language ability) available on the children.

Children raised in the institution during the first 3 years were inferior to the foster children on all tests of intelligence. Their greatest weaknesses were in the areas of concept formation, reasoning, and abstract thinking. As late as in adolescence, institution-reared children had difficulty with tests involving learning songs and stories, recalling the past clearly, or anticipating the future.

Many of the institution-reared children were subsequently adopted into foster homes that were intellectually and emotionally more stimulating than the institution. Despite this, they continued to be retarded in mental growth.

Moreover, specific language and speech difficulties, often noted among institution children (11), persisted long after the child left the institution. Apparently, the early lack of interaction resulted in a restricted capacity for language development which was not overcome in spite of long periods of ordinary school, family, and community experience (19, 23).

The behavior of the institution-reared children differed from the foster-home children in three major ways. The former were noticeably more aggressive (temper tantrums, lying, stealing, destruction of property, kicking and hitting other children), more dependent on adults (demand attention, ask for unnecessary help), and more distractible and hyperactive. Case records showed that children reared in institutions did not develop strong or affectionate personal attachments, but remained emotionally cold and isolated, capable of only the most superficial interpersonal relationships. According to the author, these social and emotional difficulties, which persisted into adolescence, were related to the severe deprivations experienced in infancy when "strong anchors to specific adults were not established" (21, 22, 25).

Although language development and social responsiveness appear to be most adversely affected as a result of deprived institutional care, other areas of development may not be impaired to the same degree. For example, Dennis (10) investigated institutionalized children between 2 and 12 months of age and between 4½ and 6 years of age. Both groups were living in a Lebanese institution, called the Creche, in which personal care was minimal. Although the children 2 to 12 months of age did not perform as well as normals on standard mental test items, the 5-year-olds were not markedly inferior to normal subjects in tests of memory and drawing. Dennis believes that the institutionalized infants performed more poorly than normals because they had no opportunity to learn the skills necessary to solve the memory and drawing test items at 1 year of age. That is, the restriction of activity and absence of stimulation and materials may have temporarily prevented the institutional children from practicing the tasks that they were required to do on the test at 1 year of age. This retardation was not so permanent as it appeared during the first 12 months, for the 5-year-olds in the institution were not seriously retarded in memory and drawing. Dennis acknowledges, however, that the language retardation shown by the institutional children was more permanent for it was present in the 5-year-old institutionalized children as well as in the younger group.

One of the most famous follow-up studies of children raised in institutions (44) involved a group of infants who had been raised in an orphanage until the age of 2 and then separated into two groups. One group of 13 seriously retarded children was transferred from this orphanage to institutions for the mentally retarded before they were 3 years old. The contrast group consisted of 12 children who were matched with the experimental group, but the contrast group remained in the orphanage until placement at a later time. During childhood the transferred children raised by *older mentally retarded children* showed a greater increase in IQ than did the contrast group who were still in the orphanage, being cared for in the usual institutional way. These two groups of children were studied again when they were adults, 20 years after their transfer from either the orphanage or the institution for the mentally retarded. (Unfortunately, there was a disproportionate number of girls in the transferred group and boys in the contrast group.) In adulthood, all 13 children of the transferred children were self-supporting, and none was a ward of any institution. In the contrast group, 1 person had died in adolescence following continued residence in a state institution; 4 were still wards of institutions. Four members of the transferred group had one or more years of college, and 1 had received a bachelor's degree and taken some graduate training. The average IQ of the children of the transferred group was much higher than that of the contrast group (44).

In sum, lack of a consistent interaction with a caretaker—which is one of the major deficits in an institutional setting—leads to depressed and abnormal social behavior and retarded language development. Institutional living, however, does not retard all aspects of psychological development. These children do eventually develop motor skills and their memory and drawing performances are at least satisfactory. Socially isolated monkeys also seem to perform in a satisfactory manner on simple problems requiring discrimination or memory—despite their very abnormal patterns of social behavior. The responses that are primarily maturational, especially the perceptual and motor skills of object manipulation and postural development, are least likely to be permanently affected by severe deprivation of consistent interactions with an adult. Responses that are acquired through and involved in social interaction, such as language and social responsiveness, appear to be most vulnerable to deprivation experiences. The lack of sufficient interaction with an adult specifically affects language, social responsiveness, emotional involvement with others, and a desire to work at problems in order to obtain adult approval and praise.

In a test situation with an adult, most children will be eager to do well in order to obtain acceptance and praise from the adult examiner. The deprived child does not view the adult as a potential source of acceptance. Thus the deprived child will not be highly motivated on the test and will appear sullen, apathetic, or indifferent. In time, the severely deprived child may become incapable of an emotional involvement with people.

One aspect of institutional living that should be emphasized is the lack of distinctive stimulation and the lack of variability in stimulation. The institutional environment is monotonous, but this is not the same as *no* stimulation. Some psychologists have suggested that lower-class children from so-called deprived environments do not have enough sensory stimulation and, as a result, are retarded mentally (see p. 566). Compare the quiet bedroom of a suburban middle-class home in the country with an urban one-room ghetto apartment. If one measured the *amount* of stimulation in physical terms, the environment of the city child would contain much more stimulus energy than that of the middle-class infant. But the middle-class infant lives in a stimulus environment that is highly variable and distinctive. Moreover, the infant attends to and learns most from distinctive stimulation—stimuli that attract his attention. A mother's voice breaking the quiet of the bedroom and addressed directly to the infant when he is alert has the maximal probability of attracting the young infant's attention, and therefore, of teaching him something. A voice yelling over a television set in a sea of noise is less distinctive and is less likely to recruit the infant's attention.

The importance of distinctiveness of stimulation is illustrated in the observations of lower- and upper-middle-class mothers of 4-month-old girls (29). When the upper-middle-class mothers vocalized to their infants, they were likely to be face-to-face with them and not providing any other stimulation. They were not tickling them, touching them, or patting them. The mother's vocalization to the infant was maximally distinctive. The lower-class mother was apt to talk to her infant when she was feeding, diapering, or burping the baby. As a result, the vocalization was less distinctive, for the infant may have been attending to the tactile or kinesthetic stimuli that accompanied the diapering or burping. It is probably more than coincidence that the upper-middle-class girl produces more variable sounds and shows precocious language development during the first 2 years of life.

It is helpful to take a relativistic view of the stimulus events that occur during the first year. The issue is not the amount of sensory stimulation the infant receives, but its variety and distinctiveness—i.e., quality rather than quantity.

Cultural Factors

Child-rearing techniques vary from one culture to another. Whiting and Child (47) found a wide variety of feeding practices in 51 cultural groups for which they had data. The Marquesans, for example, do not indulge their children, and nurse them only a short time. Marquesan mothers, fearing disfigurement of their breasts, generally wean their infants within the first year. At the other extreme, the Chenchu tribe of India allow their children to nurse until they are 5 or 6. The Lepcha of India ordinarily wean their children by the age of 3, but youngest children are occasionally allowed to nurse until puberty.

There are also great cultural differences in the severity of the weaning process. Thus, among the Baiga, weaning is accomplished entirely by techniques of punishment, whereas the Kurtatchi attempt a gradual build-up of the child's satisfactions in eating like an adult, without actively discouraging him from nursing.

Subgroups within our own culture employ different feeding practices with their children. About 25 years ago, Davis and Havighurst (9) studied the child-rearing practices of lower- and middle-class white and Negro mothers. Their data, obtained from intensive interviews with 200 women, showed that permissive feeding and weaning treatment was more characteristic of lower-class than of middle-class mothers. More lower-class children were fed only by breast, nursed for longer periods of time and on self-demand schedules, and allowed to use pacifiers. Negro mothers tended to be more lenient than whites in their feeding procedures, nursing their children longer, feeding on demand, and weaning more gradually.

Research done about 15 years ago challenged these findings on the greater permissiveness of lower-class parents (30, 31, 46). A staff of investigators at the Laboratory of Human Development at Harvard University conducted interviews with 198 upper-middle- and 173 upper-lower-class mothers in the Boston area (31). They found few differences between the social classes in infant-feeding practices. Middle-class mothers breast-fed somewhat more frequently, and scheduled feedings slightly more rigidly, but neither of these differences was significant.

Recent studies in the Boston area suggest that the well-educated middle-class mother is more likely to breast-feed than the lower-class, poorly educated one (29). Thus between the periods of these investigations there seems to be a complete reversal in the ratio of middle- to lower-class mothers choosing to nurse their babies.

Several recent studies point up differences in child-rearing practices within Europe and between Japan and the United States. For example, mothers from Stockholm and London breast-fed their children for a longer period of time than the mothers from Zurich or Brussels, but the majority of mothers had stopped breast-feeding before the child was 6 months old. The attitudes of doctors, nurses, and mothers in the country were important determinants of how long the mothers would breast-feed (28).

When it came to the age at which toilet training was started, London and Paris mothers started early, while Stockholm mothers started late. Thus the Stockholm mothers tended to be permissive with respect to elimination training as well as breast-feeding. However, 50 percent of the mothers in all cities started toilet training before the child was 1 year old, several months *before* the majority of American mothers usually start such training (28).

An intriguing study compared 30 Japanese and 30 American mothers and their 3- to 4-month-old first-born infants (7). The Japanese child lives and sleeps typically in the same room with the mother and father and the Japanese mother is always close to her infant. When the infant cries, the mother is apt to respond quickly and feed him soon after he begins to fret. In contrast, the American child usually has a room of his own, and the mother often lets him cry for a few minutes before she comes to feed him.

Second, the Japanese mother feels the need to soothe and quiet her baby, while the American mother more often wants to stimulate him and make him vocalize or smile. The American mother plays with her baby and talks to him; the Japanese mother soothes and rarely talks to her baby. The Japanese baby is less active than the American baby, and much less vocal. There is, therefore, a reasonable association between the maternal practices and the child's behavior.

The differences in maternal behavior seem to derive from different philosophies, or attitudes, about the infant. The American mother believes that her child is basically passive, and it is her job to mold him—to make him into an active, independent child. As a result, she feels she must stimulate him. The Japanese mother believes her infant is basically independent and active and it is her job to soothe him and make him dependent upon her and the family. She sees "the infant as a separate biological organism, which from the beginning, in order to develop, needs to be drawn into interdependent relations with others" (7).

To put it simply, the American mother sees her infant as fundamentally dependent. She must make him independent and achieving, and she stimulates him to babble and does not rush to soothe him at the first cry. The Japanese mother sees her infant as already independent and she must make him more dependent. Therefore, she soothes him and hastens to care for him as quickly as possible. One could not ask for a clearer example of the importance of cultural attitudes on the rearing practices of the mother and, subsequently, on the behavior of the infant and older child.

SUMMARY

The infant is born with the capacity to emit behaviors toward the person caring for it. These responses include clinging, vocalizing, smiling, scanning, and following the caretaker. Moreover, the caretaking adult typically provides pleasant experiences and reduces the infant's pain and distress. As a result, the infant becomes attached to the caretaker and becomes upset and fearful when it is separated from the caretaker. This process occurs in many animal species in ways that are markedly similar to the process in the human infant. The pattern of responses developed toward the caretaking adult generalizes to other adults and leads to a socialized child.

In addition to emitting behaviors, the infant is developing schemata about the environment and becomes distressed when he encounters objects or events that are moderate distortions of these schemata, especially if he has no response to make to the unusual stimulus. These encounters with a surprising event are one of the most important sources of vigilance and alertness in the infant. If he can interpret or deal with the surprise he will grow psychologically. If he cannot, he may withdraw or in some cases show panic. Thus the child passes through periods of gaining familiarity with people, objects, and events which permit him, in turn, to understand events at the next level of complexity or difficulty. And the repetition of this process is a good definition of psychological growth. The institutionalized infant is in a monotonous and impersonal environment and development of schemata is retarded. He does not react to human beings in the socialized way that is so characteristic of family-reared children.

INTRODUCTION OF CASE HISTORIES

In order to illustrate the major points in the chapters of this book we shall trace the personality development of two normal boys as they pass through the various periods of growth. One of the basic principles herein is that the child's motives, values, and behaviors are, in considerable measure, a function of the pattern of rewards and punishments that come from the parents, and the values and attitudes that the parents indirectly communicate to the child through their everyday behavior. We have chosen to illustrate this principle by selecting a pair of boys whose parents emphasized different behaviors and goals. Both were born to accepting parents; both were born healthy; both showed average mental and motor development during the first few years of life; both had one sister and no brothers. In each case, the father was a middle-class businessman in a small town, and the mother had had some college training.

Jack's parents, however, were anxious that he be a "man"—tough, strong, and independent. They did not want a sissy for a son, and they conscientiously avoided catering to his every whim.

Peter, on the other hand, was born to a family that was less concerned with pressuring their son into adopting conventional standards of masculinity. In fact, they punished any evidence of aggression in Peter and pampered him excessively. Both his father and mother were protective and indulgent.

Although Jack and Peter appeared to be alike during the first year of life, we shall see how these differences in parental values and attitudes influenced the behaviors of the boys as they progressed through childhood and into adolescence.

References

1. Ainsworth, M. D. S. *Infancy in Uganda*. Baltimore: Johns Hopkins Press, 1967.
2. Bakwin, H. Emotional deprivation in infants. *J. Pediat.*, 1949, *35*, 512–521.
3. Bateson, P. P. G. The characteristics and context of imprinting. *Biol. Rev.*, 1966, *41*, 177–220.
4. Brackbill, Y. Extinction of the smiling response in infants as a function of reinforcement schedule. *Child Develpm.*, 1958, *29*, 114–124.
5. Brackbill, Y. *Research and clinical work with children*. Washington, D.C.: American Psychological Association, 1962.
6. Bronfenbrenner, U. Socialization and social class through time and space. In

E. E. Maccoby, T. M. Newcomb, & E. L. Hartley (Eds.), *Readings in social psychology.* New York: Holt, Rinehart and Winston, 1958, 400–425 (3rd ed.).

7. Caudill, W., & Weinstein, H. Maternal care and infant behavior in Japanese and American urban middle class families. In R. Konig & R. Hill (Eds.), *Yearbook of the International Sociological Association,* 1966.

8. Collard, R. R. Fear of strangers and play behavior in kittens with varied social experience. *Child Developm.,* 1967, *38,* 877–891.

9. Davis, A., & Havighurst, R. J. Social class and color differences in child-rearing. *Amer. sociol. Rev.,* 1946, *11,* 698–710.

10. Dennis, W., & Najarian, P. Infant development under environmental handicap. *Psychol. Monogr.,* 1957, Vol. 71 (Whole No. 436).

11. Dennis, W. Causes of retardation among institutional children: Iran. *J. genet. Psychol.,* 1960, *96,* 47–59.

12. Dittrichova, J., & Lapackova, V. Development of the waking state in young infants. *Child Develpm.,* 1964, *35,* 365–370.

13. Freedman, D. G. The effects of kinesthetic stimulation on weight gain and on smiling in premature infants. Presented at the annual meeting of the American Orthopsychiatric Association, San Francisco, 1966.

14. Freud, A., & Burlingham, D. T. *Infants without families.* New York: International Universities Press, 1944.

15. Gardner, D. B., & Swiger, M. K. Developmental status of two groups of infants released for adoption. *Child Develpm.,* 1958, *29,* 521–530.

16. Gardner, D. B., Pease, Damaris, & Hawkes, G. R. Responses of two-year-old adopted children to controlled stress situations. Paper read at a meeting of the Society for Research in Child Development, Washington, D.C., March, 1959.

17. Gewirtz, J. L. The cause of infant smiling in four child-rearing environments in Israel. In B. M. Foss (Ed.), *Determinants of infant behavior.* Vol. III. London: Methuen, 1965, 205–260.

18. Goldfarb, W. Infant rearing and problem behavior. *Amer. J. Orthopsychiat.,* 1943, *13,* 249–266.

19. Goldfarb, W. The effects of early institutional care on adolescent personality. *J. exp. Educ.,* 1943, *12,* 107–129.

20. Goldfarb, W. The effects of early institutional care on adolescent personality (graphic Rorschach data). *Child Develpm.,* 1943, *14,* 213–225.

21. Goldfarb, W. Effects of early institutional care on adolescent personality: Rorschach data. *Amer. J. Orthopsychiat.,* 1944, *14,* 441–447.

22. Goldfarb, W. Infant rearing as a factor in foster home placement. *Amer. J. Orthopsychiat.,* 1944, *14,* 162–167.

23. Goldfarb, W. Effects of psychological deprivation in infancy and subsequent stimulation. *Amer. J. Psychiat.,* 1945, *102,* 18–33.

24. Goldfarb, W. Psychological privation in infancy and subsequent adjustment. *Amer. J. Orthopsychiat.,* 1945, *15,* 247–255.

25. Goldfarb, W., & Klopfer, B. Rorschach characteristics of "institution children." *Rorschach Res. Exch.,* 1944, *8,* 92–100.

26. Harlow, H. F., & Zimmermann, R. R. Affectional responses in the infant monkey. *Science,* 1959, No. 3373, *130,* 421–432.

27. Harlow, H., & Harlow, M. H. Learning to love. *Amer. Scientist,* 1966, *54,* No. 3, 244–272.

28. Hindley, C. B., Filliozat, A. M., Klackenberg, G., Nicolet-Meister, D., & Sand, E. A. Some differences in infant feeding and elimination training in four European longitudinal samples. *J. child psychol. Psychiat.,* 1965, *6,* 179–201.

29. Kagan, J. Continuity in development in the first year. Unpublished manuscript.
30. Littman, R. A., Moore, R. C. A., & Pierce-Jones, J. Social class differences in child-rearing: a third community for comparison with Chicago and Newton. *Amer. sociol. Rev.,* 1957, *22,* 694–704.
31. Maccoby, E. E., Gibbs, P. K., & the staff of the Laboratory of Human Development, Harvard University. Methods of child-rearing in two social classes. In W. E. Martin, & C. B. Stendler (Eds.), *Readings in child development.* New York: Harcourt, Brace & World, 1954, 380–396.
32. Marquis, D. P. Learning in the neonate. The modification of behavior under three feeding schedules. *J. exp. Psychol.,* 1941, *29,* 263–282.
33. Mason, W. A. Motivational aspects of social responsiveness in young chimpanzees. In H. W. Stevenson, E. H. Hess, & H. L. Rheingold (Eds.), *Early behavior.* New York: Wiley, 1967.
34. Miller, D. R., & Swanson, G. E. *The changing American parent.* New York: Wiley, 1958.
35. Morgan, G. A., & Ricciuti, H. N. Infants' responses to strangers during the first year. In B. M. Foss (Ed.), *Determinants of infant behavior.* Vol. IV. London: Methuen, 1967.
36. Moss, H. A. Maternal influences and early social visual behavior. Presented at the annual meeting of the American Orthopsychiatric Association, 1967.
37. Provence, S., & Lipton, R. C. *Infants in institutions.* New York: International Universities Press, 1962.
38. Rabin, A. I. Personality maturity of kibbutz (Israeli collective settlement) and non-kibbutz children as reflected in Rorschach findings. *J. proj. Tech.,* 1957, *31,* 148–153.
39. Rabin, A. I. Behavior research in collective settlements in Israel: infants and children under conditions of "intermittent" mothering in the kibbutz. *Amer. J. Orthopsychiat.,* 1958, *28,* 577–586.
40. Rheingold, H. L. The effect of a strange environment on the behavior of infants. Personal communication.
41. Rheingold, H. L. The modification of social responsiveness in institutional babies. *Monogr. Soc. Res. Child Develpm.,* 1956, *21,* No. 2 (Serial No. 63).
42. Rose, J. B., & McLaughlin, M. N. *A portable medieval reader.* New York: Viking Press, 1949. Cited in L. J. Stone, A critique of studies of infant isolation. *Child Develpm.,* 1954, *25,* 9–19.
43. Sackett, G., Porter, M., & Holmes, H. Choice behavior in rhesus monkeys. *Science,* 1965, *147,* 304–306.
44. Skeels, H. M. Adult status of children with contrasting early life experiences. *Monogr. Soc. Res. Child Develpm.,* 1966, *31,* No. 3.
45. Spitz, R. A., & Wolf, K. M. Anaclitic depression: an inquiry into the genesis of psychiatric conditions in early childhood, II. In A. Freud *et al.* (Eds.), *The psychoanalytic study of the child.* Vol. II. New York: International Universities Press, 1946, 313–342.
46. White, Martha A. Social class, child-rearing practices and child behavior. *Amer. sociol. Rev.,* 1957, *22,* 704–712.
47. Whiting, J. W. M., & Child, I. L. *Child training and personality.* New Haven: Yale Univer. Press, 1953.
48. Yarrow, L. J. Maternal deprivation. *Psychol. Bull.,* 1961, *58,* 459–490.

7

Development in the Second Year

During the second year of life, the human child progresses from the status of *infant*—responsive to stimuli but basically dependent on others for the satisfaction of most of his wants—to that of a *child*, with some measure of independence. The swift and exciting changes of this year, both quantitative and qualitative, have repercussions on almost all aspects of behavior. The combined forces of physical growth, maturation, and learning, produce remarkable gains in size, in motor skills, and in language and cognitive abilities. Inevitably, these factors lead to new and different self-perceptions and perceptions of the environment, new motivations, and new approaches to problems. Moreover, the reactions of significant people in the child's world are considerably different from what they were when he was an infant. In short, the child's psychosocial world changes dramatically in the second year and by the end of this year he is a much more capable and complex individual than he was at the age of 1.

The nature of the child's relationship with his mother—quality of stimulation, patterns of rewards and nurturance—continues to be of major significance for the child's development. In our culture, the second year seems to be characterized by much more active and vigorous parental efforts to begin the socialization of the child. Socialization refers to "the whole process by which an individual, born with behavioral potentialities of an enormously wide range, is led to develop actual behavior which is confined within a much narrower range—the range of what is customary and acceptable for him according to the standards of his group" (11, 655). In brief, it is the process by which the individual becomes a member of his social group through acquisition of the group's values, motives, and behaviors. During this period, socialization training is likely to be centered on cleanliness, control of anger and temper, moderation of incipient tendencies toward autonomy, and restriction of exploratory activities.

The child's progress in physical, motor, cognitive, and language development are critical determinants of the ease and speed of socialization. For this reason, we will consider these areas first.

GENERAL PHYSICAL DEVELOPMENT

American infants of this generation gain more rapidly in height and weight than those of the last generation. Physical development in the second year proceeds rapidly, although more slowly than in the first year. For example, the average infant grows about 4 inches and gains 4 to 5 pounds during the second year, as opposed to height increases of 8 to 9 inches and weight gains of 14 to 15 pounds during the first year (60). At 2, the average child is 32 or 33 inches tall and weighs approximately 28 pounds (59, 60). Children who are tall and heavy for their age on the first birthday are likely to maintain their relative standing at age 2 (45).

There is also a positive relation between amount of fat and height, with the fatter children being slightly taller than the leaner ones. Moreover, this association between fat and stature is evident through 12 years of age (27).

The infant's skeletal structure also changes during the second year. Bones increase in size and number and more of them become calcified. The fontanelles, or soft membrane spots in the skull, generally close (i.e., the bones become hardened and fused) somewhere between the ages of 18 and 24 months, and most of the child's temporary teeth erupt during the second year (59).

Body Proportions

It will be recalled that, compared with adult body proportions, the newborn infant is top-heavy. His head is too large for his body, and his cranium is out of proportion to his face; his arms are too long, and his legs, hands, and feet are too short. Differential rates of development of the various body parts during the first 2 years produce a body build more like the adult's. For instance, the head grows a good deal more slowly than the rest of the body and assumes more adultlike proportions as the facial skeleton becomes relatively larger. Between birth and 2 years of age, both the arms and legs develop rapidly, the former becoming comparatively longer.

Muscular and Nervous Systems

The child increases markedly in strength during the second year, as his muscles develop more, accounting for a greater proportion of body weight. His potential for making new, finer, and more precise movements is also increased as his nervous system develops. His brain becomes heavier, increasing from an average of 350 grams at birth to about 1000 grams (three-quarters of its total adult weight) at age 2. His nervous system becomes more complex and more highly differentiated. Immature nerve fibers which have not been entirely separated, now become insulated from one another by developing protective fatty shields. This process is called *myelinization*.

MOTOR DEVELOPMENT

Walking

As the child's general physical status advances, his motor response capacities become correspondingly enlarged. The locomotor phases preceding independent walking—sitting, crawling, creeping, standing, walking with support—were discussed in Chapter 5. Apparently neuromuscular maturation, rather than specific practice, is the chief antecedent of these responses. Available evidence suggests that this holds true of independent walking, too. In other words, it again appears that physical maturation—or, more specifically, changed body proportions, advanced neural development, and increased muscle strength—is far more crucial than practice in determining the child's progress from one locomotor stage to another. However, complete absence of any opportunity to practice creeping or standing may retard the child's locomotor development (14).

As already stated, by 12 months of age, the average child is able to pull himself to a standing position and walk with support. By 14 months he can stand alone, and by 15 months he walks awkwardly and cautiously, but unassisted. These, of course, are normative, average data, and there are wide individual differences among perfectly normal children. Some children walk independently as early as 10 months; others not until they are almost 2 years old. In general, babies born prematurely and those suffering from severe illness during the first 2 years may be slightly delayed in beginning to creep and walk (57). There is no evidence to support the popular opinion that heavy infants are "slower" sitters, standers, or walkers than lighter ones (47). In the recent cross-cultural study of age of onset of walking in five European cities (Paris, London, Brussels, Stockholm, and Zurich) that we have discussed previously, it was found that there were no significant sex or social-class differences in this response in any of the cities (31). However, as Fig. 7.1 shows, there were significant mean differences between geographical areas. Swedish babies walked earliest, on the average, and Parisians latest. It is difficult to account for these national differences. They may be attributable to differences in racial-genetic factors, in nutrition, or perhaps even in maternal handling or encouragement of locomotion.

According to one large-scale investigation, the average child can walk up and down stairs with help at about 19 months, and without assistance at 23 months. Initiation of stair-climbing, like beginning other locomotor activities, seems to be more influenced by maturation than by learning experiences. In a co-twin study, Gesell and Thompson (29) gave one of a pair of identical

United Nations

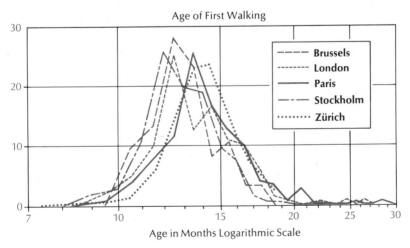

Fig. 7.1. Age of first walking in five sample groups. (From C. B. Hindley, A. M. Filliozat, G. Klackenberg, D. Nicolet-Meister, E. A. Sand. Differences in walking in the European longitudinal samples. *Human Bio.*, December, 1966, *38*, 369. By permission of the Wayne State University Press.)

Table 7.1. Some Second-Year Items in Bayley's Scales of Psychomotor Development.

Item	Age Placement (Months)
Walks alone	11.7
Throws a ball	13.3
Walks sideways	14.1
Walks backward	14.6
Walks upstairs with help	16.1
Walks downstairs with help	16.4
Tries to stand on walking board	17.8
Walks with one foot on walking board	20.6
Walks upstairs alone; marks time	25.1

Source: N. Bayley. Bayley's infant scales of development. New York: By permission of The Psychological Corporation, 1968.

twins (T) 6 weeks of daily practice sessions in stair-climbing, beginning at the age of 46 weeks. Her twin sister (C) had no contact with stairs until she was 53 weeks old and, at that time, she was given a brief 2-week training course. Twin C climbed more rapidly and efficiently than her sister who had been trained for a longer period of time at an earlier age (29, 116). Until the child's neuromuscular apparatus is sufficiently mature, efforts to "teach" him loco-motor responses are bound to meet with failure.

After the child becomes capable of these basic locomotor responses, however, practice brings improvements. For example, in walking and stair-climbing, coordination improves; waste movements are eliminated; steps become longer, straighter, and more rapid.

Bayley's Scales of Psychomotor Development, standardized recently on a large, national sample of children, measures many motor and perceptual abilities. Table 7.1 shows some of the motor tasks the child becomes capable of performing during the second year and gives their age placement in months—i.e., the average age at which these capabilities are manifested. Thus we can see that at 13 months, the average child can throw a ball; at 16 months he can walk upstairs with help; and at 20½ months he tries to stand on a walking board (4).

The child's impressive advances in motor abilities during the second year seem to be accompanied by a real urge to experiment. He seems intent on exercising his new skills and capabilities for the sheer pleasure of it. As casual and systematic observations attest (58, 22), the youngster is absorbed in testing and perfecting his recently acquired motor, manual, and manipu-lative skills.

Robert W. White has suggested that these testing and practice activities are manifestations of the child's *need for competence.* Competence is an inclusive term,

> a suitable word to describe such things as grasping and exploring, crawling and walking, attention and perception, language and thinking, manipulating and changing the surroundings, all of which promote an effective—a competent—

interaction with the environment. . . . There is a competence motivation as well as competence in its more familiar sense of achieved capacity. The behavior that leads to the building up of effective grasping, handling, and letting go of objects, to take one example, is not random behavior produced by a general overflow of energy. It is directed, selective, and persistent, and it is continued not only because it serves primary drives, which indeed it cannot serve until it is almost perfected, but because it satisfies an intrinsic need to deal with the environment (62, 318–319).

As we shall see later, parental reactions to the child's emerging need for competence and to his manifestations of newly developed skills become extremely significant factors in his socialization.

LANGUAGE

Perhaps the most remarkable and exciting development of the second year, the one with the most far-reaching implications, is the child's enormous progress in language. During this year, the child begins to associate many symbols (words) to objects and to use words meaningfully; his comprehension of questions and commands increases; his speech becomes more complex and more comprehensible. With the development of language, the child launches into a whole new world of learning and understanding, and he deals with his experiences and his environment in new ways. He begins to respond to simple commands at about 10 months. The first word—generally a single or duplicated syllable such as bye-bye, mama, or dada—is spoken around the first birthday, on the average.

There is a vast difference between language production (performance) and comprehension (competence); the child understands more than he can express. The increase in word knowledge during the second year is phenomenal. The effective vocabulary (words spoken or understood) of the average 1-year-old is 3 words; by 15 months, the average is 19; by 18 months, 22 words; by 21 months, 118, and by 2 years, 272 (56; see also Fig. 7.2).

It is much more difficult to study the child's active vocabulary accurately. In one investigation the average 2-year-old spoke 37 words in the presence of an examiner (54). There were marked individual differences, of course, the range being from 6 to 126 words. These are hardly accurate estimates of the children's verbal achievements, however, for the data are based only on spontaneous talk during periodic routine examinations.

It is clear that some aspects of language development (but, as we shall see, certainly not all) may be stimulated and encouraged by direct training and by practice. In a Russian study referred to earlier, babies between 9 and 18 months of age were taught to comprehend new words simply by orienting them to objects, naming the objects, and repeating this procedure several times. Providing a young child with different experiences with an object and repeating its name (for example, showing a ball, telling the child to throw the ball, take the ball, kick the ball, pick the ball up, roll the ball) also facilitates learning its name (41).

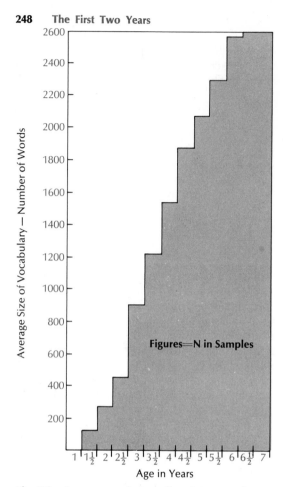

Fig. 7.2. Average vocabulary size of ten samples at various ages. (Data from M. E. Smith. An investigation of the development of the sentence and the extent of vocabulary in young children. *Univer. Iowa Stud. Child Welf.,* 1926, Vol. 3, No. 5.)

In one American study, a group of lower-class mothers, who ordinarily would not read to their children, were persuaded to read aloud to their babies, who were just over a year old, for 10 to 15 minutes a day. At 20 months of age, these youngsters were more advanced than a matched control group (who had no special experiences) in phoneme development and in word comprehension.

Ruth Weir's ingenious study demonstrates that young babies spontaneously "practice" speaking correctly (61). The investigator attached a microphone to her 2½-year-old son's crib and recorded all the sounds made when he was alone before falling asleep. The child clearly enjoyed playing with words, and the play seemed purposeful: The child was practicing and perfecting his linguistic skills. In the course of his monologue, he was correcting his own pronunciation, drilling himself on sounds, particularly consonants with which he had difficulty, and practicing using his vocabulary in sentence-like phrases. The child's ability to correct his own errors in the course of his verbal play suggests rather strongly that he must know a great deal more than he is actually producing during the day (61).

Psycholinguistics.   While the infant's sound production and vocabulary growth have been traditional subjects of research, some other complex problems of language acquisition have only recently been investigated systematically. The new and dynamic field of psycholinguistics, devoted to "the study of the acquisition and use of structured language" (20), has emerged during the last decade and has already made many significant contributions to our understanding of early language development. The major focus of psycholinguistic research has been the acquisition of grammar or syntax, the rules for putting words together.

Every language has two major aspects: *structure* (the basic units, words and sounds, and rules for arranging them) and *meaning* (conventional, arbitrary signs for referents, for objects and events). The structural aspects consist essentially of the sound system (phonology), rules for formation of words from sounds (morphology), and rules for word combination (grammar or syntax). These aspects, the *linguistic system,* rather than the social-communicative functions of language, are studied by psycholinguists. Let us again review some basic information about this field.

Recall that the elementary sounds of a language are phonemes—"for the most part, vowels and consonants, . . . correspond roughly to the letters of an alphabetic writing system" (8, 247; see pp. 188–189). Phonemes are arranged into larger units called morphemes which are "similar to, but not the same as, words" (8, 247). "Free morphemes" can stand alone, e.g., the words *ask* and *cat.* The words *asked* and *cats* are *not* single morphemes, however. *Asked* is composed of a verb and the ending -*ed,* indicating past time; *cats* is made up of a noun and the ending -*s,* which signifies plurality. These endings are morphemes that cannot stand alone; they are called "bound morphemes."

Each language has its own rules governing the combination of phonemes, permitting some combinations, and prohibiting others. In English there are no morphemes beginning with *ng* and the sequence *zb* never occurs, although these combinations occur in other languages.

At the next descriptive level, "the elements are morphemes, the smallest units of meaning. From morphemes, words are composed by morphological rules and sentences by syntactic rules" (8, 252). Grammar, or syntax, refers to the set of rules for creating sentences from words—that is, with syntax, phrases and sentences can be generated.

The study of semantics, which concerns meanings or referents, is generally separated from the study of phonology and grammar. Obviously, understanding language requires understanding both meaning and structure; the syntatic description of a sentence consists of both "deep structure" and a "surface structure." "Every sentence, however simple, has some kind of deep structure related to some kind of surface structure by means of certain transformations" (42).

The "deep structure" of a sentence is related to its underlying meaning; it is an abstract representation of the relations involved in the semantic interpretation of a sentence. The "surface structure" refers to the overt, observable orderlings and relations among the words, the "sound" of the sentence. "The deep structure contains all information relevant to semantic interpretation; the surface structure, all information relevant to phonetic interpretation" (13, 406).

> That sound and meaning are separate, and so need relating, is evident from paraphrase, where the same meaning is expressed in different patterns of sound [the child caught the ball and the ball was caught by the child] and from ambiguity, where the same pattern of sound has different meanings. . . . [The sentence *Flattering women amused him* may have two quite different underlying meanings: either *it amused him to flatter women* or *he was amused by women who were flattering*.] Between sound and meaning stands syntax (42).

The transformational grammar proposed by Chomsky (12) was designed to formulate rules that tie together deep and surface structures, specifying how the underlying meaning is transformed into sounds (surface structure). It "attempts to characterize in an explicit way the intrinsic association of phonetic form and semantic content in a particular language" (13, 407).

Acquisition of Grammar. Rich systematic observations by psycholinguists of very early language development have provided compelling evidence that even the very young child possesses a kind of basic, elementary grammar. While the very first words spoken at the end of the first year are generally simple labels for persons, objects, or acts, the child soon begins to make requests or to describe the environment. Single words may stand for entire sentences. "Shoe" may mean "take off my shoe" or "eat" may mean "is baby going to eat now?"

At about 18 months of age, on the average, children begin putting two words together to make simple sentences. These early sentences "seem to be abbreviated or telegraphic versions of adult sentences. 'That's the ball' becomes 'that ball,' 'where is the ball' becomes 'where ball.' Function words [such as *and, at, the, his*] are almost completely lacking at this stage" (19, 119). Nevertheless, we can begin analyzing the structure or grammar of the child's language as soon as "he has at least two systematically contrasted meaningful words" (19, 109).

Braine's data (6) on the development of two-word sentences in two young children came from their mothers' complete and detailed written records of the children's spontaneous comprehensive utterances (any utterances that were not direct imitations or repetitions of something someone else said in the previous few seconds). The two children manifested strikingly similar sequences of development. After the first word combinations were uttered, the number of different word combinations increased slowly and then suddenly surged upward after a few months. For example, Gregory, one of the subjects, spoke 14 different two-word combinations during his nine-

Table 7.2 Gregory's Word Combinations: First 4 Months

14 combina-	*my mommy*	*nightnight office*	*hi plane*	*allgone vitamins*
tions with *see*	*my daddy*	*nightnight boat*	*hi mommy*	*allgone egg*
(—) e.g.,	*my milk*			*allgone lettuce*
see boy		31 combinations	*big boss*	*allgone watch*
see sock	*do it*	with *bye-bye* (—)	*big boat*	
see hot	*push it*	e.g.,	*big bus*	20 unclassified,
	close it	*bye-bye plane*		e.g.,
pretty boat	*buzz it*	*bye-bye man*	*more taxi*	*mommy sleep*
pretty fan	*move it*	*bye-bye hot*	*more melon*	*milk cup, ohmy*
			allgone shoe	*see*

Source: M. D. S. Braine. The ontogeny of English phrase structure: the first phase. *Language,* 1963, 39. Published by the Linguistic Society of America. By permission.

teenth month, the first month in which he uttered a two-word sentence. In the following 6 months, the cumulative number of recorded different two-word combinations were 14, 24, 54, 89, 350, 1400, 2500, "and undoubtedly the sampling was more complete in the earlier than the later months" (6, 2).

These early sentences contain some typical structural properties—that is, systematic regularities of word order. Even at this age, the child seems to have his own grammar, his own set of rules for forming sentences. The grammar is of course a relatively simple one, and, according to Braine, consists of two classes of words: *pivots* (or *operators*) and X-words. Consider a few of Gregory's first two-word combinations. His third word combination was "see hat," and the next three were "see sock," "see horsie," and "see boy." Ten of his first 13 two-word combinations contain the word "see" in the first position. "In the development of Gregory's language, it appears that from time to time a particular word is singled out, placed in a certain position, and combined with a number of other words in turn, often in quick succession. The words that are singled out in this way are the pivots" (6, 10). The pivots, then, are a few words that tend to occur in a number of word combinations and are associated with a particular position, initial or final. They do not ordinarily occur alone. The X-class is a large open one consisting of the child's entire vocabulary except for some of the pivots. "X-words tend to recur in relatively few combinations and do not appear to be tied to a particular utterance position; they occur alone or in the position complementary to that of the pivot word" (6, 8).

Table 7.2 summarizes 89 word combinations uttered by Gregory during the first 4 months that he used two-word combinations.

Notice that over two-thirds of these two-word combinations contain one or another of a small group of pivot words in the first position. Thus, "bye-bye" occurs in 31 combinations, always in the first position; "see" occurs in 14 combinations.

The child continues to use this kind of two-word combination, or pivotal construction, as new words are added and new two-word sentences are generated. About 5 or 6 months after beginning to use pivotal construction, children are likely to begin to use more two-word sentences in which an X-word (e.g., an English noun) occupies both utterance positions. Examples are "man car" ("the man is in the car"), "car bridge" ("the car is under the bridge"), "coffee daddy" ("coffee for daddy"). These are not pivotal constructions but seem rather to exemplify a primitive sentence form in which both components can be expanded . . . e.g., "man car" expanded to "other man car" ["the other man is in the car"] or "man other car" ["the man is in the other car"] (see 6, 10).

It is very difficult to explain how the child acquires grammar so early and how he uses this to generate new "sentences." Psycholinguists argue strongly that the usual kind of explanations based on learning theory—i.e., explanations based on imitation, practice, and reinforcement—are inadequate. Many of the child's pivotal constructions have never been heard before; the child generates them himself. Moreover, the young child's grammar does not seem to be acquired by direct training. Brown's extremely careful longitudinal observations of language development indicate that parents do not necessarily reward grammatically correct sentences. In fact, ungrammatical but true utterances are often rewarded, while grammatically correct but factually untrue statements are not rewarded. In spite of this, correct grammar is acquired relatively early.

> The contingencies governing approval and disapproval were not grammatical at all. If approval and disapproval are not governed by grammar they cannot very well teach grammar. The principal operating contingency is the truth value of the proposition which the parent fits to the child's often incomplete or defective sentence. When Eve said: "Mama isn't boy. He is a girl," the answer was: "That's right." Eve used the wrong pronoun but mother knew what she meant and what she meant was true. On the other hand, when Adam said in perfect English, "Walt Disney comes on, on Tuesday," his mother said "That's not right" because Walt Disney doesn't. The parents we have studied positively reinforce true statements and punish false ones and disregard grammar. Which makes rather paradoxical the usual product of child training—a speaker who is highly grammatical but not notably truthful (9, quoted in 55).

Perhaps the most telling argument against imitation as a crucial variable in the acquisition of grammar is the fact that even the very young child creates (generates) new, grammatically correct sentences that he has never heard before.

As another psycholinguist sees it:

> If a child were to spend a lifetime imitating the sentences he heard, we could never account for the outstanding ability of every human being to speak and understand sentences he has clearly never heard before but which are nevertheless acceptable as sentences of his language. And, indeed, recent careful observers of child language have heard the child speak many utterances which

he could never have heard—which could not be imitations or reduced imitations of adult utterances—but which seem to be explainable in terms of an inferred structure, in terms of the child's idiosyncratic grammar. For example, drawing from the studies of Braine [6] and Brown and his co-workers [10], we have utterances like: "allgone pacifier," "put on it," and "a this truck." Such examples are simply a more dramatic way of making the same point: almost all utterances are novel (55, 437–438).

If imitation is not *necessary* for acquiring grammar, does it help in the process? Some observers have compared the grammar used in children's spontaneous speech with the syntactic structure of their sentences spoken in imitation of others. The two types of grammar do not differ in complexity or structure (18, 19, 43)—i.e., young children tend to use their own grammars even when imitating adult models. Such findings would seem to be a strong argument against the hypothesis that grammar is learned by imitation.

In spite of these findings, one particular kind of imitation may be effective in promoting syntactical development. While interacting with her child, a mother frequently "expands" what the child says, filling in and clarifying his telegraphic speech. Thus, the child may say, "Daddy bye-bye," and the mother responds (expands) by saying, "Yes, Daddy has gone bye-bye." Brown and Bellugi noted this phenomenon in their intensive longitudinal observations and recordings of the language development of two children, Adam and Eve. About 30 percent of the children's utterances elicited expansions from their mothers, and the children in turn often imitated their mothers' expansions. In fact, about 15 percent of the child's speech in the last half of the second year consisted of this kind of imitation. But what is most pertinent to the argument about imitation is that, in 50 percent of these imitations, the child added "something to his original utterance, something he picked up from the expansion" (55, 440). The items added were precisely those generally missing from the youngster's telegraphic speech—articles, pronouns, copulative verbs, prepositions, inflections.

> Expansions would seem to be an excellent natural teaching device. The mother gives the child a correct model for his own speech, at a time when his attention is engaged and in which the semantic content—the situation—remains unchanged (55, 440).

This kind of evidence may suggest that expansions are capable of encouraging linguistic development, but it hardly constitutes systematic evidence that "adult expansion of child speech play[s] any essential or even facilitative role in normal grammatical development" (55, 441–442).

As the principles of learning do not seem to be adequate to explain the acquisition of grammar, some psycholinguists (such as Chomsky and his collaborators) suggest that perhaps the human organism's nervous system is "programmed" or "wired" in such a way that there is, in effect, a mental structure with an "innate conception of 'human language' that makes language acquisition possible" *(13,* 401). A model is proposed in which a hypothesized language acquisition device (LAD)—a fiction or model; *not* a device, specific organ, or part of the brain—receives as input all the language heard by the child. Many of the utterances received are grammatically correct, many are not.

> Given such a corpus, LAD is so constructed that it can develop a theory of the regularities that underlie the speech to which it has been exposed. It can exclude the non-grammaticality in the corpus by constructing a theory about the regularities it contains. This theory is LAD's grammatical competence, its knowledge of the language behind the corpus. Having developed such a grammatical theory, LAD becomes able to go far beyond the corpus with which it began. LAD can distinguish the infinitely many grammatical sentences in its language from the infinitely many non-grammatical alternatives, and it can judge how far from full grammaticality each of the latter deviates (42).

Here is a diagram of the model:

Linguistic data ⟶ | LAD | ⟶ Grammatical competence

Of course, LAD

> must be universally applicable. For LAD must be able to acquire any language; it cannot be biased toward some languages and away from others for reasons of internal structure. Thus LAD may contain information and procedures bearing on the general form of language, but presumably contains nothing bearing on the form of any particular language (42).

A number of fascinating, though indirect, kinds of supportive evidence are cited by proponents of this theory of syntactic acquisition. For example, considering the almost infinite number of possible grammatical errors and overgeneralizations children could make when they are learning to speak, it is truly amazing that only a small number actually occur. This argues, they maintain, for a built-in mechanism of some sort that limits the range of grammatical structures. Secondly, it seems that all children go through the same stages of grammatical acquisition, regardless of the particular language they are exposed to. A third type of evidence cited is neurological: There are special structures in the human brain that control language functions. While these facts are consistent with the hypothesis of some language processing mechanism, it would be exceedingly difficult to make empirical tests of a hypothesis about a structure with an "innate conception of human language."

It must therefore be concluded that at present there is no satisfactory explanation for the phenomenally rapid acquisition of grammatical structure. The traditional accounts, phrased in learning theory terms, are admittedly inadequate. On the other hand, there is no alternative explanatory hypothesis that is supported by substantial direct scientific evidence.

INTELLIGENCE AND ITS MEASUREMENT

Do these second-year gains in language ability influence the child's thought processes? Certainly words are used, overtly or covertly, in thinking and problem-solving by adults and children who have already acquired language. But it is difficult to determine whether language is a necessary condition for cognitive functioning in young children. After a thorough review of recent relevant research on this problem, Flavell and Hill concluded that "linguistic ability does not appear to be either synonomous with or a necessary precondition for cognitive processing of at least low . . . levels of developmental maturity. . . . sensory-motor intelligence clearly evolves without it " (24).

Piaget's brilliant naturalistic observations of the early development of intelligence in his own three children—sometimes supplemented by experimental manipulations altering a situation to see what the infants would do—are a major source (48) of our understanding of early cognitive functioning.

It will be recalled that the first broad period of cognitive development, the sensorimotor, extends from birth to the appearance of language—that is, approximately through the first two years of life. During this time the child is basically a perceiving and acting organism, acquiring many perceptual-motor coordinations that are the precursors of further intellectual development. From these, the child develops a concept of permanent objects—objects really existing "out there," independent of him. But he does not make use of internal representation until the end of this period.

In Chapter 5, the sensorimotor period was discussed and outlined. Recall that this period consists of a progression of six major stages, with gradual changes in mental structures or intellectual organizations as a consequence of continuous child-environment interaction. The early stages are precursors of the later ones, but they are not supplanted by more advanced developments. Rather, as he progresses in cognitive ability, the child retains earlier forms of intelligence. At each more advanced stage, however, new intellectual elements and capabilities are added. These are incorporated into, and integrated with, the previously existing attainments to form new mental structures, new organizations of the intellect. The child's stage of development is defined by the most advanced performances of which he is capable.

The first four stages of the sensorimotor period are generally achieved during the first year (see pp. 194–197), although for Piaget the ages at which the stages occur are not of primary importance. All children go through the same *succession* of stages, progressing from earlier to later in the same order, but the rate of progress will vary from child to child.

During the two final stages of the sensorimotor period, which generally characterize the second year, the child's cognitive functioning becomes more complex, more objective, and increasingly oriented toward reality. Intention, directionality, and goal orientation of behavior, already evident in the fourth stage of this period (cf. p. 195), become more marked and definite in the fifth and sixth stages. In addition, the child begins to react "to new situations with a decidedly active and versatile program of experimentation" (23, 105). At the end of the sensorimotor period, more trial-and-error is evident, and a primitive kind of representation—imagery—becomes manifest. Moreover, objects may be used as instruments in obtaining goals, thus giving evidence of "genuine intentionality." The infant makes deliberate adaptations to new situations and is able to use previously developed schemata flexibly, combining them in different ways to achieve his goals.

Thus, in Piaget's stage five,—"tertiary circular reaction and the discovery of new means by active experimentation," generally between the ages of 12 and 18 months— the child manifests more advanced and effective ways of exploring new objects. Novel and interesting events are repeated with variations in the movements he makes. Trial-and-error exploration of the environment is prominent as the child seeks new means of attaining goals and new ways of solving problems. In this stage, the child begins to manifest the constructive, original elements that Piaget regards as characteristic of intelligence.

In stage six of the sensorimotor period—the final, most advanced stage—the child develops a primitive form of representation, a kind of imagery that is used in problem-solving. He invents new means of obtaining what he wants by "internal experimentation, an inner exploration of ways and means" (23, 119).

Representation and invention are the major processes of the sixth stage, and the kind of inventiveness the child demonstrates at this time requires symbolic images: the ability to imagine actions or events *before acting them out in reality.* Furthermore, the child at this stage is able to "defer imitation," i.e., to reproduce a model's behavior from memory.

The Measurement of Intelligence in Infancy

As we have seen, Piaget's chief interest is the regularities in the development of mental functioning from infancy to adulthood. His focus is on the processes by which children solve problems—on the *incorrect* solutions that precede correct ones. Thus he studies the nature of the child's ability to adapt, and the organization of his thinking as it becomes more complex and objective. Of course, Piaget is aware of individual differences in the rate of moving from one stage of mental functioning to the next, but norms of development are not of crucial concern to him and his collaborators.

American interest in intelligence and cognitive functioning, on the other hand, is, to a great extent, centered on intellectual achievements and, more specifically, on the individual child's intellectual standing relative to other children of his age. For this purpose, a number of so-called infant intelligence tests have been developed, e. g., California Preschool Mental Scale, Bayley's Scales of Infant Development, Cattell Intelligence Test for Infants and Young Children, Merrill-Palmer, Minnesota Preschool Scale, and Gesell Developmental Schedules (see Fig. 7.3).

These tests consist of large numbers of items that presumably sample

Fig. 7.3. Materials used with the Gesell Developmental Schedules. (By permission of The Psychological Corporation.)

important aspects of intellectual ability. Each test is "standardized" by trying it out on a large, representative sample of the population from which norms or standards (averages or median ages at which items are passed by infants) are derived. It is then possible to assess the rates of progress of individual children as relatively rapid, average, or slower than average.

Let us look briefly at a new and particularly well-standardized infant intelligence test, Bayley's Scale of Mental Development, which consists of 163 items (4). The following list taken from the scale, illustrates the kinds of items used in infant tests. Numbers in parentheses refer to the age placement (months) of the items—that is, the age in months at which 50 percent of the children tested passed the items.

imitates words (12.5)
builds tower of two cubes (13.8)
says two words (14.2)
uses gestures to make wants known (14.6)
attains toy with stick (17.0)
imitates a stroke (17.8)
places two round and two square blocks in a board (19.3)
follows directions in pointing to parts of a doll (19.5)
points to three pictures (21.9)
builds tower of six cubes (22.6)
names two objects (23.0)
mends broken doll (23.6)
names three pictures (24.0)
names three objects (24.9)
names five pictures (25.5)

The child's score is based on his performance on these items. Clearly, most of them—like the items of most infant tests—tap sensorimotor functions, although many of them involve an elementary understanding and use of language.

Negro and white infants of 15 months of age or younger do *not* differ in their performances on this test (4), nor do the scores on infant tests correlate with socioeconomic status of the child's family (3, 4, 35). Such findings are particularly interesting because studies of older children (of preschool age and over) have repeatedly shown that Negro children score lower than whites on intelligence tests, and children from the lower socioeconomic groups score lower than their peers from higher status groups (see pp. 313–315).

Mental testers are, of course, interested in predicting the future mental status of the children they test. Does performance on these infant tests relate to later-tested intelligence? Unfortunately for most infants, the answer is *no*. The lack of relationship is due, in large part, to the vastly different kinds of abilities sampled at earlier and later ages. While the infant tests consist largely of sensorimotor tasks, tests for preschool and school-age children are heavily weighted with items dealing with language, abstract thinking, reasoning, and memory.

In Bayley's longitudinal studies, children were examined at frequent intervals beginning in early infancy. During the first few years, an earlier version of her infant tests (a 185-item scale) was used, and at 6 and 7 the subjects were given the Stanford-Binet. Correlations between scores on the infant tests and on later tests were insignificant. The writer therefore concluded that "scores made before 18 months are completely useless in the prediction of school age abilities" (2, 100).

Moreover, test performance at 21 months gives a negligible prediction of success on the Stanford-Binet at 6 or 7 years (34). These findings emphasize the difficulty of making an accurate prognosis of the future ability of a child on a mental test administered before the age of 2.

Nevertheless, the tests may have some predictive or diagnostic value in differentiating between normal and retarded functioning. This is particularly true when the tests are supplemented by careful clinical observations and case history data. On the basis of extensive experience, one clinical researcher concluded that these tests "can succeed in detecting the mentally deviant at a very early age, often before pathology becomes manifest through pediatric or neurological examinations" (21, 120).

SOCIALIZATION IN THE SECOND YEAR

The Nature of Socialization

During the second year, the child's new skills and abilities, together with his increased understanding of the world and his improved abilities to cope with it, permit him to take a much more active role in relation to his environment. He is intensely curious about his surroundings, moves about more freely, and explores vigorously. He can manipulate objects, solve problems in new ways, and make some changes in his situation. By the age of 2 he can use language, at least in a rudimentary way, to communicate with others. He explores cupboards, spills paint, shuffles daddy's papers, and calls for more food. Unfamiliar things seem to intrigue him; he seeks out novelty and attempts to deal with new situations. The child is learning about himself and his skills—learning that, although he has severe limitations, he can sometimes gratify motives independently, without parental aid.

At the same time most parents in our culture initiate major socialization training during this period. The parents' goal in socialization—which they may accept self-consciously or without much awareness—can be stated rather simply. It is to guide the child's acquisition of personality characteristics, behavior, values, and motives, that the culture considers appropriate. Essentially, as agents of socialization, the parents direct the child's learning of what the culture defines as desirable characteristics and behavior, at the same time encouraging him to inhibit undesirable motives and behavior.

Cultures, of course, vary with respect to the behavior expected, permitted, and prohibited. Within American culture, different social classes maintain and encourage different responses, motives, and values. The amount of aggressive and dependent behavior permitted varies with the sex of the child, his culture, and, within American culture, among social classes. Japanese girls are socialized to be shy and unassertive, American boys to be outgoing and exuberant. Socialization for some culturally approved characteristics begins very early, but training of other important aspects of behavior does not begin until the child becomes older and is more "ready." Thus, in American culture, the child of school age is encouraged to become proficient in reading and writing, to do well in school, and eventually to become independent of his family. The middle-class girl of this age is supposed to acquire the social graces—poise, politeness, and charm. The Mayan Indian boy in Guatemala learns to help his father in his work on the coffee plantation, to remain close to his family, and to contribute to his family's financial well-being.

However, socialization training during the second year is generally focused on the inhibition of undesirable behaviors—that is, parents begin to impose restrictions on activities that are unacceptable but that the child normally finds pleasurable; they demand that he inhibit certain kinds of behavior that he enjoys. The child is asked to stop making so much noise at dinner, to stop messing his food, to stop jumping up and down on the bed, and to delay urination and defecation until he can get to an appropriate place. Toilet and cleanliness training, and the tasks of curbing of tantrums, destructive activities, and unrestricted exploration and wandering are generally initiated when the child is between 12 and 18 months of age.

The difficulties in this training are due largely to the facts that exploration of closets, fingering of expensive china vases, and spontaneous urination seem to be inherently gratifying to the child. The demand to delay or curb these behaviors may be one of the first major sources of friction between parent and child. Moreover, the mother's role in relation to the child may now begin to change. During feeding training, and in general during the first year, the mother is supportive to the child, giving, providing, and bringing things to him. But in the second year she becomes more of a "teacher," expecting him to assume some independence and responsibility for his own care and behavior. The situation is further complicated by the fact that many socialization demands are made simultaneously.

Successful socialization of any aspect of behavior depends not only on training techniques but also on the child's physical, cognitive, and emotional status—his "readiness" for acquiring (or inhibiting) certain behavior. Thus, the Guatemalan boy cannot learn to help his father in his work until he is physically and intellectually capable of doing the tasks that are required. Analogously, the middle-class American girl cannot acquire social poise until she understands what this means and what its components are. But even when the child is sufficiently mature, the parents' task—promoting socialized behavior with minimal parent-child conflict—is an extremely difficult one. How can this be achieved? Unfortunately, there are few solid facts about the "best" ways to socialize the child. The principles of learning theory and some clinical evidence, however, provide some basis for making inferences about the possible consequences of various types of parental reactions during this training period. Fortunately, very early in life, the child acquires certain motives that facilitate the socialization process. By the end of the first year, the child appears to be highly motivated (1) to please parents and thus insure continued affection and acceptance and, in addition and, related to this, (2) to avoid the unpleasant feelings generated by punishment or rejection. These motives are very strong in the first 2 years, and for this reason, parental rewards and punishment are the major techniques used in early socialization. In a sense, successful socialization involves an exchange in which the child gives up his desire to "do as he pleases" in return for the continued love and affection of his mother and father. But this exchange will work best if the child is receiving sufficient nurturance to make it attractive to him. The parent who has not been nurturant during the first year of life does not have sufficient reward value to motivate the child to adhere to parental values. Thus, parental warmth and acceptance are necessary conditions for effective socialization.

Later on, beginning in the preschool period, the child is more likely to be motivated by his desire to be like someone he respects, loves, and admires—the process of *identification* (see pp. 356–366). In addition, the child has a general tendency to imitate others—but this, too, may be a more powerful mechanism in later socialization than it is in early training. In short, all of these motivations or processes—desire for acceptance, fear of punishment and rejection, identification, and imitation—are involved in the socialization process, but their relative roles vary, depending on the period of development. Early acquisition or inhibition of overt behavior is probably most readily accomplished through social rewards and punishments, while later acquisition of values and motives is more likely to be a product of identification with a model.

But these conditions are not sufficient by themselves to insure that socialization demands are fulfilled, that more mature responses develop, and that subsequent adequate psychological and social adjustment are facilitated. To achieve these goals, the child must have some feeling of confidence in his ability to deal effectively with the environment.

Socialization and Autonomy

Erik Erikson, a psychoanalyst, sees this early period as a critical one for the child's development of a sense of autonomy, of self-reliance, and of competence. This depends on the child's growing capabilities during the period and, more particularly, on his mastery of the physiological functions of elimination and his increased skills in manipulation, locomotion, and exploration. These factors may bring him into direct conflict with the social environment, for as the child becomes aware of his control of body functions and of his abilities to move about and explore, he also learns that there are certain rules related to these functions.

If the child is to develop a meaningful sense of autonomy—

it is necessary that he experience over and over again that he is a person who is permitted to make choices. He has to have the right to choose, for example, whether to sit or whether to stand, whether to approach a visitor or to lean against his mother's knee, whether to accept offered food or whether to reject it, whether to use the toilet or wet his pants. At the same time he must learn some of the boundaries of self-determination. He inevitably finds that there are walls he cannot climb, that there are objects out of reach, that, above all, there are innumerable commands enforced by powerful adults (17, 208).

Parental frustration of the child's attempts to explore and investigate may have some immediate and enduring effects on personality and adjustment. Overprotective mothers may be warm and permissive when their children are infants, but become restrictive and overly cautious when they begin to show signs of independence. Then they attempt to "infantilize" their children and prevent independent behavior, thus retarding the acquisition of mature responses (39).

But if parents are accepting and reasonably permissive, granting moderate degrees of autonomy (freedom in exploration, manipulation, and investigation), the child is likely to derive some satisfaction from his own discoveries and from the pleasurable exercise of his new skills. Such a child is likely to become self-confident and spontaneous in his behavior, approaching new situations without anxiety and reacting enthusiastically to novel and challenging situations.

Socialization and Toilet Training

There are wide cultural variations in the time of beginning toilet training. While lower-class American mothers tend to begin this training early (7), middle-class mothers begin the baby's toilet training during the second year—at the same time they are trying to socialize his strong needs for autonomy and exploration as well as his seemingly irrepressible curiosity. Among the middle-class mothers interviewed in one study (52) the majority initiated toilet training when the child was between 9 and 14 months, and completed it at approximately 1½. In general, those who started the training later required less time to accomplish their goals than those who started earlier.

Europeans tend to start training earlier. According to the data of one cross-cultural study, the median age of starting regular toilet training in London is 4.6 months, in Paris 7.8 months, and in Stockholm 12.4 (32). Only in London was there a significant social-class difference (although a small one), mothers of higher social classes making their first toilet training attempts earlier than those of the lower class. There were no class differences in the other groups sampled.

Toilet training may be a major source of friction between parent and child, for the mother's role in relation to the child begins to change as she becomes a teacher and trainer. Earlier, she was primarily a feeder and caretaker, comforting and supporting the infant, ministering to his needs, providing his basic necessities, and requiring almost nothing of him. She now expects him to begin to assume some independence, to take some responsibility for his own care, to retain or withhold elimination until appropriate times, rather than evacuating whenever he has the urge. More than this, she expects the child to accomplish a difficult task, the substitution of voluntary control for what is initially an involuntary, reflex process. Originally, when the bladder and bowel are full, strong tensions are produced and urethral and anal sphincters are automatically released, expelling the urine or feces.

> To meet cultural demands this sequence must be rearranged. The connection between bowel stimulus and the evulsion response must be weakened. The child must learn to suppress the evulsion response to the bowel drive stimulus alone. It must then insert other responses in the sequence. At first it must learn to call to the parents. It must later learn to insert walking, unbuttoning, and sitting on the toilet chair while it is still suppressing the urgent evulsion response. Only to a new pattern of cues—the bowel stimulus, the cues of the proper room, the sense of freedom of clothes, the pressure of the toilet seat on the child's thighs—may the evulsion response occur without anxiety.

> In short, this response occurs not only to the pressure of the primary drive involved but also to the complex stimulus pattern just named. If one can once get the child to order the responses correctly, the strong tension reduction produced by defecation will reinforce the response to the pattern of cues enumerated. The real problem, therefore, is getting the child to suppress the naive evulsion response and to insert a considerable series of responses into the sequence before evulsion (16, 137).

Pediatricians and child psychologists generally agree that training should be delayed until the child is "ready" for it, i.e., until his neuromuscular apparatus is mature. He should be able to sit up comfortably, to understand, and to communicate. This means that stable acquisition of bowel and bladder control is not ordinarily possible until the child is about 18 months old. Otherwise, he is placed under too great a burden from both a psychological and a physiological point of view.

There is very little systematic research on the timing and techniques of toilet training, but learning theory provides a framework for predicting possible immediate and long-term outcomes of various types of training procedures. According to the principles of learning, a child may learn to inhibit a response such as evacuation if he is rewarded frequently for inhibiting it successfully. Theoretically it is possible for a child to become trained through consistent rewards for the response of withholding elimination until he is at the toilet. But, because most parents in our culture expect the child to be trained by the age of 3, they are forced to rely on a combination of reward for successful inhibition of reflex excretion and some punishment for accidents. In most instances, therefore, some anxiety about potential punishment or withdrawal of parental affection becomes attached to the urge to urinate or defecate. The child's anxiety motivates him to call for the parents, to run to the bathroom, and to initiate all the behaviors that are involved in control.

In general, toilet training is likely to proceed most smoothly, and be achieved with a minimum of conflict, if parents encourage the gradual acquisition of control. By watching for signs that the child needs to urinate or defecate, and taking him to the bathroom immediately, the parent has the opportunity to reward the child for using the toilet. If this is done frequently, the connections between the pattern of internal cues (bowel and bladder tensions) and the external cues (the bathroom) and the responses of excretion become strengthened. On subsequent occasions, the child is likely to withhold elimination until he gets to the bathroom. If the child is able to talk or signal his needs in some other way, the learning process will be easier. In toilet training their children, many mothers also attempt to capitalize on the young child's tendency to imitate, often using imitation as a supplement to rewards for withholding elimination until the proper time and place, and punishments for soiling. Parents or older children may take the child to the toilet with them to demonstrate the expected behavior, instructing the child to imitate. In one African tribe, "some mothers instead of teaching, simply tell the child to imitate what the older children do" (38, 154). Moreover, the mother who has previously established close relationships with her child will have fewer training difficulties than others, since her approval has already become an important kind of reward for him.

Women who are generally severe and punitive with their children are likely to be harsh in toilet training as well. Such women are also likely to be severe and controlling about obedience, masturbation, and sex play. On the basis of their interviews of over 300 middle-class mothers, Sears, Maccoby, and Levin noted:

> We get the impression of a rather pervasive quality of strictness in the mothers who are most severe in toilet training. They seem to have been seeking to

achieve more mature standards of conduct at a faster pace than other mothers. They had more of a tendency to drive rather than to lead their children and they used a more punitive kind of discipline (52, 121–122).

On the basis of the principles of learning theory we would also predict a number of undesirable consequences of training that is too early, too rigid, and overly severe or punitive. Such training may produce intense anxiety in the child, associated with feelings of anxiety and aggression toward the parents, together with a predisposition to develop a variety of symptoms or maladaptive behaviors. If the mother has been nurturant during the first year of life, her positive value might be sufficient to neutralize some of the negative feelings produced by socialization demands without inducing a marked change in the child's perception of her. But if the mother has been cold and rejecting, then use of strict toilet training is much more likely to have a deleterious effect on the child, and lead to negative feelings toward her (52).

The child's response to overly severe or punitive toilet training may be hostility—and even aggressive behavior—directed toward the parent doing the training. The child may scream, bite or kick, or he may express his hostility by refusing to do what he is supposed to do—that is, by refusing to evacuate while sitting on the toilet.

Maladaptive behaviors such as temper tantrums, irritability, and temporary lapses in control are not uncommon immediate reactions to severe training, and they may persist into later childhood. Chronic, continued enuresis (bedwetting) occurs most frequently in boys "whose training by energetic mothers was started too early, maturationally, to be followed by success" (40, 84).

Clinical studies suggest that severe, traumatic toilet training may have other lasting deleterious effects. In one study, over one-half of the children referred to a guidance clinic for a variety of emotional problems (e.g., restlessness, ticks, body manipulation, speech disturbances, psychosomatic ailments, or school failure despite adequate intelligence) had been bowel trained prematurely or by coercive methods. A majority of these children had reacted to their toilet training immediately with one or more of the following symptoms of emotional distress: continuation of wetting, fear of the toilet, temper tantrums, defiance, anger, and overconcern with cleanliness. Many of them (58 percent) were still enuretic (bedwetters) after they were 3 years old (36). In another investigation, children who were trained too early or too rigidly became highly compulsive, aggressive, negativistic, and fearful in later childhood (15, 40, 53, 63).

Excessive timidity and overconformity may also stem from unduly severe toilet training. If the child is punished too frequently, he will feel that it is safe to make responses only when he is certain that they are correct (i.e., in conformity with his parents' expectation of him). He may become inhibited, timid, and afraid to attempt responses that are not specifically approved by his parents (16).

Such findings and theoretical statements suggest that severe toilet training may have unfortunate consequences for the child. However, they do not establish that there are any invariant relationships between specific techniques and specific symptoms. As with feeding practices, it appears quite likely that specific toilet-training disciplines employed are not ordinarily of critical significance in themselves. They may, however, be important in terms of their intimate connection with parent-child relationships in general. As we pointed out earlier, toilet training is a learned situation in which the mother-child relationship may deteriorate, handicapping subsequent healthy emotional and social adjustment.

ADDITIONAL MOTIVES OF THE 2-YEAR-OLD

In centering our attention on the growth of autonomy and independence —and the achievement of some degree of socialization—during the second year, we must not overlook the obvious fact that most children of this age are highly susceptible to fears and anxieties and, at the same time, are strongly attached to and dependent on their parents in many ways. The child looks to his mother for assistance and signals for her help when he is in trouble. Unless the child was extremely deprived in infancy, his mother's mere presence has acquired great reward value quite independent of her functions of supplying food, warmth, and comfort. The association between the mother's presence and feelings of satisfaction and lack of tension has become firmly established by the end of the first year. For these reasons, the child's need for her presence is intense.

Moreover, as was suggested in our discussion of *separation anxiety* (anxiety responses elicited by the mother's absence) during the first year, there may also be some other underlying factors involved in this response (see Chapter 6, pp. 225–228). It may be that the mother's absence implies a discrepancy from the child's schema in which his mother is included as an essential part of every situation. This discrepancy, plus the fact that the mother's absence means a disruption of habitual responses to her and inability to make responses that will bring contact with her, may be important sources of separation anxiety. Consequently, the child of this age is apt to show signs of anxiety and emotional upset if his mother leaves him, even temporarily.

As we also learned in Chapter 6, babies in Western culture manifest the greatest intensity of separation anxiety toward the end of the first year. A team of English psychologists traced the course of social attachment, longitudinally, from early infancy to 18 months of age (50, 51). By rating the reactions of 60 children to seven separation situations (e.g., being left alone in a room, being left in a crib at night), they obtained a measure of "separation protest" which they considered an index of attachment to the mother. These investigators found that after reaching a high point of about 40–45 weeks of age, "separation protest" decreased.

This kind of protest reaches another peak at 18 months (51) and at this age, long separations from the mother may result in more drastic and enduring emotional upsets. Freud and Burlingham (25, 26) worked with a group of English children whose home life was disrupted, either by World War II or other events necessitating their removal from their own families. Those between 1 and 2 years of age reacted most violently to parting from the mother.

> The child feels suddenly deserted by all the known persons in its world to whom it has learned to attach importance. Its new ability to love finds itself deprived of the accustomed objects, and its greed for affection remains unsatisfied. Its longing for its mother becomes intolerable and throws it into states of despair which are very similar to the despair and stress shown by babies who are hungry and whose food does not appear at the accustomed time (25, 50).

Emotional upsets in children this age are likely to be reflected in disturbances in physical health. During World War II, a substantial proportion of English children under 2 did not "make satisfactory progress on admission to a day nursery, as judged by their weight gains in three monthly periods" (44, 500). This was true in spite of the fact that, compared with children remaining at home, those in nurseries had almost double rations and dietetically better-balanced meals. Their failure to gain weight adequately may therefore be attributed to emotional upset stemming from separation from the mother.

Another English research team, under the direction of John Bowlby, observed healthy children between 15 and 30 months of age who had to be separated from their mothers for a period of time either to enter a hospital or because the mother was forced to work. These children typically passed through three stages in meeting this situation. In the first stage, the child *protests:* i.e., he frets over the loss of the mother, shakes his crib, cries loudly, and looks eagerly for any sight or sound that might prove to be the missing parent. The warmer the mother-child relation, the longer the duration of this protest phase.

During the next phase, *despair,* he begins to accept the care, food, and gifts of the nurses, and he may even show some social responsiveness to others. But when his mother visits him he seems indifferent and he is likely to turn away from her. He seems to have lost interest in his mother.

If the child remains in the hospital or residential nursery school for a prolonged period of time, or if he becomes attached to a series of nurses who leave him after a short period of time, the child will eventually (third phase) act as if neither mothering nor contact with humans were important to him.

> A child living in an institution or hospital who has reached this state will no longer be upset when nurses change or leave. He will cease to show feelings when his parents come and go on visiting day; and it may cause them pain when they realize that, although he has an avid interest in the presents they bring, he has little interest in them as special people. He will appear cheerful and adapted to his unusual situation and apparently easy and unafraid of anyone. But this sociability is superficial; he appears no longer to care for anyone (5, 90).

A small group of children did not protest separation from their mothers. The researchers maintained that these children already had a low degree of attachment to their mothers as a result of ". . . inadequate previous experience of maternal care. None of these children behaved in a way typical of the normal family child whose dependency on the mother is at a peak at this age" (49, 133).

A more detailed behavioral study compared the response to separation of two groups of 2-year-olds (31). One group spent their days in a day nursery but went home to their parents in the evening. The second group lived continuously at a residential nursery and thus were more intensely deprived of parental nurturance. The children in this group, as compared with the day-nursery children, were generally more upset, showed a stronger desire for physical contact with the nursery staff, displayed more outbursts of aggression, more bowel and bladder accidents, indulged in more finger and thumb sucking, and acted out more themes of hostility in doll play. These behaviors (i.e., desire for contact with adults, overt aggression, loss of bowel training, hostile fantasies) are all expected consequences of the combination of an increased desire for parental love and continued frustration of this important motive. The child whose need for love is frustrated is apt to show very low tolerance for any frustration, and to react with heightened aggression and temper outbursts if things do not go as he wishes.

Influence of the Mother's Presence on Reactions to New Situations

In order to study the influence of the mother's presence or absence on the child's reactions, Arsenian (1) placed 24 children (between 11 and 30 months of age) in a new "insecure" situation—specifically, a strange room. Some of them were accompanied by their mothers; others were alone. Each child spent 11 5-minute periods in the strange room, which was attractively decorated and contained many toys and pictures.

The behavior of each child at each session was observed through a one-way vision mirror. The child's reactions were classified as adaptive or goal-directed (e.g., playing, locomotion, talking) or emotional, maladaptive, and nongoal-directed (e.g., crying, autistic gestures, thumbsucking, fingering parts of body, waving arms, stamping feet). Security in the situation was also rated on the basis of the type of response made (withdrawal and crying, agitated movement, retreat, attack, play, free approach).

It may be hypothesized that if the child's security is dependent on his mother's presence, he should manifest few symptoms of fear and anxiety, i.e., he should behave adaptively, when she is in the room with him. However, if he is placed there alone or if his mother leaves the room, the child should become distressed and behave maladaptively. On the other hand, a child who becomes disturbed when he is alone in the unfamiliar room should feel more secure, and behave more adaptively, when his mother accompanies him there later.

Arsenian's findings generally confirmed these hypotheses. Children who were left alone for the first few sessions spent most of their time crying and making autistic gestures. On the other hand, the majority of the children who faced the "insecure situations" accompanied by their mothers were secure from the start. During the first session they displayed three times as as much adaptive behavior and only one-third as much emotional behavior as did children who were left alone in the room. On the average, the mother-present group was rated as more secure in the *initial* session than the mother-absent group was in its *final trials* (after they had presumably become accustomed to the strange room). In summary, the mother's presence elicited positive, adaptive responses, while her absence brought out immature, mal-adaptive responses.

Subjects whose mothers were present *only* during the first few sessions became much less secure during later sessions when their mothers were absent. Apparently personal security in this situation, as in the English war-time evacuation centers or nurseries, was based on the mother's presence. Hence her absence evoked responses indicative of anxiety over absence of a nurturant figure.

The children who experienced early mother-absent sessions and later mother-present sessions became only slightly more mature and adaptive in their responses when their mothers accompanied them. The author concluded that:

> the behavior of [this] group points to the difficulty of increasing the security of the child in a situation where he has been permitted to become truly insecure. Children who were accompanied by an adult from the outset were immediately or rapidly secure in the strange situation but children who were allowed to become insecure before the adult arrived did not respond rapidly to the new source of protection (1, 203).

In summary, most 1- and 2-year-olds are anxious in new situations they face alone. The mother's presence ordinarily reduces the insecurity and anxiety, and hence enables the child to react adaptively. For reasons we discussed above (pp. 265–266), anxiety over absence of or separation from the mother is probably most intense between 1 and 3 years of age. Signs of disturbance when the mother leaves should not be interpreted as evidence of overdependency, abnormality, or pathology. They may simply indicate a normal, close mother-child relationship.

Fear and Anxiety

Separation from the mother is an important, but not the only, source of anxiety in the young child. Fear and anxiety are typically responses to the anticipation of unpleasant events. Many situations and stimuli become sources of fear and anxiety through learning, i.e., through their association with an unpleasant experience (and the accompanying physiological reactions). Pain, sudden, dramatic changes in level or quality of stimulation, or an unexpected surprise are capable of eliciting fear.

There is obviously an enormous range of variation among children in susceptibility to fear, but the factors underlying these individual differences are not well understood. Innate factors similar to those underlying individual differences in the amount of activity displayed by neonates may be involved. Very young infants differ in susceptibility to pain, and

> there could be individual differences in the capacity of the mechanism producing fear so that people would differ in the strength of their maximum fear responses just as they differ in the strength of grip. The strength of the innate connections between pain and fear could also differ so that fear would be more readily elicited in some people than it would be in others (16, 70).

Anxiety may be aroused by any stimulus associated with a fear-arousing condition or any new situation that involves anticipation of loss of attention from those who satisfy needs and provide security, nurturance, and pleasant stimulation. Consequently, there are many sources of fear and anxiety for young children. In one study, parents, using standardized forms, recorded all situations in which their children displayed fears during a 21-day observation period (37). Data were available on 136 children ranging in age from 3 to 97 months.

During the first year, fear occurred most frequently in response to noises and events previously associated with them, falling or displacement, sudden or unexpected movement, flashes of light, persons or objects previously associated with pain, as well as animals, and strange persons, objects, and events.

In the second year, fear reactions were elicited primarily by noises, strange events, and falling or danger of falling. Sudden movements and flashes of light were less frightening than they were previously, but fears of animals and persons or objects associated with pain increased. Some children in the second year were afraid of the dark or of being alone, although they had not shown these fears earlier.

Aggression

Aggression in childhood seems to be universal, and learning to control aggression is an important aspect of socialization in all cultures. The potential for behaving aggressively—and even some of the components of aggressive expression—may be innate. The nature and form of aggressive expression, and its timing, depend on learning, however. Aggression (responses intended to harm others)

> develops because the child discovers that he can secure compliance with his wishes, i.e., rewards from the social environment, by hurting. As his knowledge of others' motivation increases, he becomes more and more skilled at utilizing this method of control. The devices he learns are a function of what the parents and others respond to, and the extent or degree to which he develops such a

motive is a function of their rewarding responsiveness when he behaves injur-
iously—i.e., aggressively (53, 179).

Anger and aggression may be expressed in many diverse ways. During the individual's life, certain aspects of the original anger responses are
rewarded and repeated, while others are punished and eliminated. New responses (such as swearing, name calling, expressing feelings of jealousy or
hate) may be inserted into the pattern of angry and aggressive behavior.

Early Manifestations of Anger.   Most systematic and experimental studies
of aggression and the conditions that elicit it have been conducted with nursery school or older subjects. However, Goodenough's study demonstrates
how the expression of anger in the home and other natural settings becomes
modified through learning in the very early years (38). She collected data
from 45 mothers who recorded a total of 1878 instances of anger outbursts in
their children (aged 7 months to 8 years) during a period of 1 month. The
precipitating conditions and environmental factors involved were also noted.
Within the first 2 years, the greatest proportion of boys' and girls' manifestations of anger consisted of tantrums and other undirected outbursts of
motor activity.

> Such apparently unserviceable acts as those of screaming, kicking, or holding
> the breath may have proved themselves to be the most effective means for
> getting one's own way. On later occasions, therefore, such devices may have
> been more or less deliberately adopted by the child as methods of accomplish-
> ing his purposes (30, 53).

Directed motor and language responses soon begin to play a part in
the expression of anger. While motor or verbal resistance constituted only
14 percent of the anger responses of children under age 1, 56 percent of the
outbursts of those between ages 1 and 2 fell into these categories. Since such
behavior is more likely to be accepted and rewarded (or even encouraged)
among boys, boys manifested this kind of response more frequently than
girls did.

Peevishness, whining, and sulking became more common expressions of
anger as children grew older, and displays of simple undirected energy decreased in frequency.

> With advancing age the forms of behavior displayed during anger become more
> definitely directed toward a given end, while the primitive bodily responses of
> the infant and young child are gradually replaced by substitute reactions com-
> monly of a somewhat less violent and more symbolic character (30, 69).

Among children under 2 years of age, being forced to remain on the
toilet, restrictive clothing, and being put to bed frequently precipitated anger
outbursts. Denial of permission to carry out some desirable activity, or verbal
or physical restraints on such activities, were the antecedents of 20 percent
of the total aggressive outbursts among children between 1 and 2 years of

age, while disagreements between playmates accounted for only 10 percent of the anger manifestations.

Greater irritability and proneness to aggression were associated with visitors in the home (and, consequently, deprivation of some of the child's accustomed attention and sources of satisfaction), restless sleep or bedwetting during the previous night, colds, constipation, illness, hunger, and fatigue. All of these circumstances entail either intrinsic or extrinsic frustrations, and the child reacts in ways that have been successful in overcoming interference in the past, i.e., with anger and aggression.

In attempting to control and socialize their children's aggression, parents used a great variety of techniques. Ignoring, spanking or slapping, removing the source of trouble, diversion of attention, and coaxing were used most frequently by parents of children under 2, while scolding, threatening, and isolation were most typically used with their older children. The number of different techniques attempted during the course of a single outburst depended on the duration and violence of the child's behavior.

The methods which appeared to be most useful in bringing the outburst to an end often included removal of interferences with motivated activities—for example, granting the child's desire, removing the source of trouble, diverting the child's attention, providing a substitute activity, ignoring the outburst, and imposing isolation. Coaxing, soothing, reasoning, and scolding were effective only if employed in conjunction with other methods. As would be predicted on the basis of learning principles, "giving the child his own way" led to more frequent temper displays subsequently. In other words, if the child finds that his aggressive responses are rewarded, i.e., get him what he wants, he will repeat them.

On the basis of her investigations and appraisal of the children's total home situation, Goodenough concluded that:

> The control of anger in children is best achieved when the child's behavior is viewed with serenity and tolerance, when the standards set are within the child's ability to achieve, and when the standards are adhered to with sufficient consistency to permit the child to learn through uniformity of experience, without such mechanical adherence to routine that the child's emotional and physical well-being is sacrificed to the demands of an inflexible schedule. However, when departures from the established schedules are made, they should be determined by a recognition of the needs [i.e., taking into account the motivated, previously rewarded habits] of the child and not simply by the convenience or mood of the adult in charge. Self control in the parents is, after all, likely to be the best guarantee of self control in the child (30, 248).

SUMMARY

As a consequence of continued maturation and learning—and their interactions—the child manifests impressive advances in motor skills, language, and cognition during his second year. Many new locomotor responses (e.g., walking) emerge, apparently as a consequence of maturation; until the child's neuromuscular apparatus is sufficiently mature, efforts to teach these responses meet with failure.

During this year, the child begins to associate symbols (words) to objects and to use words meaningfully. At the same time, his understanding of language increases phenomenally, and his speech becomes more complex and more comprehensible. Fascinating psycholinguistic data and analyses indicate that, during the second year, the child begins to generate novel sentences with real, though elementary, grammar. Early language acquisition cannot be adequately explained in terms of reinforcement theory or direct training.

Between the ages of 1 and 2, the child is still in the sensorimotor period of cognitive development, acquiring knowledge of the world by means of perceptual-motor activities. During the final stages of this period, generally the second half of the second year, the child's cognitive functioning becomes more complex, more objective, and increasingly oriented toward reality, while his behavior shows definite intention, directionality, goal-orientation, and—in new situations—active experimentation.

Socialization training by parents ordinarily begins in earnest during this period and it is at first centered on the inhibition of undesirable behaviors —toilet training, curbing tantrums and destructive activities, and restricting free exploration. The effectiveness of socialization training depends on the child's relationship to his parents and his motivation to please them and to avoid the unpleasant feelings generated by punishment or rejection. Toilet training will proceed with minimum conflict if the mother is warm and loving and encourages gradual acquisition of control. If this training is given too early, too rigidly, or too severely, the child may become intensely anxious or feel highly aggressive toward his parents.

Parental acceptance and a reasonably permissive attitude toward the child's exploration and emerging autonomy are likely to foster the development of self-confidence, independence, and spontaneity. The overprotected or restricted child is more likely to become anxious and dependent, avoiding novel and challenging situations.

During this period, attachment to the mother is still intense, reaching a peak at about 18 months of age; the child will manifest strong "separation protests" when she is absent. Long separations from the mother at this time may result in enduring emotional maladjustments.

At this age, fear reactions are commonly elicited by noises, strange events, falling (or danger of falling), animals, and persons or objects associated with pain. Anger and aggression appear to be aroused by many everyday occurrences (e.g., bedwetting or fatigue) and are manifested in a variety of forms, such as screaming or holding the breath.

Case Material. Peter B and Jack L in the Second Year

It will be recalled that at 1 year of age Peter and Jack were quite similar in their rate of physical growth, mental ability, and personality tendencies.

However, during the second year, the major differences in the attitudes and behaviors of each set of parents began to be manifested in their treatment of the children and, subsequently, in the children's overt behavior.

Peter B.   Both of Peter's parents were overly concerned about his health, growth, and general maturation. They were apprehensive about his inability to walk or talk by 14 months of age. They decided not to take a summer vacation because they didn't want to take Peter with them, and were reluctant to leave him with relatives for fear that something unexpected might happen. Peter's mother rarely allowed him to roam in the backyard. She feared he might dirty or injure himself; hence Peter's activity was largely restricted to the house and porch.

Peter's grandmother was more permissive with him. However, this leniency angered Mrs. B, who felt that "routine" was the most important part of child training. She, therefore, ruled that Peter would not be allowed to go to his grandmother's during his "habit formation period."

Peter's father was a mild-mannered man with chronic asthma. He was dominated by his wife and approved of Mrs. B's babying and protective attitude toward Peter.

Mrs. B exemplified the *affectionate* and *restrictive* mother. She was afraid to let Peter explore his environment and he acceded to her wishes with a minimum of rebellion. However, this pattern of maternal attitudes is likely to lead to fear and caution in novel situations. Because the child has not learned how to handle new stresses, he tends to withdraw when complex and novel stimuli occur.

When Peter came to the Fels nursery school at age 2, he behaved in just this way. Initially, he was afraid to leave his mother, and he whimpered when he thought that she might leave. During the first days of school, he would sit in the sand and cry. Most of the time he played alone, and seemed afraid of entering into activities with the other children. He was markedly cautious on the sliding board, swing, and in other games which involved gross motor activity. He seemed afraid to try anything that contained an element of novelty or danger.

As one might expect, he was extremely conforming and obedient with adults and usually associated with them, rather than with his age-mates. Peter's speech at this time consisted of only a few grunts, and one word, "mama." At home Mrs. B anticipated all of Peter's needs and satisfied his desires before he had to ask for the object he wanted. Since speech was not a necessary tool in obtaining desired goals, Peter had not bothered to learn to communicate verbally with other people.

Jack L.   While Jack's parents were also concerned about the child's development, the focus of their concern was in a very different direction. Their main concern was that Jack should be a "real boy" and not a sissy. Mr. L became angry if Jack's mother bought him clothes with ruffles, velvet, or any accessory that appeared feminine. Both parents wanted Jack to be rough, tough, and prepared for all eventualities. Although Jack was punished for wandering far from home, there was not the strict control over exploration that Peter experienced. Jack was allowed to play outside with peers, and minor rebellion was accepted because his misbehavior was viewed as "boyish." His mother was affectionate and accepting but more permissive of autonomy and exploration than Mrs. B.

In nursery school at age 2, Jack's behavior was almost the complete opposite of Peter's. Jack spent his time on the slide, the bikes, and any apparatus he could find that would allow him to test his motor skills and abilities; Peter sat in the sandbox and cried. Jack had an air of self-confidence and, when attacked, he defended himself and his property. Peter, on the other hand, avoided any contact with peers and retreated in the face of attack.

Jack's manner reflected confidence, assurance, and minimal fear. Peter was afraid of separation from his mother, apprehensive about violation of adult rules, and cautious in his approach to new situations. It might appear at this point that Peter had all the problems, while Jack had none.

Such, however, was not the case. Although Jack was bold in his relations with the environment, he was beginning to feel a different kind of anxiety which would eventually cause him much tension. Jack was afraid of being passive, afraid of not being masculine. His parents became anxious and uncomfortable when he displayed any behavior they would regard as "not boyish." They strongly believed that a boy must be tough, athletic, aggressive, and independent. They were not ready to accept crying, occasional dependence, or any other behavior that suggested passivity and weakness. Jack's parents were communicating these standards to him, and his behavior began to reflect these steady pressures.

References

1. Arsenian, J. M. Young children in an insecure situation. *J. abnorm. soc. Psychol.,* 1943, *38,* 225–249.
2. Bayley, N. Mental growth during the first three years. In R. G. Barker, J. S. Kounin, & H. F. Wright (Eds.), *Child behavior and development.* New York: McGraw-Hill, 1943, 87–106.
3. Bayley, N. Comparisons of mental and motor test scores for ages 1–15 months by sex, birth order, race, geographical location, and education of parents. *Child Develpm.,* 1965, *36,* 379–411.
4. Bayley, N. Bayley's Scales of Infant Development. New York: The Psychological Corporation, 1968.
5. Bowlby, J. Separation anxiety. *Int. J. Psychoanal.,* 1960, *41,* 89–113.
6. Braine, M. D. S. The ontogeny of English phrase structure: the first phase. *Language,* 1963, *39,* 1–13.
7. Bronfenbrenner, U. Socialization and social class through time and space. In E. E. Maccoby, T. M. Newcomb, & E. L. Hartley (Eds.), *Readings in social psychology.* New York: Holt, Rinehart and Winston, 1958 (3rd ed.), 400–425.
8. Brown, R. *Social psychology.* New York: Free Press of Glencoe, 1965.

9. Brown, R. The dialogue in early childhood. Unpublished paper, Harvard University, 1966.
10. Brown, R., & Bellugi, U. Three processes in the child's acquisition of syntax. *Harvard Educ. Rev.*, 1964, *34*, 133–151.
11. Child, I. L. Socialization. In G. Lindzey (Ed.), *Handbook of social psychology.* Reading, Mass.: Addison-Wesley, 1954, 655–692.
12. Chomsky, N. *Syntactic structures.* The Hague: Mouton, 1957.
13. Chomsky, N. The formal nature of language. In E. Lenneberg (Ed.), *Biological foundations of language.* New York: Wiley, 1967, 397–442.
14. Dennis, W. Causes of retardation among institutional children: Iran. *J. genet. Psychol.*, 1960, *96*, 47–59.
15. Despert, J. L. Urinary control and enuresis. *Psychosom. Med.*, 1944, *6*, 294–307.
16. Dollard, J., & Miller, N. E. *Personality and psychotherapy.* New York: McGraw-Hill, 1950.
17. Erikson, E. H. A healthy personality for every child: a fact finding report: a digest. Midcentury White House Conference on Children and Youth. In J. Seidman (Ed.), *The adolescent: a book of readings.* New York: Dryden (Holt, Rinehart and Winston), 1953.
18. Ervin, S. M. Imitation and structural changes in children's language. In E. H. Lenneberg (Ed.), *New directions in the study of language.* Cambridge: M.I.T. Press, 1964, 163–190.
19. Ervin, S. M., & Miller, W. R. Language development. In H. Stevenson (Ed.), *Child psychology. (62nd Yearb. nat. Soc. Stud. Educ.)* Chicago: Univer. of Chicago Press, 1963, 108–143.
20. Ervin-Tripp, S. M., & Slobin, D. I. Psycholinguistics. *Ann. Rev. Psychol.*, 1966, *17*, 435–474.
21. Escalona, S. The use of infant tests for predictive purposes. In W. E. Martin & C. B. Stendler (Eds.), *Readings in child development.* New York: Harcourt, Brace & World, 1954, 95–103.
22. Federov, V. K. Cited in H. L. Rheingold & W. C. Stanley, Developmental psychology. *Ann. Rev. Psychol.*, 1963, *14*, 1–28.
23. Flavell, J. H. *The developmental psychology of Jean Piaget.* Princeton, N.J.: Van Nostrand, 1963.
24. Flavell, J. H., & Hill, J. P. Developmental psychology. *Ann. Rev. Psychol.*, 1969, *20*.
25. Freud, A., & Burlingham, D. T. *War and children.* New York: Medical War Books, 1943.
26. Freud, A., & Burlingham, D. T. *Infants without families.* New York: International Universities Press, 1944.
27. Garn, S. M., & Haskell, J. A. Fat thickness and development status in childhood and adolescence. *Amer. J. Dis. Child.*, 1960, *99*, 746–751.
28. Gesell, A., Halverson, H. M., Thompson, H., Ilg, F. L., & Costner, C. S. *The first five years of life: a guide to the study of the preschool child.* New York: Harper & Row, 1940.
29. Gesell, A., & Thompson, H. Learning and growth in identical infant twins: an experimental study of the method of co-twin control. *Genet. Psychol. Monogr.*, 1929, *6*, 1–124.
30. Goodenough, F. L. Anger in young children. *Inst. Child Welf. Monogr.* Minneapolis: Univer. of Minnesota Press. 1931.
31. Heinecke, C. M. Some effects of separating two-year-old children from their parents: a comparative study. *Human Relat.* 1956, *9*, 106–176.

32. Hindley, C. B., Filliozat, A. M., Klackenberg, G., Nicolet-Meister, D., & Sand, E. A. Some differences in infant feeding and elimination training in five European longitudinal samples. *J. child Psychol. Psychiat., 6,* 1965, 179–201.

33. Hindley, C. B., Filliozat, A. M., Klackenberg, G., Nicolet-Meister, D., & Sand, E. A. Differences in age of walking in the European longitudinal samples. *Human Biol., 38,* 1966, 364–379.

34. Honzik, M. P. The constancy of mental test performance during the preschool period. *J. genet. Psychol.,* 1938, *52,* 285–302

35. Honzik, M. P. A sex difference in the age of onset of the parent-child resemblance in intelligence. *J. educ. Psychol.,* 1963, *54* (5), 231–237.

36. Huschka, M. The child's response to coercive bowel training. *Psychosom. Med.,* 1942, *4,* 301–308.

37. Jersild, A. T., & Holmes, F. B. Children's fears. *Child Develpm. Monogr.,* 1935, No. 20, 358.

38. LeVine, B., & LeVine, R. Nyansongo: a Gusii community in Kenya. In B. Whiting (Ed.), *Six cultures: studies of child rearing.* New York: Wiley, 1963, 15–202.

39. Levy, D. M. *Maternal overprotection.* New York: Columbia Univer. Press, 1943.

40. Macfarlane, J. W., Allen, L., & Honzik, M. P. *A developmental study of the behavior problems of normal children between twenty-two months and fourteen years.* (University of California Publications in Child Development, Vol. II.) Berkeley: Univer. of California Press, 1954.

41. Mallitskaya, M. K. A method for using pictures to develop speech comprehension in children at the end of the first and in the second year of life. *Voprosy Psikhol.,* 1960, No. 3, 122–126.

42. McNeill, D. The development of language. In P. Mussen (Ed.), *Manual of child psychology.* New York: Wiley, in press.

43. Menyuk, P. Syntactic rules used by children from preschool through the first grade. *Child Develpm.,* 1964, *35,* 533–546.

44. Menzies, H. F. Children in day nurseries with special reference to the child under two years old. *Lancet,* 1946, 251, 499–501.

45. Meredith, H. V. Change in the stature and body weight of North American boys during the last 80 years. In L. Lipsitt & C. Spiker (Eds.), *Advances in child development and behavior.* Vol. I. New York: Academic Press, 1963, 69–114.

46. Miller, G. A., & McNeill, D. Language. In G. Lindzey (Ed.), *Handbook of social psychology.* Reading, Mass.: Addison-Wesley, 1968 (2nd ed.).

47. Peatman, J. G., & Higgons, R. A. Relation of infants' weight and body build to locomotor development. *Amer. J. Orthopsychiat.,* 1942, *12,* 234–240.

48. Piaget, J. *The origins of intelligence in children.* New York: Norton, 1963.

49. Robertson, J., & Bowlby, J. Responses of young children to separation from their mothers: II. Observations of the sequences of response of children aged 18 to 24 months during the course of separation. *Courrier,* 1952, *2,* 131–142.

50. Schaffer, H. R., & Emerson, P. E. Patterns of response to physical contact in early human development. *J. child Psychol. Psychiat.,* 1964, *5,* 1–13.

51. Schaffer, H. R., & Emerson, P. E. The development of social attachments in infancy. *Monogr. Soc. Res. Child Develpm.,* 1964, *29,* No. 3.

52. Sears, R. R., Maccoby, E. E., & Levin, H. *Patterns of child-rearing.* New York: Harper & Row, 1957.

53. Sears, R. R., Whiting, J. W. M., Nowlis, V., & Sears, P. S. Some child-rearing antecedents of aggression and dependency in young children. *Genet. Psychol. Monogr.,* 1953, *47,* 135–234.

54. Shirley, M. M. The first two years: a study of twenty-five babies. Vol. II. Intel-

lectual development. *Inst. Child Welf. Monogr.* No. 7, Minneapolis: Univer. of Minnesota Press, 1933.

55. Slobin, D. Imitation and grammatical development in children. In N. Endler, L. Boulter, & H. Osser (Eds.), *Contemporary issues in developmental psychology.* New York: Holt, Rinehart and Winston, 1968, 437–443.

56. Smith, M. E. An investigation of the development of the sentence and the extent of vocabulary in young children. *Univer. Iowa Stud. Child Welf.,* 1926, *3,* No. 5.

57. Smith, S. Influence of illness during the first two years on infant development. *J. genet. Psychol.,* 1931, *39,* 284–287.

58. Stott, D. H. An empirical approach to motivation based on the behavior of the young child. *J. child Psychol. Psychiat.,* 1961, *2,* 97–117.

59. Thompson, H. Physical growth. In L. Carmichael (Ed.), *Manual of child psychology.* New York: Wiley, 1954 (2nd ed.), 292–334.

60. Watson, E. H., & Lowrey, G. H. *Growth and development of children.* Chicago: Year Book Publishers, 1958 (3rd ed.).

61. Weir, R. H. *Language in the crib.* The Hague: Mouton, 1962.

62. White, R. W. Motivation reconsidered: the concept of competence. *Psychol. Rev.,* 1959, *66,* 297–333.

63. Wittenborn, J. R. A study of adoptive children. *Psychol. Monogr.,* 1956, *70* (No. 408–410), 1–115.

part III
The
Preschool
Years

8

The Preschool Years: Motor and Cognitive Development

During the period from 2 to 5 years of age, personality differences among children become increasingly evident and, by the age of 5, are well defined. Furthermore, longitudinal observations on children from the Fels Research Institute's population indicate that, by age 5, several clear-cut personality traits are established which, in some cases, persist into adolescence and adulthood.

The next three chapters will describe the physical, cognitive, and personality developments that occur during the preschool period. The term cognition (adjectival form, cognitive) is a broad one referring to the processes by which knowledge is acquired and utilized. Thus it includes the processes of perceiving, learning, thinking, concept formation, and problem-solving. The critical developments during this period include (1) rapid growth of language and cognitive capacities, (2) the beginning of sex-typing, (3) identification with parental models, (4) emergence of a superego or conscience, and (5) the initial establishment of defensive behaviors in reaction to anxiety-arousing situations.

The physical, motor, and cognitive changes of these years will be summarized first.

PHYSICAL GROWTH

By age 3, the average boy stands about 38 inches tall and weighs about 33 pounds. The average girl is almost as tall (37.6 inches), and nearly as heavy

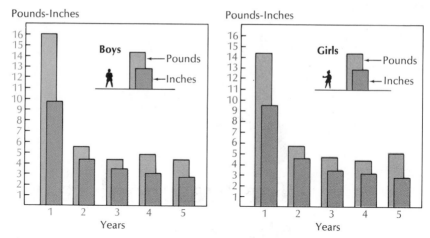

Fig. 8.1. Average gain in heights and weights of boys and girls from birth to 5 years.

(32.5 pounds) (67). Figure 8.1 shows the average yearly gain in pounds and inches of boys and girls from birth to 5 years of age.

As a result of gradual increases, the average 5-year-old boy has attained a height of 43.6 inches and a weight of 42.8 pounds. At age 5, the average girl's measurements are roughly comparable—although, again, the boy is slightly taller and heavier (67).

Children tend to maintain their relative standing in height and weight during the preschool period. Those who are tall and heavy for their age at 2 years are likely to be tall and heavy, compared with other 5-year-olds, when they are 5. The correlation between heights at ages 2 and 5 is over .80, and the correlation between weights at these ages is about the same (51).

The child's stature during the preschool period is a moderately good predictor of his height in early adulthood, the correlation between heights at these two stages being about .70 (51). A correlation of this magnitude, although highly significant, indicates that quite a few individuals *do* shift in relative height between these two age periods; many who are short preschoolers, compared with their peers, become medium-tall or tall adults.

During this period the child's body form is also becoming more mature. As the upper parts of the body begin to approximate adult size, their growth slows down and eventually stops, giving the lower extremities a chance to catch up by continued growth. Thus, during the preschool years, head growth is slow, limb growth is rapid, and trunk growth is intermediate (59). The nursery school child generally has a relatively large, round, and protruding stomach, but by the time the child reaches his sixth birthday, his body proportions are a great deal more like those of an adult.

Although the boys are only slightly heavier than the girls, there are marked sex differences in body composition—the girls have more fatty tissue, while the boys have more muscle tissue (22, 23).

Along with these changes in body proportions, the child's skeletal, muscular, and nervous systems are becoming more mature. More and more of the cartilage in the child's skeletal system is becoming replaced by bone; the size and number of bones in the body increase, and they become harder. Between 2 and 3, the child's set of temporary teeth is generally completed, and he is adequately equipped to eat adult food.

Significant changes in muscular development also occur during this period. Up until about 4 years of age, growth in the muscular system is roughly proportional to the growth of the body as a whole. Thereafter, the muscles develop at a faster rate, so that about 75 percent of the child's weight increase during the fifth year can be attributed to muscular development (59). Throughout this period, however, the larger muscles remain better developed than the small, fine muscles—partly accounting for the fact that the young child is more skillful in activities involving large movement than in those involving finer coordinations. Needless to say, individual differences in strength and muscular development will depend on many factors, such as the child's constitution, general health, and habits of eating, sleeping, and activity.

Other physiological changes also increase the child's endurance and enable him to participate in more strenuous activities. During this period, respiration becomes deeper and slower; heart rate also slows down and becomes less variable; conversely, blood pressure increases steadily (59).

The nervous system grows rapidly in the nursery school years. For example, the child's brain has reached 75 percent of its adult weight by the end of the second year; by age 6 it has increased to 90 percent of its adult weight (36). Myelinization of the nerve fibers, which has already been nearly completed in the lower portions of the body, is generally completed in the higher brain centers during this period.

During these years, the child's reaction to infection changes. Infections generally produce less of a temperature increase than they did during infancy, but the duration of the illness is generally longer. Moreover, the possibility of serious heart symptoms following a disease is smaller than it was during the first 2 years of life.

Physique and Personality

The question of whether physical build is related to personality is a very old and intriguing one. In recent years, Sheldon (57) proposed a system of categorizing somatotypes (body types) into three major categories: (1) endomorphs, who are generally soft and round, with relatively underdeveloped bone and muscle tissue; (2) mesomorphs, who have strong muscles and bones and strong, tough bodies resistant to injury; and (3) ectomorphs, who tend to be tall and thin, fragile and lightly muscled. Each body type is said to be associated with a particular pattern of personality characteristics and motivations. Endomorphs have tendencies toward gregariousness, relaxation, and physical comfort. Mesomorphs are supposedly assertive, courageous, adventurous, and bold. Ectomorphs tend to introverted, restrained, and socially inhibited.

While the empirical evidence is not strongly supportive of Sheldon's theory, the theory has excited a great deal of interest in the relationship of physique and personality. As we shall see later, there are some interesting relationships between body build and personality during middle childhood and adolescence (see pp. 613–616).

Even during the preschool years there are some significant associations between boys' body builds, on the one hand, and their personality and behavior on the other. Preschool age boys who were short and round, with relatively small bone and muscle development (endomorphs), were rated by nursery school teachers as self-assertive and aggressive. Tall, thin preschool boys, with small muscles and delicate physiques (ectomorphs), were relatively considerate and kind, introverted, and lacking in self-assertion and daring, sociability, aggressiveness, self-reliance, and energy. Such boys tended to daydream a lot, seemed generally to lack boyish interests, and were not likely to be leaders. Preschool boys with good muscle and bone development and athletic physiques (mesomorphs), tended to be leaders in play, masculine in interests, quarrelsome, easily angered, daring, self-assertive, energetic, and self-confident. These mesomorphs seemed to be future "all-American boys"—perhaps because they have a great deal of strength, vigor, and energy, or perhaps because they have learned that they can be successful if they assert themselves. Moreover, it is quite possible that other children and adults perceive well-built, muscular boys as assertive, dominant, and masculine, and react to them in accordance with these perceptions.

It should be noted that the correlations between body build and personality traits, although significant, were not generally high. This means that it is very difficult to make predictions from physique to personality; in spite of the overall statistical relationship, many ectomorphs *are* self-assertive and many mesomorphs are not. A boy's personality cannot really be judged by his physique.

Psychomotor Development

The progressive maturation of the preschool child's neuromusculature lays the foundation for increased skill in psychomotor activities. Learning plays an increasingly greater role in these improvements, but as with younger children, expansion of the repertoire of motor skills must await neuromuscular development.

By age 3, the persisting traces of infancy in the child's motor behavior have about disappeared (24).

> He runs with more smoothness, accelerates and decelerates with greater ease, turns sharper corners, negotiates sudden stops. Can go upstairs unaided alternating his feet. He can jump down from the bottom tread with both feet together, whereas the child aged two leaps down with one foot leading. [A] three [year-old] can jump upward with both feet as much as twelve inches . . .

Steven Conger

he can stand on one foot for a precarious second or more. . . . In the eyes of the three-year-old child himself, his psychomotor development has one especially significant ramification—he is now ready for a tricycle, instead of a "mere kiddy-car with its primitive propulsion" (24, 41–42).

There are other indications of the average 3-year-old's expanding psychomotor development. He can build a tower of 9 or 10 cubes as opposed to the 2-year-old's 6 or 7. In drawing, his strokes are becoming better defined, less diffuse, and less repetitive. He can fold a piece of paper vertically or horizontally, but still not diagonally, even with the aid of a model (24).

By 4, the child's psychomotor skills have increased still further. He can run more smoothly, and is better able to break up the regular rhythms of his stride. Unlike the 3-year-old, who usually is able merely to jump up and down, the 4-year-old is able to make moderately good running and standing broad jumps. He can also skip, though he is still unable to hop. His new athletic feats are partially a function of greater independence of his leg musculature:

Here, as elsewhere, the principle of individuation is at work. There is less totality in his bodily responses; legs, trunk, shoulder, arms react somewhat less in unison. This makes his joints seem more mobile. Where at two and three, he would merely toss or hurl a ball in a propulsive manner (with much torso participation), he can now swing back a more independent arm and execute a strong, over-hand throw (24, 47).

The average 4-year-old has gained sufficient spatial orientation and precision of movement to be able to trace on paper a diagonal-shaped pathway between parallel lines a centimeter apart, and can at last fold a piece of paper diagonally. He is still unable to copy a diamond from a model, but can draw a circle and a cross.

By 5 years of age, the average child has a fairly mature sense of balance, which is reflected in a more self-reliant abandon in his motor behavior. While still unable to hop, he skips and jumps more smoothly. Fine movements have also become better differentiated. Again according to Gesell,

he can pluck a dozen pellets one by one and drop them deftly into a bottle in about 20 seconds, typically with a preferred hand. In drawing, while the five-year old still has some awkwardness in handling diagonal lines, he is capable of straight strokes in all directions; can copy a square and a triangle (though not a diamond); and can at last do a recognizable picture of a man (24, 52).

The athletic skills of most nursery school children are restricted to large muscle coordinations such as climbing, balancing, running, pushing, and pulling. Skill in throwing a ball is much more complex, requiring "a fine sense of static and dynamic balance, accurate timing of delivery and release, good eye-hand coordination, and appropriate functioning of the fingers, as well as the arm, trunk, head, and legs, in controlling the trajectory of the ball" (24, 85). Most children do not master this combination of skills and abilities until they are about 6 years old (32).

Perceptual Development

As he grows in size and strength, and gains in motor skills and abilities, the child's perceptions of the environment are also modified. Perception refers to the individual's selection, organization, and initial interpretation or categorization of sensory impressions—that is, of what he sees, hears, touches, smells, or feels. Initial organizations and interpretations change as a function of learning, labeling, and experience.

Looking at an unstructured stimulus, like an ink blot, the engineer is likely to select and attend to portions of the block that he perceives as resembling engineering instruments; the musician is more likely to select portions that resemble musical instruments. A person who is musically untrained will listen to a piece of music he has never heard before and find it pleasant but completely unfamiliar; a musically trained person, listening to the same music, may select patterns of notes that are organized into themes.

Analogously, the child will select those parts of his sensory impressions that are most salient to him. For example, suppose we present a photograph of a picnic scene in which people are happily engaged in various sports. Boys are much more likely to focus their attention on (i.e., select) those parts of the picture that show boys playing ball, while girls are more likely to be attracted to those parts that show girls at play. A 4-year-old would be quite likely to describe the scene simply as, "boys and girls playing, people talking" while an older child, differentiating more aspects of the stimulus, is more likely to organize his perceptions and integrate the scene, labeling it "a happy church picnic."

As a result of their observations and experimental work, psychologists are able to describe the major trends in perceptual development during the preschool period. These changes are not independent; in fact, each change is closely related to the others.

Greater Differentiation and Accuracy in Visual Perception. The way in which the child organizes what he sees is one of the primary processes which undergo change with age.

Increasing differentiation in perception implies more accuracy and specificity—that is, greater precision in recognizing similarities and differences in physical stimuli. With increasing experience and practice (learning), and as a result of having acquired appropriate language labels, the child tends to make more differentiations among stimuli in his environment. For example, the 5-year-old perceives the stimuli that comprise a typical kitchen as a set of discrete objects (sink, stove, table, chairs, refrigerator). The 1-year-old has not yet learned the labels applied to each of the objects and does not differentiate (or separate out) these discrete elements. For him the kitchen

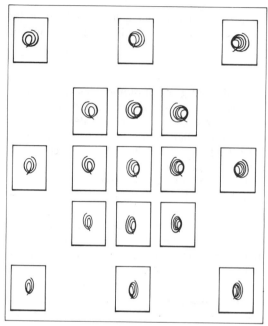

Fig. 8.2. "Scribbles" used in the Gibson & Gibson experiment. (From J. J. Gibson & E. J. Gibson. Perceptual learning: differentiation or enrichment? *Psychol. Rev.,* 1955, Vol. 67. Copyright 1955 by the American Psychological Association. By permission.)

is perceived largely as a conglomeration of different colors and shapes. As the child's perception becomes more differentiated and he has more distinctive labels to apply to objects and events he begins to make different responses (generally more appropriate from the adult point of view) to various stimuli.

The phenomenon is neatly illustrated by a systematic study of the Gibsons (27), who used scribbles as standard stimuli and constructed variations of these standards, differing in number of coils, degree of compression or looseness, and orientation (see Fig. 8.2). The standard was presented to the subject, then withdrawn. Then a pack of cards containing all the variations, as well as four duplicates of the standard, was presented item by item. The subject simply told the experimenter whether each item was the same or different from the standard. At the end of the run through the pack, the subject was shown the standard again, told to observe it carefully, and another run followed. This procedure was repeated until there were no more incorrect identifications.

Compared with older subjects, the younger ones identified many more of the variations incorrectly, or as "same" as the standard, on the first trial. In other words, with advancing age, there was increased ability to distinguish similarities and differences among stimuli immediately.

As the runs continued, errors were eliminated, and, as would be anticipated, the younger children took much longer than the older ones to achieve an errorless run. The youngest child in this study was 4 years old, and it may safely be assumed that younger children would find this task even more difficult. But it is important to note that, with practice, even the youngest subjects were able to do the task—to differentiate between stimuli the same as, and different from, the standard. "The class of undifferentiated items was thus reduced for all the subjects with repetition—the specificity of subjects identifying responses increased. What the subject was learning here, it seemed, was the ways in which the variable items differed from the standard" (26, 186).

In this investigation, experience and practice in differentiation were provided experimentally by requiring each child to repeat the task until he differentiated the stimuli perfectly. This is analogous to what happens "in nature" as the child becomes more mature and has more experience perceiving the world about him. E. J. Gibson proposes a theory of "distinctive features" to explain the phenomenon. "The increasing differentiation of the child's world—objects, sounds, pictures—is, at least in part, a result of learning to respond to the distinctive features of objects, of phonemes, . . . and so on" (26, 186).

The child's increasing skill in detecting what Gibson calls "distinctive features" is demonstrated in a study in the discrimination of letterlike forms called *graphemes*. The study traced the development of grapheme differentiation in relation to certain critical or distinctive features of letters. These are the characteristics or features of each letter (e.g., horizontal, vertical, or oblique orientation; open or closed curved; symmetry or asymmetry) that, in combination, make it unique, identifiable, and distinguishable from other letters (see Fig. 8.3).

In the study, 12 standard, letterlike stimuli were drawn. Half of them were symmetrical, half were asymmetrical; half of them were open, and half were closed. Some combined straight and curved lines; some were composed only of straight lines, others only of curves.

Then 12 transformations or variants were made for each standard form. Some of these were transformations of line to curve or curve to line; of rotation and reversal (45°, 90°, and 180° rotations; left-right reversals and upside-down reversals); breaking or closing letters. Figure 8.4 illustrates the letters and the transformations.

The subjects, 165 children between the ages of 4 and 8, were each presented with a standard grapheme and were then given a wooden frame containing a duplicate of the standard form together with the 12 variants of that form. The child's task was to match the standard with all its variants, selecting out only the exact copy of the standard, removing it from the frame, and giving it to the experimenter. The child's error score was the number of times he chose as "same" an item that did not match the standard. Errors were classified according to the type of transformation.

As might be expected, errors decreased rapidly from ages 4 to 8. Furthermore, some transformations proved to be harder to discriminate

Features	A	B	C	E	K	L	N	U	X	Z
Straight Segment										
Horizontal	+			+		+				+
Vertical		+		+	+	+	+			
Oblique	+				+				+	+
Oblique					+			+	+	
Curve										
Closed		+								
Open vertically								+		
Open horizontally			+							
Intersection	+	+		+	+				+	
Redundancy										
Cyclic change		+		+						
Symmetry	+	+	+	+	+			+	+	
Discontinuity										
Vertical	+				+				+	
Horizontal				+		+	+			+

Fig. 8.3. One possible set of distinctive features for some letters of our alphabet. Each letter is characterized by those features marked "+" in its column. (From E. J. Gibson. Learning to read. *Science,* May, 1965, Vol. 148. Copyright 1965 by The American Association for The Advancement of Science. By permission.)

from the standard than others, and improvement occurs at different rates for different kinds of transformations. Thus, even at the preschool ages tested, ages 4 and 5, there were relatively few break and close errors—e.g., graphemes like O and C were seldom confused. Many 4-year-olds have difficulties with line-to-curve transformations (transformations from U to V), but 5-year-olds have much less trouble with these. Errors of rotation (M to W) and reversal (d to b) follow generally the same pattern as line-to-curve transformations. Errors for transformation in perspective (slanting or tilting a line that previously had not been slanted or tilted) were common and remain so even until age 8, the highest age tested in the study.

It should also be noted that there were marked individual differences at all ages studied. Although the extent of individual differences decreased as the children grew older, tremendous individual differences occurred at ages 4, 5, and 6. Some 4-year-olds, for example, made fewer errors than some 6-year-olds. Findings such as these have implications for practical problems such as those of teaching the child to read.

These findings may be explained in terms of distinctive characteristics or distinctive features of graphemes—"characteristics which are invariant and critical for distinguishability." Thus breaks and closes (O versus C), transformations from line to curve (U versus V), rotations (M versus W), and reversals (d versus b) are all distinctive features which help differentiate graphemes or letters. These characteristics often occur in some combination

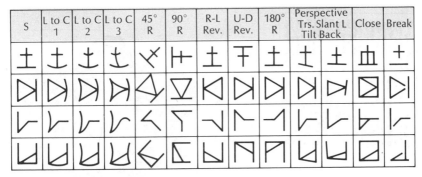

S	L to C 1	L to C 2	L to C 3	45° R	90° R	R-L Rev.	U-D Rev.	180° R	Perspective Trs. Slant L Tilt Back	Close	Break

Fig. 8.4. Matching board for studies of discrimination of graphic forms. (From E. J. Gibson. Development of perception: discrimination of depth compared with discrimination of graphic symbols. In J. C. Wright & J. Kagan [Eds.], Basic cognitive processes in children. *Monogr. Soc. Res. Child Develpm.*, copyright 1963 by The Society for Research in Child Development, Inc., *28*, 18. By permission.)

or "bundles" of distinctive features. For instance, *A* versus *V* includes both rotation and closure as critical differences.

Identifying graphemes and letters accurately involves "a process of isolating and focusing on those features . . . that are both invariant and critical for rendering each one unique" (*25*, 21). Gibson postulates that these distinctions are made on the basis of previous learning. Some distinctions are easier to make than others because the child has had more experience making these distinctions. For example, the distinction between linear and curvilinear forms is a relatively "easy" one because from early infancy (during the sensorimotor period), children probably use curves and straight lines as criteria (distinctive features) for differentiating among various solid objects.

Acquired Distinctiveness. The acquisition of language—which we shall discuss at length shortly—helps in the process of learning that things have different distinctive features, unique characteristics or combinations of characteristics that differentiate them from other things.

The fact that objects are given distinctive names facilitates their being perceived as separate and different from each other. Because a sink and a stove, although both white and shiny, are called by different names, they are perceived as different. *Stimuli become more distinctive when specific language labels are applied to them.* Once the child learns the words "red" and "pink," he is more likely to notice (i.e., perceive) the differences between red and pink material or different sunsets than if he had learned neither word or only one of them. Through learning, labels become attached to differentiated aspects of sensory experience. This learning predisposes the child to attend to the attributes to which the labels refer. These two basic principles of perceptual development—*differentiation of stimuli* and *attaching language labels to specific stimuli*—are associated with three more specific perceptual processes that develop during the preschool and early school years.

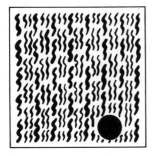

Fig. 8.5

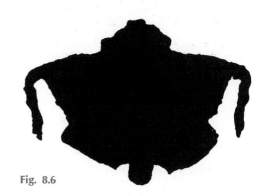

Fig. 8.6

Whole-Part Perception. The 3-year-old child has a tendency to categorize and react to an entire stimulus, rather than to label its separate parts. *This is particularly true of unfamiliar or nonmeaningful stimuli.* Thus, if a 4-year-old child is shown the design in Fig. 8.5 and asked to describe what he sees, he is apt to say, "A box with lines" or "A design." A 7-year-old is more likely to mention the black circle, "There's a black circle and some lines" or "There's a design with a black hole at the bottom."

If the stimulus is an ambiguous ink blot, the 5-year-old is likely to attend to the whole, and to ignore the parts of the stimulus. Thus, to the ink blot shown in Fig. 8.6 the 4-year-old child is apt to say "dirt" or "rock" or "ink." The 8-year-old child is more apt to say, "Butterfly with the wings and head" or "Man with arms and no feet." The older child attends to and labels *component parts of the stimulus* to a greater degree than the younger child.

Of course, if the child has not yet learned the word that applies to an entire stimulus, but has learned labels for the parts, he may name the parts of the stimulus. Thus, if a 4-year-old child is asked to describe a landscape scene with trees and cows in the foreground he may say, "Trees, cows, grass," because he has not yet learned the words "landscape" or "country scene" and because the trees and cows have salience for him. We might formulate a tentative rule about the child's categorizations during the period 4 to 7 years of age. If the internal parts of a stimulus are not distinctive (as in an ink blot), the older child is more likely than the younger to differentiate the stimulus. Moreover, if the younger child has a popular label to apply to the whole stimulus, even though the internal parts might be distinctive, he will be more likely than the older child to categorize the whole, rather than the parts. It is only when the younger child has difficulty identifying or labeling the whole, and does not have any difficulty with the parts, that he will attend to the latter rather than the former.

The young child's preference for reacting to the whole stimulus rather than the parts interferes with his ability to *notice* changes in the internal parts of a stimulus (56). Children were initially shown complete outlines of objects, but with succeeding exposures, inner detailed parts were added, and the child had to specify which internal part had been added. The younger children (age 4) were much inferior to 8-year-olds in recognizing the parts that had been added to the picture. With age, the child became increasingly more capable of attending to both the *whole* and the *part* (56). As most problems require the separation of parts from the whole, the young child is at a disadvantage in many problem situations.

Differentiation is a major component of progress in Heinz Werner's stimulating organismic theory (63, 64). According to this theory, the course of development of perception, thinking, and language involves progress from the global, undifferentiated, and unarticulated to the discrete, highly differentiated, specific, and integrated. As Werner saw it, "wherever development occurs it proceeds from a state of relative globality and lack of differentiation to a state of increasing differentiation, articulation, and hierarchic integration" (64, 126). The child's thought and language, like his perception, are at first vague and diffuse; but, with development, they become differentiated into parts. These parts are then articulated with each other into new, differentiated and integrated wholes—wholes in which the parts are separate, yet coordinated, and a higher level of organization is achieved.

Perception of Spatial Orientation. It is a common observation that young children will look at pictures either rightside up or upside down, and this does not seem to make any difference in their understanding. Moreover, they tend to confuse letters which are mirror-image reversals of each other, such as *p* and *q*, and *b* and *d*. One might therefore conclude that preschool children disregard orientation in their perceptions. The reader will recall that the 4- and 5-year-old subjects in the Gibson study, summarized above, found it difficult to differentiate reversals and rotations of graphemes.

Recently this view of the child's difficulties in handling spatial orientation has been challenged, however. According to the data of one study, children as young as 4 or 5 years of age can quite readily learn to differentiate between a stimulus which is identical with a standard or sample figure (a line drawing), and one that is a reversal of this figure. In the first part of the experiment, 4- and 5-year-old subjects were given a number of "pretest trials." On each trial, the subject was presented with a card with a standard stimulus (e.g., ⟋▽⟍) and two other stimuli below it, one identical with the standard and one different (e.g., a picture of a familiar object). Subjects were rewarded by the flashing of a bright red light if they touched the identical stimulus. This was of course a very easy task. Following the pretraining, subjects were presented with the test cards. These contained a standard figure, some geometric form, and below it an identical figure and one that was an up-side-down, or left-right reversal of the standard. Subjects made very few errors in choosing between the correct and the reversed figure. In other words, preschool children "have little difficulty, on the average, in discriminating stimuli on the basis of their spatial orientation *provided the task requires a response to this cue*" (67, 1120, italics ours). Perhaps, as Gibson suggests, children at this age do not ordinarily attend to or detect reversals because these are not critical in object differentiation. When one is dealing with objects, reversals "indicate not a different object but a change in the position of the same object. They must be tolerated in order for size and shape constancy to be possible" (26, 181–182).

Apparently the young child, although often failing to pay heed to the orientation of objects, is *capable* of detecting and reacting to spatial orientation if his attention is specifically called to this dimension and if he is rewarded for attending to this. Thus many 5-year-olds appear to have difficulty detecting the differences between a letter and its mirror image, such as *b* and *d*, *p* and *q*. However, as the study summarized above indicates, young children can *learn* to make these distinctions quite easily if they are rewarded for differentiating.

This brings us to a very important general point about the young child's responses. In dealing with many perceptual, cognitive, and language phenomena, we must make a clear distinction between the child's *capacity* and his *performance*. In the case of the geometric figures and their reversals, it is clear that the child is capable of making the distinction—he is able to perceive the differences between *b* and *d*, for example—but his overt responses do not ordinarily reflect this ability. However, he will make a response based on this discrimination only if he regards it as relevant (for example, if making the distinction is rewarding) or he has already learned a specific response to either of the stimuli. (The linguists make an analogous distinction, pointing out that children's *performance* in speech is not a valid index of his linguistic *competence*, i.e., his fundamental comprehension of the language and underlying knowledge of the rules of syntax.)

With increasing age, the child comes to regard spatial orientation of objects as a relevant dimension. This advance is probably due to further experience in which the dimensions of upright and upside-down are relevant, and also, in part, to learning labels such as *right, left, up, down,* and therefore attending to these directions.

Amount of Information Necessary for Recognition. Compared with older children or adolescents, the 4-year-old child requires more *clues* in order to recognize an object (66). Thus, if a 10-year-old is shown a series of dots as in Fig. 8.7 he is likely to perceive it as a rabbit's face. The 4-year-old will require many more dots to be filled in before he recognizes this pattern as resembling a rabbit. With age, *less* stimulus support is necessary to allow the child to recognize familiar objects. In effect, the young child requires a great deal of extra information in order to come to the same perceptual conclusion as that arrived at by the older child with less information.

These are some of the perceptual processes that develop during the preschool and early school years. Little has been said about perception of sound, touch, or smell because most of the research has involved visual perception. However, it is reasonable to assume that similar changes occur in other sensory modalities. That is, the child learns to differentiate streams of speech into individual words. If the mother calls the baby in the family

Fig. 8.7

"Little Bobby," the 4-year-old child behaves as if these two words were one; and if asked what his baby brother's name is he will say, "Little Bobby." With age, he perceives this pattern of sounds as *two discrete* units.

It should be obvious that what is perceived (or experienced via sensory information) is very much related to the language labels the child has acquired. In fact, some social scientists believe that the language of a culture exerts a powerful influence on the way the world is experienced. For example, the Eskimos have several words to describe snow (i.e., depending on whether it is composed of large, wet flakes or small, powdered ones), and these specific words probably help sensitize the Eskimo child to these different aspects of snow; American children are apt to perceive only one kind of snow.

LANGUAGE DEVELOPMENT

As we have already indicated in Chapter 7, pp. 247–254, language is a critical factor in cognitive development, and the child's progress in language during the preschool years is astounding. Between the ages of 3 and 5 the child adds over 50 new words to his vocabulary each month, on the average. Data collected during the 1920s indicated that the average 2-year-old had an effective vocabulary (words he can use or understand) of 272 words; the average 3-year-old had an effective vocabulary of 896 words; the average 4-year-old, 1540; and the average 5-year-old, over 2000.

A more recent investigation, conducted in the late 1950s, indicated that children had larger vocabularies than children of 30 years ago, and that they talked in lengthier clauses and sentences. Thus 3-year-olds in 1930 used 3.4 words per "sentence" on the average, but children of the same age in 1957 averaged 4.0 words. Four-year olds of 1930 averaged 4.3 words per sentence in contrast with an average of 5.3 in 1957. While it is difficult to explain this kind of increase in sentence length and vocabulary size during two decades, it has been suggested that this is at least partially attributable to

> the advent of radio and television, fewer foreign born and bilingual children, the rise of nursery schools affording more opportunities for language stimulation outside the home for the formerly underprivileged groups of children, more leisure time for parents to spend with their children, and better economic conditions allowing parents even in lower income brackets to provide more stimulating environments for their children (50, 15).

Increases in vocabulary size or sentence length are not the only bases for assessing capacity to use language and to communicate. In addition to acquiring an immense number of new words between the ages of 2 and 5, the child learns to use them far more efficiently and flexibly. As the child advances through the preschool years, he talks more and his speech becomes richer, more comprehensible, better articulated, and more complex in grammatical structure.

The 2-year-old child is at an "early sentence stage" characterized by a predominance of nouns and a pronounced absence of articles, auxiliaries, verbs, prepositions, and conjunctions. This stage gradually gives way to the short sentence stage, with sentences of 3.5 to 4.5 words having the same general structural characteristics as those of the preceding stage, but to a lesser degree. Inflections have not yet been mastered, and only one or two sentences out of fifty are likely to be compound or complex. At about 4 years, the child begins to enter the complete sentence stage, using 6- to 8-word sentences "characterized by greater definiteness and complexity, as shown by an increased use of relational words and a fairly good mastery of inflections" (49, 552).

Different areas of language develop at different rates (62). For example, only 32 percent of the average 2-year-old's sounds are clearly articulated, and the greatest increase in articulation proficiency occurs between ages 3 and 3½. By 8, the child's articulation has attained essentially mature form. Vocabulary level, on the other hand, continues to increase into adulthood (62).

Grammar. While the syntactic (grammatical) system of any language is complex, children as young as 3 or 4 have clearly mastered certain fundamental grammatical rules. This is an impressive accomplishment, "one of the most complicated intellectual achievements of children" (16, 116). Paradoxically, the young child's mastery of grammar is most evident from certain grammatical errors (unlawful utterances) he is likely to make. By studying these errors we find that the child is in fact making use of rules of grammar which permit him to generate new sentences.

> Suppose a child comes in from the yard and says, "I digged a hole," or comes back from a drive in the country and says, "We saw some sheeps and oxes."

In saying *digged, sheeps, and oxes,* he produced words that are not actual utterances in English. We can be fairly sure, therefore, that he has not heard these from anyone and so is not simply imitating. As long as a child speaks correctly he may only be producing utterances he has heard. We cannot after all, keep track of every morpheme, word, and sentence a child has had a chance to learn to imitate. When he speaks incorrectly or unlawfully he is not likely to be imitating.

In the case of such unlawful utterances as *digged* and *sheeps,* we are, in addition, able to guess the source of the creations. They seem to be overgeneralizations of the regular forms of the past and the plural. As it happens English verbs and nouns do not all follow the regular inflectional paradigms. By treating irregulars as if they were regulars the child exposes the inductive operations of his mind and reveals to us his possession of a productive formula (7, 297).

To study the child's acquisition of grammar more systematically, Berko designed an interesting "game" in which children reveal their knowledge of grammatical rules. For example, the child is shown a picture of a small animal and is told:

"This is a *wug.* Now there are two of them. There are two_____." The experimenter holds her voice up to signal the child that he is to complete the sentence; he will usually supply *wug/-z/.* For a different animal the word is *bik* and the correct plural *bik/ -s/.* For a third animal it is *niss* and the plural *niss/ -iz/* (7, 297–298).

Printed English uses the letter *s* for all these endings; but as attention to pronunciation will reveal, the endings are distinct and pronounced differently.

Other materials, presented as a picture-book game, provided an opportunity to make an inventory of young children's knowledge of grammatical rules relating to plural and possessive endings; simple past, third person indicative, and progressive verbs; comparative and superlative forms of adjectives.

The use of the regular inflections for children seems to be more general than it is for adults. Both kinds of subjects were shown a picture of a man swinging something about his head and told: "This is a man who knows how to gling. He glings every day. Today he glings. Yesterday he_____." Adults hang suspended among *gling, glang, glung,* and even *glought* but children promptly say *glinged.* Dr. Berko also tested to see whether children who generalize the regular inflection would correctly imitate irregular forms or would assimilate them to the rules. She showed a picture and said, for instance, "Here is a goose and here are two geese. There are two_____." Most of her subjects said *gooses* and performed similarly with other irregular forms. These observations suggest that rules of great generality may survive and override a number of counter instances (7, 298).

Berko's youngest subjects were 4 years old, and all of them had mastered the inflectional rules of English. Even younger children know grammatical rules. Brown and Fraser (8) recorded 500 spontaneous utterances made by each of 13 children between the ages of 2 and 3, who were in their homes under conditions as natural as possible. These utterances were then analyzed in various ways to determine their grammatical structure. The speech of each child was found to be "a systematic reduction of adult speech, largely accomplished by omitting function words [such as articles and prepositions] which carry little information" (8, 79). But these reduced sentences revealed that the child had acquired grammatical rules, that he had induced the formulas that govern the construction of new utterances.

These swift strides in language development are immensely significant from several points of view. First of all, in acquiring grammatical rules (even though he can't state them), the young child gives evidence of remarkable intellectual ability and accomplishment. Certainly it is difficult to account for this accomplishment in terms of learning, rewarded responses, generalization, or imitation. While in our opinion no adequate explanation is available at present, apparently some kind of active process of concept formation and/or processing of complex information must be involved. The acquisition of complex language skills, occurring so early and so rapidly, presents a major challenge to the usual learning-theory explanations about how knowledge is acquired. More importantly, language plays a key role in the development of cognitive processes.

Language and Cognitive Development. As the child's facility in language improves by leaps and bounds, his cognitive abilities also undergo radical modifications. The preschool child of 3 or 4 learns, perceives, thinks, reasons, and solves problems in ways that are vastly different from those that characterize the 1- or 2-year-old.

Once a basic understanding of language is acquired, subsequent learning becomes increasingly controlled and regulated by words. The famous Russian psychologist Luria points out that "in the early stages of child development, speech is only a means of communication with adults and other children. . . . Subsequently it becomes also a means whereby he organizes his experience and regulates his own actions. So the child's activity is mediated through words" (47, 116).

A series of Russian experiments, conducted in Luria's laboratory, show how language—and particularly, the child's own verbalizations—become increasingly effective in controlling the child's behavior during the preschool period. In one experiment the child is seated before a red and green light, and he is given a rubber bulb which he can press, "If you see a red light, press. If you see a green light, do not press."

Children of 2, 3, 4½, and 5½ respond differently to these instructions. The experimenter's words seem to have little or no effect on the behavior of subjects under 2 years of age, who squeeze the bulb in response to either light. According to Luria's data, which are not reported in detail, the child of 2½ or 3 responds appropriately to the experimenter's instructions and can repeat them, but can not regulate his behavior by his own speech—that is, he is unable to instruct himself, and he cannot effectively command himself to inhibit a motor act that he has begun (47).

While these Russian findings are provocative, other researchers have concluded that the young child *is* capable of controlling his own behavior and of inhibiting responses by means of self-commands (1, 37). In one study, 3-year olds were able to establish effective self-instruction— instructing themselves to respond to stimuli (lights) and to terminate or inhibit motor (lever-pressing) responses—after only a brief period of training. In a pretest (before training), these children gave little evidence of being able to generate their own commands.

Nevertheless, Luria has made one fundamental generalization: as the child matures his own speech becomes more powerful in controlling his behavior and at the same time the child shifts from loud, overt speech to covert, primarily internal, subvocal speech.

> the child's speech, which directs his solution of a problem, is at first unabbreviated and full; but . . . later, as he masters his actions, it becomes increasingly abbreviated and contracted. First, the child ceases to say everything aloud and in full; his speech sinks to a whisper, its grammatical structure becomes contracted and broken, he begins to utter only separate words indicating necessary objects or actions at critical points; after a certain time his speech ceases, and he begins to perform his task in silence. Occasionally, when children utter stray remarks, the fact that speech has not disappeared, but has only taken new concealed forms, is revealed. Full, overt speech, therefore, gradually becomes transformed into contracted, internal speech. This internal speech, however, continues to fulfill the same function, that of mobilizing the systematized connections of past experience, which may be useful for orientation in the new conditions and for the regulation of future actions. The child's speech, in this contracted form, is indissolubly linked with his thinking . . . (47, 116).

This last statement of Luria's is most important. Advances in language pave the way for progress in complex learning, concept formation, thinking, reasoning, and problem-solving. These high-level cognitive activities are considerably enhanced by verbal mediation or mediated generalization, and this, in turn, is closely linked to the acquisition of language.

Verbal Mediation.   When the child can use speech efficiently for self-instruction, words become mediators of actions. What is a mediator or mediated response? According to Kendler, it "is a response, or a series of responses, which intercedes between the external stimulus and the overt response to provide stimulation that influences [the] eventual course of behavior. These responses may be overt, but they are usually presumed to be covert" (41, 34).

In mediated generalization, the child may apply the same label to two or more objects and, consequently, react to the objects in the same way. For example, the 4-year-old child has learned to apply the word "candy" to certain stimuli. Because candy stands for something good to eat he is apt to behave in a predictable way toward all things he labels candy. When an adult introduces a new object the child has never seen and says, "Have a piece of candy," the child will transfer the behavior he has learned for the word candy to this novel stimulus. In all probability he will take this new object and pop it into his mouth. Thus, mediated generalization is usually adaptive and allows the child to behave appropriately to new stimuli on first contact.

A number of excellent experimental studies suggest that verbal mediation is of major importance in learning and problem-solving. In transposition experiments, children learn to make choices on the basis of the *relationships* among stimuli rather than on the basis of their absolute qualities, e.g., rewards are given for choosing the largest of three black squares. Later these children are presented with three new squares, the smallest of them being exactly the same size as the largest (rewarded) one in the previous trials. Young children, with limited language ability, find it very difficult to "transpose"—that is, to learn to choose in terms of the *relative* sizes of the new stimuli. Instead, they continue, for many trials, to select the square that had been associated with rewards earlier, although it is the smallest—incorrect and unrewarded—stimulus in this phase of the experiment (46). Kindergarten children can tell themselves "It is the largest one," and respond accordingly, regardless of the absolute magnitude of the stimuli. In other words, they can use words (verbal mediators) and can thus learn transposition or relational problems without difficulty.

Reversal Shifts.   A child capable of using verbal mediators and abstracting can perform successfully in reversal learning or reversal-shift problems (40–44). In these problems, he must learn to switch his responses, to do the opposite of what he has done previously in the same situation. The task involves a simple discrimination, e.g., discovering which of two different squares varying both in size (large and small) and color (black and white) is correct and brings the reward (a marble). The subject is consistently reinforced or rewarded only for choosing in terms of one dimension. Thus, if size is the relevant dimension, choosing the larger of two squares, regardless of its color, will bring a reward. (Color would be irrelevant and must be ignored.) After learning this discrimination, the child is presented with a new problem: he must make a reversal shift and choose the *small* rather than the *large* square to obtain a reward. In another kind of shift, a nonreversal shift, the subject would be required to choose what was previously the irrelevant dimension—that is, to make his choice on the basis of color (black or white) rather than of size.

If children can make mediated verbal responses—if they can say something like "the size is what's important,"—they find it relatively easy to learn this reversal shift. Many nursery school children do not give themselves verbal instructions and have difficulty with reversal shifts; nonreversal shifts are easier for them. Children over 7 make reversal shifts easily, but only about half of the children of kindergarten age do. Among the latter, fast learners (who probably have greater verbal facility and are more advanced in using verbal mediation) achieve reversal shifts more easily than slow learners, who presumably have less verbal ability (41–43). These findings suggest that ages 5 to 7 may be an extremely important transition period during which verbal mediation is becoming a powerful process in problem-solving. Some children progress more rapidly than others in the use of verbal mediators in solving difficult problems such as reversal shifts (40, 41).

It seems clear that children with verbal ability can use some form of language in solving cognitive problems. Undoubtedly, verbal ability can enhance cognitive functioning. But, despite these findings, we cannot state conclusively that language is a *necessary* condition for thought and problem-solution. For some children, other kinds of mediators, such as imagery, pictorial representations, or nonverbal symbols, may serve the same purpose that labels or other linguistic symbols do for verbal children. Thus, deaf children who are deficient in verbal skills can solve transposition problems readily (20, 21), and there are no differences between hearing and deaf children in their performance on reversal shift problems (68). While the kinds of symbols used by the deaf are not known, "successful performance on these tasks (e.g., reversal shift) by deaf persons implies an *efficient function-ing of a symbolic system other than verbal*" (20, 160, italics ours). In short, symbols and particular words may be mediators of choice in thinking and problem-solving, but they are not the only possible ones. "Versatile crea-tures that we are, other symbolic means are apparently exploited when lan-guage is denied us, as with the young deaf" (19).

In a recent discussion of mediation, Kendler and Kendler gave a broad definition of mediators, stating that:

> representational responses are not synonymous with linguistic labels. As far as we know, any response with adequate feedback could serve the purpose. . . . It . . . seems likely that, among articulate humans, verbal labels are among the most common responses used for representation simply because they are so well suited to this function. They are so available, discriminable, easily frac-tionated, can occur without interference with any other ongoing activity, and can so easily move forward in the behavior sequence (43, 188).

It should also be noted that, among children, the absence of verbal mediation in problem-solving does not necessarily imply an *inability* to use words. Thus, in a simple picture recall test (pointing to pictures, chosen from a larger group, that the experimenter had earlier pointed out), kinder-garten children are much less likely than second graders to use verbal codes and rehearse the names of the depicted objects spontaneously. The kinder-garten child clearly " 'knows' the relevant words and . . . he can and does produce them in some situations; his deficiency here consists solely in the fact that this particular task (or perhaps tasklike situations in general) fails to elicit them." (18, 284) In other words, the child of this age can *produce* appropriate mediators but he does not necessarily utilize words effectively in cognitive tasks.

Viewed in this way, our kindergarten Ss may have failed to talk to themselves for reasons having nothing whatever to do with their level of linguistic development. That is, they may simply have been too young to engage in the kinds of intellectual activities which assume the guise in this particular task of verbal coding and rehearsal (18, 297–298).

Moreover, preschool children who do not ordinarily use verbal mediators in problem-solving may use this kind of mediation in many other situations. Observe any group of nursery school children at play and you will find plentiful evidence that practically all children, even 3-year-olds of average intelligence, use verbal mediators. In their imaginative play, children will act as though a wooden box is a fort, a twig is a gun, and peers are Indians. The preschool child's activities and statements clearly indicate that he is *capable* of using verbal mediators.

Young children who do not spontaneously use words as mediators in solving cognitive problems can easily *learn* to do so with very little training. This is true in the cases of performance in simple, delayed recall tests and in reversal-shift problems. In recall tests, rehearsal of the names of the stimulus objects considerably enhances performance and children who do this spontaneously perform better than those who do not (39). But, as has been shown experimentally, nonrehearsers can, with very little difficulty and only brief training, learn to rehearse; having learned this, they recall as well as spontaneous rehearsers (39).

Kendler (41) taught 4-year-olds to verbalize the relevant dimension, size, in a reversal-shift problem simply by instructing them to tell the experimenter which stimulus was correct, the *large* square in this case. The children in control groups were not required to say anything, or the irrelevant dimension was verbalized. After learning the initial discrimination, subjects were presented with a reversal shift: the *small* square, regardless of brightness, became the rewarded one. The children in the experimental group—those who verbalized the relevant dimension—mastered the reversal shift much more easily than those in the control groups.

Clearly then, with only a little training, the preschool child can *learn* to use verbal mediation to solve these kinds of problems. He will make use of this capability if he finds the use of verbal mediators relevant to the situation, i.e., if the results of using these mediators are rewarding.

PIAGET'S VIEW OF COGNITIVE DEVELOPMENT DURING THE PRESCHOOL YEARS

Piaget's brilliant observations and analyses provide a framework for understanding the child's overall strategies in thinking during the preschool period. In his view, cognitive or intellectual activities are adaptive; they function in the individual's adaptation to his environment. Intelligence is seen as an aspect of biological adaptation, of coping with the environment, and organizing and reorganizing thought and action. This adaptation involves an interaction between the processes of assimilation and accommodation. Assimilation refers to the fact that the child relates what he perceives to his existing knowledge and understanding. It "operates whenever the organism sees something new in terms of something familiar, whenever it acts in a new situation as it has acted in other situations in the past, whenever it invests anything with familiarity (recognition), importance, or value" (35, 112). New perceptions are incorporated into the child's own understanding of the world, fitting unfamiliar stimuli into his own available "mental structures" or "organizations" in Piaget's terms. New perceptions or new knowledge may be distorted in order to fit neatly into his existing view of the world. An example of assimilation would be the child's interpretation of a novel stimulus, for example, a flying squirrel. If in his comprehension, all flying objects are classified as birds, the child may perceive the squirrel as more birdlike in shape than it actually is, and regard it as a bird. He may fail to notice that the animal has no wings, and no feathers, and does have four legs. These perceptual distortions occur as the child *assimilates* the stimulus of the flying squirrel into his notion of "bird."

At a more complex level, the child who had never seen a dog bite a child might distort such a scene, interpreting it as an affectionate licking gesture. The perception of the dog biting a child does not fit (i.e., is not congruent with) his conceptualization of dogs and their relation to people.

Accommodation, which is complementary to assimilation, "operates as the variations in the environmental circumstances demand coping which modifies existing schemata [ways of organizing or structuring the world]" (35, 112). In this process, environmental circumstances acting on the child compel him to change his conceptual understanding to fit new perceptions. That is, the person modifies his reference system so that it is congruent with external reality. To illustrate, suppose a 4-year-old, who expects to see girls dressed in skirts and boys in pants, sees a child with both long hair and pants playing with a doll. He will probably "accommodate" to the stimulus and perceive this new person as a girl, thus altering his conception of the world to take account of the new experience. One of the clearest instances of accommodation occurs when the child faithfully imitates the behavior of a parent. In this case, he is attempting to perceive the behavior of another with maximal accuracy and alter his own behavior so that it matches that of another. Accommodation and assimilation are present in all perceptual experiences and intelligent behavior, and there is always a balance between the two processes.

The reader will recall that during the sensorimotor period (between birth and 18 months or 2 years of age), environmental stimuli—and the child's perception of them—elicit motor responses, actual manipulations of concrete objects. By and large, these activities do not require symbolic mediators, or words.

By the end of the sensorimotor period, however, the child gives some evidence of reasoning or insight, inventing new methods to solve problems by "mental combination." For example, at 16 months of age, Piaget's son Laurent used a stick to obtain a toy that was otherwise out of reach, although he had never used a stick in this way before. This kind of action, which seems to involve some symbolic imagery, marks the emergence of genuine intelligence.

The next broad phase of cognitive development in Piaget's categorization is the *preoperational*, which extends from the end of Stage six of the sensorimotor period, approximately 1½ to 2 years of age, up to the ages of 6 or 7. During the preconceptual phase, which lasts roughly until the age of 4, the child constructs symbols, uses language, and indulges in make-believe play. It is during this period that the child develops his "symbolic function, imagery, and genuine representation." He begins to distinguish between signifiers (words and images) and the things signified (significates, or perceptually absent events).

The connection between the signifiers and the signified "is mediated by images that intervene in the development of imitation, play, and cognitive representation." As a result of these developments, the child is no longer restricted to overt actions dealing with real objects (as he was during the sensorimotor period), but can think about objects and activities, manipulating these symbolically. Thus the range of his cognitive functioning and thinking is immeasurably expanded. As Piaget states it:

> Towards 1½ to 2 years, the symbolic function appears: language, symbolic play (the beginning of fictional invention), deferred imitation, i.e., occurring sometime after the original event, and that kind of internalized imitation which gives rise to mental imagery.

> However, the child cannot immediately construct such operations; several years of preparation and organization are still required. In fact, it is much more difficult to reproduce an action correctly in thought than to carry it out on the behavioral level. The child of 2 years, for example, is able to coordinate his movements from place to place (when he walks about the room or in the garden) into a group, as well as his movements when he turns objects round. But a lengthy period of time will elapse before he will be able to represent them precisely in thought; in reproducing, for example, from memory with the help of objects, a plan of the room or garden, or in inverting the positions of objects in thought by turning the plan around (54, 10–11).

When compared with the thinking of mature adults and older children, preconceptual thinking is not of a high order. The child possesses only "preconcepts." He does not understand the nature of classes and class membership. To cite one of Piaget's examples, the child regards every snail he sees as an instance of "snail." He does not understand that each snail is a member of a class of snails, having some characteristics in common with other snails, as well as unique characteristics that make it an individual.

In a study of concept formation, children were given a mixed set of objects—geometric forms, plastic models of people, toy kitchen equipment, plastic animals—and asked to put together those that "go together" (55).

Adults would sort these objects in groups according to some rule of membership in a class—that is, possession of some common attribute by all members of the group, e.g., people, triangles, four-legged animals. Children generally do not sort this way, however. They are more likely to classify on a part-whole basis. Thus a child might group together toy pots, a woman, a plant, and a dog, labelling it, "a kitchen." A few children may sort on the basis of similarity, but even these children cannot usually give a rule that accurately describes their grouping. In short, the preschool child's preconcepts lack real generality; the child does not go from particular to the general, as in inductive reasoning, nor from the general to the particular, as in deductive reasoning. He is essentially without genuine concepts.

As may be expected, preconceptual thought is extremely concrete rather than abstract; "the young child simply runs off reality sequences in his head just as he might do in overt action" (17, 158).

Furthermore, preconceptual thought and speech are strikingly egocentric. The child is unable to take the role of another person or to see that his viewpoint is only one of many possible points of view. Asked what the moon does when he goes for a walk, the child states that it follows him. When a child of this age with two brothers is asked, "How many brothers are there in your family?" he is likely to reply "two." He sees things from only his own point of view.

The child of this age makes little effort to adapt his speech to the needs or interests of his listeners. Hence, he cannot explain things clearly to others. He finds it "exceedingly difficult to treat his own thought processes as an object of thought" (17, 156)—that is, to think about his thinking, and he does not look for possible contradictions in his thinking.

The preschool child's thinking tends to be static, focusing on one feature at a time: "impressionistically and sporadically on this or that momentary . . . condition" (17, 157). Sets of successive conditions or events are not combined into integrated patterns. This is related to the notion that preconceptual thought is *centered,* in Piaget's terms; the child characteristically attending to one salient aspect of a problem, neglecting other important ones, and thus distorting his reasoning. There is the famous example of Piaget's experiment in which the child is faced with two identical tall, thin vases containing equal amounts of water. The child will deny that the quantities are identical if the contents of one of these vases is poured, before his eyes, into a short, broad jar. He will assert that the amount of water in the tall vase is greater than the amount of water in the other. Apparently the child has "centered" solely on the height of the first container (or the height of the liquid column) and says that it contains more liquid because it is taller. He has failed to *decenter* and to consider both width and height simultaneously and thus reason that the height of one is compensated by the width of the next.

The next stage, the period of intuitive thought, lasts from age 4 to 7 or 8. During this time, the child conceptualizes more, elaborates his concepts, and constructs more complex representations, thoughts, and images.

He becomes able to group objects together into classes according to his own perceptions of similarity. He now has some notions of class membership and the objects included in the particular class. This is evidenced by his use of quantifiers such as "some" and "all." But his ability to draw logical conclusions is still extremely limited.

The child's understanding at this stage is still largely restricted to his own perceptions, and his comprehension of objects or situations is still based on single salient perceptual aspects of the stimulus. This was illustrated in Piaget's famous conservation experiments, such as the one involving water in vases of different shapes. The child of 2 knows that objects exist even when they are hidden from view, but the child of 4 does not yet understand that a quantity of liquid remains the same regardless of the container into which it is poured. Recall what the child says when, in the example given above, water from one vase is poured into another having a different shape. His comprehension of the abstract concept *amount* or *quantity* is highly dependent on *one* perceptual aspect of the stimulus—in this case, the *height* of the jar or the liquid column. It is as if he intuitively equates the height of a container with the amount of liquid it can hold—as if the child had learned an equation that reads "tall = big = more."

This example also illustrates what is for Piaget the most significant characteristic of preoperational thinking, that is, its irreversibility (the child's failure to realize that if, in the example above, the water were poured back into the taller, thinner container, it would again reach its original height). Every logical or mathematical operation is reversible in the sense that in thought, steps can be retraced, actions can be canceled, and the original situation can be restored. Thus in pouring the water from a tall, thin vase to a broader, shorter one, the diminution in the height of the column of water is compensated for by the increase in the width of the column so that the same amount of water is maintained, i.e., the amount of water is invariant despite the shape of the vessel into which it is poured. The diminution in the height of the column of water is compensated for by the increased width of the vessel into which it has been poured. In reversible thinking, the individual can retrace these steps mentally to see that the amount of water has not been changed.

> . . . a thought form which is reversible is one which is flexible and mobile . . . able to correct for distorting superficials by means of successive, quick-moving decenterings, but the turgid, slow-paced, and extremely concrete mental experiment of preoperational thought is not reversible, parroting, as it does, irreversible events in reality (17, 159).

Many of these changes, advances in conceptualization and the ability to group objects together into classes, may be related to the improvements in the child's language abilities at this age—for, as we saw earlier, these improvements in language are very important in verbal mediation, concept formation, and problem-solving.

Intelligence Measured by Intelligence Tests

As has been mentioned, Piaget's concern is clearly with how knowledge is acquired and changes—essentially with the problems of the operations or processes underlying the manifestations of cognitive or intellectual functioning, such as reasoning or problem-solving. His emphasis is on the lawful sequences in the development of intellectual and cognitive activities and adaptations, on the typical and modal. He is *not* interested in range or variation in intellectual performance.

American psychologists, on the other hand, have a long tradition of preoccupation with individual differences—with comparisons among people—in cognitive abilities and, particularly, in intelligence. Intelligence, as it is used in psychological literature, often refers not to intellectual activity or adaptation, but specifically to performance on standardized intelligence tests. Such tests yield a score, the IQ, which is commonly considered an index of intellectual capability and, in the case of children, of potential for intellectual achievement. By and large, the items in these tests measure language acquisition and comprehension, immediate memory, perceptual organization, reasoning, and problem-solving—the outcomes, results, or manifestations of the basic processes that concern Piaget.

Numerous factors influence scores on intelligence tests: genetic make-up, parental esteem for intellectual achievement, cultural opportunities, language skills, motivation to do well in school or on tests (which are made up of items that resemble school tasks).

Intelligence tests given to infants under 2 years of age sample functions which are very different from those tapped by the usual adult intelligence tests. Infant tests are made up primarily of items measuring motor skills and sensorimotor development, e.g., placing pegs in a peg board; placing blocks in a form board; building towers of cubes; attaining toys with a stick; imitating gestures. In contrast to these kinds of items, adult intelligence tests emphasize verbal ability, cognitive functioning, and abstract thinking. It is easy to see why the correlations between performance on infant (below 2) tests and scores on adult intelligence tests have been found to be insignificant.

As the child develops greater language facility, however, it becomes possible to use tests with more items involving knowledge of words, abstractions, and problem-solving processes. Intelligence tests given at ages 2 and 3 are generally composite tests, having both psychomotor and cognitive-verbal tasks. More and more verbal items and relatively fewer tests of sensorimotor functions are included with each succeeding year throughout the preschool period. For example, the norms for the Stanford-Binet, one of the best-known intelligence tests with both verbal and performance tasks, indicate that the average 2-year-old can do the following: place simple blocks properly in a three-hole form board; identify models of common objects, such as a cup, by their use; identify major parts of a doll's body; and repeat two digits.

Four-year-level items, involving much more language, include naming pictures that illustrate a variety of common objects; naming objects from memory; discriminating visual forms such as squares, circles, and triangles; defining words like "ball" and "bat"; repeating a ten word sentence; and counting four objects.

Because intelligence tests given to preschool children are more heavily weighted with language, children who have achieved high levels of language skills will do well in these tests; others will not.

In the next section of this chapter, we will discuss the culturally deprived or disadvantaged preschool child who is quite likely to be deficient in language skills. Consequently he does not ordinarily do well in intelligence tests. It is interesting to note that Negro and white babies 40 weeks of age did not differ significantly in their scores on infant intelligence tests (largely psychomotor and sensorimotor), but that the white group scored 16 points higher, on the average, in intelligence (largely verbal) test scores at the age of 3 (45; cf. also pp. 314–316).

Intelligence test items for preschoolers, older children, and adults are largely verbal, and in this sense, alike. It is therefore understandable that preschool intelligence test scores are better predictors of future IQ than are scores obtained from infant tests (34).

As part of an extensive longitudinal guidance study carried out at the University of California, subjects were given intelligence tests periodically beginning when they were 21 months old. During the preschool period the California Preschool Schedule was used, and the Stanford-Binet was administered to each child during later childhood and adolescence. At age 18, the subjects were given the Wechsler Adult Intelligence Scale. Table 8.1 shows the correlation between intelligence test scores at each of the preschool years and at ages 10 and 18. This table shows that as children advance in age through the preschool period, their test scores become increasingly more predictive of later performance.

Benjamin Bloom of the University of Chicago has made a fascinating analysis of these and other longitudinal data (5). He concluded that correlations between early and later intelligence would be much higher *if* the psychomotor portions of the earlier tests are held constant or suppressed. Thus the correlation between intelligence, when ideally measured, at age 3 (with the sensorimotor portions eliminated) and age 17 is about 65; between intelligence measured at age 5 (psychomotor tasks excluded) and age 17, about .80 (5).

It should be noted, however, that while the correlations reported in Table 8.1 and those reported by Bloom are statistically significant, they are not high enough to preclude the possibility that many children undergo significant changes in IQ between early childhood and later ages. In fact, there are many marked changes—sometimes as much as 20 points—between the nursery school period and later childhood. As we shall see later, many factors such as extremely favorable or unfavorable changes in environmental

Table 8.1   Correlations Between Intelligence Test Scores
During the Preschool Years and IQ at Ages 10 and 18

Age	Correlation with IQ (Stanford-Binet) at Age 10	Correlation with IQ (Wechsler) at Age 18
2	.37	.31
2½	.36	.24
3	.36	.35
3½	.59	.42
4	.66	.42

Source: M. P. Honzik, J. W. Macfarlane, & L. Allen. The stability of mental test performance between two and eighteen years. *J. exp. Educ.,* 1948, *17.* By permission.

circumstances may produce such shifts in intellectual performance. Similar data from the Fels Research Institute reveal the same pattern (*38*).

The stability of intelligence test scores is greater for shorter than for longer periods of time; the shorter the interval between tests, the higher the correlation between the IQ's derived. For example, the correlation between IQ's obtained at ages 3 and 5 is higher than the correlation between IQ's measured at ages 3 and 7. Moreover, the IQ becomes more stable (less likely to change) with increasing age. Thus, the correlation between IQ's at ages 3 and 5 is .72; the correlation between IQ's at ages 8 and 10 is .90 (*38*).

In general, in cases of very low IQ (below 70, for instance), test scores obtained during the preschool years are much more reliable (more consistent with later scores) than IQ's in the normal or above-normal range. For many children in these ranges, the IQ does not become sufficiently stable for accurate prediction of future intellectual performance until age 6.

The early years are apparently critical in the development of intelligence as measured by standard tests. A thorough review of studies of stability of intelligence led Bloom to hypothesize that extreme environmental conditions can have far greater effects in the early years of development than they do later. For example,

deprivation in the first 4 years of life can have far greater consequences than deprivation [or extremely rich environments and enriched opportunities] in the 10 years between 8 and 17. . . .

The effects of the environments, especially of the extreme environments, appear to be greatest in the early (and more rapid) periods of intelligence development and least in the later (and less rapid) periods of development. . . . The evidence so far available suggests that marked changes in the environment in the early years can produce greater changes than will equally marked changes in the environment at later periods of development (*5, 72, 88–89*).

CONDITIONS AFFECTING LANGUAGE DEVELOPMENT
AND COGNITIVE FUNCTIONS

Thus far our discussion has been restricted to what is *typical* or generally true for preschool children: the normal course of language acquisition, the processes underlying further gains in cognitive functioning, the nature and predictive efficiency of intelligence tests administered during this period. Obviously, all children do not make equal progress in these areas or progress at the same rate. Some are highly advanced compared with their peers; others are woefully retarded.

What are the factors influencing rate and level of cognitive development? The question has particularly great force in American society today, for psychologists and educators, responding to pressures from an enlightened public, are conscientiously searching for ways to improve the social and educational status of the culturally—i.e., socially and economically—disadvantaged. Children from these backgrounds tend to be markedly deficient in basic cognitive skills, and, consequently, in school performance. Greater educational achievement depends upon the acquisition of more high-level cognitive skills. To promote this acquisition requires knowledge of how cognitive skills are affected by family and environmental conditions and by educational intervention.

Language, one of the chief agents of cognitive development, appears to be the key to the problem and, fortunately, considerable research attention has been paid to factors that promote or retard language development. Since language development and cognitive functioning are so intimately linked, it is virtually impossible to consider one without discussing the other, and we will make no attempt to separate them in the following discussion.

One broad, general conclusion emerges from all the available evidence: "The quality of a child's early linguistic environment is the most important external factor affecting the rate of language development" (9, 749). A stimulating linguistic environment—one offering good language models, together with variety, novelty, and rewards for verbal responses—enhances learning and cognitive development; a dull, unstimulating environment seems to inhibit development in these areas. From early infancy on, children reared in institutions are less advanced in language development, vocalizing less frequently and making fewer types of speech sounds than infants reared in homes with families—presumably because institutional attendants do not stimulate or respond to children's speech as parents do (6). Preschool children in institutions where they are neither highly motivated to speak nor rewarded frequently or consistently for their speech responses are also handicapped in many areas of language development—including speech sounds, intelligibility, and level of language organization (28–30).

Twins and triplets are relatively slow in speech development because they are probably not so highly motivated as other children to learn speech responses—many of their needs (particularly social needs) are satisfied without verbal communication. Of all groups studied, singletons—especially only-girls—are the most advanced in all aspects of language development (10–12, 14, 15), for they generally come from "environments . . . affording greater association with adults, broader experience, and greater opportunities for practice in the use of language under optimum conditions" (49, 589). Children from bilingual homes, in general, have greater difficulty than those from monolingual homes in learning language (49). However, if the children from bilingual homes are strongly encouraged to master the language taught in school, the potentially deleterious effects of a bilingual atmosphere are likely to be reduced.

Rate of language acquisition is obviously influenced by the degree to which the child's language leads directly to rewarding and gratifying goal states. Some parents insist that their 3-year old begin to ask for "the cookie" by name rather than pointing to the cookie jar and saying "uh-uh." This technique of making the acquisition of desired goals dependent upon the use of speech is a clear example of how parental behavior influences language learning. Peter, one of the two boys whose case histories are given in the text (see p. 417), was grossly retarded in speech development at this age, partially because his mother consistently anticipated Peter's needs and did not wait for him to ask for what he wanted.

In this connection, it is interesting to note that a mother's concern with language development during the first 3 years of life—which is undoubtedly related to her interest in the child's achievement—is correlated with the child's IQ at age 3 (52). The mother usually spends more time with the child than the father during the preschool years, and consequently probably exerts more influence than the father on the child's early intellective development.

Social Class, Language Development, and Cognitive Functioning. The most striking—and from several points of view, most significant—finding about language development concerns social-class differences, which are evident in almost all studies of language development from infancy onward. It will be recalled that infants from working-class families vocalize less than those from middle-class homes. Recent studies show that from age 1 through age 5, middle- and upper-class children are superior to those of the lower class in all aspects of language behavior: vocabulary scores, sentence structure, sound discrimination, and articulation (58). These well-documented differences seem to be largely attributable to the contrast between middle- and lower-class homes in quality of verbal stimulation.

The most relevant research dealing directly with social-class differences in language training is that of the English educational sociologist Basil Bernstein, of the University of London. His findings were based on British subjects but they would seem to be valid for American lower- and middle-class families as well. Bernstein's systematic observations highlight the sharp contrasts between what he has labeled the *restricted* language of the lower class and the *elaborated* codes or messages of the middle class. In dealing with her child, the lower-class mother uses language primarily to denote things and actions. Sentences are short and simple, grammatically uncomplicated, and easily understood. There is little pressure on the child to verbalize his unique or personal experiences. Lower-class language "focuses on the inhibiting function of speech" (3, 97). Only low levels of conceptualization and differentiation are involved, and attention is directed toward "the concrete here and now—toward the direct, immediate, the descriptive, the global" (3, 97). In this kind of speech there is little evidence of reasoning; conclusions and authoritarian commands are simply stated.

In contrast:

> Inherent in the middle-class linguistic relationship is a pressure to verbalise feeling in a relatively individual manner and this process is guided by a speech model which regularly and consistently makes available to the child the formal means whereby this process is facilitated.

> It can be said that for the middle-class child there is a progressive development towards verbalising and making explicit, subjective intent, whilst that is *not* the case for the working-class child (3, 93).

Elaborated language, typical of the middle class, is more individualized, specific to a particular situation or person, more differentiated, and more precise than the language of the lower class. A wider, more complex range of thought is communicated, and cognitive and affective contents are differentiated and expressed. Restricted codes are highly stereotyped and limited, lacking in specificity and in the exactness needed for precise conceptualization and differentiation.

Bernstein presents a pointed illustration of the social class contrasts in language by citing two hypothetical mother-child conversations on a bus. In each case, the mother has a child on her lap. The first mother is lower class; the second, middle class.

MOTHER:	Hold on tight.
CHILD:	Why?
MOTHER:	Hold on tight.
CHILD:	Why?
MOTHER:	You'll fall.
CHILD:	Why?
MOTHER:	I told you to hold on tight, didn't I?

MOTHER:	Hold on tightly, darling.
CHILD:	Why?
MOTHER:	If you don't you will be thrown forward and you'll fall.
CHILD:	Why?
MOTHER:	Because if the bus suddenly stops you'll jerk forward on to the seat in front.
CHILD:	Why?
MOTHER:	Now darling, hold on tightly and don't make such a fuss (3, 97).

Even casual analysis of these two conversations reveals a striking contrast between the two mothers in number of words used and in the complexity of language structure. In addition, there are some other impressive differences—in the nature of the mother-child relationship and in factors closely related to cognitive functioning, that is, in encouragement of curiosity and questions, and in the models of thinking and reasoning presented.

> In the first example a whole range of potential learning and connections have been cut out by the categoric statement. The natural curiosity of the child has been blunted. There is no causal chain between the mother's request and the child's expected response. The change in the behaviour has been brought about by a process akin to verbal conditioning rather than through instrumental learning. If the child challenges the statement then in a short period he is challenging the *right* of the mother to issue the request, that is, he is challenging the authority which inheres in the status of the mother. The potential social power in the form of the relation is revealed very quickly.

> In the second example the child is exposed to an area of connection and sequence. If this is challenged then another set of reasons are elicited. Of course, after a time the categoric statement is applied but an order of learning has been made available in between. It should be noted that as the result of the linguistically elaborated relationship the initial challenges are of the reasons given to support the request. The challenge of the mother comes much *later* in the relationship and the latent social power is revealed later *and* under different conditions. If the categoric statement is used frequently in a *public* language then it limits learning and curiosity and induces a sensitivity towards a particular type of authority in which social power is quickly and nakedly revealed. The categoric statement becomes part of a language which narrows the range of stimuli to which the child responds (3, 97–98).

As would be expected from Bernstein's observations and comments, and from findings on class differences in children's language abilities, lower-class children perform relatively more poorly than their middle-class peers on tasks involving cognitive functioning (thinking, reasoning, conceptualization), and on standardized intelligence tests which are highly dependent on language skills. Moreover, the gap between the abilities of middle- and lower-class children, already evident during the preschool period, widens and becomes more pronounced with increasing age. Culturally deprived or culturally disadvantaged environments seem conducive to producing and maintaining "cumulative deficits" or progressive retardation in the areas of cognitive development, intelligence, and school achievement.

A thorough survey of the literature on these deficits shows that

> children from deprived backgrounds score well below middle-class children on standard individual and group measures of intelligence (a gap that increases with age); they come to school without the skills necessary for coping with first grade curricula; their language development, both written and spoken, is relatively poor; auditory and visual discrimination skills are not well developed; in

scholastic achievement they are retarded an average of 2 years by grade 6 and almost 3 years by grade 8; they are more likely to drop out of school before completing a secondary education; and even when they have adequate ability are less likely to go to college (33, 869–870).

Some recent American research, conducted by Hess and Shipman (33) confirmed and extended Bernstein's findings. At the same time, it demonstrated concretely the effects of social class language patterns on a number of aspects of cognitive functioning. The subjects were urban Negro mothers and their preschool (4-year-old) children. Three social classes were represented: upper-middle (college-educated professional, executive, and managerial occupational levels), upper-lower (skilled blue-collar occupational levels), and lower-lower (two groups: unskilled or semiskilled occupational levels and predominantly elementary school education, and another group from the same occupational levels with father absent and families supported by public assistance).

The mothers were interviewed in their homes, and each mother was observed in interaction with her child while teaching him three simple standardized tasks. Tests of several aspects of cognitive functioning were administered to both mothers and children.

The mothers in the three social status groups differed relatively little, on the average, in the emotional aspects and qualities of their interaction with their children. But gross differences appeared in the verbal and cognitive environments that they presented to their children.

Like English middle-class mothers, American middle-class mothers consistently used more words in responding to children's questions and in carrying out the assigned teaching tasks. They also offered more "opportunities for labeling, for identifying objects and feelings and adult models who . . . demonstrate the usefulness of language as a tool for dealing with interpersonal interaction and for ordering stimuli in the environment" (33, 875).

Furthermore, even controlling for total verbal output, middle-class mothers' sentences were much more subtle and complex grammatically and contained more abstraction and concepts. From this type of interaction the child learns to recognize the possibilities and subtleties of the language not only for communication but also for thinking and problem-solving.

When approaching cognitive tasks, such as sorting pictures of humans into categories or classes, the mothers in different social-class groups behaved in vastly different ways. Lower-class mothers gave "relational-contextual" responses (e.g., a husband and a wife) which require less reflection, less attention to detail, and less evaluation of alternative classifications than other kinds of responses. Middle-class mothers gave more descriptive, (e.g., "all lying down") and categorical-inferential responses (e.g., "all handicapped people") indicative of more reflection, more objectivity, greater complexity of thought, and more highly developed abilities for abstraction and organization of thinking.

The children apparently learned and emulated their mother's approaches to problems. Thus, in sorting tests similar to those given to their mothers, lower-class children gave relatively more nonverbal responses and relational responses, and fewer descriptive or categorical responses, indicating impaired verbal and conceptual abilities. These children had not learned to reflect about alternative solutions to problems, nor had they acquired the capacity to delay their responses long enough to analyze a problem into its component parts.

> A problem-solving approach requires reflection and the ability to weigh decisions, to choose among alternatives. The effect of restricted speech and of status orientation is to foreclose the need for reflective weighing of alternatives and consequences; the use of an elaborated code, with its orientation to persons and to consequences (including future), tends to produce cognitive styles more easily adapted to problem-solving and reflection (33, 885).

The evidence, then, seems compelling. For preschool children, cultural deprivation or disadvantage results in definite deficiencies in language and in cognitive functioning which is closely dependent on language. These deficiencies appear to be attributable, at least in large part, to inadequate stimulation and the relative paucity of verbal interaction in lower-class homes. And, as noted earlier, the impairments are likely to become more marked as the child grows older. The question of utmost significance is: Are the effects of early deprivation fixed and permanent, or can they be reversed? As we shall see in Chapter 12, there are enduring effects of deprivation, reflected in impaired performance later on in school (see pp. 565–573).

In recent years, many governmental and social agencies have concentrated tremendous amounts of time and effort on proposed solutions to this vast educational and social problem. The goals are very broad ones: to ameliorate the conditions of the culturally disadvantaged, so that children from these backgrounds can develop competencies and motivational patterns that would enable them to share more fully in our complex society and to reap a fairer share of the social rewards. The question of the reversibility (or irreversibility) of the effects of early deprivation is therefore of paramount importance.

The reader will recall the results of one study in which children were transferred from a deprived orphanage environment to a situation in which they were at all times given individual care by mentally retarded older children. These children gained considerably in IQ, but they had been transferred before they were 3 years old (see p. 235).

But what about the child who is raised in a deprived environment and continues to live in this environment beyond the age of 3? Can the so-called compensatory education projects (such as Head Start, sponsored by the United States Office of Education)—designed to raise the educational level of economically and culturally deprived children—help him? Can enriched training programs, applied early, offset cognitive deficiencies? It is impossible to answer these questions definitively at this time, but a few studies suggest that it is possible, although difficult, to achieve such goals.

In our opinion, the available data permit cautious optimism. With great efforts on the part of nursery school teachers and interested parents and welfare workers, and with much special, individual attention, some of the adverse effects of early deprivation can be overcome. This opinion is based on the findings of a number of systematic studies. A few of them will be reviewed briefly here.

In one, a long-term Russian experiment (48), the objective was simply improvement in verbal ability, but the outcomes were more far-reaching. The subjects were a pair of twins with retarded language development owing, in large measure, to restricted experience with language. They had little need to develop language skills because they communicated with each other very well through gestures, pointing, and other signal systems. Having poor language ability, they could not use verbal mediators effectively to solve problems. At ages 5 and 5½, "their intellectual operations . . . remained very limited; even such operations . . . as elementary classification were beyond them" (48, 121).

To improve their language skills, the twins were separated and placed in different kindergarten classes. In addition, one twin was trained systematically in a variety of speech functions. Both twins improved substantially in language and in general cognitive ability, the twin with special training surpassing the other.

> [The] whole structure of the mental life of both twins was simultaneously and sharply changed. Once they acquired an objective language system, the children were able to formulate the aims of their activity verbally and after only three months we observed the beginnings of meaningful play; there arose the possibility of productive, constructive activity in the light of formulated aims and to an important degree there were separated out a series of intellectual operations which shortly before this were only in an embryonic state.

> In the course of further observations we were able to note cardinal improvements in the structure of the twins' mental life which we could only attribute to the influence of the one changed factor—the acquisition of a language system (48, 122–123).

Needless to say, this kind of treatment, requiring a thoroughly individualized training program, is exceedingly difficult, expensive, and time-consuming. It could not be readily used in teaching in public schools with large numbers of children. But the study is important for our purposes because it demonstrates clearly that with concentrated, individualized training, the effects of early deprivation can be overcome.

The results of a fascinating, well-conducted American study recently published (4) indicate that daily, short (15–20 minutes), individual tutoring sessions may produce marked gains in the intellectual functioning of socially disadvantaged preschool children. In the tutoring sessions, designed to generate an "abstract attitude," the child becomes actively involved with the stimuli "so as to comprehend their significance." The training tasks, conducted by a professionally trained nursery school teacher, were focused on improving the child's "ability to organize thoughts, to reflect upon situations, to comprehend the meaning of events, and to structure behavior so as to be able to choose among alternatives" (4, 380).

To accomplish each training task the child had to understand and use language, to produce relevant responses independently, and to discuss hypothetical situations related to the task (e.g., past, future, and alternative courses of action). "By structuring the teaching time in this way, the teacher made maximum use of every opportunity to aid the child in developing his budding ability to think and to reflect" (4, 382).

The 22 children in the study, ranging in ages from 3 years 3 months to 4 years 7 months, were divided into four groups, matched as closely as possible for IQ, age, and sex. One group was tutored five times a week, and another group received the same training three times a week. There were two control groups: one of them had daily individual sessions with the teacher, but no tutoring, and the other experienced only the regular nursery school program. The study lasted 4 months and all subjects were tested before and after the training period.

The average IQ gains for the group that had 5 days of tutoring a week was 15, and for the group that had three days of tutoring per week, 7. The two control groups averaged gains of only 2.0 and 1.3 points. Thus, improvement in intelligence test performance appears to be correlated with the amount of tutoring per week. Some of the children in the tutored groups manifested other dramatic changes in behavior. Several children who were originally excessively withdrawn, spoke incoherently, and manifested symptoms of emotional upset began to speak clearly and coherently, and their symptoms diminished.

> The most striking gains in the program were the apparent joy in learning and the feeling of mastery which the children displayed as the tutoring progressed. The untutored children, even those who received individual attention, showed none of these attitudes. This result is extremely important in that it strongly suggests that exposure to materials, a school-like situation, and an interested adult is not sufficient for learning. Both mastery and enthusiasm for learning will come only when the child can be shown how to become actively involved in the learning process (4, 388).

But can these effects, achieved in individual tutoring, also be accomplished by group procedures, by techniques that can be applied to large numbers (totaling hundreds of thousands) of children? Again, there is some evidence that this is possible.

Dawe (13) worked with preschool and kindergarten children of low-normal intelligence (average IQ about 81), who were living in an orphanage. There were 11 experimental subjects and 11 control subjects, matched in sex, chronological and mental age, intelligence, and vocabulary.

The children in the experimental group were given speech and language training on weekends for a total of 92 hours. They were trained in understanding words and concepts, discussing pictures in books, and listening to poems and stories. The control subjects did not have any special training.

After the training period, which lasted about 7 months, the experimental group showed an average gain in IQ of 14 points, while the control dropped an average of 2 points. Both groups gained in vocabulary and information scores (which was to be expected, in view of the fact that the subjects were 7 months older at the end of the study), but the experimental subjects surpassed the controls by a substantial margin. Moreover, the experimental group showed marked advances in motivational characteristics related to cognitive functioning, e.g., attentiveness and intellectual interest. Clearly, the special training was effective, at least temporarily, in promoting the cognitive abilities of these children.

The recently awakened attention to the educational problems of culturally deprived children is the source of an upsurge in systematic studies of special early childhood training and its effects. A bold and exciting program for preschoolers, operated by Carl Bereiter and Siegfried Engelmann of the University of Illinois (2), has been called "an intellectual pressure cooker for children from the slums." In this setup, about 15 children are drilled intensively by 3 teachers for 2 hours a day on basic arithmetic and language skills—not just on vocabulary, idioms, or accents, but on language as a tool of thinking and learning. The major activities of most middle-class nursery schools—playing, group singing, puzzles, listening to stories—are scarcely in evidence at this school. Instead, children are continually being challenged to solve problems geared to their capabilities and are given the feeling that they are succeeding at something tough.

Since only a small number of children have completed the program, it is difficult to assess results. Many psychologists are highly critical of these high-pressure methods, but the directors of the nursery school claim that the children make impressive gains. Improvements in language are said to be particularly startling, scores on tests of linguistic ability increasing spectacularly. At the beginning of the program, the children spoke in single words or grunts; by the end of the year, they spoke, and fully understood, complex sentences. Moreover, they gained 17 points in IQ and, at the end of the year, scored at the first-grade level in reading and arithmetic (2).

The Early Training Project, directed by Gray and Klaus at Peabody College and sponsored by the United States Office of Education, is one of the most successful and suggestive systematic attempts to work with disadvantaged children (31). The purpose of the project was "to see whether it is possible, by specially planned techniques, to offset the progressive retardation in cognitive development and school achievement that characterizes the culturally deprived child as he passes through his years of schooling" (31, 887).

The investigators worked with a total of 87 Negro preschool subjects who came from poverty stricken families; their parents were unskilled or, at most, semiskilled workers with only elementary school educations. There were two experimental and two control groups. One of the experimental groups attended three special summer sessions of preschool, while the other attended two such sessions. The controls received no special training.

The experimental subjects participated in a stimulating, concentrated program designed to promote stronger motivation toward achievement and to foster the development of behaviors and characteristics correlated with achievement—such as persistence, ability to delay gratification, and interest in school materials such as books, puzzles, and pencils.

> The materials and activities used in the summer sessions did not differ radically from those of conventional nursery school and kindergarten. The difference lies rather in the way in which materials were used, the self-conscious attempt to focus on the experimental variables—for example, to promote achievement motivation, to stimulate language development, to encourage the child to order and classify the objects and events of his work (31, 892).

In addition, the mothers of the experimental subjects met weekly with a specially trained teacher who attempted to make them aware of children's motives and to encourage them to reward strivings for achievement.

At the end of the training period, the trained children were superior to the controls in tests of vocabulary, language ability, and reading readiness. Both experimental groups showed modest but significant gains in IQ and maintained these gains for 27 months, while the two control groups showed small losses in IQ. In other words, without special training, children from these backgrounds showed progressive retardation or cumulative deficit as they became older, while the specially trained group improved in cognitive functioning.

This special training program for preschool children was obviously effective in counteracting some of the usual outcomes of cultural disadvantage, at least for a short period of time. Will these effects last? It is frankly too early to say. "It is not until the children have been in school for several years . . . that we can know whether we have been able by this massive attack to offset the effect of a culturally deprived environment as it affects school performance" (31, 897).

However, even at the minimum, programs such as these provide evidence that specialized experiences and training can give underprivileged children a head start—some real advantage in cognitive abilities that they would not ordinarily have when they begin school. As a result of such training, these children seem to be better prepared for handling schoolwork, and they perform at a higher level in tasks known to be related to school achievement.

SUMMARY

Height and weight increase gradually but continuously during the preschool period, and the preschool child's height is a moderately good predictor of how tall he will be in early adulthood. Simultaneously, psychomotor skills improve significantly and, with maturation and practice, visual perception becomes more differentiated, accurate, and precise. The acquisition of language aids in the process of learning the *distinctive characteristics* of objects and visual stimuli such as letters of the alphabet.

This period is also marked by dramatic increases in vocabulary and sentence length; greater flexibility and efficiency in the use of language; richer, more comprehensible speech; and more complex grammatical structures. By the age of 4, most children have clearly mastered the fundamental rules of grammar. As the child's verbal abilities improve, his learning becomes increasingly controlled and regulated by words, for they can readily become mediators of self-instruction and action.

According to Piaget's theory and observations, the preschool child is in the preoperational phase of cognitive development. His thinking is not yet of a high level: he has only "preconcepts"—his thought is concrete rather than abstract, and like his speech, highly egocentric. He does not yet understand the nature of categories or classes (or the criteria of class membership), and, in attempting to solve problems, he characteristically attends to only one salient aspect of the problem, neglecting other important features and thus distorting his reasoning.

Intelligence tests appropriate for children of this age are more heavily weighted with verbal items than infant intelligence tests. As children advance in age, their test scores become increasingly predictive of later performance, although many children change significantly in IQ between this and later periods.

A stimulating linguistic environment—one that offers good language models together with linguistic variety, novelty, and rewards for verbal responses—enhances verbal ability, cognitive development, and intelligence test scores; dull, unstimulating environments have the opposite effects. Thus middle-class children are superior to those of the lower class in all aspects of language development (vocabulary sentence structure, and articulation), presumably because homes of the former provide more and better verbal stimulation.

Among preschool children, the culturally deprived are relatively deficient in language and cognitive abilities. However, individual attention and tutoring can help youngsters to overcome some of the adverse effects of their early cultural deprivation.

References

1. Bem. S. L. Verbal self-control: the establishment of effective self-instruction. *J. exp. Psychol.,* 1967, *74,* 485–491.
2. Bereiter, C., & Englemann, S. *Teaching disadvantaged children in the preschool.* Englewood Cliffs, N.J.: Prentice-Hall, 1966.
3. Bernstein, B. Social structure, language and learning. In J. P. De Cecco (Ed.), *The psychology of language, thought, and instruction.* New York: Holt, Rinehart and Winston, 1967, 89–103.
4. Blank, M., & Solomon, F. A tutorial language program to develop abstract thinking in socially disadvantaged preschool children. *Child Develpm.,* 1968, *39,* No. 2, 379–389.

5. Bloom, B. *Stability and change in human characteristics.* New York: Wiley, 1964.
6. Brodbeck, A. J., & Irwin, O. C. The speech behavior of infants without families. *Child Develpm.,* 1946, *17,* 145–165.
7. Brown, R. *Social psychology.* New York: Free Press of Glencoe, 1965.
8. Brown, R., & Fraser, C. The acquisition of syntax. In U. Bellugi & R. Brown (Eds.), The acquisition of language. *Monogr. Soc. Res. Child Develpm.,* 1964, *29,* No. 1, 43–79.
9. Carroll, J. B. Language development. In C. W. Harris (Ed.), *Encyclopedia of educational research.* New York: Macmillan, 1960, 744–752.
10. Davis, E. A. The development of linguistic skill in twins, singletons with siblings, and only children from age five to ten years. *Inst. Child Welf. Monogr.* (Ser. No. 14). Minneapolis: Univer. of Minnesota Press, 1937.
11. Davis, E. A. Mean sentence length compared with long and short sentences as a reliable measure of language development. *Child Develpm.,* 1937, *8,* 69–79.
12. Davis, E. A. The mental and linguistic superiority of only girls. *Child Develpm.,* 1937, *8,* 139–143.
13. Dawe, H. C. A study of the effect of an educational program upon language development and related mental functions in young children. *J. exp. Educ.,* 1942, *11,* 200–209.
14. Day, E. J. The development of language in twins: I. A comparison of twins and single children. *Child Develpm.,* 1932, *3,* 179–199.
15. Day, E. J. The development of language in twins: II. The development of twins: their resemblances and differences. *Child Develpm.,* 1932, *3,* 298–316.
16. Ervin, S. M., & Miller, W. R. Language development. In H. W. Stevenson (Ed.), *Child psychology.* (62nd Yearb. nat. Soc. Stud. Educ.) Chicago: Univer. Chicago Press, 1963, 108–143.
17. Flavell, J. H. *The developmental psychology of Jean Piaget.* Princeton, N.J.: Van Nostrand, 1963.
18. Flavell, J. H., Beach, D. R., & Chinsky, J. M. Spontaneous verbal rehearsal in a memory task as a function of age. *Child Develpm.,* 1966, *37,* No. 2, 283–299.
19. Flavell, J. H., & Hill, J. P. Developmental psychology. *Ann. Rev. Psychol.,* 1969, in press.
20. Furth, H. G. Research with the deaf: implications for language and cognition. *Psychol. Bull.,* 1964, *62,* 145–164.
21. Furth, H. G. *Thinking without language: psychological implications of deafness.* New York: Free Press of Glencoe, 1966.
22. Garn, S. M. Roentgengrammetric determinations of body composition. *Human Biol.,* 1957, *29,* 337–353.
23. Garn, S. M. Fat, body size, and growth in the newborn. *Human Biol.,* 1958, *30,* 265–280.
24. Gesell, A., Halverson, H. M., Thompson, H., Ilg, F. L., Castner, B. M., Ames, L. B., & Amatruda, C. S. *The first five years of life: a guide to the study of the preschool child.* New York: Harper & Row, 1940.
25. Gibson, E. Development of perception: discrimination of depth compared with discrimination of graphic symbols. In J. C. Wright & J. Kagan (Ed.), Basic cognitive processes in children. *Monogr. Soc. Res. Child Develpm.,* 1963, *28,* No. 2, 5–32.
26. Gibson, E. Perceptual development. In H. W. Stevenson (Ed.), *Child psychology.* (62nd Yearb. nat. Soc. Stud. Educ.) Chicago: Univer. Chicago Press, 1963, 144–195.

27. Gibson, J. J., & Gibson, E. J. Perceptual learning: differentiation or enrichment? *Psychol. Rev.,* 62, 1955, 32–41.
28. Goldfarb, W. Infant rearing and problem behavior. *Amer. J. Orthopsychiat.* 1943, 13, 249–266.
29. Goldfarb, W. Effects of psychological deprivation in infancy and subsequent stimulation. *Amer. J. Psychiat.,* 1945, 102, 18–33.
30. Goldfarb, W. Psychological privation in infancy and subsequent adjustment. *Amer. J. Orthopsychiat.,* 1945, 15, 247–255.
31. Gray, S. W., & Klaus, R. A. An experimental preschool program for culturally deprived children. *Child Develpm.,* 1965, 36, No. 4, 887–898.
32. Gutteridge, M. A study of motor achievement of young children. *Arch. Psychol.,* 244, 1939.
33. Hess, R. D., & Shipman, V. C. Early experience and the socialization of cognitive modes in children. *Child Develpm.,* 1965, 36, No. 4, 869–886.
34. Honzik, M. P., Macfarlane, J. W., & Allen, L. The stability of mental test performance between two and eighteen years. *J. exp. Educ.,* 1948, 17, 309–324.
35. Hunt, J. McV. *Intelligence and experience.* New York: Ronald Press, 1961.
36. Hurlock, E. B. *Child development.* New York: McGraw-Hill, 1950.
37. Jarvis, P. E. The effect of self-administered verbal instructions on simple sensory-motor performance in children. Unpublished doctoral dissertation, University of Rochester, 1963.
38. Kagan, J., & Moss, H. A. *Birth to maturity: a study in psychological development.* New York: Wiley, 1962.
39. Keeney, T. J., Cannizzo, S. R., & Flavell, J. H. Spontaneous and induced verbal rehearsal in a recall task. *Child Develpm.,* 1967, 38, 953–966.
40. Kendler, H. H., & Kendler, T. S. Vertical and horizontal processes in problem solving. *Psychol. Rev.,* 1962, 69, 1–16.
41. Kendler, T. S. Development of mediating responses in children. In J. C. Wright & J. Kagan (Eds.), Basic cognitive processes in children. *Monogr. Soc. Res. Child Develpm.,* 1962, 28, No. 2, 33–52.
42. Kendler, T. S. Verbalization and optional reversal shifts among kindergarten children. *J. verb. Learn. verb. Behav.,* 1964, 3, 428–436.
43. Kendler, T. S., & Kendler, H. H. Experimental analysis of inferential behavior in children. In L. Lipsitt and C. Spiker (Eds.), *Advances in child development and behavior.* Vol. 3. New York: Academic Press, 1967, 157–190.
44. Kendler, T. S., Kendler, H. H., & Wells, D. Reversal and non-reversal shifts in nursery school children. *J. comp. physiol. Psychol.,* 1960, 53, 83–88.
45. Knobloch, H., & Pasamanick, B. Exogenous factors in infant intelligence. *Pediatrics,* 1960, 26, 210–218.
46. Kuenne, M. R. Experimental investigation of the relation of language to transportation behavior in young children. *J. exp. Psychol.,* 1946, 36, 471–490.
47. Luria, A. R. The role of language in the formation of temporary connections. In B. Simon (Ed.), *Psychology in the Soviet Union.* Stanford: Stanford Univer. Press, 1957.
48. Luria, A. R., & Yudovich, F. *Speech and the development of mental processes in the child.* London: Staples (MacGibbon & Kee), 1959.
49. McCarthy, D. Language development in children. In L. Carmichael (Ed.), *Manual of child psychology.* New York: Wiley, 1954 (2nd ed.), 492–630.
50. McCarthy, D. Research in language development: retrospect and prospect. *Monogr. Soc. Res. Child Develpm.,* 1959, 24, No. 5 (Whole No. 74), 3–24.
51. Meredith, H. V. Selected anatomic variables analyzed for interage relationships of

the size-size, size-gain, and gain-gain varieties. In L. P. Lipsitt & C. C. Spiker (Eds.), *Advances in child development and behavior.* Vol. 2. New York: Academic Press, 1965, 221–256.

52. Moss, H. A., & Kagan, J. Maternal influences on early IQ scores. *Psychol. Rep.,* 1958, *4,* 655–661.

53. Neisser, U. *Cognitive psychology.* New York: Appleton-Century-Crofts, 1967.

54. Piaget, J. *Logic and psychology.* New York: Basic Books, 1957.

55. Piaget, J., & Inhelder, Barbel. *La genèse des structures logiques elementaires: classifications et sériations.* Neuchâtel: Delchaux et Niestlé, 1959.

56. Schober, G., & Schober, A. Über Bilderkennungs- und Ünterscheidungsfahigkeit bei kleinen Kindern. *Beih. Z. angew. Psychol.,* 1919, *19,* 94–137.

57. Sheldon, W. H. (with S. S. Stevens). *The varieties of temperament.* New York: Harper & Row, 1942.

58. Templin, M. C. Certain language skills in children. *Inst. Child Welf. Monogr.* (Ser. No. 26). Minneapolis: Univer. of Minnesota Press, 1957.

59. Thompson, H. Physical growth. In L. Carmichael (Ed.), *Manual of child psychology.* New York: Wiley, 1954 (2nd ed.), 292–334.

60. Walker, R. N. Some temperamental traits in children as viewed by their peers, their teachers, and themselves. *Monogr. Soc. Res. Child Develpm.,* 1967, *32,* No. 6, 1–36.

61. Watson, E. H., & Lowrey, G. H. *Growth and development of children.* Chicago: Year Book Publishers, 1958 (3rd ed.).

62. Wellman, B. L., Case, I. M., Mengert, I. G., & Bradbury, D. E. Speech sounds of young children. *Univer. Iowa Stud. Child Welf.,* 1931, *5,* No. 2.

63. Werner, H. *Comparative psychology of mental development.* Chicago: Follet, 1948 (rev. ed.).

64. Werner, H. The concept of development from a comparative and organismic point of view. In D. Harris (Ed.), *The concept of development: an issue in the study of human behavior.* Minneapolis: Univer. of Minnesota Press, 1957.

65. Werner, H., & Kaplan, E. The acquisition of word meanings: a developmental study. *Monogr. Soc. Res. Child Develpm.,* 1952, *15,* No. 1 (Serial No. 51).

66. Wohlwill, J. F. Developmental studies of perception. *Psychol. Bull.,* 1960, *57,* 249–288.

67. Wohlwill, J. F., & Wiener, M. Discrimination of form orientation in young children. *Child Develpm.,* 1964, *35,* No. 4, 1113–1125.

68. Youniss, J. Concept transfer as a function of shifts, age, and deafness. *Child Develpm., 34,* 1964.

9 The Preschool Years: Personality Development

I. Social Learning in the Family

As the child progresses in motor coordination and in language, and as his conceptual facility in the preschool years improves, his personality becomes more highly differentiated. Look at any group of preschool-age children, and one is struck by the vast range of personal characteristics and behavior. The shy, retiring child and the outgoing, boisterous one are easily distinguished in even the most casual observations. The striking diversity of behaviors at age 5, in comparison with age 2, is due in large part to the rapid acquisition of new habits, expanding perceptions, increasingly extensive social interactions, and heightened awareness of the social environment.

For many reasons, these are critical years for personality development; and during this time, many characteristics of paramount importance are established or modified. Included among these characteristics are sexual curiosity, dependence (or independence), aggression, achievement motivation or mastery, sex typing, anxiety, and conscience. These dimensions of personality are considered crucial in understanding human personality dynamics. Each characteristic is a pervasive one—manifested in many forms and in diverse situations, and affecting many aspects of behavior. The significance of these variables is attested to by the large number of theoretical writings and empirical studies devoted to them. As we shall see, some of these traits become stable and enduring early in life, and thus predictive of subsequent behavior. For example, the socially anxious 5-year-old boy is likely to become a shy adolescent.

In the first part of this chapter, these significant characteristics are defined and examined, their manifestations delineated, and methods of assessment presented. The "normal" course of development of each characteristic is described, and age changes in the nature and forms of its expression (and conflicts related to overt expression) are specified. In addition, we will discuss basic processes—learning by rewards and punishments, imitation, and identification—that are involved in the acquisition and development of these traits.

In the last part of the chapter, the focus of attention will shift to the family: the principal and primary determinant—or set of determinants—of personality structure and of individual variations in these characteristics. The child's personality emerges and develops in the context of the earliest complex social relationships, particularly those involving the family. Consequently, the final sections of the chapter will review some significant data on the effects of different types of family atmospheres and parent-child relationships on many aspects of the preschool child's personality and on the patterning and organization of his characteristics and motives.

Motives and Behavior. Before examining specific characteristics, the reader must be alerted to the important distinction between *behavior* and underlying *motives*. We can speak of an aggressive *motive* (a desire to hurt someone) or aggressive *behavior* (hitting someone). And, as we shall see, there is not necessarily a direct link between motives and overt responses.

Motives cannot be seen or measured directly. A motive (or need) is a construct or mediating variable referring to the desire for a particular goal. Motives must be inferred from behavior, and more specifically, individual differences in strength of motives are typically inferred from the directionality of the individual's behavior and his perseverance in trying to obtain the desired goal. To illustrate, two boys may desire to achieve an important athletic goal—to set a new record in swimming 100 meters. The boy who practices diligently and persists in his attempts to perform this feat—in spite of handicaps, obstacles and failures—appears to be more highly motivated for success than the boy who gives up after some perfunctory efforts and a few practice trials.

But, can we be sure that our inferences about the motives of the two boys (based on our observations) are valid? It is not difficult to think of reasons why they may not be. The first boy may want to break the record not because he desires athletic success per se, but because he wants to win the love and approval of his athlete father. This example shows that a particular response may appear to gratify a particular motive, but may in fact be in the service of another need.

The second boy may give up easily not because he lacks motivation for success in swimming—in fact, he may be strongly motivated to achieve this kind of success—but because he is dreadfully afraid of failure. This case illustrates that (1) a motive can be strong and yet not lead directly to behavior that gratifies that motive, and (2) fear or anxiety may inhibit goal-directed behavior in spite of a strong motivation to achieve the goal.

The first boy's primary, most powerful motive was getting approval from his father and he had learned that the response of "trying hard in athletics" brought parental love and approval, the goal he strongly desired. A child readily learns the responses that lead directly to gratification of his motives. Analogously, a girl with strong dependency needs will manifest dependent behavior (e.g., clinging to others, asking for help) if she has learned that such behavior leads to gratification of this motive. In short, a motive will be expressed directly in overt behavior if that behavior effectively gratifies needs—that is, if the child expects to achieve his goals as a result of this behavior.

Consider some other instances in which inferences from behavior to motive are misleading. Not all aggressive behavior reflects underlying hostile motivation, i.e., a desire to injure or hurt someone else. A hyperactive or clumsy boy may inflict physical pain on others or destroy valued property even though he has no intention of being aggressive. Some "aggressive" behavior may be purely accidental, such as tripping someone unintentionally. A boy may behave aggressively not because he wants to injure anyone particularly, but because he wants to assert his masculinity. A preadolescent girl may make dependent overtures toward a handsome boy in her class—acting quite helpless, and asking him to help her with her work—because she wishes to appear feminine, not because she is expressing dependency needs. To cite an extreme example, a boy may strive for good grades in school not as a result of strong motives for academic achievement but primarily as an expression of hostility toward his uneducated father who derogates school achievement and is threatened by the boy's academic accomplishments. Few people would consider hard work in school to be aggressive behavior, yet in this case the boy uses this behavior (perhaps unconsciously) to satisfy hostile motives.

Let us return to the case of the boy who gave up rather easily in athletic competition in spite of strong motivation toward the goal of setting a record. His motives were not expressed in overt behavior. In spite of his high level of motivation, his anxiety or fear of failure—his expectancy that he would not achieve the desired goal—led him to inhibit his goal-directed behavior. In a similar way, a child may have strong dependency needs but not approach others in a dependent way if previous dependent responses have frequently been rejected. Such a child does not expect to gratify his strong dependency needs by behaving in dependent ways.

Many of the motives of the 5-year-old involve what is termed an *approach-avoidance conflict*. This means that there will be, on the one hand, a desire to approach a goal and, on the other, anxiety associated with the attainment of the goal. For example, the desire to disobey the mother openly is part of an approach-avoidance conflict. The child wants to rebel against the mother's demand that he drink his milk, but he is anxious about this and fears punishment or disapproval if he refuses her request. There are, therefore both forces impelling him to disobey (i.e., approach motives) and counterforces (anxiety and fear) which oppose the direct expression of rebellion (i.e., avoidance motives). The actual behavior displayed by the child will be a function of the interaction of these two forces: the desire to gratify the motive and the anxiety that interfered with gratification. Whether the child will attempt to obtain the desired goal will depend on the relative strengths of the approach and avoidance tendencies.

In the course of his socialization training, the child learns that he must inhibit certain forbidden acts and that he must delay the fulfillment of many of his desires. In the 1-year-old child, the arousal of a motive is likely to lead immediately to behavior aimed at gratifying the motive directly. Babies have not yet learned to delay or to inhibit gratification of their needs. The preschool child, however, is expected to exert some control over his aggressive, dependent, and sexual impulses—to modify them and to express them only in acceptable ways. Some kinds of responses, such as physical aggression toward parents, must be inhibited because they will invoke punishment whenever they occur.

The child also learns that the gratification of some motives must be postponed until the appropriate time and place. A 4-year-old girl may find that her nurturant mother generally gratifies her dependency needs (hugging her, helping her) as soon as they arise, but does not do so at all times. For example, if she is engaged in an important discussion with the father, she may postpone her dependency-gratifying reactions toward the child, perhaps telling the little girl, "I'll be with you in just a little while." Under these circumstances, the child learns to postpone or delay gratification until a later time when the mother is able to gratify the child's needs freely. The dependency responses are not inhibited, but the child has learned to delay gratification. This growing ability to delay immediate gratification of a motive is an important aspect of ego development.

Thus the fact that dependent or aggressive behavior occurs infrequently does not always indicate that the child's dependent or aggressive motivation is low. Rather, it may only signify the acquisition of controls and inhibitions of these behaviors.

SEXUAL MOTIVES AND CURIOSITY

Sexual motives include many kinds of wishes related to pleasurable— usually genital—sensations. There is some genital interest or activity before the preschool period. Male infants have erections, and masturbation and sex-play occur in very young children of both sexes, but erotic stimulation from the genitals becomes more intense during the preschool period. Many children discover that stimulation of the genitals produces pleasant sensations and may practice some modified form of masturbation (touching and manipulation of the genitals) during these years. According to the data of one large interview study of mothers of kindergarten children (70), about half of middle-class preschool children indulge in sex-play or genital handling. As many mothers are probably reluctant to report this kind of information, and because many children masturbate only in secret, these figures undoubtedly represent conservative estimates of the frequency of masturbation in young children.

As pleasant sensations and gratification are associated with masturbation, the child's interest in the genitals increases. Moreover, the child is likely to have opportunities to notice the differences between his own genitals and those of adults and of the opposite sex. The discrepancies elicit curiosity about and interest in the genitals of others—especially those of the opposite sex—and a desire to understand the differences. Questions about sex—particularly about the origins of babies and anatomical sex differences —are common between the ages of 2 and 5 (34).

Instances of exhibitionism (exposing genitals), voyeurism (looking at others' genitals), and persistent curiosity about the anatomy of the opposite sex have been observed frequently among nursery school children. In more permissive cultures, children may be much more open and spontaneous in their sexual behaviors. For example, Malinowski observed that in the Trobriand Islands, where sexual exploration is not punished or restricted, children of preschool age are highly active at a genital level and a large proportion of their play is sexually oriented (53).

In Western culture, however, parents are under strong pressure to suppress signs of sexual activity, interest, excitability, or curiosity in their young offspring. Of a large group of mothers interviewed, only 5 percent were completely permissive about masturbation, and less than 15 percent permitted the child to run about the house naked (70). Typically, mothers spank or scold if they discover the child masturbating openly. The genitals may then become the focus for conflict because they supply uniquely pleasant sensations, and, at the same time, evoke the anticipation of punishment and anxiety.

A second, less punitive type of response to the child's sexual activity frequently used by American mothers is to "nonlabel" or "mislabel" the child's sexual behavior when she observes it by distracting the child from what he is doing and suggesting tasks that might be more enjoyable. "In the case of sex behavior, a major method of training and control was the avoidance of stimulation; the avoidance of labels for sexual matters seems to have been one rather notable method of achieving this aim" (70, 214).

Discussing possible consequences of this handling of the child's sexual curiosity and activity, the investigators note:

> there may be some side-effects of these methods that many people would consider undesirable. . . . The child who has not been provided with proper labels for certain parts of his body, or for behavior related to sex, or for sexual feelings, may be somewhat handicapped in developing an understanding of sexual matters and an acceptance of his own sexual feelings without anxiety.

Mislabeling may have still other consequences. If a child is told not to touch his genitals because they are "dirty" from going to the toilet or if he is sent to the toilet whenever he is seen holding himself, on the assumption that he needs to eliminate, he may attach to sex some of the emotions he feels in connection with toileting: for example, disgust. Or, when sexually stimulated, he may experience anxiety that will be reflected in disturbances in toileting activities. And possibly the common warning to the child that he will "hurt himself" if he touches his genitals may strengthen an association between his sexual feelings and a feeling of impending injury or danger. None of these associated attitudes would be helpful to his sexual adjustment either in childhood or later (70, 214–215).

Sexual activity of any kind may become a source of conflict because, on the one hand, the activity provides pleasant sensations and, on the other, evokes anxiety and anticipation of punishment. Many instances of adolescent and adult sexual anxiety, misunderstandings, and handicapping ignorance about sex undoubtedly have their roots in punishment for early sexual activity or mislabeling of sexual acts and feelings in early childhood. "There is substantial evidence that the experiences of the child early in life have lasting and defining influences on the way in which he conducts his sexual life" (27, 216).

A child is not likely to develop anxiety associated with sexual feelings and sexual behavior if parents handle his sexual curiosity realistically, acting neither embarrassed nor secretive about questions or, on the other hand, overwhelming the child with too much information.

When the child becomes interested in problems pertaining to sex and birth, his questions should be answered frankly, truthfully, and without embarrassment as they come up. That is not so difficult a job as one might think because children need and want very little information at any one time. If children ask where they come from, and they are told that babies grow within the mother's body, that answer will satisfy most children for that particular day, and, perhaps, for several weeks or months to come. . . . Very often parents make a problem for themselves by feeling that when the child asks the first question about sex, they are obligated to tell him everything. . . . Obviously this is neither necessary nor advisable (20, 72).

AGGRESSION

Aggressive behaviors are actions that are intended to cause injury or anxiety to others, including hitting, kicking, destroying property, quarreling, derogating others, attacking others verbally, and resisting requests. *Hostile motivation* refers to the individual's wish or desire to cause injury or anxiety to others, and a very wide variety of behaviors can gratify hostile motives. For example, a nursery school boy who is hostile toward a peer may strike him. An older boy who is hostile toward his academically oriented father may do poorly in school because he knows that his poor performance will hurt his father's feelings.

Biological Factors

Observations of animals in their natural habitats have led some ethologists to postulate that aggressive drives have an innate, biological ("instinctive") basis (1, 18, 51). Konrad Lorenz speaks of aggression as a "true, primarily species-preserving instinct" (51, 50) in humans as well as in animals. According to him, certain stimuli or configurations of stimuli innately elicit aggressive reactions from animals, the eliciting stimuli and forms of aggression varying from species to species.

While these observations of animals' aggressive behavior suggest the *possibility* that certain stimulus situations may innately evoke aggression from humans, generalizations about innate aggressive drives in humans hardly seem warranted. Moreover, in many subhuman species the patterns of aggression may be significantly modified through experience (67). A thorough review of the relevant research led Feshbach to conclude that

> [generalizations] from an animal species to the human species are . . . highly questionable. The animal data may suggest the kinds of physiological mechanisms and situational variables that should be investigated in humans but cannot substitute for direct empirical studies of human aggression. It is also apparent that there are major differences between animal aggression and human aggression. Animal aggression is, on the whole, regulated by immediate stimulus changes. Human aggression can be maintained by mediating cognitive structures and is, to a much smaller degree, stimulus bound (25).

While the question of the biological basis of aggressive drives is a debatable one, there is a strong possibility that constitutional factors play a significant role in aggressive behavior. It seems quite likely, for example, that sex differences in aggressive expression have a biological basis. The male young of many animal species (e.g., rats, guinea pigs, monkeys) are much more aggressive than their female siblings. Experimental administration of male hormones to females of these species makes them much more aggressive in their approaches to others—more threatening, more "rough-and-tumble" in their play, and less likely to withdraw from the threats and approaches of other animals.

Furthermore, children's aggression appears to be intimately related to activity level, which is strongly influenced by constitutional makeup (63). Active children interact more frequently and more intensely with their peers and become involved in more situations that are likely to elicit aggressive responses. There is, furthermore, a positive correlation between activity level and frequency of initiation of aggressive behavior, and active children are likely to be reinforced by their peers for socially aggressive behavior (see pp. 398–399).

Social Experience and Aggression

Psychological theory and research are focused on the interpersonal and social factors affecting the child's tendency to behave aggressively. The forms and degrees of aggression a child will exhibit depend on many factors, such as intensity of his motivation (his desire to hurt others), the degree of environmental frustration, his observation and imitation of aggressive models, and the amount of anxiety and guilt associated with the expression of aggression. Let us turn our attention first to situations that are likely to give rise to aggression.

Effects of Frustration

Frustration and Aggression. According to the popular frustration-aggression hypothesis, aggression is a prepotent, if not inevitable, reaction to frustration. While there is no general agreement on a definition of frustration, most investigators and theorists agree that frustrating events are those which block the individual's goal-seeking behavior, threaten his self-esteem, or deprive him of the opportunity to gratify some salient motive. The sources of frustration may be (1) externally imposed barriers that prevent or delay the achievement of an important goal, or (2) internal conflicts between incompatible responses or (3) feelings of inadequacy or anxiety that inhibit or prevent the pursuit of important goals.

An event can be considered frustrating only if it actually disturbs or upsets the child. Young children encounter many situations that seem to be frustrating from an adult observer's point of view, but most of these are inconsequential, producing no reaction, or only minor, transient responses. Fawl (23) made meticulous observations of the incidence, intensity, and duration of interferences and unpleasant events in the everyday lives of children in their natural habitats (e.g., home, nursery school, playground). Preschool youngsters experienced more than 90 "goal blockages" (impositions, thwarting of enjoyable activities, loss of a valued toy) per day on the average, but most of these were "neither sufficient nor necessary conditions for producing states of disturbance in the child" (23, 100).

Reactions to these interferences were typically very mild in intensity, and of brief duration—usually less than a few minutes. Minor interferences seldom elicited strong, enduring, or intense reactions. Goal blockages that are really upsetting to the child are more likely, however, to arouse behaviors directed at eliminating the source of the interference or diminishing its effects.

It must be recognized that children differ markedly in their assessments of how frustrating a particular "interference" is. For example, a highly dependent child may be very much frustrated by the brief absence of his mother, which may entail some minor deprivations. However, such a child, being quite passive, may feel very little frustration by another child's domination of social play activities. A more independent child may not feel deprived because of his mother's absence, but may feel very frustrated by another child's "taking over" on the playground.

There is a great range of individual differences in reaction to frustration, both in the intensity and in the form of reaction. Some children seem to have "low frustration tolerance," reacting very readily to any frustration.

Children with "high frustration tolerance" may be remarkably unperturbed by events that most would regard as highly frustrating.

It is not clear how the aggressive response to frustration is acquired. Sears (68) has suggested that the infant finds that aggressive acts are often effective in eliminating frustration (e.g., the infant's thrashing about and hitting when he is being held uncomfortably may bring relief and a more relaxed, comfortable position). At the same time, these aggressive responses may evoke pain in the individual who is the source of frustration. This association between the perception of pain in others and the reduction of frustration is then learned and repeated. Feshbach (24) postulated that aggression stems from the child's frequent exposure to behaviors and cultural norms which indicate that injuring others is an appropriate response when the individual is frustrated or in pain—that is, the association between frustration and aggressive behavior is a kind of internalized cultural standard. But, as has been pointed out, both these explanations "are largely speculative, there being little in the way of empirical evidence that directly bears on this issue" (25).

While we do not understand how the frustration-aggression linkage is acquired, it is clear that frustrating situations and events often give rise to increased aggressive behavior (78). This was demonstrated experimentally in the study of 60 preschool children—30 boys and 30 girls—from lower-middle-class and professional families who were divided into three groups. Each subject was observed in two half-hour doll-play sessions. In the first session, all subjects were allowed to play freely with the dolls. However, immediately before the second session, one group, the failure group, was given very difficult tasks to accomplish and was left with feelings of failure and frustration. The second group was given pegboards and encouraged to manipulate the pegs for 20 minutes. This induced states of "satiation," which may also be regarded as frustrating. The third group, the control, had neither frustration nor satiation experiences before their second doll-play session. All aggressive responses (e.g., arguing, scolding, threatening, deprivation, spanking, hitting, kicking) were recorded.

In the second session, all three groups displayed more total aggression than they had in the first session and shorter delays (latencies) before the first expression of aggression. The permissive atmosphere of the doll-play situation apparently weakened inhibition against the expression of aggression; consequently, such behavior increased.

Nevertheless, the influence of frustration and satiation on aggressive behavior was clear. Subjects who were frustrated or satiated immediately preceding the second session showed significantly *greater* increases in aggression than the control group. Thus, as predicted from the frustration-aggression hypothesis, frustration produced heightened subsequent aggression.

Frustration and Regression. Aggression, though perhaps a prepotent reaction to frustration, is not the only common one. Regression (resorting to immature response patterns) is another frequent immediate consequence. In one highly significant investigation, Barker, Dembo, and Lewin (6) observed the behavior of 30 nursery school children under two conditions: first, free-play, and later, frustration. Regression was measured in terms of decreases in productivity, creativity, and constructiveness of play after frustration.

In the free-play situation, the children played alone for half an hour in a room which contained a standard set of play materials arranged on three large squares of paper. Behavior was recorded and units of play were scored on a 7-point scale of constructiveness from 2 (superficial examination of the playthings) to 8 (highly original, elaborate game or story involving the toys).

The frustration situation was divided into three parts. During the first stage, prefrustration, the child was brought into the experimental room, where he found the standard play material of the free-play period incorporated into an elaborate, highly attractive set of new toys. When the child had become thoroughly involved in play with these new toys, the experimenter collected all the less attractive, standard toys. He arranged them, as they had been earlier, on three squares of paper in another part of the room. The child was led to that part of the room, and a wire screen separating the standard toys from the new ones was lowered and locked. This marked the beginning of the second phase of the frustration period. During this time (30 minutes), the child could play only with the less attractive play materials while the more desirable toys remained visible but inaccessible (see Fig. 9.1).

Following the frustration period, the partition was lifted and the child was allowed to play with the new toys for as long as he wished. This final period served no experimental purpose, but was designed to mitigate any undesirable consequences of the frustration.

Children's reactions during the second phase of the frustration period differed greatly from their behavior during free play with the same toys. When frustrated, the children displayed significantly more barrier or escape activities (e.g., physically approaching the inaccessible regions, pleading with the experimenter to be allowed out of the room, talking about outside regions, and aggressive behavior toward experimenter or barriers). In addition, their play was appreciably less creative and constructive than it had been during free play. In other words, a marked reduction in the level of maturity of play was a consequence of frustration. Furthermore, the children who seemed to be most severely frustrated, i.e., those most occupied with barrier and escape behavior during the frustration situation, regressed most in their play.

As is the case with respect to tendencies to become aggressive, there are striking individual differences in "frustration tolerance" which affect children's ability to control regression as a reaction to frustration. In one interesting study (12), the investigators assessed the frustration tolerance of a group of preschool children by means of two behavioral tests. In addition, each child was observed in a separate session in the frustration situation described above in which he was first allowed to play with attractive

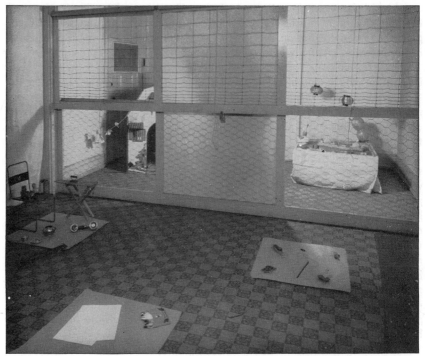

Fig. 9.1. The frustration situation. (From R. G. Barker, T. Dembo, & K. Lewin. *Univer. Iowa Stud. Child Welf., 18,* 56. By permission.)

toys, and then was prevented by a barrier from playing with them. The children who seemed low in "frustration tolerance" could not adequately control their regressive reactions to frustration. After being frustrated, they were unable to play constructively with the ordinary toys, and often kicked the barrier aggressively, while children who had been able to tolerate frustration on the two tests did not become less constructive in their play with the ordinary toys (12).

It may be concluded that children differ in their ability to tolerate frustrating situations. For those who have a low tolerance for frustration, aggression and immature play are likely to be elicited by frustration.

Situational Factors Affecting Reactions to Frustration.   Situational factors, such as the presence of friends, may also influence the child's reactions to frustration. Pairs of close friends and of casual friends of preschool age were tested together in the frustration situation used in the study described above (77). During free play, close friends spent more time in social play activities than casual friends did, and their play was generally more mature and constructive. While both groups regressed under conditions of frustration, strong friends showed significantly *less* decrement in creativity of play than casual friends. In other words, the differences in the play of pairs of strong and weak friends, observed during free play, became more marked under conditions of frustration. The presence of a close associate fostered highly constructive play under ordinary conditions and limited the adverse influence of frustration on creativity (77).

In addition, as another study indicated, the presence of close friends may attenuate aggressive reaction to frustration. In fact, close friends may actually become more socially outgoing and cooperative in their play under frustrating circumstances, reacting with less hostility toward each other and with more joint aggression against the experimenter, the source of their frustration. These data demonstrate that social cohesiveness and the presence of friends—and the personal security associated with these—not only mitigate aggressive and regressive responses to frustration but may actually promote socially desirable behavior, such as cooperation.

Such findings may be applied in situations to which parents and teachers can anticipate that the child will become frustrated. If the child can meet difficulties or potentially frustrating situations accompanied by a person with whom he feels secure, he will probably behave in more constructive, mature ways—that is, with less aggressive and regressive behavior than he would if he were alone.

Learning, Imitation, and Aggression.   We have seen that frustration may be a potent factor in eliciting aggressive behavior. But not all children react aggressively—or with equal degrees of aggression—to blocking and deprivation. The probability that any particular preschool child will manifest aggression, as well as the strength and intensity of his aggressive behavior, depend on a number of factors in his experience—such as the degree to which he has been rewarded or punished for such behavior in the past, and the availability and influence of aggressive models.

In empirical studies of aggression, investigators typically observe and record all instances of acts that are culturally defined as aggressive, but they do not differentiate between those that are actually intended to injure or hurt others (i.e., acts mediated by aggressive motivation) and those that do not have this goal. The distinction is a very difficult one to make, and it could be argued that human aggression does hurt others—regardless of whether that is the primary intention—and that what is most important, theoretically and practically, is the discovery of the antecedents of expression and inhibition of aggressive responses (25).

The Effects of Rewards.   Rewards for aggressive behavior lead to increases in overt expression of aggression and generalization of aggressive responses to other situations. In one straightforward experimental study, 7 preschool children received trinkets as rewards for verbal aggression while playing with dolls (calling the dolls "dirty," "bad"), while 7 other subjects, the control group, were rewarded for nonaggressive verbal responses. Following this training period, all subjects were then observed in another play situation with other toys. During the training session, the children who were rewarded for verbal aggression made significantly more of these responses than did the controls, and, in the subsequent play period, they also manifested significantly greater amounts of *nonverbal* aggression. "The importance of this study lies in its demonstration that reinforcement of verbal aggression in one play setting has effects that are manifested in nonverbal aggression in a different play setting" (5, 384).

The principle that reward for aggression will produce increased aggressiveness has been applied in socialization in cultures in which the individual, usually the male, is expected to behave aggressively. Among the Kwoma, for example, the adult male fights and expresses hostility freely toward many people, and from early childhood the male is prepared for his adult role largely through direct rewards for aggression (74).

The effects of permissiveness of aggression—allowing the child to express aggression overtly and freely—are comparable to the effects of direct reward. Thus, with a permissive adult present, aggressive responses increase from the first half to the second half of a 10-minute doll-play session and from one session to the next (5, 391). All the preschool subjects in one doll-play study displayed more aggression in the second of two sessions than they had in the first and shorter delays (latencies) before the first expression of aggression (40). Apparently the permissive atmosphere of the doll-play situation leads the child to infer that aggression is suitable or appropriate in this situation and decreases his inhibitions against aggressive expression. That is, "adult behavior which is intended by the adult to be 'acceptant' is seen by the child as permission-giving, and an adult attempt at being 'nonjudgmental' is interpreted by the child as being in fact affirmatively judgmental" (72, 133). Thus, when the child encounters such a permissive situation again, he behaves more aggressively.

It may be inferred from these findings that if parents are clearly permissive of, or reward, aggression, children are likely to behave highly aggressively at home, and, by generalization, in other settings where they feel aggression is permitted, expected, or encouraged.

It should be noted, however, that if the child does not regard a particular setting as specifically permissive, he is less likely to manifest overt aggression. This was demonstrated in one study in which children participated in two free-play sessions with a young friend (72). For half of the subjects, an adult was present throughout, but for the other half, this was not the case. Two-thirds of the children observed with the permissive adult present showed more aggression in the second session than they had in the first. However, in the adult-absent group—i.e., the group without specific permission to be aggressive—all the subjects showed *less* aggression in the second session. Apparently, the accepting adult was seen as granting permission for aggressive expression, but in the absence of an adult the child's own internalized standards (his inhibitions against the expression of aggression) were invoked. The child controls himself when no adult is available to tell him what to do, but abdicates this control when an adult is present—acting as he thinks this adult expects him to.

Modeling

Exposure to an aggressive model (or models) is likely to elicit imitation of aggression in children. In the stimulating research of Bandura and his associates at Stanford University, the subjects, usually preschool children, are first exposed to aggressive real-life or fantasy (movies or television) models. In one experiment, for example, an adult model was observed by preschool children while she "solved" a discrimination-learning problem (4). During her trials, she made many incidental, irrelevant responses that had nothing to do with the discrimination learning including behaving aggressively toward dolls located on the discrimination boxes. When she was with the control subjects, she did not behave in those aggressive ways.

Subsequently, the subjects were given the same discrimination problem. Ninety percent of the children in the experimental group imitated the aggressive responses of the model, whereas none of the control children displayed such behavior. The authors point out that these findings demonstrate that mere observation of aggressive models is *sufficient* to stimulate imitative aggressive behavior in children. Frustration is not a *necessary* antecedent condition for the occurrence of aggressive responses.

Imitative aggressive responses, acquired from a model, as in the experiment described above, may also generalize to other settings. In another experiment, the subjects were 48 nursery school children (24 boys and 24 girls). Some of the subjects observed aggressive models behaving in distinctive aggressive ways toward an inflated balloon painted to resemble a clown; others observed nonaggressive models. A control group of 24 children were not exposed to any adult models in the experimental situation.

Following their exposure to the model, the children experienced a mild frustration before being tested for delayed imitation of the model's behavior. Then they spent 20 minutes in a room playing with a variety of toys. The subjects who had been exposed to aggressive models displayed significantly more imitative physical and verbal aggression than the controls or the children who observed nonaggressive models. Other kinds of aggression, not displayed by the model, were also more common among those who observed an aggressive model. Clearly, exposure to human models behaving aggressively has a great deal of influence in eliciting aggressive behavior regardless of whether it is preceded by frustrating experiences.

The frequency of aggressive *acts* apparently increases after exposure to aggressive models and as a result of rewards for these responses. But note that these studies tell us nothing about aggressive *motivation* because there is no evidence that the child desired to hurt or injure the dolls.

Punishment for Aggression. While reward for aggression, frustration, and observation of aggressive models may stimulate the child's aggressive behavior, punishment for aggression should, according to the principles of learning, lead to inhibition of overt aggression. There is good experimental evidence to support this expectancy. In one study, the investigators recorded and rated all instances of aggression exhibited by 23 nursery school children during four doll-play sessions. During the second session, 12 children, the experimental group, were punished verbally (e.g., "No, John, don't you know nice boys don't do things like that?") every time they made an aggressive response. The control group, 11 children, were allowed complete freedom to express aggressive behavior without punishment.

None of the subjects was punished during the third session. Nevertheless, the experimental subjects who had been punished during the second session manifested significantly fewer and less intense aggressive responses than they had in the first, or "baseline," session. The control group, on the other hand, increased steadily in both frequency and intensity of doll-play aggression from the first to the fourth sessions. In short, punishment for aggression led to inhibition of aggression while permissiveness reduced anticipation of punishment and weakened inhibitions against aggressive expression (40).

These findings should be applicable to the home situation. If aggression is punished there, fear and anxiety become attached to hostile responses and the child learns to *inhibit* such responses at home and, by generalization, in situations resembling the home.

The effects of parental punishment on children's aggressive behavior appear to be more complex than this, however. Sears and his coworkers observed the aggressive responses of three groups of nursery school children in free-play situations. The first group had nonpunitive mothers; the second group, mildly punitive mothers; and the third group, severely punitive mothers. The mildly punished children manifested the greatest number of aggressive responses. The first group had relatively few aggressive responses, presumably because they were seldom frustrated at home and consequently did not have strong aggressive *drives*. The third group, having experienced severe punishment for aggression, inhibited their aggressive *responses* (71).

The investigators' interpretation of their findings is that:

> punishment serves as a form of frustration and hence increases the total instigation to aggression, but when punishment becomes sufficiently severe, it inhibits the specific actions punished; in such cases, the increased aggressive instigation would be manifested only in forms of aggressive activity different enough from those punished not to suffer from inhibition by means of stimulus or response generalization (69, 475).

Displacement.   If aggressive *motives* are of considerable strength—perhaps as a result of severe frustration at home—they will not necessarily be eliminated, even if aggressive *responses* are punished. Under these circumstances aggression may be *displaced,* that is, expressed in situations that are quite different from the home (e.g., in permissive doll play).

Specific predictions about the expression and displacement of aggression, derived from these theoretical considerations, were tested in a study of the effects of *home punishment and frustration* on children's doll-play aggression. The mothers of the 30 nursery school subjects were intensively interviewed about restrictive rules, responsiveness to the child's needs or requests, and enforcement of compliance with mother's wishes. Measures of *home frustration* were derived from the mothers' responses, and *punishment of aggression* in the home was also rated on the basis of mothers' statements about the frequency and intensity of spanking, threatening, and scolding.

As would be predicted on the basis of theory, highly frustrated children (those above the median in *home frustration)* were more aggressive in permissive doll play than mildly frustrated children were. Moreover, highly punished children (above the median in *home punishment)* exhibited more doll-play (i.e., displaced) aggression than those who were mildly punished. Homes rated high in both frustration and punishment produced children who manifested considerably more frequent and more intense expressions of displaced aggression than children from homes rated low in both these variables.

Inconsistent handling of the child's aggression may also stimulate aggressive expression. Mothers who permit aggression on some occasions and punish it at other times are likely to have highly aggressive children (70). When parents permit occasional aggression, the child probably experiences some reduction in anxiety about this response. In addition, inconsistency in discipline creates a frustrating situation which instigates aggressive behavior. Probably

> the way for parents to produce a non-aggressive child is to make abundantly clear that aggression is frowned upon, and to stop aggression when it occurs, but to avoid punishing the child for aggression. . . . When the parents punish— particularly when they employ physical punishment—they are providing a living example of the use of aggression at the very moment they are trying to teach the child not to be aggressive. The child who copies his parents in many ways, is likely to learn as much from this experience of successful aggression on his parents' part as he is from the pain of punishment. Thus, the most peaceful home is one in which the mother believes aggression is not desirable and under those circumstances is never to be expressed toward her, but relies mainly on non-punitive forms of control. The home where children show angry, aggressive outbursts frequently are likely to be homes in which the mother has a relatively tolerant (or careless) attitude toward such behavior, or where she administers severe punishment for it, or both (70, 266).

Sex and Age Differences in Aggression

The form, style, frequency, and intensity of the child's aggressive responses seem to be, to a very great extent, functions of his social learning experiences. "In the area of aggression, social training consists largely in teaching a child to be aggressive only *in certain ways*. For example, he may be taught to 'defend his principles' (or his parents) but not to attack his opponent physically" (5, 402).

There is no doubt that in American culture, as in almost all cultures (17), boys receive more encouragement (reward) and less punishment for aggressive behavior than girls do. Many parents believe that the ideal boy should be able to fight back and defend himself when attacked (70), and boys are generally not made as anxious about aggressive behavior as girls are. As would be anticipated, during the preschool years, boys express more aggression than girls in play and fantasy. Physical attacks, fighting, negativistic behavior, quarreling, lying, tackling, verbal aggression, destructiveness, and temper tantrums are all more common among boys than among girls (52, 323–324).

These sex differences become more marked with increasing age during the preschool period. According to the data of one observational study, 2-year-old boys and girls hit, scream, and cry with approximately equal frequency. By the age of 4, however, boys do more hitting, and relatively less screaming than girls do (45). This increase in sex differences with age probably reflects stronger, more thorough learning of patterns of aggressive expression that are appropriate for one's own sex.

With increasing age and experience, the child learns to display those forms of aggression that are defined as culturally acceptable, and to inhibit aggressive expressions (usually gross, violent types) that are considered less acceptable. Thus, in doll play, older nursery school children manifest more prosocial aggression (aggression for socially desirable purposes, e.g., verbal disapproval of antisocial acts) and fewer antisocial responses (e.g., destruction, hitting) than younger children.

Stability of Aggressive Expression

The level of the child's aggression appears to be another characteristic that is established early; data from nursery school teachers' ratings indicate that it tends to remain relatively stable between the ages of 3 and 5 (19). A follow-up observational study also revealed that the child's proneness to aggression while in nursery school was a good predictor of his aggressive behavior in kindergarten. Children ordinarily maintain their relative position in the group with respect to frequency of aggressive outbursts (45).

The data from the Fels longitudinal study are most relevant for the problem of long-term stability or continuity of aggressive behavior (48). The sample consisted of 36 men and 35 women (age range, 20 to 29) who had been studied and observed from birth through adolescence. During the early years, the subjects had been interviewed and observed in their homes, in the Fels experimental nursery school and day camp, and in public schools. Their mothers were interviewed at the Fels Institute and observed at home in order to assess their attitudes and child-rearing practices.

A psychologist, who had no knowledge of the adult subjects' personalities studied all the observations on these children for four separate age periods: birth to age 3; 3 to 6; 6 to 10; and 10 to 14 years. After studying all the material for each child from birth to age 3, he rated each of them on a variety of behaviors, and then rated them all for ages 3 to 6, 6 to 10, and finally, 10 to 14. A second psychologist, who had no knowledge of the subjects' childhood behavior, interviewed each of the subjects and rated their adult behavior on variables similar to those rated during childhood (e.g., aggression, dependency, withdrawal response to stress, mastery, sex-typed interests, and involvement in intellectual activities).

In order to assess the stability or continuity of childhood characteristics, the ratings of each of the four childhood periods were intercorrelated and correlated with assessments of the adult's personality. The correlations showed that aggressive behavior is more stable for boys than for girls during childhood and adolescence (48). Rage and tantrum behaviors are more stable for boys than for girls from ages 3 through 14, and these aggressive expressions during preschool were predictive of adolescent and adult irritability and aggression for males, but not for females. Boys who showed extreme degrees of rage and tantrum behavior during the preschool and early school years became men who were easily angered and likely to express verbal aggression when frustrated.

The most reasonable interpretation of this finding is that aggressive behavior is an accepted component of traditional masculine behavior (i.e., sex-typed behavior) but not of feminine behavior. Aggression in girls typically meets with more punishment than it does in boys, and the role-models young girls choose are less likely to be overtly aggressive. For these reasons, young girls who are aggressive will gradually learn to inhibit aggressive manifestations, while boys have more freedom to express their hostile feelings and will continue to manifest aggressive behaviors.

DEPENDENCY

The dependency *motive* is the wish to be nurtured, aided, comforted, and protected by others, or to be emotionally close to or accepted by others. There are numerous types and forms of dependent behavior: seeking assistance, attention, recognition, approval, reassurance, contact; clinging to adults or other children; resisting separation from adults; soliciting affection and support.

> But each one of these goals (attention, for example) may be sought in numerous ways. One child may shout to the teacher, "See me!" Another child may silently force his way to the front row in order to be directly under the eyes of his teacher. A third may smear his neighbor's drawing and then make sure this comes to the teacher's attention (30, 335).

As was true in the case of aggression, there is no one-to-one relationship between dependency motivation and dependent behavior. A child with high dependency motivation will probably manifest a great deal of dependent behavior *if* (but only if), in his experience, these responses have been rewarded and are not associated with punishment, anxiety, or conflict. But a child with strong dependency needs may find that his dependency responses give rise to rejection by his parents and/or peers. Or, his parents may discourage dependent behavior by telling him that it is "babyish." Under these circumstances, the manifestation of dependent behavior will make the child feel inadequate and anxious and he is not so likely to exhibit such behavior.

Another 4-year-old boy with strong dependency motivation may be undergoing rather intensive socialization for independence. This may precipitate an approach-avoidance conflict because, on the one hand, he wants to ask his parents for help in obtaining some goals, and, on the other (because of his independency motives), he is anxious about expressing dependency. As a result of this conflict, he is quite likely to avoid the expression of this behavior except in situations in which he desperately needs help (when the approach motives are very strong).

Some dependent behavior may be impelled by motives other than dependency. For example, the child's attention-seeking may be based on his need for greater self-esteem or social status rather than on a desire for help or reassurance. Ironically, seeking help and assistance may also serve the child's motives for independence: the child, wanting to solve a difficult and challenging problem himself, may realize that he can do so only if others supply him with some necessary information or techniques.

Unfortunately, investigations of dependency seldom involve efforts to assess motivational aspects. Typically, investigators observe and measure dependent *behavior* and then look for the antecedents of various degrees of this behavior. In the present section we will examine evidence on the development, antecedents, and correlates of dependent behavior during the preschool period.

As would be expected, the predominant forms of expressing dependency, as well as the objects of the child's dependency, change during the preschool period. Observational studies of nursery school children show that 2-year-olds are likely to be significantly more dependent upon their teachers, while dependency on peers is more common among 4-year-olds (35). The form of dependent behavior also changes with age: 2-year-olds cling more and seek affection more frequently, relative to attention- or approval-seeking, than 4-year-olds, while 4-year-olds seek both reassurance and positive attention less frequently than 5-years-olds do. Apparently attention- and approval-seeking are more mature forms of dependency expression than direct bidding for affection by clinging, touching, crying (30, 348).

In one recent short-term longitudinal study (19), 53 middle-class nursery school children were rated by their teachers on a number of behavior scales. Ratings were made each semester of their 2 years of nursery school attendance. The scales dealt with dependent behavior: e.g., seeks recognition from children, seeks to be near teacher, seeks help from teacher, seeks attention from teacher. Factor analysis of the data revealed marked individual stability in dependency during this period, leading the author to conclude that dependency is an attribute of personality that becomes "established early in life and tend[s] to be sustained in [its] original forms" (19, 21).

Interestingly, *instrumental dependency* (help-seeking—seeking out the teacher, not for herself, but as a means of obtaining assistance) was closely associated with *emotional* dependency (essentially *affiliation* or *attachment*, manifested by such behavior as clinging and seeking affection) in the first year (age 3–4), but not during the second (age 4–5). On the other hand, instrumental dependency and autonomy (independence), though not related during the first year, were highly *negatively* correlated during the second year. Apparently, then, dependency "increasingly came to signify an *alternative* to autonomy" (19, 22). By the age of 4, self-reliance and help-seeking are "alternative habits or 'strategies' used by the child in his goal-directed and problem-solving efforts" (19, 23).

As dependency is obviously a fairly stable and pervasive attribute during the nursery school period, it is unfortunate that we have so little understanding of its origins and antecedents. Theoretically, the amount of dependent behavior manifested by the child will be a function of the extent to which he is rewarded and punished for such behavior, the strength of his dependency motives, and imitation of dependent models. A mother who consistently and frequently rewards and rarely punishes dependent behavior should produce a dependent child, while punishment for dependency should discourage this behavior in the child. Some data consistent with this expectation come from studies of children reared in an extremely rejecting, institutional environment in which experiences of nurturant mothering are either absent or very infrequent during the earliest years. Under these conditions, affiliative (attachment) and dependent responses are rarely rewarded, and the children manifest very little of such behavior. The genesis of dependency, then, seems to depend upon early experiences of relatively consistent gratification of dependency needs from some other person.

Among the mothers of kindergarten children interviewed in the Sears, Maccoby, and Levin study (70), those who punished dependency but ultimately gave the child the attention or help he was demanding had the most dependent children.

> Reward for dependency had a tendency to increase dependency *only* when it was superimposed on punishment for the same behavior.

> The situation in which the mother sometimes loses her temper over the child's dependency and sometimes responds sweetly and nurturantly, or in which she becomes irritated but nevertheless turns her attention to the child and gives him what he wants, is one ideally calculated to produce conflict in the child. On the one hand, he anticipates unpleasant consequences to his behavior, and this anticipation produces anxiety. On the other hand, he simultaneously anticipates reward. When he has an impulse to be dependent, the impulse makes him both anxious and hopeful; the fear of the mother's irritation may make him inhibit his impulse temporarily, but the hope of getting the mother's attention through dependent behavior is still there. If eventually the dependent behavior does show itself, it will be of an "overdetermined" sort—exceptionally intense, doubly irritating to the mother, and impossible to ignore. Thus the mother's double response of giving the desired attention in the midst of irritation is made more probable and a vicious circle is established (70, 173–174).

Most mothers gradually begin to encourage independence during the preschool period. By the time the child is 5 years old, his mother expects some self-reliance and independent behavior; he should be able to dress himself, to attend to himself in the bathroom, to solve minor problems without help, to initiate and complete some activities, and to be able to play alone without constant supervision. If the mother is warm, accepting, and nurturant while she encourages independence, her child will be motivated to be more self-reliant, and excessively dependent behavior will diminish.

Many 5-year-olds give abundant evidence of *both* strong dependent and independent, autonomous motivations (9, 10, 11, 35). Apparently many children of this age are in conflict about seeking nurturance from others and dealing with the world independently. It is important to recognize that dependent behavior alone may not be an accurate index of the intensity of the child's basic needs for help and support. Some children have learned that it is important to be independent, and they try to inhibit overt help-seeking behavior in many situations.

Like dependency, autonomy or independence has been found to be a general, highly salient factor of marked stability during the preschool years. In Emmerich's study (19), measures of autonomy were derived from teachers' ratings of behaviors such as: "overcomes obstacles by himself,""gets intrinsic satisfaction from his work," "completes activities." There was considerable behavioral continuity while the children were in nursery school—i.e., they tended to maintain their relative standing in these behaviors throughout the four semesters of attendance. Moreover, children's achievement efforts which are related to independence are negatively correlated with help-seeking.

As we shall see shortly, maternal rewards for achievement behavior at home, which are closely linked with the development of independence and self-reliance, also foster a child's achievement efforts in nursery school. Not surprisingly, there is an inverse relationship between the mother's tendency to reward dependency and to reward achievement.

Relation of Dependency to Other Aspects of Socialization. During early childhood, manifestations of dependency (and, presumably, dependent motivation) are more frequent and more intense among girls than among boys. Nursery school teachers consistently rate girls higher than boys in dependency throughout the nursery school years (19). In free-play settings, girls 3 to 8 years of age show more dependent overtures to adults than boys do (16). Moreover, in contrast to aggression, dependent behavior is more stable for girls than for boys from the age of 3 to the age of 14 (47, 48). For example, a dependent 5-year-old girl is apt to become a dependent adolescent and young adult, but it is more difficult to predict adolescent dependency for boys from their preschool behavior. Perhaps this is because girls have less intense anxiety over expressing dependency, an accepted component of traditional feminine behavior, while conflict over violating sex-role standards for dependency may lead to inhibition of this type of behavior among boys.

Not surprisingly, highly dependent children become more upset and aggressive when their direct attempts to get help from others are frustrated. On the other hand, when subjected to relatively mild frustration, highly dependent preschool children (as measured by affection-seeking and clinging to the teacher) have been found to be less aggressive than nondependent children (62). Apparently, frustration has a differential effect on the child, depending on the child's initial level of dependency. A highly dependent child may be less likely to react with aggression because he is anxious about possible rejection or loss of love and nurturance if he behaves in prohibited, aggressive ways.

Similarly, children who are dependent upon peers, seeking them out for help and support, are more compliant when peers request them to do something, and they tend to be nurturant toward other children, giving sympathy and helping others (32). Nevertheless, highly dependent children, especially those dependent on adults, are *not* popular with other children in school, according to findings achieved through sociometric techniques (54).

Dependency on adults may be useful in "teaching," for children highly dependent on adults appear to be highly motivated to learn when rewarded with adult approval. In one study (29), the nurturance needs of two groups of preschool children were experimentally manipulated. One group was consistently nurtured by a female experimenter who played and talked with each child individually. In the second group, each child was first nurtured, and then the nurturance was suddenly withdrawn. It was assumed that the treatment of the second group would increase the child's motive for nurturance as a consequence of deprivation of a pleasant goal. Finally, each child was asked to learn a simple task and was verbally praised by the experimenter for a good performance. The group that experienced nurturance-withdrawal—and presumably had a stronger need for adult approval and attention—learned the task more rapidly with adult approval than the other group did. Moreover, highly dependent boys were more strongly influenced than relatively independent boys by this treatment. Apparently, the child's need for attention and nurturance was heightened by the experience of nurturance-withdrawal. Consequently, the experimenter's praise, after withdrawal, was a particularly effective reward and led to harder work and faster learning.

Men and women are differentially effective in gratifying boys' and girls' needs for nurturance. Boys performed best in the learning task described above with a woman experimenter who was nurturant at first and then rewarded the performance. Apparently, nurturance from a woman was "worth more" to a preschool boy than nurturance from a man, but nurturance from a man was more effective with preschool girls. This phenomenon may not be true of older children; school-age boys, who regard men as ego ideals, should be more likely to prize the approval and praise of a man more highly than that of a woman.

It may be concluded that a child with a strong need for nurturance (high dependency motivation) will work hard to learn various tasks in order to obtain adult nurturance and praise, but this varies to some extent with the sex of the child and the experimenter. As the school situation is one in which the child is asked to learn a task in order to obtain the teacher's praise, boys who are highly dependent on their mother may do better in the first few years of school with female teachers than extremely independent boys will do. The data from the Fels longitudinal study indicate that boys rated as highly dependent during the first 6 years of life were less highly motivated in school than the more independent boys.

MASTERY AND ACHIEVEMENT MOTIVATION

Only relatively recently have psychologists interested in personality become seriously concerned with man's motivation to deal effectively with his environment—*effectance motivation,* as it has been labeled by Robert W. White (73). The development of competence as an attribute of personality is closely linked to the basic and pervasive motives for mastery and achievement—that is, the child's desire to master problems and increase his skills and abilities (e.g., gross motor tasks, reading, writing, painting).

It must be recognized, however, that this kind of behavior may also gratify other motives. Getting good grades in school, one important kind of achievement behavior in our culture, may bring the child recognition from peers, thus helping to gratify his needs for social status, or perhaps for power. Achievement in athletics may bring the boy the love and affection he desires from his parents. Mastery behavior may even, in some cases, help satisfy aggressive motives. A boy who is hostile to his older sister may find that he can hurt her feelings and injure her pride by earning better school grades than she does.

In investigations of mastery motivation, psychologists have arbitrarily delimited the criteria of achievement to the areas of intellectual attainment and physical skills. It is, of course, possible to achieve in other areas—in social skills, interpersonal relations, altruism, charity, religious or political activities—but success and achievement in these areas have not been the foci of empirical study.

Correlates of High Achievement Behavior. As noted earlier, the independent, self-reliant child is the one most likely to be highly motivated to achieve, and, like independence, the motive is acquired early. The data from one study indicate that nursery school children who spend most of their time and effort in achievement activities (coloring, painting, making clay models, reading books) were generally less dependent upon adults and less frequently sought help and emotional support than their peers who participated in few "achievement" activities.

Shackman from Monkmeyer

Mothers of the "high achievement" children revealed in interviews that, from the child's infancy onward, they had rewarded and encouraged attempts at achievement and tended to ignore the child's requests for help. "Moreover, the mothers who usually spontaneously praised and rewarded their children's achievement efforts, even when the children did not seek approval, had children who displayed especially strong and frequent achievement efforts outside the home" (15, 429).

In American culture, as in most societies, achievement is more strongly stressed and reinforced in the training of boys than of girls (70). It is, there-fore, not surprising that in the primary grades, boys manifest more achieve-ment motivation than girls on many criteria (e.g., interest in solving a puz-zle they had previously failed), although these sex differences are not so evident during the preschool years (16).

The early development of high achievement motivation during preschool has prolonged and enduring effects. Winterbottom contrasted the early child-training procedures used by the mothers of preadolescent (8–10 years old) boys high in achievement motivation (as revealed in projective tests) with those used by mothers of boys low in achievement motivation. The former expected self-reliant and independent behavior at earlier ages, from nursery school age onward, and from the earliest years gave frequent and substantial rewards for independent accomplishment (76, 478).

Moreover, mothers who encouraged their children's early mastery of such basic skills as walking and talking had children with higher levels of school achievement than children whose mothers did not encourage early mastery (40). Reinforcement for early accomplishment seems to facilitate the development of a general motive for achievement and, more specifically, the desire to learn new intellectual skills and to perform well in school. Clearly, "early training in independence and mastery contributes to the de-velopment of strong achievement motivation in preadolescents" (76, 478).

Girls whose mothers rewarded their intellectual accomplishments during the first 3 years gained substantially in IQ between the ages of 6 and 10, and personality tests showed that they were highly concerned with mastery and competition. For example, a girl with an achievement-rewarding mother responded to a picture of a boy with a violin by telling a story in which a boy is "practicing the violin and wants to be good so he can play in Carnegie Hall." In contrast, a girl with a nonachievement-rewarding mother would reply, "The boy doesn't want to practice and wants to go out and play" (55).

Achievement behavior, especially in the intellectual area, is one of the most stable aspects of a child's personality. Girls and boys who show a strong desire to perfect and master intellectual skills during the preschool years tend to retain this motivation during adolescence and early adulthood. (55). The child who enters school with high achievement motivation—a strong desire to do well—is likely to develop into the adolescent and adult who is concerned with intellectual competence.

While the subjects of these studies were mostly from the middle class, the findings are probably applicable to other groups as well. The disadvantaged child grows up in a home almost completely lacking in intellectual stimulation and achievement orientation; generally he receives little or no encouragement or reward for independent achievements. Understandably, he acquires a low level of achievement motivation and, since achievement motivation is critical for success in school, he is likely to perform poorly there.

FEAR AND ANXIETY

Everyone sometimes experiences fear and anxiety in one form or another, and in varying degrees. The distinction between these emotions is not clear-cut. Both involve a pattern of physiological and psychological reactions, including unpleasant and stressful feelings and emotions. Both are anticipatory internal responses—basically anticipations of danger or of an unpleasant event, feeling or reaction.

Fear is generally considered the more specific emotion, a response to particular, specifiable objects and stimuli such as fast-moving vehicles or wild animals. Anxiety, a more diffuse, unfocused, and less clearly perceived emotional state, differs from fear primarily in its "free-floating" quality— its lack of objective or realistic foci characteristic of fears of, say, moving vehicles and uncaged wild animals. However, as Erikson points out, it is difficult to maintain a rigorous distinction or differentiation between fear and anxiety, particularly in the case of young children, because young children do not differentiate between inner and outer, real and imagined dangers (21).

From a clinician's perspective,

> anxiety is not a pathological condition in itself but a necessary and normal physiological and mental preparation for danger. . . . Anxiety is necessary for the survival of the individual under certain circumstances. Failure to apprehend danger and to prepare for it may have disasterous results . . . Further, . . . anxiety can serve the highest aims of man (26, 11).

In terms of learning theory, stimuli capable of eliciting anxiety are those that were present on previous occasions when strong feelings of fear were elicited. Later, thinking about the fear-evoking event leads to anticipation of the unpleasant feelings that were associated with it originally. Furthermore, as we learned earlier, certain other antecedent conditions, e.g., uncertainty about the future and inability to cope with strange stimuli (see pp. 268–269), may also elicit anxiety.

Preschool Children's Fears

Every child learns a variety of fears or sources of anxiety. Some of these serve a "self-preservation" function—that is, fears attached to certain kinds of stimuli (e.g., highways, fierce animals, dangerous tools, moving automobiles) motivate effective avoidance responses. Moreover, fears may serve as a basis for learning new responses. For example, fear of speeding cars can motivate the child to learn the rules of crossing streets—the appropriate place and the signals to be observed. Fear of wild animals or natural events, such as thunderstorms, may stimulate the child's interest in learning more about nature and about natural science.

But extensive, overly intense, and very frequent fear reactions (e.g., crying, retreating, withdrawing, cringing, trembling, protesting, appealing for help, cowering, clinging to parents) are incompatible with stable or constructive behavior. If the child is to achieve adequate emotional adjustment, many of these responses must be replaced by mature, purposeful reactions to stimuli that previously elicited fear.

According to one study in which parental records were the source of data, fears of actual objects or unusual stimuli (e.g., sudden unexpected movements; strange objects, settings, or people) declined with age during the preschool years. However, fears of anticipated, imaginary, or supernatural dangers (such as the possibility of accidents, darkness, dreams, ghosts) increased. Apparently the child's cognitive development—his increased understanding of the world and greater use of representations and symbols—influence his emotional reactions. In general, the frequency and intensity of the overt signs of fear decreased with age (e.g., crying, panic, withdrawal) between ages 2 and 5.

Childhood fears are highly unpredictable, and, at all age levels, there are marked individual differences in susceptibility to fear. The same stimulus may be extremely frightening to one child but leave another completely unperturbed. Moreover, a child may be much disturbed by a particular stimulus in one situation, but pay no attention to it in another.

Some of the parents in this study were interviewed between 13 and 35 months after the original records had been made. By this time, more than half of the fears had dropped out and only a third persisted in their original form. There were numerous instances of modifications in form, of new fears growing out of older ones. For example, a child who was afraid of a balloon used in administering an anesthetic during an operation became fearful of all balloons and objects resembling them. Another child, frightened by a mouse running through his bedroom, began to fear all scratching sounds at night. In brief, fears seem to spread by the process of stimulus generalization.

Intelligence may also influence the acquisition of fear. Among children between the ages of 2 and 5, the number of fears displayed correlated positively with IQ, the relationship being most marked at the youngest age levels (24 to 35 months of age). A significantly higher proportion of girls than of boys show fear responses (42, 43, 44). Apparently intelligent children are able to recognize "potential danger" more readily than duller ones, have livelier imaginations, and probably think and reflect more about dangers.

Relationships Between Mothers' and Children's Fears

Most fears are acquired, and since the young child's most important learning occurs in the home, it is not surprising to find that there is a marked tendency for a child to adopt his mother's fears. This is most clear in the cases of fears of dogs, insects, and storms (28).

The parent's fears are acquired by the child through identification or observational learning. Moreover, if the mother herself is afraid of an object or event, she cannot do anything to make it less fear-provoking for her child. Consequently, he continues to fear this stimulus and to make avoidance and withdrawal responses which may be tension-reducing in the sense of removing him from the object of his fear. This is reinforcing, and the responses tend to be repeated, thus preventing the learning of new, more mature reactions. For these reasons, fears which the child shares with his mother are particularly resistant to treatment and extinction.

Techniques of Eliminating Fears

Children cannot be expected to "outgrow" their fears automatically. Unless new responses to fear-eliciting stimuli are learned, fears are not eliminated. Fortunately the principles of learning theory, particularly the concept of extinction, may be applied with success in reducing children's fears. For example, a stimulus the child fears, such as a rat, may be presented at the same time the child receives something pleasant, such as candy. After several such pairings, the child may begin to have more positive reactions to the object he had previously feared (46). If fear responses (feelings of fright or withdrawal, for example) fail to occur after many presentations of the stimulus, these stimulus-response connections will be weakened and the response may disappear (i.e., be extinguished) eventually.

These principles were applied by one investigator in experimental attempts to overcome children's fears (41). Youngsters who were afraid of the dark were accompanied into a dark room by a friendly adult or were encouraged to become active explorers in dark places where they found valuable prizes. In these situations, the connections between the feared stimulus (the dark) and the anxiety and fear responses are weakened, and withdrawal responses are eliminated. In addition, as the child grows older and better able to use language, or verbal mediators, it becomes possible to supplement these conditioning techniques with verbal explanations.

Mothers can reduce their children's fears most effectively by techniques of explaining *plus* gradually encouraging the child to confront the situation he fears. Explanation alone has not been found to be a useful method with very young children since they have not yet learned to associate words with the fear-provoking stimuli. On the other hand, when subjection is accompanied by explanation, the fear-eliciting stimuli became associated with the parent's calming presence, encouragement, and gentle words of explanation. In addition, in this situation the child is rewarded for *inhibiting* fear responses, and new, more mature responses to the stimuli may become dominant over fear responses learned earlier (28). The use of therapeutic techniques for the reduction of intense, irrational fears (phobias) is discussed in the next chapter (see pp. 400–401).

Anxiety and Defense

Like fear, anxiety impels the individual to action of some sort. Minimal anxiety may, and often does, serve constructive purposes, acting as a spur to creativity, problem-solution, and inventive accomplishments; but it may be emotionally crippling—tying the individual in knots, rendering him ineffectual and desperate.

> The inability to cope with danger may result in a sense of helplessness and inadequacy, in reactions of fright, in neurotic symptoms or in antisocial behavior. Only in such cases can we speak of anxiety as pathological, but it would be more direct to say that the solution or attempt at solution [of his problems or conflicts] was a pathological one (26, 12).

Antecedents of Anxiety

The preschool years seem to be a critical period for the development of anxiety, for every young child has to deal with many sources of anxiety and consequently has numerous opportunities to acquire anxiety reactions. He may become anxious about expressing freely his aggressive, sexual, or dependent feelings. The possible loss or dilution of parental love when a new baby arrives may be perceived as threatening, or the child may become apprehensive about real or imagined rejection by parents or peers.

Intense and frequent anxiety among young children has its roots in early parent-child relationships. According to clinical observations, the significant antecedents are overly severe punishment and restrictions; parental efforts to impose standards of behavior that are too high for the child to attain; harsh negative evaluations of the child's behavior and accomplishments; or inconsistency in parental treatment of the child, together with frequent and intense changes in mood and in reactions to the children (49, 64).

Seymour Sarason and his colleagues at Yale University have conducted the most systematic work on the antecedents and correlates of anxiety in young children (66). The subjects were primary school children and the child's anxiety was assessed by means of a questionnaire dealing primarily with reactions to taking tests in school. It consisted of items such as, "Are you afraid of the teacher asking you questions about how much you have learned in school?" "Does your heart begin to beat faster when the teacher calls on you?" The test is valid and scores on it are positively correlated with teachers' ratings of anxiety, with tests of general anxiety, and with children's manifest anxiety in interviews and other kinds of situations (64).

Sarason and his colleagues did not study preschool children, and their method of testing probably limits the extent to which their findings can be generalized. Nevertheless, many of their findings are directly relevant for understanding anxiety in preschoolers. They present convincing data that

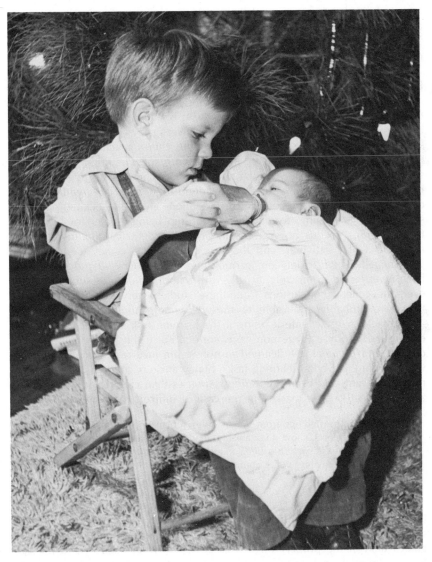

John Conger

children's anxieties are "the result of a complex interaction between the parental threat of negative evaluation of the child's performance and the child's conflicting feelings of aggression toward his parents and his needs to be dependent upon them" (66 190). The anxious child experiences his greatest difficulties in situations which he views as evaluative—that is, situations in which he is required to act independently. Moreover, interviews revealed that mothers of highly anxious children, in contrast to the other mothers, responded to and evaluated the child's behavior not in terms of his capabilities or his own needs but in terms of the mother's own standards and values. The child cannot fulfill the mother's demand, and his failures "result in experiencing negative evaluations and the development of a derogatory self-image" (66, 232).

Behavioral Correlates of Anxiety

The pervasive effects of anxiety in preschool children are evident in social behavior and in cognitive functioning. It is difficult to assess the degree of a preschool child's anxiety objectively. Investigators generally use criteria such as teachers' ratings, observations of the child's reactions in the classroom or in situational tests (e.g., in a strange or new setting). Thus, in one study, high levels of anxiety among nursery school children, as judged by their responses in a strange new room, were found to be associated with frequent dependency reactions of both active (attention- and help-seeking) and passive (touching, clinging) forms, the relationship being greater for boys than for girls (35). Anxious boys give evidence of inadequacy and insecurity in their social play activities, and they prefer immature games (64, 501).

The effects of anxiety on learning and other cognitive processes have been investigated extensively, usually with school children as subjects. However, the general conclusions from these studies—very briefly summarized here—are probably applicable to nursery school children.

Anxiety may facilitate learning if the learning task is simple and a well-established response (or responses) is correct. But if the task is complex and difficult and/or previously learned responses are incorrect, anxiety interferes with learning. In verbal learning tasks, highly anxious children tend to make more irrelevant, and even interfering responses than children low in anxiety, and the effect is most marked in the case of difficult problems.

> In general, the findings from . . . studies [of anxiety in relation to problem-solving processes] show that anxiety tends to impair children's performance on verbal tasks. Anxiety has been found to impair certain speech characteristics, such as voice quality, voice comprehensibility and the like, as well as the use of abstract concepts (64, 499).

Since school learning tasks and assignments generally become more difficult and require more ability to abstract as the child advances through school, anxiety is more likely to hinder academic achievement in the higher grades than in the primary ones. This is exactly what Sarason and his colleagues found in a longitudinal study: "Over time, anxiety scores become increasingly and negatively related to indices of intellectual and academic performance" (36, 57).

Defense Mechanisms

Because anxiety is so stressful and painful, everyone develops techniques of coping with it or defending against it. The *defense mechanisms*—learned responses used to avoid or reduce feelings of anxiety—are commonly used to enable the individual to live reasonably comfortably. Typically the individual is unaware of the presence of the defense, or defense mechanism, which helps him avoid problems that he cannot deal with adaptively.

When a defense is used, some aspect of reality is usually distorted. For example, a child may have provoked a friend's anger by attempting to dominate him. Because it would be anxiety-arousing to admit to himself that he was responsible for what happened, the child may blame the other boy, explaining that "Johnny is a bad boy." In this case, we say that the child has distorted the situation and has *projected* the blame for the social friction onto his friend.

Many children of this age have "imaginary playmates" to whom they turn for solace in times of crisis (e.g., after being punished by a parent). For some children, the playmate is "there," an obvious distortion of reality.

Everyone uses defense mechanisms. But strong dependence on these mechanisms—and their pervasiveness in the individual's behavior—may be associated with frequent and gross distortions of reality and failure to cope adaptively with psychological problems and with the real world. Used in these ways, the defense mechanisms may have consequences that are extremely deleterious for mental health and adequate emotional adjustment.

> In most children, after anxiety takes on its signaling functions, the ego learns to react to this danger signal in various ways which are probably also both constitutionally and environmentally determined. These defensive reactions take many forms and may be utilized flexibly or rigidly. It also seems likely that these early-learned reactions to anxiety are basic determinants of personality and characterological differences in later life. In addition, the defensive maneuvers of an individual may be adaptive or maladaptive in different situations. When the defensive processes available to a particular individual are varied and flexible, the chances are high that they will be adaptive in most situations. But when an individual's defensive structure is rigid and limited, it follows that his defensive reactions will usually not be appropriate to a particular situation and thus will be maladaptive in the sense that they will interfere with adaptive functioning. Such defensive processes are usually labeled symptoms, although we are learning that even where the defenses are not clearly pathological they can still interfere with performance if they are inflexible and inappropriate to the particular task (66, 31–32).

A few defense mechanisms seem to be particularly prominent among preschool children. These are withdrawal, regression, denial, repression, and projection.

Because these defense mechanisms, plus some others, are more prominent (and easier to detect and identify) among children of the middle childhood years, full discussion is reserved for the chapter on adjustment during
the school years (see pp. 516–518). Here we will merely define and describe
them briefly.

Behavioral withdrawal, one of the most frequently used defenses of
preschool children, involves avoidance of, or flight from, threatening situations or people. *Regression* is the adoption of a response that was characteristic of an earlier phase of development (e.g., thumb sucking or bed
wetting). *Denial* is seen in the child's insistence that an anxiety-arousing
event or situation (e.g., the death of a beloved pet) is not true, and he believes his denial is accurate. When *repression* is used, the child refuses to
remember the anxiety-producing event. In *projection,* the child attributes his
own undesirable thoughts or actions to someone else.

Hill and Sarason (36) investigated parent-child relationships as antecedents of extreme defensiveness—that is, of frequent, inflexible, overcon-
trolled use of defense mechanisms. Highly defensive boys do not have
adequate communication with their parents about either emotional or
cognitive matters. They

> do not openly indicate their pleasure or displeasure to their mothers; they do
> not ask questions about sex nor receive information about it; there is a reluc-
> tance by the mothers to discuss death; the mothers don't openly show their
> own feelings toward the boys. The expression of feelings and curiosity about
> emotionally tinged topics appears to be discouraged by the parents, and the
> motivation to communicate honestly and fully appears to be interrupted (36, 66).

IDENTIFICATION

In our review of theories and data on the development and modification of such characteristics as aggression, dependency, and anxiety, we have
frequently used reinforcement and imitation as explanatory concepts. But
many aspects of the child's behavioral development cannot be readily explained by the principles of reward learning or of simple, direct imitation.
For example, many complex reactions, personal idiosyncrasies, patterns of
personality characteristics, motives, attitudes, and moral standards appear
to be acquired by the child spontaneously, without direct training or reward
—without anyone's "teaching" and without the child's intending to learn.
In short, some acquired characteristics do not seem to yield readily to analysis in terms of reward and punishment. A more subtle process, identification,
is involved.

Identification, a concept derived from psychoanalysis and introduced
by Freud, refers to the process that leads the child to think, feel, and behave as though the characteristics of another person (called the *model* or

identificand)—usually a parent in the case of a young child—belong to him. Identification is not ordinarily a consciously initiated process, like learning to ride a bicycle or to read.

It is not difficult to think of many real events that illustrate the complex concept of identification. A 6-year-old boy feels proud as he watches his father defeat a rival in tennis. A young girl feels grown-up when she puts on her mother's apron and attempts to bake a pie. A 10-year-old girl feels ashamed when the police arrest her father, or put her mother in a mental institution. In each of these examples, the child acts as if he or she possessed some of the characteristics, feelings, or emotions of the parent with whom he is identified.

Identification with a strong parent may be a very important source of security for a young child. By means of this identification, the child in effect incorporates in himself the parent's strength and adequacy—that is, he feels himself to be more adequate and self-controlled. On the other hand, a child identified with an inadequate model (e.g., a psychotic father) feels less secure and more anxious because, in his perception, he has absorbed the identificand's undesirable attributes.

Identification, then, is a hypothesized process by means of which the child incorporates or absorbs some of the model's *complex integrated patterns of behavior, personal attributes and characteristics, and motives.* Moreover, responses acquired by identification seem to be emitted spontaneously, without any specific training or direct rewards for imitation, and they are generally relatively stable and enduring rather than transient.

In his excellent review of concepts of identification, Bronfenbrenner clarifies Freud's conception of the process:

> In concerning himself with identification, Freud was not asking why and how a child might learn an isolated piece of behavior from his parent. He was interested in what he felt to be a more sweeping and powerful phenomenon— the tendency of the child to take on not merely discrete elements of the parental model but a total pattern. Moreover, as Freud saw it, this acquisition was accomplished with an emotional intensity which reflected the operation of motivational forces of considerable power (13, 27).

The Development of Identification

Most behavioral scientists—whether or not they are strongly influenced by psychoanalytic theory—regard identification as a basic process in the socialization of the child. Unfortunately, scientific understanding of the development of identification is far from complete, although there are various theories and speculations and some relevant empirical evidence, as we shall see in the following section.

Two conditions appear to facilitate the development of identification with a model. First, the child must be *motivated* to identify with the model—that is, he must want to possess some of the model's attributes. Second, he must have some basis for believing that he and the model are similar in some ways, that they share some physical or psychological attribute.

The Positive Attributes of the Parents as Models

Most children feel that their parents have numerous desirable characteristics, skills, and privileges. They give and receive love, are strong and have power, and they possess areas of competence the child would like to have. These are characteristics and goals the child wants to possess and areas of pleasure, power, and mastery he would like to control. The discrepancy between his perception of adults and his perception of his own lack of power and mastery act as an impetus for attempting to acquire the parents' attributes.

There are of course many desirable goal states that parents control. Three important ones are: (1) power over the child and other people; (2) mastery of the environment; and (3) love. The desire to possess these goals fosters an identification with the parents.

The child seems to assume that if he possessed some of the characteristics of the model, that is, if he were similar to the model, he would also possess the model's desirable psychological characteristics and command the model's resources: power, affection from others, skills, and competence; he would vicariously enjoy the emotions enjoyed by the model.

The process of identification will be facilitated if the model is a highly desirable and attractive person. A nurturant parent is more likely to be taken as a model than a rejecting one. The nurturant parent gratifies the child's needs and comes to stand for pleasure. In short, his actions, behaviors, and personal characteristics acquire positive reward value. Therefore, the child's imitations of his actions may, according to some psychologists, also be a source of reward. That is, by reproducing (i.e., imitating) some of the parent's behavior himself, the child experiences the acquired positive reward value associated with the parent. For example, a 3-year-old girl may care for her doll in the same way her mother cared for her. The motive for this behavior may be the desire to reproduce the positive acts of the mother that have acquired reward value. As the child imitates the mother's behavior and characteristics, she believes that she experiences the feelings and emotions—the warmth, happiness, and pride— that the mother experiences in caring for her. At the same time as she acts "as though she were the mother," she feels that she actually possesses the power, skills, and pleasures of the mother. If the mother is highly rejecting, her behaviors will not have positive reward value and the child will not be motivated to practice them. When parents are warm and accepting, the child views their behavior as rewarding and, consequently, will want to be like them and act as they do.

Perception of Similarity to the Parents

It is now necessary to make a crucial assumption that links the child's desire for these prized goals with his adoption of parental behaviors. The assumption states that in the mind of the child similarity to the parent or model implies possession of the parent's (or model's) traits and privileges.

There are two major ways in which the child may come to feel similar to the model: through adoption of the model's attributes, behavior, and gestures; and as a result of communication with others who tell the child he is similar to the model.

Thus the child imitates parental behaviors in order to increase the basis of similarity between himself and the parents and to possess vicariously the parents' traits. In so doing, his identification is strengthened. When a 5-year-old boy tries to mow the lawn "like daddy" he may be attempting to make himself similar to his father. The child behaves as though he believed that if he were similar to his father in this respect he would possess some of the father's desirable characteristics—strength, competence, and power over the environment. The child behaves as though the more numerous the bases of similarity between himself and the model, the greater the likelihood that he will possess the model's desirable attributes.

Each time the child perceives some similarity with the model, the identification with the model is strengthened. The crucial events in the development of identification are perceptions of similarity with the model. These perceptions may be derived from the child's own observations, or through communications from others who tell the child that he and the model possess similar attributes. These experiences occur regularly in the child's day. For example, a little girl notices that she and her mother wear the same kind of dress or cut their hair similarly. The fact that a girl and her mother have the same family name makes her feel more similar to her mother than to mothers with different family names. The child may be told by its grandmother or neighbor, "Mary, you're just like your mother" or "Bob, you have a memory just like your father." These are just a few of the countless ways in which a child perceives similarities between himself and a parent. These experiences aid the development of the identification.

When both parents are perceived as nurturant, powerful, and competent, the child will identify to some extent with both of them. Typically, however, the child will perceive greater similarity to the parent of the same sex, rather than to the one of the opposite sex, and will therefore identify more strongly with the former.

To summarize briefly: initially, the child becomes aware of the discrepancies between his perceptions of his parents' power, privileges, and desirable characteristics and his perceptions of himself. He begins to behave as though he believes that if he were similar to the parents he would share vicariously in their emotions and possess some of their envied qualities. He may therefore imitate and adopt parental actions in order to increase the similarity between himself and the model. This process is aided by others telling the child that he is similar to the parent, and by the child's own perception of his similarity to that parent in clothing, anatomy, personality, name, or even type of haircut.

As the child's identification becomes stronger, he begins to behave as though he does indeed possess some of the model's characteristics. The behaviors that he imitated earlier become automatic and are more firmly entrenched aspects of his character and personality.

Finally, it should be emphasized that identification is not an all-or-none phenomenon. Each child identifies, to some degree, with both parents, and as his social contacts become wider, with adults and peers outside the family.

As we noted earlier, it is impossible to determine what aspects of personality or what proportions of the individual's vast behavior repertoire are the consequents of identification and how much can be attributed to reinforcement learning. A little girl may develop strong dependency needs as a consequence of either reward for dependent behavior, identification with her highly dependent mother, or both. The school boy who mainfests a high level of motivation for achievement may have been rewarded frequently during early childhood for independent, self-reliant behavior (see pp. 348–350). At the same time, the manner in which he manifests high achievement needs—for example, in striving for academic or social success—may be, at least in part, a product of his identification with his achievement-oriented father. In any case, it is reasonable to infer that identification is a central process in the acquisition of a very wide range of behavior patterns and attributes of personality.

Consequents of Parental Identification

Freud delineated two major products of identification that are of great relevance during the preschool period: sex-typing (adoption of behavior, values, attitudes, and interests appropriate to one's own sex) and the development of the *superego*, or conscience. Both of these are broad, pervasive multifaceted aspects of psychological organization.

Sex-Typing

During the preschool years, sex-typing figures prominently in the socialization of the child. Most parents pay considerable attention to the sex-appropriateness of their child's behavior, rewarding responses that are appropriate to his sex and discouraging those that are not. Thus, parents are likely to encourage a boy to "fight back" if attacked by a peer, but they are more likely to punish this kind of behavior in their daughter (70). If a preschool girl cries after losing a game, this reaction is likely to be accepted as appropriate for the "weaker sex," but a boy who shows tears is likely to be reminded that "little men don't cry." By age 5, most children are keenly aware of sex-appropriate interests and behavior. Presented with pictures illustrating sex-typed toys, objects, and activities (e.g., guns, dolls, cowboys, Indians, kitchen utensils), most 3-, 4-, and 5-year-olds prefer those appropriate for their sex (14, 22, 33).

Social pressures also foster appropriate sex-typing of behavior. The culture provides considerable reward for accepting one's own sex role and punishment for the manifestation of traits appropriate to the opposite sex. Thus the boy is pressured to model himself after his father, the girl, after her mother.

The basic components of sex-typing are undoubtedly acquired at home, largely through identification with, and imitation of, the parent of the same sex.

> In the ideal family constellation, a little boy finds it very natural and highly rewarding to model himself in his father's image. The father is gratified to see this re-creation of his own qualities, attitudes, and masculinity; and the mother, loving the father, finds such a course of development acceptable in her son. Tentative explorations, conscious and unconscious, in the direction of being "like mother" quickly convince the boy that this it not his proper or approved destiny; and he speedily reverts to his identification with father. In the well-ordered, psychologically healthy household, much the same picture, in reverse, holds for the little girl (56, 596).

Theoretically, the degree to which the child adopts a parent's behavior is a function of that parent's nurturance and affection, competence, and power. If the parent did not possess these characteristics, the child would not want to be like him, and would not acquire a positive identification with him. The ideal situation for the adoption of culturally approved, appropriate sex-role behaviors would be one in which (1) the same-sex parent is seen as nurturant and possessing desirable characteristics, and (2) both parents consistently reward sex-appropriate responses and discourage inappropriate ones.

A number of studies have yielded data supporting these hypotheses. One experimental study tested the effects of nurturance by a model—originally a stranger to the child—on the child's tendency to imitate the model's behavior. With one group of preschool subjects, the model behaved in a pleasant, interested and nurturant way; with the other group, she was aloof and disinterested. Following her first interaction with each child, the model demonstrated to him the solution to a number of discrimination-learning problems, and while doing so, made some novel verbal, motor, and gestural responses that were irrelevant to the task. Subjects in the nurtured group imitated the model's novel responses to a significantly greater extent than those in the other group. Apparently, then, nurturant, warm, and rewarding relationships with the model do in fact foster the child's identification with (imitation of) that model (4).

In a somewhat similar experiment, groups of generally nurturant and nonnurturant mothers (categorized on the basis of their responses to an interview on child-rearing practices) served as models, teaching their daughters to solve maze problems (60). During the teaching session, the mother made novel, irrelevant responses in accordance with directions from the experimenter. For example, the mother drew her lines very slowly, hesitated at each choice point, made some comment before each trial (e.g. "Here we go")and made unnecessary marks in her tracing (e.g., loops or curves in her lines).

As would be predicted from theory, the daughters of the nurturant group imitated many of their mother's irrelevant responses, but the nonnurtured girls copied relatively few. This is what would be predicted from the hypothesis that nurturance is related to identification and the tendency to imitate the nurturant model's behavior (60).

Studies of the relationship between parental nurturance and sex-typing also show that, as the hypothesis would predict, boys identify with their fathers if the latter are perceived as strong, powerful, and nurturant (58, 59, 61). The subjects of this study, 38 5-year-old boys, were given a projective test of sex-role preferences. The 10 most masculine and the 10 least masculine boys were selected for further study on the assumption that the former had strong masculine identifications, presumably based on iden-tification with the father, while the latter were only weakly identified with that parent. These 20 boys were seen in doll-play sessions in which they supplied endings to some incomplete stories designed to assess the child's perception of the father as nurturant, warm, punitive, and powerful. The responses of the highly masculine boys—i.e., those highly identified with their fathers—indicated that, compared with boys who are low in mascu-linity, they perceive their fathers as more nurturant and more rewarding.

Interviews with the boys' mothers yielded data that corroborated these findings. The mothers of the highly masculine boys reported that the boys' fathers were warmer, more interested in their sons, and more affectionate toward them than the fathers of less masculine boys. All these findings, of course, support the hypothesis that identification stems from warm parent-child relationships (59).

Analogously, femininity in preschool girls seems to be related to warm, nurturant mother-daughter interactions. In one investigation, girls high in femininity and girls low in femininity, as judged by a test of sex-role prefer-ences, were observed completing doll-play stories of the sort used in the study described above, and their mothers were interviewed. The findings were parallel to those for boys high and low in masculinity. In comparison with the other girls, highly feminine, appropriately sex-typed girls portrayed their mothers in doll-play as significantly warmer, more nurturant, affec-tionate, and gratifying. Similarly, their mothers reported, highly feminine girls have more intense and warmer interactions with their mothers than the less feminine girls do.

Cognitive-Development Theory of Sex-Typing. Kohlberg (50) has pre-sented a much different and intriguing theory of sex-typing based on "the child's cognitive organization of his social world along sex role dimensions" (50, 82). The most significant factor in sex-typing, according to this theory, is the child's cognition—his selection and organization of perceptions, knowledge, and understanding of the sex role concept.

Sex-typing is said to be initiated by the sex labeling of the child as a boy or girl, which occurs very early in life. The child's basic gender self-concept, his categorization of himself as a boy or girl, becomes the major organizer and determinant of his activities, values, attitudes, and motives. A boy in effect says, "I am a boy, therefore, I want to do boy things." and therefore the opportunity to do boy things (and to gain approval for doing them) is rewarding (50). The child's self-concepts about his sex role become stabilized at about 5 or 6 years, according to Kohlberg, and, once established, these basic sex role concepts generate new sex-typed values and attitudes.

Sex-typing is not viewed as a product of identification; quite the contrary, identification is seen as a consequence of sex-typing. Boys model themselves after males because they already have masculine interests and values; therefore, masculine ways of behaving, thinking, and feeling are more interesting and hence are imitated and adopted.

Although the theory does not deal with antecedent-consequent relationships in sex-typing, and pays little attention to individual differences, it does call attention to an aspect of the sex-typing process that learning theory and psychoanalytic theory neglect. There can be little doubt that the child's perceptions and understanding of his environment strongly influence the development of his sex role behavior.

Conscience Development

During the preschool years the child begins to show evidence of conscience development—that is, of having a set of standards of acceptable behavior, acting in accordance with these standards, and feeling guilty if he violates them. He has, at least to some extent, adopted his parents' moral values and standards for evaluating his own and others' behavior. Freud regarded the development of conscience—or superego as he labeled it—as a product of identification: "When, by the process of identification he demands from himself conformity to a standard of conduct, the superego is said to be making its appearance" (57, 543).

The child striving to be similar to the parent will absorb parental moral standards, behaviors, and prohibitions in the same way that he adopts other parental behaviors. The adoption of parental standards makes him feel similar to his parents and, therefore, strengthens his identification with them. He then begins to punish himself whenever he has done something for which he believes his parents might punish him (75). According to psychoanalytic theory, this demonstrates that ". . . through identification with the parent, he has taken over and incorporated within himself the attitudes of condemnation of those who transgress" (57, 541).

Conscience is obviously a very broad, pervasive component of the individual's psychological organization. The term subsumes a wide variety of responses, opinions, and judgments: e.g., being honest; obeying rules and regulations; resisting temptations to cheat, lie or steal; acting in kind, considerate, altruistic ways; considering the rights and welfare of others; treating people in egalitarian rather than authoritarian ways; making moral judgments in which justice is tempered with mercy.

The establishment and development of conscience are, of course, very complex phenomena and not simply products of identification. Unfortunately there have been very few systematic studies of moral behavior or of its antecedents. Consequently we have relatively few "hard facts."

It does seem clear, however, that when the child's behavior conforms with his parents' standards it is likely to be rewarded and hence repeated. Imitation of a model's standards and behavior may be an effective way of increasing resistance to temptation or incorporating honest and altruistic responses.

Anxiety about punishment or loss of love may motivate the acquisition of moral standards and behavior that please the parents. Guilt about transgression is frequently used as an index of conscience development; according to the data from a number of studies, a child's tendency to feel guilty about "doing something wrong" is related to a number of parental practices: frequent use of praise, expression of affection, and infrequent use of physical punishment. Maintaining a close relationship with the child and using training techniques that are "capable of arousing unpleasant-feeling reaction in the child about his misbehavior, independently of external threat, and which encourage the child to accept responsibility for his actions" (8, 183) promote the development of a high level of conscience.

In general the research findings indicate that parental discipline which is based on a close, affectionate relationship with the child is likely to foster the development of internalized reactions to transgression (feelings of guilt, self-responsibility, confession). The use of "power-assertive" techniques in controlling the child (physical punishment, yelling, threatening) are more likely to be associated with externalized reactions to transgression—that is, fear of punishment or anxiety. Older boys with internalized standards of morality report that their parents were affectionate and did not use force or threats in disciplining them, but emphasized the effects of the child's misbehavior on the parents' feelings (39).

Sears, Maccoby, and Levin (70) describe the behavior of a little girl during a transition period between fear of punishment and development of a real conscience.

> Martha's parents brought her along one Sunday afternoon when they came for a visit. She was seventeen months old, full of curiosity and mischief. While we had coffee and cookies, she thirstily drank down a glass of milk, ate half a cookie, and began an eager exploration of her surroundings. Toddling most of the time, crawling occasionally, she left trails of crumbs and tipped over cups wherever she went. One of the floor lamps fascinated her especially. It was tall and straight, made of a single, glossy round of wood just the right size for Martha to get a good grip on. When she stood up against it, clutching happily, the lamp teetered and swayed in what was obviously an entrancing fancy for Martha.

> Twice her father had to put down his cup and leap across the room to prevent a crash. Twice he said, clearly and distinctly, "Now Martha, don't touch." Each time he took her by the hand and led her over to some toys. These distracted her only briefly.

> After the second interruption, Martha began a general exploration of the room again. Now she went a little more slowly, and several times glanced at her

father. As she came closer to the lamp, however, she stopped looking his way and her movements were all oriented toward the lamp. Deliberately she stepped toward it, came within a couple of feet of it, and lifted her arm partly, a little jerkedly, and then said sharply, commandingly, "Don't touch."

There was an instant of struggling silence, then she turned and stumbled across the room, flopped down on the floor, and started laughing excitedly. Her father laughing with her, and obviously adoring, reached out and hugged and snuggled her for minutes.

Why was this a beginning of conscience? Why not assume, more simply, that Martha was afraid her father would punish her if she touched the lamp again? The difference between fear and conscience lies in the self-instruction and the incorporation in the child herself of the values expressed by the parents. Martha was playing the parental role when she said sternly to herself, "Don't touch." Had she continued to look furtively at her father as she got close to the lamp— had she oscillated back and forth in her approach—had she been whimpery or silent and withdrawn after the moment of decision—we would have said she was responding to the dangers of the situation by simple avoidance. But at the crucial moment, she did not have to look at her father, she looked to herself for guidance and the behest she followed was her own (70, 365–366).

The association between high levels of conscience development in the child and warm, rewarding nurturant parent-child relationships is consistent with the hypothesis that conscience development or morality is—at least in part—a consequent of identification. But identification seems to be only one of several factors that influence conscience development. For example, in one study, maternal warmth and acceptance were found to be positively correlated with strength of conscience (70). In this study, mothers' reports of their kindergarten children's reactions to "doing something wrong" were the sources of data on conscience development. Boys with accepting fathers—with whom they were presumably identified—manifested more guilt following wrongdoing and higher levels of conscience development than boys with rejecting fathers. The use of withdrawal of love as a technique of discipline was also associated with strongly developed conscience among young children. But this technique could only be used effectively if strong, affectionate mother-child relationships had already been established.

The patterns most calculated to produce "high conscience" should be that of mothers who are usually warm and loving and, as a method of control, threaten this affectionate relationship. The children most prone to behave in the ways we have considered indicative of having a well developed conscience were those whose mothers were relatively warm toward them, and who made their love contingent on the child's good behavior. These were the children who truly were risking the loss of love when they misbehaved (70, 388–389).

One recent study examined the relationship between warmth and nurturance of the parent (as perceived by the child) and generosity—a positive, socially oriented kind of moral behavior. Nursery school boys were presented with a bowl of candies and told they could share any or all of them with two friends. Analysis of responses to incomplete doll-play stories showed that generous boys (those who shared a substantial portion of the candies) perceived their fathers as warmer, more nurturant, and more rewarding than nongenerous boys who kept almost all the candies for themselves (65).

This finding is generally supportive of the hypothesis that conscience development is influenced by the nature of the child's interactions with his parents and thus by the strength of his identification with them. But it must be recognized that this is only one of many factors influencing the child's moral judgments and behavior. Clearly, the level of the child's cognitive development is one of the crucial determinants of his moral judgments and behavior (50; see also pp. 510–512). The details of conscience formation are not fully understood and there is a real need for more research on the many factors that may influence moral development.

PERSONALITY AND SOCIAL LEARNING IN THE HOME

Up to this point in this chapter, we have centered our attention on particular personality and social characteristics, examining individual differences and their antecedents, as well as the major processes involved in their development and modification: learning, imitation, and identification. In this last section, we shall examine more closely various broad aspects of the social environment of the home—including parent-child relationships—as they affect the development of specific traits and motives, and the general pattern or structure of personality. This subject is a critical one and, consequently, there have been numerous studies of the relationship between family atmosphere or parental attitudes and the personal and social adjustment of children. Here we will summarize only a few of the many highly relevant investigations.

Let us digress a bit to consider some of the methodological problems involved in this kind of research. The reader will recall that almost all relevant investigations of the effects of very early parent-child interactions center on the mother's role in satisfying the infant's basic needs, in toilet training him, and in reacting to manifestations of aggression, sexuality, dependency, and independence (see pp. 261–266). But as the child matures, his relationships with his parents become more intensive, more complex, and more subtle. Investigations of parent-child relations during the preschool years focus not on specific interactions in restricted situations, but on very broad, global characteristics of the home and parental behavior. Examples of such inclusive, "molar" qualities are parental warmth (or coldness), nurturance, permissiveness and control, expression of affection, democracy and authoritarianism in the home, and ease of communication between parent and child. The student of personality development is concerned with variations in these dimensions as antecedents of children's social behavior, personality characteristics, motives, and attitudes.

Unfortunately from the researcher's point of view, these general, comprehensive dimensions are very difficult to evaluate and to measure objectively. Interviews with parents or questionnaires about parent-child relations are the most commonly used methods. But data from these sources are not entirely satisfactory because parents are not ordinarily reliable and objective observers of either their own or their children's behavior. Their reports are likely to be biased, and important information may be forgotten, withheld, or (consciously or unconsciously) distorted. However, because the interview method is, in many ways, efficient and convenient, there have been some interesting attempts to increase objectivity of interview data, e.g., by asking a parent to describe in great detail everything that took place between him and the child throughout the day preceding the interview (37, 38). Interviews used for research purposes are generally taped and transcribed. The information given may then be coded according to specific categories of behavior (e.g., parental assertion, child submission) or rated on salient dimensions such as warmth, affection, communication, control.

A *home visit* is sometimes used to observe and record family interactions in their natural setting. A home visitor, a specially trained observer, goes to the subject's home for a specified period, say 2 hours, and watches the family members engaged in their customary activities, presumably interacting naturally and in their habitual ways. The observations are recorded fully and subsequently, as with interview data, coded into categories or rated.

In *structured observation,* a parent and child may be brought together in a standard setting and presented with a task or a problem. For example, the mother may be given instructional material or educational toys and instructed to teach her child how to use these. The spontaneous interactions between parent and child are observed and subsequently coded and/or rated. The situation presumably provides an opportunity to observe the mother's habitual, "natural"

> way of enforcing rules, her directiveness in teaching, her ability to motivate the child and secure his compliance, her use of praise and disapproval in success and failure experiences (the child almost always had both during the teaching period), her methods of dealing with the child's anxiety, her ability to follow and facilitate the child's thought processes and to answer his questions, her degree of involvement with him, her supportiveness, patience, handling of dependency, and her intellectual expectations of the child (7, 69).

Unfortunately, most of the studies in this area have used middle-class parents and children as subjects, so it is difficult to know whether the findings can be generalized to members of other social classes. For example, upper-middle-class children may react quite differently from those of the lower class to a rigid, authoritarian home atmosphere. In the middle class, this kind of atmosphere may be relatively uncommon and frequently associated with lack of parental affection. In the lower class, on the other hand, such authoritarian atmosphere may be more usual, but often accompanied by genuine expressions of affection. If this is true, the implications of authoritarian control would, of course, be different for children in different social classes.

Another problem in interpreting data in this area of research stems from the fact that the home variables considered most salient—e.g., permissiveness, control, democracy, nurturance—are not defined in the same way by all investigators. For example, "control" is a dimension investigated in two studies reported below. In one of them, high control—viewed as the opposite pole of high democracy in the home—is characterized by dictatorial, arbitrary parental rules; high domination of children by parents; lack of permissiveness; authoritarian parental attitudes; rigid, clear-cut rules and strong restrictions on the child's behavior; and relative absence of discussion about disciplinary procedures (2).

In the other study, however, "control" refers *not* to rigidity or authoritarian rules, but rather to

> the socializing functions of the parent: that is, to those parental acts that are intended to shape the child's goal-oriented activity, modify his expression of dependent, aggressive, and playful behavior, and promote internalization of parental standards. Parental control as defined here is not a pressure of restrictiveness, punitive attitudes, or intrusiveness. Parental control included such variables as consistency in enforcing directives, ability to resist pressure from the child, and willingness to exert influence upon the child (7, 54).

Not surprisingly, the two studies found quite different patterns of child behavior correlated with high parental control. The two sets of findings were not really contradictory, however, and the differences obtained are probably attributable in large measure to the vastly different definitions —and methods of evaluation—of control.

Effects of Democratic and Controlled Home Atmospheres. In studies conducted by Baldwin (2, 3) at the Fels Research Institute, a "home visitor" visited the children's homes, observed the general family atmosphere and parent-child interactions, wrote a critical summary of the findings, and rated the home on 30 carefully defined scales.

These scales, called the Fels Parent Behavior Rating Scales, are shown in Fig. 9.2. Taken together, they provide objective, well-rounded descriptions of the domestic situation. Moreover, they permit systematic examination of the relationships between home environment and children's characteristics.

Of course, the 30 scales are not entirely independent of each other: many of them are positively intercorrelated. Groups of related variables, called *clusters* or *constellations,* are assumed to measure some common aspect or area of parent behavior. In Fig. 9.2, the scales are grouped into clusters listed in the left column (3).

Two of these clusters, *democracy* and *control,* represent opposite poles of parent-child relationships. The democratic home atmosphere, as defined

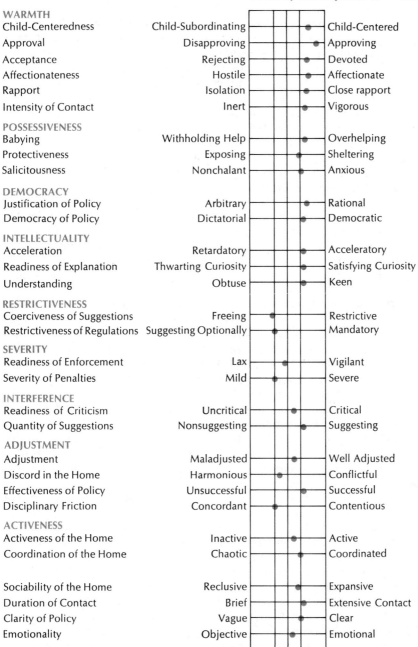

WARMTH
Child-Centeredness — Child-Subordinating ● Child-Centered
Approval — Disapproving ● Approving
Acceptance — Rejecting ● Devoted
Affectionateness — Hostile ● Affectionate
Rapport — Isolation ● Close rapport
Intensity of Contact — Inert ● Vigorous

POSSESSIVENESS
Babying — Withholding Help ● Overhelping
Protectiveness — Exposing ● Sheltering
Salicitousness — Nonchalant ● Anxious

DEMOCRACY
Justification of Policy — Arbitrary ● Rational
Democracy of Policy — Dictatorial ● Democratic

INTELLECTUALITY
Acceleration — Retardatory ● Acceleratory
Readiness of Explanation — Thwarting Curiosity ● Satisfying Curiosity
Understanding — Obtuse ● Keen

RESTRICTIVENESS
Coerciveness of Suggestions — Freeing ● Restrictive
Restrictiveness of Regulations — Suggesting Optionally ● Mandatory

SEVERITY
Readiness of Enforcement — Lax ● Vigilant
Severity of Penalties — Mild ● Severe

INTERFERENCE
Readiness of Criticism — Uncritical ● Critical
Quantity of Suggestions — Nonsuggesting ● Suggesting

ADJUSTMENT
Adjustment — Maladjusted ● Well Adjusted
Discord in the Home — Harmonious ● Conflictful
Effectiveness of Policy — Unsuccessful ● Successful
Disciplinary Friction — Concordant ● Contentious

ACTIVENESS
Activeness of the Home — Inactive ● Active
Coordination of the Home — Chaotic ● Coordinated

Sociability of the Home — Reclusive ● Expansive
Duration of Contact — Brief ● Extensive Contact
Clarity of Policy — Vague ● Clear
Emotionality — Objective ● Emotional

Fig. 9.2. Ratings of a warm, democratic home on the Fels Parent Behavior Rating Scales. (After A. L. Baldwin, J. Kalhorn, & F. H. Breese. Patterns of parent behavior. *Psychol. Monogr.*, 1945, *58*, No. 3. Copyright 1945 by the American Psychological Association. By permission.)

here, is characterized by general permissiveness, avoidance of arbitrary decisions, and a high level of verbal contact between parents and child (consultation about decisions, explanations of reasons for family rules, supplying answers to satisfy the child's curiosity). "Controlled" homes emphasize clearcut restrictions on behavior, and consequently, friction over disciplinary procedures is low.

The subjects in this study were 67 4-year-old nursery school pupils whose homes had been visited and evaluated. Nursery school teachers and observers rated the children's behavior in school.

As would be anticipated, children from democratic and controlled homes manifested strikingly divergent personality structures. Those from democratic homes were generally active, competitive, and outgoing. They ranked high in aggressiveness, leadership, planfulness, and cruelty, and tended to be more curious, disobedient, and nonconforming. If, in addition to democracy, there was a great deal of parent-child interaction (activity) in the home, these characteristics were most pronounced. In democratic, but relatively inactive, homes, characterized by more detachment, fewer verbal interchanges, and less leadership in the parent-child relationship, the consequences of democratic atmosphere were less marked.

Children from homes rated high in control presented the opposite kind of personality picture. They showed relatively little quarrelsomeness, negativism, disobedience, aggression, playfulness, tenacity, or fearlessness. Homes characterized by authoritarian control (high control together with low democracy) produced quiet, well-behaved, nonresistant children who were socially unaggressive. Apparently in these homes, conformity, which was associated with restricted curiosity, originality, and fancifulness, was obtained at the expense of freedom of expression. Of course, democratic parents run the risk of producing too little conformity to cultural demands in their children. However, in the groups of homes investigated in this study, there was a positive correlation between democracy and control—that is, most democratic parents practiced enough control to avoid the pitfalls of extreme nonconformity.

In a supplementary study, this same investigator (2) described the consequents of three clusters of home variables—democracy, warmth, and indulgence—on children's personalities. The subjects were 56 nursery school children between the ages of 36 and 60 months who were rated on a battery of 45 behavior and personality variables.

Democracy in the home was found to be associated with warmth—that is, most highly democratic families provided strong emotional support for the child. As in the previous study, children from these homes were socially outgoing in both friendly and hostile ways, participating actively in school events, expressing aggression, and generally asserting themselves quite strongly. Their bossing and aggressiveness seemed to be socially successful and they enjoyed superior status in their own group. Moreover, the democratic home environment seemed to promote intelligence, curiosity, originality, and constructiveness.

Indulgence (babying, protecting) appeared to foster the development of the opposite kinds of personality characteristics. Children from these homes were relatively inactive, unaggressive, lacking in originality, and of inferior social status. In addition, indulged children were apprehensive of physical activity and lacked skill in muscle activities.

Thus "the effect of the democratic home as contrasted to the non-democratic one is to stimulate the child in such a way that he is more actively engaged in peer-centered activities, that he is more successful in those activities, and that he is better able to contribute original creative ideas to the groups with which he interacts" (2, 62).

The general conclusions of these studies have major practical as well as theoretical significance. Apparently certain socially valuable behaviors and personality characteristics are produced by the use of democratic child-rearing procedures, but these techniques can be effective only if they are consistent with the parents' personalities and attitudes (3). If rigid, authoritarian parents attempt to employ democratic procedures, they are likely to find them difficult and frustrating—producing tensions that may be detrimental to the emotional health of the preschool child.

The contrasting personality structures of children from different types of homes may be interpreted as the outcomes of differential patterns of rewards and punishments. In the democratic home, the child is rewarded for curiosity and independent activity; for spontaneous, relatively uninhibited expression of ideas, feelings, and opinions; and for participation and self-assertion in family discussions and decision-making. These rewarded responses become strong and habitual at home, and consequently they are generalized to other settings, such as the nursery school and playground.

In contrast, children growing up in homes high in control, as defined here, are *not* rewarded (and may be punished) for manifesting curiosity, spontaneity, or self-assertion. Further, rewards are associated with obedience to parents, conformity with parental standards, and suppression of curiosity and expression of feelings and opinions. Again, these responses of compliance and conformity become strong habits, and they generalize to the social world outside the home.

The child who is highly indulged, babied, and overprotected is not rewarded for independent action, for expressing himself freely, or for experimenting with new activities. Fearing for his safety or threatened by his growing independence, his parents may punish (or at least discourage) outgoing responses and independent efforts. Consequently, in the nursery school and on the playground, the child is timid, awkward, and apprehensive.

Child-Rearing Antecedents of Competence and Maturity. Baumrind's study was centered on three groups of nursery school children who differed markedly in patterns of behavior and personality characteristics (7). The child-rearing practices used by their parents and the family atmospheres in which they were raised were thoroughly investigated.

The basic data came from extensive and intensive observations of 110 nursery school children made by trained observers and teachers. Five child-behavior dimensions were assessed: *self-control* (the tendency "to suppress, redirect, inhibit, or in other ways control the impulse to act in those situations where self-restraint is appropriate" [7, 52]); *approach tendencies* (the tendency to approach "stimuli that are novel, stressful, exciting, or unexpected . . . in an explorative and curious fashion" [7, 52]); *subjective mood* (predominant degree of pleasure and zest); *self-reliance* (the ability to act independently); and *peer affiliation* ("ability and desire to express warmth toward others of his own age" [7, 53]).

Three groups of children of different personality structures were selected for further study on the basis of these observations and assessments. Pattern I children, a group of 13, were the most mature, competent, content and independent. Compared with the others, they were the most realistic, self-reliant, self-controlled, explorative, affiliative, content, and self-assertive. The 11 Pattern II children were rated as moderately self-reliant and self-controlled, but relatively discontent, insecure and apprehensive, withdrawn, distrustful, uninterested in peer affiliation, and more likely than Pattern I children to become hostile or regressive under stress. Pattern III children, a group of the 8 most immature, were highly dependent, had less self-control or self-reliance than the children in the other two groups, and tended to retreat from novel or stressful experiences.

To investigate the possible antecedents of these three patterns of children's behavior, the child-rearing practices of the three groups of parents were contrasted, using a variety of assessment procedures, including home visits, observations in structured situations, and parental interviews. Four aspects of parental relationships to children were evaluated: *control*, which, as noted above, referred to parental efforts to influence "the child's goal-oriented activity, modify his expression of dependent, aggressive, and playful behavior, and promote internalization of parental standards" (7, 54); *maturity demands*, i.e., pressures on the child to perform at the level of his ability, and freedom to make some of his own decisions; *clarity of parent-child communication*, e.g., use of reason to obtain compliance, asking the child's opinions and feelings; and *parental nurturance*, including both warmth (love, caretaking, and compassion) and involvement (praise and pleasure in the child's accomplishments).

The "scores" of the parents of the three groups of children on these four child-rearing dimensions, assessed on the basis of home visit reports, are shown in Fig. 9.3. Observation of mother-child interaction in structured situations in which the mother taught the child something and played games with him yielded findings very nearly identical with those derived from the home visit.

As may be seen in Fig. 9.3, the parents of mature, competent children were uniformly high on all four dimensions in comparison with other parents. Parents of Pattern I children were highly consistent, warm, loving, conscientious, and secure in their interactions with their children. While respect-

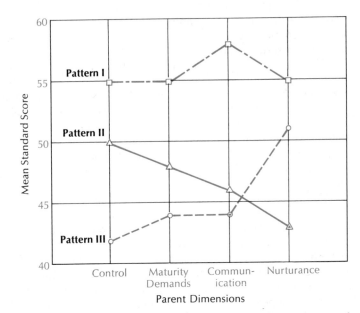

Fig. 9.3.   Parent dimension scores from the home visit data for three patterns of child behavior. (From Diana Baumrind. Child care practices anteceding three patterns of preschool behavior. *Genet. Psychol. Monogr.*, 1967, Vol. 75. By permission.)

ing their youngsters' independence and decisions, they generally held firm in their own positions, and they were clear and explicit about the reasons for directives they gave.

In the structured situations, the mothers of Pattern I children demonstrated both firm control and strong demands for high levels of performance. . At the same time, they were more supportive, and communicated more clearly and directly than the mothers in the other two groups. In general, the mothers of mature, competent children seemed able to balance nurturance and control, high demands and clarity of communication. Baumrind concludes that "by using reason to accompany a directive and by encouraging verbal give and take, these parents [of Pattern I children] were able to maintain control without stimulating rebellion or passivity" (7, 80).

Clearly, such parents as those of Pattern I children provide a learning setting conducive to the acquisition of behavior that is both socialized and independent. These parents appear to do a great deal of "teaching," integrating attempts to control their children's behavior with giving information and reasoning. Their efforts promote the child's learning of self-direction consistent with parental expectations, advance his social skills, encourage independence in decision-making, and stress mature ways of thinking and reasoning. Since they are also warm and nurturant, these parents are probably very effective reinforcers of the child's mature, independent behavior—using love and approval as rewards. At the same time, these parents also provide excellent models of competent, decisive, reasonable, calm, self-assertive, and mature behavior.

The parents of Pattern II children (relatively discontent, insecure children who interacted very little with their peers) were by comparison with the other two groups of parents less nurturant toward their children and less involved with them. While they were firm in their control and used power freely, they were not supportive or affectionate toward their children. Communication between them and their children was poor, attempts to convince their children through reason to obey their directives were infrequent, and the children were not encouraged to express themselves when they disagreed.

The parents of the least mature (Pattern III) children are also warm and nurturant, but they are *low in control* of the children. They make relatively few and relatively weak maturity demands and pay little attention to independence training. Compared with the other parents studied, they are lax in both discipline and reward, and more overprotective of their children. They did not motivate, teach, or reward the child's mature, self-reliant, independent behavior. Consequently, in the nursery school setting, the Pattern III children appeared immature, lacking independence and self-reliance.

Baldwin's and Baumrind's investigations, based on different conceptualizations and using markedly different techniques of assessment, yielded findings that are in many ways consistent. The data of both studies indicate that in young children, the qualities of competence, independence, affiliation, outgoingness, self-control, and self-reliance are fostered by nurturant, warm home environments in which independent actions and decision-making, as well as responsible and self-reliant behavior, are encouraged and rewarded. Baumrind's data further suggest that in the context of the nurturant home, parental control or firmness, together with high maturity demands—but *not* authoritarian discipline, high punitiveness, high restrictiveness, or overprotection—promote young children's maturity and competence.

SUMMARY

The combined forces of maturation, learning through reinforcement, imitation, and identification, lead to greater differentiation and complexity of personality during the preschool years. Personality characteristics may be regarded from the points of view of underlying motives or overt behavior, and the two are not necessarily directly linked.

Aggressiveness, one of the most salient and thoroughly studied personality variables, may be affected by biological, constitutional factors, but the amount and form of a child's aggression depend primarily upon his social experience. Although frustration is a common antecedent of aggression, children differ widely in their ability to tolerate frustration and in the intensity and frequency of their aggressive reactions to it. Direct rewards for aggressive behavior and the presence of aggressive models tend to raise the level of aggression. Wtih increasing age and experience, the child learns to express his aggression in culturally acceptable ways and to inhibit socially unacceptable responses. Boys are more likely than girls to receive strong reinforcement for aggression, and it becomes a fairly stable characteristic—that is, boys who are highly aggressive during the pre-school period are also likely to be highly aggressive in adolescence.

The predominant ways of expressing dependency and the objects of the child's dependency change during the preschool period. Two-year-olds appear to be more dependent on adults, 4-year-olds on peers. Dependency, autonomy, and independence tend to be markedly stable during the preschool years.

Achievement motivation—the desire to master problems and to increase skills and abilities—also develops very early as a consequence of the mother's rewards and encouragement of the child's early efforts to behave independently. Children who have strong achievement motivation during the preschool years tend to retain this motive in adolescence and adulthood.

While there are marked individual differences among preschoolers in susceptibility to fear, every child has some fears, and there is a marked tendency for a child to adopt his mother's fears. Intense anxiety among young children often stems from parental attempts to impose standards of behavior that are too high for the child to attain. The child's anxieties are likely to be strongest in situations which he views as evaluative and requiring independent actions.

Some motives and personal characteristics appear to be acquired on the basis of reinforcement or simple imitation. However, complex integrated patterns of behavior and personal characteristics seem to be incorporated by means of *identification* with a model, usually a parent. Sex-typing (adoption of behavior, values, and interests appropriate to one's own sex) and conscience development are two major products of the process of identification, which is motivated by the child's desire to possess goals that his parents control—e.g., power, mastery of the environment, and love. Nurturant parents are more likely to be taken as models than rejecting ones.

Children from homes that are high in *control* show relatively little negativism, disobedience, playfulness, spontaneity, or fearfulness. Democratic home environments tend to produce preschool children who are active, competitive, outgoing, aggressive, curious, and nonconforming. The parents of the most mature, competent, and independent preschool children are highly consistent, warm, loving, and secure. They respect their child's independence, but hold firm to their own positions, giving clear and explicit reasons for their decisions.

References

1. Ardrey, R. *The territorial imperative.* New York: Atheneum, 1966.
2. Baldwin, A. L. The effect of home environment on nursery school behavior. *Child Developm.*, 1949, *20*, 49–62.
3. Baldwin, A. L., Kalhorn, J., & Breese, F. H. The appraisal of parent behavior. *Psychol. Monogr.*, 1949, *63*, No. 299.
4. Bandura, A., & Huston, A. C. Identification as a process of incidental learning. *J. abnorm. soc. Psychol.*, 1961, *63*, 311–318.
5. Bandura, A., & Walters, R. H. Aggression. In H. W. Stevenson (Ed.), *Child psychology. (62nd Yearb. nat. Soc. Stud. Educ.)* Chicago: Univer. Chicago Press, 1963, 364–415.
6. Barker, R. G., Dembo, T., & Lewin, K. Frustration and regression. In R. G. Barker, J. S. Kounin, & H. F. Wright (Eds.), *Child behavior and development.* New York: McGraw-Hill, 1943, 441–458.
7. Baumrind, D. Child care practices anteceding three patterns of preschool behavior. *Genet. Psychol. Monogr.*, 1967, *75*, 43–88.
8. Becker, W. C. Consequences of different kinds of parental discipline. In M. L. Hoffman & L. W. Hoffman (Eds.), *Review of child development research.* New York: Russell Sage Foundation, 1964.
9. Beller, E. K. Dependency and independence in young children. *J. genet. Psychol.*, 1955, *87*, 25–35.
10. Beller, E. K. Dependency and autonomous achievement striving related to orality and anality in early childhood. *Child Developm.*, 1957, *28*, 287–315.
11. Beller, E. K. Exploratory studies of dependency. Trans. N. Y. Acad. Sci., 1959, *21*, 414–426.
12. Block, J., & Martin, B. Predicting the behavior of children under frustration. *J. abnorm. soc. Psychol.*, 1955, *51*, 281–285.
13. Bronfenbrenner, U. Freudian theories of identification and their derivatives. *Child Developm.*, 1960, *31*, 15–40.
14. Brown, D. G. Sex-role preference in young children. *Psychol. Monogr.*, 1956, No. 421, *70*, 1–19.
15. Crandall, V. J. Achievement. In H. W. Stevenson (Ed.), *Child psychology (62nd Yearb. nat. Soc. Educ.)* Chicago: Univer. Chicago Press, 1963, 416–459.
16. Crandall, V. J., & Rabson, A. Children's repetition choices in an intellectual achievement situation following success and failure. *J. genet. Psychol.*, 1960, *92*, 161–168.
17. D'Andrade, R. G. Sex differences and cultural institutions. In E. E. Maccoby (Ed.), *The development of sex differences.* Stanford, Calif.: Stanford Univer. Press, 1966, 173–203.
18. Eibl-Eibesfeldt, I. The fighting behavior of animals. *Scientific Amer.* 1961, *205*, 112–122.
19. Emmerich, W. Continuity and stability in early social development: II. Teacher ratings. *Child Developm.*, 1966, *37*, 17–28.
20. English, O. S., & Pearson, G. H. J. *Emotional problems of living.* New York: Norton, 1945.
21. Erikson, E. H. Toys and reason. In M. R. Haworth (Ed.), *Child psychotherapy: practice and theory.* New York: Basic Books, 1964, 3–11.

22. Fauls, L., & Smith, W. D. Sex-role learning of five-year-olds. *J. genet. Psychol.,* 1956, *89,* 105–117.
23. Fawl, C. L. Disturbances experienced by children in their natural habitats. In R. G. Barker (Ed.), *The stream of behavior.* New York: Appleton-Century-Crofts, 1963, 99–126.
24. Feshbach, S. The function of aggression and the regulation of aggressive drive. *Psychol. Rev.,* 1964, *71,* 257–272.
25. Feshbach, S. Aggression. In P. Mussen (Ed.), *Manual of child psychology.* New York: Wiley, in press.
26. Fraiberg, S. H. *The magic years.* New York: Scribner, 1959.
27. Gagnon, J. H. Sexuality and sexual learning in the child. *Psychiatry,* 1965, *28,* No. 3, 212–228.
28. Hagman, R. R. A study of fears of children of preschool age. *J. exp. Educ.,* 1932, *1,* 110–130.
29. Hartup, W. W. Nurturance and nurturance-withdrawal in relation to the dependency behavior of preschool children. *Child Develpm.,* 1958, *29,* 191–201.
30. Hartup, W. W. Dependence and independence. In H. W. Stevenson (Ed.), *Child psychology. (62nd Yearb. nat. Soc. Stud. Educ.)* Chicago: Univer. Chicago Press, 1963, 333–363.
31. Hartup, W. W. Peers as agents of social reinforcement. In W. W. Hartup & N. L. Smothergill (Eds.), *The young child: reviews of research.* Washington, D.C.: National Association for the Education of Young Children, 1967, 214–228.
32. Hartup, W. W., & Keller, E. D. Nurturance in preschool children and its relation to dependency. *Child Develpm.,* 1960, *31,* 681–690.
33. Hartup, W. W., & Zook, E. A. Sex-role preferences in 3- and 4-year-old children. *J. consult. Psychol.,* 1960, *24,* 420–426.
34. Hattendorf, K. W. A study of the questions of young children concerning sex: a phase of an experimental approach to parental education. *J. soc. Psychol.,* 1932, *3,* 37–65.
35. Heathers, G. Emotional dependence and independence in nursery-school play. *J. genet. Psychol.,* 1955, *87,* 37–58.
36. Hill, K. T., & Sarason, S. B. The relation of test anxiety and defensiveness to test and school performance over the elementary-school years: a further longitudinal study. *Monogr. Soc. Res. Child Develpm.,* 1966, *31,* No. 2.
37. Hoffman, M. L. An interview method for obtaining descriptions of parent-child interaction. *Merrill-Palmer Quart.* 1957, *3,* No. 2, 76–83.
38. Hoffman, M. L. Parent discipline and the child's consideration for others. *Child Develpm.,* 1963, *34,* 573–588.
39. Hoffman, M. L., & Saltzstein, H. D. Parent discipline and the child's moral development. *J. pers. soc. Psychol.,* 1967, *5,* 45–57.
40. Hollenberg, E., & Sperry, M. Some antecedents of aggression and effects on doll play. *Personality,* 1950, *1,* 32–43.
41. Holmes, F. B. An experimental investigation of a method of overcoming children's fears. *Child Develpm.,* 1936, *7,* 6–30.
42. Jersild, A. T., & Holmes, F. B. Children's fears. *Child Develpm. Monogr.,* 1935, No. 20.
43. Jersild, A. T., & Holmes, F. B. Some factors in the development in childrens' fears. *J. exp. Educ.,* 1935, *4,* 133–141.
44. Jersild, A. T., & Holmes, F. B. Methods of overcoming children's fears. *J. Psychol.,* 1935–36, *1,* 75–104.

45. Jersild, A. T., & Markey, F. V. Conflicts between preschool children. *Child Develpm. Monogr.,* 1935, No. 21.
46. Jones, M. C. A laboratory study of fear: the case of Peter. *Ped. Sem.,* 1924, *31,* 308–315.
47. Kagan, J., & Moss, H. A. The stability of passive and dependent behavior from childhood through adulthood. *Child Develpm.,* 1960, *31,* 577–591.
48. Kagan, J., & Moss, H. A. *Birth to maturity: a study in psychological development.* New York: Wiley, 1962.
49. Kessler, J. W. *Psychopathology of childhood.* Englewood Cliffs, N.J.: Prentice-Hall, 1966.
50. Kohlberg, L. A cognitive-developmental analysis of children's sex-role concepts and attitudes. In E. E. Maccoby (Ed.), *The development of sex differences.* Stanford, Calif.: Stanford Univer. Press, 1966.
51. Lorenz, K. *On aggression.* New York: Harcourt, Brace & World, 1966.
52. Maccoby, E. E. (Ed.), *The development of sex differences,* Stanford, Calif.: Stanford Univer. Press, 1966.
53. Malinowski, B. Prenuptial intercourse between the sexes in the Trobriand Islands, N.W. Melanesia. *Psychoanal. Rev.,* 1927, *14,* 20–36.
54. McCandless, B. R., & Marshall, H. R. Sex differences in social acceptance and participation of preschool children. *Child Develpm.,* 1957, *28,* 421–425
55. Moss, H. A., & Kagan, J. The stability of achievement and recognition seeking behaviors. *J. abnorm. soc. Psychol.,* 1961, *62,* 504–513.
56. Mowrer, O. H. *Learning theory and personality dynamics.* New York: Ronald Press, 1950.
57. Murphy, G. *Personality.* New York: Harper & Row, 1947.
58. Mussen, P., & Distler, L. Masculinity, identification and father-son relationships. *J. abnorm. soc. Psychol.,* 1959, *59,* 350–356.
59. Mussen, P., & Distler, L. Child rearing antecedents of masculine identification in kindergarten boys. *Child Develpm.,* 1960, *31,* 89–100.
60. Mussen, P., & Parker, A. Mother nurturance and girls' incidental imitative learning. *J. pers. soc. Psychol.,* 1965, *2,* 94–97.
61. Mussen, P., & Rutherford, E. Parent-child relations and parental personality in relation to young children's sex-role preferences. *Child Develpm.,* 1963, *34,* 589–607.
62. Otis, N. B., & McCandless, B. R. Responses to repeated frustrations of young children differentiated according to need area. *J. abnorm. soc. Psychol.,* 1955, *50,* 349–353.
63. Patterson, G. R., Littman, R. A., & Bricker, W. Assertive behavior in children: a step toward a theory of aggression. *Monogr. Soc. Res. Child Develpm.,* 1967, *32,* No. 5, 1–43.
64. Ruebush, B .K. Anxiety. In H. W. Stevenson (Ed.), *Child psychology (62nd Yearb. nat. Soc. Stud. Educ.)* Chicago: Univ. Chicago Press, 1963, 460–516.
65. Rutherford, E., & Mussen, P. Generosity in nursery school boys. *Child Develpm.,* 1968, *39,* 755–765.
66. Sarason, S. B., et al. *Anxiety in elementary school children.* New York: Wiley, 1960.
67. Scott, J. P. *Aggression.* Chicago: Univer. Chicago Press, 1958.
68. Sears, R. R. Personality development in the family. In J. M. Seidman (Ed.), *The child: a book of readings.* New York: Holt, Rinehart and Winston, 1958.
69. Sears, R. R. Relation of early socialization experiences to aggression in middle childhood. *J. abnorm. soc. Psychol.,* 1961, *63,* 466–492.

70. Sears, R. R., Maccoby, E. E., & Levin, H. *Patterns of child rearing.* New York: Harper & Row, 1957.
71. Sears, R. R., Whiting, J. W. M., Nowlis, V., & Sears, P. S. Some child rearing antecedents of aggression and dependency in young children. *Genet. Psychol. Monogr.,* 1953, *47,* 135–234.
72. Siegel, A., & Kohn, L. Permissiveness, permission and aggression: the effect of adult presence or absence on children's play. *Child Develpm.,* 1959, *30,* 131–141.
73. White, R. Motivation reconsidered: the concept of competence. *Psychol. Rev.,* 1959, *66,* 297–333.
74. Whiting, J. W. M. *Becoming a Kwoma.* New Haven: Yale Univer. Press, 1941. 1941.
75. Whiting, J. W. M., & Child, I. L. *Child training and personality.* New Haven: Yale Univer. Press, 1953.
76. Winterbottom, M. R. The relation of need for achievement to learning experience in independence and mastery. In J. W. Atkinson (Ed.), *Motives in fantasy, action and society.* Princeton, N.J.: Van Nostrand, 1958, 453–478.
77. Wright, M. E. The influence of frustration upon the social relationships of young children. Unpublished doctoral dissertation, State University of Iowa, 1940.
78. Yarrow, L. J. The effect of antecedent frustration on projective play. *Psychol. Monogr.,* 1948, *62,* No. 6.

10

The Preschool Years: Personality Development

II. Extrafamilial Influences

The last chapter dealt with the acquisition and development of a number of crucially important dimensions of personality—such as aggression, dependency, mastery, anxiety, sex-typing, and conscience. These characteristics are considered pervasive in the sense that they have some generality (i.e., they are reflected in many aspects of behavior and social relationships) and stability (i.e., they are not transient characteristics, but endure over some prolonged period of time). For example, the child who has strong dependency motives may manifest them in many relationships: with parents, with teachers, with peers; in the home, in the nursery school, and in the playground. His approach to new social situations, to new people and to new environments, to frustration, and to problem-solution will also be strongly influenced by his desires for gratification of his dependency needs.

The major determinants of the development of these early characteristics are to be found in the home—particularly in the child's relations with his parents. But, obviously, all of the child's behavior cannot be explained simply as consequents of his past history in the family. While the family continues to be the primary agent of socialization during the preschool period, as it was earlier, extrafamilial factors—experiences, situations, and people outside the family—begin to have significant impacts on the child's behavior. In this chapter, we will discuss some major factors that may change or modify patterns of behavior and motivations acquired at home.

As the child becomes more mature, his social world begins to broaden, expanding beyond the boundaries of his home into the neighborhood and nursery school, where he establishes relationships with new adults and peers. The nursery school presents a new social setting and vast new opportunities for learning. Here, some well-established responses acquired in the home are reinforced and strengthened, while other behaviors are modified or extinguished. Peers begin to play a more important role in the child's life, and, as we shall see, they may serve as reinforcers (positive or negative) and as models for imitation of new and different responses. In this chapter we will examine the nature of the nursery school and of peer interactions and their impacts on the child's development. Finally we will consider emotional problems and maladjustment during the preschool years and briefly survey techniques for modifying maladaptive responses.

NURSERY SCHOOL ATTENDANCE AND SOCIAL BEHAVIOR

The nursery school introduces the child to a new and different social world, and to new agents of socialization, formal and informal, such as teachers and peers. He must adapt to a "way of life" that differs in many ways from his home life. The child spends a great deal of time in this new social setting, which will make significant impacts on him, giving rise to modifications in his established behavior patterns and characteristics, and perhaps fostering new kinds of adjustment.

The central figure in the nursery school is the teacher, almost always a woman, who is in charge of many children. Middle-class children are likely to find that she is not as responsive to their needs and desires as mothers are, nor can she give them the attention they get at home. In some ways, the teacher will respond to the child as his mother does—although perhaps not as often or promptly—but in other ways her re· actions, as well as her perceptions and expectancies, will be far different. For example, in the view of many nursery school youngsters, the teacher expects much more independence and is much less tolerant of dependent behavior.

In view of the teacher's importance in the child's life, she can hardly avoid becoming an agent of socialization. As part of her work, she attempts to enhance the child's personal adjustment and, at the same time, to foster increased social skills and sensitivity. To accomplish these goals, she encourages or reinforces certain behavioral responses and personal characteristics while discouraging, ignoring, or punishing others. Often, but not always, the teacher rewards the behaviors that the child's parents are trying to instill in him, and fails to reward responses the parents want him to eliminate. Her reactions, strengthening some established responses and weakening others, inevitably lead the child to modify his behavior in some significant ways. Moreover, she is a readily available, as well as a generally powerful and attractive, model for imitation and identification.

At the same time, the child must adjust to the presence of many other children who are together for long periods of time. These new companions interact in different ways at different times, playing peacefully and contentedly much of the time, but also frequently acting competitively and aggressively. The child will be encouraged to interact with these others who are strangers to him at the time he enters school, and to form friendships with at least a few of them. Most children respond to the teacher's (and probably parents') pressures for sociability and their thoughts and activities become increasingly oriented toward their peers who inevitably become agents of socialization.

Over the last 20 years, enrollments in nursery schools and kindergartens have soared, but there has been surprisingly little systematic investigation of the role of these institutions in the socialization process. There is relatively little reliable information about the actual outcome of attendance in these schools and classes on children's personality, behavior, and cognitive development. In this section we will attempt to evaluate whatever data are available about the immediate and persisting effects of nursery school attendance in these early years.

A word of caution in interpreting the studies seems appropriate. Many of the studies compare children who attend nursery school with those who do not. In general the groups are matched with respect to a number of important variables such as age, intelligence, and socioeconomic status. But there are probably other important factors—for example, parental attitudes and the child's personality characteristics—on which the two groups cannot be matched. These factors may be intimately related to whether the child goes to nursery school at all, and to whether his behavior changes as a result. Therefore, observed differences between children attending and those not attending nursery school may not be attributable so much to the variable of attendance as to differences in the family backgrounds and children's personalities.

Effects on Cognitive Development

As we learned in Chapter 8, special attention in the nursery school, particularly individualized "tutoring," may raise the intelligence test scores of culturally disadvantaged children significantly (see pp. 315–319). While the results of these studies are not yet completely analyzed, there is apparently a tendency for children to show initial gains far greater than those of control groups. While the evidence is not clear-cut, some researchers feel that kindergarten or nursery school experience provides enduring benefits for the school performance of children of low socioeconomic status.

What about the influence of nursery school and kindergarten attendance on the cognitive development of the large majority of children who are not culturally deprived? The results on intelligence, as measured by standard tests, are equivocal. Some studies have reported moderate but consistent and enduring gains in intelligence test scores for children attending nursery school (66, 67); other reports indicate that nursery school attendance does not produce any significant gains in intelligence (11, 25, 39).

A recent longitudinal study in England yielded inconclusive but somewhat pessimistic results. The subjects were 224 children who attended nursery school at age 4 and were members of the National Survey of Health and Development, which included more than 5000 subjects. In tests of intelligence and educational performance (measuring attainment as well as ability) given at ages 8, 11, and 15, children who had been at nursery schools made higher scores at age 8 than the average survey child, although the differences were not statistically significant. By the age of 11, however, these children had lost their initial advantage, and by 15 they had actually fallen slightly, although not significantly, behind the other children in the survey (20).

Immediate Effects on Adjustment

The objectives of nursery school experience have not usually been stated in cognitive terms but rather in terms of personal and social adjustment. Nursery school is viewed as "a social situation that will constitute a real learning situation resulting in learning to adjust and conform to others as well as maintaining [one's] own freedom as an individual in a group" (37). Furthermore, "successful adjustment to the social situation may be considered one of the tool subjects in nursery school" (37). Most workers in the field agree that the basic aims of the nursery school include increasing the "general security" of the child, promoting his personal adjustment, and enhancing his social relations (4). In many cases, the nursery school affords the child his first contact with groups of peers and thus marks the beginning of peer influences.

Some responses learned at home are likely to be reinforced further in nursery school and hence to acquire greater habit strength, while others fail to bring rewards from peers or teachers and thus lose habit strength. It might therefore be anticipated that some aspects of the child's behavior will change as a consequence of his nursery school experience.

Systematic observations confirm this expectation, at least as far as social behavior is concerned. Immediately after entering nursery school, most children make rapid gains in social participation. As early as the latter part of the fall term of their first year of attendance, they make almost as many interpersonal contacts as children who already had a year of nursery school experience, and by the end of the school year, they are equal in social activity. Apparently these children discover quickly that their peers can provide important gratifications and that social relationships can be rewarding. Moreover, the program in the nursery school probably includes many group activities which are satisfying to all the children.

Rapid, positive modifications in personality characteristics have also been noted. In one of the earliest studies of the problem, 22 nursery school children were compared with 21 youngsters matched in age, intelligence, physical development, and socioeconomic background, who did not attend nursery school. All were rated on a series of behavior items at the beginning of the school year and again six months later (64).

During the intervening period, the nursery school children became less inhibited, more spontaneous, and more socialized. They gained more than the other children in initiative, independence, self-assertion, self-reliance, curiosity, and interest in the environment. According to the investigator, these changes are "probably due to the influence of the social force of a large group of children who had to adjust to each other constantly" (64, 72).

A great many "undesirable" infantile and dependent habits may be eliminated and an even greater number of "desirable" habits—many of them indicative of emancipation from adults—may be acquired during a year of nursery school attendance (41). Nursery school experience seems to facilitate social adjustment and the development of improved routine habits, at the same time reducing social inhibitions, nervous tendencies, and maladaptive reactions such as avoiding strangers, shrinking from notice, giving in easily, tenseness, enuresis, leaving tasks incomplete, and dawdling with food (31, 41). According to the data of one study, however, preschool training probably does not affect the degree of underlying anxiety, for "emotional" behaviors—such as "cries easily," twitching, sulking, temper tantrums—occur with equal frequency among children with little and with extensive nursery school experience. The author concluded that "the influence of nursery school may be greater for social behavior and routine adjustments than for emotional traits per se" (31, 188).

In brief, the outstanding consequents of nursery school attendance seem to be advances in sociability, self-expression, independence, initiative, social adaptability, and interest in the environment. As we pointed out earlier, it is not always possible in these studies on changes in behavior to separate the influences of home atmosphere from the influences of nursery school attendance itself. Nevertheless, it seems reasonable to conclude that nursery school attendance itself may play an important part in strengthening such responses as social outgoingness, independence, and self-expression, for these are the responses which are generally highly rewarded in these schools.

Influences of Different Nursery School Atmospheres

It should be pointed out that the nursery schools involved in the above studies very likely constituted a select sample of well-conducted schools with professionally trained personnel. Unfortunately, not all nursery schools are of this level. A well-designed experimental study shows how the impact of nursery school attendance on the child's personality and social adjustment varies with the general atmosphere, teaching techniques, and programs of the school (63). The investigator studied two groups of 4-year-olds—equated in IQ, socioeconomic status, and general personality characteristics (as judged by teachers)—who had different kinds of nursery school experiences. With one group of 12 subjects, the teachers were understanding and interested but somewhat detached, allowing the children to plan their own activities and assisting them only when they specifically requested help. With the other group, 11 subjects, these same teachers were warm, friendly, and cooperative, maintaining a great deal of personal contact with the children, guiding their activities, and spontaneously giving help and information.

After eight months of nursery school experience, the children who had a great deal of teacher guidance improved more in personal and social adjustment, became more dominant, and participated more actively in social relationships than the others. They were also less hostile, rejecting, persecuting, threatening, attacking, and destructive. Frequent warm, friendly interactions with teachers also fostered more leadership and greater constructiveness when the children were faced with possible failure, and a lower incidence of nervous habits. In short, from the points of view of the preschool child's social and emotional adjustment, active teacher guidance and participation are more beneficial than detachment. The favorable changes in children's behavior following nursery school training, noted in the studies cited above, may be attributable to the "high teacher guidance, active participation" qualities of the schools they attended.

Long-Term Effects

Are the generally beneficial effects of nursery school attendance enduring ones? Research, using different techniques and different populations, has again, yielded equivocal results. In general, it may be concluded that nursery school attendance may foster the development of certain characteristics associated with good personal and social adjustment, but there is no evidence that these characteristics persist or remain stable.

For example, one study of the emotional adjustment of kindergarten children used 42 *pairs* of children as subjects. In each pair, drawn from the same class, one of the children had attended nursery school for at least a year, the other had not. The pairs were matched for social status, sex, ordinal position in the family, and IQ.

Teachers rated all of the children on four graphic rating scales: adjustment to usual kindergarten routines and activities; adjustment to peers; adjustment to authority (in routine relations with the teacher); and personal or "inner" adjustment, characterizing the child "as a person."

According to these ratings, children who had *not* attended nursery school surpassed those who had attended in personal adjustment, relations with other children, and participation in group activities. The investigators therefore concluded that there is no support for "the hypothesis that nursery school attendance will enhance later school adjustment" (12, 592).

It is not simple to account for these negative results, but some plausible explanations may be offered. Nursery school attendance may result in a kind of independence, freedom, and spontaneity that makes it difficult for youngsters to adjust to the greater conformity pressures of the kindergarten class. Or perhaps the redundancy of nursery school and kindergarten activities produces frustration, boredom, and consequently primitivization (regression) of the child's behavior, especially in the cases of brighter children—and the subjects of this study were highly intelligent. Moreover, it is possible that those who attended nursery school were more maladjusted originally. Perhaps more "problem" children are sent to these schools because their parents encounter difficulties in rearing such children at home and feel that perhaps nursery school will help solve their difficulties.

This was in fact true of the children in the longitudinal English study mentioned earlier. Compared with the others, those who attended nursery school came from "more difficult home backgrounds" and were consequently more likely to be "more emotionally and educationally vulnerable than an unselected group of the same population" (20, 75). At ages 13 and 15, more of the latter were considered "highly maladjusted" by their teachers.

> At first sight . . . it looks as if attendance at nursery school is not associated with good adjustment assessments in later school life and that it may be associated with worse. . . . [However] at least some children are sent to nursery schools because they have problems of behaviour which, it is thought, would be helped by the atmosphere and social contacts these schools are expected to provide. If this was the reason for sending any considerable proportion of these children to nursery schools, it is clear that some have remained maladjusted, and it may well be that they (and the others) would have been more disturbed if they had not gone (20, 79).

The Nursery School Teacher as "Therapist"

Simply attending nursery school and participating in routine activities will not ordinarily solve a child's deep-lying emotional problems or diminish well-established anxieties or their manifestations. But there is an impressive, growing body of evidence that indicates that *individualized* treatment by the nursery school teacher may have some startling effects, reducing maladaptive reactions and strengthening desirable responses. Essentially the "treatment" consists of application of the principles of learning (rewarding certain responses and failing to reward others) in planned, systematic ways. In theory, this kind of "treatment" can be carried out by the nursery school teacher. In practice, however, this may be extremely difficult to accomplish because nursery school teachers are generally overworked and there are numerous, relentless demands on their time and energy which are incompatible with highly "individualized" work.

In one type of treatment the child is given special "training" from which he learns new responses that are to be substituted for established, undesirable habits. For example, after observing a large group of nursery school children, one investigator selected 12 subjects (the experimental group) who showed withdrawal and regressive response to failure in problem-solving situations (e.g., retreating or giving up almost at once, crying, whining, sulking). Each was given special training designed to teach him "to persist longer in the face of tasks that were difficult for him, to depend less on an adult for help in solving a problem, and to attack a problem and see it through with some composure" (42, 34). The control group of 12 children, who gave slightly less evidence of immaturity, received no special training.

During a 16-week training period, the experimenter met with each child in the experimental group in individual sessions lasting between 8 and 33 minutes, until the child was able to finish the training tasks (e.g., completing picture puzzles of progressively increasing complexity). No direct assistance was given during these sessions, but independent behavior was praised by statements such as "That was fine! You are learning to try hard. . . . You did that one all by yourself" (42). In addition to this, the experimenter occasionally gave encouragement or suggestions for problem solutions.

Although the level or difficulty of the tasks increased regularly as training progressed, the subjects showed continuous gains in independence and interest in the problems, requesting help less frequently and persisting longer in the more difficult tasks. Spontaneous verbalizations by the subjects also revealed increased self-confidence and ability to sustain effort.

After completion of the training, the children were tested again in difficult problem-solving tasks. The trained group made significantly more constructive reactions and "attempts to solve alone" than they had before training. They asked for assistance less frequently and manifested no exaggerated emotional responses such as crying, yelling, whining, sulking, or destructive behavior. In short, the composed, mature, independent responses learned in training generalized to other problem situations. The group who had no special training did not show any significant improvement in handling frustration (43).

The study just summarized shows how "frustration tolerance" may be increased through a series of specialized, individual training sessions. Submissive-withdrawal behavior may be reduced, while dominating and cooperative behavior may be increased by analogous means. In one experiment, *pairs* of nursery school children were observed playing with a sandbox and toys in an experimental room, and all dominant reactions were recorded.

Nursery school behavior records revealed that the 6 children who were most self-directed and dominant in the experimental situations were generally self-confident, while the 6 who were least dominant lacked this characteristic. The investigator, therefore, reasoned that building up the child's confidence might raise his dominance level. To test this hypothesis, she chose the 5 most submissive children as an experimental group and gave them special training designed to increase self-confidence. This consisted of a series of individual training sessions in which the subject was taught all the knowledge and skills necessary to master three difficult tasks. A control group, 5 other submissive children, did not receive any special training.

Following these sessions, each child was observed in four pairings—each time with a different, originally more dominant child—in situations resembling those used in training. In these interactions, the trained children were more dominant than their companions (taking the lead in instructing them, demonstrating the use of materials, etc.).

About 10 weeks after the initial tests were made, the trained children were again paired with peers in the original experimental situation. They showed significantly greater gains in dominance than untrained children did, 4 of the 5 showing marked changes. The dominance scores of the control group did not change significantly between the initial and final experimental tests (35).

These findings support the investigator's hypothesis that a child may gain in dominant behavior if his self-confidence is elevated. Moreover, this increase in confidence may transfer from the immediate situation in which the new learning occurs to other settings.

Just as submissive children can be trained to be more dominant, extremely dominating children can readily be trained to become more cooperative. In one training program which consisted of eleven 15-minute doll-play periods, the child and the experimenter discussed and analyzed several situations involving social difficulties or conflicts, attempting to decide upon the most desirable ways of resolving the problems. Occasionally the child was asked to work out a solution by himself.

After the training period, the dominating behavior of trained children was considerably diminished, and they made more cooperative responses. On the other hand, the behavior of a control group of equally dominating children was essentially unchanged. The decrease of domination in the trained group—which was maintained for at least a month—was not accompanied by either an increase in submission or a decrease in general social participation. Apparently, socially desirable behavior can be fostered without restricting the child's social activity or his ability to maintain his standing with his peers. Children can be helped to become more cooperative without becoming victims of the domination of others (16).

In the foregoing studies behavior modification involved individual training sessions—that is, the experimenter (who in theory could have been the nursery school teacher) worked with one child at a time outside the classroom. More recently there have been a number of successful attempts at guiding nursery school teachers in applying the principles of "behavior therapy" to modify the behavior of their pupils in the course of their ordinary work. Basically, this consists of the teachers' rewarding certain desirable responses, and not rewarding maladaptive ones, *whenever they occur* in the classroom or on the playground.

A simple, straightforward experiment on modification of aggression and cooperation in nursery school boys demonstrates the use and usefulness of these techniques. The purpose was "to control the aggressive behavior of all of the boys [27 3- and 4-year-olds] in an entire nursery school class, by using as techniques the removal of positive generalized reinforcement (attention for aggression) while giving attention to cooperative acts" (13, 103).

During the training (experimental manipulation), the nursery school teachers tried, as much as possible, to ignore aggression and to reward cooperative and peaceful behavior by attention and praise. Ratings of the children's aggression were made for a week before the training period began, to determine a base or reference rate of aggressive responses. Similar ratings were made again after the first week of a 2-week training period, and again, three weeks later to assess the persistence of the effects of training.

This simple treatment was successful and apparently had enduring effects. The number of acts of physical and verbal aggression decreased significantly in the second week of training, and the number of cooperative acts increased. Although the effects on verbal aggression were enduring, physical aggression increased after the brief training period, decreasing again with further training. The success of the "experiment" was particularly dramatic to the nursery school teachers, the real "experimenters"— who were at first skeptical about its efficacy—because "two extremely aggressive boys became friendly and cooperative to a degree the teachers had not thought possible following the training" (13).

Applying the principles of "behavior therapy," a nursery school teacher may serve as a "therapist" in cases of problem children with complex symptoms, as the following case study (2) demonstrates. The subject was a 4-year-old pupil at a university nursery school where she was in a group of 8 boys and 8 girls, homogeneous in age, intelligence, and family background (upper middle class).

> During the first days of school, Ann interacted freely with adults but seldom initiated contact with children or responded to their attempts to play with her. She did not seem severely withdrawn or frightened; instead she revealed a varied repertory of unusually well-developed physical and mental skills that drew the interested attention of adults but failed to gain the companionship of children. Teachers gave warm recognition to her skilled climbing, jumping, and riding; her creative use of paints and clay; her original songs and rhythmic interpretations of musical selections; her collections of nature objects; her perceptive and mature verbalizations; and her will and thorough help-with-cleanup behaviors.

> With passing days she complained at length about minute or invisible bumps and abrasions. She often spoke in breathy tones at levels so low that it was difficult to understand what she said. . . . She spent increasing time simply standing and looking. Frequently she retired to a make-believe bed in a packing box in the play yard to "sleep" for several minutes. Mild, tic-like behaviors such as picking her lower lip, pulling a strand of hair, or fingering her cheek were apparent (2, 512).

Clearly, for many complicated reasons, Ann wanted to isolate herself. To reduce Ann's tendencies to isolate herself from the other children

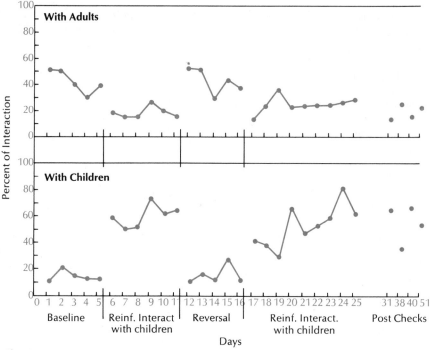

Fig. 10.1. Percentages of time Ann spent in social interaction during approximately 2 hours of each morning session. (From K. Eileen Allen, Betty Hart, Joan S. Buell, Florence R. Harris, & M. M. Wolf. Effects of social reinforcement on isolate behavior of a nursery school child. *Child Developm.*, copyright 1964 by The Society for Research in Child Development, Inc., *35*, No. 2, 310. By permission.)

and to seek adult attention, and simultaneously, to foster peer interactions, the investigators instituted a plan in which the teacher rewarded her with maximum attention whenever she played with another child. At the same time, she did not reward her isolated behavior or interactions with an adult alone, but tried to extinguish these responses by withdrawing attention when they occurred.

Meticulous observations of Ann's behavior were made throughout the study, beginning with a 5-day period before training procedures began. During this "baseline" period, she spent little more than 10 percent of her nursery school time interacting with children, about 40 percent with adults, and for at least half of the time she was essentially alone, either quiet, or playing by herself (see Fig. 10.1).

During the training procedures,

> the teacher made comments and directed other attending behaviors to Ann, not individually, but as a participant in the ongoing group play; whenever possible, the adult approached the group prepared to give Ann an appropriate material or toy to add to the joint play project. A sample amended operation

was, "You three girls have a cozy house! Here are some more cups, Ann, for your tea party." Whenever Ann began to leave the group, the teacher turned away from her and became occupied with some other child or with equipment. This procedure, which extended over 6 days, seemed to bring Ann into interaction with other children more frequently and for longer periods (2, 514).

On the first day of training, there was an immediate change in Ann's behavior. As Fig. 10.1 shows, she spent almost 60 percent of her time that day first in "approximations to interaction" and then in active play with other children, while adult-child interactions, which were not rewarded, decreased to less than 20 percent. These levels of interaction were maintained, with little variation, throughout the 6-day training period.

Then, to test the effects of reinforcement, the procedures were reversed after the sixth day of the training period. Beginning on this day, solitary pursuits and interactions with adults were rewarded by adult attention, while interactions with children were disregarded and ignored. Under these conditions, Ann's previous behavior reappeared immediately (see Fig. 10.1), and for the 5 days of the "reversal" period, she averaged less than 20 percent of her time in interaction with children and about 40 percent with adults.

After 5 "reversal" days, a final shift was made. Adult attention and reward again became contingent upon interaction with children. The change in Ann's behavior was dramatic and immediate. For this final reinforcement period of 9 days, interactions with adults decreased to about 25 percent of the total session, and interactions with children rose to about 60 percent.

Checks on Ann's behavior 6 days after the last reinforcements had been given and at intervals after this time showed that Ann's behavior was fairly stable. She spent about 60 percent of her time with children and less than 15 percent in interaction with adults. Moreover, according to teachers' reports, her complaining, babyish behavior disappeared. In general, she seemed to become a happy, confident, sociable member of the school group.

Although this is a study of a single case, it points up the efficacy of basic reinforcement techniques applied by nursery school teachers in the course of their regular professional work in modifying complex "problem" behavior. Another convincing demonstration of the usefulness of these techniques comes from the study of a 3-year-old girl who regressed to crawling (after she had been walking for a long time) when she entered nursery school. Presumably, the new environment, including many new children and adults, and the prospect of separation from her mother were powerful frustrations that led to regressive behavior. Through a planned program of reinforcement every time she stood up or walked, and ignoring her whenever she sat or crawled, her teachers accomplished some remarkable changes in the child's behavior. After 2 weeks of training (1 month after she entered school), her behavior was indistinguishable from the behavior of the other children. She walked and ran as other children did, talked readily, smiled often, and used outdoor equipment with vigor and enthusiasm. She seemed to enjoy all the nursery school activities, playing and working in spontaneous, animated ways with both peers and adults.

It is impossible at this time to assess fully the potential uses and limitations of these techniques, for they have only recently been applied to behavior problems; however, it is clear that they are extremely promising. There are undoubtedly cases of deep-seated anxiety, as well as other maladaptive and neurotic characteristics, that are probably more resistant to change by these methods. But the range of problems for which these techniques are appropriate and efficacious has not been fully explored. As we shall see later, some investigators have achieved notable success using these techniques with profoundly disturbed, psychotic children (see pp. 408–410).

PEER INTERACTIONS AND PEER INFLUENCES

Teachers are not the only new agents of socialization the child encounters in nursery school. The child's peers also become agents of socialization—although unwittingly—as reinforcers of certain behaviors, as models for imitation and identification, as a group pressuring the child to make some modifications in his behavior.

Peer influences on personality development and behavior are probably second in importance only to those of the parents. Before examining these influences in detail, we will examine the nature of the social setting and interactions among nursery school children as well as age changes in personal relationships during the preschool years.

Typically, the child comes to nursery school with little or no experience in interacting with large groups of children for long periods of time. Thus the nursery school provides a setting for learning to adjust to *groups* of people—both in intimate interactions (such as friendships) and in more extensive relationships (the entire nursery school group). In effect, the child is introduced to society at large, albeit a miniature version.

In approaching his new social relationships, the child generalizes the responses, characteristics, and social behavior he has acquired at home, trying them out at school and testing the reactions of peers and teachers. But he is likely to find that the expectancies of the nursery school teachers and other children are not identical with those of parents and siblings. Hence the child must continuously assess himself and his established patterns of behavior, noting which ones are effective—i.e., give rise to positive responses from others—and which ones simply will not work in this new setting and may perhaps bring rejection or aggression from others.

The child learns a great deal from these testing experiences and their consequences. Many of his well-established responses also bring him acceptance from his peers and enhanced social status; hence these become strengthened. Other responses in the child's repertoire are relatively weak when he enters nursery school, but if these responses bring rewards from peers, they will become stronger and more prominent. Still other responses acquired through learning at home may prove unacceptable at nursery school, bringing rejection or punishment from others—these will be weakened or extinguished. New responses may also be acquired by imitation of or identification with peers or teachers, as we shall see shortly. In brief, the nursery school may provide the child with a novel and different system of rewards and punishments, and in response to these, his behavior may undergo significant modifications.

Furthermore, during the preschool period, the child continues to mature physically and intellectually and thus has more substantial bases for prolonged and complex social interactions—e.g., longer attention span, increased comprehension of games, greater imagination—than he was capable of when he was younger. The child's cognitive structures also advance and become more complicated as a result of maturation and a broadened range of social experiences. At this age, the child does not readily view things from the perspective of another person, but clearly his perceptions and understanding of social interactions change and become more accurate. In a rudimentary way, the child begins to realize the kinds of behavior that are acceptable and unacceptable in the broader social world, or more specifically, in the new social settings he encounters.

Changes in Social Behavior During Preschool Years

While the young child is at home, he is oriented primarily toward his mother. So it is not surprising to find he may spend a great deal of time during his first few weeks of nursery school seeking attention and approval from teachers and other adults. It soon becomes evident, however, that he is expected to interact with the other children, and the child soon becomes more oriented toward his peers.

Parten (54) made detailed records of 20 1-minute observations of 42 nursery school children between the ages of 2 and 5. Social participation during each sample was classified and scored according to six categories: unoccupied behavior, solitary play, onlooker behavior (watches, but does not enter play), parallel play (plays alongside, but not with, other children using the same playthings), associated play (plays with others and shares materials), and cooperative or organized play.

Parallel play, the most rudimentary form of social behavior, was much more characteristic of young preschool children, while older ones participated more frequently in associated or cooperative play. Composite social participation scores were highly correlated with chronological age (r = +.61). This indicates that as they grow older, children generally spend more time in social interactions of an associated or cooperative sort and less time in idleness, solitary play, and onlooker behavior.

These changes in social behavior may be partially attributable to increased ability to participate in more complex, cooperative activities, and the teacher's and peers' pressures to take part. In addition to this, however, the older child probably has had more experiences in which outgoing social responses have been rewarded. Attendance at nursery school and playgrounds gives him more opportunities to learn that group-centered behavior can bring gratifications. As a consequence of many experiences, socially oriented responses become stronger and the child is likely to engage in more group activities. His social interactions become more frequent, and more complex.

A number of outgoing responses become more prominent in the child's behavior repertoire. Systematic observations show that 4-year-olds exceed 3-year-olds in four types of socially reinforcing interactions: *giving positive attention and approval, giving affection and personal acceptance, submission,* and *giving tangible objects (15)*. Children who display high frequencies of these behaviors are not restricted in their relationships with peers; rather, they tend to distribute their reinforcements widely (29). Moreover, tendencies to be socially reinforcing appear to be reasonably stable—that is, children who were high social reinforcers during the fall sessions behaved in the same way in the spring. The amount of social reinforcement given by a child was strongly correlated with the amount he received from others $(r = +.75)$.

Between the ages of 2 and 5, the child forms his first friendships, generally with members of his own sex. Similarities in chronological age, sociability, and physical activity influenced friendships among boys. Girls who became friends were alike in social participation, chronological age, sociability, and physical activity (14).

Friendship patterns change with age during this period. Between the ages of 2 and 3, there was generally an expansion in the number of playmates a child had. After this age, the primary increase was in strength of friendship for a few particular children, rather than in total number of friends (26). This shift in friendship patterns may be viewed as a consequence of the child's learning in these new interpersonal situations. In his first experiences outside the home, the child may interact with many different children. Some of these early relationships do not bring rewards and may even bring punishment. With time, the child learns that relationships with certain children are gratifying, and he forms closer attachments to these children.

Competition

In our competition-oriented culture, excelling others and striving for higher status are frequently and consistently rewarded at home and in school. Hence, as the child becomes increasingly socialized, and as he identifies more strongly with his parents and others in his society, he adopts the socially approved competitive values. Many of the conflicts that occur during the preschool years may be related to the growth of competitive responses.

In one classic study of competition (27), children between 2 and 7 years of age were brought into a room in pairs and seated opposite each other at a table on which there was a pile of blocks. After playing and

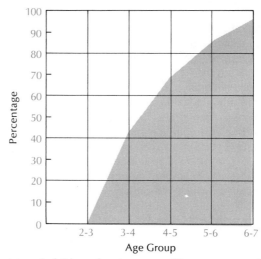

Fig. 10.2. Percentage of children showing competitive responses at various ages. (From P. J. Greenberg. Competition in children: an experimental study. *Amer. J. Psychol.*, 1932, *44*, 239. By permission.)

building freely for awhile, they were challenged to compete, to build something "prettier" and something "bigger" than their companion.

Figure 10.2, taken from data of this study, shows the increase which occurs with age in the percentage of children exhibiting competitive responses (e.g., grabbing blocks or making competitive remarks). Two-year-olds did not compete and made only "undirected, nonspecific" movements toward the materials. Competitive responses began between the ages of 3 and 4, when the children became more aware of the material, and, more significantly, of the social relationships with their companions. Competition became much more intense between the ages of 4 and 6, when grabbing materials from the other child, disregarding his feelings, and making self-flattering remarks increased, and giving materials or help to the companion decreased (27).

There are, of course, wide individual variations in competitiveness among children within our own culture. Some youngsters are highly and violently competitive; others are only mildly and calmly so; still others do not seem to be competitive at all (27). Nursery school children from democratic, freedom-giving homes tended to be both more outgoing and more rivalrous than those from authoritarian homes (7, 8). Children who got along well with their siblings were less rivalrous than others.

Sex and socioeconomic status are also related to competition among youngsters of this age (49). Nursery school children were brought in pairs to a playroom in which there were two piles of toy construction blocks, and all their competitive and aggressive responses, including verbalizations, were recorded. The data revealed that there were more instances of competition among older than among younger children, those from the lower-middle class competed more than those from the upper-middle group, and boys competed more than girls. It may be inferred that the lower-middle-class children had been rewarded by their parents for competition, while the upper-middle parents of this group discouraged competition in play. Apparently, masculine sex-typing, even at this age, includes learning to be more highly competitive, while feminine sex-typing does not include this characteristic. Competition and hostile aggression were not closely related, i.e., highly competitive children were not necessarily highly aggressive (49).

The role of cultural rewards in the development of rivalry may be clarified by comparing Americans' attitudes with those of individuals from societies in which competition is discouraged. For the American,

> self-esteem has become conditioned to excelling. Excelling is a secondary (learned) drive in his personality. On the other hand, in the village of the Zuni, the ideal man "sees his activities in those of the group" and avoids both leadership as well as the competitive execution of tasks. Asch has several times been quoted as observing Hopi children to consistently belittle their own work. . . . Apparently the Zuni and Hopi modal personality lacks an acquired motivation of competitiveness (34, 190).

Despite the general approval in our society, an overemphasis on competition may be damaging to the child and to those with whom he associates. For example, competition may be unhealthy "if the child's own estimate of himself and of his worth is tied to the extent to which he can outdo others. It is unhealthy if the child has a tendency to regard himself as contemptible and inferior unless he can prove his superiority to all comers" (36, 226).

Aggressive and Ascendant Interactions

Ascendant behavior in peer interactions also increases during the preschool years, while submissiveness diminishes. One study (62) indicated that ascendant behaviors reached a peak when the child is 5 years old, and changed little during the elementary school years, while *forms* of aggressive expression change in several respects. Screaming, weeping, hitting, and physical attack decline, while verbal aggression increases (38). Older preschoolers participate in fewer but longer quarrels, generally with others of their own sex but of different ages (19). Total frequencies of aggressive peer interactions tend to increase between the ages of 2 and 4 and then to decline (65), while sex differences in aggression become more pronounced. These qualitative changes may be of greater significance than changes in total amount of peer aggression.

Peers as Socializers

These general trends in social behavior during the preschool years may be regarded as the joint outcomes of group and teacher pressures often accomplished by rewards and punishments, and of the child's greater cognitive maturity. As the preschool child's social interactions increase in scope and intensity, his peers play increasingly prominent and significant roles in the socialization process. Basically, they act as socialization agents in two ways: as reinforcers (and punishers) of behavior, and as models for imitation and identification.

The extent to which a child's behavior, values, attitudes, and motivations may be influenced and modified by his peers' reactions depends on a whole host of factors. One of the most important sets of factors is the child's own social and personality characteristics—e.g., his outgoingness or avoidance of social contacts; his relative dependence or his independence from his parents; his attachments to peers; the flexibility or rigidity of his already established behavior patterns; his tendency to be dominant or passive in social interactions; his attractiveness as a friend or companion.

A peer's power as an influencer will be a function of such factors as his attractiveness to the child; the degree of affection, attachment or friendship between them; his tendency to dominate or submit; his ability to satisfy the child's motives (e.g., giving help and support when needed).

Situational factors will also affect the child's "influenceability." The presence of friends may keep the child secure and calm in his activities, outgoing in his orientation, working contentedly at his tasks. On the other hand, the presence of disliked peers may have quite different effects, giving rise to frustration, discontent, and avoidance reactions. If the child is engaged in structured activities or in tasks requiring concentrated attention (e.g., solving a puzzle or listening to a story), he is not likely to be receptive to the influence of others. In situations in which he feels secure and confident, the child will make appropriate responses, uninfluenced by his peers' reactions; but in a strange setting, not knowing what is expected, he may imitate the response of a peer—especially a dominant or popular one. Or, under these circumstances, he may, in a very tentative way, try out some available response, observing peers' reactions for indications of approval (rewards) or disapproval (punishment).

Peers as Agents of Reinforcement

While it is obvious that peers have significant impact on the child's learning, systematic study of peers as agents of reinforcement has only begun relatively recently. The most relevant research has been conducted by Hartup and his colleagues at the University of Minnesota (*15, 28–30*) and is related to types and frequency of reinforcement by peers and effects of these factors on nursery school children. In one study, four kinds of peer reinforcement were recorded in the natural setting of the nursery school: giving attention and approval; giving affection and personal acceptance; showing submission (passive acceptance, imitation, sharing, accepting another's idea or help); and token-giving (giving tangible, physical rewards such as toys or food spontaneously). Reinforcements were given more frequently during dramatic play than during any other kind of activity, which suggests that "activities which involve attending to a project or an adult do not elicit as large a quantity of social reinforcement from peers" as free activities do (29, 1001). Boys reinforced other boys significantly more often than they did girls, and girls gave more reinforcement to other girls than to boys.

The investigators also noted a marked increase with age in children's use of reinforcers in their interactions with peers, 4-year-olds reinforcing peers much more frequently than 3-year-olds. Moreover, older children distributed their reinforcement more widely—that is, to a larger number of other children. Reinforcement appeared to be a reciprocal process, for those who gave the most reinforcement also received the most. Giving positive reinforcement is significantly associated with social acceptance and high social status. Popular children give and receive more positive reinforcement than those who are disliked (29, 1022). It may be inferred that nursery school children, especially older ones, are most likely to be influenced by popular peers of the same sex.

Most significant and most directly related to the problem of influence of peer reinforcements was the finding that reinforcement was generally followed by continuation of the responses that were reinforced. In other words, the child tended to continue—and presumably to strengthen—the activities he was engaged in when he received reinforcement from peers. Clearly, then, peers' reactions to the child's behavior will be an important determinant of whether he maintains or changes his behavior.

This brings us to the problem of the kinds of behavior peers are likely to reinforce and thus strengthen. Recent research seems to support many parents' contention (or complaint) that their children become more assertive and aggressive after they attend nursery school. In one intensive investigation, full data on a total of 2583 aggressive acts (bodily attack, attack with an object, invasion of territory) and their consequences were recorded in the natural settings of two nursery schools (55).

The most striking finding of the study is that in both nursery schools, aggressive behavior was frequently and strongly reinforced by other children who yielded to the aggressor's wishes, withdrawing from the conflict, thereby permitting him to attain what he wanted, or giving him something (e.g., a toy, a place in line). Consequently, "it is unlikely that the nursery school setting will provide a basis for the *extinction* of aggressive behaviors for children who enter the school with these behaviors already at high strength" (55, 20).

Very often the victim of aggression himself provided the positive reinforcement for the aggressor's actions. This reinforcement increased the probability that the victim would soon be attacked again by the same peer using the same kind of aggressive techniques. On the basis of this finding the investigators concluded that the "social setting provided substantial support for the maintenance of already existing assertive-aggressive behaviors" (55, 22).

Moreover, and perhaps even more interesting, the nursery school setting clearly "provided an extremely efficient program for training in the *acquisi-*

tion of assertive behavior" (*55, 22*). Children who were passive or only moderately aggressive when they entered the nursery school became more aggressive during the period of their attendance there if they interacted frequently with their peers. Passive children who participated in social activities were at first frequent victims of aggression, but eventually they counterattacked, and their counterattacks were reinforced. Subsequently, they began to initiate assertive-aggressive actions and increased their output of these responses significantly. Children who were originally passive and, in addition, socially inactive ("bumps on a log"; "wallflowers") did not show significant increases in aggressive initiations. Some other passive children who did interact but were unsuccessful in their counterattacks against aggressive peers did not become significantly more aggressive. In short, peer reinforcements may result in substantial changes in this important aspect of the child's personality, but the extent of peer impact is mediated by the child's past history and personality.

Peers as Models

Perhaps even more important than their roles as agents of reinforcement is the peers' ready availability to serve as *models* whose behavior will be imitated. Peer aggression is likely to be imitated by nursery school children. An experimental group of nursery school children was shown a film in which a peer makes many aggressive responses, such as hitting an inflated plastic doll with a bat, throwing plastic balls at a doll, striking the doll with a mallet or punching it in the nose (*32*).

Following exposure to the film, each subject was subjected to a mildly frustrating experience and then taken to an experimental room, which contained a variety of play materials, some of which could be used for imitative aggression. The subject's imitation score was the number of his responses that were identical with those made by the peer model in the film.

Analysis of the data revealed that exposure to aggressive peer models was an important antecedent in determining the subsequent form of the child's behavior, boys showing more direct imitation than girls. The power of peer models is further attested to by the finding that adult models of aggressive responses were not emulated as frequently as peer models (*32*).

The level of more positive social behavior may also be elevated by imitating peers. Exposure to an altruistic model will result in increases in the child's altruistic responses. A most relevant experimental study dealt with modeling itself, and (1) the possible differential effects of rewarding and nonrewarding models and (2) the child's history of reinforcement from peers (*30*).

Extensive observations of the nursery school subjects interacting with other children yielded data on the frequencies of their being "givers" or "receivers" of reward from peers. Some children became confederates of the experimenters, serving as models. Some of these were frequent givers of reward, others were relatively nonrewarding.

In the actual modeling situation, the subject watches the model solving some simple maze puzzles and receiving six trinkets as a prize for each correct solution. The trinkets could then be deposited in either of two bowls on the table, one designated as the subject's, and the other designated as belonging to another boy in the class. The model always put five of the trinkets in the "other" boy's bowl. After the model had finished his turn, he left the room, and the subject played the game himself. His altruism was indexed by the number of trinkets he gave the other boy.

Subjects who observed the model were significantly more altruistic and sharing than control subjects who were not exposed to a model (30). Moreover,

> the amount of imitative sharing depended on the child's past experience in the group and his past experience with the particular child who was the model. Children who had a history of frequent reinforcement from their peers imitated a *rewarding* child significantly more than a child who was not usually a source of reinforcement in nursery school. On the other hand, children who received generally little reinforcement from their peers in nursery school imitated *nonrewarding* models significantly more than rewarding models.

> Thus, there is evidence to suggest that the determinants of peer imitation include the child's previous experience with reinforcement from other children. Apparently, not all children choose to imitate peers who have been attentive and supportive. On the contrary, nonparticipating, noninteracting children are more influenced by other children with whom they have had little or no experience. These findings indicate, then, that the kinds of interactions a child has with other children in the nursery school have far-reaching effects on his responsiveness to social influence (28, 226).

Peers as Models for Behavior Modification.   Peers may serve as effective models of calm, approach responses to stimuli (e.g., a dog) that the child fears, and repeated exposure to a model behaving this way may be very effective in reducing the observer's fears and avoidance behavior. In one experimental demonstration the subjects were 24 boys and 24 girls, 3 to 5 years old, who were fearful of dogs (9). The strength of their fears was measured before "treatment" by means of a graded sequence of tasks in which the children were required to engage in increasingly intimate interactions with a dog (e.g., simply looking at a dog confined in a playpen, patting the dog, walking him on a leash, and, finally, climbing into a playpen and remaining there alone with him).

Each fearful child was then assigned to one of four treatment groups Group 1, the *model-positive context* group, participated in a series of eight enjoyable parties. During each one, a 4-year-old model was ushered into the room and exhibited progressively longer, closer, and more intense interactions with a dog. Group 2, the *model-neutral context* group, observed the same peer model performing the same sequence of approach responses with the dog, but without parties. The other two groups were controls. Group 3, the *exposure-positive context* group, attended parties during which a dog was brought into the room, but did not observe any modeling. Group

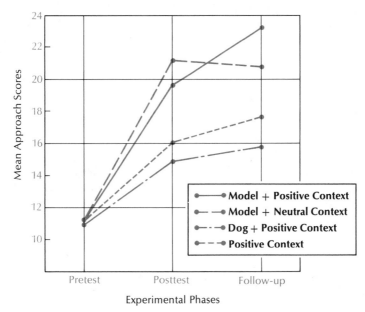

Fig. 10.3. Mean approach scores achieved by children in each of the treatment conditions on the three different periods of assessment. (From A. Bandura, Joan E. Grusec, & Frances L. Menlove. Vicarious extinction of avoidance behavior. *J. pers. soc. Psychol.*, 1967, Vol. 5. Copyright 1967 by the American Psychological Association. By permission.)

4, the *positive-context* group, participated in the parties but they were never exposed to either the dog or the model.

On the day after completion of the treatment series, and a month later, the children were again given the graded sequence of interaction tasks with two dogs, the one used in the original test, and, to test the generalization effects, an unfamiliar one.

Figure 10.3 shows the performance of the four groups on the pretest, the post-test (given 1 day after training was completed), and the follow-up (1 month later). It is obvious that the subjects in both modeling conditions (in positive and neutral contexts) displayed significantly greater and more stable, lasting reduction in avoidance behavior than the children in the control conditions. In addition, significantly more of the children exposed to models performed the terminal approach behavior in the test (that is, were willing to get into the playpen with the dog even with no one else in the room). The increment in approach responses (or the extinction of avoidance behavior) was generalized from a familiar to an unfamiliar dog. Clearly, then, gradual exposure to models coping with feared stimuli produces extensive, enduring therapeutic fear-reduction outcomes, although the nature of the context of modeling does not have any significant effect (9).

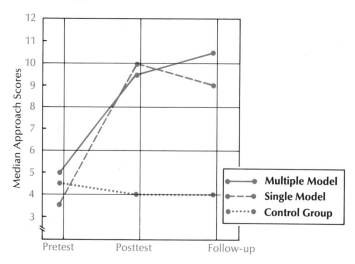

Fig.10.4. Median approach scores obtained by children in each of three conditions at different phases of the experiment. (From A. Bandura & Frances L. Menlove. Factors determining vicarious extinction of avoidance behavior through symbolic modeling. *J. pers. soc. Psychol.*, 1968, Vol. 8. Copyright 1968 by the American Psychological Association. By permission.)

In a related study (*10*), nursery school boys and girls who feared dogs watched a series of movies of models display progressively bolder approach responses to a dog. One group was exposed to a *single model condition,* in which the same model, a 5-year-old boy, interacted with a cocker spaniel. Another group of children saw movies with *multiple modeling,* i.e., several girls and boys of varying ages interacted with dogs ranging from tiny, gentle breeds to larger, more threatening ones. Children in the control condition were shown movies of Disneyland for equivalent periods of time. Approach tests were given, as in the experiment described above, 1 day and 1 month after completion of the film series.

Figure 10.4 presents a summary of the performance of the three groups at three phases of the study. Children in the control group showed no change in their avoidance of dogs, while those from both other groups showed striking increases in approach behavior the day after the completion of the film series and 1 month later. As is clear from Fig. 10.4, the two modeling conditions did not produce differential effects on total approach scores. The multiple modeling treatment was more effective than single modeling, however, in bringing children to the level of terminal performance (remaining confined with the dog in the playpen). One month after the completion of treatment, twice as many children in the *multiple modeling* group as in the other two groups completed the terminal task.

The results of the two experiments converge in demonstrating that observation of fearless peer models, either "in person" or filmed, resulted in generalized, stable reductions in the child's avoidance behavior. Some other data on the children's fears, collected as part of the second study, make it clear that this kind of treatment has some distinct limitations. Children who were generally anxious and fearful (according to mothers' interviews and questionnaire reports) benefited somewhat less from exposure to models than less fearful subjects. This led the authors to conclude that

> modeling procedures must be further modified or supplemented with additional techniques to effect substantial reduction of avoidance tendencies in subjects who display generalized patterns of anxiety. Such persons are unlikely to experience marked decrements in emotional responsiveness on the basis of a single exposure to a graded series of modeling situations (10, 106).

Dependence on Peers

Under extraordinary circumstances, peers may serve more general functions than those of reinforcing and modeling; even in the very early years they can become the chief objects of the child's attachment and emotional dependence. This was dramatically illustrated in the unusual study conducted by Anna Freud and a colleague (24) of 6 German-Jewish orphans whose parents were killed in the gas chambers during World War II. These children arrived at the same concentration camp when they were a few months old, and were always together as a group thereafter. When they were all between 3 and 4 years old, they were taken to live together in a large country house in England, where they were systematically observed for a year. By this time, the dependence these children had on each other appeared to be similar to the kind of attachment normal children have toward their mothers.

> The children's positive feelings were centered exclusively in their own group. It was evident that they cared greatly for each other and not at all for anybody or anything else. They had no other wish than to be together and became upset when they were separated from each other, even for short moments. No child would consent to remain upstairs while the others were downstairs, or vice versa, and no child would be taken for a walk or on an errand without the others. . . .

> The children's unusual emotional dependence on each other was borne out further by the almost complete absence of jealousy, rivalry, and competition, such as normally develop between brothers and sisters or in a group of contemporaries who came from normal families. There was no occasion to urge the children to "take turns"; they did it spontaneously since they were eager that everybody should have his share. Since the adults played no part in their emotional lives at the time, they did not compete with each other for favors or for recognition. They did not tell on each other and they stood up for each other automatically whenever they felt that a member of the group was unjustly treated or otherwise threatened by an outsider. They were extremely considerate of each other's feelings . . . (24, 133).

During the year's observation, the children never formed as close or strong ties with adults as they had with each other. It appears that the reward value of the other children continued to be higher than that of adults. In the authors' words, "their companions of the same age were their real love objects. . . . This explains why the feelings of the six children toward each other show a warmth and spontaneity which is unheard of in ordinary relations between young contemporaries" (24, 166).

SOCIAL STRUCTURE OF NURSERY SCHOOL GROUPS

With these quantitative and qualitative changes in peer interactions—particularly increased social participation—the children in a nursery school constitute a social group. Every social group is characterized by a differentiated hierarchical system of positions which gives some order and regularity to the interactions among members of the group. This system of positions constitutes the structure of the group. In the nursery school, as in all social groups, hierarchies of status positions emerge very shortly after the group is formed and can be detected easily (29).

The factors that determine the child's position in the social hierarchy in nursery school are parallel to those that determine an individual's status in any social group. Certain personality characteristics, skills, and abilities fit the individual for particular roles. Some seem to be "leaders," interacting with many children, winning friends and influencing people easily. As we have already seen, some children are "general reinforcers," giving attention, approval, and affection to many other children. Some are—and remain—aggressive and dominant, even at the cost of unpopularity and friendlessness; others are submissive and dependent, orienting themselves toward the teacher, rejecting other children, withdrawing from social interaction, and remaining socially isolated.

Even the child's physical characteristics may affect his social status during the preschool years. The strong, good-looking, competent boy is generally more socially successful than his immature-looking, unattractive peer. Ugliness, physical deformity, and even skin color or a different way of speaking may put the child in an inferior social status position.

The correlates of popularity and unpopularity (high and low social status) are generally investigated by means of observational and/or sociometric techniques. In the latter technique, children are interviewed and asked to name (or choose from a board containing pictures of all the children in the nursery school), for example, the children they especially like to play with, sit next to, never want to play with.

Popularity or high status in nursery school, as measured by sociometric techniques, is correlated with frequency of friendly approaches to others and extent of participation in associative play (48). Data from other observational studies indicate that popular children—those frequently chosen as "liked" by their peers—are more likely than unpopular children to provide their peers with nurturance and social reinforcements (e.g., giving attention or approval, giving affection, indicating acceptance, imitating another child, willingly complying with another's request, and giving tokens of friendship; *51, 235*). Furthermore, they tend to be positively socially reinforcing to many children; they "spread their joy around" (*51, 235*). In contrast, children frequently chosen as "disliked" were more likely to manifest rejection-exclusion behaviors (e.g., denying participation, refusing to share or cooperate, ignoring, criticizing, insulting, blaming, tattling, or engaging in more openly aggressive behaviors such as demanding, annoying, physically attacking, or threatening to attack), and they gave this negative reinforcement to many of their peers (*15*).

Not surprisingly, children with high sociometric status are frequently designated by their peers as "friendly to others," "liking to play near others," "helping others when they are hurt or sad," and "talking with other children a lot" (*50*). On the other hand, children who are disliked are perceived by peers as displaying a great deal of aggressive behavior—such as fighting, hitting, yelling at others and at the teacher, and hurting others.

Two other variables related to reactions to the nursery school situation are also correlated with high social status. Compared with their relatively unpopular peers, popular children are cooperative and comply readily with school routines. Their peers regard them as cooperative, helpful, and compliant with the teacher's wishes. These data do not imply that the popular child is overly compliant or submissive to authority, but rather that he is willing "to modulate his own behavior and to make necessary compromises toward the peaceful and efficient operation of the group" (*51, 235*).

Emotional dependence on adults (seeking attention, comfort, and support from teachers, for example), however, is significantly and negatively related to social participation and popularity. Constant seeking of affection and attention from adults (e.g., wanting to sit on laps, clinging to adults) will obviously interfere with maintaining active relationships with peers.

But peer-oriented dependency seems to contribute to popularity—that is, this characteristic is correlated with sociometric status. A child who needs help, affection, and support from his companions actually raises his social status. Perhaps young children are somewhat flattered at having companions come to them for this type of nurturance. In short,

> a child's peer status will not suffer because of his dependency-striving and may even be enhanced if: a) the child directs many of his appeals to members of the peer group rather than to adults; b) his appeals for help, affection, and support are not so intense as to interfere with active peer participation; c) he expresses his needs in school-appropriate ways such as through help- and approval-seeking rather than affection-seeking (*51, 244*).

Prejudice Among Preschoolers. Most behavioral scientists agree that the accomplishment of children's thorough, meaningful racial integration depends on having satisfying interactions with peers of different racial groups from the very early years onward. In theory, at least, nursery school should provide opportunities for such interactions—although, unfortunately, some children develop race prejudice very early in life.

Awareness of race differences and negative reactions toward black children are common among white 3-year-olds (60). The positive value attached to white skin and negative reactions to dark skin, characteristic of American culture, are clearly discernible among preschool children, both white and black. In doll-play situations, for example, preschool white boys tend to attribute many undesirable characteristics and behaviors (aggressive, bad, stupid) to blacks, and this trend increases between ages 2 and 5 (3).

The effects of prejudice on the black child's self-image are reflected in his high evaluation of white skin. When shown pictures of boys of different skin colors and asked "Which is your brother?" over 40 percent of black 3- and 4-year-olds chose a picture of a white boy (17, 18). In another study, black and white children in the North and the South were presented with pictures and asked to indicate the children they would like to be and the ones they would like as playmates. Of all the groups studied, Southern black children made the fewest choices of children of their own race (53). Black children frequently expressed negative attitudes toward self and toward their race in completing incomplete stories involving social problems depicted in colored drawings. They seldom depicted blacks as leaders or winners in games, but often described them as aggressors or "bad guys." A relatively small proportion of black children made choices of pictures of children of their own race in selecting playmates, companions to go home with, and guests for a birthday party (61).

Can integrated nursery schools help solve the critical social problem of race prejudice that, as these data indicate, has already been acquired by the preschool period? At least tentatively, the answer seems to be positive.

Evidence for this may be found in one intensive study of an interracial nursery school in the South, in which 5 black and 5 white children between 2½ and 3½ years of age were systematically observed for a total of over 15 hours. None of the children had had any real experience with children of the other race before entering nursery school. During the first few weeks of attendance at school, the children were intrigued with their new surroundings and spent their time exploring and playing. Racial characteristics did not seem to influence their thinking or activities.

After several weeks, however, several children gave evidence of awareness of the racial characteristics differentiating the group, some of them responding positively and some negatively. For example, one little girl stood next to a black boy and placing her arm beside his said, "Pink and brown are very pretty together." There was little evidence of strong rejection of black children by the whites, but some beginnings of race prejudice were noted, as the following recorded behavioral sequence demonstrates.

Lyle (white) and Dan (Negro) were in the bathroom washing their hands. Without immediate provocation, Lyle looked up at Dan and said, "I don't like black and you're black. I don't like your nose and I won't play with you."

Later in the period . . . Lyle and Dan were lying next to each other during rest period, Lyle said, "I don't like black and brown." He repeated this, "I don't like black and brown." Dan said, "I like _____." Lyle: "I don't like your face, I don't like your nose." (60, 60).

Fortunately, integration seemed to be effective in overcoming prejudice. No strong, lasting rejection of black children was observed in this integrated group. In fact, by the middle of the school year, children no longer commented about race or mentioned racial similarities or differences, nor were the children's social roles determined by racial group membership. Instead,

> The interaction between children appeared to depend, as it does in most types of social interaction, upon the degree to which the relationship between individuals satisfied each other's needs. The results indicated no general differences in the behavior of the two races in the types of behavior shown or in the relative amounts of time spent in own-race and other-race interaction (59, 207).

Apparently race prejudice can be overcome, and racial integration can be achieved relatively easily at this age. This may be accomplished simply by providing opportunities and training so that children of different races learn to interact in mutually satisfying ways. Racial integration in preschool may indeed be a vital first step, paving the way for complete and effective integration in all schools.

MALADJUSTMENT AND PSYCHOTHERAPY

A full discussion, or even a brief survey, of the vast range and variety of children's maladjustments, behavior problems, and psychological symptoms is beyond the scope of this book. It should be noted, however, that almost all preschool children display some minor behavior "problems," fears, or anxieties. In one longitudinal study, the incidence of each of 63 "problem" behaviors at each half-year interval during the preschool period was investigated (47). The average child of this age manifested between four and six problems. For most problems, incidence varied with age. For example,

> thumbsucking decreased as nail biting increased. Overt tempers, fears, jealousy, and . . . oversensitiveness increased to around four and four and one half years and then began subsiding. Since temper tantrums, fears, and overt jealousy occur at one age level in more than 50 per cent of our children, they cannot sensibly be regarded as neurotic behavior when occurring in these early years, as so commonly assumed, but rather as evidence of tension or as adjustive devices (47, 313).

Many of the nursery school child's problems seem to appear and then disappear after awhile, even without any treatment. And, as we learned earlier, some of these symptoms—tantrums and withdrawal, for example— seem to be readily amenable to change by the nursery school teacher's (or experimenter's) application of techniques of "behavior therapy" (see pp. 386–392). A child is considered "neurotic" or a "problem" only if the behaviors are persistent and if the frequency and/or intensity of these reactions interfere with effective functioning or the enjoyment of normal social interactions.

Infantile Autism

Even a very young child may manifest profound and enduring symptoms of emotional disturbance. One severe and dramatic form of maladjustment, *early infantile autism,* has attracted a great deal of attention recently from both clinicians and theorists. Autistic children are characterized by an extreme degree of isolation and aloneness, evident even in earliest infancy. As babies they do not respond with normal anticipatory gestures when adults reach to pick them up, and they do not adapt at all to the bodies of those who hold them. Their communication systems are badly impaired, and speech is not ordinarily used for interaction with others. Some autistic children are entirely mute or have only echolalic speech (repeating another person's verbalization precisely, but without meaning). Affirmation, when expressed, generally consists of repetition of what someone has said, rather than the word "yes."

These children display a kind of obsessive insistence on "sameness"; they reveal great anxiety in new and unfamiliar environments. In addition, they engage in a tremendous amount of repetitive, ritualistic behavior such as rocking, wiggling fingers, and making faces. Objects are a source of intense fascination for autistic children, but they are not interested in people (40, 57).

O. Ivar Lovaas, who has worked extensively and intensively with autistic children, described a group of ten, with whom he has had contact, in this way:

> Some of the children were completely unresponsive to social stimuli and evidenced no social or intellectual behavior. They were so oblivious to their surroundings that they behaved as if they were blind and deaf. They were completely engrossed in self-stimulatory behaviors, such as spinning objects, rocking in sitting or standing positions, twirling, flapping their wrists, and gazing at lights and at their cupped hands. In six of the children, vocal behaviors were limited to occasional vowel productions having no discernible communicative intent. The behavior of such children could be completely recorded under two categories: self-stimulation and vocal output. Self-stimulation took up from 70 to 95 per cent of the child's waking day, and vocal behaviors anywhere from 10 to 35 per cent. . . . About 75 per cent of the children would engage in tantrum behavior which included smearing of feces, biting attending adults, and self-mutilation (46, 8–9).

In some extreme cases, self-destructive and self-mutilating behaviors included continuous, severe biting of one's own flesh—in some cases to the point of tearing the flesh away and exposing the bone—and persistent, severe head-banging.

Traditional psychotherapeutic methods, in which the therapist attempts to establish a personal bond with the child, have not generally produced noticeable improvements. It is therefore particularly remarkable to find that application of "behavior therapy" techniques of reinforcement has sometimes resulted in marked behavior changes, if not cures. The training methods employed are in many cases radical ones and even seem cruel at times, but those who apply them maintain that the results (which they say could not possibly be achieved by other methods) justify their use.

For example, Lovaas, one of the leading exponents of behavior therapy, reports that the self-destructive behavior of autistic children may be extinguished by punishment of these behaviors when they occur, either by isolation of the child or by administration of a painful shock to him each time he shows such behavior. In two children with whom Lovaas worked, self-destructive behaviors were suppressed within minutes and remained suppressed for 11 months (46). Analogously, echolalia can also be brought under control by reinforcement, and suppressed in some cases within less than a month, by punishment of its appearance while appropriate speech is rewarded by food, attention, or a hug.

Through reinforcement, autistic children may also learn to approach others. Two autistic children who were unresponsive to any form of social stimulation were placed in a room that had an electrified floor. They were given a powerful electric shock which was terminated whenever they sought the company of adults who were present. The adults became associated with pain reduction (termination of shock) and thus acquired positive, rewarding properties. After a few trials with shocks, the children began to show real interest in observing the adults. Moreover, the effects generalized, and they began to seek physical contact with adults and to make adjustments to being held by them.

By use of reinforcement techniques, these children may be "taught" to imitate many kinds of behavior. The training begins with simple imitations in which

> the child is required to attend to and match a simple bodily action (standing up, pointing) or to manipulate a single object when only that object is present (cranking a toy ukelele, dialing a telephone). Complex imitations involve matching of the adult's behavior in relationship to a whole set of objects, which may differ in color, size, and shape (such as placing a ball in a cup, instead of a bowl, or selecting one of four geometric shapes) (46, 43).

Lovaas trained autistic children in 60 such imitative tasks. In the first training task, 50 or more trials were required before mastery, but later imitations were acquired very quickly, often with one presentation. After successful training on the 60 tasks, the child had acquired a generalized tendency to imitate and would imitate many actions of the experimenter.

Another group of investigators worked intensively with two autistic children, isolated them in a room for 21 days, and used food, water, and release from physical restraint to reinforce imitative responses. They, too, found that the tendency to imitate generalized, and after some training, many responses were imitated after only the first or second presentation by the model.

Following the 3-week intensive training period,

> the ward staff and parents of the children were trained in using reinforcement techniques, which they applied two to three hours daily during training sessions with the children. Five months after the initial training period, Sonny and Becky had increased their behavioral repertoires beyond imitative responding. Both children can now print the complete alphabet, using either a pure visual model or a visual-motor model. They also know the phonetic names of many of the letters. They can cut out figures with scissors and throw a basketball through a net. They can aim and hit targets with a dart gun with considerable accuracy, and can also name various parts of the human anatomy as they are pointed out. Sonny can now spontaneously emit simple vocal requests, and can name over 200 objects and pictures upon presentation. He is now beginning to learn complete sentences and can answer certain simple questions. Although Becky has not progressed as rapidly with language, she can also name some parts of the body and some objects and pictures. The continued progress made during the months following the training period would indicate the changes in behavior are not transitory. . . .

> The major contribution of the short-term intensive imitative training period would seem to be the establishment, in a relatively short period of time, of a large number of behaviors which can be used by parents, teachers, and others as the foundation for working toward a broader and more spontaneous behavioral repertoire in the autistic child (33, 41–42).

Psychotherapy

As we have seen in the preceding discussion and in earlier sections on the treatment of certain behavior problems in nursery school, "behavior therapy" seems to be an appropriate and effective technique for reducing the frequency and intensity of some kinds of symptoms, at least for some children. But many serious emotional disturbances and behavioral symptoms reflecting profound emotional maladjustment may be much more resistant to change by such "simple" means. Treating these problems, which are generally rooted in complex, upset family relations, may require highly specialized techniques of psychotherapy that are designed to reveal the child's fundamental conflicts, conscious and unconscious, and to help him to "handle" them.

There are many "schools" of psychotherapy, each with its own theories, concepts, and techniques, and all of them claim some "success" in treating children. Regardless of the "school" to which he adheres, the highly trained psychotherapist attempts to establish close relationships with his patient, providing an atmosphere of warmth, acceptance, and security. Ordinarily, the therapist works with the child in a series of sessions, and confers with his parents. "Complete acceptance of the child is shown by the therapist's attitude. She maintains a calm, steady, friendly relationship with the child. She is careful never to show any impatience. She guards against any criticism and reproof—either direct or implied. She avoids praise for actions or words" (6, 239).

All psychotherapy can be viewed as a learning process—the therapist acting as a kind of teacher, the patient as a learner. Ideally, psychotherapeutic settings facilitate the acquisition of new, constructive, and adaptive responses, which are to be substituted for habitual, but inadequate and maladjustive reactions.

Techniques of Therapy. Play is commonly used as a therapeutic device, the disturbed child using dolls and toys to express his anxieties, problems, and emotions freely and to "break through his defenses against anxiety." This permits both the child and the therapist to arrive at deeper understanding (insights) of the child and the sources of his difficulties. This, in turn, gives him some leverage to deal with his problems in a more constructive way. Erikson suggests that "the child's play is the infantile form of the human ability to deal with experiences by creating model situations and to master reality by experiment and planning. . . . To 'play it out' in play is the most natural self-healing measure childhood affords" (22, 10–11).

Nondirective Play Therapy. In nondirective play therapy, the child is given a great deal of latitude to do or say what he wants. Throughout the sessions, the therapist is friendly and interested but gives no direct suggestions. He remains alert to what the child is expressing in play and conversation, but gives the child complete freedom "to play out his accumulated feelings of tensions, frustration, insecurity, aggression, fear, bewilderment and confusion" (5, 16).

> By playing out these feelings he brings them to the surface, gets them out in the open, faces them, learns to control them, or abandons them. When he has achieved emotional relaxation, he begins to realize the power within himself to be an individual in his own right, to think for himself, to make his own decisions, to become psychologically more mature, and, by so doing, to realize selfhood.

> The play-therapy room is good growing ground. In the security of this room where the *child* is the most important person, where he is in command of the situation and of himself, where no one tells him what to do, no one criticizes what he does, no one nags, or suggests, or goads him on or pries into his private world, he suddenly feels that here he can unfold his wings; he can look squarely at himself, for he is accepted completely; he can test out his ideas; he can express himself fully; for this is *his* world, and he no longer has to compete with such other forces as adult authority or rival contemporaries or situations where he is a human pawn in a game between bickering parents, or where he is the butt of someone else's frustrations and aggressions. He is an individual in his own right. . . .

> It is a unique experience for a child suddenly to find adult suggestions, mandates, rebukes, restraints, criticisms, disapprovals, support, intrusions gone. They are all replaced by complete acceptance and permissiveness to be himself (5, 16).

As a consequence of this therapy, "the child gains the courage to move ahead, to become a more mature and independent individual" (5, 21).

Others who use nondirective play involve the child in more discussion, generally directing his attention to the immediate situations, present activities, feelings, and emotions, rather than to past circumstances and events that have influenced his behavior. These sessions are "growth experiences" for the child because, experiencing a unique emotional relationship in which he is completely accepted, he is more likely to try new solutions to problems and to learn to deal adequately with problems which were previously upsetting (1).

According to some therapists, free and spontaneous play techniques are particularly indicated with children whose neurotic traits are of long standing. They maintain that youngsters who are inhibited, repressed, extremely hostile, excessively timid, or overly meticulous are most likely to benefit from this kind of treatment (1, 50).

Directive Play Therapy: Psychoanalytic Techniques. The use of play as a therapeutic device originated in early attempts to apply psychoanalytic techniques to children. In psychoanalytic therapy with adults, free association and dream interpretation are among the principal techniques employed to uncover the patient's basic conflicts and sources of emotional maladjustment. Since these methods require a high degree of verbal facility and comprehension on the part of the patient, they have limited value for the treatment of children.

Anna Freud, the daughter of Sigmund Freud, was one of the first to recognize the therapeutic potential of play as a partial substitute for more verbal treatment methods. In her efforts to understand the child and his conflicts, she used systematic observation of play, combined whenever possible with reports of dreams and daydreams, free associations, and direct discussion (23).

Most psychoanalytic therapists use "interpretations" of the child's behavior in the therapy sessions, although Anna Freud herself uses them sparingly. Interpretation consists of "making connections for the child where he himself sees none. Sometimes these connections are between the past and the present; sometimes, between a defense and a feeling; sometimes, between a fantasy and a feeling" (44, 379).

Through interpretation, the analyst hopes to help the child to achieve some insights into his behavior and problems.

> The therapist hopes that the child will learn enough about himself to recognize his feelings and his defenses and deal with them directly. In the process of achieving this, one tries to make the unconscious conscious to the child. . . . Child psychoanalysts work above all on the past, thereby providing a cleared and improved ground for future development (44, 380).

Psychoanalysts are convinced that their kind of treatment is essential for alleviating certain kinds of symptoms, such as acute anxiety (nightmares and night terrors, for example) and a sense of helplessness and inadequacy. For children manifesting such symptoms,

> treatment will be directed toward determining the intrapsychic conflicts that are causing the conscious feeling of anxiety. Since the conflicts are usually completely or partially unconscious, treatment will have to be by psychoanalysis or by psychotherapy that is psychoanalytically oriented. . . . such cases should be treated *only* by a child analyst because of the possibility of malignant outcome (56, 72).

Directive Play Therapy: Controlled Techniques.   Needless to say, not all therapists would agree that the long, intensive, and expensive process of psychoanalysis is required for alleviating such symptoms. David Levy, for example, advocates the use of a technique that he calls "release therapy" (45). In this approach, the therapist supplies the dolls and other play material to the child and depicts a plot concerned with what he feels is the child's major problem, e.g., separation from the mother. The technique is particularly useful in relieving severe anxiety, fear reactions, or night terrors precipitated by traumatic experiences (surgical operations, accidents, divorce of parents). According to Levy, the technique is most useful for children under 10 who present a relatively recently acquired "symptom picture, precipitated by a specific event in the form of a frightening experience" (45, 916). Moreover,

> it is important that the child is suffering from something that happened in the past and not from a difficult situation going on at the time of treatment. Release therapy cannot be applied, for example, to a child suffering from the results of maternal rejection or overprotection. In such cases the mother and not the child is the primary or even the exclusive object of therapy (45, 916).

Parent Participation.   Most therapists maintain that successful therapy requires full cooperation from the child's parents—not only in the early stages but also throughout treatment, in some cases for long periods of time. When consulted about a child's emotional problems, then, the therapist must first direct his attention to the personalities and emotional problems of the parents.

The type and amount of psychological help recommended for the parents will, of course, vary with the complexity of both the child's and the parents' problems.

> If their emotional problems are deeply ingrained and represent established neuroses or even psychoses it may then be necessary to spend a considerable period of time and effort in helping them. At times, however, parents have strayed from a proper role because of ignorance or mild emotional problems which are amenable to short-term psychotherapy easily carried out by a general practitioner or pediatrician. Obvious defects in the parental attitude may sometimes be removed by a few discussions. The overdemanding mother who has ritualized home routines may be sufficiently flexible to accept the physician's advice in the direction of more leniency. The father who spends little time with

his children, feeling that his role in the family as far as they are concerned is unimportant, may be stimulated to greater activity by a physician's well-chosen comments (21, 137).

Removal from the Home.   In some cases, the parents are so uncoop-erative or incapable of change that their interactions with the child actually counteract the therapist's efforts. Under these circumstances, if the child's maladjustment is severe enough, he may be taken away from his own family and placed in a foster home or institution.

In general, this is a "last resort" technique, "one to be avoided when-ever there are possible alternatives" (58, 401). There are many uncertainties and psychological hazards in institutionalization or foster home placement.

The child who is placed outside his home is by no means guaranteed a more stable life; more than likely, he will have to endure a succession of foster homes, placement agency workers, and institution staff. In addition to these external difficulties, placement also puts an additional strain on the child. The placed child feels rejected, guilty, and unworthy, and expects a repetition of the experience. He cannot help but blame his parents for their desertion, and one can readily imagine the problems which this angry, disappointed, and guilty child will bring to the substitute parents. His sense of identity is shaken by the loss of his parents and, all in all, his emotional turmoil is exacerbated by the separation. Some child care workers have therefore come to think that his own home, no matter how bad, is still preferable to placement (44, 456).

Institutionalization or foster home placement is so drastic a step that it should be made *only* when all other possible alternatives fail, and "the long-range goals warrant the risks and the pain" (44, 456).

SUMMARY

In nursery school, the child encounters new agents of socialization in the persons of his teachers and peers. Attendance at nursery school is not likely to stimulate the intellectual functioning of middle-class children, but may affect personality and social behavior. After entering nursery school, most children make rapid gains in social participation; compared with peers who do not attend, they become less inhibited and more spontaneous, inde-pendent, self-assertive, self-reliant, curious, and interested in the environ-ment.

Individualized attention by the teacher may reduce a child's maladaptive reactions (withdrawal, or regressive and submissive behavior), strengthen adaptive behavior, and raise the levels of the child's self-confidence, frustra-tion tolerance, and ability to persist in working on difficult problems. More-over, in the course of their regular program, nursery school teachers can apply the principles of "behavior therapy" (rewarding desirable behavior; ignoring or punishing undesirable responses) to modify the behavior of their pupils, reducing their aggression and increasing their cooperation.

Peers become agents of socialization by reinforcing certain of the child's responses and by serving as models for imitation and identification. As children advance in age, they spend more time in social interactions with peers and less time in idleness and solitary play. Four-year-olds reinforce peers' behavior more than 3-year-olds do—using attention, approval, affection, and acceptance, as well as giving objects, as reinforcements. Aggression is frequently and strongly reinforced by preschool peers, and peers may serve as models for aggressive or altruistic behavior. Moreover, a child's fears—e.g., fear of dogs—may be reduced by observing live or filmed peers responding to feared stimuli in calm, relaxed ways.

Nursery school groups manifest hierarchical structures. High status or popularity is associated with friendliness, frequent participation in cooperative play, and tendencies to provide others with nurturance and social reinforcement. Emotional dependence on adults is negatively correlated with popularity.

Almost all nursery school children manifest some "problem" behaviors, but most problems disappear after awhile without any special treatment. Severe trauma and enduring behavior problems may require specialized treatment, however. The techniques of behavior therapy have proved effective in eliminating many relatively minor behavior problems, and have also been used successfully in treating some severe maladjustments—including cases of early infantile autism. In their treatment of serious emotional problems, most psychotherapists attempt to establish close, warm, accepting, secure relationships with patients. Play is commonly used in diagnosis and therapy, although different "schools" of clinicians use and interpret the child's play in different ways.

Case Material. Peter B

The early signs of dependency on his mother, conformity to adults, and fearfulness of the environment, already present in Peter at age 2, became much stronger during the preschool period. By the time Peter was ready to begin school he was a meek and mild boy eager to please his teacher and afraid of the bustling and energetic activity of other school-age boys. Let us trace Peter's development in relation to the processes discussed in the previous two chapters.

Sex-Typing. Both of Peter's parents fostered his timidity, his interest in sedentary activities, and his avoidance of the rough play of preschool boys. They were not bothered by his corresponding passivity and fear and made no attempt to punish these behaviors. If Peter cried when a boy grabbed his toy, his mother felt sorry for him. If Peter decided to lie down in the middle of an activity, his mother usually approved and remarked, "What a good boy he is." During sunny afternoons, Peter frequently stayed indoors leafing through magazines or listening to music, and Mrs. B generally encouraged his quiet, intellectual interests.

Peter was not adopting traditional boyish interests. He preferred books to wrestling, withdrawal to retaliation, and girls rather than boys as play-mates. These tendencies were accepted by both his mother and father, and they increased in strength as he grew older.

Peter's passivity was partially related to his identification with his father. Mr. B. was himself quiet and retiring, and the masculine role-model he presented to his son was congruent with the behavior he encouraged.

At the same time, Peter was also adopting many of his mother's characteristics. Mrs. B believed in neatness, compulsive adherence to routine, and the avoidance of aggression. Peter's desire to please his mother and his partial identification with her resulted in the adoption of many of her attitudes and behaviors. By age 4, Peter was the most compulsive boy in the entire population studied at the Fels Institute. He regularly put his toys away neatly; he never failed to wash his hands when they were dirty; and he became upset if a standard routine was altered in any way. On one occasion, the man who regularly mowed the lawn left the mower out in the rain; this was the first time the mower had not been returned to the garage. Peter became agitated and cried hysterically until someone brought the mower inside—something that was "routine" in Peter's experience.

Superego Development. By age 5, Peter had developed a precociously strict superego. He cried bitterly when he was punished and ran to his mother to be kissed and pardoned after violating some rule. He acceded to all of the major demands that were made of him. To get Peter to obey required only a sharp, "Peter—stop that."

Patterns of Maternal Reward and Punishment. Peter's mother was relatively consistent in the administration of rewards and punishments. She characteristically rewarded dependent overtures toward her and punished independence and autonomous action. If Peter wished to walk next door to a friend's house, he had to ask permission to do so.

It is not surprising that Peter was excessively dependent. He characteristically solicited help in problem situations, whether it was getting on or off a bicycle or putting on his pajamas. Frequently he would climb on a living-room chair and, finding it difficult to get down, cry for someone to help him out of this precarious position. Any semblance of physical or verbal aggression was immediately punished, and Peter rarely expressed aggression to parents or playmates. If another child attacked him, Peter would cry or scream, but rarely defended himself.

During these years, Mrs. B was extremely restrictive, screening Peter's playmates and selecting his activities with great care. This restrictiveness strengthened the fear and timidity Peter had already shown at age 2. By 5 years of age, he was afraid to go on slides, afraid to fight, afraid to climb to high places, and afraid to ride a bike too rapidly for fear that he might hurt himself. He was clumsy and poorly coordinated—all of which led to rejection by other boys who enjoyed gross motor activity and saw Peter as a "sissy." Peer rejection, in turn, made Peter even more fearful of engaging in social interaction with other boys.

Peter's speech was still retarded at 5 years of age, largely because his mother continued to reward his infantile speech patterns. He lisped and many of his phrases were infantile in structure. For example, he said, "thore" rather than "store" or "me go home" rather than "I will go home." Rather than ignore or discourage these expressions, Mrs. B actually rewarded them by speaking to Peter in his own infantile way.

Verbatim reports of his behavior at the Fels nursery school vividly described Peter at 3½ years of age.

> Babyish in appearance—a big, baby stare, long, curly eyelashes, and a rosebud mouth. He showed extreme caution and would back away from any situation that smacked of danger. When threatened he would shake his head, clasp his hands, and beg in a frantic tone, "No—no—no." His role with peers was a sedentary, passive, and shrinking one. He stayed out of the swirl of the activity of the other children and seemed like a "clam without a shell." His play showed a great deal of *oldmaid* preciseness and prissiness. He made neat little block arrangements, spent a long time straightening up the shelves, getting things in line, and putting things into small spaces. He was very anxious about small details, becoming upset if the routine was at all changed. He would fuss at the teacher for any small variation in routine and often followed the teacher about doing his own manner of straightening up. He liked everything to be just right. With the staff of the Nursery School he was highly conforming and very dependent. He liked to help clean up, like to wash, liked to take a nap, and often told others what to do in a rather pointed way. Signs of guilt were quite apparent and whenever he dirtied something, wet himself, or committed what he regarded as a violation, he became very tense and apprehensive as if he felt that he had been a "bad boy."

One year later, at 4½ years of age, he was similarly described:

> Conforming, good, kind, and nonaggressive. One of the Nursery School teachers remarked, "Gentle Peter, meek and mild." He always showed an extreme degree of fear: fear of the unknown, fear of height, fear of being attacked by other children, fear of being hurt, and fear of doing the wrong thing. For example, some of the children in the Nursery School were being called upstairs for scientific experiments in another part of the Institute. Peter became very fearful of these experiments and when someone came down the stairs, Peter would say, "Not me—not me, today—tomorrow I'll go with you—but not today."

At age 4½ Peter was nonaggressive, very dependent, and showed little interest in mastering new problems. He was subject to many sources of anxiety. He was anxious over loss of nurturance from adults, and this contributed to his conformity to their demands. His fear of physical harm was unusually intense and this caused him to avoid many peer group activities. He typically showed signs of strong guilt following any mischievous behavior and misdeeds. The anticipation of making a mess, disobedience, or talking-back to his mother was so anxiety-provoking that Peter inhibited these reactions completely.

As we shall see later, Peter's conformity, passivity, withdrawal, and compulsivity were almost as strong at age 20 as they were at age 5.

Case Material. Jack L

Jack, like Peter, had a fairly strict superego, in that he showed concern with being obedient and doing the "right" thing. The two boys differed, however, in what they regarded as "right and proper." For Peter, passivity, dependency, and nonaggression were the proper modes of conduct. For Jack, activity, independence, and aggression were rewarded while passivity and dependence were viewed as "bad."

These two boys illustrate an important psychological principle: *Two children may have acquired dramatically different overt behaviors* (e.g., independence or dependence) *in response to the same underlying motives* (desire to please the parents and identification with parental models).

Sex-Typing. The tendency of Jack's parents to push him toward traditional masculine activities was intensified during these years. Jack's father regularly brought home cars and mechanical gadgets and encouraged Jack to play ball with the older boys. His mother encouraged him to pursue energetic activities. In her mind, boys were supposed to be active and out-of-doors, and not, as in Peter's case, strolling around the house listening to music and looking at pretty pictures. His mother was unhappy because Jack was still sleeping with a doll at 2½ years of age, and she regarded this behavior as "sissified." When Jack was 4, he ran home several times because some bigger boys had attacked him on the street. His father punished him for running away from the boys and instructed him to fight back the next time he was attacked. From then on Jack rarely retreated from the aggression of agemates. Peter's parents would have punished him for fighting back; Jack's parents punished him for running away from a fight.

When he was almost 5, Jack became ill and, on recovering, temporarily developed a mild fear of other boys. His father became apprehensive and feared that Jack might become a sissy, unable to stand up to other boys. For some time thereafter, his father routinely shadow-boxed with Jack each night in order to build up his self-confidence and to make sure he would no longer be afraid of his peers.

It is important to recognize that Jack did not have a strong desire to be aggressive. For many boys, especially those from a rejecting home, it would not be necessary for parents to encourage aggression in order to insure that their child would "fight" with other boys. Aggressive behavior is characteristic of children who feel threatened and rejected. For such children, aggressive behavior is a way of expressing retaliation to the adult world.

Jack, however, was accepted at home. He was not extremely frustrated or insecure. Consequently, he felt no strong desire to hurt or injure others. Nevertheless, as his parents felt aggressivity was an appropriate behavior for him, he was gradually acquiring an aggressive bravado with his peers. However, the motive underlying his aggressive veneer was not anger at the world, but anxiety over rejection for not behaving in accordance with parental wishes.

Identification.   Jack was strongly identified with his father, often "helping" him at his place of business and, in play, adopting the role of the typical masculine heroes of young boys—a policeman, a cowboy, a fireman, or a football player. Jack was acquiring his father's mechanical and athletic interests but, in contrast to Peter, Jack's identification with his mother was weak.

Parental Attitudes Toward Dependency.   As Jack reached his fourth year, both parents put pressure on him to become more independent. They encouraged him to take his own bath, to dress himself, and to do errands for them. When Jack would whine for help his mother would ignore him and, in this fashion, she indirectly punished dependent overtures toward her.

This persistent training in independence had its inevitable result. By the time he was 5, Jack was taking his own bath, dressing himself, and priding himself on these self-help behaviors. He did errands around the neighborhood, and was encouraged to walk downtown, a distance of many blocks, to have his monthly haircut. Contrast this degree of independence at age 5 with the clinging, timid, fearful dependence of Peter at the same age.

When Jack came to the Nursery School at 5 years of age the Fels observer noted:

> Jack is handsome, capable, and vigorous, and endowed with techniques and personal abilities that made him a popular leader. He is the kind of little boy that is often seen in breakfast food advertisements or on the cover of *Parents* magazine. He is solidly built, broad-shouldered, big-boned, sturdy, and masculine in his posture and movements. Jack is robust, full of vigor, and has lots of muscular strength. He likes high, swift swinging; likes play that is full of stress, balance, and use of the muscles. He uses his whole body to express himself, standing with legs wide apart, hands on his hips, and with his whole-self full of importance. He is uninhibited in his frankness about his body, and is boyishly crude in many of his noises.

> He was always busily employed at something. When he was outdoors he concentrated on highly organized sand-play using trucks, cars, planes; building roads, airports, and garages. He had a close gang of other boys and was usually involved in stereotyped cops-and-robbers play. Jack did excellent carpentry work and he showed good judgment in constructing various objects. He was a recognized leader and organized some of the best group-play of the session. He did not dictate to the other children, but had a knack of holding the group together in getting something done that was fun. Jack was a universal favorite among the adults in the Nursery School. In general, Jack was able to take people and things pretty much at their own value, interact freely, and maintain his identity without having to be offensive.

The picture of Jack at age 5 was in marked contrast to the one drawn for Peter. Jack was independent and prided himself on it; Peter was dependent. Jack actively dealt with new problem situations; Peter was timid and withdrawing. Jack was interested in the traditional masculine activities of mechanical games and athletics; Peter liked to read and listen to music. Jack's parents encouraged independence, aggression, and masculine activities; Peter's parents encouraged dependence, passivity, and nonmasculine behavior.

There were, however, some basic similarities between the two boys. They both came from affectionate and accepting homes and both had fairly strict superegos. Both boys conformed to adult demands and were concerned with doing the right thing, because they were anxious about loss of adult nurturance. The differences in type of potential conflict were already established. Jack was anxious over not playing the masculine role as his parents defined it for him, and this was to be a source of future conflict. For Peter, a major source of future anxiety was his haunting sense of inadequacy and a fear of being hurt and attacked by the environment.

References

1. Allen, F. *Psychotherapy with children.* New York: Norton, 1942.
2. Allen, K., Hart, B., Buell, J. S., Harris, F. R., & Wolf, M. M. Effects of social reinforcement on isolate behavior of a nursery school child. *Child Develpm.*, 1964, *35*, No. 2, 511–518.
3. Ammons, R. B. Reactions in a projective doll-play interview of white males two to six years of age to differences in skin color and facial features. *J. genet. Psychol.*, 1960, *76*, 323–341.
4. Andrus, R., & Horowitz, E. L. The effect of nursery school training: insecurity feeling. *Child Develpm.*, 1938, *9*, 169–174.
5. Axline, V. M. *Play therapy.* Boston: Houghton Mifflin, 1947.
6. Axline, V. M. Accepting the child completely. In M. R. Haworth (Ed.), *Child psychotherapy: practice and theory.* New York: Basic Books, 1964, 239–242.
7. Baldwin, A. L. Socialization and the parent-child relationship. *Child Develpm.*, 1948, *19*, 127–136.
8. Baldwin, A. L. The effect of the home environment on nursery school behavior. *Child Develpm.*, 1949, *20*, 49–62.
9. Bandura, A., Grusec, J. E., & Menlove, F. L. Vicarious extinction of avoidance behavior. *J. pers. soc. Psychol.*, 1967, *5*, 16–23.
10. Bandura, A., & Menlove, F. L. Factors determining vicarious extinction of avoidance behavior through symbolic modeling. *J. pers. soc. Psychol.*, 1968, *8*, 99–108.
11. Bird, G. E. The effect of nursery school attendance upon mental growth of children. *(39th Yeab. nat. Soc. Stud. Educ.)* Chicago: Univer. Chicago Press, 1940, Part II, 81–84.
12. Brown, A. W., & Hunt, R. G. Relations between nursery school attendance and teachers' ratings of some aspects of children's adjustment in kindergarten. *Child Develpm.*, 1961, *32*, 585–596.
13. Brown, P., & Elliott, R. Control of aggression in a nursery school class. *J. exp. child Psychol.*, 1965, *2*, 103–107.

14. Challman, R. C. Factors influencing friendships among preschool children. *Child Develpm.*, 1932, *3*, 146–158.

15. Charlesworth, R., & Hartup, W. W. Positive social reinforcement in the nursery school peer group. *Child Develpm.*, 1967, *38*, 993–1002.

16. Chittenden, G. E. An experimental study in measuring and modifying assertive behavior in young children. *Monogr. Soc. Res. Child Develpm.*, 1942, *7*, No. 1.

17. Clark, K. B., & Clark, M. K. The development of consciousness of self in the emergence of racial identification in Negro preschool children. *J. soc. Psychol.*, 1939, *10*, 591–599.

18. Clark, K. B., & Clark, M. K. Skin color as a factor in racial identification of Negro preschool children. *J. soc. Psychol.*, 1940, *11*, 159–169.

19. Dawe, H. C. A study of the effect of an educational program upon language development and related mental functions in young children. *J. exp. Educ.*, 1942, *11*, 200–209.

20. Douglas, J. W. B., & Ross, J. M. The later educational progress and emotional adjustment of children who went to nursery schools or classes. *Educ. Res.*, 1964, *7*, 73–80.

21. English, O. S., & Finch, S. M. *Introduction to psychiatry.* New York: Norton, 1954.

22. Erikson, E. H. Toys and reasons. In M. R. Haworth (Ed.), *Child psychotherapy: practice and theory.* New York: Basic Books, 1964, 3–11.

23. Freud, A. Introduction to the technique of child analysis. *Nerv. ment. dis. Monogr.*, 1928, No. 48.

24. Freud, A., & Dann, S. An experiment in group up-bringing. In R. Eisler *et al.* (Eds.), *The psychoanalytic study of the child.* Vol. 6. New York: International Universities Press, 1951, 127–163.

25. Goodenough, F. L., & Maurer, K. A. The mental development of nursery school children compared with that of nonnursery school children. *(39th Yearb. nat. Soc. Stud. Educ.)* Chicago: Univer. Chicago Press, 1940, Part II, 161–178.

26. Green, E. H. Group play and quarreling among preschool children. *Child Develpm.*, 1933, *4*, 302–307.

27. Greenberg, P. J. Competition in children: an experimental study. *Amer. J. Psychol.*, 1932, *44*, 221–249.

28. Hartup, W. W. Peers as agents of social reinforcement. In W. W. Hartup & N. L. Smothergill (Eds.), *The young child: reviews of research.* Washington, D.C.: National Association for the Education of Young Children, 1967, 214–228.

29. Hartup, W. W. Peer interactions in childhood. In P. Mussen (Ed.), *Manual of child psychology.* New York: Wiley, in press.

30. Hartup, W. W., & Coates, B. Imitation of a peer as a function of reinforcement from the peer group and rewardingness of the model. *Child Develpm.*, 1967, *38*, 4, 1003–1016.

31. Hattwick, B. W. The influence of nursery school attendance upon the behavior and personality of the preschool child. *J. exp. Educ.*, 1936, *5*, 180–190.

32. Hicks, D. J. Imitation and retention of film-mediated aggressive peer and adult models. *J. pers. soc. Psychol.*, 1965, *2*, 97–100.

33. Hingtgen, J. N., Coulter, S. K., & Churchill, D. W. Intensive reinforcement of imitative behavior in mute autistic children. *Arch. gen. Psychiat.*, 1967, *17*, 36–43.

34. Honigmann, J. J. *Culture and personality.* New York: Harper & Row, 1954.

35. Jack, L. M. An experimental study of ascendant behavior in preschool children.

In L. M. Jack, E. M. Maxwell, I. G. Mengert et al. (Eds.), Behavior of the preschool child. *Univer. Iowa Stud. Child Welf.*, 1934, No. 9, *3*, 7–65.

36. Jersild, A. T., *Child psychology.* Englewood Cliffs, N.J.: Prentice-Hall, 1954 (4th ed).
37. Jersild, A. T., & Fite, M. D. The influence of nursery school experience on children's social adjustments. *Child Develpm. Monogr.*, 1939, No. 25.
38. Jersild, A. T., & Markey, F. V. Conflicts between preschool children. *Child Develpm. Monogr.*, 1935, No. 21.
39. Jones, H. E., & Jorgensen, A. P. Mental growth as related to nursery school attendance. *39th Yearb. nat. Soc. Stud. Educ.)* Chicago: Univer. Chicago Press, 1940, Part II, 207–222.
40. Kanner, L., & Eisenberg, L. Early infantile autism. *Psychiatric Res. Repo.*, 1957, *1*, 55–65.
41. Kawin, E., & Hoefer, C. *A comparative study of a nursery school versus a nonnursery school group.* Chicago: Univer. Chicago Press, 1931.
42. Keister, M. E., & Updegraff, R. A study of children's reactions to failure and an experimental attempt to modify them. *Child Develpm.*, 1937, *8*, 241–248.
43. Keister, M. E. The behavior of young children in failure: an experimental attempt to discover and to modify undesirable responses of preschool children to failure. *Univer. Iowa Stud. Child Welf.*, 1938, *14*, 27–82.
44. Kessler, J. W. *Psychopathology of childhood.* Englewood Cliffs, N.J.: Prentice-Hall, 1966.
45. Levy, D. M. Release therapy. *Amer. J. Orthopsychiat.*, 1939, *9*, 913–936.
46. Lovaas, O. I. A behavior therapy approach to the treatment of childhood schizophrenia. In J. Hill (Ed.), *Minnesota Symposium on Child Psychology.* Minneapolis: Univer. of Minnesota Press, 1967.
47. Macfarlane, J. W. Study of personality development. In R. G. Barker, J. S. Kounin, & H. F. Wright (Eds.), *Child behavior and development.* New York: McGraw-Hill, 1943.
48. McCandless, B. R., & Marshall, H. R. Sex differences in social acceptance and participation of preschool children. *Child Develpm.*, 1957, *28*, 421–425.
49. McKee, J. P., & Leader, F. B. The relationship of socioeconomic status to the competitive behavior of school children. *Child Develpm.*, 1955, *25*, 135–142.
50. Moore, S. G. The relation between children's sociometric status and their social behaviors as perceived by peers. Unpublished manuscript, University of Minnesota, 1964.
51. Moore, S. G. Correlates of peer acceptance in nursery school children. In W. W. Hartup & N. L. Smothergill (Eds.), *The young child: reviews of research.* Washington, D.C.: National Association for the Education of Young Children, 1967, 229–247.
52. Moore, S. G., & Updegraff, R. Sociometric status of preschool children related to age, sex, nurturance-giving and dependency. *Child Develpm.*, 1964, *35*, 519–524.
53. Morland, J. K. A comparison of race awareness in Northern and Southern children. *Amer. J. Orthopsychiat.*, 1966, *36*, 22–31.
54. Parten, M. B. Social participation among preschool children. *J. abnorm. soc. Psychol.*, 1932, *27*, 243–269.
55. Patterson, G. R., Littman, R. A., & Bricker, W. Assertive behavior in children: a step toward a theory of aggression. *Monogr. Soc. Res. Child Develpm.*, 1967, *32*, No. 5, 1–43.

56. Pearson, G. H. J. *Emotional disorders of children.* New York: Norton, 1949.

57. Rimland, B. *Infantile autism.* New York: Appleton-Century-Crofts, 1964.

58. Rotter, J. B. *Social learning and clinical psychology.* Engelwood Cliffs, N.J.: Prentice-Hall, 1954.

59. Stevenson, H. W. Studies of racial awareness in young children. In W. W. Hartup & N. L. Smothergill (Eds.), *The young child: reviews of research.* Washington, D.C.: National Association for the Education of Young Children, 1967, 206–213.

60. Stevenson, H. W., & Stevenson, N. G. Social interaction in an inter-racial nursery school. *Genet. Psychol. Monogr.,* 1960, *61,* 37–75.

61. Stevenson, H. W., & Stewart, E. C. A developmental study of racial awareness in young children. *Child Develpm.,* 1958, *29,* 400–409.

62. Stott, L. H., & Ball, R. S. Infant and preschool mental tests: review and evaluation. *Monogr. Soc. Res. Child Develpm.,* 1965, 30.

63. Thompson, G. G. The social and emotional development of preschool children under two types of educational programs. *Psychol. Monogr.,* 1944, *56,* No. 5.

64. Walsh, M. E. The relation of nursery school training to the development of certain personality traits. *Child Develpm.,* 1931, *2,* 72–73.

65. Walters, J. C., Pearce, D. & Dahms, L. Affectional and aggressive behavior of preschool children. *Child Develpm.,* 1957, *28,* 15–26.

66. Wellman, B. L. Iowa studies on the effects of schooling. *(39th Yearb nat. Soc. Educ.)* Chicago: Univer. of Chicago Press, 1940, Part II, 377–399.

67. Wellman, B. L. IQ changes of preschool and nonpreschool groups during the preschool years: a summary of the literature. *J. Psychol.,* 1945, *20,* 347–368.

part IV
Middle Childhood

11 Development in Middle Childhood

I. Intellectual-Cognitive Development

During the middle-childhood years, the child continues to develop physically, and his cognitive abilities change dramatically, becoming both more complex and better differentiated. At the same time, the child's social environment expands tremendously; there is his entrance into school and his increased contact with peers and nonparental adults which widen his intellectual and social horizons, bringing him new challenges, problems, and opportunities for personal and social growth. As a consequence of the continuing interaction between the rapidly maturing child and his expanding environment, the child's personality during these years becomes both richer and more complex and he emerges even more clearly as a unique individual.

In the present chapter, we will review very briefly the child's continued physical growth during this period, devoting most of our attention to the impressive intellectual and cognitive development which characterizes these years. In the following two chapters, we will examine the child's overall personality development and problems of adjustment, and the impact of his expanding social environment as he enters the wider world of school and the peer group.

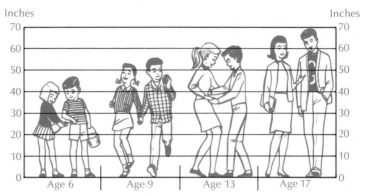

Inches   Inches

Fig. 11.1. Heights of boys and girls at various ages. (From *How Old Are You?* By permission of Metropolitan Life Insurance Co.)

PHYSICAL GROWTH FACTORS DURING MIDDLE CHILDHOOD

General Trends in Physical Development

By the age of 6, physical growth, which has been proceeding at a remarkably fast pace, has begun to decelerate. The average child of this age in America stands about 46 inches tall and weighs about 48 pounds (67). His height increases during the middle-childhood years at the rate of about 5 or 6 percent a year, his weight at the rate of somewhat over 10 percent a year. By the time he reaches the age of 12, his height has increased to about 60 inches, and his weight to about 85 pounds (67).

Up until the tenth year, boys, on the average, are slightly taller than girls. However, from then until about 15, girls are, on the average, slightly taller than boys—as any dancing school instructor can testify (69; see Fig. 11.1.) The pattern is similar with regard to weight. Until about 11 years of age, boys are slightly heavier than girls, but after that age girls weigh more.

The child's body proportions are already much like the adult's. The slight changes in build which occur in this period result largely from lengthening of the child's limbs (67).

Other changes occur, too. Because of deposits of various mineral salts, especially calcium phosphate, the 12-year-old's bones are harder, but easier to break, than the 6-year-old's. At about 6, the average child loses his first teeth, but by 12, he has most of his permanent ones (67). With advancing age from 6 to 12, blood pressure increases, and pulse rate decreases (67). The child needs more to eat and he eats more. Concomitantly, muscle tissue increases proportionately, and the child grows stronger. Sex differences in proportion of fat and muscle tissue, noted earlier, still obtain, with boys having more muscle mass and girls a greater proportion of body fat.

Although various aspects of growth (i.e., rates of development in dentition, height, weight, bone hardening) are generally correlated with one another, not all children develop in the same way or at the same rates. Some grow relatively more in height, others in weight, producing variations in general body types such as "tall and slender," or "short and stocky."

The remaining sections of this chapter will concentrate on the psychological processes and elements that are involved in cognition in the school-age child. The word cognition refers to the interpretation of sensory events, the understanding of words and numbers, the ability to manipulate these symbols in thinking, reasoning and the solving of problems, and the acquisition of beliefs about the environment. Stated in a more formal way, cognitive activity consists of the active processes of perception, memory, generation of ideas, evaluation, reasoning, and free association. These six cognitive processes—or functions—involve certain cognitive units which are manipulated in thought. The major cognitive units are images, symbols, concepts, and rules. Thus the growth of intelligence can be linked to the construction of a house. The processes involved in the building of a house include erection of a frame, laying down lines for power and plumbing, plastering, and painting; the units used in these functions are wood, wire, pipe, nails, and paint. The processes involved in the growth of intelligence include perception, memory, generation of hypotheses, evaluation, reasoning and free association; the units are images, symbols, concepts, and rules.

The Units in Cognitive Activity

Perceptual images are one kind of cognitive unit. The mental picture of your childhood home or an old friend is a perceptual image, and these images are probably the first cognitive structures to appear in the infant. (See Chapter 5 for a discussion of schema formation.)

Symbols are names for the letters, numbers, pictures, and words that have come to represent another object. In one sense, symbols are the simple associations the child has to a stimulus, be it a stop sign, the number 9, a skull and crossbones on a bottle, or the word "cat." *Concepts* are constructed from symbols and are names for a group of events, objects, or experiences that share a common set of characteristics (e.g., history, animals, happiness). *Concepts represent dimensions; symbols represent objects.*

Developmental Changes in Concepts. A concept allows a child to react similarly to different stimuli. Once a child possesses the concept "candy," he regards a variety of objects of different colors, shapes, and sizes as "candy" and reacts to them in an equivalent way (i.e., he will eat them). A concept is a symbolic way of noting similarity among events and objects that are, on the surface, different. As such, concepts allow children to bring order out of their experience.

Three attributes of a concept that change with development include the *validity* of the concept, the *status* of the concept, and the *accessibility* of the concept (12). The validity of a concept refers to the degree to which the child's understanding of the concept matches that of the larger social community. A particular 2-year-old's concept of the word "good" or "mother" is often personal and may not be similar to that of other 2-year-olds. As the child becomes older, the meaning of those concepts becomes more similar for all children. In that sense, the concept becomes more *valid*. Second, concepts improve their degree of articulation and their availability for use in thinking. A 3-year-old's concept of "size" is rather murky whereas an 8-year-old's understanding of this concept is clearer, more exact, more stable over time—and he is able to think about the size of objects. Finally, the child becomes increasingly able to talk about his concepts. They become more accessible to him and he can communicate his concepts to others. Ask a 5-year-old child about the concept of *goodness* or the concept of *number*, and he often says he doesn't know—although his behavior indicates that he does have some comprehension of these concepts. On the other hand, a 10-year-old can easily talk about these ideas and use them in his reasoning. In sum, with age, a concept increases its validity, status, and accessibility (12).

Finally, the child acquires *formal rules,* such as addition and subtraction, or *informal rules* (e.g., the belief that snakes are dangerous; that wood floats on water; that snow falls in winter). Rules are relations among concepts.

Images, symbols, concepts, and rules are the primary entities manipulated in thinking. The child is only able to understand information that either matches or is a little in advance of his own cognitive units. If a new picture, idea, equation, or word does not have some association or connection to his available cognitive units, he is apt to learn little from it.

COGNITIVE ACTIVITIES

Cognitive activity can be divided, at a very general level, into two types: *undirected* and *directed*. Undirected cognition refers to free associations, dreams, or reveries, and includes the free flow of thoughts that occur continually as the child walks home or stares out the window. There has not been much inquiry into this exciting and important kind of cognition because it is difficult to study the private, undirected associations of a child (or an adult). If one asks a child to report his free associations or to write them down, the situation is altered, and the undirected thought suddenly becomes directed. The child will view the situation as a problem and will automatically attempt to present an orderly, coherent, and even socially acceptable report of his thinking. The inquiry itself changes the nature of the phenomenon and we do not see the disorder that so often characterizes uncontrolled, free association.

Directed Thinking. Directed thinking refers to the cognitive processes that occur when the child tries to solve a problem given to him by others or one he sets for himself. The child knows there is a solution to a problem and he knows when he has arrived at an answer. The problem-solving process typically involves the following sequence: encoding, memory, generation of hypotheses, evaluation, deduction, and, when required, public report. We shall consider each of these processes in sequence. However, it is helpful to keep in mind the general changes that occur during the period between 5 and 12 years of age. The richness of the child's supply of words, concepts, and rules increases each year and this change is accompanied by a decreasing tendency to rely on images in problem-solving. The child becomes increasingly concerned with the degree of agreement between his concepts and those of other children and adults, and he becomes more apprehensive about making mistakes. Finally, his memory capacity appears to improve dramatically, and he demonstrates a greater ability to *recall* larger amounts of information.

Process 1:   Encoding

The perception and comprehension of information in the environment is the first process in all problem-solving sequences. Encoding involves selective attention to one event rather than another, and a labeling or interpreting of the information in the event. The child encodes—or interprets—information in the environment naturally and spontaneously, but the nature of his interpretation changes with age. The infant or very young child usually translates experience into images; the older child is more likely to use words and concepts. Consider the following figure: If this figure is shown to a 1-year-old he is likely to encode it as an image, for he has no other way to interpret it. The 6-year-old is likely to encode the figure using language—he might say, "It looks like a finger," or, "It looks like a pencil." If asked to reproduce it or select a figure from a set of similar ones, he might make an error that would reveal that he perceived it as resembling a finger or a pencil. He might draw it as   or   . We say that the 6-year-old assimilated the original figure to his language label. The school-age child typically uses words and concepts to interpret situations and the richer the child's repertoire of words and concepts, the more likely he will rely on them rather than images. This suggestion touches the issue of *eidetic imagery*.

Eidetic Imagery.   Only a few children and very few adults in the Western world can maintain a complete visual image of a picture so that when it is taken away the person can describe it in detail (21). The child who can do this is said to have eidetic imagery. About 5 to 10 percent of the population of American school children have eidetic imagery. They can "see" in its original color an image of a picture for 45 seconds after it is taken away from them and can report details of it. However, children and adults among nonliterate groups (the Ibo of eastern Nigeria, for example) have a frequency of eidetic imagery that is close to 20 percent (9). Moreover, occurrence of eidetic imagery among mentally retarded American children is also close to 20 percent (62). The higher frequency of eidetic imagery among the mentally

Fig. 11.2. Pairs of stimuli shown to children in the Gollin experiment. (From E. S. Gollin. Serial learning and perceptual recognition in children: training, delay, and order effect. *Percept. mot. Skills*, 1966, Vol. 23. By permission.)

retarded and the Ibo might be the consequences of inadequate language resources and the tendency to use images as the primary unit in converting experience to meaning.

Preference for Single Strategies of Encoding. The possibility that the child (or the adult) becomes accustomed to using one set of units to encode experience is part of a more general tendency toward inflexibility—a tendency to view a situation or problem in only one way. In one experiment *(15)* children had to learn to guess the animal that was represented by a set of fractionated lines (see Fig. 11.2). The child was first shown a set of lines that represented a particular animal (e.g., an elephant) and then was shown the complete drawing of the elephant. The child had to associate the two so that when only the set of fractionated lines was shown to him he could correctly guess what animal the stimulus represented. The *order* of presentation of the pairs was *always* the same. Some children were given only a few trials (i.e., a complete run through the various pairs of animals); others were given many trials. When the children were tested later with the fractionated drawings, the number of correct guesses depended on whether the order of presentation of the original stimuli remained the same as it was during the original learning or whether the order was changed. If the order was the same as earlier, the children who had been given many trials performed better. If the order was changed, the children who had been given fewer trials did better. It seems that all the children were learning both the association between the fractionated lines and the picture *as well as the order* of occurrence of each pair. The children given only a few trials had not overlearned a particular order of presentation of the animal pairs and thus did better when the order changed. They were more flexible. Intellectual development consists, in part, of the learning of codes for events. As it is often helpful for the child and adult to be able to shift codes for different events and different problems, it is helpful if he is given practice with diverse ways to code reality.

This conclusion has an important implication for educational practices. For example, many teachers have begun to use Cuisenaire rods to teach first graders the fundamentals of arithmetic and numeration. The rods are wooden sticks of different length and different colors. The number 1 is represented by a colored stick one unit long; the number 2 is represented by a stick of a different color twice as long as the one-unit stick. The advantage of this particular method of teaching numbers is that it gives the young child a concrete introduction to the concept of number as a magnitude estimator. Numbers are a new experience for the child. The stimulus $1 + 1 = \boxed{}$ is a new stimulus to be decoded. If the mental units given the child for decoding numbers are rods of different lengths and colors the child will build up quickly a strong tendency to translate all numbers and number problems into images of these rods. This method will be troublesome and disadvantageous when long division or multiplication problems are confronted. The young child should probably be weaned from the Cuisenaire representation of numbers before he becomes too strongly addicted to it and is unable to shift to a new translation system.

Encoding of Information and Attention.   The encoding process is directly related to age and individual differences in selectivity of attention; selective focusing on one particular aspect of an event rather than another. It will be recalled from Chapter 8 that both preschool and school-age children are more likely to attend to breaks and closes in lines $\pm$ than to changes in perspective.

Directed attention refers to the selected focusing of attention on one aspect of an event. Directed attention is relatively free from interference, and when a child is attending to an event his threshold for being distracted by other events is increased. It is difficult for children and adults to focus attention on more than one sensory input at any one time. A major difference between younger and older children is that the younger child may be unable to shift his focus of attention as rapidly as the older one—although the number of sensory events that can be attended to at any one time may be the same.

The Role of Expectancy.   The child's selectivity of attention is related, in part, to his *expectations*. If a child knows what events are about to happen (i.e., he has an expectancy of what he might see or hear), then he can prepare himself better for the event. Often such a preparation aids the accuracy of his perception. School-age children (kindergarten, and grades 2, 4, and 6) listened to a man's voice and a woman's voice simultaneously speaking two-word phrases (e.g., dog eat). The voices came simultaneously from two loud speakers placed 18 inches apart. One speaker was marked with the picture of a man's face, the other with a woman's face. When the child was to report the words spoken by the man's voice, the man's picture was

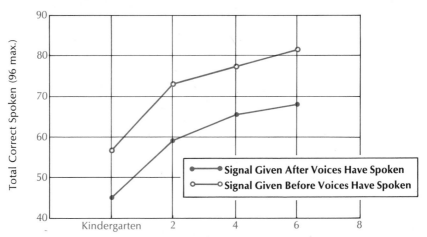

Fig. 11.3. Differences in amount of message reproduced as a function of whether the child was told to attend to the voice before or after he heard it. (From E. E. Maccoby. Selective auditory attention in children. In L. P. Lipsitt & C. C. Spiker (Eds.), *Advances in child development and behavior.* New York: Academic Press, 1967, 117. By permission.)

lighted; when the child was to report the words spoken by the woman, her picture was lighted. On some trials the picture of the face was lighted *before* the voices spoke (the child was given a preparatory signal). On other trials the picture of the face was lighted *after* the voices spoke. With age, the children became increasingly better at reporting the words spoken by the voice to which they were told to listen. However, when the child was given a preparatory set—he was told which voice to listen to *before* the voices spoke—his performance was better than if he was told after the voice spoke (*42;* see Fig. 11.3).

Capacity for Sustained Attention. Developmental changes on a variety of intellectual tasks suggest that between 6 and 7 years of age there is a dramatic increase in quality of performance on problems requiring focused and sustained attention. This generalization seems to hold for both American children and those in other cultures. The child under 5 years seems easily distracted and has difficulty maintaining attention for a long time on a problem or communication from another person. These psychological changes in cognitive functioning are associated with important biological changes in the central nervous system, including the growth of neural tissue and changes in the electrical potentials generated by the brain. It is possible that an important reorganization of the central nervous system occurs between 5 and 7 years of age, and this reorganization may be partly responsible for the dramatic increase in the child's capacity for sustained attention (*70*).

Summary. The school years are marked by three important developments in the encoding process—increasing use of words and concepts at the expense of imagery in the interpretation of the environment; the learning of expectations that direct the child's attention to relevant aspects of an event; increased ability to maintain attention on a problem without becoming distracted. The child becomes more efficient, more selective, and more accurate in his encoding of events.

Process 2:   Memory Functions

Memory refers to the storage of experiences for a period after they have ended. It had been assumed for many years that all perceived events were registered with equal strength. If a person could not remember an event that he perceived, it was assumed that the fault lay with his inability to recall it rather than with any differences in registration. Recent research suggests that it may be useful to distinguish between two memory processes—short-term memory and long-term memory. Short-term memory usually refers to a trace available for a maximum of 30 seconds, but typically for a much shorter period of time. It is believed that without special control processes, encoded information in short-term memory is not transferred to long-term memory and cannot be retrieved at a later time.

Kindergarten age children seem to have a more limited short-term memory than adults. Kindergarten children and adults were shown two, three, or four geometric forms for very brief exposures (.15 second) in a tachistoscope (i.e., a machine that allows very brief controlled exposures of visual stimuli). After the brief exposure the child looked at a card containing ten geometric forms and had to point to the forms which he had seen in the tachistoscope. The children did very well when they were exposed briefly to only two forms, but could not recall three or four geometric figures. More of the adults, by contrast, were able to recall three or four forms. It appears that the adults were coding the stimuli (i.e., saying to themselves that it reminded them of a star or a triangle or a circle) and, as a result, were able to hold more of the forms in memory (45).

As indicated earlier, the capacity of immediate memory (i.e., how much a child can report immediately after seeing or hearing a string of numbers or words) increases each year across the period 5 to 10 years of age. A 10-year-old can recall a string of six or seven numbers read to him, while the 5-year-old can typically recall only four or, at the most, five. The kindergarten child's inability to carry out a complicated instruction or provide the correct answer to an orally presented problem is sometimes caused by his forgetting the essential elements of the instruction or problem rather than by inability to do what was required. Often such forgetting is due to the fact that he does not rehearse, to himself, the essence of the instruction or problem. In one experiment, children of three ages (kindergarten and grades 2 and 5) were exposed to a set of familiar pictures; the experimenter pointed to a given number of them in a given order. Then that array of pictures was replaced with a new arrangement and the child had to point to the same pictures in the same order as he watched the experimenter touch them. The older children, in contrast to the younger ones, had better memory scores and were more likely to rehearse silently the names of the pictures as they were touched or while the child was attempting to recall them (as evidenced by distinct movements of the lips). The kindergarten children knew the names of the pictures, but their poor recall and low rehearsal were caused by a failure to use the "trick" of saying the names of the pictures to themselves in order to help memory (13). Thus possession of a vocabulary to encode objects is no guarantee that the child will use his vocabulary to help him remember information, or in other aspects of problem-solving.

Individual Differences in Memory. Differences among children of the same or different ages in their ability to remember events seem to be related, in large measure, to the capacity to sustain attention, as well as the availability of vocabulary, images, and concepts that can be associated with the events and help to hold them in memory. If the child attends to the material, the most important determinant of his ability to remember anything is the active use of available words, concepts, and images to aid both in the registration of the event and in its recall. Both memory and vocabulary size improve with age. A 9-year-old can remember a longer series of numbers of words than a 5-year-old can; and the length of the series remembered is a function of the familiarity of the words. Similarly, with each year, the child's vocabulary grows larger, and children from linguistically improverished environments perform poorly on memory tasks that involve language. Children with meager language do not comprehend or recall new information as faithfully or extensively as children with rich language resources *(3, 23)*.

Other Factors Controlling Memory. Lack of selective attention also leads to imperfect registration of the event and, therefore, to memory failure. Failure to focus attention could be the result of several factors, but the most obvious, and perhaps the most frequent, are interfering thoughts and distracting stimuli. The negative relations between quality of memory and anxiety have been well documented. Anxious children display poorer recall than less anxious children and it is believed that the anxiety creates distracting stimulation that deflects attention from relevant incoming information and, therefore, impairs memory.

In a recent study, third-grade boys were divided into three groups. One group was made anxious by causing them to fail on a word problem *(43)*. A second group was allowed to succeed on the same word problem, and a third group was not given the problem at all. Each child was then read the short story that appears below and told to remember it.

The American horse known as Man of War was a very fine horse. He ran in races in the United States, in France and in Germany. He was brown with a red mane and had very strong legs. Five times a year, he was in horse shows in Boston, where children came to see him trot and run. After watching him, the children were served hot chocolate, biscuits and fudge *(43)*.

Immediately after hearing the story, the children had to recall as much of it as possible. The children who were made anxious had markedly poorer memory for elements of the story than the other two groups, who were equal in their recall scores *(43)*.

In addition to use of available vocabulary and freedom from anxiety or distracting factors, a third source of differences in quality of memory involves motivational variables. Is the child motivated to recall material or does he stop searching after the first layer of information has been retrieved? Retrieval of information from memory is effortful and the child who works longer is likely to ferret out more information.

In sum, better techniques to store and hold information, focused attention, freedom from anxiety, and motivation to recall all lead to better recall during the school years.

Process 3:   Generation of Ideas and Hypotheses

Encoding (the comprehension of events) and the storage of information in memory are typically the first two processes in a problem-solving sequence. The third process is the generation of possible solutions: the production of alternative ideas to solve a problem. This process is occasionally called the *induction phase* of problem-solving, and is closely related to the notion of creativity.

In order to generate ideas successfully, the child must possess (1) the necessary knowledge or cognitive units, (2) a permissive attitude toward error, so that he is not afraid of making a mistake, and (3) the less palpable ingredient, *insight*. Generation of hypotheses is always involved when a child tries to find a basis of similarity among objects or attempts to figure out how to solve a problem.

The Importance of Critical Attributes.   The child's judgment that two objects are similar or alike is partly a function of the degree to which those two objects share what have been called *critical attributes*. That is, the conceptual similarity between two objects is typically based on the shared presence of a few salient elements, rather than a large number of shared elements. Adults call a chihuahua and a wolfhound both dogs because they share the critical attributes of a bark and other species-typical characteristics. However, a chihuahua shares a larger number of attributes with a Siamese cat (size, short hair, frequency of "residence" in a small apartment) than it does with a wolfhound. But because the chihuahua and the cat do not share the same critical attributes, they are not judged as being members of the same class.

The critical attributes that define specific concepts will vary with the child's learning experiences. For example, children who learn that social class and its accompanying prestige are defined by the critical attributes of *wealth* rather than *education* will probably, as adults, invest more effort in

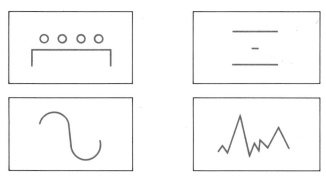

Figs. 11.4 (top) and 11.5. Drawings used to test creativity. (Drawings from Figures 2 and 3 from *Modes of thinking in young children* by M. A. Wallach & N. Kogan. Copyright © 1965 by Holt, Rinehart and Winston, Inc. Reprinted by permission of Holt, Rinehart and Winston, Inc.)

accumulating material wealth than those children whose definition of social class has education as the critical attribute. First grade children for whom straight versus curved lines are the critical attributes for letters of the alphabet may confuse small case *d* with small case *b*, but not capital *C* and capital *E*.

Generation of Hypotheses and the Concept of Creativity. The possession of a rich reservoir of knowledge is separate from the freedom to use that knowledge. Typically, the child with a rich and varied storehouse of images, words, and rules is regarded as *intelligent*. The child who uses these units in a unique and constructive way is called *creative*. Intelligent children can be either creative or noncreative. In one study, fifth grade children were given standard tests for their intelligence as well as tests of creativity. The tests for creativity required the child to generate many unusual hypotheses. For example, in one test the child would be told a characteristic and asked to name as many objects as he could that had that characteristic (e.g., name all the things that you know that are *sharp; round*). The children were also asked to think up varied uses for objects (e.g., tell me all the different ways that you would use a newspaper, a cork). In a third test the child was shown a line drawing as seen in Fig. 11.4 and asked to think up all the things each drawing might be. He was also shown a nonsense line design as shown in Fig. 11.5 and asked to say all the things the nonsense design made him think of. The child was classified creative if he gave many answers to each of the tests, some of which were very unusual—unique in comparison to the answers given by the other children. The children were grouped into four categories: highly intelligent and highly creative; highly intelligent and low in creativity; low in intelligence and highly creative; low in intelligence and low in creativity.

The girls who were both highly intelligent and highly creative were very self-confident in school and were popular with their friends. The highly creative, but low-intelligence girls, on the other hand, seemed to be just the opposite in personality. They were cautious, hesitant, and had little self-confidence. The low-intelligence, low-creative girls were slightly less cautious and hesitant than were the high-creative, low-intelligence girls, and the former were more popular and outgoing with their friends. Finally, the highly intelligent but low-creative girls were sought out by others, but they often failed to reciprocate such overtures—as if they were a little aloof or cautious with the other girls. Differences in creativity among boys did not relate closely to their social behavior with their peers.

In general, the creative child who was intelligent was willing to take a chance, to risk a "crazy" idea. He seemed to have a less severe attitude toward error. The girl who was both intelligent and creative seemed to be successful both in school and in her relationships with her peers. These children seemed to be confident and free of anxiety over generating unconventional ideas (66).

Generation of Hypotheses and Learning Set. One of the clearest demonstrations of the importance of developmental changes in the generation of ideas is seen in a phenomenon called learning set or "learning to learn." A learning set is the acquired set or attitude that is relevant to solving a particular class of problems, a disposition to attend to the relevant stimuli in the problem, and to discard incorrect classes of hypotheses. In brief, the child learns a general solution approach to a specific class of problems. Thus, if a person played 20 Questions each day for 100 days, his efficiency and the quality of his questions would improve daily, even though the specific "secret" object he was trying to guess changed each day. He would be learning to ask better questions, and learning *not* to ask questions that yield little information.

The problems used with children to explore "learning set" usually involve a series of discriminations in which a pair of objects is presented to the child. The child is told that one of the objects is correct and if he picks the correct one he will get a penny. Suppose that the first pair of objects presented to the child were a red and a yellow cube and the experimenter had decided that the yellow cube was correct. If the child picks the yellow cube he receives a penny; if he picks the red cube he receives nothing. Initially, a 5-year-old might behave as if the position of the cube, whether it is on the right or the left, is the clue to correctness. If the yellow cube were on the right and he picked it and was rewarded, he would likely pick the cube on the right on the next trial even though the yellow cube were on the left. His initial hypothesis to solve this problem was that *position* was the key to the solution. Eventually the child will solve the problem and pick the yellow cube consistently, regardless of its position. After solving this problem he is presented with a different one. Now he is shown a bird and a four-footed animal of the same size and coloration, and the experimenter has decided that the bird is correct. The key to the solution has nothing to do with color or size but rather with two versus four feet.

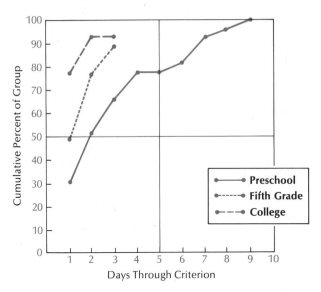

Fig. 11.6. Cumulative percentage of age groups reaching criterion on each day of testing. (From B. Levinson & H. W. Reese. Patterns of discrimination learning set in pre-school, fifth graders, college freshmen, and the aged. *Monogr. Soc. Res. Child Develpm.,* copyright 1967 by The Society for Research In Child Development, Inc. Vol. 32, 64. By permission.)

However, the 5-year-old child who had solved the yellow-red cube prob-lem earlier would be likely to solve this problem more rapidly as a result of having first had the cube problem. He has learned something from the initial problem: he has learned to disregard the initial hypothesis of posi-tion. The more rapidly he eliminates incorrect hypotheses that he ordinarily would try, the quicker he will solve the problem. Learning to learn is a combination of disregarding preferred hypotheses that are of no help, and learning to attend to the new and relevant aspects of a problem.

   In one study *(40),* learning-set problems were administered to preschool children, fifth grade children, and college students. The child was shown a pair of objects and was told to guess which one was correct. He was given several chances with a specific pair of objects and then was given a new pair of objects and, therefore, a new problem to solve. Each subject was given ten different problems each day. There was an orderly progression in the efficiency with which a learning set was acquired (see Fig. 11. 6). It took the preschool children 6 days (ten problems a day) to learn to solve each new problem quickly. The fifth grade children required only 3 days, and the college students only 2 days in order to arrive at a point where they could solve a discrimination problem within one or two trials. The increasing efficiency of the older children was due to (1) greater flexibility in eliminating incorrect hypotheses, (2) the availability of a greater number of hypotheses, and finally (3), the faith that there was a correct solution—that analysis and attention to the stimuli would result in successful solution. In addition, the child learns that the content of a problem does not have to be realistic or related to his personal life. The 6-year-old has not yet learned this principle and he occasionally brings in personal items from his own life experiences in solving problems. For example, Scottish children were administered problems of the following type:

> There are three boys, John, Bill and Pete, and they go to three different schools, the North school, the South school, and the West school. John goes to the North school, Bill goes to the South school, where does Pete go?

A 6-year-old child might say, "Pete goes to the North school because my brother Pete goes there," confusing his own personal experiences with the arbitrary content of the problem. The 10-year-old would realize that "West school" was correct. Children must learn that a formal problem can be divorced from reality and that a solution can be arrived at logically, through thinking (8). As we shall see later, this idea is central to Piaget's conception of intellectual growth during the early school years.

Generation of Hypotheses in Concept-Sorting Tasks. There are important developmental as well as individual differences in the kinds of conceptual categories the child uses to classify information. Normally we are most concerned with the content or particular meaning of the concept (e.g., Does the concept deal with people, animals, plants, cars, or school?). However, a second aspect of a concept pertains to its formal qualities. The formal aspect deals with the quality of the grouping, independent of its specific content. Some of the major formal dimensions (37) include:

1. Superordinate or categorical concepts—When a categorical concept is used it characterizes or represents a shared attribute among the objects. The child who groups pears, apples, or bananas together under the label *fruit* is using a superordinate concept.

2. Functional-relational concepts—In these concepts the basis of similarity involves the relation between or among members of the class. Examples of functional-relational concepts include grouping together four children because they play together or grouping a match with a pipe because the match lights the pipe.

3. Functional-locational—In this case the members of the class share a common location. The child who groups all animals that live on a farm is producing a functional-locational concept.

4. Analytic concepts—The basis for similarity involves a manifest or public component that is part of each stimulus in the category. An example would be to group together all living things that had legs or all objects with a vertical stripe.

There are lawful developmental changes in the use of these four conceptual categories. As the child grows he is more likely to use superordinate

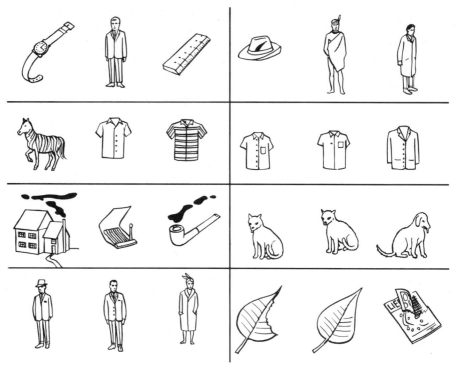

Fig. 11.7. Sample items from CST (From J. Kagan *et al.,* Information processing in the child. *Psychol. Monogr.,* 1964, Vol. 78. Copyright 1964 by the American Psychological Association. By permission.)

categorical dimensions and less likely to use functional dimensions in classifying or grouping familiar materials together.

The Meaning and Significance of Analytic Concepts. The tendency to produce analytically based concepts with visual stimuli (objects or pictures) tends to increase with age—because of both a tendency to think before acting as well as a preference to analyze the stimulus materials. Children 6 to 11 years of age were shown a set of three pictures such as in Fig. 11.7 and were asked to select two pictures that were alike in some way. With age, there was an increase in number of analytic concepts. The older children would be more likely to say that the watch and the ruler go together because they both have numbers, rather than the watch and the man go together because the man wears the watch. Similarly, the older children would be more likely to group the house and the pipe together because they both have smoke coming out, rather than to pair the match and the pipe because the former lights the latter. Analytic concepts increase with age in part because older children often pause and reflect longer in generating concepts than younger children do. In one experiment, one group of school-age children was instructed to wait 15 seconds before telling the examiner the conceptual basis they selected; a second group was told to respond quickly (34). The former group produced more analytic concepts than the latter group.

Relevance of the Material to Be Categorized. It is important to realize that the child who uses analytic or relational concepts with pictures may not do so when he is presented with words. The child's strategy of classifying information depends to a great extent on the material being classified. Subjects 6 to 19 years of age were asked to state the similarity among groups of words (49). The subject was first read a pair of words, then a third word was added to the pair, a fourth word to the trio, and so on until he had the task of explaining the similarity among eight words. The eight words—in order of their presentation—were banana, peach, potato, meat, milk, water, air, germs. The use of an analytic conceptual basis to tie the words together decreased with age; superordinate categories increased. It will be recalled that, with pictures, analytic reasons increased with age. How are we to interpret the fact that the relation of age to use of analytic or superordinate concepts depends on whether the child is working with words or pictures?

The Motive for the "Elegant" Concept. The child has standards regarding the quality of the concepts he produces on a test, just as he has standards regarding the quality of his behavior with others. The school-age child has learned, to some degree, what kinds of answers in a concept-sorting task are of high quality—i.e., "good" concepts to produce. Part of his judgment is related to the subtlety of the category, the amount of work required to produce it. An answer to a hard problem is much more valuable than an answer to an easy one. Thus the specific stimulus array shown to the child is important in determining the concepts he chooses to draw from it. If the stimulus array makes functional concepts easy to detect and analytic ones difficult, the older child is likely to select analytic concepts because he believes them to be better, more elegant. The older child may choose the analytic concept not because he failed to note the relational aspect but because he believes them to be "better," more elegant. Hence it is inappropriate to say that a child is analytic or relational without specifying the stimulus materials presented to him.

An illustration of the importance of the stimulus array on ease of conceptualization is contained in a study in which children had to learn either a relational or an absolute categorization of number. Children in grades 1, 3, 5, and 8 were presented with pairs of stimuli representing numerical amounts and told that one stimulus was correct. The children had to learn either a relational (pick the smaller number of the pair) or an absolute (always pick the number 5) conception of number.

One group of children was presented with *perceptual* representations of the numbers (e.g., five dots versus seven dots, three dots versus five dots). A second group was presented with an *abstract* representation of the numbers in terms of sets (e.g., five triangles versus seven squares, five crosses versus three circles). A third group was presented with actual pairs of numerals (the number 5 versus the number 7, the number 5 versus the number 1; 73).

Under the perceptual and abstract conditions, acquisition of the relational concept (pick the smaller) was easier than acquisition of the absolute concept. When the stimuli were numerals, the absolute concept was very easy to attain. The importance of the mode of presentation was clearest among the first grade children. The relational concept was easy to attain under the perceptual conditions; the absolute response was easy to attain under the numeral condition; but both relational and absolute concepts were very difficult to obtain under the abstract condition. It is not reasonable to conclude, therefore, that first grade children are preferentially relational or preferentially absolute in the way they think about number concepts. The ease with which they conceptualize number depends intimately on how the material is presented. A preferred conceptual response is rarely independent of the material that is being classified. Similarly, a child is not to be classified as analytic or categorical, for he may be analytic with visual stimuli containing subtle analytic cues, but superordinate when presented with verbal representations of those objects. The descriptive term *analytic* is like the term *prejudiced*. In both cases, we must know the *target of the attitude*.

Process 4:   Evaluation

We now focus on a fourth process in problem-solving, that of evaluation. Evaluation pertains to the degree to which the child pauses to evaluate the quality of his thinking, and this process influences the entire spectrum of mental work: the quality of initial encoding, recall, and hypothesis generation. Some children accept and report the first hypothesis they produce and act upon it with only the barest consideration for its appropriateness or accuracy; these children are called impulsive. Other children devote a long period of time to study and reflection and censor many hypotheses; they are called reflective. This dimension is evident as early as 2 years of age, and seems to be consistent and relatively stable (27, 29).

Matching Familiar Figures.   One of the tests used to assess the tendency for the child to be reflective or impulsive is called Matching Familiar Figures (see Fig. 11.8). A child is asked to select from the six variants one stimulus that is identical with the standard. The major scores coded are the time the child takes to select his first hypothesis and the number of errors he makes. Among American children there is a dramatic decrease in errors and a corresponding increase in response time from 5 to 12 years of age. Moreover, the faster the child's decisions, the more mistakes he makes. Children who respond quickly and make many errors, in contrast to those who respond slowly and do not make errors, tend to retain this disposition over time (i.e., this preferred tendency is stable). Moreover, the reflective children (those who respond slowly and make few errors), in contrast to the impulsive children, wait longer before they describe a picture, delay longer in answering a question posed to them by an adult, are less likely to report words that did not appear in a list that was read to them, are less likely to make

Fig. 11.8. S a m p l e items from the Matching Familiar Figures test for reflection-impulsivity in the school-age child.

errors in reading English prose, and make fewer errors in inductive reasoning tests. In one study, first grade children were given tests of inductive reasoning. On one test the child was told three attributes of an object and he had to guess the object (e.g., What is yellow, melts in the sun, and you eat it? What has doors, wheels, and moves?). The impulsive children responded more quickly to these questions and made more errors than the reflective children. If one studies the eye-tracking patterns of these two groups of children, the reflective children scan visual stimuli in a more systematic way and are more likely to search every one of the variants before offering a solution hypothesis. The impulsive children often answer before they have examined every variant, and adopt a much riskier strategy.

It appears that one can change a child's disposition to be reflective or impulsive through training. Some impulsive children were merely told to inhibit their responses on the Matching Familiar Figures test. After several 30-minute sessions of such training in inhibition, they showed longer response times than untrained, impulsive children.

The teacher's tendency to be reflective or impulsive can also influence the child. Each of 20 first grade teachers was classified as reflective or impulsive through use of an adult version of the Matching Familiar Figures task. Then a random group of children from each of the 20 classrooms was tested in the early fall and again in the late spring to determine if exposure to a teacher with a preferred strategy influenced the child's tempo. The children changed in a direction consonant with the teacher's tempo, and the effect was most marked for impulsive boys assigned to teachers who were both reflective and experienced. These boys showed the greatest increase in decision time over the course of the school year. Thus the tendency to be reflective or impulsive is stable over time, across varied tasks, and is modifiable.

The Basis for Reflection-Impulsiveness.   One of the factors causing a reflective or impulsive attitude is fear of making a mistake. The more apprehensive the child is of making an error, the more likely he will be reflective. Reflective children are concerned with error and wish to avoid it at all costs; impulsive children seem minimally apprehensive about making a mistake and respond quickly. The increase in the tendency among American children to become reflective with age seems to reflect a change in the more general disposition for American children to grow more cautious with age, to become increasingly concerned with avoiding a mistake (10).

Process 5: Implementation of Hypotheses— the Deductive Phase

The processes of hypothesis generation and deduction are often complementary and are regarded as the essence of thinking. Generation of hypotheses and deduction of conclusions typically occur together, for to realize that both air and ocean have permanent, spatially located currents is simultaneously to deduce that each flows in a specified direction and each influences the weather. Deduction refers to the application of a rule—formal or informal—to solve a problem. Hence the most important set of cognitive units controlling quality of deduction is the child's storehouse of rules, which increases with age. Some of the rules are mathematical ($8^2 = 64$, $18/3 = 6$); others are more informal (thundershowers usually occur in the summer). These rules are critical for the solution of problems. One of the important theoretical questions concerning cognitive processes centers on whether there are basic changes in the use of rules by children of different ages across the period 4 through 12 years of age. A simplistic point of view assumes that the child merely acquires new and different rules each day and stores them for future use, but there is no deductive rule that is necessarily difficult or impossible for a 5-year-old child to acquire.

An alternative assumption is that some rules are too difficult for young children to acquire and, as a result, there must be stages in the development of reasoning skills. Jean Piaget believes in this second position and we shall now consider his ideas in some detail.

PIAGET'S THEORY OF INTELLECTUAL DEVELOPMENT

As has been suggested in earlier chapters, Jean Piaget is the most influential theorist of intellectual development of this century. His writings have been prolific and his views about intelligence, although complex, have been extremely provocative and have stimulated much research.

Piaget's use of the term intelligence has a specific meaning. Intelligence is "the coordination of operations." An operation has two important characteristics: it is an *internalized* action that is *reversible*. The concept of addition is a good example of an operation. One can *add* two apples to three apples, or perform the reverse operation of subtracting two apples from three apples. Addition has the reverse operation of subtraction. One can square the number 6 and get 36, or do the operation of taking the square root of 36 and obtaining 6. In physics, one can use prisms to split light into its component parts or perform the reverse operation and combine the rays into white light again. One can boil water to produce water vapor and condense the vapor to form the same amount of water. *These are reversible operations in which nothing is lost.* The gradual acquisition of these reversible operations is, according to Piaget, the essence of intellectual growth. Note that all the statements we call rules—in the general use of that word—are *not* operations according to Piaget. For example, the 6-year-old child may know that if he hits his sister he will be punished. This knowledge is a rule. But this rule does not have a reverse operation, and Piaget would not call it an operation.

The Concern with Logical Rules. Piaget has been primarily concerned with a special set of rules that involve propositions in mathematics and physics—particularly the Newtonian concepts of mass, quantity, weight, volume, space, number, time, movement, and velocity. The 5-year-old child does not understand these concepts the way the adolescent or adult does. For example, the child does not conceive of a standard time to which all events are referred. He believes that each event has its own local time. In one experiment, the child sees two toy cars starting and stopping at the same time but one car travels at a faster velocity and, as a result, covers more distance. Although the time the cars traveled was equal, the child of 5 denies that the time was the same because the space covered was different. He confuses the notions of time and space. In a similar experiment, the child is shown two parallel race tracks on which two little men run. The men start at the same place. One of the men runs a fixed distance (say, five units) while the second man simultaneously runs a shorter distance at a slower velocity (say, two units). Immediately thereafter the second man runs again, one more unit, while the first man remains in place. Thus, the second man ran for a *longer time* but covered less space. A 5½-year-old interprets the situation as follows:

EXAMINER: What did you see?

CHILD: The yellow one [the first man] stopped and the other one walked again.

EXAMINER: Then which one stopped first?

CHILD: The second one.

EXAMINER: Which stopped first?

CHILD: The second one.

EXAMINER: Which one walked for the longest time?

CHILD: The first one.

EXAMINER: Let's say that this one [the first one] stopped at noon. Now look, did this one [the second one] stop at noon also, or before or after?

CHILD: Before noon.

For this child distance covered is proportional to time; he does not take velocity into account.

Conservation of Quantity. The most famous of Piaget's experiments is the demonstration that the 5-year-old does not believe that a quantity of water or clay remains constant (is conserved) despite changes in its shape. A 5-year-old child is shown two identical glasses of equal shape filled to the same height with colored water. The adult asks the child if the two glasses have the same amount of water or unequal amounts. The child quickly acknowledges that both have the same amount of water. The examiner then pours the water from one container into a tall, thin glass so that the water level is higher in this new container. When asked again, the 5-year-old says that the tall container contains more water; the 7-year-old insists that both have the same amount of water. However, the critical evidence that indicates that the 7-year-old has acquired the operation that Piaget calls conservation (i.e., the rule that the quantity of liquid remains constant, regardless of the shape of the container holding it) rests with the child's explanation of why the containers have the same amount of water. The older child will say, "They are the same because you can pour the water back to the other glass and then the height will be the same." *The child is aware of the reverse operation that will restore the original situation.* This awareness is the critical evidence of his possession of the operation of conservation of quantity. This same concept is shown in Fig. 11.9 in which the glasses contain solid objects instead of colored water.

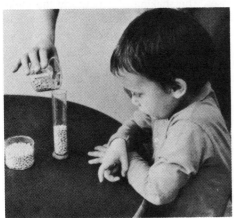

Fig. 11.9. The boy is being tested for conservation of quantity. He is deciding which jar has more objects. (Photographs by Susanna Sak.)

Piaget's Stages

As we have indicated earlier in this book, Piaget is a developmental theorist who believes that the child passes through stages on his way to achieving the end state of adult Western thought; he wants to explain how a child gradually arrives at this goal. This attitude toward psychological growth resembles Freud's view that libidinal freedom was the idealized end state toward which the child and adolescent were growing. Freud attempted to describe, in his psychoanalytic theory of development, how the child changed in his travels toward the goal of libidinal maturity. Freud and Piaget both assumed an idealized adult psychological state, and their theories describe the stages the child passes through in approaching that state.

According to Piaget, there are four major stages or periods of intelligence: sensorimotor stage (0 to 18 months of life), preoperational stage (18 months to age 7), concrete operations (7 to 12 years), and, finally, the stage of formal operations (age 12 onward).

Sensorimotor Stage. This period (see Chapter 5, pp. 194–199) deals with the time prior to the child's acquisition of language. Piaget believes that the intelligence of the infant is manifested in his actions. When a 1-year-old wants a toy resting on a blanket far from him, he pulls the blanket toward him to get the object. Piaget would regard this as an act of intelligence. The child used the blanket to achieve a goal (the prized toy). Piaget does not call this act an operation, but rather a *schema of action.* It is a generalized response that can be used to solve a variety of problems. The habit of bouncing in the crib in order to make toys attached to the crib shimmer or move is another example of a schema of action. At every age in infancy the child has a set of such schemata. The infant can suck, hit, bang, and shake, and when a new toy is presented to him he will typically exhibit one of these responses. The shaking of a new toy the child has never seen is an example of Piaget's concept of *assimilation,* which is one of the two basic dynamic principles of Piaget's theory.

Assimilation is the incorporation of a new object or stimulus into an existing schemata. At any age a child has an existing set of actions or operations, and new objects or new ideas are assimilated to the older, existing ones. The process opposed to assimilation is *accommodation.*

Accommodation is the tendency to adjust to a new object, to change one's schemata of action to fit the new object. Thus the 2-year-old child who has never been exposed to a magnet initially assimilates it to his own schemata, and acts toward the magnet as he does toward a familiar toy. He may bang it, bounce it, throw it, or try to make it produce a noise. But once he recognizes the unique qualities of the magnet—that it attracts metal—he will accommodate to it and develop new schemata of actions toward magnets.

Mental growth, for Piaget, is the resolution of the tension between assimilation and accommodation—the conflict between using old responses for new situations and acquiring new (or changing old) responses to fit new ones. *Intellectual growth is adaptation to new situations.* The learning-set experiments described earlier are good examples of this tension between assimilation and accommodation. The child initially assimilates the problem situation to his existing set of hypotheses. He may adopt a position habit and always go to the right for his reward. Eventually he accommodates to the situation and applies the correct rule. Alteration of older schemata to fit new situations, which is Piaget's definition of accommodation, is the essence of intellectual growth.

Preoperational Stage (Ages 1½ to 7). The child in the preoperational stage has language, and meanings of objects and events are manipulated as well as overt actions—a schema now consists of a symbolic unit. The 2-year-old will treat a stick as if it were a candle and blow it out, or treat a block of wood as if it were a car and move it around making a noise as he travels. This ability to treat objects as symbolic of things other than themselves is an essential characteristic of the preoperational stage. Piaget offers an illustration in which a doll is treated as if it were a live baby.

> At 2 years 1 month, J put her doll's head through the balcony railings with its face turned toward the street and began to tell it what she saw, "You see the lake and trees, you see a carriage or house." The same day she seated her doll on a sofa and told it what she herself had seen in the garden (55, 127).

Piaget does not believe that the 2- or 3-year-old who collects a group of similar forms (puts all the red blocks in a pile, for example) is necessarily showing categorization or classification. The child, according to Piaget, does not have a mental representation of a set of categories as he sorts and is not aware of any defining characteristic that unites all the members of the class. Thus the act of putting similar things together—which preoperational children often do—is not necessarily evidence for conceptual classification. Moreover, the preoperational child has difficulty taking the point of view of another child or adult. He cannot anticipate how an object will look from the point of view of another person or even realize that a scene he sees may look different in the eyes of another. Piaget regards the preoperational child as egocentric in his perspective.

Although the 3-year-old is symbolic, his words and images are not necessarily organized into firmly articulated concepts and rules. That process happens during the next stage of concrete operations.

Stage of Concrete Operations (Ages 7 to 12).   There are several important differences between the child in the preoperational stage and the 7-year-old who is in the stage of concrete operations; these differences are summarized below.

Mental Representations.   One major difference between the preoperational and the operational child is that the former does not have a *mental representation of a series of actions.* The 5-year-old can learn to walk four blocks from his home to a neighborhood store, but he cannot sit at a table with a pencil and paper and trace the route he takes. He does not have, according to Piaget, a mental representation of the entire sequence of actions. He walks to the store successfully by making certain turns at certain places along the way, the way a rat runs a maze, but he has no overall picture of the route that he travels. Adults, of course, do have such a mental plan. Try to trace your route, on paper, from your home to a favorite restaurant. Notice how you must have a mental representation of the entire route in order to accomplish this task. According to Piaget, the 4-year-old is incapable of this level of functioning.

Conservation.   A second deficit of the preoperational stage is the absence of the operation of *conservation*. The notion that liquids and solids can be transformed in shape without changing their volume or mass is manifested only when the child reaches the stage of concrete operations. The 5-year-old believes that if you change the shape of a piece of clay the amount of clay also changes—the quantity of clay is not conserved. For example, a 5-year-old child is shown two balls of clay of equal mass and shape; he acknowledges that they have the same amount of clay. The experimenter then flattens one of the balls so that it resembles a pancake and asks the child which has the greater amount of clay, or whether there is an equal amount of clay in both masses. Typically, the 5-year-old regards the ball and pancake as unequal in quantity. Two years later, he is likely to insist that the ball and pancake have the same amount of clay because "the pancake is thinner but it is wider"—indicating that he is aware of the compensatory dimensions: "I can make the pancake into the ball again." Similarly, the preoperational child does not believe that the length of a stick or the number of pennies in a pile remain constant despite changes in their arrangement or shape. If two sticks of equal length are placed side by side so that their endpoints coincide, the child will admit they are equal. But if one stick is moved forward an inch, the 5-year-old will say that it is longer while the 7-year-old will acknowledge that they are still of the same length. The young child does not realize that the attribute of length of an object is constant and not dependent on its perceptual context.

Similarly, the preoperational child does not appreciate the fact that if the number of objects in two arrays is equal, they are equal in quantity regardless of the shape of the arrays. In this experiment, two rows of five buttons each are placed one above the other so that the rows are of equal length. The child acknowledges that the two rows have the same amount of buttons. But if one row is made shorter (by regrouping the buttons) the preoperational child says that the longer row has more buttons. He behaves as if the word "more" refers to the apparent quantity—the perceptual aspect—and does not refer to the number of items.

Relational Terms.   The preoperational child does not understand relational terms, such as darker, larger, bigger; he tends to think absolutely. That is, he interprets *darker* as meaning very dark rather than darker *than* another object. If he is shown two light objects, one of which is slightly darker and asked to pick the darker one, he may not answer. Similarly, concepts such as brother of, left of, and taller than are difficult to apply. These relational expressions are understood as names for *absolute attributes of objects*, rather than as relations holding between objects. Piaget summarizes the child's conception as follows:

> The conclusion to which we are finally led is this. The child does not realize that certain ideas, even such as are obviously relative for an adult, are relations between at least two terms. Thus he does not realize that a brother must necessarily be the brother of somebody, that an object must necessarily be to the right or left of somebody, or that a part must necessarily be part of a whole, but thinks of all these notions as existing in themselves absolutely (*51*, 131).

Class Inclusion.   According to Piaget, a fourth deficit of the preoperational child is that he cannot reason simultaneously about part of the whole and the whole. If a 5-year-old child is shown eight yellow candies and four brown candies and asked, "Are there more yellow candies or more candies?", he is likely to say, "More yellow candies." Piaget believes this reply means that the child cannot reason about a part and a whole simultaneously.

Serialization.   The fifth characteristic that differentiates preoperational children from those in the stage of concrete operations is the ability to arrange objects according to some quantified dimension, such as weight or size, on an ordinal scale. This ability is called *serialization*. The 5-year-old typically cannot arrange eight sticks of differing length in a row according to their length. The student can readily see how critical serialization ability is for understanding the relation of numbers to one another and, therefore, to the learning of arithmetic.

Summary.   The child of 7, who has just entered the stage of concrete operations, has acquired an important set of rules that he did not possess a year or two earlier. He believes that length, mass, weight, and number remain constant despite superficial modification in their external appearance. He is able to produce a mental image of a series of actions and realizes that relational concepts such as darker or heavier do not necessarily refer to absolute qualities, but to a relation between two or more objects. Finally, he can reason about the whole and its parts simultaneously and can order objects on a dimension of quantity (such as size or height). In short, he has learned some central rules to aid his adaptation to his environment.

Stage Four: The Stage of Formal Operations (Age 12 on).   There are several important attributes of formal operational thinking that differentiate it from the previous stage of concrete operations. First, the adolescent is capable of considering all the possible ways a particular problem might be solved and the possible forms a particular variable might assume. If he is thinking about the shortest way to get to the seashore, he can and will review all the possible routes and he knows when he has exhausted all the possibilities. Consider the following question put to a 7-year-old and a 13-year-old.

A man was found dead in the back seat of a car which had hit a telephone pole. What happened?

The younger child thinks up a reason that satisfies him and states it: "The man hit a pole and was thrown in the back seat and was killed." The older child is more likely to generate all the possible ways this event might have happened—he could have hit a pole and been thrown into the back seat; he could have been put in the car after it crashed in order to make the scene appear to be an accident; he could have been put in the back seat by his companion after the crash; and so on. This tendency to generate and to explore systematically all the possible solution hypotheses and then carefully check each for its probable validity is one of the hallmarks of the stage of formal operations.

Second, the adolescent's thought is self-consciously deductive and resembles that of a scientist. The adolescent can think in terms of hypothetical propositions that may be fanciful and not fit reality. Consider the following question:

> They found a three-year-old skull of an animal with five feet and three heads that lived to be 50 years. What is silly about that?

The 7-year-old might object to this problem by saying that there are no animals with five feet and three heads; the adolescent is capable of accepting this fanciful hypothesis and attempting to reason out the answer.

Third, the adolescent organizes his operations into higher-order operations—ways of using abstract rules to solve a whole class of problems. For example, consider the problem:

> What number is 30 less than 3 times itself?

The 7-year-old in the stage of concrete operations is likely to begin the problem by trial and error, trying first one number and then another, using the operations of addition and multiplication until he finally arrives at the correct answer. The adolescent has learned a higher-order operation and may set up the equation: $x + 30 = 3x$ and quickly find the answer of 15. He combines the separate operations of addition and multiplication into the more complex operation of the algebraic equation. If children are given a bowl of water and a box full of objects and are asked to select the ones that float, the older child will not put each object in water one at a time but will apply a simplifying rule. He will first pick out all the wooden objects and may even apply some test (such as knocking them on wood) to see if they are primarily made of wood. These more complex units are called *combinative structures*. To know that one should use the operation of multiplication to solve the problem, "How many ways can I pair six color discs with each other?" is an example of a combinative structure, and such structures are necessary to understand algebra and higher mathematics.

Thus, formal thought is basically a generalized orientation toward problem solving. The basis of this orientation is the tendency to isolate the elements of a problem and systematically explore all the possible solution hypotheses, regardless of how hypothetical they are. Formal thought is rational and systematic. Moreover, the adolescent seems to reflect upon the rules he possesses and is aware of his own thoughts, aware of what he knows. It is not accidental that adolescence is the first time when the child begins to think about himself, his role in life, his plans, and the validity and integrity of his beliefs. The adolescent's concern with "the phoniness" of his own ideals and those of adults is acute in our time, but is rarely seen in children under 10 years of age. The child in concrete operations tends to deal largely with the present, with the here and now; the adolescent becomes concerned with the hypothetical, the future and the remote. An adolescent was overheard to remark, "I find myself thinking about my future and then I began to think about why I was thinking about my future, and then I began to think about why I was thinking, about why I was thinking about my future." Piaget believes that this preoccupation with thought is the principal component of the stage of formal operations.

Piaget's Early Work

The child's understanding of mathematical and physical concepts represents Piaget's most recent area of work during the last 25 years. During the early part of his career he was primarily concerned not with such concepts but rather with notions closer to the child's experience. He studied, for example, the child's understanding of causality, life, death, and morality. He suggested that a young child of 4 is egocentric and does not take into account the point of view of another person. Moreover, the 4-year-old has an absolute and concrete view of the world. The 5-year-old believes that dreams are external, palpable realities that are visible to other people. He attributes life to the inorganic world (animism), especially to objects that show movement (wind, cars, curtains). As the child grows he limits his animistic tendencies by restricting life to entities whose movement is self-engendered, such as the wind, but will not attribute life to movement resulting from external force, as is true of bicycles. These conclusions come from informal interviews with children. Piaget abandoned this early work in part because he began to doubt the power of informal conversations with children to reveal a faithful picture of their beliefs.

Evaluation of Piaget

An evaluation of the significance of Piaget's ideas rests most directly on the generality of his observations and his theoretical hypotheses concerning intellectual growth. There is little doubt that his statements about the developmental changes in conservation of mass, class inclusion, or seriation are generally true for Western children. The provocative suggestion that we theorize about these cognitive rules as operations (as interiorized actions that are reversible) is an ingenious and perhaps profitable way to view the gradual acquisition of such rules. Piaget's theory implies that a normally endowed child who could not use his arms or legs would have great difficulty growing intellectually, for Piaget assigns an important role to the infant's motor actions. These actions subsequently become internalized as operations. Study of the intellectual growth of thalidomide babies or babies born with paralyzed limbs would furnish an important test of this critical hypothesis.

Piaget and his followers believe that his ideas may be relevant to all aspects of mental development, not just to the phenomena Piaget has studied. That is, Piaget's writings occasionally imply that the 5-year-old child cannot serialize on any dimension; that no 7-year-old can reason without concrete objects on any issue. These stronger statements are still controversial. Most 5-year-olds will state that their father is bigger than a rabbit and a rabbit is bigger than a mouse, and acknowledge that their father is bigger than a mouse, indicating an ability to order objects on a dimension of size. The difference between this problem and those used by Piaget is that the father-rabbit problem deals with very familiar ideas.

If the child does not understand the question that is being put to him, he will obviously perform at an immature level. For example, Piaget suggests that the child of 8 years cannot classify himself on two dimensions simultaneously. That is, he cannot regard himself simultaneously as a member of a city and also as a member of a country. One reason for this deficiency is that the child does not have a complete understanding of the semantic meanings of the words "city" and "country." *He does not know that a city is part of a nation.* It can be demonstrated that a 5-year-old child is capable of double classification if he understands the two concepts. The 5-year-old knows that he can be both a member of the "Jones" family and a member of the male sex at the same time.

Piaget is interested in knowing when the child can use—or comprehend—the adult meaning of certain concepts: "Which stick is *longer?*" "Which cup has *more* water?" "Which car traveled for a *longer time?*" The answer the child gives to these questions depends on his understanding of the words *longer, more,* and *time.* In the experiment on conservation of quantity the examiner pours water from one jar into a tall thin container and asks which jar has more water. The 6-year-old child points to the tall thin jar. Piaget concludes that the child has not learned that a certain quantity remains constant despite transformation of shape. However, the young child's understanding of the word *more* in this context may be closely tied to the perception of height (i.e., higher means more). Height is synonymous with quantity for the young child. This point is nicely illustrated in a study on conservation of numbers.

The child was shown two rows of seven buttons, but one row was shorter than the other. The child said that both rows had seven buttons; they both had the same number of buttons. However, when he was asked which row had *more* buttons, he insisted that the longer row had *more* buttons (16). For this child, the word *more* was not synonymous with the arithmetic meaning of *more.*

It is possible that part of the process of acquiring the operation of conservation of length may involve learning the *arithmetic* meaning of the words for quantity and giving up the perceptual definition. Piaget has shown that the 5-year-old does not understand the meaning of words such as more, equal, and longer the way adults do. But this conclusion is not only true for concepts in mathematics or physics; it is also true for the concepts of love, justice, beauty, and evil. The critical attributes of many important concepts in our language change with development, and some of these changes do not seem easily explained in terms of changes in operations.

Piaget's emphasis on the importance of reversibility, class inclusion, serial ordering operations, and combinative structures is most relevant to mathematics and physics and less obviously relevant to many natural phenomena that do not show reversibility or obey class-inclusion rules. The relation between a whole and its parts in mathematics is usually not applicable to living things or the behavior of people. The concept of crowd is more than the sum of the number of people in the crowd. Moreover, the child discovers that death, unlike quantity of water, is not conserved and capable of a reversible operation. When a child kills a butterfly, it is not possible to perform an operation that transforms the insect back to the living state.

Piaget's observations of the sequences in cognitive development seem to be essentially correct. The controversy centers on the best way to explain the developmental changes in the child's thinking. Is the ability to conserve quantity best explained as the acquisition of an operation (that is, as an interiorized action that is reversible)? Some studies have successfully trained children to conserve quantity without requiring the child to act on any materials. These children were merely taught—or reminded—that a particular object should be regarded as possessing more than one attribute. For example, 5-year-old children who had not acquired conservation of quantity with clay or water were brought to a room where a woman showed the child various objects and encouraged the youngsters, in a group, to name many characteristics of these objects. Subsequently, the children were shown objects and asked to name all the ways in which they were similar, and the ways in which they were different. The transcript that follows conveys the flavor of these interviews (61, 305).

Portion of Verbatim Transcript of a Training Session Dealing with Multiple Attributes of Objects

TEACHER: Can you tell me what this is, Mary?
MARY: A banana.
TEACHER: What else can you tell me about it?
MARY: It's straight.
TEACHER: It's straight. What else?
MARY: It has a peel.
TEACHER: It has a peel. . . . Tom, what can you tell me about it?
TOM: Ummm . . . It has some dark lines on it.
TEACHER: Uh-huh.
TOM: It has some green on it.
TEACHER: What can you do with it?
TOM: You can eat it!
TEACHER: That's right! . . . Now let's see . . .
CHILDREN: . . . I love bananas!
TEACHER: What is this?
CHILDREN: An orange.
TEACHER: Is it really an orange?
CHILDREN: Uh-huh. . . . Yes.
CHILD: Look at it closely.
TEACHER: It's an artificial one.
CHILDREN: Oh, that's right, it's an artificial one. . . . But, what else can you tell me about it?

TEACHER: You can eat it. . . . It is round . . .
CHILDREN: Uh-huh.
TEACHER: That's right!
CHILD: It has a stem.
TEACHER: Now, look at this one . . . What's this?
CHILDREN: An orange . . . orange.
TEACHER: And what can you do with it?
CHILDREN: You can eat it . . . and it's round . . .
TEACHER: It is round . . .
CHILD: It has a peel . . .
TEACHER: It has a peel. . . . Now, look at these two things. Are they the same?
CHILDREN: No.
TEACHER: What's different?
CHILDREN: This one . . . this one here is pressed in on the side a little . . . this one is lighter.
TEACHER: Do you know what this really is? This is a tangerine . . . and this is an orange. Now tell me in what ways they are alike.
CHILDREN: This is smaller and that's bigger.
TEACHER: I said, "In what way are they alike?"
CHILDREN: They are both round . . . they both have a stem . . . both orange.

In essence, the children were taught that objects possess many characteristics simultaneously. Following several half-hour training sessions, each child was individually tested again on the original tasks for conservation of quantity. After training, most of them were able to conserve quantity, whereas they were unable to do so prior to the training. The experience of noting the multiple attributes of objects facilitates the child's ability to conserve quantity (67). As the training did not teach the child reversibility directly, we are faced with the problem of explaining why the training helped the child to believe in conservation of quantity, for this result is not congruent with Piaget's explanation of the phenomenon. It is of vital importance to determine the theoretical validity of Piaget's suggestion that changes in *operations* are the most profitable way to conceptualize the public phenomena. But regardless of the results of future research on this issue, it is clear that Piaget's contributions have been epochal and his influence on developmental psychology without parallel.

THE CONCEPT OF INTELLIGENCE
AND THE INTELLIGENCE TEST

It is characteristic of people to think that because many words stand for things, all words necessarily do. But many words, such as the concepts of time and force in physics, are simply useful scientific fictions which help us to explain observable events. They do not stand for objects in the way words such as trees and chairs do. No one has ever seen, heard, or touched intelligence. It is a scientific invention to help explain and predict aspects of behavior. Presently the word intelligence has several different meanings, depending on the scientist using it. To Piaget, intelligence is the acquisition of operations that facilitate adaptation.

To Professor J. P. Guilford of the University of Southern California, intelligence consists of at least five different types of cognitive processes or operations. These are called recognition, memory, divergent production, convergent production, and evaluation. Notice how similar these are to our earlier categories of encoding, memory, generation of hypotheses, deduction, and evaluation (*17, 18, 19, 20*).

Recognition involves sensitivity to aspects of the environment, awareness of changes in external stimuli, and the ability to label or name the environment accurately. *Memory* is the ability to remember or retain information. *Divergent production* refers to the individual's facility in generating a variety of hypotheses or hunches in problem situations. *Convergent production* involves grouping divergent ideas into one unifying concept (e.g., grouping all women who have children into the conceptual category "mothers"). *Evaluation* refers to the ability to make a decision about a problem without persistent vacillation, and to assess the quality of the decision.

Guilford believes that these five basic cognitive processes can be applied to four different kinds of contexts with differing success. The four contexts are *figures, symbols* (letters and numbers), *semantics* (words and sentences), and *behaviors*. Some children are more intelligent with objects, others with numbers, others with ideas. The mechanic, mathematician, and philosopher would be representative of optimal skill with these different types of contexts.

Finally, Guilford suggests that the five processes act on the four units to produce one of six cognitive products. The six products are *units*—a single word or idea; *classes*—a concept that represents a set of units; *relations*— a relationship between or among units or classes; *systems*—an organized sequence of ideas; *transformations*—a change or redefinition of a unit or class; and *implications*—predictions of the future.

Guilford believes that each person is a unique composite of a great many different intellectual abilities. Each intellectual ability, according to Guilford, involves three components: a cognitive operation, a specific content, and a specific product. A child who is exceptionally good at memorizing long poems would illustrate the operation of memory, with a semantic content and a relational product. Guilford visualizes intelligence as a cube containing 120 cells, each cell representing a unique intellectual ability (see Fig. 11.10). This theoretical idea of the cube is, itself, an example of a convergent cognitive process with semantic content and a system as a product.

It is important to note that the differences between Piaget and Guilford stem, in part, from the source of their primary observations. Piaget works with children individually and in a natural context; he infers the concepts they use from their overt behavior and speech. Guilford, on the other hand, administers long paper-and-pencil tests to large groups of adolescents and adults and uses factor analysis (a mathematical procedure) to ar-

Operations
Evaluation
Convergent production
Divergent production
Memory
Cognition

Products
Units
Classes
Relations
Systems
Transformations
Implications

Contents
Figural
Symbolic
Semantic
Behavioral

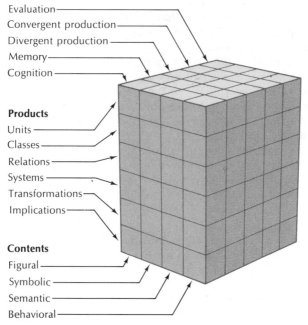

Fig. 11.10. A cube with each "cell" representing a unique intellectual ability. (From J. P. Guilford. *The nature of human intelligence.* New York: McGraw-Hill, 1967, 63. By permission.)

rive at his concepts. Unlike Piaget, Guilford does not have an idealized adult state toward which he thinks intelligence is developing, and he is not concerned with the development of intellectual abilities.

Both Piaget and Guilford have produced theoretical and research-based descriptions of the concept of intelligence, despite the differences in their points of view. There is, however, a special meaning of the word intelligence which is more practical than theoretical, and defines intelligence as a score on a test. The test is called the intelligence test and the score is called the IQ.

The Concept of the IQ

The concept of the IQ, based on the intelligence test, has gained wide acceptance by Americans. Typical American parents are anxious about their child's IQ, and attribute more value and mystique to a high IQ score than to almost any other individual characteristic possessed by their child. There is a zealous and often fanatic belief in the fundamental nature of the IQ.

Some people believe that a person's IQ is inherited, that an IQ does not change very much over the course of a lifetime, that IQ can be measured in the first year of life, and that a high IQ is associated with a large financial income, mental health, and a happy life. These assumptions are not generally true.

As Guilford, Piaget, and others have suggested, intelligence is best defined as the ability to benefit from experience, the ease with which a child learns a new idea or a new set of behaviors, and the limit to which a person might profit from experience. It is generally assumed that everyone has a ceiling, a point above which he will not be able to profit from experience in a particular activity, and that this ceiling is governed by hereditary factors. However, a psychologist who evaluates a child's IQ by giving him a Stanford-Binet intelligence test does not ask many questions that require the child to learn anything new. The majority of the questions on an intelligence test measure a skill or a piece of knowledge that the child already possesses, rather than his ability to learn a new skill or fact. The IQ test, therefore, may not measure the basic attribute that most people acknowledge as the central meaning of intelligence.

The reason for this paradox is that the IQ test was invented initially to solve a practical problem, not a theoretical one. At the turn of the century the public schools in Paris were overcrowded and there were many mentally retarded children who could not profit from schooling. The city fathers decided that they needed some practical way to identify the mentally retarded so they could be removed from regular public school classes. They commissioned a psychologist—Alfred Binet—to construct a test that would be a fair and sensitive predictor of the child's ability to profit from academic instruction. The test was constructed with this specific goal in mind. The test that Binet produced did the job for which it was intended. There have been remarkably few basic changes in that early IQ test, and the test used today resembles, in large measure, the one used more than 60 years ago.

The Binet Scale

Construction.   Binet did not start with a preconceived idea of an entity called intelligence. He started with the fact that on a number of kinds of tasks, some children seemed capable of doing better than others. He further observed that children who did better on one type of test were also likely to do better on others. From these observations he derived a generalized concept of intelligent behavior. He also assumed that individuals differed in their innate capacity for such behavior. His job was to find measures of intelligent behavior that he thought were relatively independent of special training and experiences, and differences in motivation, and which would therefore reflect differences in native potential. An additional requirement of the job was to arrive at objective scores which would show the relative ranks of individuals on a continuum from bright to dull.

The final form of the Stanford-Binet includes a wide variety of items including measures of information and past learning, verbal ability, perceptual-motor coordination, memory, perception, and logical reasoning.

For example, at the sixth-year level in the 1960 revision of the test, the child must define at least six words, such as orange, envelope, and puddle; state the differences between a bird and a dog, a slipper and a boot; recognize parts that are missing in pictures of a wagon, a shoe, a rabbit; count up to nine blocks; and trace the correct path through a maze. (For sample test items at an earlier age level, see pp. 307–308.)

Administration and Scoring.   After establishing a certain rapport with the child to be tested, the examiner begins with items which are below the expected level of the child and gradually proceeds to those of greater difficulty.

The test is scored in terms of mental age, determined as follows: First, a *basal mental age* is established. This is the year level on the scale at which the child can pass all the test items. For example, a 10-year-old who passed all the items scaled at year 9, but failed some items at year 10, would receive a basal mental age of 9 years. The examiner would then proceed to add to this basal age when items of higher levels are passed. The amount added will depend on the total number of higher items correctly answered. The examiner stops when he reaches an age level at which all items are failed. To illustrate, if the 9-year-old in the above example passed half the items at year 10, one-fourth of the items at year 11, and no items at year 12, he would receive six months credit at year 10, three months credit at year 11, and zero months credit at year 12. Adding these scores to his basal age, he would receive an overall mental age of 9 years, plus 6 months, plus 3 months, or 9 years 9 months.

Since the particular items a child is given on the Binet will depend on the range of his ability, the same items are not given to all children. The test has been developed to cover the years from 2 to adulthood. While some of the items given normal 4- and 5-year-olds would overlap, normal 5- and 12-year-olds would be given completely different items.

Intelligence Quotients

We have already mentioned the term Intelligence Quotient, or IQ. On the Binet the IQ is simply a ratio of mental age over chronological age multiplied by 100:

$$IQ = \frac{MA}{CA} \times 100$$

Thus a child of 10 years zero months who obtained a mental age of 10 years zero months on the Binet would be given a score of 10.0/10.0 × 100, or an IQ of 100. It can be seen that an IQ of 100 will be characteristic of the average child from the group on which the test is based. The 10-year-old previously described, whose mental age was 9 years 9 months, would receive an IQ of 9.75/10 × 100, or 97.5.

Distribution of IQ's.   Figure 11.11 shows the distribution of IQ scores for the population used in standardizing the Stanford-Binet. As may be seen, the distribution centers around IQ 100, with higher and lower IQ's about

Table 11.1 The Meaning of Various IQ's Obtained with the Revised Stanford-Binet Scale

The Child Whose IQ Is:	Equals or Exceeds	The child Whose IQ Is:	Equals or Exceeds
136	99 percent	98	45 percent
135	98	97	43
134	98	96	40
133	98	95	38
132	97	94	36
131	97	93	34
130	97	92	31
129	96	91	29
128	96	90	27
127	95	89	25
126	94	88	23
125	94	87	21
124	93	86	20
123	92	85	18
122	91	84	16
121	90	83	15
120	89	82	14
119	88	81	12
118	86	80	11
117	85	79	10
116	84	78	9
115	82	77	8
114	80	76	8
113	79	75	6
112	77	74	6
111	75	73	5
110	73	72	4
109	71	71	4
108	69	70	3
107	66	69	3
106	64	68	3
105	62	67	2
104	60	66	2
103	57	65	2
102	55	65	2
101	52	64	1
100	50	63	1
99	48	62	1

160	1 out of 10,000
156	3 out of 10,000
152	8 out of 10,000
148	2 out of 1,000
144	4 out of 1,000
140	7 out of 1,000

Source: Reprinted from *Supplementary Guide for the Revised Stanford-Binet Scale* (Form L) by Rudolph Pinter, Anna Dragositz, & Rose Kushner. With permission of the Stanford University Press.

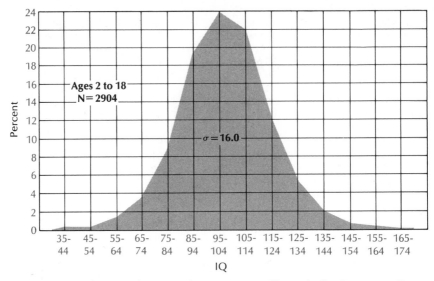

Fig. 11.11 Distribution of IQ's in the Terman-Merrill standardization group (From L. M. Terman & M. A. Merrill. *Measuring intelligence: a guide to the administration of the new revised Stanford-Binet tests of intelligence.* Boston: Houghton Mifflin, 1937. By permission.)

equally common. Table 11.1 shows the percentage of individuals at each IQ level, and is probably the most helpful guide to understanding the meaning of a particular score.

Constancy of the IQ. The practical utility of an intelligence test score will depend partly upon its stability or constancy—that is, upon its capacity for yielding similar scores on future retestings. How confidently can we predict that a child who obtains a superior score at one age will also obtain a comparable score at a later age? It will be recalled that tests given to infants under 2 have little value for the prediction of future intelligence scores. Tests given to older children are more highly predictive.

Table 11.2 shows the correlations between intelligence test scores during the middle-childhood years and at ages 10 and 18. As may be seen, during the middle school years, the correlation between Stanford-Binet test scores given one or two years apart (for example, at ages 8 or 9, and again at 10) is very high (around .90). Moreover, tests given during this period are fairly good predictors of intellectual status in early adulthood (age 18). Nevertheless, despite the fact that the IQ becomes more stable at later ages, we must be cautious in using test scores for predicting the future status of individual children because "the correlations are not sufficiently high so that the possibility of marked changes in the IQ's of individual children is precluded" (24). Repeated testings of a large group of children between the ages of 6 and 18 revealed that the IQ of over half the children "showed

Table 11.2   Correlations Between Stanford-Binet IQ During the
Middle-Childhood Years and IQ at Ages 10 and 18 (Wechsler-Bellevue)

Age	Correlation with IQ at Age 10	Correlation with IQ at Age 18
6	.76	.61
7	.78	.71
8	.88	.70
9	.90	.76
10	—	.70
12	.87	.76

Source: Adapted from M. P. Honzik, J. W. Macfarlane, & L. Allen, The stability of mental test performance between two and eighteen years. *J. exp. Educ.*, 1948, 17. By permission.

a variation of 15 or more points . . . at some time during the school years, and a third group varied as much as 20 points . . ." (24).

The Usefulness of IQ's. What do we actually know when a child obtains an IQ of, for example, 132 on the Stanford-Binet? At the very least, we know that he can do the items on this test better than 97 percent (see Table 11.1) of the large group of persons of his age on whom the test was standardized. And we know that these items are probably representative of a large variety of tasks commonly met by people in their daily lives. In this sense, the authors of the test feel justified in calling it a measure of *general intelligence.* But how useful is such knowledge? Few teachers, for example, are particularly interested in whether a child can do the particular tasks on the Binet. They want to know if he will be able to do satisfactory work in reading, writing, and arithmetic.

The only way of settling the question is by examination of the actual relationship between IQ and school success. In general, IQ scores have been found to be fairly good predictors of academic performance. One investigator (1), for example, lists the following correlations between the Stanford-Binet Intelligence Test and school grades:

IQ and reading comprehension   .73
IQ and reading speed   .43
IQ and English usage   .59
IQ and history   .59
IQ and biology   .54
IQ and geometry   .48

The fairly high relationship between school success and IQ scores may be partly attributed to the similarity of the kinds of behavior measured in both cases. And, indeed, when it comes to predicting success in less academic fields—such as mechanical trades, music, and art—the intelligence test does a less adequate job.

Fig. 11.12. Administrating the Wechsler Intelligence Scale for Children. (By permission of The Psychological Corporation.)

Other Types of Intelligence Tests

Next to the Binet, the Wechsler Intelligence Scale for Children, or WISC (68), is probably the most frequently used test for older children. The IQ's for children from 5 through 15 years may be derived from this test. While, on the Binet, children are given different items at the various age levels, on the WISC the items are the same for children of all ages. Also on the WISC, mental age is not used in deriving an IQ. Instead, the child's performance is compared with that of other children in his own age group. His IQ is merely a function of his percentile rank in comparison with his peers. To illustrate, let us say that a child of 6 obtains a WISC IQ of 79. This simply means (if one consults the appropriate table in the WISC manual) that this child has done better on the test than about 10 percent of 6-year-olds in the standardization group and less well than about 90 percent.

The most important difference between the Binet and WISC is that the latter has special tests for verbal in contrast to perceptual organization skills (often called performance tests). Thus, the child's score on five language tests yields a *Verbal Scale IQ*. Similarly, the score for five perceptual organization tests allows the psychologist to compute a *Performance Scale IQ*. The five verbal tests measure general information, comprehension of judgment regarding everyday situations, vocabulary, arithmetic skills, and reasoning. The perceptual organization and performance tests include various puzzles, speed of performance on a simple copying task, comprehension of pictorial representations of situations, construction of complex designs from blocks (which requires conceptualization of spatial relationships), and recognition of missing elements in pictures. One of the advantages of the WISC over the Binet is that the child's differential ability in verbal and nonverbal areas can be assessed objectively.

Despite the differences in test items and method of computing the IQ, Binet and WISC IQ's tend to be highly correlated (48). In general the WISC is somewhat easier to administer and score (see Fig. 11.12) than the Binet. At present, the Binet is used more frequently for younger children (ages 3–6), and the WISC for older children (ages 7–12).

Group Tests of Intelligence. The intelligence tests described thus far must be individually administered. There are, however, a number of group tests available for use by teachers and others. Such tests have the advantages that they do not require intensive training to administer and they are economical of time.

On the other hand, they also have serious limitations. The results they yield are not so useful for prediction as those from individual tests administered by a skilled clinician. Practical decisions about children who deviate on these tests should not be made without individual follow-up testing by a competent psychologist, together with an investigation of other factors within the individual's life which may be affecting his performance (including his general health and sensory functioning). Too frequently erroneous diagnoses of mental deficiency have been made on the basis of low scores on group intelligence tests.

Tests of Reading Readiness

There is another group of tests which deserve mention in connection with a discussion of children's intelligence and school adjustment—namely, tests of so-called reading readiness (7, 46, 47). While not in themselves measures of intelligence, the readiness tests correlate quite highly with IQ scores (44). They have been designed, however, for a much more specific purpose—namely, to gauge the proper time for the child to begin reading instruction, and also to detect possible difficulties which may be holding the child back in learning to read. These aims have been achieved remarkably well, and for this reason the tests have been widely adopted in elementary school programs. Parents are likely to hear a good deal about readiness tests at the time their children are beginning school.

The Reading Aptitude Tests (Primary Form) designed by Marion Munroe (47) will serve to illustrate the contents of readiness tests in general. Included in her battery are visual tests (designed to measure orientation of forms, ocular-motor control, and visual memory), auditory tests (including measures of pronunciation, discrimination of sounds, and auditory memory), language tests, articulation tests, and tests of motor skills (including both speed and steadiness).

From an overall knowledge of a child's competence in these basic skills, it is possible to establish with some accuracy how well the child will do in learning to read.

Influences on Intelligence Test Performance

It should be evident by now that the intelligence test—which gives rise to the IQ—is a good measure of what a child knows, and what he has taken from his culture. It is a good predictor of the child's grades and test scores in school. If the child has strong motivation to improve the quality of his intellectual skills and has high standards for intellectual mastery, he is likely to have a higher IQ score than a child who is not highly motivated or has low standards. As middle-class children are more consistently encouraged than lower-class children to learn to read, spell, add, and write, one expects that a child's intelligence test score, social class, and school grades will be all positively related to each other. This is, in fact, the case. Moreover, the personality correlates of school success (i.e., persistence, nonaggression, responsible behavior) are similar to the correlates of social class, IQ, and grades in school.

Parental Influences on IQ and Mastery of Intellectual Tasks. Because a child's IQ score is related, in part, to the desire to improve his knowledge and problem-solving skills, family experiences which encourage the development of this motive (i.e., the desire to master intellectual problems) would also lead to high IQ scores, better grades, and stronger motivation for intellectual mastery. This expectation is confirmed.

In a study of motivation for intellectual achievement, 20 boys and 20 girls from the first 3 grades were given a variety of tests and observed in a free-play situation. In addition, both the mothers and fathers were extensively interviewed (5). In the free-play situation, the children could choose from a variety of activities (e.g., reading, riding bicycles, building with blocks, playing house). The girls who showed an intense interest in intellectual activities (read books, worked at puzzles) had parents who encouraged intellectually oriented behavior. This relation was positive, but was not so marked for the boys.

A similar study furnishes some specific hypotheses regarding the father's role in the development of achievement motivation in young boys (58). A group of 40 boys, 9 to 11 years of age, was divided into two sections—those who told many achievement stories and those who told few achievement stories. The investigator visited the home of each of these boys and asked the boy to perform some problem tasks while the parents were watching. The boys who told many achievement stories (high achievement motivation) performed more efficiently than those who told very few achievement stories (58).

In addition, the behavior of both parents toward the child was observed while he was performing the task. Characteristically, the mothers of high achievement boys were involved with their sons and identified with them. These mothers felt close to their sons, wanted them to be competent, and made demands for achievement. However, these demands were associated with a feeling of affection for the child. The fathers of these boys were not overly demanding and gave the boys autonomy and freedom. The boys who told few achievement stories had more demanding and authoritarian fathers who did not give freedom of action and mothers who were less affectionate. The data suggest that boys with low achievement motivation experienced greater degrees of rejection from both parents than the high achievement boys.

> To begin with, the observer's subjective impressions are that the parents of a high achievement boy tend to be more competitive, more involved, and seem to take more pleasure in the problem solving experiments. They appear to be more interested and concerned with their son's performance; they tend to give him more things to manipulate rather than fewer; on the average they put out more effective acts. More objective data show that the parents of a boy with high achievement tend to have higher aspirations for him to do well at any given task, and they seem to have a higher regard for his competence at problem solving. They set up standards of excellence for the boy even when none is given, or if a standard is given, they would expect him to do better than average. As he progresses they tend to react to his performance with warmth and approval, or in the case of the mother especially, with disapproval if he performs poorly (58, 215).

These specific relationships for boys cannot be generalized to girls. Information on the Fels children supports the conclusion that middle-class boys with mothers who are protective, affectionate, and encourage school achievement obtain good grades in school. The girls who do well in school, on the other hand, have mothers who are not overly affectionate and push their daughters toward independent behavior (6, 33).

Another investigation of the families of children whose schoolwork reflected strong achievement motives has yielded results similar to those described above. The investigators (38) employed a series of interviews with parents, teachers, and children to study the home backgrounds of 40 under-achievers and 40 overachievers in academic work. Overachievers were defined as children whose scholastic achievement was "well above" what would have been predicted from their intelligence test scores. Underachievers were children whose achievement was "definitely below expectation" on the basis of their scores. In general, marked differences were found between the two groups.

> Pride, confidence, affection, and interest of parents in their children as shown in instances in which parents read to their children, play with them, build for them, or attend school with them, appear to be in greater evidence for plus-achievers (overachievers) than for minus-achievers (underachievers). On the part

of children, there is a tendency among plus-achievers to respect their parents, to take them into their confidence, to be concerned about pleasing them, and to return the love their parents show.

Minus-achievers appear to have a comparatively limited place in the home. There does not appear to be so much exchange of affection, or mutual respect, desire to measure up to expectations. In fact even expectations appear limited for minus achievers . . . *(38).*

The Determinants of Change in IQ Score. Children who show large increases in IQ during the early school years tend to be similar in personality and family background to those who have high IQ scores. They work hard in school, obtain good grades, and care about intellectual mastery. Thus, one can use amount of increase in IQ as a rough index of the child's desire to master academic skills.

The major results of investigations on the antecedents and correlates of IQ change can be summarized briefly. The correlation between a child's IQ score at age 6 and his score at age 10 approximates $+.70$, suggesting that some children show significant changes in intelligence test score between first and fifth grades.

Investigators at the Fels Research Institute have made an analysis of changes in IQ and related these changes to personality variables *(30, 63).* Their subjects were a group of 140 boys and girls for whom annual IQ scores and behaviorial observations were available. Graphs of the Stanford-Binet IQ scores of these children from ages 3 through 12 showed striking differences among children in the patterns of their scores. Some children's scores remained the same; others decreased; and still others increased. Figure 11.13 illustrates some of the individual curves which were obtained *(63).*

It may be noted that the scores of Case 64 hover around 90 with very little variation over time. On the other hand, Case 139 dropped steadily from an IQ of 140 at age 3 to an IQ of 110 at age 12. Case 2 gained 50 points during the same period; his IQ rose from 110 to 160. Approximately one-half of the group showed a stable IQ pattern with little change over the 10-year period. The other children showed either increases or decreases in IQ score.

What do these changes mean? Are they related to other aspects of the child's psychological functioning? From the total group of 140, the investigators selected 35 children who showed the greatest increase in IQ during the ages 6 through 10, and 35 children who showed the greatest decrease during these years. Ratings based on behavioral observations of these children at home and school during the first 10 years of their lives were then analyzed. A number of interesting discoveries were made.

Twice as many boys as girls showed large increases in IQ. Boys were more likely to gain in IQ score, whereas girls were more likely to lose in IQ. Compared with children who decreased in IQ, those who increased were, according to their behavioral ratings, more independent, more competitive, and more verbally aggressive. While there was no relation between the pattern of IQ changes and the degree of friendliness with age-mates,

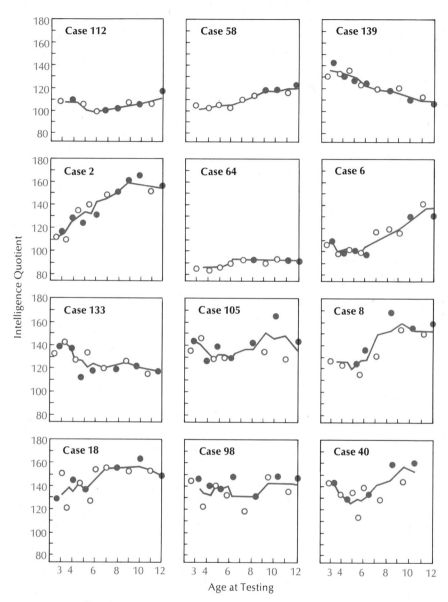

Fig. 11.13. Illustrative cases of changes in IQ scores over time. (From L. Sontag, C. Baker, & V. Nelson. Mental growth and personality development: a longitudinal study. *Monogr. Soc. Res. Child Develpm.*, copyright 1958 by The Society for Research in Child Development, Inc. Vol. 23, No. 2. By permission.)

those who gained in IQ worked harder in school, showed a strong desire to master intellectual problems, and were not likely to withdraw from difficult problem situations. Apparently children who attempt to master challenging problems are more likely to show increases in IQ than children who withdraw from such situations (63).

The mothers of a group of Fels children were rated with respect to the degree to which they encouraged their children to talk and to walk during the first three years of life (31). For the girls, there was a positive relation between maternal concern with the child's early developmental progress and the amount of IQ increase the girls showed during the years 6 through 10. The correlation for boys was positive, but much lower. The lack of a strong relationship between maternal encouragement of walking and talking and IQ increases in boys may be a function of sex differences in the degree of identification with the mother. Girls are more likely than boys to identify with the mother and, hence, more likely to adopt her values. This finding suggests that, although a mother's concern for intellectual mastery influences both boys and girls, this effect may be greater for daughters than for sons. This interpretation is supported by the fact that, even though the relation between mothers' formal education and children's IQ is positive for both sexes, mothers' education is a better predictor of girls' than of boys' IQ scores at ages 3, 6, and 10 (31). For example, the correlation between maternal education and children's IQ at age 10 was .66 for girls, but only .39 for boys. If it is assumed that well-educated mothers are more apt than poorly educated ones to encourage mastery of intellectual skills, it would appear that the mother's emphasis on perfecting intellectual proficiency influences both the level as well as increases in IQ among girls.

How should the IQ score be viewed in the light of this discussion? This question can best be answered by first asking, "What use do we want to make of the IQ score?" If we are interested primarily in predicting the child's success in school subjects, then this test is the best instrument psychologists have devised, for it does a creditable job of predicting who is likely to obtain good grades in elementary school, high school, and college.

Educators have ordinarily not been interested in predicting nonacademic behaviors from IQ scores. For special skills, such as music or art, there are special tests that are more appropriate. The controversy over the meaning of the IQ concept exists partly because many people assume there is a general factor of intelligence (measured by the IQ test) rather than a set of more specific talents. If Binet had viewed his test as an index of "academic potential" rather than "intellectual potential" there would probably be less controversy.

The Child's Personality and His Performance on Intellectual Tests

Increases in IQ score, a strong desire to master intellectual problems, and superior school performance appear to be facilitated by a parental emphasis on and reward of intellectual achievement, as well as the establishment of independence. Moreover, the desire to excel in intellectual skills is a highly stable phenomenon. The Fels longitudinal study revealed that the first 5 years of school furnished important clues to the child's later intellectual strivings, for the desire to master intellectual tasks becomes established during middle childhood. The child who did not develop strong achievement motivation by age 11 or 12 was not likely to change during adolescence. The Fels children who were concerned with intellectual competence during the early school years (e.g., were involved in schoolwork; worked on intellectual projects after school) pursued intellectual vocations and interests in adulthood (33).

In order to integrate the existing data into a tentative concluding statement, three factors appear to be crucial. The first involves the child's motivation.

Motives. If a child believes that mastery of an intellectual task will help him obtain a desired goal, the child will work at mastery. At a general level, most children have strong desires for recognition, affection, and approval from adults; dominance over peers; hostility, power, and mastery. If the child believes that working hard at intellectual tasks will help him attain one or more of these goals, he will do so. Some environments teach the child that attainment of athletic skills will lead to power; others teach that intellectual competence will provide the same goal. The specific behaviors the child chooses in order to gratify his motives are obviously a function of the values espoused by his family. The greater the parental emphasis on intellectual mastery, the stronger will be the child's motivation to master these skills. A parent who is accepting but encourages popularity, beauty, or athletic prowess will not foster the development of a desire to excel in school. The child develops a motive to maintain and increase his similarity to desired models. This process of identification can facilitate intellectual mastery (see pp. 357–363). If intellectual competence is one of the model's central attributes, the child will attempt to increase his mastery in order to increase his similarity to the desired model.

Expectancy. Expectancy of success at intellectual tasks is a second factor controlling quality of performance on IQ or school tests. As a child approaches his third year he becomes more acutely conscious of his ability— or lack of ability—to complete certain tasks or solve particular problems. He seeks to avoid the unpleasant feelings that accompany task failure. He approaches those tasks he expects to master successfully, and avoids tasks he expects to fail. A balance of successes and failures accumulates over time and gradually leads to the establishment of a relatively stable expectancy of success for varied classes of problems. The presence of an excessively competent parent may lead to expectancy of failure if the child cannot identify with the parent. The child is likely to feel that he can never be as powerful or as competent as the parent. Under such circumstances, the child may doubt his ability to succeed and he may withdraw from intellectual challenges.

Anxiety. Finally, the degree of anxiety associated with intellectual mastery is important. Anxiety is most likely to occur under two conditions—when expectancy of success (or failure) is moderate and when motivation is high but expectancy is low. In the first instance the child is maximally uncertain about how he will perform on a test and the uncertainty generates anxiety. The child would be much less anxious if he knew definitely he would pass or fail. In the second instance, the child values competence on a particular intellectual task but expects to fail. When there is a discrepancy between a valued goal and the expectancy of obtaining that goal, anxiety is likely to be generated.

Interaction of Psychodynamic Factors. Motives, expectancies, and anxiety are intimately related to each other and each is related to quality of cognitive performance. The most important relation ties expectancy of success with motivation to master the task. If expectancy of success remains low, motive strength often becomes weak; if expectancy of success is high, motivational strength may increase (25, 26). In general, the child with a high expectancy of success will perform better on an intellectual task than one whose expectancy of success is low.

A child's IQ may rise if his teacher is led to believe that the child is academically superior. The teacher's greater confidence in the child probably increases the child's expectancy of success which, in turn, increases the quality of his performance on the intelligence test (59). In a provocative experiment, all of the children in a public elementary school were given a group intelligence test which was disguised as a test that predicted which children would show a dramatic growth in academic ability. Each teacher was given the names of a few children who "would show unusual academic development" during the coming school year. Actually, these children were no different in ability from the other children in the class, but the teacher was led to expect that they were of "greater capacity." At the end of the school year, all the children were retested with the same group intelligence test given almost a year earlier.

The children in grades 1 and 2 whose teachers expected them to gain in academic ability showed larger gains in IQ than the other children. This effect did not hold for the older children in grades 3 through 6 (59; see Table 11.3).

The author writes: ". . . if teachers can, then probably healers, parents, spouses, and other ordinary people also can affect the behavior of those with whom they interact by virtue of their expectations of what that behavior will be" (59, 412).

Expectancy of success, motivation, and quality of performance are interrelated. Thus in one study children 7 to 9 years of age were asked to state whether they could solve mazes and memory tasks of differing difficulty and were later observed in a situation in which observers coded how long each child played with intellectual games and puzzles. The children who had stated that they could solve difficult problems (high expectancy of suc-

Table 11.3   Excess of IQ Points Gained by Children
Who Were Expected to Perform Well over Other Children

| | Ability Level | | |
	Bright	Average	Below Average
Grade 1	+11.2	+9.6	+24.8
Grade 2	+18.2	−2.9	+6.1
Grade 3	−4.3	+9.1	−6.3
Grade 4	0.0	0.2	+9.0
Grade 5	−0.5	—	+1.2
Grade 6	−1.3	+1.2	−0.5

Source: From R. Rosenthal. *Experimenter effects in behavioral research.* Copyright © 1966 by Meredith Publishing Company. Reprinted by permission of Appleton-Century-Crofts.

cess) approached the intellectual materials frequently (4). As might be expected there is a consistent, positive relation between a child's expectancy of good grades and his actual report card grades. However, girls' expectancy estimates are consistently lower than boys'—despite equal IQ scores and equivalent grades. It is likely that boys feel they should state a higher expectancy for success on intellectual tasks than girls, as task competence is more appropriate for the male than for the female sex role.

These sex differences in expectancy of success in school seem to persist despite equivalent objective performance over a year. In one interesting study the entire entering freshman class at a small college was studied over four academic quarters. At the beginning of each of the academic quarters the students were asked to list each course they would take and the grade they expected to receive in each of their courses. The men always stated that they would receive better grades than the girls for each quarter, although examination of the grades received revealed no sex differences. The expectancy statements of the students and their actual grades remained generally constant over the four quarters. Thus the positive relation between expectancy of success and quality of performance had some permanence. It is possible that high expectancies cause a better academic performance. It is just as reasonable, however, to conclude that quality of performance leads to high expectancies. The child's expectancy derives, in part, from his assessment of how well he is doing. It is likely that actual performance and expectancy are wedded intimately, each influencing the other, and the simultaneous resolution of these two forces affecting the child's motivation.

The Power of Expectancy of Failure.   Expectancy of failure exerts a powerful role on the child's motivation to master or perform on a task, and it can be seen in clear form as early as 2 years of age. Two-year-old children can become very involved in certain problems. If the initial problems are easy and correct solutions come after a brief expenditure of effort, motivation is maintained and obvious indexes of delight punctuate the child's performance. But after one failure, or at most two (children seem to know when they have failed without being told), there is a sudden sullen withdrawal from the task which is difficult to overcome. The child knows which answers are correct and which incorrect and he prefers to avoid the pain of possible failure rather than risk the possible delight of success. It is difficult to explain why expectancy of failure is so strong a force in governing the Western child's behavior. Perhaps the responses of inhibition and withdrawal are easier to elicit than the acts that characterize task involvement. Moreover, failure leaves the child with no response to make. The child who has failed is uncertain as to what he should do and withdrawal is a likely reaction. Prior to failing, the child had been issuing responses that were accepted and led to positive outcomes. Suddenly these responses are not accepted any more; they do not lead to the expected positive outcome. The child feels pressured to behave but he does not know what to do. The prepotent reaction in such a situation is to withdraw. This interpretation of withdrawal as a response to failure places the burden of explanation as much on the avail-ability of task-related responses as on the unpleasant feeling generated by failure or disapproval. The Western child is driven to avoid failure and the quality of his performance on any cognitive task is continually monitored by his guess as to how well he will perform on the task.

The Significance of the Child's Public Test Behavior

Most of this chapter has been concerned with the child's overt problem-solving behavior—his IQ score or his answer to a question. But an answer—spoken, written, drawn, or acted out in gesture—may not be an absolutely faithful index of the quality of the child's thought. Psychologists and teachers must, of course, use the child's actual performance to make educated guesses about the quality of the child's cognitive processes. But we must view these performances with wisdom. Absence of a correct response does not neces-sarily mean the child is not capable of the correct answer. If the child says "sheeps" not sheep, or "wented" instead of went, this error does not neces-sarily mean that he could not tell you that the latter are correct and the former incorrect. If a child of 4 years is asked to draw a man as best he can, he is likely to draw the arms attached to the head. But if the child is shown a drawing of a well-formed man and a drawing of one with arms attached to the head and is asked to point to the man, the child quickly points to the correct representation, not the incorrect one. *He knows much more than he can produce.* A child who cannot reproduce a geometric design has no trouble identifying the correct design when it is presented along with a group of similar ones.

Children also differ in their preferred behavioral reactions to difficult problem situations. Some children persist, others directly refuse to go on with the task, still others become quietly passive (neither speaking nor acting). A recent study compared 3-year-old lower-class Puerto Rican chil-dren with middle-class non-Puerto Rican children of the same age (22).

There were two interesting differences between the groups in their behavioral reaction to intellectual problems. The middle-class children were more likely to work at a problem than the Puerto Rican children, and when problems became difficult the middle-class subjects were more likely to shake their head or push the material away. The Puerto Rican children just sat passively, saying or doing nothing.

The content of a child's answer, his drawing, or his spontaneous speech are under the control of many factors. A careless attitude toward a drawing can yield a poor reproduction; an inability to coordinate lines can yield a gross pictorial distortion; immature syntax can destroy effective communication of a well-formed idea. Psychologists and teachers have been forced to use the child's actions and speech as the primary sources of information about the quality of his thought because of the absence of more sensitive procedures. But each action is the result of multiple forces. Behavior is the result of motivation, language proficiency, expectancy of success, anxiety, preferred strategies for perceptual analysis, and degree of evaluation, to name only a few elements. The child's final performance is an inadequate index of each of these processes for it is a unique composite of them all. The child has many ways to produce a wrong answer. The invention of procedures which will allow separate evaluation of each of these components of a child's public performance has the highest priority for the future. Perhaps one day we will have more direct access to the child's thoughts and not have to guess their form from his hesitant speech or the cryptic messages he writes on paper.

SUMMARY

Cognitive activity involves the five basic processes of comprehension of information (called *encoding*); memory; production and implementation of ideas and rules; and evaluation of the accuracy and appropriateness of cognitive products. These activities, or mental functions, involve a small set of hypothetical mental entities which we have called images, symbols, concepts, and rules. In a sense, one can regard these mental functions and entities as the physiology and anatomy of thought. As in physiological and anatomical development, there are important changes in the nature of the interaction between the functions and the mental units. The major changes involve increasing richness of symbols, concepts, and rules, which, in turn, produce more efficient comprehension, better retention of information, and more flexible and more adequate hypothesis generation. In addition, the rules and concepts become combined into more complicated rules, much as simple chemical elements become combined into complex molecules. As in chemistry, the more complex forms—built from the simpler ones— have unique properties that are not characteristic of the simpler elements. Thus the 12-year-old's realization that he can multiply the speed of a car by the time it travels in order to find the total distance between two points is a forceful and powerful rule that is not given by knowing the meaning of the concept of speed or time alone.

In the early days of medicine and physiology, most people were concerned with the general health of the individual rather than with the functioning of specific parts of his body (such as the thyroid or the efficiency of his sugar metabolism). Similarly, psychology has been concerned during the last 20 years with a gross function which has been called "general intelligence." Like general health, this concept tends to ignore the many separate entities and functions that make up mental activity. The work of Guilford, Piaget, and those concerned with the multidetermined facets of intellectual activity are gradually reshaping our thinking about intelligence. It may be that a century hence, the concept of IQ or intelligence will, like the notion of general health, play a less important role than it does today.

The present task is to gain more exact knowledge about the separate cognitive functions and how they are combined in thought. Finally, it must be realized that the public use or overt manifestation of mental acquisitions will depend on the motives, fears, and expectations of the child. The relation between the answers he gives in the classroom and the mental processes that produce these answers is still largely a mystery.

References

1. Bond, E. A. *Tenth grade abilities and achievements.* New York: Columbia Univer. Press (Teachers College, Bureau of Publications), 1940.
2. Castaneda, A., McCandless, B. R., & Palermo, D. S. The children's form of the Manifest Anxiety Scale. *Child Develpm.,* 1956, *27,* 317–327.
3. Cazden, C. B. Subcultural differences in child languages, *Merrill-Palmer Quart.,* 1966, *12,* 185–219.
4. Crandall, V. J., Katkovsky, W., & Preston, A. Motivational and ability determinants of young children's intellectual achievement behaviors. *Child Develpm.,* 1962, *33,* 643–666.
5. Crandall, V. J., Katkovsky, W., & Preston, A. Parent behavior and children's achievement development. Presented at the annual meeting of the American Psychological Association, Chicago, 1960.
6. Crandall, V. J., Dewey, R., Katkovsky, W., & Preston, A. Parents' attitudes and behaviors and grade school children's academic achievement. *J. genet. Psychol.,* 1964, *104,* 53–66.
7. Cronbach, L. J. *Essentials of psychological testing.* New York: Harper & Row, 1949.
8. Donaldson, M. *The study of children's thinking.* London: Tavistock, 1963.
9. Doob, L. W. Eidetic images among the Ibo. *Ethnology,* 1964, *3,* 357–362.
10. Draguns, J. G., & Multari, G. Recognition of perceptually ambiguous stimuli in grade school children. *Child Develpm.,* 1961, *32,* 541–550.
11. Elkind, D., Koegler, R. R., & Go, E. Studies in perceptual development, *Child Develpm.,* 1964, *35,* 81–90.
12. Flavell, J. H. Concept development. In P. H. Mussen (Ed.), *Handbook of child psychology.* New York: Wiley, in press.

13. Flavell, J. H., Beach, D. R., & Chinsky, J. M. Spontaneous verbal rehearsal in a memory task as a function of age. *Child Develpm.*, 1966, *37*, 284–299.

14. Foulkes, D., Tivik, T., Steadman, H. S., Spear, P. S., & Symonds, J. E. Dreams of the male child: an EEG study. *J. abnorm. Psychol.* 1967, *72*, 457–467.

15. Gollin, E. S. Serial learning and perceptual recognition in children: training, delay, and order effects. *Percept. mot. Skills,* 1966, *23*, 751–758.

16. Greco, P. Quantité et quotité. In P. Greco & A. Morf (Eds.), *Structures numeriques elémentaires. Etudes d'Epistémologie Génétique* (Vol. 13). Paris: Presses Universitaires de France, 1962, 1–70.

17. Guilford, J. P. The structure of intellect. *Psychol. Bull.*, 1956, *53*, 267–293.

18. Guilford, J. P. Three faces of intellect. *Amer. Psychol.*, 1959, *14*, 469–479.

19. Guilford, J. P. *The nature of human intelligence.* New York: McGraw-Hill, 1967.

20. Guilford, J. P. Intelligence has three facets. *Science,* 1968, *160*, 615–620.

21. Haber, R. N., & Haber, R. B. Eidetic imagery. *Percept. mot. Skills,* 1964, *19*, 131–138.

22. Hertzig, M. E., Birch, H. G., Thomas, A., & Mendez, O. A. Class and ethnic differences in the responsiveness of preschool children to cognitive demands. *Monogr. Soc. Res. Child Develpm.,* 1968, *33*, No. 1 (Serial 117).

23. Hess, R. D., & Baer, R. M. (Eds.), *Early education.* Chicago: Aldine, 1968.

24. Honzik, M. P., Macfarlane, J. W., & Allen, L. The stability of mental test performance between two and eighteen years, *J. exp. Educ.,* 1948, *17*, 309–324.

25. Irwin, F. W. Stated expectations as functions of probability and desirability of outcomes. *J. Pers.,* 1953, *21*, 329–335.

26. Jessor, R., & Readio, J. The influence of the value of an event upon the expectancy for its occurrence. *J. genet. Psychol.,* 1957, *56*, 219–228.

27. Kagan, J. Individual differences in the resolution of response uncertainty. *J. pers. soc. Psychol.,* 1965, *2*, 154–160.

28. Kagan, J. Reflection impulsivity and reading ability in primary grade children. *Child Develpm.,* 1965, *36*, 609–628.

29. Kagan, J. Generality and dynamics of conceptual tempo. *J. abnorm. Psychol.,* 1966, *71*, 17–24.

30. Kagan, J., Sontag, L. W., Baker, C. T., & Nelson, V. L. Personality and I.Q. change. *J. abnorm. soc. Psychol.,* 1958, *56*, 261–266.

31. Kagan, J., & Moss, H. A. Parental correlates of child's I.Q. and height: a cross-validation of the Berkeley Growth Study results. *Child Develpm.,* 1959, *30*, 325–332.

32. Kagan, J., & Moss, H. A. Stability and validity of achievement fantasy. *J. abnorm. soc. Psychol.,* 1959, *58*, 357–364.

33. Kagan, J., & Moss, H. A. *Birth to maturity.* New York: Wiley, 1962.

34. Kagan, J., Rosman, B. L., Day, D., Albert, J., & Phillips, W. Information processing in the child. *Psychol. Monogr.,* 1964, *78*, No. 1 (Whole Number 578).

35. Kagan, J., Pearson, L., and Welch, L. Conceptual impulsivity and inductive reasoning. *Child Develpm.,* 1966, *37*, 583–594.

36. Kagan, J., Pearson, L., and Welch, L. The modifiability of an impulsive tempo. *J. educ. Psychol.,* 1966, *57*, 359–365.

37. Kagan, J., Moss, H. A., & Sigel, I. E. Psychological significance of styles of conceptualization. In J. C. Wright and J. Kagan (Eds.), Basic cognitive processes in children. *Monogr. Soc. Res. Child Develpm.,* 1963, *28*, No. 2 (Serial No. 86), 73–112.

38. Kurtz, J. J., & Swenson, E. G. Factors related to overachievement and underachievement in school. *School Rev.,* 1951, *59*, 472–480.

39. Lee, L. C., Kagan, J., & Rabson, A. Influence of a preference for analytic categorization upon concept acquisition. *Child Develpm.*, 1963, *34*, 433–442.
40. Levinson, B., & Reese, H. W. Patterns of discrimination learning set in preschool children, fifth graders, college freshmen, and the aged. *Monogr. Soc. Res. Child Develpm.*, 1967, *32*, No. 7 (Serial No. 115).
41. Maccoby, E. E. Sex differences in intellectual functioning. In E. E. Maccoby (Ed.), *The development of sex differences.* Stanford, Calif.: Stanford Univer. Press, 1966, 25–55.
42. Maccoby, E. E. Selective auditory attention in children. In L. P. Lipsitt & C. C. Spiker (Eds.), *Advances in child development and behavior.* New York: Academic Press, 1967, 99–124.
43. Messer, S. B. The effect of anxiety over intellectual performance on reflective and impulsive children. Unpublished doctoral dissertation Harvard University, 1968.
44. Milner, E. A. A study of the relationship between reading readiness in grade one school children and patterns of parent-child interaction. *Child Develpm.*, 1951, *22*, 95–112.
45. Morrison, F., Eisenberg, K., Haith, M. M., & Mindes, P. Short term memory for visual information in children and adults. Paper presented at a meeting of the Eastern Psychological Association, Washington, April, 1968.
46. Munroe, M. Reading aptitude tests for the prediction of success and failure in beginning reading. *Education*, 1935, *56*, 7–17.
47. Munroe, M. *Reading aptitude tests, primary form.* Boston: Houghton Mifflin, 1935.
48. Mussen, P. H., Dean, S., & Rosenberg, M. Some further evidence on the validity of the WISC. *J. consult. Psychol.*, 1952, *16*, 410–411.
49. Olver, R. R., & Hornsby, J. R. On equivalence. In J. S. Bruner, R. R. Olver, & P. M. Greenfield (Eds.), *Studies in cognitive growth.* New York: Wiley, 1966, 68–85.
50. Piaget, J. *The language and thought of the child.* London: Routledge & Kegan Paul, 1926.
51. Piaget, J. *Judgment and reasoning in the child.* New York: Harcourt, Brace & World, 1928.
52. Piaget, J. *The child's concept of the world.* New York: Harcourt, Brace & World, 1929.
53. Piaget, J. *The child's conception of physical causality.* London: Routledge & Kegan Paul, 1930.
54. Piaget, J. *The moral judgment of the child.* London: Routledge & Kegan Paul, 1932.
55. Piaget, J. *Play, dreams, and imitation in childhood.* New York: Norton, 1951.
56. Piaget, J. *The origins of intelligence in children.* New York: International Universities Press, 1952.
57. Piaget, J. *Logic and psychology.* New York: Basic Books, 1957.
58. Rosen, B. D., & D'Andrade, R. The psychosocial origins of achievement motivation. *Sociometry*, 1959, *22*, 185–218.
59. Rosenthal, R. *Experimenter effects in behavioral research.* New York: Appleton-Century-Crofts, 1966.
60. Sarason, S. B., Davidson, K. S., Lighthall, F. F., Waite, R. R., & Ruebush, B. K. *Anxiety in elementary school children.* New York: Wiley, 1960.
61. Sigel, I. E., Roeper, A., & Hooper, F. H. A training procedure for acquisition of Piaget's conservation of quantity. *Brit. J. educ. Psychol.*, 1966, *36*, 301–311.

62. Siipola, E. M., & Hayden, S. D. Scoring eidetic imagery among the retarded. *Percept. mot. Skills,* 1965, *21,* 275–286.
63. Sontag, L. W., Baker, C. T., & Nelson, V. L. Mental growth and personality: a longitudinal study. *Monogr. Soc. Res. Child. Develpm.,* 1958, *23,* No. 68, 1–143.
64. Terman, L. M., & Merrill, M. A. *Measuring intelligence: a guide to the administration of the new revised Stanford-Binet tests of intelligence.* Boston: Houghton Mifflin, 1937.
65. Tyler, L. E. The development of vocational interests: I. The organization of likes and dislikes in ten-year-old children. *J. genet. Psychol.,* 1955, *86,* 33–44.
66. Wallach, M. A., & Kogan, N. *Modes of thinking in young children.* New York: Holt, Rinehart and Winston, 1965.
67. Watson, E. H., & Lowrey, G. H. *Growth and development of children.* Chicago: Year Book Publishers, 1967 (5th ed.).
68. Wechsler, D. *Wechsler intelligence scale for children.* New York: The Psychological Corporation, 1952.
69. Weinstein, E. A. Weights assigned by children to criteria of prestige. *Sociometry,* 1956, *19,* 126–132.
70. White, S. H. Changes in learning processes in the late pre-school years. Presented at a meeting of the American Education Research Association, Chicago, 1968.
71. Winker, J. B. Age trends and sex differences in the wishes, identification, activities and fears of children. *Child. Develpm.,* 1949, *20,* 191–200.
72. Winterbottom, M. R. The relation of need for achievement to learning experiences in independence and mastery. In J. W. Atkinson (Ed.), *Motives in fantasy, action and society.* Princeton, N.J.: Van Nostrand, 1958, 450–478.
73. Wohlwill, J. F. The learning of absolute and relational number discriminations by children. *J. genet. Psychol.,* 1963, *101,* 217–228.
74. Yando, R. M., & Kagan, J. The effect of teacher tempo on the child. *Child Develpm.,* 1968, *39,* 27–34.

12

Development in Middle Childhood

II. Personality Development and Problems of Adjustment

As the child enters the school years, his horizons are expanded, and he is subjected to an ever-widening series of influences—teachers, peers, books, television. Nevertheless, the kinds of parents a child has, and the kinds of relationships he has with them, remain, for the average child, the most significant environmental factors in determining the kind of person he will become, the problems he will face in his quest for maturity, and the ways in which he will deal with these problems.

In this chapter, we will turn our attention first to the continuing influences of the family on the child's personality and social development. Following this, we will examine the growth of conscience and moral standards, which assume critical importance during this age period. Finally, we will consider some of the more common problems of adjustment that may occur in the middle-childhood years and their significance.

INFLUENCE OF THE FAMILY IN MIDDLE CHILDHOOD

Parent-Child Relationships

There is probably no area of child development in which public opinion is characterized by more misconceptions and myths than the area of the effects of parental behaviors in child-rearing. Thus we frequently hear statements such as: "You can say what you want to about the influence of parents on their children's development, but I know it's really all in the genes they're born with"; or "I know psychologists don't believe in discipline, but in my opinion that's what's wrong with today's children. Look at all those hippies and college dissenters!" From listening to such popular critics, one could easily gain the impression that the field contains no substantive research information, and that psychologists are merely responding to shifting fads, in much the same way that women raise or lower the hemlines of their dresses in response to current fashions.

Much popular thinking is deficient in several respects: (1) it oversimplifies the complexities and variations possible in parental behavior; (2) it assumes that any assertion that parental practices affect the child's development is tantamount to declaring that other factors, including individual biological differences, have no effects; and (3) it assumes that it is not possible to investigate the potential effects of parental practices in a systematic, reliable manner. As we shall attempt to show, all of these assumptions are in error. While we still have much to learn about the interacting effects of various influences on the course of the child's personal and social development (especially about possible interactions between genetically based temperamental characteristics and parent behaviors), considerable progress has been made in the past decade in our knowledge of the effects of parent behavior on children.

Dimensions of Parent Behavior.   Parent behavior is not unidimensional; it does not consist simply of variations along a single axis, as popular oversimplifications (such as those examples cited above) sometimes seem to imply. Parents may love their children, or they may reject them. They may also, however, be loving *and* controlling, or loving *and* permissive; rejecting *and* controlling, or rejecting *and* permissive. The response of the child will not depend simply on one aspect of the parents' behavior and personality, but rather on the combined effect of many aspects.

A number of investigators (15, 165, 166) have attempted to conceptualize meaningful dimensions of parental behavior, and their relationships to one another. There is, of course, no magic in these theoretical models; they are to an extent arbitrary. Furthermore, as we have already noted (see pp. 366–374), even after one has abstracted a potentially meaningful dimension (e.g., permissiveness or rejection), the task of defining what is meant by the dimension remains. "Permissiveness," for example, may mean one thing to one investigator and something else to another. We have already seen that apparently conflicting results regarding the effects of parental behavior may be caused largely by differences in definition. Thus, it becomes important to make clear what is meant by particular terms. Nevertheless, as we shall see, these theoretical models may prove extremely helpful both in conceptualizing variations in parent behavior in an orderly manner, and in permitting us to design meaningful research and to interpret its findings.

Two dimensions that consistently emerge in such theoretical schemes

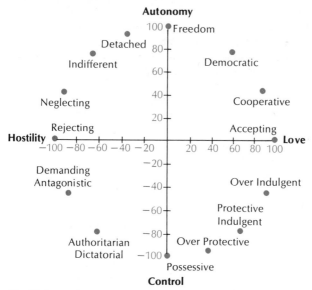

Fig. 12.1. A hypothetical circumplex of maternal behavior concepts. (From E. S. Schaefer. A circumplex model for maternal behavior. *J. abnorm. soc. Psychol.,* 1959, 59, 232. Copyright 1959 by the American Psychological Association. By permission.)

(or models) are *love-hostility* (or *warmth-hostility*) and *control-autonomy.* One such hypothetical model, formulated by Schaefer (*166*) is shown in Fig. 12.1. Wesley Becker, a psychologist at the University of Illinois, has indicated that it might be desirable to add an additional third dimension to such models by distinguishing two aspects of the control-autonomy axis: *restrictiveness-permissiveness* and *anxious emotional involvement-calm detachment.* He notes, for example, that two different parents may both be restrictive (or permissive), yet differ in their emotional involvement. Thus,

> both the democratic parent and the indulgent parent (by definition) are high on the dimensions of warmth and permissiveness, but the indulgent parent is high on emotional involvement while the democratic parent tends to be low on this dimension (calm-detached). Both the organized-effective parent and the overprotective parent are high on warmth and restrictiveness, but the overprotective parent again shows more emotional involvement than the organized-effective parent (*15, 174*).

While this extra refinement has potential value for lending additional precision to future research, little work on it has been done to date, and it will not be developed further here.

Warmth-Hostility. For present purposes, this dimension of parental behavior is defined at the warm end by such characteristics as: "accepting, affectionate, approving, understanding, child-centered, frequent use of explanations, positive response to dependency behavior, high use of reasons in discipline, high use of praise in discipline, low use of physical punishment" (15, 174). The hostility end of this dimension is defined, in general, by the opposite of these characteristics.

Control-Autonomy (i.e., Restrictiveness-Permissiveness).   This dimension is defined at the restrictive end by: "many restrictions and strict enforcement of demands in the area of sex play, modesty behavior, table manners . . . neatness, orderliness, care of household furniture, noise, obedience, aggression to sibs, aggression to peers, and aggression to parents" (15, 174). As already noted above, these parental behaviors can be carried out in a rather calm, detached fashion or in an excitable, emotionally overinvolved manner.

It is possible to make some meaningful (though rather limited) generalizations about the probable effects of variations in parental behavior along one of these dimensions considered separately, without regard to variations on the other. Thus, most studies (15, 169, 188) suggest that hostility on the part of the parents tends to produce counterhostility and aggression, either in feelings or behavior, on the part of children. Similarly, restrictiveness tends to foster inhibited behaviors, while permissiveness encourages less inhibited behaviors (10, 15, 89, 109, 115, 168). However, more precise and more meaningful generalizations become possible when interactions between these two dimensions are considered. Thus, while the child of a hostile, permissive parent and the child of a hostile, restrictive, and controlling parent may both have deep-seated feelings of hostility, the extent to which (and the directions in which) the hostility is expressed in behavior may vary greatly. The former is likely to express his aggression directly and with little control. In the latter, the aggression may be expressed in certain "safe" areas (e.g., with peers), "but it is more likely to be inhibited and turned against the self, or to be revealed in manifestation of internal conflict" (15, 198). It is not likely to be expressed openly or directly against the parents, despite the fact that they may be the primary source of the child's hostile or aggressive feelings. A number of the probable effects upon the child of various combinations of parental *warmth-hostility* and *restrictiveness-permissiveness (control-autonomy)* are shown in Fig. 12.1.

The Warm-Permissive Parent.   The parent who is both warm *and* permissive probably comes closest to the popular stereotype of the recommendations of child-rearing specialists, whether this stereotype serves as a source of assurance or outraged alarm. The child of such parents is likely to be rather active, outgoing, socially assertive, and independent (10, 15, 89, 121, 188), as well as friendly, creative, and lacking in hostility toward others or himself (10, 89, 168). He may also be somewhat aggressive and bossy and, on occasion, somewhat disobedient and disrespectful, particularly at home (10, 110). However, these kinds of aggressive manifestations appear to emerge largely because of feelings of security and a lack of severe punitive responses from parents, and to be "more easily turned on and off in response to reinforcing conditions" (15, 197), rather than reflecting chronic anger and frustration, or uncontrollable explosions of deep-seated but dammed-up feelings of hostility (15).

In a study by Levin (109), another important possible consequence of warm-permissive parental behavior is suggested. Levin measured the relative frequency with which children preferred to use adult dolls in a doll-play situation under different conditions. It was found that maximum preference for adult role-taking (i.e., maximum use of adult dolls) occurred under warm-permissive conditions. If adult role-taking is assumed to reflect a positive modeling of the parent and the learning of adult ways of doing things, these findings appear consistent with other studies indicating greater autonomy and mastery motivation among permissively reared children (15, 89, 188). It would appear that while the child of warm-permissive parents may be "somewhat of a handful," there are offsetting bonuses for the parent in his self-confidence, friendliness, and development of autonomy, independence, and desire for mastery of his environment.

The Warm-Restrictive Parent. A parent who is warm may nevertheless be restrictive in child-rearing practices, particularly if the restrictiveness is not extreme. It has been found that children reared in warm-restrictive homes, as compared with those reared in warm-permissive homes, were likely to be: more dependent, less friendly, less creative, more hostile in their fantasies, and either very high or very low in persistence. These results in many ways parallel those of Kagan and Moss (89) in their longitudinal study of the Fels population (pp. 340–341), although these latter investigators did not consider restrictiveness specifically in relation to the variable of warmth. In their study, maternal restrictiveness was evaluated by means of extended home observations and interviews, and averaged ratings were obtained for three age periods: birth to age 3, 3 to 6, and 6 to 10. Restrictiveness was defined as the degree to which the mother attempted to force the child— through punishment or threat—to adhere to her standards, and the degree to which deviations from these standards were punished. In general, it was found that early maternal restrictiveness, particularly during the first three years, tended to have lasting effects upon the child. Children of restrictive parents were more conforming, less aggressive, less dominant and competitive with their peers, and less likely to display mastery behavior. There were, however, a number of interesting variations revealed by this study. For one thing, early restrictiveness (when the child was under 3) appeared to have a much greater inhibitory effect throughout childhood and adolescence than later restrictiveness (ages 3 to 6 and 6 to 10). Secondly, mothers tended to be more consistent over time in their restrictiveness with girls than was the case with boys. Thus, among girls, early maternal restrictiveness was highly correlated with later restrictiveness, while among the mothers of boys, it was not—although positive correlations were obtained among *older* age periods. It appears that this difference between boys and girls may be accounted for, at least in part, by the greater sex-role acceptability of restrictiveness and its effects among girls than among boys. Third, restrictiveness at later ages tended to produce more hostility in the child than at earlier ages, regardless of whether this restrictiveness resulted in a conforming, dependent child. In the period between 6 and 10 years of age, maternal restrictiveness toward boys tended to produce both dependency and aggressive reactions to the mother, related to her restrictiveness (89).

Further, consistent data emerge from a study by Maccoby (115) which showed that parents who were both warm and restrictive in the child's early years tended to have sons who, at age 12, were strict rule-enforcers with their peers. These rule-enforcing boys also manifested less overt aggression (based on teacher ratings), less misbehavior when the teacher was out of the room, and greater motivation toward schoolwork, although similar findings were not obtained for girls.

In general, it would appear that the more extreme types of behavior disorders, such as neurotic disability or delinquency, are not so likely to occur when there is adequate parental warmth. However, within the context of warmth, significant differences in behavior may result, depending upon whether the parent is basically permissive or restrictive. The permissively reared child is more likely to be active, outgoing, friendly, creative, independent, and socially assertive; the restrictively reared child is more likely to be submissive to parents, conforming, dependent, compliant, polite and neat, lacking in aggression and competitiveness with peers, and less oriented toward mastery in the assumption of autonomy and independence (89, 123, 168, 189). Further research is needed, particularly in determining differences between boys and girls in their responses to parental permissiveness and restrictiveness within the context of overall warmth (15).

The Hostile-Restrictive Parent. The parent who is both hostile *and* restrictive tends to promote counterhostility within the child without allowing it to be expressed in behavior. Sometimes the child may not even be able to admit his hostile feelings to conscious awareness. Under such conditions, it is perhaps not surprising that this parental behavior pattern is often found among neurotic children (93, 158, 159). The combination of low permissiveness and high punishment (i.e., restrictive-hostile) leads to self-punishment, suicidal tendencies, and accident proneness (168) as well as to shyness and social withdrawal, difficulties in relating to peers, and little confidence in or motivation toward adult role-taking (89, 110, 188). "By and large, these studies suggest that the combination of restrictiveness and hostility fosters considerable resentment, with some of it being turned against the self, or, more generally, experienced as internalized turmoil and conflict" (15, 19).

The Hostile-Permissive Parent. While restrictiveness combined with hostility tends to maximize self-aggression, social withdrawal, and symptoms of internal conflict (particularly when parental hostility is covert and difficult for the child to label), permissiveness combined with hostility appears to maximize "aggressive, poorly controlled behavior" (15, 193). As we shall see in our discussion of delinquency (pp. 734–746), parents of a significant percentage of delinquents generally lack parental warmth and are either neglectful in exercising parental control or highly inconsistent and quixotic in the use of discipline. While the child who is subjected to covertly hostile, restrictive parental motives is more likely to "internalize" his angry feelings, the child who is reared under lax-hostile conditions is more likely to "act out" his resentment.

Studies of nondelinquent children tend to yield similar findings. Among the children of working-class mothers, nonaggressive boys came most frequently from homes where the mother was overcontrolling and domineering; normally assertive, self-confident boys came most often from homes in which the mother used a normal, flexible sort of discipline (121). In contrast, aggressive, "acting-out" boys came most frequently from homes where the mother was lacking in control or where she attempted to impose overcontrol. In the latter case, aggression occurred most often where the mother, while attempting to be strict, was not consistent about imposing discipline. Maximum overt aggression is most frequently the consequence of conditions of high permissiveness-high punishment—analogous to the lax-hostile condition of the delinquency studies (123, 169).

Effects of Inconsistent Discipline.   Perhaps the most frequently asked question with which psychologists are confronted by parents is "Do you believe in discipline?"—often with the implication that the answer will be "no." In actuality, of course, the question is a meaningless one. The question is not one of discipline or no discipline, but of how much discipline, of what kind, at what stage in the child's development, for what purpose, and in what sort of parental emotional climate (i.e., loving-hostile). Socialization of the child obviously requires the imposition of controls. Without controls the skills, attitudes, and behaviors necessary for a satisfactory interdependent existence in a complex society could not be learned. On the other hand, excessive control and discipline, as we have already seen, threaten the child's development of autonomy, self-confidence, and self-reliance—qualities which are equally necessary for social effectiveness. The studies reviewed above appear to indicate that the most effective balance between cooperative, responsible, disciplined behavior, on the one hand, and self-confidence, autonomy, self-reliance, and emotional freedom, on the other hand, occur where discipline is flexible but firm and consistent. Discipline is also most beneficial when it is applied only in the child's own interest in terms of his development, and only to the extent necessary to achieve its purpose, rather than as an expression of the parents' hostility or need to control or dominate the child.

It appears further that inconsistent or erratic discipline may be as harmful as too little or too much discipline. Whether stemming from parental hostility or indifference (as in the case of the parent who only imposes discipline for his own convenience—e.g., no "back-talk" and keeping quiet or out of the way when father is around), or from parental uncertainty and lack of confidence or mood swings, inconsistency in parental discipline tends to contribute to maladjustment, conflict, or aggression in the child (*163, 179*).

Parent-Child Relationships and the Child's Self-Concept

A favorable self-concept (self-esteem) is essential to personal happiness and effective functioning, both in the child and in the adult. Persons who seek psychological and psychiatric help frequently acknowledge that they suffer from feelings of inadequacy and unworthiness (*195*). They tend to perceive themselves as helpless and inferior (*153*), have difficulty in either giving or receiving love (*56*), and tend to feel isolated and alone (*34*). They are likely to feel guilty, ashamed, or depressed, and to derogate their own potential and accomplishments (*34*). Not surprisingly, a high anxiety level and a negative conception of the self tend to be correlated (*17, 23, 42, 112, 135, 186*). Furthermore, the anxious child's tendency to derogate himself tends to generalize and affect his image of his bodily integrity and adequacy as well (*162, 186*). A negative self-concept appears to promote defensiveness in the child's reactions to himself and others (*150, 161*). Finally, a negative self-concept appears to impair initial school adjustment and subsequent academic progress (*17, 48, 137, 189*).

While, as we have already seen, the child's self-concept is affected by the way in which his peers and teachers respond to him, it appears likely that for most children the way in which they are treated by parents is of overriding importance in determining their perceptions of themselves (*177*). How is the child's self-esteem related to the patterns of parental behaviors described above? Some interesting recent studies (*34, 156*) help to shed considerable light on this question.

What Is Self-Esteem? For purposes of this discussion, "self-esteem is a *personal* judgment of worthiness that is expressed in the attitudes the individual holds toward himself. It is a subjective experience which the individual conveys to others by verbal reports and other overt expressive behavior" (*34, 5*).

In a study of a large number of preadolescent children attending the public schools of central Connecticut, Coopersmith (*34*) found marked differences in the experiential worlds and social behaviors of children differing in self-esteem. Children high in their estimation of themselves approached tasks and persons with the expectation that they would be well-received and successful:

> They have confidence in their perceptions and judgments and believe that they can bring their efforts to a favorable resolution. Their favorable self-attitudes lead them to accept their own opinions and place credence and trust in their reactions and conclusions. This permits them to follow their own judgments when there is a difference of opinion and also permits them to consider novel ideas. The trust in self that accompanies feelings of worthiness is likely to provide the conviction that one is correct and the courage to express those convictions. The attitudes and expectations that lead the individual with high

self-esteem to greater social independence and creativity also lead him to more assertive and vigorous actions. They are more likely to be participants than listeners in group discussions, they report less difficulty in forming friendships, and they will express opinions even when they know these opinions may meet with a hostile reception. Among the factors that underlie and contribute to these actions are their lack of self-consciousness and their lack of preoccupation with personal problems. Lack of self-consciousness permits them to present their ideas in a full and forthright fashion; lack of self-preoccupation permits them to consider and examine external issues.

The picture of the individual with low self-esteem that emerges from these results is markedly different. These persons lack trust in themselves and are apprehensive about expressing unpopular or unusual ideas. They do not wish to expose themselves, anger others, or perform deeds that would attract attention. They are likely to live in the shadows of a social group, listening rather than participating, and preferring the solitude of withdrawal above the interchange of participation. Among the factors that contribute to the withdrawal of those low in self-esteem are their marked self-consciousness and preoccupation with inner problems. This great awareness of themselves distracts them from attending to other persons and issues and is likely to result in a morbid preoccupation with their difficulties. The effect is to limit their social intercourse and thus decrease the possibilities of friendly and supportive relationships (34, 70–71).

What patterns of parental characteristics and behaviors distinguished between children high and low in self-esteem? In general, children with high self-esteem tended to have parents who were also high in self-esteem. These parents, in contrast to parents of children low in self-esteem, also tended to be more emotionally stable and more self-reliant, resilient, and effective in their attitudes and actions regarding child care. Interactions between the parents of high self-esteem children tended to be marked by greater compatibility and ease, with clearer definitions of each parent's areas of authority and responsibility. While these parents tended to have high expectations of their children, they also provided sound models for them and gave their children consistent encouragement and support.

Mothers of children high in self-esteem were more accepting of their children, and, even more importantly, tended to express their acceptance through specific, everyday manifestations of concern, affection, and close rapport. These mothers were likely to express agreement with such statements as "Children would be happier and better behaved if parents would show an interest in their affairs" and "When you do things together, children feel close to you and talk easier"; and to disagree with such statements as "Children should not annoy their parents with the unimportant problems" and "The trouble with giving attention to children's problems is they usually just make up a lot of stories to keep you interested." In contrast, mothers of children low in self-esteem were "more likely to withdraw from their children, and by their inattentive and neglectful treatment to produce a milieu that is physically, emotionally, and intellectually impoverished" (34,

179). Low self-esteem mothers were likely to depreciate their children and to treat them as a burden. Their emotional responses to their children tended to range from hostility to indifference.

Interestingly, mothers of high self-esteem children were *more* likely to enforce established rules carefully and consistently. They used reward as the preferred mode of affecting behavior, but used straightforward and appropriate punishment rather than harsh treatment or loss of love when some sort of punishment was required (34). The fathers of these boys were usually the ones to administer punishment, although they frequently shared that responsibility with the mother. Furthermore, these punishments tended to be perceived as justifiable by the high self-esteem subjects.

In contrast, lack of parental guidance and relatively harsh and disrespectful treatment of children were characteristic of the parents of children low in self-esteem. Apparently these parents either did not know or did not care to establish and enforce guidelines for their children:

> They are apt to employ punishment rather than reward, and the procedures they do employ lay stress on force and loss of love. The mothers are more likely to administer punishment to these boys, which may have negative connotations and significance for children in this age group. There is an inconsistent and somewhat emotional component in the regulatory behaviors of these parents. They are less concerned, on the one hand, and inclined to employ more drastic procedures, on the other. They propose that punishment is a preferred method of control, yet state that they find it generally ineffective. Their children apparently smart under such a regimen and believe that the control behaviors of their parents are often unwarranted (34, 196–197).

While parents of high self-esteem children were more likely to provide carefully defined standards and limits on behavior for their children, within these limits parental treatment was noncoercive and emphasized the rights and opinions of the child. Typically, the child's views were sought, his opinions respected, and concessions were often granted to him if differences existed. The freedom that prevailed within broad limits permitted the child to enter into discussions as a true participant and to gain confidence from the assertion of his own views. Thus parents of high self-esteem children were more likely to agree with such statements as "Children should have a say in the making of family plans" and "A child has a right to his own point of view and ought to be allowed to express it." (In the case of the latter statement, 90.3 percent of the parents of high self-esteem children, as compared with only 9.7 percent of the parents of low self-esteem children, were in agreement!) Further, while most parents of high self-esteem children tended to stress "discussion and reasoning" as methods of obtaining the child's cooperation and compliance, most parents of low self-esteem children tended to stress "force and autocratic" measures.

Finally, in their encouragement of independence, parents of high self-esteem children tended to fall between the parents of children with low self-esteem and parents of those with moderate self-esteem. Parents of children with high self-esteem seemed to be trying to establish a reasonable balance between protectiveness and encouragement of autonomy. For example, they were less likely than parents in other groups to express anxiety about the child's sleeping outside the home. On the other hand, they were more likely than low-esteem parents and less likely than middle-esteem parents to agree with the statement: "A child should be protected from jobs which might be too trying or too hard for him."

In summary, it appears that the kinds of parental practices which appeared in our earlier discussion to promote desirable social behaviors are also those that promote a confident self-image in the child. It is not surprising that high self-esteem has also been found to be positively related to academic accomplishment, and low self-esteem to academic and learning difficulties (4, 25, 113).

Social Background and Self-Esteem. In Coopersmith's study (34) and others (156), positive but modest relationships between a child's level of self-esteem and his socioeconomic status have been found, with high-status children manifesting higher self-esteem. One factor which may play a role in determining the lower self-esteem of lower-status children involves discrepancies between the social-class-related traits developed by the child and the traits most valued by the wider society. If the particular combination of traits a child possesses happens to be highly valued and rewarded by the culture, his self-esteem will be enhanced. On the other hand, if the child possesses traits that might be valued in some other culture, but not in his own, his self-esteem may suffer. For example, a cooperative, self-effacing, noncompetitive boy might be highly valued in the culture of the Zuni Indians. But if this same boy moves into the wider "Anglo" culture, his lack of aggressiveness may be scorned, and his self-esteem may suffer.

It is clear, however, that the specific nature of the child's relationships with his parents is far more influential in determining his self-image than is the class status of the parents and children. Jewish children are more likely than either Protestants or Catholics to have favorable self-images (34, 156)—possibly owing in part to traditionally warm, supportive parent-child relationships in Jewish culture. A father's work history also appears related to his son's self-esteem. Children with low self-esteem were more likely to have fathers who had been unemployed for extended periods. Interestingly, maternal employment did not appear to have any adverse effects on the child's self-esteem. In fact, mothers of high self-esteem children were more likely to have worked for long periods and were more likely to express favorable attitudes toward their work (34).

Parental Absence. Thus far, we have been discussing the effects of parental influences on the child in the intact family setting. Increasingly, however, families are being broken up for long periods of time, or in some instances permanently, by death, divorce, abandonment, or involuntary separation (because of military service, job demands, or other obligations). What are the effects of prolonged absence of either parent on the child's personality development and adjustment in the middle-childhood years?

Broken homes occur more frequently in the backgrounds of delinquents and children suffering from emotional disorders, as contrasted with non-disturbed peers (*4, 8, 24, 167, 175*). Perhaps not surprisingly—in view of the importance of the same-sex parent as an identification model—absence of the same-sex parent appears particularly important. One study showed a significantly higher-than-average rate of delinquency among boys living with their mothers following the loss of the father through death, parental separation, or divorce (*61*). When the boy lived with his father following the loss of the mother, however, only an average rate of delinquency was found.

In an effort to explain the relation to delinquency of father absence among boys, a number of investigators "have concluded that the exaggerated toughness, aggressiveness, and cruelty of delinquent gangs reflect the desperate effort of males in lower-class culture to rebel against their early over-protective, feminizing environment and to find a masculine identity" (*21, 915*).

According to one author:

> The genesis of the intense concern over "toughness" in lower class culture is probably related to the fact that a significant proportion of lower class males are reared in a predominantly female household, and lack a consistently present male figure with whom to identify and from whom to learn essential components of a "male" role. Since women serve as a primary object of identification during preadolescent years, the almost obsessive lower class concern with "masculinity" probably resembles a type of compulsive reaction-formation. . . . A positive overt evaluation of behavior defined as "effeminate" would be out of the question for a lower class male (*126, 9*).

Delinquency rates were also higher for girls who had lost their mothers, but not among those who had lost their fathers. The same types of relations were found for frequency of high school dropouts. In brief, it appears that "the identification model and source of control functions provided by a parent of the same sex were thus more crucial in preventing these social problems than was any aspect of the child's relationship with a parent of the opposite sex" (*21, 914*).

Much of the research on parental separation during the early childhood period dealt with separation from the mother—a not surprising fact, in view of the dependency of the young child on direct maternal care (cf. pp. 265–267). In studies of the effects of parental separation upon development during the middle-childhood years, the greatest emphasis has been on the absence of the father, as this is the most common social pattern. In our society, children are usually awarded to the mother following divorce or separation of the parents. In disadvantaged families, desertion by the father is a far more frequent occurrence than abandonment by the mother; in these families, the matriarchal tradition is much the stronger. Finally, it is the father who is most likely to be separated involuntarily from the family—through military service, the demands of his job, and even premature death.

The separation of many young fathers from their families during World War II permitted a number of studies comparing middle-class children from father-absent homes with those from father-present homes (*8, 167, 175*).

The results of these investigations suggested that boys from father-absent households behaved in a less masculine way both in fantasy and overt behavior, especially with respect to producing very little aggression. Even boys whose fathers had been absent early, but who later returned, continued to be more effeminate in their overt behavior (175). However, there was a marked change in the boys' fantasy expressions. They now produced the maximum amount of aggression and fantasy. The author concludes that father absence during the initial years, followed by later imposition of control by an adult man tends to produce frustration and conflict over sexual identification.

Similarly, the sons of Norwegian sailors who are often away on extended voyages of two or more years have been studied (62,114,182). Among 8- and 9-year-old boys in these sailor families, prolonged absences of the father were linked with lessened adequacy of peer adjustment, infantile and dependent characteristics, and manifestations of conflict over identification through compensatory or overly masculine behavior. Their mothers were more isolated from social contacts, more overprotective, and more concerned with obedience than with happiness and self-realization for their children. This was much less characteristic of father-present households.

The effects of paternal absence on the child's development are also reflected in school performance. One study found that lower-class Negro children from broken homes were much more likely to score below grade level on measures of academic achievement than their classmates from intact families—in fact, the higher frequency of broken homes among Negro families accounted for most of the achievement difference between the black and white samples (40).

The age of separation from father also appears to be important. Heatherington (73) found that both early-separated Negro and white boys (age 4 or earlier) and late-separated boys (after age 6) were more dependent on their peers and somewhat less dependent on adults than boys whose fathers lived at home. But only early-separated boys differed significantly from father-present boys on a number of measures of sex-typing. The former had lower scores in masculine aggressiveness, masculine sex-role preference, and involvement in competitive, physical-contact games. Early-separated boys spent significantly more time in nonphysical, noncompetitive activities, such as reading, working on puzzles, and collecting things. Similar patterns were obtained for both Negro and white boys, although Negro boys as a total group showed a somewhat greater involvement in competitive, contact sports than their white peers did. The results of this study suggest that boys who lose their fathers early, before identification can be assumed to have been clearly established, have greater difficulty in establishing a masculine sex-role identification and in acquiring sex-typed traits, while absence of the father after the child reaches age 5 has far less effect.

Social-Class Differences in the Mother-Child Relationship

Although the extrafamilial environment (teachers and peers) exerts a strong influence on the motives and behaviors of the school-age child, the attitudes and practices of the family are still of major significance. The models that the parents present to the child, and the pattern of rewards and punishments they exercise are determined, in large measure, by two sets of factors: the unique personalities of the parents and the values of the social-class setting in which the family lives. Every family belongs to a number of subcultural groups (racial, religious, social class). Members of these groups share many attributes and differ in many ways from the members of other groups. In earlier chapters we reviewed studies indicating that middle- and lower-class families differ in their infant- and child-training practices.

Subcultural influences continue to be effective during middle childhood. Within any particular community, parents of a particular class usually join the same clubs, have similar interests and attitudes, band together against outsiders from other classes, and work together at the same kinds of jobs. Consequently, their ideas about acceptable and unacceptable behavior, including the techniques of child-rearing and discipline, are usually much alike (187). For example, physical punishment of children is more often condoned among lower-class than among middle-class parents (124) and, therefore, is used more frequently. The reward of artistic interests, on the other hand, is more frequent among middle- than among lower-class families. Honesty, however, is less clearly related to social-class values, being rewarded in all social-class groups. The child's tendency to adopt honesty as a value is, therefore, more dependent upon the degree of honesty displayed by the same-sex parent (identification) and the parental encouragement of this behavior (reward) than upon his social-class membership.

Social-Class Differences in Child-Rearing Practices

Child behavior which is encouraged and rewarded by one social class may be disapproved and punished by another. Through an intricate system of selective rewards and punishments, parents teach their children the responses, values, and beliefs appropriate for their own social class.

> Class training of the child ranges all the way from the control of the manner and ritual by which he eats his food to the control of his choice of playmates and of his educational and occupational goals. The times and places for his recreation, the chores required of him by his family, the rooms and articles in the house which he may use, the wearing of certain clothes at certain times, the amount of studying required of him, the economic control to which he is subjected by his parents, indeed his very conceptions of right and wrong, all vary according to the social class of the child in question (38, 609).

Most of the evidence indicates that middle-class mothers are more affectionate and less punitive than those of the lower classes. For example, interviews of 198 white, upper-middle- and 178 upper-lower-class mothers of kindergarten children indicated that upper-middle-class mothers "are somewhat warmer and more demonstrative . . . than upper-lower mothers" (80, 395). Moreover, "upper-lower parents employed physical punishment, deprivation of privileges, and ridicule as techniques of controlling their children more commonly than did upper-middle parents. It appears likely that the upper-middle parents used reasoning and praise more often. . . ." (*116,* 395). These findings were corroborated by another investigation (*13*) in which lower-middle-class mothers were found to be less affectionate and more punitive and restricting than upper-middle-class mothers. Still another investigation of the mothers of preadolescent boys (*24*) found that lower-class mothers were more likely than middle-class mothers of similar ethnic and regional background to lose their temper and employ physical punishment. Clearly the basic maternal dimensions of love-hostility and restrictive-permissiveness are associated with the social class of the mother. Differences in personality among children of different classes are no doubt related to these differences in child-rearing practices.

Class Differences in Children's Attitudes to Parents

If the findings of these studies are valid, lower-class children would be expected to perceive their parents' disciplinary procedures as harsh and punitive, while those in the middle-class should see their parents as more lenient. Several investigations indicate that this is so. In one study, two groups of 21 fifth grade children, one lower-class and one upper-middle-class, were asked to write compositions concerning a 10-year-old boy's reactions to his younger brother's misbehavior and interference. It was assumed that through the medium of the story, the child would reveal his perceptions of his parents' disciplinary procedures (*41*).

Twice as many lower- as middle-class children wrote stories involving nonconstructive solutions to the problem (e.g., appealing to authority). The vast majority of the solutions suggested by the higher social-class group, but only half of those given by the lower-class children, were constructive, amicable settlements. In general, children of low socioeconomic status were more inclined to use punishment and to avenge misdeeds.

Each subject in this study was also interviewed privately and asked ten questions relating to routine discipline problems in school, at home, or in the neighborhood (e.g., Should children ever talk back to their parents?). The socioeconomically more-favored children revealed positive attitudes toward their parents' treatment and toward authority in general. Lower-class children viewed authority, including their parents, as unreasonable and severe. Hence they revealed more rigid compliance and greater fear of deviating from fixed rules and regulations (*41*).

Somewhat similar results were obtained in another study of the influences of social-class variations in discipline procedures on children's attitudes toward parents. The subjects, three groups of 50 children each in grades 5 to 8, were drawn from three schools representing upper-, middle-, and lower-class economic levels. Each child was seen individually, and after good rapport had been established, he was asked to speak out the first ten ideas (associations) that came to him when he thought of his mother and father. These data were analyzed to determine children's notions and descriptions of their parents; nature and degree of attachment and dependence; feeling tone, and degree of repression of expressiveness (*122*).

Although there was great variability in each group, children of different economic levels generally revealed fairly distinct attitudes toward their parents. For example, as a group, middle-class children manifested pleasant feelings, accepting and respecting their parents, whom they regarded as helpful and permissive. Few of these children appeared to be overly dependent or hostile to their parents.

Lower-class children, on the other hand, had the greatest number of unfavorable reactions. Of the three groups, they were the most ambivalent (had mixed love and hostility) toward the parents and were the most insecure. Although they had relatively few feelings of rejection or over-dependence, they felt that their parents were generally repressive and gave them little companionship. The upper-class group was the most variable, but as a group they expressed the most severe feelings of rejection and over-dependency. Hostility was less common in this group than among the lower-class subjects, but adoration, together with fear and guilt, was more prevalent.

Influence of Siblings

Although the personalities of the parents and their behavior toward the child are of primary importance in shaping his development, the child's relationship with his siblings, if he has any, may also exert some influence on the development of his personality.

More than 80 percent of American children have siblings. In the child's interactions with them, he may learn patterns of loyalty, helpfulness, and protection; or of conflict, domination, and competition—and these may be generalized to other social relationships. The number of siblings a child has and his relationship to them constitute an important aspect of the child's learning situation, and hence may strongly affect what, and how, the child learns at home. A number of systematic studies have been concerned with the consequents of ordinal position (oldest, youngest, middle child), and "oneliness" on the personality and behavior of the school-age child.

The social learning situation encountered by the first-born child obviously differs from that of his younger siblings. For example, oldest children may be handicapped by the relative inexperience of their parents. They may be overstrained or pushed too hard to accomplish, or they may have to care for younger children before they are ready for such responsibility. They alone must face the difficult adjustment involved in losing "only child" status.

The psychological influence of siblings on the child's development is likely to be felt most keenly when the child is between 3 and 9 years of age. The arrival of a new sibling at this time provides the greatest threat to the first-born. From the perspective of the second-born, it is the time when the older sibling is perceived as an omnipotent and invulnerable competitor, with special privileges and status. Thus each of the ordinal positions carries with it its own set of advantages and disadvantages.

Kagan (83) has recently hypothesized the following sequelae for first-born, in contrast to later-born children.

1. First-borns have higher standards surrounding competences and attributes that are positively valued by parents and the adult society. If the parents value academic skills, for example, the first-born will use adult levels of competence as his reference for setting a standard of quality. These standards are likely to be excessively high. The child does not have a clear notion of how "good" he is supposed to be at a task. He must discover this standard and he does so by orienting to his family for a guide as to what level of competence he should try to attain. If his major experience is with adults, as is likely with first-borns, a higher standard will be set than if the child is exposed to the performance of older children. The later-born child is exposed to less demanding standards because he can compare himself to his older siblings as well as to his parents. The later-born is therefore likely to be more realistic in his standards.

2. The first-born has only adult models available to him and he is prone to identify primarily with them and as he grows older to choose older adults as models. As adults have in fact, more power and competence than children, the first-born child is more likely to pass through a period of intense identification with an adult. The later-born has an older child as an available model and this condition dilutes the later-born's motivation to identify with the adult parental models.

3. The first-born is more likely to experience an orderly world—he is exposed to coherent and orderly explanations to his questions. The first-born child usually asks his parents about events that puzzle him and he is likely to get a relatively rational and consistent explanation. In contrast, consider the situation of a typical second-born. He is playing with a toy when his older brother suddenly races toward him and grabs at the toy without explanation. A later-born asks his brother why it is raining and receives one answer one time and a different answer on the next occasion. The world should appear less orderly and less predictable; less knowable and less rational for the later-born child. In the extreme, the later-born may develop a picture of a predatory world in which one must vigilantly protect one's possessions against the onslaughts of the unpredictable older sibling.

In view of these three potential influences, generally regarded as "advantages," it is not surprising that a series of investigations (6, 82, 152) have yielded the finding that first-born children are more likely to achieve eminence, and are overrepresented in such listings as Who's Who (82). Moreover, a disproportionate number of first-born children attain very high scores on intelligence and aptitude tests (3). As the first-born is also more likely to view the world as a potentially orderly and knowable place, rather than a chaotic jungle where social predators lie waiting at every turn, it is probably more than coincidental that the personality and intellectual ideologies of first- and later-born men tend to be congruent with these presumed attributes (65). Freud, for example, tried all his life to construct a theory that would explain all of human behavior. Such an attempt reflects a faith in the possibility of explaining human behavior in one grand scheme. Freud was a first-born boy. As one might expect, so was Einstein.

While these first three influences are usually regarded as "advantages," Kagan (83) postulates two other less positive influences:

4. The first-born is subjected to anxiety over loss of parental attention in a more traumatic way than the later-born child. The first-born becomes accustomed to the exclusive affection of his parents. He is not required to share this resource and he has come to expect a certain level of intense attention. The inevitable attenuation of attention that must occur when the next baby is born represents a dramatic loss for him and he is likely to become highly anxious over it. The later-born enters a world in which he is always sharing his parents with his older siblings and he grows up expecting and accepting this situation. The first-born, therefore, is more vulnerable to anticipated rejection and possible loss of nurturance than later-borns. And because he normally received nurturance from adults, he tends to turn to others for help when he is anxious. In short, he is more likely to be overtly dependent in time of stress if an adult is around on whom he can become dependent.

5. Finally, the first-born is predisposed to experience more guilt over hostility than the later-born. This expectation is based on the assumption that the first-born will be naturally jealous of the new baby and his special status. However, the first-born has no way to rationalize his hostility. He knows and is told repeatedly that babies are entitled to extra attention and his hostility is not appropriate and cannot be justified. The inability to justify his resentment leads to guilt (for he has violated a standard) and self-derogation. The later-born will have an easier time justifying his hostility to his older sibling for the first-born is, in fact, aggressive toward him and does enjoy privileges he does not possess. As the later-born is better able to rationalize his resentment, he is less likely to experience strong guilt over these hostile thoughts.

In view of the latter hypotheses, it is not surprising that research studies of the problem show general agreement that oldest children are likely to be less aggressive and more prone to feelings of guilt than their peers (28, 58, 92, 167) and more conforming (14). They are also more likely to fear physical harm and to avoid dangerous sports (71, 72, 133, 134). Moreover, at least two independent studies show that there are disproportionately large numbers of first-born children among the patients at child guidance clinics (157, 191). Surveys of elementary school children also indicate that oldest children manifest more nervous symptoms than either intermediate or youngest children (57, 92, 181).

Among normal school children, first-born boys seem to have more problems involving anxiety, withdrawal, mood swings, and oversensitiveness (51, 92, 118, 181). They are also more likely than later-born children to respond to anxiety-provoking situations by seeking the support and comfort of others ("affiliative tendency"). In contrast, under nonanxious conditions, first-born children are, if anything, less "sociable" than later-born children (164).

On the average, youngest children seem to present a sharply contrasting picture. Compared with other children, they appear to be highly striving (92, 151) and more defiant (28). Middle children are generally socially gregarious, rather easily influenced by suggestion, and eager for physical demonstrations of affection (18).

The results of a comprehensive study by Koch of the effects of ordinal position, sex, and spacing of siblings on personality development support the less systematic findings summarized above. In this study (94–96) there were 384 subjects (ages 5 to 6), from two-children families. The four types of sibling combinations (older boy-younger girl; older girl-younger boy; two sisters; two brothers) were equally represented, and there were groups of siblings separated by 1 to 2 years, 2 to 4 years, and 4 to 6 years. Teachers of these children observed and rated the children on a variety of traits. All of the major variables—sex, ordinal position, and spacing of the sibling— influenced the child's personality, with the sex of the sibling being one of the most important determinants of the adoption of sex-typed behaviors.

Sex of Sibling.   In general, children with brothers had more masculine traits than children with sisters. The girls with brothers, as compared with the girls with sisters, were more ambitious, more aggressive, and did better on tests of intellectual ability. Girls with older brothers had more "tomboyish" traits than girls with older sisters. Boys with older sisters were less aggressive and less daring than boys with older brothers. These results would be expected from our knowledge of the identification process and the imitation that occurs between siblings. In many cases, the older sibling is viewed by the younger as stronger, more competent, and in control of important goals that the younger one wants but does not yet possess. The older child can stay up later, eat adult foods, and may even be perceived as the family favorite. The younger sibling would strive, therefore, to become similar to the older by attempting to adopt the latter's behaviors.

Ordinal Position.   First-born children tend to have stronger consciences than second-borns; they tend to be more responsible, less aggressive, and more intellectually curious. However, the effect of ordinal position is very much dependent on the sex of the siblings and the spacing between them. When siblings were of the same sex and separated by less than 2 years, there were few differences between them. When the spacing increased to 4 years or the sibs were of the opposite sex, behavioral differences between them were more marked. For example, if a boy had a brother 4 years younger, he was less aggressive and more responsible than a boy with a sister 4 years younger than himself.

Spacing.   Koch feels that a 2- to 4-year difference between siblings is the most threatening to the older child. If the first-born is 3 years old when the new baby arrives, he is apt to become anxious over possible loss of nurturance. If the first-born is only a year old when the new sib arrives, his self-image is still so diffuse and unclear that he will probably not regard the baby as a major threat or competitor for his mother's affection. If the older child is 7 or 8 when the new sibling arrives, he is much more independent of his parents and is less threatened by the newcomer in the family. Moreover, the older child in this case is more likely than a sibling only 2 years older to become a hero figure or identification model for the younger child.

It appears that sibling position is an important psychological variable because it duplicates, in microcosm, many of the significant social interaction experiences of adolescence and adulthood. To be first or second, to have high or low power, to side with the authority or rebel against it, to feel guilt over hostility, or to be able to "place the blame" are tendencies that begin to be differently strengthened during early childhood as a result of the child's sibling position.

SEX-TYPING AND SEX-ROLE IDENTIFICATION

As we have already seen (cf. pp. 360–363), sex differences in motives, attitudes, interests, and behavior have already begun to crystallize by the time the child enters school. As he continues to develop in the years between school entrance and adolescence, boy-girl differences become more numerous, more highly differentiated, and more stable. Furthermore, the *agents* that play a role (through identification and direct reinforcement) in the child's adoption of appropriate sex-role motives, attitudes, and behaviors become more numerous and their influence greater. Thus, as in other areas of the socialization process, the primary agents promoting sex-typing in the preschool years are the parents. In middle childhood, however, other agents play an increasingly stronger role—including peers and nonparental adults representing the broader culture in the social institutions to which the child is exposed. When youngsters between the ages of 8 and 18 were asked to write an essay on, "The person I would like to be," those below 10 most frequently said they wanted to emulate their parents. Older children often named real or imaginary glamorous adults (69). In general, girls are more likely to idealize people they know, whereas boys indicate respect for people having status in the society at large (193).

As the child grows older, new heroes emerging from newspapers, television, movies, books, and magazines may appear stronger, more daring, more intriguing, and more attractive than plain old Mom and Dad. The movie star, the football hero, the pilot, the airline hostess, the scientist, the missile expert, the professor, the doctor, and the nurse have dramatic appeal for the child, and he may see these figures as models to emulate. In his attempt to identify with them, he begins to imitate the behavior of these people, or at least his conception of their behaviors. The model a particular child finds most attractive will be a function, in part, of his own skills and personality at the time, prior parent-child relationships, and the degree of pressure exerted by his family and friends toward adopting sex-appropriate roles.

Increasingly, as the child grows older, he is expected to progress toward the assumption of the adult role generally, and also more specifically, to the sex-appropriate role of *male* or *female*. The demands of society for the gradual assumption of these roles tend to become internalized as standards that the child sets for himself. His success in meeting these external and internal demands will influence both the degree to which his behavior is rewarded by society, his self-image, and his confidence in himself. In some instances sex-appropriate motives, attitudes, and behaviors developed through parental identifications and direct reinforcement of specific behaviors will be further strengthened and expanded through experiences with other adults and with peers. In other instances—in which sex-appropriate parental identifications may have failed to develop or may have been distorted, or when parental models themselves do not exhibit culturally accepted sex-typed characteristics—the child may develop attributes that do not conform with the expectations of peers and nonparental adults, and he may suffer negative reinforcement from society, as well as internal anxiety, conflict, and confusion.

The Development of Sex-Role Standards

A sex-role standard "refers to a learned association between a class of selected attributes on the one hand, and the concepts male and female, on the other" (83). A sex-role standard summarizes the culturally approved characteristics for males and females. Consequently, the acquisition of relatively well-developed standards requires that the child be capable of a sufficient degree of abstract thinking to classify people or objects with common characteristics into meaningful categories—including, of course, the categories male and female. As Lawrence Kohlberg points out, the preschool child aged 2 to 4 "is very uncertain of the constancy of his sexual identity, and the label 'boy' is for him as arbitrary as the label 'Johnny'" (97, 87). While he may refer to himself and to peers as "boy" because he has been taught this direct association, the younger child does not have a clear conception of the term "boy" as representing a category with definable common attributes, within which some persons are clearly included and others excluded. Nor has he established the notion of the constancy of these attributes. By age 3, for example, most children can properly label themselves as "boy" or "girl" (97); and by age 4, they are able to label both themselves and a variety of dolls of different ages correctly by sex, principally on the basis of clothing and hair style (32, 91, 97). Even by age 5, however, most children are not certain of the constancy of sex identity.

Thus, in the study by Kohlberg (97) children aged 4 to 8 were asked whether a pictured girl could be a boy if she wanted to, or if she played boy games, or if she wore a boy's haircut or clothes. "Most 4-year-olds said that she could be a boy if she wanted to, or if she wore the appropriate hair-cut or clothes. By age 6–7, most children were quite certain that a girl could not be a boy regardless of changes in appearance or behavior" (97, 95).

These findings correspond to more ancedotal observation. The following comments were made by Jimmy, just turning 4, to his 4½ year-old friend Johnny, as reported by Kohlberg (97, 95):

JOHNNY: I'm going to be an airplane builder when I grow up.
JIMMY: When I grow up, I'll be a Mommy.
JOHNNY: No, you can't be a Mommy. You have to be a Daddy.
JIMMY: No, I'm going to be a Mommy.
JOHNNY: No, you're not a girl, you can't be a Mommy.
JIMMY: Yes, I can.

Kohlberg emphasizes that the young child's difficulties in establishing gender-identification are not the result of emotional difficulties regarding sex, as implied by some psychoanalysts. Instead, they "closely parallel his difficulties in establishing stable definitions of physical concepts in general" (97, 94) and reflect his overall level of cognitive development.

Once the child has reached a stage of cognitive development wherein meaningful categorization by gender is possible, as is the case with the school-age child, he can then go on to develop increasingly differentiated perceptions of the characteristics associated with the concepts male and female. In general, in our culture, these fall into several categories, as discussed below.

Physical Attributes.   Even at ages 5 to 6, most children have developed a view of the male as physically more powerful and invulnerable than females. Almost every one of 24 first grade children in one study (97) said that boys fight more than girls. When asked why, the most frequent response was "because girls get hurt more easily than boys." At this age, boys are also seen as having shorter hair, and wearing different clothes (apparently indicating that recent adolescent fads have not yet pervaded the school-beginner group). Rather interestingly, differences in sexual anatomy, upon which the society bases male-female differentiations, only gradually enter clearly into the child's concept of sexual identity. Thus, in a study by Katcher (91), children were asked to put together correctly and identify the gender of several cut-out figures that were separated into head, trunk, and below-the-trunk sections. The figures to be assembled were a clothed boy, girl, man, and woman, and an unclothed boy, girl, man, and woman. Few errors were made by children over 3 in assembling and identifying the sex of the clothed figures. In contrast, children age 3 to 6 made many more errors in identifying the gender of the genital section, and in matching it with the gender of the hair and trunk sections of the unclothed figure. Some error in genital assignment was made by 88 percent of the 3-year-olds, by 69 percent of the 4-year-olds, and by 31 percent of the 6-year-olds. Taken together with the results of other investigations (31, 32), this study suggests that children do not form clear general concepts of genital differences until the period between 5 and 7 years of age, even when they are extensively enlightened by parents (97).

As the child continues through the school years, other characteristics become increasingly associated with idealized, sex-linked stereotypes regarding appearance. Studies of preadolescent and adolescent youth reveal that American girls regard an attractive face, hairless body, a small frame, and moderate-sized breasts as the most desirable characteristics for a girl; boys regard height, large muscle mass, and facial and body hair as the most desirable characteristics for boys. A girl should be pretty and small; a boy large and strong (29, 52, 63, 79, 132).

Behavioral Characteristics. While perhaps not so clearly delineated as physical attributes, patterns of behavioral characteristics are also subject to sex-typing in our culture. As Mischel (127) points out, two of the broadest, most pervasive, and most carefully studied sex-type behavioral patterns are aggression and dependency.

Typically, boys are expected to be strong, courageous, assertive, and ambitious. Girls, in contrast, are expected to be sociable, well-mannered, and neat, but to inhibit verbal and physical aggression. Available data clearly support the view that this expectation is fulfilled even in relatively young children. Thus, in virtually every relevant study of preschool and school-age children, aggressive behavior has been found to be more frequent among boys than girls (11, 12, 39, 68, 117, 131). Boys also show more negativistic attention-getting and antisocial behavior than girls, although girls tend to show greater "prosocial" aggression (e.g., stating of rules with threats of punishment for breaking them; 127). Even in their fantasies, as indicated by story-telling, play, or drawings and paintings, boys indicate a greater preoccupation with aggressive themes (9, 138, 167, 190).

Such findings appear to be consistent with reported sex differences in the characteristics of parental identification models as perceived by children, and in the behaviors differentially rewarded by parents. In the case of the former, it has been found that if children are asked which parent is more dangerous or more punitive (i.e., more aggressive), both boys and girls agree that the father is more aggressive than the mother (47, 86, 87, 88). This perception of father as more aggressive also holds when aggressive and nonaggressive animals are used as stimuli (e.g., a tiger versus a rabbit, an alligator versus a bird). In each case, fathers tend to be associated with the more aggressive animal (87).

With relation to the differential rewarding of the behavior of boys and girls by parents, Sears, Maccoby, and Levin (169) found that parents made the greatest distinctions in the rearing of boys and girls in the area of aggression. Significantly more boys were permitted to express aggression toward their parents. They were also allowed to show more aggression to other children, and were more frequently encouraged to fight back if another child started a fight. In contrast, girls obtained somewhat more praise for "good" behavior, and were more often subjected to withdrawal of love for "bad" behavior. As Mischel (127) has observed, these relationships are consistent with the view that physical or antisocial aggression is less sanctioned for girls than for boys in our culture, and, indeed, that physical aggression is expected and rewarded for boys more than it is for girls. In contrast, " 'prosocial' aggression, which is tolerated in girls, is probably more readily labeled 'sissy stuff' and is unlikely to be rewarded either by peers or by parents when displayed by boys" (127, 73).

A second broad class of sex-typed behavior "includes the correlated trio of dependency, passivity, and conformity" (83). While the data are not so clear-cut as in the case of aggression (83, 127), a majority of studies do report this trio of characteristics to be more common among females than among males, particularly at older ages (16, 36, 78, 89, 111, 120, 169–171). These findings appear reasonable in light of the fact that dependent behaviors tend to be less rewarded for males (160), and physically aggressive behaviors are less rewarded for females (in our culture and probably by individual parents as well). Furthermore, girls are more likely than boys to display interest in nurturant behavior, and a preoccupation with harmonious interpersonal relationships (59, 74, 77, 103, 180, 190, 193).

Emotional Expression.   Closely related to the above behavioral characteristics are traditional sex differences in the expression of emotions. Boys are increasingly expected through the middle childhood and adolescence years to suppress fear and to control expression of emotion in times of stress (84). In contrast, expressions of fear, hurt feelings, and general emotional upset are considered more acceptable for girls. While boys are expected to deal more pragmatically, calmly, and effectively with stress situations, "helplessness" is more permissible for girls. While there are suggestions that contemporary parents are less rigid than those of earlier generations, the "little-boys-don't-cry" attitude is still far more general, even today, than a similar attitude toward girls.

Problem-Solving and Intellectual Mastery.   Even in the early childhood years, boys tend to take a more analytical, independent approach to problem-solving than girls. They are more likely to ask "how" and "why" questions spontaneously; in contrast, girls are more likely to ask questions about social rules and the "correct" ways of doing things (172). Boys are also more likely to be persistent in problem situations. Crandall and Rabson (35) gave school-age children two puzzles, one of which they were able to solve, while failing the other. When the children were later asked which puzzle they wanted to return to, more boys than girls chose the failed puzzle. In light of such differences in orientation, it is not surprising that boys tend to show a greater preference for science and mathematics, while girls more often move toward the arts and humanities (83).

It is well known that in the early school years, girls outperform boys, although by late adolescence and adulthood, the picture is reversed. There is some indication that school work tends to be viewed as more feminine in the early years. In a recent study at the Fels Research Institute, second and third grade children were taught different nonsense syllables to stand for maleness and femaleness. They were then shown pictures of school-related objects (i.e., blackboard, page of arithmetic, book, school desk, library), as well as nonacademic stimuli. The results indicated that second grade boys and girls were more likely to label the school objects feminine than masculine (85). This tendency diminished with age, especially for boys (the labeling of the nonacademic objects was in accord with expectation—e.g., the children called a cub feminine and a lion masculine). The greater emphasis in girls on being cooperative and socially compliant, as contrasted to greater tolerance of aggressiveness, restlessnesss, and rambunctiousness in boys, may also contribute to the superior performance of girls in the early school years.

Expression of Standards Through Games.   Sex-typed standards of behavior are also reflected in the games, hobbies, and sports which children of the two sexes prefer. Boys have greater interest in playing such games as soldiers, cops-and-robbers, contact sports, and in using tools and building things such as radios and model airplanes (154). In contrast, girls show a significantly greater preference for playing with dolls, dressing up, playing house, and activities such as hopscotch, stoop tag, and jumping rope (see Table 12.1). Other studies (77, 155) also indicate that boys prefer activities associated with construction, aggression, speed, and power, while girls prefer those associated with social relationships and feminine occupations. While boys' sex-typed activities tend to become relatively stereotyped fairly early, girls are slower to narrow their interests. The "tomboy" at grades 4, 5, and 6 is far more common than the "sissy" (155). It is perhaps not surprising that girls continue to display interest in "masculine" activities longer than boys do in "feminine" activities, inasmuch as the male role in our society still tends to be associated with greater freedom, privileges, and in some respects, status. While girls would sometimes prefer to have been boys, the reverse is seldom the case (22).

There is some evidence to suggest that sex-differences in interests and behavior are less marked currently than they were in earlier generations; certainly parents generally appear less preoccupied with stressing sex-limited behavior at every turn. The little girl today is more apt to be wearing the same blue jeans and T-shirt as her male counterpart, rather than always having to wear a dress and being instructed not to roughhouse or get dirty. This is particularly true among middle-class children, and especially girls. Lower-class mothers tend to encourage sex-typing more consistently than middle-class mothers do (101, 145).

Sex-Role Identity

Thus far we have been discussing the development of sex-differences in motivation, feelings, attitudes, interests, and behavior related to sex-typing

Table 12.1   Game Choices Differentiating
Between Boys (N = 928) and Girls (N = 973)[a]

Masculinity		Femininity	
Item No.	Game	Item No.	Game
8	bandits	1	dolls
9	soldiers	2	dressing up
10	cowboys	3	houses
13	cops-and-robbers	4	store
14	cars	5	school
18	spacemen	6	church
53	marbles	16	actors
64	bows & arrows	17	actresses
65	throw snowballs	30	stoop tag
113	darts	34	ring-around-the-rosy
128	wrestling	35	London bridge
129	baseball	36	farmer in the dell
131	football	38	in & out the window
133	basketball	41	drop the handkerchief
135	boxing	44	mulberry bush
139	shooting	47	hopscotch
157	fish	48	jump rope
158	hunt	49	jacks
164	use tools	87	Mother, may I?
168	climbing	156	dance
170	make radio	159	sewing
171	model aeroplane	161	cooking
172	toy trains	162	knit
174	work machines	163	crochet
178	build forts	175	cartwheels

[a] All items differentiate between the sexes beyond the .01 level.
Source: From B. G. Rosenberg & B. Sutton-Smith. The measurement of masculinity and femininity in children: an extension and revalidation. *J. genet. Psychol.*, 1964, *104*, 260. By permission of The Journal Press.

in our culture. A related but separate question involves the factors that influence the individual child's sex-role identity—that is, his conceptualization of his own degree of masculinity or femininity. In general, it would appear that in our culture identification with the male role, and a perception of one's self as possessing (at least to some degree) masculine characteristics would facilitate the development of a positive self-concept in the boy, just as feminine identification and self-perception might be expected to facilitate a positive self-image in the girl.

Several influences appear to be involved in fostering the development of an appropriate sex-role identity in the school-age child. As in the case of the preschool child (cf. pp. 356–360), positive identification with a parent of the same sex, preferably a parent who himself represents a sex-appropriate model, continues to facilitate sex-role identity. In addition to parents, same-sex peers, siblings, relatives, and other important adults may increasingly play a role in fostering the school-age child's assumption of an appropriate sex-role identity.

In addition to identification with an appropriate model, sex-role identity may also be facilitated, or even altered, by the acquisition of desirable sex-typed attributes. The boy who learns to be dominant with peers or competent on the athletic field often begins to regard himself as more masculine. Similarly, the girl who acquires feminine skills, is socially poised with adults, and is capable of engaging in nurturant activities may see herself as becoming more feminine. If one assumes that the strength of a sex-role identity is a function of the discrepancy between the inventory of actual sex-typed attributes and the "ideal" attributes prescribed by the culture, then acquisition of appropriate attributes can reduce this discrepancy and lead to corresponding modifications in one's self-perception. The opposite effect is, of course, also possible. "Loss of attributes or goal states that are essential parts of the self label, 'I am (masculine, feminine),' can widen the gap between actual attributes and the ideal, and make a sex-role identity more vulnerable" (83).

In a related vein, experiences with other people in ways that are congruent with sex-type standards may also alter a child's perceptions of himself with respect to his sex-role identity. Thus, if adults and other children consistently react to a boy as though he were dominant and strong, the boy is likely to begin to perceive himself in a similar fashion. By the same token, if a girl continually hears praise of herself as feminine, pretty, and attractive, her tendency to view herself in a similar light will be increased. In sum, differential identification with parents and parent-surrogate models; acquisition of sex-type skills; and sex-role congruent experiences are each influential in determining the degree to which an individual perceives and labels himself as masculine or feminine.

DEVELOPMENT OF CONSCIENCE AND MORAL STANDARDS

While the precursors of conscience and moral standards may be seen in the preschool years (cf. pp. 363–366), the middle-childhood years represent a critical period during which conscience develops at a rapid rate. While the older preschool child may gradually begin to abandon the relative hedonism of the 2- or 3-year-old—whose behavior is pretty much governed by doing whatever he wants to do at a particular moment—his early conscience development tends to be erratic, largely confined to prohibitions against specific behaviors, and based on external rather than internal sanctions. If this situation persisted into later childhood and adult life, we would have to have a host of "vigilant authorities keeping an eagle eye on the activities of us all" (20, 58) if organized society were to survive. Gradually, however, from about 4 to 6 years on into middle childhood, conscience in most children becomes less confined to specific behaviors and begins to involve the development of more generalized abstract standards; it becomes less exclusively determined by external rewards and punishments, and more by internal sanctions; and it begins to involve not only the avoidance of prohibitions but also the pursuit of what one *should* do.

Piaget believes that from ages 5 to 12 the child's concept of justice passes from a rigid and inflexible notion of right and wrong, learned from his parents, to a sense of equity in moral judgments that takes into account the specific situation in which a moral violation has occurred. For example, the 5-year-old is apt to view lying as bad, regardless of the situation of the circumstances in which it occurs. With increasing age, the child becomes more flexible and realizes that there are exceptions to this strict rule (i.e., that there are some circumstances under which lying may be justifiable; 136). Piaget's techniques of investigation included conversing with children and asking them questions about moral issues or about the ethics of characters and events in short stories. For instance, in a conversation with a child he would ask, "Why shouldn't you cheat in a game?" Or, after telling a story about a mother who gives the biggest piece of cake to her most obedient child, he would question the subject about the justice of her action.

Piaget's observations suggest that as the child becomes a member of larger, more varied peer groups, rules and moral judgments may become less absolute and authoritarian, and more dependent on the needs and desires of the group. "Moral relativism," based on cooperation and respect for others, eventually replaces "moral realism": "For very young children, a rule is a sacred reality because it is traditional; for the older ones it depends upon a mutual agreement" (136, 192). For example, 150 children between the ages of 6 and 12 were told stories involving a conflict between obedience to parents and a sense of justice or equality, and were asked to solve the conflict. The percentage of children who chose solutions involving "obedience to adults" decreased steadily with advancing age. Thus 95 percent of the 6-year-olds favored this type of solution.

In another phase of this investigation, children were asked to give examples of what they regarded as unfair. "Behaviors forbidden by parents" were mentioned by 64 percent of the children between 6 and 8 years of age, but only by 7 percent of those in the 9- to 12-year-old group. On the other hand, inequality in punishment and treatment were mentioned by 73 percent of the 9- to 12-year-olds, but only 27 percent of those 6 to 8 years of age.

On the basis of numerous studies of this sort, Piaget concluded that

> there are three great periods in the development of the sense of justice in the child. One period, lasting up to the age of 7–8 during which justice is subordinated to adult authority; a period contained approximately between 8–11, and which is that of progressive equalitarianism; and finally a period

which sets in toward 11–12, and during which purely equalitarian justice is tempered by considerations of equity (*136*, 314).

Other investigators have tried to repeat some of Piaget's studies (*44, 45, 106, 119, 176*). For example, in one study, 101 boys and girls in grades 2, 5, and 8 were questioned about the correct thing to do if one child hit a second child (*44*). The older children were more apt than the younger ones to ask for the particular circumstances of the moral violation and the motive for the aggressive act. This finding supports Piaget's hypothesis that the older child views a moral violation in the total context in which it appears and his reaction is influenced by situational factors.

Using both American and Swiss children as subjects, Lerner (*105, 106*) confirmed Piaget's findings regarding age changes in moral judgments, especially among children of a lower socioeconomic status. He found a progressive decline in suggestions for solving conflicts by subordination to adult demands or acceptance of authority (including majority opinion) between the ages of 6 and 13. During the same period, solutions based on moral relativism, reciprocity, and equality increased. Summarizing these changes in moral concepts, Murphy says: "Moral realism yields gradually during childhood to an ethics of reciprocity; what is right is now defined not in terms of self-evident and inherent necessity but in terms of a sense of balance or justice. Rightness is a matter of the mutual consideration of needs" (*128*, 386).

One investigator attempted to test directly the relationship between the nature of the child's moral concepts and his interactions with parents and peers (*119*). Moral judgment tests and questionnaires about parents and peers were administered to 244 American boys between 5 and 14 years of age. From the boys' answers to the questionnaire items, the investigator derived measures of several aspects of authority and peer relations.

Analysis of the questionnaire data revealed that boys who were strictly controlled by their parents, currently or in the past, tended to conform rigidly to adult-dictated regulations. Compared with the children of less strict parents, these boys were more likely to make moral judgments primarily on the basis of "such moral prescriptions as . . . respect for property, obedience to teachers, and veracity" (*119*, 17). They were less likely than the other boys to be influenced by the obligations of friendship and peer-group membership.

It is probable that the children of strict parents were more afraid of violating parental prohibitions than were the children of more permissive parents. As we saw earlier, the children who were least likely to be influenced by peer values feared withdrawal of parental acceptance for the commission of prohibited acts.

Recently, Kohlberg (*99*) studied the development of children's capacity to judge action in terms of moral standards as opposed to sanctions "by asking them to evaluate deviant acts which they were told were followed by reward, and conforming acts which they were told were followed by punish-

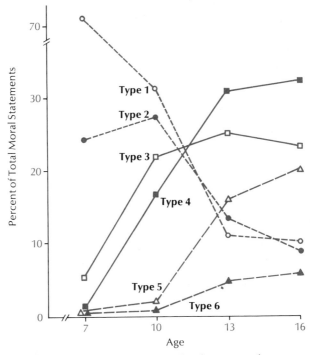

Fig. 12.2. Use of six types of moral judgments at four ages. (From L. Kohlberg. The development of children's orientation toward a moral order: I. Sequence in the development of moral thought. *Vita Humana*, 1963, 6, 16. By permission.)

ment" (99, 321). A careful analysis of individual responses led them to define six developmental types grouped into three moral levels. At the lowest ("pre-moral") level, the child was guided by an orientation toward punishment and obedience (Type I), or a naive kind of hedonism (Type II). At an intermediate level ("morality of conventional rule-conformity"), morality was viewed as a matter of trying to maintain the approval of others and good relations with them—a "good boy morality" (Type III), or a reliance on the precepts of authority (Type IV). At the highest level ("morality of self-accepted moral principles"), the child was able to view morality in terms of contractual obligations and democratically accepted law (Type V), or, finally, "morality of individual principles of conscience" (Type VI).

Four-year-olds tended to judge the act as good or bad in terms of its reinforcement rather than in terms of the rule. By age 5 to 7, the children evaluated the act in terms of its moral label rather than in terms of its reinforcement in the story. These older children continued to give the possibility of punishment as reasons for an act being bad, however, so that the distinction between badness and situational reinforcement was in terms of long-range as opposed to short-range reinforcement. By preadolescence, a majority of children made "disinterested" moral judgments and formulated some concept of a morally good self (99).

Kohlberg views his findings as supporting the general developmental view of morality espoused by Piaget, although he differs on specifics. He found considerable overlap at various ages in the use of his six moral types (see Fig. 12.2), although the frequency of the more primitive types declined with age, and that of the more mature types increased with age.

> As opposed to Piaget's view, the data suggest that the "natural" aspects of moral development are continuous and a reaction to what the whole social world rather than a product of a certain stage, a certain concept . . . or a certain type of social relations . . . (99, 322–323).

Unless a reasonable degree of conscience development takes place during the middle-childhood years—that is, unless standards of right and wrong are established—the child, and later the adult, is apt to yield to asocial temptations offered by others or to his own urges for uncontrolled aggressive, sexual, and regressive behavior. On the other hand, if the learning of internal standards and prohibitions (superego development) is unduly strong, crippling guilt may develop in association with a wide variety of behaviors and thoughts. Furthermore, as we shall see later, defenses erected against painful guilt feelings may lead to the development of psychological and psychosomatic symptoms.

Obviously, mature conscience development requires cognitive maturation, as well as a number of complex psychological processes based on learning. As Kohlberg points out, without the sort of cognitive development described in Chapter 11, the child is unable to carry out the degree of abstract thinking required for the development of generalized standards, as opposed to highly specific, concrete prohibitions (98, 100). Nor would he become capable of shifting from absolute and rigid standards, to more flexible and relative ones in which, for example, motivational intent, rather than simply the act itself, is taken into account in assessing blame or determining guilt (cf. pp. 509–510). Many cognitive functions play a role in conscience development. As the child develops concepts "of time, of future gratifications, of consequences, of right and wrong, of values and ideals," he becomes increasingly aware of the effects of his actions (93, 58). His perception of the feelings of others also becomes more acute, and he begins to see the logical necessity for people to cooperate with one another in the interests of all (93).

However, conscience development is far from being solely, or even primarily, a function of cognitive maturation. A variety of studies (2, 7, 70, 76, 108, 169, 184, 185, 191) indicate that the development of conscience—as manifested by internal reactions to transgression in the form of guilt, or by the adoption of moral standards which the child feels responsible for maintaining—is fostered by the presence of parental warmth and love (15). This appears reasonable in terms of two mechanisms that appear to be involved in conscience development: *identification* (pp. 356–357) and *fear of loss of love or approval*. If a responsible parent, because of his parental warmth and love, is a rewarding figure for the child to identify with and model himself after, adoption of the parent's standards as his own ("internalization") is more likely to occur, and violations of these standards then become painful and to be avoided because they result in an impaired self-image. The second probable mechanism is more negative in character: if the child has been rewarded by parental love and approval, transgressions against parental standards may produce anxiety based upon fear of parental disapproval or withdrawal of love. Most children have at least some anxiety over possible loss of love from their parents, and acquire the standards their parents practice at least partly in order to keep the anxiety low and under control. This process, of course, assumes that the parent, as a socializing agent, has acquired reward value in the first place through parental warmth and nurturance. In other words, fear of withdrawal of love can hardly serve as a motivation when there is no love to lose (*2, 15, 70*).

It is interesting to note that, contrary to popular stereotypes, children who tend to have internalized standards rather than merely a fear of detection and punishment report that their mothers are less likely to use physical threats of force, deprivation, or direct commands as disciplinary techniques, and are more likely to use love-oriented methods (e.g., how much the child's behavior "hurt them"; *76*).

The former techniques are more likely to produce counteraggression from the child, and while they may sometimes prevent transgressions in the immediate situation out of fear of retribution, they appear relatively ineffective in promoting the development of internal moral standards.

Parenthetically, it has been suggested (*15*) that love-oriented techniques of discipline may also facilitate the development of conscience by providing a child with a better learning situation for the development of standards—through increased opportunities for identifying the nature of transgressions; providing cues for labeling of transgressions, including self-critical statements; and use of reinforcements carefully geared to the specific behaviors involved (as opposed, for example, to generally punitive parental behaviors, poorly directed parental yelling and screaming, and so on). Becker notes:

> the parent who talks and reasons with the child about his misbehavior is more likely to provide the child with a clear understanding of what he did wrong, so that the anxiety of that misbehavior is connected to the right cues. Secondly, as Aronfreed has suggested, explanations and reasons provide the child with internal resources for evaluation of his own behavior; that is, the child gains explicit training in making moral judgments (*15, 185*).

It has also been asserted (*75*) that one of the critical factors involved in love-oriented techniques of discipline may be the reinforcement by the parent of explicit reactions from the child:

> Love-oriented discipline is likely to continue till the child makes some symbolic renunciation of his wrong-doing. Thus self-admission and verbal recognition

of wrong-doing may be reinforced by regaining parental approval and ending the punishment. Physical punishment is more likely to occur all at once and be over, and what the child does toward the end of preventing future occurrences is not related to the ending of punishment (15, 18).

Parent-Child Relationships and Conscience Development. From the foregoing, it appears clear that the standards of parents themselves and the nature of parent-child relationships play a crucial role in determining whether a child's developing conscience will be seriously deficient, normal, or overly strict and punitive. The parent whose own conscience is defective—either in terms of a deficit or in terms of excessive rigidity and harshness—can hardly serve as an appropriate model for normal superego development in the child. Furthermore, the nature of the parent-child relationship will determine, in large measure, whether adoption by the child of parental standards as his own will be rewarding. Ideally, it would appear that optimal superego development in the child is facilitated if (1) the parent's own conscience and moral standards are mature and reasonable, but not overly rigid, harsh, and inflexible, and (2) adoption of the parent's standards by the child is based on positive identification and modeling. Whether anxiety over loss of love as a mechanism for the child's adoption of parental standards will also be helpful, rather than harmful, will depend in great measure on how this mechanism is employed by the parent. When disapproval and disappointment are confined to the child's transgressions themselves, rather than extended to the child as a whole, and when the disapproval is not extreme, harsh, impulsive, or otherwise inappropriate, socialization may be fostered without crippling effects on the child. But if it is used, as unfortunately is sometimes the case, as a kind of "emotional blackmail" to control and dominate the child, it may result not only in an overly anxious, superego-ridden child, but a child whose development of autonomy, self-confidence, and self-reliance is impaired.

As we shall see later, the child whose superego development is deficient—either because his parents' standards are themselves deficient or because disturbed parent-child relationships mitigate against identifying positively with parental values, or both—may become delinquent or otherwise lacking in responsible social behavior. Rather than responding to mature internal standards, he may be guided primarily by external considerations of probable reward and punishment. On the other hand, the child whose superego is unusually harsh and rigid as a result of strict and emotionally constricting demands on the part of parents who themselves possess rigid, punitive standards, may encounter severe psychological problems. Some of these problems may become especially evident in the later years of middle childhood, as even normal children tend to have difficulty integrating conscience demands into their developing personality structures in this age period.

By about 6 or 7, the child has acquired the capability of feeling guilt. The standards he sets for himself, and the particular causes for guilt, will continue to change and develop as he grows older.

PSYCHOLOGICAL AND PSYCHOSOMATIC PROBLEMS
OF MIDDLE CHILDHOOD

As anxiety, frustration, and conflict are a part of the human condition, all children will encounter some psychological problems, at one time or another, during middle childhood. These problems will usually be transient and limited in their severity if the child's parents provide good role models, are warm and accepting, and are consistent and flexible in their disciplinary techniques, but not so controlling or dominating that they thwart the child's development of autonomy, self-reliance, and mastery behavior. In the former case, the child will typically have needs which are reasonable, and will, in considerable measure at least, possess the means for satisfying them. He will have a conscience which can serve as a reliable internal guide to responsible and rewarding personal and social behavior, rather than one which is either seriously defective in providing him with appropriate internal controls, or so harsh, punitive, and arbitrary that it conflicts with the child's normal impulses and needs. Finally, the psychologically favored child will encounter a social environment—in his neighborhood, school, and home, in his peer group, and in society at large—that values him as an individual, provides for his basic needs, and offers an opportunity for optimal development of his potential.

In contrast, the child whose parents and society have seriously failed him in one way or another may be expected to encounter psychological or psychosomatic problems which are more severe, more chronic, and more refractory to treatment. This book is not a treatise on the psychopathology of childhood, and adequate reviews are available elsewhere (30, 53, 90, 93). Nevertheless, it may be valuable to discuss briefly some of the more common forms of psychological and psychosomatic symptomatology that may occur in middle childhood.

The Nature of Symptoms. Some of the manifestations of psychological problems in childhood are relatively easily understood: The child whose efforts at mastery behavior have met consistently with criticism or ridicule for his ineptness may be anxious and uncertain in the face of new and challenging situations, and inclined to withdraw and avoid them. The child who has been subjected to an endless series of injustices or rejections, and who, at the same time, has had only harsh, arbitrary, or inconsistent discipline, and has not developed strong internal superego controls, may emerge as angry, rebellious, unmanageable, and generally lacking in conformity to the social patterns one would expect of his age group. The child with overly meticulous, compulsive, overprotective parents who inhibit any evidence of spontaneous emotion and who place great emphasis on being controlled, orderly, and cautious, may well end up being overly meticulous, cautious, and lacking in spontaneity himself.

It is not difficult to appreciate, at least in a general sense, the transient depression of the bereaved child, or the anxiety and bad dreams of a child who has just been through a terrifying real-life experience. Other kinds of symptoms, however, are not always so easily understood: Phobias (strong fears) that seem unrealistic or fantastic, and appear to have no basis in actual experience; motoric disturbances, such as tics, in which a child constantly and without apparent awareness blinks his eyes or shrugs his shoulders; obsessional, recurrent, apparently absurd thoughts that won't go away; compulsive behaviors, such as a need constantly to wash one's hands; and psychosomatic symptoms of various sorts.

Anxiety and the Mechanisms of Defense. In most cases, the original source of such symptoms lies in the child's anxiety about something—fear of loss of love, or separation; of having angry, hostile feelings; of sexual impulses; of personal inadequacy; of punishment or retribution. The antecedents of his anxiety in the early years were discussed in Chapter 9 (cf. pp. 349–355). Frequently, the anxiety also involves guilt, in that the child's impulses are unacceptable to his conscience—that is, to the internal standards he has developed about what is "right" and "wrong," "good" and "wicked." One of the difficulties in understanding these anxieties arises from the fact that the sources of the child's true concerns are not directly expressed. Instead, the child may unconsciously erect psychological defenses against their expression, because allowing such disturbing impulses and feeling to find conscious expression would produce painful anxiety and guilt, and sometimes even panic. The basic function of these *mechanisms of defense* (55) is to help the child avoid painful feelings of anxiety. Some defense mechanisms may have the additional advantage of allowing some gratification of unconscious impulses while still allowing the individual to remain unaware of them. Thus the blue-stocking censor of "obscene" literature, may convince himself by virtue of his dedication to suppressing such literature that he has no illicit sexual impulses himself, but at the same time he may gain secret satisfactions from having to read this material in order to "protect" others.

The kinds of defenses people are most likely to employ will vary, depending on the individual's personality structure and specific learning experiences. A number of these defense mechanisms are more easily observed in children than in adults, because of the child's relative lack of sophistication and the immaturity of his ego.

In *repression,* the most basic underlying defense, anxiety-producing impulses, memories, and the like are simply kept from conscious awareness. When the individual's associations begin to encroach on such painful areas, anxiety is increased, and the individual's thoughts move off in another direction, with the result that anxiety then decreases. Thus repression as a defense tends to be employed and learned because it is rewarded. The total inability of an individual to recall a particularly painful experience provides one example; the transient block in remembering the name of a familiar person whom one dislikes provides another. In a closely related, but more primitive defense, *denial,* obvious reality factors are treated by the child as if they did not exist; an amusing, if touching, example might be the little girl who while sobbing her heart out, keeps insisting, "I am not unhappy!"

In denial, the child insists that an anxiety-arousing event or situation is not true, and he believes his denial is accurate. For example, the child who has been openly rejected by his mother may deny that she is hostile, and insist that she is a kind and loving person. Some children who have been rejected by their families deny that these people are their parents. The child insists that he is adopted and that his true parents love him.

When repression is used, the child blots out the anxious or frightening event by removing it completely from awareness. Repression is neither a refusal to remember an event nor a denial of its reality. Rather the thought or event has been removed from consciousness by forces beyond the child's control. For example, the child may repress his memory of a violent argument between his parents or of resentful thoughts he has felt toward one of his parents. Although he was clearly aware of these thoughts at one time, after repression the child is unaware of them, and questioning him will not bring them to light.

There is a subtle distinction between denial and repression. In repression the child has no awareness of the frightening or painful thought (e.g., he cannot recall his parents' heated argument). In denial, the anxiety-arousing thought is denied (e.g., he actively denies having heard the argument).

In *projection* and *displacement,* an unacceptable feeling or impulse is acknowledged, but is attributed to other sources. *Projection* is the ascription of an undesirable thought or action to another person, when, in reality, the thought or action applies to one's self. The child of 5 often projects aggression and blame for misdeeds onto other people. For example, a child may be running after a playmate and in so doing bump into an adult. The child may project (i.e., attempt to place) the blame on the child he was chasing by saying, "He made me chase him. If he didn't make me chase him, I wouldn't have bumped into you." The plea, "He started the fight, Mother, not me," is one of the most common examples of projection in young children.

In *displacement,* the child has the appropriate emotional response, but it is not attributed to its true source, as we shall see in discussing childhood phobias. A child's fear of his father, for example, may be too painful for him to acknowledge, but he *is* fearful, and therefore, he may attribute the fear to an acceptable symbolic substitute for the father (e.g., lions). A little girl's intense fear of snakes, or even perhaps of objects, such as pencils, may conceal her underlying fear of masculine sexuality.

Rationalization is a comforting defense that all of us—not only children, but adults as well—engage in. It involves providing one's self with socially acceptable reasons for his behavior or attitudes, when the real reason would not be acceptable to one's conscience, and hence would, if permitted into awareness, lead to painful anxiety and guilt. The parent who harshly punishes his child because of his own intense anger toward the child, but who then says he is "doing it for his [i.e., the child's] own good" is engaging in rationalization.

Reaction formation, as it is termed by psychoanalysts, has already been illustrated in the case of the censor of obscene literature described above. Similarly, the child who is overly preoccupied with being spotlessly clean and tidy may actually be defending himself against strong and unacceptable wishes to be dirty and messy, either literally or symbolically (e.g., sexually). It is as though the child were saying, "I can't have any desire to be messy or dirty, because look how preoccupied I am with being clean." As we shall see, reaction formation frequently plays a role in childhood compulsions.

Behavioral withdrawal is one of the most frequently used defenses of preschool children; it is the direct avoidance of, or flight from, threatening situations or people. The child will hide his eyes or run to his room when a stranger enters the house; he will refuse to approach a group of strange children despite his desire to play with them; he will shy away from a jungle gym if he doubts his ability to climb it successfully.

The withdrawal response temporarily removes the child from the feared situation, but the tendency to withdraw becomes stronger each time the child practices this behavior. This defense is therefore often maladaptive, for the child who refuses to cope with stressful situations may eventually become fearful of all problems and stresses, and may never learn to handle adequately the crises that are inevitable in the course of development.

Regression is the adoption—or, more accurately, the readoption—of a response that was characteristic of an earlier phase of development. Thumb sucking or bedwetting are examples of regressive behavior in children who have stopped such behavior for some period of time. In regression, the child is attempting to withdraw from a current anxiety-arousing situation to the more gratifying and less anxious state of infancy.

Regressive behavior frequently occurs when a new baby is brought into the home. Some 4-year-olds are made anxious by the anticipation that a new baby will displace them and obtain the love and attention that they have been receiving. By adopting infantile behaviors they attempt to gain attention and to retain desired parental nurturance.

As already stated, the ultimate function of these and other defense mechanisms is to protect the child from impulses, thoughts, and feelings that would lead to painful anxiety if the child became aware of them.

Fears and Phobias in Middle Childhood

The importance of fears (i.e., sources of anxiety) in the mental life of the 10-year-old child is seen in a study (49) in which children were asked to draw the most important events in their lives. Almost one-third of the drawings illustrated fear experiences. Although many childhood fears are a function of direct experience with frightening events (being bitten by a dog, being hit by a car) or a product of parental warnings about certain objects (stay away from the fire, watch out for snakes), there are also many fears that are symbolic in nature. The work of Jersild, Markey, and Jersild (80) revealed that many of the fears held by children (about 20 percent) are unrealistic and deal with imaginary creatures, the dark, and being alone. Dangerous animals, like lions and tigers, are also frequently named as objects of fear. Dunlop (43) asked a group of children, ages 9 to 12, about the things they feared and the intensity of their fears of specific objects. Feared objects were classified as realistic (i.e., could have happened to the child), remote, unrealistic, or mystical. The fear of falling off a ladder is possible, realistic, and in the child's immediate experience. The fear that a lion will hurt the child is remote and unrealistic. The children tended to be only *moderately* afraid of immediate and possible dangers (i.e., getting hit by a car) but were *strongly* afraid of remote or impossible events (lion attack, ghosts). The remote fears of ghosts, lions, witches, which usually involve being seriously hurt or killed, may be symbolic substitutes of feared parental punishment.

Let us elaborate this hypothesis. The typical child learns from the first year of life that a misdemeanor is followed by some form of parental punishment. That is, the child learns that he must pay for the pleasure of a misdemeanor with some form of punishment. Fear of attack by ghosts, snakes, crocodiles, and witches may be symbolic of anticipated parental punishment, rejection, or chastisement—a fear which the child cannot admit to himself directly. The evidence of strong and persistent fears in a 10-year-old, especially when they are excessively unrealistic, may be an index of the amount of guilt and conflict the child is experiencing.

In such cases, a rational attempt to reduce the child's fear of ghosts by pointing out that ghosts do not actually exist is not likely to be successful. After all, the ghosts, in this case, are merely a symbol for the child's unrecognized fear of the parent. Unlike realistic fears (being hit by a car, burned in a fire), unrealistic or symbolic fears can be ameliorated best by attacking the actual source of the fear.

Nightmares and Sleep Disturbances. All childhood fears, anxieties, and troublesome feelings are not manifested, either directly or symptomatically, during the child's waking state. Some may remain adequately repressed during the day, only to emerge in nightmares or "bad dreams."

Nightmares tend to reach a peak between ages 4 and 6 (93). According to one investigator, however, more than 25 percent of 6- to 12-year-olds studied were still having nightmares (104). Occasional bad dreams, or even nightmares, need not necessarily be a source of parental alarm, despite the fact that they indicate the presence of at least transient anxiety and conflict in the child—concerns that may be repressed during waking hours, but that emerge when the child's defenses are lowered by sleep. However, when nightmares become frequent, unusually severe, and recurrent, an effort should be made, through psychotherapy or otherwise, to determine the source of the child's anxiety and to ameliorate it. This course should also be followed in the case of recurrence of an extreme form of nightmare, called night terror or *pavor nocturnus*, following which the child has great difficulty reorienting to reality. He is hard to waken, his panic does not abate, and waking does not help him to regain control. "In such night terrors, the child is often reliving a traumatic event" (93, 237).

Often the content of nightmares provides some clue as to their source. For example, a child who repeatedly dreams that his father has been killed, and who wakes up terrified, may well be reflecting hostile wishes toward his father, wishes that he would find too anxiety-producing to be able to admit to himself. The child might also be reflecting a deep fear of losing the father.

One of the reasons that nightmares are more frequent in young children than in adults is that children's defense systems are not so well developed as those of adults, and consequently are more likely to fail under stress. In addition, the strength of conflicting desires and fears may be greater in childhood. Difficulty in going to sleep and difficulty in maintaining sleep may also reflect the child's anxieties and conflicts. Lying alone in the darkened room, with nothing but his own rambling thoughts, and with his controls lowered by approaching sleep, the child may be more vulnerable than in an active waking state to anxiety-inducing desires and concerns. Sometimes sexual feelings and thoughts may be involved, sometimes angry or hostile ones, sometimes fears of his own inadequacy or powerlessness.

School Phobias.   One of the relatively common childhood fears of greatest concern to parents is that of *school phobia*—a fear, which may approach panic, of leaving home and going to school. While occasional mild reluctance against going to school is common among children of this age—and the source of any number of dubious physical ills that clear up promptly when it is evident that the child can stay home—persistent morbid fear of school is a significant symptom; it indicates either a dread of some aspect of the school situation, or concerns with leaving home, or, frequently, both. Interestingly, while boys outnumber girls in most child guidance clinics, a majority of clinicians report that school phobias are more common among girls (93). While many problems may be symbolized by a school phobia, the most widely observed pattern involves *separation anxiety,* a fear of separation shared equally by parent and child (26, 33, 46, 81, 93, 107). Mothers of school-phobic children frequently are threatened by any loss of the child's dependency on them, and many reveal unresolved dependency problems with their own mothers (81). Furthermore, these mothers are themselves likely to see the school as a cold, forbidding place, and go to great lengths to protect their children, not only from it, but from virtually all of the painful facts of existence (93). The child, in turn, perceives—at least unconsciously—the mother's real desire to keep the child dependent, and responds to it (46). Further, the child is likely to fear separation from the mother because of both dependent and hostile needs (33, 93).

School phobias may be more common in girls at least partly because of the greater social acceptability of dependency in girls. It should be stressed, however, that while the pattern of parent-child relationships described above appears relatively common, there may be many other factors involved. In a case encountered by one of the authors in his clinical work, an elaborate school phobia in a young boy eventually turned out to involve a vaguely perceived fear of seductive approaches by a male teacher. Leventhal and others have suggested that school-phobic children commonly overvalue themselves and overestimate their own power and achievements, and then try to hold onto their unrealistic self-image. "When this is threatened in the school situation, they suffer anxiety and retreat to another situation where they can maintain their narcissistic self-image. This retreat may very well be a running to a close contact with mother" (107, 686).

Interestingly, children with school phobias generally have at least average ability (26).

Death Phobias. Pronounced fear of death has sometimes been referred to by clinicians as "8-year anxiety" because it tends to occur fairly commonly at this age. Freud was one of the first investigators to note this phenomenon, and he also referred to the eighth year as a kind of "boundary line" separating different periods of childhood. In Piaget's earlier studies, the eighth year was also seen as a boundary line "between the egocentric child with his magical, animistic, 'realistic' tendencies associated with a precausal, prelogical mode of thinking and the 'operational' child who sees the world logically and rationally" (5, 1395). We have already seen that conscience tends to become increasingly severe among children around ages 8, 9, or 10.

In a considerable number of children, there occurs at this age period what James Anthony, a child psychiatrist, refers to as an "existential crisis" (5). The child becomes increasingly preoccupied with ideas that either he or his parents will die. The child's concept of death, like many of his other ideas develops gradually during the whole period of growth:

> At an early age, death is thought of mostly in animistic terms in which the dead see, hear, and feel. Later it is viewed as separation, or rather desertion, and, still later, death becomes personified as a dreaded figure removing a loved person. Before the age of 7, death is reversible. At about 8 years, death, for many children, becomes irreversible, and, therefore, death wishes, both conscious and unconscious, take on a new emotional coloring. At the time of the crisis, the child becomes aware of a peculiar kind of helplessness in the face of the inevitability of death, with the additional feeling that no one can help, since everyone also is in the same predicament (5, 1395).

Actual experiences of death may sometimes be instrumental in precipitating a death phobia, or may bring it out at an earlier age. However, preexisting conflicts, frequently involving anxiety about separation from parents or fears of punishment and retribution, are usually present. As the condition improves, the sense of personal immunity to death reasserts itself.

Tics. One of the most commonly observed symptoms of psychological tension during the middle-childhood years is the tic. "A tic is a repetitious, involuntary, and seemingly purposeless movement of interconnected muscles" (50, 118). Usually tics involve repeated motor responses of the face, neck, and head, of which the child is largely unaware; the actions may include blinking of the eyes, nose-wrinkling, throat-clearing, yawning, shoulder-shrugging, head-shaking, and the like. Tics frequently are symptoms of repressed needs and conflicts, and sometimes the nature of a tic serves as a clue to the underlying conflict.

> Some facial grimaces, for instance, look suspiciously as if the person is aggressively making a face at somebody. The head-shaker is saying "No" to some unconscious wish. Wrinkling of the nose seems to say "Something doesn't smell good around here." Blinking the eye seems to suggest an attempt to blot out something which was seen. The child has no awareness either of the tic or the feelings or memory which prompts it. He can neither stop it nor explain it (93, 247).

Tics are more common in tense children with fairly strict parents (173).

> There may be too much pressure at home. Sometimes a mother or father is going at the child too hard, directing him, correcting him whenever he is in sight. Or the parents may be showing constant disapproval in a quieter way, or setting standards that are too high, or providing too many activities. . . . If the child were bold enough to fight back, he would probably be less tightened up inside. But being, in most cases, too well brought-up for that, he bottles up his irritation, and it keeps "backfiring" in the tic (173, 302–303).

As tics are involuntary, it is important that the child should not be scolded or corrected because of them. Except for brief intervals of awareness, they are practically out of his control. Effort should be made to make the child's life at home as relaxed and agreeable as possible, and with the least possible nagging, and his school and social life should be reasonably satisfying and not overstrenuous. When tics persist, despite such efforts, it is important to seek psychological help in order to gain a more specific understanding of the source of the child's tension, with the aim of ameliorating it.

While tics are isolated disturbances of motility, they tend to be closely related to the fidgeting and restlessness which plague school teachers and parents. They may be no more than a sign of diffuse anxiety, a kind of general movement that is an effort to restore a feeling of ease. However, at other times such restless moving about may serve as a defense against some other motor act which is forbidden, such as masturbation or aggressive behavior. As in the case of tics, generalized restlessness and fidgeting seem to be more common among children subject to strict parental restrictions (93).

Obsessions and Compulsions

Conscience development during the middle-childhood years is likely to pose some difficulty for many children. On the one hand, the child's desires to do what he wants to do when he wants to do it are still strong. On the other hand, his growing conscience, his increasingly internalized set of moral standards, dictates that many of these impulses are "wrong."

Under these circumstances, anxiety is produced in the child. Because unresolved anxiety is a particularly painful state, the child may attempt to erect psychological defenses against it. In the case of conflicts between his needs and the demands of a strict conscience, the child may attempt to ward off his unacceptable impulses, and hence control his anxiety, by the "occurrence of thoughts (obsessions), acts or impulses to act (compulsions), or mixtures of both which are all isolated from the original, unacceptable impulse" (53, 1401). Often the obsessive thought or compulsion serves not only to help control and to prevent awareness of unacceptable impulses, but, as a kind of double insurance, to emphasize the opposite of the unacceptable impulse. Thus a child with desires to be dirty and messy or to indulge in "dirty" sexual practices, such as masturbation, may develop compulsions to be extremely clean or to engage in repeated hand-washing. Obsessive, constantly recurring thoughts about being clean may serve a similar purpose. As previously noted, it is as though the child were saying to himself, "Look, I can't possibly have these impulses to engage in dirty behavior. See how concerned I am with being clean" (reaction formation).

Similarly, in the case of the childhood ritual of avoiding cracks in the sidewalk while chanting "Step on a crack, break your mother's back" the child seems to be saying, "I cannot really be hostile to my mother, because I am carefully avoiding an action which would harm her" (i.e., stepping on the crack). Mild obsessions and compulsions are common among children in the middle-childhood years, particularly around ages 8, 9, and 10 (50, 93, 173), and are not necessarily a source of serious concern. Most adults can remember periods when they had "foolish" recurrent thoughts they could not get out of their heads, or when they engaged in such activities as touching every third picket in the fence, avoiding cracks in the sidewalk, or having to do some other activity in a special way (173). On the other hand, when obsessions and compulsions are more severe, sustained, or unusual (e.g., hand-washing compulsions), psychological or psychiatric help appears indicated. Not unexpectedly, serious obsessive-compulsive neuroses are more frequent in the children of overly strict, fastidious, demanding parents, who pressure the child for accomplishment, hold him to overly severe standards of thought and behavior, and allow him little room for the expression of normal childhood impulses and desires (53, 93). Current research also indicates that the parental milieu most conducive to high guilt is one in which there has existed an affectionate relationship between parent and child, and wherein withdrawal of love is the most frequent method of socialization. Under these conditions, the child values the parent's nurturance and is made anxious by contemplation of withdrawal of love resulting from any violation, in thought or deed, of strict parental standards.

Hostility to Parents

Strong hostility to parents may generate symptoms in the preadolescent child. Often the intent of the symptom is to cause anxiety to the agent who is the source of the child's resentments. The methods of expression depend, in part, on the models of aggressive behavior to whom the child has been exposed. The most direct form is physical aggression toward the parents. Instances of homicide are essentially absent in children under 10 years of age, and are rare even among young adolescents. Direct verbal aggression is the most common form of hostility during the early years and, if not subject to strong punishment, is an effective way for the child to have immediate gratification of his hostile feelings. Many of the maladaptive responses that result from strong wishes occur when the child is not able to express his hostility verbally and is forced to choose more indirect means. The indirect strategies typically involve choosing a behavior that will cause the parent anxiety or frustration, but one in which the aggressive component of the behavior is not obvious. There are not many responses that fit this requirement. By failing in school, violating parental standards for social conduct, regression, or acting dishonestly, the child elicits anger and emotional upset in the parent and, as a result, gratifies his hostile wishes. The child is, of course, unaware of the intent of his actions and must suffer the realistic pain and anxiety that accompany school failure or peer rejection.

Psychophysiological Symptoms

Psychological problems of the school-age child may also be reflected in psychophysiological (psychosomatic) symptoms of one sort or another. A psychophysiological symptom means a bodily disease or disorder in function that is determined, in part, by psychological disturbance. Although constitutional predisposition appears to play a significant role in psychosomatic disorders, psychological factors often act to precipitate the disorder. Some of the more common psychosomatic disorders of middle childhood include asthma, ulcerative colitis, skin disorders, and rheumatoid arthritis.

In a recent study, mothers of children (ages 6–12) with psychosomatic disorders (mainly asthma, rheumatoid arthritis, and ulcerative colitis) were compared with mothers of children with purely physical ailments (poliomyelitis, heart malfunction, blood disorders) and mothers of neurotic children (frequent aggression, anxiety attacks). Interviews with the mothers revealed that those of the psychosomatic group were less accepting and more controlling particularly during their children's first year of life than the mothers of the physically ill or neurotic children. The mothers also told stories in response to pictures showing mothers and infants; the stories of mothers of the psychosomatic and neurotic children indicated that these mothers were probably less accepting and more controlling than the mothers of the physically ill children (57).

In another study (125) it was found that children with allergies (hay fever, asthma, skin disorders) were not likely to express aggression overtly and directly, indicating high anxiety over this behavior. Parents of allergic children are often inconsistent in their giving of nurturance; they are giving at one moment and rejecting at another. The child is, therefore, never quite sure about the reliability of parental love. This condition leads to strong hostility toward the parent, but the child is afraid to express his anger because he fears complete rejection and loss of love. It is hypothesized that this combination of high anxiety over loss of love and high conflict over expressing resentment toward the parents produces a state of tension which may precipitate a variety of psychophysiological symptoms. However, it appears that the likelihood of precipitating a particular psychosomatic condition is influenced by constitutional predisposition, and, further, that even in a particular symptom complex, such as asthma, the relative importance of psychological, as contrasted to constitutional factors may vary. Thus in some children with this disorder, constitutional factors may be more significant while in others, psychological factors may play a more important role.

In a recent series of studies, Purcell and his collaborators (140–143) have investigated the interesting clinical observation that some children with intractable (i.e., severe) asthma had a rapid remission in symptoms, even without medication ("rapid remitters") as soon as they were referred to a children's residential treatment center. Other children, however, continued to require maintenance doses of corticosteroid drugs ("steroid dependent") while at the center. It was found that rapidly remitting children reported significantly more often than steroid-dependent children that emotions such as anger, anxiety, and depression triggered their asthma. Furthermore, both mothers and fathers of rapidly remitting children displayed authoritarian and punitive attitudes to a greater degree than the parents of the steroid-dependent children, according to their responses to a questionnaire (144).

The investigators concluded that among rapidly remitting children, in contrast to steroid-dependent children, the symptom of asthma may be more intimately associated with neurotic conflict and affective reactions. The asthmatic symptom of steroid-dependent children, on the other hand, was viewed as a response more regularly linked to the influences of allergic and infectious factors. However, "the differences between these groups are regarded as relative rather than absolute" (144).

Many severely asthmatic children become essentially asymptomatic without any medication when they leave their homes and enter the new environment of a treatment center. Most of the rest of these children show substantial, although not so dramatic, improvement. Thus there appears to be clear evidence that removal from the family and placement in an institutional setting often has a profoundly ameliorative effect on asthma in children.

Minority-Group Membership and Anxiety in the Child

All children experience some conflict over the commission or contemplation of aggressive or sexual behavior, and all share some anxiety over possible rejection by parents and friends. However, a small number of children carry an additional psychological burden—membership in a minority group that is vulnerable to hostile prejudice and rejection from peers and adults.

The reader will recall that, beginning in preschool, children are aware of an increasing number of differences, and there has been, at least in the recent past, a preference among both whites and blacks for white skin (cf. pp. 405–407). However, strong racial prejudice is not common at that age.

Identification with Ethnic Groups. In the same way that the child becomes identified with his parents and his social class, he also learns to identify with the other subcultural groups (ethnic, religious, racial) to which he belongs. These identifications develop gradually and usually become firmly established during the school years. In one of the earlier studies of the problem, 86 Protestant, Catholic, Jewish, and Negro children were interviewed and asked questions such as "What are you?" "What kinds of people live around your house?" "What is Daddy? Mommy?" (66, 67). With advancing age, ethnic designations were used more frequently.

From the age of about 5½ on, the child's conception both of himself and others in terms of names is virtually abandoned. Reference to ethnic group membership becomes widespread, and, in a lesser degree, references to personal qualities are increasingly utilized. As exemplified by the responses secured in the 6½ to 8½ and 8½ to 10½ groups, both the child and his neighbors are most frequently viewed as "American," "Negro," "Jewish," "Catholic," "Italian," "Spanish" (66, 374).

Children generally describe their parents in the same ethnic identification terms they use for themselves.

Young children answered questions like "What does it take to be Catholic, Jewish?" "What does it mean to be Catholic, Jewish?" primarily in terms of concrete activities, e.g., "talking Jewish," "going to a synagogue," "making communion." Older children more frequently make use of abstractions. Thus a 10-year-old Jewish boy said, "Jewish is a religion just like Christian. You go to Hebrew (school) and you see the star in the Talmud Torah. It means to believe in these things, to respect your parents. You shouldn't steal" (67).

Negro Children's Identification. The definition of who is black is, after all, a cultural one, dictated largely by the majority group. In our culture, anyone with even a small amount of black ancestry is defined as Negro. Hence identification with blacks means acceptance of oneself as a member of a so-called racial group.

In one study of minority-group identification, 253 black children between the ages of 3 and 7 were the subjects (27). In order to determine whether these children understood the word Negro, the examiner presented each child with Negro and white dolls and asked him to "give me the doll who looks like a Negro child." Apparently the word was not well understood in the early years, but by the age of 6, a substantial proportion (78 percent) of Negro children chose a brown-skinned doll.

Of course, the fact that a child is aware of the differences between blacks and whites does not necessarily mean that he has made a personal identification with Negroes. In order to determine whether the children identified themselves with blacks, the experimenter also requested each child to "give me the doll that looks like you." Again the youngest children were not certain in their choices. However, with increasing age, there was a marked rise in the percent of subjects who chose (and presumably identified with) the Negro doll. Thus 36 percent of the 3-year-olds, 49 percent of the 5-year-olds, and 87 percent of the 7-year-olds chose the Negro doll as the one "that looks like you" (27).

By the age of 7, all children appear to be aware of the concept of "Negro" (174), and black as well as white children in a study a few years ago showed a tendency to assign undesirable traits to the blacks, as was discussed in an earlier chapter. The Negro child appeared to be identified with a group that he regarded as possessing negative and undesirable traits. This type of anxiety-arousing identification is apt to make the black child feel insecure and resentful toward the white majority, and hopefully the picture is changing. The incidence of Negro delinquency, while involving many other factors (cf. pp. 734–746), is probably at least in part a result of hostility to the white "establishment" and an attempt to deny feelings of insecurity through aggressive and rebellious behavior. Certainly, as the 1968 report of the National Advisory Commission on Civil Disorders makes evident, discrimination is still a fact of life in this country, both North and South. While steps have been taken toward restoring civil and legal rights, social and economic injustice remains largely unresolved.

Black children's perception of a hostile white environment is evidenced in the stories they tell about pictures they are shown (37, 129). In one study, the Thematic Apperception Test (a set of pictures used to elicit stories) was given to 50 white and 50 black preadolescent boys. Analysis of this test showed that the minority-group children described the general environment as more hostile than did the white subjects (129). The central figures of the stories told by black youths were often hated, scolded, reprimanded, or physically attacked.

Apparently the blacks perceived the social environment as basically inhospitable, unfriendly, and threatening, and they revealed strong feelings of personal inferiority and helplessness. Relatively few Negro boys depicted the central figures in their stories as leaders or as friendly and considerate individuals who respect others. This perception of the world as hostile is largely attributable to personal encounters with race prejudice, to general awareness of discrimination against Negroes, and to identification with a disadvantaged minority group.

The evidence suggests that identification with ethnic, racial, and religious groups becomes well established during the middle-childhood years. These identifications, if firmly implanted, become a permanent part of the individual's psychological make-up and continue to influence his behavior for many years to come.

It may be hoped that current attempts on the part of the white majority not only to remedy social and economic injustices but also to recognize the cultural and historical contributions of minority groups to American life will help to provide more positive identification models for minority-group children. Certainly, the increasingly strong emphasis on Negro culture among blacks themselves should also aid in this process. It is interesting that much of the emphasis has properly been on the *unique* contributions rather than those in "me too" areas.

Ultimately, however, the values of *uniqueness* must be recognized within the framework of equal opportunity and *shared* values for all. In an interesting study made in 1966 (25), the self-concepts of both white and black children attending a *de facto* segregated (predominantly Negro) school were compared with the self-concepts of black and white children attending recently desegregated and long-term desegregated schools in a small city in New Jersey. Children attending the *de facto* segregated school had fewer positive self-concepts than children attending the newly desegregated or long-term desegregated schools, and also had lower levels of aspiration than children attending the newly desegregated school. Further, pride in themselves *as related to the school situation* and levels of aspiration of both white and black children attending the *de facto* segregated school were significantly lower than those of children attending the newly desegregated or long-term desegregated schools. Apparently it is not only minority-group children but also children of the white majority who are the victims of racism in our society.

The Development of Prejudice

By kindergarten, many children have developed hostile attitudes toward minority groups. During the early school years more children acquire these prejudices, which become more crystallized and conform more closely to adult patterns of prejudice (147–149). Children's prejudices are rarely based on their own experiences. Their verbalizations about minorities typically reflect negative attitudes learned from the direct or indirect teaching of adults (147, 148). Parents may make statements in support of democratic values and intercultural education and express opposition to racial or religious segregation in the schools. However, they often have little insight into their own underlying feelings toward minority groups or the implications of their own group membership, and make no direct or planned attempts to teach their children ethnic attitudes. Instead, such attitudes are conveyed to the children by restricting social relationships in the home, neighborhood, and school, and by disapproving of friendships with members of certain groups (149).

Background and Personality of Prejudiced Children. Children may acquire the prejudices of those with whom they identify—parents, peers, their social group. Children of prejudiced parents may become bigoted, while those emulating tolerant parents may develop democratic attitudes. However, more is involved in the development of prejudice than simple imitation of attitudes. Studies of anti-Semitic and anti-Negro adults show that their prejudices are components of broader patterns of attitudes and are related to basic personality structure. Compared with tolerant people, prejudiced adults tend to be rigid, authoritarian, highly conforming, and overly moralistic (1).

An excellent study by Frenkel-Brunswik "designed to throw light on the determinants of susceptibility to racial or ethnic prejudice and allied forms of undemocratic opinions and attitudes" (54, 295) demonstrates that children's ethnic prejudices are also related to general personality structure. About 1500 California boys and girls between the ages of 11 and 16 were given tests measuring attitudes toward Jews, Negroes, Japanese, Mexicans, and out-groups in general. A series of statements about these groups was presented and the subjects were asked to express their agreement or disagreement with each. Some contained stereotypical accusations: Japanese cruelty, Negro laziness, Jewish radicalism and money-mindedness, etc. Others involved sharing activities with minority-group members (e.g., eating in the same restaurants, living in the same neighborhood, socializing together). From the larger group, the 120 most and least prejudiced children were selected for further study, including personality tests and interviews.

Ethnocentric (prejudiced) children revealed selfish orientations toward America and indifference toward other countries. They agreed with generally intolerant statements (e.g., "Only people who are like myself have the right to be happy"; "We should not send any of our food to foreign countries, but should think of America first") much more frequently than unprejudiced children did.

Other generalized attitudes typical of the prejudiced child, but not the unprejudiced, were: rejection of all that is weak or different; rigid conceptions of appropriate sex roles, together with intolerance of passive or feminine behavior in boys and masculine or tomboyish behavior in girls; admiration of the strong, tough, powerful, and in the boys, a fear of weakness in themselves; rigid conformity to approved social values and moralistic condemnation of others; feelings of helplessness in a world thought to be full of chaos and destruction. All these attitudes were considered indicative of "narrow and rigid personality" (54).

In discussing relationships with parents, the tolerant children frequently mentioned affection, cooperation, and companionship, while the prejudiced children complained of lack of affection and submission to stern, harsh, punitive treatment. Interviews with the parents offered evidence that the tolerant child "learns at home the equalitarian and individualized approach to people, as the ethnocentric child learns the authoritarian and hierarchical way of thinking" (54, 302).

From these data, Frenkel-Brunswik concluded:

From the point of view of society as a whole, the most important problem . . . seems to be the child's attitude toward authority. Forced submission to authority produces only surface conformity countermanded by violent underlying destructiveness, dangerous to the very society to which there seems to be conformity. Only a frightened and frustrated child will tend to gain safety and security by oversimplified black-white schematizations and categorizations on the basis of crude, external characteristics. Deliberately planned democratic participation in

school and family, individualized approach to the child, and the right proportion of permissiveness and guidance may be instrumental in bringing about the
attitude necessary for a genuine identification with society and thus for international understanding (*19, 306*).

Prejudiced children show significantly poorer self-concepts than unprejudiced children and less satisfaction with their own mental abilities;
impaired social relations with members of the same- and opposite-sex
parents and teachers; and overconcern with their own personality and with
school subjects. Interestingly, no relations were obtained between prejudice
and actual school achievement (*178, 183*).

Such findings are not restricted to the dominant white majority. In a
study of black 9- to 18-year-old pupils in three schools in New York City,
it was found that black children who were most self-accepting expressed
significantly more positive attitudes toward *both* blacks and whites than
did children who were least self-accepting (*183*).

In another investigation of the relationship between personality and
ethnic attitudes, a variety of tests were given to fourth, fifth, and sixth
grade pupils (*60*). Subjects were asked to indicate agreement or disagreement with a variety of statements related not only to minority-group prejudice or acceptance, but also to *general* tolerance or intolerance. The high
correlations obtained between general intolerance and attitudes toward
Jews and Negroes indicated that there is a generalized prejudiced attitude.
Compared with the tolerant children,

> the more prejudiced child favors his own immediate group over any larger
> society, he thinks categorically of "weak" and "strong," he declares himself in
> favor of authoritarianism on the part of teachers, he is suspicious of integrity
> of others. . . . In general, the picture one gets of the prejudiced child . . .
> suggests fear and distrust of others, lack of confidence in himself, feelings of
> guilt and uneasiness, insecurities and doubts about the larger physical and
> social world and possibly a reactive hostility toward people who are "weak"
> or "different" (*51, 89*).

"Moreover, intolerant children . . . have cynical, distrustful opinions of
others, have fears of being exploited or duped, or have feelings of having
been treated unfairly" (*60, 91*).

These two investigations are in essential agreement about the nature
of the personality structure of the prejudiced child. In general, as Frenkel-
Brunswik's study indicates, personality characteristics associated with intolerance are established in early parent-child relationships.

In a further study of the antecedents of children's prejudices, one team
of investigators made a direct test of the hypothesis that "authoritarian
and disciplinary attitudes of parents concerning child training practices
would be related to a greater incidence of ethnic bias in the children of
these parents" (*64, 170*).

The subjects were 154 mothers of children whose attitudes toward
minority groups had been tested. The mothers answered questionnaires

consisting of 81 items grouped into five scales: authoritarian attitudes and practices; pèrmissiveness, parent-child integration (evidence of a close, affectionate parent-child relationship); parental rigidity or fussiness; general good judgment. The correlations between the parental behavior scales and children's attitude scores generally substantiated the original hypothesis. There was a distinct tendency for more of the mothers of prejudiced children (as contrasted with mothers of nonprejudiced children) to score in the higher ranges of the authoritarian and rigidity scales. Correspondingly, fewer of the mothers of low-prejudice children scored low on permissiveness, parent-child integration, and "good judgment" (64).

> Prejudice in children appears to be associated with the complex of parental attitudes which is involved in authoritarian handling of control and with lack of tolerance of children's "annoyance value." It appears that attitudes of tolerance and good judgment in child rearing are possibly part of a personality and attitude complex on the parents' part which is associated with freedom from ethnic prejudice in children (64, 180).

What children learn is not a specific attitude, but a whole "complex of attitudes and personality characteristics, which reveal themselves in interpersonal relationships of various sorts" (64, 180).

Prejudice and Mental Functioning. The prejudiced child tends to think in terms of discrete categories. He tends to be rigid in his approach to problems and has difficulty altering his original conception of a problem. Thus we might expect his approach to intellectual tasks to be less effective than that of a less prejudiced child. In one study (102), 26 boys and 34 girls, 7 years of age, first designated their agreement or disagreement with statements that contained intolerant or prejudiced statements about Mexicans, Catholics, Jews, and Negroes. On the basis of their answers to the test, the children were categorized as prejudiced or unprejudiced. These children were then given a series of tasks to assess their approach to problems and their ability to solve them. For example, in one test a child was confronted with 16 objects that differed in color, shape, and size (four colors, three shapes, and two sizes). He was asked to divide the 16 blocks into two equal groups. The only correct solution was to divide the blocks on the basis of size. The prejudiced children, in comparison with the unprejudiced, had more difficulty solving the problem; they tended to persist with a poor hunch or hypothesis, and showed an inability to make use of the hints that the examiner gave them.

On the basis of this and other tests, the author concluded that the prejudiced child tried to look for simple solutions and had difficulty changing his original approach or idea. The prejudiced child performed poorly when the problems were ambiguous and he had to structure the meaning of the problem. In brief, the rigidity of attitude that is present in maintaining a prejudice is also reflected in an individual's approach to intellectual problems (102).

Modification of Racial Attitudes

As intolerance is related to firmly established characteristics, it might be inferred that intolerance could be reduced only by changing the basic personality structure of the prejudiced person. This, of course, would require intensive clinical treatment.

It would be a serious mistake, however, to assume that there is a one-to-one correspondence between personality and prejudice. If they live among bigoted people, well-adjusted children may learn to behave intolerantly—that is, in accordance with the standard or accepted attitudes of their own social group. In such cases, prejudice might be viewed as a reflection of the child's identification with his group rather than as displacement of his hostility toward his parents. Pehaps those whose prejudice has this kind of basis, but who in general are well adjusted and not essentially hostile, would become more tolerant if they were transferred to an environment that promoted "democratic living" and an equalitarian philosophy. On the other hand, those who *need* scapegoats as an outlet for deep-lying aggressive feelings may not be able to relinquish their prejudices, even in a democratic setting. To test these hypotheses, one investigator (130) studied changes in boys' attitudes toward Negroes after a four-week vacation at an interracial camp where blacks and whites lived, ate, and played together. The subjects were 106 white New York City boys ranging from 8 to 14 years of age.

An indirect test of prejudice was administered to each boy less than 24 hours before he left home—that is, before intimate contact with Negro boys at camp. In this test the child was given 12 photographs of boys' faces, eight of them black, four of them white. In the first part of the test, the child simply indicated his order of preference for these faces. In the second part, he selected the pictures of boys he would like to go to the movies with, invite home to lunch, etc. The extent of discrimination against the pictures of Negroes constituted the measure of prejudice. This test was given again just before the children left the camp.

Personality structure was evaluated by analyzing responses to a picture-story test (the Thematic Apperception Test) in which the subject's underlying needs and attitudes were reflected in the kinds of stories he told. Data about personal and social adjustment at camp were collected from two sources: a brief interview with each child and a camp social worker's report.

Following the camp experience, some of the boys increased significantly in prejudice whereas others decreased. As hypothesized, these changes were related to personality structure. In general, the boys who increased in prejudice were hostile, defiant youngsters who perceived the world as cruel and unpleasant and felt they were frequent victims of aggression. Because, for them, the expression of aggression led to punishment, retaliation, and restraint, they probably did not "act out" their hostile feelings. Hence they had greater needs to displace their aggression by means of anti-Negro prejudice.

Moreover, these boys were dissatisfied with the camp itself, the other campers, and interpersonal relations there. The child who was poorly adjusted socially in the situation and did not find the experience rewarding probably did not identify with the camp or accept its attitudes. Under the circumstances, he may have felt more frustrated, and may have become more, rather than less, prejudiced against blacks.

Children who decreased in prejudice presented a sharply contrasting picture. They manifested fewer aggressive needs, less hostility toward their parents, fewer feelings of restraint, and generally favorable attitudes toward society. Consequently, they had little need to displace aggression through prejudice.

In the camp, they were well accepted by their peers, and their counselors judged them to be high in "ability to relate to others." They complained less about interpersonal relations, were more satisfied with the camp experience and their fellow campers, and probably formed more intimate friendships (130). It may be assumed that they found the experience rewarding and, consequently, identified more closely with the camp, accepting its tolerant philosophy.

In another extensive study on the modification of racial attitudes (146), more than 1000 children 8 to 13 years of age were observed at a summer camp. Some of the children, both white and black, lived in desegregated cabins for a two-week period. The behavior of the children in the desegregated situation was compared with the behavior of children who lived in segregated cabins.

Signs of tension (enuresis, nightmares, crying, physical symptoms, repeated accidents) were more frequent among the children living in the desegregated cabins. Moreover, the white children initially became vigilant to possible aggression from the black children. As might be expected from earlier work, both the black and white children viewed the latter as more desirable for friends and assigned higher status to the whites. However, there was a general trend for both black and white children to view the blacks as more desirable after the two weeks of desegregated living.

Although the experience of living in a biracial setting decreased suspicion and hostility between the groups, the most important catalyst for change was the counselor. His attitudes and personality, particularly his warmth and personal security, facilitated the establishment of good interpersonal relation between the black and white children.

Apparently both personality and social situational factors are involved in changes in race attitudes. The study suggests that prejudice may be reduced by educational measures, such as encouraging contacts between members of various races. Moreover, this study highlights the importance of the attitudes of authority figures, such as teachers, in promoting more positive feelings toward minority groups in a desegregated setting, whether it is a camp or a school. Modification of the mutual fears, suspicions, and resentments of black and white children is most apt to occur when the adult in charge favors desegregation and is admired and liked by the children (146).

The above-described study suggests that even a modest change in the social milieu (a summer camp experience) may help to reduce prejudice. While tensions between various ethnic and cultural groups have recently come to the surface and emerged into public consciousness, the very acknowledgment of their existence and some of the reasons for them is likely to lead to increased efforts to overcome them. It appears probable that we are currently witnessing the troubled beginnings of fundamental changes in the social structure of our entire society, which hopefully will begin to sound the death knell of prejudices that our society can ill afford if it is to survive—socially, politically, or economically.

SUMMARY

During the middle-childhood years, the child is exposed to an ever-expanding series of extrafamilial influences. Nevertheless, relationships with parents remain, for most children, the most important factor in determining the kind of person the child will become, and the kinds of problems he will face in his quest for maturity.

Parent behavior is not unidimensional. While many theoretical dimensions for conceptualizing parent behavior are possible, the two axes most consistently employed in research to date are *warmth-hostility* and *control-autonomy*. The child of warm-permissive parents is likely to be active, independent, friendly, and socially assertive, but may also be somewhat aggressive, bossy, and disobedient. The child of warm-restrictive parents, in contrast, is likely to be more dependent, less creative, more conforming, less dominant and competitive, but more polite and neat. Hostile parents tend to impair the child's adjustment and to arouse counter-hostility, whether manifested internally or externally. While restrictiveness combined with hostility tends to maximize self-aggression, social withdrawal, and symptoms of internal conflict in the child, permissiveness combined with hostility appears to maximize aggressive, poorly controlled behavior, of a kind frequently seen in delinquent or "acting-out" children.

The child's development of self-esteem is fostered by parents whose own self-esteem is high, who are warm and accepting and interested in the child's activities, who encourage autonomy without being excessively demanding, and who have definite and consistent standards of conduct for the child, while respecting his rights and opinions. Absence of either father or mother from the home may make the child's adjustment and development of a clearly defined sex-role identification more difficult, particularly when parental absence occurs early in life (and when the same sex parent is absent).

Studies of social-class differences in child-rearing practices indicate that middle-class mothers tend to be more affectionate and less punitive than those of lower classes; and middle-class children generally have more favorable perceptions of their parents. Sibling status also influences the child's personality development. Oldest children are more likely to achieve eminence and to identify more closely with adults; they are also more likely, however, to be oversensitive, anxious, and fearful of physical harm. In contrast, younger children tend to be more gregarious, defiant, and eager for physical demonstrations of affection. Sex of siblings also appears to influence personality characteristics; thus, for example, girls with older brothers have more "tomboyish" traits than other girls.

The development of sex-role standards is increasingly fostered during middle childhood. Thus boys are expected to be strong, courageous, ambitious, and assertive; while girls are expected to be sociable, well mannered, and neat, but to inhibit verbal and physical aggression. General emotional expressiveness is considered more appropriate in girls, while analytical, independent approaches to problem-solving are expected more from boys.

The middle-childhood years represent a critical period for conscience development. According to Piaget, before age 7 or 8 the child's concept of justice is based on rigid and inflexible notions of right and wrong learned from parents. Between the ages of 8-11, a progressive equalitarianism develops; and beginning about age 11-12, "purely equalitarian justice is tempered by considerations of equity." Conscience development is dependent both upon the child's level of cognitive maturation (Kohlberg), and also upon parental and other influences to which the child is subjected. Optimal conscience development is facilitated if (1) the parent's own conscience and moral standards are mature and reasonable, but not overly rigid, harsh and inflexible; and (2) adoption of the parent's standards by the child is based on positive identification and modeling. Love-oriented discipline appears more effective in fostering conscience development than physical punishment.

All children encounter some psychological problems during middle childhood. These will usually be transient and limited in severity if the child's parents provide good role models, are warm and accepting, and are consistent and flexible in disciplinary techniques; but not so controlling or dominating that they thwart his development of autonomy, self-reliance, and mastery behavior. In contrast, the child whose parents and society have seriously failed him in one way or another may be expected to encounter psychological or psychosomatic problems which are more severe, more chronic, and more refractory to treatment. Many psychological symptoms involve manifestations of defense mechanisms employed to ward off painful feelings of anxiety (e.g., repression, denial, projection, rationalization, regression, etc.). Among the most frequent problems of middle childhood are: nightmares and sleep disturbances, school phobias, death phobias, tics and related disturbances of motility, obsessions and compulsions (often related to the child's increasingly strict conscience during this period), hostility to parents, and various psychophysiological symptoms.

Ethnic, racial, and religious identifications become well established during middle childhood, and prejudice can have serious consequences for the child's personality development and self-concept. While prejudiced attitudes among children of this age are typically learned from parents, peers, and society, individual personality factors play a role. In comparison with other children, prejudiced children tend to be more egocentric, rigid, inflexible in mental functioning, fearful of authority, and frustrated; and to have poorer self-concepts and poorer relations with peers of both sexes. Modification of racial prejudice is essential for optimal personality development of all children in contemporary society.

References

1. Adorno, T. W., Frenkel-Brunswik, E., Levinson, D. J., & Stanford, R. N. *The authoritarian personality.* New York: Harper & Row, 1950.
2. Allinsmith, W. Moral standards: II. The learning of moral standards. In D. R. Miller & G. E. Swanson (Eds.), *Inner conflict and defense.* New York: Holt, Rinehart and Winston, 1960, 141–176.
3. Altus, W. D. Birth order and its sequellae. *Science,* 1966, *151,* 44–49.
4. Andrews, R. J. The self-concept and pupils with learning difficulties. *Slow learn. Child,* 1966, *13,* 47–54.
5. Anthony, E. J. Psychoneurotic disorders. In A. M. Freedman & H. I. Kaplan (Eds.), *Comprehensive textbook of psychiatry.* Baltimore: Williams & Wilkins, 1967.
6. Apperly, F. L. A study of America's Rhodes scholars. *J. Hered.,* 1939, *30,* 494–495.
7. Aronfreed, J. The nature, variety, and social patterning of moral responses to transgression. *J. abnorm. soc. Psychol.,* 1961, 63, 223–240.
8. Bach, G. R. Father-fantasies and father-typing in father-separated children. *Child Develpm.,* 1946, *17,* 63–79.
9. Bach, G. R. Young children's play fantasies. *Psychol. Monogr.,* 1945, *59,* No. 2.
10. Baldwin, A. L. The effect of home environment on nursery school behavior. *Child Develpm.,* 1949, *20,* 49–61.
11. Bandura, A. Social learning through imitation. In M. R. Jones (Ed.), *Nebraska symposium on motivation,* Vol. X. Lincoln: Univer. of Nebraska Press, 1962, 211–268.
12. Bandura, A., Ross, D., & Ross, S. A. Transmission of aggression through imitation of aggressive models. *J. abnorm. soc. Psychol.,* 1961, *63,* 575.
13. Bayley, N., & Schaefer, E. S. Relationships between socioeconomic variables and the behavior of mothers toward young children. *J. genet. Psychol.,* 1960, *96,* 61–77.
14. Becker, S. W., Lerner, M. J., & Carroll, J. Conformity as a function of birth order and type of group pressure: a verification. *J. pers. soc. Psychol.,* 1966, *3,* 242–244.
15. Becker, W. C. Consequences of different kinds of parental discipline. In M. L. Hoffman & L. W. Hoffman (Eds.), *Review of child development, Vol. I.* New York: Russell Sage Foundation, 1964.
16. Beller, E. K., & Turner, J. LeB. A study of dependency and aggression in early childhood. Unpublished report from progress report on NIMH Project M-849.
17. Bledsoe, J. C. Self concepts of children and their intelligence, achievement, interests, and anxiety. *J. indiv. Psychol.,* 1964, *20,* 55–58.
18. Bonney, M. E. Relationships between social success, family size, socioeconomic

home background and intelligence among school children in grades III and IV. *Sociometry*, 1944, 7, 26–39.

19. Bonney, M. E. A study of social status on the second grade level. *J. genet. Psychol.*, 1942, 60, 271–305.

20. Bonney, M. E. A study of the relation of intelligence, family size, and sex differences with mutual friendships in the primary grades. *Child Develpm.*, 1942, 13, 79–100.

21. Bronfenbrenner, U. The psychological costs of quality and equality in education. *Child Develpm.*, 1967, 38, 909–925.

22. Brown, D. G. Masculinity-femininity development in children. *J. consult. Psychol.*, 1957, 21, 197–202.

23. Bruce, P. Relationship of self acceptance to other variables with sixth grade children oriented in self understanding. *J. educ. Psychol.*, 1958, 49, 229–238.

24. Burton, R. V., & Whiting, J. W. M. The absent father and cross-sex identity. *Merrill-Palmer Quart.*, 1961, 7, 85–95.

25. Caplin, M. D. The relationship between self concept and academic achievement and between level of aspiration and academic achievement. *Dissert. Abstr.*, 1966, 27, 979–980.

26. Chazan, M. School phobia. *Brit. J. educ. Psychol.*, 1962, 32, 209–217.

27. Clark, K. B., & Clarke, M. P. Racial identification, and preference in Negro children. In T. M. Newcomb & E. L. Hartley (Eds.), *Readings in social psychology*. New York: Holt, Rinehart and Winston, 1947.

28. Cobb, E. A. Family press variables. *Monogr. Soc. Res. Child Develpm.*, 1943, 8, 327–361.

29. Cobb, H. V. Role wishes and general wishes of children and adolescents. *Child Develpm.*, 1954, 25, 161.

30. Committee on Child Psychiatry, *Psychopathological disorders in childhood: theoretical considerations and a proposed classification.* New York: Group for the Advancement of Psychiatry, 1966.

31. Conn, J. H. Children's reactions to the discovery of genital differences. *Amer. J. Orthopsychiat.*, 1940, 10, 747–755.

32. Conn, J. H., & Kanner, L. Children's awareness of sex differences. *J. child Psychiat.*, 1947, 1, 3–57.

33. Coolidge, J. C., Tessman, E., Waldfogel, S., & Willer, M. L. Patterns of aggression in school phobia. *Psychoanal. Study Child*, 1962, 17, 319–333.

34. Coopersmith, S. *The antecedents of self-esteem.* San Francisco: W. H. Freeman, 1967.

35. Crandall, V. J., & Rabson, A. Children's repetition choices in an intellectual achievement situation following success and failure. *J. genet. Psychol.*, 1960, 97, 161–168.

36. Crutchfield, R. S. Conformity and character. *Amer. Psychologist*, 1955, 10, 191.

37. Dai, B. Some problems of personality development among Negro children. In C. Kluckholm & H. A. Murray (Eds.), *Personality in nature, society, and culture.* New York: Knopf, 1953, 545–566.

38. Davis, A. Child training and social class. In R. G. Barker, J. S. Kounin, & H. F. Wright (Eds.), *Child behavior and development.* New York: McGraw-Hill, 1943.

39. Dawe, H. C. An analysis of 200 quarrels of preschool children. *Child Develpm.*, 1934, 5, 139.

40. Deutsch, M. Minority group and class status as related to social and personality factors in scholastic achievement. *Monogr. soc. appl. Anthrop.*, 1960, 2, 1–32.

41. Dolger, L., & Ginandes, J. Children's attitudes toward discipline as related to socio-economic status. *J. exp. Educ.*, 1946, *15*, 161–165.

42. Doris, J. Test anxiety and blame-assignment in grade school children. *J. abnorm. soc. Psychol.*, 1959, *58*, 181–190.

43. Dunlop, G. M. Certain aspects of children's fears. Unpublished doctoral dissertion, Columbia University, 1951.

44. Durkin, D. Children's concepts of justice: a comparison with the Piaget data. *Child Develpm.*, 1959, *30*, 59–67.

45. Durkin, D. Children's acceptance of reciprocity as a justice principle. *Child Develpm.*, 1959, *30*, 289–296.

46. Eisenberg, L. School phobia: a study in communication of anxiety. *Amer. J. Psychiat.*, 1958, *114*, 712–718.

47. Emmerich, W. Young children's discriminations of parent and child roles. *Child Develpm.*, 1959, *30*, 403.

48. Engel, M., & Raine, W. J. A method for the measurement of the self-concept of children in the third grade. *J. genet. Psychol.*, 1963, *102*, 125–137.

49. England, A. O. Nonstructured approach to the study of children's fears. *J. clin. Psychol.*, 1946, *2*, 363–368.

50. English, O. S., & Finch, S. M. *Introduction to psychiatry.* New York: Norton, 1954.

51. Fenton, N. The only child. *J. genet. Psychol.*, 1928, *35*, 546–556.

52. Frazier, A., & Lisonbee, L. K. Adolescent concerns with physique. *School Rev.*, *58*, 397.

53. Freedman, A. M., & Kaplan, H. I. *Comprehensive textbook of psychiatry.* Baltimore: Williams & Wilkins, 1967.

54. Frenkel-Brunswik, E. A study of prejudice in children. *Human Relat.*, 1948, *1*, 295–306.

55. Freud, A. *The ego and the mechanisms of defense.* New York: International Universities Press, 1946.

56. Fromm, E. Selfishness and self-love. *Psychiatry*, 1939, *2*, 507–523.

57. Garner, A. M., & Wenar, C. *The mother-child interaction in psychosomatic disorders.* Urbana: Univer. of Illinois Press, 1959.

58. Goodenough, F. L., & Leahy, A. M. Effects of certain family relationships upon the development of personality. *Ped. Sem.*, 1927, *34*, 45–71.

59. Goodenough, F. W. Interest in persons and aspects of sex differences in the early years. *Psychol. Monogr.*, 1957, *55*, 287.

60. Gough, H. G., Harris, D. B., Martin, W. E., & Edwards, M. Children's ethnic attitudes: I. Relationship to certain personality factors. *Child Develpm.*, 1950, *21*, 83–91.

61. Gregory, I. Studies of parental deprivation in psychiatric patients. *Amer. J. Psychiat.*, 1958, *115*, 432–442.

62. Gronseth, E. The impact of father absence in sailor families upon the personality structure and social adjustment of adult sailor sons. Part I. In N. Anderson (Ed.), *Studies of the family*, Vol. 2. Gottingen: Vandenhoeck and Ruprecht, 1957, 97–114.

63. Harris, D. B. Sex differences in the life problems and interests of adolescents, 1935 and 1957. *Child Develpm.*, 1959, *30*, 453.

64. Harris, D. B., Gough, H. G., & Martin, W. E. Children's ethnic attitudes. II. Relationship to parental beliefs concerning child training. *Child Develpm.*, 1950, *21*, 169–181.

65. Harris, I. D. *The promised seed.* London: Macmillan, 1964.

66. Hartley, E. L., Rosenbaum, M., & Schwartz, S. Children's use of ethnic frames of references: an exploratory study of children's conceptualization of multiple ethnic group membership. *J. Psychol.*, 1948, *26*, 367–386.
67. Hartley, E. L., Rosenbaum, M., & Schwartz, S. Children's perception of ethnic group membership. *J. Psychol.*, 1948, *26*, 387–398.
68. Hattwick, B. A. Sex differences in behavior of nursery school children. *Child Develpm.*, 1937, *8*, 343.
69. Havighurst, R. J., Robinson, M. Z., & Door, M. The development of ideal self in childhood and adolescence. *J. educ. Res.*, 1946, *40*, 241–257.
70. Heinecke, C. M. Some antecedents and correlates of quiet and fear in young boys. Unpublished doctoral dissertation, Harvard University, 1953.
71. Helmreich, R. L. Prolonged stress in Sealab. II: A field study of individual and group reactions. Unpublished doctoral dissertation, Yale University, 1966.
72. Helmreich, R. L., & Collins, B. E. Situational determinants of affiliative preference under stress. *J. pers. soc. Psychol.*, 1967, *6*, 79–85.
73. Hetherington, E. M. Effects of paternal absence on sex typed behaviors in Negro and white preadolescent males. *J. pers. soc. Psychol.*, 1960, *1*, 87–91.
74. Hildreth, G. The social interests of young adolescents. *Child Develpm.*, 1945, *16*, 119.
75. Hill, W. F. Learning theory and the acquisition of values. *Psychol. Rev.*, 1960, *67*, 317–331.
76. Hoffman, M. L., & Saltzstein, H. D. Parent practices and the child's moral orientation. Paper read at meeting of American Psychological Association, Chicago, 1960.
77. Honzik, M. P. Sex differences in the occurrence of materials in the play constructions of preadolescents. *Child Develpm.*, 1951, *22*, 15.
78. Hovland, C. I., & Janis, I. L. (Eds.), *Personality and persuasibility*. New Haven, Conn.: Yale Univer. Press, 1959.
79. Jersild, A. T. *In search of self*. New York: Columbia Univer. Press, 1952.
80. Jersild, A. T., Markey, F. V., & Jersild, C. L. Children's fears, dreams, wishes, daydreams, likes, dislikes, pleasant and unpleasant memories. *Child Develpm. Monogr.*, 1933, No. 12.
81. Johnson, A. M. School phobia. *Amer. J. Orthopsychiat.*, 1941, *11*, 702–711.
82. Jones, H. E. The environment and mental development. In L. Carmichael (Ed.), *Manual of child psychology*. New York: Wiley, 1954 (2nd ed.), 668.
83. Kagan, J. Personality development. In I. J. Janis (Ed.), *Personality dynamics*, Harcourt, Brace & World, in press.
84. Kagan, J. Acquisition and significance of sex typing and sex role identity. In M. L. Hoffman & L. W. Hoffman (Eds.), *Review of child development research*, Vol. 1. New York: Russell Sage Foundation, 1964, 137–168.
85. Kagan, J. The child's sex role classification of school objects. *Child Develpm.*, 1964, *35*, 1051.
86. Kagan, J. The child's perception of the parent. *J. abnorm. soc. Psychol.*, 1956, *53*, 257.
87. Kagan, J., Hosken, B., & Watson, S. The child's symbolic conceptualization of the parents. *Child Develpm.*, 1961, *32*, 625.
88. Kagan, J., & Lemkin, J. The child's differential perception of parental attributes. *J. abnorm. soc. Psychol.*, 1960, *61*, 446.
89. Kagan, J., & Moss, H. A. *Birth to maturity: the Fels study of psychological development*. New York: Wiley, 1962.
90. Kanner, L. *Child psychiatry*. Springfield, Ill.: Thomas, 1957 (3rd ed.).

91. Katcher, A. The discrimination of sex differences by young children. *J. genet. Psychol.,* 1955, *87,* 131–143.

92. Kawin, E. *Children of the preschool age.* Chicago: Univer. Chicago Press, 1934.

93. Kessler, J. W. *Psychopathology of childhood.* Englewood Cliffs, N.J.: Prentice-Hall, 1966.

94. Koch, H. L. Attitudes of children toward their peers as related to certain characteristics of their siblings. *Psychol. Monogr.,* 1956, *70,* No. 426, 1–41.

95. Koch, H. L. Some emotional attitudes of the young child in relation to characteristics of his siblings. *Child Develpm.,* 1956, *27,* 393–426.

96. Koch, H. L. Sissiness and tomboyishness in relation to sibling characteristics. *J. genet. Psychol.,* 1956, *88,* 231–244.

97. Kohlberg, L. A cognitive-developmental analysis of children's sex-role concepts and attitudes. In E. E. Maccoby (Ed.), *The development of sex differences.* Stanford, Calif.: Stanford Univer. Press, 1966, 82–173.

98. Kohlberg, L. Development of moral character and moral ideology. In M. L. Hoffman & L. W. Hoffman (Eds.), *Review of child development,* Vol. I. New York: Russell Sage Foundation, 1964, 383–431.

99. Kohlberg, L. The development of children's orientations toward a moral order: I. Sequence in the development of moral thought. *Vita Humana,* 1963, *6,* 11–33.

100. Kohlberg, L. Moral development and identification. In H. W. Stevenson (Ed.), *Child psychology,* Part I. (62nd Yearb., nat. Soc. Stud. Educ.) Chicago: Univer. Chicago Press, 1963.

101. Kohn, M. L. Social class and parental values. *Amer. J. Sociol.,* 1959, *64,* 337.

102. Kutner, B. Patterns of mental functioning associated with prejudice in children. *Psychol. Monogr.,* 1958, *72,* No. 460.

103. Lansky, L. M., Crandall, V. J., Kagan, J., & Baker, C. T. Sex differences in aggression and its correlates in middle class adolescents. *Child Develpm.,* 1961, *32,* 45.

104. Lapouse, R., & Monk, M. A. Fears and worries in a representative sample of children. *Amer. J. Orthopsychiat.,* 1959, *29,* 803–818.

105. Lerner, E. *Constraint areas and moral judgment of children.* Menasha, Wis.: Banta, 1937.

106. Lerner, E. The problem of perspective in moral reasoning. *Amer. J. Sociol.,* 1937, *43,* 249–269.

107. Leventhal, T., & Sills, M. Self-image in school phobia. *Amer. J. Orthopsychiat.,* 1964, *34,* 685–695.

108. LeVine, B. B. Punishment techniques and the development of conscience. Unpublished doctoral dissertation, Northwestern University, 1961.

109. Levin, H. Permissive child rearing and adult role behavior. In D. E. Dulany, R. L. DeValois, D. C. Beardsley, & M. R. Winterbottom (Eds.), *Contributions to modern psychology.* New York: Oxford Univer. Press, 1958, 307–312.

110. Levy, D. M. *Maternal overprotection.* New York: Columbia Univer. Press, 1943.

111. Lindzey, G., & Goldberg, M. Motivational differences between males and females as measured by the TAT. *J. Pers.,* 1953, *22,* 101.

112. Lipsitt, L. P. A self-concept scale for children and its relationship to the children's form of the manifest anxiety scale. *Child Develpm.,* 1958, *29,* 463–472.

113. Lourenso, S. V., Greenberg, J. W., & Davidson, H. H. Personality characteristics revealed in drawings of deprived children who differ in school achievement. *J. educ. Res.,* 1965, *59,* 63–67.

114. Lynn, D. B., & Sawrey, W. L. The effects of father-absence on Norwegian boys and girls. *J. abnorm. soc. Psychol.,* 1959, *59,* 258–262.

115. Maccoby, E. E. The taking of adult roles in middle childhood. *J. abnorm. soc. Psychol.,* 1961, *63,* 493–503.

116. Maccoby, E. E., Gibbs, P. K., & the staff of the Laboratory of Human Development, Harvard University. Methods of child-rearing in two social classes. In W. E. Martin & C. B. Stendler (Eds.), *Readings in child development.* New York: Harcourt, Brace & World, 1954, 380–396.

117. Maccoby, E. E., & Wilson, W. C. Identification and observational learning from film. *J. abnorm. soc. Psychol.,* 1957, *55,* 76.

118. Macfarlane, J. W., Allen, L., & Honzik, M. P. A developmental study of the behavior problems of normal children between twenty-one months and fourteen years. *Univer. of Calif. Publ. in Child Develpm.,* 1954, No. 2.

119. MacRae, D. A test of Piaget's theories of moral development. *J. abnorm. soc. Psychol.,* 1954, *49,* 14–18.

120. McCandless, B. R., Bilous, C. B., & Bennett, H. L. Peer popularity and dependence on adults in preschool age socialization. *Child Develpm.,* 1961, *32,* 511.

121. McCord, W., McCord, J., & Howard, A. Familial correlates of aggression in non-delinquent male children. *J. abnorm. soc. Psychol.,* 1961, *63,* 493–503.

122. Meltzer, H. Economic security and children's attitudes to parents. *Amer. J. Orthopsychiat.,* 1936, *6,* 590–608.

123. Meyers, C. E. The effect of conflicting authority on the child. *Univer. Iowa Stud. Child. Welf.,* 1944, *20,* No. 409, 31–98.

124. Miller, D. R., & Swanson, G. E. *Inner conflict and defense.* New York: Holt, Rinehart and Winston, 1960.

125. Miller, H., & Baruch, D. W. A study of hostility in allergic children. *Amer. J. Orthopsychiat.,* 1950, *25,* 506–519.

126. Miller, W. B. Lower class culture as a generating milieu of gang delinquency. *J. soc. Issues,* 1958, *14,* 5–19.

127. Mischel, W. A social-learning view of sex differences in behavior. In E. E. Maccoby (Ed.), *The development of sex differences.* Stanford, Calif.: Stanford Univer. Press, 1966, 56–81.

128. Murphy, G. *Personality.* New York: Harper & Row, 1947.

129. Mussen, P. H. Differences between the TAT responses of Negro and white boys. *J. consult. Psychol.,* 1953, *17,* 373–376.

130. Mussen, P. H. Some personality and social factors related to changes in children's attitudes toward Negroes. *J. abnorm. soc. Psychol.,* 1950, *45,* 423–441.

131. Muste, M. H., & Sharpe, D. F. Some influential factors in the determination of aggressive behavior in preschool children. *Child Develpm.,* 1947, *18,* 11.

132. Nash, H. Assignment of gender to body regions. *J. genet. Psychol.,* 1958, *92,* 113.

133. Nisbett, R. E. Birth order and participation in dangerous sports. *J. pers. soc. Psychol.,* 1968, *8,* 351–353.

134. Nisbett, R. E., & Schacter, S. Cognitive manipulation of pain, *J. exp. soc. Psychol.,* 1966, *2,* 227–236.

135. Phillips, B. N., Hindsman, E., & Jennings, E. Influence of intelligence on anxiety and perception of self and others. *Child Develpm.,* 1960, *31,* 41–46.

136. Piaget, J. *The moral judgment of the child.* London: Routledge & Kegan Paul, 1932.

137. Piers, E. V., & Harris, D. B. Age and other correlates of self-concept in children. *J. educ. Psychol.,* 1964, *55,* 91–95.

138. Pintler, M. H., Phillips, R., & Sears, R. R. Sex differences in the projective doll play of preschool children. *J. Psychol.*, 1946, *21*, 73.
139. Purcell, K. Distinctions between subgroups of asthmatic children: Children's perceptions of events associated with asthma. *Pediatrics*, 1963, *31*, 486–494.
140. Purcell, K., Bernstein, L., & Bukantz, S. C. A preliminary comparison of rapidly remitting and persistently "steroid dependent" asthmatic children. *Psychosom. Med.*, 1961, *23*, 305–310.
141. Purcell, K., Brady, L., & Chai, H. Effect of experimental separation from the family on asthma in children. Paper read at symposium on research in asthma, Denver, April, 1967.
142. Purcell, K., & Metz, J. R. Distinctions between subgroups of asthmatic children: some parent attitude variables related to age of onset of asthma. *J. psychosom. Res.*, 1962, *6*, 251–258.
143. Purcell, K., Turnbull, J. W., & Bernstein, L. Distinctions between subgroups of asthmatic children: psychological test and behavior rating comparisons. *J. psychosom. Res.*, 1962, *6*, 283–291.
144. Purcell, K., & Weiss, J. H. Emotions and asthma: assessment and treatment. In C. G. Costello (Ed.), *Symptoms of psychopathology*. New York: Wiley, in press.
145. Rabban, M. Sex role identification in young children in two diverse social groups. *Genet. Psychol. Monogr.*, 1950, *42*, 81–158.
146. Radke-Yarrow, M. Interpersonal dynamics in a desegregation process. *J. soc. Issues*, 1958, *14*, 3–63.
147. Radke, M. J., & Trager, H. G. Children's perception of the social roles of Negroes and whites. *J. Psychol.*, 1950, *29*, 3–33.
148. Radke, M. J., Trager, M. G., & Davis, H. Social perceptions and attitudes of children. *Genet. Psychol. Monogr.*, 1949, *40*, 327–447.
149. Radke-Yarrow, M., Trager, H. G., & Miller, J. The role of parents in the development of children's ethnic attitudes. *Child Develpm.*, 1952, *23*, 13–53.
150. Riley, J. E. The self concept and sex-role behavior of third and fourth grade boys. *Dissert. Abstr.*, 1966, *27*, 680.
151. Roberts, C. S. Ordinal position and its relation to some aspects of personality. *J. genet. Psychol.*, 1938, *53*, 173–213.
152. Roe, A. A psychological study of eminent psychologists and anthropologists and a comparison with biological and physical scientists. *Psychol. Monogr.*, 1953, *67*, No. 2.
153. Rogers, C. R., & Dymond, R. F. *Psychotherapy and personality change*. Chicago· Univer. Chicago Press, 1954.
154. Rosenberg, B. G., & Sutton-Smith, B. The measurement of masculinity and femininity in children: an extension and revalidation. *J. genet. Psychol.*, 1964, *104*, 259–264.
155. Rosenberg, B. G., & Sutton-Smith, B. A revised conception of masculine feminine differences in play activities. *J. genet. Psychol.*, 1960, *96*, 165–170.
156. Rosenberg, M. *Society and the adolescent self-image*. Princeton, N.J.: Princeton Univer. Press, 1965.
157. Rosenow, C., & Whyte, A. H. The ordinal position of problem children. *Amer. J. Orthopsychiat.*, 1931, *1*, 430–434.
158. Rosenthal, M. J., Ni, E., Finkelstein, M., & Berkwits, G. K. Father-child relationships and children's problems. *AMA Arch. gen. Psychiat.*, 1962, *7*, 360–373.
159. Rosenthal, M. J., Finkelstein, M., Ni, E., & Robertson, R. E. A study of mother child relationships in the emotional disorders of children. *Genet. Psychol. Monogr.*, 1959, *60*, 65–116.

160. Rothbart, M. K., & Maccoby, E. E. Parents' differential reactions to sons and daughters. *J. pers. soc. Psychol.*, 1966, *3*, 237–243.

161. Ruebush, B. K. Anxiety. In H. W. Stevenson (Ed.), *Child Psychology, Part I*. (62nd *Yearb. nat. Soc. Stud. Educ.*) Chicago: Univer. Chicago Press, 1963.

162. Ruebush, B. K. Children's behavior as a function of anxiety and defensiveness. Unpublished doctoral dissertation, Yale University, 1960.

163. Sanford, R. N., Adkins, M. M., Miller, R. B., & Cobb, E. Physique, personality and scholarship: a cooperative study of school children. *Monogr. Soc. Res. Child Develpm.*, 1943, *8*, No. 1.

164. Schacter, S. *The psychology of affiliation: experimental studies of the sources of gregariousness*. Stanford, Calif.: Stanford Univer. Press, 1959.

165. Schaefer, E. S. Converging conceptual models for maternal behavior and for child behavior. In J. C. Glidewell (Ed.), *Parental attitudes and child behavior*. Springfield, Ill.: Thomas, 1961.

166. Schaefer, E. S. A circumplex model for maternal behavior. *J. abnorm. soc. Psychol.*, 1959, *59*, 226–235.

167. Sears, P. S. Doll play aggressions in normal young children: influence of sex, age, sibling status, father's absence. *Psychol. Monogr.*, 1951, *65*, No. 6.

168. Sears, R. R. The relation of early socialization experiences to aggression in middle childhood. *J. abnorm. soc. Psychol.*, 1961, *63*, 466–492.

169. Sears, R. R., Maccoby, E. E., & Levin, H. *Patterns of child rearing*. New York: Harper & Row, 1957.

170. Sears, R. R., Whiting, J., Nowlis, V., & Sears, P. S. Some child rearing antecedents of aggression and dependency in young children. *Genet. Psychol. Monogr.*, 1953, *47*, 135.

171. Siegel, A. E., Stolz, L. M., Hitchcock, A. E., & Adamson, J. Dependence and independence in the children of working mothers. *Child Develpm.*, 1959, *30*, 553.

172. Smith, M. E. The influence of age, sex and situation of the frequency and form and function of questions asked by preschool children. *Child Develpm.*, 1933, *3*, 201.

173. Spock, B. *Baby and child care*. New York: Pocket Books, 1946.

174. Stevenson, H. W., & Stewart, E. C. A developmental study of racial awareness in young children. *Child Develpm.*, 1958, *29*, 399–410.

175. Stolz, L. M. *Father relations of warborn children*. Stanford, Calif.: Stanford Univer. Press, 1954.

176. Strauss, A. L. The development of conception of rules in children. *Child Develpm.*, 1954, *25*, 193–208.

177. Swift, J. W. Effects of early group experience: the nursery and day nursery. In M. L. Hoffman & L. W. Hoffman (Eds.), *Review of child development*, Vol. I. New York: Russell Sage Foundation, 1964.

178. Tabachnick, R. Some correlates of prejudice toward Negroes in elementary age children. *J. genet. Psychol.*, 1962, *100*, 193–203.

179. Terman, L. M., et al. *Psychological factors in marital happiness*. New York. McGraw-Hill, 1938.

180. Terman, L. M., & Miles, C. C. *Sex and personality studies in masculinity and femininity*. New York: McGraw-Hill, 1936.

181. Thurstone, L. L., & Jenkins, R. L. *Order of birth, parent age, and intelligence*. Chicago: Univer. Chicago Press, 1931.

182. Tiller, P. O. Father absence and personality development of children in sailor families: a preliminary research report. Part II. In N. Anderson (Ed.), *Studies of the family*, Vol. 2. Gottigen: Vandenhoeck and Ruprecht, 1957, 115–137.

183. Trent, R. D. The relation between expressed self-acceptance and expressed attitudes toward Negroes and white among Negro children. *J. genet. Psychol.*, 1957, *91,* 25–31.
184. Unger, S. M. Antecedents of personality differences in guilt responsibility. *Psychol. Rep.*, 1962, *10,* 357–358.
185. Unger, S. M. On the development of guilt response systems. Unpublished doctoral dissertation, Cornell University, 1960.
186. Walsh, A. M. *Self-concepts of bright boys with learning difficulties.* New York: Columbia Univer. Press (Bureau of Publications, Teachers College), 1956.
187. Warner, W. L., & Lunt, P. S. *Social life in a modern community.* New Haven, Conn.: Yale Univer. Press, 1941.
188. Watson, G. A comparison of the effects of lax versus strict home training. *J. soc. Psychol.*, 1934, *5,* 102–105.
189. Wattenberg, W. W., & Clifford, C. Relation of self-concepts to beginning achievement in reading. *Child Develpm.*, 1964, *35,* 461–467.
190. Whitehouse, E. Norms for certain aspects of the Thematic Apperception Test on a group of nine- and ten-year-old children. *Personality,* 1949, *1,* 12.
191. Whiting, J. W. M., & Child, I. L. *Child training and personality.* New Haven, Conn.: Yale Univer. Press, 1953.
192. Wickman, E. K. Children's behavior and teachers' attitudes. Commonwealth Fund, 1928.
193. Winker, J. B. Age trends and sex differences in the wishes, identification, activities and fears of children. *Child Develpm.*, 1949, *20,* 191–200.
194. Wirt, R. D., & Briggs, P. F. Personality and environmental factors in the development of delinquency. *Psychol. Monogr.*, 1959, *73,* No. 15, 1–47.
195. Wylie, R. *The self-concept.* Lincoln: Univer. of Nebraska Press, 1961.

13

Development in Middle Childhood

III. Expansion of Social Environment

During the middle-childhood years, from school entrance to the beginning of adolescence, the child's social environment expands tremendously. At the same time, as we saw in Chapter 11, the child continues to develop physically, and his cognitive abilities increase and become more complex and better differentiated. As a consequence of the continuing interaction between the developing child and his expanding environment, some motives become strengthened and more clearly articulated while others diminish in importance; new standards are set, and the child is confronted with new problems and challenges. If he is prepared to confront and eventually master these problems, his self-image becomes clearer and his self-esteem strengthened. In contrast, if the demands are too great, too sudden, too poorly defined, or inconsistent and contradictory—or if the child is too poorly prepared, psychologically, socially, or intellectually—to meet even reasonable demands, crippling conflicts and anxieties may develop and lead to a variety of psychological and psychosomatic symptoms, as we saw in Chapter 12.

Among the major developmental tasks confronting the child during the middle-childhood years are: the development of various intellectual and academic skills, and the motivation to master them; learning how to interact with peers; the crystallization of sex-role identification; increased autonomy and independence; development of moral standards and conscience; and learning to deal appropriately with anxiety and conflict. These psychological developments are precursors of the problems that adolescents and adults have to face. Thus the ways in which the child handles the tasks of middle childhood will significantly affect his later behavior. The changing adjustments required of him during this period reflect in great measure his movement away from the home as the one central focus of his activities, interpersonal relationships, struggles, and satisfactions, and into the wider world of school, the neighborhood, and, in a more limited sense, society itself. In turn, however, his readiness to take on the new demands of this expanded environment will depend largely on both his prior and his continuing experiences in the family setting.

The School Situation

Once a child has entered kindergarten or first grade, school becomes for more than a decade the center of his extrafamilial world, occupying almost half of his waking hours.

It would be difficult to overestimate the importance of the school's role in the child's life. Not only does it strengthen some of the social and cognitive responses that the child's parents may be teaching him; it also teaches him many new responses. The number, variety, and complexity of learned responses required of adults in our culture are so great that even the most remarkable parents could hardly accomplish the task of instilling, without assistance, all such responses in their children. As one of the principal socializing agents of our society, the school should be in a uniquely favorable position to supplement—and sometimes to compensate for—parental training. By teaching the child academic skills, by broadening his store of cultural information, by stimulating his needs for achievement and mastery, and by giving him supervised practice in social relationships both with adults and a wider range of peers, the school should make him better able to deal comfortably with the ever-widening range of challenges and opportunities, as well as problems that lie ahead of him on the road toward psychological maturity. While in many instances the school succeeds remarkably well in carrying out these functions, there are, as we shall see, some circumstances in which its success to date has been far from optimal (e.g., in meeting the special needs and problems of culturally disadvantaged children).

In examining the influence of the school setting upon the child's continuing development, we shall be concerned with the ways in which school adjustment is influenced both by differences among children and by differences in school experiences. As we shall see later, such considerations assume critical importance in any meaningful discussion of the problems of special groups of children, such as the culturally disadvantaged.

ADJUSTMENT TO SCHOOL

For many children, school entrance marks the first separation from the mother for a large part of the day, almost every day. The school, therefore, plays an important part in helping the child to reduce his dependent ties to his home. It also presents him with a new adult whom he must obey and whose acceptance he may court. This new adult will require the child to learn certain responses which are not initially rewarding. Hopefully, the school will contribute to the development of a desire to master intellectual skills, to acquire a pride in one's work, to persevere in solving problems, and to formulate long-range goals. Finally, the school provides the child with increased opportunities to establish more extensive and more meaningful relationships with age-mates.

Many new behaviors are learned during the elementary school years. Previously established but inefficient responses (e.g., crying in stress situations) must be extinguished, while existing motives (e.g., mastery) must be stimulated and strengthened. The elements involved in this new learning situation and their effects will be analyzed in subsequent sections. In addition, an effort will be made to show how the child's earlier experiences influence his reactions to the school setting.

The Role of the Teacher

Among the situational factors affecting the child's adjustment and progress within the school setting, probably none is as important as the teacher-pupil relationship. This is particularly evident at school entrance. At this stage, the teacher is likely to be the first adult outside the immediate family who plays a major role in the child's life. However, the teacher also continues to have a significant influence on the child's development throughout the school years. The kinds of teachers a child has will determine in great measure whether his school experience will foster his overall development, or will simply increase his difficulties and frustrations. Having the right teacher may help a child to overcome handicaps and make the most of his talents and interests, while having a teacher who is ill-suited to working with children generally, or with a particular child or group of children, may have serious and sometimes disastrous consequences. This may be especially true of teachers working with culturally disadvantaged, minority-group children, as will become evident later.

The Child's First Teacher as a Substitute Mother. In almost every instance, the child's first teacher is a woman. She helps the child to dress and undress when necessary; she praises good behavior and punishes bad; she is a source of nurturance; and she encourages honesty, perseverance, and maturity. The teacher's appearance, attitudes, and actions are usually similar to those of the child's mother, especially if teacher and mother are from the same social class. Hence it is not unreasonable to assume that many children react to the teacher as though she were a substitute mother.

It will be recalled (see Chapter 4) that, according to the principles of generalization and mediated generalization, the individual will transfer attitudes and reactions learned in response to one stimulus to others that are viewed as similar to the original. Similarities between teacher and mother in sex, age, and salient behaviors are usually sufficiently numerous to support a high degree of generalization from one to the other. Consequently, the motives, attitudes, fears, and overt behaviors that the child has developed in relation to his mother are likely to generalize to the teacher. If the child desires the nurturance of the mother and views her as accepting, he is likely to approach the teacher with the same positive attitude. If, on the other hand, the child has hostile feelings toward a rejecting mother and has generally behaved aggressively toward her, he may transfer these responses to the teacher. In a recent study (59) of school beginners, it was found that children tended to have similar perceptions of their mothers and teachers. If one was perceived as a disciplinarian or helper, the other tended to be also. Interestingly, this correlation persisted throughout the year, even among those children whose perceptions of mother and teacher were unstable; thus, while a child's perceptions regarding adult helpfulness or disciplinary qualities might change, the changes tended to occur together for both mother and teacher (59).

Is having the child's first teacher a woman a wise choice? As mothers are generally viewed by young children as more nurturant and less fear-arousing than fathers, there are probably advantages in having a woman as the child's first contact with an adult in the school environment. The kindergarten atmosphere and school performance might be quite different if all kindergarten and first grade teachers were men. Under such conditions, some children might experience more tension and anxiety. Furthermore, most male teachers do not view themselves as possessing the necessary personality characteristics for being the primary teacher of very young children; and studies of the differences in desirable behavior between teachers of younger and older children indicate that more "feminine" behavior is associated with the former—for example, "warmth" and expressive interaction versus emphasis on rational thought, substantive content, and instrumental interaction (25).

Nevertheless, there might be some positive results, especially for boys, in having greater exposure to males in the early school years. The typical 6-year-old boy is establishing an identification with his father and other male role models, and, in some cases, his attempts to increase similarity between himself and adult males may involve some rebellion against the mother. Most boys regard the father as the dominant figure in the household, and boys are encouraged to de-emphasize the power and competence of adult females in attempting to establish an independent masculine identity. The more frequent mischievous behavior of first and second grade boys suggests that they are less anxious than girls about rejection by the female teacher; girls are typically more obedient and conscientious with women teachers. The fact that problems in reading, spelling, and conduct are more frequent among boys than girls in the elementary school years may be indirect evidence that boys enter school with somewhat greater resistance than girls do. There is also evidence that some female teachers tend to provide fewer learning opportunities and more negative admonitions to boys (113). It is at least theoretically possible that if some of the boys' first teachers were male, there might be less resistance and a greater desire to gain the teacher's acceptance. Finally, boys might be more likely to associate the act of acquiring knowledge with masculinity if more of their elementary grade teachers were men rather than being almost exclusively women.

Certainly, the traditional degree of masculinity or femininity associated with any activity "is a function primarily of the sex of the person who normally performs the behavior" (94). Cooking, sewing, and caring for children are considered feminine largely because women typically do them. Repairing fences, mowing the lawn, and fishing are viewed as masculine because men usually perform them. As elementary school classes are conducted by women, young children may have a tendency to view school work as more closely related to femininity than to masculinity and, therefore, as more appropriate for girls than for boys (cf. pp. 505–506). This attitude may increase the girl's motivation to master reading and spelling, and may help to account for her relatively greater achievement in the early school years, but it may inhibit involvement for some boys, particularly those for whom stereotyped sex roles are especially important.

What are the major responses to be learned during the first five years of school? There are, of course, the intellectual skills of reading, arithmetic, spelling; the kindergarten and first grade activities of coloring, painting, and pasting; and the social skills, habits, and attitudes which play an important role in our culture.

In the United States and Western Europe the teacher's values are usually middle-class in content. She rewards neatness, obedience, cooperation, and cleanliness; she punishes waste, lack of responsibility, lying, aggressiveness. Many teachers feel that stealing, cheating, lying, and disobedience are the most serious crimes a young child can commit (11). It is easy to see that prior patterns of familial rewards and punishments may facilitate the girl's initial adjustment to the teacher's values. For example, as we have already seen, neatness and inhibition of aggressive behavior are characteristic sextyped responses generally required of girls during the preschool years. Sloppiness and mischievous behavior are more often expected of boys, and boys are less likely to be punished for indulging in them. It might be anticipated, therefore, that boys will be more frequently subjected to disapproval by the teacher, and friction is more likely to develop between boys and their teachers than between girls and their teachers. As we shall see, data on social-class differences indicate that lower-class boys, whose backgrounds reflect different attitudes from those of most teachers, are least likely to adopt the values that are encouraged by the traditional middle-class-oriented school (neatness, obedience to a woman, perseverance, desire to master school subjects). Hence it is not surprising that lower-class boys show poorer performance in school subjects than middle-class boys and middle- and lower-class girls.

Despite the formidable adjustments that the child must make upon entering school, the—perhaps surprising—fact is that most children still react to the beginning of school with favorable anticipation, and these positive feelings are maintained by most children at least through the earliest school years (93, 149, 150). Parents, older siblings, and neighborhood chums provide a great deal of information about school ahead of time, and this pervasive "cultural dramatization" of the event stimulates interest and eagerness to begin. In one study (149, 150), 212 mothers of first grade children were interviewed three times. The first interview, conducted before the child entered school, dealt with attitudes toward beginning school. Almost all the mothers (197 out of 212) reported that their children looked forward eagerly to school. After the children had attended school for two months, mothers were again interviewed to determine the behavioral and attitudinal changes occurring in the intervening period. An overwhelming majority (86 percent) noted definite changes in the child's self-concept and behavior after two months of school attendance. These included enhanced feelings of self-importance and bigness, manifestations of increased independence (such as dressing one's self and beginning work without special instructions), and a general improvement in behavior. For example, the children were reported to be more responsible, helpful, cooperative, and reasonable; better-humored and more self-controlled; and less irritable and explosive.

The third interview was held eight months after the beginning of school. Mothers were asked to compare their children's behavior with what it had been before they went to school. An analysis of the data showed that most mothers felt that their children had improved significantly in traits such as maturity, self-control, helpfulness, responsibility, self-confidence, and ability to get along with playmates—but not in obedience and patience. Almost 60 percent of the mothers said it was easier to deal with the child than it had been during the preceding year.

But while reactions to school were generally positive, the picture was not entirely blissful. For example, although 92 percent of the children in this study were reported to like school, 42 percent criticized both the school and teacher, and 39 percent occasionally did not want to go to school within the first two months. Obviously, all children did not react to school in the same way.

Furthermore, the reactions of children to school and to their teachers do not remain static. Unfortunately, in most instances, and particularly in the case of disadvantaged children, the child's enthusiasm for his teachers and for the school tends to decline in the later years of middle childhood. Children in the early grades tend to have rather stereotyped and generally positive feelings about teachers, but those in grades 4, 6, 8, 10, and 12 have less favorable attitudes and attribute less relative prestige to the occupation of teacher in comparison with others, such as nurse and airline stewardess (1). It is obvious that factors other than simply the quality of teachers and curriculum are at work here, including the influence of parents and the general social environment, and the propensity of children at any particular moment to want to do what they want to do—which frequently may not include learning axioms in plane geometry or declensions of nouns. Nevertheless, the quality of teachers and teaching is vital, and in view of the ever-increasing importance of the school in the socialization of today's children, it appears unfortunate that the interest and excitement with which most children begin school cannot be better maintained. The necessity for continuing to make education interesting, challenging, and relevant to children throughout the school years can hardly be overstressed.

According to the results of one survey, children in our culture tend to prefer teachers who possess the following characteristics: (1) *human qualities*—kind, cheerful, natural, even-tempered; (2) *disciplinary qualities*—fair, consistent, impartial, respected; (3) *pleasing physical appearance*—well-groomed, nice voice, and generally attractive; (4) *good teaching qualities*—helpful, democratic (gives children voice in class affairs), interesting, and enthusiastic (*91*). The same sorts of characteristics seem to be preferred by older as well as younger children (*74, 101*). Similar qualities also are stressed by school administrators and teachers themselves as desirable teacher characteristics. Thus one survey (*62*) summarizes the following as desirable teacher behaviors: *warmth; cognitive organization* ("a clear and valid cognitive organization of the subject matter or discipline"); *orderliness; indirectness* ("good teachers tend more often than others to influence pupils indirectly, through asking questions and otherwise evoking participation in classroom activity"); *ability to solve instructional problems* ("ability to solve problems requiring technical knowledge of teaching methods").

Teacher Behavior and Student Progress. A number of studies have investigated the relationship between teacher characteristics and children's academic and social progress in the school situation. In one such study (*80*) involving fourth, fifth, and sixth graders, three broad teacher-types were isolated on the basis of psychological testing.

Turbulent teachers appeared to be turbulent in both feeling and thought, with aggressive and sexual impulses close to consciousness. While these impulses tended to be expressed primarily in fantasy and verbal aggression, they sometimes resulted in overt action. This type of teacher did not appear to feel a strong need for acceptance by others; did not identify closely with others; and did not appear to be ambitious for leadership. She had little interest in orderliness or self-discipline, and her likes and dislikes tended to be sharper than those of other types. "Her main interest is in thinking, imagining, and conjecturing. She is not, therefore, especially warm or empathic. To others, she is likely to seem blunt, impulsive, and unpredictable. She may often seem tense. She wants to be independent of authority and to be free to do uninhibited and unconventional thinking" (*80*, 402–403).

The *self-controlled* teacher, in contrast, emerged as methodical, self-disciplined, not particularly interested in the opposite sex, and not interested in displaying wit at the expense of others. Such a teacher "feels most secure when things run smoothly. She likes to keep her thoughts and feelings to herself. She does not like to listen to 'hot' arguments, to be around people who forget themselves and talk freely, nor does she like 'to stick by the truth no matter whom it hurts' " (*80*, 403).

The self-controlled teacher, while ambitious and desiring leadership, does not like to be in the limelight. In her zeal to have things run smoothly, she sometimes tends to be apprehensive and even rigid about making on-the-spot changes in her plans. She tends to be sensitive to the reactions of others, and can be relied upon to accept responsibility and execute effectively ideas which have been formulated by others. While somewhat submissive to authority herself, she may also tend to be authoritarian toward subordinates.

The *fearful* teacher stands in rather marked contrast to both of the other types. She appeared fearful of contamination by her environment, afraid of being alone, and afraid of her sexual impulses. "She tends to feel helpless, dependent, and defensive. She is very conscientious, likes to 'stick by the truth no matter whom it hurts,' to have rules by which to abide, and is irritated by those who do not abide by the rules. She is afraid of doing the wrong thing" (*80*, 403).

The relation of type of teacher personality to academic growth (as measured by the Stanford Achievement Test) and to social development was then investigated.

It was found that children, *in general,* made the greatest academic progress under the self-controlled teacher and least under the fearful teacher; children under self-controlled teachers averaged about half again as much academic progress as those under fearful teachers. Similarly, growth in "friendliness" during the school year was significantly greater under self-controlled teachers than under either turbulent or fearful teachers (*80*). Other studies (*19, 62, 100*) suggest that students generally prefer and progress more under teachers who are: "warm"; possessed of a high degree of "ego strength"; enthusiastic; able to display initiative; creative; reactive to suggestions; poised and adaptable; planful; interested in parental and community relations; and aware of individual differences in children and oriented toward individual guidance.

In contrast, teachers who are hostile or dominating generally appear to affect pupil adjustment adversely. In a series of related studies (*3–8*), Anderson and Anderson and their coworkers undertook to study "The nature and degree of relationship between . . . children's behavior . . . and . . . teacher's dominative and socially integrated contacts." These investigators were interested in testing two hypotheses which they felt could be applied to teacher-child relations. The first of these, referred to as "The Hypothesis of the Growth Circle," was that "Integrative [i.e., give-and-take, democratic] behavior in one person tends to increase integrative behavior in others" (*5*). The second hypothesis, referred to as "Hypothesis of the Vicious Circle," was that "Dominative [i.e., authoritarian] behavior in one person tends to incite domination in others" (*5*).

In their observations of teacher-pupil interactions, these investigators considered dominative behavior on the part of teachers to be evidenced by such behaviors as use of force, commands, threats, shame, blame, and rigid insistence upon conformity. Integrative behaviors, on the other hand, included approval, extending invitations to activity, questioning the child about his interests, sympathy, and mutual participation of children and teachers in activities (5).

In one of these studies, the reactions of the pupils of two second grade teachers from the same elementary school were observed (8). One of the teachers was found to be consistently more integrative or democratic, and less dominative; the other was consistently more dominative or authoritarian. The children in each of the teacher's groups had been assigned randomly in the first grade, and had been promoted as a room. Thus there was no reason to assume that the two classroom groups differed significantly in any important respects.

It was found that the children with the more integrative teacher tended to behave more integratively than did the children of the more dominative teacher. They displayed a significantly greater number of behaviors reflecting spontaneity, initiative, and constructive social attitudes relating to others. The findings "were consistent with the hypothesis that *integration in the teacher induces integrative behavior of the child*" (7).

On the other hand, the children with the more dominating teacher showed significantly higher frequencies of nonconforming behavior. This supported directly the hypothesis that domination incites resistance. In addition, the children with the more dominating teacher paid less attention to their work, engaging more in such activities as looking around and whispering to their companions (7). "If it is a pedagogical objective for a teacher to reduce the conflict and increase the harmony in her school room, then the study showed that [the dominating teacher] was defeating her own purpose" (7).

These same teachers and children were studied a year later (6). The children by this time were, of course, in the third grade. It was found that the teachers tended to behave in a similar manner year after year, regardless of the kinds of pupils they encountered. The children, on the other hand, did not. They showed far greater flexibility, reacting dominatively if they had a dominative teacher, but shifting readily to integrative behavior if their next teacher happened to be an integrative individual.

These studies suggest that the behavior of school children is highly dependent on the behavior of their teachers, and that teachers who use democratic (integrative) techniques with their children will generally be rewarded by greater cooperation, spontaneity, interest, and initiative on the part of their pupils. On the other hand, teachers who attempt to force compliance through aggressive dictatorial techniques will only be encouraging greater resistance on their pupils' part—whether manifested by whispering, doodling, lack of attention, or through more direct opposition. In general the integrative teacher more often helps to satisfy the child's needs and less often frustrates him.

The dominative teacher, on the other hand, through her lack of concern for the child's needs and her narrower conception of socially acceptable behavior, more frequently frustrates the child in his attempts to satisfy his needs. Because, as we have already seen, frustration may produce aggression, the dominative teacher is likely to become a target for hostility rather than a source of reward. Thus she is likely to encounter more difficulty in her attempts to instill socialized responses than the integrative teacher. She may be able to inhibit overtly aggressive responses on the part of her pupils through the use of fear and punishment, but she is not able to instill a positive desire for cooperation.

Somewhat similar conclusions were reached in other investigations (107, 138). A study of "group atmosphere" by Lewin, Lippitt, and White (107), although it dealt with the relation of boys' club members to adult leaders rather than with those of pupils to a teacher, appears to have similar implications. In this study, four recreational clubs, each consisting of 5- to 11-year-old boys were subjected to three different types of adult leadership in group atmosphere: *democratic, authoritarian,* and *laissez-faire.* It was found that boys were freer, more friendly, less rebellious and irritable, more creative, more constructive, and more productive under *democratic* leadership (when the adult leader gave assistance, encouragement, and advice, while allowing the boys to participate actively in the determination of group policy and goals and their implementation) than under either rigid, unilateral *authoritarian* leadership or indifferent, passive *laissez-faire* conditions.

In summary, most children appear to do best under well-trained democratic teachers who know their subject matter, are interested in their pupils, and are not overly concerned with their own problems. Such teachers encourage the student to participate actively in the learning process, while maintaining leadership, direction, and, when necessary, reasonable discipline. In contrast, optimal academic and personal growth will not be stimulated in most students by the teacher who is either rigidly authoritarian, hostile, or unresponsive to student needs, or the teacher who is indecisive and uncertain, poorly trained, too overly narcissistic, or too preoccupied with her own anxieties and personal problems.

Variations in Teacher Effectiveness. As might be anticipated, the same teacher may not be equally effective with all kinds of students. Nor, indeed, is she even necessarily perceived in the same way by all children. For example, *overachieving* students tend to perceive their teachers as "warm, affable, and deferring [to the student's needs]" (172), while *underachieving* students perceived the same teachers as "cold, unfriendly, and unconcerned" (172).

Similarly, in a study (34) of discrepancies between pupils' perceptions of their own teachers and their "ideal" teacher, it was found that: (1) high-achieving students showed smaller discrepancies than low-achieving students; (2) boys showed larger discrepancies than girls, and (3) children socially accepted by their peers showed smaller discrepancies than those who were rejected.

Recall the study of teacher-types—turbulent, self-controlled, fearful Their pupils were similarly differentiated into four general types: *conformers, opposers, waiverers,* and *strivers.* The three types of teachers did not have identical effects on the four general types of students. For example, while self-controlled teachers were *generally* most effective, *conforming* children (possibly already overly self-controlled, orderly, etc.) made slightly more progress under turbulent teachers. In contrast, *opposers* made significantly greater progress under self-controlled teachers and showed wider differences than other groups between the effectiveness of self-controlled and fearful teachers. Presumably, these children, unlike the conformers, had a need for control and order which they could not obtain from the fearful, insecure teacher *(80).*

There were differences, too, in the areas in which each of the three types of teachers performed best, at least relatively. Thus self-controlled teachers were at their best in reading and spelling; turbulent teachers were most effective in arithmetic and science; fearful teachers did best in the presumably less structured area of social studies.

Another recent study investigated the hypothesis that children would be more likely to imitate *rewarding* teachers than *critical* ones *(129).* Children aged 8 to 10 watched movies of a rewarding (positive) or critical (negative) teacher teaching a lesson. Subsequently, the children were observed teaching a lesson to a doll. While there was generally much more imitation of the rewarding teacher than of the critical teacher, the effects were not the same for all children. There was much more imitation by girls than by boys, and more imitation by middle-class than by lower-class children. Middle-class girls imitated positive teachers most.

Teachers may influence their pupils in other ways. First grade children taught by *impulsive* teachers tend to become more impulsive and hasty themselves in responding to school tasks; those taught by *reflective* teachers tend to become more careful, orderly, and slower in their own responses *(175).* The effect is more marked for boys than for girls.

It would appear that thought should sometimes be given to tailoring tempo of teacher to tempo of child. Boys have greater difficulty than girls in mastering reading, and previous research has indicated that part of the problem can be attributed to boys' more impulsive attitudes *(95).* Placement of extremely impulsive boys with teachers who are temperamentally reflective might promote the adoption of a more reflective disposition on the part of the boy and facilitate his reading progress.

As will be seen later, the effectiveness of the teacher—not merely for students in general, but for particular types of students—becomes especially important when one considers the culturally disadvantaged student, whose needs and social perceptions may vary markedly from those of the average middle-class teacher.

Variations in Teaching Methods

The effectiveness of different teaching methods, as well as differences among teachers, will vary from one child to another. A variety of studies

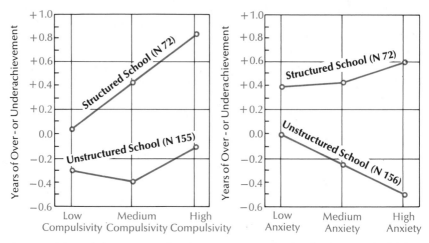

Fig. 13.1 (above left) Test results showing mean school achievement of children categorized as to compulsivity. (From J. W. Grimes & W. Allinsmith. Compulsivity, anxiety, and school achievement. *Merrill-Palmer Quart.*, 1961, 7, 259. By permission.)

Fig. 13.2. (above right) Test results showing mean school achievement of children categorized as to anxiety. (From J. W. Grimes & W. Allinsmith. Compulsivity, anxiety, and school achievement. *Merrill-Palmer Quart.*, 1961, 7, 261. By permission.)

(55, 60, 82, 96, 131, 135, 148) indicate that high levels of *anxiety* tend to impair academic achievement. In general, moderate levels of *compulsivity* in children would appear to foster academic achievement, at least in some kinds of school settings, as this type of child tends to place a high value on carefulness, orderliness, conformity, meeting adult expectations, and attention to detail (72). But the effects of anxiety and compulsivity upon the child's performance may depend in great measure on the type of learning experience to which the child is exposed, as a recent study demonstrates (72). It was hypothesized that highly anxious or highly compulsive children who were initially taught reading by traditional "structured" methods stressing phonics would show more achievement by the third grade than similar children taught in other schools in which the "unstructured" word-recognition ("whole-word" or "look-and-say") approach to beginning reading was used. (Moreover, "in the structured schools, the classroom atmosphere was found to be more authoritarian and cold, and the curriculum more traditional. In the unstructured schools, child expression and meaningful experience were emphasized throughout the curriculum, and the teachers were more democratic and permissive" [72, 254].) It was also hypothesized that the relative levels of performance of high- and low-anxiety and of high- and low-compulsivity students would vary in the two settings.

The criterion score used in testing these hypotheses was an index of over- or underachievement, based on the discrepancy between the child's achievement test score and the score that would be predicted by his IQ. As Figs. 13.1 and 13.2 indicate, the hypotheses were supported. Highly compulsive children in the structured school setting did far better than equally compulsive children in the unstructured setting. Furthermore, while high-compulsive children did significantly better than low-compulsive children in the structured setting, no significant difference between the two groups was found in the unstructured setting (Fig. 13.1). High-anxious children also performed better in the structured setting (see Fig. 13.2). Here, however, the most striking finding was that while high-anxiety children achieved significantly less well in the unstructured school setting than low-anxiety children did, they appeared to do at least as well as the average in the structured classroom.

In qualifying their findings, the authors note (72, 141) two factors that may be effective in relieving anxiety: (1) the availability of a pattern of behavior (the authors assumed that a structured program should excel in offering a guide to behavior), and (2) the availability of a pattern of relationship, i.e., dependence upon some other person. In the present study, apparently the structuring of what was expected of him had a positive effect for the anxious child, despite the greater impersonality of the teacher in this setting. The authors postulate that "if the highly anxious children in the structured schools had experienced a greater degree of warmth and security in interpersonal relationships, they might have made even greater gains" (72, 262).

The authors of this study also cautioned that:

> The continuance of structuring too far in later schooling may perpetuate dependence upon those in authority positions. Because of this danger, McKeachie [72, 112] wrote of structured techniques, ". . . we still may not grant that it is the most desirable method to be used in our educational system which has as its aim preparation for life in a democracy." We suggest that if particular children's desperate need for structure in certain types of learning can be satisfied during the early school years with failure prevented and their literacy assured, ways to reduce the need for continuance of such structure may be gradually introduced later (72, 267).

At any rate, while the overall merits of structured versus unstructured approaches at varying ages require additional investigation, this study does appear to demonstrate clearly and ingeniously that different teaching methods may have very different effects upon different kinds of children.

Influences of Children's Textbooks

While the teacher's own attitudes and behavior undoubtedly exert a more profound effect on the child's development than do the texts she uses, the latter also play an important role. It is, of course, obvious that textbooks contribute to a child's development of academic skills. What has probably been less evident, at least until very recently, is that they may also influence his development of social and emotional attitudes (39, 40, 63).

Within the past five years, however, there has been increasing emphasis on investigating the content as well as the formal characteristics of children's readers. This interest has been stimulated by a variety of factors, including a greater interest in the special educational and social needs of lower-class, culturally disadvantaged, urban children (166); and by a growing awareness of and concern with the far higher incidence of reading difficulties among boys than among girls (117).

It appears reasonable to hypothesize that the desire to learn to read and to continue reading will be influenced by the interest aroused by elementary readers, and that the degree of such interest will be a function of the age- and sex-appropriateness of the content of the reader, its meaningfulness in relation to the child's everyday life experiences, and its appeal to his personal need systems, including fantasy needs. It also appears reasonable to assume that the course of the child's socialization—his developing view of the world, the strengthening of some motives and the weakening of others, the encouragement or discouragement of sex-role identifications— will also be influenced by the content of the books to which he is exposed in the early school years.

Before examining specific hypotheses about the effects of textbooks, however, it may be useful to discuss briefly the general tone of typical elementary school readers. Comprehensive historical reviews of children's readers (48, 178, 179) present a generally discouraging picture to anyone concerned with the educational requirements of our pluralistic, conflict-laden society. Despite the growing need for all children—both in the dominant middle class and the disadvantaged—to gain a better understanding of and sympathy for cultural diversity and for the real-life problems of themselves and others, the average children's reader still presents a world that is largely unrelated to the real needs and experiences of children (not only children with special problems, but all flesh-and-blood children). Unfortunately, despite some encouraging recent trends, a majority of children's early readers are still primarily of the "Dick and Jane" variety:

> Dick and Jane's world is a friendly one, populated by good, smiling people who are ready and eager to help children whenever necessary. Strangers, therefore, are not to be mistrusted but are viewed as potential helpmates. Human nature and physical nature are also cooperative and friendly rather than competitive and conspiring. There are no evil impulses to be controlled. Instead, free rein and encouragement is given for seeking more and more fun and play. Life in general is easy and comfortable; frustrations are rare and usually overcome quite easily. Combining work with play, seeking out new friends, and giving generously are all amply rewarded by nature, adults and one's peers (178).

In a similar vein, DeCharms and Moeller (48) have found a steady decline in achievement-oriented themes in children's readers since 1900. The facts that real-life children, even favored middle-class children, struggle with anxieties and conflicts; that obstacles are not always easy to overcome; that parents and children are not always sweet and reasonable (nor should they be expected to be); and that all life, as Frank Jennings (90) notes, does not consist of a "sun-drenched Sunday afternoon," do not seem to have occurred to authors of such texts. Furthermore, many of these books display a marked ethnocentrism and sociocentrism which are increasingly inappropriate in today's pluralistic society:

> One might conclude from these books that Americans are almost exclusively Caucasian, North European in origin and appearance, and are quite well-to-do. Poverty does exist but only in stories set in a foreign environment or in fairy tales. Foreign nationalities as well as American minority groups are placed in either an unfavorable light or are treated inadequately.

> Religion is rarely mentioned, but Christian religious observance is over-emphasized with no hint of the range or variety of observances found among different religious groups (48, 99).

In addition, "despite the fact that 60 percent of Americans now live in cities, city life is largely ignored in these readers" (90). And it is not only the urban, or lower-class, or racially different child who is ignored in the sunny, Caucasian, suburban world of children's readers: "Kids from large families, or one-parent homes, children who wear glasses, youngsters who are short, tall, slim, or stocky—they all belong in any but a falsely glamorized fantasy world" (116). Finally, as Zimet (178) observed, "And if all this isn't bad enough, it is also felt that unnecessary barriers to the intellectual development of children are perpetuated by the adherence to out-dated vocabulary lists and readability formulas, as well as to the proliferation of anthropomorphism and animism in the content of the readers" (178; see also 99).

To understate the case, it hardly appears that readers such as those described above are likely to broaden the contemporary child's understanding of the pluralistic, complex world in which he will have to live, nor do they seem likely to help him to understand and to struggle more effectively with his own needs, anxieties, and conflicts.

While a number of publishers have attempted recently to overcome some of the obvious liabilities of traditional readers for urban, racially mixed schools by producing texts which "would focus on the life of a working-class family, living in a typical, racially mixed, urban neighborhood (110, 305), their success to date has not been striking. Studies of such readers (21, 165) indicate that with a few notable exceptions, we see the "same Pollyannaish stories about essentially the same smiling unreal children in the same sunshiny, idealized middle-class situations" (165, 8). It appears that only the color and shape of the faces have been changed to provide the illusion of multi-ethnic relevance. In the case of black-oriented, supposedly "urban" readers, "what is depicted is a Negro family living in a happy, stable, white suburban neighborhood" (21, 179).

More specific hypotheses regarding the content of children's readers and its possible effect on academic progress and socialization have also been investigated recently. It has been noted that boys are three times as likely as girls to encounter difficulty in learning to read (117). One of a series of investigations of children's readers *(166)* investigated the possibility that one contributing factor to the greater difficulty encountered by boys might involve the content of children's readers. Specifically, they hypothesized that typical readers depict activities that are most frequently engaged in by girls, rather than boys, in American culture, and that such masculine activities as are depicted more frequently end in failure in these stories than is the case with feminine activities. Somewhat to the authors' surprise, it was found that, while both hypotheses tended to be confirmed in readers produced before 1961, no significant differences were obtained in subsequent readers. It was also found that the story level in readers produced after 1961 tended to be age-appropriate, while earlier readers tended to be written at too young an age level to interest today's sophisticated 6-year-olds *(166)*. Hopefully, these findings indicate some progress in increasing the relevance of elementary readers to the needs and interests of children.

In several investigations of the possible influence of children's readings on the socialization of the child *(20, 36)*, the feelings, personal characteristics, and activities of the male and female characters in the stories were markedly different. Thus story themes involving active or aggressive play, pranks, and work projects were related to boy activity. Quiet activities, school, folk tales, and "real life with positive emotions" (i.e., "Pollyannaish" themes) were related to girl activity *(20, 36)*. Interestingly, twice as many girl activity stories (63 percent) as boy activity stories (37 percent) involved school activities. Although literacy and formal education were primarily masculine prerogatives in the early period of American history, this is no longer the case, as is reflected in readers of that era and the contemporary association of school with girl activities in children's readers; this appears inappropriate if we are concerned with promoting positive relationships between school and boy-associated activities. The fact that female teachers predominate in the elementary school years only heightens the need for encouraging boys to view school activities as appropriate for males.

Furthermore, the feelings, personal characteristics, and activities of the male and female characters in the stories are markedly different. Compared with males, females are more frequently portrayed as sociable, outgoing, kind, timid, easily frightened, but inactive, unambitious, and uncreative. "To the extent that boys identify with male characters and girls with female characters, this difference both in itself and as a reflection of facts that hold true of many sources of influence on children, must have a profound significance for the differential development of personality in the two sexes" *(36)*.

The schools and educational methods align themselves with other familial and social forces in making clear distinctions between males and females with respect to appropriate behavior and personality. As the authors conclude, "there is clear evidence that the education [of the two sexes] is not the same, even at early levels of grammar school and even when boys and girls are mixed together, as they usually are, in the same classroom. Not only does the informal training of boys and girls at the home and in the community differ, but even the formal education they are receiving in the classroom differs" (36).

SOCIOECONOMIC STATUS AND SCHOOL ACHIEVEMENT

Parental Rewards for School Achievement

Middle-class parents typically display marked interest in the child's reports of his school activities, praise him for his first stumbling attempts at reading, and may even provide more tangible rewards, in the form of movies, bicycles, or spending money for accomplishments in school. Furthermore, as he grows older, the middle- and upper-class child is able to see for himself the delayed rewards to which academic skills may lead, by noting the important part they play in the success of his doctor-father, his businessman-uncle, or his accountant-older brother. Of course, we would not expect these distantly anticipated rewards to be very effective if the child's immediate experiences were punishing, but when these latter are favorable, the prospects of additional future rewards may provide increased impetus for the child to try to do well in school.

Parental interest in the school is less common among the lower socioeconomic groups. Upper-middle-class parents are great believers in education as the solution to many problems—economic, social, and personal. Lower-middle- and upper-lower class parents tend to look upon school more as a way of getting children ready for adulthood (77, 78). They are not great believers in education per se, but see it as necessary for vocational success. Nevertheless, all these groups, in contrast to lower-lower class groups (particularly those subject to ethnic segregation and discrimination), reinforce the value of school to some degree because they expect the school to do something for their children (149).

Several factors seem to be meaningfully related to the more positive attitudes toward academic success shown by children and parents of the higher socioeconomic group. For one thing, the school child's social-class identification tends to be strong, and threats to his membership status in a particular social class will be tremendously anxiety-producing. School success is much more important in maintaining class membership in the higher classes than in the lower, and consequently middle- and upper-class children will be more motivated to achieve it. They see that the kinds of jobs to which they and other members of their social class aspire depend heavily on the acquisition of academic skills. Obviously school success is much more important to the future banker, lawyer, or business executive than it is to the laborer or farm hand.

Moreover, upper- and middle-class parents are likely to encourage their children to work hard in school because of their genuine interest in the child's academic progress and because of the threat to their own social status of having a child who "couldn't make the grade." However, parents of any class may desire to have their children improve their social status beyond that of their own. The school may provide the best route toward social mobility, not only because it increases academic skills but because it also offers an opportunity for imitation of higher-class children.

Finally, children of middle-class parents are more likely to see their parents engage in intellectual work. That is, the child of a doctor, lawyer, architect, accountant, or engineer has the opportunity to watch his father read books or journals and show a personal interest in intellectual matters. His mother also is likely to read books or manifest an interest in study or in community lectures. Thus middle-class parents often present themselves as intellectual *models for identification*—as people who not only encourage intellectual goals for the child but also value them in their own lives. They practice what they preach. Lower-class parents, on the other hand, are less likely to engage in intellectual activities and, consequently, provide no models for intellectual interests or mastery.

Socioeconomic differences in parental attitudes toward school are not restricted to the white, native-born majority group in our culture. Social-class differences and attitudes seem to cut across racial and other minority-group lines. For example, among middle-class Negroes, the concern of parents for their child's scholastic success, and, consequently, their approval of responses in this direction are, if anything, stronger than among middle-class whites *(46)*.

On the other hand, lower-class children, particularly those in the lower-lower class and those suffering the double jeopardy of ethnic group segregation and discrimination as well, are likely to be far less highly motivated and to have lower aspirations for academic achievement than middle-class children *(115)*. As Deutsch *(49, 52)* notes, these children generally have much less opportunity than middle-class ones to perceive relationships between academic achievement and success in life; consequently they are likely to adopt a "so what" attitude toward school. Their parents frequently feel isolated from, fearful of, or indifferent or antagonistic to the school as an institution, often viewing it simply as another extension of the middle-class "establishment" from which they have been excluded.

Ethnic Differences in Academic Skills. In addition to social-class differences in motivation and in intellectual and academic skills, there are also differences that are associated with membership in a particular ethnic group. First grade children from four different ethnic groups (Chinese, Negroes, Jews, and Puerto Ricans) from both lower- and middle-class families were given four different kinds of tests: verbal ability, reasoning, knowledge about numbers, and spatial ability. Although lower-class children from all four ethnic groups performed more poorly than middle-class children on all tests, each ethnic group had a unique profile whose shape was similar for both middle- and the lower-class children in the group (see Fig. 13.3). As may be seen, the Jewish children did best on the verbal tests and poorest on the space tests. Chinese children demonstrated the reverse profile; they per-

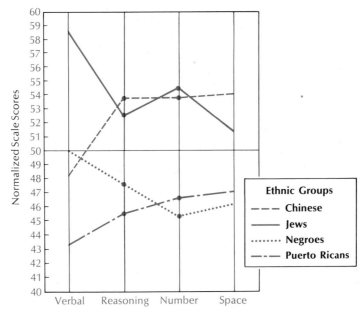

Fig. 13.3 Patterns of normalized mental-ability scores for each ethnic group. (From G. S. Lesser, F. Fifer, & D. H. Clark. Mental abilities of children from different social class and different cultural groups. *Monogr. Soc. Res. Child Develpm.*, copyright 1965 by The Society for Research In Child Development, Inc. *30,* No. 4, 64. By permission.)

formed most poorly on the verbal test and best on the space test. The Negro children resembled the Jewish children in being better on verbal than on space measures, while the Puerto Ricans resembled the Chinese and did better on space measures than on the verbal *(105).*

Peer-Group Influences on Motivation

As we have already seen, one of the pressing needs of school children is to gain acceptance by their peers. Depending upon the particular values of the peer group, the child's motivation for scholastic success may be either strengthened or reduced. In many middle- and upper-class groups, scholastic success—or at least the absence of scholastic failure—is positively valued and explicitly rewarded, not only by teachers and parents but also by the children themselves. Thus, for example, in a number of studies involving primarily middle-class children *(26, 29),* the children who were most popular in school were better students and were more conforming and cooperative. Lower-class, and particularly slum children, are not likely to be rewarded either by parents or peers for scholastic achievement, as many discouraged teachers from marginal-area schools can readily testify.

Davis *(45)* makes the following point.

Whereas the middle class child learns a socially adaptive fear of receiving poor grades in school, of being aggressive toward the teacher, of fighting, of cursing, and of having early sex relations, the slum child learns to fear quite different social acts. His gang teaches him to have a fear of being taken in by the teacher, of being a softie with her. To study homework seriously is literally a disgrace. Instead of boasting of good marks in school, one conceals them if he ever receives them (45, 30).

Parental Practices, Anxiety, and Intellectual Performance

Parents who create a high level of anxiety in their children and a strong concern about failing to measure up in evaluative situations may affect not only the child's overall adjustment and self-concept but his intellectual performance and academic achievement as well. The child's ability to solve problems efficiently and to acquire knowledge is influenced not only by his achievement motivation but also by his anxiety about intellectual activities. Many individuals have an unusually intense fear of failure; they doubt their ability to pass a test and to solve problems. For some, this anxiety can be so intense that it obstructs clear thinking and results in withdrawal of interest from academic tasks. There are, therefore, many bright children who possess a strong desire to improve their intellectual skills but fail to do so. Strong anxiety and doubts about their ability interfere with their effectiveness on tests, cause them to become easily discouraged, and, therefore, make concentration and new learning difficult.

Special questionnaires or scales have recently been devised to measure children's anxiety—the degree to which children admit apprehension and fear in school and in other situations (32, 136). Some of the questions related to anxiety about school performance include: "Are you afraid of school tests?" "Do you worry about being promoted?" "Do you have butterflies in your stomach when you have to take a test?" "Do you worry a lot while you are taking a test?" "When the teacher says she is going to find how much you have learned, does your heart begin to beat faster?" Other questions were related to sources of fear that seemed unrelated to school (i.e., nightmares, fears of the dark, fears of being hurt). Some sample questions included: "Do you get scared when you have to walk home alone at night?" "Are you afraid of things like snakes?" "Do you worry that you are going to get sick?" (136).

There is a positive relation between *test anxiety* and general anxiety—for example, anxiety over the dark, ghosts, or illness (71, 82, 136, 137). Moreover, anxiety scores have been found to be significantly and negatively related to a wide variety of measures, such as IQ, achievement-test scores for reading and arithmetic, and school performance (55, 60, 71, 82, 131, 137, 151). The strength of these relationships tends to increase with age (82). Also, while individual children may increase or decrease in anxiety with age, test performance tends to parallel these changes. Thus for children who become more anxious, performance declines; for those whose anxiety decreases, performance improves (82).

The extent to which the child feels free to acknowledge anxiety in himself will be a function of how defensive he feels about the acceptability of expressing anxiety (82). Thus test anxiety scores that can be adjusted to take into account defensiveness on the part of the subject should be better predictors of achievement than straight anxiety scores, and this is indeed the case. It has recently been found that while test anxiety scores alone can significantly predict performance across grade levels and sex of subjects (82, 151), prediction is consistently improved by adjusting anxiety scores (through a partialing-out technique) to take account of the effect of scores on measures of defensiveness (82).

It has also been widely assumed from informal observation that boys may be more likely to be defensive about expressing anxiety than girls (44), as a result of greater cultural pressures against the expression of anxiety in boys (cf. p. 505). Some support for this notion is provided in the recent work of Hill and Sarason (82) on text anxiety, which indicates that girls score higher on test anxiety while boys score higher on defensiveness (82). Further, as the boys grow older, defensiveness scores are better predictors of their performance than anxiety scores, while for girls, anxiety scores are the better predictors—although both anxiety and defensiveness interfere with intellectual functioning (82, 135).

The pattern of results indicates that the degree of anxiety the child experiences exerts an important influence on the quality of his intellectual behavior. Anxious children apparently become more flustered in problem-solving situations and their performance, therefore, is negatively affected. Anxiety is a painful and distracting feeling that can interfere with concentrated thought and with the accurate solution of problems.

THE SCHOOL AND THE CULTURALLY DISADVANTAGED STUDENT

The culturally disadvantaged student is likely to be poorly prepared to enter and to progress in the traditional school setting. Largely as a result of developmental influences in the family and in his overall social milieu, which are markedly different from those of the middle- and upper-class child, he is likely to be handicapped in approaching academic tasks requiring a variety of basic cognitive abilities (38). His language development tends to be limited: a variety of studies indicate that disadvantaged children use fewer words per remark (157, 158), less mature sentence types, less complex sentence construction, and less detailed concepts (2). While the middle-class child's language is elaborated in form and serves "to communicate ideas, relationships, feelings, and attitudes" (67, 13), the disadvantaged child's language tends to be restricted in form, serving to communicate signals and directions, and generally confining thinking to a relatively low level of repetitiveness (18). Furthermore, social-class differences in language associated with social class tend to increase with the age of the child (51, 83). As the disadvantaged child grows older, he falls further and further behind middle-class children (51, 67). It has been demonstrated that by the end of first grade, more than one-half of children who will be failing in arithmetic in grade 6 can be identified on the basis of their social class, their intelligence test scores, and their achievement in arithmetic. By the end of the second grade, two-thirds of failing children can be identified (152).

If it is true that "the acquisition of language is a prerequisite to concept formation and problem-solving, then the presence of this language deficiency would indicate a tremendous lower-class deficit in conceptual function" (67, 14). In fact, disadvantaged children perform relatively well on motor tasks, on tasks requiring a short time span, and on tasks which can easily be related to concrete objects and services, but they are generally inferior to middle-class children in abstract thinking (10, 51). The importance of language ability is also suggested by repeated findings that the performance of disadvantaged children tends to be less depressed in tests of arithmetic than in basic reading skills (52, 66).

In general, it would appear that disadvantaged children "tend to depend more on real life encounters than on symbolic experience in developing ideas and skills" (67, 15). Their functioning tends to be slower (134), their time orientation shorter (103), and their ability to attend to and concentrate on sustained academic tasks poorer (51, 67). In addition, as we have already seen (pp. 561–562), they are likely to be less highly motivated and to have lower aspirations for academic achievement than middle-class children, and receive little academic encouragement from either parents or peers. The disadvantaged child's progress in school may also be further limited by feelings of inadequacy and a depressed self-concept resulting from the greater difficulties he encounters and from feelings of not "belonging" in a social setting characterized by unfamiliar or foreign goals and codes of behavior (67, 70, 102, 122, 164).

Another problem presented by the disadvantaged child in the school setting, particularly in the changing urban environment, is that of transiency (92, 106). As people become more affluent and move out of urban slums, their places are taken by a constant stream of newcomers, largely from poor rural backgrounds: Negroes, Appalachian whites, Puerto Ricans, Mexican-Americans, and others. In many slum schools the turnover of pupils may approach 100 percent in a single year (42, 106).

Given the problems that the disadvantaged child faces in meeting traditional academic demands, it seems reasonable to conclude that, if anything, he should be provided greater assistance in school than the better prepared middle-class youth. Yet the fact of the matter is that the reverse is usually the case. The school the culturally disadvantaged child attends is far more likely to be physically deteriorated (often to the point of posing real dangers to his health and safety), overcrowded, lacking in essential physical facilities (i.e., playgrounds, shops, laboratories, cafeterias, even adequate lavatories), inadequately staffed, and lacking in the most basic kinds of equipment, such as teaching aids and books (42, 98).

It would be a mistake, however, to assume that what is required to meet the educational needs of the disadvantaged child is simply more of what has traditionally been provided the average middle- and upper-class child. Certainly, the disadvantaged child, like all children, needs decent physical surroundings and educational facilities, and dedicated, skillful teachers. But he also needs new and imaginative kinds of approaches to education and curricular development; to vocational, social and personal guidance; and to community involvement with the schools. All of these things are necessary, not merely to help the disadvantaged child to compensate for his general academic deficiencies, as judged by traditional measures of performance but also to respond to his specific life problems and, it should be added, to take maximum advantage of his particular assets and aptitudes, whether they fit traditional middle-class patterns or not. After all, not all of the characteristics of the disadvantaged child represent liabilities, even when these characteristics may pose difficulties within the framework of traditional middle-class oriented educational systems.

The Teacher and the Culturally Disadvantaged Student. In view of the greater difficulties encountered in working with disadvantaged children, and the need for special skills and understanding on the part of the teacher, it might seem logical to expect that these children would be exposed to the most highly trained and experienced teachers within the school system. While there are many superb, dedicated teachers in ghetto schools, working against what must often seem like insurmountable odds to provide their pupils a meaningful start in life, the reverse is frequently the case. In all too many school systems, it is the youngest, the least experienced, and the least skilled teacher who is most likely to be assigned to the ghetto or slum school. Furthermore, while some of these teachers may go on to make a permanent adjustment to such a setting, typically those who were first assigned to culturally disadvantaged schools become dissatisfied and frustrated and leave for a "more desirable" (i.e., middle-class) school as soon as possible (16, 35, 58).

Some of the reasons for these attitudes are not hard to understand. As already mentioned, the ghetto school itself is likely to be dilapidated, poorly equipped, overcrowded, and understaffed—the stepchild of the school system. Further, it is likely to lack support and prestige, not only within the administration of the school system and among older teachers, but also in the neighborhood and among parents and pupils. With these factors taken together, it is not difficult to see why even an optimistic, dedicated teacher might be discouraged.

In addition, given her own values and cultural background, the average middle-class teacher's attempts to teach disadvantaged children are almost bound to be an exercise in frustration, particularly if the teacher has had no special prior training in understanding such students' needs (the usual situation in most schools of education, at least until very recently). Such a teacher feels most rewarded when her efforts to instill traditional academic skills yield the greatest gains; this is what she perceives as her basic job. When the disadvantaged child does not appear capable of responding to instruction in ways that she expects he should, or when he does not appear to share her own *need* for achievement, the teacher is likely to become frustrated, discouraged, or resentful.

A study of the biographies of 50 women teachers *(156)* showed that the need for achievement, inherent in the teacher herself, frequently gave rise to personality problems and clashes in the classroom. "This need to achieve on the part of middle-class oriented teachers is often frustrated when teachers attempt to put achievement into operational effect in the deprived school classrooms" *(35, 85)*.

The middle-class teacher is also likely to be confused and puzzled by the values, attitudes, and behaviors she encounters in children whose whole cultural background differs so widely from her own. In one study *(73)*, 294 teachers of disadvantaged children were asked what they thought was the main reason for the high turnover among teachers of these children.

> 40% of the responses pointed to "peculiarities" in the personalities of culturally deprived children as the major cause of the dissatisfaction that leads to turnover. 37% highlighted deficiencies in the administration or organization of the teachers themselves. Problems of discipline or negative behavior, classes that were too large, and lack of understanding and acceptance of deprived children by teachers headed the list of specifics *(73, 66)*.

Finally, in all too many instances, the teacher's preoccupation with middle-class status leads her to look upon a disadvantaged child not as *different* (and hence potentially challenging), but as *inferior* (and, by inference, unrewarding; *35*). The danger posed by her preconceived notions about a child's potential, whether right or wrong, is that they may lead to a self-fulfilling prophecy (cf. pp. 474–475).

In view of the discrepancies between the middle-class teacher's values and cultural background, and those of the disadvantaged, minority group student, there has recently been an increased emphasis on recruiting teachers for the disadvantaged among persons who themselves come from lower-class backgrounds At first glance, this might appear as a ready solution to the problem. A recent investigation of the comparative job satisfactions and dissatisfactions of white, predominantly middle-class teachers and Negro, predominantly working-class teachers working with culturally disadvantaged Negro students indicated that Negro teachers were more likely than white teachers to express satisfaction with their jobs and a desire to continue *(68)*. In explaining job dissatisfactions, the Negro teachers tended primarily to blame "inadequate materials and poor facilities" and "crowded classrooms," while the white teachers placed the greatest blame on "behavior-discipline problems" and "lack of parental interest." Furthermore, when the two groups of teachers were asked to describe the outstanding characteristics of their pupils by checking adjectives on a checklist, white teachers most frequently checked: *talkative, lazy, fun-loving, high strung,* and *rebellious.* In contrast, the five items most frequently selected by Negro teachers were: *fun-loving, happy, cooperative, energetic,* and *ambitious.* It would appear from these findings that Negro teachers tended to be less critical and less pessimistic in their evaluations of these disadvantaged students than the white teachers, possibly because many of them had themselves come from backgrounds similar to those of their students *(68).*

Unfortunately, however, attempting to recruit more teachers from disadvantaged backgrounds does not provide a simple answer to the problem. Both white *and* Negro teachers become progressively more dissatisfied working with culturally disadvantaged children as they continue in their jobs *(68).* In addition, greater difficulties are encountered in recruiting teachers from the ranks of the underprivileged *(35),* and there is no assurance that many such teachers will be truly oriented to the needs and problems of the disadvantaged children. In a significant number of cases, the lower-class individual who violates class expectancies by becoming a teacher does so because of his or her dedication to stereotyped middle-class values, and a need for upward social mobility. As a consequence, he may, despite his background, adopt middle-class expectations of his pupils that are not unlike those of middle-class teachers.

What Is Needed?   If our rapidly changing society is to remain viable, we can no longer afford a *laissez-faire* approach to the education of culturally and economically disadvantaged children. It is true, as some have argued, that inadequate schools are not a new phenomenon, nor is "the presence in our schools of children whose background of experience and whose readiness for the traditional demands of the school differ from those of white, middle-class United States Nationals" *(67, 2).*

> We have had large numbers of such children in the past, particularly during the period of great migrations to this country. History reveals that the schools were challenged at that time just as they are today, and it further reveals that they failed in their attempt at providing for the educational needs of many of these children. But the school's failures in previous years had far less serious consequences for the children and for society than do our failures today *(67, 2).*

In the 1800s, and even in the early part of the present century, there was considerable room in the job market for relatively uneducated individuals with strong backs and willing hands. The existence of such opportunities provided access for members of earlier generations of immigrants, such as the Irish and Italians, into the socioeconomic structure of the nation. Currently, however, as we shall see (cf. pp. 676–677), the situation is changing rapidly. With the growth of automation, and the increasing complexity of our technological society, ever fewer jobs are open to the poorly educated individual lacking even basic technical or vocational skills. Ironically, in contrast, for those with superior ability, education, and skills, vocational opportunities are probably greater than at any other period in history. Consequently, it is essential to provide maximal educational opportunities consistent with the youngsters' abilities and potential, for all children. Furthermore, this education must be geared to the actual needs—intellectual, social, and vocational—of the child, particularly the disadvantaged child *(50)*.

A further difference between our present and earlier eras must be noted. Educational needs and vocational demands do not exist in a vacuum. As Gordon and Wilkerson further note:

> The growing crisis in intellectual resources and the management of knowledge has been paralleled by a social crisis involving civil, or more properly, human rights. A social revolution is in progress, led by the Negroes, other poverty-stricken people, and their allies—a revolution in which these dispossessed members of our affluent society are demanding total and meaningful integration into the mainstream and an opportunity to share in the wealth of the nation. More than any other factor, equality of educational opportunity and, ultimately of educational achievement, is viewed as crucial in achieving this end *(67, 3–4)*.

What Can Be Done? Among the items most highly stressed in the recent report of the National Advisory Commission on Civil Disorders *(132)* was the need for better schools for deprived, ghetto children. In many ways, the school as the single social institution most involving all children represents the best opportunity for breaking the relentless cycle of the "culture of poverty" and the institutionalization of "separate, but unequal" ways of life for the deprived and nondeprived. It has been argued that the nation cannot afford the price of bringing disadvantaged children back into the mainstream of society after centuries of neglect. Our contention is that we cannot afford to do otherwise if the fabric of a truly democratic society is to be preserved.

Not only do we need schools that in their construction, physical facilities, and equipment are the equal of those in white suburbia *(42, 98)*, we also need a "total push" approach to upgrading the educational effort directed at the children of poverty in order to bring them up to a level at which they can profit by more traditional learning experiences. Such an effort must be based on a sophisticated understanding of the problems that these children face—cultural, intellectual, psychological, physical, and motivational.

At the simplest level, such steps mean ensuring that a child is not handicapped in his ability to profit from his school experience because he has had no breakfast, as is all too frequently the case in both rural and urban slums *(23)*. Even the widely heralded school lunch programs are denied many children today because a small, but still prohibitive, charge is made for this service *(23)*. Children in a number of areas in this affluent society still either do not go to school because they do not have proper clothes, or they are shamed in school by their peers because of the inadequacy of their clothes. Many have never had physical examinations, and suffer from poor vision or hearing, malnutrition, or chronic, low-grade illnesses that make already difficult school work even more difficult *(23, 67)*.

When the parents or society are otherwise unable or unwilling to meet such basic needs of children, these needs must, as a matter of simple justice, be provided by the schools.

We have already discussed the need for preschool training programs, such as Head Start, which attempt to compensate partially for deficiencies in school readiness among disadvantaged children (pp. 311–319). Such programs need to be extended and multiplied. But if we are to be ultimately effective and if gains made are not to be soon lost, special academic programs directed at the specific needs of deprived children must be continued into the school years. A large number of scattered but varied and imaginative efforts are beginning to be made in different parts of the country. They include: programs of early admission (15, 67) to get the children ready for regular school; extending the school day and providing evening assistance for pupils and parents (67); summer schools and camps, and year-around schooling (15, 24, 67); smaller classes for the disadvantaged (15, 23); special programs for transient or immigrant youth (15); team teaching, including the use of multiple teachers and teachers' aides (67, 79); cultural enrichment programs and specially designed field trips (67); the use of staffs of expert consultants and tutors in such fields as clinical psychology and psychiatry, speech pathology, audiology, and remedial reading (15, 67); use of "non-grading" (in which grade-level divisions in the curriculum are erased to allow for "continuous progress" at the students' own rate in various subject matter areas (67, 69, 79, 125, 170). Increasing attention is being paid to the use of programmed instruction, "teaching machines" (cf. p. 125), and other audio visual aids that simplify critical learning tasks or, importantly, allow the child through supervised self-instruction to proceed at his own pace (15, 67, 113, 114, 143). In our opinion, in all of these kinds of efforts (separately or in combination), of *primary importance* is the need to provide all children with the basic tools of language, reading, writing, simple arithmetic, and logical reasoning—without which further academic work becomes merely an exercise in frustration, and hopes of competing realistically and meaningfully in today's increasingly complex world of work and social interaction are doomed. It is impossible adequately to review all of the many innovative compensatory education programs for the disadvantaged that are currently being explored, but adequate reviews are available elsewhere (4, 15, 20, 154, 168). Indicative of some of the possibilities, however, are recent efforts by psychologists to develop extensive educational television programming for disadvantaged preschoolers.

It should be noted that it is too early, in most cases, to tell which kinds of programs will be most productive. The important thing at this juncture is to experiment on a broad scale and to build into such efforts adequate means of evaluation.

If the kinds of programs briefly described above are to have any hope of being successful, and if they are to become capable of being applied on a wide scale, there is a great need for upgrading the training of teachers. Not only will teachers require broader training in better understanding the psychological, cultural, and intellectual needs and problems of the disadvantaged, and general ways to deal more effectively with them, they will also require specific training in carrying out special curricular programs (e.g., language arts training), programmed instruction, and the like. Fortunately, a few schools of education are responding more adequately and imaginatively to such needs, both in their curricula and in field experiences (15, 67, 154). The latter range from supervised practice in ghetto schools to home and community visits (67, 154). However, much more is needed; most teacher-training programs are still geared to the imagined needs of the average, responsive, middle-class student. A number of efforts, also still far too few, are under way to provide special training and in-service experience for teachers already on the job (15, 67, 154). It might be added that, even under optimal conditions of training and experience, the job of the teacher of the culturally disadvantaged child is a difficult one. For this reason alone, these teachers need maximum support from administrative and supervisory personnel and from school boards; and, if anything, they need *more* rather than less status, financial reward, and additional educational opportunity than the average teacher (15, 67, 154). To date, with few exceptions, they are not getting such recognition.

Finally, if school programs for the culturally disadvantaged are to work, they must gain the confidence of parents and community (65, 67, 154). Decades of discrimination, exploitation, and lack of concern on the part of the middle-class majority have led urban and rural slum dwellers to be suspicious and fearful of, or antagonistic to, the middle-class "establishment" and its institutions—ranging from welfare and the police to the schools themselves. Greater efforts must be made to get to know parents and their often crushing problems, not as representatives of the "establishment" in a scheduled school interview, which just spells trouble to most slum dwellers, but as concerned equals in informal settings and in the home. Neighborhood and community representatives must become involved in planning and carrying out school programs; school activities and courses for parents themselves must be provided, and the schools must become active with parents and others in the neighborhood in nonschool community projects. In short, the school must be made a meaningful, relevant part of the community (67) rather than an irrelevant or threatening outside agency superimposed by the "establishment" on the community. This change is essential if compensatory education is to work, and if the school is to carry out its function of serving as a bridge between society and the deprived child and his parents. For older youth, as we shall see in our discussion of adolescence (pp. 729–734), still other kinds of efforts must be made, not only to reduce "dropping out" of school but also to provide meaningful and rewarding programs and practical transitions for youth from school to the world of work.

Unless broad enough and widespread enough programs can be developed in all of these areas—school facilities, academic programs, teacher training, and parental and community involvement—to compensate for the cultural deprivations of the poor (and, especially, the ethnically penalized poor who suffer double jeopardy in our society), there is a real question, as the National Advisory Commission of Civil Disorders points out, as to whether democracy as we know it can survive *(132)*. At the least, unless adequate steps are taken, millions of children will enter adulthood unprepared to lead reasonably happy, self-sustaining, and productive lives.

RELATIONS WITH PEERS

The child of school age is confronted with two new socialization agents: teachers and peers. As we have already seen, the teachers that a child is exposed to may have a significant effect on his subsequent development. The peer group, too, plays an increasingly important role in influencing development as the child moves out of the home for a greater percentage of his waking hours—a percentage which increases steadily from kindergarten to high school *(30)*. Among most middle-class children there is usually greater similarity between teachers' and parents' values than between those of peers and parents. The adoption of peer-group values will depend on the degree to which the child needs and wants acceptance by age-mates as well as by his identifications with peer heroes.

When peers, parents, and teachers are in agreement about the appropriateness of certain values or actions, few problems arise. However, in many cases, the behaviors encouraged by the peer group are in direct opposition to those rewarded by parents and teachers. In these instances, the child will experience conflict. How this conflict is resolved will depend largely on the differential reward value of authority figures and peers. If acceptance by peers in achieving a particular goal is more important than parental acceptance, the child probably will adopt peers' standards and behaviors.

The peer group also provides an opportunity to learn how to interact with age-mates, how to deal with hostility and dominance, how to relate to a leader, and how to lead others. It also performs a psychotherapeutic function for the child by helping him deal with social problems. Through discussions with peers the child may learn that others share his problems, conflicts, and complex feelings, and this may be reassuring. The discovery that other boys are also angry at their fathers or are concerned with sexuality relieves tension and guilt.

Finally, the peer group helps the child develop a concept of himself. The ways in which peers react to the child, and the bases upon which he is accepted or rejected, give him a clearer, and perhaps more realistic, picture of his assets and liabilities.

It is fair to say that the crucial arena for self-esteem is the arena of one's age-mates. At home there is an age hierarchy. Even the siblings are bigger or smaller, so that differences of competence are expected. The home, moreover, continues to be the source of love and provision of basic wants, even when the child ventures forth to play-ground and school. At home he must be *love-worthy:*

this may include being competent but it is heavily weighted on the side of being good, obedient and affectionate. On the play-ground the values are different; he must be *respect-worthy*, able to command respect because he shows competence and handles himself with ease. It is a sharp strain for many children when they pass from the atmosphere of a child-centered home into the competitive realities of even a friendly play group. They must now show what they have in the way of physical prowess, courage, manipulative skill, outgoing friendliness, all in direct comparison with other children of their age. The penalties for failure are humiliation, ridicule, rejection from the group (171, 144–145).

The influence of the peer group as a socializing agent appears stronger in American culture at the present time than in some other societies, or than in our own society in earlier eras (30). For example, it has been found that Mexican youth (111) and Chinese youth living in Hawaii (86) are far less under the "tyranny of their peers" than American youth because, in comparison with the American child, they "live far more in the family and less in peer society" (30, 295). The same is true of many European youth. In contrast, however, children living in an Israeli kibbutz or within the Soviet educational system are, through conscious design on the part of society, reared under maximal peer (rather than family) contact, although there is considerable nonfamily supervision (53, 147).

The rapidity of social change within American society also affects the influence of the peer group. Davis points to the significance of rapid social change as a factor "creating a hiatus between one generation and the next, thus contributing to the role of age mates in the socialization process" (47, 523). Keniston makes a similar observation: "the relations between the generations are weakened as the rate of social innovation increases" (97, 153). This change will become especially evident in our later discussions of adolescence and the relationships between generations.

Integration into New Peer Groups

When the child starts school, he quickly discovers that many of his satisfactions are dependent on establishing himself as a member of a peer group. His opportunities for companionship, and his chance of being asked to play favored roles—or even to participate in various play activities— vary with the degree of his acceptance by the group. Furthermore, physical retreat from the peer-group situation is practically impossible now. In the past, if the child failed to enjoy playing with his peers, he could always "pick up his marbles and go home," but now no such solution is available. Happy or not, he must remain in school.

It is therefore not surprising to find that most children of school age are intensely motivated to gain peer-group acceptance. At the same time, they are rather tentative and cautious in their initial attempts to become group members. A new social situation has a great deal of potential for both reward and punishment. Yet, in most instances, children have little prior knowledge of what will be considered the correct and incorrect responses in the new setting and hence must rely to a great extent on trial and error.

In an attempt to study the process of assimilation into peer society, one team of investigators *(124)* introduced four 6-and-7-year-old children individually into well-established, "nucleus" play groups of three children their own age. The new child did not know the other children or the experimenter.

They found that the newcomers made real efforts to relate to the nucleus group and to become part of it "on a par with other members." Apparently, most of them had already learned that group activities (being a member of a group) may be very rewarding, and they were therefore eager to play with the others.

In these groups, the new arrival had to take the initiative in interacting with other children. Established members of the group rarely tried to adopt his interests, put him at ease, or take him into account in their activities. The same sort of behavior has often been observed in the schoolroom where "new" children often seek the teacher's aid in dealing with other pupils before they initiate direct social contacts.

The usual technique of relating to the group consisted of imitating the remarks, actions, and gestures of the most active member. Progress in becoming integrated was gradual and continuous. For example, only 5 percent of the average newcomer's responses during his first meeting with the group were classified as "successful initiation and direction of group activities." Four sessions later, he made almost as many contacts of this type as "nucleus" members did (25 percent of his contacts).

The children who had been together longer knew how to interact successfully, i.e., they had learned the important cues and the responses which were likely to be reinforced by their peers. The new child did not know what behavior would be rewarded by these strangers, and hence was at a tremendous disadvantage. Under the circumstances, he turned to an adult for help, probably because parents or teachers had been helpful in such situations previously. In short, he may have generalized earlier rewarded responses of looking to adults for help. When this was not possible and when there were no specific instructions, the child's best tactics were to observe the behavior patterns of successful children and to imitate them. It has also been found that children are more readily assimilated into the peer group at grades 1, 2, and 3 than in grades 4, 5, and 6, and that girls are more readily assimilated than boys *(177)*.

Peer Culture in Middle Childhood

In a very real sense, the child lives in two worlds—that of his parents and other adults, and that of his peers. Even when these worlds exist side by side, there is often remarkably little overlap between them. The world of peers seems often to be a subculture of its own, influenced in a number of ways by the larger culture of which it is a part, but also having its own history, its own social organization, and its own means of transmitting its folklore from one generation to another. Much of the ritual of the childhood years is transmitted by peers, not by parents, even though the rituals themselves may have changed little over the years (153). When adults overhear children at their games, they are likely to be nostalgically reminded of the forgotten years of their own childhoods.

Similarly, while enthusiastic parents may coach their children in Little League baseball or football, such eternal avocations as hopscotch, marbles, tag, hide-and-seek, Red Rover, jacks, and London Bridge are carefully preserved and transmitted from one generation to another within the childhood culture itself (153). Much the same thing appears to apply to the changing nature of children's groups over the middle-childhood years, and to their sometimes amusingly elaborate—though frequently violated—rules, regulations, and initiation ceremonies.

The changing adult culture may act to set limits on peer associations. Thus the suburban, middle-class, Protestant, white child or the urban, lower-middle-class, Negro child may each have little opportunity for interaction with children of other cultural, ethnic, or socioeconomic backgrounds—often to the detriment of both. Parents may restrict, even among available opportunities, the other children with whom he allows his child to associate. Segregation of boys and girls in peer groups in the middle-childhood years may be partially encouraged by the adult culture in its efforts to promote sex-typed identification. However, within the limits set by the social circumstances of the larger adult culture, the structure, function, and membership of children's groups, and their changes with age, tend to occur in a largely autonomous fashion, with marked similarities from generation to generation.

During the early years of middle childhood, informal groups, formed by the children themselves, predominate, and the school-aged child is likely to refer to "the gang." The gang has few formal rules for governing itself, and there is a rapid turnover in membership. Expediency plays a large role in determining group membership.

Later, however, between the ages of 10 and 14, there is a tendency for children's groups to become more highly structured. Aspects of formal organization, such as special membership requirements and elaborate rituals for conducting meetings, appear. Even so, the personnel may change frequently and the group itself may not last long. At this time, formal organizations such as the Boy Scouts, Girl Scouts, or Campfire Girls become more important, especially with middle-class children.

The group play of children from 7 to 11 years differs in important ways from that of children 5 to 6 years of age. In the younger period, a boy may play—or fight—with either boys or girls. Their games may be feminine (e.g., playing house) or masculine (playing ball or building). Beginning at age 7 or 8, however, children begin to associate primarily with same-sex peers. The boys now chase and tease girls, rather than play with them. The boy seeks out other boys and is likely to be embarrassed if he is found alone with a group of girls. From age 9 through 11, there is usually considerable anxiety over associations with girls or revealing any interest in them.

Throughout the middle-childhood years, age, as well as sex, plays an important role in determining the nature of peer group relations (*30, 33, 84, 161*). Both boys and girls tend to associate primarily with peers of the same age, although prepubertal girls—with their earlier growth spurt—may begin to express an interest (although a rather tenuous one) in somewhat older boys, in contrast to their "grubby" male contemporaries.

It is obvious that age- and sex-groupings are not merely historical accidents, or designed simply to meet unrelated whims of the adult culture. As Linton has observed, similar groupings exist throughout both ·literate and preliterate societies (*108*). They also occur among other primates and additional infrahuman species. Sex and age groupings meet the needs both of society and the child himself. The society may feel a need to inculcate sex- and age-appropriate skills and attitudes in the course of the child's socialization. The child himself, however, needs the experience of interacting with other children who share, at his particular stage of life and level of cognitive development, his interests, needs, abilities, skills, and problems. Increasingly, as the child moves away from his former relatively exclusive ties with his parents during the early school years, he also needs a compensatory feeling of belongingness in a peer group in which he can feel comfortable. The average amount of time spent in family settings decreases, time spent in peer settings consequently increases from kindergarten to adolescence (*173*), and the interdependence of peer group members in many situations increases steadily with age (*144*).

Sex cleavages in interests and activities become increasingly evident throughout the school years. While there is still much overlap—e.g., girls show an increasing interest in masculine games and activities during grades 3 to 6 (*155*)—there is nevertheless growing separation of interests, activities, and concerns of boys and girls during these years, with some areas of interest being almost entirely masculine and others almost entirely feminine:

> In general, boys tend to be doers and girls talkers. Boys tend to be oriented to things, with a special emphasis on things mechanical, and girls to people and social relations. Girls engage in sports (including touch football), but boys in addition read about them, idolizing the heroes and clustering in search of autographs around the hotel where the visiting team is staying. Girls like to ride bicycles, but boys also enjoy taking bicycles apart and putting them back together. In school, girls perform better than boys in the early years but gradually slip back into second place (*153, 387*).

During the middle-childhood years, boys tend to be somewhat more involved with gang and other peer-group activities than girls, who tend to remain somewhat more closely tied to parents during these years. However, girls tend to have more intimate, individual interpersonal relationships than boys even at these ages—a precursor of later lifelong interpersonal orientations.

As we shall see, these different interests are closely associated with the sex-typed identifications of children which are developing during middle childhood (cf. pp. 501–508).

FACTORS AFFECTING PEER ACCEPTANCE AND STATUS

From our discussion thus far, it is clear that the peer group plays an important role during middle childhood—not simply in providing the child with immediate satisfactions, but in implementing his integration into the broader social world. It can help to train him to become a competent and knowledgeable individual, secure in his sex identifications and possessed of the interests, attitudes, and skills expected of his sex group. In addition, relationships with peers teach him to work cooperatively toward the achievement of mutually rewarding goals.

When we consider the scope of these functions, we can appreciate the advantages that accrue to the youngster who is accepted by his peers, and the penalties to which the rejected child is subject. It is therefore important to understand both the factors which promote and those which militate against peer-group acceptance. What determines whether a child will be popular in his group, treated indifferently, or avoided by others? On what basis are friendships among children formed? What variables are related to leadership? What are the consequents of high or low social standing in the group?

Social Status with Peers

Several techniques of measurement have been used in studies of the social status of children. In the sociometric approach (also discussed in an earlier chapter), youngsters are asked to list their preferences and rejections among the other children of the group with respect to some definite criterion. For example, each child in a camp cabin might be asked to name three children he would like to have as team mates, as swimming buddies, or as neighbors at home. From these data, a composite diagram of all the children's choices, known as a *sociogram*, can be constructed. This shows the relative social status of each child, from the most popular (i.e., most frequently chosen) to the "social isolates" (never chosen).

As outlined earlier, Bonney (26–28) used the technique to differentiate socially successful and unsuccessful fourth grade children in three schools. On the basis of his classmates' response to a series of sociometric questions (e.g., Whom would you like to serve with on committees?), each child received a composite social acceptance score.

Classmates and teachers rated the 20 most popular (i.e., highest in social acceptance) and 20 least popular children on a battery of 20 personality variables. Popular children were rated much higher in socially aggressive and outgoing characteristics. In general, they manifested either of two personality syndromes (groups of characteristics which go together). The first was composed of strong, positive, aggressive characteristics such as leadership, enthusiasm, and active participation in recitations. The second, which was less definite, involved cheerful disposition and friendly attitudes (tidy, good-looking, frequent laughter, happy, and friendly) [27, 28]. By and large, the characteristics associated with popularity showed a great resemblance to those which have been found to be the consequents of gratifying and rewarding early interactions in the family setting.

Other studies of school-age children (162) indicate that popular children in most groups are considered good-looking, friendly, good sports, and best friends. The relationships of other attributes to popularity varies with sex and age. For example, among first grade girls, popularity is closely associated with the characteristics "acting like a little lady," "being quiet," "not quarrelsome," and "not bossy." The importance of "acting like a little lady" declines as girls grow older, until by the fifth grade this trait has little to do with social prestige. At this age, good looks, good sportsmanship, friendliness, tidiness, and lack of quarrelsomeness are most highly correlated with girls' popularity.

The most highly esteemed first grade boys tend to be those whom their peers consider good sports, good at games, "real boys," not bashful, and daring. Fairness in play and leadership ability are the most important correlates of popularity among third grade boys. Fifth grade boys with high prestige also tend to be viewed as best friends, good-looking, not bashful, and "real boy." In this group, friendliness, good sportsmanship, and tidiness were somewhat less closely linked to popularity; characteristics such as "not bossy," "doesn't get mad," "not quarrelsome," and "doesn't fight" had little to do with prestige position.

In the area of skills and abilities, "the picture continues to build up that the more intelligent and creative are generally more accepted by their age mates; the slow learners and the retarded, less well accepted" (30, 305; see also 13, 14, 64, 120, 123, 128, 174). Significant relationships have also been obtained between peer status and reading achievement at every socioeconomic level of the school community (128, 146). Arithmetic ability and general academic achievement have also been found to be significantly related to peer acceptance (81, 85, 87, 140). Body size, muscular strength, and athletic ability also appear as criteria for acceptance among boys (37, 162).

On the negative side, anxiety, uncertainty, social indifference, withdrawal, rebelliousness, aggressiveness, and hostility emerge as attributes of low-status or rejected children (41, 81, 85, 119, 145, 159), as do physical liabilities, such as obesity and facial disfigurement (133). Rather interestingly, in view of predominant same-sex preferences during this age period, one investigator found that in comparison with other children, anxious and defensive children more frequently reported that they wanted to play with peers of the opposite sex (81). In this study (81), it was found that anxious children tended to be less frequently chosen by children of either sex.

It may be concluded that the responses and characteristics most likely to be rewarded by social acceptance vary according to age and sex. In general, however, the characteristics which conform to the cultural stereotypes of masculine behavior—athletic skills, leadership, and daring—are associated with popularity in boys, while typically feminine characteristics, such as docility and unassertiveness, are associated with popularity in girls. From these findings it may be inferred that high prestige with peers is at least partially a product of adequate sex-typing. It also appears that the extent to which a child's behavior is rewarding to others influences the way in which they treat him in return, and the extent to which he is accepted by others.

Social Class and Peer-Group Status

As we might expect, peer-group status is related to social class. In one study of 63 children in two school classes, social acceptance (as defined by sociometric questions) was found to be highly related to objective measures of family socioeconomic status (27, 29, 30). The child's social-class background was apparently of major importance in determining his social prestige among peers.

Other findings from sociometric studies indicate that lower-class children are more likely to have poor reputations among their peers of all social classes, including their own. They are likely to have few friends and are generally considered poorly dressed, plain-looking, unpopular, aggressive, not liking school, dirty, bad-mannered, unhappy, and unfair in play (27, 28).

Economic factors may partially account for the relatively poor social standing of lower-class children. Poverty may mean poor health, poor clothes, and little participation in social activity. Any of these factors may reduce the child's opportunities for establishing stable peer relationships, and may thus handicap him in learning good social techniques. Moreover, the lower-class child's awareness of his lack of social know-how may produce feelings of inferiority and inadequacy, and hence withdrawal from social interactions.

The specific behaviors associated with social status and popularity vary from class to class because the "ego ideals" for boys and girls differ among the classes. One investigator (127) compared boys and girls from lower- and middle-class families with respect to the clusters of traits they would regard as necessary for a good reputation. The lower-class boys respected two masculine types. The first was the aggressive, belligerent youngster who had earned the respect of his peers because he was tough and strong. The second included boys who were outgoing and sociable but not overly aggressive. The personality pattern that led to rejection was that of the "sissy" who conformed to the teacher's request and obtained good grades. The lower-class boy who does well in school makes himself vulnerable to alienation from his peers, and hence he may be conflicted over becoming involved in schoolwork.

Lower-class girls were willing to accept the rowdy, verbally aggressive girl who showed a strong interest in boys. However, in contrast to boys, they also respected the friendly, pretty, neat, and studious girl who was not necessarily a leader or overly interested in the opposite sex. Thus a lower-class girl, like the middle-class girl, could be a good student without alienating her friends.

Middle-class boys accepted boys who were skilled in competitive games but who were neither overly bossy nor blatantly aggressive. Friendly, handsome, and popular boys were also admired, as were good students. As in the lower class, the effeminate and frightened middle-class boy was rejected by his peers. There was only one acceptable stereotype for middle-class girls—that of the pretty, friendly, and vivacious girl. Girls in this class rejected the aggressive, rowdy, and sexually forward girl that some lower-class girls admired. Although there were some class differences, the boys in both social classes rejected the "sissy," and the girls in both classes valued beauty, neatness, and sociability.

The marked social-class differences in attitude toward aggression make lower-class children more receptive to the "heroes" who appear on television, in movies, and in comic books. One investigator (12) obtained data on children's exposure to television, movies, and comic books and their effects on the child. There was a tendency for the boys who were (1) from working-class homes, (2) of lower IQ, and (3) rebelliously independent to adopt the aggressive adventurers of television (Superman, detectives, pirates) as ego-ideal figures. This tendency was less evident among boys who were (1) from white-collar homes, (2) of higher IQ, and (3) less rebellious and independent.

There is much current concern among parents and social scientists over the degree to which the public media influence the habits and long-range goals of growing children. It appears that television and movies can strengthen an attitude (e.g., positive value of aggression) that is already present when the child's background and personality are such as to make him receptive to the attitude communicated by the public media (54, 118). When the attitudes and values communicated by television or movies conflict with the pre-existing values of the child and his family, he will be much less influenced by these communication sources. Thus the heavy emphasis on violence and aggression in movies and on television has its maximum effect on children who already have lowered anxiety over aggression and are predisposed to accept aggressive behavior as generally appropriate. Children from homes that discourage aggression and who, therefore, view it as bad are not likely to have their standards changed by aggressive stories and movies.

In view of the fact that from ages 3 through 16, the average American child spends about one-sixth of his waking hours watching television, and in view of the extensive amount of information and the values to which he is subjected through this experience (139), one might well hope that the television industry would take a more responsible approach to children's programming. Not only would less programming of objectionable (or simply poor) material be desirable, even more importantly, great opportunities for presenting imaginative, informative, and socially meaningful, as well as genuinely entertaining, subject matters are being missed. Under the circumstances, it is not surprising that brighter children spend considerably less time viewing television than their less intelligent peers, or that television-viewing, after reaching a peak around the sixth through eighth grades declines significantly thereafter (139).

Status with Peers and Social Behavior

The child's status among his peers, which depends to a great extent on his personality and class background, strongly affects the course of his socialization. A social psychological study illuminated the relationship between the child's prestige position among his peers and his ability to exercise influence over others as well as his proneness to be influenced by others (126). The subjects of the investigation were eight groups of boys and eight groups of girls (with 7 to 9 members each) ages 11 to 15, in a summer camp. Observers recorded all interactions involving attempts to influence others either indirectly or directly (being demanding, using force or threats, pleading, suggesting). They also noted all instances of behavior contagion—spreading of behavior—initiated by one of the children, even though the initiator did not communicate any intention to be imitated.

Each child's group influence was assessed in terms of frequencies of both initiation of contagion and successful direct attempts to influence others. The frequency of the child's compliance with the attempts of others at direct influence and the number of contagion incidents he "picked up" were used as measures of susceptibility to social influence. Counselors rated the children on feeling of acceptance in the group, adult relatedness, group relatedness, and group belongingness need. Prestige position was evaluated directly by means of cabinmates' rankings on strength and ability in athletics; independence of adults; having ideas for fun; sex sophistication ("knowing the score"); independence of social pressure.

Status position correlated significantly with ratings on feelings of acceptance in the group, contagion initiation, and successful direct influence attempts. In other words, children who were accorded high status felt more secure and accepted in the group and were able to sway the behavior of others by means of both direct and indirect techniques. Others responded by following their leads, thus rewarding their leadership activities.

Children with high status were less likely to accept others' commands and suggestions, but were more susceptible than the average to behavior contagion. Because they were secure in their group, they were free to "pick up" contagion if they wished, but could also resist direct attempts at influencing them. Their peers, aware of the high-status children's position in the social hierarchy, more frequently made indirect rather than direct approaches to them when attempting to influence their behavior.

By and large, those children to whom prestige position is attributed are aware of the fact; their awareness is facilitated by the behavior of others toward them in a variety of ways including, among other things, a readiness to be influenced either directly or "contagiously." They tend to act on the basis of this awareness by making more direct attempts at influencing, and by other behavior indicative of freedom to act spontaneously in the group (126, 334).

While the greatest influence on others is possessed by high-status children, and interest understandably tends to focus on them, influence is not entirely confined to such children. A single impulsive child, given the right potential situation, may be an important determiner of group action. A "contagious" response which extends rapidly throughout the group may result when the impulsive child "triggers off an action that the group is ready for, but has not yet done" (30, 313). Such children may exert a surprisingly dramatic influence in stressful situations when their expressive emotionality parallels needs of the group at the moment (126).

Effects of Adults and Situational Factors on Peer-Group Relationships

While many children's groups are informal and relatively independent of adult influence, there are other situations in which adults may be involved, and in which they can exert significant influences both on general group atmosphere and effectiveness, and on individual peer relationships—for good or ill. Neither the idyllic events in *Peter Pan* nor the frightening denouement of William Golding's *Lord of the Flies* would have taken the same course with adult participation.

The roles played by adult leaders can significantly affect the outcome of peer-group efforts (56, 109, 176). One investigation of racial desegregation in preadolescent campers (176) showed that adults significantly affected the young campers' reactions to the initial ambiguity of the interracial situation "by structuring activities, defining behavioral possibilities, and setting the tone of affective relations" (30, 314). In another study of tenth grade students (56), the teacher restricted praise for participants in a discussion session to students sitting in odd-numbered seats; the method was not known to the participants. Subsequent sociometric ratings by the children indicated that the praised students received more positive choices.

Environmental factors may also influence peer relationships and peer acceptance (30). Among preadolescent campers, all of whom were initially strangers, it was found that friendship preferences within the cabin setting were significantly influenced by the physical structure of the cabin. Not only did cabin membership tend to solidify peer relationships, but even such factors as proximity of bunks within the cabin played a role (22, 31). Other studies have indicated that pre-existing social structure of groups; their size; the extent to which a group shares a common purpose; and reward structures that require cohesive group effort may all influence the degree and patterning of peer acceptance (30). Obviously many socially isolated children could be helped to gain group acceptance and self-confidence and could begin to initiate socially successful behavior if they were provided assistance from appropriately structured peer-group situations.

Friendships

Of all his peers, the child's close friends are probably his most important "teachers," exerting the most potent and direct influences on his development and behavior. Hence it is important to understand how he selects them.

When asked to name their best friends, children of school age choose others of their own sex almost exclusively (160). This is hardly surprising in view of the sex-segregation characteristic of this period. Propinquity is also an important situational determinant of friendship choice. Most pairs of friends live in the same neighborhood or are in the same classroom at school (61).

Furthermore, personal characteristics appear to play a significant part in the formation of friendships. In one study, data on 62 pairs of boy chums were analyzed to determine the ways in which friends resemble each other (61). Pairs of friends resembled each other most in "'developmental age" (a measure of social maturity) and were also somewhat alike in chronological age, height, weight, and intelligence. The investigator concluded that resemblances in nonintellectual traits are probably more crucial in friendship ties than similarities in intelligence (61).

In a series of studies of grammar school children, mutual and unreciprocated pairs of friends were compared (26, 29). Mutual friendships were those in which two children named each other frequently in response to sociometric questions such as: Who would you like as a partner for a trip to the zoo? In unreciprocated pairs, one child showed attraction for another who practically ignored him.

In general, mutual friendship had little relationship to academic achievement, but mutual friends resembled each other in socioeconomic background and in general intelligence. Only-children, who generally came from families of higher socioeconomic status, were more successful in maintaining reciprocal relationships than those from large (four or more children) or medium-sized (two or three children) families. In the lower grades of elementary school, girls appeared to be more sociable than boys. They chose more companions for the suggested activities, and were involved in more mutual friendships (29).

Among fourth-graders, mutual friends tended to possess strong, positive, aggressive personality traits and to be outstanding in leadership and class recitation. In at least half of the pairs of mutual friends, both members were rated above average by their classmates in quietness, tidiness, daring, leadership, friendliness, desirability as companions, good looks, enthusiasm, frequent laughter, and activity in recitations (26).

Apparently, capable, alert, energetic, responsive children are ordinarily attracted to each other. This may be attributed to their ability to understand and satisfy each other's needs. Associations with listless, unresponsive children are not rewarding to them, and they do not generally form friendships with such children. Other children are often attracted to those with more positive traits, but their friendship is usually rejected (26).

In another study, 400 sixth grade children were asked to list the names of their three best friends, together with their reasons for choosing them (9). Frequent associations (for example: living nearby; selling papers together), similarity of interests or tastes (such as reading books together; having the same hobbies), cheerful ("have fun with him"; good-natured), nice and friendly ("nice guy"; "swell girl") were the four most frequently mentioned reasons.

Friendships were quite unstable at this age. A few weeks after the initial lists were made, these subjects were again asked to name their best friends. Sixty percent of the subjects rejected at least one of the children they had chosen originally, usually giving lack of recent contact ("don't see him very much") or a quarrel as the reason for the changed relationship (9).

The instability of friendships is probably related to rapid fluctuations in interests at this age. Two children with similar interests are likely to form an alliance, for they can understand and satisfy each other's needs, and their relationship is rewarding to both children. However, when interests change, they no longer provide mutual gratifications and the friendship is likely to be discontinued.

With increasing age, interests generally become more crystallized, and as we would expect, friendships become more enduring. Among seventh and eighth grade children, there is a high degree of consistency of friendship choices over a period of the 1½ years of study (142). Similar findings were obtained in an investigation of week-to-week friendship patterns in a summer camp setting. After an initial brief period of adjustment, preferences tended to become crystallized and stable throughout the remainder of the summer (88).

Emotional factors, as well as age, and level of cognitive development may influence the stability of a child's friendship patterns. Hospitalized, emotionally disturbed boys between 7 and 13 years of age manifested significantly less stable friendship patterns than a comparable group of campers and school boys of approximately the same age (43). In general, persisting mutual interests give a substantial basis for maintaining friendship. As with any other learned behavior, friendship responses tend to be repeated if they are continually reinforced.

SOCIALIZATION FUNCTIONS OF THE PEER GROUP

The peer group obviously provides an opportunity for the child to gain many immediate satisfactions. Here he finds companions who can keep up with his restless energy in a way that tired fathers with aching joints never could. He finds others of his own level of intellectual and social development with whom to talk and to compare notes. He finds the personnel necessary for group sports and games.

It would be a mistake, however, to dismiss the peer group as simply a way of keeping the child happy during this period of his life, for it serves much more extensive purposes in the child's socialization. One of the major functions of the peer group involves changing some of the child's attitudes. The peer group may strengthen existing attitudes, establish new ones, or weaken those that are in conflict with peer-group values. When peer-group values are in conflict with existing attitudes, the child's susceptibility to change will depend on the relative importance of peer acceptance.

There are two reasons why some children might be particularly susceptible to peer-group influences that conflict with parental values. The child who comes from a nonnurturant home atmosphere will be insecure and will have a strong need for acceptance and nurturance by others. In such a case, the child will not be too anxious about disappointing his parents, for they have not been nurturant. If the group will accept the child, he may adopt their values eagerly.

A second antecedent of susceptibility to peers has its origin in the failure to form a strong same-sex identification with a parent during the years 3 to 6. If the child has not made such an identification, he will be looking for substitute models with whom to identify, and he will be motivated to adopt the attitudes of peer-group leaders. Children who will be most likely to resist the peer group's values, if they contradict the parents', are those who view parents as nurturant, are anxious about violating parental standards, and have identified with these adult models (104). Moreover, boys who feel that they are not popular with peers are more subject to persuasion than children who feel liked and accepted by peers (104). Apparently a child who views his parents as accepting and the peer group as rejecting is, as might be expected, most likely to agree with the opinions of adults.

Conformity to Peers

The tendency to adopt the values and attitudes of others (conformity) is a personality variable that varies with age and is of different strength in different children. The special power of the peer group was clearly demonstrated in one study in which children were shown a single, black line (standard) and three black lines of different lengths (reference lines) and asked to state which of the three reference lines was equal in length to the standard (17). When tested alone, most children were accurate in their judgments. Some time after being tested alone, however, each child was placed in the same test situation with eight other peers who were "stooges." The subject was not aware that all the stooges had been instructed ahead of time by the experimenter to report aloud the wrong answer. The child under study was seated in the room so that five of the stooges reported their judgments before the subject did. Under these conditions all children showed an increased tendency to "go along" with the majority and make objectively inaccurate judgments. The younger children (ages 7-10) were more influenced by the incorrect majority than the older children (ages 10-13).

In a second experiment with different children, a teacher served as the "stooge" instead of peers. The teacher first made her judgment aloud, after which the child responded. It was found that these children were less influenced by a single teacher than the first group had been by a group of eight peers. Again, however, the younger children were much more influenced than the older children. The 7-year-old child would say,

"Miss —— is a teacher. She should have it most right" or "My teacher is bigger, she knows. Big people know better."

A 10-year-old boy said,

"I suppose they just look different to different people. She just don't see correctly—bad eyesight."

The results suggest that the child is more susceptible to the opinion of a group of peers than to one important adult but that, with age, susceptibility to both teacher and peers decreases.

Girls are more likely to conform to peer-group suggestions than boys are (30, 121, 163). This is perhaps not surprising in terms of the greater importance of interpersonal relationships with girls, and the lesser concern with activities for their own sake. As might be expected, the susceptibility of a child to peer influence is linked to his status in the group, with leaders being clearly less subject to influence than low-status group members (30, 75, 76, 169). Finally, individual personality factors may play a role in determining the strength of a child's conformity tendencies. On the one hand, dependent (89) and anxious (167) boys are more conforming than nondependent, nonanxious peers; on the other hand, hyperaggressive boys are more rigid and less susceptible to influence than normal boys (130): "The reasonable implication is that 'conformity' is not solely the province of the anxious, the dependent, the maladjusted; unwitting conformity in the face of ambiguity may be so, but conformity to the socially accepted demands of clearly defined situations seems a perfectly healthy response for a child . . ." (30, 312).

SUMMARY

The child's social environment expands markedly during the middle-childhood years. In the continuing interaction between the developing child and his expanding environment, some motives become strengthened and more clearly articulated, while others diminish in importance; new standards are set; and the child is confronted with new problems and challenges. The changing adjustments required of him during this period reflect in great measure his movement away from home as the one central focus of his activities. Beginning with kindergarten or first grade, the school becomes the center of the child's extrafamilial life, occupying almost half of his waking hours. The kinds of teachers he has, the teaching methods he encounters, and the types of textbooks he is exposed to, will have important effects not only on his academic progress, but upon his general capacity to meet and master new problems and challenges, and consequently his self-confidence and self-esteem. Teachers, teaching methods, and textbooks vary widely not only in overall quality, but in their appropriateness for individual children. While children generally prefer teachers who are kind, cheerful, fair and consistent in discipline, and enthusiastic, some children may progress better with a quiet, self-controlled teacher, while others may benefit more from a gregarious, outgoing, and less orderly teacher. Similarly, highly compulsive and highly anxious children may respond differently to highly structured teaching methods than children low in compulsivity and anxiety.

The child's school progress is also influenced by his family background. Parental interest in school and rewards for school achievement occur more frequently among middle-class than among lower-class parents. In addition, the middle-class child, having been exposed to a higher level of intellectual activity in the home, is likely to enter school better prepared to profit from the learning experiences to which he will be exposed.

In contrast, the culturally disadvantaged student, deprived of such experiences, is likely to be handicapped in approaching academic tasks. He tends to be limited in language development and basic cognitive abilities. In addition, both he and his parents may be less highly motivated and have lower aspirations for academic achievement. The disadvantaged child's progress in school may be further limited by feelings of inadequacy and a depressed self-concept resulting from the greater difficulties he encounters and from feelings of not "belonging" in a social setting characterized by middle-class goals and codes of behavior. There is an urgent need for the development of curricular approaches geared to the needs of disadvantaged students; better preparation of teachers for working with these children; and much more adequate physical facilities and support of services (e.g., remedial reading, speech pathology, psychological counseling, cultural enrichment and early admission programs).

The child's contact with his peers also expands greatly during the school years. The peer group provides an opportunity to learn to interact with age-mates, to deal with hostility and dominance, to relate to a leader, to lead others, to deal with social problems, and to develop a concept of himself. The child whose school experiences and interactions with peers are constructive and rewarding, and whose relationships with parents are favorable will develop a clearer self-image, increased competencies, and enhanced self-esteem. Unfavorable experiences in any of these areas is likely to limit the child's development of his potential, and to foster crippling conflicts, anxieties, and an impaired self-image.

The influence of the peer group appears stronger in America than in some other societies, where children live more in the family and less in peer society. The current rapidity of social change also affects the influence of the peer group, creating a hiatus between one generation and the next, and thus contributing to the role of age-mates in the socialization process. During the early years of middle childhood, informal groups, such as "the gang," formed by children themselves, predominate; between 10 and 14, however, children's groups tend to become more highly structured. Beginning at age 7 or 8, children begin to associate primarily with same-sex peers. This persists through middle childhood, although prepubertal girls—with their earlier growth spurt—may begin to express a tenuous interest in somewhat older boys. Sex cleavages and interest in activities also become increasingly evident throughout the school years, despite considerable overlap. Boys tend to be more involved with gang and other peer-group activities, while girls tend to have more intimate, individual interpersonal relationships.

Children having high social status with peers tend to be more socially aggressive, outgoing, enthusiastic, cheerful, intelligent, and friendly. In contrast, anxiety, uncertainty, social indifference, withdrawal, and hostility emerge as attributes of low-status or rejected children. The relationship of other attributes to popularity varies wih sex and age. Peer-group status is also related to social class, with lower-class children generally having lower status than their middle-class peers. Finally, a number of studies indicate that the roles played by adult leaders can significantly affect the likelihood of a child's profiting from peer-group experiences. Many socially isolated children could be helped to gain group acceptance and self-confidence if provided proper assistance.

Friendships tend to become more stable and enduring as middle childhood progresses. Mutual friends are likely to resemble each other in socioeconomic background, sex, maturity, general intelligence, personality characteristics, and mutual interests.

While there is a general tendency for children to conform to the values and attitudes of other members of the peer group, there are wide variations in the strength of this tendency. Girls are more likely to conform to peergroup suggestions than boys, and low status group members are more likely to conform than leaders. Furthermore, individual personality factors may play a role. On the one hand, dependent and anxious children are more conforming than nondependent, nonanxious peers; on the other hand, hyperaggressive children are more rigid and less susceptible to influence than normal children. Conformity is not solely the province of the anxious, dependent, or maladjusted child; unwitting conformity may be so, but conformity to the socially accepted demands of clearly defined situations is a perfectly healthy response for a child during this period.

Case Material. Peter B

Relations with Peers. During the early school years, Peter's adjustment to age-mates was clearly related to the passivity, dependency, and fear that characterized his personality during the preschool years. His lack of interest in boyish activities and his avoidance of stressful situations gradually led to social isolation from his peers. He seemed to find enjoyment in gardening, collecting rocks and flowers, and playing the piano. On several occasions he indicated that he might like to be a florist or a baker, occupations which do not require competitiveness or extensive social interaction with others.

When the boys and girls divided into play groups, Peter was usually found with the girls. Furthermore, he seemed oblivious to the teasing that resulted from this "siding with the girls." He enjoyed racing with them and willingly took part in the game of "house" which they initiated. He would willingly play father, milkman, horse, or any other role they suggested for him—finding special pleasure in the domestic details associated with the games that girls typically choose. Peter enjoyed flowers, and when the group went on a hike he pointed out every new variety, often gathering a straggly bouquet to which he clung during the excursion.

Peter was a follower, and was usually on the periphery of the group. His fear of fighting and competitive athletics prevented him from entering most of the play of boys his age and, finding himself alone so often, he became increasingly involved in his music, his garden, and his pretty rocks. Failure to obtain peer recognition and acceptance made it even more important that he retain the acceptance of his parents and teachers.

Adjustment to School.   Peter transferred his dependent and obedient relationship with his mother to his teacher and became a conforming and studious young boy. He chattered constantly about his teacher during supper and before bedtime, and waited after school so that he might walk home with her. Peter parroted his teacher's views on many issues, interposing phrases like, Miss A said this; or Miss A said that; or "Miss A's victrola is just like mine except that hers is brown and white."

Peter needed the teacher's praise and acceptance, and the possibility of failure in school was a major source of anxiety for him. He frequently told his mother, "I am afraid that I won't do everything right at school." Failure on a test represented potential rejection by the teacher, and Peter's concern over "doing well" in school resulted from his strong need to retain the teacher's approval.

Superego Development and Sources of Conflict.   During this period, Peter's conscience was excessively strict. Any act that was not specifically permitted by adults was viewed as "taboo." He often behaved like a policeman—informing a staff member of the day camp that "somebody was climbing the poles of the swing," or ". . . taking off their shoes," or ". . . carrying a toy outside." Peter interpreted all adult prohibitions literally, and he became the model of a "good" boy. He repressed any temptations to lie or to act aggressively. Perhaps he had guilt feelings about such dangerous thoughts, for he manifested many irrational fears of danger and unusually strong fears of being hurt. He would come into his mother's room at night, lean over her, and talk to her. As his mother phrased it, "Peter would be very close to me as if he wanted to tell me something."

Occasionally, Peter became frightened and upset before bedtime and he sought reassurance from his parents. He would ask rhetorically, "Nothing is going to hurt me tonight; I shall be all right, won't I?"

Peter also developed a number of psychosomatic symptoms. He had difficulty in keeping food down and often complained of cramps. He was hypochondriacal and became unduly concerned when he became ill. One particularly warm day, he insisted on wearing a sweater to Bible School because he was afraid he might catch cold, despite the fact that his mother assured him that he would not need it.

Peter had recurrent nightmares, and for a period of six months he had a strong fear of turtles. His excessive concern with injury to living things was dramatically illustrated one day while he was inspecting his plants in the family garden. He screamed whenever he found a worm that was eating a leaf or a leaf that was dying.

As might be anticipated, Peter never retaliated when attacked; he was afraid of fighting because it was bad and because he might be hurt.

During an interview at Fels, Peter said, "Some of the boys fight, but I never fight; I just pray that no one ever hits me."

When Peter was 8 years old, his day camp report described him as,

> . . . a pale youngster, very clean and neat looking, and rather girlish in his attitudes. He likes both his school and his teacher. When asked what he wanted to do when he grew up, Peter said, "I might play an instrument." His voice is shrill and he has many prissy mannerisms. In playing, he never seems to do anything quite right; his knees are at an angle when he runs, he wobbles when he hops, and is particularly futile in his attempts to catch a ball. He automatically makes a warding-off gesture first, ducking his head, and closing his hands after the ball has passed. Peter preferred to play "house" rather than engage in sports, but if someone yelled for him to join in a game he would prance over.
>
> Peter is an exceedingly "good" boy. He did a great deal of tattle-telling on all of the minor infractions committed by other children.

At age 10, much of Peter's adult personality was already determined. His orientation to authority was obedience; to peers it was fear and avoidance. His preferred reaction to stress was withdrawal rather than an attempt to deal with the problem. He had not developed traditional masculine interests or skills and his identification with a weak father had promoted the adoption of a passive and dependent attitude in problem situations. His major source of mastery gratification came from the school, and his musical interests and school success became the primary determinants of his vocational choice.

Case Material. Jack L

Relations with Peers. In contrast to Peter, Jack enjoyed peer activities and actively sought acceptance and leadership positions with his age-mates. He shunned solitary play and was only happy when he was surrounded by his "gang." Jack's popularity owed, in large measure, to his competence at traditional masculine skills; he was a fighter, an athlete, and a leader. He was a hero to the other boys because he incorporated the bravado, confidence, and aggression that represent, as we have seen, the ego-ideal of the average young boy.

At 9½ years of age, the following day camp report was written.

> Jack was in one of his most charming moods throughout the day camp session. He is becoming increasingly interested in athletics with a desire to learn new techniques. Several times he did his best to get a baseball game going, but turned down the chance to join in with the girls, considering that beneath his dignity. On the tennis court he was the swaggering male and at any suggestions from the girls he bellowed out, "Shut your mouth." He seems confident of his ability, amiable and poised in competition and occasionally teasing. He was the best swimmer in the group and the only child who could really dive. Jack was one of the more vivid and popular members of the group.

Jack's father conscientiously encouraged Jack's interest in sports, leadership, and fighting prowess. His father started a basketball and baseball team and, of course, Jack played on both teams. His father participated in these athletic groups and rewarded Jack for his efforts at mastery of gross motor skills.

School Achievement.   Although Jack's wholehearted adoption of traditional masculine activities led to success with his peers, it interfered with his motivation to excel at school. Jack's parents encouraged rebellion toward women. They felt that a man should not be submissive to a woman, and they transmitted this value to their son. Moreover, Jack's peers viewed conformity to the teacher as characteristic of the "sissy," and as Jack wanted their acceptance he was reluctant to become too studious or overly obedient. Jack told the Fels interviewer that he tries not to cry if someone hits him: "I take it, I have to; though when I'm hit in the belly hard, it hurts. They call you sissy if you cry." He was aware of the fact that his friends would not approve of a boy who was too smart, and he told the interviewer that he did not "care much for boys who study too hard." The implication was that this behavior was not appropriate for a "real" boy. Thus, Jack became rebellious in school and was one of the poorer students.

He typically made every effort to be the constant center of attention. One day he kept his four-buckle boots on with all the buckles undone and flapping, and visited the other children's desks, proudly displaying the Air Force insignia on his shirt. While the class gave answers to arithmetic problems, Jack rested his head on his desk, and yawned and stretched with a dramatic flair. He was sent to the board to do problems and, when told that he didn't need to take his book, he made a pretense of slamming it on his desk. He clowned at the board, pretended to dust the erasers, and rolled his eyes in order to get the attention of the class. On one occasion, the teacher went out of the room briefly and instructed the children to put down their heads and rest. Suddenly she heard screams from the room. When she returned, Jack was standing on his desk doing a comic dance and the class was in stitches.

Superego and Sources of Conflict. Unlike Peter, Jack was not guilty over his aggressive behavior, and he enjoyed fighting and wrestling. However, his conscience did not allow him to express passive or dependent behavior. He was afraid to cry or show his inner feelings. He put on a facade of independence and denied any need for help or affection from others. Jack and Peter each placed strong prohibitions on specific behaviors, but, while Jack inhibited dependence, Peter inhibited aggression. Nevertheless, the bases for these inhibitions were similar—the desire to retain parental acceptance.

The major differences we saw emerging in Peter and Jack at age 3 had become crystallized and magnified by age 10. The pattern of sex-role interests, relationship to authority, reactions to stress, concern with intellectual competence, and major conflicts were relatively fixed. The future behavior of these two boys will be guided, in large measure, by the needs, conflicts, and reaction patterns laid down during the first decade of their lives.

References

1. Allen, B. H. Development of children's stereotype of the female school teacher. *Dissert. Abstr.*, 1962, *23*, 231–232.
2. Anastasi, A., & D'Angelo, R. Y. A comparison of Negro and white preschoolers in language development and Goodenough, Draw-a-man I.Q. *J. genet. Psychol.*, 1952, *81*, 147–165.
3. Anderson, H. H. An experimental study of dominative behavior and integrative behavior in children of preschool age. *J. soc. Psychol.*, 1937, *8*, 335–345.
4. Anderson, H. H. Domination and integration in the social behavior of young children in an experimental play situation. *Genet. Psychol. Monogr.*, 1937, *19*, 341–408.
5. Anderson, H. H., & Anderson, G. L. Social development. In L. Carmichael (Ed.), *Manual of child psychology.* New York: Wiley, 1954 (2nd ed).
6. Anderson, H. H., Brewer, J. E., & Reed, M. F. Studies of teachers' classroom personalities. III. Follow-up studies of the effects of dominative and integrative contacts on children's behavior. *Appl. Psychol. Monogr.*, 1946, No. 11.
7. Anderson, H. H., & Brewer, J. E. Studies of teachers' classroom personalities. II. Effects of teachers' dominative and integrative contacts on children's classroom behavior. *Appl. Psychol. Monogr.*, 1946, No. 8.
8. Anderson, H. H., & Brewer, J. E. Studies of teachers' classroom personalities. I. Dominative and socially integrative behavior of kindergarten teachers. *Appl. Psychol. Monogr.*, 1945, No. 6.
9. Austin, M. C., & Thompson, G. C. Children's friendship: a study of the bases on which children select and reject their best friends. *J. educ. Psychol.*, 1948, *39*, 101–116.
10. Ausubel, D. P. How reversible are the cognitive and motivational effects of

cultural deprivation? Implications for teaching the culturally deprived child. *Urban Educ.,* 1964, *1,* 16–38.

11. Ayers, L. P. The effect of physical defects on school progress. *Psychol. Clin.,* 1909, *3,* 71–77.

12. Bailyn, L. Mass media and children: a study of exposure habits and cognitive effects. *Psychol. Monogr.,* 1959, *73,* 1–48.

13. Baldwin, W. K. The social position of the educable mentally retarded child in the regular grades in the public schools. *Except. Child.,* 1958, *25,* 106–108.

14. Barbe, W. B. Peer relationships of children of different intelligence levels. *Sch. Soc.,* 1954, *80,* 60–62.

15. Beck, J. M., & Saxe, R. W. (Eds.) *Teaching the culturally disadvantaged pupil.* Springfield, Ill.: Thomas, 1965.

16. Becker, H. The career of the Chicago public school teacher. *Amer. sociol. Rev.,* 1952, *17,* 470–476

17. Berenda, R. W *The influence of the group on the judgments of children.* New York: King's Crown Press, 1950.

18. Bernstein, B. Social class, linguistic codes and grammatical elements. *Lang. Speech,* 1962, *5,* 221–240.

19. Blake, M. T. Factors influencing teacher success. *Dissert. Abst.,* 1966, *27,* 990.

20. Blom, G. E., Waite, R. R., & Zimet, S. Content of first grade reading books. *The read. Teach.,* 1968, *21,* 317–323.

21. Blom, G. E., Waite, R. R., & Zimet, C. F. Ethnic integration and urbanization of a first grade reading textbook: a research study. *Psychol. Sch.,* 1967, *4,* 176–181.

22. Blood, R. O., & Livant, W. P. The use of space within the cabin group. *J. soc. Issues,* 1957, *13,* 47–53.

23. Bloom, B. S., Davis, A., & Hess, R. *Compensatory education for cultural deprivation.* New York: Holt, Rinehart and Winston, 1965.

24. Bradman, M., & Kelley, K. C. Summertime and the learning wasn't easy. *New York State Educ.,* 1963, *50,* 20–22.

25. Brown, O. H., Fuller, F. F., & Richek, H. G. A comparison of self-perceptions of prospective elementary and secondary school teachers. *Psychol. Sch.,* 1967, *4,* 21–24.

26. Bonney, M. E. Relationships between social success, family size, socioeconomic home background, and intelligence among school children in grades III to V. *Sociometry,* 1944, *7,* 26–39.

27. Bonney, M. E. Sex differences in social success and personality traits. *Child Develpm.,* 1944, *15,* 63–79.

28. Bonney, M. E. The constancy of sociometric scores and their relationship to teacher judgments of social success and to personality self-ratings. *Sociometry,* 1943, *6,* 409–424.

29. Bonney, M. E. A study of the relation of intelligence, family size, and sex differences with mutual friendships in the primary grades. *Child Develpm.,* 1942, *13,* 79–100.

30. Campbell, J. D. Peer relations in childhood. In M. L. Hoffman & L. W. Hoffman (Eds.), *Review of child development research,* Vol. I. New York: Russell Sage Foundation, 1964, 289–322.

31. Campbell, J. D., & Yarrow, M. R. Personal and situational variables in adaptation to change. *J. soc. Issues,* 1958, *14,* 29–46.

32. Castaneda, A., McCandless, B. R., & Palermo, D. S. The children's form of the Manifest Anxiety Scale. *Child Develpm.,* 1956, *27,* 317–327.

33. Challman, R. C. Factors influencing friendships among preschool children. *Child Develpm.*, 1932, *3*, 146–158.

34. Cheong, G. S. C., & DeVault, M. V. Pupils' perceptions of teachers. *J. educ. Res.*, 1966, *59*, 446–449.

35. Cheyney, A. B. Teachers of the culturally disadvantaged. *Except. Children*, 1966, *33*, 83–88.

36. Child, I. L., Potter, E. H., & Levine, E. M. Children's textbooks and personality development: an exploration in the social psychology of education. *Psychol. Monogr.*, 1946, *60*, No. 3.

37. Clarke, H. H., & Clarke, D. H. Social status and mental health of boys as related to their maturity, structural, and strength characteristics. *Res. Quart. Amer. Ass. Hlth. Phys. Educ. Recr.*, 1961, *32*, 326–334.

38. Coleman, J. S., et al. *Equality of education opportunity.* Washington, D.C.: U.S. Government Printing Office, 1966.

39. Collier, M. J., & Gaier, E. L. The hero in the preferred childhood stories of college men. *Amer. Imago*, 1959, *16*, 177–194.

40. Collier, M. J., & Gaier, E. L. Adult reactions to preferred childhood stories. *Child Develpm.*, 1958, *29*, 97–103.

41. Commoss, H. H. Some characteristics related to social isolation of second grade children. *J. educ. Psychol.*, 1962, *53*, 38–43.

42. Conant, J. B. Social dynamite in our large cities. In *Social dynamite: the report of the conference on unemployed, out-of-school youth in urban areas.* Washington, D.C.: National Committee for Children and Youth, 1961.

43. Davids, A., & Parenti, A. N. Time orientation and interpersonal relations of emotionally disturbed and normal children. *J. abnorm. soc. Psychol.*, 1958, *57*, 299–305.

44. Davidson, K. S., & Sarason, S. B. Test anxiety and classroom observations. *Child Develpm.*, 1961, *32*, 199–210.

45. Davis, A. *Social class influences upon learning.* Cambridge, Mass.: Harvard Univer. Press, 1948.

46. Davis, A., & Dollard, J. *Children of bondage: the personality development of Negro youth in the urban South.* Washington, D.C.: American Council of Education, 1940.

47. Davis, K. The sociology of parent youth conflict. *Amer. sociol. Rev.*, 1940, *5*, 523–535.

48. DeCharms, R., & Moeller, G. H. Values expressed in American children's readers: 1800–1950. *J. abnorm. soc. Psychol.*, 1962, *64*, 136–142.

49. Deutsch, M. The role of social class in language development and cognition. *Amer. J. Orthopsychiat.*, 1965, *35*, 78–88.

50. Deutsch, M. Social and psychological perspectives on the development of the disadvantaged learner. *J. Negro Educ.*, 1964, *33*, 232–244.

51. Deutsch, M. The disadvantaged child and the learning process. In A. H. Passow (Ed.), *Education in depressed areas.* New York: Columbia Univer. Press, 1963, 163–179.

52. Deutsch, M. Minority group and class status as related to social and personality factors in scholastic achievement. *Monogr. soc. appl. Anthrop.*, 2, 1960.

53. Diamond, S. Kibbutz and shtetl: the history of an idea. *Soc. Probl.*, 1957, *5*, 68–100.

54. Eron, L. D. Relationship of TV viewing habits and aggressive behavior in children. *J. abnorm. soc. Psychol.*, 1957, *64*, 359–372.

55. Feldhusen, J. F., & Klausmeier, H. J. Anxiety, intelligence, and achievement in

children of low, average, and high intelligence. *Child Develpm.*, 1962, *33*, 403–409.

56. Flanders, N. A., & Havumaki, S. The effect of teacher-pupil contacts involving praise on the sociometric choices of students. *J. educ. Psychol.*, 1960, *51*, 65–68.

57. Flavell, J. H., et al. *Development of role taking and communication in children.* New York: Wiley, 1968.

58. Foley, W. J. Teaching disadvantaged pupils. In J. M. Beck & R. W. Saxe (Eds.), *Teaching the culturally disadvantaged pupil.* Springfield, Ill.: Thomas, 1965, 89–107.

59. Franco, D. The child's perception of "The Teacher" as compared to his perception of "The Mother." *Dissert. Abstr.*, 1964, *24*, 3414–3415.

60. Frost, B. P. Intelligence, manifest anxiety, and scholastic achievement. *Alberta J. educ. Res.*, 1965, *11*, 167–175.

61. Furfey, P. H. Some factors influencing the selection of boys' chums. *J. appl. Psychol.* 1927, *11*, 47–51.

62. Gage, N. L. Desirable behaviors of teachers. *Urban Educ.*, 1965, *1*, 85–95.

63. Gaier, E. L., & Collier, M. J. The latency-stage story preferences of American and Finnish children. *Child Develpm.*, 1960, *31*, 431–451.

64. Gallagher, J. J. Social status of children related to intelligence, propinquity, and social perception. *Elem. sch. J.*, 1958, *58*, 225–231.

65. Goldberg, M. L. Teachers for disadvantaged children. In A. Kerber & B. Bommarito (Eds.), *The schools and the urban crisis.* New York: Holt, Rinehart and Winston, 1966.

66. Gordon, E. W. Educational achievement in the Prince Edward County Free School, 1963–1964. In E. W. Gordon & D. A. Wilkerson (Eds.), *Compensatory education for the disadvantaged. Programs and practices: preschool through college.* New York: College Entrance Examination Board, 1966.

67. Gordon, E. W., & Wilkerson, D. A. *Compensatory education for the disadvantaged. Programs and practices: preschool through college.* New York: College Entrance Examination Board, 1966.

68. Gottlieb, D. Teaching and students: the views of Negro and white teachers. *Sociol. Educ.*, 1964, *37*, 345–353.

69. Graham, K. A., Mathematics for the disadvantaged child. In J. M. Beck & R. W. Saxe (Eds.), *Teaching the culturally disadvantaged pupil.* Springfield, Ill. Thomas, 1965.

70. Greenberg, J. W., Gerver, J. M., Chall, J., & Davidson, H. H. Attitudes of children from a deprived environment toward achievement-related concepts. *J. educ. Res.*, 1965, *59*, 57–62.

71. Greer, D. R. Test anxiety, psychological arousal and test performance of first grade children. *Dissert. Abstr.*, 1966, *27*, 953.

72. Grimes, J. W., & Allinsmith, W. Compulsivity, anxiety, and school achievement. *Merrill-Palmer Quart.*, 1961, *7*, 247–269.

73. Groff, P. J. Dissatisfactions in teaching the culturally deprived child. *Phi Delta Kappa,* 1963, *45*, 76.

74. Hart, F. W. Ten thousand high school seniors. In F. W. Hart, *Teachers and teaching.* New York: Macmillan, 1936.

75. Harvey, O. J., & Consalvi, C. Status and conformity to pressures in informal groups. *J. abnorm. soc. Psychol.*, 1960, *60*, 182–187.

76. Harvey, O. J., & Rutherford, J. Status in the informal group: influences and influencibility at differing age levels. *Child Develpm.*, 1960, *31*, 377–385.

77. Havighurst, R. J. & Breese, F. H. Relation between ability and social status in a midwestern community. III. Primary mental abilities. *J. educ. Psychol.*, 1947, *38*, 241–247.

78. Havighurst, R. J., & Janke, L. L. Relations between ability and social status in a midwestern community. I. Ten-year-old children. *J. educ. Psychol.*, 1944, *35*, 357–368.

79. Heathers, G. School organization; non grading, dual progress, and team teaching. In J. I. Goodlan (Ed.), *The changing American school,* Part II. (*65th Yearb. nat. Soc. Stud. Educ.*) Chicago: Univer. Chicago Press, 1966.

80. Heil, L. M., & Washburne, C. Characteristics of teachers related to children's progress. *J. teacher Educ.*, 1961, *12*, 401–406.

81. Hill, K. T. Relation of test anxiety defensiveness and intelligence to sociometric status. *Child Develpm.*, 1963, *34*, 767–776.

82. Hill, K. T., & Sarason, S. B. The relation of test anxiety and defensiveness to test and school performance over the elementary-school years: a further longitudinal study. *Monogr. Soc. Res. Child Develpm.*, 1966, *31*, No. 2, 1–76.

83. Hilliard, G. H., & Troxwell, E. Informational background as a factor in reading readiness and reading progress. *Elem. sch. J.*, 1957, *38*, 255–263.

84. Hollingshead, A. B. *Elmtown's youth: the impact of social class on youth.* New York: Wiley, 1949.

85. Horowitz, F. D. The relationship of anxiety, self-concept, and sociometric status among fourth, fifth, and sixth grade children. *J. abnorm. soc. Psychol.*, 1962, *65*, 212–214.

86. Hsu, F. L. K., Watrous, B. G., & Lord, E. M. Culture pattern and adolescent behavior. *Int. J. soc. Psychiat.*, 1960/61, *7*, 33–35.

87. Hudgins, B. B., Smith, L. M., & Johnson, T. J. The child's perception of his classmates. *J. genet. Psychol.*, 1962, *101*, 401–405.

88. Hunt, J. McV., & Solomon, R. L. The stability and some correlates of group-status in a summer-camp group of young boys. *Amer. J. Psychol.*, 1942, *55*, 33–45.

89. Jakubczak, L. F., & Walters, R. H. Suggestibility as dependency behavior. *J. abnorm. soc. Psychol.*, 1959, *59*, 102–107.

90. Jennings, F. Textbooks and trapped idealists. *Saturday Rev.*, January 18, 1964, 57–59, 77–78.

91. Jersild, A. T. Characteristics of teachers who are "liked best" and "disliked most." *J. exp. Educ.*, 1940, *9*, 139–151.

92. Justman, J. Academic aptitude and reading test scores of disadvantaged children showing varying degrees of mobility. *J. educ. Measmt.*, 1965, *2*, 151–155.

93. Kabasakalian, L. The grade school from childhood reality to school reality. *Dissert. Abstr.*, 1964, *25*, 615.

94. Kagan, J. Personality development. In I. J. Janis (Ed.), *Personality dynamics.* Harcourt, Brace & World, in press.

95. Kagan, J. Reflection-impulsivity: the generality and dynamics of conceptual tempo. *J. abnorm. Psychol.*, 1966, *71*, 17–24.

96. Keller, E. D., & Rowley, V. N. Anxiety, intelligence, and scholastic achievement in elementary school children. *Psychol. Rep.*, 1962, *11*, 19–22.

97. Keniston, K. Social change and youth in America. *Daedalus*, Winter, 1962, 145–171.

98. Kerber, A., & Bommarito, B. (Eds.) *The schools and the urban crises.* New York: Holt, Rinehart and Winston, 1966.

99. Klineberg, O. Life is fun in a smiling, fair-skinned world. *Saturday Rev.*, February 16, 1963, 75–77 & 87.

100. Kosier, K. P., & DeVault, M. V. Effects of teacher personality on pupil personality. *Psychol. Sch.*, 1967, *4*, 40–44.

101. Leeds, C. P., & Cook, W. W. The construction and differential value of a scaie for determining teacher pupil attitudes. *J. exp. Educ.*, 1947, *16*, 149–159.

102. Lefevre, C. Inner-city school—as the children see it. *Elem. sch. J.*, 1966, *67*, 8–15.

103. LeShan, L. L. Time orientation and social class. *J. abnorm. soc. Psychol.*, 1952, *47*, 589–592.

104. Lesser, G. S., & Abelson, R. P. Personality correlates of persuasibility in children. In I. C. Janis, C. I. Hovland *et al.* (Eds.), *Personality and persuasibility*, New Haven, Conn.: Yale Univer. Press, 1959, 187–206.

105. Lesser, G. S., Fifer, G., & Clark, D. H. Mental abilities of children from different social class and different cultural groups. *Monogr. Soc. Res. Child Develpm.*, 1965, *30*, No. 4.

106. Levine, M., Wesolowski, J. C., & Corbett, F. J. Pupil turnover and academic performance in an inner city elementary school. *Psychol. Sch.*, 1966, *3*, 153–158.

107. Lewin, K., Lippitt, R., & White, R. K. Patterns of aggressive behavior in experimentally created "social climates." *J. soc. Psychol.*, 1939, *10*, 271–299.

108. Linton, R. Age and sex categories. *Amer. sociol. Rev.*, 1942, *7*, 589–603.

109. Lippit, R., & White, R. K. An experimental study of leadership and group life. In T. M. Newcomb & E. L. Hartley (Eds.), *Readings in social psychology*. New York: Holt, Rinehart and Winston, 1947, 315–330.

110. Marburger, C. L. Consideration for educational planning. In A. H. Passow (Ed.), *Education in depressed areas*. New York: Columbia Univer. Press, 1963, 298–321.

111. Maslow, A. H., & Diaz-Guerrero, R. Delinquency as a value disturbance. In J. G. Peatman & E. L. Hartley (Eds.), *Festschrift for Gardner Murphy*. New York: Harper & Row, 1960, 228–240.

112. McKeachie, W. J. Anxiety in the college classroom. *J. educ. Res.*, 1951, *55*, 153–160.

113. McNeil, J. D. Programed instruction versus usual classroom procedures in teaching boys to read. *Amer. educ. Res. J.*, 1964, *1*, 113–119.

114. McNeil, J. D., & Keislar, E. R. Individual differences and effectiveness of auto instruction at the primary grade level. *Calif. J. educ. Res.*, 1961, *12*, 160–164.

115. Merbaum, A. D. Need for achievement in Negro and white children. *Dissert. Abstr.*, 1962, *23*, 693–694.

116. Michalak, J. City life in primers. New York: *The Herald Tribune*, January 26, 1965.

117. Money, J. (Ed.) *Reading disability: progress and research needs in dyslexia.* Baltimore: Johns Hopkins Press, 1962.

118. Mussen, P., & Rutherford, E. Effects of aggressive cartoons on children's aggressive play. *J. abnorm. soc. Psychol.* 1961, *62*, 461–464.

119. Northway, M. L. Outsiders: a study of the personality patterns of children least acceptable to their age mates. *Sociometry*, 1944, *7*, 10–25.

120. Northway, M. L., & Rooks, M. McC. Creativity and sociometric status in children. *Sociometry*, 1956, *18*, 450–457.

121. Patel, A. E., & Gordon, J. E. Some personal and situational determinants of yielding to influence. *J. abnorm. soc. Psychol.*, 1960, *61*, 411–418.

122. Pavenstedt, E. A comparison of the child-rearing environment of upper-lower and very low-lower-class families. *Amer. J. Orthopsychiat.*, 1965, *35*, 89–98.
123. Peck, R. F., & Galliani, C. Intelligence, ethnicity, and social roles in adolescent society. *Sociometry*, 1962, *25*, 64–72.
124. Phillips, E. L., Shenker, S., & Revitz, P. The assimilation of the new child into the group. *Psychiatry*, 1951, *14*, 319–325.
125. Podendorf, I. Science for the disadvantaged child. In J. M. Beck & R. W. Saxe, (Eds.), *Teaching the culturally disadvantaged pupil.* Springfield, Ill.: Thomas, 1965.
126. Polansky, N., Lippitt, R., & Redl, F. An investigation of behavioral contagion in groups. *Human Relat.*, 1950, *3*, 319–348.
127. Pope, B. Socioeconomic contrasts in children's peer culture prestige values. *Genet. Psychol. Monogr.*, 1950, *42*, 81–158.
128. Porterfield, O. V., & Schlichting, H. F. Peer status and reading achievement. *J. educ. Res.*, 1961, *54*, 291–297.
129. Portuges, S. H., & Feshbach, N. D. The effects of teacher's reinforcement style upon imitative behavior of children. Paper read at the meeting of the American Educational Research Association, Chicago, February, 1968.
130. Raush, H. L., Farbman, I., & Llewellyn, L. G. Person, setting, and change in social interaction: II. *Human Relat.*, 1960, *13*, 305–322.
131. Reese, H. W. Manifest anxiety and achievement test performance. *J. educ. Psychol.*, 1961, *52*, 132–135.
132. *Report of the National Advisory Commission on Civil Disorders.* New York: Bantam Books, 1968.
133. Richardson, S. Personal communication.
134. Riessman, F. The culturally deprived child. New York: Harper & Row, 1962.
135. Ruebush, B. K. Children's behavior as a function of anxiety and defensiveness. *Dissert. Abstr.*, 1966, *27*, 971.
136. Sarason, S. B., Davidson, K. S., Lightfall, F. F., Waite, R. R., & Ruebush, B. K. *Anxiety in elementary school children.* New York: Wiley, 1960.
137. Sarason, S. B., Hill, K. T., & Zimbardo, P. G. A longitudinal study of the relation of test anxiety to performance on intelligence and achievement tests. *Monogr. Soc. Res. Child Develpm.*, 1964, *29*, No. 7.
138. Schmuck, R. Some aspects of classroom social climate. *Psychol. Sch.*, 1966, *3*, 59–65.
139. Schramm, W., Lyle, J., & Parker, E. B. *Television in the lives of our children.* Stanford, Calif.: Stanford Univer. Press, 1961.
140. Sears, P. S. *The effect of classroom conditions on the strength of achievement motive and work output on elementary school children.* U.S. Dept. of HEW, Office of Educ., Cooperative research project. No. 873. Stanford, Calif.: Stanford Univer. Press, 1963.
141. Shands, H. C. Anxiety, anaclitic object, and the sign function: Comments on early developments in the use of symbols. *Amer. J. Orthopsychiat.*, 1954, *23*, 84–97.
142. Singer, A., Jr. Certain aspects of personality and their relation to certain group modes, and constancy of friendship choices. *J. educ. Res.*, 1951, *45*, 33–42.
143. Skinner, B. F. Teaching machines. *Scientific Amer.*, 1961, *205*, 90–107.
144. Smith, A. J. A developmental study of group processes. *J. genet. Psychol.*, 1960, *97*, 29–30.
145. Smith, G. H. Sociometric study of best-liked and least-liked children. *Elem. sch. J.*, 1950, *51*, 77–85.

146. Spaulding, R. L. Personality and social development: peer and school influences. *Rev. educ. Res.*, 1964, *34*, 588–598.
147. Spiro, M. E. *Children of the kibbutz.* Cambridge, Mass.: Harvard Univer. Press, 1958.
148. Stakenas, R. G. Evaluative stress, fear of failure and academic achievement. *Dissert. Abstr.*, 1966, *27*, 401.
149. Stendler, C. B. Social class differences in parental attitudes toward school at grade I level. *Child Develpm.*, 1951, *22*, 36–46.
150. Stendler, C. B., & Young, N. Impact of first grade entrance upon the socialization of the child: changes after eight months of school. *Child Develpm.*, 1951, *22*, 113–122.
151. Stevenson, H. W., & Odom, R. D. The relation of anxiety to children's performance on learning and problem-solving tasks. *Child Develpm.*, 1965, *36*, 1003–1012.
152. Stodolsky, S. S., & Lesser, G. Learning patterns in the disadvantaged. *Harv. educ. Rev.*, 1967, *37*, 546–593.
153. Stone, L. J., & Church, J. *Childhood and adolescence.* New York: Random House, 1968 (2nd ed.).
154. Strom, R. D. (Ed.) *The inner-city classroom: teacher behaviors.* Columbus, Ohio: Merrill, 1966.
155. Sutton-Smith, B., Rosenberg, B. G., Morgan, E. F., Jr. Development of sex differences in play choices during preadolescence. *Child Develpm.*, 1963, *34*, 119–126.
156. Symonds, P. M. Personality adjustment of women teachers. *Amer. J. Orthopsychiat.*, 1941, *11*, 14–20.
157. Templin, M. C. Norms on screening test for articulation for ages three through eight. *J. Speech & Hearing Disorders*, 1953, *8*, 323–331.
158. Thomas, D. R. Oral language, sentence structure and vocabulary of kindergarten children living in low socioeconomic urban areas. *Dissert. Abstr.*, 1962, *23*, 101.
159. Toigo, R. Social status and schoolroom aggression in third-grade children. *Genet. Psychol. Monogr.*, 1965, *71*, 221–268.
160. Tuddenham, R. D. Studies in reputation: I. Sex and grade differences in school children's evaluation of their peers. II. The diagnosis of social adjustment. *Psychol. Monogr.*, 1952, *66*, No. 333.
161. Tuddenham, R. D. Studies in reputation: I. Sex and grade differences in school children's evaluation of their peers. *Psychol. Monogr.*, 1951, *66*, No. 1.
162. Tuddenham, R. D. Studies in reputation: III. Correlates of popularity among elementary school children. *J. educ. Psychol.*, 1951, *42*, 257–276.
163. Tuma, E., & Livson, N. Family socio-economic status and adolescent attitudes to authority. *Child Develpm.*, 1960, *31*, 387–399.
164. Vosk, J. S. Study of Negro children with learning difficulties at the outset of their school careers. *Amer. J. Orthopsychiat.*, 1966, *36*, 32–40.
165. Waite, R. R. Further attempts to integrate and urbanize first grade reading textbooks: a research study. *J. Negro Educ.*, in press.
166. Waite, R. R., Blom, G. E., Zimet, C. F., & Edge, S. First-grade reading textbooks. *Elem. sch. J.* 1967, *67*, 366–374.
167. Walters, R. H., Marshall, W. E., & Shooter, J. R. Anxiety, isolation, and susceptibility to social influence. *J. Pers.*, 1960, *28*, 518–529.
168. Wilkerson, D. A. Programs and practices in compensatory education for disadvantaged children. *Rev. educ. Res.*, 1965, *35*, 426–440.

169. Wilson, R. S. Personality patterns, source attractiveness, and conformity. *J. Pers.*, 1960, *28*, 186–199.
170. Wittick, M. L. Language arts for the disadvantaged. In J. M. Beck & R. W. Saxe (Eds.), *Teaching the culturally disadvantaged pupil.* Springfield, Ill.: Thomas, 1965.
171. White, R. W. *The abnormal personality: a textbook.* New York: Ronald Press, 1948.
172. White, W. F., & Dekle, O. T. Effect of teacher's motivational cues on achievement level in elementary grades. *Psychol. Rep.*, 1966, *18*, 351–356.
173. Wright, H. F. Psychological development in Midwest. *Child Develpm.*, 1956, *27*, 265–286.
174. Yamamoto, L., Lembright, M. L., & Corrigan, A. M. Intelligence, creative thinking, and sociometric choice among fifth-grade children. *J. exp. Educ.*, 1966, *34*, 83–89.
175. Yando, R. M., & Kagan, J. The effect of teacher tempo on the child. *Child Develpm.*, 1968, *39*, 27–34.
176. Yarrow, L. J., & Yarrow, M. R. Leadership and interpersonal change. *J. soc. Issues*, 1958, *14*, 47–50.
177. Ziller,. R. C., & Behringer, R. D. A longitudinal study of the assimilation of the new child in a group. *Human Relat.*, 1961, *14*, 121–133.
178. Zimet, C. F. A sociological review of the content of American elementary reading textbooks: 1600–1967. *Teachers Coll. Rec.*, in press.
179. Zimet, C. F. Sex role models in primary reading texts of the U.S.A.: 1600–1966. A lecture in education at the University of Denver, 1967.

part V
Adolescence

14
Adolescence

I. Physical Change, Sex, and Social Development

Adolescence has traditionally been viewed as a critical period in development, not only in America but in many other cultures as well—particularly the more technologically advanced societies. References to the "storm and stress" of the years between childhood and nominal adulthood have been common, both in popular discussion and in the writings of novelists, dramatists, and poets. Behavioral scientists have also tended to agree that adolescence represents a period of particular stress in our society. Some, particularly the more biologically oriented, have emphasized the adjustments required by the physiological changes associated with puberty, including increases in sex hormones and changes in body structure and function. Others have tended to hold the culture primarily responsible for the adolescent's difficulties, emphasizing the numerous, highly concentrated demands which our society has traditionally made upon youth at this time —demands for independence, for heterosexual and peer adjustments, for vocational preparation, for the development of a basic, guiding philosophy of life. In many cultures in which these demands are neither as complex nor as restricted to one limited age period as in our society, adolescence is not viewed as a particularly difficult period of adjustment.

While we encounter differences of opinion regarding the relative importance of biological, social, and psychological factors, there is nevertheless general agreement that the adolescent period has traditionally presented special adjustment problems in our society. In contrast, there is currently a good deal of disagreement, even among acknowledged authorities in child development, about whether the problems of adolescents have become more acute in recent years, with a consequent heightening of adolescent difficulties and conflicts with the adult culture. Popular magazines, newspapers, and television programs are replete these days with conflicting accounts of the values, attitudes, and behavior of today's adolescents.

We are told by some alarmed observers that youth today is more rebellious, more troubled emotionally, more promiscuous sexually, less idealistic, and more critical of the values and standards of the adult culture and more "disengaged" from them. All manner of plausible sounding "evidence" is cited in support of this "distressing" state of affairs: adolescent rampages at holiday resorts; riots in minority group ghettos; sit-ins on school and college campuses; increased use of drugs—from "pep" pills and glue-sniffing to marijuana and LSD; pregnancy among adolescent girls, venereal disease, and suicide; highly vocal demonstrations, initially for social concerns, such as civil rights, and increasingly at present in support of personal freedom from parental or other established social constraints. Even teenage music and fashions in dress and personal appearance are cited as examples of this presumably deteriorating state of affairs.

In contrast, we are told by other observers, and with equal assurance, that adolescents today are brighter and better informed than their parents; less sentimental, but more genuinely idealistic; more serious; no more promiscuous in sexual behavior than their elders were at adolescence, but more open, honest, and tolerant; and less hypocritical, obsessed, or troubled in their sexual attitudes and beliefs. We are informed that youth are more serious about the fundamental purposes of education and less satisfied merely to "get by" with acceptable grades; that they feel a greater sense of social responsibility and concern for the welfare of others; and that, if anything, they come closer to having a sense of their own identity and are less emotionally conflicted than their parents were at the same age.

Still a third group of observers feel that presumed differences—good or bad—between today's adolescents and those of earlier generations are largely illusory, and are more a matter of form than of substance, or that they stem from unwarranted generalizations based upon the behavior of vocal, but relatively small, numbers of atypical youth. Protagonists of this latter view remind us that every generation of adults has tended to view its successors with alarm, and that there have always been differences between generations in social and political beliefs, tastes and fashions, and fundamental liberalism or conservatism.

It will be one of our major aims in this and the following chapter to examine the evidence behind these conflicting views, and to try to arrive at a balanced judgment about the problems confronting adolescents and their responses to these problems. In order to approach this task, however, it will be necessary to consider separately the problems facing youth in general and those confronting special subgroups of adolescents within American culture. In our opinion, much of the current confusion regarding adolescence stems from the widespread tendency to assume that all adolescents are alike, face the same problems and demands, and react to them in similar fashion. Thus, if some late adolescents engage in conspicuous demonstrations against the dominant values of the adult culture, it is frequently concluded that a majority of today's youth are in active rebellion against society, and to a degree unprecedented in earlier generations. Or if an adolescent crime wave occurs in one of our larger urban ghettos, we can anticipate a sudden rash of television programs and articles in the popular press encouraging the view that an entire generation stands on the brink of lawlessness.

Available evidence, however, does not support such deceptive oversimplifications. It is certainly true, as we shall see, that adolescents share a number of common experiences and problems. For example, all undergo the physiological and physical changes of puberty and later adolescent growth. All face the need for establishing an identity of their own—some kind of personal answer to the age-old question, "Who am I?" All are ultimately confronted with the need to earn a living and to make their own way as independent members of society.

But the fact remains, despite such similarities, that adolescents clearly are not all alike and do not all face the same environmental demands. The problems confronting a socioeconomically deprived youth from a broken home living in a segregated urban ghetto are vastly different from the problems faced by an economically favored adolescent from a loving and protective suburban family; and the responses of youths from such widely disparate environments may be expected to differ significantly.

An appreciation of the problems and developmental demands facing adolescents in general, and of those confronting particular subgroups in our society, is necessary if we are to avoid misleading oversimplifications regarding adolescent behavior and adjustment. In this chapter our attention will be directed primarily to considerations of adolescent growth and development, the adjustment demands facing youth generally in our culture and the responses of adolescents to these demands. We shall consider the development of independence, sexual maturation, peer relations, and preparation for a vocation. In the final chapter, we shall examine the problems confronting young people generally in developing a system of values and a sense of ego identity, as well as the special problems of those who for one reason or another—social, psychological, economic, or ideological—find themselves outside the mainstream of adolescent culture in America.

PHYSICAL CHANGES IN ADOLESCENCE

Among the most dramatic of all developmental events, and one to which all youth must adjust, is the host of interrelated physiological and morphological changes occurring during the early adolescent period of eleven to fifteen years of age. The term puberty, which is applied to these years, is derived from the Latin word *pubertas* meaning *age of manhood*. Puberty refers to the first phase of adolescence during which the reproductive apparatus matures. Usually puberty, or onset of sexual maturity, is dated from the first menstrual period (i.e., the menarche) in girls, and the emergence of pigmented pubic hair in boys (*182*).

Glandular Changes

The physiological and bodily changes that occur at this time are due, in part, to an increased output of the *gonadotropic* hormones of the anterior pituitary gland. This gland, located in the brain, governs and controls the hormone balance of the body. The gonadotropic hormone stimulates the activity of the gonads or sex glands, thus increasing the production of sex hormones and the growth of mature sperm and ova in males and females. These sex hormones—testosterone in males and estrogen in females—in combination with other hormones of the body, stimulate the growth of bone and muscle and lead to the growth spurt (*182*).

Growth Spurt

The growth spurt refers to the accelerated rate of increase in height and weight that occurs during adolescence. This increase varies widely in intensity, duration, and age of onset from one child to another, even among perfectly normal children—a fact often poorly understood by adolescents and their parents and, consequently, too often a source of needless concern.

In boys, the growth spurt may begin as early as 9½ years or as late as 13½ years (*122*). For the average boy, however, rapid acceleration in growth begins at about 13 years, reaching a peak rate of growth between 13½ and 14 years, and then declining sharply to pregrowth-spurt rates by age 15½. Further slow growth may continue for several years thereafter (see Fig. 14.1; also *122, 182*).

In girls, the adolescent growth spurt may begin as early as 7½ years of age or as late as 11½ (*122*). However, for the average girl rapid acceleration in growth begins about age 11, reaches a peak between 11½ and 12 years, and then decreases rapidly to pregrowth-spurt rates by about age 13, with slow continued growth for several additional years (*122, 182*).

The popular belief that girls mature earlier than boys stems primarily from the fact that girls obtain their adult height and weight about two years earlier than boys. During the adolescent growth spurt, boys increase only slightly more than girls in height. The common notion that the greater eventual height of males owes primarily to greater growth during this period is incorrect; actually, it is primarily because of the fact that boys are older and, therefore, taller at the beginning of their adolescent growth spurt (*122*).

As puberty approaches, the body proportions of both boys and girls undergo change also, although, again, the change is later among boys. The baby face of childhood begins to disappear. The low forehead becomes higher and wider. The mouth widens and the flat lips become fuller. The slightly receding chin of childhood begins to jut out. Moreover, the relatively

Fig. 14.1. Adolescent spurt in height and growth for girls and boys. The curves are from subjects who have had their peak velocities during the modal years 12–13 for girls, and 14–15 for boys. (Actual mean increments, each plotted at center of its one-half-year period.) (Data from F. K. Shuttleworth. The physical and mental growth of girls and boys, age six to nineteen, in relation to age at maximum growth. *Monogr. Soc. Res. Child Develpm.*, copyright 1939 by The Society for Research in Child Development, Inc. Vol. 4, No. 3, tables 23 and 32. By permission.)

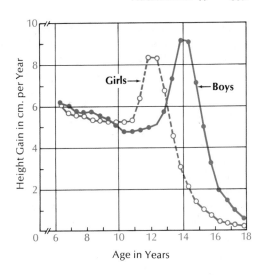

Lymphoid type: thymus, lymph nodes, intestinal lymph masses.

Brain and head type: brain and its parts, dura spinal cord, optic apparatus, head dimensions.

General type: body as a whole, external dimensions (except head), respiratory and digestive organs, kidneys, aortic and pulmonary trunks, musculature, blood volume.

Reproductive type: testis, ovary, epididymis, prostate, seminal vesicles, Fallopian tubes.

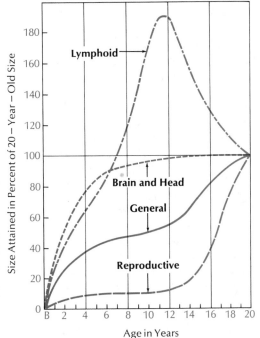

Fig. 14.2. Growth curves of different parts and tissues of the body, showing the four chief types. All the curves are of size attained and plotted to that size at age 20, which is 100 on the vertical scale. (Data from F. K. Shuttleworth. The physical and mental growth of girls and boys, age six to nineteen, in relation to age at maximum growth. *Monogr. Soc. Res. Child Developm.*, copyright 1939 by The Society for Research in Child Development, Inc. Vol. 4, No. 3. By permission).

large head, characteristic of childhood, continues to become smaller in proportion to total body length, in large measure because of the fact that throughout development the extremities are growing at a faster rate than the head. By age 10, the average child's head has achieved 90 percent of its mature length, and by age 15 it has practically reached adult size. During these years the extremities are still growing rapidly.

Along with the increases in height and weight during this period, less obvious physical changes are occurring, too. Almost every part of the body undergoes some change at adolescence and many tissues increase in size (182). The heart grows faster (122), and all aspects of the reproductive system increase in size; however, brain size does not change noticeably. In boys, there is a decrease during adolescence in the width of the fatty tissue that lies underneath the skin, and the proportion of bodily weight that is attributable to fat decreases during this period (122, 182). The picture varies for girls, however. They have thicker fatty tissue than boys at all ages, "but the prepubescent spurt in boys is followed by a sharp drop in fat widths during and after adolescence, while fat widths in girls continue to increase in size during the prepubescent and adolescent years" (121, 154).

As we have already seen, the bones change in size, proportion, and shape as the child grows older. Bone-width differences between boys and girls are minimal during childhood, but growth is clearly greater in the male during adolescence (121). The bones change internally also. It will be recalled that in early childhood the composition of the bones is such that there is relatively more cartilage and fibrous tissues, and less mineral matter than is found later. This makes the bones somewhat spongy and soft. But as the bones increase in size, the cartilage begins to calcify, making the bones harder, denser, and more brittle. This process of ossification speeds up at puberty. By the age of 17, the average girl's bones "should be mature not only in size, but also in ossification" (86).

In girls, the appearance of the breast bud (about 11 years of age) is one of the first clear, external signs of reproductive change. The breast bud consists of an increase in the diameter of the areola and growth of breast tissue, which form a small mound on the chest. The next three stages of growth involve increased growth of the breast and the projection of the papilla (nipple). The breast bud usually appears a year or two prior to the time of menarche (about age 13), and close to the time when uterine growth and the first appearance of pubic hair are noted.

Age of Menarche

The average age at which American girls reach menarche (i.e., begin menstruation) is about 13 years. However, there is considerable variation and, although 97 percent of girls reach menarche between 11 and 15, some reach it as early as the ninth or as late as the twentieth year (42, 123). It has been widely assumed that menarche occurs earlier today than it did fifty or one hundred years ago (182). However, earlier information was based largely on retrospective data which have proved notably vulnerable to error (*123, 147*). In a recent, carefully controlled study (*123*) using actual measurement of onset in comparable populations, the mean age of menarche in 1965 was found to be the same as that in 1930—13.17 years, with a range from 10 years, 6 months, to 15 years, 1½ months. It may be of anecdotal, though hardly of much scientific interest, to note that in ancient China the menarche was said to occur at the age of 13 years (*123*).

There is also a widespread belief that girls in tropical countries reach puberty earlier than those in more temperate zones, such as the United States. Even in 1855, one author (*123*) asserted that "the menarche came as early as 8 or 9 in hot climates, between the 13th and 15th years in temperate climates and as late as 20 in cold climates." This was still taught in the 1940s in spite of the fact that examination of the evidence failed to support any influence of climate on the rate of maturation (*123, 105*). The reported age of menarche from various tropical and semitropical countries ranges from 13.5 to 14.5 years, though much of the data is of doubtful quality. On the other hand, girls from far northern countries are frequently assumed to mature rather late. The available data, however, are conflicting, and largely dependent on inadequate sampling or based on retrospective recall which has been found to be subject to considerable error (*123*).

Much more convincing than the hypotheses either of an evolutionary change in age of menarche or a direct relationship between menarche and climate is the assertion that age of menarche reflects the individual's general physiological state (*179*). Thus fairly sound data indicate that during periods of widespread malnutrition in various European countries during World War II, age of menarche was significantly retarded. It also appears clear that menarchial age may be related to genetic factors which may vary from individual to individual (*179*).

Most important from a psychological point of view, however, is an awareness of the widespread variation in age of menarche among girls with no associated physical abnormality. Much unnecessary concern among adolescent girls could be avoided if there were a broader recognition of the fact that such variations in menarchial age are perfectly normal and do not presage later difficulties in either general physical growth or specific sexual development and functioning—although there is a tendency for late-maturing girls to have somewhat more slender (ectomorphic) physiques, and for early-maturing girls to have somewhat less slender, more rounded (endomorphic) physiques (*126, 203*).

Pubertal Age in Boys

Information about the onset of puberty is not so extensive in the case of boys as it is for girls. However, in a relatively complete study (*164*), the status of primary and secondary sexual development in 1475 normal representative New York males ranging in age from birth to 25 years was investigated. Each subject was classified as either (1) prepubescent; (2) in one of four stages of pubescence (progressively greater pubic hair development, in-

crease in size of penis and testes); or (3) fully mature. Marked individual variations were noted in the rates at which normal boys mature sexually. For
example, while 17 percent of the 20- to 21-year-old males were still in the
last stage of pubescence, 7 percent of the 14-year-olds were already fully
mature. Similarly, while 6 percent of the 14-year-olds had not yet reached
pubescence, 4 percent of the 10-year-olds were already pubescent.

The limited number of other studies of pubertal age available are in
essential agreement with these findings. In general, they show that boys
develop noticeable pubic hair about the same time that girls begin their
menses—again between 13 and 14 years, on the average; and that they
show the same sorts of individual variations in age of pubescence as girls
(a range from 10 to 15 years [3, 42, 43]). If we were to assume that the
development of pigmented pubic hair in boys is really equivalent to the
menarche in girls, it would appear that both boys and girls reach comparable stages of adolescence at approximately the same age. But as we
have already emphasized, the selection of these two events as criteria of
puberty has arisen mostly from convenience, and there is no necessary
reason for assuming their equivalence.

Adolescent Fertility

Perhaps the age at which the adolescent achieves fertility (i.e., the
ability to have children) might be considered a more convincing criterion
of maturity. Unfortunately, however, such data are extremely difficult to
obtain. There is some evidence to suggest that both boys and girls tend
to remain sterile for a considerable period after the development of
pubescent hair or the menarche, but precise information is lacking, particularly in the case of boys (179). One team of investigators (131) recorded
the ages of the menarche and of the first conception in various groups
among which promiscuity was frequent from an early age. They found that

> conception is extremely unlikely to occur during the first year following the
> menarche, and that for a period of four to six years it is less likely than after
> full maturity but does occur with increasing frequency. This period of adolescent
> physiologic sterility progressively shortens as the menarche is delayed. Concep-
> tion can occur very early, but it seldom does so before the age of 16, regardless
> of the age at the menarche (131, 611).

Interrelationships Among Growth Factors

Although we have discussed the changes in skeletal, muscular, and
reproductive growth separately, the timing of these processes is highly correlated. Thus the correlation between age of height spurt and time of
beginning testes growth in boys is .86. For girls, the correlation between
age of menarche and beginning breast-bud appearance is also .86, and the
correlation between age of menarche and time of appearance of pubic
hair is .70. These correlations suggest that in any one adolescent there is
likely to be a close correspondence between the age at which he reaches
his maximum rate of growth in height and weight and the age at which

he reaches puberty (*42, 170, 171*). Thus the boy who shows the growth spurt early will develop pubic hair early; the girl who has early menarche will show early breast development.

Even before maximum growth rate is achieved, measures of skeletal activity are predictive of age of menarche (*171*). During the preadolescent period, the bones of the legs, arms, hands, and feet increase in length and begin to join together or fuse. The rate at which this fusion of the bones occurs is closely related to the reproductive maturity of the adolescent. Greulich has studied the skeletal changes that occur in the hand by X-ray analyses, and has found that there is a close correspondence between age of menarche in the girl and the age at which the bones of the fingers become fused (*73*). Similarly, appearance of pubic hair in boys is closely associated with skeletal development of the hand (*73*). Similar relationships seem to hold among other aspects of skeletal and muscle growth on the one hand, and primary and secondary sexual development, on the other. In brief, there tends to be a general "going togetherness" of various maturational factors at this period of the individual's life (*140*).

RELATION BETWEEN PHYSICAL DEVELOPMENT AND PERSONALITY

In previous chapters we have referred to the term *self-concept*. This phrase refers to the individual's assessment, partly unconscious, of his position on a variety of dimensions that the social environment regards as important. Every culture has certain arbitrary rules about the desirability or undesirability of certain bodily characteristics. Possession of desirable characteristics is typically associated with sexual attractiveness and other aspects of group acceptance. Failure to develop bodily characteristics that the culture judges to be desirable is apt to lead to social rejection and feelings of sexual inadequacy. Members of Western culture equate certain anatomical attributes with strength or weakness and with sexual attractiveness or unattractiveness.

Through a complex set of mediated generalizations, the adolescent equates his ability to have dates and to establish satisfying heterosexual relationships with aspects of his physique and appearance. Thus the boy in American culture is concerned with his height, the breadth of his chest and shoulders, his muscular development, and the amount of facial and bodily hair. The girl is concerned with facial features and her figure.

> Since possession of acceptable or unacceptable bodily characteristics is so important for the adolescent's self-confidence, there is an important relation between his rate of physical maturation and his personality. The adolescent's concern with his body is fostered by . . . increasing identification with culturally determined ideals concerning appropriate physical characteristics for men and women.

Since the peer group becomes the chief source of his status and prestige, the adolescent desires to conform to the specific norms of body proportions and growth prevailing in his own limited circle. Now, for the first time, physical attractiveness becomes a crucial determinant of the girl's sociometric status among her peers of both sexes. In similar fashion, the boy's sociometric status is largely governed by his relative degree of masculinity in athletic prowess (1, 161).

The important role of physical characteristics in the adolescent's self-evaluation was demonstrated in a study by Jersild (91). When junior high school students were asked what they did and did not like about themselves, they mentioned physical characteristics more often than either intellectual or social characteristics. This trend was much less marked in senior high school.

Interviews with a group of 1925 girls from 11 to 18 years of age also revealed an unusually strong concern with appearance. To the question, "What would you like to change about yourself if you could—your looks, your personality, or your life?" 59 percent mentioned some aspect of their physical appearance, whereas only 4 percent mentioned a desire for greater ability (46).

Furthermore, there is evidence to suggest that when they compare themselves with the stereotyped ideal of their own peer groups, most adolescents are not entirely satisfied with the results. When tenth grade boys and girls were asked whether they desired a change in their physical selves, the majority of both sexes replied that they did (69).

The commonest complaint among both boys and girls concerned facial defects, principally skin disturbances. Other desired changes reflected quite clearly stereotyped masculine and feminine ideals. Thus there was a distinct association in the minds of boys between masculinity and a large, rugged physique (136). Girls wanted to be small and delicate in build, and to have "a good figure" (35). The adolescent who perceives himself as deviating from these cultural stereotypes is likely to have an impaired self-concept, and to worry about his capacity to attract members of the opposite sex.

In this connection, it is interesting to note that in one study (191), adolescent boys of slender ("linear") physique pictured themselves more frequently than their less linear peers as seeking approval by giving in to the demands of others and tending to place a higher value on remaining as inconspicuous as possible in most situations. In contrast, heavier, more muscular ("nonlinear") boys were more likely to picture themselves in the role of manipulator—one who makes decisions, gives directions, and controls the activity of others (191). In other studies, "linear" males have been found to be more restrained in movement, whereas "nonlinears" tended to be more vigorous and assertive in their posture and actions (168).

Inasmuch as masculinity of build and other characteristics of the masculine stereotype are related to overall rate of maturation (203), the age at which physical maturity is reached may have significant psychological consequences. A late-maturing boy who has no facial hair and is slight of build at 15 years is likely to feel inferior to his peers. He may be reluctant to ask girls for dates for fear that they will reject him. He may avoid athletic participation because he is afraid that he will make mistakes and be humiliated in front of others.

Investigators at the University of California (96, 97, 134, 135) have compared the fantasies and behavior of adolescents who matured very early with those who matured late. In one intensive study of the relation of physical maturing to behavior among boys, skeletal age was used as an index of maturity (94). The subjects included 16 boys, ages 12 to 17, who were currently accelerated, and 16 boys who were currently retarded in maturing. Using social observational data and peer-group ratings as measures of behavior, the investigators found that the later maturers tended to engage in more attention-getting behaviors, and were rated more restless, talkative, and bossy. They were also less popular than the early maturers, fewer of them were leaders, fewer were able to laugh at themselves, and fewer were considered matter-of-fact and unaffected. The authors concluded that:

> Those who are physically accelerated are usually accepted and treated by adults and other children as more mature. They appear to have relatively little need to strive for status. From their ranks come the outstanding student-body leaders in senior high school. In contrast, the physically retarded boys exhibit many forms of relatively immature behavior: this may be in part because others tend to treat them as the little boys they appear to be. Furthermore, a fair proportion of these boys give evidence of needing to counteract their physical disadvantage in some way—usually by greater activity in striving for attention, although in some cases by withdrawing (94, 148).

Thus it appears that the boys who mature late are anxious about their deviant status, and this anxiety leads to a variety of maladaptive behaviors designed to gain attention and recognition from others. Moreover, boys who matured late, in contrast to early maturers, revealed in their stories deeper feelings of inadequacy and anticipations of rejection by the social environment (135). They were also rated as having stronger needs for social acceptance (134).

The authors concluded:

> The boy whose physical development is retarded is exposed to a sociopsychological environment which may have adverse effects on his personality development. Apparently being in a disadvantageous competitive position in athletic activities, as well as being regarded and treated as immature by others, may lead to negative self-conceptions, heightened feelings of rejection by others, prolonged dependent needs, and rebellious attitudes to parents. . . .

> The physically accelerated boys, on the other hand, are likely to experience environmental circumstances which are much more conducive to good psychological adjustment (135, 252–253).

Early maturation (as measured by age of menarche) tends *initially* (grade 6) to be a handicap socially, but it soon turns into a social advantage (grade 7) and remains so throughout the junior high school years *(62).* In the sixth grade, when most girls are prepuberal, the largest number of prestige associated personality characteristics (such as "popular," "friendly," "assured with adults") is assigned to other prepuberal girls. However, beginning in the seventh grade, when the average girl is beginning to cope with the demands of puberty herself, girls who are already postpuberal are assigned the largest number of prestige-associated traits, with the highest scores going to girls whose development is most advanced *(62).* Apparently:

> for girls neither physical acceleration nor physical retardation is consistently advantageous. It is not until the junior high school years that the early-maturing girl "comes into her own" and reaps the benefit of her accelerated development. Until that time her precocious development is somewhat detrimental to her social status. The adjustments which inevitably must be made to losses and gains in status during the adolescent period . . . may be partly a function of this discontinuity in the relationship between developmental maturity and prestige during the adolescent period. . . .

> After the transition to junior high school, girls begin to ascribe prestige to classmates who have been physically mature for a longer period of time and to girls whose interests and activities are undoubtedly more advanced. Perhaps these more mature girls satisfy a requirement for prestige in the group because of their "advanced standing" with respect to the new developmental tasks which the less mature girls are facing *(62, 181).*

Early- and late-maturing boys and girls also appear to differ in their interests. In a study of pre- and postmenarchial girls of matched ages, Stone and Barker *(13)* found that the postmenarchial girls were more interested in social activities with the opposite sex, in personal adornment, display of person, and in daydreaming. On the other hand, menarchial girls were less interested in games and sports requiring vigorous activity. On a test of masculinity-femininity, early-maturing boys obtain more masculine interest scores, and early-maturing girls more feminine interest scores than their later-maturing peers. Similarly, a study of adolescent boys revealed a relatively high correlation (.51) between amount of male hormone in the urine and maturity of interests and attitudes *(174).*

While late maturing generally appears to have a handicapping effect, we must not forget that many other factors will also affect the individual adolescent's social and emotional adjustment. As we shall see, the early maturer who is nagged by skin blemishes or other physical disturbances, by membership in a minority group, or by adverse factors in the home may have a more difficult time adjusting socially than the slightly late maturer, who is more fortunate in other respects.

Significance of Menstruation

Menstruation means much more to the adolescent girl than just a simple physiological readjustment. It is a symbol of sexual maturity—of her future role as a wife and mother. As the reactions of the girl to menstruation may generalize so broadly, it is vital that her initial experience with this phenomenon be as favorable as possible.

Many girls look forward calmly to the onset of menstruation, and some receive it proudly, as a sign of increased status. Unfortunately, because many notions concerning the shamefulness or even dangerousness of menstruation have persisted in our time, there are other girls who fear and hate it. In a study of the emotional reactions of 475 girls to the onset of their menses, it was found that 51 percent reported their reaction as one of indifference; 4 percent said they were curious and interested; 12 percent were chagrined; 1 percent were terrified; and only 6 percent were delighted and proud (38). In a similar study of white and Negro girls, a majority of white girls again reported reactions of indifference, with most of the remainder expressing such generally negative feelings as "upset," "worried," and "unhappy," or "ashamed." Among Negro girls, only one-fifth reported reacting indifferently, and almost all of the remainder expressed predominantly negative feelings. Only about 19 percent of white girls, and an even smaller percentage of Negro girls expressed "happiness." The author suggests that at least a part of the difference between Negro and white girls in their reactions, at least in this population, may have been caused by poorer preparation of the Negro girls for the onset of menarche (78).

Probably one of the main reasons that girls may react negatively to menstruation is that they are influenced by the negative attitudes of others. Thus, if a menstruating girl's parents and friends act as though she requires sympathy for her "plight"—an attitude implied in such prevalent euphemisms for menstruation as "the curse," "being unwell," etc.—the girl herself is likely to adopt similar attitudes toward her menstruation.

Negative reactions to menstruation may also stem in part from physical discomfort. During the early years of menstruation, when the menses are likely to be quite irregular, a number of girls experience disturbing symptoms in relation to their menstrual period. Among the more common of these are: headaches, backaches, cramps, and severe abdominal pain (1, 86). However, in most cases where such initial disturbances occur, they tend to disappear as puberty progresses and menstruation becomes more regular.

Another factor which may adversely affect the girl's reaction to her first menstruation arises from the similarity between menstruation and other physical reactions. As the menstrual flow may be similar to other types of bleeding, the girl who has been inadequately prepared for menstruation may, and too frequently does, gain the impression that she has been injured (58).

There are, of course, other reasons why the adolescent girl may react negatively to menstruation. For example, if she has been unable to establish a satisfactory feminine identification, she may be disturbed by having her attention bluntly directed by the onset of menstruation to the fact that she is a woman and can do nothing about it.

Many of these negative reactions could be avoided or alleviated if the parent employed a wise and understanding approach to the problem. By seeing that the girl receives adequate medical care in the case of physical difficulties; by explaining to her the naturalness of the phenomenon; and by showing pride and pleasure in her greater maturity, the parents—particularly the mother—can help to make the onset of menstruation a happy, rather than a feared or hated event. This of course will have consequent benefits for the girl's whole future sexual and social role as a woman.

Nocturnal Emission

Just as the onset of menstruation may cause concern to the pubescent girl, so may the appearance of nocturnal emission surprise and worry the pubescent boy. By nocturnal emission is meant ejaculation of the seminal fluid during sleep. According to Kinsey (106), approximately 83 percent of males report experiencing nocturnal emissions at some time in their lives, tending usually to begin a year or two after the onset of puberty. Frequently, but by no means always, these emissions are accompanied by erotic dreams. Nocturnal emission occurs more frequently among youth who are headed for college (95 percent) than those with grade school education (67 percent), possibly because sexual intercourse as a primary sexual outlet occurs earlier in the latter group (106, 151). The female equivalent of nocturnal emissions, nocturnal dreams with orgasm, is far less frequent (probably never exceeding 10 percent), and tends not to reach a peak until after adolescence.

It seems to be true that boys as a group worry less about nocturnal emissions than girls do about menstruation, perhaps partly because boys are more often able to talk freely among themselves about such matters. It also appears that current adolescents are better informed and less likely to be concerned about nocturnal emissions than were boys of earlier generations. Nevertheless, many boys, especially in the early and middle years of adolescence, do not gain proper instruction from their peers or parents, and torture themselves with unnecessary fears (108).

Cognitive Development in Adolescence

The dramatic physical and physiological changes that occur in adolescence may tend to obscure the fact that impressive changes in cognitive development are taking place at the same time. Indeed, it is fair to state that adolescence is "the period during which the capacity to acquire and to utilize knowledge reaches its peak efficiency" (54, 130). This is particularly evident in tests of mental ability that involve relatively pure measures of high level mental processes, such as mathematical reasoning and analogies. Scores on such tests tend to peak in late adolescence or early adulthood, after which they begin to decline. In contrast, tests such as vocabulary ones that depend to a significant extent on "the mere accumulation of verbal or factual inventories" tend to show little deterioration (93). This is especially likely in the case of persons of higher intelligence who continue to follow academic pursuits, thus "keeping their hand in" (5, 26, 141). It has also been found that mental test scores in adolescence are better predictors of adult functioning than those obtained at earlier ages (23; cf. pp. 464–465).

It appears that the level of intellectual functioning achieved by late adolescence or early adulthood and the extent to which this capacity is exploited during this period will determine in great measure the future course of adult cognitive functioning (54). As Alfred North Whitehead once remarked, "The imagination is most active between the ages of nineteen and thirty-five and we must keep going thereafter on whatever fizz we have experienced then" (195, 132).

Sex Differences in Cognitive Functioning. While boys and girls show no demonstrable difference in overall intelligence, there are sex differences in the areas of greatest relative competence. Thus girls tend to do best on verbal measures while boys do best on quantitative or spatial problems (183). Not surprisingly, on tests of academic achievement, girls are superior in languages while boys are superior in science and mathematics (183). The fact that these differences are not apparent in the preschooler, but become marked by adolescence (56, 57, 105), suggests that they "reflect differences in interest, rather than differential mental abilities" (54, 138).

Qualitative Changes in Adolescent Cognitive Development

The changes that take place in cognitive functioning during adolescence are reflected qualitatively as well as quantitatively. It will be recalled that, according to Piaget's theory (pp. 451–455), the adolescent shifts from the stage of *concrete operations*, which characterizes thinking during middle and late childhood, to the stage of *formal operations*. While the older pre-adolescent child is capable of relatively elementary deductive reasoning and of dealing with *relational terms, class inclusion, serialization,* and the principles of *reversibility* and *conservation,* the sophistication of his reasoning is still quite limited, in comparison with that of the adolescent (144).

> . . . the child can only reason about those things with which he has had direct personal experience. He has difficulty as soon as he has to deal with any hypothetical or contrary-to-fact proposition [cf. pp. 451–453]. In addition, while he can deal with two classes, relations, or quantitative dimensions at the same time, this is about the limit of his capabilities. As soon as more variables than two have to be taken into account in a systematic way, he flounders because he lacks an operational system appropriate to such situations. This is the fundamental deficiency of concrete operational thought (54, 141).

With the advent of *formal operations,* however, the adolescent gains a number of important new capabilities: "He can take his own thought as an object and reason about it" (54, 141). He can consider not merely one possible answer to a problem, or explanation of a situation, but many possible alternatives. (The younger child, when he has thought of one possible solution, is likely immediately to adopt it as fact.) For example, in attempting to work out possible combinations of objects or propositions, the adolescent is not limited to combinations that spontaneously occur to him; he can logically exhaust all possible combinations *(54)*. "Furthermore, while the child's concrete operational system enables him to distinguish between reality and appearance, between how things look and how they really are, formal operational thought enables the young person to distinguish between truth and falsity, i.e., to judge hypotheses against fact *(54, 142)*.

The ability to generate hypotheses systematically and to test them against the evidence—in brief, to think scientifically and objectively—vastly increases the adolescent's capacity to deal with himself and the world about him. While the elementary school child raises hypotheses about events, he does not appear aware of their arbitrariness, and does not feel the need to test them against the facts *(54)*.

> It is for this reason that the child appears to be more rigid than the adolescent in certain problem-solving tasks. The adolescent, with his awareness of the arbitrariness of his hypothesis and of their mental quality, is ready to give them up to produce others. This ability to discriminate between thought and reality is derived from the capacity to take all of the possibilities in the situation into account, and it is the awareness of *possibility* that marks the true differentiation between thought and reality *(54, 146)*.

Adolescent thought also becomes more abstract (i.e., more general and more divorced from immediate experience) than that of the younger child. Thus, in defining *time,* the younger child is likely to say that it is "something that the watch tells," or "time means the clock" *(72)*. A 15-year-old, on the other hand, may say that "time is sort of like an interval of space" *(72)*. While the younger child's thinking is concrete, the adolescent can deal readily with metaphors. For example, Shaffer *(167)* found that it was not until ages 12–14 that children could go beyond the literal meaning of a cartoon to its metaphorical meaning.

Consequences of Adolescent Cognitive Development

It is easy to appreciate the fact that without the quantitative and qualitative changes in cognitive functioning that take place during adolescence, the young person would be unable to deal adequately with many of the intellectual demands made upon him during this period—mastering academic skills, preparing for a vocation, and gaining a factual knowledge of the world around him. Perhaps less obvious, however, is the fact that many of the social and emotional concerns of the adolescent—his preoccupation with values, his characteristic dissatisfactions with the world in general and his parents in particular, even much of his egocentrism *(55)*—are to some extent a function of his new-found capacity for formal operational thought.

In a highly perceptive essay, David Elkind, a psychologist at the University of Rochester, notes that the younger child lives primarily in the present. He is concerned about the world as it is and about learning how to function in this world.

With the advent of adolescence, however, and the emergence of formal operational thought, all of this changes. The adolescent is now able not only to grasp the immediate state of things but also the possible states they might or could assume. This new awareness of the discrepancy between how things are and how they might be—at home, at schol, with themselves—probably underlines many of the recurrent adolescent feelings of depression and dissatisfaction. . . . The awareness of the discrepancy between the actual and the possibble also helps to make the adolescent a rebel. He is always comparing the possible with the actual and discovering that the actual is flagrantly wanting (54, 152).

The development of formal operational thought also affects the adolescent's approach to himself. He begins to turn his new powers of thought inward and becomes introspective, analytical, and self-critical. "This he does with a certain equanimity since he now recognizes the private character of thought and that he need not share the results of his self examination with others" (54, 153). Without the capacity for abstract thought, for conceptualizing hypothetical alternatives to existing reality and for evolving criteria to distinguish between truth and falsity (87), many of the characteristic concerns of adolescents that we shall examine in this and the following chapter would not be possible. The development of values and moral principles, the preoccupation with introspection and self-criticism, the self-consciousness that is reflected in relations with the self and others, and the development of future goals and life plans that characterize adolescents, all depend in considerable measure on the cognitive maturation taking place in adolescence.

ADJUSTMENT DEMANDS OF ADOLESCENCE

As we have seen, physical and intellectual maturation play a necessary and vital role in the adolescent's transition from childhood to adult status in our society. But meaningful maturity—socially and psychologically—cannot be achieved unless the adolescent is also able to master successfully a number of critically important, interrelated developmental tasks. If the adolescent is to become truly adult, and not just physically mature, he must—in the few short years between childhood and nominal adulthood—gradually achieve independence from his family; adjust to his sexual maturation; establish cooperative and workable relationships with his peers, without being dominated by them; and decide on and prepare for a meaningful vocation. In the process, he must develop a philosophy of life—a set of guiding moral beliefs and standards which can lend some order and consistency to the many decisions he will have to make and the actions he will have to take in a diverse, changing, sometimes chaotic world. And he must develop a sense of his own identity. Before the adolescent can safely abandon the security of childhood dependence on others, he must have some idea of who he is, where he is going, and what the possibilities are of getting there.

In many ways, the question "Who am I?" is the central problem of adolescence, a problem celebrated in poetry, in novels, and autobiographies over many centuries. Recently, however, it has become the focus of increased psychological concern through the writings of the gifted psychoanalyst, Erik Erikson, who has discussed the problem in terms of "ego identity." Perhaps it is no coincidence that Erikson came to psychoanalysis with a broad background in literature and the arts. In Erikson's words:

> The identity the adolescent seeks to clarify is who he is, what his role in society is to be. Is he a child or is he an adult? Does he have it in him to be someday a husband and father? What is he to be as a worker and an earner of money? Can he feel self-confident in spite of the fact that his race or religious or national background makes him a person some people look down upon? Overall, will he be a success or a failure? By reason of these questions adolescents are sometimes morbidly preoccupied with how they appear in the eyes of others as compared with their own conception of themselves, and with how they can make the rules and skills learned earlier jibe with what is currently in style . . . (60, 9).

The danger of this developmental period is self-diffusion. As Biff puts it in *Death of a Salesman,* "I just can't take hold. I can't take hold of some kind of a life." A boy or girl can scarcely help feeling somewhat diffuse when the body changes in size and shape so rapidly, "when genital maturity floods body and imagination with forbidden desires, when adult life lies ahead with such a diversity of conflicting possibilities and choices" (60, 9).

Thus a sense of ego identity is necessary for a secure footing in life, for it leads to "a sense of knowing where one is going, and an inner assuredness of anticipated recognition from those who count" (59, 118–119).

Let us consider in detail the major developmental tasks facing the adolescent in our society—the establishment of independence, sexual adjustment, peer relations, and preparation for a vocation. However, as we shall see in the next chapter, the individual adolescent's ability to meet each of these requirements, the directions he takes, and the degree of success he has in integrating these complex and varied demands, will be intimately related to his success in establishing a workable set of personal values and a strong sense of his own ego-identity. That some adolescents—for personal, social, or other reasons—succeed while others fail will become painfully evident in the final chapter's discussion of alienated youth.

DEPENDENCE AND INDEPENDENCE

Establishing true independence from his parents is not a simple matter for the adolescent, for, as we shall see, opposing motivations and external pressures for independence and for continued dependence are both strong, thus producing conflict and vacillating behavior.

Cultural Pressures for Independence

Parents, teachers, relatives, and other authority figures generally encourage a certain amount of independent behavior during the preadolescent years. They show increasing disapproval if the child consistently relies on adults for advice and support. Therefore, the desire to please adults may motivate the adolescent to inhibit the dependent behaviors typical of childhood.

However, our society also imposes certain obstacles to complete independence from the family. Preparation for a vocation may require prolonged training, frequently involving college and sometimes post-graduate education. The adolescent is often forced, therefore, to remain financially dependent upon his parents for a long period of time. Furthermore, as marriage does not usually occur in early adolescence, the individual generally continues to live with his parents. This situation is, by definition, a dependent one because food and shelter are usually provided by the family. Consequently, the goal of independence fostered by society is blocked by mores and rules that are inconsistent with complete independence. This inconsistency is a source of anxiety and conflict.

Identification with Adult Independence

Social pressures for independence are not the only determinants of the adolescent's motivation to inhibit dependence. Intrapsychic forces, only indirectly related to social reward and punishment, facilitate the development of this motive. During the years 3 to 6, the child's imitations of adult behavior necessarily had a gamelike quality because of the vast differences between the child and his parents. The adolescent, however, is seriously trying to be an adult. He has the height, weight, and many of the skills of an adult. In order to achieve adult status, he must acquire the salient psychological characteristics of an adult. Independence and autonomy are clearly two of the most important of these characteristics. The adult decides what to wear, what to eat, when to sleep, and what to buy. As a result, the adolescent strives to make these independent behaviors part of his own repertoire, in the hope that this will insure his status as an adult. In brief, the strong motivation for independent behavior in the adolescent stems from at least two sources: social pressures and identification with the independence of adult role-models.

Establishment of Independence in Other Cultures

In a number of nonliterate societies the task of establishing independence may be less difficult than it is in our culture. In some societies, the child may be prepared more gradually for independence, being given increasing freedom from early childhood on, with no discernible spurt at puberty. In others, true independence from the parents may be postponed until long after puberty, and may occur slowly. Among the Arapesh people of New Guinea, for example, the adolescent takes over much of the responsibility for supporting and managing the household, but there are few marked changes in basic family relationships at this time. The Arapesh girl does not suddenly leave home during adolescence to go to live in a strange household with strange people, in order to undergo the joint uncertainties of married life, sex, and child-bearing. In this culture, the girl has been chosen as a wife by her husband's parents many years prior to the consummation of the marriage, and she has been allowed during the interim to wander confidently back and forth between her own home and her future husband's. By the time her marriage is consummated she has come to think of her parents-in-law as an additional mother and father. She has known her husband almost as an older brother, whose responsibility it has been to look after her, to feed her, to help her grow up.

As time goes on, the Arapesh girl takes on increasing responsibility in her new home. However, many of the problems which occur frequently in American marriages do not exist in Arapesh culture. There is none of the atmosphere of confusion, of sudden complete separation from parents, of moving into a new house and beginning a separate existence with a relatively unknown male, and of bearing and caring for her babies by herself.

Similarly, the independence problems faced by the Arapesh boy are likely to be less severe than those faced by American boys. Once the Arapesh youth has passed through the initiation ceremony following pubescence, he assumes added responsibility. "From one who has been grown by the daily carefulness and hard work of others, he now passes into the class of those whose care is for others' growth" (128, 76). He takes on new responsibilities toward those "who after years devoted to his growth are now growing old themselves, and toward his younger brothers and sisters, and his young betrothed wife" (128, 76). But he does not need to go out into a new community on his own, somehow obtain an unfamiliar job, and complete his emotional independence from his parents. He continues, but with new responsibility, to till the family's garden. He still sees his parents daily, and when at last he consummates his marriage, it is with a girl he has known, whom he has cared for, and to whom he has to adjust his personality over a long period of time.

Among the Mixtecan Indians of Mexico, socialization is also a gradual and rather informal process. Younger children, both boys and girls, have few assigned duties, and are treated with relatively great leniency—"They should play when they want to and help when they want to" (132, 196). Girls may learn relatively early to do simple tasks like going for water, picking up dishes after meals, and running small errands. Boys start to learn animal care and feeding, and to follow their fathers into the fields. Around the sixth or seventh year, the girl begins caring for younger siblings, going to market, helping to serve food and wash the dishes, and perhaps caring for small domestic animals. At about the same age, boys begin gathering produce or fodder in the fields, and caring for large animals such as goats or burros.

In such informal ways, largely through example, Mixtecan children gradually learn to take increasing responsibility and to perform the tasks they will assume as adults. There is little anxiety about the child's learning these tasks, either on the part of parents or children. Parents assume that their children will learn to do such basic necessary jobs *adequately,* and there is no demand or expectation for achievement beyond this. Aggressive competition would be considered unseemly, and nurturance plays a strong role among these people.

In contrast to the Arapesh and Mixtecan youth, the Mundugumor adolescent finds the problem of orderly transition from dependence on the parents to the setting up of an independent household infinitely more difficult. This increased difficulty is at least partially attributable to the fact that "Mundugumor social organization is based on a theory of a natural hostility between all members of the same sex . . ." (128, 176). Fathers and sons view each other almost as natural enemies, as do mothers and daughters. Moreover, relations between husband and wife are notably poor. Fathers band together with daughters, while mothers band together with sons. Between the two subfamily groups rivalry and distrust are characteristic.

Consequently, it seems likely that the Mundugumor boy approaches adolescence close psychologically only to his mother, hostile toward his father, and distrustful of girls his own age. The girl, on the other hand, has strong ties to her father, resentment toward her mother, and distrust of her male contemporaries. Furthermore, the girl's problem is magnified because of the jealous father's attempts to keep his hold on her as long as possible (128).

There seems little doubt that Mundugumor children, who grow up in a culture that contains so much hostility and so little tenderness, early develop a kind of hardy independence that prepares them somewhat for the demands they must face in adolescence. But this advantage is virtually negated by the fact that the independence demanded of the Mundugumor adolescent is so much more extreme than in most cultures. The prospect of establishing independence is unpleasant, and in many ways threatening. In fact its only really attractive aspects seems to be escape from the hostility of the same-sexed parent.

Problems of Independence in American Culture

In setting up his own household the American adolescent certainly encounters more stress than the Arapesh or Mixtecan youth, though he is spared much of the violence of the Mundugumor's independence struggles.

In contrast to the Arapesh adolescent and those in many other primitive cultures (132, 196, 197), the American adolescent is expected, in the years between puberty and adulthood, to pass from a state of relatively great dependence on his family to one of considerable independence. Middle-class Americans begin independence training somewhat earlier than most primitive societies (132, 196, 197). However, they generally complete this training relatively late, requiring a high degree of continued dependence into adolescence (132, 196, 197).

Not until the adolescent is nearing adulthood do the demands for true independence become really strong. In other words, the American adolescent is asked to assume real independence suddenly after having developed strongly rewarded dependence responses over a long period of time. As a consequence of strong societal demands for independence, in the face of incompatible and well-established dependence responses, the adolescent is likely to be in conflict. And the fact that this conflict is timed to coincide with so many other demands related to puberty and adolescence only increases its stressfulness.

Moreover, no clear pattern of transition from dependence to independence is spelled out for the adolescent by our society as a whole. There is little agreement as to the forms this greater independence should be allowed to take. We have no formalized procedures in our culture comparable to the puberty ceremonies or *rites de passage* of many primitive cultures which can serve as guides both to the parents and to the adolescent as to when and how independence should be granted and assumed.

About all our culture has in the way of institutionalized forms of recognizing the adolescent's increasing independence are a number of laws, often internally inconsistent and varying a great deal in their content from one area of our culture to another. For example, there are sizable variations from state to state in the age at which the child becomes legally responsible for his own actions, and at which the parent is no longer held responsible. There are differences, too, in the ages at which the adolescent is considered competent to drive a car, to marry, to own property, to carry firearms, to drink alcoholic beverages, and to purchase tobacco.

Thus the adolescent who must face the problems of transition from childish dependency to adult independency is likely to be impressed, not with the solidarity of the expectations of the adults in this regard, but with their divisiveness. In one instance, or with one set of people, he is likely to find that independent responses are rewarded. In other instances, or with other people, he may just as easily find that they are punished. The church, the school, the members of the various social classes, even the adolescent's own parents may have different notions as to the time when adult protection and guidance should be relinquished in favor of greater individual responsibility.

The adolescent is likely to observe that one of his peers is allowed by his parents to decide how to spend his money, to use the family car, to date, to choose his own vocation, to do part-time work, to choose his own companions, to go off on trips by himself or with his friends. Another adolescent, even of the same age and social group, may be allowed to do none of these things.

Moreover, the adolescent finds numerous inconsistencies in the ways in which people react to him as an individual. The young high school student's employer usually expects him to be independent and responsible more often than do his parents. The same thing usually holds true for male peers and his sweetheart. It is also true of the law in most instances.

A mother and father may have differing independence expectations with regard to their child. In addition, either or both parents may possess mixed feelings over their child's growing independence. These mixed feelings are likely to be reflected in inconsistent patterns of parental behavior—as, for example, demanding independence and at the same time punishing it when it occurs.

The adolescent himself is likely to be uncertain and confused about the problem of achieving independence. He may desire to be a free agent, but he may just as truly want the security and lack of responsibility that are associated with continuing dependence. As a result, he may suffer personal conflict over independence needs. When all the above environmental inconsistencies with regard to independency-dependency expectations are added to the adolescent's own uncertainties, it is not surprising to find that the adolescent's path to independence should often be a stormy one both for the adolescent himself and for his parents (162).

Parent-Child Relationships and the Development of Independence. The severity of the adolescent's conflicts over independence-dependence, and the ease with which they are resolved in the direction of greater independence will depend to a large extent on previous and current parent-child relationships. One important factor obviously involves the parents' overall predispositions along the dimension of authority and control *versus* freedom and autonomy.

The parent who encourages increasing autonomy as the child grows older, but who still retains an interest in and some responsibility for the adolescent's decisions, is likely to encourage both responsibility and independence (51, 52). Autocratic or authoritarian parents, on the other hand, will tend to stifle the orderly acquisition of independence responses; while indifferent, *laissez-faire,* or completely permissive parents may fail to encourage the development of responsibility.

In a study of 7400 adolescents in a southern and a midwestern state, one investigator (52) employed adolescent ratings of parents' behavior to study parental variations in child-rearing techniques, ranging from complete parental domination to complete self-direction. Seven parental structures were defined:

Autocratic. No allowance is provided for the youth to express his views on a subject nor for him to assert leadership or initiative in self government.

Authoritarian. Although the adolescent contributes to the solution of problems, his parents always decide issues according to their own judgment.

Democratic. The adolescent contributes freely to discussion of issues relevant to his behavior, and may even make his own decisions; however, in all instances the final decision is either formulated by parents or meets their approval.

Equalitarian. This type of structure represents minimal role differentiation. Parents and the adolescent are involved to a similar degree in making decisions pertaining to the adolescent's behavior.

Permissive. The adolescent assumes a more active and influential position in formulating decisions which concern him than do his parents.

Laissez-Faire. The position of the adolescent in relation to that of his parents

Table 14.1 The Fairness of Parental Child-Rearing Policy
as Related to Types of Child-Rearing Structures

Parent	Percent of Adolescents by Types of Child-Rearing Structures				
	Autocratic	Authoritarian	Democratic	Equalitarian	Permissive
Mother	55.1 (367)	58.9 (667)	85.5 (2237)	82.8 (1081)	80.4 (1471)
Father	50.7 (668)	74.9 (942)	85.1 (1966)	77.1 (817)	74.6 (1051)

Source: From G. H. Elder, Jr. Structural variations in the child rearing relationship. *Sociometry,* 1962, *25,* 258. By permission of the American Sociological Association.

in decision making is clearly more differentiated in terms of power and activity. In this type of relationship the youth has the option of either subscribing to or disregarding parental wishes in making his decisions.

Ignoring. This type of structure, if it can be legitimately considered as such, represents actual parental divorcement from directing the adolescent's behavior.

Moving from the autocratic to the ignoring structure involves a gradual increase in the participation of the adolescent in self-direction and a concurrent decrease in the participation of parents in making decisions concerning him. Just as these types of interdependence, as perceived by adolescents, represent variations in the allocation of power between parents and the adolescent, they also represent different patterns of communication. Communication is primarily from parent to child in the autocratic structure and from child to parent in the permissive structure *(52).*

A number of other interesting findings emerge from this study, despite sources of error inherent in using adolescent ratings rather than independent means of categorizing parent behaviors. As might be expected, fathers were more likely to be rated as authoritarian or autocratic (35 percent) than mothers (22 percent). This is consistent with findings in other studies which indicate that normal adolescents tend to view their fathers as more strict in discipline and more aggressive, and their mothers as more emotionally supportive, expressive of affection, child-centered, and protective *(47, 48, 65, 129).* Also, as one might anticipate, both mothers and fathers tended to treat older adolescents more permissively than younger ones, although there is a greater shift toward permissiveness with age in the case of mothers than with fathers. Parents in larger families tended to be slightly more autocratic or authoritarian than those in smaller families, even when social class was held constant.

How did adolescents respond to these varying patterns of parental control ("child-rearing structures")? Subjects were asked, "Do you think your (mother's/father's) ideas, rules, or principles about how you should behave are good and reasonable, or wrong and unreasonable?" As may be seen from Table 14.1, children exposed to *democratic* practices considered their parents most fair (approximately 85 percent for both mother and father),

Table 14.2   Feelings of Maternal and Paternal Rejection
as Related to Types of Child-Rearing Structures

Parent	Percent of Adolescents by Types of Child-Rearing Structures					
	Autocratic	Authoritarian	Demo- cratic	Equalitarian	Permissive	Laissez- Faire Ignoring
Mother	41.7 (277)	25.7 (239)	10.9 (283)	11.0 (143)	11.1 (190)	56.8
Father	40.1 (525)	17.6 (220)	8.4 (193)	11.1 (117)	11.0 (140)	58.0

Source: From G. H. Elder, Jr. Structural variations in the child rearing relationship.
Sociometry, 1962, *25,* 259. By permission of the American Sociological Association.

with *equalitarian* parents ranking next. Autocratic parents (those who "just tell" their children what to do) ranked lowest. These results are consistent with other findings (39) and with the hypothesis that communication between parents and children (e.g., democratic, equalitarian) fosters *identification,* while a unilateral exercise of power without communication (e.g., autocratic) is more likely to produce *resentment (34).* Interestingly, however, it may be observed that more favorable ratings on fairness were given to authoritarian fathers than to authoritarian mothers; in contrast, more favorable ratings were given to permissive mothers than to permissive fathers. As these results held up when sex and social class were controlled, it appears that a father, even though he makes the basic decisions, will generally be considered fair if he is willing to listen (authoritarian), but not if he lays down the law without listening (autocratic). In other words, acceptance of parental dictates is greater if the parent makes some effort to "legitimatize his power" *(79).* Further, being the "law giver" (provided he is willing to listen) is generally considered by adolescents as a more socially appropriate role for fathers than for mothers. In contrast, permissiveness is considered a somewhat more appropriate role for mothers than for fathers. This, of course, is consistent with other findings *(47, 139, 189).*

Adolescents were also asked whether they ever thought that their parents made them feel as if they were unwanted. As Table 14.2 shows, by far the largest percentages of adolescents who reported that they had felt unwanted were found among those youths with autocratic or laissez-faire and ignoring parents. Thus about 40 percent of the youths with either an autocratic mother or father reported that they had felt unwanted by them, whereas only around 10 percent of adolescents with democratic, equalitarian, or permissive parents expressed similar feelings. This relationship was also analyzed with the age, sex, and social class of the adolescent controlled, and the nature and degree of the relationship remained essentially unchanged. "In essence, child rearing structures which represent considerable adolescent participation in self-direction appear least provocative of rejection feelings" *(52, 260).*

In a related study, Elder *(51)* examined the relation between *autocratic, democratic,* and *permissive* parental practices and adolescent autonomy (for purposes of this investigation, *laissez-faire* and *ignoring* parents were included in the permissive category). Each of the three categories of parental practice was further subdivided into those parents who frequently explained their rules of conduct and expectations, and those who did not. (As might have been expected, democratic and permissive parents were far more likely than autocratic parents to provide explanations.) The author reasoned that infrequently explaining parents would be perceived as coercive, while explaining parents would be seen as providing "legitimacy" in the exercise of power *(70, 149, 150).* When parental power was perceived as legitimate, it was anticipated that adolescents would have more positive feelings toward parents, be more likely to model themselves after parents, and be more likely to act on the basis of internalized standards of behavior *(70, 79, 145, 149).* On the other hand, "the possible effects of non-explaining parents on the autonomy of the child are considerable" *(51, 53).*

The author reasoned that:

> The non-explaining parent is . . . apt to undermine the self-confidence of the adolescent in his ability to make his own decisions as well as weaken his desire for such independence. While adolescent autonomy may be positively related to the parental practice of explaining rules and requests, it is likely to be inversely related to parental power. By definition, the autocratic type of parent-child interdependence severely limits opportunities for adolescents to acquire wisdom and confidence in independent decision making *(51, 54).*

Therefore, it was hypothesized that *autonomy would be most common among children of parents who were more permissive and less autocratic in the exercise of parental power, and who frequently explained their reasons for rules of conduct and expectations.*

Autonomy was indicated by (1) *confidence* in one's own values, goals, and awareness of rules, and (2) *independence*—a desire to make up one's own mind, with or without listening to others' ideas. As may be seen in Table 14.3, adolescent *confidence* and *independence* occurred most frequently among the children of democratic and permissive parents who also frequently provided parental explanations. *Lack of confidence* and *dependence* occurred most frequently among autocratic parents who infrequently provided parental explanations of rules of conduct and expectations; they occurred *least frequently* among democratic, explaining parents.

In brief, it appears that democratic practices, with frequent explanations by parents of the reasons for their rules of conduct and expectations, foster responsible independence learning in several ways: (1) by providing opportunities for increasing autonomy, guided by interested parents who communicate with the child and exercise appropriate degrees of control; (2) by promoting positive identification with the adult parent, based on love and respect for the child, rather than rejection or indifference; and (3) by themselves providing models of reasonable independence, i.e.,

Table 14.3 Levels of Parental Power and Frequency of Explanation in Relation
to Types of Adolescent Dependence-Independence Behavior

| Level of Parental Power | Parental Explana-tions | N | Types of Adolescent Dependence-Independence Behavior[a] | | | | Total Per-cent |
| | | | Lack of Confidence | | Confidence | | |
			Dependent	Independent	Dependent	Independent	
Autocratic	Freq.	139	27.3	6.5	37.4	28.8	100
	Infreq.	231	34.2	14.7	20.3	30.3	100
Democratic	Freq.	1233	10.5	6.7	37.6	45.2	100
	Infreq.	194	22.7	9.8	35.6	31.9	100
Permissive	Freq.	729	13.2	7.2	29.8	49.8	100
	Infreq.	177	28.2	13.6	24.9	33.3	100

[a] The degree of self-confidence in personal ideas and values was measured by the following item: How confident are you that your own ideas and opinions about what you should do and believe are right and best for you? [Lack of confidence] (1) Not at all confident, (2) Not very confident, (3) I'm a little confident. [Confidence] (4) I'm quite confident, (5) I'm completely confident.

Self-reliance in problem-solving and decision making was measured by the following item: When you have a really important decision to make, about yourself and your future, do you make it on your own, or do you like to get help on it? [Dependent] (1) I'd rather let someone else decide for me, (2) I depend a lot upon other people's advice, (3) I like to get some help. [Independent] (4) Get other ideas then make up my own mind, (5) Make up my own mind without any help.
Source: From G. H. Elder, Jr. Parental power legitimation and its effect on the adolescent. Sociometry, 1963, 26, 61. By permission of the American Sociological Association.

autonomy within the framework of a democratic order (178). In contrast, the child of autocratic or indifferent parents is not presented with models of responsible, cooperative independence; he is not so likely to be encouraged by parental acceptance to identify with adults, and is not given graded experiences in the orderly assumption of responsible autonomy (4).

Sociocultural Influences and Parental Power Practices. In both of the studies described above, the relationship of parental power practices to social class, religious affiliation, educational level of parents, and size of family were also investigated (51, 52). With respect to social-class effects, differences (though present) were not uniformly so large as might have been expected, perhaps partly as a result of bias in using adolescent ratings of parental behavior. Overall, there was a slight tendency for middle-class parents to be viewed as more democratic, equalitarian, or permissive, and for lower-class parents to be viewed as more autocratic and authoritarian (52). The largest differences occurred in the case of younger girls. Proceeding from these younger females to the younger males, older females, and older males, successively smaller social-class differences are observed (52).

Recent research has suggested that Catholic parents engage in independence training later than Protestant parents do (124, 251). It appears that Catholic parents may be more reluctant to give their adolescents freedom in self-direction than Protestants. If so, one would have expected to find proportionately more Catholic than Protestant parents in these studies who were autocratic or authoritarian in child-rearing. Further, on the basis of differences in Catholic and Protestant family-life literature on the role of the husband-father in the family, one might have expected that differences in the power wielded by parents in child-rearing by religious affiliation would be chiefly between Catholic and Protestant fathers (53).

Results of these studies indicated that Catholic and Protestant parents were similar in the control they exercised over their *younger* sons and daughters, and that only Catholic and Protestant fathers (but not mothers) differed in relating to their *older* adolescents. When the children were of older ages, proportionately more Protestant fathers were viewed as democratic, equalitarian, or permissive in rearing their older children, and proportionately more Catholic fathers were seen as either autocratic or authoritarian. This suggests that there is a tendency among Catholic fathers, but not Catholic mothers, to increase their control and restrictiveness as their children become older—a tendency which is reversed among Protestant fathers.

When class differences in frequency of parental explanations were examined, it was found that lower-class autocratic mothers and middle-class democratic and permissive mothers were more likely to explain rules and policies (51). Also, mothers were more likely to explain frequently to younger than to older adolescents, and to girls rather than boys. (51).

In summary, autocratic and authoritarian parents, according to the ratings of adolescent children, were most likely to be fathers with older sons and daughters; to be of lower-class status; to possess a high school education or less; to be Catholic; and to have three or more children living at home. In contrast, parents defined as democratic and equalitarian were most apt to be mothers; to be parents of older youths; to be of middle-class status; to have had at least some college education; to be Protestant fathers of high school-age children; and to have one or two children living at home. In brief, middle-class Protestant parents in one- or two-child families were most inclined to allow their children of high school age some responsibility in directing their own behavior in life.

Individual Influences on Parental Attitudes Toward Adolescent Independence. We have already seen that there are likely to be contradictions in attitudes toward adolescent independence, not only *between* various agents of the adult culture, but also *within* the individual parent. It is this second type of contradiction which is likely to be most difficult for the adolescent to cope with because of its elusiveness. When one voice of the culture, such as the church, issues a particular set of directives for adolescent behavior, and another voice, such as the peer group, issues another, the adolescent may be in conflict, and he will be forced to choose between them. But at least in this situation he has a clear recognition of the attitudes with which he is dealing. On the other hand, when a parent proclaims, for example, that he wants his son to be independent, but covertly does everything he can to prolong dependency, the result is likely to be confusion for the adolescent. His position becomes similar to Alice's in her encounter with the Mad Hatter—nothing is ever quite what it seems. Because of the difficulty of identifying and labeling parental attitudes correctly, he finds it almost impossible to deal with them rationally.

Parental inconsistencies with regard to emancipation may simply reflect confusion on the part of the parent as to the role society expects him to play. (When *should* he permit a child to date, to have his own spending money, to drive a car, to make his own decisions?) If so, the problem of helping the parent to achieve consistency may be merely one of education. More often, however, a parent's inconsistencies seem to result from his own contradictory needs—needs that are deeply rooted and not infrequently unconscious. Many parents, for example, genuinely want their children to become able to handle their own affairs because they realize that ultimately this will be necessary. But, at the same time, they are likely to want to continue to protect their children from the unpleasant realities of existence—an impossible task (58).

There are of course many other possible sources of a parent's inconsistencies. A parent with strong needs to be all-powerful and all-wise in the eyes of others may in reality have gained little recognition from the world at large. As a result, he may be unwilling to grant his child independence, because an inevitable corollary of independence is a renunciation of the idea that any one, including one's parent, is always right and can be trusted to run one's life adequately.

Similarly, those parents who feel unloved by their marriage partners or their friends may be reluctant to see their children begin leading their own lives. For they realize, either consciously or unconsciously, that another of the inevitable consequences of independence is a shift in primary affectional goals from parents to other important life figures—whether sweetheart, marriage partner, or one's own offspring. As Meyers states:

> Allowing a child to achieve emancipation, will be difficult in proportion as the parent has achieved satisfaction, knowingly or not, for his own wants by loving and controlling his child. If the child is providing gratification and compensation for frustrations arising elsewhere, he will be surrendered reluctantly, surrendered at a cost, or not surrendered at all (130).

The parent who possesses secret needs for sexual delinquency may project these desires on to the child, and hence become fearful of what the child may do if left to his or her own devices. As a result, the parent may become unduly repressive in controlling the child's activities.

Many parents, while consciously desirous that their children lead a happy and rewarding life, often keep them tied to their parental apron strings through jealousy. Unconsciously, they do not want their children to enjoy good times that they themselves have missed *(58)*.

There are, of course, many other reasons why parents may be reluctant to grant their children independence, such as fearing that they may marry too young and thus require a longer period of financial support. Parents may also fear that a young person will marry unwisely, or marry the wrong person, or someone beneath him—whatever that may mean to the particular family. Moreover, they fear there is a real danger of sexual indulgence before marriage and that even friendly proximity is going to be a temptation to sexual intercourse, with the resultant danger of illegitimate pregnancy or disease and the consequent disgrace *(58)*. Despite the current availability of birth-control pills, they are not employed in most initial instances of premarital intercourse.

In general, it appears that the most common source of parental ambivalence (mixed feelings) toward the child's assumption of independence is the realization on the one hand that the child must someday stand on his own feet, but the coexistent fear that in learning to do so he will be deeply hurt. A great many of these fears, however, are unfounded.

Children will, of course, make mistakes, and they may even be hurt. This is unfortunate. But the chances of their being seriously harmed seem to us much less if they are allowed to learn independency responses gradually, while they are still able to turn to their parents for support, than if they are suddenly thrust out into the world at the age of 21, totally unprepared to act independently.

Horrocks offers a worthwhile caution, however, in regard to parents' attempts to help their children achieve emancipation: he points out that extremes can be exceedingly dangerous, and that while it is necessary for the parent to promote independence, "there is danger that a child may be emancipated too early, or that emancipation may be vigorously or too harshly promoted" *(84, 47)*. He points out:

> Emancipation cannot be achieved overnight and the wise parent will make it a gradual process of induction over a period of time so that the adolescent will not lose his sense of security, or misunderstand the motives of his parents. . . . The problem seems to be that of striking a golden mean between overprotection and overrestriction on the one hand, and absolute independence on the other *(84, 47–48)*.

Stability of Dependent and Independent Behavior

Study of the Fels children from early childhood through adulthood revealed that those girls who had achieved relative independence from the family during adolescence continued to be independent and self-sufficient as adults: the dependent adolescent girls were, as women, still dependent on their families *(99)*. As preadolescents and adolescents, these girls were observed at home and at the Institute and were interviewed by Fels' psychologists. In contrast to girls who showed self-sufficiency during adolescence, those who frequently relied on their mothers for help with problems were, as women, still dependent upon their family. These women consulted with their mothers before making major purchases, preferred to live close to their family, and felt a strong need to keep a close tie to their family *(99)*.

Dependent or independent behavior was less stable for the boys because society encourages the adolescent boy to become independent. Thus, if he has previously been overly dependent, parents and peers will put pressure on him to develop more independent behavior. This pressure forces some boys to inhibit overt dependent behavior, thus making it more difficult to predict the degree of dependent behavior in an adult man from observations of his behavior as an adolescent. Dependent behavior is socially more acceptable for girls, and a girl who is excessively dependent as an adolescent is more likely to remain dependent through the early adult years *(98, 99)*.

SEXUAL BEHAVIOR IN THE ADOLESCENT

Increased sexual drive, influenced by hormonal and anatomical changes, is, of course, a major physiological concomitant of adolescence. However, the forms it takes, and the manner in which it is expressed will vary, depending on the sex of the adolescent and also upon a wide variety of psychological and cultural forces. There is little question that for most boys, the rapid increase in sexual drive which accompanies adolescence is difficult, if not impossible, to deny. In boys this drive is "imperious and biologically specific. . . . He must confront [it] directly, consciously, find within himself the means of obtaining sexual discharge without excessive guilt, and means of control without crippling inhibitions" *(45, 110)*.

In contrast, among girls sexual drive is likely to be more diffuse and ambiguous. For many girls, a limited temporary denial of sexual impulses may not only be feasible but may also often provide a comfortable adaptation *(45)*. Regardless of the underlying reasons for these sex-differences (pp. 636–638), sexual impulses among girls appear to be more easily transformed and displaced into a great many other disguises: "Sexuality is then not experienced as such; it very easily becomes spiritualized, idealized, etherealized" *(45, 111)*. Obviously, as adolescence proceeds, girls experience a greater increase in conscious awareness of sexual impulses, but even then erotic gratification *as such* is likely to remain secondary to—or at least closely related to—the fulfillment of other needs such as self-esteem, reassurance, affection, and love. For most girls, the overall relationship with the individual boy whom she loves—the extent to which this relationship is characterized by trust, concern, and a mutual sharing of life experiences—takes precedence over specific sexual release. Consequently, control of impulses is likely to constitute a considerably less urgent problem for girls.

Virtually all available data indicate that, while there is a significant increase in specifically sexual interests and behavior during adolescence, sexual activity is considerably greater among boys than girls *(106, 107, 151)*. Girls also display somewhat more conservative attitudes toward sexual morality. In the light of the differences between boys and girls mentioned above, these findings do not appear surprising. The underlying reasons for such differences are, however, far from clear. Several theories have been advanced —some primarily physiological in nature, others primarily cultural.

One possibility is that females are less likely than males to discover sexual responses spontaneously because the girl's sexual organs are less prominent. Some authors have advanced such an argument to account partially for the greater incidence of masturbation among adolescent males than among females. As Mead says:

> The human female shows a lesser capacity for sexual stimulation, and it might be argued that the lesser frequency of masturbation among young females that is reported in our own society, and characteristic of all South Sea societies I have studied is merely a structural matter. The female child's genitals are less exposed, subject to less maternal manipulation and self-manipulation. If masturbation is not socially recognized and taught either by parents to children or by older children to younger, it may escape the spontaneous learning of the female child *(128, 47)*.

It is also possible that there may be basic physiological differences in sexual motivation between male and female adolescents, as some authors have suggested. Such differences may be quantitative (i.e., sex drive may be "stronger" in males; *50, 177*), or qualitative (i.e., different in form), as suggested earlier, or both. It is also interesting to note that sexual behavior (e.g., frequency of orgasm) may vary within wider ranges among girls than boys *(106, 107)*. That biological differences between males and females in sexual motivation exist is suggested both by the lesser amount of specifically sexual behavior found in females in widely varying cultures *(127)* and by the persistence of sex differences across human and animal species (e.g., generally greater aggressiveness of the male, greater responsiveness of the male to visual and other sexual stimuli, etc.).

Nevertheless, it also appears probable that the lesser sexual responsiveness of female adolescents, and to some extent the qualitatively different nature, is attributable at least partially to our culture's more restrictive social attitudes toward sexual gratification for girls. As we shall see, sexual attitudes and behavior vary widely from one culture to another.

CULTURAL INFLUENCES ON SEXUAL ATTITUDES AND BEHAVIOR

In the light of the role that learning plays in determining the sexual response patterns which are adopted as ways of gratifying sexual drives, it is not surprising to find that sexual behavior during adolescence varies markedly from one culture to another. There are important differences between cultures, not only in the amount and type of sexual behavior that is socially accepted, but also in the consistency of the society's sexual standards as development proceeds. A culture may be restrictive with regard to sexual activity throughout childhood, adolescence, and even to some extent in adulthood. It may be fairly permissive at all ages. Or it may be highly restrictive during childhood and adolescence, and then suddenly become much more permissive about, and, of course, in many cases demand, sexual activity in adulthood.

Thus, Dakota Indians do not expect children to be interested in sexual behavior until they have reached puberty and are capable of reproduction. Among the Melanesian cultures of New Guinea, on the other hand, sex play among preadolescent children is taken lightly.

Moreover, the culture's attitude toward sexuality will depend, in part, on whether the culture views sex primarily as a source of pleasure or as reserved for reproduction. The Marquesans stress the pleasure value of sex and are permissive of sexual behavior in children. The Zuni of New Mexico are less encouraging of sex among preadolescents because children of this age are not capable of reproduction (12).

In our own society the formal adult culture has tended generally to view sex behavior as appropriate only among marriage partners and, therefore, to discourage it among children and adolescents. While there is evidence that cultural attitudes are now becoming somewhat more liberal, we have typically spent a great many years teaching the individual to inhibit sexual responses in order to prepare him for a time when he will be expected to make these responses. We have taught him to respond to sex with anxiety when he was a child, and then demanded that he not respond anxiously after he is married.

> The man or woman who learned during childhood and adolescence that it was "wrong" to examine or stimulate his or her own genitals, that it was "even worse" to have any contact with those of another person, and, particularly, that attempts at heterosexual relations were immoral, is expected to reverse completely at least some of these attitudes on the wedding night or shortly thereafter. This expectation is difficult to fulfill. If the initial lessons have been well learned, the unlearning is bound to take a long time and may never be completed (67, 195).

It would be a mistake to assume that such contradictory cultural expectations have been confined to our own society. For example, "in sexual matters the Manus boy is in much the same position as our middle-class adolescent male" (1). While the male physiological sex drive is recognized as natural in this New Guinea tribe, sexual behavior is strongly tabooed until marriage. Apparently such release of tension as does occur is achieved primarily through covert homosexual activity and through solitary masturbation "surrounded by shame" (1). The Manus girl's position is highly reminiscent of that of a female of the Victorian era. She is taught that sex is not gratifying to women, and, in fact, that it is "loathsome, shameful, and repugnant" (7). The consequent difficulties in adjusting to intercourse after marriage can easily be imagined.

In some nonliterate societies, the inconsistencies of social attitudes toward sex are even more extreme than in our own. For example, among the Ashanti, sexual intercourse with a girl who has not undergone the puberty ceremony is considered so harmful to the community that the offense is punishable by death for both parties (67).

In contrast, there are many cultures, such as the Hopi, the Siriono, and the Alorese, which are highly tolerant of sexual behavior in childhood. In most cases, this tolerance persists into adolescence and adulthood. Under such conditions, sex play increases in both sexes, beginning with casual masturbation and extending, as the child grows older, to handling the genitals of the same and opposite sex, and to intercourse (67).

Among the Ila-speaking people of Africa, "childhood is regarded as a time of preparation for adult life and mature sexual functions. At harvest time, each girl is given a house to which she takes a boy of her choice, and there they play as man and wife. It is reported that there are no virgins among these people after the age of 10" (67, 191). "The Lepcha of India believe that girls will not mature without benefit of sexual intercourse. Early sex play among boys and girls characteristically involves many forms of mutual masturbation and usually ends in attempted copulation. By the time they are 11 or 12 years old, most girls regularly engage in full intercourse" (67, 191).

Obviously, adolescent sexual attitudes and practices vary widely from one culture to another. These attitudes and practices, in turn, will have a marked influence on the ease with which the adolescent is able to adjust to adult heterosexuality.

Sexual Attitudes in Relation to the Total Culture

The type of sexual training an individual receives during childhood and adolescence helps to determine whether he will show great or little interest in sexual behavior, and whether he will tend to view sex as a pleasant and matter-of-fact affair; as sinful and dangerous; extremely exciting; or as a matter of aggressive conquest, or even rape. Sex-training practices in turn are intimately related to broad cultural attitudes. Among the Zuni, for example, the relations—sexual and otherwise—between husband and wife tend to be pleasant, cooperative, and untainted by feelings of guilt. This is true not simply because of cultural attitudes toward sex but also because of cultural attitudes toward living generally. The sense of sin, for example, is not absent only with regard to sexual behavior. As Benedict says, "It is unfamiliar to them not only in sex but in any experience" (13). Sexual intercourse is a cooperative, rather than a competitive, matter to the Zunis, "not simply because of specific sex training, but because cooperation is an integral part of the whole Zuni way of life" (13).

Romney and Romney, in Whiting's *Six cultures: studies of child rearing* (196) have recently called attention to a similar attitude among the Mixtecan Indians of Mexico: ". . . sex is regarded as necessary and natural. From [their] point of view, the use of sex for exploitative purposes is inconsistent with their attitudes, just as are all other forms of exploitation of human beings. Sexual power does not add to the luster of the individual. . . (*196*, 565–566).

In other societies, such as the Mundugumor, aggression and competition play an important part in the individual's sexual relations largely because they pervade the whole Mundugumor way of life.

The data on cultural variations in sexual behavior presented in the preceding sections provide impressive evidence of the modifiability of human sexual behavior. These data also demonstrate the tremendously important role of cultural differences in determining the individual's sexual attitudes and beliefs, the frequency and direction of his sexual responses, and, to the degree that actual behavior deviates from beliefs, the degree of anxiety and conflict associated with such behavior. Thus it becomes important to consider whether current social attitudes are changing and, if so, what effects they may be having on present and future patterns of sexual behavior of adolescent boys and girls. We hear much these days about the "new morality" of the adolescent subculture. Does this phenomenon, in fact, exist and, if so, what are its effects upon behavior? Does the sexual behavior of today's adolescents differ from that of their parents and grandparents at the same age? Each question will be taken up in turn.

Sexual Attitudes and Values of American Adolescents

If one asks adolescents themselves whether they think there is a "new morality" regarding sex, the answer—at least among middle- and upper-class youth—definitely appears to be "yes." In a recent nationwide questionnaire interview of 550 adolescents, aged 13 to 20, 75 percent stated the belief that they were developing a new sexual morality. However, they do not view this change as a *lowering* of morals; 82 percent of the sample viewed their morals as "no lower than their parents" (*184*, 48). In the words of one adolescent girl, "Adults are just plain phonies about sex."

What then does the "new morality" involve for the average adolescent? Most clearly, it appears to involve a desire for a greater openness and honesty about sex (*28, 77, 184*). In the study cited above, 84 percent of the sample thought that there should be sex education classes in their high schools (*184*). Apparently, the much-publicized doubts of some current parent groups in the United States regarding the wisdom of such classes are not shared by their children. There also appears to be a greater tendency to view decisions about individual sexual behavior as primarily a *personal* rather than a *public* concern (*184*). There is less manifest tendency to judge others; 80 percent of the sample felt that "a pregnant girl should not marry if she didn't love the boy." (In a national sample of college students, 37 percent of both boys and girls approved prescription of oral contraceptives in student health centers [*28*], although few universities have concurred in this view, particularly in the case of unmarried girls.) Regardless of whether they would become involved themselves, 66 percent of the adolescent sample expressed the view that sex before marriage is accepted by their contemporaries. Forty-five percent of the total sample (34 percent of girls) agreed that it is "all right for a boy and girl who are in love to live together" (184, 48).

In a recent poll of college campuses in the United States, two-thirds of the students expressed the belief that prevailing campus standards encouraged sexual activity; and more than four out of five said that their experiences in college had made them take a more tolerant attitude toward those who defied traditional sexual morality (28).

In the opinion of today's adolescents, the acceptability of heterosexual behavior is highly dependent on the degree of closeness of the relationship shared by the couple. In one study (153) an attempt was made to develop a scale of premarital sexual permissiveness, involving three levels of progressively more intimate sexual activity (kissing, petting, and coitus). At each level, subjects were asked to rate the acceptability of the activity before marriage under four conditions: (1) engaged to be married, (2) in love, (3) strong affection felt for partner, and (4) not particularly affectionate toward partner. Ratings ranged from strongly agree to strongly disagree. Each subject, regardless of sex, was asked to complete rating scales on acceptable standards both for males and for females.

These scales were initially administered to (1) 1028 students in five high schools and colleges (a white and a Negro high school, a white and a Negro college, all in Virginia, and a predominantly white "liberal" college in New York), and (2) to a representative national sample of the adult population of the United States (N = 1515).

In every case, students ranked an activity as most acceptable when the couple were engaged and least acceptable when no particular affection was felt for the partner. Percentage agreement with each item in the male and female scales for the five school sample is shown in Table 14.4.

In the view of these students, premarital intercourse, accompanied by affection or love, is considered more acceptable than petting when no particular affection is felt. In contrast, adults found intercourse, even between engaged couples, far less acceptable than petting, even when affection was absent. Obviously, these students (both males and females) placed a greater emphasis on the meaningfulness of the personal relationship between the partners than on what they viewed as arbitrary social standards of right and wrong. These findings appear consistent with the emphasis among today's adolescents upon finding viable personal relationships between individuals and meaningful personal standards of morality, rather than relying on traditional social mores (particularly those of the adult culture), or on a fear of the consequences (e.g., pregnancy).

It should be noted that in no study available to us did a majority of students approve of premarital sexual relations for couples who are not in love or engaged, and in most studies, less than 50 percent approved even when there was a formal engagement. Percentages of students approving

Table 14.4 Percentage Agreement with Sexual Permissiveness Scale Items in Male and Female Scales for National Adult Sample and Five School Sample[a]

Question	National Sample Total Percent Male	Five School Sample Total Percent Male	National Sample Total Percent Female	Five School Sample Total Percent Female
I believe that kissing is acceptable for the male before marriage when he is engaged to be married.	95.3	97.5	95.0	98.5
I believe that kissing is acceptable for the male before marriage when he is in love.	93.6	98.9	93.3	99.1
I believe that kissing is acceptable for the male before marriage when he feels strong affection for his partner.	90.2	97.2	88.1	97.8
I believe that kissing is acceptable for the male before marriage even if he does not feel particularly affectionate toward his partner.	58.6	64.2	50.1	55.2
I believe that petting is acceptable for the male before marriage when he is engaged to be married.	60.8	85.0	56.1	81.8
I believe that petting is acceptable for the male before marriage when he is in love.	59.4	80.4	52.6	75.2
I believe that petting is acceptable for the male before marriage when he feels strong affection for his partner.	54.3	67.0	45.6	56.7
I believe that petting is acceptable for the male before marriage even if he does not feel particularly affectionate toward his partner.	28.6	34.3	20.3	18.0
I believe that full sexual relations are acceptable for the male before marriage when he is engaged to be married.	19.5	52.2	16.9	44.0
I believe that full sexual relations are acceptable for the male before marriage when he is in love.	17.6	47.6	14.2	38.7

Table 14.4   (*Continued*)

Question	National Sample Total Percent Male	Five School Sample Total Percent Male	National Sample Total Percent Female	Five School Sample Total Percent Female
I believe that full sexual relations are acceptable for the male before marriage when he feels strong affection for his partner.	16.3	36.9	12.5	27.2
I believe that full sexual relations are acceptable for the male before marriage even if he does not feel particularly affectionate toward his partner.	11.7	20.8	7.4	10.8
	1,390	811	1,411	806

a N equals those who answered all scale questions. Those who failed to answer one or more questions were dropped.
Source: From I. L. Reiss. The scaling of premarital sexual permissiveness. *J. Marriage Fam.*, 1964, Vol. 26. By permission. Reprinted in I. L. Reiss. *The social context of premarital sexual permissiveness.* New York: Holt, Rinehart and Winston, 1967, 29.

intercourse between couples who did not "share any particular affection" or who "were merely willing" ranged from a high of 20.8 percent for older adolescent males in one study (*153*) to a low of 4 percent among younger teen-age girls and 8 percent among girls 18 to 20 in another national survey (*112*). Contrary to popular adult stereotypes, it appears reasonably clear that promiscuity is widely disapproved by both adolescent boys and girls of all ages.

While only a minority—although a substantial and increasing minority—of adolescents agree on the personal acceptability of premarital intercourse, even when love or engagement are involved, petting appears to be widely accepted by most older adolescents of both sexes (*112, 153*), particularly if the couple are in love or engaged (*112, 153*). When there is any degree of affection, kissing and necking appear to meet with virtually universal acceptance—up to 98 percent (*153*).

On the basis of the (admittedly limited) data reported above, it would appear that adolescent attitudes and values regarding sex are changing (*152*). There also appears to be little doubt that, for some subgroups of adolescents, the findings reported here would appear conservative. At the same time, there are other subgroups in which we have no doubt they would appear exaggerated. There is, however, a real and often ignored danger in generalizing too widely from specialized subgroups (e.g., a particular college campus or a particular urban high school) to youth in general.

In brief, these findings, combined with general social observation, do suggest an emerging "new morality" among adolescents, at least as far as attitudes and values are concerned (*154*). Obviously, there are dangers, particularly for girls, in assuming that sexual involvement is "okay as long as you're in love." Encouraged by such a philosophy among peers, a girl or boy may become more deeply involved emotionally than he or she can responsibly handle at a particular stage of maturity (*190*). An adolescent may also consciously think that his attitudes are more "liberal" than they actually are, and involvement may lead to unanticipated feelings of guilt, anxiety, or depression. There also still remain such very practical problems as the possibility of pregnancy. Many girls today express the opinion that "now that science has given us the [birth control] pill, we no longer have to be frightened about pregnancy. We just have to decide what is right." Noble as this sentiment may be, the facts indicate that only a small percentage of unmarried girls having intercourse have used the contraceptive pill to prevent pregnancy (*74, 112*), and a disturbingly high percentage, at least in their first experience, have used no contraceptive device whatever (*112*). Currently, the number of illegitimate births in the United States is running about 300,000 a year and is continuing to rise. More than 70 percent of these babies are born to girls under 25 years of age. It is also estimated that approximately 20 percent of all new brides, and 30 to 50 percent of high-school-age brides are pregnant when they marry (*188*). Furthermore, the danger of venereal disease from promiscuous sexual relations cannot be ignored. Despite popular notions to the contrary, current strains of gonorrhea are highly resistant to the treatments now available. And rates of venereal disease are soaring among adolescents, just as are the rates for illegitimate births. In their faith in the magical properties of drugs, modern adolescents sometimes tend to ignore the fundamentals of biology.

Parent-Child Differences in Sexual Attitudes. It would appear from the above discussion that there are indeed generational differences in sexual values, although they have probably been exaggerated. Parents, in general, tend to express more conservative and more traditional attitudes than their adolescent sons and daughters on such topics as necking, petting, and premarital intercourse (*9*). They also differ regarding the ages and the circumstances (e.g., in love, engaged, married) under which various forms of sexual intimacy are acceptable (*153*).

In the study by Reiss cited above, the largest single difference between the generations came on the item, "I believe that full sexual relations are acceptable for the male (female) before marriage when he (she) is engaged to be married." In the case of the male, 52.2 percent of students, but only 19.5 percent of adults, expressed agreement. In the case of the female, similar results were obtained, although both the overall percentages agreeing and the size of the adult-student difference were somewhat smaller (44.0 percent of students and 16.9 percent of adults replied affirmatively).

It is also interesting to note a trend toward a single standard of morality among both adults and students—away from the destructiveness of the widely accepted double standard of the last century and, indeed, much of the present century. Thus among students, intercourse between engaged persons is considered acceptable by 52.2 percent in the case of boys and 44.0 percent in the case of girls; among adults, the comparable percentages are 19.5 percent and 16.9 percent, respectively (Table 14.4). Similarly, among students, petting between engaged couples is considered acceptable by 85.0 percent in the case of boys, and 81.8 percent in the case of girls. Comparable percentages for adults were 60.8 percent and 56.1 percent, respectively (153).

In another recent study, 217 coeds and their mothers served as subjects. Both mothers and daughters were asked to respond to the question, "How important do you think it is that a girl be a virgin when she marries?" Of the mothers, 88 percent answered "generally important" and 0 percent "not important," compared with 34 percent and 13 percent of the daughters (10, 391). In response to the question, "Do you think sexual intercourse during engagement is very wrong; generally wrong; right in many situations?" the responses were "very wrong" for 83 percent of the mothers but for only 35 percent of the daughters (10, 391). Both of the questions "show sharp differences between the value responses of the mothers and daughters with reference to premarital chastity" (10), and other studies yield results similar to those cited above (9, 153).

Granted that there is a generational gap in sexual values and attitudes, is this gap increasing or decreasing? In the opinion of the authors, it appears more likely to be decreasing, primarily because adult values are becoming more liberal rather than because youth's values are becoming more conservative (although for reasons to be discussed later, it appears probable that some gap will always exist between generations). Certainly adult values, particularly adult middle-class values, have become more liberal in this century. They are also better rooted in factual scientific information. Perhaps of most general importance, a majority of today's parents do not believe and do not, either directly or indirectly, lead their children to believe that sex per se is bad. In fact, there is a general acknowledgment, publicly and privately, that it is pleasurable and can, under favorable circumstances, be deeply meaningful both for boys and for girls. This clearly represents a significant shift in parental attitudes and values in this century.

Sexual Behavior of Contemporary Adolescents

Given the changing sexual values of adolescents, one might also be led to conclude that changing sexual values would be dramatically reflected in changed sexual behavior among adolescents. Paradoxically, the available evidence suggests that the sexual behavior of today's adolescents, while more open and in some respects probably freer, is not so strikingly different from that of their parents at the same age.

Investigations of sexual behavior over the past fifty years have consistently indicated that boys engage in a greater amount of specifically sexual (as distinguished from romantic) activity than girls, and this still appears to be the case. In Kinsey's study (106), 95 percent of boys had their first orgasm by age 15, two-thirds of them through masturbation. Other authors give similar estimates.

Kinsey found that as adolescence progressed, the average boy's frequency of orgasm increased, reaching a lifetime peak of about 3.4 per week between 16 and 17 years of age (25). This frequency tended to persist with only slight diminution until the age of 30, after which there was a gradual tapering off (106).

In contrast, fewer girls than boys experienced orgasm in adolescence. Even at age 20, only 53 percent of girls had experienced orgasm, and incidence did not reach a lifetime maximum of around 90 percent until age 35. The maximum frequency of orgasm (1.8 per week) did not occur until the period of 26 to 30 years (106, 107).

There were also marked sex differences in the source of first orgasm. In contrast to boys, only 37 percent of girls who had achieved orgasm had done so through masturbation. On the other hand, while premarital petting to climax was an insignificant source of first orgasm in boys, it accounted for almost 20 percent in girls. Again, while premarital intercourse was a minor source of first orgasm in boys, it accounted for 30 percent in girls. Other sources of sexual outlet accounted for only a minor proportion of girls' initial orgasms (107). Although nearly 100 percent of boys had reached orgasm by the time of marriage (through a variety of methods), only 30 percent of females had done so.

While the evidence is admittedly inadequate, such information as is available indicates relatively little if any change in the past few decades in the incidence of either male or female masturbation (106, 107). Masturbation among adolescent males prior to age 20 has remained fairly stable over the years, with an estimated incidence of about 95 percent (106, 151). By the same age, less than half as many females have engaged in masturbation (probably somewhere around 40 percent). Furthermore, *frequency* of masturbation is much greater among males. By late adolescence, well over four-fifths of adolescent males masturbate with a frequency of one to four times a week; in contrast, girls show both a much lower frequency and much more variability. Some girls report a frequency of masturbation as low as once or twice a year, or even less, while others may masturbate as many as ten to twenty times a week. The modal frequency for girls is probably less than once a month (151). It would appear that the greatest changes occurring among present-day youth with respect to masturbation are probably not in behavior itself, but in reduced fear and guilt, and increased objectivity and scientific information.

Petting does appear to have increased significantly in the past century (151), and it tends to occur earlier (106, 107, 151). However, a considerable portion of these changes were already accounted for by the time today's parents were themselves adolescents. According to Kinsey's data (107), about 94 percent of today's mothers had engaged in petting as adolescents. In contrast, the incidence for *their* mothers varied between 66 percent (for those born before 1900) to 81 percent (for those born between 1900 and 1909). Today's average mother began petting between ages 15 and 16; *her* mother, in contrast, began between 16 and 17 (younger group) or 17 and 18 (older group). Thus, at least as far as accumulative incidence is concerned, today's mothers did differ from *their* mothers; however, they do not differ markedly from their daughters on this measure. (Today's fathers yielded data very similar to that for mothers, both in incidence of adolescent petting and age of beginning petting; 106, 107.) Today's adolescents are very similar to their parents in frequency of petting and average age of beginning petting (112, 153). There is some reason to believe, however, that frequency of petting, degree of intimacy in terms of techniques involved, and, certainly, frankness about this activity have continued to increase among today's youth (153).

A similar picture exists with respect to premarital intercourse. Inconceivable as it may seem to today's adolescents, if anything that could properly be called a sexual revolution in behavior has occurred in this century, it was probably initiated by their parents and grandparents. Kinsey's data indicate that only 8 percent of females born before 1900 had premarital intercourse prior to age 20, and only 14 percent prior to age 25; in contrast, the corresponding figures for today's parents and grandparents (those born after 1900) are approximately 21 percent and 37 percent, respectively. Interestingly, these incidence figures changed little between those born in the period 1900–1909 and those born in the period 1920–1929. Such inadequate data as are available suggest that, among girls *currently,* incidence of premarital intercourse before age 20 may fall between 25 and 30 percent, and by age 25, between 30 and 40 percent (17, 112), although there are wide cultural and geographic differences as well as indications that incidence is rising among couples who are in love or engaged (71). To date, however, the really significant difference in incidence of premarital intercourse is not to be found between today's mothers and daughters, but between *both* generations and those women born before 1900.

The picture for males is probably similar to that for females, although for all generations the incidence of premarital intercourse among males is higher (106). Approximately 45 percent of today's fathers had engaged in premarital intercourse by age 20. By age 25, the figure had risen to 65 percent. While comparable data for today's male adolescents are not currently available, it seems likely that similar, though probably slightly higher, incidence percentages obtain.

Again, the greatest differences occur not between today's adolescents and their parents, but between today's parents and *their* parents. As in the case of petting, however, it appears that secrecy regarding premarital intercourse has continued to decrease, particularly in the case of couples who are engaged or deeply (and publicly) committed to each other.

Socioeconomic Differences.   In addition to differences between adolescent males and females in overall sexual responsiveness and some, though more limited, differences between today's adolescents and their parents, there are also differences in responsiveness related to social-class membership (106–107).

It is interesting to note that the effects of social-class membership apparently are considerably less for females than for males. In their report of female sex behavior, Kinsey and his associates pointed out: "There seems to have been no correlation at all between occupational classes of the parental homes in which the females in the sample have been raised and the incidences and frequencies of their total [sexual] outlet" (107, 529). There also appeared to be little relationship between social-class background of females and incidence or frequency of most types of sexual response.

In contrast to the rather negligible influences of social-class membership upon sexual behavior in females, religious affiliations seem to play a strong role, both during adolescence and in later life. Kinsey found regularly that inactive members of the Protestant, Jewish, and Catholic faiths were consistently more sexually active both before and after marriage than were moderately active church members, while devout members, in turn, were consistently the least active sexually. Other investigators have obtained similar results (117).

Among boys, on the other hand, implicit standards of acceptable sexual behavior vary from one social-class level to another (11). Among upper-middle-class older adolescent boys, masturbation and petting to climax, while not specifically approved, are generally viewed as more acceptable than actual intercourse. Conversely, there is a general tendency among lower-class adolescents and adults to consider these practices abnormal (106). As a result, masturbation and petting are more common among the higher social-class groups than among the lower.

In contrast, actual intercourse, which is more anxiety-arousing among upper- and middle-class boys, is considered entirely normal by those of lower status: "They have nothing like the strong (higher-level) tabu against premarital intercourse, and, on the contrary, accept it as natural and inevitable and as a desirable thing. Lower-level tabus are more often turned against an avoidance of intercourse and against any substitution for simple and direct coitus" (106, 379). As a reflection of these disparate attitudes, Kinsey found that by age 15 nearly half of lower-class boys but only 10 percent of higher-status boys had engaged in intercourse (106). Among college males, less than one-half had intercourse during the adolescent years, while over three-quarters of the adolescents who did not finish grade school had premarital coitus (80, 157).

The reasons for these social-class differences are multiple and complex. They are not simply the result, for example, of greater parental punishment for sexuality by middle-class parents. It is likely that these differences owe, in part, to the identification models available to the child, and the degree to which the child adopts traditional sex-role values. We have suggested in other chapters of this book, that the child attempts to model himself after the adults in his immediate life space who are viewed as powerful, competent, and prestigeful. It is likely that the lower-class child has traditionally been exposed more often to adults (relatives, older friends, older brothers) who openly boast about sexual conquests and promiscuous relations. Thus the lower-class adolescent attempting to identify with these adult models may be motivated to have sexual experiences in order to strengthen his identification with them.

Moreover, lower-class boys are more concerned with the cluster of traits that define masculinity. As noted in Chapter 12, working-class mothers more vigorously encourage the adoption of traditional sex-typed behaviors in their sons, and in a more stereotyped fashion than middle-class mothers (pp. 506–507). The traditional characteristics of masculinity in our culture include, among other things, strength, courage, aggressivity, sexual potency, and conquests. Lower-class boys more often view sexual experience as an index of masculinity. This conclusion points up an important fact about sexual behavior—namely, that it is often used as a means of proving maturity. Initiation of sexual behavior sometimes is less related to the desire for sexual gratification per se than to the desire to establish one's adult status, as defined by the adolescent's immediate cultural milieu.

Parent-Child Conflicts in Sexual Values

Thus far we have seen that a significant attitudinal gap between generations regarding sexual values does exist, even though behavior at comparable ages is fairly similar. Why the discrepancy?

While the grandparents and parents of today's youth may have engaged in generally similar sexual behavior, they probably did so with more conflicting emotions. After all, their break with *their parents* was more clearly revolutionary as far as actual behavior was concerned. Consequently, it seems reasonable to assume that it was accompanied by more doubt and anxiety, and such indeed appears to have been the case (154). Thus it should not be too surprising to find less consonance between behavior, on the one hand, and values and attitudes, on the other hand, in the older generation than among their children. Today's youth may be perceiving such a lack of consonance when they accuse the adult culture of being "hypocritical" in its sexual attitude and values. Furthermore, parents and children stand in a different relationship to one another, and differ in their responsibilities. As Robert R. Bell notes in a thoughtful article on parent-child conflicts in sexual values:

> Given their different stages in the life cycle, parents and children will almost always show differences in how they define appropriate behavior for a given role. Values as to single "proper" premarital sexual role behavior from the perspective of the parents are greatly influenced by the strong emotional involvement of the parent with his child. Youth, on the other hand, are going through a life cycle stage in which the actual behavior occurs, and they must relate the parent values to what they are doing or may do. There is a significant difference between defining appropriate role conduct for others to follow and defining proper role conduct to be followed by one's self. Even more important for actual behavior, there is often more than one significant group of role definers to which the young person can turn as guide for his sex role behavior (8, 34).

The young person who has only to decide his own values and behavior is in a very different position from the parent concerned about the welfare of his child. In addition to being freer of the strong pressures (both physiological and social) that their adolescent sons and daughters are confronted with, they have, as Bell says, "a strong emotional involvement with their children." They do not wish to see them hurt, either by becoming involved in sexual and emotional relationships they may not be prepared to handle, or by becoming pregnant or involved in early, ill-considered marriages. In many respects, these concerns of parents are part of the larger problem of independence-dependence (cf. pp. 622–635). Parents want their child ultimately to grow up and be independent, but they do not wish to see him hurt in the process.

Factors Affecting Attitudes Toward Opposite-Sex Peers

It is not surprising that some adolescents have trouble making satisfactory heterosexual adjustments. The ease with which the child will be able to progress from antagonism to a positive interest in the opposite sex will depend largely on his previous parent-child relationships. The attitudes which the child develops in his early relations with his mother and father may persist into adolescence and may be generalized to other males and females. For example, as a child a girl may have learned to expect love and admiration from her father. She may have been rewarded by her mother for exhibiting feminine traits. Such a girl will tend to grow up expecting that relations with males in general can also lead to love and admiration. She will not be resentful of playing a feminine role in relation to male contemporaries during adolescence and adulthood.

On the other hand, the girl whose father has rejected her is likely, also on the basis of generalization, to anticipate rejection from all men. Similarly, the boy whose mother has exploited him or dominated him is likely to anticipate exploitation and domination from all women.

The above, of course, are simply examples of the ways in which attitudes developed in relation to parents are likely to be generalized to same- or opposite-sex contemporaries in adolescence, with either a facilitating or damaging effect upon the child's chances for reaching an adequate heterosexual adjustment.

Antagonism toward the opposite sex, stemming from the differential treatment of boys and girls, is another factor which may handicap the adolescent in his heterosexual relationships. The adolescent girl who finds boys able to do things she is unable to do, or receiving rewards she does not receive, may become resentful toward them.

Resentment toward the opposite sex is probably more prevalent among girls than among boys, as boys seem to have a preferred status in our society which is tacitly acknowledged by both sexes. In one study, it was found that while boys seldom, if ever, wished they were girls, girls were not infrequently envious of and wished they were boys (*194*). Factors which may further magnify this sex antagonism and prolong it, possibly permanently, include learned fears of sexuality, shyness, fear of social relationships, and, of course, poor parental identification patterns.

The longitudinal study of the Fels population indicated that the pattern of sexual behavior displayed by boys during early adolescence was indicative of amount and pattern of sexual behavior in adulthood. Boys who did not date during the early high school years were less likely to have established a gratifying heterosexual relationship by the mid-twenties than boys who had been frequent daters. Moreover, the boys who adopted traditional masculine interests (sports, mechanics, competitive games) engaged in more erotic activity in late adolescence and adulthood than the boys whose activities and interests were not traditionally masculine (e.g., music, reading, art; *98*).

Boy-Girl Relationships

As they mature, boys and girls begin to pay more attention to one another. Earlier sex antagonisms and crushes begin to wane, and heterosexual interests increase.

Dating. In our society, dating is both a rather ritualized social institution within which heterosexual skills may be perfected and also one of the principal forms of heterosexual behavior. Because the dating institution is so ubiquitous in America, we often tend to take it for granted, neglecting the fact that dating tends to occur earlier and to play a more dominant role in adolescent peer relations here than in many other countries. According to a recent survey, most girls in the United States begin dating at age 14, while most boys begin between 14 and 15 (*45*).

Among the positive functions presumably served by dating are: developing social and interpersonal skills in relations with members of the opposite sex; providing an opportunity to meet opposite-sex peers and explore mutual compatibility within a social framework that allows for terminating unwanted relationships (and for finding new ones) with a minimum loss of face (*45*); aiding in the finding and testing of identity; providing occasions for sexual experiment and discovery within mutually acceptable limits; and, perhaps most important as far as future marriage is concerned, allowing for the development of reciprocal relationships of genuine trust, love, and mutual concern between opposite-sex peers.

Middle-class dating patterns in this country do, in fact, appear to facilitate at least some of these goals. In comparison with many of their European contemporaries, American adolescents exhibit "a degree of poise and nonchalance which stands in vivid contrast to the shyness, embarrassment, and even gaucherie of the European youngster of equivalent years" (*45*, 207). If the adolescent does not begin going steady with one person too early and for too long a period of time, the dating institution permits him to gain experience with a variety of opposite-sex peers. The depth and maturity of interpersonal relationships encouraged by the dating pattern appear more open to question. Particularly in the earlier years of adolescence, there seems to be less emphasis on the development of warm, spontaneous, meaningful interactions between two individuals and more emphasis on the development of the so-called "dating personality." Many aspects of the so-called "good date"—superficial social and conversational skills; personal charm; the ability to affect a bright, interested manner without letting mood variations show through; keeping the conversation from getting "too serious"; manipulating sexual attractiveness—all seem somewhat irrelevant if not inimical to later development of more honest, direct, complex, deeper emotional relationships, particularly if dating is begun too early. Overeager pursuit of "popularity" and "success" can sometimes work against the development of a richer personal identity and inner resourcefulness.

There does seem to be a growing number of contemporary adolescent boys and girls who seem less impressed with the superficial aspects of the "dating game" and are more concerned with the development of meaningful interpersonal relationships with peers of both sexes than their elders were at the same age (cf. pp. 699–703). Nevertheless, because of dating's peculiar admixture of positive and negative features, both the youth who begins dating too early and displays too much emphasis on it (especially if it involves "going steady" with one person) and the late adolescent who has little or no experience with dating appear to be penalized in their development, although in different ways.

This was demonstrated by the data of one study (45) which showed that girls who started dating and going steady early (ages 11–14) tended to be active, energetic, and self-confident, but also immature, superficial, unimaginative, and limited in their interests and friendships, especially with other girls. In contrast, the late adolescent who did not date tended to be retarded in social development, overly dependent on parents, insecure, and self-absorbed.

In neither case are we (or the investigators) attributing these personality patterns solely to the dating pattern. In fact, it appears more likely that the situation is primarily the reverse, with pre-existing personality structure influencing dating patterns—although once the patterns are begun, a reciprocal feedback pattern, or vicious cycle, appears to be set in motion, further reinforcing the girl's particular liabilities.

The average girl appears to go through three general stages with respect to dating:

> The preadolescent group treats dating as a more or less intellectual issue and gives no real indication of emotional involvement with boys except for occasional signs of anxiety about their imminent introduction to dating. Early adolescents are very much involved in beginning dating, have considerable anxiety about it, and take a defensive rather than an interactive stance toward boys. Only in late adolescence, as initial anxiety subsides, do girls begin to have true interactive relationships with boys, and bring understanding, sensitivity, and feeling to these relationships. In her early dating, the girl is likely to be absorbed

Shackman from Monkmeyer

with the problem of integrating new role demands and an image of femininity to this self-concept. As she gains some assurance that she is measuring up to a style of feminine behavior, the girl can begin to seek and find emotional gratification in friendships with boys (45, 210).

Somewhat similar patterns exist with boys, although, as in other areas, boys tend to place somewhat less stress on the intimate, emotional, interpersonal aspects of boy-girl relationships, and more on commonly shared activities and interests (45). They probably also have a somewhat greater involvement in vocational plans, which for them are more distinct from heterosexual relationships; for girls, even vocational plans are likely to involve heterosexual relationships (i.e., marriage and a family).

In brief, it would appear that the young person who will be best prepared for both his social and vocational responsibilities in adult life, and also for the intimate, emotional demands for marriage, will be one who in the early years of adolescence has been able to try out a variety of social and personal roles, both with opposite-sex peers and with close friends of the same sex, and who, in the later years of adolescence, has an opportunity to develop meaningful, trusting, and mutually supportive relationships with an opposite-sex peer.

Socioeconomic Status and Dating. Rather interestingly, early dating appears to be more a middle-class than a lower-class phenomenon in this country. Early dating tends to be associated with: higher educational level of parents (some college versus high school or less); higher economic and social status; native-born parents; small family; and region of residence (e.g., earlier dating in the South; 120). This group tends not only to engage in earlier dating but also to "play the field" more before settling finally on a steady partner. In contrast, adolescents from large families of lower socioeconomic status, and of recent foreign origin, with less education, tend to begin dating later and to start "going steady" relatively quickly without much experience in dating (120).

Socioeconomic status also influences the opposite-sex peers whom adolescents date. In one comprehensive study (83), boys and girls of all classes tended to date primarily within their own social class. This was most conspicuously true of lower-class youth. None of the boys and girls in the two highest social classes dated youth of the lowest class, nor did any of the boys or girls in the lowest class date youth in the highest class. Thus it may be seen that, while dating may permit some degree of upward social mobility, the opportunities are severely limited. Even when an individual dates outside his social class, he rarely goes farther than an immediately adjoining class.

Adolescent Marriages.   The role of married adults in our society is a complex one. The young husband has to meet complicated cultural demands both in social relationships with others, and in the increasingly complex and changing world of work. The girl, whether working or not, has to meet the responsibilities of social interactions and the complex tasks of running a home and child-rearing, often without the aid and support of the extended family of an earlier day.

In addition, the emphasis in our society on marriage as a continuing romantic affair may burden what is already a very complex, intimate, and emotional interaction with unrealistic expectations. Considerable personal maturity and prior integration into other adult roles would appear desirable if a couple's chances for a successful marriage are to be enhanced. In the first five years of marriage, the divorce rate of girls who are married under the age of 20 is more than twice that of girls married at later ages, and the rate remains consistently higher throughout life (119, 187).

Adolescent marriages are often complicated further by the fact that they are more likely than older marriages to have resulted from pregnancy. According to one Midwestern study, 70.9 percent of premaritally pregnant brides were 18 or younger; 95.3 percent were 21 or younger (119). A majority of 16-year-old girls who married were pregnant, and more than one-third of 17-year-olds. Clearly, as the author notes, "premarital pregnancy . . . is largely a phenomenon characteristic of the young." In such cases, the young couple may not be marrying the person he or she would ultimately choose, and even if they are, they have less time following marriage to become adjusted to each other and to the other demands of marriage before undertaking the responsibilities (and restrictions) of parenthood.

Nevertheless, significant numbers of adolescent marriages are successful. Those that achieve stability and happiness involve partners who are personally well-adjusted and relatively mature (61). It is interesting to note that in a recent study of teenage marriages (61), 60 percent of the subjects stated that if they had it to do over again, they would marry at the same age, although only 23 percent felt they would advise their children to marry at the age they married. Wives were more willing than their husbands to marry at the same age, as well as to advise their children to marry at their age (61).

THE ADOLESCENT AND HIS PEERS

In adolescence, relations with peers perform many of the same functions that they do for the child, providing him an opportunity to learn how to interact with agemates, to control social behavior, to develop age-relevant skills and interests, and to share similar problems and feelings. If anything, however, the role peers play in adolescence is an even more important one for a variety of reasons. For one thing, relations both with same- and opposite-sex peers in this period come closer to serving as prototypes for later adult relationships—in social relations, in work, and in interactions with members of the opposite sex. The male who has not yet learned how to get along with others of his own sex, in work and in play, by the time he reaches adulthood faces serious obstacles. The girl who reaches adulthood without having learned how to get along with other women of her own age and how to establish satisfactory heterosexual relationships—ranging from friendship to love—is similarly handicapped.

Adolescents are also more dependent upon peer relationships simply because ties with parents have become progressively looser as greater independence from parents is achieved. Furthermore, relationships with family members are frequently so charged with conflicting emotions during the adolescent period—dependent yearnings existing alongside independent strivings, hostility mixed with love, and conflicts over cultural values and social behavior—that many areas of the adolescent's inner life and outward behavior become difficult to share with parents. Also, it appears that parents themselves, having finally come to terms with their own prior adolescent struggles to achieve a sense of ego-identity and impulse control, tend frequently to "let the past bury its dead." They may not desire or, in most cases, be capable of reviving the intense, shifting, and sometimes painful feelings of adolescence. Reawakening such feelings may be discomforting, and may also endanger the arduously achieved repression of underlying impulses and feelings which appear inappropriate to an adult role (45). Consequently, parents may have difficulty in understanding and sharing the problems of adolescents, even though they may make an effort to do so.

And yet the adolescent needs, perhaps more than at any time in his life, to be able to share his strong and often confusing emotions, his doubts, and his dreams. Adolescence is generally a time of intense sociability, but it is also often a time of intense loneliness. Merely being with others does not solve the problem; frequently the adolescent may feel most alone in the midst of a crowd, at a party or a dance (90). Under such circumstances, being accepted by his peers generally and, especially, having one or more close friends may make a great difference in the life of the adolescent.

Finally, the role of the peer group in helping the adolescent to define his own identity assumes particular importance at this age because at no other age is the individual's sense of identity so fluid: no longer a child, but not yet fully accepted as an adult, the adolescent must prepare, with few clear guidelines, to meet society's demands for social independence, for vocational competence, for a responsible role as a citizen, for marriage and a family, and for a workable philosophy of life. At the same time,

> . . . he is in process of breaking (or recasting) his ties to the family and desperately needs the support, approval and security, as well as the norms, of a peer group. He is discovering, and trying to interpret and control, a changed body, and with it new and frightening impulses, and so requires both the example and communion of peers. He is about to crystallize an identity, and for this needs others of his generation to act as models, mirrors, helpers, testers, foils (45, 178–179).

Conformity to Peer Culture

Under such circumstances as have been noted, the adolescent may be under considerable pressure to conform to the values, customs, and fads of peer culture—much has been made of the presumed excessive conformity of adolescents. While the *manifestations* of peer-group conformity change rapidly in our society, there can be little doubt that the adolescent needs to conform (although whether adults are as relatively free of similar conformity needs as they seem to imply when talking about adolescent conformity is open to some question). According to one national survey of adolescent attitudes and opinions, conducted over many years, American adolescents show significant social-class differences in many aspects of values, needs, and behavior, but ". . . in their desire for popularity and their conformist attitude they are as one: low-income or high-income, their concern is to be liked" (155, 267). Only about one young person in four in the survey claimed that he often disagreed with the prevailing opinion in the group to which he belonged.

There are other reasons for adolescent conformity to peer-group culture. One is related to the very reasons for the existence of a peer culture at all. The adolescent in our society has left the world of childhood forever but he has not yet been admitted to the world of adults. In those societies in which the young person is accepted without fanfare into adult society as early as his maturing abilities permit, "youth culture" as we know it either does not exist or is highly attenuated in its extent. But this is not the case in our society, with its ever greater prolongation of dependency, related in considerable measure to the constantly expanding educational requirements of a complex, technological culture. Faced by this potential vacuum between childhood and adult status, the adolescent is virtually forced to create at least a semblance of an "interim culture" of his own. He needs a group which he can understand, to which he can relate, and which can provide him with the status denied him by adult society.

Parents are typically mystified, and in some cases deeply threatened, by the shifting external trappings of adolescent peer culture, from fashions in clothes and music to special and rapidly shifting vocabularies. Parents may wonder why adolescents need to look so "different" and act so "bizarrely." But, of course, that is one of the principal reasons for the existence of adolescent fads: to establish, at least superficially, a clear line of demarcation from adults. Once adults have recovered from their anguished cries of imminent disaster and have, rather ironically, gone on to incorporate adolescent fashions and tastes into adult culture (as is currently happening in dress, in music, and even to some extent in language), adolescents will have to turn to new fads to preserve their separateness.

Actually, it appears to us, parents and other adults might take some comfort from the presence of these outward trappings of the "differentness" of adolescents. By achieving the semblance of a group identity of their own in these relatively superficial ways, adolescents may satisfy some of the need to be different from their parents in more fundamental matters. While, as we shall see, adolescent values and behavior are changing and are different to some degree—and sometimes to an important degree—from those of adults (cf. pp. 699–703), there is also, in most cases, a fundamental continuity in the values and beliefs of parents and children that is often overlooked, probably for valid psychological reasons on the part of both parents and children.

Relative Influence of Parents and Peers.   The common view that parental and peer group influences represent clearly defined opposing forces, each struggling for supremacy in the battle for the adolescent's loyalty, is misleading for several reasons. In the first place, as implied above, there is usually considerable overlap between the values of an adolescent's parents and those of his peers, for the simple reason that his acquaintances and friends tend to come from the same sociocultural background as his parents. Thus, in many cases, the peer group serves to reinforce fundamental parental attitudes, values, beliefs, and interests. For example, the emphasis of middle- and upper-class parents on academic accomplishment is generally shared by peers of the same social class. While many of today's middle-class adolescents raise more questions than their parents about the validity of educational methods and the continued pressure for grades and academic success (cf. p. 700), they still share an underlying belief in the value of education for its own sake—a belief which is largely absent among parents and children in the lower socioeconomic classes (cf. p. 731). We should be cautious about overemphasizing differences and underemphasizing similarities, and against being misled by relatively conspicuous but actually rather superficial differences (e.g., musical tastes, fashions, fads) as opposed to more basic matters (e.g., fundamental moral or social values and codes of behavior).

Another factor tending to limit potential conflict between parental and peer influences lies in the uncertainty of many parents as to the behavior they *should* expect from adolescents. Parents ". . . are likely to be impressed (probably over-impressed) by social change, likely to feel that parent and child live in different worlds, and that they themselves lack the experience to teach the child how to meet and manage his world. We have here something similar to a self-fulfilling prophecy. Half believing he cannot really guide his child, the parent helps the child in his turn to the peer group" (*45*, 200).

In other words, while bemoaning the adolescent's conformity to the peer group, parents often, at the same time, contribute to this conformity. Furthermore, many parents—particularly upper- and middle-class parents—place a great emphasis on popularity and success, and thus strengthen the adolescent's motivation to conform to peer expectations (*45*).

Another consideration that is often overlooked is that neither parental nor peer influence is monolithic, extending to all areas of adolescent decision-making and behavior. Whether parental or peer influence is more likely to win out when a conflict between them arises is likely to depend on the specific situation involved and the adolescent's appraisal of the relative value of parental and peer opinion in that situation (*25, 175*). Parental influence is likely to be stronger when the situation is one in which the adolescent views parental knowledge and authority as more reliable than that of peers (*25*). In general, however, peer influences appear to be strongest in the more superficial areas noted above, while parental influence appears greatest in determining underlying moral and social beliefs, attitudes and behavior (*45*).

As might be expected, the greatest conflict between parental and peer values is likely to occur when, for one reason or another, the adolescent's parents and his peers come from dissimilar backgrounds. Thus, the first generation son of immigrant parents from another culture, the lower-class boy or girl sent to school with middle-class peers, the middle-class youth whose peer associations come largely from a lower socioeconomic level, and the adolescent from a fundamentalist religious background who grows up among liberal Protestant peers or among disbelievers, all are likely to encounter increased conflict between parental and peer influences.

Finally, there is considerable individual variation among adolescents in the extent of their need for a rigid conformity to *either* parents or peers. The adolescent who is approaching true maturity and a sense of his own identity may be able to profit from the views and the learning experiences provided by both parents and peers on a selective basis, without being strongly dependent on either or being unduly troubled by parent-peer differences. Ironically, the adolescent who has gained most confidence in his own self-image and who is least concerned with popularity, "and goes his own way may find that his peers flock around him as a tower of strength" (*177*, 291).

Shackman from Monkmeyer

The Nature of Adolescent Peer Groups

While we have tended to speak of the adolescent "peer group" or "peer culture," these terms actually represent an oversimplification. In reality, the developing adolescent is involved in complex ways with a number of overlapping peer groups that vary in size and in the degree of intimacy among group members. Furthermore, the nature of these groups and the functions they serve change with age.

In the preadolescent period, the child's peer relationships tend, as we have seen, to center about same-sex "gangs" (49). However, as he enters the wider world of adolescence and spends less and less time at home, the range of his acquaintances broadens: "Where the school-age child's peer group was peopled with friends, best friends, and faceless strangers, the adolescent has a wider circle of casual acquaintances as well" (177, 285).

In general, the adolescent's peer relationships fall into three broad categories: The "crowd" or "set," the "clique," and individual friendships. The most inclusive of these categories is the crowd. It is also the least personal: "It is a 'forced group' comprised of individuals selected because of mutual interests, likes, and social ideals. The members meet on the basis of *activities,* not because of mutual attraction as is true of chums and, to a lesser extent, of cliques" (85, 126).

A recent study of adolescent peer groups (49) in an urban setting confirmed that the two basic groups consisted of large *crowds* and smaller *cliques.*

He found further that *the crowd is essentially an association of cliques.* "Clique membership appears to be a prerequisite of crowd membership" (*49,* 234). No subject in the study belonged to a crowd without also belonging to a component clique.

Cliques and crowds perform different functions for their members. In this study, for example, it was found that the clique centered heavily around talking (frequently on the telephone!), while the crowd served as the center of larger and more organized social activities, such as parties and dances. The crowd "acts as a reservoir of acceptable associates who can be drawn on to the extent required by any social activity" (*49,* 235).

In contrast, the clique, with its more intimate interpersonal relationships, performs "an important instrumental function in that it is the center for the preparation of crowd activities, for dissemination of information about them, and for their evaluation after they are over" (*49,* 235). Not surprisingly, it was found that crowd settings occurred primarily on weekends, while clique settings occurred principally on weekdays.

Structural Change.   As adolescence proceeds, structural changes in the nature of peer groups take place, and these in turn are related to the changing socialization processes of adolescence, including, in particular, the development of heterosexual relationships. An abstract outline of this structural development is shown in Fig. 14.3. As may be seen, Stage 1 reflects the persistence of the preadolescent "gang" into the adolescent period. Stage 2 indicates the first tentative movement toward heterosexuality in group structure. At this stage, unisexual cliques previously unrelated to similar cliques of the opposite sex now interact—but only with the protection found in having the support of one's same-sex clique members as one approaches this new adventure.

It is not until Stage 3 that the function of the heterosexual clique is seen for the first time. Rather interestingly, the individual-to-individual heterosexual interaction tends to be begun by upper-status members of each unisexual clique, and in this fashion the new heterosexual clique begins to develop.

> Those adolescents who belong to these emergent heterosexual groups still maintain a membership role in their unisexual clique, so that they possess dual membership in two intersecting cliques. This initiates an extensive transformation of group structure by which there takes place a reorganization of unisexual cliques and the reformation of their membership into heterosexual cliques (stage 4). While the cliques persist as small intimate groups, their membership now comprises both sexes (*49,* 237).

Beginning in Stage 5, in late adolescence, when the need for the support and convenient resources of the crowd for larger-group activities begins to diminish, we see the "slow disintegration of the crowd and the formation of cliques consisting of couples who are going steady or engaged" (*49,* 238).

As this study points up, one of the principal functions served by the crowd is the role that it plays in making possible the transition from the

660   Adolescence

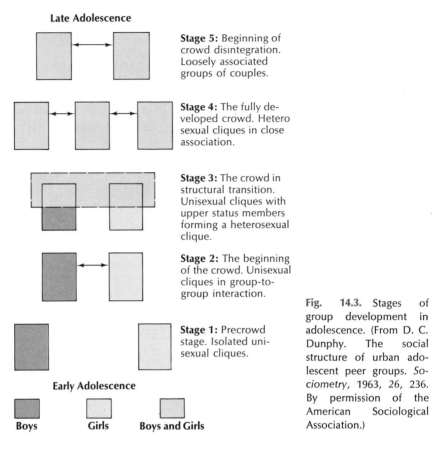

Late Adolescence

Stage 5: Beginning of crowd disintegration. Loosely associated groups of couples.

Stage 4: The fully developed crowd. Hetero sexual cliques in close association.

Stage 3: The crowd in structural transition. Unisexual cliques with upper status members forming a heterosexual clique.

Stage 2: The beginning of the crowd. Unisexual cliques in group-to-group interaction.

Stage 1: Precrowd stage. Isolated unisexual cliques.

Early Adolescence

Boys   **Girls**   **Boys and Girls**

Fig. 14.3. Stages of group development in adolescence. (From D. C. Dunphy. The social structure of urban adolescent peer groups. *Sociometry*, 1963, *26*, 236. By permission of the American Sociological Association.)

unisexual cliques of early adolescence to the heterosexual cliques of older adolescence (49). At the same time, it should be recognized that associations with individuals and groups of same-sex members continue, though somewhat less in the foreground, throughout adolescence and into adult life—whether in the form of small circles of friends, individual close friends, fraternities, sororities, clubs, or interest groups.

Both crowd and clique membership are influenced by a wide range of variables: geographic, educational, and social, as well as those involving mutual interest. Popularity also affects entrance into cliques, clubs, and more formal organizations, such as sororities and fraternities.

Socioeconomic status also plays a significant role in determining crowd and clique membership. There is little cutting across class lines, particularly in the case of girls, whose cliques tend generally to be closer, more impregnable to outsiders, and rather more enduring (37, 102, 104, 143, 199). Somewhat more democracy and flexibility is found in male groups, where athletic skills and overall sociability tend to have a leveling influence

(36). In many high schools there tends to be a fairly sharp division between those students (usually of somewhat higher socioeconomic status) planning to go on to college and those planning to go directly to work after high school. Common interests and hobbies, close residential proximity and similar school environment, degree of social and personal maturity, and degree of heterosexual interest all are influential in determining clique and crowd membership.

Friendships

Among the peer relationships of adolescents, friendships hold a special place and perform, at least to some extent, a special function. In comparison with other broader and more general interactions with peers, friendships are more intimate, involve more intense feelings, and are more honest and open and less concerned with self-conscious attempts or role-playing aimed at greater social acceptance. Consequently, close friends can contribute to the adolescent's development in ways not open to him in his relations with the broader peer group.

As we have already seen, the adolescent who is attempting to adjust to a changing self (psychologically and physiologically) and to rapidly changing external demands may often experience doubts, anxieties, and, not infrequently, strong resentments. In most situations, these reactions must be concealed. To admit them to any but one's closest friends opens the door to possible misunderstanding, lack of acceptance, or worst of all, amusement or scorn. When a meaningful friendship exists, however, such defensiveness is not necessary. In such a relationship, "there is trust, there is no need to pretend, no necessity for being on guard against betrayal of shared secrets. Adolescents who have a relationship of this kind can reprove each other without condemning each other" (90, 254).

Under favorable circumstances, adolescents may reveal a talent for friendships not shared by younger children or by most adults. A major distinction between both the younger child and the adult, on the one hand, and the adolescent, on the other, is that the adolescent often enters friendships with a considerable degree of *flexibility* and *readiness for change*. The younger child may not be happy with himself as he is, but he tends to accept the situation as an unfortunate fact of life (45). With the beginning of adolescence, however, the young person becomes more aware of himself as a social stimulus, and one which can be changed by conscious intent (45). In fact, this discovery of "the tractable self" by adolescents has provided the basis for adult promotion of an enormously profitable and, unfortunately, sometimes rather cynical and exploitative "self-help" industry, ranging from grooming aids and equipment for muscle development and figure control to charm courses and newspaper columns on manners and morals. Aware of the possibility of change, the adolescent

 . . . enters friendship with an eagerness to make good, and the conviction that the self can be transformed to that end.

> Along with this almost conscious, almost deliberate openness to change, we have another level of openness . . . , the openness to the inner states of experience; with it comes a psychic fluidity, a vulnerability to conflict, an affective liability which together give adolescent intimacies so much of their characteristic flavor (45, 180).

At their best, friendships may help the adolescent in dealing with his own complex feelings and those of others. They can serve as a kind of "therapy" both by allowing the freer expression of suppressed feelings of anger or anxiety and by providing evidence that others have many of the same doubts, hopes, fears, and seemingly dangerously strong feelings. In the freedom that close friends may have to criticize each other, the adolescent may also learn to modify his behavior, tastes, or ideas, without the necessity of learning only from painful experiences of rejection by others.

Friendships are most likely to develop between adolescents who share at least a number of the more obvious characteristics—age, intelligence, socioeconomic status, common interests, and common career goals. While friendships may sometimes involve "the attraction of opposites" (e.g., a shy, inhibited girl and an extroverted, "wild" one), similarities are generally more evident than differences (45).

Friendship patterns tend to vary with age and sex. As the young person moves through adolescence, he tends to develop "an increasing emotional investment in friendship, greater sophistication and subtlety in . . . conceptions about it, a growing capacity for disinterested appreciation of the friend, and greater tolerance of differences within the relationship" (45, 185). Girls' friendships tend to be more frequent, deeper, and more dependent than those of boys (15, 45), and in their friendships, girls reveal greater nurturance needs, desire for and ability to sustain deep intimate relationships, and concern about defection (15). Boys in contrast, tend to place more stress on the results of friendship, such as having a congenial companion with whom one shares a common interest in activities oriented to reality (45).

The differences in emphasis between girls' and boys' friendships do not appear too surprising in view of the fact that throughout adolescent and adult life, women tend to maintain a strong interpersonal orientation in adjusting to life. A girl or woman is more likely than a man to have drives for love and nurturance as dominant motives, and fear of loss of love as a major anxiety (92, 114, 125). When threatened, the girl is more likely to appeal for support and nurture from persons important to her. Adolescent and adult males, on the other hand, are more likely than females to be motivated by a need for autonomy, and for relying on one's self or on a broader group of peers (the "gang" or the "clique") in dealing with the competitive demands of the world about them (92, 125). As we have seen, even in sexual motivation boys are more likely to perceive sex as a specific, biologically imperious but relatively independent motive. In contrast, for girls the interpersonal and erotic aspects of love are more likely to be closely linked (45, 50, 177).

Factors Affecting Social Acceptance by Peers

Not surprisingly, personal as well as sociological and other characteristics influence the likelihood that an adolescent will be accepted by his peers. In general, as indicated by a variety of sociometric studies, accepted adolescents are viewed by their peers as: liking other people and being tolerant, flexible, and sympathetic; being lively, cheerful, good-natured, and possessed of a sense of humor; acting "naturally" and self-confidently without being conceited; and possessing initiative, enthusiasm, drive, and plans for group activity (18, 88, 95, 115, 116, 185). Adolescents who are favorably selected in sociometric choices tend to be those who contribute to others—by making *them* feel accepted and involved, by promoting constructive interaction between peers, or by planning and initiating interesting or enjoyable group activities (103).

Adolescent characteristics which are least admired and most likely to lead to rejection are in many ways the antitheses of those leading to acceptance. The adolescent who is ill-at-ease and lacking in self-confidence, and who tends to react to his discomfiture either by timidity, nervousness, or withdrawal, or by a compensatory overaggressiveness, conceit, or demands for attention, will court rejection. Similarly, the adolescent who is self-centered and unable or unwilling to perceive and act to meet the needs of others, who is sarcastic, tactless, inconsiderate, and contributes little to the success of the group efforts, will receive little consideration in return.

In addition to an adolescent's personality characteristics, there are many other factors which may affect his acceptance by his peers. Among these are included his intelligence and ability, social-class status, and ethnic-group membership.

It is frequently assumed that Americans in general, and adolescents in particular, shun any appearance of being "too bright" or "intellectual." From this, it might be inferred that superior intelligence is actually a detriment to adolescent social acceptance. The reverse, however, appears to be the case (142, 201). Other factors being equal, intelligence is positively and significantly related to age-mate acceptance (142). Intelligence and ability may affect social acceptance indirectly as well as directly. An awareness that he is of below-average ability and is having school difficulties, and that others are also aware of this, may lead an adolescent to develop personality characteristics—insecurity, withdrawal, compensatory demands for attention, or aggressiveness—that may in themselves lead to rejection.

Social acceptance is also easiest for members of the culturally dominant majority in any peer group. Thus members of ethnic minorities and socio-economically deprived subgroups are less likely to be accepted, both by the dominant majority, and, interestingly, by other minority-group members (83, 142, 165, 177).

Few adolescents (or adults) are immune to a lack of social acceptance. While a few individuals, confident of their own goals and interests and possessed of a strong sense of ego identity, may neither need nor seek the

acceptance of peers, most adolescents, judging their own worth in terms of others' reactions to them, are dependent on the approval and acclaim of others.

Unfortunately, the unpopular adolescent is likely to be caught in a vicious circle. If he is already emotionally troubled, self-preoccupied, and lacking in a secure self-concept, he is likely to meet with rejection or indifference from his peers. In turn, an awareness that he is not accepted by his peers and a lack of opportunity to participate in and learn from peer group activities only further undermines his self-confidence and increases his sense of social isolation. The result is likely to be still further inappropriateness in his behavior with peers. While social acceptance is obviously desirable, particularly if based on mutual helpfulness and shared interests, there is, in our opinion, an overemphasis, particularly among upper- and middle-class parents, on the pursuit of popularity for their children. David Riesman (156) has suggested that people in our culture are too much the products of "other-directedness"—concerned with "fitting-in," with superficial appearances, with "not rocking the boat" in an organization-minded society, rather than with pursuing our own private "inner-directed" dreams and goals (101). There is some encouraging evidence that today's adolescents may be beginning to swing the pendulum back in the direction of a more tolerant individualism wherein each person is freer, as members of the recent "hippie" movement have phrased it, "to do his own thing." But to expect the developing adolescent—unsure of his own identity and unclear about the demands that will be made upon him in a confused, rapidly changing society—to be immune to the favor of his peers would be unrealistic and inappropriate. Most adolescents, at one time or another, feel that they "do not belong," and the pain, however temporary, can be very real; parents' overdetermined insistence on "popularity" can further compound the adolescent's difficulties.

VOCATIONAL CHOICE

The problem of deciding on a vocation is probably more critical for adolescent boys than for girls, for a variety of reasons. In the first place, boys are more likely than girls to have to work for the greater portion of their adult lives. Most girls expect to go to work for a period of time following graduation from school or college, and to be economically independent during this period (202). Most, however, expect to marry before too many years, and indeed they do. And while an increasing number of women also work at some time during their married lives, the fact remains that in most cases a family's standard of living, its place in the community, and its financial security will depend primarily on the earning capacity of the husband and the kind of position he has.

For most women, identification with an adult role still primarily involves assuming successfully the roles of wife and mother, and only secondarily, if at all, that of breadwinner. It is probably for this reason that girls as a group, regardless of social-class status, set their sights lower than boys in their vocational aspirations, and have less commitment to vocational goals (46). The social-class status of the average girl will be dependent more on her husband's occupation than on her own. Even in the case of the unmarried girl, it is likely to depend more on the status of her family and friends, and less on the prestige level of her own occupation, than would be the case for a boy. Thus many girls, regardless of social class, will list as their vocational aims such positions as secretary, nurse, teacher, stewardess, and so on (46, 200).

In contrast, the adolescent boy and his parents are both aware that his future financial security and status, and that of his family, will rest primarily in his own hands. Most adult males are deeply involved with making a living, and in order to assume the role of adult, the boy must make a meaningful vocational commitment. Consequently, parents, teachers, and peers are likely to place greater pressure on the boy than on the girl to make a vocational decision during this period. The extent and the kinds of pressures exerted will, of course, vary with social class and ethnic group status, as well as with a number of other factors.

A vocation also offers adolescent boys and girls (boys more strongly) a socially approved way to achieve direct or indirect satisfaction for motives which may have been strong, but not fully gratified during the preceding decade. These may involve what Anne Roe (*159, 160, 161*), a prominent psychologist and vocational theorist, calls "lower order needs," such as safety and security; generalized "higher order needs," such as self-esteem, independence, and self-actualization; or other needs more directly related to specific occupations. For example, motives such as dominance over others, aggression, nurturance, and, occasionally, sexual curiosity can be at least partially gratified in one or another occupation (e.g., army officer, policeman, social worker, physician, or nurse). Various specific acquired interests, personality traits, and life-styles may also be better served by some occupations than others *(181)*.

More broadly, choice of a vocation and subsequent participation in it, may help, through a kind of reciprocal feedback mechanism, to crystalize and reinforce the adolescent's self-concept (*20, 33, 181*). Specific vocational choice may also reflect the particular kinds of identification patterns that a youth, either boy or girl, has formed with his mother and father within the family setting.

Vocational Adjustment in American Culture

In many nonliterate societies, the vocational problems of the adolescent are much simpler than in our own culture. The number of vocations supported by the culture are fewer, and the adolescent is already likely to be familiar with them—either through observation or apprenticeship. The Arapesh youth, for example, gradually takes over from his father responsibility for tilling the family garden as he enters adolescence (cf. pp. 623–625). Furthermore, many, but by no means all, nonliterate societies lack the involvement in aggressive competitiveness and concern with social status characteristic of American culture (cf. pp. 624–625).

The typical adolescent in our own society does not share the advantages of the Arapesh youth. He knows that many of his important satisfactions will depend on his ability to find and keep a job, including his chances for full emancipation from his parents, for acceptance as an equal by his peers, and for getting married and maintaining a home.

But despite the importance of vocational adjustment for the American adolescent, he typically has only a vague idea of the nature of the various jobs available in the society. He does not know which he would be able to do successfully and would enjoy doing, the prior training required for a specific job, or the present or future demands for workers in the various occupations.

This problem, rather than becoming easier, is becoming increasingly difficult as our entire society grows more complex, more specialized, and more technologically oriented. The kinds of skills society requires are changing ever more rapidly as new technologies are developed. With the growth of automation, there is less and less room for the unskilled or semiskilled worker; prior education and training are becoming increasingly necessary for admission to the world of work. Further, as machines take on more of the jobs formerly performed by workers, there is a significant movement away from production and into service occupations. We shall have more to say later about some of these critical problems and their implications for the adolescent, including the socioeconomically deprived youth. For the present, we only wish to emphasize the increasing difficulties faced by most adolescents today in planning for their vocational futures.

Ordinarily, as the adolescent leaves his childhood behind, and the time when he must support himself approaches, he begins to spend more of his time thinking about vocational goals.

He also becomes progressively more realistic about these goals. As a child, he is likely to have preferred occupations which seemed active and exciting to him, such as those of cowboy, fireman, airplane pilot, or detective. The social status of his preferred occupation is not likely to have had much influence on him. However, as he grows older, he is likely to begin to prefer occupations of marked prestige in the adult world—being a famous doctor, scientist, or lawyer. Finally, as adulthood approaches, he is likely to settle upon some occupation that represents a realistic reconciliation between what he would like to do and what he thinks he might actually be able to do (76, 133).

As the child's vocational interests become progressively more realistic, more influenced by status and less by glamour and excitement, they also become more stable. For example, it has been shown that the older the adolescent, the more stable (i.e., the less changeable) his vocational interests become (as measured by vocational interest tests repeated after a given interval of time) (32). By middle adolescence, vocational interest has become fairly stable, though changes may still occur. By age 25, practically complete stability is achieved.

Despite the increasing stability and realism of the adolescent's vocational interests, there is considerable evidence that he cannot be left to his own devices in dealing with his vocational problems. In a complex society such as ours, in which the actual requirements of most jobs and their availability in the labor market are not matters of common knowledge, the adolescent needs help.

In our culture, the young person's vocational interests usually develop in a rather unsystematic fashion, guided by such influences as parental desires, relationships with parents, accidental contact with various occupations, and the kinds of jobs his friends choose. Class and sex-typed standards also play a role.

Subcultural Influences on Vocational Choice

Up to this point in the discussion, we have been dealing with broad problems of vocational choice as they affect adolescents in our culture. There are, however, two subcultural influences which affect vocational goals differentially, and which seem to us important enough to merit special consideration.

Socioeconomic Factors and Vocational Goals. Social-class membership operates to influence vocational goals in a variety of ways. For one thing, it helps to determine the kinds of occupations with which the individual will be familiar, and hence which he will be likely to consider in formulating his occupational aims. In addition, it plays an important role in determining the social acceptability (i.e., the reward value) of a given occupation to the young person and to his peers. Certain types of occupations are considered appropriate to the members of a particular social class, others inappropriate. The individual who deviates from class expectancies for occupational choice is likely to be subjected to anxiety-producing disapproval from his peers, particularly if this deviation is in the direction of jobs associated with lower-class status. The very young upper-class child who wants to be an iceman, or fireman, or policeman, may be indulged or even encouraged. After the attainment of adolescence, however, when the problem of vocational choice becomes a serious one with practical implications, the child's parents are not likely to find such notions amusing (1).

Choices of lower-status occupations run counter to the parents' ideas about appropriate behavior for a member of their social class, and consequently are likely to be discouraged. The parents may also fear that such a choice will lead to general social disapproval both of their child and indirectly of themselves. Also, when economic rewards are involved in the occupation chosen, they may fear that the child will not be able to live in the same neighborhood as other members of his social class, to afford the same social, recreational and educational advantages for himself and his family.

Aspirations toward higher-social-status occupations may also lead to social disapproval (particularly if they are flaunted openly) because such aspirations may be viewed as a threat by other members of the individual's social class. In this case, however, the disapproval is likely to be much less strong and, in the child's view, may be more than outweighed by the prospect of increased rewards associated with higher-class status. This observation is supported by the fact that actually most young people wish for jobs having a somewhat higher socioeconomic status than those of their parents (109).

The relation of social-class membership to vocational aspiration is clearly demonstrated in a study by Hollingshead (83). Adolescents in a small midwestern city were asked to list the occupations they would like to follow as adults. The results, subdivided according to social-class membership, are shown in Fig. 14.4. As may be seen, while 77 percent of the children of the highest two social classes listed business and professional occupations, only 7 percent of the children in the lowest social class made these choices. Similarly, while only 1 percent of Class I and II (higher social class) members listed the various services and trades, 25 percent of Class V (lower social class) did. It is interesting to note that the number of youths undecided about their vocational aspirations increased regularly as socioeconomic class decreased.

In attempting to account for such social-class differences in vocational goals, several hypotheses have been offered. One is that there are differences in the evaluation of the relative values assigned by adolescents to various occupations, and that these value differences account largely for social-class

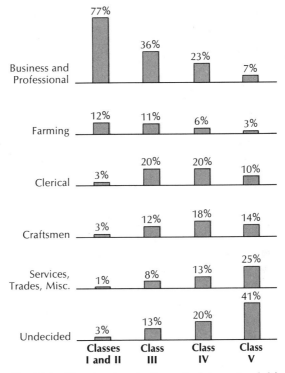

Fig. 14.4. Vocational aspirations of adolescents of different social classes. (From Karl C. Garrison. *Psychology of adolescence*, 5th ed. Englewood Cliffs, N.J.: Prentice-Hall. © 1956, p. 418. By permission. [After A. B. Hollingshead. *Elmtown's youth: the impact of social classes on youth.* New York: Wiley, 1949.])

differences in vocational goals *(30)*. Other theorists, however, have argued that both middle-class and "working-class" youth agree on the relative desirability and prestige of various occupations, and that differences in goals stem not primarily from values but rather from class-associated perceptions of differences of opportunities and general life chances *(176)*. While adolescents may be somewhat unrealistic about their vocational goals, they nevertheless possess some awareness of practical obstacles which may modify their vocational aspirations, and these are certainly affected by social-class status.

A lower-class boy whose parents are unable or uninterested in helping him to go to college, much less to medical school, is less likely to aspire to be a doctor than one whose parents encourage such a vocational choice and who are in a position to help him. Similarly, the boy whose parents expect him to go to work upon completion of the ninth grade is not likely to spend much time contemplating the idea of becoming an engineer.

In addition to limiting the adolescent's opportunity for training in a particular occupation, social-class factors are also likely to influence his chances of obtaining some jobs, even if he is qualified. Persons in a particular social class tend to pick others from the same social class as their colleagues and successors. While this is often done without conscious awareness, it is nevertheless done. The employer may say that a person from another social class does not have the right sort of personality for a particular job, when he means that he does not have the same sets of class-learned social traits as others holding that position.

To a certain extent, such attitudes may be justified in that people with similar social backgrounds may find it easier to deal with one another in the job situation. But it appears that the importance of socially derived personality characteristics is often exaggerated by employers. This may be attributable in part to their need to maintain their own status as members of a particular social class.

Value Stretch

Rodman has introduced a concept of what he calls "value stretch," arguing that ". . . the lower-class person, without abandoning the general values of society, develops an alternative set of values. Without abandoning the values placed upon success . . . he stretches the values so that lesser degrees of success also become desirable (158, 209)." In the stretched value system there is a "low degree of commitment to all values within the range, including the dominant, middle-class values (158, 209)." The alternative values help the lower-class person to adjust to his deprived circumstances.

In a test of Rodman's hypotheses, 71 "working-" and 73 middle-class male high school seniors, were asked to describe the desirability of two sets of occupations on a seven-point scale (30). The first set consisted of such high-prestige positions as lawyer, factory owner, and educator; a second set included such medium-prestige positions as policeman, machine operator, and bookkeeper. Students were then asked to estimate the relative probability of their actually ending up in one group or the other, under various conditions. The results indicated that students from both middle- and working-class backgrounds tended to prefer the set of high-prestige positions to those of medium prestige, but middle-class students ranked high-prestige occupations higher and medium-prestige occupations lower than working-class students did (see Table 14.5). It appears that middle-class students have strong preferences for high-prestige occupations while working-class students are more flexible or less immediately concerned about their occupational futures.

With respect to probable actual job outcome, middle-class students perceived themselves as more likely than working-class students actually to achieve a high-prestige occupation. Incidentally, both groups also viewed college as increasing the chances of a high-prestige job; however, working-class students perceived college as less likely to insure such a result, and they showed only a slight preference for college over work as an immediate

Table 14.5   Desirability Ratings of Sets of Occupations
by Social Class[a]

(Means)

| | Social Class | | t | p |
Sets of Occupations	Working (N = 71)	Middle (N = 73)	t	p
High prestige	3.01	2.29	4.09	<.01
Medium prestige	3.49	4.30	3.90	<.01
t	2.12	17.60		
p	<.05	<.01		

[a] 1 = highly desirable
7 = highly undesirable
Source: From F. G. Caro, Social class and attitudes of youth relevant for the realization of adult goals. Soc. Forces, 1966, 44, 495. By permission of the University of North Carolina Press.

post-high school activity. In contrast, middle-class students showed a strong preference for college.

Working-class students, perceiving high-prestige occupations as less accessible to them, tend to protect themselves from possible disappointment both by placing less value on high-prestige positions and more value on medium-prestige positions (30, 31). Nevertheless, like their middle-class peers, they still tend to view high-prestige positions as more desirable, though the differences are not nearly so wide as in the case of middle-class students.

Parental Influences on Vocational Choice

One of the more obvious parental influences on vocational choice is that of *parental motivation,* and a good deal of variation in parental motivation occurs within all social classes. It has been hypothesized that a working-class boy is relatively likely to seek advanced education and occupational mobility if his parents urge him to do so, and unlikely to seek mobility if they do not exert pressure in this direction (172; see also 21, 66, 100, 118). Indeed, such a boy with strong parental support may prove more ambitious than a middle-class boy without such parental support and urging. According to the data of one study, *ambitious middle-class boys* showed the highest percentage of parental support; *mobile working-class boys* ranked a close second. In contrast, *unambitious middle-class boys* and *nonmobile working-class boys* ranked far behind in percentage of parental support (172). These results provide considerable support for the hypothesis that parental influence is associated with mobility aspiration among working-class boys, and also with ambition among middle-class boys. Indeed, as the author points out, parental advice may be a better predictor of high ambition than is the boy's social class alone.

Parental motivation has been found to be significantly related to student's aspiration level, even when social-class status and IQ are held constant. In general, students whose parents ranked high on aspirational motivations (i.e., held high educational and occupational goals for their children and rewarded good school work) tended to have a high aspiration level themselves (i.e., a "desire for an occupation above that of their parents' social class level"; 7, 183). Interestingly, however, this positive relationship was particularly strong among students scoring high on personality measures of *authoritarianism* and *conformity*. Apparently, nonauthoritarian and non-conforming adolescent males are less susceptible than their more dogmatic, conforming peers to the motivational directives of parents.

The specific occupation held by the father also exerts a significant influence on the career choice of sons, though not daughters (women seldom choose a male career such as their fathers might follow; 193). The number of sons following in their father's footsteps greatly exceeds what one would expect by chance, even if social-class influences are taken into account. For example, 43.6 percent of physicians' sons choose medicine and 27.7 percent of lawyers' sons choose law (193). This can probably be accounted for on several grounds, including (1) greater opportunity to become familiar with father's occupation, as compared with others; (2) greater likelihood of access to the occupation; (3) at least in some cases (e.g., physicians) strong parental motivation—and sometimes pressure—for the son to enter that occupation; and (4) *identification* with the parent, encouraging the development of similar interests, values, and goals.

Further, data from one study demonstrated that boys identifying *primarily* with their fathers are more likely to have masculine vocational interests, while those identifying *primarily* with their mothers were more likely to have typically feminine interest patterns (e.g., verbal-linguistic). Boys with *mixed-sex* identifications (mother *and* father) were somewhat more likely to have vocational interests permitting the expression of both masculine and feminine interests, e.g., social service field, "which allows for the expression of both masculine (e.g., doing research) and feminine (e.g., helping people) preferences" (40, 264).

Personality Characteristics and Interest Patterns. Personality characteristics, interests, and needs are related to vocational interests. Thus, for example, it was found in one study that adolescent boys with vocational interests in artistic fields are relatively more likely than boys with other interests to perceive themselves as: introspective, intuitive, disorderly, imaginative, original, sensitive, unconventional, enthusiastic, rebellious, and impractical. In contrast, boys expressing interest in scientific vocations were more likely to perceive themselves as: analytical, curious, "hard-headed," imaginative, quiet and reserved, and scholarly. Those with entrepreneurial interests (such as sales manager) were relatively more apt to perceive themselves as: aggressive, striving, dominant, conventional, energetic, extroverted, industrious, practical-minded, persuasive, and not particularly interested in artistic, idealistic, scholarly, or scientific pursuits (82). College students who are not anxious and do not fear failure, and who have a strong need for achievement, tend to choose high-prestige occupations on tests of vocational choice. In contrast, those with a high level of anxiety and fear of failure, but a weak need for achievement, make lower choices (27). Similarly introverted adolescents tend to exhibit a narrower, more rigid range of possible vocational choices than extroverts do (173).

Of course, many factors other than personality characteristics and needs alone will affect choice of a career, as we have already seen. It is also obvious that the adolescent may not consciously recognize all of the motives that help to direct his selection of a career. However, most adolescents have a fantasy or stereotyped picture of what an engineer, army officer, physicist, secretary, assembly line worker, lawyer, accountant, social worker, nurse, actor, or psychiatrist is like and what he or she does—a daydream that contains some of the gratifications that are being sought, and usually has at least some relationship to reality (44, 81). To illustrate, the most frequent attributes assigned to engineers by high school seniors of superior ability were found to be (in order of frequency): practical, builders, useful, intelligent, inventive, important, interesting, and hard-working (81). Teachers, in contrast, were seen as underpaid, dedicated, indispensable to society, patient, and helpful. Accountants—fairly or unfairly—were seen as dull, precise, mathematically inclined, boring, methodical, and unimaginative, but necessary! Stereotypes can obviously be misleading, and the chances of a student's selecting an occupation consonant with his own needs (consciously or unconsciously) will be greatly enhanced by possessing actual knowledge of a variety of careers.

Peer Group and School Influences

The adolescent will, of course, also be influenced in his career choice by other factors—including his school environment, his teachers, and, in particular, the peers with whom he associates (6, 7, 41, 172, 186, 198). Thus a boy from a lower-class home is more likely to have upwardly mobile educational and vocational aspirations if he happens to attend a largely middle-class school than if he attends one whose students come primarily from a lower-class background (22). Partly this may be a function of the generally greater educational opportunities provided by such a school, but in all likelihood it will also be a function of greater opportunity for involvement with peers who themselves have higher educational and vocational aspirations, and who share other values, interests, and behavior patterns associated with middle-class culture (6, 172, 198), thus providing the lower-class adolescent with a great opportunity for what has been called "anticipatory socialization" (186).

Even within a particular school setting, those lower-class boys who associate frequently with middle-class boys are more likely to aspire to higher status, including a desire for a college education and for a prestige career. It might also be argued that working-class boys who engage in a substantial amount of schoolwide extracurricular activities that bring them into contact with middle-class interests and values will be more likely than those not so

Table 14.6   Occupational Aspirations of Middle-Class and Working-Class Boys
by Extent of Parental and Peer-Group Influence Toward Ambition

	Percent Aspiring to High-Status Occupations			
Source and Extent of Influence	Working-Class		Middle-Class	
	(N)	%	(N)	%
1 Both high	(28)	71.4	(94)	81.9
2. Parents high, peers low	(45)	55.6	(50)	78.0
3. Peers high, parents low	(70)	35.7	(109)	72.5
4. Both low	(168)	25.6	(113)	30.1

Chi-squares, 1 d.f.: *Within middle class:* group 1 vs. group 2, one-tail test, .32, p<.35; group 2 vs. group 3, two-tail test, .55, p<.50; group 3 vs. group 4, one-tail test, 39.92, p<.001. *Within working class:* group 1 vs. group 2, one-tail test, 1.185, p<.10; group 2 vs. group 3, two-tail test, 4.39, p<.05; group 3 vs. group 4, one-tail test, 2.48, p<.10. *Between classes, one-tail tests:* group 1, 1.46, p<.15; group 2, 5.45, p<.01; group 3, 23.68, p<.001; group 4, .69, p<.25.
Source: From R. L. Simpson. Parental influence, anticipatory socialization, and social mobility. *Amer. sociol. Rev.,* 1962, *27,* 521. By permission of the American Sociological Association.

engaged to seek higher-status careers. Again, the rationale would be that increased contact with middle-class peers fosters "anticipatory socialization" into middle-class values.

A number of investigations have supported this hypothesis *(7, 172).* Thus, among working-class boys, those with middle-class (as opposed to working-class) friends tended to be upwardly mobile in their educational and vocational aspirations; among middle-class boys, those with working-class friends were less ambitious. It was also found that mobile working-class boys approached the ambitious middle-class boys in the extent of their extracurricular participation "substantially more than the unambitious middle-class boys did and much more than the nonmobile working-class boys did" *(172, 520).*

In an effort to see whether parents and peers influenced the boys' aspirations independently of each other, Simpson classified boys as "high" or "low" in the extent to which they had been subjected to each type of influence toward high occupational aspirations. They were rated as high or low in *parental influence* and high or low in *peer influence.* Thus it was possible to define the boys as high in both types of influence, high in one but low in the other, or low in both. The results are shown in Table 14.6. As may be seen, these results support the hypothesis of independent effects strongly and consistently for working-class boys and less strongly for middle-class boys. Among working-class boys, almost three-fourths of those high in both parental and peer influence aspired to high-level occupations, compared

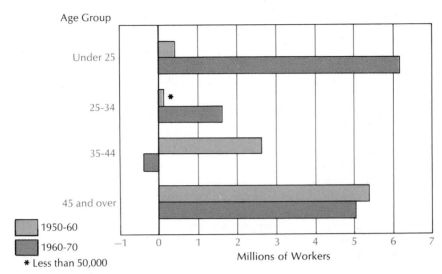

Fig. 14.5. Changes in the number of workers, by age group, 1950–1960 and 1960–1970. (From *Manpower Research Bulletin*, No. 2, March, 1963.)

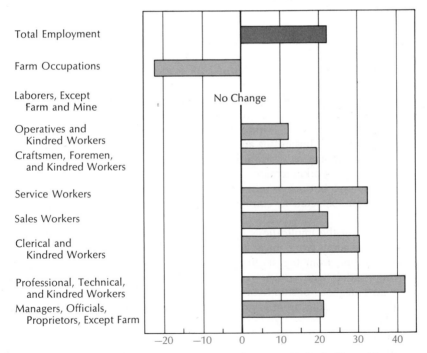

Fig. 14.6. Employment by occupation, percent change, 1960–1970. (From *Manpower Research Bulletin*, No. 2, March, 1963.)

with only about one-fourth of those low in both types of influence—the boys high in one influence but low in the other being intermediate.

> Among middle-class boys, the rank order of the four groups in percentage aspiring to top-level occupations was the same as among working-class boys, but the differences between groups were small and statistically insignificant, with one exception: boys low in both types of influence were less than half as likely as those high in either or both influences to have high aspirations (172, 521).

These results also suggest that parental influence is more strongly related to aspirations than is peer influence. It is also interesting to note that when *both* types of influence were either high or low, they came close to nullifying the effects of social class background on career aspiration.

Vocational Choice in a Changing Society

Any discussion of the problem of vocational choice must take into account the changing nature of the job market in contemporary society, and its effects on adolescents. There can be little doubt that current changes will have their primary impact on today's adolescents and young adults. In the present decade, the greatest change in the number of persons in the work force in the United States is occurring in the under-25 age group (see Fig. 14.5).

It has already been made clear that establishing a viable and meaningful occupational role is essential for the adolescent, particularly the boy. Not only does he need to prepare himself for a job in order to support himself and, at some point, his family, but also to achieve an adequate identification with the male role in our society. What then are the kinds of changes that are taking place, and what are their implications for today's adolescent? In recent years, we have witnessed a rapid growth in automation, the consolidation of small businesses and farms into larger ones, increased urbanization, and a gradual shift toward service occupations and away from farm and production work. Increases are needed in professional service, and white collar positions, but not in unskilled and semiskilled laborers (Fig. 14.6). This trend can be expected to continue and probably be magnified in the coming decade.

What are the implications of these changes for our emerging adults? It is already evident from the scramble on our campuses for capable college graduates, and from the starting salaries offered them, that the adolescent or young adult with advanced education is finding himself in an increasingly advantageous position vocationally. At the same time, poorly educated youth with few skills are finding themselves increasingly penalized. Not only are their opportunities limited, particularly in the case of minority-group members, but there are wide and shifting geographical differences in degree of opportunity as well. The result has been that in some areas, unemployment among youthful minority-group members of the work force has run as high as 40 percent. To the extent that particular subgroups in our society (e.g., minority-group dropouts in urban ghettos) find themselves unable not only to achieve upward mobility in the world of work but even to gain entrance to it, the way is open to serious social unrest as well as to individual frustration, maladjustment, and ineffectiveness.

The trends discussed above may involve not only a quantitative but also a significant qualitative change in the capacity of our society to absorb new minority groups into its socioeconomic mainstream, inasmuch as the traditional route followed by such groups in the past was from initially unskilled to increasingly more-skilled occupations. Unless corrective social measures can be applied, there appears to be a very real danger that communication among and mobility between various elements of our population will continue to decline.

Our immediate interest, however, is in whether these social changes in job demands are reflected in the vocational aspirations and career plans of youth generally. If youth is to keep up with these increasingly sophisticated demands, it will have to aspire to occupations higher on the socioeconomic scale than those of parents. This indeed appears to be the case, at least for most adolescents, not only in the United States but also in other countries that are developing more complex economic, social, and technological systems (14, 16, 113).

The most difficult vocational problem facing our society, but the one most urgently in need of solution, remains that of the deprived youth. Penalized by an inadequate home environment, serious problems of social adjustment, and poor motivation, he is likely to enter a school system unequipped to meet his needs. After falling farther behind as he progresses from grade to grade, and receiving few rewards for such efforts as he does make, he is likely to drop out of school as soon as he is able—only to find barriers at every turn in a job market that is becoming increasingly dependent on highly educated or skilled workers, with less and less need for unskilled, poorly educated youth. The accumulated frustration which results can be disastrous, not only for the individual himself but for our whole society as well.

SUMMARY

In addition to having to adjust to the physical and physiological changes associated with puberty, adolescents in our society must meet a variety of demands in the years between childhood and nominal adulthood. These include the establishment of independence, adjustment to same- and opposite-sex peers, vocational preparation, and development of a sense of ego identity and a basic, guiding philosophy of life. Consequently, adolescence has traditionally been viewed as a critical period of development in our society. In contrast, in many simpler cultures, with less complex societal demands during this age period, adolescence is not viewed as presenting particularly difficult problems. Whether contemporary American adolescents face more or less complex problems of adjustment than earlier generations is currently a matter of some dispute.

Adolescence is a period of dramatic physical and physiological change. The adolescent growth spurt begins at about age 11 in girls and about age 13 in boys, although there are wide individual variations. Body proportions change and become more like those of adults, and rapid maturation occurs in the reproductive system and in secondary sex characteristics. The physical changes of adolescence may produce a variety of concerns, including anxiety over early or late maturation, worry about deviations from idealized masculine and feminine stereotypes in appearance, and fear, guilt, or rejection associated with new physiological events (e.g. menstruation).

Impressive changes in cognitive development also take place during adolescence. Scores on tests that involve relatively pure measures of high-level mental processes tend to reach a peak in adolescence or early adulthood. Qualitatively, there is a shift in cognitive functioning from the stage of *concrete operations* characterizing middle and late childhood to the stage of *formal operations* (Piaget). The adolescent becomes able to generate hypotheses systematically and flexibly, and to test them against evidence. This vastly increases his capacity to deal with himself and the world about him. He becomes more capable of meaningful introspection, as well as of perceiving differences between how things are and how they might be.

One of the major adjustment demands of adolescence in American culture is the establishment of independence. This task is complicated by a number of factors, including prolongation of childhood dependence in our society; variations among important individuals and institutions (e.g., parents, peers, the law, teachers) in their independency expectations for youth at various ages; and ambivalent attitudes and conflicts regarding dependence-independence *within* parents and *within* adolescents themselves. In a number of nonliterate societies, there is a much more gradual and orderly transition from childhood dependence to complete adult independence. In our own culture, children of democratic and equalitarian parents rank higher in autonomy (independence) and self-confidence than children of autocratic parents; they also perceive their parents as more fair and more fond of their children.

Increased sexual drive is a major physiological concommitent of adolescence. While there appear to be basic physiological differences between boys and girls in the nature and expression of sexual drive, anthropological evidence of wide variations in the sexual behavior of both sexes from one society to another clearly indicates the importance of cultural influences as well, both on attitudes and behavior.

Is there currently emerging a "new morality" among adolescents? Available evidence suggests that changes are occurring, but probably more in the area of attitudes than of behavior. Contemporary adolescents appear less conservative than their parents, and more open and honest about sex. They also appear more concerned with meaningful interpersonal relationships and with developing a personal morality than relying on arbitrarily imposed public standards. Changes in overt sexual behaviors between generations are not nearly as dramatic as those in attitudes. In fact, if a real revolution in behavior has taken place in this century, it probably was initiated by today's parents and grandparents.

Virtually all forms of sexual behavior occur more frequently among males. Social class membership also significantly affects the sexual behavior patterns of males, but not females. On the other hand, religious affiliation is correlated with level of sexual behavior among both males and females. Sexual attitudes and adjustment of adolescents are also influenced by the rewarding or unrewarding nature of previous parent-child relationships and by parental attitudes toward sex.

In America, dating is a much more common and a more heavily emphasized institution than in many other countries. While dating may provide helpful social experience in establishing boy-girl relationships, it also may encourage superficiality, particularly if begun too soon. Girls who date very early and those who are very delayed in dating both appear less mature and well-adjusted than girls falling between these two extremes.

In adolescence, relations with peers perform many of the same functions that they do for the child, providing him an opportunity to learn how to interact with age-mates, to control social behavior, to develop age-relative skills and interests, and to share similar problems and feelings. If anything, however, the role peers play in adolescence is an even more important one for a variety of reasons. Relations both with same- and opposite-sex peers in this period come closer to serving as prototypes for later adult relationships—in social relations, in work, and in interactions with the opposite sex.

The nature of adolescent peer groups changes with age, moving from the preadolescent "gang" to tentative interactions between male and female cliques, to heterosexual cliques, and finally to the formation of cliques consisting of couples who are going steady or who are engaged. Individual friendships also play an important role in adolescence, and may help the adolescent to deal with his own complex feelings and those of others, as well as providing opportunities for sharing interests and activities with like-minded peers. In view of the importance of the peer group, social acceptance by peers is actively sought by most adolescents. In general, accepted adolescents are more likely to be viewed by their peers as: tolerant, flexible, and sympathetic; lively, cheerful, good-natured, and possessed of a sense of humor; natural and self-confident, without being conceited; and possessed of initiative, enthusiasm, drive, and plans for group activities.

Deciding on a vocation is an increasingly important and difficult task in our complex, technologically oriented society. While opportunities for those who are educated are expanding rapidly, there is also less and less room for the unskilled and uneducated. Vocational choice is influenced by a wide variety of factors: sex (girls generally having lower vocational goals than boys); social class; individual personality characteristics, interests, and needs of the adolescent; identification with parents, parental motivation, and vocational models provided by parents; and peer group and school influences. The most difficult vocational problem facing our society, but the one most urgently in need of solution, remains that of providing appropriate educational and vocational opportunities for socioeconomically and culturally deprived youth.

References

1. Ausubel, D. P. *Theory and problems of adolescent development.* New York: Grune & Stratton, 1954.
2. Baldwin, A., Kalhorn, J., & Breese, F. Patterns of parent behavior. *Psychol. Monogr.,* 1945, *58,* 1–75.
3. Baldwin, B. T. A measuring scale for physical growth and physiological age. *(15th Yearb. nat. Soc. Stud. Educ.)* Chicago: Univer. Chicago Press, 1916, *15,* 11–23.
4. Baumrind, D. Effects of authoritative control on child behavior. *Child Develpm.,* 1966, *37,* 887–907.
5. Bayley, N., & Oden, M. H. The maintenance of intellectual ability in gifted adults. *J. Gerontology,* 1955, *10,* 91–107.
6. Beilin, H. The pattern of postponability and its relation to social class mobility. *J. soc. Psychol.,* 1956, *44,* 33–48.
7. Bell, G. D. Processes in the formation of adolescents' aspirations. *Soc. Forces,* 1963, *42,* 179–195.
8. Bell, H. M. *Youth tell their story.* Washington, D.C.: American Council on Education, 1938.
9. Bell, R. R. Parent-child conflict in sexual values. *J. soc. Issues,* 1966, *22,* 34–44.
10. Bell, R. R., & Buerkle, J. V. Mother-daughter attitudes to premarital sexual behavior. *Marriage Fam. Living,* 1961, *23,* 390–392.
11. Bene, E. Suppression of heterosexual interest and of aggression by middle class and working class grammar school boys. *Brit. J. educ. Psychol.,* 1958, *28,* 226–231.
12. Benedict, R. Continuities and discontinuities in cultural conditioning. In W. E. Martin & C. B. Stendler (Eds.), *Readings in child development.* New York: Harcourt, Brace & World, 1954, 142–148.
13. Benedict, R. *Patterns of culture.* Boston: Houghton Mifflin, 1934.
14. Berdie, R. F., & Hood, A. B. *Decisions for tomorrow: plans of high school seniors for after graduation.* Minneapolis: Univer. of Minnesota Press, 1965.
15. Berlin, J. C. Adolescent friendship patterns in relation to anxiety and dominance. *Dissert. Abstr.,* 1966, *27,* 298.
16. Bertrand, A. L. School attendance and attainment: function and dysfunction of school systems. *Soc. Forces,* 1962, *40,* 228–233.
17. Blaine, G. B., quoted in C. Kirk, The new sexual freedom. *Coronet,* July, 1967, 62.
18. Bonney, M. E. A sociometric study of some factors to mutual friendships on the elementary, secondary, and college levels. *Sociometry,* 1946, *9,* 21–47.
19. Bonney, M. E. Personality traits of socially successful and socially unsuccessful children. *J. educ. Psychol.,* 1943, *34,* 449–472.
20. Bordin, E. S. A theory of interests as dynamic phenomena. *Educ. psychol. Measmt.,* 1943, *3,* 49–66.
21. Bordua, D. J. Educational aspirations and parental stress on college. *Soc. Forces,* 1960, *38,* 262–269.

22. Boyle, R. P. The effect of the high school on students' aspirations. *Amer. J. Sociol.,* 1966, *71,* 628–639.
23. Bradway, K. P., & Thompson, C. W. Intelligence at adulthood: a twenty-five year follow-up. *J. educ. Psychol.,* 1962, *53,* 1–14.
24. Bretsch, H. S. Social skills and activities of socially accepted and unaccepted adolescents. *J. educ. Psychol.,* 1952, *43,* 449–458.
25. Brittain, C. V. Adolescent choices and parent-peer cross-pressures. *Amer. sociol. Rev.,* 1963, *28,* 385–391.
26. Burns, R. B. Age and mental ability: re-testing with thirty-three years' interval. *Brit. J. educ. Psychol.,* 1966, *36,* 116.
27. Burnstein, E. Fear of failure, achievement motivation, and aspiring to prestigeful occupations. *J. abnorm. soc. Psychol.,* 1963, *67,* 189–193.
28. Campus '65. *Newsweek,* March 22, 1965, 43–54.
29. Cannon, K. L. Stability of sociometric scores of high school students. *J. educ. Res.,* 1958, *52,* 43–48.
30. Caro, F. G. Social class and attitudes of youth relevant for the realization of adult goals. *Soc. Forces,* 1966, *44,* 492–498.
31. Caro, F. G., & Pihlblad, C. T. Aspirations and expectations: a reexamination of the bases for social class differences in the occupational orientations of male high school students. *Sociol. soc. Res.,* 1965, *49,* 465–475.
32. Carter, H. D. The development of interests in vocations. In *Adolescence.* Part I. *(43rd Yearb. nat. Soc. Stud. Educ.)* Chicago: Univer. Chicago Press, 1944.
33. Carter, H. D. The development of vocational attitudes. *J. counsel. Psychol.,* 1940, *4,* 185–191.
34. Chorost, S. B. Parental child rearing attitudes and their correlates in adolescent hostility. *Genet. Psychol. Monogr.,* 1962, *66,* 49–90.
35. Cobb, H. V. Role wishes and general wishes of children and adolescents. *Child Develpm.,* 1954, *25,* 161–171.
36. Coleman, J. S. Athletics in high school. *Ann. Amer. Acad. Pol. Soc. Sci.,* 1961, *338,* 33–43.
37. Coleman, J. S. *The adolescent society.* New York: Free Press of Glencoe, 1961.
38. Conklin, E. S. *Principles of adolescent psychology.* New York: Holt, Rinehart and Winston, 1933.
39. Cooper, J. B. Parent evaluation as related to social ideology and academic achievement. *J. genet. Psychol.,* 1962, *101,* 135–143.
40. Crites, J. O. Parental identification in relation to vocational interest development. *J. educ. Psychol.,* 1962, *53,* 262–270.
41. Day, S. R. Teacher influence on the occupational preferences of high school students. *Voc. Guid. Quart.,* 1966, *14,* 215–219.
42. Dennis, W. The adolescent. In L. Carmichael (Ed.), *Manual of child psychology.* New York: Wiley, 1946, 633–666.
43. Dimock, H. S. *Rediscovering the adolescent.* New York: Association Press, 1937.
44. Dipboye, W. J., & Anderson, W. F. Occupational stereotypes and manifest needs of high school students. *J. counsel. Psychol.,* 1961, *8,* 296–304.
45. Douvan, E. A., & Adelson, J. *The adolescent experience.* New York: Wiley, 1966.
46. Douvan, E. A., & Kaye, C. *Adolescent girls.* Ann Arbor: Publication of Survey Research Center, Univer. of Michigan, 1957.
47. Droppleman, L. F., & Schaefer, E. S. Boys' and girls' reports of maternal and paternal behavior. Paper read at a meeting of the American Psychological Association, 1961.
48. Dubbé, M. C. What parents are not told may hurt: a study of communication

between teenagers and parents. *Family Life Coordinator,* 1965, *14,* 51–118.

49. Dunphy, D. C. The social structure of urban adolescent peer groups. *Sociometry,* 1963, *26,* 230–246.
50. Ehrmann, W. *Premarital dating behavior.* New York: Holt, Rinehart and Winston, 1959.
51. Elder, G. H., Jr. Parental power legitimation and its effect on the adolescent. *Sociometry,* 1963, *26,* 50–65.
52. Elder, G. H., Jr. Structural variations in the child rearing relationship. *Sociometry,* 1962, *25,* 241–262.
53. Elder, G. H., Jr. Family structure and the transmission of values and norms in the process of child rearing. Doctoral dissertation, University of North Carolina, 1961.
54. Elkind, D. Cognitive development in adolescence. In J. F. Adams (Ed.), *Understanding adolescence.* Boston: Allyn and Bacon, 1968, 128–158.
55. Elkind, D. Egocentrism in adolescence. *Child Develpm.,* 1967, *38,* 1025–1034.
56. Elkind, D. Children's discovery of the conservation of mass, weight, and volume. *J. genet. Psychol.,* 1961, *98,* 219–277.
57. Elkind, D. Quantity conceptions in junior and senior high school students. *Child Develpm.,* 1961, *32,* 551–560.
58. English, O. S., & Pearson, G. H. J. *Emotional problems of living.* New York· Norton, 1955.
59. Erikson, E. H. Identity and the life cycle. *Psychol. Issues,* 1959, *1,* 1–165.
60. Erikson, E. H. *A healthy personality for every child. A fact finding report: a digest.* Midcentury White House Conference on Children and Youth. Raleigh, N.C.: Health Publications Institute, 1951, 8–25.
61. Eshleman, J. R. Mental health and marital integration in young marriages. *J. Marriage Fam.,* 1965, *27,* 255–262.
62. Faust, M. S. Developmental maturity as a determinant in prestige of adolescent girls. *Child Develpm.,* 1960, *31,* 173–184.
63. Feinberg, M. R. Relation of background experience to social acceptance. *J. abnorm. soc. Psychol.,* 1953, *48,* 206–214.
64. Feinberg, M. R., Smith, M., & Schmidt, R. An analysis of expressions used by adolescents at varying economic levels to describe accepted and rejected peers. *J. genet. Psychol.,* 1958, *93,* 133–148.
65. Fitzgerald, M. P. Sex differences in the perception of the parental role for middle and working class adolescents. *J. clin. Psychol.,* 1966, *22,* 15–16.
66. Floud, J. E., Halsey, A. H., & Martin, F. M. (Eds.) *Social class and educational opportunity.* London: Heinemann, 1956, 93–95, 107–108.
67. Ford, C. S., & Beach, F. A. *Patterns of sexual behavior.* New York: Harper & Row, 1951.
68. Foshay, A. W. The teacher and children's social attitudes. *Teachers Coll. Rec.,* 1951, *52,* 287–296.
69. Frazier, A., & Lisonbee, L. K. Adolescent concerns with physique. *Sch. Rev.,* 1950, *58,* 397–405.
70. French, J. R. P., Jr., Morrison, H. W., & Levinger, G. Coercive power and forces affecting conformity. *J. abnorm. soc. Psychol.,* 1960, *61,* 93–101.
71. Gebhard, P. Personal communication.
72. Gesell, A., Ilg, F. L., & Ames, L. B. *Youth: the years from ten to sixteen.* New York: Harper & Row, 1956.
73. Greulich, W. W. The rationale of assessing the developmental status of chil-

dren from roentgenograms of the hand and wrist. *Child Develpm.*, 1950, *21*, 33–44.

74. Grinder, R. E., & Schmitt, S. S. Coeds and contraceptive information. *J. Marriage Fam.*, 1966, *28*, 471–479.

75. Gronlund, N. E., & Anderson, L. Personality characteristics of socially accepted, socially neglected, and socially rejected junior high school pupils. *Educational Admin. Supervis.*, 1958, *44*, 255–260.

76. Gunn, B. Children's conceptions of occupational prestige. *Personnel Guid. J.*, 1964, *42*, 558–563.

77. Harris, L. The teenagers. *Newsweek*, March 21, 1966, 57–77.

78. Henton, C. L. The effect of socio-economic and emotional factors on the onset of menarche among Negro and white girls. *J. genet. Psychol.*, 1961, *98*, 255–264.

79. Hoffman, M. L. Power assertion by the parent and its impact upon the child. *Child Develpm.*, 1960, *31*, 129–143.

80. Hohman, L. B., & Schaeffner, B. The sex lives of unmarried men. *Amer. J. Sociol.*, 1947, *52*, 501–507.

81. Holland, J. L. Explorations of a theory of vocational choice: Part I. Vocational images and choice. *Voc. Guid. Quart.*, 1963, *11*, 232–239.

82. Holland, J. L. Explorations of a theory of vocational choice: Part II. Self descriptions and vocational preferences. *Voc. Guid. Quart.*, 1963, *12*, 17–24.

83. Hollingshead, A. B. *Elmtown's youth: the impact of social classes on youth.* New York: Wiley, 1949.

84. Horrocks, J. E. *The psychology of adolescence.* Boston: Houghton Mifflin, 1962.

85. Hurlock, E. B. *Adolescent development.* New York: McGraw-Hill, 1967 (3rd ed.).

86. Hurlock, E. B. *Adolescent development.* New York: McGraw-Hill, 1949.

87. Inhelder, B., & Piaget, J. *The growth of logical thinking from childhood through adolescence.* New York: Basic Books, 1958.

88. Jennings, H. H. Leadership and sociometric choice. *Sociometry*, 1947, *10*, 32–49.

89. Jennings, H. H. Structure of leadership. *Sociometry*, 1937, *1*, 99–143.

90. Jersild, A. T. *The psychology of adolescence.* New York: Macmillan, 1963 (2nd ed.).

91. Jersild, A. T. *In search of self.* New York: Columbia Univer. Press, 1952.

92. Johnson, T. J., & Smith, L. M. Achievement, affiliation, and power motivation in adolescents. *Psychol. Rep.*, 1965, *16*, 1249–1252.

93. Jones, H. E. Age changes in adult mental abilities. In H. S. Conrad (Ed.), *Studies in human development.* New York: Appleton-Century-Crofts, 1966.

94. Jones, H. E. The environment and mental development. In L. Carmichael (Ed.), *Manual of child psychology.* New York: Wiley, 1954, 631–696.

95. Jones, H. E. *Motor performance and growth.* Berkeley: Univer. of California Press, 1949.

96. Jones, M. C. The later career of boys who were early or late maturing. *Child Develpm.*, 1957, *28*, 113–128.

97. Jones, M. C., & Mussen, P. H. Self conceptions, motivations and interpersonal attitudes of early and late maturing girls. *Child Develpm.*, 1958, *29*, 491–501.

98. Kagan, J., & Moss, H. A. *Birth to maturity.* New York: Wiley, 1962.

99. Kagan, J., & Moss, H. A. The stability of passive and dependent behavior from childhood through adulthood. *Child Develpm.*, 1960, *31*, 577–591.

100. Kahl, J. A. Educational and occupational aspirations of "common-man" boys. *Harv. educ. Rev.*, 1953, *23*, 186–203.

101. Kallen, D. J. Inner direction, other direction, and social integration setting. *Human Relat.,* 1963, *16,* 75–87.
102. Keedy, T. C. Factors in the cohesiveness of small groups. *Sociol. soc. Res.,* 1956, *40,* 329–332.
103. Keislar, E. R. Experimental development of "like" and "dislike" of others among adolescent girls. *Child Develpm.,* 1961, *32,* 59–66.
104. Keislar, E. R. Differences among adolescent social clubs in terms of members' characteristics. *J. educ. Res.,* 1954, *48,* 297–303.
105. King, W. H. The development of scientific concepts in children. *Brit. J. educ. Psychol.,* 1963, *23,* 240–252.
106. Kinsey, A. C., Pomeroy, W. B., & Martin, C. E. *Sexual behavior in the human male.* Philadelphia: Saunders, 1948.
107. Kinsey, A. C., Pomeroy, W. B., Martin, C. E., & Gebhard, P. H. *Sexual behavior in the human female.* Philadelphia: Saunders, 1953.
108. Kirkendall, L. A. Sex concerns of adolescent boys. *Marriage Hygiene,* 1948.
109. Kroger, R., & Louttit, C. M. The influence of father's occupation on the vocational choices of high school boys. *J. appl. Psychol.,* 1935, *19,* 203–212.
110. Kuhlen, R. G., & Bretsch, H. S. Sociometric status and personal problems of adolescents. *Sociometry,* 1947, *10,* 122–132.
111. Kuhlen, R. G., & Lee, B. J. Personality characteristics and social acceptability in adolescence. *J. educ. Psychol.,* 1943, *34,* 321–340.
112. Lake, A. Teenagers and sex: a student report. *Seventeen,* July, 1967, 88.
113. Lambert, W. E., & Klineberg, O. Cultural comparisons of boys' occupational aspirations. *Brit. J. clin. soc. Psychol.,* 1963, *3,* 56–65.
114. Lansky, L. M., Crandall, V. J., Kagan, J., & Baker, C. T. Sex differences in aggression and its correlates in middle-class adolescents. *Child Develpm.,* 1961, *32,* 45–58.
115. Latham, A. J. The relationship between pubertal status and leadership in junior high school boys. *J. genet. Psychol.,* 1951, *78,* 185–194.
116. Laughlin, F. *The peer status of sixth and seventh grade children.* New York: Columbia Univer. Press, 1954.
117. Lindenfeld, F. A note on social mobility, religiosity, and students attitudes towards premarital sexual relations. *Amer. sociol. Rev.,* 1960, *25,* 81–84.
118. Lipset, S. M., & Bendix, R. *Social mobility in industrial society.* Berkeley· Univer. of California Press, 1959.
119. Lowrie, S. H. Early marriage: premarital pregnancy and associated factors. *J. Marriage Fam.,* 1965, *27,* 48–57.
120. Lowrie, S. H. Early and late dating: some conditions associated with them. *Marriage Fam. Living,* 1961, *23,* 284–291.
121. Maresh, M. M. Changes in tissue widths during growth. *Amer. J. Dis. Child.,* 1966, *3,* 142–155.
122. Maresh, M. M. Variations in patterns of linear growth and skeletal maturation. *J. Amer. phys. Ther. Ass.,* 1964, *44,* 881–890.
123. McCammon, R. W. Are boys and girls maturing physically at earlier ages? *Amer. J. Publ. Hlth.,* 1965, *55,* 103–106.
124. McClelland, D. C., Rindlisbacher, A., & DeCharms, R. Religious and other sources of parental attitudes toward independence training. In D. C. McClelland (Ed.), *Studies in motivation.* New York: Appleton-Century-Crofts, 1955, 389–397.
125. McDonald, R. L., & Gynther, M. D. Relationship of self and ideal self descriptions. *J. pers. soc. Psychol.,* 1965, *1,* 85–88.

126. McNeill, D., & Livson, N. Maturation rate and body build in women. *Child Develpm.*, 1963, *34*, 25–32.
127. Mead, M. *Male and female*. New York: Morrow, 1939.
128. Mead, M. *From the south seas: Part III. Sex and temperament in three primitive societies*. New York: Morrow, 1939.
129. Meissner, W. W. Parental interaction of the adolescent boy. *J. genet Psychol.*, 1965, *107*, 225–233.
130. Meyers, C. E. Emancipation of adolescents from parental control. *Nerv. Child*, 1946, *5*, 251–262.
131. Mills, C. A., & Ogle, C. Physiologic sterility of adolescence. *Human Biol.*, 1936, *8*, 607–615.
132. Minturn, L., & Lambert, W. W., et al. *Mothers of six cultures: antecedents of child rearing*. New York: Wiley, 1964.
133. Montesano, N., & Geist, H. Differences in occupational choice between ninth and twelfth grade boys. *Personnel Guid. J.*, 1964, *43*, 150–154.
134. Mussen, P. H., & Jones, M. C. The behavior inferred motivations of late and early maturing boys. *Child Develpm.*, 1958, *29*, 61–67.
135. Mussen, P. H., & Jones, M. C. Self conceptions, motivations, and interpersonal attitudes of late and early maturing boys. *Child Develpm.*, 1957, *28*, 243–256.
136. Nash, H. Assignment of gender to body regions. *J. genet. Psychol.*, 1958, *92*, 113–115.
137. Neugarten, B. L. Social class and friendship among school children. *Amer. J. Sociol.*, 1946, *51*, 305–313.
138. Northway, M. L., & Wigdor, B. T. Rorschach patterns related to the sociometric status of school children. *Sociometry*, 1947, *10*, 186–199.
139. Nye, I. Adolescent-parent adjustment: age, sex, sibling, number, broken homes and employed mothers as variables. *Marriage Fam. Living*, 1952, *14*, 327–332.
140. Olson, W. C., & Hughes, B. O. Growth of the child as a whole. In R. G. Barker et al. (Eds.), *Child behavior and development*. New York: McGraw-Hill, 1943, 199–208.
141. Owens, W. A., Jr. Age and mental abilities: a longitudinal study. *Genet. Psychol. Monogr.*, 1953, *48*, 3–54.
142. Peck, R. F., & Gallini, C. Intelligence, ethnicity and social roles in adolescent society. *Sociometry*, 1962, *25*, 64–72.
143. Phelps, H. R., & Horrocks, J. E. Factors influencing informal groups of adolescents. *Child Develpm.*, 1958, *29*, 69–86.
144. Piaget, J. *The construction of reality in the child*. New York: Basic Books, 1954.
145. Pikas, A. Children's attitudes toward rational versus inhibiting parental authority. *J. abnorm. soc. Psychol.*, 1961, *62*, 315–321.
146. Polansky, N., Lippit, R., & Redl, F. The use of near-sociometric data in research on group treatment processes. *Sociometry*, 1950, *13*, 39–62.
147. Poppleton, P. K., & Brown, P. E. The secular trend in puberty: has stability been achieved? *Brit. J. educ. Psychol.*, 1966, *36*, 95–100.
148. Potashin, R. Sociometric study of children's friendships. *Sociometry*, 1946, *9*, 48–70.
149. Raven, B. H., & French, J. R. P., Jr. Group support, legitimate power and social influence, *J. Pers.*, 1958, *26*, 400–409.
150. Raven, B. H., & French, J. R. P., Jr. Legitimate power, coercive power, and observability in social influence. *Sociometry*, 1958, *21*, 83–97.
151. Reevy, W. R. Adolescent sexuality. In A. Ellis & A. Abarband (Eds.), *The encyclopedia of sexual behavior*, Vol. I. Englewood Cliffs, N.J.: Hawthorn, 1961.

152. Reiss, I. L. (Ed.) The sexual renaissance in America. *J. soc. Issues,* 1966, *22,* No. 2.
153. Reiss, I. L. The scaling of premarital sexual permissiveness. *J. Marriage Fam.,* May, 1964, 188–199.
154. Reiss, I. L. *Premarital sexual standards in America.* New York: Free Press of Glencoe, 1960.
155. Remmers, H. H., & Radler, D. H. *The American teenager.* Indianapolis: Bobbs-Merrill Co., 1957.
156. Riesman, D. *Individualism reconsidered.* New York: Free Press of Glencoe, 1954.
157. Rockwood, L. D., & Ford, M. E. N. *Youth, marriage, and parenthood.* New York: Wiley, 1945.
158. Rodman, H. The lower class value stretch. *Soc. Forces,* 1963, *42,* 205–215.
159. Roe, A. Early determinants of vocational choice. *J. counsel. Psychol.,* 1957, *4,* 212–217.
160. Roe, A. *The psychology of occupations.* New York: Wiley, 1956.
161. Roe, A., & Siegelman, M. *A study of the origin of interests.* Cambridge, Mass.: Harvard Graduate School of Education, Harvard University, 1962.
162. Rue, P. A. Friction between adolescents and parents. *Education,* 1960, *81,* 225–227.
163. Ryan, F. R., & Davie, J. S. Social acceptance, academic achievement, and aptitude among high school students. *J. educ. Res.,* 1958, *52,* 101–106.
164. Schonfeld, W. A. Primary and secondary sexual characteristics: study of their development in males from birth through maturity, with biometric study of penis and testes. *Amer. J. Dis. Child.,* 1943, *65,* 535–549.
165. Sewell, W. H., & Haller, A. O. Factors in the relationship between social status and the personality adjustment of the child. *Amer. sociol. Rev.,* 1959, *24,* 511–520.
166. Sewell, W. S., & Orenstein, A. M. Community of residence and occupational choice. *Amer. J. Sociol.,* 1965, *70,* 551–563.
167. Shaffer, L. F. *Children's interpretations of cartoons.* Contributions to Education No. 429. New York: Columbia Univer. Press, 1930.
168. Sheldon, W. H. *The varieties of temperament: a psychology of constitutional differences.* New York: Harper & Row, 1942.
169. Shoobs, N. Sociometry in the classroom. *Sociometry,* 1947, *10,* 154–164.
170. Shuttleworth, F. K. The physical and mental growth of girls and boys, age six to nineteen, in relation to age at maximum growth. *Monogr. Soc. Res. Child Develpm.,* 1939, *4,* No. 3.
171. Simmons, K. The Brush Foundation study of child growth and development: II. Physical growth and development. *Monogr. Soc. Res. Child Develpm.,* 1944, *9,* No. 1.
172. Simpson, R. L. Parental influence, anticipatory socialization, and social mobility. *Amer. sociol. Rev.,* 1962, *27,* 517–522.
173. Sinha, A. K., Prasaa, M. S., & Madhukar, R. P. Extraversion-introversion and rigidity of vocational aspirations. *Guidance Rev.,* 1964, *2,* 88–94.
174. Sollenberger, R. T. Some relationships between the urinary excretion of male hormone by maturing boys and their expressed interests and attitudes. *J. Psychol.,* 1940, *9,* 179–189.
175. Solomon, D. Influences on the decisions of adolescents. *Human Relat.,* 1963, *16,* 45–60.
176. Stephenson, R. Mobility orientation and gratification of 1,000 ninth graders. *Amer. sociol. Rev.,* 1957, *22,* 203–212.

177. Stone, L. J., & Church, J. *Childhood and adolescence: a psychology of the growing person.* New York: Random House, 1957.
178. Straus, M. A. Conjugal power structure and adolescent personality. *Marriage Fam. Living,* 1962, *24,* 17–25.
179. Stuart, H. C. Normal growth and development during adolescence. *New England J. Med.,* 1946, *234,* 666–672, 693–700, 732–738.
180. Super, D. E. A theory of vocational development. *Amer. Psychologist,* 1953, *8,* 185–190.
181. Super, D. S., Starishevsky, R., Matlin, N., & Jordaan, J. P. *Career development: self concept theory.* New York: College Entrance Examination Board, 1963.
182. Tanner, J. M. *Growth at adolescence.* Springfield, Ill.: Thomas, 1955.
183. Terman, L. M., & Tyler, L. E. Psychological sex differences. In L. Carmichael (Ed.), *Manual of child psychology.* New York: Wiley, 1954 (2nd ed.).
184. The open generation. *Look,* 1966, *30.*
185. Tryon, C. M. Evaluation of adolescent personality by adolescents. *Monogr. Soc. Res. Child Develpm.,* 1939, *4,* No. 4.
186. Turner, R. H. Sponsored and contest mobility and the school system. *Amer. sociol. Rev.,* 1960, *25,* 855–867.
187. Venables, E. Proposed affinities in British-American perspectives of adolescence. *J. Marriage Fam.,* 1965, *27,* 148–155.
188. Vincent, C. E. Teen-age unwed mothers in American society. *J. soc. Issues,* 1966, *22,* 22–33.
189. Vogel, W., & Lauterbach, C. G. Relationships between normal and disturbed sons' percepts of their parents' behavior and personality attributes of the parents and sons. *J. clin. Psychol.,* 1963, *19,* 52–56.
190. Walters, P. A., Jr. Promiscuity in adolescence. *Amer. J. Orthopsychiat.,* 1965, *35,* 670–675.
191. Washburn, W. C. The effects of physique and intrafamily tension on self-concepts in adolescent males. *J. consult. Psychol.,* 1962, *26,* 460–466.
192. Watson, E. H., & Lowrey, G. H. *Growth and development of children.* Chicago: Year Book Publishers, 1954 (2nd ed.).
193. Werts, C. E. Social class and initial career choice of college freshmen. *Sociol. Educ.,* 1966, *39,* 74–85.
194. West, J. *Plainville, U.S.A.* New York: Columbia Univer. Press, 1945.
195. Whitehead, A. N., cited in Elkind, D. Cognitive development in adolescence. In J. F. Adams (Ed.), *Understanding adolescence.* Boston: Allyn and Bacon, 1968.
196. Whiting, B. B. (Ed.) *Six cultures: studies of child rearing.* New York: Wiley, 1963.
197. Whiting, J. W. M., & Child, I. L. *Child training and personality: a cross-cultural study.* New Haven, Conn.: Yale Univer. Press, 1953.
198. Wilson, A. B. Residential segregation of social classes and aspirations of high school boys. *Amer. sociol. Rev.,* 1959, *24,* 836–845.
199. Wittenberg, R. M., & Berg, J. The stranger in the group. *Amer. J. Orthopsychiat.,* 1952, *22,* 89–97.
200. Witty, P. A study of pupils' interests, grades 9, 10, 11, 12. *Education,* 1961, *82,* 169–174.
201. Yamamoto, K. Creativity and sociometric choice among adolescents. *J. soc. Psychol.,* 1964, *64,* 249–261.
202. *Youth and the world of work.* East Lansing: Social Research Service, Michigan State College, 1949.
203. Zuk, G. H. The plasticity of the physique from early adolescence through adulthood. *J. genet. Psychol.,* 1958, *92,* 205–214.

15

Adolescence

II. Ego Identity, Values, and Alienation

Central to the task of becoming an adult is the development of a sense of one's own identity, of what defines him as a person (cf. pp. 689–695). This conception of oneself need not be all positive; it can, as Erikson notes *(42)* contain negative elements as well. But there is *something there*—a frame of reference within which the individual can view with some perspective the varied, often seemingly accidental influence and events of a rapidly changing, often chaotic world. Without some sense of his own identity, of who he is and where he is headed, the adolescent faces virtually insurmountable odds in attempting to cope with the demands of adolescence reviewed in the last chapter—the demands for independence, for integrating his new-found sexual maturity, for establishing meaningful and workable relations with peers of both sexes, and for deciding on his life work and his goals.

The problem of ego identity cannot be separated from that of values. We live in a world and at a period in history characterized by rapid change. This is particularly true in America, with its accelerated technological trans-formations and its continually shifting (socially and geographically) popula-tion. As Erikson says, "This is *the* country of changes; it is obsessed with change" *(42, 29)*. If the individual is to be able to maintain some stability in his conception of himself and in his internal guides to action in a changing world, he must have *fidelity* to some basic values. He may have to adopt new ways of implementing these values to meet changing circumstances. But if the values are there, and are sound, he will be able to be flexible in adapting to change while remaining constant in his conception of himself and faithful to his central values. In Erikson's words: "I would . . . claim that we have almost an instinct of fidelity—meaning that when you reach a certain age you can and must learn to be faithful to some ideological view.

Speaking psychiatrically, without the development of a capacity for fidelity the individual will either have what we call a weak ego, or look for a deviant group to be faithful to (42, 30).

In this final chapter, we will examine some of the antecedents and correlates of ego identity, and then turn to the problem of values. The prevailing values of the average adolescent will be examined first. Following this, we will consider the special problems faced by youth who in one way or another have become alienated from the dominant values of contemporary American society.

EGO IDENTITY

The adolescent or adult with a strong sense of ego identity sees himself as a distinctive individual in his own right. Indeed, the very word "individual," as a synonym for "person," implies a universal need to perceive one's self as somehow separate from others, no matter how much one may share motives, values, and interests with others. Closely related is the need for self-consistency—for a feeling of "wholeness." When we speak of the *integrity* of the self, we imply both a separateness from others *and* unity of the self— a workable integration of one's needs, motives, and patterns of responding. In order to have a clear sense of ego identity, the adolescent or adult requires a self-perceived consistency, not only at a particular moment but also over time. He needs to perceive the person that he is today as, if not the same person he was yesterday, at least similar to and having consistent links with the person he was yesterday. Any developmental influences which contribute to confident self-perceptions of one's self as separate and distinct from others, as reasonably consistent and integrated in his definition of himself, and as having a continuity of the self over time, also contribute to an overall sense of ego identity. By the same token, influences which impair any of these self perceptions foster ego diffusion.

Ibsen's *Peer Gynt* is essentially a depiction of Peer's search for identity. In his encounter with the Onion Man, Peer felt threatened because he felt himself, like an onion, to be merely a series of layers, of transient and shifting roles. When all the layers were peeled off, Peer wondered, would there be any central core, or true identity, left? Many adolescents have similar feelings. Not only do they find themselves playing roles which shift from one situation, or one time to another, and worry about "Which, if any, is the *real* me?", they also self-consciously try out different roles in the hope of finding one which seems to "fit." An adolescent girl had three distinctly different handwriting styles. When asked why she did not simply have one consistent style, she replied, "How can I only write one way till I know who I am?" (38).

The problem of ego identity becomes acute at adolescence for a variety of reasons. Change occurs during the middle-childhood years. But for the most part, it is gradual and regular, without abrupt shifts from day to day, or month to month. "But in puberty and adolescence all sameness and continuities relied on earlier are more or less questioned again, because of a rapidity of body growth which equals that of early childhood and because of the new addition of genital maturity" (41, 261). As Erikson notes, the rapidly changing adolescent, confronted with this physiological revolution within himself and with the varied intellectual, social, and vocational demands of adulthood that lie directly ahead, is concerned with how he appears in the eyes of others, compared with how he feels he actually is, and with the question of how to connect the roles and skills cultivated earlier with the demands of tomorrow. "In their search for a new sense of continuity and sameness, adolescents have to refight many of the battles of earlier years, even though to do so they must artificially appoint perfectly well-meaning people to play the roles of adversaries; and they are ever ready to install lasting idols and ideals as guardians of a final identity" (41, 261).

The ease with which the adolescent establishes a clear sense of ego identity will depend upon many factors: the kinds of parent-child relationships he has had and the previous identifications he has developed; his ability to integrate these identifications with his new-found sexual maturity; the aptitudes and skills he has developed out of his ability and experience; and the opportunities offered in social roles (41). Establishing a strong ego identity will be facilitated if (1) a sufficiently rewarding, interactive relationship exists between parent and child to permit a positive identification with the parent (e.g., an affectionate, nurturant relationship between father and son); also if (2) the same-sex parent serves as an adequate model for appropriate sex-role behavior (9, 23, 62, 80, 81, 83, 91, 102). Such an adolescent or young adult will be likely to have a favorable and clearly defined perception of himself, and will also be less likely to encounter conflicts between his perception of himself and both the internal demands of approaching sexual maturity and the external demands of society for sex-appropriate behavior. Consistent with this reasoning, it has been shown that, over a variety of interpersonal situations, adolescent boys with more nurturant fathers perceive themselves as having a greater role-consistency than sons of less nurturant fathers (67). That is, they perceive themselves as responding in similar ways to parents, friends, employers, casual acquaintances, children, and members of the opposite sex. Thus, if they view themselves as being relaxed or formal, warm or indifferent, independent or dependent in one kind of relationship, they tend to view themselves as responding in similar fashion in other relationships. Furthermore, greater nurturance in more masculine fathers is related to greater role-consistency, but stronger nurturance in more feminine fathers is associated with lower role-consistency (67).

In addition, it has been found that the adolescent boy's sense of ego identity is likely to be stronger when the father is seen as the dominant parental figure; when both parents are similar in their behavior toward the adolescent; and when the mother supports the boy's identification with the father, while herself avoiding an intrusive, demanding kind of orientation to the boy (95).

Among late adolescent girls, those scoring high in identification with their mothers tend to perceive themselves as "calm," "reasonable," "reserved," "self-controlled," "confident," and "wise." In contrast, those scoring low in identification tend to view themselves as "changeable," "impulsive," "rebellious," "restless," "dramatic," "touchy," and "tactless" (9). In Erikson's terms, the former self-descriptions appear more closely related to emerging *ego identity*, while the latter appear more related to ego *diffusion*. In the same study of adolescent girls (9), it was found that girls who saw themselves as more like their mothers (i.e., identified with their mothers) perceived their actual and "ideal" selves as more similar and consistent than did girls who viewed themselves as less like their mothers.

Sex-Typing and Ego Identity. We have indicated that development of a strong sense of ego identity is likely to be facilitated by identification with a parent who serves as an adequate model for sex-appropriate behavior. However, in view of the complex and shifting demands on the adolescent and young adult in our society, it appears important to qualify what is meant by "appropriate sex-role behavior" if we are to avoid misunderstanding and confusion.

Generally, the boy or girl who has developed a secure sex-role identification that he views as consistent with his image of himself and with the expectations of his peers and society will have an easier time establishing a confident ego identity. Thus it is not surprising that a generally positive relationship has been found between sex-stereotyped behavior in adolescent males and ego identity, as measured by self-perceived role consistency (61).

Furthermore, boys with highly masculine interests show more positive self-conceptions and more self-confidence than boys with relatively feminine interests (89). They appear more carefree, more contented, more relaxed, more exuberant, happier, calmer, and smoother in social functioning than those with less masculine interests (89).

However, the picture does not appear to be so simple as one might initially expect. When these same boys are examined again as young adults, comparisons of the two groups show that highly masculine boys tend to remain more traditionally "masculine" in their interests, but they appear less confident in their perception of themselves:

> During adolescence, highly masculine subjects possessed more self-confidence and greater feelings of adequacy than the other group, but as adults, they were relatively lacking in qualities of leadership, dominance, self-confidence, and self-acceptance. In general, there seems to have been a shift in the self-concepts of the two groups in adulthood, the originally highly masculine boys apparently feeling less positive about themselves after adolescence; and, correlatively, the less masculine group changing in a favorable direction (88, 440).

How can these shifts be explained? It appears that the personality traits associated with a *high* degree of masculinity of interests may be maximally rewarding in the culture of the adolescent peer group, with its greater emphasis on masculine stereotypes and with relatively fewer culturally approved social and vocational roles available. In contrast, in adulthood, less stereotypy in the "masculinity" of one's social and vocational role is necessary. Admittedly, highly "feminine" roles, such as ballet dancer, interior decorator, or women's hairdresser may continue to be viewed with suspicion, but many vocational roles that combine "masculine" demands for independence and aggressiveness and "feminine" demands for nurturance and interpersonal sensitivity and orientation (e.g., physician, psychologist, author, teacher, personnel director) are highly rewarded in adulthood. In fact, to some degree at least, highly stereotyped "masculine" vocational roles may be relatively low in social and financial reward value (e.g., cowboy, truck driver, miner, laborer in heavy industry). In adulthood, personality characteristics that may have developed partly as defenses among less stereotypically masculine youths in adolescence—such as efforts to be sociable and sensitive to the interests of others, development of introspectiveness and inner resources, and a need to prove one's self—may contribute to social and vocational success, and hence may result in increased security, socially and vocationally, and a more confident adjustment. One is reminded of the "Big Man on Campus" who never again finds the world so rewarding or compliant, and who becomes an increasingly pathetic example of the "perennial sophomore"—really happy only at college or school reunions. In contrast, one recalls the "invisible" undergraduates, unrecognized and perhaps somewhat lonely in school or college, who go on to become leaders in business, science, and the arts.

In short, despite the relatively greater consistency in our society's sex-role expectations for boys than for girls, an *extremely stereotyped* masculine identification does not appear to be the best guarantee of a stable, long-term sense of ego identity, even in one's role as a male. It appears less likely to lead to a diffuse sense of identity than an extreme feminine identification, but it would appear that the most desirable identification is one that, while basically masculine, allows for some flexibility and an avoidance of extreme stereotypes. Rather interestingly, in one study (60) it was found that even in adolescence, boys whose fathers provided a *moderately* masculine role-model and who were *moderately* nurturant had less difficulty in establishing appropriate and consistent sex-role behavior in adolescence and showed fewer discrepancies between their expressed social values and their social behavior than boys whose fathers fell at the extremes.

The situation with respect to sex-role stereotypes and identity is even more complex for girls. In our opinion, there are more ways, even in adolescence, in which a girl can successfully establish a feminine ego identity than is the case with boys, although not necessarily with less difficulty. For one thing, as we have already noted (cf. p. 506), the girl is permitted considerably more freedom as a child to engage in cross-sex behaviors (13). There is also increasing evidence that the traditional feminine role is in a state of transition (13, 80). This means that the girl may be exposed to conflicting social rewards and punishments "no matter whether she assumes the traditional feminine role or the 'modern' masculinized role" (*61*, 352). In these circumstances the outward forms which her role-behavior takes may be less important than (1) the kind of parental identification on which it is at least in part based and (2) whether, despite cultural variations, her role-behavior is consistent with her basic biological nature as a girl (i.e., a potential heterosexual partner, wife, and mother). Thus both the girl who is identified with a very traditional "feminine" mother and the girl who is identified with a socially assertive, intellectual, highly independent mother may achieve a relatively conflict-free adjustment and a strong sense of ego identity, even though the girl in the latter case may score low on a relatively stereotyped measure of "femininity." On the other hand, a girl whose sex-role behavior is based on rejection of a nonnurturant mother (regardless of whether the mother is "traditional" or "modern") or on identification with a mother who rejects her basic biological identity (e.g., resents her sexual nature or her childbearing role, or who is hostile to her own or the opposite sex), will have difficulty in establishing a stable, secure ego identity.

This viewpoint appears to receive support in Douvan and Adelson's study of adolescent experience (*38*), in which a variety of groups of adolescent girls were investigated. Girls with a strong and *unambivalent* (i.e., without mixed feelings) *feminine sex-role identification* appeared clearly identified with their mothers, and apparently had close and amiable relationships with strong, traditional parents. Of all groups of girls analyzed, the *unambivalent feminine girls* most often chose their mothers or some other feminine relative as an adult ideal. This group reported fewer disagreements with their parents than other girls, and they more often spent part of their leisure time in family activities. These girls

> are distinguished by a compliant, dependent relationship to their parents (for example, they also gain self-esteem from being praised by adults more often than do ambivalent feminine girls), they observe parental regulations with caution and in a spirit of identification with the parents' point of view. Apparently compliance is also an important part of the parents' expectations—this group reports, more often than any other, that their parents expect them to be obedient and "respect authority" (*38*, 245).

On the other hand, their parents were not harsh, and these girls were rarely punished physically. Their parents apparently were strong and clear in stating requirements, and because the girls complied with their demands, little occasion for conflict or harshness occurred (*38*, 245). These girls, who represented one extreme along a dimension of relative femininity, also expressed a *clear sense of their own identity* and were "most thoroughly focused on the social and personal aspects of reality" (*38*, 244).

> Compared even to other feminine girls, she is consistently outstanding in this respect. She gains self-esteem from helping others and playing a succorant role; she typically chooses an adult ideal on the basis of interpersonal warmth and

sensitivity. She shows little motivation for personal achievement. She prefers security to success, she does not daydream about achievement, but rather exclusively about popularity, dating, marriage, and family goals (*38*, 244).

At the opposite extreme, girls with *antifeminine identifications* were least likely to choose women at all (including mother, other feminine relatives, or unrelated women) as ideal adults. Their parents tended to be traditional and restrictive toward their daughters, and were considerably more punitive than the parents of any other group. Over a third of these girls reported that they were physically punished when they did something wrong, compared with less than half that number in the total sample. The antifeminine girls viewed parents as suspicious and lacking in trust, and expressed an almost unanimous wish for less restriction when asked how a girl might want her parents to be different. Parents of girls in this group discouraged autonomy, seldom allowed their daughters to take part in rule-making at home, and demanded unquestioning obedience and respect for authority. An atmosphere of conflict typically pervaded the family setting in this group.

These girls, in turn, responded with resentment against their parents' regulation; rejected the feminine role model as restricting freedom, demanding attention to clothes and grooming, and, in some cases, as "subjecting" the girl to feminine biological functions, such as menstruation and childbirth. They appeared to have little self-esteem, and to be insecure and self-rejecting. They displayed few interests, had difficulty with friendships, had a low activity level, and generally appeared to have a *poorly defined sense of their own ego identity (38).*

Falling between these two extremes, but clearly nearer to the feminine-identification end of the continuum, was a third group of girls. These were girls who, although strongly feminine, could and did recognize attractions in the masculine role. While they were similar to the unambivalent feminine girls in their concern with marriage and motherhood, in their articulated ideas about marriage, and in general social development, they also maintained a lively interest in personal achievement, and were focused on individual development.

Again, as in the case of unambivalent feminine girls, girls in this latter group appeared to be modeling themselves after parents with whom they had experienced positive, generally rewarding relationships. Mothers in this group were likely themselves to be ambitious, highly educated, and working outside the home. They encouraged their daughters toward independence and self-reliance to a greater extent than parents of unambivalent feminine girls, and typically allowed their daughters a significant share in making rules and regulations regarding conduct (*71*).

In brief, development of a strong and stable sense of ego identity and a relatively conflict-free sex-role adjustment in adolescence will depend to an important degree on the nature of previous parent-child relationships and the kinds of parental identification patterns that have been established.

However, as Erikson observes, "the integration now taking place in the form of ego identity is . . . more than the sum of the childhood identifications. It is the accrued experience of the ego's ability to integrate all identifications with the vicissitudes of the libido, with aptitudes developed out of endowment, and with the opportunities offered in social roles" (41, 261).

Development of a secure sense of identity can be made easier or more difficult by the values, expectations, and opportunities of the society in which youth is expected to adjust. In a complex society such as our own, which is in rapid transition and in which ever larger minorities are disenfranchised from society's rewards while having to bear the burden of its failures, the development of ego identity can be a formidable task indeed, as we shall see later in this chapter.

VALUES

Probably at no time in his life is the average individual more likely to be concerned about the problem of moral values and standards than during adolescence. There appear to be a number of reasons for this heightened concern. For one thing, the realistic demands which the adolescent faces are changing, and this fact in itself requires a reappraisal of his value system. The average younger child lives in a world which, at least relatively, is more homogeneous, more immediate, and more limited than that of the adolescent. As a result, he faces fewer demands for making moral choices. Living according to a fairly circumscribed set of rules, established for the most part by parents, he and his peers learn to find satisfaction of their needs from day to day within this context. Granted, the child must learn to establish *internal controls* as a necessary part of the socialization process. He cannot do what he wants whenever he wants to do it. And, certainly, as we shall see, controls are related to the problem of values. But establishing controls is not synonymous with learning to make value decisions, often under ambiguous circumstances.

In contrast with the younger child's position, the adolescent must make choices. He himself is changing, and this change requires a rethinking of former childhood values, which may have been adopted over time with little conscious intent. For example, increases in sexual drive may confront the adolescent with a whole new set of value choices for which his childhood experiences have provided little preparation. Similarly, in his increased sophistication, the adolescent can no longer adopt without question the social or political beliefs of his parents in the happy conviction that solely because his parents have particular beliefs, all right-thinking persons must necessarily share them.

Not only is the adolescent himself changing—physiologically, socially, and psychologically—he is also confronted with an increasingly diverse world in which the opportunities and the necessity for choice are multiplied. He finds, for example, that there are many ways to live his life and that he must make choices. Does he want to be a businessman, a doctor, an artist, a Peace Corps worker, a minister, a soldier? Does a girl want to be a nurse, teacher, social worker, secretary, scientist, airline stewardess, or entertainer? Such vocational choices cannot be made independently of personal values, although, of course, many other factors also play a role (cf. pp. 665–677). If a particular adolescent is strongly convinced of the necessity for helping others, he may make a different career choice than if he places a high valuation on material success. If he believes more in freedom and autonomy than in security, he may likewise choose differently. If he believes that honesty is the best policy, he may be less likely to enter certain occupations than if he believes that there is a sucker born every minute, and that the main responsibility (hence the main value of a man *as a man*) is survival in a social jungle. Girls face value judgments in comparing the prospective merits of work and marriage.

The time perspective of adolescents becomes greatly extended, as contrasted to that of children; this, too, increases the urgency of developing a set of values. The adolescent who is beginning to look forward to an entire lifetime is much more in need of a set of guiding moral principles— if his life is to have a semblance of order, consistency, and meaning— than the child whose principal preoccupation at a given moment may be whether he is going to an amusement park the next day or to the dentist.

To complicate matters further, the adolescent is confronted with a wider range of conflicting pressures in the adoption or modification of personal values than the average younger child. As we have seen, the peer group may be urging one set of values and the parents another. The adolescent may be motivated to conform to the values of his peers in order to gain acceptance or to avoid rejection. Increasingly, too, other influences enter the arena of moral choice—teachers, books, and representatives of conflicting groups in the broader society.

Furthermore, as Anna Freud (46) and others (38) have noted, the adolescent may need to become engaged in matters of broad philosophical concern and conflicts about moral values—not *simply* for their own sake, but as a way of struggling with more personal and less cosmic, but no less real problems.

> [It] would be wrong to suppose that most adolescents caught in normative conflicts have these imposed on them by circumstance. On the contrary, value conflicts are often "chosen" by adolescents for internal, and usually unconscious, reasons. Intrapsychic factors may play the leading role, in that the struggle between family and extrafamily standards and values expresses an internal crisis, although a crisis which may have "external" referents, as when a boy chooses lower-class friends to torment his ambitious parents. It is often difficult to disentangle the interaction between genuine conflicts in values and the personal dispositions which lead the youngster to use the "conflict of generations" motif in resolving some part of the adolescent crisis; and it is easy to be "bamboozled" by the rhetoric which these conflicts occasion (38, 85).

Douvan and Adelson cite as an example the case of an adolescent boy, highly gifted intellectually, who suddenly lost interest in schoolwork, opted for the "hippie" life, and was preparing to go on the road:

> When he was taken to a psychological clinic by his parents, he offered a compelling indictment of the fakeries of the "Organization" society, sounding very much like Paul Goodman, and the intake interviewer (also *au courant* in these matters) was persuaded that this was a social-philosophical rather than a personal crisis. The clinic staff thought something was fishy, nevertheless, and urged a more searching interview, which revealed that the boy's loss of interest had been preceded by a homosexual seduction by one of his teachers. Going on the road was simultaneously a flight from homosexual arousal, an unconscious seeking to repeat and master the trauma, a way of punishing the "elders," a self-punishment for having yielded, and no doubt much else. This tale is not told to debunk Paul Goodman, or anyone else who believes that the prevailing ideology of adolescent discontent tells a great deal about the culture and about those adolescents attracted to it; nor is it meant to refute the "reality" of the protest or of adolescent values in general. Rather we mean to caution against simplistic appraisals of parent-peer conflicts, which are always a mixture of the "social" and "psychological," the real and the unreal, the objective and the personal (58, 86).

In a similar fashion, an adolescent boy may become an ardent, even eloquent advocate of liberal (or conservative) political views primarily in order to prove to himself his independence from his autocratic, conservative (or liberal) father, or to express a deep-lying resentment toward him. Withdrawal from political interest and involvement may also be a function of hostility toward the father (5). Similarly, a girl may develop a highly intellectualized philosophy of "free love," or become a vigorous crusader against traditional middle-class values, principally as a way of reassuring herself that she does not feel guilty about her own sexual impulses, or in order to punish her dogmatic, domineering mother.

The role of underlying psychological mechanisms need not, of course, be confined to reactions *against* others, in or outside the family. In a more positive sense, adolescent beliefs may be formed as a result of the selection of a hero or heroine and the subsequent adoption of the hero's moral standards in order to strengthen an identification with this model. Thus, some adolescents may adopt the liberal religious or sexual views of a young adult whom they admire. The maintenance of a value that is identical to one held by the respected hero strengthens the youth's identification with this idealized figure, and makes the adolescent feel stronger and more adequate.

Finally, the adolescent may change one or more of his moral standards as a result of certain experiences, sometimes traumatic and sometimes involving interpersonal relations, which lead him to question the consistency of his value system. Most individuals have a strong need to regard their collection of attitudes as logical and rational. It is disturbing to discover that one holds values that are inconsistent.

Of course, many individuals delude themselves into thinking that their values are consistent when, in fact, this is not the case. However, the important thing is that the individual *consciously* believe that his values are consistent with one another. If a series of experiences causes him to question this consistency, he is likely to change one or more of his values in order to restore consistency. Thus one adolescent may evolve a value system that emphasizes the importance of rationality. No value would be taken seriously unless it matches rational laws or experience. This value might clash with a pre-existing belief in a formal religion. In order to maintain consistency, the youth's attitudes about religion might undergo some change.

Conscience and Shifting Moral Standards

By the time the American child reaches adolescence, his conscience has had a good many years in which to develop (cf. pp. 508–514). Guilt has become associated with a great number of responses. As long as he can continue to avoid making such responses, all is reasonably well. But when incompatible motives are aroused—motives which can be reduced only by making responses previously associated with increases in guilt—then conflict and tension must inevitably result. For example, a child may have learned to associate guilt with sexual responses. As long as the child's sexual needs are not too strong, little conflict may result, as the responses which are necessary to gratify sexual needs will also lead to increases in guilt. The adolescent would encounter minimal emotional strain if the society consistently demanded that certain responses be carried out, and always rewarded them; and also if when certain other responses were *not* carried out, always prescribed punishment. Unfortunately, our society is not nearly so consistent.

Inconsistencies are evident in the area of sexual behavior and they occur also in many other areas. A child may be expected, for example, to believe in the code of doing unto others as he would have others do unto him. He may often be taught that it is wrong to be aggressive, to compete, to question authority, to play cards, to smoke, to swear, and to lie. And yet when the same child grows up, he is often expected suddenly to change and to be sexually responsive; "one of the boys" with respect to smoking, swearing, card playing, and similar activities; not to be too "naive" in his religious beliefs; and, "when necessary," to be aggressive and competitive regardless of the consequences to others, and even at times to lie and cheat a bit. Having once adopted at face value the parable of the Good Samaritan, he is faced with the task of renouncing this belief with the newer dictum that "business is business." Having been taught that "Thou shall not kill," he may now be expected to engage in wars he does not understand involving civilian populations in remote lands. Whereas previously he was exhorted to be an idealist, he is now exhorted with equal vigor to be "practical." As we shall see later in this chapter, not all youth make such adjustments without either active rebellion, disillusionment and withdrawal, or emotional difficulties. However, most ultimately do make some sort of adjustment to such shifting standards—though frequently not without some difficulty. The average adolescent may share, in attenuated form, a number of the concerns of political or social activist youth groups or of "social dropouts," but, in general, as we shall see, most still find life reasonably rewarding and happy, and are not in active rebellion against the social order.

Changes in Religious Beliefs During Adolescence

Religious beliefs tend to become more abstract and less literal between the ages of 12 and 18 (75). For example, God comes to be seen more frequently as an abstract power than as a fatherly human being. Religious views also become more tolerant and less dogmatic (75).

In an attempt to determine the nature of changes in religious beliefs during adolescence, one team of investigators prepared a list of 70 statements dealing with religious issues, and asked a group of 547 12-, 15-, and 18-year-old students to indicate, for each statement, whether they believed it, didn't believe it, or wondered about it (75). The results indicate that many adolescents change at least some aspects of their religious beliefs. For example, the percentage of adolescents believing that "only good people go to heaven" or "every word in the Bible is true" decreases with age.

The greatest changes appear to take place among students in their late teens, and particularly among students attending college. While 75 percent of a recent national sample of college students acknowledged a belief in God, in many cases this belief became increasingly tenuous or more abstract during the course of their college careers (16). Among freshmen, 53 percent stated that college had not changed their religious beliefs, 23 percent said it had increased their faith, and 23 percent said it had raised doubts about their faith. In contrast, among college seniors, only 34 percent said there had been no change and 45 percent said college had raised doubts about their beliefs; only 20 percent said it had increased their faith. Fifty percent of graduating college seniors characterize themselves as "fairly religious," with an additional 20 percent stating that they are "very religious." Only 16 percent feel that they are either "fairly" or "very" nonreligious, with 13 percent not committing themselves to any point of view.

There is some indication, however, that today's adolescents are placing a somewhat greater emphasis than previous generations on *personal*, rather than *institutionalized* religion (107). This would appear consistent with the greater stress among adolescents generally on personal values and relationships, and on individual moral standards, with less reliance on traditional social beliefs and institutions. In a recent study (107), 40 percent of adolescents aged 13–20 expressed the opinion that clergymen are not keeping in touch with youth. In the words of one respondent, "The clergy are still caught up in the Victorian outlook. They're afraid to come out of it because they're afraid of what's happening to religion today" (107, 45–46).

Current Trends in Adolescent Values

Adolescent concerns with moral standards and values vary not only with age but also from generation to generation. While there are important continuities in values between parents and children, it is also obvious that values may become modified over time. It is also important to recognize that all moral values are not held with equal intensity. Values that are strongly held give way to expediency when the pressure for compromise is great. More strongly held, central values, however, may be much more resistant to external pressures.

Adolescents currently appear to place a relatively high value on open and meaningful interpersonal relationships. As we have seen in the previous chapter, they tend to view sexual relationships without love as far less acceptable morally than those in which love is present. As a group, they seem genuinely opposed to promiscuity, not only in principle, but for the most part in behavior.

In contrast, while a majority of adolescents would probably acknowledge *in principle* that cheating in school was wrong, this conviction does not appear to be strongly held for a variety of reasons (and rationalizations). It is frequently argued that our system of education, with its large classes, impersonality, and machine-scoring of standardized tests, is itself essentially false and does not truly measure the individual's knowledge or ability. In a recent national survey of teenage students, 65 percent expressed the view that their teachers were "cheating" them—by playing favorites, padding grades for colleges, giving true-false quizzes, and not preparing for classes (107).

Pressure for grades is viewed as a doubtful value by many students, although they see themselves as yielding to it in order to advance, to get into college, to obtain a job, or simply, as one student phrased it, "to stay on the treadmill." Influenced by such views—both genuine and rationalized—and by the increased academic pressures to which contemporary youth is exposed, increasing numbers of students appear to be involved in cheating (56). In a recent study of high school and college students, 96 percent admitted cheating on school tests. Not surprisingly, 75 percent stated that an honor system would not work in their school or college (107). Moreover, the guilt associated with cheating appears to be diminishing.

What values do adolescents currently hold? As stated above, they place a relatively strong emphasis on being natural, open, and honest in relations with peers of both sexes. They decry "phoniness," as adolescents have traditionally done, but probably with even more vigor. Only a minority are activists on social or political issues (16, 56, 107), but most do appear to have more concern with issues such as discrimination and civil rights than their parents did. In their attitudes they seem to be reflecting flexibility, tolerance, and lack of prejudice as much as, or more than, crusading zeal. In two recent studies, broadly representative of parents and adolescents nationally, almost 50 percent of the parents, but only 25 percent of adolescents, said they would object to a Negro family as next-door neighbors (56). Most young people expressed no objection to sharing classrooms or churches with blacks; even in the South, 62 percent stated they had no objection to sitting next to a Negro in school. Fifty-eight percent of the adolescent sample saw war as a major problem confronting the country (56).

At the same time, today's adolescents do not appear to be a generation of hero-worshipers. In a recent study, adolescents were asked whom
they admired most. With the exception of John F. Kennedy (the overwhelming favorite of 47 percent of boys and 50 percent of girls), only Abraham
Lincoln, with George Washington running a poor third, got more than 5
percent of the vote (56). In a similar survey (107), virtually no heroes
emerged with the exception again of President Kennedy (one 17-year-old
girl mentioned "Babe Ruth, because he's so cool"). Among both high
school (56) and college students (16), Kennedy appears to have come closest
to symbolizing the aspirations of the current generation. Most prominently
mentioned by students in both surveys were his "youthfulness," "intelligence," "spirit of vitality," "practical optimism," "progressive rather than expedient values," and "coolness" (an ironic detachment, fatalism, wit, and an
ability to avoid taking himself too seriously).

In terms of their confidence in the social institutions of our society, older
adolescents appear to place a "great deal" of faith (over 64 percent) in the
scientific community, medicine, banks, the United States Supreme Court,
and higher education (16). In contrast, they show little confidence in political
parties, the press, advertising, organized labor, and television (only 12–25
percent express a "great deal" of faith in these institutions).

Adolescents speak frequently of their opposition to "materialistic values,"
but paradoxically they seem to accept readily this generation's relative affluence, which is by all odds the greatest in history. It is estimated that allowances and part-time and summer jobs put twelve billion dollars annually in the
pockets of today's adolescents, of whom more than 60 percent own records,
transistor radios, record players, and encyclopedias. While 18 percent of boys
and 8 percent of girls have cars, another 44 percent and 37 percent, respectively, want them (56). Seventy-six percent of a national sample of adolescent youth regarded shopping as "one of the experiences they most enjoy"
(56). It would appear more accurate to say that many adolescents are finding
that materialistic goals are insufficient to produce a sense of personal fulfillment rather than to say that adolescents generally are opposed to material
values.

While a number of relatively small subgroups of today's adolescents are
either strong activists, dedicating their efforts to causes with which they are
deeply concerned, or are "social dropouts," disillusioned with what they view
as the inability of an immoral, unjust, and impersonal society to change,
most adolescents are far more docile. They go their own way with values
that are in many respects admirable, troubled by some aspects of their society (pressure, war, the draft, civil rights, economic injustice), but largely
uninterested in "making waves" and generally fairly satisfied with themselves
and with their way of life (16, 56, 107).

In a broad survey conducted by Louis Harris for Newsweek magazine
(56), American adolescents between the ages of 13 and 17 were asked to
describe their feelings about the world in which they were growing up.
At all ages, adolescents perceived the world about them as "modern" and

"fast-moving." Increasingly, as they grew older, they viewed the world as "competitive," "warlike," and "impersonal." Nevertheless, the average adolescent was far more likely, despite these pressures, to see himself as "happy" than "sad," and to feel that there is "lots to do" rather than "nothing to do." Of course, no direct comparisons with the results of his particular survey are available from earlier generations of adolescents. However, results from other studies suggest that today's adolescents, despite the problems they face, may be less troubled generally than youth of earlier generations. For example, the same questions put to a sample 20 years earlier were recently asked of 2000 Catholic high school boys. In general, youth in the most recent group evidenced significantly less anxiety on a variety of measures. They pictured themselves far less frequently as "being discouraged easily," "feeling so conscious of your faults you can't enjoy anything," feeling sad, depressed, and lonely, and worrying about school progress or vocational success in the future (84). There are also indications that American adolescents have fewer worries than those in a number of other cultures (e.g., India and Germany) although there is a high degree of similarity of rankings of problems across cultures (101).

Summary. It appears that the generation of adolescents which is currently emerging sees the world as proceeding at an ever faster pace; growing increasingly competitive and impersonal; and becoming more and more diverse and conflicted in its values, beliefs, and proposed solutions to social, political, and economic problems. In response, some youths have become social or political activists, while others have "dropped out"—either from disillusionment or defeat, or in order to build what they view as a private but more meaningful world of their own. The majority of adolescents, however, have remained, and intend to continue to remain, in the mainstream of society and its overall evolution, and they are interested in "success" as conventionally defined. They are aware of the pressures and the accelerated, often hectic pace of modern life, but for the most part they feel they can cope. They are learning to live with uncertainty and ambiguity in many spheres and they are neither activists nor dropouts. Despite the pressures and contradictions of their era, most find more satisfaction than dissatisfaction in their daily lives. They appear at least as happy as earlier generations, and possibly more so than many. If anything, they appear less anxious than their parents were at the same age.

In achieving such adjustment, they have tended to rely somewhat more than earlier generations on such values as honesty and "openness" in interpersonal relationships, with members of both the same and opposite sex; a belief in the importance and dignity of the individual; a greater emphasis on personal, relativistic, individualized codes of morality and behavior, and less on the institutionalized, arbitrary, and frequently inconsistent dictates of society. We do not mean to imply that today's youth are lacking in the often contradictory impulses and actions of past generations of adolescents or that they do not still share many of the traditional concerns of adolescence—with belonging, with intermittent loneliness and isolation, with self-preoccupation and occasional narcissism, with achieving a sense of identity, and with a feeling of separateness from adult society. But they do appear to us to be relatively more ready than their more self-conscious predecessors of earlier generations to put into practice a philosophy of "live and let live" and of pragmatic idealism. More than earlier generations they appear to be sophisticated and critical exponents of the art of the possible—not illusioned, but not disillusioned either. With considerable justification, it seems to us, James A. Wechsler, editor of *The New York Post,* has termed today's adolescents as a generation of "flaming moderates" (16).

ALIENATION

It is fashionable these days to speak of youth who in one way or another do not "fit in" as being "alienated." By such labeling, we gain the illusion that we have said something significant about these adolescents. However, as Kenneth Keniston points out in his thoughtful study of uncommitted college youth, all we have really done is to imply that "something is wrong somewhere," and to suggest the loss or absence of a previously desirable relationship. Unless we can go further and specify what relationships the individual has lost, what he is alienated *from,* we have accomplished little. Further, it is important to know whether the alienation has been imposed on the individual largely by obvious external forces, or whether it originates primarily within the individual himself. Finally, we need to know what new relationships, if any, have replaced those which have been lost; and we need to know how the alienation is expressed.

> In one sense the revolutionary and psychotic are both highly alienated from the norms and values of their society—both reject these norms and values. Yet there is a vast difference in the way their rejection is expressed: the revolutionary actively attempts to transform his society; the psychotic has undergone a regressive self-transformation that leaves his society relatively unaffected. One major way of classifying alienations is therefore according to their *mode;* e.g., whether they are alloplastic (i.e., they involve an attempt to transform the world) or autoplastic (they involve self-transformation) (74, 454).

Varieties of Alienation

Viewed in this context, it becomes obvious that alienations differ in important ways. While particular alienated individuals and groups rarely represent "pure cases" of a particular form of alienation, there are important differences in emphasis, as we shall see.

Some aspects of alienation tend to be relatively widespread in a particular culture, while others tend to be more limited to particular subgroups. With the rapid decline in clearly defined religious faith in the past century, there is a feeling of alienation from what previously had appeared to be a

meaningful and orderly universe, with a personal God at its center. This feel- ·
ing of "existential outcastness" (74), of the essential lack of any absolute
meaning in the universe as a whole, can be painful indeed, and can result
in feelings of deprivation and outrage—particularly among adolescents, with
their relatively greater sensitivity, need for absolute values, and lack of repressive defenses.

Many adolescents share what Keniston (74) calls *developmental estrange-
ments:* a sense of alienation or loss that comes with the abandonment of
childish ties to one's parents, one's childhood self, and, indeed, the whole
world of childhood—an egocentric world which, as many readers can no
doubt recall, seems to have been created specifically for *us,* with ourselves at
its center. How difficult this sense of estrangement will be to deal with will
depend in great measure, as we have already seen, both on the particular
kinds of childhood experiences the individual has had, and also on what he
finds to take their place. The other side of the coin of childhood dependence
is emancipation, and for the youth who can find new emotional ties and
new challenges and rewards in living, the loss of his childhood world will
be much less painful.

Alienation may also take the form of a sense of estrangement from what
is vaguely felt to be one's "real self." Whether as a result of unfortunate
developmental experiences or the demands of society, the individual feels
that somehow he has lost touch with his real self, and that much of what
he does is empty, flat, and devoid of meaning (74).

While significant numbers of our youth may share all of these and other
forms of alienation, the most prominently emphasized alienation currently
involves an *"explicit rejection of traditional American culture"* (74, 465).
Although they often are obviously alienated in other ways as well, most of
the adolescents we will discuss in the remainder of this chapter share a
common disillusionment with the goals, values, practices, and accomplishments of contemporary society. However, as previously noted, there may be
important differences in the sources of alienation and in the ways in which
it is expressed. Furthermore, it is important to know whether abandoned
values are replaced by new ones. In the case of lower-class youth who have
suffered economic deprivation and ethnic discrimination, the alienation may,
to an important degree, be imposed by society from without. An important part of the deprived youth's disillusionment with, and resentment against,
contemporary American society may stem from society's failure to permit him to share equally in its material and social rewards. In contrast, the
economically favored, or even overindulged middle- or upper-class youth may
be reacting against what he perceives as the ultimate futility of materialistic
rewards and social status, and the shallowness and hypocrisy of many of the
values and practices of contemporary society.

It is also important to note the way in which the adolescent responds
to his alienation from society. Does he actively attempt to change his world
into a better one, either within or outside the framework of traditional political, economic, or social mechanisms, or does he simply withdraw? Further,

if he withdraws, is it into a personal but still meaningful and satisfying world with its own private values and rewards, or into a vacuum of boredom, despair, or defeat?

The New Alienation

We have long been familiar with the alienation of individuals from a society that has rejected, ignored, or exploited them. Such alienation "makes good sense and requires no very complex explanation. . . . the rejected have no reason to embrace their society: it offers them little" (74, 7).

What is "new," at least relatively, and what is more difficult to understand, is the special kind of alienation that has increasingly affected the "non-rejected" in recent years: "an alienation that has few apparent roots in poverty, exclusion, sickness, oppression, lack of choice and opportunity" (74, 8). While a minority of hard-core rural and urban poor is, as we shall see, becoming ever more isolated from the mainstream of our complex, technologically oriented, rapidly changing society, the majority of young Americans, particularly middle- and upper-middle-class individuals, in many respects have "never had it so good." They are living in and are the principal beneficiaries of the most affluent society the world has ever known. The average American adolescent takes for granted material possessions and recreational activities that only the truly rich could afford in an earlier generation. He has better health care, a higher level of education, and more personal freedom than his parents. And his chances for employment in a wide variety of occupations, with relatively high salaries or wages, are excellent once his education is completed.

Under such circumstances, we might expect the privileged majority of American adolescents to be generally satisfied with themselves and their way of life, and, indeed, most are. However, even they are not without some social concerns—the preservation of individuality and meaningful interpersonal relationships in a mass society, pressures for accomplishment, as well as concern over the draft, the war, civil rights, and economic injustice. With all of these matters, they show greater concern than their elders. Nevertheless, for the most part they are uninterested in "making waves"; they are content to remain in the mainstream of society and its overall evolution.

In contrast, however, a growing minority of privileged middle- and upper-class youth are not going along. Why? Obviously, there is no single answer. For some, the roots of their alienation derive to an important degree from particular kinds of developmental experiences—experiences that would be likely to result in alienation in most societies. In a number of the articulate, frequently brilliant alienated college youth studied by Keniston, particular kinds of parent-child relationships and particular childhood experiences played a crucial, though certainly not an exclusive role (cf. pp. 713–714). Among other youth, the special characteristics and conflicts of contemporary society play a major role in their alienation (i.e., it could be anticipated that these individuals would not manifest conspicuous alienation under other, but still realistically possible, cultural conditions).

For some youth, the alienation may be quite specific: it may involve a rejection of a specific aspect of the culture (e.g., war, discrimination), while accepting as egosyntonic the climate of society as a whole. For others, it may be both deep and pervasive.

Obviously, too, there are differences in the individual's response to alienating aspects of society. Some youths may find positive substitutes for alienation, and may pursue them within the framework of the established social order. Others may feel that the only way to attack and modify the social structure lies outside the traditional processes of social change (e.g., some of the advocates of civil disobedience in relation to the draft and the war in Vietnam, or some of the Black Power advocates of the more extreme "Burn, baby, burn" variety).

Still other youth may respond to their alienation by withdrawing from the society as a whole. For some, this may involve deep despair, apathy, or defeat, without any meaningful substitute to take the place of their alienations. A number of the youthful psychiatric casualties of our time fall in this category. Others may find only a blind, angry, disorganized, self-defeating striking back—if this can be properly called a substitute, as in the case of some kinds of delinquents. Still other youth may, while expressing their alienation from society, continue to search for meaningful private alternatives within themselves, or within a separate subculture of like-minded individuals. Here one may find youths who, while perhaps outwardly inconspicuous, are attempting to find meaning as individuals in inner-exploration, in meditation, in Eastern religions, in the private pursuit of art, music, or poetry, or in a return—or an escape—to the "simple life" (the Vermont farm or the Pacific island). In Keniston's terms these are "autoplastic" as opposed to "alloplastic" youth, viewed in terms of the *mode* of their alienation. Here one may also find the more visible social dropouts, the "beats" of an earlier generation or, more recently, the hippies—the flower children—individual or tribal. As we shall see, a number of the latter have attempted not merely to "drop out" but also to live by values alternative to those which they find and reject in the dominant culture. The appeal of many of these values (at least as they are proclaimed), and the fact that they have aroused an almost obsessional interest among adults, probably indicates a good deal more about deficiencies in contemporary society than about what is actually positive, viable, or practical about hippie culture as a way of life.

All of these various kinds of alienation that may and do occur among middle-class youth make meaningful generalizations difficult. Nevertheless, there do appear to be some basic trends which emerge when one compares contemporary alienations and the relation of today's youth to their parents and to adult society. After discussing briefly some representative examples of various kinds of alienated middle-class youth, we will return to a discussion of some of these trends, both for the light it may shed on modern-day alienated youth, and also on the problems of our rapidly changing society of which they (and all youth) are the inheritors.

The Peace Corps—an Alternative Within the System

It is perhaps misleading to speak of youthful volunteers for the Peace Corps, VISTA, and similar programs as being "alienated." Such alienations as participants have felt are seldom deeply pervasive; further, these young volunteers have generally found positive, personally satisfying alternatives; and they have done so within the system—currently, at least, with considerable social approval. Nevertheless, it should be noted that a significant aspect of the appeal of these programs probably has stemmed from a feeling that the society as a whole is lacking in an energetic commitment to meaningful social ideas.

> Perhaps overseas service for two years does fulfill a need for them, but our society has failed to provide alternative, socially approved, useful ways in which this need could be met.
>
> In fact, the very success of the Peace Corps—the response it has evoked from the best of our youth—may well be an indication that something is lacking in our society as it relates to youth. . . . if other meaningful channels had been open to these young people, the Peace Corps might not have worked (72, 155).

The Peace Corps, originally dismissed out-of-hand by former President Eisenhower and many congressmen as the "Kiddie Korps," proved capable of turning many talented, psychologically well-integrated young men and women away from apathy (or, at least, a restless dissatisfaction) to spirited and ego-rewarding purposefulness and a broadened conception both of themselves and of their world.

Despite the rapid transition most Peace Corps workers have had to make in going to live and work in almost totally unfamiliar cultures; despite the physical hardships with which they have frequently been faced; and despite the psychological stress of knowing that many people were expecting or even hoping for their failure, especially at the beginning of the program, the record of accomplishment has been impressive. Psychiatric casualties have been minimal, as have been social failures. Perhaps the best evidence of this is that each of the fifteen countries in which Peace Corps workers first served asked for additional workers (72).

From his observations of the program, and the response of volunteers to it, Kaufman lists three of the kinds of opportunities to which these young men and women appeared eager to respond:

> 1. The volunteer senses or perceives that he will have an opportunity to apply what is *theoretically* the ideal in our value system but which rarely has an opportunity to be expressed—namely the blending of sensitivity, patience, and the humane and ethical virtues with the qualities of courage or manliness. . . .
>
> 2. The volunteer has the opportunity to feel honestly needed and to perform vital tasks that require his skill and training. . . .
>
> 3. The opportunity to learn, about others as well as one's self, is clearly a part

of the Peace Corps experience and young people have responded knowingly to the fact. . . (72, 156).

In the words of a young woman teacher in a remote area of Nigeria: "One can almost feel one's self growing and expanding one's perspective and understanding. In some ways, it is like going through the adolescence experience again with both its rewards and frustrations. The important things to come with are three main attitudes: of learning, of unfailing optimism, and of flexibility" (72, 157).

In addition, it appears likely that the novelty of the Peace Corps experience, the chance to "get out of a rut," and, sometimes, the opportunity to delay decisions regarding ultimate life goals, may serve to attract youth to the program.

The Student Activist

In recent years, the individual whose knowledge of campus life is limited to what he reads in a newspaper or magazine or what he sees on television is likely to have reached the conclusion that the American campus is a hotbed of political and social protest, frequently noisy or even violent in its manifestations. And he is likely to have been surprised at this apparent new development. As Sampson comments: "Given the relatively quiet campus years of the fifties, with the Silent Generation, born in war, bred in war, participants in war, seeking only security and income, home and career, one would not think to look to the university campus for leadership in national protest and dissent" (105, 1).

There can be little doubt that college youth, like other youth, have changed and are changing, or that the campus of the late 1960s differs in many ways from its predecessors of earlier decades. However, it would be a mistake to conclude that student activism is currently rampant, and commands the time and energy of the majority of students. At most only a small percentage, probably not more than 9–15 percent, of any student body were involved in recent protest movements, and percentages of even this magnitude were limited to a few select colleges (63, 98, 114, 115). Widespread impressions of broad participation can be attributed largely to the overzealousness of the press, bent on finding a "good story"; to the talent, often very skillfully—sometimes professionally—developed by activist minorities, for dramatizing dissent or producing disruptions; and to the apathy or inarticulateness of the majority of students. There may also have been a more subtle influence at work in fostering a heightened awareness of student protest among members of the adult culture. Significant numbers of adults may find in the well-publicized concerns of student activists confirmation of some of their own latent or poorly articulated anxieties about the directions of contemporary society.

What are the concerns of the activist minority? How are these concerns expressed? And, perhaps of greatest interest; how do the activists differ—in their backgrounds, in family influences, and in personality characteristics—from their nonactivist peers?

The concerns of the activist vary considerably from individual to individual, from one campus to another, and from one time period to another. Characteristically the activist feels that some injustice has been done, and that it is his duty to "take a stand." "The initial concern of the protester is almost always immediate, ad hoc and local . . ." (73, 111). The issues likely to be involved range from protest against perceived restrictiveness on personal freedoms by "paternalistic" college administrations and by what are viewed as the depersonalization, rigidities, or irrelevancies of the educational process, to dissent from the nation's foreign and military policies and the draft, as well as indignation about social injustice, whether defined as racial discrimination, exploitation, and neglect of the poor, or some other concern.

In all such protests, the activists indicate an alienation from current values or practices in the majority culture, and a rejection of traditional structures of authority. But their alienation does not lead to defeat or withdrawal— to a loss of some values with nothing to replace them. Rather, they have adopted values of their own that are strongly held and which lead them to action, either within the traditional social and political process or at its fringes. In fact, as Timothy Leary, a proponent of the "hippie" movement, argues, the student who "fights for power, argues, debates, protests, seeks to negotiate, strikes, pickets, etc." (106, 6), is still very much involved with the "system"—a situation that Leary characteristically deplores.

Themes of Student Protest. The self-conscious student protest movement that has emerged in the past seven years or so began primarily as a response to the efforts by southern black students to break the barriers of legal segregation in public accommodations, and expanded rapidly "to include such issues as nuclear testing and the arms race, attacks on civil liberties, the problems of the poor in urban slum ghettos, democracy and educational quality in universities, the war in Vietnam, conscription" (106, 52).

What are the underlying themes of such protests? On the basis of his research into the problem, Flacks (45) lists: (1) *romanticism*—a quest for "free" self-expression, an emphasis on "experiencing" and "knowing," unconstrained by highly rational pursuits and attitudes; (2) *anti-authoritarianism* —a strong antipathy toward what is perceived as arbitrary rule, centralized decision-making, or "manipulation" by the "establishment"; (3) *egalitarianism, populism*—a strong belief in the need for direct participation in the making of decisions by those affected by them; (4) *antidogmatism*—a strong resentment against doctrinaire ideological interpretations of events (obviously a factor in producing the "generation gap" between the dogmatist of the "Old Left" politics of the 1930s and their restless, questioning successors of the current "New Left"); (5) *moral purity*—a strong antipathy to self-serving behavior, which many view as pervading the older adult culture, as well as a particularly strong aversion to "phoniness"; (6) *community*—a strong need to break through traditional barriers that threaten the establishment of warm, open, and honest human relationships; and (7) *anti-institutionalism*—a vigorous distrust of involvement with conventional institutional roles, whether in industry, the professions, science, or politics.

Who are the activists? The popular stereotype of the student activist, nourished by the mass media, is extremely misleading.

> The "stereotypical" dissenter as popularly portrayed is both a Bohemian and political activist. Bearded, be-Levi-ed, long-haired, dirty and unkempt, he is seen as profoundly disaffected from his society, often influenced by "radical" (Marxist, Communist, Maoist, or Castroite) ideas, an experimenter in sex and drugs, unconventional in his daily behavior. Frustrated and unhappy, often deeply maladjusted as a person, he is a "failure" (or as one U.S. Senator put it, a "reject"). Certain academic communities like Berkeley are said to act as "magnets" for dissenters, who selectively attend colleges with a reputation as protest centers. Furthermore, dropouts or "non-students" who have failed in college cluster in large numbers around the fringes of such colleges, actively seeking pretexts for protest, refusing all compromise and impatient with ordinary democratic processes.

> According to such popular analyses, the sources of dissent are to be found in the loss of certain traditional American virtues. The "breakdown" of American family life, high rates of divorce, the "softness" of American living, inadequate parents, and, above all, overindulgence and "spoiling" contribute to the prevalence of dissent. Brought up in undisciplined homes by parents unsure of their own values and standards, dissenters channel their frustration and anger against the older generation, against all authority, and against established institutions (73, 110).

This popular stereotype is misleading in a variety of ways. For one thing, it confuses the *activist* with the *culturally alienated* and the *social dropouts*, whom we will discuss later. This view also assumes that the activist is a maladjusted, confused individual reacting against breakdowns in his family or rebelling against parental values. While there is evidence of a profound "generation gap" and rebellion against parents in some forms of alienation, recent research indicates that the activist tends in many ways to share rather than to oppose parental values.

The student activist tends to come from an upper-status family with a relatively high income (45, 114). Both parents are likely to be highly educated (119). His father tends to be a professional (college faculty, lawyers, doctors), and his mother tends to have "a career" (45). Student activism obviously is not a response, as in the case of many of the culturally deprived, to social rejection and exploitation.

Of particular interest is the finding that the views of activist students, rather than being in diametric opposition to those of their parents, tend to parallel them. For example, Table 15.1 shows the views of students and their fathers—among both activist college students involved in protest movements and nonactivists—on a variety of social issues investigated in one recent study (45). As may be seen, there are wide differences in viewpoints between the fathers of activist and nonactivist students—with the fathers of activists being far more liberal. Activist sons tend to share their father's liberal values, but they tend to carry them further, and to act on them in

Table 15.1   Students' and Fathers' Attitudes on Current Issues

Issue	Activists		Nonactivists	
	Students	Fathers	Students	Fathers
Percent who approve:				
Bombing of North Vietnam	9	27	73	80
American troops in Dominican Republic	6	33	65	50
Student participation in protest demonstrations	100	80	61	37
Civil disobedience in civil rights protests	97	57	28	23
Congressional investigations of "un-American activities"	3	7	73	57
Lyndon Johnson	35	77	81	83
Barry Goldwater	0	7	35	20
Full socialization of industry	62	23	5	10
Socialization of the medical profession	94	43	30	27
N	34	30	37	30

Source: R. Flacks. The liberated generation: an exploration of the roots of student protest. *J.soc. Issues,* 1967, *23,* No. 3, 67. By permission of The Society for the Psychological Study of Social Issues.

a more militant or "radical" fashion. This picture is reflected in other findings as well. Forty percent of nonactivists' fathers said they were Republican, while only 13 percent of activists' fathers were Republican. Only 6 percent of nonactivists' fathers were willing to describe themselves as "highly liberal" or "socialist," whereas 60 percent of the activists' fathers accepted such designations. Forty percent of the nonactivists' fathers described themselves as conservatives; none of the activists' fathers endorsed that position. Thus the popular notion, even among behavioral scientists, that activist students are involved in "conversion" or "rebellion" against the values of their parents is not supported. "A more supportable view suggests that the great majority of activist students are attempting to fulfill and renew the political traditions of their parents" (45, 68). Activist fathers and sons share different value patterns from those of nonactivists. As compared with nonactivists, activist fathers and their sons tended to score higher on measures of (1) *romanticism*—aesthetic and emotional sensitivity; (2) *intellectualism*—high valuation of intellectual creativeness; and (3) *humanitarianism*—concern with the plight of others in society. In contrast, nonactivist fathers and sons scored higher on (4) *moralism and self-control*—concern about the importance of strictly controlling personal impulses, opposition to impulsive or spontaneous behavior, value on keeping tight control over emotions, adherence to conventional authority, etc. (45).

Interestingly, parents of activists appeared to be more "permissive" in child-rearing practices than those of nonactivists. In rating their treatment in childhood, activist sons and daughters tended to rate their parents as milder, warmer, more lenient, and less strict (45). The likelihood of parents' "intervening strongly" in the decisions of their adolescent sons and daughters was found to be much greater among nonactivist parents.

Student activists, in comparison with nonactivists, have been found to be significantly brighter, more successful academically, more flexible, more individualistic, and more autonomous (63, 110, 119). They were also found to be more anxious; more imaginative; more tolerant of ambiguity; more concerned with reflective and abstract thinking in the areas of art, literature, music, and philosophy; and more liberal and less conventional in religious values (45, 63).

If activists "are not, on the whole, repudiating or rebelling against explicit parental values and ideologies" (73, 119); if they come from affluent rather than deprived backgrounds; and if they are generally brighter and more successful academically than their peers, how can we explain their proneness to protest? On the basis of the available evidence, it would appear likely that activist youth are living out expressed but unimplemented values of their liberal, socially conscious parents—values that, if put into action, may well lead to conflicts with institutionalized representatives of the majority culture. In a number of instances, there are indications that the youthful protester is more likely to criticize his parents' failure to put their values into practice than he is to criticize the values themselves. There is also, in some cases at least, the possibility that parents may be "secretly proud of their children's eagerness to implement the ideals they as parents have only given lip-service to" (73, 119–120).

Further, the kinds of values encouraged by activist parents—humanitarianism, nurturance, autonomy, permissiveness, self-expression, and intellectual independence—are likely to encourage both activist goals and efforts to implement them, whether these goals are socially popular or not (106).

Given the ingredients of the "protest-prone" personality, it seems probable that certain environments are more likely to encourage such active expression than others. It does not seem surprising that the centers of student protest have most often been "progressive" or "liberal" colleges and universities with high standards of academic excellence and a strong tradition of academic freedom. Such institutions not only provide a more receptive institutional climate for protest but they also are more likely to attract the kind of protest-prone student described above in sufficient numbers to create "the critical mass" for an "activist subculture" (14, 106).

Finally, one cannot overlook the interaction between historical and cultural trends and the protest-prone individual's personality and developmental history. Much of current student protest involves, not so much a need to change traditional American values as it does impatience or anger at the slowness with which these values are viewed as being implemented in practice, or anger at what is viewed as a betrayal of them. In the recent past, internal civil strife—involving civil rights, poverty, the crisis of the cities, and other acute social problems—has forced an intimate awareness of social problems on the national consciousness. Middle-class youth, and especially the alert, sensitive, protest-prone middle-class youth, can no longer remain unaware of these problems. And they are likely to respond vigorously to what are perceived as violations not merely of private or personal values but of traditional, textbook American values as well. Similarly, the self-image of America developed in peacetime may suffer considerable buffeting under the stresses of war, particularly such confusing, ill-understood, fundamentally political wars as those recently taking place in underdeveloped countries such as Vietnam.

Still further, one cannot overlook the fact that, except for the disenfranchised poor, ours is currently a society unparalleled in history in its affluence. Such limited goals as sheer survival become of secondary importance only when one is economically secure. Unlike some of their parents who lived through the Depression, the affluent, middle-class dissenter can look beyond survival to broader social values and goals—at least partly because economic security is taken for granted. Also, the fact of the enormous gap between his own relative affluence and security and the grinding poverty of the hard-core poor is difficult to escape. Secure himself, he can psychologically more easily afford a nurturant identification with the deprived. He may also, in some cases at least, feel a conscious or unconscious obligation to respond to the poor's needs in order to avoid or assuage feelings of guilt about his own favored position.

In brief, middle-class student activism has roots not only in the individual's family background and influences, and in his own personality, but also in his immediate social environment and the broader cultural conditions of our times. We cannot simply focus on the special personal characteristics of the protester without also asking ourselves whether there are not, indeed, social conditions that are legitimately protestable.

The Culturally Alienated

Not all bright, talented, sensitive American middle-class youth who find a good deal wrong with "the establishment" respond to their discontent with activism. In contrast to the politically involved or socially concerned protester is the *culturally alienated* youth who is far too pessimistic and too firmly opposed to

> "the System" to wish to demonstrate his disapproval in any organized public way. His demonstrations of dissent are private: through nonconformity of behavior, ideology and dress, through personal experimentation and above all through efforts to intensify his own subjective experience, he shows his distaste and disinterest in politics and society. The activist attempts to change the world around him, but the alienated student is convinced that meaningful change of the social and political world is impossible. . . (73, 112–113).

While alienated students and activists appear to be drawn largely from the same social-class and educational backgrounds, there are important differences, psychologically and ideologically. Unlike the activist, who is likely to share his parents' values—though he may carry them a step further and may also be more likely to act on them—the culturally alienated student appears to reject his parents' values, viewing his father "as a man who has 'sold out' to the pressures for success and status in American society" (73, 113). Among both activist and culturally alienated youth, there appear to be deep emotional ties with the mother. In the case of the activist, the mother is likely to be a highly individuating force, pushing her son toward independence and autonomy. But the mother of the culturally alienated student is apt to be controlling and intrusive—oversolicitous and limiting. Furthermore, "The most common family environment of the alienated student-to-be consists of a parental schism supplemented by a special mother-son alliance of mutual understanding and maternal control and depreciation of the father" (73, 113; see also 116).

Perhaps not surprisingly, culturally alienated students appear more likely to be disturbed psychologically. Though they may frequently, like the activist, be talented and academically gifted, they are typically less committed to academic values and intellectual achievement.

What appear most conspicuous in the personality and attitudes of the truly culturally alienated student are his distrust of any real commitment; his pervasively pessimistic, nihilistic, chaotic view of the world; his egocentric scorn and contempt for society and, perhaps paradoxically, for himself as well; and his emphasis on inner experience and aesthetic awareness, as opposed to success-oriented, "practical," rational, and disciplined "doing" (74). Fragmented in his perception of himself, holding all values to be subjective and, hence, shifting and uncertain, he is likely to be anxious, "confused, disoriented, and unhappy. . . . The defiant public face of scorn and opposition soon gives way to clear unhappiness, depression, self-doubt, and apprehensiveness" (74, 101–102).

In Erikson's terms, the truly culturally alienated young man is suffering from *identity diffusion*—"from an intense feeling of the precariousness and disunity of the self, from doubt about [his] own continuing capacity to 'cope,' coupled with a relentless search for some trustworthy foundation for selfhood" (74, 102).

The fact that both the activist and the culturally alienated are confronted with similar historical forces and similar elements of cultural change and conflict; that both share membership in an affluent middle-class subculture; and that to a considerable extent both possess unusual talents and opportunities, and nevertheless respond so differently, all suggest the inadequacy of purely historical or cultural explanations of alienation. Other more personal influences, such as the impact of differing family influences seen above, must also be taken into account.

The Social Dropouts

While the culturally alienated students described above may be said to have "dropped out" spiritually and intellectually from middle-class culture, they have not found a substitute for it. Nihilistic and pervasively pessimistic, they remained in, but not of, the familiar middle- and upper-class world. In contrast, the "social dropout," as defined here, has physically abandoned the conflicts and constraints of his middle-class surroundings and moved to a life outside the formal structure of society.

While the obsession of the public and the press with the recent hippie movement might appear to suggest otherwise, the social dropout is not a new phenomenon. In every society, there have been those who did not share the values of the dominant social order and who, rather than trying actively to change the order, or even to drift along with it, elected to find their own way of life outside it. Even in our own time, the "beat" generation antedated that of the "hippies." What is perhaps most notable about the recent hippie movement is its source, the nature of its values, and, above all, the response of society to it—a response that appears wholly disproportionate to the actual size or significance of the movement itself.

Who is the hippie and where does he come from? Contrary to public opinion, there is no single type of hippie. Nevertheless, a few salient features stand out. "They are predominantly white, middle-class, educated youths, ranging in age from 17 to 25" (15, 4), though one may encounter an occasional, and often rather pathetic, 40- or even 50-year-old. There are the serious, philosophically oriented hippies, and the "groovers" and recent graduates of the teeny-bopper crowd—drifting, aimless, searching principally for "kicks." There are rural hippies and urban hippies, although the latter predominate (15, 55). There are those who are attempting to live at least minimally planned communal existences (the tribal hippies) and, in greater number, the floaters (15). Also, as the movement has become publicized and commercialized, there are increasing numbers of pseudohippies and "plastic" or part-time hippies.

Nevertheless, there are some characteristics that "true" hippies are likely to share, at least to a significant degree. As already noted, they tend to come not from the already disenfranchised poor, but from the relatively affluent, socially conforming, success-oriented middle class. Their parents, more often than not, are the kinds of people who are viewed as "pillars of the community." These youth possess a common aversion to what they perceive as the aggressive, highly competitive, conformity-demanding nature of modern society, with its emphasis on social status and material success. Not only do they view these values as hollow and meaningless—"a real hang-up"—but as inimical to other values that they do hold, or believe they hold: love; gentleness; honesty; an immediate relatedness and sharing between people, unencumbered by competition or role-playing; an emphasis on individual self-expression ("doing your own thing"); heightened sensory awareness, typically aided by drugs; an appreciation of nature and direct experience—an antirational, anti-intellectual orientation; and a presumed lack of inhibitions, social or sexual (15, 35, 59, 117).

When one surveys this list of values proclaimed by the hippies, it is not difficult to perceive some of the reasons why this so-called movement has attracted such obsessional concern on the part of "square" society. Quite simply, these are values that many adults either admire or envy, but which they find it difficult or impossible to express or fulfill within the context of active participation and survival in contemporary society. Confronted by a seemingly endless succession of cold and hot wars, many adults hark back nostalgically to the Judeo-Christian traditions of childhood—of "love thy neighbor as thyself," "thou shalt not kill," and "peace on earth, good will to men." Many older adults, familiar with the anxiety about mere survival engendered by the Depression, have struggled long and hard to achieve financial security and social status in our highly competitive society, only to discover, once they have achieved these goals, that they are not enough to produce a sense of meaningful personal fulfillment. Caught up in the seemingly ever more frantic pace of work and daily living—their senses overloaded by constant, almost random stimulation from the environment and their perceptions "staled by custom"—they may envy the child (or the hippie) who can apparently sit staring appreciatively at the complex simplicity of a leaf. Faced by the necessity of "role-playing"—of "preparing a face to meet the faces that you meet," as T. S. Eliot has phrased it—in order to meet the competitive demands of contemporary society, many adults long for a renewal of the direct and open relationships between people that most adults have experienced less and less often since childhood and adolescence. The current generation of middle-class adults, having struggled (frequently at considerable psychological cost) to cast off some of the rigid sexual inhibitions and anxieties inherited from a Victorian past, may envy or resent the ease with which the hippies appear—at least from a distance—to have done so. For those adults who can accept such unfulfilled longings in themselves, and who are not wholly committed to present-day society as representing the best of all possible worlds, the hippie legend can be an appealing one, or at least a source of considerable ambivalence.

In contrast, for those adults whose psychological defenses require that such errant unfulfilled longings be repressed, and who are completely committed to the values and practices of contemporary culture, the "hippie" represents a psychological threat extending far beyond the actual social problems he presents—though such problems do exist and are a legitimate basis for concern.

In either case, the recent obsessional concern with the hippie movement appears clearly to have been excessive and stems principally, in our view, from the fact that the hippies have touched upon the most exposed and sensitive nerve endings of our society, sometimes with a skill that belies their supposedly "naive" approach to life. As Judson Gooding states, "The hippies have an instinct for the jugular vein of society" (15, 204). This, then, is one side of the coin, and it probably tells us more about the deficiencies of our society than about the hippies themselves. But there is, unfortunately, another side.

While many of the loudly proclaimed values of the hippie movement may be laudable, they are, in the long run, probably no easier to achieve outside of the organized social system than within it. Further, the hippie culture suffers from several inherent, and probably ultimately fatal flaws. For one thing, the awkward fact is that hippie society is for the most part parasitic; it depends upon the continued existence of the society it rejects. Like other mortals, hippies must eat, though they are often found to suffer from severe malnutrition *(15, 117)*. This means that most must either get part-time jobs in the "system," panhandle, or solicit checks from "square" parents back home. It is true that some hippies have come close to having it both ways—notably the more successful acid-rock musicians, and some artists and craftsmen. But most have not, nor, indeed (with the dread of social and vocational "hang-ups"), have they tried. They also require services from the "establishment," such as medical care. A high incidence of hepatitis (often the result of dirty needles used in administering drugs), of venereal disease, of deficiency diseases, of psychological problems, of drug reactions, and the like, stands in disheartening contrast to the hippies' happy slogans about the good life. Such social, educational, and health services unfortunately do not grow like flowers, but require many of the commitments that the hippies reject: discipline, intellectual dedication, long training, and social and economic organization. In its ultimate dependence on the continuation of a society it claims to reject, the hippie movement appears to contain the seeds of its own destruction.

Another central factor of the hippie movement has been its dependence on drugs. In fact, one of the distinguishing characteristics of this particular movement, as opposed to those of earlier social dropouts, is that it is basically a *drug culture*—a fact appreciated by hippies themselves, but frequently not fully grasped by outsiders. Dr. David E. Smith of the University of California Medical Center, who has personally treated hundreds of patients from the Haight-Ashbury district of San Francisco, remarks "In Haight-Ashbury, you would have to say the drug culture is 100 per cent. . . . everyone of them had smoked marijuana and taken LSD at least once" *(15, 184)*. In a survey of 200 hippies in the Haight-Ashbury district, it was found that the group had taken an average of 26 psychedelic trips on LSD, though the range was from 1 to 300. The average hippie had smoked hashish or marijuana 6.7 times per week, with the range from complete abstinence to as many as 35 times. About two-thirds said they had also used stimulants such as methadrine and dexadrine *(15)*. Aside from the obvious dangers of some of these drugs (which will be discussed in a later section), there is a real question as to whether there is any chemical short cut to true creativity and meaningfully heightened inner experience, a point emphasized even by sympathetic observers. For the chronic drug user, it is often too easy to confuse self-indulgence, impulsivity, a lack of intellectual discipline, a loss of the critical function, and even apathy, with creativity.

Further, the proclaimed values of the hippies cannot always be taken at face value. If there is one word which occupies a central place in the ideological firmament of the hippie movement, it is *love*. There are certainly some hippies, particularly the more mature, who do indeed appear to display "love" in the traditional Judeo-Christian sense, not only through gentleness and tolerance, but through a concern for the welfare of others—trying to provide food and shelter for homeless hippies, trying to protect confused, vulnerable young teenage runaways and getting them back to their parents, trying to get needed help for hippies who are ill or coming down from a "bad trip." But in a number of cases, "love" seems to emerge in practice more as a matter of simple tolerance—or sometimes even indifference—regarding others; or a relatively simple way of relating directly and with a minimum of competitive role-playing to others, and of sharing common experiences: turning on with drugs, listening to music, walking in the park. A stranger may be welcome to drop into someone's pad, such food or drugs as there are may be shared with him, and no one will demand to know who he is or where he is from. However, this same stranger may leave a day, a week, or a month later, and there may be little feeling of loss. Indeed, it sometimes appears that the kind of "love" displayed by some hippies may actually be a *defense against* rather than a manifestation of an enduring *commitment* to the welfare of others and an intimate psychological involvement with them. Many hippies may proclaim, as one stated, that "Christ was a very groovy cat" *(15)*, but too often they appear to lack the discipline, stable sort of psychological commitment and the capacity for true identification and ego-involvement with others that being "your brother's keeper" or "loving others as yourself" requires.

The apparent, proudly proclaimed happiness of the hippie—the assertion that everything is "groovy"—while no doubt true for some, is largely a matter of self-deception for many, if not a majority. Despite the off-beat clothes, the gay beads, the psychedelic designs, the flowers, the put-ons, the often perceptive humor, the leisure, the self-indulgence, the frequently proclaimed (but not as frequently achieved) sexual freedom, the drug highs, and the freedom from "the rat race," many hippies appear to the more detached clinical observer as aimless, depressed, bored, or anxious and "up tight"; and smaller numbers may impress one as being seriously confused mentally, apathetic, or physically ill. They can get hung up on drugs, are highly vulnerable to disease and malnutrition, may be harried by the police, and are too often susceptible to the blandishments of psychopaths, or physical attacks from petty criminals or neighborhood gangs, particularly in urban slums.

Another major source for concern, which has not yet been adequately investigated, is the increasing number of children of hippie couples. While in some instances these children appear to receive as great or greater affection, attention, and concern for their well-being as children of "square" parents, many do not. What are the long-range prospects, psychologically and physically, for a child whose existence is almost completely unstructured, and whose parents are frequently on trips or on marijuana highs, or who may have been given drugs himself—in some cases at ages as low as 2 or 3? Many children of hippies, like their parents, also suffer from malnutrition, physical neglect, and disease. Certainly, this is a topic deserving of further investigation, not only for its scientific but also for its social and humanitarian implications.

Such black linings to a silver cloud often seem a high price to pay for the privilege of dropping out and turning on. And rather sad, too, because so many of the hippies' bravely asserted values, at least in theory, are needed antidotes to some of the "hang-ups" of contemporary society.

It would appear to us that the ultimate significance of the hippies lies not in the movement itself, which even at the time of this writing appears to be in considerable disarray. It does not appear likely that a movement with the inherent weaknesses of this one will sweep the world, despite the lure of some of its slogans. It seems probable that most hippies, except the psychologically crippled, will eventually find their way back to home and society, or to a new kind of life based on firmer foundations. What appears far more important is the appeal that aspects of the movement have had for many youths who have remained within the system, and for many troubled adults as well. In the words of one observer, "The hippies are a symptom of the fundamental crisis in American society. . . . the country has lost its youth—that is, it has lost the commitment of its youth to society's values. These are moral expatriates who have stayed at home" (15, 196).

Drug Use Among Adolescents

A problem of mounting concern over the past decade has been the rapid rise in the use of drugs by adolescents on college campuses, in senior and even junior high schools, and among school dropouts. Exact incidence figures are not available, and there are regional and interschool variations in the nature and extent of drug consumption, but it appears likely that at least 10 to 15 percent of all adolescents have experimented with illicit drugs of one kind or another (53). In considering college students, the greatest attention has focused on the use of marijuana, both because of the relative frequency of its use and the serious legal and social sanctions associated with the drug. More recently, attention has been directed to the still rather limited but increasing use of LSD (lysergic acid diethylamide) and related strong hallucinogens, such as psilocybin, mescaline, and DMT or "Speed" (dimethyl-tryptamine), all of which produce radically altered states of consciousness and perceptual distortions.

Among college students, use of both marijuana and LSD is greatest on the campuses of large, cosmopolitan universities—particularly those located in urban areas and those drawing a high percentage of their students from urban populations (10, 120, 121). Drug usage is generally less—or even, in some cases, virtually absent—in smaller colleges with relatively homogenous student populations drawn from rural areas and small towns. It is also less in the South.

While other drugs, notably the "pills" (including sedatives, "pep" pills, and tranquilizers) are also used by college students, occasionally with serious consequences including death, the popularity of these pills as a "fad" has been more characteristic, at least up until recently, of high school and junior high school students (53). One investigator (53) argues that perhaps partly because of their relative popularity among high school students, the "hip" college student drug taker may tend to dismiss pill-taking as "kid stuff," despite its potential danger. It is also obvious, however, that the minority of students who use drugs will not be convinced that they should avoid them by moralistic propaganda, often offered by adults who know less about these drugs than the users. What are the admittedly incomplete scientific facts?

Marijuana.   Despite its linkage in federal and many state laws with the opiates, marijuana is not a narcotic, nor is it physiologically addicting. Actually, it is a mild hallucinogen. On the basis of currently available evidence, use of marijuana is not likely to progress to use of heroin and other opiates, at least among middle- and upper-class individuals living outside ghettos. Nor is there any evidence that the use of marijuana is associated in the United States with crimes of violence, despite claims to the contrary. Most marijuana users, particularly among college students, fall in the category of "dabblers," who may try it a few times out of curiosity or feelings of rebellion, and then give it up. Only a small percentage can be described as "potheads" (repeated frequent or chronic users).

Nevertheless, convictions for sale or even use of marijuana may result in 2- to 10-year federal sentences for a first offense, and 5 to 25 years for a second offense. In 44 states, the maximum possible sentence is 5 years to life. To use the drug is to subject oneself to possible (even if infrequently given) sentences of this severity, or to a lifetime police record as a felon—hardly a very good way to maintain one's "cool." Secondly, as a hallucinogen, marijuana may occasionally in some persons produce all the untoward effects attributed to more potent hallucinogens, including confused, uncontrolled behavior and psychosis *(47)*. Even though the risk of such consequences may not be great in most cases, it cannot be dismissed. Further, use of marijuana, like the use of alcohol, may impair judgment, perception, and coordination, and such disruption may be particularly dangerous if one is engaged in any skilled activity, such as driving.

The actual mechanisms by which marijuana produces its effects in the brain are not yet known, and it is also possible that there are long-term physiological or psychological effects of which we are still ignorant. At present, however, it appears that a few deaths occur from the depressant effects of marijuana taken in extremely large doses; "by contrast, cirrhosis of the liver, heart conditions and other disorders brought about by alcoholism claim some twenty thousand lives in the United States every year *(121, 47)*. Chronic "potheads," who are usually already suffering from some form of psychiatric disorder, may, of course, in their prolonged semistupors, fail to take adequate care of themselves physically, including failure to gain adequate nutrition.

The "Pills."   The problems posed by the "pills"—barbiturates, tranquilizers, and amphetamines—vary from one category to another. The barbiturates (sleeping pills) account for three thousand accidental or intentional deaths a year, but habituation and addiction are far greater problems *(47)*. Barbiturate addiction is characterized by intellectual impairment, self-neglect, slurred speech, tremor, defective judgment, drowsiness, emotional lability, bizarre behavior, and ataxia *(47, 53)*. Withdrawal symptoms are actually more acute for barbiturate addiction than for heroin, and, if withdrawal is abrupt, may include nausea, high fever, delirium, hallucinations, and most dangerous of all, convulsions, stupor, and coma that may be fatal *(47, 53)*.

A number of nonbarbiturate sedatives and tranquilizers may also be physiologically, as well as psychologically, addictive. The amphetamines (pep pills) do not produce true physiological addiction, but they may be psychologically habituating and dangerous. Judgment and intellectual impairment, aggressive behavior, incoordination and hallucinations, may all occur during habituation *(47, 53)*. Suspicious or paranoid feelings frequently accompany chronic high dosages of the amphetamines. Combinations of these drugs, with each other or with alcohol, may be particularly dangerous, and have led to increasing numbers of deaths in recent years.

Of course, use of these drugs is not restricted to adolescents, but is widespread among adults. While the taking of "pep" pills ("Bennies" and "Dex") for "kicks" as part of a cult is more a phenomenon of adolescents and some young adults, the use of all of these drugs for "medical" reasons is growing alarmingly among adults; sedatives and tranquilizers are used with increasing frequency. A recent cartoon contained an all too troublesome element of truth. It showed two young women returning to their apartment after work; one of them was remarking to the other, "I don't know whether to take a Dexedrine and go out for the evening, or a Nembutal and go to bed." If ours is getting to be a "drug culture," it is not, at least in the broader sense, simply an adolescent phenomenon.

LSD and Other Hallucinogens.   The hallucinogens may vary from mild (e.g., aeroplane glue, nutmeg, marijuana, morning glory seeds) to moderate (e.g., psilocybin, mescaline, peyote—the Indian ceremonial drug) to highly potent (e.g., LSD-25). As already noted, sniffing of glue and similar substances remains a persistent and probably growing problem among school children *(48, 108)*. Use of LSD and other strong and moderate hallucinogens, while still not widespread, appears to have increased in recent years among late adolescents, both on and off college campuses, and particularly in the larger, urban-oriented universities. There is some suggestion, however, that recent reports of chromosomal aberrations and genetic defects resulting from the use of LSD may be reducing interest in this and related drugs, particularly among college students.

There appear to be two broad extremes of users of LSD-type drugs: intellectuals, artists, and other creative or pseudocreative middle-class individuals who view these hallucinogenic experiences as providing an aesthetic religious and mystical experience (an "expansion of consciousness" and a deepening of insight into themselves); and nonacademic, rootless adolescents, often including school dropouts in large cities, who see these experiences not in the context of a philosophical cult but simply as an explosive way of becoming "high" or "getting their kicks."

LSD was originally derived from a fungus growing on wheat and rye, and was first used scientifically as a "psychomimetic" research drug—that is, a drug thought to produce a model psychosis-like state experimentally. Subsequently it has been tried with uncertain success in the treatment of various mental disorders, ranging from alcoholism to schizophrenia. Most recently, as the reader is aware, it has become the basis of a new philosophical or religious cult, in the hands of some of its intellectual enthusiasts, such as Timothy Leary, a former Harvard psychologist.

Use of LSD may lead to experiences of a sense of timelessness, vivid panoramic visual hallucinations of fantastic brightness and depth, a heightening and blocking of sensory experience, and feelings of a loss of individual identity, together with a feeling of unity with other human beings, animals, inanimate objects, and the universe in general. It is argued by the proponents of LSD that such experiences give one a new, superior, and lasting insight into oneself and the universe, under proper conditions. While there is little doubt that many LSD users sincerely have these feelings, there is also no evidence that its use increases creativity or artistic productivity.

The effects of LSD vary from one individual and from one situation to another, and are highly unpredictable. An LSD "trip" may also produce bizarre and frightening images, a sense of isolation and depersonalization, acute panic, and paranoia (a pathological suspiciousness). In a 10-month period in 1965, 65 persons were admitted to the Psychiatric Division at Bellevue Hospital in New York with acute psychoses induced by LSD (79). Some of these people may have already been psychotic or prepsychotic, and in some cases the acute psychoses cleared up within 48 hours. On the other hand, 5 of these persons who appeared to be functioning adequately prior to taking LSD required long-term hospitalization in a psychiatric institution. Many large urban hospitals and university medical centers are currently reporting alarming increases in the incidence of victims of "bad trips." In some of these institutions in 1967, rates doubled in a period of a year.

Further, there is the still unresolved question of the long-term physiological or psychological effects of LSD "trips." Recent research (2, 4, 25, 65) indicates that LSD and related drugs may cause chromosomal aberrations and genetic defects.

Longer-term psychological effects of the steady use of LSD have also been studied (10). Users tend to view themselves as becoming less constricted, less anxious, more relaxed, more creative, more loving, and generally more "open" to experience, as well as being freer in their interpersonal relationships. On the other hand, to outside observers, many of these presumed assets are viewed differently; many long-term users appear to others as showing "poor judgment insofar as they are overly trusting and euphoric" (10, 267). Not only may they be less anxious in responding to what previously were neurotic sources of anxiety; they may also fail to respond appropriately to more realistic sources of concern or danger—e.g., the possibility of arrest, loss of a job, exploitative or aggressive intents of others, physical danger. Their "creativeness" may involve increased pre-occupation with the self and with inner experience, and with a somewhat impulsive openness to the experiences of the moment, rather than with increased creativity as demonstrated in disciplined aesthetic productions.

Among many users of LSD and related hallucinogens, there is a vocal, and at times monotonous, insistence upon getting away from what they view as competitive and meaningless role-playing (i.e., what Richard Alpert and Timothy Leary refer to as "games," such as the "student game," "the executive game," "the parent game," "the neurotic game," and so on), which separates people from direct and meaningful experience of one another in a sterile society, and turning toward open and honest relationships characterized by "love." However, this "lovingness" needs to be qualified in terms of its meaning to LSD users. For one thing, shared experience, trust, and love are likely to become increasingly difficult if not impossible to achieve except with other users; thus the individual is likely to become ever more narrowly ethnocentric, retreating from interaction with people in general in a "square" society to a small band of fellow users. Further:

> This lovingness need not be manifest to others. For one thing, the mystically oriented person may not be actively benevolent. He may be disinterested in those overt forms of charity and aggressively helpful intervention of those who subscribe to the conventions of philanthropy and humanitarianism. These acts are themselves part of the other-directed motifs of an ethical and rational society. Thus, what the LSD user feels to be loving and what the observer requires as "proof of love" are quite different (*10*, 284).

To an observer who views "love" primarily as a heightened concern for all men, and an active dedication to their welfare, the "love" extolled by the LSD disciple may seem more like psychological dependency on others with similar views, or withdrawal from competitiveness and an active confrontation of social problems into greater passivity, narcissism, and a reduction in socialized anxiety (*87*).

Why Do Adolescents Take Drugs? Why does an increasing number (even if a minority) of adolescents take drugs? At the simplest level, the broader society, of which adolescents are a part, is increasingly becoming a "drug culture." Technological development has multiplied the number even of medically sanctioned drugs into the thousands and "normal" adults show a mounting use of drugs to rest, to sleep, to calm anxiety, to induce euphoria, to restore a feeling of energy, and to alleviate pain. The commercial slogan "Better living through chemistry" appears to have been adopted by our society in more ways than were intended, as recent "hippie" badges proclaim.

Against this background, drug use by adolescents may serve a number of special motivations. There may be a simple urge to rebel against adult constraints by using disapproved drugs—particularly those, such as marijuana, that appear to many adolescents to alarm adults unreasonably, demonstrating adult ignorance or hypocrisy. Or simple adolescent curiosity may be at work, manifested by exploration of new experience of many kinds.

At a deeper level, however, adolescent drug users may reflect a rejection of the values of an adult society perceived as increasingly impersonal ("don't fold, spindle, or mutilate"), often cruel, and lacking in genuine concern for the individual. Many young middle-class drug users view society as overly concerned with materialistic goals and lacking in opportunities for creative experience, for achieving or restoring a sense of beauty and wonder, and for finding personally meaningful values and beliefs. Hence some adolescents will renounce the "rewards" of organized society and turn inward to the self-preoccupied world of mind-altering drugs, such as LSD and, to a lesser extent, marijuana, in order—however mistakenly—to seek a renewal of wonder, trust, beauty, and meaning. Perhaps it is not too surprising either that other more "disadvantaged" adolescents—facing a future without hope and confronted with economic, social, and racial discrimination, with impossible living conditions, and with a breakdown in their social environment and in their own families—may give up the search for meaning and a sense of ego identity entirely, and seek the escape and oblivion of the "hard" narcotics, such as heroin.

However, the fact remains that, while drugs may produce oblivion or temporary escape, they have not produced, and have frequently impaired, creativity. Further, they have never produced a better and more responsible world, in which all people will have an opportunity for food, shelter, health, a little joy, and a sense of purpose. The challenge to adolescents, and to adults as well, is not to "turn on with drugs and drop out" of life, but to find a way to make life itself more just, more creative, and more genuinely meaningful—so that the individual can turn away from the myriad drugs of our age, turn on with life itself, and drop out of social isolation, personal anonymity, or hopelessness and despair.

THE CULTURALLY DEPRIVED

There can be little doubt, that unlike middle- and upper-class whites, the alienation from the dominant culture of increasing numbers of the "hardcore" poor is largely imposed from without, whether directly or indirectly. The great majority of these adolescents are born into "the culture of poverty," whether in rural slums or urban ghettos. Even at birth, the odds are against them; the infant mortality rate among the 20 percent of Americans living below the poverty level is far higher than that of the rest of the population. Among blacks alone, the infant mortality rate is nearly twice that for whites, and the discrepancy in mortality rates continues in all later age periods (64). In their developing years, the hard-core poor are exposed to hunger and malnutrition; inadequate or nonexistent health care; overcrowded, deteriorated, rat and vermin infested housing, often without heat,

Roy Stevens for the Ford Foundation

electricity, or adequate plumbing; harassment both by police and other authorities and by petty criminals, slum landlords, and dishonest merchants. The guidance they might as children expect from parents is often limited by the fact that the father is absent. Those parents—often only the mother—who do remain in the home are frequently so poorly educated, so worn down, or so powerless to cope with the "establishment" themselves that they can be of little assistance in helping their children to cope with our increasingly complex society.

Poorly prepared intellectually, psychologically, and socially, these young people enter overcrowded, rundown schools, frequently manned by over-burdened, harassed, or cynical teachers who have little understanding of their students' special problems. Under these conditions, deprived children fail to make normal school progress, and often drop out of school, either from choice or necessity, as soon as they are able to. By the beginning of secondary school, the typical culturally disadvantaged student is reading at a level approximately 3½ years below his grade level. His problem-solving abilities and abstract thinking are at a very low level as compared with others of his age or grade level (52, 94, 108). Needless to say, among such youth there is a typically strong disaffection with school, and their approach to learning experiences is likely to be apathetic or even hostile.

When such a youth does leave school, he finds few jobs available at his skill level. Unemployment among out-of-school youth under 20 years of age is nearly three times greater than the nationwide rate for all workers (28). In one slum section of a large northern city, it was found that a total of 59 percent of the male youth between the ages of 16 and 21 were out of school and unemployed. An even worse state of affairs was found in another special study in a different city. "In a slum area of 125,000 people, mostly Negro, a sampling of the youth population shows that roughly 70 percent of the boys and girls age 16–21 are out-of-school and unemployed" (28). If, further, the adolescent is a member of an ethnically segregated minority, he finds himself discriminated against even in jobs for which he may be quali-fied. For such a youth, the idea of the American dream becomes merely a nightmare.

The tragic irony—not only for the hard-core poor themselves, but for the nation as a whole—is that while the majority of American youth are sharing an ever greater affluence and unparalleled job opportunities, the posi-tion of the poor, particularly the ethnically rejected poor, has tended to worsen. Millions of middle- and lower-class Americans, including millions of blacks, are making steady advances, but millions of others are falling even further behind. The impending crisis of this country is that, as the gap between the affluent majority and the deprived minorities continues to widen, the possibilities for communication, for meaningful interaction, and for access of the poor into the power structure of society by the conventional political and economic paths of the past have narrowed. Unless the dom-inant, increasingly affluent, predominantly white middle-class in this country is willing to take major steps without delay—economically, politically, and socially—to reverse this trend, America seems destined to face what will possibly be its greatest crisis since the Civil War. Our culturally deprived youth may once have accepted their fate, if not willingly or uncomplainingly, at least apathetically and nonviolently. As recent events, including the riots in more than a hundred American cities, make clear, that day is largely past.

Alienation of the Culturally Deprived... With the growth of the civil rights movement, and somewhat later with the beginnings of the war on poverty, increasing numbers of young people, both white and black, set about the task of establishing for the first time the Negro's most elementary rights—to ride in the front of a bus, to eat in the only restaurant in town, to play or swim in community parks, simply to hold up their heads on the streets, and, most importantly, to strive for a decent education, to obtain a decent job, and to vote as American citizens.

The idealism of these young people, their courage and patience, their renunciation of hate and violence in the face of the crudest provocation, and their ability to survive verbal abuse, physical assault, jailings, humiliation, and even torture, is one of the most inspiring, if saddest chapters in the history of American youth, and indeed of the nation. At few other times in our history has youth so clearly led, while adults timorously followed. The struggle was not without its psychological toll; here are some of the voices of these youth, as interviewed by Dr. Robert Coles, an informed and perceptive Harvard psychiatrist:

A young student wife:

"I'm prepared to give up my life. . . . I've made that decision, and it's almost as if I'm no longer in my body. The body can be sacrificed. I just look at myself and say to myself 'Man, you can lose your body, but they can't take your soul away. They can just lose theirs. And I'm going to help them . . .' " (27, 206–207).

A young girl who wants to be a teacher hesitates, then starts with:

"Every time I feel afraid I just remind myself that we've got nothing to lose. I think of all the things I've had to put up with in my life. I think of all the movies I can't go to, all the restaurants I can't eat in, all those separate rest rooms and water fountains, and, I tell you, I can get so angry they could have atom bombs on their clubs and police dogs and I'd keep on walking or sitting. We've got our rights as human beings to gain, and absolutely nothing to lose, not a thing. So, why not? Oh, I have to get myself to thinking about this sometimes, when I get nervous, or when the jail is a bad one, and you don't know what they're going to do . . . you can do that, though, get yourself primed, like a pump or something . . ." (27, 207).

In a sensitive clinical analysis of adolescent activists of this period, Fishman and Soloman (44) commented:

we would emphasize that one can find in the student sit-in movement patterns of adolescent identity strivings similar to those in many other adolescent groups. These young people, however, are caught on a wave of psychosocial transition and upheaval. For the Negroes, inferiority, submission and deprivation are their childhood experience; passive-aggressive resolutions their heritage; Christianity their normal background; the Supreme Court decision and the coming of age of new African nations part of the tempo of change. Through these influences are filtered the typical internal pressures and new ego capacities of early and late adolescence. Public action for social goals is their way of at least temporarily resolving issues of identity formation, conscience and aggression. They see themselves as prodders of the national conscience, and derive satisfaction and self-esteem from this role. As a result, they have been forced into synthesizing a new social character with its new problems and anxieties, with its risks and violence, but also with a vitality and optimism for a future that they feel they have had a hand in shaping (44, 881).

Recently, however, the climate has changed. In the minds of increasing numbers of young people, it has become evident that—despite some of the decisions of the Supreme Court and important legal changes in civil rights, and despite widely heralded, but essentially token or pilot programs in the war on poverty—the basic plight of the poor did not just remain but was in fact deteriorating. Hence alienation from the dominant American culture is once again increasing. Among some minority youth, simple despair has taken the place of hope. As one young Negro, who had emigrated from the South, told Dr. Coles:

"You come here hoping, but you find you've put out too much hope on the line, and you're not going to get anything back. So you just sit and make yourself at home; you and the rats, and you and the broken glass. We were fed up long ago, to tell the truth. . . .

We didn't want to go back, and we don't find it any good up here. They don't want us here anymore than they did down there. They used us down there until they had nothing more for us to do, and then they were glad to be rid of us. So we came up here, and there was some work in the factories while the war was going on; but then things started to slump, and now they don't want us up here either. Then, the last few years, we thought it might somehow get better, because of the Civil Rights movement, you know. But nothing happened. They got the vote back home, and up here they made a few jobs for younger kids, and they said we could have the hydrants open for the little children, if we wanted, and they said to wait, and everything would be O.K. by the year 2000 or 3000, or sometime like that. Well, if it does get better by then, I know one thing now, it won't be because of anything the white people in this city do. Maybe God will come and clean up this mess the way He promised He would. That's the only time it'll get better in this neighborhood, if you ask me" (18, 105).

Other youth express their nihilism and outrage in rioting and rebellion. As one young Oakland, California gang leader stated:

"I can't lose by rioting. Done lost. Been lost. Gonna be lost some more. I'm sayin' to the Man: 'You includin' me in this game or not?' And I know his answer, so I'm getting ready to get basic" (27, 41).

The greatest need of the black and other minority-group youth is not to achieve "integration" in the limited sense. It is to find his rightful place in an otherwise affluent society, and with pride in his own identity. To help him achieve this rightful place will require a massive but long overdue commitment on the part of the dominant middle-class, working in partnership with minorities, in the fields of health, of housing, of jobs, of local government, and, especially, of education—beginning at the earliest levels and continuing throughout the educational process.

SCHOOL DROPOUTS

In a society characterized by rapid technological change, increasing automation, and ever greater specialization, the school dropout is very seriously disadvantaged. Although the society as a whole may be affluent, although overall unemployment rates may be low, and although there may be manpower shortages in jobs requiring specialized skills or advanced education, the opportunities for those without either education or vocational skills continue to decline. The proportion of young people who are unemployed is currently greater than it was during the depression of the 1930s. Many of the kinds of jobs that in an earlier era provided immigrants and the native-born poor an opportunity to gain a foothold on the socioeconomic ladder no longer exist. Farm laborers, unskilled workers in heavy industry, and even many basic service workers have been replaced by machines. Many traditional occupations that still demand human effort have been upgraded and require ever higher levels of skill. And most of the new kinds of jobs that are constantly being generated by our rapidly changing society require complex—frequently very complex—backgrounds of training and education.

The result, as we have seen (cf. pp. 676–677), is that highly educated young people currently face unparalleled opportunities in the world of work, while the uneducated are in serious danger of becoming something new and explosive in our "open society"—a permanent and restive proletariat (22). Of the seven and a half million youth who will drop out of school in the present decade, 2.3 million or 30 percent will have completed less than the eighth grade (112).

The tragic irony of the school dropout is that he is most likely to come from segments of our society already disadvantaged economically and discriminated against socially (8, 34). Thus, the dropout rate is highest in slums and among members of minority groups. The dropout rate among blacks is double that for whites (22, 197), even though four out of five dropouts are white.

Already unemployment rates among adolescents seeking work approximate 70 percent in some restricted urban areas, and a large percentage of these young people are school dropouts. From the dropout group come the many delinquents and criminals, drug addicts, and the welfare-dependent, irresponsible, and illegitimate parents of tomorrow (22, 197). The incidence

Hugh Rogers from Monkmeyer

of delinquency is already ten times higher for dropouts than for those who remain in school (22, 197).

Antecedents of Dropping Out

Both sociological and psychological factors appear to be involved in the adolescent's dropping out of school. The dropout rate is highest among ethnically segregated youth living in urban slums. It is higher among the poor in general than among the more well-to-do (6, 98). However, extensive investigations indicate that economic need per se is seldom a major factor in dropping out (22). In one such study of 2579 youths dropping out of school between 1960 and 1961 in a large urban community, only 3 out of 100 students withdrew primarily because of financial need or because they were needed at home (22, 99).

Among upper-upper-class families, only one youth in fifty—and among lower-uppers, only one in ten—fails to finish high school. Among upper-middle-class youth, the proportion of dropouts is one in six, and among lower-middle and upper-lower class youth, it is one in four. At the bottom of the socioeconomic ladder, one in two lower-lower-class youth dropped out prior to completing high school (22, 97).

School Experience and the Dropout. A greater number of dropouts than graduates are below average in intelligence and the probability of dropping out of school prior to completion of high school varies inversely with intelligence (22, 36). In one large scale study, it was found that nine out of ten students in the upper one-third in intelligence went on to graduate from high school, as compared with seven out of ten in the lowest third (111). Apparently a high level of intelligence favors graduation, but intelligence per se is not a decisive factor in most cases of dropping out of school. A majority of dropouts are of at least average intelligence (22 101; 39).

School difficulties, both academic and social, play a prominent role in the history of most dropouts. The typical dropout, even though of average IQ, is two years behind in reading and arithmetic at the seventh grade level, and a majority of his grades are below average. He is likely to have failed one or more school years (8, 22). In one study of dropouts, 85 percent were behind one year, and 53 percent were behind two or more years (22, 198). In another recent study, it was found that future dropouts and graduates differed significantly even in the early school years (19, 22). In tests given at grade 2, only about 10 percent of future graduates scored below grade level on a measure of *reading,* while about 90 percent of future dropouts performed below grade level. Similar results were obtained for *spelling* and for a measure of *word discrimination* (19). Students "dropped out earlier and more abundantly in direct ratio to their low scholastic ranks, when categorized into quarters" (19, 343), and in direct proportion to the number of times that they had been held back in grade level (19).

There are many reasons for discrepancies between the potential dropout's intelligence and his basic academic skills: deficiencies in home background, in motivation, in emotional adjustment, in the appropriateness of his teaching, and the like. Once academic difficulties have developed, however, they exert a formidable influence of their own (54). The student who cannot keep up academically or who finds much of the curriculum puzzling and irrelevant to his needs is likely to find his school experience frustrating, unrewarding, and in a significant number of instances, humiliating. A frequent theme expressed by dropouts in various studies is "feeling goofy" with those "little kids." In such a situation, the decision to drop out is at least likely to be guided by a desire to *escape from* the burdens of his school experience as by any positive attraction of external goals. Most dropouts, in fact, acknowledge that they would have been better off vocationally and socially if they had been able to complete school, and few have any well-defined goals when they leave school *(78)*.

Failures in being able to keep up academically, or in finding relevance and challenge in the school curriculum, are not the only factors that may make continuance in school a frustrating and unrewarding experience. As we have already seen, for many lower-class youth (among whom the largest numbers of dropouts are found), school is an unrewarding experience *socially* as well as *academically*. They do not participate to the same degree as other youth in the social life and activities of the school; they do not share the values of their largely middle-class teachers; and they are likely to feel inadequate or resentful when confronted with the social, as well as the academic, demands of the school setting *(8)*. Similar reactions may affect dropouts from other social classes; and they also appear to affect the lower-class dropout more than the lower-class youth who stays in school. Even while still in school, future dropouts tend more frequently than nondropouts to associate with peers who have already dropped out *(22, 39)*.

> One note that comes through loud and clear when listening to the life stories of the dropout is that he did not feel identified with the school. It is characteristic of the lower class not to participate in school activities to the same extent as do the upper classes [31] but the dropout seems to have been utterly without ties of identity at the time he dropped out. In another study it was found that "not one person who dropped out of high school before the third year had engaged in even one activity. Of those who had finished the third year, eighty-nine per cent had engaged in extracurricular activities" *(22, 103)*.

The one fact which emerges most clearly at this juncture is that the school experience, as currently constituted, is failing to meet the needs—personal, social, and vocational—of an increasing number of our youth, particularly in the lower-class large urban ghettos. This is not to say that the fault lies solely with the schools themselves—obviously, larger social and personal factors are also involved.

Influence of Family and Peers. Not all dropouts come from deprived backgrounds, and many students who do come from deprived backgrounds (over 50 percent) successfully complete high school. Furthermore, in one study in which dropouts were matched in age, sex, school background, family socioeconomic status, and minority-group membership, significant differences still emerged in family and peer influences and in individual psychological characteristics of the students themselves *(22)*. Communication between parents and children, and mutual acceptance and understanding among family members are all significantly poorer in the families of dropouts than of graduates. For example, when asked, "Would you say that your whole family both understands and accepts each other?", 84 percent of dropouts gave responses of "little" or "very little," while 82 percent of graduates gave replies ranging from "moderate" to "very much" *(21)*. To this question, Edward, a dropout, responded, "Very little. Like before you all came. We was having a big argument. My sister keeps dogging me. When I come in she tells me to get out or go to work or something like that. She is stupid. She don't understand me. And my mother doesn't understand me. She just don't have time to understand me. She's got to be worried with my brothers and sisters and I can take care of myself. I can look after myself and make my own decisions and all . . ." *(21, 219)*.

There also appeared to be far less communication within the families of dropouts than within the families of graduates, and the latter were far more likely to share leisure-time activities as a family. Furthermore, "the different climate of happiness in the homes of the dropouts as contrasted with the graduates is startling. Unhappiness is the characteristic of the one group, happiness that of the other" *(21, 222)*.

The families of dropouts tended to be more isolated than those of graduates. Dropout families had fewer friends, and such friendships as they had tended to be more superficial. These families tended to view friends simply as people you "can have fun with" or "who will help you." In contrast, families of graduates tended to view friendships more in terms of *reciprocal* assistance and mutual understanding. In addition, friends of graduate families tended to be more stable and more *homogeneous* in terms of socioeconomic status, region of origin, religion, and occupational aspirations.

Psychological Characteristics of Dropouts.   Dropouts appear more troubled emotionally, less confident of their own worth, more lacking in a clearly defined self-image and sense of identity, and less likely to have structured values and goals—personal, social, or occupational—than those who graduate from high school. They are more likely to have hostile, angry feelings and to be resentful of authority in any form—"home authority, civil authority, intellectual authority, occupational authority" *(22, 192)*. Influenced more by frustrations from which they are trying to escape than by longer-term goals toward which they are striving, these adolescents tend to live more for the moment—responding impulsively, planning little, showing little sustained, goal-directed activity, and seeking immediate gratification *(22)*.

According to projective tests and interview material, dropouts are more likely to view the world as an unpredictable place, characterized by violence, hostility, strife, cheating, faithlessness, and exploitation of other people *(22)*. In this world, as perceived by the dropouts, longer-term goals are relatively meaningless. Plans were likely to go astray or to be doomed from the start. In the dropout's approach to life,

> Human relations are characteristically brittle, haphazard, unpremeditated, affectless, and exploitative . . . . Gratitude is a superflous theme. Fun, pleasure, spontaneity, and emotional upheavals of various types are much in evidence but not as integrated with the superphysical or with life's goals. Our dropout protocols seem more interlaced with the impulse ridden, the nondeferred grati-

fication, the unconventional (from the host culture's viewpoint), the unrealistically romantic, the loosely structured, the shallow, the predestined, the fateful.

. . . the mind of the dropout seems to exhale feelings of inadequacy, worthlessness, frustration, and failure. A dropout, by that very fact, is more clearly cast in the role of outcast and pariah (22, 192–193).

Summary

The typical dropout is likely to come from an emotionally troubled, socially isolated, lower-class home—most frequently located in an ethnically or economically segregated urban ghetto. He is likely to have friends of whom his parents do not approve, who share his aversion to school, and who have already dropped out or soon will drop out themselves. He has probably had academic difficulty in school (particularly in reading and related skills) for many years, even though he may be of average intelligence. He is likely to have been held back in one or more grades. At school, he has not only felt academically frustrated but also socially isolated.

Psychologically, he is troubled by feelings of inadequacy, by resentment of authority, and by lack of a clear sense of ego identity. Lacking well-defined goals or values, he tends to be a creature of the moment—impulsive, low in frustration tolerance, and seeking immediate gratification.

A number of imaginative beginnings in trying to solve the dropout problem have been made in a few isolated areas: summer and school work programs in a few cities; attempts by government and industry to provide training and to find jobs for small numbers of deprived dropouts; special school training programs with a strong vocational orientation and individualized counseling; the Job Corps and the Teacher Corps; preschool health and social enrichment programs, such as Head Start; and so on (cf. pp. 570–572). However, at least to date, these programs have been undertaken on only a token basis, and even then have frequently been withdrawn or reduced in scope soon after they were begun. Sufficiently intensive and extensive programs, especially in our deteriorating cities, will be enormously expensive. In the words of one authority on the subject:

We are confronted, therefore, by a choice as to how we spend our public funds. Shall we continue to pay out large sums for idle workers, leading to desertion and nonsupport, or shall we develop government-supported work programs that will enable our young people to have the satisfaction of being needed by their communities and of working for a living? If we continue to place the major responsibility for these youth upon our schools, we shall experience continued distress. The schools cannot go it alone. The responsibility must be shared by business and labor as well as the community as a whole (112, 504).

JUVENILE DELINQUENCY

Juvenile delinquency is basically a legal concept, defined in different ways in different times and places. In our culture, the term *juvenile delin-*

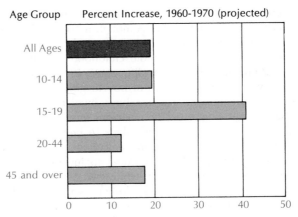

Age Group   Percent Increase, 1960-1970 (projected)

Fig. 15.1. Population growth: the greater increase in our population during the 1960s is in the age range most vulnerable to delinquency and youth crime. (From U.S. Bureau of Census.)

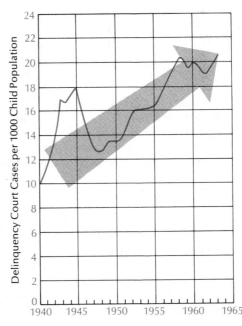

Fig. 15.2. Rates in juvenile delinquency, 1940–1963, per child population ages 10–17. (Data from I. R. Perlman, Juvenile delinquency and some social and economic trends. *Welfare in Review*, 1963, *1*, 13.)

quent is generally applied to children under 16 or 18 who exhibit behavior which is punishable by law. Although most delinquents are adolescents when they come to the attention of the authorities, they generally begin their illegal activities during middle childhood *(43, 49, 50)*.

There are striking sex differences in the incidence of recorded delinquency. Typically, the ratio of boy to girl offenses is 4 or 5 to 1. The most frequent delinquent acts for boys involve active or aggressive behaviors, such as joy-riding, burglary, malicious mischief, larceny, and auto theft. Girls, on the other hand, are more likely to become involved in such offenses as running away from home and engaging in illicit sexual behavior. It is also interesting to note that, according to juvenile authorities, boys are usually apprehended by the police, while girls are frequently reported to the court by parents (particularly the mother) who assert that they cannot control the girl's behavior *(30)*.

The incidence of juvenile delinquency cases began to increase substantially after 1948, and has continued to rise ever since *(96)*. According to current estimates, at least 12 percent of all children, and 22 percent of boys alone, are likely to turn up in juvenile court records before the end of adolescence. Part of this staggering increase appears related to the disproportionately large increases currently occurring in that part of the population aged 15 and 16 (see Fig. 15.1). This trend may be expected to continue throughout the present decade. However, as Fig. 15.2 makes evident, the incidence of delinquency is expanding even faster than the child population.

Social Change and Delinquency

Current increases in delinquency appear to be related at least in part to changes in the structure of society: our increased mobility as a people, with its consequent disruption of well-established cultural patterns and family ties; the increased population growth and social disorganization of large cities; and the lack of a clear sense of national purpose and concern with social problems.

Delinquency rates are highest in deteriorated neighborhoods near the centers of large cities *(29, 49, 50)*. In such areas—characterized by economic privation, rapid population turnover, and general social disorganization—delinquency is often an approved tradition and there are many opportunities for learning antisocial behavior from delinquent peers. Consequently, the continuing migration of Americans—particularly disadvantaged, poorly prepared, rural minority-group members—to the cities is a matter of serious concern. And it is young people who are most heavily affected. Perlman *(96)* notes that the number of youth age 10 to 17 in urban areas increased by 72 percent in the decade from 1950 to 1960, whereas the number in rural areas increased only 11 percent. Much of the urban increase was from rural areas due to migration, and the proportion of nonwhites was slightly greater than that of whites.

Many delinquents come from broken or economically substandard homes. Moreover, delinquency occurs about twice as frequently among the children of immigrants as among those of native-born parents. In native-born minority groups, such as Negroes and Spanish-Americans, it is more frequent among the children of parents moving from a relatively simple rural environment to crowded cities than among children of parents already long established in the city environment. Children of parents in both groups experience a great deal of conflict produced by the contrasting standards of their homes, on the one hand, and the neighborhood and school, on the other. Moreover, the prestige of these children and their parents in the community may be relatively low. In addition, such families are more likely to live in deteriorated neighborhoods, and thus the children are more likely to be exposed to delinquent practices. Finally, such parents may themselves lack the knowledge and skills necessary to deal successfully with their environment, and hence may serve as inadequate role models for their children. They are also likely to be too preoccupied or defeated by their own problems to give their children adequate attention.

The problem presented by such general environmental factors is particularly acute in the ethnically segregated, economically deteriorated areas of a few large cities, such as New York. It is in such areas that delinquency is most likely to take the form of gang, rather than individual, offenses. Current headlines about gang warfare and the more brutal and apparently senseless juvenile crimes, such as "thrill-killing," come most frequently from these areas.

Delinquents are more often lower-class boys who are highly motivated to obtain material possessions and comforts, who have less innate ability to see what limited legitimate opportunities are available to them, and who do not accept middle-class proscriptions against illegitimate avenues to the rewards they desire (20, 24). Gang membership among lower-class youth also plays an important role in meeting needs common to all youth, for a sense of personal worth, and for peer-group acceptance. In some lower-class groups, gang membership may be the only avenue available for satisfying such needs (20). Furthermore, some investigators maintain that the need for peer-group participation among socioeconomically deprived male delinquents may be heightened by the frequent absence of a stable father-figure in lower-class households (86).

> Not every boy who joins a gang need be motivated by . . . status discontent. Once groups of disaffected boys *are* formed, then additional members may join them out of a variety of motives—fun, fellowship, protection, even conscription (11, 4).

Harrison Salisbury, the perceptive correspondent of *The New York Times,* in his reports on youth gangs in deprived sections of the greater New York area, points out that in such locales many youths are almost forced—not only by lack of more attractive alternative activities but by social pressures from the peer group—to engage in gang behavior. At times, in fact, gang membership may be almost a condition for self-preservation (104).

While an adolescent in a gang area may at times avoid gang membership by paying tribute to the gang leader, or simply by being an outstanding boy in the neighborhood, this does not often happen. The function of the gang, in turn, is seen by the group as providing a social life for its members and protection for them, particularly in their own territory or "turf."

In less severely deprived areas, or in smaller cities and towns, group pressures toward delinquency are usually less extreme (97), and other social and psychological factors may play a correspondingly greater role. Even in severe delinquency areas, however, such other factors are frequently involved to an important degree.

Not all children who grow up in poverty, live in deteriorating neighborhoods, or who have culturally displaced parents become delinquent. Conversely, many children who are not economically deprived, who come from well-established middle-class homes, and whose parents are neither culturally displaced nor members of struggling minority groups, do become delinquent.

Personality and Delinquency

The facts noted above have led a number of investigators (3, 6, 7, 12, 29, 32, 33, 51, 57, 58, 82, 92, 93, 99, 118) to examine the child's individual personality characteristics and parent-child relationships within the home to explain why, for example, one child from a particular neighborhood, school, social class, and ethnic background becomes delinquent, whereas another— apparently subject to the same general environmental influences—does not.

In approaching this problem, investigators have typically used a research design in which delinquents and nondelinquents from the same general background are compared with respect to personality characteristics and parent-child relationships at various ages.

In their classic study of the personality structures and motivations of delinquents, Healy and Bronner (58) compared each delinquent subject with a nondelinquent brother or sister near his own age. Despite the fact that they had the same parents and came from the same background and environmental milieu, delinquents and controls differed markedly in their personality characteristics, attitudes, and interpersonal relationships. More delinquents than controls manifested "personality deviations" and symptoms indicative of maladjustment. Their academic records were inferior to their brothers' or sisters', and they felt they were unpopular with schoolmates.

The most striking difference between the two groups, however, involved "familial attitudes and emotional experiences." Most of the delinquents gave clear evidence of being or having been very unhappy and discontented in their life circumstances, or extremely disturbed because of emotion-provoking situations or experiences. Many felt keenly either rejected, deprived, insecure, not understood in affectional relationships, unloved, or that love had been withdrawn. Others showed deep feelings of being thwarted other than affectionately, as in normal impulses or desires for self-expression or other self-satisfactions. Still others felt strongly either real or fancied inadequacies or inferiorities in their home life, in school, or in relation to companionship or to sports. In contrast, Healy and Bronner found similar evidences of inner stresses in only a small minority of the controls.

Analyses of projective test responses have suggested that, as a group, delinquents are much more socially assertive, defiant, ambivalent to authority, resentful, hostile, suspicious and destructive, impulsive, independent, and extroverted. At the same time, they appear significantly less self-controlled, less submissive to authority, less conventional in ideas and behavior, less cooperative, and less fearful of failure and defeat (49).

Intelligence of Delinquents

Although there is a somewhat larger proportion of mentally deficient children among juvenile delinquents than among the population at large, there is a wide range of intelligence in the delinquent group (90). A comparison of the Stanford-Binet Intelligence Test scores of 500 juvenile delinquents and a representative sample of 3000 children showed similar distributions for the two groups, although the average IQ of the delinquents was 92.5 as compared with 101.8 for the nondelinquents (85). As the average difference between the two groups is not a large one, and as there is a great deal of overlap between the delinquent and nondelinquent groups, low intelligence, *in and of itself,* cannot be considered a major factor in determining most cases of delinquency (17, 29, 57, 76).

Personality Characteristics, Social Class, and Intelligence

As we have already seen, a considerable number of studies have investigated the relationship between delinquency and variables such as social class, intelligence, and area of residence. Many others have investigated the relationship of personality traits to delinquency within various populations.

In a recent study at the University of Colorado School of Medicine (29, 30), an attempt was made to determine not only whether overall personality differences exist between future delinquents and nondelinquents at various ages but also whether personality traits may be differentially related to delinquency, depending on the intelligence and social-class status of the child. The investigators used the entire tenth grade of all high schools in a large western city as subjects. Personality test data and teacher ratings of behavior for all these subjects were available for various ages from kindergarten through the ninth grade. All youths in this population who became delinquent prior to age 18 were subsequently located through Juvenile Court records. Each delinquent youth was individually matched with a nondelinquent peer of the same age, sex, IQ (within 10 points), socioeconomic status, residence area (frequently the same block), ethnic-group membership, educational background, and school environment (junior and senior high school).

Two matched groups, one of 384 boys and another of 170 girls, were obtained. Each of these groups was then divided into six subgroups, comprising three levels of intelligence (below average, average, and above average) and two levels of socioeconomic status (deprived, nondeprived), with each subgroup containing an equal number of delinquents and matched nondelinquents. As a result, it became possible to determine not only whether there were overall personality and behavioral differences between delinquents and a matched group of nondelinquents in this population at various ages, but also whether there were variations from one subgroup to another in the personality characteristics distinguishing delinquents from nondelinquents. For example, are the personality characteristics which distinguish *average IQ–socioeconomically deprived* delinquents from nondelinquents the same as those which distinguish *above average IQ–nondeprived* delinquents from nondelinquents? Results obtained to date indicate that it may be misleading to speak of differences between delinquents and nondelinquents without taking into account the youths' intelligence and socioeconomic levels.

Findings for Boys.   Overall differences between future delinquents and nondelinquents in personality characteristics and social behavior began to emerge in the early school years. Differences continued and, indeed expanded over the years

> despite the fact that delinquent-nondelinquent pair members were of the same age and sex; had grown up in similar neighborhoods (not infrequently the same block); had faced similar socioeconomic problems; had, in the case of minority group members, encountered similar problems of discrimination and sociocultural isolation; were of comparable intelligence (at least as measured by IQ tests); and had attended the same schools (29, 185).

By the end of the period from kindergarten through third grade, future delinquents were already viewed by their teachers as more poorly adapted than their classmates. They appeared less considerate and fair in dealing with others, less friendly, less responsible, more impulsive, and more antagonistic to authority. In return, they were less well liked and accepted by their peers.

In their schoolwork, they were much more easily distracted, daydreamed more, and, in general, had greater difficulty in maintaining attention and sticking to the task at hand until it was completed. They were less likely to display any special ability or interest. Not surprisingly, these social and academic problems appeared to reflect underlying emotional problems, and in the opinion of their teachers, future delinquents more often came from a disturbed home environment, and were considered overly aggressive.

Although this general picture continued into the period covering grades 4 to 6, some additional differences and some changes in emphasis emerged. Thus in the middle school years inconsistent academic performance among delinquents became increasingly evident. They were more likely to be viewed as underachieving, and showed poorer work habits. Socially, future delinquents demonstrated less overall leadership ability and had a narrower range of general interests—although, relatively, they were becoming more and more attention-seeking. On the other hand, resentment toward and rejection of school authority began to differentiate less clearly between delinquents and nondelinquents at this age, "possibly because problems with authority are *generally* more common at this age than among school beginners" (29, 186).

By the end of the ninth grade, when these boys were entering the period in which delinquent acts are most common, the delinquents manifested differences from their nondelinquent peers in virtually every area of personality functioning and behavior measured through either personality tests or teacher ratings and comments. They continued to display significantly less respect and consideration for the rights of others—both teachers and peers—than the nondelinquents. Not surprisingly, they were much less cooperative in observing school rules and regulations, and in meeting their responsibilities as members of a social group. Moreover, at this age the delinquents showed a much greater antagonism toward authority in comparison with nondelinquent peers than was true in grades 4 to 6. Apparently in the years between middle childhood and adolescence the attitudes of the nondelinquents toward authority improved considerably, while among delinquents, they continued to deteriorate.

Peer relations remained significantly poorer among the delinquents in adolescence. The delinquents were less friendly and pleasant toward classmates, and, in return, were less well liked and accepted by their peers. In their academic activities, the delinquents continued "to have greater difficulty than their nondelinquent matches. Their work habits were still significantly poorer; they were more careless in their work, appeared more often to be working below their capabilities, and needed much more supervision from teachers. Attendance was more often a problem among these youths" (29, 187). The delinquents appeared more distractible; they manifested much less capacity for sustained attention, daydreamed more, and, when challenged academically, tended to give up more easily.

In adolescence, the delinquents were rated as less well adjusted generally, more lacking in self-confidence and self-respect, less cheerful and happy, less able to get along with members of their own and the opposite sex, and were more attention-seeking. Again, home problems were evident, with delinquents much more likely to have "disturbed home environment" mentioned spontaneously by their teachers as a significant problem.

Interestingly, these impressions of poorer adjustment among the delinquents seemed to find support in the reports of the boys themselves, as judged from the psychological testing at the end of junior high school. In the various group tests, the delinquents emerged as clearly less well adjusted.

In particular, they appeared to feel less capable of establishing close personal relationships with either peers or adults, especially the latter. They described themselves as having fewer interests in life, and emerged as generally lacking in enthusiasm. Not unexpectedly, they appeared significantly less impressed by the dominant ethical values and goals of American middle-class culture than their nondelinquent matches.

Perhaps somewhat more surprisingly, in the areas of emotional stability, general maturity, and behavior symptomatology, the delinquents also tended to view themselves in much the same way as their teachers had pictured them. Thus the delinquents emerged in the testing as more: egocentric, childishly demanding, inconsiderate, thoughtless, and given to petty expressions of pique (although they might not have cared to use these particular labels for the implicit and explicit attitudes they expressed). They also acknowledged feelings of depression and discouragement, mood swings, daydreaming, and oversensitivity more frequently than their nondelinquent peers. And they admitted more often to a variety of somatic and behavioral expressions of anxiety and hypochondriacal preoccupations. Finally, they also appeared significantly more likely than the nondelinquents to respond to environmental pressures (particularly from parents or other authority-figures) with hostility, rejection, or simply withdrawal from the situation, rather than by acceptance, either for their own sake or that of others (29, 188).

Findings for Girls.   Somewhat similar results were obtained for girls, significant differences between future delinquents and nondelinquents emerging as early as the period from kindergarten to the third grade. Increasingly, it became evident that future delinquents were significantly less well adjusted socially, emotionally, and academically than their nondelinquent matches. They were less poised and more unstable emotionally; less likely to be cheerful, happy, or friendly; and less likely to possess "a good sense of humor." They had more difficulty in relating to same- and opposite-sex peers. They were less likely to show respect and consideration for the rights of others and, in return, were less well liked and accepted by others.

The delinquent girls also displayed significantly more antagonism toward adult authority of any kind, including the school, and were much less cooperative in observing rules and regulations. At the same time, they appeared to have greater difficulty in learning to think for themselves, and in developing a clear set of values of their own, or realistic, planful goals. They showed less creative ability generally, and fewer special abilities or interests. Their work habits were significantly poorer than those of their nondelinquent peers.

Many of these differences are similar to those obtained for boys. There did, however, appear to be some variations of emphasis. Thus the *largest* differences between delinquent and nondelinquent girls appeared in the areas of overall emotional adjustment and conformity; among boys, the largest delinquent-nondelinquent differences occurred in the areas of conformity, creative ability, self-reliance, and relations with peers. Furthermore, though differences were somewhat smaller, *negative affect* (i.e., feelings of unhappiness, moodiness, humorlessness, and discouragement) differentiated significantly for girls, but not for boys, while *leadership ability* differentiated for boys but not for girls. On *self-reports* (i.e., group psychological tests), many more differences emerged for boys than for girls. This is consistent with the findings of other investigators (57) that delinquent girls are more likely than delinquent boys to be aware of social expectations, and to respond on self-reports and psychological tests in terms of these expectations—even though their actual behavior, feelings, and attitudes may be quite different.

Differential Effects of Socioeconomic Status and Intelligence.   Interestingly, while the above rather marked differences in personality and behavior distinguish delinquent and nondelinquent boys and girls *as a whole*, it became clear that these findings could not be applied indiscriminately to all subgroups of children at all ages, regardless of intellectual and socioeconomic status. For example, Figs. 15.3 and 15.4 show the distribution of average D- ("delinquency") scores (a general measure of social, emotional, and academic adjustment) by social-class status (deprived, nondeprived) and intelligence level (below average, average, and above average) for delinquent and nondelinquent boys and girls in the period from kindergarten through third grade.

As may be seen, future delinquents (both male and female) obtained higher D-scores than nondelinquents, overall and in *most* subgroups. However, by far the largest delinquent-nondelinquent differences occurred in the deprived-average IQ subgroup. In contrast, among deprived subjects of below-average IQ, differences either did not exist (girls) or were actually in the opposite direction from those of other subgroups (boys), although not significantly so. At this age, at least, youths in this subgroup not only did *not* contribute to the significance of the overall delinquent-nondelinquent differences, but actually tended to reduce these differences. It is also interesting to note that *deprived* future nondelinquents of average intelligence were rated more favorably by teachers on D-score than subjects in any other subgroup—delinquent or nondelinquent. Contrary to some assertions, it appears that teachers do not necessarily rate deprived children more unfavorably than nondeprived children if they are of average IQ and if their behavior is not suggestive of future delinquency.

The above example of possible subgroup variations in delinquent-nondelinquent differences is intended merely as an illustration. Throughout this study it became evident that the nature, extent, and direction of delinquent-nondelinquent differences may vary from one personality or behavioral trait to another; from one age level to another; and from one social-class IQ subgroup to another (29). While we still have much to learn about the nature of such differences, this study does make clear that it may be misleading to assume that overall mean scores and mean score differences in personality and behavioral measures between future delinquents and nondelinquents are necessarily equally applicable to all social-class IQ subgroups at all ages.

Parent-Child Relationships

In a study of the home backgrounds and family influence of delinquents and nondelinquents by Sheldon and Eleanor Glueck (49), all the available data indicated that the nondelinquents were better handled by their parents than the delinquents. For example, the early disciplinary techniques to which the delinquents had been subjected were typically found to have been "lax" and "erratic." Fathers of delinquents were more frequently considered "over-strict," and a smaller proportion of them were considered "firm but kindly." Physical punishment was the favorite disciplinary method used by the delinquent boys' parents, while the controls' parents more frequently reasoned with their children about their misconduct.

In general, the delinquents' parents were less affectionate, more indiffer-

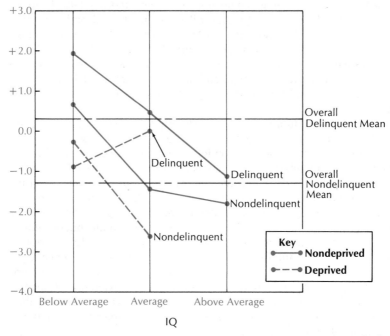

Fig. 15.3. Distribution of mean D-scores for male delinquents and matched nondelinquents by social class-IQ subgroup (K–3). (By permission of J. J. Conger and W. C. Miller.)

ent and hostile toward them, and showed less warmth, sympathy, and affection. Compared with the control group, relatively few of the delinquents had close ties to their fathers, and more of them expressed open hostility toward both parents. Many of them felt that their fathers were wholly unacceptable as models for their conduct. Obviously, they must have found it difficult to identify with them, or learn acceptable patterns of social behavior from them.

In brief, "the delinquent boys, far more than the nondelinquents, grew up in a family atmosphere not conducive to the development of emotionally well-integrated, happy youngsters, conditioned to obedience to legitimate authority" (49, 133).

The apparent role of disturbed family relationships in the genesis and repetition of delinquency is suggested in several other studies. In one investigation of high delinquency areas in New York City (32, 33), three factors were found to be related to increased likelihood of delinquency in boys: (1) careless or inadequate supervision by mother or mother substitute; (2) erratic or overstrict discipline; and (3) lack of cohesiveness of the family unit.

Somewhat similar findings emerged in a study by Bandura and Walters (6) of 26 delinquent boys and an equal number of nondelinquents from the same social class and IQ range. Both the boys and their parents were inter-

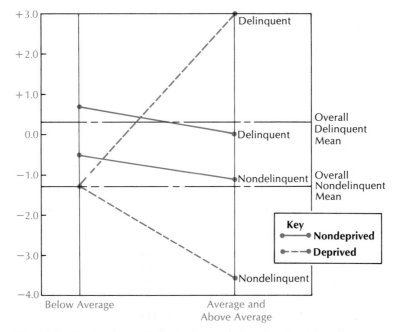

Fig. 15.4. Distribution of mean D-scores for female delinquents and matched nondelinquents by social class-IQ subgroup (K–3). (By permission of J. J. Conger and W. C. Miller.)

viewed and rated for a variety of psychological variables. The parents of the delinquents were found to be more rejecting and less affectionate than those of the nondelinquents. According to the authors, the boys' relations with their fathers constituted a more important factor in development than their relationships with their mothers. The fathers of the delinquent boys were prone to ridicule them when they made a mistake, and there was typically an atmosphere of ill will between father and son. Somewhat similarly, it has been found that the incidence of criminal convictions was higher among boys whose fathers were rated "cruel" or "neglecting" than among those rated "passive" or "warm." Furthermore, the likelihood of crime was increased if the child was disciplined in an erratic fashion or left undisciplined. Investigators also found a higher incidence of criminal convictions when the mother was rated as "nonloving" than when she was rated as "loving." Incidence was lowest when mothers were both "loving" and manifested consistent discipline.

Social Class, Delinquency, and Emotional Disturbance

In their interesting book, *Delinquent behavior: culture and the individual,* Kvaraceus and Miller (77) postulate that "a nonlower-class youth who

becomes involved in delinquency is much more likely to be emotionally disturbed than not" (77, 55), whereas the opposite is the case with lower-class
children. The investigators' basic assumption is that delinquency is much less
likely to involve "norm-violating" behavior in lower-class groups, and is
thus less likely to be based on emotional disturbance. They assert that "the
preponderant portion of our 'delinquent' population consists of emotionally
'normal' lower-class youngsters" (77, 55).

Another prominent investigator, Adelaide Johnson, distinguishes between
the "sociologic delinquent" and the "individual delinquent" (66–70). In her
opinion, "What makes the sociologic delinquent group is that it is largely
molded by community and home forces more or less *consciously* in opposition to the whole other social world" (66, 852). She cites as an example a
youngster who grows up in a gypsy society in which stealing from villagers
is permissible. Thus some lower-class children are seen as acquiring delinquency as an acceptable activity of their own social group. In contrast, the
individual delinquent's antisocial behavior is seen as stemming not from an
untroubled conformity to parental and social norms, but from disturbed
parent-child relationships—frequently including an *unconscious* fostering by
the parents of defects of conscience and related distortions in the child's
capacity to evaluate the environment realistically.

There is little question that many lower-class youth are subjected to
greater cultural pressures toward delinquency than their more socioeconomically favored peers. But does this mean that lower-class delinquents as a
group are necessarily freer of emotional problems than middle- and upper-
class delinquents? In a study of a large group of delinquents, Reiss (100)
encountered a type of lower-class delinquent youth (the *integrated delinquent*) who tended to come from a stable family and who did not appear
particularly troubled emotionally. Rather, like Johnson's *sociologic delinquent,* he came from a high-delinquency area, and simply tended to adopt the
asocial values of the delinquent group with whom he interacted. However,
Reiss also found another type of lower-class delinquent who would not be
likely to be described as emotionally "normal."

In the study by Conger and Miller cited above, it was noted that *both*
lower-class and middle-class delinquents emerged as more poorly adjusted
than nondelinquents—either deprived or nondeprived. On some traits, at some
ages, and at some IQ levels, deprived delinquents scored *more* unfavorably
than nondeprived delinquents, while in some other instances the reverse was
the case. In general, however, deprived delinquents tended to score more like
nondeprived delinquents than like nondelinquents, either deprived or nondeprived.

> It would appear more meaningful, and probably more accurate, to emphasize
> the greater accomplishment—emotionally, socially, and academically—of the
> deprived youth who manages to remain *nondelinquent,* in comparison to his
> nondeprived counterpart, than to assert that the *nondeprived delinquent* is
> much more likely to be emotionally disturbed than the *deprived delinquent,*

or to assert that the latter is generally "normal," that is, similar to nondelinquents generally in his degree of emotional stability (29, 216).

SUMMARY

An essential element in the task of becoming a mature adult is the development of a sense of one's own identity. The adolescent or adult with a strong sense of ego identity sees himself as distinctive and separate from others, but also as self-consistent, with a workable integration of his own needs, motives, and patterns of responding. The problem of ego identity becomes particularly acute at adolescence, partly as a function of the rapid physical and physiological changes of puberty, but also because of increased and changing social demands. The ease with which a strong and stable sense of ego identity and a relatively conflict-free sex-role adjustment is achieved in adolescence will depend to an important degree on the nature of previous parent-child relationships. This task will also be made easier or more difficult, depending upon the values, expectations, and opportunities of the society in which the youth is expected to adjust.

The problem of ego identity cannot be separated from that of values, and adolescents are particularly concerned with issues of conscience and with moral values and standards. The nature of these concerns, however, vary from generation to generation. The average current adolescent tends to view society as becoming more fast-paced, competitive, conflicted in its values and beliefs, complex, and impersonal. Nevertheless he intends to remain in the mainstream of society, is interested in "success" as conventionally defined, and is reasonably happy.

In achieving such adjustment, the average adolescent has tended to rely somewhat more than earlier generations on such values as: honesty and "openness" in interpersonal relationships with members of both the same and opposite sex; a belief in the importance and dignity of the individual; a greater emphasis on personal, relativistic, and individualized codes of morality and behavior, and less emphasis on the institutionalized, arbitrary, and frequently inconsistent dictates of contemporary society. Today's average adolescent appears more ready than his more self-conscious predecessors of earlier generations to put into practice the philosophy of "live and let live" and of pragmatic idealism. More than his counterparts in earlier generations, he appears to be a sophisticated and critical exponent of the art of the possible—not illusioned, but not disillusioned either. One commentator has termed today's adolescents as a generation of "flaming moderates."

In contrast, important minorities in the adolescent subculture have become alienated from the values and practices of contemporary society. In some instances, alienation is imposed primarily *from without,* and represents a reaction of frustration and resentment to deprivation and discrimination imposed by the larger society (as in the case of the culturally deprived and the school dropout). This sort of alienation is more traditional, and has been a part of society over many centuries.

On the other hand, there is increasingly a "new" alienation taking place among economically and socially favored middle-class youth, based upon an *explicit rejection of contemporary American culture*, with its emphasis on competition and materialistic values, and its apparent lack of concern for social justice, equality of opportunity, and civil rights, as well as its continued involvement in wars, both hot and cold. Some of these middle-class youth react by trying to change "the system," either within or outside traditional political mechanisms (e.g., Peace Corps workers, student activists); while others attempt to establish a more compatible way of life for themselves outside the system (e.g., social dropouts and hippies). Still others, partly as a result of disturbed parent-child relationships in the past as well as current social conditions, are far too pessimistic, nihilistic, and despairing to look for a new way of life, either within the system or outside of it (e.g., the culturally alienated).

A problem of mounting concern is the increasing use of drugs among adolescents, ranging from marijuana, glue sniffing, and the "pills" (amphetamines, tranquilizers, barbiturates) to LSD and other highly potent mind-altering drugs. For some adolescents, the use of drugs may simply reflect an urge to rebel against adult constraints or to seek novelty. For others, drug use may represent a rejection of contemporary society, and an attempt to seek a creative subjective experience, to restore a sense of beauty and wonder, or to find meaningful personal values. For still others, such as the slum-dwelling user of the "hard" narcotics such as heroin, drug use may simply reflect an attempt to escape into oblivion from an intolerable existence. However, the fact remains that drugs, while they may produce a temporary escape, frequently create new problems and have never been shown to increase creativity, and, in fact, have frequently impaired it.

Another problem of major concern is the rising incidence of juvenile delinquency. This phenomenon has both sociological and psychological roots. While delinquency rates are higher among youth who grow up in poverty, live in deteriorating neighborhoods of large cities, and have culturally and economically deprived parents, not all such youth become delinquent. Conversely, many children who are not deprived, who come from well-established middle-class homes, and whose parents are neither culturally deprived nor members of struggling minorities, do become delinquent.

Obviously, personality characteristics and parent-child relationships are also important in the development of delinquency. For example, as compared to nondelinquents, delinquents have been shown to be more poorly adjusted generally and more lacking in self-confidence; more impulsive, distractible, aggressive, unhappy, and resentful; and less well-liked and accepted by their peers. In general, parents of delinquents are less affectionate and more indifferent or hostile toward their children. They are also likely to provide less supervision, to be more erratic or unduly harsh in discipline, and to lack cohesion as a family unit.

Case Material

In the adolescent and early adult personalities of Peter and Jack, we can see clearly the cumulative effects of the divergent psychological and social forces that operated on these two very different boys over the years. We can see, too, the remarkable consistency in the unique patterns of behavior each boy displayed as he grew toward adulthood. In both boys, the embryonic manifestations of many of their behaviors were present, even in the preschool years.

Of course, not all children show such consistency. There is little doubt that in these particular cases, it was fostered by the consistency, over time, of the influences to which they were subjected, particularly those of the parents. Nevertheless, one cannot help but be impressed by the regularity with which personality development follows the principles of learning discussed in this book. Nor can one help but be impressed—and hopefully, perhaps, rather sobered—by the truth of the time-worn cliché, "as the twig is bent, so grows the tree."

Peter B. It will be recalled that during the school years, Peter was closely tied to his parents and eager to please adult authorities. He was conscientious and was, of course, doing well in school. His teachers unanimously described him as a conforming and friendly child.

Peter's interests and activities still deviated markedly from the traditional masculine ego ideal, and he was not involved in competitive sports, roughhousing or gang behavior, or dating. When he was 10, he had decided to be a florist or a baker, but by age 15 he felt sure that he wanted to be a teacher.

During adolescence, Peter remained cautious in all problem situations, constantly weighing all the possible eventualities before making a decision and rarely quarreling or fighting. Peter dealt with the five problem areas of adolescence with differential success. He had decided on teaching as a vocation and felt moderately confident of his abilities in this area. He had a strict and well-defined set of moral standards that prohibited sexual and aggressive behavior and dictated unquestioning obedience to his family and adults. His desires for sexual activity were suppressed and he did no dating. As he was still very dependent on his parents, the task of establishing independence from his family was a most troublesome problem.

At age 15, Peter was still dependent, timid, conforming, and effeminate in his interests. While he had established some degree of ego identity, there were several areas (such as dependence on family and sexual adequacy) that were colored with anxiety.

At age 21, Peter had not changed very much. He was frail of build and spoke in a soft and high-pitched voice. His face and physique made him appear much younger than his 21 years. When interviewed, he had difficulty elaborating many of his answers; he often meditated for several minutes before answering, and there was a prevailing air of caution and insecurity in his manner.

Peter had decided to teach English at a high school. Although he was primarily interested in teaching at a college, he was afraid to begin there because he doubted his ability to handle college courses. As usual, Peter preferred to avoid the challenge of the more difficult job, even if it was more gratifying.

He admired all his high school and college teachers and retained a dependent tie to them. He felt close to many of them "because," he said, "they were all willing to help me." His major hobbies were painting and growing flowers; athletics and competitive activities were avoided as strongly as ever.

Peter did not want to marry until he was financially secure, and he had serious doubts about his ability to support a family. He felt tense and uncomfortable when with girls and he preferred not to date. Sexual behavior was still a source of fear and, in characteristic fashion, his preferred reaction to fear was withdrawal.

Peter had few friends and most of his leisure time was spent alone. Because he felt tense with strange people, he avoided clubs and social groups. If someone irritated Peter, he walked away, and he rarely insulted or became sarcastic with anyone.

With his parents he was close and conforming, and he enjoyed talking over his problems with them. Fearing a feeling of isolation from his family, Peter decided to attend a college close to his home.

On the brink of adulthood, his behavior was, in many ways, similar to the reactions he showed when he was 4 years old. Let us quote again from a description of his behavior at 3½ years.

> Babyish in appearance—a big, baby stare, long, curly eyelashes, and a rosebud mouth. He showed extreme caution and would back away from any situation that smacked of danger. When threatened he would shake his head, clasp his hands, and beg in a frantic tone, "No—no—no." His role with peers was a sedentary, passive, and shrinking one. He stayed out of the swirl of the activity of the other children and seemed like a "clam without a shell." . . . With the staff of the Nursery School he was highly conforming and very dependent. He liked to help clean up, liked to wash, liked to take a nap, and often told others what to do in a rather pointed way. Signs of guilt were quite apparent and whenever he dirtied something, wet himself, or committed what he regarded as a violation, he became very tense and apprehensive; as if he felt that he had been a "bad boy."

Peter's development is not typical, for this degree of consistency in personality is unusual. However, it demonstrates how stable the reactions of dependency, passivity, and fear can be if the forces that determine personality development arrange themselves in this particular configuration.

Jack L. At age 10, Jack had identified with traditional masculine role models. By adolescence, he was a leader among his peers, competitive and mischievous. He had achieved some degree of independence from his family and was confident of his ability to establish a heterosexual relationship.

However, Jack was plagued with two problems: poor school grades and anxiety over the possibility of not being "masculine." Over the years, his parents had stressed the importance of being independent and competitive, and had punished any display of the "childish" traits of dependency or loss of emotional control. As all adolescents have some desire to behave childishly, Jack had to repress these urges. This struggle was a continuing source of tension.

Jack's resistance to school continued through preadolescence and adolescence. He still viewed "studiousness" as nonmasculine, and this attitude prevented the development of any strong motivation to master academic subjects. On the other hand, his interest in sports and other masculine activities intensified, and at 20 he was saving all his money to buy a car. He had developed into a good athlete who was proud of his ability.

Jack began to date early in high school and both parents encouraged his heterosexual interests. He entered into the traditional kissing games at parties with the typical ambivalence of a 12-year-old.

When Jack was interviewed at age 17, he was still unsure about a vocational choice and he was not highly motivated to go to college. He was dating regularly and enjoyed the usual forms of romantic activity. In short, Jack was a rather typical middle-class American adolescent.

In comparison with Peter, he was less sure of his intellectual competence. His failure to do well in school subjects made him fearful of attending college, and this anxiety prevented his choosing any one of a variety of vocations that he might have found appealing.

By 21 years of age, Jack's earlier confidence and aggressivity had diminished. He appeared a bit more subdued and less sure of himself than he did at age 10. He did not attend college because he was afraid of failure and, instead, entered the business world. His avocations were still traditionally masculine, and cars and sports were his primary recreational interests. He was unmarried but dating steadily a girl whom he had met in high school. Jack had not yet established complete independence from his parents, and he was reluctant to leave the security and familiarity symbolized by his home.

The areas of consistency in Jack's personality over the years included the strong identification with his father, the adoption of traditional masculine values, and the rejection of intellectuality. The major aspect of his personality that changed during adolescence was a slight decrease in the apparent independence, bravado, and confidence that he showed during middle childhood.

Jack's developmental history is more representative than Peter's, in that some traits remained constant, whereas others changed. However, one important principle applies in both cases. The changes in behavior at each new developmental stage were directly related to the child's total personality at that time. When Peter had to make a vocational choice at adolescence, it was unlikely that he would consider becoming a football coach or a pilot. His choice was limited by the pattern of skills, interests, and fears he had acquired over the years. Similarly, Jack's poor school performance and negative attitude toward intellectual activity seriously limited the vocational directions he could take.

Development is not always reversible. The individual cannot completely return to an earlier stage and start life afresh. It is hoped that the presentation of these cases has made this one lesson clear—human development is punctuated with "points of no return."

EMOTIONAL MATURITY—EPILOGUE

It should be possible at this juncture to cast a long look backward over the whole course of the child's development. Such a longitudinal survey should certainly serve to convince us that no one's behavior can be explained by easy platitudes. As we maintained at the outset, people do not behave as they do simply because "their mothers spoiled them," because "they were born that way," or because "they are underprivileged." Our personalities are the result of too many complex interacting forces ever to be adequately explained in terms of any one of them.

In the course of this book, we have reviewed many of the kinds of forces that, taken together, determine the unique personality that the individual develops. We have seen that his development is bound to be affected, for good or ill, by his genetic inheritance; by his prenatal environment; by his physical and psychological environment; by the attitudes and behavior of his parents, teachers, and peers; by the "alarums and excursions" of his own particular era in history; and by his culture and subculture—economic, religious, or social.

When one attempts to translate this breathtaking expanse of possible developmental influences into personal terms, one question often arises. How do we want our children to develop?

Every parent will have his own answer, determined largely by his own unique set of values and life experiences. The parent who has himself fought against great economic odds may want financial security for his children. The parent who was unloved or rejected may want affection and love. The parent who had to leave school at 14 in order to go to work may feel that a proper education is all-important. Specific frustrations may play a role too. How many parents want their children to realize their own unfulfilled dreams: to be an artist, or banker, or doctor, or general, or statesman, or movie actress?

It does not seem a naive oversimplification, however, to state that probably most of all, most parents want their children "to be happy." But wherein lies the key to happiness; and how can we gain it for our children? By helping them to become financially secure? By looking out for their health? By protecting them from tragedy and misfortune? Certainly we can make efforts in these directions; but we cannot, in this most unpredictable of worlds, be sure of success. In spite of our efforts, fortunes may crumble, health may fail, tragedy—at one time or another—will surely strike.

When we look unsparingly at reality, it seems that the best insurance that we can try to pass on to our children is what the minister probably would call "inner strength" and what the psychologist and psychiatrist would term "emotional maturity" or ego identity. Life brings many crises and disappointments to all of us, but the emotionally mature person will at the least be better prepared to cope with them than the immature, the rigid and inflexible, or the neurotic.

But what actually do we mean by "emotional maturity"? According to English and Finch, ". . . a person with a mature personality has worked out a harmonious relationship between his basic needs, his conscience and ideals, and the environment which enables him to make maximum use of his psychic energies in constructive work, heterosexual adjustment, and altruistic living" (40, 39).

The first responsibility of those who are entrusted with the task of socialization—parents, teachers, or others—is to understand the structure of the adult society which the child is to enter. Without such knowledge, the process of socialization becomes a hit-or-miss affair. With such knowledge, intelligent training can be undertaken.

No individual can avoid encountering conflicts between his needs and the demands of reality, and between opposing needs within himself. Nor would such a state of affairs probably be desirable, even if it were possible, because a reasonable degree of conflict often provides the impetus for the further development of the individual. One of the useful functions parents can perform is to help their children learn to tolerate conflict and frustration, and to deal with them effectively. However, through proper parental guidance, the child can be helped to avoid learning conflicting needs which are too strong and which, instead of promoting maturity, tend to handicap the individual's adjustment. Thus the child may be helped to avoid conflicts based on extreme needs for both dependency and independency, on intense desires for social or sexual contact and paralyzing fears of them, on wishes to exploit others and to serve them. The child can also be taught those responses in the form of knowledge, social and performance skills, and cultural attitudes, which are likely to lead in his particular culture to satisfaction of his existing needs, both primary and learned.

In these last two chapters, we have reviewed many of the needs and response patterns which are necessary for successful adaptation to adult life in American culture. We have seen, for example, that the individual must have learned to be reasonably independent and capable of foresightful planning. He must have been motivated to gain satisfaction from fulfilling the roles he must play in his own society. He must have developed the skills necessary for performance of a vocation which is needed by the culture. He must have learned to compete and to cooperate, to assert himself when necessary without paralyzing fear, and to gain satisfaction from being helpful to others. He must have learned to tolerate frustration and anxiety—for no individual's life is without painful stress and at times seemingly insurmountable obstacles. And he must be flexible, able to try out new responses when old ones fail as environmental situations change—for change is inevitable.

Probably more than anything else, he needs to have developed a realistic knowledge of himself, his capabilities and limitations, his predominant needs, his fears, his sources of conflict. For without a reasonable degree of such knowledge, he is like a man trying to put together a jigsaw puzzle when several of the most important parts are missing. He may attempt goal responses of which he is incapable, thus wasting his energy and becoming discouraged or defeated. Conversely, he may neglect to try out those responses of which he is capable, and which could lead to the satisfaction of his basic needs.

He may also deny to himself the existence of needs that he actually has, because he has been taught that they are wrong. But because denying that one has needs does not lead to their extinction, the person may learn to cope with them in maladaptive or neurotic rather than in realistic ways. Thus instead of admitting and expressing his anger toward his boss, a young man may displace his angry feelings to his sweetheart, unnecessarily alienating her. The young person with extreme dependency needs may run from friendship to friendship, always concluding that "people are no damn good," simply because they have not been able to meet his insatiable needs for dependence. The individual with secret needs for status may deny them to himself, but he may become an antiminority hate monger in an effort to achieve some kinds of prestige. In the words of Franz Alexander, "The Greek maxim, 'Know yourself,' may once have been a luxury. Today it is a necessity. Man can adjust himself to his changing environment only by knowing himself, his desires, impulses, motives, and needs. He must become wiser, more judicious and self-reliant; in one word, more mature" (1, 3).

The task of guiding the child's development so that he will be able to meet the demands of life maturely is not an easy one. And although parents have a critically important role to play, they cannot be expected to do the job alone. Particularly in the case of disadvantaged youth, it is unrealistic to expect parents—frequently poorly prepared themselves—to be able alone to counteract the crippling effects on their children's development of poverty, malnutrition, inadequate education, discrimination, and social disorganization. Only through a far more determined effort by all of us than has been evident to date can we hope to ameliorate these conditions, and give all of our children a fighting chance—not merely for physical survival but for a reasonable degree of happiness and social effectiveness.

References

1. Alexander, F. From adolescence to adulthood. *Ment. Health Bull.* (Illinois Society for Mental Hygiene), 1948, *26*, 1–4.
2. Alexander, G. LSD: injection early in pregnancy produces abnormalities in offspring of rats. *Science*, 1967, *157*, 459–460.
3. Andry, R. G. Paternal and maternal roles in delinquency. In *Deprivation of*

maternal care. Public Health Paper No. 14. Geneva: World Health Organization, 1962, 31–43.

4. Auerback, R., & Rugowski, J. Lysergic acid diethylamide: effect on embryos. *Science,* 1967, *157,* 1325–1326.
5. Ball, D. W. Covert political rebellion as resentment. *Soc. Forces,* 1964, *43,* 93–101.
6. Bandura, A., & Walters, R. H. *Adolescent aggression.* New York: Ronald Press, 1959.
7. Bender, L. Psychopathic behavior disorders in children. In R. M. Linder (Ed.), *Handbook of correctional psychology.* New York: Philosophical Library, 1947, 360–377.
8. Bertrand, A. L. School attendance and attainment: function and dysfunction of school and family social systems. *Soc. Forces,* 1962, *40,* 228–233.
9. Block, J., & Turula, E. Identification, ego control, and adjustment. *Child Develpm.,* 1963, *34,* 945–953.
10. Blum, R. *Utopiates: the use and users of LSD-25.* New York: Atherton Press, 1964.
11. Bordua, D. J. *Sociological theories and their implications for juvenile delinquency.* Washington, D.C.: U.S. Government Printing Office (Children's Bureau), 1960.
12. Bowlby, J. Forty-four juvenile thieves. *Int. J. Psychoanal.,* 1944, *25,* 1–57.
13. Brown, D. G. Sex-role development in a changing culture. *Psychol. Bull.,* 1958, *55,* 232–242.
14. Brown, D. R. Student stress and the institutional environment. In E. E. Sampson (Ed.), *J. soc. Issues,* 1967, *22,* No. 3, 92–107.
15. Brown, J. D. (Ed.) *The Hippies.* New York: Time-Life, Inc., 1967.
16. Campus '65. *Newsweek,* March 22, 1965, 43–54.
17. Caplan, N. S., & Siebert, L. A. Distribution of juvenile delinquent intelligence test scores over a thirty-four year period (N = 51,808). *J. clin. Psychol.,* 1964, *20,* 242–247.
18. Carmichael, S., & Hamilton, C. Dynamite. *Atlantic Monthly,* 1967, *220,* No. 4, 98–102.
19. Carrino, C. A. Identifying potential dropouts in the elementary grades. *Dissert. Abstr.,* 1966, *27,* 343.
20. Cartwright, D. S., Howard, K. I., & Short, J. F., Jr. The motivation of delinquency. Unpublished manuscript.
21. Cervantes, L. F. Family background, primary relationships, and the high school dropout. *J. Marriage Fam.,* 1965, *5,* 218–223.
22. Cervantes, L. F. *The dropout: causes and cures.* Ann Arbor: Univer. of Michigan Press, 1965.
23. Chorost, S. B. Parental child rearing attitudes and their correlates in adolescent hostility. *Genet. Psychol. Monogr.,* 1962, *66,* 49–90.
24. Cloward, R. A., & Ohlin, L. E. *Delinquency and opportunity: a theory of delinquent gangs.* New York: Free Press of Glencoe, 1960.
25. Cohen, M. M., & Marinello, M. J. Chromosomal damage in human leukocytes induced by lysergic acid diethylamide. *Science,* 1967, *155,* 1417–1419.
26. Coles, R. Maybe God will come and clean up this mess. *Atlantic Monthly,* 1967, *220,* No. 4, 103–106.
27. Coles, R. Serpents and doves: non-violent youth in the South. In E. H. Erikson (Ed.), *Youth: change and challenge.* New York: Basic Books, 1963.
28. Conant, J. B. Social dynamite in our large cities. In *Social dynamite: the*

report of the conference on unemployed, out-of-school youth in urban areas. Washington, D. C.: National Committee for Children and Youth, 1961.

29. Conger, J. J., & Miller, W. C. *Personality, social class, and delinquency.* New York: Wiley, 1966.

30. Conger, J. J., Miller, W. C., & Walsmith, C. R. Antecedents of delinquency, personality, social class and intelligence. In P. H. Mussen, J. J. Conger, & J. Kagan (Eds.), *Readings in child development and personality.* New York: Harper & Row, 1965.

31. Coster, J. K. Some characteristics of high school pupils from three income levels. *J. educ. Psychol.,* 1959, *50,* 55–62.

32. Craig, M. M., & Glick, S. J. *A manual of procedures for application of the Glueck Prediction Table.* New York: New York City Youth Board, 1964.

33. Craig, M. M., & Glick, S. J. Ten years' experience with the Glueck Social Prediction Table. *Crime and Delinq.,* 1963.

34. Dentler, R. A. Dropouts, automation, and the cities. *Teachers Coll. Rec.,* 1964, *65,* 475–483.

35. Didion, J. The hippie generation: slouching towards Bethlehem. *Saturday Evening Post,* 1967, *19,* 27–31, 88–94.

36. Dillon, H. J. *Early school leavers.* New York: National Child Labor Committee, Publication No. 401.

37. Dinitz, S., Karpith, F. R., & Reckless, W. C. Delinquency vulnerability: a cross group and longitudinal analysis. *Amer. sociol. Rev.,* 1962, *27,* 515–517.

38. Douvan, E. A., & Adelson, J. *The adolescent experience.* New York: Wiley, 1966.

39. Elliott, D. S., Voss, H. L., & Wendling, A. Dropout and the social milieu of the high school: a preliminary analysis. *Amer. J. Orthopsychiat.,* 1966, *36,* 808–817.

40. English, O. S., & Finch, S. M. *Introduction to psychiatry.* New York: Norton, 1954.

41. Erikson, E. H. *Childhood and society.* New York: Norton, 1950.

42. Evans, R. I. *Dialogue with Erik Erikson.* New York: Harper & Row, 1967.

43. Fenton, N., et al. *The delinquent boy and the correctional school.* Claremont, Calif.: Claremont College Guidance Center, 1935.

44. Fishman, J. R., & Solomon, F. Youth and social action: 1. Perspectives on the student sit-in movement. *Amer. J. Orthopsychiat.,* 1963, *33,* 872–882.

45. Flacks, R. The liberated generation: an exploration of the roots of student protest. *J. soc. Issues,* 1967, *22,* No. 3, 52–75.

46. Freud, A. *The ego and the mechanisms of defense.* New York: International Universities Press, 1946.

47. Gershon, S., & Angrist, B. Drug-induced psychoses: II. *Hospital Practice,* 1967, *2,* 50–53.

48. Glaser, H. H., & Massengale, O. M. Glue sniffing and children. *J. Amer. Med. Ass.,* 1962, *181,* 300–303.

49. Glueck, S., & Glueck, E. T. *Unraveling juvenile delinquency.* New York: Commonwealth Fund, 1950.

50. Glueck, S., & Glueck, E. T. *One thousand juvenile delinquents.* Cambridge, Mass.: Harvard Univer. Press, 1934.

51. Gold, M. *A social-psychology of delinquent boys.* Ann Arbor: Inst. for Soc. Res., Univer. of Michigan, 1961.

52. Goldberg, M. L. Factors affecting educational attainment in depressed urban areas. In A. H. Passow (Ed.), *Education in depressed areas.* New York: Columbia Univer. Press, 1963.

53. Goldstein, R. *1 in 7: drugs on campus.* New York: Walker, 1966.
54. Gowan, J. C., & Demos, G. D. (Eds.) *The disadvantaged and potential drop-out: compensatory educational programs. A book of readings.* Springfield. Ill.: Thomas, 1966.
55. Gruen, J. *The new Bohemia.* New York: Grosset & Dunlap, 1966.
56. Harris, L. The teen-agers. *Newsweek,* March 21, 1966, 57–72.
57. Hathaway, S. R., & Monachesi, E. D. (Eds.) *Analyzing and predicting juvenile delinquency with the MMPI.* Minneapolis: Univer. of Minnesota Press, 1953.
58. Healy, W., & Bronner, A. F. *New light on delinquency and its treatments.* New Haven, Conn.: Yale Univer. Press, 1936.
59. Hedgepeth, W. Inside the hippie revolution. *Look,* 1967, *31,* 58–64.
60. Heilbrun, A. B., Jr. Parental model attributes, nurturant reinforcement, and consistency of behavior in adolescents. *Child Develpm.,* 1964, *35,* 151–167.
61. Heilbrun, A. B., Jr. Conformity to masculinity-femininity stereotypes and ego identity in adolescents. *Psychol. Rep.,* 1964, *14,* 351–357.
62. Heilbrun, A. B., Jr., & Fromme, D. K. Parental identification of late adolescents and level of adjustment: the importance of parent-model attributes, ordinal position and sex of the child. *J. genet. Psychol.,* 1965, *107,* 49–59.
63. Heist, P. Intellect and commitment: the faces of discontent. In O. W. Knorr & W. J. Minter (Eds.), *Order and freedom on the campus: the rights and responsibilities of faculty and students.* Boulder, Colo.: Western Interstate Commission for Higher Education, 1965, 61–69.
64. Huyck, E. E. (Ed.) *White-nonwhite differentials in health, education, and welfare.* Washington, D.C.: Department of Health, Education, and Welfare, 1965.
65. Irwin, S., & Egozcue, J. Chromosomal abnormalities in leukocytes from LSD-25 users. *Science,* 1967, *157,* 313–314.
66. Johnson, A. M. Juvenile delinquency. In S. Arieti (Ed.), *American handbook of psychiatry.* New York: Basic Books, 1959.
67. Johnson, A. M. Collaborative psychotherapy: team setting. In M. Heiman (Ed.), *Psychoanalysis and social work.* New York: International Universities Press, 1953, 79–108.
68. Johnson, A. M. Some etiological aspects of repression, guilt, and hostility. *Psychoanal. Quart.,* 1951, *20,* 511.
69. Johnson, A. M. Sanctions of superego lacunae of adolescents. In K. R. Eissler (Ed.), *Searchlights on delinquency.* New York: International Universities Press, 1949, 225–245.
70. Johnson, A. M., & Szurek, S. A. The genesis of antisocial acting out in children and adults. *Psychoanal. Quart.,* 1952, *21,* 233.
71. Kagan, J., & Freeman, M. Relation of childhood intelligence, maternal behaviors, and social class, to behavior during adolescence. *Child Develpm.,* 1963, *34,* 899–911.
72. Kauffman, J. F. Youth and the Peace Corps. In E. H. Erikson (Ed.), *Youth: change and challenge.* New York: Basic Books, 1963.
73. Keniston, K. The sources of student dissent. *J. soc. Issues,* 1967, *22,* No. 3, 108–137.
74. Keniston, K. *The uncommitted: alienated youth in American society.* New York: Dell, 1960.
75. Kuhlen, R. G., & Arnold, M. Age differences in religious beliefs and problems during adolescence. *J. genet. Psychol.,* 1944, *65,* 291–300.
76. Kvaraceus, W. C. *Juvenile delinquency and the school.* New York: Harcourt, Brace & World, 1945.

77. Kvaraceus, W. C., Miller, W. B., et al. *Delinquent behavior: culture and the individual*. Washington, D.C.: National Educ. Assn., 1959.
78. Lichter, S. O., Rapien, E. B., Seibert, F. M., & Slansky, M. A. *The drop-outs*. New York: Free Press of Glencoe, 1962.
79. Louria, D. *Nightmare drugs*. New York: Pocket Books, 1966.
80. Lynn, D. B. A note on sex differences in the development of masculine and feminine identification. *Psychol. Bull.*, 1959, *66*, 126–135.
81. McBride, B. E. The parental identifications of adolescents. *Alberta J. educ. Res.*, 1962, *8*, 204–210.
82. McCord, W., McCord, J., & Zola, I. K. *Origins of crime*. New York: Columbia Univer. Press, 1959.
83. Medinnus, G. R. Adolescents' self-acceptance and perceptions of their parents. *J. consult. Psychol.*, 1965, *29*, 150–154.
84. Meissner, W. W. Comparison of anxiety patterns in adolescent boys: 1939–1959. *J. genet. Psychol.*, 1961, *99*, 323–329.
85. Merill, M. A. *Problems of child delinquency*. Boston: Houghton Mifflin, 1947.
86. Miller, W. Lower class culture as a generating milieu of gang delinquency. *J. soc. Issues*, 1968, *23*, 5–19.
87. Morimoto, K., cited by H. A. Abrahamson, *Neuropharmacology: transactions of the 2nd conference*. New York: Josiah Macy, Jr. Foundation, 1955.
88. Mussen, P. H. Long-term consequents of masculinity of interests in adolescence. *J. consult. Psychol.*, 1962, *26*, 435–440.
89. Mussen, P. H. Some antecedents and consequents of masculine sex-typing in adolescent boys. *Psychol. Monogr.*, 1961, *75*, No. 506.
90. Mussen, P. H., Conger, J. J., & Kagan, J. *Child development and personality*. New York: Harper & Row, 1963 (2nd ed.).
91. Mussen, P. H., Young, H. B., Gaddini, R., & Morante, L. The influence of father-son relationships on adolescent personality and attitudes. *J. child Psychol. Psychiat.*, 1963, *4*, 3–16.
92. Nye, F. I. *Family relationships and delinquent behavior*. New York: Wiley, 1958.
93. Oltman, J., McGarry, J., & Friedman, S. Parental deprivation and the "broken home" in dementia praecox and other mental disorders. *Amer J. Psychiat.*, 1952, *108*, 685–694.
94. Osborne, R. T. Racial differences in mental growth and school achievement: a longitudinal study. *Psychol. Rep.*, 1960, *7*, 233–239.
95. Pable, M. W. Some parental determinants of ego identity in adolescent boys. *Dissert. Abstr.*, 1965, *26*, 3480–3481.
96. Perlman, I. R. Juvenile delinquency and some social and economic trends. *Welfare in Review*, 1963, *1*, 12–21.
97. Perlman, I. R. Delinquency prevention: the size of the problem. *Assn. Amer. Acad. pol. soc. Sci.*, 1959, *322*, 1–9.
98. Peterson, R. E. *The scope of organized student protest in 1964–1965*. Princeton, N.J.: Educational Testing Service, 1966.
99. Powers, E., & Witmer, H. *Prevention of delinquency: the Cambridge-Somerville youth study*. New York: Columbia Univer. Press, 1951.
100. Reiss, A. J. Social correlates of psychological types of delinquency. *Amer. sociol. Rev.*, 1952, *17*, 710–718.
101. Remmers, H. H. Cross cultural studies of teenagers' problems. *J. educ. Psychol.*, 1962, *53*, 254–261.

102. Rosenberg, M. Parental interest and children's self-conceptions. *Sociometry,* 1963, *26,* 35–49.
103. Rubin, T., & Thomas, L. G. *Presentations of a conference on inhalation of glue fumes and other substance abuse practices among adolescents.* Denver, Colo.: Denver Juvenile Court, 1967.
104. Salisbury, H. E. *The shook-up generation.* New York: Harper & Row, 1959.
105. Sampson, E. E. (Ed.) Student activism and the decade of protest. *J. soc. Issues,* 1967, *23,* No. 3, 1–33.
106. Sampson, E. E. (Ed.) Stirrings out of apathy: student activism and the decade of protest. *J. soc. Issues,* 1967, *23,* No. 3.
107. Shepherd, J. The *Look* youth survey. *Look,* September 20, 1966, 44–49.
108. Siller, J. Socioeconomic status and conceptual thinking. *J. abnorm. soc. Psychol.,* 1957, *55,* 365–371.
109. Smith, Kline, & French Labs. *Drug abuse: escape to nowhere.* Philadelphia: S.K.F. Labs, 1967. (Addressed to educators; available from National Education Assn.)
110. Somers, R. H. The mainsprings of the rebellion: a survey of Berkeley students in November 1964. In S. M. Lipset & S. S. Wolin (Eds.), *The Berkeley student revolt: facts and interpretations.* Garden City, N.Y.: Anchor (Doubleday), 1965.
111. Stice, G. Talent losses before high school. Princeton, N.J.: Research Memorandum, Educational Testing Service, January, 1960, p. 5 (mimeographed).
112. Taber, R. C. The critical dilemma of the school dropout. *Amer. J. Orthopsychiat.,* 1963, *33,* 501–508.
113. Thomas, R. J. An empirical study of high school dropouts in regard to ten possibly related factors. *J. educ. Psychol.,* 1954, *28,* 17.
114. Trent, J. W., & Craise, J. L. Commitment and conformity in the American college. *J. soc. Issues,* 1967, *22,* No. 3, 34–51.
115. Trent, J. W., & Medsker, L. L. *Beyond high school: a study of 10,000 high school graduates.* Berkeley: Center for Research & Development in Higher Education, Univer. of Calif., 1967.
116. Vogel, W., & Lauterbach, C. G. Relationships between normal and disturbed sons' percepts of their parents' behavior, and personality attributes of the parents and sons. *J. clin. Psychol.,* 1963, *19,* 52–56.
117. Waters, H., Porter, G. B., & Zimmerman, P. Trouble in hippieland. *Newsweek,* October 30, 1967, 84–90.
118. Wattenberg, W. W. *The adolescent years.* New York: Harcourt, Brace & World, 1955.
119. Watts, W. A., & Whittaker, D. N. Some socio-psychological differences between highly-committed members of the Free Speech Movement and the student population at Berkeley. *J. appl. behav. Sci.,* 1966, *2,* 41–62.
120. Young, W., & Hixson, J. *LSD on campus.* New York: Dell, 1966.
121. Zimmerman, P., Clark, M., & Coleman, K. Marijuana: the pot problem. *Newsweek,* July 24, 1967, 46–52.

Indexes

Index
of Names

Index
of Subjects

Body proportions (*Continued*)
  in preschool years, 283–284
  in second year, 243
Bound morphemes, 249
Boy-girl relationships in adolescence, 650–654
  adolescent marriages, 653–654
  dating, 650–652; socioeconomic status and, 652–653

Caesarian section, 80
California Preschool Mental Scale, 256
California Preschool Schedule, 308
Capacity, performance and, distinction between, 294
Caretaker, attachment to, consequences of, 217–221
  primary, lack of, 228–233
Case histories, introduction to, 239
Categorical concepts, 441
Cattell Intelligence Test for Infants and Young Children, 256
Cell division, 34–35, 37, 38–39
Cell metabolism, 85
Cephalocaudal trend, 180
Cerebral palsy, 87
Chorion, 67
Chromosomal aberration, 51
Chromosomes, 35, 36–37, 38, 39, 42, 43, 51, 55, 65–66
Class, social, alienation in relation to, 704–705, 713, 724–734
  children's textbooks, content of, and, 557–561
  dating behavior and, 652–653
  delinquent behavior and, 737–738, 742–743
  differences in, attitudes to parents, 496–497; child-rearing practices and, 495–496, 631–632; mother-child relationship and, 494–495
  drug usage and, 724
  juvenile delinquents and, 739–743; emotional disturbances and, 745–747
  language development, cognitive functioning and, 311–319
  peer-group membership and, 660–661
  peer-group status and, 580–582, 663–664
  rewards for school achievement and, 561–563
  school problems and, 565–573
  self-esteem and, 492
  sexual behavior and, 646–648
  teacher's values and, 549, 567–569

vocational choice and, 667–671, 673–677
  See also Socioeconomic status
Classical conditioning, 103-105, 106, 113, 127
Class inclusion, 453, 619
Cognitive activities in middle childhood, 430-447
  encoding, 431–435; eidetic imagery, 431–432; expectancy, role of, 433–434; information and attention, 433; single strategies of, preference for, 432–433; sustained attention, capacity for, 434–435
  evaluation, 444-446
  ideas and hypotheses, generation of, 437-444; concept of creativity and, 438-439; concept-sorting tasks in, 441-443; critical attributes, importance of, 437-438; learning set and, 439-441; material to be categorized, relevance of, 443
  implementation of hypotheses, 446-447
  memory functions, 435-437; differences in memory, individual, 436; factors controlling memory, 436-437
  types of, 430
  units in, 429-430
Cognitive development, 24
  in adolescence, 618-619; consequences of, 620-621; qualitative changes, 619-620; sex differences in cognitive functioning, 619
  in first year, 192-199; Piaget's view of, 194-199
  in middle childhood, see Cognitive activities in middle childhood; Intellectual-cognitive development
  nursery school attendance and, 382-383
  in preschool years, 295-320; conditions affecting, 310-319; language and, 298-299; Piaget's view of, 302-309
  in second year, 255-258; measurement of intelligence, 256-258
  social class, language development and, 311-319
Cognitive theory, 3, 17-18
Colic, 85
Competence, child-rearing antecedents of, 371-374
  motive for, 135
Competition, personality development, in preschool years, 394-396
Compulsions in middle childhood, 522-523

73 74 75   20 19 18 17 16 15 14 13 12 11